THE OXFORD POPULAR
FRENCH DICTIONARY

THE
OXFORD POPULAR
FRENCH
DICTIONARY

Edited by
EDWIN CARPENTER
DORA CARPENTER

Based on
The Oxford French
Minidictionary

Oxford   New York
OXFORD UNIVERSITY PRESS
1995

Based on The Oxford French Minidictionary
© Oxford University Press 1993
This abridged edition published 1995 by Paragon Book Services and
Magpie Books, an imprint of Robinson Publishing Ltd.; by
arrangement with Oxford University Press

Oxford is a trade mark of Oxford University Press

ISBN 0-75250-032-5

Typeset by Pentacor PLC

Contents

Proprietary terms

Pronunciation of French

Phonetic symbols

Vowels

i	v*ie*	y	vêt*u*
e	pr*é*	ø	p*eu*
ɛ	l*ai*t	œ	p*eu*r
a	pl*a*t	ə	*de*
ɑ	b*a*s	ɛ̃	m*a*t*in*
ɔ	m*o*rt	ɑ̃	s*ans*
o	m*o*t	ɔ̃	b*on*
u	gen*ou*	œ̃	l*un*di

Consonants and semi-consonants

p	*p*ayer	ʒ	*j*e
b	*b*on	m	*m*ain
t	*t*erre	n	*n*ous
d	*d*ans	l	*l*ong
k	*c*ou	r	*r*ue
g	*g*ant	ɲ	a*gn*eau
f	*f*eu	ŋ	campi*ng*
v	*v*ous	j	*y*eux
s	sa*l*e	w	*ou*i
z	*z*éro	ɥ	h*u*ile
ʃ	*ch*at		

Notes: ' before the pronunciation of a word beginning with *h* indicates no liaison or elision.

An asterisk immediately following an apostrophe in some words like **qu'*** shows that this form of the word is used before a vowel or mute 'h'.

Abbreviations · Abréviations

abbreviation	*abbr., abrév.*	abréviation
adjective(s)	*a. (adjs.)*	adjectif(s)
adverb(s)	*adv(s).*	adverbe(s)
American	*Amer.*	américain
anatomy	*anat.*	anatomie
approximately	*approx.*	approximativement
archaeology	*archaeol.,*	archéologie
	archéol.	
architecture	*archit.*	architecture
motoring	*auto.*	automobile
auxiliary	*aux.*	auxiliaire
aviation	*aviat.*	aviation
botany	*bot.*	botanique
computing	*comput.*	informatique
commerce	*comm.*	commerce
conjunction(s)	*conj(s).*	conjonction(s)
cookery	*culin.*	culinaire
electricity	*electr., électr.*	électricité
feminine	*f.*	féminin
familiar	*fam.*	familier
figurative	*fig.*	figuré
geography	*geog., géog.*	géographie
geology	*geol., géol.*	géologie
grammar	*gram.*	grammaire
humorous	*hum.*	humoristique
interjection(s)	*int(s).*	interjection(s)
invariable	*invar.*	invariable
legal, law	*jurid.*	juridique
language	*lang.*	langue
masculine	*m.*	masculin
medicine	*med., méd.*	médecine
military	*mil.*	militaire
music	*mus.*	musique
noun(s)	*n(s).*	nom(s)
nautical	*naut.*	nautique
oneself	*o.s.*	se, soi-même
proprietary term	P.	marque déposée
pejorative	*pej., péj.*	péjoratif
philosophy	*phil.*	philosophie

photography	*photo.*	photographie
plural	*pl.*	pluriel
politics	*pol.*	politique
possessive	*poss.*	possessif
past participle	*p.p.*	participe passé
prefix	*pref., préf.*	préfixe
preposition(s)	*prep(s)., prép(s).*	préposition(s)
present participle	*pres. p.*	participe présent
pronoun	*pron.*	pronom
relative pronoun	*pron. rel.*	pronom relatif
psychology	*psych.*	psychologie
past tense	*p.t.*	passé
something	*qch.*	quelque chose
someone	*qn.*	quelqu'un
railway	*rail.*	chemin de fer
religion	*relig.*	religion
relative pronoun	*rel. pron.*	pronom relatif
school, scholastic	*schol., scol.*	scolaire
singular	*sing.*	singulier
slang	*sl.*	argot
someone	*s.o.*	quelqu'un
something	*sth.*	quelque chose
technical	*techn.*	technique
television	*TV*	télévision
university	*univ.*	université
auxiliary verb	*v. aux.*	verbe auxiliaire
intransitive verb	*v.i.*	verbe intransitif
pronominal verb	*v. pr.*	verbe pronominal
transitive verb	*v.t.*	verbe transitif

FRANÇAIS–ANGLAIS
FRENCH–ENGLISH

A

a /a/ *voir* **avoir**.

à /a/ *prép.* (*à + le = au, à + les = aux*) in, at; (*direction*) to; (*temps*) at; (*jusqu'à*) to, till; (*date*) on; (*époque*) in; (*moyen*) by, on; (*prix*) for; (*appartenance*) of; (*mesure*) by. **donner**/*etc.* **à qn.,** give/*etc.* to s.o. **apprendre**/*etc.* **à faire,** learn/*etc.* to do. **l'homme à la barbe,** the man with the beard. **à la radio,** on the radio. **c'est à moi,** it is mine. **dix km à l'heure,** ten km. per hour.

abaisser /abese/ *v.t.* lower; (*levier*) pull *ou* push down; (*fig.*) humiliate. **s'∼** *v. pr.* go down, drop; (*fig.*) humiliate o.s. **s'∼ à,** stoop to.

abandon /abɑ̃dɔ̃/ *n.m.* abandonment; desertion; (*sport*) withdrawal; (*naturel*) abandon. **à l'∼,** in a state of neglect. **∼ner** /-ɔne/ *v.t.* abandon, desert; (*renoncer à*) give up, abandon.

abat-jour /abaʒur/ *n.m. invar.* lampshade.

abats /aba/ *n.m. pl.* offal.

abattement /abatmɑ̃/ *n.m.* (*comm.*) allowance.

abattoir /abatwar/ *n.m.* abattoir.

abattre† /abatr/ *v.t.* knock down; (*arbre*) cut down; (*animal*) slaughter; (*avion*) shoot down; (*affaiblir*) weaken; (*démoraliser*) dishearten. **s'∼** *v. pr.* come down,

fall (down). **se laisser ∼,** let things get one down.

abbaye /abei/ *n.f.* abbey.

abbé /abe/ *n.m.* priest.

abcès /apsɛ/ *n.m.* abscess.

abdi|quer /abdike/ *v.t./i.* abdicate. **∼cation** *n.f.* abdication.

abdom|en /abdɔmɛn/ *n.m.* abdomen. **∼inal** (*m. pl.* **∼inaux**) *a.* abdominal.

abeille /abɛj/ *n.f.* bee.

aberrant, ∼e /abɛrɑ̃, -t/ *a.* absurd.

abîmer /abime/ *v.t.* damage, spoil. **s'∼** *v. pr.* get damaged *ou* spoilt.

abject /abʒɛkt/ *a.* abject.

aboiement /abwamɑ̃/ *n.m.* bark (ing). **∼s,** barking.

abol|ir /abɔlir/ *v.t.* abolish. **∼ition** *n.f.* abolition.

abominable /abɔminabl/ *a.* abominable.

abond|ant, ∼ante /abɔ̃dɑ̃, -t/ *a.* abundant, plentiful. **∼amment** *adv.* abundantly. **∼ance** *n.f.* abundance; (*prospérité*) affluence.

abonn|er (s') /(s)abɔne/ *v. pr.* subscribe (**à,** to). **∼é, ∼ée** *n.m., f.* subscriber; season-ticket holder. **∼ement** *n.m.* (*à un journal*) subscription; (*de bus, théâtre, etc.*) season-ticket.

abord /abɔr/ *n.m.* access. **∼s,** surroundings. **d'∼,** first.

abordable /abɔrdabl/ *a.* (*prix*) reasonable; (*personne*) approachable.

abordage /abɔrdaʒ/ *n.m.* (*accident: naut.*) collision.

aborder /abɔrde/ *v.t.* approach; (*lieu*) reach; (*problème etc.*) tackle. —*v.i.* reach land.

aboutir /abutir/ *v.i.* succeed, achieve a result. ~ **à**, end (up) in, lead to. **n'** ~ **à rien**, come to nothing.

aboyer /abwaje/ *v.i.* bark.

abrasi|f, ~**ve** /abrazif, -v/ *a. & n.m.* abrasive.

abréger /abreʒe/ *v.t.* (*texte*) shorten, abridge; (*mot*) abbreviate, shorten; (*visite*) cut short.

abreuv|er /abrœve/ *v.t.* water; (*fig.*) overwhelm (**de**, with). **s'**~**er** *v. pr.* drink.

abréviation /abrevjasjɔ̃/ *n.f.* abbreviation.

abri /abri/ *n.m.* shelter. **à l'**~, under cover. **à l'**~ **de** sheltered from.

abricot /abriko/ *n.m.* apricot.

abriter /abrite/ *v.t.* shelter; (*recevoir*) house. **s'**~ *v. pr.* (take) shelter.

abrupt /abrypt/ *a.* steep, sheer; (*fig.*) abrupt.

abruti, ~**e** /abryti/ *n.m., f.* (*fam.*) idiot.

absence /apsɑ̃s/ *n.f.* absence.

absent, ~**e** /apsɑ̃, -t/ *a.* absent, away; (*chose*) missing. —*n.m., f.* absentee.

absenter (s') /(s)apsɑ̃te/ *v. pr.* go ou be away; (*sortir*) go out, leave.

absolu /apsɔly/ *a.* absolute. ~**ment** *adv.* absolutely.

absor|ber /apsɔrbe/ *v.t.* absorb; (*temps etc.*) take up. ~**bant**, ~**bante** *a.* (*travail etc.*) absorbing; (*matière*) absorbent. ~**ption** *n.f.* absorption.

absten|ir (s') /(s)apstənir/ *v. pr.* abstain. **s'**~**ir de**, refrain from.

abstr|aire /apstrer/ *v.t.* abstract. ~**action** *n.f.* abstraction. ~**ait**, ~**aite** *a. & n.m.* abstract.

absurd|e /apsyrd/ *a.* absurd. ~**ité** *n.f.* absurdity.

abus /aby/ *n.m.* abuse, misuse; (*injustice*) abuse. ~ **de confiance**, breach of trust.

abuser /abyze/ *v.t.* deceive. —*v.i.* go too far. ~ **de**, abuse; misuse; (*profiter de*) take advantage of; (*alcool etc.*) over-indulge in.

académ|ie /akademi/ *n.f.* academy; (*circonscription*) educational district. **A**~**ie**, Academy. ~**ique** *a.* academic.

acajou /akaʒu/ *n.m.* mahogany.

accablement /akablǝmɑ̃/ *n.m.* despondency.

accabl|er /akable/ *v.t.* overwhelm. ~**ant**, ~**ante** *a.* (*chaleur*) oppressive.

accaparer /akapare/ *v.t.* monopolize; (*fig.*) take up all the time of.

accéder /aksede/ *v.i.* ~ **à**, reach; (*pouvoir*, *requête*, *trône*, *etc.*) accede to.

accélér|er /akselere/ *v.i.* (*auto.*) accelerate. —*v.t.*, **s'**~**er** *v. pr.* speed up. ~**ateur** *n.m.* accelerator. ~**ation** *n.f.* acceleration; speeding up.

accent /aksɑ̃/ *n.m.* accent; (*sur une syllabe*) stress, accent; (*ton*) tone. **mettre l'**~ **sur**, stress.

accent|uer /aksɑ̃tɥe/ *v.t.* (*lettre, syllabe*) accent; (*fig.*) emphasize, accentuate. **s'**~**uer** *v. pr.* become more pronounced, increase.

accept|er /aksɛpte/ *v.t.* accept. ~**er de**, agree to. ~**able** *a.* acceptable. ~**ation** *n.f.* acceptance.

accès /aksɛ/ *n.m.* access; (*porte*)

entrance; (de fièvre) attack; (de colère) fit; (de joie) (out)burst. **les ~ de,** (voies) the approaches to. **facile d'~,** easy to get to.

accessible /aksesibl/ a. accessible; (personne) approachable.

accession /aksesjɔ̃/ n.f. **~ à,** accession to.

accessoire /akseswar/ a. secondary. —n.m. accessory; (théâtre) prop.

accident /aksidɑ̃/ n.m. accident. **~ de train/d'avion,** train/plane crash. **par ~,** by accident. **~é** /-te/ a. damaged ou hurt (in an accident); (terrain) uneven, hilly.

accidentel, ~le /aksidɑ̃tɛl/ a. accidental.

acclam|er /aklame/ v.t. cheer, acclaim. **~ations** /-asjɔ̃/ n.f. pl. cheers.

accommodant, ~e /akɔmɔdɑ̃, -t/ a. accommodating.

accommoder /akɔmɔde/ v.t. adapt (à, to); (cuisiner) prepare; (assaisonner) flavour.

accompagn|er /akɔ̃paɲe/ v.t. accompany. **s'~er de,** be accompanied by. **~ateur, ~atrice** n.m., f. (mus.) accompanist; (guide) guide. **~ement** n.m. (mus.) accompaniment.

accompli /akɔ̃pli/ a. accomplished.

accompl|ir /akɔ̃plir/ v.t. carry out, fulfil. **~issement** n.m. fulfilment.

accord /akɔr/ n.m. agreement; (harmonie) harmony; (mus.) chord. **être d'~,** agree (pour, to). **se mettre d'~,** come to an agreement, agree. **d'~!,** all right!

accordéon /akɔrdeɔ̃/ n.m. accordion.

accord|er /akɔrde/ v.t. grant; (couleurs etc.) match; (mus.) tune. **s'~er** v. pr. agree. **s'~er avec,** (s'entendre avec) get on with.

accotement /akɔtmɑ̃/ n.m. roadside, verge; (Amer.) shoulder.

accouch|er /akuʃe/ v.i. give birth (de, to); (être en travail) be in labour. —v.t. deliver. **~ement** n.m. childbirth; (travail) labour.

accoud|er (s') /(s)akude/ v. pr. lean (one's elbows) on. **~oir** n.m. armrest.

accoutumance /akutymɑ̃s/ n.f. habituation; (méd.) addiction.

accro /akro/ n.m./f. (drogué) addict; (amateur) fan.

accroc /akro/ n.m. tear, rip; (fig.) hitch.

accroch|er /akroʃe/ v.t. (suspendre) hang up; (attacher) hook, hitch; (déchirer) catch; (heurter) hit; (attirer) attract. **s'~er** v. pr. cling, hang on; (se disputer) clash. **~age** n.m. hanging; hooking; (auto.) collision; (dispute) clash; (mil.) encounter.

accroissement /akrwasmɑ̃/ n.m. increase (de, in).

accroître /akrwatr/ v.t., **s'~** v. pr. increase.

accroup|ir (s') /(s)akrupir/ v. pr. squat. **~i** a. squatting.

accru /akry/ a. increased, greater.

accueil /akœj/ n.m. reception, welcome.

accueill|ir /akœjir/ v.t. receive, welcome; (aller chercher) meet. **~ant, ~ante** a. friendly.

accumul|er /akymyle/ v.t., **s'~** v. pr. accumulate, pile up. **~ateur** n.m. accumulator. **~ation** n.f. accumulation.

accusation /akyzasjɔ̃/ n.f. accusation; (jurid.) charge. **l'~,** (magistrat) the prosecution.

accus|er /akyze/ v.t. accuse (de, of); (blâmer) blame (de, with); (jurid.) charge (de, with); (fig.) show, emphasize. **~é, ~ée** a. marked; n.m., f. accused.

acharn|é /aʃarne/ *a.* relentless, ferocious. **~ement** *n.m.* relentlessness.

acharner (s') /(s)aʃarne/ *v. pr.* **s'~ sur,** set upon; (*poursuivre*) hound.

achat /aʃa/ *n.m.* purchase. **~s,** shopping. **faire l'~ de,** buy.

achet|er /aʃte/ *v.t.* buy. **~er à,** buy from; (*pour*) buy for. **~eur, ~euse** *n.m., f.* buyer; (*client de magasin*) shopper.

achèvement /aʃɛvmɑ̃/ *n.m.* completion.

achever /aʃve/ *v.t.* finish (off). **s'~** *v. pr.* end.

acid|e /asid/ *a.* acid, sharp. —*n.m.* acid. **~ité** *n.f.* acidity.

acier /asje/ *n.m.* steel. **aciérie** *n.f.* steelworks.

acné /akne/ *n.f.* acne.

acompte /akɔ̃t/ *n.m.* deposit, part-payment.

acqu|érir† /akerir/ *v.t.* acquire, gain; (*biens*) purchase, acquire. **~éreur** *n.m.* purchaser. **~isition** *n.f.* acquisition; purchase.

acquiescer /akjese/ *v.i.* acquiesce, agree.

acquis, ~e /aki, -z/ *n.m.* experience. —*a.* acquired; (*fait*) established; (*faveurs*) secured. **~ à,** (*projet*) in favour of.

acquit /aki/ *n.m.* receipt. **par ~ de conscience,** for peace of mind.

acquitt|er /akite/ *v.t.* acquit; (*dette*) settle. **s'~er de,** (*promesse, devoir*) carry out. **s'~er envers,** repay. **~ement** *n.m.* acquittal; settlement.

acrobate /akrɔbat/ *n.m./f.* acrobat.

acrobatie /akrɔbasi/ *n.f.* acrobatics. **acrobatique** /-tik/ *a.* acrobatic.

acte /akt/ *n.m.* act, action, deed;

(*théâtre*) act; (*de naissance, mariage*) certificate.

acteur /aktœr/ *n.m.* actor.

actif, ~ve /aktif, -v/ *a.* active. —*n.m.* (*comm.*) assets. **~vement** *adv.* actively.

action /aksjɔ̃/ *n.f.* action; (*comm.*) share; (*jurid.*) action. **~naire** /-jɔnɛr/ *n.m./f.* shareholder.

actionner /aksjɔne/ *v.t.* work, activate.

activer /aktive/ *v.t.* speed up; (*feu*) boost. **s'~** *v. pr.* hurry, rush.

activité /aktivite/ *n.f.* activity.

actrice /aktris/ *n.f.* actress.

actualiser /aktɥalize/ *v.t.* update.

actualité /aktɥalite/ *n.f.* topicality. **l'~,** current events. **les ~s,** news. **d'~,** topical.

actuel, ~le /aktɥɛl/ *a.* present; (*d'actualité*) topical. **~lement** *adv.* at the present time.

acupunct|ure /akypɔ̃ktyr/ *n.f.* acupuncture.

adapt|er /adapte/ *v.t.* adapt; (*fixer*) fit. **s'~er** *v. pr.* adapt (o.s.); (*techn.*) fit. **~ateur** *n.m.* (*électr.*) adapter. **~ation** *n.f.* adaptation.

additif /aditif/ *n.m.* (*note*) rider; (*substance*) additive.

addition /adisjɔ̃/ *n.f.* addition; (*au café etc.*) bill. **~ner** /-jɔne/ *v.t.* add; (*totaliser*) add (up).

adepte /adɛpt/ *n.m./f.* follower.

adéquat, ~e /adekwa, -t/ *a.* suitable.

adhérent, ~e /aderɑ̃, -t/ *n.m., f.* member.

adhé|rer /adere/ *v.i.* adhere, stick (à, to). **~rer à,** (*club etc.*) be a member of; (*s'inscrire à*) join. **~sif, ~sive** /-zif, -ziv/ *a.* adhesive. **~sion** *n.f.* membership; (*accord*) adherence.

adieu (*pl.* **~x**) /adjø/ *int. & n.m.* goodbye, farewell.

adjacent, ~e /adʒasã, -t/ a. adjacent.

adjectif /adʒɛktif/ n.m. adjective.

adjoint, ~e /adʒwɛ̃, -t/ n.m., f. & a. assistant. ~ **au maire,** deputy mayor.

admettre† /admɛtr/ v.t. let in, admit; (tolérer) allow; (reconnaître) admit; (candidat) pass.

administrati|f, ~**ve** /administratif, -v/ a. administrative.

administr|er /administre/ v.t. run, manage. ~**ateur,** ~**atrice** n.m., f. administrator, director. ~**ation** n.f. administration. **A~ation,** Civil Service.

admirable /admirabl/ a. admirable.

admirati|f, ~**ve** /admiratif, -v/ a. admiring.

admir|er /admire/ v.t. admire. ~**ateur,** ~**atrice** n.m., f. admirer. ~**ation** n.f. admiration.

admissible /admisibl/ a. admissible; (candidat) eligible.

admission /admisjɔ̃/ n.f. admission.

adolescen|t, ~**te** /adɔlesã, -t/ n.m., f. adolescent. ~**ce** n.f. adolescence.

adopt|er /adɔpte/ v.t. adopt. ~**ion** /-psjɔ̃/ n.f. adoption.

adopti|f, ~**ve** /adɔptif, -v/ a. (enfant) adopted; (parents) adoptive.

adorable /adɔrabl/ a. delightful, adorable.

ador|er /adɔre/ v.t. adore; (relig.) worship, adore.

adouci|r /adusir/ v.t. soften. **s'~r** v. pr. soften; mellow; ease; (temps) become milder. ~**ssant** n.m. (fabric) softener.

adresse /adrɛs/ n.f. address; (habileté) skill.

adresser /adrese/ v.t. send; (écrire l'adresse sur) address; (remarque

etc.) address. ~ **la parole à,** speak to. **s'~ à,** address; (aller voir) go and ask or see; (bureau) enquire at; (viser, intéresser) be directed at.

adroit, ~e /adrwa, -t/ a. skilful, clever. ~**ement** /-tmã/ adv. skilfully, cleverly.

adulte /adylt/ n.m./f. adult. —a. adult.

adultère /adyltɛr/ a. adulterous. —n.m. adultery.

adverbe /adverb/ n.m. adverb.

adversaire /adverser/ n.m. opponent, adversary.

adverse /advers/ a. opposing.

aér|er /aere/ v.t. (texte) lighten. **s'~er** v. pr. get some air. ~**ation** n.f. ventilation. ~**é** a. airy.

aérien, ~**ne** /aerjɛ̃, -jɛn/ a. air; (photo) aerial; (câble) overhead; (fig.) airy.

aérobic /aerɔbik/ m. aerobics.

aérodrome /aerɔdrom/ n.m. aerodrome.

aérodynamique /aerɔdinamik/ a. streamlined, aerodynamic.

aérogare /aerɔgar/ n.f. air terminal.

aéroglisseur /aeroglisœr/ n.m. hovercraft.

aérogramme /aerɔgram/ n.m. air-mail letter; (Amer.) aerogram.

aéronautique /aerɔnotik/ a. aeronautical. —n.f. aeronautics.

aéronavale /aerɔnaval/ n.f. Fleet Air Arm; (Amer.) Naval Air Force.

aéroport /aerɔpɔr/ n.m. airport.

aérosol /aerɔsɔl/ n.m. aerosol.

affaibl|ir /afeblir/ v.t. s'~**ir** v. pr. weaken. ~**issement** n.m. weakening.

affaire /afɛr/ n.f. matter, affair; (histoire) affair; (transaction) deal; (occasion) bargain; (firme) business; (jurid.) case. ~**s,** affairs; (*comm.*) business; (*effets*) belongings. **avoir ~ à**, (have to) deal with. **ce sont mes ~s**, that is my business. **faire l'~**, do the job. **tirer qn. d'~**, help s.o. out.

affairé /afere/ *a.* busy.

affaissement /afɛsmɑ̃/ *n.m.* subsidence.

affaler (s') /(s)afale/ *v. pr.* slump (down), collapse.

affamé /afame/ *a.* starving.

affect|é /afɛkte/ *a.* affected. **~ation**[1] *n.f.* affectation.

affect|er /afɛkte/ *v.t.* (*feindre, émouvoir*) affect; (*destiner*) assign; (*nommer*) appoint. post. **~ation**[2] *n.f.* assignment; appointment, posting.

affecti|f, ~ve /afɛktif, -v/ *a.* emotional.

affection /afɛksjɔ̃/ *n.f.* affection; (*maladie*) ailment. **~ner** /-jɔne/ *v.t.* be fond of.

affectueu|x, ~se /afɛktɥø, -z/ *a.* affectionate.

affiche /afiʃ/ *n.f.* (public) notice; (*publicité*) poster; (*théâtre*) bill.

affich|er /afiʃe/ *v.t.* (*annonce*) put up; (*événement*) announce; (*sentiment etc., comput.*) display. **~age** *n.m.* billposting; (*électronique*) display.

affiner /afine/ *v.t.* refine.

affirmati|f, ~ve /afirmatif, -v/ *a.* affirmative. **—***n.f.* affirmative.

affirm|er /afirme/ *v.t.* assert. **~ation** *n.f.* assertion.

affligé /afliʒe/ *a.* distressed.

affluence /aflyɑ̃s/ *n.f.* crowd(s).

affluent /aflyɑ̃/ *n.m.* tributary.

afflux /afly/ *n.m.* influx, flood; (*du sang*) rush.

affol|er /(s)afole/ *v. pr.* panic. **~ant, ~ante** *a.* alarming. **—***n.m.* panic.

affranch|ir /afrɑ̃ʃir/ *v.t.* stamp; (*à*

la machine) frank; (*fig.*) free. **~issement** *n.m.* (*tarif*) postage.

affréter /afrete/ *v.t.* charter.

affreu|x, ~se /afrø, -z/ *a.* (*laid*) hideous; (*mauvais*) awful. **~sement** *adv.* awfully, hideously.

affront /afrɔ̃/ *n.m.* affront.

affront|er /afrɔ̃te/ *v.t.* confront. **s'~er** *v. pr.* confront each other.

afin /afɛ̃/ *prép. & conj.* **~ de/que**, in order to/that.

africain, ~e /afrikɛ̃, -ɛn/ *a. & n.m., f.* African.

Afrique /afrik/ *n.f.* Africa. **~ du Sud**, South Africa.

agacer /agase/ *v.t.* irritate, annoy.

âge /aʒ/ *n.m.* age. **quel ~ avez-vous?**, how old are you?

âgé /aʒe/ *a.* elderly. **~ de cinq ans**/*etc.*, five years/*etc.* old.

agence /aʒɑ̃s/ *n.f.* agency, bureau, office; (*succursale*) branch. **~ d'interim**, employment agency. **~ de voyages**, travel agency.

agenc|er /aʒɑ̃se/ *v.t.* organize, arrange. **~ement** *n.m.* organization.

agenda /aʒɛ̃da/ *n.m.* diary.

agenouiller (s') /(s)aʒnuje/ *v. pr.* kneel (down).

agent /aʒɑ̃/ *n.m.* **~ (de police)**, policeman. **~ de change**, stockbroker.

agglomération /aglɔmerasjɔ̃/ *n.f.* built-up area, town.

aggloméré /aglɔmere/ *n.m.* (*bois*) chipboard.

agglomérer /aglɔmere/ *v.t.*, **s'~** *v. pr.* pile up.

agglutiner /aglytine/ *v.t.*, **s'~** *v. pr.* stick together.

aggraver /agrave/ *v.t.*, **s'~** *v. pr.* worsen.

agile /aʒil/ *a.* agile, nimble. **~ité** *n.f.* agility.

agir /aʒir/ *v.i.* act. **il s'agit de faire**, it is a matter of doing; (*il* *faut*) it is necessary to do. **dans ce livre il s'agit de,** this book is about. **dont il s'agit de,** in question.

agité /aʒite/ *a.* restless, fidgety; (*trouble*) agitated; (*mer*) rough.

agit|er /aʒite/ *v.t.* (*bras etc.*) wave; (*liquide*) shake. **s'∼er** *v. pr.* bustle about; (*enfant*) fidget; (*foule, pensées*) stir. **∼ateur,** **∼atrice** *n.m., f.* agitator. **∼ation** *n.f.* bustle; (*trouble*) agitation.

agneau (*pl.* **∼x** /aɲo/ *n.m.* lamb.

agraf|e /agraf/ *n.f.* hook; (*pour papiers*) staple. **∼er** *v.t.* hook (up); (*robe*) do up. **∼euse** *n.f.* stapler.

agrand|ir /agrɑ̃dir/ *v.t.* enlarge. **s'∼ir** *v. pr.* expand, grow. **∼issement** *n.m.* extension; (*de photo*) enlargement.

agréable /agreabl/ *a.* pleasant. **∼ment** /-əmɑ̃/ *adv.* pleasantly.

agré|er /agree/ *v.t.* accept. **∼é** *a.* authorized.

agress|er /agrese/ *v.t.* attack. **∼eur** /-esœr/ *n.m.* attacker; (*mil.*) aggressor. **∼ion** /-esjɔ̃/ *n.f.* attack; (*mil.*) aggression.

agressi|f, ∼ve /agresif, -v/ *a.* aggressive. **∼vité** *n.f.* aggressiveness.

agricole /agrikɔl/ *a.* agricultural; (*ouvrier etc.*) farm.

agriculteur /agrikyltœr/ *n.m.* farmer.

agriculture /agrikyltyr/ *n.f.* agriculture, farming.

agripper /agripe/ *v.t.,* **s'∼ à,** grab, clutch.

agroalimentaire /agroalimɑ̃ter/ *n.m.* food industry.

agrumes /agrym/ *n.m. pl.* citrus fruit(s).

ah /a/ *int.* ah, oh.

ahur|ir /ayrir/ *v.t.* dumbfound. **∼issement** *n.m.* stupefaction.

ai /e/ *voir* **avoir.**

aide /ɛd/ *n.f.* help, assistance, aid. —*n.m./f.* assistant. **à l'∼ de,** with the help of. **∼-mémoire** *n.m. invar.* handbook of facts. **venir en ∼ à,** help.

aider /ede/ *v.t./i.* help, assist. **∼ à faire,** help to do. **s'∼ de,** use.

aïe /aj/ *int.* ouch, ow.

aigle /ɛgl/ *n.m.* eagle.

aigr|e /ɛgr/ *a.* sour, sharp; (*fig.*) sharp. **∼eurs** **d'estomac,** heartburn.

aigrir /egrir/ *v.t.* embitter; (*caractère*) sour. **être aigre,** be embittered.

aigu, ∼ë /egy/ *a.* acute; (*objet*) sharp; (*voix*) shrill. (*mus.*) **les ∼s,** the high notes.

aiguillage /eguijaʒ/ *n.m.* (*rail.*) points; (*rail., Amer.*) switches.

aiguille /eguij/ *n.f.* needle; (*de montre*) hand; (*de balance*) pointer.

aiguill|er /eguije/ *v.t.* shunt; (*fig.*) steer. **∼eur** *n.m.* pointsman. **∼eur du ciel,** air traffic controller.

aiguiser /eg(ɥ)ize/ *v.t.* sharpen; (*fig.*) stimulate.

ail (*pl.* **∼s**) /aj/ *n.m.* garlic.

aile /ɛl/ *n.f.* wing.

ailé /ele/ *a.* winged.

aille /aj/ *voir* **aller**[1].

ailleurs /ajœr/ *adv.* elsewhere. **d'∼,** besides, moreover. **par ∼,** moreover, furthermore. **partout ∼,** everywhere else.

ailloli /ajɔli/ *n.m.* garlic mayonnaise.

aimable /ɛmabl/ *a.* kind. **∼ment** /-əmɑ̃/ *adv.* kindly.

aimant[1] /ɛmɑ̃/ *n.m.* magnet. **∼er** /-te/ *v.t.* magnetize.

aimant[2]**, ∼e** /ɛmɑ̃, -t/ *a.* loving.

aimer /eme/ *v.t.* like; (*d'amour*) love. **j'aimerais faire,** I'd like to do. ~ **bien**, quite like. ~ **mieux** *ou* **autant**, prefer.

aine /ɛn/ *n.f.* groin.

aîné, ~**e** /ene/ *a.* eldest; *(entre deux)* elder. —*n.m., f.* eldest (child); elder (child).

ainsi /ɛ̃si/ *adv.* thus; *(donc)* so. ~ **que**, as well as; *(comme)* as. **et** ~ **de suite**, and so on. **pour** ~ **dire**, so to speak, as it were.

air /ɛr/ *n.m.* air; *(mine)* look, air; *(mélodie)* tune. ~ **conditionné**, air-conditioning. **avoir l'** ~ **de**, look like. **avoir l'** ~ **de faire**, appear to be doing. **en l'** ~, (up) in the air; *(promesses etc.)* empty.

aire /ɛr/ *n.f.* area. ~ **d'atterrissage**, landing-strip.

aisance /ɛzɑ̃s/ *n.f.* ease; *(richesse)* affluence.

aise /ɛz/ *n.f.* joy. —*a.* **à l'** ~, *(sur un siège)* comfortable; *(pas gêné)* at ease; *(fortuné)* comfortably off. **mal à l'** ~, uncomfortable; ill at ease. **se mettre à l'** ~, make o.s. comfortable.

aisé /eze/ *a.* easy; *(fortuné)* well-off. ~**ment** *adv.* easily.

aisselle /ɛsɛl/ *n.f.* armpit.

ait /ɛ/ *voir* **avoir**.

ajourn|er /aʒurne/ *v.t.* postpone; *(assemblée)* adjourn. ~**ement** *n.m.* postponement; adjournment.

ajout /aʒu/ *n.m.* addition.

ajouter /aʒute/ *v.t.* & ~ *v. pr.* add (à, to). ~ **foi à**, lend credence to.

ajust|er /aʒyste/ *v.t.* adjust; *(vêtement)* alter; *(cible, coup)* aim at; *(adapter)* fit. **s'** ~**er** *v. pr.* fit. ~**é á** close-fitting. ~**ement** *n.m.* adjustment. ~**eur** *n.m.* fitter.

alarme /alarm/ *n.f.* alarm. **donner l'** ~, sound the alarm.

alarmer /alarme/ *v.t.* alarm. **s'** ~ *v. pr.* become alarmed (**de**, at).

alarmiste /alarmist/ *a. & n.m.* alarmist.

albatros /albatros/ *n.m.* albatross.

album /albɔm/ *n.m.* album.

albumine /albymin/ *n.f.* albumin.

alcool /alkɔl/ *n.m.* alcohol; *(eau de vie)* brandy. ~ **à brûler**, methylated spirit. ~**ique** *a. & n.m./f.* alcoholic. ~**isé** *a. (boisson)* alcoholic. ~**isme** *n.m.* alcoholism.

alcootest /alkɔtɛst/ *n.m.* (P.) breath test; *(appareil)* breathalyser.

alcôve /alkov/ *n.f.* alcove.

alentour /alɑ̃tur/ *adv.* around. ~**s** *n.m. pl.* surroundings. **aux** ~**s de**, round about.

alerte /alɛrt/ *n.f.* alert. ~ **à la bombe**, bomb scare. —*a.* agile. *(vif)* alert.

alerter /alɛrte/ *v.t.* alert.

alg|èbre /alʒɛbr/ *n.f.* algebra. ~**ébrique** *a.* algebraic.

Alger /alʒe/ *n.m./f.* Algiers.

Algérie /alʒeri/ *n.f.* Algeria.

algérien, ~**ne** /alʒerjɛ̃, -jɛn/ *a. & n.m., f.* Algerian.

algue /alg/ *n.f.* seaweed. **les** ~**s**, *(bot.)* algae.

alias /aljas/ *adv.* alias.

alibi /alibi/ *n.m.* alibi.

aligner /aliɲe/ *v.t. (objets)* line up, make lines of; *(chiffres)* string together. **s'** ~ *v. pr.* line up. **s'** ~ **sur**, align o.s. on. **alignement** /-ɔmɑ̃/ *n.m.* alignment.

aliment /alimɑ̃/ *n.m.* food. ~**aire** /-tɛr/ *a.* food; *(fig.)* bread-and-butter.

aliment|er /alimɑ̃te/ *v.t.* feed; *(fournir)* supply; *(fig.)* sustain. ~**ation** *n.f.* feeding; supply(ing); *(régime)* diet.

allaiter /alete/ *v.t.* feed. ~ **au biberon**, bottle-feed. ~ **au sein**, breast-feed; *(Amer.)* nurse.

allée /ale/ *n.f.* path, lane; *(menant à une maison)* drive(way). ~**s et venues**, comings and goings.

allégation /alegɑsjɔ̃/ *n.f.* allegation.

allég|er /aleʒe/ *v.t.* make lighter;

(*poids*) lighten; (*fig.*) alleviate. **~e** *a.* (*diététique*) light.

Allemagne /alman/ *n.f.* Germany.

allemand, ~e /almɑ̃, -d/ *a.* & *n.m., f.* German. —*n.m.* (*lang.*) German.

aller[1]† /ale/ (*aux. être*) *v.i.* go. **s'en ~** *v. pr.* go away. **~ à,** (*convenir à*) suit; (*s'adapter à*) fit. **~ faire,** be going to do. **comment allez-vous?, (comment) ça va?,** how are you? **ça va!,** all right! **il va bien,** he is well. **il va mieux,** he's better. **allez-y!,** go on! **allez!, allons-y!,** let's go!

aller[2] /ale/ *n.m.* outward journey; **~ (simple),** single (ticket); (*Amer.*) one-way (ticket). **~ (et) retour,** return journey; (*Amer.*) round trip; (*billet*) return (ticket); (*Amer.*) round trip (ticket).

allerg|ie /alerʒi/ *n.f.* allergy. **~ique** *a.* allergic.

alliance /aljɑ̃s/ *n.f.* alliance; (*bague*) wedding-ring.

allié, ~e /alje/ *n.m., f.* ally.

alligator /aligator/ *n.m.* alligator.

allô /alo/ *int.* hallo, hello.

allocation /alɔkasjɔ̃/ *n.f.* allowance. **~ (de) chômage,** unemployment benefit. **~s familiales,** family allowance.

allongé /alɔ̃ʒe/ *a.* elongated.

allongement /alɔ̃ʒmɑ̃/ *n.m.* lengthening.

allonger /alɔ̃ʒe/ *v.t.* lengthen; (*bras, jambe*) stretch (out). **s'~** *v. pr.* get longer; (*s'étendre*) stretch (o.s.) out.

allum|er /alyme/ *v.t.* light; (*radio, lampe, etc.*) turn on; (*pièce*) switch the light(s) on in. **s'~er** *v. pr.* (*lumière*) come on. **~age** *n.m.* lighting; (*auto.*) ignition. **~e-gaz** *n.m. invar.* gas lighter.

allumette /alymɛt/ *n.f.* match.

allure /alyr/ *n.f.* speed, pace;

(*démarche*) walk; (*prestance*) bearing; (*air*) look. **à toute ~,** at full speed. **avoir de l'~,** have style.

allusion /alyzjɔ̃/ *n.f.* allusion (**à,** to); (*implicite*) hint (**à, at**). **faire ~ à,** allude to.

alors /alɔr/ *adv.* then. —*conj.* so, then. **~ que,** when, while; (*tandis que*) whereas. **ça ~!,** well! **et ~?,** so what?

alouette /alwɛt/ *n.f.* lark.

alourdir /alurdir/ *v.t.* weigh down.

aloyau (*pl.* **~x**) /alwajo/ *n.m.* sirloin.

Alpes /alp/ *n.f. pl.* **les ~,** the Alps.

alpestre /alpɛstr/ *a.* alpine.

alphab|et /alfabɛ/ *n.m.* alphabet. **~étique** *a.* alphabetical.

alpinis|te /alpinist/ *n.m./f.* mountaineer. **~me** *n.m.* mountaineering.

altér|er /altere/ *v.t.* falsify; (*abîmer*) spoil. **s'~er** *v. pr.* deteriorate.

alternati|f, ~ve /alternatif, -v/ *a.* alternating. —*n.f.* alternative. **~vement** *adv.* alternately.

altern|er /altɛrne/ *v.t./i.* alternate. **~ance** *n.f.* alternation. **en ~ance,** alternately.

altitude /altityd/ *n.f.* altitude, height.

aluminium /alyminjɔm/ *n.m.* aluminium.

amabilité /amabilite/ *n.f.* kindness.

amaigr|ir /amegrir/ *v.t.* make thin(ner). **~issant, ~issante** *a.* (*régime*) slimming.

amalgam|e /amalgam/ *n.m.* combination. **~er** *v.t.* combine, amalgamate.

amande /amɑ̃d/ *n.f.* almond; (*d'un fruit à noyau*) kernel.

amant /amɑ̃/ *n.m.* lover.

amarr|e /amar/ *n.f.* (mooring)

rope. **~es**, moorings. **~er** v.t. moor.

amas /ama/ n.m. heap, pile.

amasser /amase/ v.t. amass, gather; (empiler) pile up.

amateur /amatœr/ n.m. amateur. **~ de**, lover of. **d'~**, amateur; (péj.) amateurish.

Amazonie /amazɔni/ n.f. Amazonia.

ambassade /ãbasad/ n.f. embassy.

ambassa|deur, **~drice** /ãbasadœr, -dris/ n.m., f. ambassador.

ambiance /ãbjãs/ n.f. atmosphere.

ambigu, **~ë** /ãbigy/ a. ambiguous. **~ïté** /-ɥite/ n.f. ambiguity.

ambitieu|x, **~se** /ãbisjø, -z/ a. ambitious.

ambition /ãbisjɔ̃/ n.f. ambition.

ambre /ãbr/ n.m. amber.

ambulanc|e /ãbylãs/ n.f. ambulance. **~ier**, **~ière** n.m., f. ambulance driver.

ambulant, **~e** /ãbylã, -t/ a. itinerant.

âme /am/ n.f. soul.

amélior|er /ameljɔre/ v.t., s'**~er** v. pr. improve. **~ation** n.f. improvement.

aménag|er /amenaʒe/ v.t. (arranger) fit out; (transformer) convert; (installer) fit up; (territoire) develop. **~ement** n.m. fitting out; conversion; fitting up; development; (modification) adjustment.

amende /amãd/ n.f. fine.

amendement /amãdmã/ n.m. (de texte) amendment.

amener /amne/ v.t. bring; (causer) bring about. **~ qn. à faire**, cause sb. to do. s'**~** v. pr. (fam.) come along.

amer, **amère** /amɛr/ a. bitter.

américain, **~e** /amerikɛ̃, -ɛn/ a. & n.m., f. American.

Amérique /amerik/ n.f. America. **~ centrale/latine**, Central/Latin America. **~ du Nord/Sud**, North/South America.

amertume /amɛrtym/ n.f. bitterness.

ami, **~e** /ami/ n.m., f. friend; (de la nature, des livres, etc.) lover. —a. friendly.

amiable /amjabl/ a. amicable. **à l'~** adv. amicably; a. amicable.

amiante /amjãt/ n.m. asbestos.

amic|al (m. pl. **~aux**) /amikal, -o/ a. friendly. **~alement** adv. in a friendly manner.

amicale /amikal/ n.f. association.

amidon /amidɔ̃/ n.m. starch.

amincir /amɛ̃sir/ v.t. make thinner. s'**~** v. pr. get thinner.

amir|al (pl. **~aux**) /amiral, -o/ n.m. admiral.

amitié /amitje/ n.f. friendship. **~s**, kind regards.

ammoniac /amɔnjak/ n.m. (gaz) ammonia.

ammoniaque /amɔnjak/ n.f. (eau) ammonia.

amnésie /amnezi/ n.f. amnesia.

amnistie /amnisti/ n.f. amnesty.

amoindrir /amwɛ̃drir/ v.t. diminish.

amonceler /amɔ̃sle/ v.t., s'**~** v.pr. pile up.

amont (en) /(ã)amɔ̃/ adv. upstream.

amorc|e /amɔrs/ n.f. bait; (début) start. **~er** v.t. start; (hameçon) bait; (pompe) prime.

amortir /amɔrtir/ v.t. (choc) cushion; (bruit) deaden; (dette) pay off; (objet acheté) make pay for itself.

amortisseur /amɔrtisœr/ n.m. shock absorber.

amour /amur/ n.m. love. **~-propre** n.m. self-respect.

amoureu|x, **~se** /amurø, -z/ a. (ardent) amorous; (vie) love.

—n.m., f. lover. **~x de qn.**, in love with s.o.

amovible /amɔvibl/ a. removable.

ampère /ɑ̃pɛr/ n.m. amp(ere).

amphithéâtre /ɑ̃fiteatr/ n.m. amphitheatre; (d'université) lecture hall.

ample /ɑ̃pl/ a. ample; (mouvement) broad. **~ment** /-əmɑ̃/ adv. amply.

ampleur /ɑ̃plœr/ n.f. extent, size; (de vêtement) fullness.

ampli /ɑ̃pli/ n.m. amplifier.

amplif|ier /ɑ̃plifje/ v.t. amplify; (fig.) expand, develop. **s'~ier** v.pr. expand, develop. **~icateur** n.m. amplifier.

ampoule /ɑ̃pul/ n.f. (électrique) bulb; (sur la peau) blister; (de médicament) phial.

amput|er /ɑ̃pyte/ v.t. amputate; (fig.) reduce. **~ation** n.f. amputation; (fig.) reduction.

amuse-gueule /amyzgœl/ n.m. invar. appetizer.

amus|er /amyze/ v.t. amuse. **s'~er** v. pr. enjoy o.s.; (jouer) play. **~ant, ~ante** a. funny.

amygdale /amidal/ n.f. tonsil.

an /ɑ̃/ n.m. year. **avoir dix/etc. ans**, be ten/etc. years old.

analgésique /analʒezik/ a. & n.m. analgesic.

analog|ie /analɔʒi/ n.f. analogy. **~ique** a. analogical, (comput.) analogue.

analogue /analɔg/ a. similar.

analphabète /analfabɛt/ a. & n.m./f. illiterate.

analy|se /analiz/ n.f. analysis; (de sang) test. **~ser** v.t. analyse. **~ste** n.m./f. analyst. **~tique** a. analytical.

ananas /anana(s)/ n.m. pineapple.

anarch|ie /anarʃi/ n.f. anarchy. **~ique** a. anarchic.

anatom|ie /anatɔmi/ n.f. anatomy. **~ique** a. anatomical.

ancêtre /ɑ̃sɛtr/ n.m. ancestor.

anchois /ɑ̃ʃwa/ n.m. anchovy.

ancien, ~ne /ɑ̃sjɛ̃, -jɛn/ a. old; (de jadis) ancient; (meuble) antique; (précédent) former, ex-, old; (dans une fonction) senior. —n.m., f. senior; (par l'âge) elder.

ancre /ɑ̃kr/ n.f. anchor.

âne /ɑn/ n.m. donkey, ass; (imbécile) ass.

anéantir /aneɑ̃tir/ v.t. destroy; (accabler) overwhelm.

aném|ie /anemi/ n.f. anaemia. **~ié, ~ique** adjs. anaemic.

anesthés|ie /anɛstezi/ n.f. (opération) anaesthetic. **~ique** a. & n.m. (substance) anaesthetic.

ange /ɑ̃ʒ/ n.m. angel.

angine /ɑ̃ʒin/ n.f. throat infection.

anglais, ~e /ɑ̃glɛ, -z/ a. English. —n.m., f. Englishman, Englishwoman. —n.m. (lang.) English.

angle /ɑ̃gl/ n.m. angle; (coin) corner.

Angleterre /ɑ̃glətɛr/ n.f. England.

anglicisme /ɑ̃glisism/ n.m. anglicism.

anglo- /ɑ̃glɔ/ préf. Anglo-.

anglophone /ɑ̃glɔfɔn/ a. English-speaking. —n.m./f. English speaker.

angoiss|e /ɑ̃gwas/ n.f. anxiety. **~ant, ~ante** a. harrowing. **~é** a. anxious. **~er** v.t. make anxious.

anguleux, ~se /ɑ̃gylø, -z/ a. (traits) angular.

anim|al (pl. **~aux**) /animal, -o/ n.m. animal. —a. (m. pl. **~aux**) animal.

anima|teur, ~trice /animatœr, -tris/ n.m., f. organizer, leader; (TV) host, hostess.

animé /anime/ a. lively; (affairé) busy.

animer /anime/ v.t. liven up; (mener) lead; (mouvoir, pousser)

drive; (*encourager*) spur on. **s'~**
v. pr. liven up.

anis /anis/ *n.m.* (*parfum, boisson*)
aniseed.

anneau (*pl.* **~x**) /ano/ *n.m.* ring;
(*de chaîne*) link.

année /ane/ *n.f.* year.

annexe /anɛks/ *a.* attached;
(*question*) related. (*bâtiment*) adjoining. —*n.f.* annexe; (*Amer.*)
annex.

annexer /anɛkse/ *v.t.* annex;
(*document*) attach.

anniversaire /anivɛrsɛr/ *n.m.*
birthday; (*d'un événement*) anniversary. —*a.* anniversary.

annonc|e /anɔ̃s/ *n.f.* announce-
ment; (*publicitaire*) advertise-
ment; (*indice*) sign. **~er** *v.t.*
announce; (*dénoter*) indicate.

annuaire /anɥɛr/ *n.m.* year-book.
~ (**téléphonique**), (telephone)
directory.

annuel, ~le /anɥɛl/ *a.* annual,
yearly. **~lement** *adv.* annually,
yearly.

annul|er /anyle/ *v.t.* cancel.
~ation *n.f.* cancellation.

anodin, ~e /anɔdɛ̃, -in/ *a.* insignificant; (*blessure*) harmless.

anomalie /anɔmali/ *n.f.* anomaly.

anonyme /anɔnim/ *a.* anonymous.

anorak /anɔrak/ *n.m.* anorak.

anorexie /anɔrɛksi/ *n.f.* anorexia.

anorm|al (*m. pl.* **~aux**) /anɔrmal,
-o/ *a.* abnormal.

antagonis|me /ɑ̃tagɔnism/ *n.m.*
antagonism. **~te** *n.m./f.* an-
tagonist; *a.* antagonistic.

antarctique /ɑ̃tarktik/ *a.* & *n.m.*
Antarctic.

antenne /ɑ̃tɛn/ *n.f.* aerial; (*Amer.*)
antenna; (*d'insecte*) antenna;
(*succursale*) agency.

antérieur /ɑ̃terjœr/ *a.* previous,
earlier; (*placé devant*) front. **~ à**,
prior to.

anthologie /ɑ̃tɔlɔʒi/ *n.f.* antho-
logy.

anthropolo|gie /ɑ̃trɔpɔlɔʒi/ *n.f.*
anthropology. **~gue** *n.m./f.*
anthropologist.

anti- /ɑ̃ti/ *préf.* anti-.

antiadhésif, ~ve /ɑ̃tiadezif, -v/
a. non-stick.

antibiotique /ɑ̃tibjɔtik/ *n.m.* antibiotic.

anticonceptionnel, ~le /ɑ̃ti-
kɔ̃sɛpsjɔnɛl/ *a.* contraceptive.

anticorps /ɑ̃tikɔr/ *n.m.* antibody.

anticyclone /ɑ̃tisyklɔn/ *n.m.* anticyclone.

antidote /ɑ̃tidɔt/ *n.m.* antidote.

antigel /ɑ̃tiʒɛl/ *n.m.* antifreeze.

antihistaminique /ɑ̃tiistaminik/
a. & *n.m.* antihistamine.

antillais, ~e /ɑ̃tije, -z/ *a.* & *n.m.,
f.* West Indian.

Antilles /ɑ̃tij/ *n.f. pl.* **les ~**, the
West Indies.

antilope /ɑ̃tilɔp/ *n.f.* antelope.

antipath|ie /ɑ̃tipati/ *n.f.*
tipathy. **~ique** *a.* unpleasant.

antiquaire /ɑ̃tikɛr/ *n.m./f.* antique dealer.

antiqu|e /ɑ̃tik/ *a.* ancient. **~ité**
n.f. antiquity; (*objet*) antique.

antiseptique /ɑ̃tisɛptik/ *a.* & *n.m.*
antiseptic.

antivol /ɑ̃tivɔl/ *n.m.* anti-theft lock
ou device.

anus /anys/ *n.m.* anus.

anxiété /ɑ̃ksjete/ *n.f.* anxiety.

anxieu|x, ~se /ɑ̃ksjø, -z/ *a.*
anxious. —*n.m., f.* worrier.

août /u(t)/ *n.m.* August.

apaiser /apeze/ *v.t.* calm down,
(*douleur, colère*) soothe (*faim*)
appease.

apath|ie /apati/ *n.f.* apathy.
~ique *a.* apathetic.

apercevoir† /apɛrsəvwar/ *v.t.* see.
s'~ de, notice. **s'~ que**, notice
ou realize that.

apéritif /aperitif/ n.m. aperitif.

à-peu-près /apøprɛ/ n.m. invar. approximation.

apeuré /apœre/ a. scared.

aphte /aft/ n.m. mouth ulcer.

apitoyer /apitwaje/ v.t. move (to pity). **s'~oyer sur**, feel pity for. **~oiement** n.m. pity.

aplatir /aplatir/ v.t. flatten (out). **s'~** v. pr. (s'allonger) lie flat; (s'humilier) grovel; (tomber: fam.) fall flat on one's face.

aplomb /aplɔ̃/ n.m. balance; (fig.) self-possession.

apparaître† /aparɛtr/ v.i. appear.

appareil /aparɛj/ n.m. apparatus; (électrique) appliance; (anat.) system; (téléphonique) phone; (dentaire) brace; (auditif) hearing-aid; (avion) plane; (culin.) mixture. **l'~ du parti**, the party machinery. **c'est Gabriel à l'~**, it's Gabriel on the phone. **~-(photo)**, camera. **~ électroménager**, household electrical appliance.

appareiller /apareje/ v.i. (navire) cast off, put to sea.

apparemment /aparamɑ̃/ adv. apparently.

apparence /aparɑ̃s/ n.f. appearance.

apparent, ~e /aparɑ̃, -t/ a. apparent; (visible) conspicuous.

appariteur /aparitœr/ n.m. (univ.) attendant, porter.

apparition /aparisjɔ̃/ n.f. appearance; (spectre) apparition.

appartement /apartəmɑ̃/ n.m. flat; (Amer.) apartment.

appartenance /apartənɑ̃s/ n.f. membership (à, of), belonging (à, to).

appartenir† /apartənir/ v.i. belong (à, to) **il lui/vous/etc. appartient de**, it is up to him/you/etc. to.

appât /apa/ n.m. bait; (fig.) lure. **~er** /-te/ v.t. lure.

appauvrir /apovrir/ v.t. impoverish. **s'~** v. pr. grow impoverished.

appel /apɛl/ n.m. call; (jurid.) appeal; (mil.) call-up. **faire ~**, appeal. **faire ~ à**, (recourir à) call on; (invoquer) appeal to; (évoquer) call up; (exiger) call for. **~ d'offres**, (comm.) invitation to tender. **faire un ~ de phares**, flash one's headlights.

appeler /aple/ v.t. call; (nécessiter) call for. **s'~er** v. pr. be called. **il s'appelle**, his name is. **~lation** /apelasjɔ̃/ n.f. designation.

appendice /apɛ̃dis/ n.m. appendix. **~ite** n.f. appendicitis.

appétissant, ~e /apetisɑ̃, -t/ a. appetizing.

appétit /apeti/ n.m. appetite.

applaudir /aplodir/ v.t./i. applaud. **~ir à**, applaud. **~issements** n.m. pl. applause.

appliquer /aplike/ v.t. apply; (loi) enforce. **s'~** v. pr. apply o.s. (à, to). **s'~ à**, (concerner) apply to.

appoint /apwɛ̃/ n.m. contribution. **d'~**, extra. **faire l'~**, give the correct money.

apport /apor/ n.m. contribution.

apporter /aporte/ v.t. bring.

apposer /apoze/ v.t. affix.

appréciable /apresjabl/ a. appreciable.

apprécier /apresje/ v.t. appreciate; (évaluer) appraise. **~iation** n.f. appreciation; appraisal.

appréhension /apreɑ̃sjɔ̃/ n.f. apprehension.

apprendre† /aprɑ̃dr/ v.t./i. learn; (être informé de) hear of. **~ qch. à qn.**, teach s.o. sth.; (informer) tell s.o. sth. **~ à faire**, learn to do. **~ à qn. à faire**, teach s.o. to do. **~ que**, learn that; (être informé) hear that.

apprentissage /aprɑ̃tisaʒ/ *n.m.* apprenticeship; (*d'un sujet*) learning.

apprivoiser /aprivwaze/ *v.t.* tame.

approba|teur, ~trice /aprɔbatœr, -tris/ *a.* approving.

approbation /aprɔbasjɔ̃/ *n.f.* approval.

approchant, ~e /aprɔʃɑ̃, -t/ *a.* close, similar.

approcher /aprɔʃe/ *v.t.* (*objet*) move near(er) (**de**, to); (*personne*) approach. —*v.i.* ~ (**de**), approach. s'~ **de**, approach, move near(er) to.

approfond|ir /aprɔfɔ̃dir/ *v.t.* deepen; (*fig.*) go into thoroughly. ~**i** *a.* thorough.

approprié /aprɔprije/ *a.* appropriate.

approprier (s') /saprɔprije/ *v. pr.* appropriate.

approuver /apruve/ *v.t.* approve; (*trouver louable*) approve of; (*soutenir*) agree with.

approvisionn|er /aprɔvizjɔne/ *v.t.* supply. s'~**er** *v. pr.* stock up. ~**ement** *n.m.* supply.

approximati|f, ~ve /aprɔksimatif, -v/ *a.* approximate. ~**vement** *adv.* approximately.

appui /apɥi/ *n.m.* support; (*de fenêtre*) sill; (*pour objet*) rest.

appuyer /apɥije/ *v.t.* lean, rest; (*presser*) press; (*soutenir*) support, back. —*v.i.* ~ **sur**, press (on); (*fig.*) stress. s'~ **sur**, lean on; (*compter sur*) rely on.

après /aprɛ/ *prép.* after; (*au-delà de*) beyond. —*adv.* after(wards); (*plus tard*) later. ~ **avoir fait, après doing.** ~ **qu'il est parti**, after he left. ~ **coup**, after the event. ~ **tout**, after all. **d'~**, (*selon*) according to. ~-**demain** *adv.* the day after tomorrow. ~-**midi** *n.m./f. invar.* afternoon. ~-**rasage** *n.m.* aftershave.

aquarelle /akwarɛl/ *n.f.* watercolour, aquarelle.

aquarium /akwarjɔm/ *n.m.* aquarium.

aquatique /akwatik/ *a.* aquatic.

aqueduc /akdyk/ *n.m.* aqueduct.

arabe /arab/ *a.* Arab; (*désert*) Arabic; (*désert*) Arabian. —*n.m./f.* Arab. —*n.m.* (*lang.*) Arabic.

Arabie /arabi/ *n.f.* ~ **Séoudite**, Saudi Arabia.

arachide /araʃid/ *n.f.* peanut.

araignée /arɛɲe/ *n.f.* spider.

arbitraire /arbitrɛr/ *a.* arbitrary.

arbitr|e /arbitr/ *n.m.* referee; (*cricket, tennis*) umpire; (*maître*) arbiter; (*jurid.*) arbitrator. ~**age** *n.m.* arbitration; (*sport*) refereeing. ~**er** *v.t.* (*match*) referee; (*jurid.*) arbitrate.

arbre /arbr/ *n.m.* tree; (*techn.*) shaft.

arbuste /arbyst/ *n.m.* bush.

arc /ark/ *n.m.* (*arme*) bow; (*voûte*) arch. ~ **de cercle**, arc of a circle.

arcade /arkad/ *n.f.* arcade, arches.

arc-en-ciel (*pl.* **arcs-en-ciel**) /arkɑ̃sjɛl/ *n.m.* rainbow.

archéolo|gie /arkeɔlɔʒi/ *n.f.* archaeology. ~**gique** *a.* archaeological. ~**gue** *n.m./f.* archaeologist.

archet /arʃɛ/ *n.m.* (*mus.*) bow.

archevêque /arʃəvɛk/ *n.m.* archbishop.

archi- /arʃi/ *préf.* (*fam.*) tremendously.

architecte /arʃitɛkt/ *n.m.* architect.

architecture /arʃitɛktyr/ *n.f.* architecture.

arctique /arktik/ *a. & n.m.* Arctic.

ardoise /ardwaz/ *n.f.* slate.

are /ar/ *n.m.* are (= *100 square metres*).

arène /arɛn/ *n.f.* arena. ~**(s)**, (*pour courses de taureaux*) bullring.

arête /aret/ *n.f.* (*de poisson*) bone; (*bord*) ridge.

argent /arʒɑ̃/ *n.m.* money; (*métal*) silver. ∼ **comptant**, cash. ∼ **de poche**, pocket money.

argenté /arʒɑ̃te/ *a.* silver(y); (*métal*) (silver-)plated.

argenterie /arʒɑ̃tri/ *n.f.* silverware.

argentin, ∼**e** /arʒɑ̃tɛ̃, -in/ *a.* & *n.m.*, *f.* Argentinian, Argentine.

Argentine /arʒɑ̃tin/ *n.f.* Argentina.

argile /arʒil/ *n.f.* clay.

argot /argo/ *n.m.* slang.

argument /argymɑ̃/ *n.m.* argument. ∼**er** /-te/ *v.i.* argue.

aride /arid/ *a.* arid, barren.

aristocrate /aristokrat/ *n.m./f.* aristocrat.

aristocrat|ie /aristokrasi/ *n.f.* aristocracy. ∼**ique** /-atik/ *a.* aristocratic.

arithmétique /aritmetik/ *n.f.* arithmetic. —*a.* arithmetical.

arme /arm/ *n.f.* arm, weapon.

armée /arme/ *n.f.* army. ∼ **de l'air**, Air Force. ∼ **de terre**, Army.

armement /arməmɑ̃/ *n.m.* arms.

armer /arme/ *v.t.* arm; (*fusil*) cock; (*photo.*) wind on. **s'**∼ **de**, arm o.s. with.

armoire /armwar/ *n.f.* cupboard; (*penderie*) wardrobe; (*Amer.*) closet.

aromatisé /aromatize/ *a.* flavoured.

arôme /arom/ *n.m.* aroma.

arracher /araʃe/ *v.t.* pull out *ou* off; (*plante*) pull *ou* dig up; (*page*) tear *ou* pull out. ∼ **à**, (*enlever à*) snatch from; (*fig.*) force *ou* wrest from.

arrangement /arɑ̃ʒmɑ̃/ *n.m.* arrangement.

arranger /arɑ̃ʒe/ *v.t.* arrange, fix

up; (*réparer*) put right; (*régler*) sort out; (*convenir à*) suit. **s'**∼ *v. pr.* (*se mettre d'accord*) come to an arrangement; (*se débrouiller*) manage (**pour,** to).

arrestation /arɛstasjɔ̃/ *n.f.* arrest.

arrêt /arɛ/ *n.m.* stopping (**de,** of); (*lieu*) stop; (*pause*) pause; (*jurid.*) decree. **à l'**∼, stationary. **sans** ∼, without stopping. ∼ **maladie**, sick leave. ∼ **de travail**, (*grève*) stoppage; (*méd.*) sick leave.

arrêté /arete/ *n.m.* order.

arrêter /arete/ *v.t./i.* stop; (*date, regard*) fix; (*appareil*) turn off; (*appréhender*) arrest. **s'**∼ *v. pr.* stop. **(s')**∼ **de faire**, stop doing.

arrhes /ar/ *n.f. pl.* deposit.

arrière /arjer/ *n.m.* back, rear; (*football*) back. —*a. invar.* back, rear. **à l'**∼, in *ou* at the back. **en** ∼, behind; (*marcher*) backwards. **en** ∼ **de**, behind. ∼-**goût** *n.m.* after-taste. ∼-**pays** *n.m.* backcountry. ∼-**pensée** *n.f.* ulterior motive. ∼-**plan** *n.m.* background.

arriéré /arjere/ *a.* backward. —*n.m.* arrears.

arrivage /arivaʒ/ *n.m.* consignment.

arrivée /arive/ *n.f.* arrival; (*sport*) finish.

arriver /arive/ *v.i.* (*aux. être*) arrive, come; (*réussir*) succeed; (*se produire*) happen. ∼ **à**, (*atteindre*) reach. ∼ **à faire**, manage to do. **en** ∼ **à faire**, get to the stage of doing. **il arrive que**, it happens that. **il lui arrive de faire**, he (sometimes) does.

arrogan|t, ∼**te** /arɔgɑ̃, -t/ *a.* arrogant. ∼**ce** *n.f.* arrogance.

arrondir /arɔ̃dir/ *v.t.* (make) round; (*somme*) round off.

arrondissement /arɔ̃dismɑ̃/ *n.m.* district.

arros|er /aroze/ *v.t.* water; (*repas*) wash down; (*rôti*) baste; (*victoire*) celebrate with a drink. **~oir** *n.m.* watering-can.

arsen|al (*pl.* **~aux**) /arsənal, -o/ *n.m.* arsenal; (*naut.*) dockyard.

art /ar/ *n.m.* art. **~s et métiers**, arts and crafts.

artère /arter/ *n.f.* artery. **(grande) ~**, main road.

arthrite /artrit/ *n.f.* arthritis.

arthrose /artroz/ *n.f.* osteoarthritis.

artichaut /artiʃo/ *n.m.* artichoke.

article /artikl/ *n.m.* article; (*comm.*) item, article.

articul|er /artikyle/ *v.t.* articulate. **~ation** *n.f.* articulation; (*anat.*) joint.

artificiel, ~le /artifisjɛl/ *a.* artificial. **~lement** *adv.* artificially.

artisan /artizɑ̃/ *n.m.* artisan, craftsman. **~al** (*m. pl.* **~aux**) /-anal, -o/ *a.* of *ou* by craftsmen, craft; (*amateur*) home-made. **~at** /-ana/ *n.m.* craft; (*classe*) artisans.

artist|e /artist/ *n.m./f.* artist. **~ique** *a.* artistic.

as¹ /a/ *voir* **avoir**.

as² /ɑs/ *n.m.* ace.

ascendant /asɑ̃dɑ̃/ *n.m.* influence. **~s**, ancestors.

ascenseur /asɑ̃sœr/ *n.m.* lift; (*Amer.*) elevator.

aseptis|er /asɛptize/ *v.t.* disinfect; (*stériliser*) sterilize. **~é** (*péj.*) sanitized.

asiatique /azjatik/ *a. & n.m./f.* Asian

Asie /azi/ *n.f.* Asia.

asile /azil/ *n.m.* refuge; (*pol.*) asylum; (*pour malades, vieillards*) home.

aspect /aspɛ/ *n.m.* appearance; (*fig.*) aspect. **à l'~ de**, at the sight of.

asperge /aspɛrʒ/ *n.f.* asparagus.

asperger /aspɛrʒe/ *v.t.* spray.

asphalte /asfalt/ *n.m.* asphalt.

asphyxie /asfiksi/ *n.f.* suffocation.

asphyxier /asfiksje/ *v.t.*, **s'~** *v. pr.* suffocate, asphyxiate; (*fig.*) stifle.

aspirateur /aspiratœr/ *n.m.* vacuum cleaner.

aspir|er /aspire/ *v.t.* inhale; (*liquide*) suck up.

aspirine /aspirin/ *n.f.* aspirin.

assaillir /asajir/ *v.t.* assail.

assainir /asenir/ *v.t.* clean up.

assaisonn|er /asɛzɔne/ *v.t.* season. **~ement** *n.m.* seasoning.

assassin /asasɛ̃/ *n.m.* murderer; (*pol.*) assassin.

assassin|er /asasine/ *v.t.* murder; (*pol.*) assassinate. **~at** *n.m.* murder; (*pol.*) assassination.

assaut /aso/ *n.m.* assault, onslaught.

assemblée /asɑ̃ble/ *n.f.* meeting; (*gens réunis*) gathering; (*pol.*) assembly.

assembl|er /asɑ̃ble/ *v.t.* assemble, put together; (*réunir*) gather. **s'~er** *v. pr.* gather, assemble. **~age** *n.m.* assembly; (*combinaison*) collection; (*techn.*) joint.

asseoir† /aswar/ *v.t.* sit (down), seat; (*affermir*) establish; (*baser*) base. **s'~** *v. pr.* sit (down).

assez /ase/ *adv.* enough; (*plutôt*) quite, fairly. **~ grand/rapide** *etc.*, big/fast/*etc.* enough (**pour,** to). **~ de**, enough. **j'en ai ~ (de)**, I've had enough (of).

assid|u /asidy/ *a.* (*zèle*) assiduous; (*régulier*) regular. **~u auprès de**, attentive to. **~uité** /-ɥite/ *n.f.* assiduousness; regularity. **~ûment** *adv.* assiduously.

assiéger /asjeʒe/ *v.t.* besiege.

assiette /asjɛt/ *n.f.* plate; (*équilibre*) seat. **~ anglaise**, assorted cold meats. **~ creuse/plate**, soup-/dinner-plate.

assimil|er /asimile/ *v.t.*, **s'~er** *v. pr.* assimilate. **~er à**, liken to; (*classer*) class as. **~ation** *n.f.* assimilation; likening; classification.

assis, ~e /asi, -z/ *voir* **asseoir**. —*a.* sitting (down), seated.

assistance /asistãs/ *n.f.* audience; (*aide*) assistance. **l'A~** (**publique**), government child care service.

assistant, ~e /asistã, -t/ *n.m., f.* assistant; (*univ.*) assistant lecturer. **~s**, (*spectateurs*) members of the audience. **~ social, ~e sociale**, social worker.

assist|er /asiste/ *v.t.* assist. —*v.i.* **~er à**, attend, be (present) at; (*scène*) witness. **~é par ordinateur**, computer-assisted.

association /asɔsjasjɔ̃/ *n.f.* association.

associé, ~e /asɔsje/ *n.m., f.* partner, associate. —*a.* associate.

associer /asɔsje/ *v.t.* associate; (*mêler*) combine (**à**, with). **~ qn. à**, (*projet*) involve s.o. in; (*bénéfices*) give s.o. a share of. **s'~ à**, (*projet*) take part in.

assoiffé /aswafe/ *a.* thirsty.

assommer /asɔme/ *v.t.* knock out; (*tuer*) kill; (*animal*) stun; (*fig.*) overwhelm; (*ennuyer: fam.*) bore.

assorti /asɔrti/ *a.* matching (*objets variés*) assorted.

assort|ir /asɔrtir/ *v.t.* match (**à**, with, to). **~iment** *n.m.* assortment.

assoupir (s') /(s)asupir/ *v. pr.* doze off.

assouplir /asuplir/ *v.t.* make supple; (*fig.*) make flexible.

assourdir /asurdir/ *v.t.* (*personne*) deafen; (*bruit*) deaden.

assumer /asyme/ *v.t.* assume.

assurance /asyrãs/ *n.f.* (self-)assurance; (*garantie*) insurance;

(*contrat*) insurance. **~-maladie** *n.f.* health insurance. **~s sociales**, National Insurance. **~-vie** *n.f.* life assurance.

assuré, ~e /asyre/ *a.* certain, assured; (*sûr de soi*) (self-)confident, assured. —*n.m., f.* insured.

assur|er /asyre/ *v.t.* ensure; (*fournir*) provide; (*exécuter*) carry out; (*comm.*) insure; (*stabiliser*) steady. **~ à qn. que**, assure s.o. that. **~ la gestion de**, manage. **s'~ de/que**, make sure of/that. **~eur** /-œr/ *n.m.* insurer.

asthm|e /asm/ *n.m.* asthma. **~atique** *a. & n.m./f.* asthmatic.

asticot /astiko/ *n.m.* maggot.

astiquer /astike/ *v.t.* polish.

astringent, ~e /astrẽʒɑ̃, -t/ *a.* astringent.

astrolo|gie /astrɔlɔʒi/ *n.f.* astrology. **~gue** *n.m./f.* astrologer.

astronaute /astrɔnot/ *n.m./f.* astronaut.

astronom|ie /astrɔnɔmi/ *n.f.* astronomy. **~e** *n.m./f.* astronomer. **~ique** *a.* astronomical.

astuce /astys/ *n.f.* smartness; (*truc*) trick.

astucieu|x, ~se /astysjø, -z/ *a.* smart, clever.

atelier /atəlje/ *n.m.* workshop; (*de peintre*) studio.

athé|e /ate/ *n.m./f.* atheist. —*a.* atheistic. **~isme** *n.m.* atheism

athl|ète /atlɛt/ *n.m./f.* athlete. **~étique** *a.* athletic. **~étisme** *n.m.* athletics.

atlantique /atlãtik/ *a.* Atlantic. —*n.m.* **A~**, Atlantic (Ocean).

atlas /atlɑs/ *n.m.* atlas.

atmosph|ère /atmɔsfɛr/ *n.f.* atmosphere. **~érique** *a.* atmospheric.

atome /atom/ *n.m.* atom.

atomique /atɔmik/ *a.* atomic.

atomiseur /atɔmizœr/ *n.m.* spray.

atout /atu/ *n.m.* trump (card); (*avantage*) great asset.

atroc|e /atrɔs/ *a.* atrocious. **~ité** *n.f.* atrocity.

attabler (s') /(s)atable/ *v. pr.* sit down at table.

attachant, ~e /ataʃɑ̃, -t/ *a.* likeable.

attache /ataʃ/ *n.f.* (*agrafe*) fastener; (*lien*) tie.

attaché /ataʃe/ *a.* être **~ à**, (*aimer*) be attached to. —*n.m., f.* (*pol.*) attaché. **~-case** *n.m.* attaché case.

attacher /ataʃe/ *v.t.* tie (up); (*ceinture, robe, etc.*) fasten; (*étiquette*) attach. **~ à**, (*attribuer à*) attach to. **~ à**, (*culin.*) stick. **s'~ à**, (*se lier à*) become attached to; (*se consacrer à*) apply o.s. to.

attaque /atak/ *n.f.* attack. **~ (cérébrale)**, stroke. **il va en faire une ~**, he'll have a fit. **~ à main armée**, armed attack.

attaquer /atake/ *v.t./i.*, **s'~ à**, attack; (*problème, sujet*) tackle.

attarder (s') /(s)atarde/ *v. pr.* linger.

atteindre† /atɛ̃dr/ *v.t.* reach; (*blesser*) hit; (*affecter*) affect.

atteint, ~e /atɛ̃, -t/ *a.* **~ de**, suffering from.

atteinte /atɛ̃t/ *n.f.* attack (**à**, on). **porter ~ à**, make an attack on.

attelle /atɛl/ *n.f.* splint.

attendant (en) /(ɑ̃n)atɑ̃dɑ̃/ *adv.* meanwhile.

attendre /atɑ̃dr/ *v.t.* wait for; (*bébé*) expect; (*être le sort de*) await; (*escompter*) expect. —*v.i.* wait. **~ que qn. fasse**, wait for s.o. to do. **s'~ à**, expect.

attendr|ir /atɑ̃drir/ *v.t.* move to pity. **s'~ir** *v. pr.* be moved to pity. **~issant, ~issante** *a.* moving.

attendu /atɑ̃dy/ *a.* (*escompté*) expected; (*espéré*) long-awaited. **~ que**, considering that.

attentat /atɑ̃ta/ *n.m.* murder attempt. **~ (à la bombe)**, (bomb) attack.

attente /atɑ̃t/ *n.f.* wait(ing); (*espoir*) expectation.

attenter /atɑ̃te/ *v.i.* **~ à**, make an attempt on; (*fig.*) violate.

attenti|f, ~ve /atɑ̃tif, -v/ *a.* attentive; (*scrupuleux*) careful. **~f à**, mindful of; (*soucieux*) careful of. **~vement** *adv.* attentively.

attention /atɑ̃sjɔ̃/ *n.f.* attention; (*soin*) care. **~ (à)!**, watch out (for)! **faire ~ à**, (*professeur*) pay attention to; (*marche*) mind. **faire ~ à faire**, be careful to do.

atténuer /atenɥe/ *v.t.* (*violence*) tone down; (*douleur*) ease; (*faute*) mitigate. **s'~** *v. pr.* subside.

atterr|ir /aterir/ *v.i.* land. **~issage** *n.m.* landing.

attestation /atɛstasjɔ̃/ *n.f.* certificate.

attester /atɛste/ *v.t.* testify to. **~ que**, testify that.

attirail /atiraj/ *n.m.* (*fam.*) gear.

attirance /atirɑ̃s/ *n.f.* attraction.

attirant, ~e /atirɑ̃, -t/ *a.* attractive.

attirer /atire/ *v.t.* draw, attract; (*causer*) bring. **s'~** *v. pr.* bring upon o.s.; (*amis*) win.

attitude /atityd/ *n.f.* attitude; (*maintien*) bearing.

attrait /atrɛ/ *n.m.* attraction.

attraper /atrape/ *v.t.* catch; (*habitude, style*) pick up; (*duper*) take in; (*gronder: fam.*) tell off.

attrayant, ~e /atrɛjɑ̃, -t/ *a.* attractive.

attrib|uer /atribɥe/ *v.t.* award; (*donner*) assign; (*imputer*) attribute. **~utions** *n.f. pl.* attributions.

attrister /atriste/ *v.t.* sadden.

attroupe|r (s') /(s)atrupe/ *v. pr.* gather. **~ement** *n.m.* crowd.

au /o/ *voir* à.

aubaine /obɛn/ *n.f.* (stroke of) good fortune.

aube /ob/ *n.f.* dawn, daybreak.

aubépine /obepin/ *n.f.* hawthorn.

auberg|e /obɛrʒ/ *n.f.* inn. **~e de jeunesse,** youth hostel. **~iste** *n.m./f.* innkeeper.

aubergine /obɛrʒin/ *n.f.* aubergine; (*Amer.*) egg-plant.

aucun, ~e /okœ, okyn/ *a.* no, not any; (*positif*) any. —*pron.* none, not any; (*positif*) any. **~ des deux,** neither of the two.

audace /odas/ *n.f.* daring; (*impudence*) audacity.

audacieu|x, ~se /odasjø, -z/ *a.* daring.

au-delà /odla/ *adv.,* **~ de** *prép.* beyond.

au-dessous /odsu/ *adv.,* **~ de** *prép.* below; (*couvert par*) under.

au-dessus /odsy/ *adv.,* **~ de** *prép.* above.

au-devant (de) /odvã(də)/ *prép.* **aller ~ de qn.,** go to meet s.o.

audience /odjãs/ *n.f.* audience; (*d'un tribunal*) hearing; (*intérêt*) attention.

audio-visuel, ~le /odjovizɥɛl/ *a.* audio-visual.

audi|teur, ~trice /oditœr, -tris/ *n.m., f.* listener.

audition /odisjɔ/ *n.f.* hearing; (*théâtre, mus.*) audition.

auditoire /oditwar/ *n.m.* audience.

auditorium /oditɔrjɔm/ *n.m.* (*mus., radio*) recording studio.

augment|er /ogmãte/ *v.t./i.* increase; (*employé*) increase the pay of. **~ation** *n.f.* increase. **~ation (de salaire),** (pay) rise; (*Amer.*) raise.

augure /ogyr/ *n.m.* (*devin*) oracle. **être de bon/mauvais ~,** be a good/bad sign.

aujourd'hui /oʒurdɥi/ *adv.* today.

aumône /omon/ *n.f.* alms.

auparavant /oparavã/ *adv.* before(hand).

auprès (de) /oprɛ(də)/ *prép.* by, next to; (*comparé à*) compared with; (*s'adressant à*) to.

auquel /okɛl/ *voir* **lequel.**

aura, aurait /ora, orɛ/ *voir* **avoir.**

auréole /oreɔl/ *n.f.* halo.

aurore /orɔr/ *n.f.* dawn.

ausculter /oskylte/ *v.t.* examine with a stethoscope.

aussi /osi/ *adv.* too, also; (*comparaison*) as; (*tellement*) so. —*conj.* (*donc*) therefore. **~ bien que,** as well as.

aussitôt /osito/ *adv.* immediately. **~ que,** as soon as. **~ arrivé/levé/***etc.***,** as soon as one has arrived/got up/*etc.*

aust|ère /ostɛr/ *a.* austere. **~érité** *n.f.* austerity.

Australie /ɔstrali/ *n.f.* Australia.

australien, ~ne /ɔstraljɛ̃, -jɛn/ *a. & n.m., f.* Australian.

autant /otã/ *adv.* (*travailler, manger, etc.*) as much (que, as). **~ (de),** (*quantité*) as much (que, as); (*nombre*) as many (que, as); (*tant*) so much; so many. **~ faire,** one had better do. **d'~ plus que,** all the more since. **en faire ~,** do the same. **pour ~,** for all that.

auteur /otœr/ *n.m.* author. **l'~ du crime,** the person who committed the crime.

authentifier /otãtifje/ *v.t.* authenticate.

authenti|que /otãtik/ *a.* authentic. **~cité** *n.f.* authenticity.

auto /oto/ *n.f.* car. **~s tamponneuses,** dodgems, bumper cars.

auto- /oto/ *préf.* self-, auto-.

autobiographie /otɔbjɔgrafi/ *n.f.* autobiography.

autobus /otɔbys/ *n.m.* bus.

autocar /otɔkar/ *n.m.* coach.

autocuiseur /otɔkyizœr/ *n.* pressure cooker.

autodéfense /otɔdefɑ̃s/ *n.f.* self-defence.

autodidacte /otɔdidakt/ *a.* & *n.m./f.* self-taught (person).

auto-école /otɔekɔl/ *n.f.* driving school.

automatique /otɔmatik/ *a.* automatic. **~ment** *adv.* automatically.

automne /otɔn/ *n.m.* autumn; (*Amer.*) fall.

automobil|e /otɔmɔbil/ *a.* motor, car. —*n.f.* (motor) car. **l'~e**, (*sport*) motoring. **~iste** *n.m./f.* motorist.

autonom|e /otɔnɔm/ *a.* autonomous. **~ie** *n.f.* autonomy.

autopsie /otɔpsi/ *n.f.* post-mortem, autopsy.

autoradio /otɔradjo/ *n.m.* car radio.

autorisation /otɔrizasjɔ̃/ *n.f.* permission, authorization; (*permis*) permit.

autoriser /otɔrize/ *v.t.* authorize, permit; (*rendre possible*) allow (of).

autoritaire /otɔriter/ *a.* authoritarian.

autorité /otɔrite/ *n.f.* authority.

autoroute /otɔrut/ *n.f.* motorway; (*Amer.*) highway.

auto-stop /otɔstɔp/ *n.m.* hitchhiking. **faire de l'~**, hitch-hike. **prendre en ~**, give a lift to. **~peur, ~peuse** *n.m., f.* hitch-hiker.

autour /otur/ *adv.,* **~ de** *prép.* around. **tout ~**, all around.

autre /otr/ *a.* other. **un ~ jour/etc.**, another day/etc. —*pron.*

un ~, une ~, another (one). **l'~**, the other (one). **les autres**, the others; (*autrui*) others. **d'~s**, (some) others. **l'un l'~**, each other. **l'un et l'~**, both of them. **~ chose/part**, sth./somewhere else. **qn./rien d'~**, s.o./nothing else. **quoi d'~?**, what else? **d'~ part**, on the other hand. **vous ~s Anglais**, you English. **d'un jour/etc. à l'~**, (*bientôt*) any day/etc. now. **entre ~s**, among other things.

autrefois /otrəfwa/ *adv.* in the past.

autrement /otrəmɑ̃/ *adv.* differently; (*sinon*) otherwise; (*plus*) far more. **~ dit**, in other words.

Autriche /otriʃ/ *n.f.* Austria.

autrichien, ~ne /otriʃjɛ̃, -jɛn/ *a.* & *n.m., f.* Austrian.

autruche /otryʃ/ *n.f.* ostrich.

aux /o/ *voir* **à**.

auquel|s, ~les /okɛl/ *voir* **lequel**.

aval (en) /(ɑ̃n)aval/ *adv.* downstream.

avalanche /avalɑ̃ʃ/ *n.f.* avalanche.

avaler /avale/ *v.t.* swallow.

avance /avɑ̃s/ *n.f.* advance; (*sur un concurrent*) lead. **~ (de fonds)**, advance. **à l'~, d'~**, in advance. **en ~**, early; (*montre*) fast. **en ~ (sur)**, (*menant*) ahead (of).

avancement /avɑ̃smɑ̃/ *n.m.* promotion.

avanc|er /avɑ̃se/ *v.i.* move forward, advance; (*travail*) make progress; (*montre*) be fast; (*faire saillie*) jut out. —*v.t.* (*argent*) advance; (*montre*) put forward. **s'~er** *v. pr.* move forward, advance; (*se hasarder*) commit o.s. **~é, ~ée** *a.* advanced; *n.f.* projection.

avant /avɑ̃/ *prép* & *adv.* before. —*a. invar.* front. —*n.m.* front;

(*football*) forward. ~ de faire, before doing. ~ qu'il (ne) fasse, before he does. en ~, (*mouvement*) forward. en ~ (de), (*position, temps*) in front of. ~ peu, before long. ~ tout, above all. bien ~ dans, very deep(ly) ou far into. ~-dernier, dernière &. *n.m.*, *f.* last but one. ~-guerre *n.m.* pre-war period. ~-hier /-tjɛr/ *adv.* the day before yesterday. ~-veille *n.f.* two days before.

avantag|e /avɑ̃taʒ/ *n.m.* advantage; (*comm.*) benefit. ~er *v.t.* favour; (*embellir*) show off to advantage.

avantageu|x, ~se /avɑ̃taʒø, -z/ *a.* attractive.

avar|e /avar/ *a.* miserly. —*n.m./f.* miser. ~ice *n.f.* avarice.

avec /avɛk/ *prép.* with; (*envers*) towards. —*adv.* (*fam.*) with it ou them.

avènement /avɛnmɑ̃/ *n.m.* advent; (*d'un roi*) accession.

avenir /avnir/ *n.m.* future. à l'~, in future. d'~, with (future) prospects.

aventur|e /avɑ̃tyr/ *n.f.* adventure; (*sentimentale*) affair. ~eux, ~euse *a.* adventurous; (*hasardeux*) risky. ~ier, ~ière *n.m.*, *f.* adventurer.

aventurer (s') /(s)avɑ̃tyre/ *v. pr.* venture.

avenue /avny/ *n.f.* avenue.

averse /avɛrs/ *n.f.* shower.

avert|ir /avɛrtir/ *v.t.* inform; (*mettre en garde, menacer*) warn. ~i *a.* informed. ~issement *n.m.* warning.

avertisseur /avɛrtisœr/ *n.m.* (*auto.*) horn.

aveu (*pl.* ~x) /avø/ *n.m.* confession. de l'~ de, by the admission of.

aveugl|e /avœgl/ *a.* blind. —*n.m./f.* blind man, blind woman. ~er *v.t.* blind.

aviation /avjɑsjɔ̃/ *n.f.* (*industrie*) aviation; (*mil.*) air force.

avid|e /avid/ *a.* greedy (de, for); (*anxieux*) eager (de, for). ~e de faire, eager to do. ~ité *n.f.* greed; eagerness.

avion /avjɔ̃/ *n.m.* plane, aeroplane, aircraft; (*Amer.*) airplane.

aviron /avirɔ̃/ *n.m.* oar. l'~, (*sport*) rowing.

avis /avi/ *n.m.* opinion; (*renseignement*) notification; (*comm.*) advice. à mon ~, in my opinion. changer d'~, change one's mind.

avocat¹, ~e /avɔka, -t/ *n.m.*, *f.* barrister; (*Amer.*) attorney; (*fig.*) advocate.

avocat² /avɔka/ *n.m.* (*fruit*) avocado (pear).

avoine /avwan/ *n.f.* oats.

avoir† /avwar/ *v. aux.* have. —*v.t.* have; (*obtenir*) get; (*duper: fam.*) take in. —*n.m.* assets. je n'ai pas de café, I haven't (got) any coffee; (*Amer.*) I don't have any coffee. est-ce que tu as du café?, have you (got) any coffee?; (*Amer.*) do you have any coffee? ~ à faire, have to do. tu n'as qu'à l'appeler, all you have to do is call her. ~ chaud/faim/*etc.*, be hot/hungry/*etc.* ~ dix/*etc.* ans, be ten/*etc.* years old. ~ lieu, take place. en ~ assez, have had enough. en ~ pour une minute/*etc.*, be busy for a minute/*etc.* il en a pour cent francs, it will cost him one hundred francs. qu'est-ce que vous avez?, what is the matter with you? on m'a eu!, I've been had.

avort|er /avɔrte/ *v.i.* (*projet etc.*)

miscarry. **(se faire) ~er**, have an abortion. **~é** *a.* abortive. **~ement** *n.m. (méd.)* abortion.

avouer /avwe/ *v.t.* confess (to). —*v.i.* confess.

avril /avril/ *n.m.* April.

axe /aks/ *n.m.* axis; *(essieu)* axle. **~ (routier)**, main road.

ayant /εjᾶ/ *voir* avoir.

azote /azɔt/ *n.m.* nitrogen.

B

baba /baba/ *n.m.* **~ (au rhum)**, rum baba.

babiole /babjɔl/ *n.f.* knick-knack.

bâbord /babɔr/ *n.m.* port (side).

baby-foot /babifut/ *n.m. invar.* table football.

baby-sitt|er /bebisitœr/ *n.m./f.* baby-sitter. **~ing** *n.m.* **faire du ~ing**, babysit.

bac[1] /bak/ *n.m.* = baccalauréat.

bac[2] /bak/ *n.m. (bateau)* ferry; *(récipient)* tub; *(plus petit)* tray.

baccalauréat /bakalɔrea/ *n.m.* school leaving certificate.

bâch|e /baʃ/ *n.f.* tarpaulin. **~er** *v.t.* cover (with a tarpaulin).

bacheli|er, ~ière /baʃəlje, -jɛr/ *n.m., f.* holder of the *baccalauréat*.

bachot /baʃo/ *n.m. (fam.)* = baccalauréat.

bâcler /bakle/ *v.t.* botch (up).

bactérie /bakteri/ *n.f.* bacterium.

badiner /badine/ *v.i.* joke **(sur, avec,** about).

badminton /badmintɔn/ *n.m.* badminton.

baffe /baf/ *n.f. (fam.)* slap.

baffle /bafl/ *n.m.* speaker.

bafouer /bafwe/ *v.t.* scoff at.

bafouiller /bafuje/ *v.t./i.* stammer.

bagage /bagaʒ/ *n.m.* bag; *(fig.)* (store of) knowledge. **~s**, luggage, baggage. **~s à main**, hand luggage.

bagarr|e /bagar/ *n.f.* fight. **~er** *v.i.*, **se ~er** *v. pr.* fight.

bagnard /baɲar/ *n.m.* convict.

bagnole /baɲɔl/ *n.f. (fam.)* car.

bagu|e /bag/ *n.f. (anneau)* ring. **~er** *v.t.* ring.

baguette /bagɛt/ *n.f.* stick; *(de chef d'orchestre)* baton; *(chinoise)* chopstick; *(magique)* wand; *(pain)* stick of bread. **~ de tambour**, drumstick.

baie /bɛ/ *n.f. (géog.)* bay; *(fruit)* berry. **~ (vitrée)**, picture window.

baign|er /beɲe/ *v.t.* bathe; *(enfant)* bath. —*v.i.* **~er dans**, soak in; *(être enveloppé dans)* be steeped in. **se ~er** *v. pr.* go swimming *(ou)* bathing. **~é de**, bathed in; *(sang)* soaked in. **~ade** /bɛɲad/ *n.f.* bathing, swimming. **~eur, ~euse** /bɛɲœr, -øz/ *n.m., f.* bather.

baignoire /beɲwar/ *n.f.* bath(-tub).

bail *(pl.* **baux)** /baj, bo/ *n.m.* lease.

bâill|er /baje/ *v.i.* yawn. **~ement** *n.m.* yawn.

bailleur /bajœr/ *n.m.* **~ de fonds**, *(comm.)* backer.

bain /bɛ̃/ *n.m.* bath; *(de mer)* bathe. **~(s) de soleil**, sunbathing. **~marie** *(pl.* **~s-marie)** *n.m.* double boiler. **~ de bouche**, mouthwash. **mettre qn. dans le ~**, *(au courant)* put s.o. in the picture.

baiser /beze/ *n.m.* kiss. —*v.t. (main)* kiss; *(fam.)* screw.

baisse /bɛs/ *n.f.* fall, drop. **en ~**, falling.

baisser /bese/ *v.t.* lower; *(radio, lampe, etc.)* turn down. —*v.i.* go down, fall; (santé, forces) fail. se ~ v. pr. bend down.

bal (pl. ~s) /bal/ n.m. dance; (habillé) ball.

balad|e /balad/ n.f. stroll; (en auto) drive. ~er v.t. take for a stroll. se ~er v. pr. (go for a) stroll. se ~er (en auto), go for a drive.

baladeur /baladœr/ n.m. personal stereo.

balai /balɛ/ n.m. broom.

balance /balɑ̃s/ n.f. scales. la B~, Libra.

balancer /balɑ̃se/ v.t. swing; (doucement) sway; (lancer: fam.) chuck; (jeter: fam.) chuck out. —v.i., se ~ v. pr. swing; sway.

balancier /balɑ̃sje/ n.m. (d'horloge) pendulum.

balançoire /balɑ̃swar/ n.f. swing; (bascule) see-saw.

balay|er /balɛje/ v.t. sweep (up); (chasser) sweep away; (se débarrasser de) sweep aside. ~age n.m. sweeping; (cheveux) highlights. ~eur, ~euse n.m., f. road sweeper.

balcon /balkɔ̃/ n.m. balcony; (théâtre) dress circle.

baleine /balɛn/ n.f. whale.

balis|e /baliz/ n.f. beacon; (bouée) buoy; (auto.) (road) sign. ~er v.t. mark out (with beacons); (route) signpost.

balistique /balistik/ a. ballistic.

ballast /balast/ n.m. ballast.

balle /bal/ n.f. (projectile) bullet; (sport) ball; (paquet) bale.

ballet /balɛ/ n.m. ballet.

ballon /balɔ̃/ n.m. balloon; (sport) ball. ~ de football, football.

ballottage /balɔtaʒ/ n.m. second ballot (due to indecisive result).

balnéaire /balneɛr/ a. seaside.

balustrade /balystrad/ n.f. railing(s).

bambou /bɑ̃bu/ n.m. bamboo.

ban /bɑ̃/ n.m. round of applause. ~s, (de mariage) banns.

banal (m. pl. ~s) /banal/ a. commonplace, banal. ~ité n.f. banality.

banane /banan/ n.f. banana.

banc /bɑ̃/ n.m. bench; (de poissons) shoal. ~ des accusés, dock.

bancaire /bɑ̃kɛr/ a. banking; (chèque) bank.

bancal (m. pl. ~s) /bɑ̃kal/ a. wobbly; (raisonnement) shaky.

bandage /bɑ̃daʒ/ n.m. bandage.

bande¹ /bɑ̃d/ n.f. (de papier etc.) strip; (rayure) stripe; (de film) reel; (radio) band; (pansement) bandage. ~ (magnétique), tape. ~ dessinée, comic strip. ~ sonore, sound-track.

bande² /bɑ̃d/ n.f. (groupe) bunch, band, gang.

bandeau (pl. ~x) /bɑ̃do/ n.m. headband; (sur les yeux) blindfold.

bander /bɑ̃de/ v.t. bandage. ~ les yeux à, blindfold.

bandit /bɑ̃di/ n.m. bandit. ~isme /-tism/ n.m. crime.

bandoulière (en) /(ɑ̃)bɑ̃duljɛr/ adv. across one's shoulder.

banlieu|e /bɑ̃ljø/ n.f. suburbs. de ~e, suburban. ~sard, ~sarde /-zar, -zard/ n.m., f. (suburban) commuter.

bannière /banjɛr/ n.f. banner.

bannir /banir/ v.t. banish.

banque /bɑ̃k/ n.f. bank; (activité) banking. ~ d'affaires, merchant bank.

banqueroute /bɑ̃krut/ n.f. (fraudulent) bankruptcy.

banquet /bɑ̃kɛ/ n.m. dinner; (fastueux) banquet.

banquette /bɑ̃kɛt/ *n.f.* seat.

banquier /bɑ̃kje/ *n.m.* banker.

baptême /batɛm/ *n.m.* baptism; christening; **~iser** *v.t.* baptize, christen; (*appeler*) christen.

bar /bar/ *n.m.* (*lieu*) bar.

baraque /barak/ *n.f.* hut, shed; (*boutique*) stall; (*maison: fam.*) house. **~ments** *n.m. pl.* huts.

baratin /baratɛ̃/ *n.m.* (*fam.*) sweet *ou* smooth talk.

barbar|e /barbar/ *a.* barbaric.

barbe /barb/ *n.f.* beard. **~ à papa**, candy-floss; (*Amer.*) cotton candy.

barbecue /barbəkju/ *n.m.* barbecue.

barbelé /barbəle/ *a.* **fil ~**, barbed wire.

barbiche /barbiʃ/ *n.f.* goatee.

barbiturique /barbityrik/ *n.m.* barbiturate.

barboter /barbɔte/ *v.i.* paddle, splash.

barbouill|er /barbuje/ *v.t.* (*souiller*) smear; (*griffonner*) scribble. **avoir l'estomac ~é** *ou* **se sentir ~é** feel liverish.

barbu /barby/ *a.* bearded.

barème /barɛm/ *n.m.* list, table; (*échelle*) scale.

bariolé /barjɔle/ *a.* motley.

barman /barman/ *n.m.* barman; (*Amer.*) bartender.

baromètre /barɔmɛtr/ *n.m.* barometer.

baroque /barɔk/ *a.* baroque.

barque /bark/ *n.f.* (small) boat.

barrage /baraʒ/ *n.m.* dam; (*sur route*) road block.

barre /bar/ *n.f.* bar; (*trait*) line, stroke; (*naut.*) helm.

barreau (*pl.* **~x**) /baro/ *n.m.* bar; (*d'échelle*) rung. **le ~**, (*jurid.*) the bar.

barrer /bare/ *v.t.* block; (*porte*) bar; (*rayer*) cross out; (*naut.*) steer. **se ~** *v. pr.* (*fam.*) hop it.

barrette /barɛt/ *n.f.* (hair-)slide.

barricad|e /barikad/ *n.f.* barricade. **~er** *v.t.* barricade. **se ~er** *v. pr.* barricade o.s.

barrière /barjɛr/ *n.f.* (*porte*) gate; (*clôture*) fence; (*obstacle*) barrier.

baryton /baritɔ̃/ *n.m.* baritone.

bas, basse /bɑ, bɑs/ *a.* low; (*action*) base. —*n.m.* bottom; (*chaussette*) stocking. —*adv.* low. **à ~**, down with. **en ~**, down below; (*dans une maison*) downstairs. **en ~ âge**, young. **en ~ de**, at the bottom of. **plus ~**, further *ou* lower down. **~-côté** *n.m.* (*de route*) verge; (*Amer.*) shoulder. **~ de casse** *n.m. invar.* lower case.

bascule /baskyl/ *n.f.* (*balance*) scales. **cheval/fauteuil à ~**, rocking-horse/-chair.

basculer /baskyle/ *v.t./i.* topple over; (*benne*) tip up.

base /baz/ *n.f.* base; (*fondement*) basis; (*pol.*) rank and file. **de ~**, basic.

baser /baze/ *v.t.* base. **se ~ sur**, base o.s. on.

basilic /bazilik/ *n.m.* basil.

basilique /bazilik/ *n.f.* basilica.

basket(-ball) /baskɛt(bɔl)/ *n.m.* basketball.

basque /bask/ *a. & n.m./f.* Basque.

basse /bɑs/ *voir* **bas**.

basse-cour (*pl.* **basses-cours**) /baskur/ *n.f.* farmyard.

bassesse /basɛs/ *n.f.* baseness; (*action*) base act.

bassin /basɛ̃/ *n.m.* bowl; (*pièce d'eau*) pond; (*rade*) dock; (*géog.*) basin; (*anat.*) pelvis. **~ houiller**, coalfield.

bat /ba/ *voir* **battre**.

bataill|e /bataj/ *n.f.* battle; (*fig.*) fight. **~er** *v.i.* fight.

bataillon /batajɔ̃/ n.m. battalion.

bateau (pl. ~x) /bato/ n.m. boat. ~-mouche (pl. ~x-mouches) n.m. sightseeing boat.

bâti /bɑti/ a. **bien** ~, well-built.

bâtiment /bɑtimɑ̃/ n.m. building; (navire) vessel; (industrie) building trade.

bâtir /bɑtir/ v.t. build.

bâtisse /bɑtis/ n.f. (péj.) building.

bâton /bɑtɔ̃/ n.m. stick.

battant /batɑ̃/ n.m. (vantail) flap. **porte à deux** ~s, double door.

battement /batmɑ̃/ n.m. (de cœur) beat(ing); (temps) interval.

batterie /batri/ n.f. (mil., électr.) battery; (mus.) drums. ~ **de cuisine**, pots and pa~s.

batteur /batœr/ n.m. (mus.) drummer; (culin.) whisk.

battre† /batr/ v.t./i. beat; (cartes) shuffle; (faire du bruit) bang. **se** ~ v. pr. fight. ~ **des ailes**, flap its wings. ~ **des mains**, clap. ~ **pavillon britannique**/etc., fly the British/etc. flag. ~ **son plein**, be in full swing.

battue /baty/ n.f. (chasse) beat; (de police) search.

bavard, ~**e** /bavar, -d/ a. talkative. —n.m., f. chatterbox.

bavard|er /bavarde/ v.i. chat; (jacasser) chatter, gossip. ~**age** n.m. chatter, gossip.

bav|e /bav/ n.f. dribble, slobber; (de limace) slime. ~**er** v.i. dribble, slobber.

bavette /bavɛt/ n.f., ~**oir** n.m. bib.

bazar /bazar/ n.m. bazaar; (objets: fam.) clutter.

BCBG abrév. (bon chic bon genre) posh.

BD abrév. (bande dessinée) comic strip.

béant, ~**e** /beɑ̃, -t/ a. gaping.

beau ou **bel***, **belle** (m. pl. ~x) /bo, bɛl/ a. fine, beautiful; (femme) beautiful; (homme) handsome; (grand) big. ~, n.m.; (sport) deciding game. **au** ~ **milieu**, right in the middle. **bel et bien**, well and truly. **on a** ~ **essayer/insister**/etc., however much one tries/insists/etc., it is no use trying/insisting/etc. ~**x-arts** n.m. pl. fine arts. ~**frère** (pl. ~**x-frères**) n.m. brother-in-law. ~**père** (pl. ~**x-pères**) n.m. father-in-law; stepfather. ~**x-parents** n.m. pl. parents-in-law.

beaucoup /boku/ adv. a lot, very much. —pron. many (people). ~ **de**, (nombre) many; (quantité) a lot of. ~ **plus**/etc., much more/etc. ~ **trop**, much too much. **de** ~, by far.

beauté /bote/ n.f. beauty.

bébé /bebe/ n.m. baby. ~-**éprouvette**, test-tube baby.

bec /bɛk/ n.m. beak; (de bouilloire) spout; (bouche: fam.) mouth.

bécane /bekan/ n.f. (fam.) bike.

bécasse /bekas/ n.f. woodcock.

bêche /bɛʃ/ n.f. spade.

bêcher /beʃe/ v.t. dig.

bécoter /bekɔte/ v.t., **se** ~ v. pr. (fam.) kiss.

becquée /beke/ n.f. **donner la** ~ **à**, (oiseau) feed; (fig.) spoonfeed.

bedonnant, ~**e** /bədɔnɑ̃, -t/ a. paunchy.

beffroi /befrwa/ n.m. belfry.

bégayer /begeje/ v.t./i. stammer.

bègue /bɛg/ n.m./f. stammerer. **être** ~, stammer.

béguin /begɛ̃/ n.m. **avoir le** ~ **pour**, (fam.) have a crush on.

beige /bɛʒ/ a. & n.m. beige.

beignet /bɛɲɛ/ n.m. fritter.

bel /bɛl/ voir **beau**.

bêler /bele/ v.i. bleat.

belette /bəlɛt/ n.f. weasel.

belge /bɛlʒ/ a. & n.m./f. Belgian.

Belgique /bɛlʒik/ n.f. Belgium.
bélier /belje/ n.m. ram. **le B~**,
Aries.
belle /bɛl/ voir beau.
belle-fille (pl. **~s-filles**) /bɛlfij/
n.f. daughter-in-law; (remariage)
stepdaughter. **~-mère** (pl. **~s-
mères**) n.f. mother-in-law; step-
mother. **~-sœur** (pl. **~s-sœurs**)
n.f. sister-in-law.
bémol /bemɔl/ n.m. (mus.) flat.
bénédiction /benediksjɔ̃/ n.f. bless-
ing.
bénéfice /benefis/ n.m. (gain)
profit; (avantage) benefit.
bénéficiaire /benefisjɛr/ n.m./f.
beneficiary.
bénéficier /benefisje/ v.i. **~ de**,
benefit from.
bénéfique /benefik/ a. beneficial.
Bénélux /benelyks/ n.m. Benelux.
bénévole /benevɔl/ a. voluntary.
bén|in, ~igne /benɛ̃, -in/ a.
mild, slight; (tumeur) benign.
bénir /benir/ v.t. bless.
bénitier /benitje/ n.m. stoup.
benne /bɛn/ n.f. (de grue) scoop;
(amovible) skip. **~ (bas-
culante)**, dump truck.
berceau (pl. **~x**) /bɛrso/ n.m.
cradle.
bercer /bɛrse/ v.t. (balancer) rock.
berceuse /bɛrsøz/ n.f. lullaby.
béret /berɛ/ n.m. beret.
berge /bɛrʒ/ n.f. (bord) bank.
berg|er, ~ère /bɛrʒe, -ɛr/ n.m., f.
shepherd, shepherdess.
berlingot /bɛrlɛ̃go/ n.m. boiled
sweet; (emballage) carton.
berne (en) /(ɑ̃)bɛrn/ adv. at half-
mast.
besogne /bəzɔɲ/ n.f. task, job,
chore.
besoin /bəzwɛ̃/ n.m. need. **avoir
~ de**, need. **au ~**, if need be.

bestiole /bɛstjɔl/ n.f. creepy-
crawly.
bétail /betaj/ n.m. farm animals.
bête[1] /bɛt/ n.f. animal. **~ noire**,
pet hate, pet peeve.
bête[2] /bɛt/ a. stupid. **~ment** adv.
stupidly.
bêtise /betiz/ n.f. stupidity;
(action) stupid thing.
béton /betɔ̃/ n.m. concrete. **~
armé**, reinforced concrete.
betterave /bɛtrav/ n.f. beetroot. **~
sucrière**, sugar-beet.
beur /bœr/ n.m./f. & a. (fam.)
young French North African.
beurr|e /bœr/ n.m. butter. **~er** v.t.
butter. **~ier** n.m. butter-dish.
~é, a. buttered; (fam.) drunk.
bévue /bevy/ n.f. blunder.
biais /bjɛ/ n.m. de **~, en ~**, at an
angle. **de ~**, (fig.) indirectly.
bibelot /biblo/ n.m. curio.
biberon /bibrɔ̃/ n.m. (feeding-)
bottle. **nourrir au ~**, bottle-
feed.
bible /bibl/ n.f. bible. **la B~**, the
Bible.
bibliographie /biblijɔgrafi/ n.f.
bibliography.
bibliophile /biblijɔfil/ n.m./f.
book-lover.
bibliothè|que /biblijɔtɛk/ n.f.
library; (meuble) bookcase;
~caire n.m./f. librarian.
biblique /biblik/ a. biblical.
bic /bik/ n.m. (P.) biro (P.).
bicarbonate /bikarbɔnat/ n.m. **~
(de soude)**, bicarbonate (of soda).
biceps /bisɛps/ n.m. biceps.
biche /biʃ/ n.f. doe.
bicyclette /bisiklɛt/ n.f. bicycle.
bidet /bidɛ/ n.m. bidet.
bidon /bidɔ̃/ n.m. can. —a. invar.
(fam.) phoney.
bidonville /bidɔ̃vil/ n.f. shanty
town.
bidule /bidyl/ n.m. (fam.) thing.

bielle /bjɛl/ n.f. connecting rod.

bien /bjɛ̃/ adv. well; (très) quite, very. —n.m. good; (patrimoine) possession. —a. invar. good; (passable) all right; (en forme) well; (à l'aise) comfortable; (beau) attractive; (respectable) nice, respectable. —conj. ~ que, (al)though. ~ que ce soit/qu' ça ait, although it is/it has. ~ du, (quantité) a lot of, much. ce n'est pas ~ de, it is not right to. ~ sûr, of course. ~s de consommation, consumer goods. **bien-être** n.m. well being.

bienfaisance /bjɛ̃fazɑ̃s/ n.f. fête de ~, fête.

bienfait /bjɛ̃fɛ/ n.m. (kind) favour; (avantage) benefit.

bienfai|teur, ~trice /bjɛ̃fɛtœr, -tris/ n.m., f. benefactor.

bientôt /bjɛ̃to/ adv. soon. à ~, see you soon.

bienveillan|t, ~te /bjɛ̃vɛjɑ̃, -t/ a. kind(ly). **~ce** n.f. kind(li)ness.

bienvenu, ~e /bjɛ̃vny/ a. welcome. —n.f. welcome.—n.m., f. être le ~, être la ~e, be welcome. **souhaiter la ~e à** q., welcome.

bière /bjɛr/ n.f. beer; (cercueil) coffin. ~ **blonde**, lager. ~ **brune**, stout, brown ale. ~ **pression**, draught beer.

bifteck /biftɛk/ n.m. steak.

bifur|quer /bifyrke/ v.i. branch off, fork. **~cation** n.f. fork, junction.

bigot, ~e /bigo, -ɔt/ n.m., f. religious fanatic. —a. over-pious.

bijou (pl. ~x) /biʒu/ n.m. jewel. **~terie** n.f. (boutique) jeweller's shop; (comm.) jewellery. **~tier, ~tière** n.m., f. jeweller.

bikini /bikini/ n.m. bikini.

bilan /bilɑ̃/ n.m. outcome; (d'une catastrophe) (casualty) toll; (comm.) balance sheet. **faire le ~ de,** assess. **~ de santé,** check-up.

bile /bil/ n.f. bile. **se faire de la ~,** (fam.) worry.

bilingue /bilɛ̃g/ a. bilingual.

billard /bijar/ n.m. billiards; (table) billiard-table.

bille /bij/ n.f. (d'enfant) marble.

billet /bijɛ/ n.m. ticket; (lettre) note; (article) column. ~ **(de banque),** (bank)note. ~ **d'aller et retour,** return ticket. ~ **aller simple,** single ticket.

billetterie /bijɛtri/ n.f. cash dispenser.

bimensuel, ~le /bimɑ̃sɥɛl/ a. fortnightly, bimonthly.

biochimie /bjɔʃimi/ n.f. biochemistry.

biodégradable /bjɔdegradabl/ a. biodegradable.

biograph|ie /bjɔgrafi/ n.f. biography. **~e** n.m./f. biographer.

biolog|ie /bjɔlɔʒi/ n.f. biology. **~ique** a. biological. **~iste** n.m./f. biologist.

bis /bis/ a.invar. (numéro) A, a. —n.m. & int. encore.

biscotte /biskɔt/ n.f. rusk.

biscuit /biskɥi/ n.m. (salé) biscuit; (Amer.) cracker; (sucré) biscuit; (Amer.) cookie.

bise[1] /biz/ n.f. (fam.) kiss.

bise[2] /biz/ n.f. (vent) north wind.

bison /bizɔ̃/ n.m. (American) buffalo, bison.

bisou /bizu/ n.m. (fam.) kiss.

bistouri /bisturi/ n.m. lancet.

bistro(t) /bistro/ n.m. café, bar.

bit /bit/ n.m. (comput.) bit.

bitume /bitym/ n.m. asphalt.

bizarre /bizar/ a. odd, peculiar. **~ment** adv. oddly. **~rie** n.f. peculiarity.

blafard, ~e /blafar, -d/ a. pale.

blague /blag/ n.f. joke. **~er** v.i. joke; v.t. tease.

blaireau /blɛro/ *n.m.* (*pl.* ∼**x**) shaving-brush; (*animal*) badger.

blâm|e /blɑm/ *n.m.* rebuke, blame. ∼**er** *v.t.* rebuke, blame.

blanc, blanche /blɑ̃, blɑ̃ʃ/ *a.* white; (*papier, page*) blank. —*n.m.* white; (*espace*) blank. —*n.m., f.* white man, white woman. —*n.f.* (*mus.*) minim. ∼ **(de poulet)**, breast. **le** ∼, (*linge*) whites. **laisser en** ∼, leave blank.

blancheur /blɑ̃ʃœr/ *n.f.* whiteness.

blanch|ir /blɑ̃ʃir/ *v.t.* whiten; (*linge*) launder; (*personne: fig.*) clear; (*culin.*) blanch. —*v.i.* turn white. ∼**ir (à la chaux)**, whitewash. —*v.i.* turn white. ∼**issage** *n.m.* laundering. ∼**isserie** *n.f.* laundry.

blasé /blaze/ *a.* blasé.

blasphème /blasfɛm/ *n.m.* blasphemy.

blatte /blat/ *n.f.* cockroach.

blazer /blɛzœr/ *n.m.* blazer.

blé /ble/ *n.m.* wheat.

bled /blɛd/ *n.m.* (*fam.*) dump, hole.

blême /blɛm/ *a.* (sickly) pale.

bless|er /blese/ *v.t.* injure, hurt; (*par balle*) wound; (*offenser*) hurt, wound. **se** ∼**er** *v. pr.* injure ou hurt o.s. ∼**é, ∼ée** *n.m., f.* casualty, injured person.

blessure /blesyr/ *n.f.* wound.

bleu /blø/ *a.* (*culin.*) very rare. ∼ **marine**, navy blue. —*n.m.* blue; (*contusion*) bruise. ∼**(s)**, (*vêtement*) overalls.

bleuet /bløɛ/ *n.m.* cornflower.

blindé /blɛ̃de/ *a.* armoured; (*fig.*) immune (**contre**, to); *n.m.* armoured car, tank.

bloc /blɔk/ *n.m.* block; (*de papier*) pad; (*système*) unit; (*pol.*) bloc. ∼**notes** (*pl.* ∼**s-notes**) *n.m.* notepad.

blocage /blɔkaʒ/ *n.m.* (*des prix*) freeze, freezing; (*des roues*) locking; (*psych.*) block.

blocus /blɔkys/ *n.m.* blockade.

blond, ∼e /blɔ̃, -d/ *a.* fair, blond. —*n.m., f.* fair-haired ou blond man ou woman. ∼**eur** /-dœr/ *n.f.* fairness.

bloquer /blɔke/ *v.t.* block; (*porte, machine*) jam; (*freins*) slam on; (*roues*) lock; (*prix, crédits*) freeze. **se** ∼ *v. pr.* jam; (*roues*) lock.

blottir (se) /(sə)blɔtir/ *v. pr.* snuggle, huddle.

blouse /bluz/ *n.f.* smock.

blouson /bluzɔ̃/ *n.m.* lumberjacket; (*Amer.*) windbreaker.

blue-jean /bludʒin/ *n.m.* jeans.

bluff /blœf/ *n.m.* bluff. ∼**er** *v.t./i.* bluff.

blush /blœʃ/ *n.m.* blusher.

boa /bɔa/ *n.m.* boa.

bobine /bɔbin/ *n.f.* reel; (*sur machine*) spool; (*électr.*) coil.

bobo /bobo/ *n.m.* (*fam.*) sore, cut. **avoir** ∼, have a pain.

boc|al (*pl.* ∼**aux**) /bɔkal, -o/ *n.m.* jar.

body /bodi/ *n.m.* leotard.

bœuf (*pl.* ∼**s**) /bœf, bø/ *n.m.* ox; (*viande*) beef. ∼**s**, oxen.

bogue /bɔg/ *n.m.* (*comput.*) bug.

boire† /bwar/ *v.t./i.* drink; (*absorber*) soak up.

bois¹ /bwa/ *voir* **boire**.

bois² /bwa/ *n.m.* (*matériau, forêt*) wood. **de** ∼, **en** ∼, wooden.

boisé /bwaze/ *a.* wooded.

boisson /bwasɔ̃/ *n.f.* drink.

boit /bwa/ *voir* **boire**.

boîte /bwat/ *n.f.* box; (*de conserves*) tin, can; (*firme: fam.*) firm. ∼ **à gants**, glove compartment. ∼ **aux lettres**, letter-box. ∼ **de nuit**, night-club. ∼ **postale**, post-office box. ∼ **de vitesses**, gear box.

boiter /bwate/ *v.i.* limp; (*meuble*) wobble.

boiteu|x, ～**se** /bwatø, -z/ *a.* lame; (*meuble*) wobbly; (*raisonnement*) shaky.

boîtier /bwatje/ *n.m.* case.

bol /bɔl/ *n.m.* bowl. **avoir du ～**, (*fam.*) be lucky.

Bolivie /bɔlivi/ *n.f.* Bolivia.

bolivien, ～**ne** /bɔlivjɛ̃, -jɛn/ *a. n.m.,f.* Bolivian.

bombard|er /bɔ̃barde/ *v.t.* bomb; (*par obus*) shell. ～**ement** *n.m.* bombing; shelling.

bombe /bɔ̃b/ *n.f.* bomb; (*atomiseur*) spray, aerosol.

bombé /bɔ̃be/ *a.* rounded; (*route*) cambered.

bon, bonne /bɔ̃, bɔn/ *a.* good; (*qui convient*) right; (*prudent*) wise. ～ **à/pour**, (*approprié*) fit to/for. **tenir ～**, stand firm. ～ (*billet*) voucher, coupon; (*comm.*) bond. **du ～**, some good. **pour de ～**, for good. **à quoi ～?**, what's the good *ou* point? **bonne année**, happy New Year. ～ **anniversaire**, happy birthday. ～ **appétit/voyage**, enjoy your meal/trip. **bonne chance/nuit**, good luck/night. **bonne femme**, (*péj.*) woman. ～ **sens**, common sense. ～ **vivant**, bon viveur. **de bonne heure**, early.

bonbon /bɔ̃bɔ̃/ *n.m.* sweet; (*Amer.*) candy.

bonbonne /bɔ̃bɔn/ *n.f.* demijohn; (*de gaz*) canister.

bond /bɔ̃/ *n.m.* leap. **faire un ～**, leap in the air; (*de surprise*) jump.

bonde /bɔ̃d/ *n.f.* plug; (*trou*) plughole.

bondé /bɔ̃de/ *a.* packed.

bondir /bɔ̃dir/ *v.i.* leap; (*de surprise*) jump.

bonheur /bɔnœr/ *n.m.* happiness. **par ～**, luckily.

bonhomme (*pl.* **bonshommes**) /bɔnɔm, bɔ̃zɔm/ *n.m.* fellow. ～ **de neige**, snowman.

bonjour /bɔ̃ʒur/ *n.m. & int.* hallo, hello, good morning *ou* afternoon.

bon marché /bɔ̃marʃe/ *a. invar.* cheap. —*adv.* cheap(ly).

bonne[1] /bɔn/ *a.f. voir* **bon**.

bonne[2] /bɔn/ *n.f.* (*domestique*) maid. ～ **d'enfants**, nanny.

bonnet /bɔnɛ/ *n.m.* hat; (*de soutien-gorge*) cup. ～ **de bain**, swimming cap.

bonneterie /bɔnɛtri/ *n.f.* hosiery.

bonsoir /bɔ̃swar/ *n.m. & int.* good evening; (*en se couchant*) good night.

bonté /bɔ̃te/ *n.f.* kindness.

bonus /bɔnys/ *n.m.* (*auto.*) no claims bonus.

bord /bɔr/ *n.m.* edge; (*rive*) bank. **à ～ (de)**, on board. **au ～ de la mer**, at the seaside. **au ～ des larmes**, on the verge of tears. ～ **de la route**, roadside.

bordeaux /bɔrdo/ *n.m. invar.* Bordeaux (wine), claret. —*a. invar.* maroon.

border /bɔrde/ *v.t.* line, border; (*personne, lit*) tuck in.

bordereau (*pl.* ～**x**) /bɔrdəro/ *n.m.* (*liste*) note, slip; (*facture*) invoice.

bordure /bɔrdyr/ *n.f.* border. **en ～ de**, on the edge of.

borne /bɔrn/ *n.f.* boundary marker. ～ (**kilométrique**), (*approx.*) milestone. ～**s**, limits.

borner /bɔrne/ *v.t.* confine. **se ～** *v. pr.* confine o.s. (**à**, to).

bosquet /bɔske/ *n.m.* grove.

bosse /bɔs/ *n.f.* bump; (*de chameau*) hump.

bosser /bɔse/ *v.i.* (*fam.*) work (hard). —*v.t.* (*fam.*) work (hard) at.

bossu, ～**e** /bɔsy/ *n.m., f.* hunchback.

botanique /bɔtanik/ n.f. botany. —a. botanical.

botte /bɔt/ n.f. boot; (de fleurs, légumes) bunch; (de paille) bundle, bale. ∼ s de caoutchouc, wellingtons.

Bottin /bɔtɛ̃/ n.m. (P.) phone book.

bouc /buk/ n.m. (billy-)goat; (barbe) goatee. ∼ émissaire, scapegoat.

boucan /bukã/ n.m. (fam.) din.

bouche /buʃ/ n.f. mouth. ∼ bée, open-mouthed. ∼ d'égout, manhole. ∼ d'incendie, (fire) hydrant. ∼ de métro, entrance to the underground ou subway (Amer.). ∼-à-bouche n.m. mouth-to-mouth resuscitation.

bouché /buʃe/ a. c'est ∼, (profession, avenir) it's a dead end.

bouchée /buʃe/ n.f. mouthful.

boucher[1] /buʃe/ v.t. block; (bouteille) cork. se ∼ v. pr. get blocked. se ∼ le nez, hold one's nose.

bouch|er[2], ∼ère /buʃe, -ɛr/ n.m., f. butcher. ∼erie n.f. butcher's (shop); (carnage) butchery.

bouchon /buʃɔ̃/ n.m. stopper; (en liège) cork; (de bidon, tube) cap; (de pêcheur) float; (de circulation: fig.) hold-up.

boucle /bukl/ n.f. (de ceinture) buckle; (forme) loop; (de cheveux) curl. ∼ d'oreille, ear-ring.

boucl|er /bukle/ v.t. fasten; (terminer) finish off; (enfermer: fam.) shut up; (encercler) seal off; (budget) balance. —v.i. curl. ∼é a. (cheveux) curly.

bouclier /buklije/ n.m. shield.

bouddhiste /budist/ a. & n.m./f. Buddhist.

bouder /bude/ v.i. sulk. —v.t. steer clear of.

boudin /budɛ̃/ n.m. black pudding.

boue /bu/ n.f. mud.

bouée /bwe/ n.f. buoy. ∼ de sauvetage, lifebuoy.

boueu|x, ∼se /bwø, -z/ a. muddy.

bouff|e /buf/ n.f. (fam.) food, grub. ∼er v.t./i. (fam.) eat.

bouffée /bufe/ n.f. puff, whiff; (méd.) flush; (d'orgueil) fit.

bouffi /bufi/ a. bloated.

bouffon, ∼ne /bufɔ̃, -ɔn/ a. farcical. —n.m. buffoon.

bougeoir /buʒwar/ n.m. candlestick.

bougeotte /buʒɔt/ n.f. la ∼, (fam.) the fidgets.

bouger /buʒe/ v.t./i. move; (agir) stir. se ∼ v. pr. (fam.) move.

bougie /buʒi/ n.f. candle; (auto.) spark(ing)-plug.

bouillie /buji/ n.f. (pour bébé) baby food; (péj.) mush.

bouill|ir† /bujir/ v.i. boil. —v.t. (faire) ∼ir, boil. ∼ant, ∼ante a. boiling; (très chaud) boiling hot.

bouilloire /bujwar/ n.f. kettle.

bouillon /bujɔ̃/ n.m. (aliment) stock. ∼ cube, stock cube.

bouillotte /bujɔt/ n.f. hot-water bottle.

boulang|er, ∼ère /bulãʒe, -ɛr/ n.m., f. baker. ∼erie n.f. bakery.

boule /bul/ n.f. ball; (de machine à écrire) golf ball. ∼s, (jeu) bowls. jouer aux ∼s, play bowls. ∼ de neige, snowball.

bouleau (pl. ∼x) /bulo/ n.m. (silver) birch.

boulet /bulɛ/ n.m. (de canon) cannon-ball; (de forçat: fig.) ball and chain.

boulette /bulɛt/ n.f. (de papier) pellet; (aliment) meat ball.

boulevard /bulvar/ n.m. boulevard.

boulevers|er /bulvɛrse/ v.t. turn

upside down; (*pays, plans*) disrupt; (*émouvoir*) distress, upset. **~ant, ante** *a.* deeply moving. **~ement** *n.m.* upheaval.

boulimie /bulimi/ *n.f.* compulsive eating; (*méd.*) bulimia.

boulon /bulɔ̃/ *n.m.* bolt.

boulot[1] /bulo/ *n.m.* (*travail: fam.*) work.

boulot[2], **~te** /bulo, -ɔt/ *a.* (*rond: fam.*) dumpy.

boum /bum/ *n.m. & int.* bang.

bouquet /bukɛ/ *n.m.* (*de fleurs*) bunch, bouquet; (*d'arbres*) clump.

bouquin /bukɛ̃/ *n.m.* (*fam.*) book.

bourdon /burdɔ̃/ *n.m.* bumble-bee.

bourdonn|er /burdɔne/ *v.i.* buzz. **~ement** *n.m.* buzzing.

bourgeois, ~e /burʒwa, -z/ *a. & n.m., f.* middle-class (person); (*péj.*) bourgeois. **~ie** /-zi/ *n.f.* middle class(es).

bourgeon /burʒɔ̃/ *n.m.* bud. **~ner** /-ɔne/ *v.i.* bud.

bourgogne /burgɔɲ/ *n.m.* burgundy. **—***n.f.* la B**~**, Burgundy.

bourrade /burad/ *n.f.* prod.

bourrasque /burask/ *n.f.* squall.

bourrati|f, ~ve /buratif, -v/ *a.* filling, stodgy.

bourreau /buro/ *n.m.* (*pl.* **~x**) executioner. **~ de travail**, workaholic.

bourrer /bure/ *v.t.* cram (de, with). **~ de coups**, thrash.

bours|e /burs/ *n.f.* purse; (*subvention*) grant. **la B~e**, the Stock Exchange. **~ier, ~ière** *a.* Stock Exchange; *n.m., f.* holder of a grant.

bousculer /buskyle/ *v.t.* (*pousser*) jostle; (*presser*) rush.

bouse /buz/ *n.f.* (cow) dung.

bousiller /buzije/ *v.t.* (*fam.*) mess up.

boussole /busɔl/ *n.f.* compass.

bout /bu/ *n.m.* end; (*de langue, bâton*) tip; (*morceau*) bit. **à ~**, exhausted. **à ~ de souffle**, out of breath. **au ~ de**, (*après*) after. **~ filtre**, filter-tip.

bouteille /butɛj/ *n.f.* bottle.

boutique /butik/ *n.f.* shop; (*de mode*) boutique.

bouton /butɔ̃/ *n.m.* button; (*pustule*) pimple; (*pousse*) bud; (*de porte, radio, etc.*) knob. **~ de manchette**, cuff-link. **~ner** /-ɔne/ *v.t.* button (up). **~nière** /-ɔnjɛr/ *n.f.* buttonhole. **~-pression** (*pl.* **~s-pression**) *n.m.* press-stud (*Amer.*) snap.

bouture /butyr/ *n.f.* (*plante*) cutting.

bovin, ~e /bɔvɛ̃, -in/ *a.* bovine. **~s** *n.m. pl.* cattle.

bowling /boliŋ/ *n.m.* bowling; (*salle*) bowling-alley.

box (*pl.* **~** ou **boxes**) /bɔks/ *n.m.* (*jurid.*) dock.

box|e /bɔks/ *n.f.* boxing. **~er** *v.t./i.* box. **~eur** *n.m.* boxer.

boyau (*pl.* **~x**) /bwajo/ *n.m.* gut; (*corde*) catgut; (*galerie*) gallery; (*de bicyclette*) tyre.

boycott|er /bɔjkɔte/ *v.t.* boycott. **~age** *n.m.* boycott.

BP *abrév.* (*boîte postale*) PO Box.

bracelet /braslɛ/ *n.m.* bracelet; (*de montre*) strap.

brad|er /brade/ *v.t.* sell off. **~erie** *n.f.* open-air sale.

braguette /bragɛt/ *n.f.* fly.

braille /braj/ *n.m. & a.* Braille.

braire /brɛr/ *v.i.* bray.

braiser /breze/ *v.t.* braise.

brancard /brɑ̃kar/ *n.m.* stretcher; (*bras*) shaft.

branche /brɑ̃ʃ/ *n.f.* branch.

branché /brɑ̃ʃe/ *a.* (*fam.*) trendy.

branch|er /brɑ̃ʃe/ *v.t.* connect; (*électr.*) plug in. **~ement** *n.m.* connection.

branchies /brɑ̃ʃi/ *n.f. pl.* gills.

brandir /brɑ̃dir/ *v.t.* brandish.

braquer /brake/ *v.t.* aim; (*regard*) fix; (*roue*) turn; (*banque: fam.*) hold up. —*v.i.* (*auto.*) turn (the wheel). —*v. pr.* **se ∼**, dig one's heels in.

bras /brɑ/ *n.m.* arm. —*n.m. pl.* (*fig.*) labour, hands. **∼ dessus bras dessous**, arm in arm. **∼ droit**, (*fig.*) right-hand man.

brassard /brasar/ *n.m.* arm-band.

brasse /brɑs/ *n.f.* (breast-)stroke.

brass|er /brase/ *v.t.* mix; (*bière*) brew; (*affaires*) handle a lot of. **∼erie** *n.f.* brewery; (*café*) brasserie.

brassière /brasjɛr/ *n.f.* (baby's) vest.

brave /brav/ *a.* brave; (*bon*) good. **∼ment** *adv.* bravely.

braver /brave/ *v.t.* defy.

bravo /bravo/ *int.* bravo. —*n.m.* cheer.

bravoure /bravur/ *n.f.* bravery.

break /brɛk/ *n.m.* estate car.

brebis /brəbi/ *n.f.* ewe. **∼ galeuse**, black sheep.

bredouiller /brəduje/ *v.t./i.* mumble.

bref, brève /brɛf, -v/ *a.* short, brief. —*adv.* in short. **en ∼**, in short.

Brésil /brezil/ *n.m.* Brazil.

brésilien, ∼ne /breziljɛ̃, -jɛn/ *a. & n.m., f.* Brazilian.

Bretagne /brətaɲ/ *n.f.* Brittany.

bretelle /brətɛl/ *n.f.* (shoulder-)strap; (*d'autoroute*) access road. **∼s**, (*pour pantalon*) braces.

breton, ∼ne /brətɔ̃, -ɔn/ *a. & n.m., f.* Breton.

brève /brɛv/ *voir* **bref**.

brevet /brəvɛ/ *n.m.* diploma. **∼ (d'invention)**, patent.

brevet|er /brəvte/ *v.t.* patent. **∼é** *a.* patented.

bribes /brib/ *n.f. pl.* scraps.

bric-à-brac /brikabrak/ *n.m. invar.* bric-à-brac.

bricole /brikɔl/ *n.f.* trifle.

bricol|er /brikɔle/ *v.i.* do odd (do-it-yourself) jobs. —*v.t.* fix (up). **∼age** *n.m.* do-it-yourself (jobs).

bride /brid/ *n.f.* bridle.

bridé /bride/ *a.* **yeux ∼s**, slit eyes.

bridge /bridʒ/ *n.m.* (*cartes*) bridge.

briève|ment /brijɛvmɑ̃/ *adv.* briefly. **∼té** *n.f.* brevity.

brigad|e /brigad/ *n.f.* (*de police*) squad; (*mil.*) brigade; (*fig.*) team. **∼ier** *n.m.* (*de police*) sergeant.

brill|ant, ∼ante /brijɑ̃, -t/ *a.* (*couleur*) bright; (*luisant*) shiny; (*remarquable*) brilliant. —*n.m.* (*éclat*) shine; (*diamant*) diamond. **∼amment** *adv.* brilliantly.

briller /brije/ *v.i.* shine.

brimer /brime/ *v.t.* bully, harass. **se sentir brimé**, feel put down.

brin /brɛ̃/ *n.m.* **∼ d'herbe**, blade of grass. **un ∼ de**, a bit of.

brindille /brɛ̃dij/ *n.f.* twig.

brioche /brijɔʃ/ *n.f.* brioche (*small round sweet cake*); (*ventre: fam.*) paunch.

brique /brik/ *n.f.* brick.

briquer /brike/ *v.t.* polish.

briquet /brikɛ/ *n.m.* (cigarette-)lighter.

brise /briz/ *n.f.* breeze.

briser /brize/ *v.t.* break. **se ∼er** *v. pr.* break.

britannique /britanik/ *a.* British. —*n.m./f.* Briton. **les B∼s**, the British.

broc /bro/ *n.m.* pitcher.

brocant|e /brɔkɑ̃t/ *n.f.* second-hand goods. **∼eur, ∼euse** *n.m., f.* second-hand goods dealer.

broche /brɔʃ/ *n.f.* brooch; (*culin.*) spit. **à la ∼**, spit-roasted.

brochet /brɔʃɛ/ *n.m.* (*poisson*) pike.

brochette /bʁɔʃɛt/ *n.f.* skewer.

brochure /bʁɔʃyʁ/ *n.f.* brochure, booklet.

brod|er /bʁɔde/ *v.t.* embroider. ∼**erie** *n.f.* embroidery.

broncher /bʁɔ̃ʃe/ *v.i.* **sans** ∼, without turning a hair.

bronch|es /bʁɔ̃ʃ/ *n.f. pl.* bronchial tubes. ∼**ite** *n.f.* bronchitis.

bronze /bʁɔ̃z/ *n.m.* bronze.

bronz|er /bʁɔ̃ze/ *v.i.*, **se** ∼ *er v. pr.* get a (sun-)tan. ∼**age** *n.m.* (sun-)tan. ∼**é** *a.* (sun-)tanned.

brosse /bʁɔs/ *n.f.* brush. ∼ **à dents**, toothbrush. ∼ **à habits**, clothes-brush.

brosser /bʁɔse/ *v.t.* brush; (*fig.*) paint. **se** ∼ **les dents/les cheveux**, brush one's teeth/hair.

brouette /bʁuɛt/ *n.f.* wheelbarrow.

brouhaha /bʁuaa/ *n.m.* hubbub.

brouillard /bʁujaʁ/ *n.m.* fog.

brouille /bʁuj/ *n.f.* quarrel.

brouiller /bʁuje/ *v.t.* mix up; (*vue*) blur; (*œufs*) scramble; (*radio*) jam; (*amis*) set at odds. **se** ∼ *v. pr.* (*amis*) fall out.

brouillon /bʁujɔ̃/ *n.m.* (rough) draft.

broussailles /bʁusaj/ *n.f. pl.* undergrowth.

brousse /bʁus/ *n.f.* **la** ∼, the bush.

brouter /bʁute/ *v.t./i.* graze.

broyer /bʁwaje/ *v.t.* crush; (*moudre*) grind.

bru /bʁy/ *n.f.* daughter-in-law.

bruit /bʁɥi/ *n.m.* noise; (*fig.*) rumour.

bruitage /bʁɥitaʒ/ *n.m.* sound effects.

brûlant, ∼**e** /bʁylã, -t/ *a.* burning (hot); (*sujet*) red-hot.

brûl|er /bʁyle/ *v.t./i.* burn; (*essence*) use (up); (*signal*) go through ou past (without stopping). **se** ∼**er** *v. pr.* burn o.s. ∼**eur** *n.m.* burner.

brûlure /bʁylyʁ/ *n.f.* burn. ∼**s d'estomac**, heartburn.

brum|e /bʁym/ *n.f.* mist. ∼**eux**, ∼**euse** *a.* misty; (*idées*) hazy.

brun, ∼**e** /bʁœ̃, bʁyn/ *a.* brown, dark. —*n.m.* brown. —*n.m., f.* dark-haired person. ∼**ir** /bʁyniʁ/ *v.i.* turn brown; (*se bronzer*) get a tan.

brunch /bʁœnʃ/ *n.m.* brunch.

brushing /bʁœʃiŋ/ *n.m.* blow-dry.

brusque /bʁysk/ *a.* abrupt. ∼**ment** /-əmã/ *adv.* suddenly, abruptly.

brusquer /bʁyske/ *v.t.* rush.

brut /bʁyt/ *a.* (*pétrole*) crude; (*comm.*) gross.

brut|al (*m. pl.* ∼**aux**) /bʁytal, -o/ *a.* brutal. ∼**alité** *n.f.* brutality.

brute /bʁyt/ *n.f.* brute.

Bruxelles /bʁysɛl/ *n.m./f.* Brussels.

bruy|ant, ∼**ante** /bʁɥijã, -t/ *a.* noisy. ∼**amment** *adv.* noisily.

bruyère /bʁɥjɛʁ/ *n.f.* heather.

bu /by/ *voir* **boire**.

bûche /byʃ/ *n.f.* log. ∼ **de Noël**, Christmas log.

bûcheron /byʃʁɔ̃/ *n.m.* woodcutter.

budg|et /bydʒɛ/ *n.m.* budget. ∼**étaire** *a.* budgetary.

buée /bɥe/ *n.f.* mist, condensation.

buffet /byfɛ/ *n.m.* sideboard; (*réception, restaurant*) buffet.

buffle /byfl/ *n.m.* buffalo.

buisson /bɥisɔ̃/ *n.m.* bush.

bulbe /bylb/ *n.m.* bulb.

bulgare /bylgaʁ/ *a.* & *n.m./f.* Bulgarian.

Bulgarie /bylgaʁi/ *n.f.* Bulgaria.

bulldozer /byldozɛʁ/ *n.m.* bulldozer.

bulle /byl/ *n.f.* bubble.

bulletin /byltɛ̃/ *n.m.* bulletin, report. ∼ **d'information**, news bulletin. ∼ **météorologique**, weather report. **~ (de vote),** ballot-paper. **~ de salaire,** pay-slip.

buraliste /byralist/ *n.m./f.* tobac-conist; (*à la poste*) clerk.

bureau (*pl.* **~x**) /byro/ *n.m.* office; (*meuble*) desk; (*comité*) board. **~ de location,** booking-office; (*théâtre*) box-office. **~ de poste,** post office. **~ de tabac,** tobac-conist's (shop). **~ de vote,** polling station.

bureaucratie /byrokrasi/ *n.f.* bureaucracy.

burlesque /byrlɛsk/ *a.* ludicrous; (*théâtre*) burlesque.

bus /bys/ *n.m.* bus.

buste /byst/ *n.m.* bust.

but /by(t)/ *n.m.* target; (*dessein*) aim, goal; (*football*) goal. **avoir pour ~ de,** aim to. **dans le ~ de,** with the intention of.

butane /bytan/ *n.f.* butane, Calor gas (P.).

buté /byte/ *a.* obstinate.

buter /byte/ *v.i.* **~ contre,** knock against; (*problème*) come up against. —*v.t.* antagonize. **se ~** *v. pr.* (*s'entêter*) become obstinate.

butin /bytɛ̃/ *n.m.* booty, loot.

butiner /bytine/ *v.i.* gather nectar.

butte /byt/ *n.f.* mound.

buvard /byvar/ *n.m.* blotting-paper.

buvette /byvɛt/ *n.f.* (*refreshment*) bar.

buveu|r, ~se /byvœr, -øz/ *n.m., f.* drinker.

C

c' /s/ *voir* **ce**[1].

ça /sa/ *pron.* it, that; (*pour désigner*) that; (*plus près*) this. **ça va?,** (*fam.*) how's it going? **ça va!,** (*fam.*) all right! **où ça?,** (*fam.*) where? **quand ça?,** (*fam.*) when? **c'est ça,** that's right.

çà /sa/ *adv.* **çà et là,** here and there.

cabane /kaban/ *n.f.* hut; (*à outils*) shed.

cabaret /kabarɛ/ *n.m.* night-club.

cabas /kaba/ *n.m.* shopping bag.

cabillaud /kabijo/ *n.m.* cod.

cabine /kabin/ *n.f.* (*à la piscine*) cubicle; (*à la plage*) (beach) hut; (*de bateau*) cabin; (*de pilotage*) cockpit. **~ (téléphonique),** phone-booth, phone-box.

cabinet /kabinɛ/ *n.m.* (*de médecin*) surgery; (*d'avocat*) office; (*clientèle*) practice; (*pol.*) Cabinet; (*pièce*) room. **~s,** (*toilettes*) toilet. **~ de toilette,** toilet.

câble /kɑbl/ *n.m.* cable; (*corde*) rope.

cabot|age /kabotaʒ/ *n.m.* coastal navigation. **~eur** *n.m.* coaster.

cabrer /kabre/ *v.t.,* **se ~** *v. pr.* (*cheval*) rear up. **se ~ contre,** rebel against.

cabriole /kabrijol/ *n.f.* (*culbute*) somersault.

cacahuète /kakaɥɛt/ *n.f.* peanut.

cacao /kakao/ *n.m.* cocoa.

cachalot /kaʃalo/ *n.m.* sperm whale.

cache /kaʃ/ *n.m.* mask; (*photo.*) lens cover.

cachemire /kaʃmir/ *n.m.* cash-mere.

cach|er /kaʃe/ *v.t.* hide, conceal (à, from). **se ~er** *v. pr.* hide; (*se trouver caché*) be hidden. **~e-cache** *n.m. invar.* hide-and-seek.

cachet /kaʃɛ/ *n.m.* seal; (*de la poste*) postmark; (*comprimé*) tablet; (*d'artiste*) fee; (*fig.*) style.

cacheter /kaʃte/ *v.t.* seal.

cachette /kaʃɛt/ n.f. hiding-place. **en ～**, in secret.

cachot /kaʃo/ n.m. dungeon.

cactus /kaktys/ n.m. cactus.

cadavre /kadavr/ n.m. corpse.

caddie /kadi/ n.m. trolley.

cadeau (pl. **～x**) /kado/ n.m. present, gift. **faire un ～ à qn.**, give s.o. a present.

cadenas /kadna/ n.m. padlock.

cadet, ～te /kadɛ, -t/ a. youngest; (entre deux) younger. —n.m., f. youngest (child); younger (child).

cadran /kadrɑ̃/ n.m. dial. **～ solaire**, sundial.

cadre /kadr/ n.m. frame; (milieu) surroundings; (limites) scope; (contexte) framework. —n.m./f. (personne: comm.) executive. **les ～s**, (comm.) the managerial staff.

cadrer /kadre/ v.t. (photo) centre.

cafard /kafar/ n.m. (insecte) cockroach. **avoir le ～**, (fam.) be feeling low.

caf|é /kafe/ n.m. coffee; (bar) café. **～é au lait**, white coffee. **～etière** n.f. coffee-pot.

caféine /kafein/ n.f. caffeine.

cage /kaʒ/ n.f. cage; (d'escalier) well; (d'ascenseur) shaft.

cageot /kaʒo/ n.m. crate.

cagoule /kagul/ n.f. hood.

cahier /kaje/ n.m. notebook; (scol.) exercise-book.

caille /kaj/ n.f. quail.

caillot /kajo/ n.m. (blood) clot.

caillou (pl. **～x**) /kaju/ n.m. stone; (galet) pebble. **～teux, ～teuse** a. stony.

caisse /kɛs/ n.f. crate, case; (tiroir, machine) till; (guichet) pay-desk; (bureau) office; (mus.) drum. **～ d'épargne**, savings bank. **～ de retraite**, pension fund.

caiss|ier, ～ière /kesje, -jɛr/ n.m., f. cashier.

cake /kɛk/ n.m. fruit-cake.

calamité /kalamite/ n.f. calamity.

calcaire /kalkɛr/ a. (sol) chalky; (eau) hard.

calciné /kalsine/ a. charred.

calcium /kalsjɔm/ n.m. calcium.

calcul /kalkyl/ n.m. calculation; (scol.) arithmetic; (différentiel) calculus. **～ biliaire**, gallstone.

calcul|er /kalkyle/ v.t. calculate. **～ateur** n.m. (ordinateur) computer, calculator. **～atrice** n.f. (ordinateur) calculator. **～ette** n.f. (pocket) calculator.

calé /kale/ a. (fam.) clever.

caleçon /kalsɔ̃/ n.m. underpants; (de femme) leggings.

calendrier /kalɑ̃drije/ n.m. calendar; (fig.) timetable.

calepin /kalpɛ̃/ n.m. notebook.

caler /kale/ v.t. wedge; (moteur) stall. —v.i. stall.

calfeutrer /kalføtre/ v.t. stop up the cracks of.

calibr|e /kalibr/ n.m. calibre; (d'un œuf, fruit) grade.

câlin, ～e /kalɛ̃, -in/ a. endearing, cuddly. **～er** /-ine/ v.t. cuddle.

calmant /kalmɑ̃/ n.m. sedative.

calm|e /kalm/ a. calm. —n.m. calm(ness). **du ～e!**, calm down! **～er** v.t., **se ～er** v. pr. (personne) calm (down); (diminuer) ease.

calomn|ie /kalɔmni/ n.f. slander; (écrite) libel. **～ier** v.t. slander; libel.

calorie /kalɔri/ n.f. calorie.

calqu|e /kalk/ n.m. tracing; (fig.) exact copy. **～er** v.t. trace; (fig.) copy. **～er sur**, model on.

calvaire /kalvɛr/ n.m. (croix) calvary; (fig.) suffering.

calvitie /kalvisi/ n.f. baldness.

camarade /kamarad/ n.m./f. friend; (pol.) comrade. **～rie** n.f. good companionship.

cambiste /kãbist/ n.m./f. foreign exchange dealer.

cambouis /kãbwi/ n.m. (engine) oil.

cambrer /kãbre/ v.t. arch. **se** ~ v. pr. arch one's back.

cambriol|er /kãbrijɔle/ v.t. burgle. ~**age** n.m. burglary. ~**eur**, ~**euse** n.m., f. burglar.

camembert /kamãbɛr/ n.m. Camembert (cheese).

caméra /kamera/ n.f. (cinéma, télévision) camera.

caméra|man (pl. ~**men**) /kameraman, -mɛn/ n.m. cameraman.

camion /kamjɔ̃/ n.m. lorry, truck. ~-**citerne** /-sitɛrn/ n.m. tanker. ~**nage** /-jɔnaʒ/ n.m. haulage. ~**nette** /-jɔnɛt/ n.f. van. ~**neur** /-jɔnœr/ n.m. lorry ou truck driver.

camoufl|er /kamufle/ v.t. camouflage. ~**age** n.m. camouflage.

camp /kã/ n.m. camp; (sport) side.

campagn|e /kãpaɲ/ n.f. country (side); (mil., pol.) campaign.

camp|er /kãpe/ v.i. camp. ~**ement** n.m. encampment. ~**eur**, ~**euse** n.m., f. camper.

camphre /kãfr/ n.m. camphor.

camping /kãpiŋ/ n.m. camping. **faire du** ~, go camping. ~-**car** n.m. camper-van. ~-**gaz** n.m. invar. (P.) camping-gaz. (**terrain de**) ~, campsite.

campus /kãpys/ n.m. campus.

Canada /kanada/ n.m. Canada.

cana|dien, ~ne /kanadjɛ̃, -jɛn/ a. & n.m., f. Canadian.

can|al (pl. ~**aux**) /kanal, -o/ n.m. (artificiel) canal; (bras de mer) channel; (techn., TV) channel. **par le** ~**al de**, through.

canalisation /kanalizasjɔ̃/ n.f. (tuyaux) main(s).

canapé /kanape/ n.m. sofa.

canard /kanar/ n.m. duck; (journal: fam.) rag.

canari /kanari/ n.m. canary.

cancans /kãkã/ n.m. pl. malicious gossip.

canc|er /kãser/ n.m. cancer. **le C~er,** Cancer. ~**éreux,** ~**éreuse** a. cancerous. ~**érigène** a. carcinogenic.

cancre /kãkr/ n.m. dunce.

candeur /kãdœr/ n.f. naïvety.

candidat, ~e /kãdida, -t/ n.m., f. candidate; (à un poste) applicant, candidate (à, for). ~**ure** /-tyr/ n.f. application; (pol.) candidacy. **poser sa** ~ **pour,** apply for.

candide /kãdid/ a. naïve.

cane /kan/ n.f. (female) duck. ~**ton** n.m. duckling.

canette /kanɛt/ n.f. (de bière) bottle.

caniche /kaniʃ/ n.m. poodle.

canicule /kanikyl/ n.f. hot summer days.

canif /kanif/ n.m. penknife.

caniveau (pl. ~**x**) /kanivo/ n.m. gutter.

cannabis /kanabis/ n.m. cannabis.

canne /kan/ n.f. (walking-)stick. ~ **à pêche,** fishing-rod. ~ **à sucre,** sugar-cane.

cannelle /kanɛl/ n.f. cinnamon.

canoë /kanɔe/ n.m. canoe; (sport) canoeing.

canon /kanɔ̃/ n.m. (big) gun; (d'une arme) barrel.

canot /kano/ n.m. boat. ~ **de sauvetage,** lifeboat. ~ **pneumatique,** rubber dinghy.

cantate /kãtat/ n.f. cantata.

cantatrice /kãtatris/ n.f. opera singer.

cantine /kãtin/ n.f. canteen.

cantique /kãtik/ n.m. hymn.

canton /kɑ̃tɔ̃/ n.m. (en France) district; (en Suisse) canton.

canular /kanylar/ n.m. hoax.

caoutchou|c /kautʃu/ n.m. rubber; (élastique) rubber band.

cap /kap/ n.m. cape, headland; (direction) course.

capable /kapabl/ a. able, capable. ~ **de qch.**, capable of sth. ~ **de faire**, able to do, capable of doing.

capacité /kapasite/ n.f. ability; (contenance) capacity.

cape /kap/ n.f. cape.

capillaire /kapilɛr/ a. (lotion, soins) hair. (vaisseau) ~, capillary.

capitaine /kapitɛn/ n.m. captain.

capit|al, ~**ale** (m. pl. ~**aux**) /kapital, -o/ a. major, fundamental; (peine, lettre) capital. —n.m. (pl. ~**aux**) (comm.) capital; (fig.) stock. ~**aux**, (comm.) capital. —n.f. (ville, lettre) capital.

capitalis|te /kapitalist/ a. & n.m./f. capitalist. ~**me** n.m. capitalism.

capitonné /kapitɔne/ a. padded.

capitul|er /kapityle/ v.i. capitulate. ~**ation** n.f. capitulation.

capor|al (pl. ~**aux**) /kapɔral, -o/ n.m. corporal.

capot /kapo/ n.m. (auto.) bonnet; (auto., Amer.) hood.

capote /kapɔt/ n.f. (auto.) hood; (auto., Amer.) (convertible) top; (fam.) condom.

câpre /kɑpr/ n.f. (culin.) caper.

caprice /kapris/ n.m. whim, caprice. ~**ieux**, ~**ieuse** a. capricious; (appareil) temperamental.

Capricorne /kaprikɔrn/ n.m. le ~, Capricorn.

capsule /kapsyl/ n.f. capsule; (de bouteille) cap.

capter /kapte/ v.t. (émission) pick up.

capti|f, ~**ve** /kaptif, -v/ a. & n.m.,f. captive.

captiver /kaptive/ v.t. captivate.

captivité /kaptivite/ n.f. captivity.

captur|e /kaptyr/ n.f. capture. ~**er** v.t. capture.

capuche /kapyʃ/ n.f. hood. ~ **on** n.m. hood; (de stylo) cap.

car¹ /kar/ conj. because, for.

car² /kar/ n.m. coach; (Amer.) bus.

carabine /karabin/ n.f. rifle.

caractère /karaktɛr/ n.m. (nature, lettre) character. ~ **d'imprimerie**, block letters.

caractéristique /karakteristik/ a. & n.f. characteristic.

carafe /karaf/ n.f. carafe; (pour le vin) decanter.

caraïbe /karaib/ a. Caribbean. les **C~s**, the Caribbean.

caramel /karamɛl/ n.m. caramel. ~**iser** v.t./i. caramelize.

carapace /karapas/ n.f. shell.

caravane /karavan/ n.f. (auto.) caravan; (convoi) caravan.

carbone /karbɔn/ n.m. carbon.

carboniser /karbɔnize/ v.t. burn (to ashes).

carburant /karbyrɑ̃/ n.m. (motor) fuel.

carburateur /karbyratœr/ n.m. carburettor; (Amer.) carburetor.

carcasse /karkas/ n.f. carcass; (d'immeuble, de voiture) frame.

cardiaque /kardjak/ a. heart. —n.m./f. heart patient.

cardigan /kardigɑ̃/ n.m. cardigan.

cardin|al (m. pl. ~**aux**) /kardinal, -o/ a. cardinal. —n.m. (pl. ~**aux**) cardinal.

Carême /karɛm/ n.m. Lent.

carence /karɑ̃s/ n.f. inadequacy; (manque) deficiency.

caress|e /karɛs/ n.f. caress. ~**er** /-ese/ v.t. caress, stroke; (espoir) cherish.

cargaison /kargɛzɔ̃/ n.f. cargo.

cargo /kargo/ *n.m.* cargo boat.
caricature /karikatyr/ *n.f.* caricature.
car|ie /kari/ *n.f.* cavity. **~ié** *a.* (*dent*) decayed.
carillon /karijɔ̃/ *n.m.* chimes.
caritati|f /karitatif, -v/ *a.* **~ve** association, **~ve**, charity.
carlingue /karlɛ̃g/ *n.f.* (*d'avion*) cabin.
carnaval (*pl.* **~s**) /karnaval/ *n.m.* carnival.
carnet /karnɛ/ *n.m.* notebook; (*de tickets etc.*) book. **~ de chèques**, cheque-book. **~ de notes**, school report.
carotte /karɔt/ *n.f.* carrot.
carpe /karp/ *n.f.* carp.
carpette /karpɛt/ *n.f.* rug.
carré /kare/ *a.* (*forme, mesure*) square; (*fig.*) straightforward. —*n.m.* square; (*de terrain*) patch.
carreau (*pl.* **~x**) /karo/ *n.m.* (window) pane; (*par terre, au mur*) tile; (*dessin*) check; (*cartes*) diamonds. **à ~x**, check(ed).
carrefour /karfur/ *n.m.* crossroads.
carrel|er /karle/ *v.t.* tile. **~age** *n.m.* tiling; (*sol*) tiles.
carrelet /karlɛ/ *n.m.* (*poisson*) plaice.
carrément /karemɑ̃/ *adv.* straight; (*dire*) straight out.
carrière /karjɛr/ *n.f.* career; (*terrain*) quarry.
carrosse /karɔs/ *n.m.* (horse-drawn) coach.
carrosserie /karɔsri/ *n.f.* (*auto.*) body(work).
carrure /karyr/ *n.f.* build; (*fig.*) calibre.
cartable /kartabl/ *n.m.* satchel.
carte /kart/ *n.f.* card; (*géog.*) map; (*naut.*) chart; (*au restaurant*) menu. **~s,** (*jeu*) cards. **à la ~,** (*manger*) à la carte. **~ de crédit,**

credit card. **~ des vins,** wine list. **~ de visite,** (business) card. **~ grise,** (car) registration card. **~ postale,** postcard.
cartilage /kartilaʒ/ *n.m.* cartilage.
carton /kartɔ̃/ *n.m.* cardboard; (*boîte*) (cardboard) box. **~ à dessin,** portfolio.
cartonné /kartɔne/ *a.* (*livre*) hardback.
cartouche /kartuʃ/ *n.f.* cartridge; (*de cigarettes*) carton.
cas /ka/ *n.m.* case. **au ~ où,** in case. **~ urgent,** emergency. **en aucun ~,** on no account. **en ~ de,** in the event of, in case of. **en tout ~,** in any case.
casan|ier, ~ière /kazanje, -jɛr/ *a.* home-loving.
casaque /kazak/ *n.f.* (*de jockey*) shirt.
cascade /kaskad/ *n.f.* waterfall.
case /kɑz/ *n.f.* hut; (*compartiment*) pigeon-hole; (*sur papier*) square.
caserne /kazɛrn/ *n.f.* barracks.
cash /kaʃ/ *adv.* **payer ~,** pay (in) cash.
casier /kazje/ *n.m.* pigeon-hole, compartment; (*meuble*) cabinet; (*à bouteilles*) rack. **~ judiciaire,** criminal record.
casino /kazino/ *n.m.* casino.
casque /kask/ *n.m.* helmet.
casquette /kaskɛt/ *n.f.* cap.
cassation /kasatjɔ̃/ *n.f.* **cour de ~,** appeal court.
casse /kɑs/ *n.f.* (*objets*) breakages. **mettre à la ~,** scrap.
cass|er /kase/ *v.t./i.* break; (*annuler*) annul. **se ~** *v. pr.* break. **~e-croûte** *n.m. invar.* snack. **~e-noisettes** *ou* **~e-noix** *n.m. invar.* nutcrackers. **~e-tête** *n.m. invar.* (*problème*) headache; (*jeu*) brain teaser.
casserole /kasrɔl/ *n.f.* saucepan.
cassette /kasɛt/ *n.f.* casket; (*de*

magnétophone) cassette; *(de video)* video tape.

cassis[1] /kasis/ *n.m.* black currant.

cassis[2] /kasi/ *n.m. (auto.)* dip.

cassoulet /kasulɛ/ *n.m.* stew (of beans and meat).

cassure /kasyr/ *n.f.* break.

caste /kast/ *n.f.* caste.

castor /kastɔr/ *n.m.* beaver.

catalogue /katalɔg/ *n.m.* catalogue.

catalyseur /katalizœr/ *n.m.* catalyst.

cataracte /katarakt/ *n.f.* cataract.

catastroph|e /katastrɔf/ *n.f.* disaster, catastrophe. **~ique** *a.* catastrophic.

catch /katʃ/ *n.m.* (all-in) wrestling. **~eur, ~euse** *n.m., f.* (all-in) wrestler.

catégorie /kategɔri/ *n.f.* category.

catégorique /kategɔrik/ *a.* categorical.

cathédrale /katedral/ *n.f.* cathedral.

catholi|que /katɔlik/ *a.* Catholic. **~cisme** *n.m.* Catholicism. **pas très ~que,** a bit fishy.

cauchemar /koʃmar/ *n.m.* nightmare.

cause /koz/ *n.f.* cause; *(jurid.)* case. **à ~ de,** because of.

causer /koze/ *v.t.* cause. —*v.i.* chat.

caustique /kostik/ *a.* caustic.

caution /kosjõ/ *n.f.* surety; *(jurid.)* bail; *(appui)* backing; *(garantie)* deposit. **sous ~,** on bail.

cautionner /kosjone/ *v.t.* guarantee; *(soutenir)* back.

caval|ier, ~ière /kavalje, -jɛr/ *n.m., f.* rider; *(pour danser)* partner. —*n.m. (échecs)* knight.

cave /kav/ *n.f.* cellar.

caveau *(pl. ~x)* /kavo/ *n.m.* vault.

caverne /kavɛrn/ *n.f.* cave.

caviar /kavjar/ *n.m.* caviare.

CD *(abrév.) (compact disc)* CD.

ce[1], **c'*** /sə, s/ *pron.* it, that. **c'est,** it *ou* that is. **ce sont,** they are. **c'est moi,** it's me. **c'est un chanteur/une chanteuse/*etc.*,** he/she is a singer/*etc.* **ce qui, ce que,** what. **ce que c'est bon/*etc.*!,** how good/*etc.* it is! **tout ce qui, tout ce que,** everything that.

ce[2] *ou* **cet*, cette** *(pl. ces)* /sə, sɛt, se/ *a.* that; *(proximité)* this. **ces,** those; *(proximité)* these.

CE *abrév.* (Communauté européenne) EC.

ceci /səsi/ *pron.* this.

céder /sede/ *v.t.* give up. —*v.i. (se rompre)* give way; *(se soumettre)* give in.

cèdre /sɛdr/ *n.m.* cedar.

CEE *abrév.* (Communauté économique européenne) EEC.

ceinture /sɛtyr/ *n.f.* belt; *(taille)* waist. **~ de sauvetage,** lifebelt. **~ de sécurité,** seat-belt.

cela /səla/ *pron.* it, that; *(pour désigner)* that.

célèbre /selɛbr/ *a.* famous.

célébr|er /selebre/ *v.t.* celebrate. **~ation** *n.f.* celebration (**de,** of).

célébrité /selebrite/ *n.f.* fame; *(personne)* celebrity.

céleri /sɛlri/ *n.m. (en branches)* celery. **~(-rave),** celeriac.

célibataire /selibatɛr/ *a.* unmarried. —*n.m.* bachelor. —*n.f.* unmarried woman.

celle, celles /sɛl/ *voir* **celui.**

cellophane /selɔfan/ *n.f.* (P.) Cellophane (P.).

cellule /selyl/ *n.f.* cell.

celui, celle *(pl. ceux, celles)* /səlɥi, sɛl, sø/ *pron.* the one. **~ de mon ami,** my friend's. **~-ci,** this (one). **~-là,** that (one). **ceux-ci,** these (ones). **ceux-là,** those (ones).

cendre /sãdr/ *n.f.* ash.

cendrier /sãdrije/ *n.m.* ashtray.

censé /sãse/ *a.* **être ~ faire**, be supposed to.

censur|e /sãsyr/ *n.f.* censorship. **~er** *v.t.* censor; (*critiquer*) censure.

cent (*pl.* **~s**) /sã/ (*generally* /sãt/ *pl.* /sãz/ *before vowel*) *a. & n.m.* hundred. **~ un** /sãœ̃/ a hundred and one.

centaine /sãten/ *n.f.* hundred. **une ~ (de)**, (about) a hundred.

centième /sãtjem/ *a. & n.m./f.* hundredth.

centigrade /sãtigrad/ *a.* centigrade.

centilitre /sãtilitr/ *n.m.* centilitre.

centime /sãtim/ *n.m.* centime.

centimètre /sãtimetr/ *n.m.* centimetre; (*ruban*) tape-measure.

centr|al (*m. pl.* **~aux**) /sãtral, -o/ *a.* central. —*n.m.* (*pl.* **~aux**). **~al (téléphonique)**, (telephone) exchange. —*n.f.* **~ale** power-station.

centr|e /sãtr/ *n.m.* centre. **~e-ville** *n.m.* town centre. **~er** *v.t* centre.

cépage /sepaʒ/ *n.m.* (variety of) vine.

cèpe /sep/ *n.m.* (edible) boletus.

cependant /səpãdã/ *adv.* however.

céramique /seramik/ *n.f.* ceramic.

cercle /serkl/ *n.m.* circle. **~ vicieux**, vicious circle.

cercueil /serkœj/ *n.m.* coffin.

céréale /sereal/ *n.f.* cereal.

cérébr|al (*m. pl.* **~aux**) /serebral, -o/ *a.* cerebral.

cérémonial (*pl.* **~s**) /seremɔnjal/ *n.m.* ceremonial.

cérémonie /seremɔni/ *n.f.* ceremony. **~(s)**, (*façons*) fuss.

cerf /ser/ *n.m.* stag.

cerfeuil /serfœj/ *n.m.* chervil.

cerf-volant (*pl.* **cerfs-volants**) /servɔlã/ *n.m.* kite.

ceris|e /sriz/ *n.f.* cherry. **~ier** *n.m.* cherry tree.

certain, ~e /sertẽ, -ɛn/ *a.* certain; (*sûr*) certain, sure (**de**, of; **que**, that). —*pron.* **~s**, certain people. **un ~ temps**, some time.

certainement /sertɛnmã/ *adv.* certainly.

certificat /sertifika/ *n.m.* certificate.

certif|ier /sertifje/ *v.t.* certify. **~ier qch. à qn.**, assure s.o. of sth. **~ié** *a.* (*professeur*) qualified.

certitude /sertityd/ *n.f.* certainty.

cerveau (*pl.* **~x**) /servo/ *n.m.* brain.

cervelas /servəla/ *n.m.* saveloy.

cervelle /servel/ *n.f.* (*anat.*) brain; (*culin.*) brains.

ces /se/ *voir* **ce²**.

césarienne /sezarjen/ *n.f.* Caesarean (section).

cessation /sesasjɔ̃/ *n.f.* suspension.

cesse /ses/ *n.f.* **sans ~**, incessantly.

cesser /sese/ *v.t./i.* stop. **~ de faire**, stop doing.

cessez-le-feu /seselfø/ *n.m. invar.* cease-fire.

c'est-à-dire /setadir/ *conj.* that is (to say).

cet, cette /set/ *voir* **ce²**.

ceux /sø/ *voir* **celui**.

chacal (*pl.* **~s**) /ʃakal/ *n.m.* jackal.

chacun, ~e /ʃakœ̃, -yn/ *pron.* each (one), every one; (*tout le monde*) everyone.

chagrin /ʃagrẽ/ *n.m.* sorrow. **avoir du ~**, be distressed.

chahut /ʃay/ *n.m.* row, din.

chaîne /ʃɛn/ *n.f.* chain; (*de télévision*) channel. **~ de montagnes**, mountain range. **~ de montage/fabrication**, assembly/

production line. ~ **hi-fi**, hi-fi system.

chair /ʃɛr/ *n.f.* flesh.

chaire /ʃɛr/ *n.f.* (*d'église*) pulpit; (*univ.*) chair.

chaise /ʃɛz/ *n.f.* chair. ~ **longue**, deck-chair.

châle /ʃɑl/ *n.m.* shawl.

chalet /ʃalɛ/ *n.m.* chalet.

chaleur /ʃalœr/ *n.f.* heat; (*moins intense*) warmth; (*d'un accueil, d'une couleur*) warmth. ~**eux**, ~**euse** *a.* warm.

challenge /ʃalāʒ/ *n.m.* contest.

chalumeau (*pl.* ~**x**) /ʃalymo/ *n.m.* blowlamp.

chamailler (se) /(sə)ʃamaje/ *v. pr.* squabble.

chambre /ʃɑ̃br/ *n.f.* (bed)room; (*pol., jurid.*) chamber. ~ **à air**, inner tube. ~ **d'amis**, spare *ou* guest room. ~ **à coucher**, bedroom. ~ **à un lit/deux lits**, single/double room.

chambrer /ʃɑ̃bre/ *v.t.* (*vin*) bring to room temperature.

chameau (*pl.* ~**x**) /ʃamo/ *n.m.* camel.

chamois /ʃamwa/ *n.m.* chamois.

champ /ʃɑ̃/ *n.m.* field. ~ **de courses**, racecourse.

champagne /ʃɑ̃paɲ/ *n.m.* champagne.

champignon /ʃɑ̃piɲɔ̃/ *n.m.* mushroom; (*moisissure*) fungus. ~ **de Paris**, button mushroom.

champion, ~**ne** /ʃɑ̃pjɔ̃, -jɔn/ *n.m., f.* champion. ~**nat** /-jɔna/ *n.m.* championship.

chance /ʃɑ̃s/ *n.f.* (good) luck; (*possibilité*) chance. **avoir de la** ~, be lucky. **quelle** ~!, what luck!

chancelier /ʃɑ̃səlje/ *n.m.* chancellor.

chanceu|x, ~**se** /ʃɑ̃sø, -z/ *a.* lucky.

chandail /ʃɑ̃daj/ *n.m.* sweater.

chandelier /ʃɑ̃dəlje/ *n.m.* candlestick.

chandelle /ʃɑ̃dɛl/ *n.f.* candle. **dîner aux** ~**s**, candlelight dinner.

change /ʃɑ̃ʒ/ *n.m.* (foreign) exchange.

changeant, ~**e** /ʃɑ̃ʒɑ̃, -t/ *a.* changeable.

changement /ʃɑ̃ʒmɑ̃/ *n.m.* change. ~ **de vitesses** (*dispositif*) gears.

changer /ʃɑ̃ʒe/ *v.t./i.* change. **se** ~ *v. pr.* change (one's clothes). ~ **de** nom, change one's name. ~ **de train**, change trains. ~ **d'avis** change one's mind. ~ **de vitesses**, change gear.

changeur /ʃɑ̃ʒœr/ *n.m.* ~ **automatique**, (money) change machine.

chanson /ʃɑ̃sɔ̃/ *n.f.* song.

chant /ʃɑ̃/ *n.m.* singing; (*chanson*) song; (*religieux*) hymn.

chant|er /ʃɑ̃te/ *v.t./i.* sing. ~**eur**, ~**euse** *n.m., f.* singer.

chantier /ʃɑ̃tje/ *n.m.* building site. ~ **naval**, shipyard.

chantonner /ʃɑ̃tɔne/ *v.t./i.* hum.

chanvre /ʃɑ̃vr/ *n.m.* hemp.

chapeau (*pl.* ~**x**) /ʃapo/ *n.m.* hat. ~!, well done!

chapelet /ʃaplɛ/ *n.m.* rosary.

chapelle /ʃapɛl/ *n.f.* chapel.

chapelure /ʃaplyr/ *n.f.* breadcrumbs.

chapiteau (*pl.* ~**x**) /ʃapito/ *n.m.* (*de cirque*) big top; (*de colonne*) capital.

chapitre /ʃapitr/ *n.m.* chapter; (*fig.*) subject.

chaque /ʃak/ *a.* every, each.

char /ʃar/ *n.m.* (*mil.*) tank; (*de carnaval*) float; (*charrette*) cart; (*dans l'antiquité*) chariot.

charbon /ʃarbɔ̃/ *n.m.* coal. ~ **de**

bois, charcoal. **~nages** /-ɔnaʒ/
n.m. pl. coal-mines.

charcuterie /ʃarkytri/ *n.f.* pork-
butcher's shop; *(aliments)*
(cooked) pork meats.

chardon /ʃardɔ̃/ *n.m.* thistle.

charge /ʃarʒ/ *n.f.* load, burden;
(mil., électr., jurid.) charge;
(mission) responsibility. **~s,** expenses; *(de locataire)* service
charges. **~s sociales,** social
security contributions.

chargé /ʃarʒe/ *a. (journée)* busy;
(langue) coated.

charg|er /ʃarʒe/ *v.t.* load; *(atta-
quer)* charge; *(batterie)* charge.
—*v.i. (attaquer)* charge. **se ~ de,**
take charge ou care of. **~ qn. de,**
entrust s.o. with. **~ement** /-əmã/
n.m. loading; *(objets)* load.

chariot /ʃarjo/ *n.m. (à roulettes)*
trolley; *(charrette)* cart.

charitable /ʃaritabl/ *a.* charitable.

charité /ʃarite/ *n.f.* charity.

charmant, ~e /ʃarmã, -t/ *a.*
charming.

charme /ʃarm/ *n.m.* charm. **~er**
v.t. charm.

charnier /ʃarnje/ *n.m.* mass grave.

charnière /ʃarnjɛr/ *n.f.* hinge.

charpente /ʃarpɑ̃t/ *n.f.* framework; *(carrure)* build.

charpentier /ʃarpɑ̃tje/ *n.m.* carpenter.

charrette /ʃarɛt/ *n.f.* cart.

charrier /ʃarje/ *v.t.* carry.

charrue /ʃary/ *n.f.* plough.

charte /ʃart/ *n.f.* charter.

charter /ʃartɛr/ *n.m.* charter
flight.

chasse /ʃas/ *n.f.* hunting; *(au fusil)*
shooting; *(poursuite)* chase; *(recherche)* hunt. **~ (d'eau),** (toilet)
flush.

châsse /ʃas/ *n.f.* shrine, reliquary.

chass|er /ʃase/ *v.t./i.* hunt; *(faire*

partir) chase away; *(odeur,
employé)* get rid of. **~e-neige**
n.m. invar. snow-plough. **~eur,
~euse** *n.m., f.* hunter.

châssis /ʃasi/ *n.m.* frame; *(auto.)*
chassis.

chaste /ʃast/ *a.* chaste.

chat, ~te /ʃa, ʃat/ *n.m., f.* cat.

châtaigne /ʃatɛɲ/ *n.f.* chestnut.

châtaignier /ʃatɛɲe/ *n.m.* chestnut tree.

châtain /ʃatɛ̃/ *a. invar.* chestnut
(brown).

château *(pl.* **~x)** /ʃato/ *n.m.*
castle. **~ d'eau,** water-tower. **~
fort,** fortified castle.

châtiment /ʃatimã/ *n.m.* punishment.

chaton /ʃatɔ̃/ *n.m. (chat)* kitten.

chatouill|er /ʃatuje/ *v.t.* tickle.
~ement *n.m.* tickling.

chatouilleu|x, ~se /ʃatujø, -z/
a. ticklish; *(susceptible)* touchy.

chatte /ʃat/ *voir* **chat.**

chaud, ~e /ʃo, ʃod/ *a.* warm;
(brûlant) hot; *(vif: fig.)* warm.
—*n.m.* heat. **au ~,** in the
warm(th). **avoir ~,** be warm; be
hot. **il fait ~,** it is warm; it is hot.

chaudière /ʃodjɛr/ *n.f.* boiler.

chauffage /ʃofaʒ/ *n.m.* heating. **~
central,** central heating.

chauff|er /ʃofe/ *v.t./i.* heat (up). **se
~er** *v. pr.* warm o.s. (up). **~e-
eau** *n.m. invar.* water-heater.

chauffeur /ʃofœr/ *n.m.* driver;
(aux gages de qn.) chauffeur.

chaum|e /ʃom/ *n.m. (de toit)*
thatch.

chaussée /ʃose/ *n.f.* road(way).

chausser /ʃose/ *v.t. (chaussures)*
put on. **~ du 35/etc.,** take a size
35/etc. shoe.

chaussette /ʃosɛt/ *n.f.* sock.

chausson /ʃosɔ̃/ *n.m.* slipper; *(de
bébé)* bootee. **~ (aux pommes),**
(apple) turnover.

chaussure /ʃosyr/ *n.f.* shoe. **~s de ski**, ski boots. **~s de marche**, hiking boots.

chauve /ʃov/ *a.* bald.

chauve-souris (*pl.* **chauves-souris**) /ʃovsuri/ *n.f.* bat.

chaux /ʃo/ *n.f.* lime.

chef /ʃɛf/ *n.m.* leader, head; (*culin.*) chef; (*de tribu*) chief. **~ d'État**, head of State. **~ de gare**, station-master. **~ d'orchestre**, conductor. **~ de service**, department head. **~-lieu** (*pl.* **~s-lieux**) *n.m.* county town.

chef-d'œuvre (*pl.* **chefs-d'œuvre**) /ʃɛdœvr/ *n.m.* master-piece.

chemin /ʃmɛ̃/ *n.m.* path, road; (*direction, trajet*) way. **beaucoup de ~ à faire**, a long way to go. **~ de fer**, railway.

cheminée /ʃmine/ *n.f.* chimney; (*intérieure*) fireplace; (*encadrement*) mantelpiece; (*de bateau*) funnel.

chemise /ʃmiz/ *n.f.* shirt; (*dossier*) folder; (*de livre*) jacket. **~ de nuit**, night-dress.

chemisier /ʃmizje/ *n.m.* blouse.

chêne /ʃɛn/ *n.m.* oak.

chenil /ʃni(l)/ *n.m.* kennels.

chenille /ʃnij/ *n.f.* caterpillar.

chèque /ʃɛk/ *n.m.* cheque. **~ de voyage**, traveller's cheque.

chéquier /ʃekje/ *n.m.* cheque-book.

cher, chère /ʃɛr/ *a.* (*coûteux*) dear, expensive; (*aimé*) dear. —*adv.* (*coûter, payer*) a lot (of money). —*n.m., f.* **mon ~, ma chère**, my dear.

chercher /ʃɛrʃe/ *v.t.* look for; (*aide, paix, gloire*) seek. **aller ~**, go and get or fetch, go for.

chéri, ~e /ʃeri/ *a.* beloved. —*n.m., f.* darling.

chérir /ʃerir/ *v.t.* cherish.

chev|al (*pl.* **~aux**) /ʃval, -o/ *n.m.* horse. **~al - (vapeur)**, horse-power. **faire du ~al**, ride (a horse).

chevalet /ʃvalɛ/ *n.m.* easel.

chevalier /ʃvalje/ *n.m.* knight.

chevelu /ʃvly/ *a.* hairy.

chevelure /ʃvlyr/ *n.f.* hair.

cheveu (*pl.* **~x**) /ʃvø/ *n.m.* (*poil*) hair. **~x**, (*chevelure*) hair. **avoir les ~x longs**, have long hair.

cheville /ʃvij/ *n.f.* ankle; (*fiche*) peg, pin; (*pour mur*) (wall) plug.

chèvre /ʃɛvr/ *n.f.* goat.

chevreau (*pl.* **~x**) /ʃvro/ *n.m.* kid.

chevreuil /ʃvrœj/ *n.m.* roe(-deer); (*culin.*) venison.

chevron /ʃvrɔ̃/ *n.m.* (*poutre*) rafter. **à ~s**, herring-bone.

chevronné /ʃvrɔne/ *a.* ex-perienced, seasoned.

chewing-gum /ʃwiŋɡɔm/ *n.m.* chewing-gum.

chez /ʃe/ *prép.* at or to the house of; (*parmi*) among; (*dans le caractère ou l'œuvre de*) in. **le boucher/etc.**, at the butcher's/*etc.* **~ soi**, at home; (*avec direction*) home. **~-soi** *n.m. invar.* home.

chic /ʃik/ *a. invar.* smart; (*gentil*) kind. **sois ~**, do me a favour.

chichis /ʃiʃi/ *n.m. pl.* (*fam.*) fuss.

chicorée /ʃikɔre/ *n.f.* (*frisée*) en-dive; (*à café*) chicory.

chien, ~ne /ʃjɛ̃, ʃjɛn/ *n.m.* dog. **~-n.f.** dog, bitch. **~ de garde**, watch-dog. **~-loup** *n.m.* (*pl.* **~s-loups**) wolfhound.

chiffon /ʃifɔ̃/ *n.m.* rag.

chiffre /ʃifr/ *n.m.* figure; (*code*) code. **~s arabes/romains**, Arabic/Roman numerals. **~ d'affaires**, turnover.

chignon /ʃiɲɔ̃/ *n.m.* bun, chignon.

Chili /ʃili/ *n.m.* Chile.

chilien, ~ne /ʃiljɛ̃, -jɛn/ *a. & n.m., f.* Chilean.

chim|ie /ʃimi/ *n.f.* chemistry. **~ique** *a.* chemical. **~iste** *n.m./f.* chemist.

chimpanzé /ʃɛ̃pɑ̃ze/ *n.m.* chimpanzee.

Chine /ʃin/ *n.f.* China.

chinois, ~e /ʃinwa, -z/ *a. & n.m., f.* Chinese. —*n.m.* (*lang.*) Chinese.

chiot /ʃjo/ *n.m.* pup(py).

chips /ʃips/ *n.m. pl.* crisps; (*Amer.*) chips.

chirurgic|al (*m. pl.* **~aux**) /ʃiryʁʒikal, -o/ *a.* surgical.

chirurg|ie /ʃiryʁʒi/ *n.f.* surgery. **~ie esthétique**, plastic surgery. **~ien** *n.m.* surgeon.

chlore /klɔʁ/ *n.m.* chlorine.

choc /ʃɔk/ *n.m.* (*heurt*) impact, shock; (*émotion*) shock; (*collision*) crash; (*affrontement*) clash; (*méd.*) shock.

chocolat /ʃɔkɔla/ *n.m.* chocolate; (*à boire*) drinking chocolate. **~ au lait**, milk chocolate. **~ chaud**, hot chocolat.

chœur /kœʁ/ *n.m.* (*antique*) chorus; (*chanteurs, nef*) choir.

chois|ir /ʃwaziʁ/ *v.t.* choose, select.

choix /ʃwa/ *n.m.* choice, selection. **au ~**, according to preference. **de premier ~**, top quality.

choléra /kɔleʁa/ *n.m.* cholera.

chômage /ʃomaʒ/ *n.m.* unemployment. **en ~**, unemployed.

chôm|eur, ~euse /ʃomœʁ, -øz/ *n.m., f.* unemployed person. **les ~s**, the unemployed.

chope /ʃɔp/ *n.f.* tankard.

choquer /ʃɔke/ *v.t.* shock.

choral /kɔʁal/ *n.f.* choir, choral society.

chorégraph|ie /kɔʁegʁafi/ *n.f.* choreography. **~e** *n.m./f.* choreographer.

choriste /kɔʁist/ *n.m./f.* (*à l'église*) chorister; (*opéra, etc.*) member of the chorus *ou* choir.

chose /ʃoz/ *n.f.* thing.

chou (*pl.* **~x**) /ʃu/ *n.m.* cabbage. **~ (à la crème)**, cream puff. **~x de Bruxelles**, Brussels sprouts.

chouchou, ~te /ʃuʃu, -t/ *n.m., f.* pet, darling. **le ~ du prof.**, the teacher's pet.

choucroute /ʃukʁut/ *n.f.* sauerkraut.

chouette[1] /ʃwɛt/ *n.f.* owl.

chouette[2] /ʃwɛt/ *a.* (*fam.*) super.

chou-fleur (*pl.* **choux-fleurs**) /ʃuflœʁ/ *n.m.* cauliflower.

chrétien, ~ne /kʁetjɛ̃, -jɛn/ *a. & n.m., f.* Christian.

Christ /kʁist/ *n.m.* **le ~**, Christ.

christianisme /kʁistjanism/ *n.m.* Christianity.

chrom|e /kʁom/ *n.m.* chromium, chrome. **~é** *a.* chromiumplated.

chromosome /kʁomozom/ *n,m.* chromosome.

chronique /kʁonik/ *a.* chronic. —*n.f.* (*rubrique*) column; (*nouvelles*) news; (*annales*) chronicle.

chronolog|ie /kʁonɔlɔʒi/ *n.f.* chronology. **~ique** *a.* chronological.

chronom|ètre /kʁonɔmɛtʁ/ *n.m.* stop-watch. **~étrer** *v.t.* time.

chrysanthème /kʁizɑ̃tɛm/ *n.m.* chrysanthemum.

chuchot|er /ʃyʃɔte/ *v.t./i.* whisper. **~ement** *n.m.* whisper(ing).

chut /ʃyt/ *int.* shush.

chute /ʃyt/ *n.f.* fall. **~ (d'eau)**, waterfall. **~ de pluie**, rainfall. **la ~ des cheveux**, hair loss.

Chypre /ʃipʁ/ *n.f.* Cyprus.

-ci /si/ *adv.* (*après un nom précédé de ce, cette, etc.*) **cet homme-ci**, this man. **ces maisons-ci**, these houses.

ci- /si/ *adv.* here. **ci-après,** hereafter. **ci-contre,** opposite. **ci-dessous,** below. **ci-dessus,** above. **ci-gît,** here lies. **ci-inclus, ci-joint, ci-jointe,** enclosed.

cible /sibl/ *n.f.* target.

ciboul|e /sibul/ *n.f.*, **∼ette** *n.f.* chive(s).

cicatrice /sikatris/ *n.f.* scar.

cicatriser /sikatrize/ *v.t.*, **se ∼** *v. pr.* heal (up).

cidre /sidr/ *n.m.* cider.

ciel (*pl.* **cieux, ciels**) /sjɛl, sjø/ *n.m.* sky; (*relig.*) heaven.

cierge /sjɛrʒ/ *n.m.* candle.

cigale /sigal/ *n.f.* cicada.

cigare /sigar/ *n.m.* cigar.

cigarette /sigarɛt/ *n.f.* cigarette.

cigogne /sigɔɲ/ *n.f.* stork.

cil /sil/ *n.m.* (eye)lash.

ciment /simɑ̃/ *n.m.* cement. **∼er** /-te/ *v.t.* cement.

cimetière /simtjɛr/ *n.m.* cemetery.

cinéaste /sineast/ *n.m./f.* film-maker.

cinéma /sinema/ *n.m.* cinema.

cinémathèque /sinematɛk/ *n.f.* film library; (*salle*) film theatre.

cinglé /sɛ̃gle/ *a.* (*fam.*) crazy.

cinq /sɛ̃k/ *a.* & *n.m.* five. **∼ième** *a.* & *n.m./f.* fifth.

cinquantaine /sɛ̃kɑ̃tɛn/ *n.f.* une **∼ (de),** about fifty.

cinquant|e /sɛ̃kɑ̃t/ *a.* & *n.m.* fifty. **∼ième** *a.* & *n.m./f.* fiftieth.

cintre /sɛ̃tr/ *n.m.* coat-hanger; (*archit.*) curve.

cintré /sɛ̃tre/ *a.* (*chemise*) fitted.

cirage /siraʒ/ *n.m.* (wax) polish.

circonférence /sirkɔ̃ferɑ̃s/ *n.f.* circumference.

circonflexe /sirkɔ̃flɛks/ *a.* circumflex.

circonscription /sirkɔ̃skripsjɔ̃/ *n.f.* district. **∼ (électorale),** constituency.

circonstance /sirkɔ̃stɑ̃s/ *n.f.* circumstance; (*occasion*) occasion.

circuit /sirkɥi/ *n.m.* circuit; (*trajet*) tour, trip.

circulaire /sirkylɛr/ *a.* & *n.f.* circular.

circul|er /sirkyle/ *v.i.* circulate; (*train, automobile, etc.*) travel; (*piéton*) walk. **faire ∼er,** (*badauds*) move on. **∼ation** *n.f.* circulation; (*de véhicules*) traffic.

cire /sir/ *n.f.* wax.

ciré /sire/ *n.m.* oilskin; waterproof.

cir|er /sire/ *v.t.* polish, wax.

cirque /sirk/ *n.m.* circus; (*arène*) amphitheatre.

cirrhose /siroz/ *n.f.* cirrhosis.

ciseau (*pl.* **∼x**) /sizo/ *n.m.* chisel. **∼x,** scissors.

citadelle /sitadɛl/ *n.f.* citadel.

citadin, ∼e /sitadɛ̃, -in/ *n.m., f.* city dweller. — *a.* city.

cité /site/ *n.f.* city. **∼ ouvrière,** (workers') housing estate. **∼ universitaire,** (university) halls of residence.

cit|er /site/ *v.t.* quote, cite. **∼ation** *n.f.* quotation.

citerne /sitɛrn/ *n.f.* tank.

citoyen, ∼ne /sitwajɛ̃, -jɛn/ *n.m., f.* citizen. **∼neté** /-jɛnte/ *n.f.* citizenship.

citron /sitrɔ̃/ *n.m.* lemon. **∼ vert,** lime. **∼nade** /-ɔnad/ *n.f.* lemon squash *ou* drink, (still) lemonade.

citrouille /sitruj/ *n.f.* pumpkin.

civet /sivɛ/ *n.m.* stew. **∼ de lièvre/lapin,** jugged hare/rabbit.

civière /sivjɛr/ *n.f.* stretcher.

civil /sivil/ *a.* civil; *n.m.* civilian. **dans le ∼,** in civilian life. **en ∼,** in plain clothes.

civilisation /sivilizasjɔ̃/ *n.f.* civilization.

civi|que /sivik/ *a.* civic. **∼sme** *n.m.* civic sense.

clair /klɛr/ *a.* clear; (*éclairé*) light,

bright; (*couleur*) light; (*liquide*) thin. —*adv.* clearly. —*n.m.* ∼ **de lune**, moonlight. **le plus** ∼ **de**, most of. ∼**ement** *adv.* clearly.

clairon /klɛrɔ̃/ *n.m.* bugle.

clan /klɑ̃/ *n.m.* clan.

clandestin, ∼**e** /klɑ̃dɛstɛ̃, -in/ *a.* secret; (*journal*) underground. **passager** ∼, stowaway.

clapier /klapje/ *n.m.* (rabbit) hutch.

clapot|er /klapɔte/ *v.i.* lap.

claque /klak/ *n.f.* slap.

claqu|er /klake/ *v.i.* bang; (*porte*) slam, bang; (*fouet*) snap, crack; (*mourir: fam.*) snuff it. —*v.t.* (*porte*) slam, bang; (*dépenser: fam.*) blow; (*fatiguer: fam.*) tire out. ∼**ement** *n.m.* bang(ing); slam(ming); snap(ping).

clarinette /klarinɛt/ *n.f.* clarinet.

clarté /klarte/ *n.f.* light, brightness; (*netteté*) clarity.

classe /klɑs/ *n.f.* class; (*salle: scol.*) class(-room). **aller en** ∼, go to school. ∼ **ouvrière/moyenne**, working/middle class.

class|er /klɑse/ *v.t.* classify; (*par mérite*) grade; (*papiers*) file; (*affaire*) close. **se** ∼**er premier/ dernier**, come first/last. ∼**ement** *n.m.* classification; grading; filing; (*rang*) place, grade; (*de coureur*) placing.

classeur /klɑsœr/ *n.m.* filing cabinet; (*chemise*) file.

classif|ier /klasifje/ *v.t.* classify. ∼**ication** *n.f.* classification.

classique /klasik/ *a.* classical; (*de qualité*) classic(al); (*habituel*) classic. —*n.m.* classic; (*auteur*) classical author.

clause /kloz/ *n.f.* clause.

claustrophobie /klostrɔfɔbi/ *n.f.* claustrophobia.

clavecin /klavsɛ̃/ *n.m.* harpsichord.

clavicule /klavikyl/ *n.f.* collarbone.

clavier /klavje/ *n.m.* keyboard.

claviste /klavist/ *n.m./f.* keyboarder.

clé, clef /kle/ *n.f.* key; (*outil*) spanner; (*mus.*) clef. —*a. invar.* key. ∼ **anglaise**, (monkey-) wrench. ∼ **de contact**, ignition key.

clémentine /klemɑ̃tin/ *n.f.* clementine.

clergé /klɛrʒe/ *n.m.* clergy.

cliché /kliʃe/ *n.m.* cliché; (*photo.*) negative.

client, ∼**e** /klijɑ̃, -t/ *n.m.*, *f.* customer; (*d'un avocat*) client; (*d'un médecin*) patient; (*d'hôtel*) guest.

cligner /kliɲe/ *v.i.* ∼ **des yeux**, blink. ∼ **de l'œil**, wink.

clignot|er /kliɲɔte/ *v.i.* blink; (*lumière*) flicker; (*comme signal*) flash. ∼**ant** *n.m.* (*auto.*) indicator.

climat /klima/ *n.m.* climate. ∼**ique** -tik/ *a.* climatic.

climatis|ation /klimatizasjɔ̃/ *n.f.* air-conditioning. ∼**é** *a.* air-conditioned.

clin d'œil /klɛ̃dœj/ *n.m.* wink. **en un** ∼, in a flash.

clinique /klinik/ *a.* clinical. —*n.f.* (*private*) clinic.

clinquant, ∼**e** /klɛ̃kɑ̃, -t/ *a.* showy.

clip /klip/ *n.m.* video.

clitoris /klitɔris/ *n.m.* clitoris.

clochard, ∼**e** /klɔʃar, -d/ *n.m.*, *f.* tramp.

cloch|e /klɔʃ/ *n.f.* bell; (*fam.*) idiot. ∼ **à fromage**, cheese-cover. ∼**ette** *n.f.* bell.

clocher[1] /klɔʃe/ *n.m.* bell-tower; (*pointu*) steeple. **de** ∼, parochial.

clocher[2] /klɔʃe/ *v.i.* (*fam.*) be wrong.

cloison /klwazɔ̃/ n.f. partition; (fig.) barrier.

cloître /klwatr/ n.m. cloister.

cloîtrer (se) /(sə)klwatre/ v. pr. shut o.s. away.

cloque /klɔk/ n.f. blister.

clore /klɔr/ v.t. close.

clos, ~e /klo, -z/ a. closed.

clôtur|e /klotyr/ n.f. fence; (fermeture) closure. **~er** v.t. enclose; (festival, séance, etc.) close.

clou /klu/ n.m. nail; (furoncle) boil; (de spectacle) star attraction. **~ de girofle,** clove. **les ~s,** (passage) zebra ou pedestrian crossing. **~er** v.t. nail down.

clouté /klute/ a. studded.

clown /klun/ n.m. clown.

club /klœb/ n.m. club.

coaguler /kɔagyle/ v.t./i., **se ~** v. pr. coagulate.

coalition /kɔalisjɔ̃/ n.f. coalition.

coasser /kɔase/ v.i. croak.

cobaye /kɔbaj/ n.m. guinea-pig.

coca /kɔka/ n.m. (P.) Coke.

cocaïne /kɔkain/ n.f. cocaine.

cocasse /kɔkas/ a. comical.

coccinelle /kɔksinɛl/ n.f. ladybird; (voiture) beetle.

cocher /kɔʃe/ v.t. tick (off), check.

cochon, ~ne /kɔʃɔ̃, -ɔn/ n.m. pig. —n.m., f. (personne: fam.) pig. —a. (fam.) filthy. **~nerie** /-ɔnri/ n.f. (saleté: fam.) rubbish; (marchandise: fam.) rubbish.

cocktail /kɔktɛl/ n.m. cocktail; (réunion) cocktail party.

cocon /kɔkɔ̃/ n.m. cocoon.

cocorico /kɔkɔriko/ n.m. cock-a-doodle-doo.

cocotier /kɔkɔtje/ n.m. coconut palm.

cocotte /kɔkɔt/ n.f. (marmite) casserole. **~ minute,** (P.) pressure-cooker.

cocu /kɔky/ n.m. (fam.) cuckold.

code /kɔd/ n.m. code. **~s, phares ~,** dipped headlights. **~ de la route,** Highway Code. **se mettre en ~,** dip one's headlights.

coder /kɔde/ v.t. code.

codifier /kɔdifje/ v.t. codify.

coéquip|ier, ~ière /kɔekipje, -jɛr/ n.m., f. team-mate.

cœur /kœr/ n.m. heart; (cartes) hearts. **~ d'artichaut,** artichoke heart. **~ de palm,** heart of palm. **avoir mal au ~,** feel sick.

coexist|er /kɔɛgziste/ v.i. coexist. **~ence** n.f. coexistence.

coffre /kɔfr/ n.m. chest; (pour argent) safe; (auto.) boot. **~-fort** (pl. **~s-forts**) n.m. safe.

coffret /kɔfrɛ/ n.m. casket, box.

cognac /kɔɲak/ n.m. cognac.

cogner /kɔɲe/ v.t./i. knock. **se ~** v. pr. knock o.s.

cohérent, ~e /kɔerã, -t/ a. coherent.

cohésion /kɔezjɔ̃/ n.f. cohesion.

cohue /kɔy/ n.f. crowd.

coiffer /kwafe/ v.t. do the hair of; (surmonter) cap. **se ~** v. pr. do one's hair. **~é de,** wearing. **bien/mal ~é,** with tidy/untidy hair. **~eur, ~euse** n.f. hairdresser; n.f. dressing-table.

coiffure /kwafyr/ n.f. hairstyle; (chapeau) hat; (métier) hairdressing.

coin /kwɛ̃/ n.m. corner; (endroit) spot; (cale) wedge. **au ~ du feu,** by the fireside. **dans le ~,** locally. **du ~,** local.

coincer /kwɛ̃se/ v.t. jam; (caler) wedge; (attraper: fam.) catch. **se ~** v. pr. get jammed.

coïncid|er /kɔɛ̃side/ v.i. coincide. **~ence** n.f. coincidence.

coing /kwɛ̃/ n.m. quince.

coït /kɔit/ n.m. intercourse.

coke /kɔk/ n.m. coke.

col /kɔl/ *n.m.* collar; (*de bouteille*) neck; (*de montagne*) pass. ∼ roulé, polo-neck. ∼ de l'utérus, cervix.

coléoptère /kɔleɔptɛr/ *n.m.* beetle.

colère /kɔlɛr/ *n.f.* anger; (*accès*) fit of anger. en ∼, angry. se mettre en ∼, lose one's temper.

colér∣eux, ∼euse /kɔlerø, -z/, ∼ique *adjs.* quick-tempered.

colibri /kɔlibri/ *n.m.* humming-bird.

colin /kɔlɛ̃/ *n.m.* (*poisson*) hake.

colique /kɔlik/ *n.f.* diarrhoea; (*méd.*) colic.

colis /kɔli/ *n.m.* parcel.

collabor∣er /kɔlabɔre/ *v.i.* collaborate (à, on). ∼er à, (*journal*) contribute to. ∼ateur, ∼atrice *n.m.,* *f.* collaborator; contributor. ∼ation *n.f.* collaboration (à, on); contribution (à, to).

collant, ∼e /kɔlɑ̃, -t/ *a.* skin-tight; (*poisseux*) sticky. —*n.m.* (*bas*) tights; (*de danseur*) leotard.

colle /kɔl/ *n.f.* glue; (*en pâte*) paste.

collect∣e /kɔlɛkt/ *n.f.* collection. ∼er *v.t.* collect.

collecteur /kɔlɛktœr/ *n.m.* (*égout*) main sewer.

collecti∣f, ∼ve /kɔlɛktif, -v/ *a.* collective; (*billet, voyage*) group. ∼vement *adv.* collectively.

collection /kɔlɛksjɔ̃/ *n.f.* collection.

collectionn∣er /kɔlɛksjɔne/ *v.t.* collect. ∼eur, ∼euse *n.m.,* *f.* collector.

collectivité /kɔlɛktivite/ *n.f.* community.

collège /kɔlɛʒ/ *n.m.* (secondary) school; (*assemblée*) college.

collègue /kɔlɛg/ *n.m./f.* colleague.

coller /kɔle/ *v.t.* stick; (*avec colle liquide*) glue; (*affiche*) stick up. —*v.i.* stick (à, to); (*être collant*) be sticky.

collier /kɔlje/ *n.m.* necklace; (*de chien*) collar.

colline /kɔlin/ *n.f.* hill.

collision /kɔlizjɔ̃/ *n.f.* (*choc*) collision; (*lutte*) clash.

colloque /kɔlɔk/ *n.m.* symposium.

collyre /kɔlir/ *n.m.* eye drops.

colmater /kɔlmate/ *v.t.* seal; (*trou*) fill in.

colombe /kɔlɔ̃b/ *n.f.* dove.

Colombie /kɔlɔ̃bi/ *n.f.* Colombia.

colon /kɔlɔ̃/ *n.m.* settler.

colonel /kɔlɔnɛl/ *n.m.* colonel.

colonie /kɔlɔni/ *n.f.* colony. ∼ de vacances, children's holiday camp.

coloniser /kɔlɔnize/ *v.t.* colonize.

colonne /kɔlɔn/ *n.f.* column. ∼ vertébrale, spine.

color∣er /kɔlɔre/ *v.t.* colour; (*bois*) stain. ∼ant *n.m.* colouring.

colorier /kɔlɔrje/ *v.t.* colour (in).

coloris /kɔlɔri/ *n.m.* colour.

colosse /kɔlɔs/ *n.m.* giant.

colza /kɔlza/ *n.m.* rape(-seed).

coma /kɔma/ *n.m.* coma. dans le ∼, in a coma.

combat /kɔ̃ba/ *n.m.* fight; (*sport*) match. ∼s, fighting.

combati∣f, ∼ve /kɔ̃batif, -v/ *a.* eager to fight; (*esprit*) fighting.

combatt∣re† /kɔ̃batr/ *v.t./i.* fight. ∼ant, ∼ante *n.m.,* *f.* fighter; (*mil.*) combatant.

combien /kɔ̃bjɛ̃/ *adv.* ∼ (de), (*quantité*) how much; (*nombre*) how many; (*temps*) how long. ∼ il a changé!, (*comme*) how he has changed!

combinaison /kɔ̃binɛzɔ̃/ *n.f.* combination; (*manigance*) scheme; (*de femme*) slip; (*bleu de travail*) boiler suit; (*de plongée*) wetsuit.

combiné /kɔ̃bine/ *n.m.* (*de téléphone*) receiver.

combiner /kɔ̃bine/ *v.t.* (*réunir*) combine; (*calculer*) devise.

comble[1] /kɔ̃bl/ a. packed.

comble[2] /kɔ̃bl/ n.m. c'est le ~!, that's the (absolute) limit!

combler /kɔ̃ble/ v.t. fill; (perte, déficit) make good; (désir) fulfil; (personne) gratify.

combustible /kɔ̃bystibl/ n.m. fuel.

combustion /kɔ̃bystjɔ̃/ n.f. combustion.

comédie /kɔmedi/ n.f. comedy. ~ **musicale**, musical. **jouer la** ~, put on an act.

comédien, ~ne /kɔmedjɛ̃, -jɛn/ n.m., f. actor, actress.

comestible /kɔmɛstibl/ a. edible. ~**s** n.m. pl. foodstuffs.

comète /kɔmɛt/ n.f. comet.

comique /kɔmik/ a. comical; (genre) comic. —n.n. (acteur) comic; (comédie) comedy; (côté drôle) comical aspect.

comité /kɔmite/ n.m. committee.

commandant /kɔmɑ̃dɑ̃/ n.m. commander; (armée de terre) major. ~ **(de bord)**, captain.

commande /kɔmɑ̃d/ n.f. (comm.) order. ~**s**, (d'avion etc.) controls.

commander /kɔmɑ̃de/ v.t. command; (acheter) order. —v.i. be in command. ~ **à qn. de**, command s.o. to.

comme /kɔm/ conj. as. —prép. like. —adv. (exclamation) how. ~ **ci comme ça**, so-so. ~ **d'habitude**, as usual. ~ **il faut**, proper(ly). ~ **c'est bon!**, it's so good! ~ **il est mignon!** isn't he sweet!

commémor|er /kɔmemɔre/ v.t. commemorate. ~**ation** n.f. commemoration.

commenc|er /kɔmɑ̃se/ v.t. begin, start. ~**er à faire**, begin ou start to do. ~**ement** n.m. beginning, start.

comment /kɔmɑ̃/ adv. how. ~?, (répétition) pardon?; (surprise) what? ~ **est-il?**, what is he like?

commentaire /kɔmɑ̃tɛr/ n.m. comment; (d'un texte) commentary.

commenter /kɔmɑ̃te/ v.t. comment on.

commerç|ant, ~e /kɔmɛrsɑ̃, -t/ a. (rue) shopping. —n.m., f. shopkeeper.

commerce /kɔmɛrs/ n.m. trade, commerce; (magasin) business. **faire du** ~, trade.

commerc|ial (m. pl. ~**iaux**) /kɔmɛrsjal, -jo/ a. commercial.

commettre /kɔmɛtr/ v.t. commit.

commissaire /kɔmisɛr/ n.m. ~ **(de police)**, (police) superintendent.

commissariat /kɔmisarja/ n.m. ~ **(de police)**, police station.

commission /kɔmisjɔ̃/ n.f. commission; (course) errand; (message) message. ~**s**, shopping.

commode /kɔmɔd/ a. handy; (facile) easy. —n.f. chest of drawers).

commun, ~e /kɔmœ̃, -yn/ a. common; (effort, action) joint; (frais, pièce) shared. —n.f. (circonscription) commune. —**al** (m. pl. ~**aux**) /-ynal, -o/ a. of the commune, local.

communauté /kɔmynote/ n.f. community. ~ **des biens** (entre époux) shared estate.

commune /kɔmyn/ voir commun.

communicati|f, ~ve /kɔmynikatif, -v/ a. communicative.

communication /kɔmynikasjɔ̃/ n.f. communication; (téléphonique) call. ~ **interurbaine**, long-distance call.

communier /kɔmynje/ v.i. (relig.) receive communion; (fig.) commune. ~**ion** n.f. communion.

communiqué /kɔmynike/ n.m. communiqué.

communiquer /kɔmynike/ v.t. pass on, communicate. —v.i. communicate.

communis|te /kɔmynist/ a. & n.m./f. communist. **∼me** n.m. communism.

commutateur /kɔmytatœr/ n.m. (électr.) switch.

compact /kɔ̃pakt/ a. dense; (voiture) compact.

compact disc /kɔ̃paktdisk/ n.m. (P.) compact disc.

compagne /kɔ̃paɲ/ n.f. companion.

compagnie /kɔ̃paɲi/ n.f. company. **tenir ∼ à**, keep company.

compagnon /kɔ̃paɲɔ̃/ n.m. companion. **∼ de jeu**, playmate.

comparaître /kɔ̃parɛtr/ v.i. (jurid.) appear (devant, before).

compar|er /kɔ̃pare/ v.t. compare. **∼er qch./qn. à** ou **et** compare sth./s.o. with ou and. **∼able** a. comparable. **∼aison** n.f. comparison.

compartiment /kɔ̃partimɑ̃/ n.m. compartment.

compas /kɔ̃pa/ n.m. (pair of) compasses.

compassion /kɔ̃pasjɔ̃/ n.f. compassion.

compatible /kɔ̃patibl/ a. compatible.

compatir /kɔ̃patir/ v.i. sympathize. **∼ à**, share in.

compatriote /kɔ̃patrijɔt/ n.m./f. compatriot.

compens|er /kɔ̃pɑ̃se/ v.t. compensate for, make up for. **∼ation** n.f. compensation.

compéten|t, **∼te** /kɔpetɑ̃, -t/ a. competent. **∼ce** n.f. competence.

compétiti|f, **∼ve** /kɔ̃petitif, -v/ a. competitive.

compétition /kɔ̃petisjɔ̃/ n.f. competition; (sportive) event.

complainte /kɔ̃plɛ̃t/ n.f. lament.

complément /kɔ̃plemɑ̃/ n.m. complement; (reste) rest. **∼ (d'objet)**, (gram.) object. **∼aire** /-tɛr/ a. complementary; (renseignements) supplementary.

compl|et[1], **∼ète** /kɔ̃plɛ, -t/ a. complete; (train, hôtel, etc.) full. **∼ètement** adv. completely.

complet[2] /kɔ̃plɛ/ n.m. suit.

compléter /kɔ̃plete/ v.t. complete; (agrémenter) complement. **se ∼** v. pr. complement each other.

complex|e[1] /kɔ̃plɛks/ a. complex. **∼ité** n.f. complexity.

complex|e[2] /kɔ̃plɛks/ n.m. (sentiment, bâtiments) complex. **∼é** a. hung up.

complication /kɔ̃plikasjɔ̃/ n.f. complication; (complexité) complexity.

complic|e /kɔ̃plis/ n.m. accomplice. **∼ité** n.f. complicity.

compliment /kɔ̃plimɑ̃/ n.m. compliment. **∼s**, (félicitations) congratulations. **∼er** /-te/ v.t. compliment.

compliqu|er /kɔ̃plike/ v.t. complicate. **se ∼er** v. pr. become complicated. **∼é** a. complicated.

complot /kɔ̃plo/ n.m. plot. **∼er** /-ɔte/ v.t./i. plot.

comporter[1] /kɔ̃pɔrte/ v.t. contain; (impliquer) involve.

comport|er[2] (se) /(sə)kɔ̃pɔrte/ v. pr. behave. **∼ement** n.m. behaviour.

composé /kɔ̃poze/ n.m., a. compound.

composer /kɔ̃poze/ v.t. make up, compose; (chanson, visage) compose; (numéro) dial. **se ∼ de**, be made up ou composed of.

composi|teur, **∼trice** /kɔ̃pozitœr, -tris/ n.m., f. (mus.) composer.

composition /kɔ̃pozisjɔ̃/ n.f. composition; (examen) test, exam.

composter /kɔ̃pɔste/ *v.t.* (*billet*) punch.

compote /kɔ̃pɔt/ *n.f.* stewed fruit. **~e de pommes**, stewed apples.

compréhensible /kɔ̃preãsibl/ *a.* understandable.

compréhensi|f, ~ve /kɔ̃preãsif, -v/ *a.* understanding.

compréhension /kɔ̃preãsjɔ̃/ *n.f.* understanding, comprehension.

comprendre† /kɔ̃prãdr/ *v.t.* understand; (*comporter*) comprise.

compresse /kɔ̃prɛs/ *n.f.* compress.

compression /kɔ̃presjɔ̃/ *n.f.* (*physique*) compression, (*réduction*) reduction. **~ de personnel**, staff cuts.

comprimé /kɔ̃prime/ *n.m.* tablet.

comprimer /kɔ̃prime/ *v.t.* compress; (*réduire*) reduce.

compris, ~e /kɔ̃pri, -z/ *a.* included; (*d'accord*) agreed. **service (non) ~**, service (not) included; (*not*) including service. **tout ~**, (all) inclusive. **y ~**, including.

compromettre /kɔ̃prɔmɛtr/ *v.t.* compromise.

compromis /kɔ̃prɔmi/ *n.m.* compromise.

comptab|le /kɔ̃tabl/ *a.* accounting. —*n.m.* accountant. **~ilité** /-ilite/ *n.f.* accountancy; (*comptes*) accounts; (*service*) accounts department.

comptant /kɔ̃tã/ *adv.* (*payer*) in cash; (*acheter*) for cash.

compte /kɔ̃t/ *n.m.* count; (*facture, à la banque, comptabilité*) account; (*nombre exact*) right number. **demander/rendre des ~s**, ask for/give an explanation. **à bon ~**, cheaply. **à son ~**, (*travailler*) for o.s., on one's own. **faire le ~ de**, count. **sur le ~ de**, about. **~ rendu**, report; (*de film, livre*) review.

compter /kɔ̃te/ *v.t./i.* count; (*prévoir*)

reckon; (*facturer*) charge for; (*classer*) consider.—*v.i.* (*calculer, importer*) count. **~ sur**, rely on.

compteur /kɔ̃tœr/ *n.m.* meter.

comptoir /kɔ̃twar/ *n.m.* counter; (*de café*) bar.

comt|e, ~esse /kɔ̃t, -ɛs/ *n.m., f.* count, countess.

comté /kɔ̃te/ *n.m.* county.

concave /kɔ̃kav/ *a.* concave.

concentr|er /kɔ̃sãtre/ *v.t., se ~er v. pr.* concentrate. **~ation** *n.f.* concentration. **~é** *a.* concentrated; (*lait*) condensed; (*personne*) absorbed; *n.m.* concentrate.

concept /kɔ̃sɛpt/ *n.m.* concept.

conception /kɔ̃sɛpsjɔ̃/ *n.f.* conception.

concerner /kɔ̃sɛrne/ *v.t.* concern. **en ce qui me concerne**, as far as I am concerned.

concert /kɔ̃sɛr/ *n.m.* concert.

concerter /kɔ̃sɛrte/ *se ~ v. pr.* confer.

concerto /kɔ̃sɛrto/ *n.m.* concerto.

concession /kɔ̃sesjɔ̃/ *n.f.* concession; (*terrain*) plot.

concessionaire /kɔ̃sesjɔnɛr/ *n.m./f.* (authorized) dealer.

concevoir† /kɔ̃svwar/ *v.t.* (*imaginer, engendrer*) conceive; (*comprendre*) understand.

concierge /kɔ̃sjɛrʒ/ *n.m./f.* caretaker.

concil|ier /kɔ̃silje/ *v.t.* reconcile. **~iation** *n.f.* conciliation.

concis, ~e /kɔ̃si, -z/ *a.* concise.

concitoyen, ~ne /kɔ̃sitwajɛ̃, -jɛn/ *n.m., f.* fellow citizen.

concl|ure† /kɔ̃klyr/ *v.t./i.* conclude. **~usion** *n.f.* conclusion.

concombre /kɔ̃kɔ̃br/ *n.m.* cucumber.

concorder /kɔ̃kɔrde/ *v.i.* agree.

concourir /kɔ̃kurir/ *v.i.* compete. **~ à**, contribute towards.

concours /kɔ̃kur/ n.m. competition; (*examen*) competitive examination; (*aide*) aid; (*de circonstances*) combination.

concr|et, **∼ète** /kɔ̃krɛ, -t/ a. concrete. **∼ètement** adv. in concrete terms.

concrétiser /kɔ̃kretize/ v.t. give concrete form to. **se ∼** v. pr. materialize.

conçu /kɔ̃sy/ a. **bien/mal ∼**, (*appartement etc.*) well/badly planned.

concurrenc|e /kɔ̃kyrɑ̃s/ n.f. competition. **∼er** v.t. compete with.

concurrent, **∼e** /kɔ̃kyrɑ̃, -t/ n.m., f. competitor; (*scol.*) candidate. **—**a. competing.

condamn|er /kɔ̃dane/ v.t. (*censurer, obliger*) condemn; (*jurid.*) sentence; (*porte*) block up. **∼ation** n.f. condemnation; (*peine*) sentence.

condens|er /kɔ̃dɑ̃se/ v.t., **se ∼er** v. pr. condense. **∼ation** n.f. condensation.

condiment /kɔ̃dimɑ̃/ n.m. condiment.

condition /kɔ̃disjɔ̃/ n.f. condition. **∼s**, (*prix*) terms. **à ∼ de** ou **que**, provided (that). **∼nel** n.m. conditional (tense).

conditionnement /kɔ̃disjɔnmɑ̃/ n.m. conditioning; (*emballage*) packaging.

condoléances /kɔ̃dɔleɑ̃s/ n.f. pl. condolences.

conduc|teur, **∼trice** /kɔ̃dyktœr, -tris/ n.m., f. driver.

conduire† /kɔ̃dɥir/ v.t. lead; (*auto.*) drive; (*affaire*) conduct. **—**v.i. drive. **se ∼** v. pr. behave.

conduite /kɔ̃dɥit/ n.f. conduct; (*auto.*) driving; (*tuyau*) main. **∼ à droite**, (*place*) right-hand drive.

cône /kon/ n.m. cone.

confection /kɔ̃fɛksjɔ̃/ n.f. making.

de ∼, ready-made. **la ∼**, the clothing industry.

confédération /kɔ̃federasjɔ̃/ n.f. confederation.

conférenc|e /kɔ̃ferɑ̃s/ n.f. conference; (*exposé*) lecture.

conférer /kɔ̃fere/ v.t. give; (*décerner*) confer.

confess|er /kɔ̃fese/ v.t., **se ∼er** v. pr. confess. **∼ion** n.f. confession; (*religion*) denomination.

confiance /kɔ̃fjɑ̃s/ n.f. trust. **avoir en**, trust.

confiant, **∼e** /kɔ̃fjɑ̃, -t/ a. (*assure*) confident; (*sans défiance*) trusting.

confiden|t, **∼te** /kɔ̃fidɑ̃, -t/ n.m., f. confidant, confidante. **∼ce** n.f. confidence.

confidentiel, **∼le** /kɔ̃fidɑ̃sjɛl/ a. confidential.

confier /kɔ̃fje/ v.t. **∼ à qn.**, entrust s.o. with; (*secret*) confide to s.o. **se ∼ à**, confide in.

confirm|er /kɔ̃firme/ v.t. confirm. **∼ation** n.f. confirmation.

confiserie /kɔ̃fizri/ n.f. sweet shop. **∼s**, confectionery.

confis|quer /kɔ̃fiske/ v.t. confiscate. **∼cation** n.f. confiscation.

confit, **∼e** /kɔ̃fi, -t/ a. (*culin.*) candied. **fruits ∼s**, crystallized fruits. **—**n.m. **∼ d'oie**, goose liver conserve.

confiture /kɔ̃fityr/ n.f. jam.

conflit /kɔ̃fli/ n.m. conflict.

confondre /kɔ̃fɔ̃dr/ v.t. confuse, mix up; (*consterner, étonner*) confound.

conforme /kɔ̃fɔrm/ a. **∼ à**, in accordance with.

conformément /kɔ̃fɔrmemɑ̃/ adv. **∼ à**, in accordance with.

conform|er /kɔ̃fɔrme/ v.t. adapt. **se ∼er à**, conform to. **∼ité** n.f. conformity.

confort /kɔ̃fɔr/ n.m. comfort. **tout**

~, with all mod cons. **~able** /-tabl/ a. comfortable.

confrère /kɔ̃frɛr/ n.m. colleague.

confront|er /kɔ̃frɔ̃te/ v.t. confront; (textes) compare. **~ation** /-asjɔ̃/ n.f. confrontation.

confus, ~e /kɔ̃fy, -z/ a. confused; (gêné) embarrassed.

congé /kɔ̃ʒe/ n.m. holiday; (arrêt momentané) time off. **~ de maladie**, sick-leave. **~ de maternité**, maternity leave. **jour de ~**, day off.

congel|er /kɔ̃ʒle/ v.t. freeze. **les ~elés**, frozen food. **~élateur** n.m. freezer.

congénit|al (m. pl. **~aux**) /kɔ̃ʒenital, -o/ a. congenital.

congère /kɔ̃ʒɛr/ n.f. snow-drift.

congestion /kɔ̃ʒɛstjɔ̃/ n.f. congestion.

congrégation /kɔ̃gregasjɔ̃/ n.f. congregation.

congrès /kɔ̃grɛ/ n.m. congress.

conifère /kɔnifɛr/ n.m. conifer.

conique /kɔnik/ a. conic(al).

conjecture /kɔ̃ʒɛktyr/ n.f. conjecture.

conjoint, ~e[1] /kɔ̃ʒwɛ̃, -t/ n.m., f. spouse.

conjoint, ~e[2] /kɔ̃ʒwɛ̃, -t/ a. joint. **~ement** /-tmɑ̃/ adv. jointly.

conjonction /kɔ̃ʒɔ̃ksjɔ̃/ n.f. conjunction.

conjonctivite /kɔ̃ʒɔ̃ktivit/ n.f. conjunctivitis.

conjoncture /kɔ̃ʒɔ̃ktyr/ n.f. circumstances; (économique) economic climate.

conjugaison /kɔ̃ʒygɛzɔ̃/ n.f. conjugation.

conjug|al (m. pl. **~aux**) /kɔ̃ʒygal, -o/ a. conjugal.

conjuguer /kɔ̃ʒyge/ v.t. (gram.) conjugate; (efforts) combine.

connaissance /kɔnɛsɑ̃s/ n.f.

knowledge; (personne) acquaintance. **~s**, (science) knowledge. **faire la ~ de**, meet. **perdre ~**, lose consciousness.

connaisseur /kɔnɛsœr/ n.m. connoisseur.

connaître† /kɔnɛtr/ v.t. know; (avoir) have. **se ~** v. pr. (se rencontrer) meet.

conne|cter /kɔnɛkte/ v.t. connect. **~xion** n.f. connection.

connu /kɔny/ a. well-known.

conquér|ir† /kɔ̃kerir/ v.t. conquer. **~ant, ~ante** n.m., f. conqueror.

conquête /kɔ̃kɛt/ n.f. conquest.

consacrer /kɔ̃sakre/ v.t. devote. **se ~** v. pr. devote o.s. (**à**, to).

consciemment /kɔ̃sjamɑ̃/ adv. consciously.

conscience /kɔ̃sjɑ̃s/ n.f. conscience; (perception) consciousness. **perdre ~**, lose consciousness. **avoir bonne/mauvaise ~**, have a clear/guilty conscience.

consciencieu|x, ~se /kɔ̃sjɑ̃sjø, -z/ a. conscientious.

conscient, ~e /kɔ̃sjɑ̃, -t/ a. conscious. **~ de**, aware ou conscious of.

consécration /kɔ̃sekrasjɔ̃/ n.f. consecration.

consécuti|f, ~ve /kɔ̃sekytif, -v/ a. consecutive.

conseil /kɔ̃sɛj/ n.m. (piece of) advice; (assemblée) council, committee; (séance) meeting; (personne) consultant. **~ d'administration**, board of directors. **~ des ministres**, Cabinet. **~ municipal**, town council.

conseiller[1] /kɔ̃seje/ v.t. advise. **~ à qn.**, advise s.o. to. **~ qch. à qn.**, recommend sth. to s.o.

conseill|er[2], **~ère** /kɔ̃seje, -ɛjɛr/ n.m., f. adviser, counsellor. **~er municipal**, town councillor.

consentir 54 contact

consent|ir /kɔ̃sɑ̃tir/ *v.i.* agree (à, to). **~ement** *n.m.* consent.

conséquence /kɔ̃sekɑ̃s/ *n.f.* consequence. **en ~**, consequently.

conséquent /kɔ̃sekɑ̃/ *a.* **par ~**, consequently.

conserva|teur, ~trice /kɔ̃sɛrvatœr, -tris/ *a.* conservative. **—**.*n.m.*, *f.* (*pol.*) conservative.

conservatoire /kɔ̃sɛrvatwar/ *n.m.* academy.

conserve /kɔ̃sɛrv/ *n.f.* tinned *ou* canned food. **en ~**, tinned, canned.

conserver /kɔ̃sɛrve/ *v.t.* keep; (*en bon état*) preserve. **se ~** *v. pr.* (*culin.*) keep.

considérable /kɔ̃siderabl/ *a.* considerable.

considération /kɔ̃siderasjɔ̃/ *n.f.* consideration; (*respect*) regard. **prendre en ~**, take into consideration.

considérer /kɔ̃sidere/ *v.t.* consider; (*respecter*) esteem. **~ comme**, consider to be.

consigne /kɔ̃siɲ/ *n.f.* (*de gare*) left luggage (office); (*ordres*) orders. **~ automatique**, (left-luggage) lockers; (*Amer.*) (baggage) lockers.

consistan|t, ~te /kɔ̃sistɑ̃, -t/ *a.* solid; (*épais*) thick. **~ce** *n.f.* consistency; (*fig.*) solidity.

consister /kɔ̃siste/ *v.i.* **~ en/dans**, consist of/in. **~ à faire**, consist in doing.

consœur /kɔ̃sœr/ *n.f.* colleague; fellow member.

consoler /kɔ̃sɔle/*v.t.* console. **se ~** *v. pr.* be consoled (**de**, for).

consolider /kɔ̃sɔlide/ *v.t.* strengthen; (*fig.*) consolidate.

consomma|teur, ~trice /kɔ̃sɔmatœr, -tris/ *n.m.*, *f.* (*comm.*) consumer; (*dans un café*) customer.

consommé /kɔ̃sɔme/ *n.m.* (*bouillon*) consommé.

consomm|er /kɔ̃sɔme/ *v.t.* consume. **—**.*v.i.* drink. **~ation** *n.f.* consumption; consummation; (*boisson*) drink. **de ~ation**, (*comm.*) consumer.

consonne /kɔ̃sɔn/ *n.f.* consonant.

constan|t, ~ante /kɔ̃stɑ̃, -t/ *a.* constant. **—**.*n.f.* constant. **~amment** /-amɑ̃/ *adv.* constantly. **~ance** *n.f.* constancy.

constat /kɔ̃sta/ *n.m.* (official) report.

constat|er /kɔ̃state/ *v.t.* note; (*certifier*) certify. **~ation** *n.f.* observation, statement of fact.

constellation /kɔ̃stelasjɔ̃/ *n.f.* constellation.

constip|é /kɔ̃stipe/ *a.* constipated; (*fig.*) stilted. **~ation** *n.f.* constipation.

constitu|er /kɔ̃stitɥe/ *v.t.* make up, constitute; (*organiser*) form; (*être*) constitute. **~é de**, made up of.

constitution /kɔ̃stitysjɔ̃/ *n.f.* constitution; (*d'une équipe*) composition; (*pol., méd.*) constitution. **~nel, ~nelle** /-jɔnɛl/ *a.* constitutional.

constructeur /kɔ̃stryktœr/ *n.m.* manufacturer.

constructi|f, ~ve /kɔ̃stryktif, -v/ *a.* constructive.

constr|uire /kɔ̃strɥir/ *v.t.* build; (*système, phrase, etc.*) construct. **~uction** *n.f.* building; (*structure*) construction.

consul /kɔ̃syl/ *n.m.* consul. **~aire** *a.* consular. **~at** *n.m.* consulate.

consult|er /kɔ̃sylte/*v.t.* consult. **se ~er** *v. pr.* confer. **~ation** *n.f.* consultation; (*réception: méd.*) surgery.

contact /kɔ̃takt/ *n.m.* contact; (*toucher*) touch. **mettre/ couper**

le ～, (*auto.*) switch on/off the ignition. ～er *v.t.* contact.

contagi|eux, ～**ieuse** /kɔ̃taʒjø, -z/ *a.* contagious. ～**ion** *n.f.* contagion.

contamin|er /kɔ̃tamine/ *v.t.* contaminate. ～**ation** *n.f.* contamination.

conte /kɔ̃t/ *n.m.* tale. ～ **de fées**, fairy tale.

contempl|er /kɔ̃tɑ̃ple/ *v.t.* contemplate. ～**ation** *n.f.* contemplation.

contemporain, ～**e** /kɔ̃tɑ̃pɔrɛ̃, -ɛn/ *a.* & *n.m., f.* contemporary.

contenance /kɔ̃tnɑ̃s/ *n.f.* (*contenu*) capacity

conteneur /kɔ̃tœr/ *n.m.* container.

contenir† /kɔ̃tnir/ *v.t.* contain; (*avoir une capacité de*) hold.

content, ～**e** /kɔ̃tɑ̃, -t/ *a.* pleased (**de**, with).

contenter /kɔ̃tɑ̃te/ *v.t.* satisfy. **se** ～ **de**, content o.s. with.

contenu /kɔ̃tny/ *n.m.* contents.

contestataire /kɔ̃testatɛr/ *n.m./f.* protester.

contest|er /kɔ̃teste/ *v.t.* dispute; (*s'opposer à*) protest against. —*v.i.* protest. ～**able** *a.* debatable. ～**ation** *n.f.* dispute; (*opposition*) protest.

contexte /kɔ̃tɛkst/ *n.m.* context.

continent /kɔ̃tinɑ̃/ *n.m.* continent. ～**al** (*m. pl.* ～**aux**) /-tal, -to/ *a.* continental.

continu /kɔ̃tiny/ *a.* continuous.

continuel, ～**le** /kɔ̃tinɥɛl/ *a.* continual. ～**lement** *adv.* continually.

continuer /kɔ̃tinɥe/ *v.t./i.* continue, go on. —*v.i.* continue, go on. ～ **à** *ou* **de faire**, carry on *ou* go on *ou* continue doing.

continuité /kɔ̃tinɥite/ *n.f.* continuity.

contour /kɔ̃tur/ *n.m.* outline, contour.

contourner /kɔ̃turne/ *v.t.* go round; (*difficulté*) get round.

contracepti|f, ～**ve** /kɔ̃trasɛptif, -v/ *a.* & *n.m.* contraceptive.

contraception /kɔ̃trasɛpsjɔ̃/ *n.f.* contraception.

contract|er /kɔ̃trakte/ *v.t.* (*maladie, dette*) contract; (*muscle*) tense, contract; (*assurance*) take out. **se** ～ *v. pr.* contract. ～**é a** *a.* tense. ～**ion** /-ksjɔ̃/ *n.f.* contraction.

contractuel, ～**le** /kɔ̃traktɥɛl/ *n.m., f.* (*agent*) traffic warden.

contradiction /kɔ̃tradiksjɔ̃/ *n.f.* contradiction.

contradictoire /kɔ̃tradiktwar/ *a.* contradictory; (*débat*) open.

contraignant, ～**e** /kɔ̃trɛɲɑ̃, -t/ *a.* restricting.

contraire /kɔ̃trɛr/ *a.* & *n.m.* opposite. ～ **à**, contrary to. **au** ～, on the contrary. ～**ment à**, contrary to.

contralto /kɔ̃tralto/ *n.m.* contralto.

contrar|ier /kɔ̃trarje/ *v.t.* annoy; (*action*) frustrate. ～**iété** *n.f.* annoyance.

contrast|e /kɔ̃trast/ *n.m.* contrast. ～**er** *v.i.* contrast.

contrat /kɔ̃tra/ *n.m.* contract.

contravention /kɔ̃travɑ̃sjɔ̃/ *n.f.* (parking-)ticket.

contre /kɔ̃tr(ə)/ *prép.* against; (*en échange de*) for. **par** ～, on the other hand. ～**indiqué** *a.* (*méd.*) contra-indicated; (*déconseillé*) not recommended. ～**plaqué** *n.m.* plywood.

contreband|e /kɔ̃trəbɑ̃d/ *n.f.* contraband. **faire la** ～**e de, passer en** ～**e**, smuggle. ～**ier** *n.m.* smuggler.

contrebasse /kɔ̃trəbas/ *n.f.* double-bass.

contredire† /kɔ̃trədir/ *v.t.* contradict. **se ~** *v. pr.* contradict o.s.

contrefaçon /kɔ̃trəfasɔ̃/ *n.f.* (*objet imité, action*) forgery.

contrefaire /kɔ̃trəfɛr/ *v.t.* (*falsifier*) forge; (*parodier*) mimic.

contremaître /kɔ̃trəmɛtr/ *n.m.* foreman.

contrepartie /kɔ̃trəparti/ *n.f.* compensation. **en ~**, in exchange, in return.

contrer /kɔ̃tre/ *v.t.* counter.

contresens /kɔ̃trəsɑ̃s/ *n.m.* misinterpretation.

contresigner /kɔ̃trəsiɲe/ *v.t.* countersign.

contretemps /kɔ̃trətɑ̃/ *n.m.* hitch.

contribuable /kɔ̃tribɥabl/ *n.m./f.* taxpayer.

contribuer /kɔ̃tribɥe/ *v.t.* contribute (**à**, to; towards).

contribution /kɔ̃tribysjɔ̃/ *n.f.* contribution. **~s,** (*impôts*) taxes; (*administration*) tax office.

contrôle /kɔ̃trol/ *n.m.* check; (*des prix, d'un véhicule*) control; (*poinçon*) hallmark; (*scol.*) test. **~e continu,** continuous assessment. **~e des changes,** exchange control. **~e des naissances** birth-control. **~er** *v.t.* check; (*surveiller, maîtriser*) control. **se ~er** *v. pr.* control o.s.

contrôleu|r, ~se /kɔ̃trolœr, -øz/ *n.m., f.* (bus) conductor ou conductress; (*de train*) (ticket) inspector.

controvers|e /kɔ̃trɔvɛrs/ *n.f.* controversy. **~é** *a.* controversial.

contusion /kɔ̃tyzjɔ̃/ *n.f.* bruise.

convaincre† /kɔ̃vɛ̃kr/ *v.t.* convince. **~ qn. de faire,** persuade s.o. to do.

convalescen|t, ~te /kɔ̃valesɑ̃, -t/ *a. & n.m., f.* convalescent. **~ce** *n.f.* convalescence.

convenable /kɔ̃vnabl/ *a.* (*correct*) decent, proper; (*approprié*) suitable.

convenance /kɔ̃vnɑ̃s/ *n.f.* **à sa ~,** to one's satisfaction. **les ~s,** the proprieties.

convenir† /kɔ̃vnir/ *v.i.* be suitable. **~ à** suit. **~ de qch.,** (*s'accorder sur*) agree on sth. **~ de faire,** agree to do.

convention /kɔ̃vɑ̃sjɔ̃/ *n.f.* convention. **~s,** (*convenances*) convention. **~né** *a.* (*prix*) official; (*médecin*) health service (*not private*). **~nel, ~nelle** /-jɔnɛl/ *a.* conventional.

convenu /kɔ̃vny/ *a.* agreed.

converger /kɔ̃vɛrʒe/ *v.i.* converge.

convers|er /kɔ̃vɛrse/ *v.i.* converse. **~ation** *n.f.* conversation.

conver|tir /kɔ̃vɛrtir/ *v.t.* convert (**à**, to; **en**, into). **~tible** *a.* convertible.

convexe /kɔ̃vɛks/ *a.* convex.

conviction /kɔ̃viksjɔ̃/ *n.f.* conviction.

convier /kɔ̃vje/ *v.t.* invite.

convocation /kɔ̃vɔkasjɔ̃/ *n.f.* (*document*) notification to attend.

convoi /kɔ̃vwa/ *n.m.* convoy; (*train*) train. **~ (funèbre),** funeral procession.

convoiter /kɔ̃vwate/ *v.t.* desire, covet, envy.

convoquer /kɔ̃vɔke/ *v.t.* (*assemblée*) convene; (*personne*) summon.

convulsion /kɔ̃vylsjɔ̃/ *n.f.* convulsion.

coopérati|f, ~ve /kɔɔperatif, -v/ *a.* co-operative. —*n.f.* co-operative (society).

coopér|er /kɔɔpere/ *v.i.* co-operate (**à**, in). **~ation** *n.f.* co-operation.

coordination /kɔɔrdinasjɔ̃/ *n.f.* co-ordination.

coordonn|er /kɔɔrdɔne/ v.t. co-ordinate. **~ées** n.f. pl. (adresse: fam.) particulars.

copain /kɔpɛ̃/ n.m. (fam.) pal; (petit ami) boyfriend.

copeau (pl. **~x**) /kɔpo/ n.m. (lamelle de bois) shaving.

cop|ie /kɔpi/ n.f. copy; (scol.) paper. **~ier** v.t./i. copy.

copieu|x, **~se** /kɔpjø, -z/ a. copious.

copine /kɔpin/ n.f. (fam.) pal; (petite amie) girlfriend.

coproduction /kɔprɔdyksjɔ̃/ n.f. coproduction.

copropriété /kɔprɔprijete/ n.f. co-ownership.

coq /kɔk/ n.m. cock.

coque /kɔk/ n.f. shell; (de bateau) hull.

coquelicot /kɔkliko/ n.m. poppy.

coqueluche /kɔklyʃ/ n.f. whooping cough.

coquet, **~te** /kɔkɛ, -t/ a. (élégant) pretty; (somme: fam.) tidy.

coquetier /kɔktje/ n.m. egg-cup.

coquillage /kɔkijaʒ/ n.m. shellfish; (coquille) shell.

coquille /kɔkij/ n.f. shell; (faute) misprint. **~ Saint-Jacques**, scallop.

coquin, **~e** /kɔkɛ̃, -in/ a. naughty.

cor /kɔr/ n.m. (mus.) horn; (au pied) corn.

cor|ail (pl. **~aux**) /kɔraj, -o/ n.m. coral.

Coran /kɔrɑ̃/ n.m. Koran.

corbeau (pl. **~x**) /kɔrbo/ n.m. (oiseau) crow.

corbeille /kɔrbɛj/ n.f. basket. **~ à papier**, waste-paper basket.

corbillard /kɔrbijar/ n.m. hearse.

corde /kɔrd/ n.f. rope; (d'arc, de violon, etc.) string. **~ à linge**, washing line. **~s vocales**, vocal cords.

cordée /kɔrde/ n.f. roped party.

cordon /kɔrdɔ̃/ n.m. string, cord. **~-bleu** (pl. **~s-bleus**) n.m. first-rate cook.

cordonnier /kɔrdɔnje/ n.m. shoe mender.

Corée /kɔre/ n.f. Korea.

coriace /kɔrjas/ a. (aliment) tough.

corne /kɔrn/ n.f. horn.

cornée /kɔrne/ n.f. cornea.

corneille /kɔrnɛj/ n.f. crow.

cornemuse /kɔrnəmyz/ n.f. bagpipes.

corner¹ /kɔrne/ v.t. (page) make dog-eared. —v.i. (auto.) hoot; (auto., Amer.) honk.

corner² /kɔrnɛr/ n.m. (football) corner.

cornet /kɔrnɛ/ n.m. (paper) cone; (crème glacée) cornet, cone.

corniche /kɔrniʃ/ n.f. cornice; (route) cliff road.

cornichon /kɔrniʃɔ̃/ n.m. gherkin.

corporation /kɔrpɔrasjɔ̃/ n.f. professional body.

corps /kɔr/ n.m. body; (mil., pol.) corps.

correct /kɔrɛkt/ a. proper, correct; (exact) correct; (tenue) decent. **~ement** adv. properly; correctly; decently.

correc|teur, **~trice** /kɔrɛktœr, -tris/ n.m., f. proof-reader.

correction /kɔrɛksjɔ̃/ n.f. correction; (punition) beating.

corrélation /kɔrelasjɔ̃/ n.f. correlation.

correspondan|t, **~te** /kɔrɛspɔ̃dɑ̃, -t/ a. corresponding. —n.m., f. correspondent; (au téléphone) caller. **~ce** n.f. correspondence; (de train, d'autobus) connection. **vente par ~ce**, mail order.

correspondre /kɔrɛspɔ̃dr/ v.i. (s'accorder, écrire) correspond; (chambres) communicate.

corrida /kɔrida/ n.f. bullfight.

corridor /kɔridɔr/ n.m. corridor.

corriger /kɔriʒe/ v.t. correct; (devoir) mark, correct; (punir) beat; (guérir) cure.

corrosi|f, **~ve** /kɔrozif, -v/ a. corrosive.

corruption /kɔrypsjɔ̃/ n.f. corruption.

corsage /kɔrsaʒ/ n.m. bodice; (chemisier) blouse.

Corse /kɔrs/ n.f. Corsica.

corse /kɔrs/ a. & n.m./f. Corsican.

corsé /kɔrse/ a. (vin) full-bodied; (scabreux) spicy.

cortège /kɔrtɛʒ/ n.m. procession.

cortisone /kɔrtizon/ n.f. cortisone.

corvée /kɔrve/ n.f. chore.

cosmétique /kɔsmetik/ n.m. cosmetic.

cosmique /kɔsmik/ a. cosmic.

cosmonaute /kɔsmonot/ n.m./f. cosmonaut.

cosmopolite /kɔsmɔpolit/ a. cosmopolitan.

cosmos /kɔsmɔs/ n.m. (espace) (outer) space; (univers) cosmos.

cosse /kɔs/ n.f. (de pois) pod.

costaud, **~e** /kɔsto, -d/ a. (fam.) strong. —n.m. (fam.) strong man.

costume /kɔstym/ n.m. suit; (théâtre) costume.

cote /kɔt/ n.f. (classification) mark; (en Bourse) quotation; (de cheval) odds (de, on).

côte /kot/ n.f. (littoral) coast; (pente) hill; (anat.) rib; (de porc) chop. **~ à côte**, side by side. **la C~ d'Azur**, the (French) Riviera.

côté /kote/ n.m. side; (direction) way. **à ~**, nearby; (voisin) nextdoor. **à ~ de**, next to; (comparé à) compared to; (cible) wide of. **aux ~s de**, by the side of. **de ~**, aside; (regarder) sideways. **mettre de ~**, put aside. **de ce ~**, this way. **de chaque ~**, on each side. **de tous les ~s**, on every side; (partout) everywhere. **du ~ de**, towards; (proximité) near; (provenance) from.

coteau (pl. **~x**) /kɔto/ n.m. hill.

côtelette /kotlɛt/ n.f. chop.

coter /kɔte/ v.t. (comm.) quote; (apprécier, noter) rate.

côt|ier, **~ière** /kotje, -jɛr/ a. coastal.

cotis|er /kɔtize/ v.i. pay one's contributions (à, to). **se ~er** v. pr. club together. **~ation** n.f. contribution(s); subscription.

coton /kɔtɔ̃/ n.m. cotton. **~ hydrophile**, cotton wool.

cou /ku/ n.m. neck.

couchant /kuʃɑ̃/ n.m. sunset.

couche /kuʃ/ n.f. layer; (de peinture) coat; (de bébé) nappy.

coucher /kuʃe/ n.m. **~ (du soleil)**, sunset. —v.t. put to bed. —v.i. sleep. **se ~** v. pr. go to bed; (s'étendre) lie down; (soleil) set.

couché a. in bed; (étendu) lying down.

couchette /kuʃɛt/ n.f. (rail.) couchette; (naut.) bunk.

coucou /kuku/ n.m. cuckoo.

coude /kud/ n.m. elbow.

coudre† /kudr/ v.t./i. sew.

couette /kwɛt/ n.f. duvet, continental quilt.

couffin /kufɛ̃/ n.m. Moses basket.

coulant, **~e** /kulɑ̃, -t/ a. (indulgent) easy-going; (fromage) runny.

couler¹ /kule/ v.t./i. flow, run; (fromage, nez) run; (fuir) leak.

couler² /kule/ v.t./i. (bateau) sink.

couleur /kulœr/ n.f. colour. **en ~s**, (télévision, film) colour.

couleuvre /kulœvr/ n.f. (grass ou smooth) snake.

coulis /kuli/ n.m. (culin.) coulis.

couliss|e /kulis/ *n.f.* runner. **∼es**, (*théâtre*) wings. **∼er** *v.i.* slide.

couloir /kulwar/ *n.m.* corridor; (*de bus*) gangway; (*sport*) lane.

coup /ku/ *n.m.* blow; (*choc*) knock; (*sport*) stroke; (*de crayon, chance, cloche*) stroke; (*de fusil, pistolet*) shot; (*fois*) time; (*aux échecs*) move. **à ∼ sûr**, definitely. **après ∼**, after the event. **boire un ∼**, have a drink. **∼ de couteau**, stab. **∼ d'état** (*pol.*) coup. **∼ de feu**, shot. **∼ de fil**, phone call. **∼ de frein**, sudden braking. **∼ de main**, helping hand. **avoir le ∼ d'main**, have the knack. **∼ d'œil**, glance. **∼ de pied**, kick. **∼ de poing**, punch. **∼ de soleil**, sunburn. **∼ de sonnette**, ring (on a bell). **∼ de téléphone**, (tele)phone call. **∼ de tête**, wild impulse. **∼ de tonnerre**, thunderclap. **∼ franc**, free kick. **d'un seul ∼**, in one go. **du premier ∼**, first go. **tenir le coup**, take it.

coupable /kupabl/ *a.* guilty. —*n.m./f.* culprit.

coupe¹ /kup/ *n.f.* cup; (*de champagne*) goblet; (*à fruits*) dish.

coupe² /kup/ *n.f.* (*de vêtement etc.*) cut; (*dessin*) section. **∼ de cheveux**, haircut.

coup|er /kupe/ *v.t./i.* cut; (*arbre*) cut down; (*arrêter*) cut off; (*voyage*) break; (*appétit*) take away; (*vin*) water down. **∼er par**, take a short cut via. **se ∼er** *v. pr.* cut o.s.; (*routes*) intersect. **∼er la parole à**, cut short. **∼e-papier** *n.m. invar.* paper-knife.

couple /kupl/ *n.m.* couple.

couplet /kuplɛ/ *n.m.* verse.

coupole /kupɔl/ *n.f.* dome.

coupon /kupɔ̃/ *n.m.* (*étoffe*) remnant; (*billet, titre*) coupon.

coupure /kupyr/ *n.f.* cut; (*billet de*

banque) note; (*de presse*) cutting. **∼ (de courant)**, power cut.

cour /kur/ *n.f.* (*court*)yard; (*de roi*) court; (*tribunal*) court. **∼ (de récréation)**, playground. **∼ martiale**, court martial. **faire la ∼ à**, court.

courag|e /kuraʒ/ *n.m.* courage. **∼eux, ∼euse** *a.* courageous.

couramment /kuramɑ̃/ *adv.* frequently; (*parler*) fluently.

courant¹, ∼e /kurɑ̃, -t/ *a.* standard, ordinary.

courant² /kurɑ̃/ *n.m.* current; (*de mode, d'idées*) trend. **∼ d'air**, draught. **être/mettre au ∼ de**, know/tell about.

courbature /kurbatyr/ *n.f.* ache.

courbe /kurb/ *n.f.* curve. —*a.* curved.

courber /kurbe/ *v.t./i.*, **se ∼** *v. pr.* bend.

coureu|r, ∼se /kurœr, -øz/ *n.m., f.* (*sport*) runner. —*n.m.* womanizer.

courge /kurʒ/ *n.f.* marrow.

courgette /kurʒɛt/ *n.f.* courgette.

courir† /kurir/ *v.i.* run; (*se hâter*) rush. —*v.t.* (*risque*) run; (*danger*) face; (*épreuve sportive*) run *ou* compete in; (*fréquenter*) do the rounds of; (*filles*) chase.

couronne /kurɔn/ *n.f.* crown; (*de fleurs*) wreath.

couronner /kurɔne/ *v.t.* crown.

courrier /kurje/ *n.m.* post, mail; (*à écrire*) letters; (*de journal*) column.

courroie /kurwa/ *n.f.* strap; (*techn.*) belt.

cours /kur/ *n.m.* (*leçon*) class; (*série de leçons*) course; (*prix*) price; (*cote*) rate; (*déroulement, d'une rivière*) course. **au ∼ de**, in the course of. **∼ d'eau**, river, stream. **∼ du soir**, evening class. **en ∼**, current; (*travail*) in progress. **en ～ de route,** on the way.

course /kurs/ *n.f.* run(ning); (*épreuve de vitesse*) race; (*commission*) errand. **～s,** (*achats*) shopping; (*de chevaux*) races.

court[1], **～e** /kur, -t/ *a.* short. **～-circuit** (*pl.* **～s-circuits**) *n.m.* short circuit.

court[2] /kur/ *n.m.* **～ (de tennis),** (tennis) court.

court|ier, ～ière /kurtje, -jɛr/ *n.m.,* *f.* broker.

courtois, ～e /kurtwa, -z/ *a.* courteous. **～ie** /-zi/ *n.f.* courtesy.

cousin, ～e /kuzɛ̃, -in/ *n.m., f.* cousin. **～ germain,** first cousin.

coussin /kusɛ̃/ *n.m.* cushion.

coût /ku/ *n.m.* cost.

couteau (*pl.* **～x**) /kuto/ *n.m.* knife.

coûter /kute/ *v.t./i.* cost.

coutume /kutym/ *n.f.* custom.

coutur|e /kutyr/ *n.f.* sewing; (*métier*) dressmaking; (*points*) seam. **～ier** /-je/ *n.m.* fashion designer. **～ière** *n.f.* dressmaker.

couvent /kuvɑ̃/ *n.m.* convent.

couver /kuve/ *v.t.* (*œufs*) hatch; (*personne*) pamper.

couvercle /kuvɛrkl/ *n.m.* (*de marmite, boîte*) lid; (*d'objet allongé*) top.

couvert[1], **～e** /kuvɛr, -t/ *a.* covered (**de,** with); (*habillé*) covered up; (*ciel*) overcast.

couvert[2] /kuvɛr/ *n.m.* (*à table*) place-setting; (*prix*) cover charge. **～s,** (*couteaux etc.*) cutlery. **mettre le ～,** lay the table.

couverture /kuvɛrtyr/ *n.f.* cover; (*de lit*) blanket.

couvr|ir† /kuvrir/ *v.t.* cover. **se ～ir** *v. pr.* (*s'habiller*) wrap up; (*ciel*) become overcast. **～e-feu** (*pl.* **～e-feux**) *n.m.* curfew. **～e-lit** *n.m.* bedspread.

cow-boy /koboj/ *n.m.* cowboy.

crabe /krab/ *n.m.* crab.

cracher /kraʃe/ *v.t. i.* spit (out).

craie /krɛ/ *n.f.* chalk.

craindre† /krɛ̃dr/ *v.t.* be afraid of, fear; (*être sensible à*) be easily damaged by.

crainte /krɛ̃t/ *n.f.* fear. **de ～ de/que,** for fear of/that.

crainti|f, ～ve /krɛ̃tif, -v/ *a.* timid.

crampe /krɑ̃p/ *n.f.* cramp.

crampon /krɑ̃pɔ̃/ *n.m.* (*de chaussure*) stud.

cramponner (se) /(sə)krɑ̃pɔne/ *v. pr.* **se ～ à,** cling to.

cran /krɑ̃/ *n.m.* (*entaille*) notch; (*trou*) hole; (*courage: fam.*) pluck.

crâne /krɑn/ *n.m.* skull.

crapaud /krapo/ *n.m.* toad.

crapule /krapyl/ *n.f.* villain.

craqu|er /krake/ *v.i.* crack, snap; (*plancher*) creak; (*couture*) split; (*fig.*) break down; (*céder*) give in. **～ement** *n.m.* crack(ing), snap(ping); creak(ing); striking.

crass|e /kras/ *n.f.* grime. **～eux, ～euse** *a.* grimy.

cratère /kratɛr/ *n.m.* crater.

cravache /kravaʃ/ *n.f.* horsewhip.

cravate /kravat/ *n.f.* tie.

crawl /krol/ *n.m.* (*nage*) crawl.

crayon /krɛjɔ̃/ *n.m.* pencil. **～ (de couleur),** crayon. **～ à bille,** ballpoint pen. **～ optique,** light pen.

créanc|ier, ～ière /kreɑ̃sje, -jɛr/ *n.m., f.* creditor.

créa|teur, ～trice /kreatœr, -tris/ *n.m., f.* creator.

création /kreɑsjɔ̃/ *n.f.* creation; (*comm.*) product.

créature /kreatyr/ *n.f.* creature.

crèche /krɛʃ/ *n.f.* day nursery; (*relig.*) crib.

crédibilité /kredibilite/ *n.f.* credibility.

crédit /kredi/ *n.m.* credit; (*banque*)

bank. **~s**, funds. **à ~**, on credit.
faire **~**, give credit (à, to). **~er**
/-te/ v.t. credit. **~eur**, **~euse**
/-tœr, -tøz/ a. in credit.

crédule /kredyl/ a. credulous.

créer /kree/ v.t. create.

crème /krɛm/ n.f. cream; (dessert)
cream dessert. —a. invar. cream.
—n.m. (café) **~**, white coffee. **~
anglaise**, fresh custard. **~ à
raser**, shaving-cream.

crémeu|x, **~se** /kremø, -z/ a.
creamy.

créole /kreɔl/ n.m./f. Creole.

crêpe[1] /krɛp/ n.f. (galette) pancake. **~rie** n.f. pancake shop.

crêpe[2] /krɛp/ n.m. (tissu) crêpe;
(matière) crêpe (rubber).

crépu /krepy/ a. frizzy.

crépuscule /krepyskyl/ n.m. twilight, dusk.

crescendo /kreʃendo/ adv. & n.m.
invar. crescendo.

cresson /kresɔ̃/ n.m. (water)cress.

crête /krɛt/ n.f. crest; (de coq)
comb.

crétin, **~e** /kretɛ̃, -in/ n.m., f.
cretin.

creuser /krøze/ v.t. dig; (évider)
hollow out; (fig.) go deeply into.

creu|x, **~se** /krø, -z/ a. hollow;
(heures) off-peak. —n.m. hollow;
(de l'estomac) pit.

crevaison /krəvɛzɔ̃/ n.f. puncture.

crevasse /krəvas/ n.f. crack; (de
glacier) crevasse; (de la peau)
chap.

crevé /krəve/ a. (fam.) worn out.

crever /krəve/ v.t./i. burst; (pneu)
puncture burst; (exténuer: fam.)
exhaust; (mourir: fam.) die; (œil)
put out.

crevette /krəvɛt/ n.f. **~ (grise)**,
shrimp. **~ (rose)**, prawn.

cri /kri/ n.m. cry; (de douleur)
scream, cry.

cric /krik/ n.m. (auto.) jack.

crier /krije/ v.i. (fort) shout (out);
(de douleur) scream; (grincer)
creak. —v.t. (ordre) shout (out).

crim|e /krim/ n.m. crime; (meur-
tre) murder. **~inel**, **~inelle** a., f.
criminal; n.m., f. criminal;
(assassin) murderer.

crin /krɛ̃/ n.m. horsehair.

crinière /krinjɛr/ n.f. mane.

crique /krik/ n.f. creek.

criquet /krikɛ/ n.m. locust.

crise /kriz/ n.f. crisis; (méd.)
attack; (de colère) fit. **~ cardiaque**, heart attack. **~ de foie**,
bilious attack.

crisp|er /krispe/ v.t., se **~er** v. pr.
tense; (poings) clench. **~é** a.
tense.

crist|al (pl. **~aux**) /kristal, -o/
n.m. crystal.

critère /kritɛr/ n.m. criterion.

critique /kritik/ a. critical. —n.f.
criticism; (article) review.

critiquer /kritike/ v.t. criticize.

croasser /krɔase/ v.i. caw.

croc /kro/ n.m. (dent) fang.

croche /krɔʃ/ n.f. quaver. **double
~**, semiquaver.

crochet /krɔʃɛ/ n.m. hook; (détour)
detour; (signe) (square) bracket;
(tricot) crochet. **faire au ~**,
crochet.

crochu /krɔʃy/ a. hooked.

crocodile /krɔkɔdil/ n.m. crocodile.

crocus /krɔkys/ n.m. crocus.

croire† /krwar/ v.t./i. believe (à,
en, in); (estimer) think, believe
(que, that).

croisade /krwazad/ n.f. crusade.

croisé /krwaze/ a. (veston) double-
breasted. —n.m. crusader.

crois|er[1] /krwaze/ v.t., se **~er** v.
pr. cross; (passant, véhicule) pass
(each other). **(se) ~er les bras**,
fold one's arms. **(se) ~er les**

jambes, cross one's legs.
∼ement *n.m.* crossing; passing;
(*carrefour*) crossroads.

crois|er² /krwaze/ *v.i.* (*bateau*)
cruise. **∼ière** *n.f.* cruise.

croissan|t¹, **∼te** /krwasᾶ, -t/ *a.*
growing. **∼ce** *n.f.* growth.

croissant² /krwasᾶ/ *n.m.* crescent;
(*pâtisserie*) croissant.

croix /krwa/ *n.f.* cross. **C∼-**
Rouge, Red Cross.

croque-monsieur /krɔkməsjø/
n.m. invar. toasted ham and
cheese sandwich.

croquer /krɔke/ *v.t./i.* crunch;
(*dessiner*) sketch.

croquette /krɔkɛt/ *n.f.* croquette.

croquis /krɔki/ *n.m.* sketch.

crosse /krɔs/ *n.f.* (*de fusil*) butt.

crotte /krɔt/ *n.f.* droppings.

crotté /krɔte/ *a.* muddy.

crottin /krɔtɛ̃/ *n.m.* (horse) dung.

croupier /krupje/ *n.m.* croupier.

croustill|er /krustije/ *v.i.* be
crusty. **∼ant, ∼ante** *a.* crusty;
(*fig.*) spicy.

croûte /krut/ *n.f.* crust; (*de
fromage*) rind; (*de plaie*) scab.

croûton /krutɔ̃/ *n.m.* (*bout de pain*)
crust; (*avec potage*) croûton.

croyable /krwajabl/ *a.* credible.

croyan|t, **∼te** /krwajᾶ, -t/ *n.m.,*
f. believer. **∼ce** *n.f.* belief.

CRS *abrév.* (*Compagnies républic-*
aines de sécurité) French state
security police.

cru¹ /kry/ *voir* **croire.**

cru² /kry/ *a.* raw; (*lumière*) harsh;
(*propos*) crude. —*n.m.* vineyard;
(*vin*) wine.

crû /kry/ *voir* **croître.**

cruauté /kryote/ *n.f.* cruelty.

cruche /kryʃ/ *n.f.* pitcher.

crudités /krydite/ *n.f. pl.* (*culin.*)
raw vegetables.

crue /kry/ *n.f.* rise in water level.
en ∼, in spate.

cruel, **∼le** /kryɛl/ *a.* cruel.

crustacés /krystase/ *n.m. pl.*
shellfish.

crypte /kript/ *n.f.* crypt.

Cuba /kyba/ *n.m.* Cuba.

cubain, **∼e** /kybɛ̃, -ɛn/ *a. & n.m.,*
f. Cuban.

cub|e /kyb/ *n.m.* cube. —*a.* (*mètre*
etc.) cubic. **∼ique** *a.* cubic.

cueill|ir /kœjir/ *v.t.* pick, gather;
(*personne: fam.*) pick up. **∼ette**
n.f. picking, gathering.

cuiller, ∼ère /kɥijɛr/ *n.f.* spoon.
∼er à soupe, soup-spoon;
(*mesure*) tablespoonful. **∼erée**
n.f. spoonful.

cuir /kɥir/ *n.m.* leather. **∼**
chevelu, scalp.

cuire /kɥir/ *v.t./i.* cook. **∼ (au**
four), bake. **faire ∼,** cook.

cuisine /kɥizin/ *n.f.* kitchen; (*art*)
cookery, cooking; (*aliments*)
cooking. **faire la ∼,** cook.

cuisin|er /kɥizine/ *v.t./i.* cook.
∼ier, ∼ière *n.m., f.* cook; *n.f.*
(*appareil*) cooker, stove.

cuisse /kɥis/ *n.f.* thigh; (*de poulet,*
mouton) leg.

cuisson /kɥisɔ̃/ *n.m.* cooking.

cuit, ∼e /kɥi, -t/ *a.* cooked. **bien**
∼, well done ou cooked. **trop ∼,**
overdone.

cuivr|e /kɥivr/ *n.m.* copper. **∼e**
(jaune), brass. **∼es,** (*mus.*)
brass. **∼é·a** *a.* coppery.

cul /ky/ *n.m.* (*derrière: fam.*)
backside, bum.

culasse /kylas/ *n.f.* (*auto.*) cylinder
head; (*arme*) breech.

culbute /kylbyt/ *n.f.* somersault;
(*chute*) tumble.

cul-de-sac (*pl.* **culs-de-sac**)
/kydsak/ *n.m.* cul-de-sac.

culinaire /kylinɛr/ *a.* culinary;
(*recette*) cooking.

culot /kylo/ *n.m.* (*audace: fam.*)
nerve, cheek.

culotte /kylɔt/ *n.f.* (*de femme*) knickers.

culpabilité /kylpabilite/ *n.f.* guilt.

culte /kylt/ *n.m.* cult, worship; (*religion*) religion; (*protestant*) service.

cultivé /kyltive/ *a.* cultured.

cultiv|er /kyltive/ *v.t.* cultivate; (*plantes*) grow. **~ateur**, **~atrice** *n.m.*, *f.* farmer.

culture /kyltyr/ *n.f.* cultivation; (*de plantes*) growing; (*agriculture*) farming; (*éducation*) culture.

culturel, **~le** /kyltyrɛl/ *a.* cultural.

cupide /kypid/ *a.* grasping.

cure /kyr/ *n.f.* (course of) treatment, cure.

curé /kyre/ *n.m.* (parish) priest.

cur|er /kyre/ *v.t.* clean. **se ~er les dents/ongles**, clean one's teeth/nails. **~e-dent** *n.m.* toothpick. **~e-pipe** *n.m.* pipe-cleaner.

curieu|x, **~se** /kyrjø, -z/ *a.* curious.

curiosité /kyrjozite/ *n.f.* curiosity.

curriculum vitae /kyrikylɔm vite/ *n.m. invar.* curriculum vitae.

curseur /kyrsœr/ *n.m.* cursor.

cutané /kytane/ *a.* skin.

cuve /kyv/ *n.f.* tank.

cuvée /kyve/ *n.f.* (*de vin*) vintage.

cuvette /kyvɛt/ *n.f.* bowl; (*du lavabo*) (wash-)basin; (*des cabinets*) pan, bowl.

CV /seve/ *n.m.* CV.

cycl|e /sikl/ *n.m.* cycle. **~ique** *a.* cyclic(al).

cyclis|te /siklist/ *n.m./f.* cyclist. **—a.** cycle. **~me** *n.m.* cycling.

cyclomoteur /syklɔmɔtœr/ *n.m.* moped.

cyclone /syklon/ *n.m.* cyclone.

cygne /siɲ/ *n.m.* swan.

cylindr|e /silɛ̃dr/ *n.m.* cylinder. **~ique** *a.* cylindrical.

cymbale /sɛ̃bal/ *n.f.* cymbal.

cystite /sistit/ *n.f.* cystitis.

cyni|que /sinik/ *a.* cynical. **—n.m.** cynic. **~sme** *n.m.* cynicism.

cyprès /siprɛ/ *n.m.* cypress.

cypriote /siprijɔt/ *a.* & *n.m./f.* Cypriot.

D

d' /d/ *voir* **de**.

d'abord /dabɔr/ *adv.* first; (*au début*) at first.

dactylo /daktilo/ *n.f.* typist. **~(graphie)** *n.f.* typing. **~graphier** *v.t.* type.

dada /dada/ *n.m.* hobby-horse.

dahlia /dalja/ *n.m.* dahlia.

daim /dɛ̃/ *n.m.* (fallow) deer; (*cuir*) suede.

dalle /dal/ *n.f.* paving stone, slab. **~age** *n.m.* paving.

daltonien, **~ne** /daltɔnjɛ̃, -jɛn/ *a.* colour-blind.

dame /dam/ *n.f.* lady; (*cartes, échecs*) queen. **~s**, (*jeu*) draughts; (*jeu: Amer.*) checkers.

damier /damje/ *n.m.* draughtboard.

dancing /dɑ̃siŋ/ *n.m.* dance-hall.

Danemark /danmark/ *n.m.* Denmark.

danger /dɑ̃ʒe/ *n.m.* danger. **en ~**, in danger. **mettre en ~**, endanger.

dangereu|x, **~se** /dɑ̃ʒrø, -z/ *a.* dangerous.

danois, **~e** /danwa, -z/ *a.* Danish. **—n.m.**, *f.* Dane. **—n.m.** (*lang.*) Danish.

dans /dɑ̃/ *prép.* in; (*mouvement*) into; (*à l'intérieur de*) inside, in; (*approximation*) about. **~ dix jours**, in ten days' time.

dans|e /dɑ̃s/ *n.f.* dance; (*art*) dancing. **~er** *v.t./i.* dance. **~eur, ~euse** *n.m., f.* dancer.

darne /darn/ *n.f.* steak (*of fish*).

date /dat/ *n.f.* date. **~ limite**, deadline; **~ limite de vente**, sellby date; **~ de péremption**, expiry date.

datt|e /dat/ *n.f.* (*fruit*) date. **~ier** *n.m.* date-palm.

daube /dob/ *n.f.* casserole.

dauphin /dofɛ̃/ *n.m.* (*animal*) dolphin.

davantage /davɑ̃taʒ/ *adv.* more; (*plus longtemps*) longer. **~ de**, more. **~ que**, more than; longer than.

de, d'* /də, d/ *prép.* (*de + le = du, de + les = des*) of; (*provenance*) from; (*moyen, manière*) with; (*agent*) by. —*article* some; (*interrogation*) any, some. **le livre de mon ami**, my friend's book. **un pont de fer**, an iron bridge. **dix mètres de haut**, ten metres high. **du pain**, (some) bread; **une tranche de pain**, a slice of bread. **des fleurs**, (some) flowers.

dé /de/ *n.m.* (*à jouer*) dice; (*à coudre*) thimble. **dés**, (*jeu*) dice.

déballer /debale/ *v.t.* unpack.

débarbouiller /debarbuje/ *v.t.* wash the face of. **se ~** *v. pr.* wash one's face.

débarcadère /debarkadɛr/ *n.m.* landing-stage.

débardeur /debardœr/ *n.m.* docker; (*vêtement*) tank top.

débarqu|er /debarke/ *v.t./i.* disembark, land; (*arriver: fam.*) turn up.

débarras /debara/ *n.m.* junk room. **bon ~!**, good riddance!

débarrasser /debarase/ *v.t.* clear (**de**, of). **~ qn. de**, take from s.o.; (*défaut, ennemi*) rid s.o. of. **se ~ de**, get rid of, rid o.s. of.

débat /deba/ *n.m.* debate.

débattre|¹ /debatr/ *v.t.* debate. —*v.i.* **~ de**, discuss.

débattre|² (se) /(sə)debatr/ *v. pr.* struggle (*to get free*).

débit /debi/ *n.m.* **~ de tabac**, tobacconist's shop; **~ de boissons**, licensed premises.

débi|ter /debite/ *v.t.* cut up; (*fournir*) produce; (*vendre*) sell; (*dire: péj.*) spout; (*compte*) debit. **~teur, ~trice** *n.m., f.* debtor; *a.* (*compte*) in debit.

déblayer /debleje/ *v.t.* clear.

débloquer /debloke/ *v.t.* (*prix, salaires*) free.

débord|er /deborde/ *v.i.* overflow. —*v.t.* (*dépasser*) extend beyond. **~é** *a.* snowed under (**de**, with).

débouché /debuʃe/ *n.m.* opening; (*carrière*) prospect; (*comm.*) outlet; (*sortie*) exit.

débouch|er /debuʃe/ *v.t.* (*bouteille*) uncork; (*évier*) unblock.

debout /dəbu/ *adv.* standing; (*levé, éveillé*) up. **être ~**, be standing, stand. **se mettre ~**, stand up.

déboutonner /debutone/ *v.t.* unbutton.

débraillé /debraje/ *a.* slovenly.

débrancher /debrɑ̃ʃe/ *v.t.* unplug, disconnect.

débray|er /debreje/ *v.i.* (*auto.*) declutch; (*faire grève*) stop work. **~age** /debrejaʒ/ *n.m.* (*pédale*) clutch; (*grève*) stoppage.

débris /debri/ *n.m. pl.* fragments; (*détritus*) rubbish, debris.

débrouill|er /debruje/ *v.t.* disentangle; (*problème*) sort out. **se ~er** *v. pr.* manage. **~ard, ~arde** *a.* (*fam.*) resourceful.

début /deby/ *n.m.* beginning.

débu|ter /debyte/ *v.i.* begin; (*dans un métier etc.*) start out. **~ant, ~ante** *n.m., f.* beginner.

déca /deka/ *n.m.* decaffeinated coffee.

décafeiné /dekafeine/ *a.* decaffeinated. —*n.m.* **du ~**, decaffeinated coffee.

deçà (en) /(ã)dəsa/ *adv.* this side. —*prép.* **en ~ de**, this side of.

décacheter /dekaʃte/ *v.t.* open.

décal|er /dekale/ *v.t.* shift. **~age** *n.m.* (*écart*) gap. **~age horaire**, time difference.

décanter /dekãte/ *v.t.* allow to settle. **se ~** *v. pr.* settle.

décap|er /dekape/ *v.t.* scrape down; (*surface peinte*) strip. **~ant** *n.m.* chemical agent; (*pour peinture*) paint stripper.

décapotable /dekapotabl/ *a.* convertible.

décapsul|er /dekapsyle/ *v.t.* take the cap off. **~eur** *n.m.* bottle-opener.

décéd|er /desede/ *v.i.* die. **~é** *a.* deceased.

décembre /desãbr/ *n.m.* December.

décennie /deseni/ *n.f.* decade.

déc|ent, ~ente /desã, -ãt/ *a.* decent. **~emment** /-amã/ *adv.* decently. **~ence** *n.f.* decency.

décentralis|er /desãtralize/ *v.t.* decentralize. **~ation** *n.f.* decentralization.

déception /desɛpsjɔ̃/ *n.f.* disappointment.

décerner /desɛrne/ *v.t.* award.

décès /desɛ/ *n.m.* death.

décev|oir† /desvwar/ *v.t.* disappoint. **~ant**, **e** *a.* disappointing.

déchaîner /deʃene/ *v.t.* (*violence etc.*) unleash; (*enthousiasme*) arouse a good deal of. **se ~** *v. pr.* erupt.

décharge /deʃarʒ/ *n.f.* **~ (électrique)**, electrical discharge. **~ (publique)**, rubbish tip.

décharg|er /deʃarʒe/ *v.t.* unload; (*arme, accusé*) discharge. **~er de**, release from. **se ~er** *v. pr.* (*batterie, pile*) go flat. **~ement** *n.m.* unloading.

déchausser (se) /(sə)deʃose/ *v. pr.* take off one's shoes; (*dent*) work loose.

déchet /deʃɛ/ *n.m.* (*reste*) scrap; (*perte*) waste. **~s**, (*ordures*) refuse.

déchiffrer /deʃifre/ *v.t.* decipher.

déchiqueter /deʃikte/ *v.t.* tear to shreds.

déchir|ant, ~ante /deʃirã, -t/ *a.* heart-breaking.

déchir|er /deʃire/ *v.t.* tear; (*diviser*) tear apart. **se ~er** *v. pr.* tear. **~ure** *n.f.* tear.

décid|er /deside/ *v.t.* decide on. **~er que**/ **de**, decide that/to. —*v.i.* decide. **~er de qch.**, decide on sth. **se ~er** *v. pr.* make up one's mind (**à**, to). **~é** *a.* (*résolu*) determined; (*fixé, marqué*) decided. **~ément** *adv.* really.

décim|al, ~ale (*m. pl.* **~aux**) /desimal, -o/ *a.* & *n.f.* decimal.

décimètre /desimɛtr/ *n.m.* decimetre.

décision /desizjɔ̃/ *n.f.* decision.

déclar|er /deklare/ *v.t.* declare; (*naissance*) register. **se ~er** *v. pr.* (*techn.*) go off. **~eur** *n.m.* (*photo.*) trigger.

déclaration *n.f.* declaration; (*commentaire politique*) statement. **~ation d'impôts**, tax return.

déclench|er /deklãʃe/ *v.t.* (*techn.*) release, set off; (*lancer*) launch; (*provoquer*) trigger off. **se ~er** *v. pr.* (*techn.*) go off. **~eur** *n.m.* (*photo.*) trigger.

déclic /deklik/ *n.m.* click; (*techn.*) trigger mechanism.

déclin /deklɛ̃/ *n.m.* decline.

déclinaison /deklinɛzɔ̃/ *n.f.* (*lang.*) declension.

décoder /dekɔde/ *v.t.* decode.

décoiffer /dekwafe/ *v.t.* (*ébouriffer*) disarrange the hair of.

décoincer /dekwɛ̃se/ *v.t.* free.

décoll|er[1] /dekɔle/ *v.i.* (*avion*) take off. **~age** *n.m.* take-off.

décoll|er[2] /dekɔle/ *v.t.* unstick.

décolleté /dekɔlte/ *a.* low-cut. **—n.m.** low neckline.

décolorer /dekɔlɔre/ *v.t.* fade; (*cheveux*) bleach.

décombres /dekɔ̃br/ *n.m. pl.* rubble.

décommander /dekɔmɑ̃de/ *v.t.* cancel.

décompos|er /dekɔ̃poze/ *v.t.* break up; (*substance*) decompose. **se ~er** *v. pr.* (*pourrir*) decompose. **~ition** *n.f.* decomposition.

décompte /dekɔ̃t/ *n.m.* deduction; (*détail*) breakdown.

décongel|er /dekɔ̃ʒle/ *v.t.* thaw. **~ation** *n.f.* thawing.

déconseill|er /dekɔ̃seje/ *v.t.* **~er qch. à qn.**, advise s.o. against sth. **~é** *a.* not advisable, inadvisable.

décontract|er /dekɔ̃trakte/ *v.t.*, **se ~** *v. pr.* relax. **~é** *a.* relaxed.

décor /dekɔr/ *n.m.* (*paysage, théâtre*) scenery; (*cinéma*) set; (*cadre*) setting; (*de maison*) décor.

décor|er /dekɔre/ *v.t.* decorate. **~ateur**, **~atrice** *n.m., f.* (interior) decorator. **~ation** *n.f.* decoration.

découdre (se) /(sə)dekudr/ *v. pr.* come unstitched.

découp|er /dekupe/ *v.t.* cut up; (*viande*) carve; (*détacher*) cut out. **~age** *n.m.* (*image*) cut-out.

décourag|er /dekuraʒe/ *v.t.* discourage. **se ~er** *v. pr.* become discouraged. **~ement** *n.m.* discouragement. **~é** *a.* discouraged.

décousu /dekuzy/ *a.* (*propos etc.*) falling apart; (*idées etc.*) disjointed.

découvert, **~e** /dekuvɛr, -t/ *a.*

(*tête etc.*) bare; (*terrain*) open. **—n.m.** (*de compte*) overdraft. **—n.f.** discovery.

découvrir† /dekuvrir/ *v.t.* discover; (*enlever ce qui couvre*) uncover; (*voir*) see; (*montrer*) reveal.

décret /dekre/ *n.m.* decree. **~er** /-ete/ *v.t.* decree.

décrire† /dekrir/ *v.t.* describe.

décrisper (se) /(sə)dekrispe/ *v. pr.* become less tense.

décroch|er /dekrɔʃe/ *v.t.* unhook; (*obtenir. fam.*) get. **—v.i.** (*abandonner. fam.*) give up. **~er (le téléphone)**, pick up the phone. **~é** *a.* (*téléphone*) off the hook.

décroître /dekrwatr/ *v.i.* decrease.

décrue /dekry/ *n.f.* going down (of river water).

déçu /desy/ *a.* disappointed.

dédain /dedɛ̃/ *n.m.* scorn.

dédale /dedal/ *n.m.* maze.

dedans /dədɑ̃/ *adv. & n.m.* inside. **au ~ (de)**, inside. **en ~**, on the inside.

dédicac|e /dedikas/ *n.f.* dedication, inscription. **~er** *v.t.* dedicate, inscribe.

dédier /dedje/ *v.t.* dedicate.

dédommag|er /dedɔmaʒe/ *v.t.* compensate (**de**, for). **~ement** *n.m.* compensation.

dédouaner /dedwane/ *v.t.* clear through customs.

déd|uire† /dedɥir/ *v.t.* deduct; (*conclure*) deduce. **~uction** *n.f.* deduction; **~uction d'impôts** tax deduction.

déesse /dees/ *n.f.* goddess.

défaillance /defajɑ̃s/ *n.f.* weakness; (*évanouissement*) black-out; (*panne*) failure.

défaire† /defɛr/ *v.t.* undo; (*valise*) unpack; (*démonter*) take down; (*débarrasser*) rid. **se ~** *v. pr.* come undone. **se ~ de**, rid o.s. of.

défaite /defɛt/ n.f. defeat.

défaut /defo/ n.m. fault, defect; (*d'un verre, diamant, etc.*) flaw; (*carence*) lack; (*pénurie*) shortage.

défav|eur /defavœr/ n.f. disfavour. **~orable** a. unfavourable.

défavoriser /defavorize/ v.t. put at a disadvantage.

défect|ueux, ~ueuse /defɛktɥø, -z/ a. faulty, defective.

défendre /defɑ̃dr/ v.t. defend; (*interdire*) forbid. **~ à qn. de**, forbid s.o. to. **se ~** v. pr. defend o.s.; (*se débrouiller*) manage; (*se protéger*) protect o.s.

défense /defɑ̃s/ n.f. defence; (*d'éléphant*) tusk. **~ de fumer**/ *etc.*, no smoking/*etc.*

défenseur /defɑ̃sœr/ n.m. defender.

défensi|f, ~ve /defɑ̃sif, -v/ a. & n.f. defensive.

déferler /defɛrle/ v.i. (*vagues*) break; (*violence etc.*) erupt.

défi /defi/ n.m. challenge; (*refus*) defiance. **mettre au ~**, challenge.

déficeler /defisle/ v.t. untie.

déficience /defisjɑ̃s/ n.f. deficiency.

déficient /defisjɑ̃/ a. deficient.

déficit /defisit/ n.m. deficit. **~aire** a. in deficit.

défier /defje/ v.t. challenge; (*braver*) defy. **se ~ de**, mistrust.

défilé /defile/ n.m. procession; (*mil.*) parade; (*fig.*) (continual) stream. **~ de mode**, fashion parade.

défiler /defile/ v.i. march (past); (*visiteurs*) stream; (*images*) flash by. **se ~** v. pr. (*fam.*) sneak off.

défini /defini/ a. definite.

définir /definir/ v.t. define.

définissable /definisabl/ a. definable.

définiti|f, ~ve /definitif, -v/ a. final; (*permanent*) definitive. **~vement** adv. definitively, permanently.

définition /definisjɔ̃/ n.f. definition; (*de mots croisés*) clue.

déflagration /deflagrasjɔ̃/ n.f. explosion.

déflation /deflasjɔ̃/ n.f. deflation. **~niste** /-jɔnist/ a. deflationary.

défoncer /defɔ̃se/ v.t. (*porte etc.*) break down.

déform|er /deforme/ v.t. put out of shape; (*membre*) deform; (*faits, pensée*) distort. **~ation** n.f. loss of shape; deformation; distortion.

défouler (se) /(sə)defule/ v. pr. let off steam.

défricher /defriʃe/ v.t. clear (for cultivation).

défroisser /defrwase/ v.t. smooth out.

défunt, ~e /defœ̃, -t/ a. (*mort*) late. —n.m., f. deceased.

dégagé /degaʒe/ a. clear.

dégager /degaʒe/ v.t. (*exhaler*) give off; (*désencombrer*) clear; (*délivrer*) free; (*faire ressortir*) bring out. **se ~** v. pr. free o.s.; (*ciel, rue*) clear; (*odeur etc.*) emanate.

dégarnir /degarnir/ **se ~** v. pr. clear, empty; (*crâne*) go bald.

dégâts /degɑ/ n.m. pl. damage.

dégel /deʒɛl/ n.m. thaw. **~er** /deʒle/ v.t./i. thaw (out). **(faire) ~er,** (*culin.*) thaw.

dégénér|er /deʒenere/ v.i. degenerate. **~é, ~ée** a. & n.m., f. degenerate.

dégivrer /deʒivre/ v.t. (*auto.*) de-ice; (*frigo*) defrost.

déglacer /deglase/ v.t. (*culin.*) deglaze.

déglingu|er /deglɛ̃ge/ (*fam.*) v.t. knock about. **se ~er** v. pr. fall to bits. **~é** adj. falling to bits.

dégonfl|er /degõfle/ *v.t.* let down, deflate. **se ~er** *v. pr.* (*fam.*) get cold feet. **~é a.** (*pneu*) flat; (*lâche: fam.*) yellow.

dégouliner /deguline/ *v.i.* trickle.

dégourdi /degurdi/ *a.* smart.

dégourdir /degurdir/ **se ~ les jambes**, stretch one's legs.

dégoût /degu/ *n.m.* disgust.

dégoût|er /degute/ *v.t.* disgust. **~er qn. de qch.**, put s.o. off sth. **~ant, ~ante** *a.* disgusting. **~é** *a.* disgusted. **~é de**, sick of.

dégradant /degradã/ *a.* degrading.

dégrad|er /degrade/ **se ~** *v. pr.* (*se détériorer*) deteriorate.

dégrafer /degrafe/ *v.t.* unhook.

degré /dǝgre/ *n.m.* degree.

dégressi|f, **~ve** /degresif, -v/ *a.* gradually lower.

dégrèvement /degrɛvmã/ *n.m.* **~ fiscal** *ou* **d'impôts**, tax reduction.

dégrever /degrǝve/ *v.t.* reduce the tax on.

dégringoler /degrɛ̃gɔle/ *v.i.* tumble (down). —*v.t.* rush down.

dégueulasse /degœlas/ *a.* (*argot*) disgusting, lousy.

déguis|er /degize/ *v.t.* disguise. **se ~er** *v. pr.* disguise o.s.; (*au carnaval etc.*) dress up. **~ement** *n.m.* disguise; (*de carnaval etc.*) fancy dress.

dégust|er /degyste/ *v.t.* taste, sample; (*savourer*) enjoy. **~ation** *n.f.* tasting, sampling.

dehors /dǝɔr/ *adv. & n.m.* outside. **en ~ de**, (*hormis*) apart from. **jeter/mettre/etc. ~**, throw/put/ *etc.* out.

déjà /deʒa/ *adv.* already; (*avant*) before, already.

déjà-vu /deʒavy/ *n.m. inv.* déjà vu.

déjeuner /deʒœne/ *v.i.* (have)

lunch; (*le matin*) (have) breakfast. —*n.m.* lunch. (**petit**) **~**, breakfast.

delà /dǝla/ *adv. & prép.* **au ~ (de)**, **en ~ (de)**, **par ~**, beyond.

délai /delɛ/ *n.m.* time-limit; (*attente*) wait; (*sursis*) extension (of time).

délation /delasjõ/ *n.f.* informing.

délavé /delave/ *a.* faded.

délayer /deleje/ *v.t.* mix (with liquid); (*idée*) drag out.

delco /dɛlko/ *n.m.* (P., *auto.*) distributor.

délégation /delegasjõ/ *n.f.* delegation.

délégu|er /delege/ *v.t.* delegate. **~é**, **~ée** *n.m.*, *f.* delegate.

délibéré /delibere/ *a.* deliberate; (*résolu*) determined. **~ment** *adv.* deliberately.

délibér|er /delibere/ *v.i.* deliberate. **~ation** *n.f.* deliberation.

délicat, **~e** /delika, -t/ *a.* delicate; (*plein de tact*) tactful; (*exigeant*) particular. **~ement** /-tmã/ *adv.* delicately; tactfully. **~esse** /-tɛs/ *n.f.* delicacy; tact.

délice /delis/ *n.m.* delight.

délicieu|x, **~se** /delisjø, -z/ *a.* (*au goût*) delicious.

délimiter /delimite/ *v.t.* determine, demarcate.

délinquan|t, **~te** /delɛ̃kã, -t/ *a. & n.m.*, *f.* delinquent. **~ce** *n.f.* delinquency.

délire /delir/ *n.m.* delirium; (*fig.*) frenzy.

délirer /delire/ *v.i.* be delirious (**de**, with); (*déraisonner*) rave.

délit /deli/ *n.m.* offence, crime.

délivr|er /delivre/ *v.t.* free, release; (*pays*) deliver; (*remettre*) issue.

déloy|al (*m. pl.* **~aux**) /delwajal, -jo/ *a.* disloyal; (*procédé*) unfair.

delta /dɛlta/ *n.m.* delta.

deltaplane /dɛltaplan/ n.m. hang-glider.

déluge /delyʒ/ n.m. flood; (pluie) downpour.

demain /dmɛ̃/ adv. tomorrow.

demande /dmɑ̃d/ n.f. request; (d'emploi) application; (exigence) demand.

demandé /dmɑ̃de/ a. in demand.

demander /dmɑ̃de/ v.t. ask for; (chemin, heure) ask; (emploi) apply for; (nécessiter) require. ∼ que/si, ask that/if. ∼ qch. à qn., ask s.o. for sth. ∼ à qn. de, ask s.o. to. se ∼ si/où/etc., wonder if/where/etc.

demandeu|r, ∼se /dmɑ̃dœr, -øz/ n.m., f. les ∼rs d'emploi job seekers.

démang|er /demɑ̃ʒe/ v.t./i. itch. ∼eaison n.f. itch(ing).

démaquill|er (se) /(sə)demakije/ v. pr. remove one's make-up. ∼ant n.m. make-up remover.

démarcation /demarkasjɔ̃/ n.f. demarcation.

démarche /demarʃ/ n.f. walk, gait; (procédé) step. faire des ∼s auprès de, make approaches to.

démarr|er /demare/ v.i. (moteur) start (up); (partir) move off; (fig.) get moving. —v.t. (fam.) get moving. ∼age n.m. start. ∼eur n.m. starter.

démasquer /demaske/ v.t. unmask.

démêlant /demelɑ̃/ n.m. conditioner.

démêler /demele/ v.t. disentangle.

déménag|er /demenaʒe/ v.i. move (house). —v.t. (meubles) move. ∼ement n.m. move; (de meubles) removal. ∼eur n.m. removal man; (Amer.) furniture mover.

démener (se) /(sə)demne/ v. pr. move about wildly; (fig.) exert o.s.

démen|t, ∼te /demɑ̃, -t/ a.

insane. —n.m., f. lunatic. ∼ce n.f. insanity.

démenti /demɑ̃ti/ n.m. denial.

démentir /demɑ̃tir/ v.t. refute; (ne pas être conforme à) belie.

demeure /dəmœr/ n.f. residence.

demeurer /dəmœre/ v.i. live; (rester) remain.

demi, ∼e /dmi/ a. half(-). —n.m., f. half. —n.m. (bière) (half-pint) glass of beer. —adv. à ∼, half; (ouvrir, fermer) half-way. à la ∼e, at half-past. une heure et ∼e, an hour and a half; (à l'horloge) half past one. une ∼-journée/-livre/etc., half a day/pound/etc. une ∼-heure, a half-hour. ∼-cercle n.m. semicircle. ∼-finale n.f. semifinal. ∼-frère n.m. stepbrother. ∼-heure n.f. half-hour, half an hour. ∼-sel a. invar. slightly salted. ∼-sœur n.f. stepsister. ∼-tarif n.m. half-fare. ∼-tour n.m. about turn; (auto.) U-turn. faire ∼-tour, turn back.

démis, ∼e /demi, -z/ a. dislocated.

démission /demisjɔ̃/ n.f. resignation. ∼ner /-jɔne/ v.i. resign.

démobiliser /demɔbilize/ v.t. demobilize.

démocrate /demɔkrat/ n.m./f. democrat. —a. democratic.

démocrat|ie /demɔkrasi/ n.f. democracy. ∼ique /-atik/ a. democratic.

démodé /demɔde/ a. old-fashioned.

démographi|e /demɔgrafi/ n.f. demography. ∼que a. demographic.

demoiselle /dəmwazɛl/ n.f. young lady.

démol|ir /demɔlir/ v.t. demolish. ∼ition n.f. demolition.

démon /demɔ̃/ n.m. demon.

démonstration /demõstrasjõ/ *n.f.* demonstration; (*de force*) show.

démonter /demõte/ *v.t.* take apart, dismantle; (*installation*) take down.

démontrer /demõtre/ *v.t.* show, demonstrate.

démoraliser /demɔralize/ *v.t.* demoralize.

démystifier /demistifje/ *v.t.* enlighten.

dénigrer /denigre/ *v.t.* denigrate.

dénivellation /denivɛlasjõ/ *n.f.* (*pente*) slope.

dénombrer /denõbre/ *v.t.* count; (*énumérer*) enumerate.

dénomination /denɔminasjõ/ *n.f.* designation.

dénommé, ~e /denɔme/ *n.m.,f.* le ~ X, the said X.

dénoncer /denõse/ *v.t.* denounce; (*scol.*) tell on. se ~er *v. pr.* give o.s. up.

dénoter /denɔte/ *v.t.* denote.

dénouement /denumã/ *n.m.* outcome; (*théâtre*) dénouement.

dénouer /denwe/ *v.t.* unknot, undo. se ~ *v. pr.* (*nœud*) come undone.

dénoyauter /denwajɔte/*v.t.* stone.

denrée /dãre/ *n.f.* foodstuff.

dens|e /dãs/ *a.* dense. ~ité *n.f.* density.

dent /dã/ *n.f.* tooth; (*de roue*) cog.

dentelle /dãtɛl/ *n.f.* lace.

dentier /dãtje/ *n.m.* denture.

dentifrice /dãtifris/ *n.m.* toothpaste.

dentiste /dãtist/ *n.m./f.* dentist.

dentition /dãtisjõ/ *n.f.* teeth.

dénué /denɥe/ *a.* ~ de, devoid of.

dénuement /denɥmã/ *n.m.* destitution.

déodorant /deɔdɔrã/ *a.m. & n.m.* (**produit**) ~, deodorant.

déontologi|e /deõtɔlɔʒi/ *n.f.* code of practice. ~que *a.* ethical.

dépann|er /depane/ *v.t.* repair; (*fig.*) help out. ~age *n.m.* repair. de ~age, (*service etc.*) breakdown. ~euse *n.f.* breakdown lorry; (*Amer.*) wrecker.

départ /depar/ *n.m.* departure; (*sport*) start. au ~, at the outset.

département /departəmã/ *n.m.* department.

dépassé /depase/ *a.* outdated.

dépass|er /depase/ *v.t.* go past, pass; (*véhicule*) overtake; (*excéder*) exceed; (*rival*) surpass; (*dérouter: fam.*) be beyond. —*v.i.* stick out; (*véhicule*) overtake. ~ement *n.m.* overtaking.

dépays|er /depeize/ *v.t.* disorientate, disorient. ~ant, ~e *a.* disorientating. ~ement *n.m.* disorientation; (*changement*) change of scenery.

dépêcher (se) /(sə)depeʃe/ *v. pr.* hurry (up).

dépendre /depãdr/ *v.i.* depend (**de**, on).

dépens (aux) /(o)depã/ *prép.* aux ~ de, at the expense of.

dépens|e /depãs/ *n.f.* expense; expenditure. ~er *v.t./i.* spend; (*énergie etc.*) expend. se ~er *v. pr.* exert o.s.

dépens|ier, ~ière /depãsje, -jɛr/ *a.* être ~ier, be a spendthrift.

dépilatoire /depilatwar/ *a. & n.m.* depilatory.

dépist|er /depiste/ *v.t.* detect. ~age *n.m.* detection.

dépit /depi/ *n.m.* resentment. en ~ de, despite. en ~ du bon sens, against all common sense.

déplacé /deplase/ *a.* out of place.

déplac|er /deplase/ *v.t.* move. se ~er *v. pr.* move; (*voyager*) travel. ~ement *n.m.* moving; travel (-ling).

déplaire /deplɛr/ *v.i.* ~ à, (*irriter*)

displease. **ça me déplaît,** I dislike that.

déplaisant, ∼e /deplɛzɑ̃, -t/ *a.* unpleasant, disagreeable.

dépliant /deplijɑ̃/ *n.m.* leaflet.

déplier /deplije/ *v.t.* unfold.

déplor|er /deplɔre/ *v.t.* (*trouver regrettable*) deplore; (*mort*) lament. ∼**able** *a.* deplorable.

déporter /depɔrte/ *v.t.* (*exiler*) deport; (*dévier*) carry off course.

déposer /depoze/ *v.t.* put down; (*laisser*) leave; (*passager*) drop; (*argent*) deposit; (*plainte*) lodge. **se** ∼ *v. pr.* settle.

déposition /depozisjɔ̃/ *n.f.* (*jurid.*) statement.

dépôt /depo/ *n.m.* (*garantie, lie*) deposit; (*entrepôt*) warehouse; (*d'autobus*) depot; (*d'ordures*) dump.

dépouiller /depuje/ *v.t.* go through; (*votes*) count.

dépourvu /depurvy/ *a.* ∼ **de,** devoid of.

dépr|imer /deprime/ *v.t.* depress. ∼**ession** *n.f.* depression. ∼**ession nerveuse,** nervous breakdown.

depuis /dəpɥi/ *prép.* since; (*durée*) for; (*à partir de*) from. —*adv.* (*ever*) since. ∼ **que,** since. ∼ **quand attendez-vous?,** how long have you been waiting?

député, ∼**e** /depyte/ *n.m.*, *f.* Member of Parliament.

déraciné, ∼**e** /derasine/ *a. & n.m.*, *f.* rootless (person).

déraill|er /deraje/ *v.i.* be derailed; (*fig., fam.*) be talking nonsense. ∼**eur** *n.m.* (*de vélo*) gear mechanism, *dérailleur.*

dérang|er /derɑ̃ʒe/ *v.t.* (*gêner*) bother, disturb. **se** ∼**er** *v. pr.* put o.s. out. **ça vous** ∼**e si . . .?,** do you mind if . . .? **en** ∼**ement,** out of order.

dérap|er /derape/ *v.i.* skid; (*fig.*) get out of control. ∼**age** *n.m.* skid.

déréglé /deregle/ *a.* (*vie*) dissolute; (*estomac*) upset; (*pendule*) (that is) not running properly.

dérégler /deregle/ *v.t.* put out of order. **se** ∼ *v. pr.* go wrong.

dériv|e /deriv/ *n.f.* **aller à la** ∼**e,** drift. ∼**er** *v.i.* (*bateau*) drift; (*détourner*) divert.

dermatolo|gie /dɛrmatɔlɔʒi/ *n.f.* dermatology. ∼**gue** /-g/ *n.m./f.* dermatologist.

dern|ier, ∼**ière** /dɛrnje, -jɛr/ *a.* last; (*nouvelles, mode*) latest; (*étage*) top. —*n.m.*, *f.* last (one). **ce** ∼**ier,** the latter. **en** ∼**ier,** last.

dernièrement /dɛrnjɛrmɑ̃/ *adv.* recently.

dérogation /derɔgasjɔ̃/ *n.f.* exemption.

dérouler /derule/ *v.t.* (*fil etc.*) unwind. **se** ∼ *v. pr.* unwind; (*avoir lieu*) take place.

déroute /derut/ *n.f.* (*mil.*) rout.

derrière /dɛrjɛr/ *prép. & adv.* behind. —*n.m.* back, rear; (*postérieur*) behind. **de** ∼, back, rear; (*pattes*) hind. **par** ∼, (from) behind, at the back *ou* rear.

des /de/ *voir* **de.**

dès /dɛ/ *prép.* (right) from, from the time of. ∼ **que,** as soon as.

désaccord /dezakɔr/ *n.m.* disagreement. ∼**é** /-de/ *a.* out of tune.

désaffecté /dezafɛkte/ *a.* disused.

désagréable /dezagreabl/ *a.* unpleasant.

désagrément /dezagremɑ̃/ *n.m.* annoyance.

désaltérant /dezalterɑ̃/ *a.* thirst-quenching, refreshing.

désamorcer /dezamɔrse/ *v.t.* (*situation, obus*) defuse.

désappr|ouver /dezapruve/ *v.t.*

disapprove of. ⁓**obation** *n.f.* disapproval.

désarçonner /dezarsɔne/ *v.t.* disconcert, throw.

désarmant /dezarmɑ̃/ *a.* disarming.

désarm|er /dezarme/ *v.t./i.* disarm. ⁓**ement** *n.m.* (*pol.*) disarmament.

désarroi /dezarwa/ *n.m.* confusion.

désastr|e /dezastr/ *n.m.* disaster. ⁓**eux**, ⁓**euse** *a.* disastrous.

désavantage /dezavɑ̃taʒ/ *n.m.* disadvantage. ⁓**er** *v.t.* put at a disadvantage. ⁓**eux**, ⁓**euse** *a.* disadvantageous.

désaxé, ⁓**e** /dezakse/ *a.* & *n.m., f.* unbalanced (person).

descendan|t, ⁓**te** /desɑ̃dɑ̃, -t/ *n.m., f.* descendant. ⁓**ce** *n.f.* descent; (*enfants*) descendants.

descendre /desɑ̃dr/ *v.i.* (*aux. être*) go down; (*venir*) come down; (*passager*) get off ou out; (*nuit*) fall. ⁓ **de**, (*être issu de*) be descended from. ⁓ **à l'hôtel**, go to a hotel. —*v.t.* (*aux. avoir*) (*escalier etc.*) go ou come down; (*objet*) take down.

descente /desɑ̃t/ *n.f.* descent; (*pente*) (downward) slope; (*raid*) raid. ⁓ **de lit**, bedside rug.

description /dɛskripsjɔ̃/ *n.f.* description.

désemplir /dezɑ̃plir/ *v.i.* **ne pas** ⁓, be always crowded.

désendettement /dezɑ̃dɛtmɑ̃/ *n.m.* getting out of debt.

désenfler /dezɑ̃fle/ *v.i.* go down.

déséquilibre /dezekilibr/ *n.m.* imbalance. **en** ⁓, unsteady.

déséquilibr|er /dezekilibre/ *v.t.* throw off balance. ⁓**é**, ⁓**ée** *a.* & *n.m., f.* unbalanced (person).

désert¹ ⁓**e** /dezɛr, -t/ *a.* deserted.

désert² /dezɛr/ *n.m.* desert. ⁓**ique** /-tik/ *a.* desert.

désert|er /dezɛrte/ *v.t./i.* desert. ⁓**eur** *n.m.* deserter. ⁓**ion** /-ɛrsjɔ̃/ *n.f.* desertion.

désespér|er /dezɛspere/ *v.i.*, **se** ⁓ *v. pr.* despair. ⁓**er de**, despair of. ⁓**é** *a.* in despair; (*état, cas*) hopeless; (*effort*) desperate.

désespoir /dezɛspwar/ *n.m.* despair. **au** ⁓, in despair.

déshabill|er /dezabije/ *v.t.* **se** ⁓**er** *v. pr.* undress, get undressed. ⁓**é** *a.* undressed; *n.m.* négligée.

désherb|er /dezɛrbe/ *v.t.* weed. ⁓**ant** *n.m.* weed-killer.

déshérit|er /dezerite/ *v.t.* disinherit. ⁓**é** *a.* (*région*) deprived. **les** ⁓**és** *n.m. pl.* the underprivileged.

déshonneur /dezɔnœr/ *n.m.* dishonour.

déshonor|er /dezɔnɔre/ *v.t.* dishonour. ⁓**ant**, ⁓**ante** *a.* dishonourable.

déshydrater /dezidrate/ *v.t.*, **se** ⁓ *v. pr.* dehydrate.

désigner /dezine/ *v.t.* (*montrer*) point to ou out; (*élire*) appoint.

désincrust|er /dezɛ̃kryste/ *v. pr.* (*chaudière*) descale; (*peau*) exfoliate. ⁓**ant** *a.* **produit** ⁓**ant**, (skin) scrub.

désinfect|er /dezɛ̃fɛkte/ *v.t.* disinfect. ⁓**ant** *n.m.* disinfectant.

désintégrer /dezɛ̃tegre/ *v.t.*, **se** ⁓ *v. pr.* disintegrate.

désintéressé /dezɛ̃terese/ *a.* disinterested.

désintoxication /dezɛ̃tɔksikasjɔ̃/ *n.f.* detoxification. **cure de** ⁓, detoxification course.

désintoxiquer /dezɛ̃tɔksike/ *v.t.* cure of an addiction; (*régime*) purify.

désir /dezir/ *n.m.* wish, desire; (*convoitise*) desire.

désirer /dezire/ *v.t.* want; (*convoiter*) desire. ⁓ **faire**, want ou wish to do.

désireu|x, **~se** /dezirø, -z/ a. **~x de**, anxious to.

désobéir /dezɔbeir/ v.i. **~ (à)**, disobey.

désobéissan|t, **~te** /dezɔbeisɑ̃, -t/ a. disobedient. **~ce** n.f. disobedience.

désodé /desɔde/ a. sodium-free.

désodorisant /dezɔdɔrizɑ̃/ n.m. air freshener.

désol|er /dezɔle/ v.t. distress. **être ~é**, (regretter) be sorry.

désordonné /dezɔrdɔne/ a. untidy; (mouvements) uncoordinated.

désordre /dezɔrdr/ n.m. disorder; untidiness.

désorganiser /dezɔrganize/ v.t. disorganize.

désormais /dezɔrmɛ/ adv. from now on.

désosser /dezɔse/ v.t. bone.

desquels, **desquelles** /dekɛl/ voir **lequel**.

dessécher /deseʃe/ v.t., se **~** v. pr. dry out ou up.

desserrer /desere/ v.t. loosen. se **~** v. pr. come loose.

dessert /desɛr/ n.m. dessert.

desservir /desɛrvir/ v.t./i. clear away; (autobus) provide a service to, serve.

dessin /desɛ̃/ n.m. drawing; (motif) design; (contour) outline. **~ animé**, (cinéma) cartoon. **~ humoristique**, cartoon.

dessin|er /desine/ v.t./i. draw; (fig.) outline. **~ateur**, **~atrice** n.m., f. artist; (industriel) draughtsman.

dessous /dəsu/ adv. underneath. —n.m. under-side, underneath. —n.m. pl. underclothes. **du ~**, (voisins) downstairs. **en ~, par ~**, underneath.

dessus /dəsy/ adv. on top (of it), on it. —n.m. top. **du ~**, top; (voisins) upstairs. **en ~**, above. **par ~**,

over (it). **~-de-lit** n.m. invar. bedspread.

destin /dɛstɛ̃/ n.m. (sort) fate; (avenir) destiny.

destinataire /dɛstinatɛr/ n.m./f. addressee.

destination /dɛstinasjɔ̃/ n.f. destination; (emploi) purpose. **à ~ de**, (going) to.

destinée /dɛstine/ n.f. (sort) fate; (avenir) destiny.

destiner /dɛstine/ v.t. **~ à**, intend for; (vouer) destine for; (affecter) earmark for.

destituer /dɛstitɥe/ v.t. dismiss (from office).

destruc|teur, **~trice** /dɛstryktœr, -tris/ a. destructive.

destruction /dɛstryksjɔ̃/ n.f. destruction.

désunir /dezynir/ v.t. divide.

détachant /detaʃɑ̃/ n.m. stain-remover.

détach|é /detaʃe/ a. detached. **~ement** n.m. detachment.

détach|er /detaʃe/ v.t. untie; (ôter) remove, detach; (déléguer) send (on assignment ou secondment). se **~** v. pr. come off, break away.

détail /detaj/ n.m. detail; (de compte) breakdown; (comm.) retail. **au ~**, (vendre etc.) retail. **de ~**, (prix etc.) retail. **en ~**, in detail.

détaillé /detaje/ a. detailed.

détaill|er /detaje/ v.t.(articles) sell in small quantities, split up. **~ant**, **~ante** n.m., f. retailer.

détartrant /detartrɑ̃/ n.m. descaler.

détaxer /detakse/ v.t. reduce the tax on.

détecter /detɛkte/ v.t. detect.

détective /detɛktiv/ n.m. detective.

déteindre /detɛ̃dr/ *v.i.* (*couleur*)
run (**sur**, on to).

détend|re /detɑ̃dr/ *v.t.* slacken;
(*ressort*) release; (*personne*) relax.
se ∼re *v. pr.* become slack,
slacken; be released; relax. **∼u** *a.*
(*calme*) relaxed.

détenir† /detnir/ *v.t.* hold; (*secret,
fortune*) possess.

détente /detɑ̃t/ *n.f.* relaxation;
(*pol.*) détente; (*saut*) spring;
(*gâchette*) trigger.

détention /detɑ̃sjɔ̃/ *n.f.* ∼
préventive, custody.

détenu, ∼e /detny/ *n.m., f.*
prisoner.

détergent /detɛrʒɑ̃/ *n.m.* detergent.

détérior|er /deterjɔre/ *v.t.*
damage. **se ∼er** *v. pr.* deteriorate.
∼ation *n.f.* damaging; deteriora-
tion.

détermin|er /detɛrmine/ *v.t.* deter-
mine. **∼ation** *n.f.* determination.
∼é *a.* (*résolu*) determined;
(*précis*) definite.

déterrer /detere/ *v.t.* dig up.

détester /detɛste/ *v.t.* hate.

déton|er /detɔne/ *v.i.* explode,
detonate. **∼ateur** *n.m.* detonator.
∼ation *n.f.* explosion, detona-
tion.

détour /detur/ *n.m.* bend; (*crochet*)
detour; (*fig.*) roundabout means.

détourné /deturne/ *a.* roundabout.

détourn|er /deturne/ *v.t.* divert;
(*tête, yeux*) turn away; (*avion*)
hijack; (*argent*) embezzle.
∼ement *n.m.* hijack(ing); em-
bezzlement.

détraquer /detrake/ *v.t.* break, put
out of order; (*estomac*) upset. **se
∼** *v. pr.* (*machine*) go wrong.

détresse /detrɛs/ *n.f.* distress.

détritus /detritys/ *n.m. pl.* rubbish.

détroit /detrwa/ *n.m.* strait.

détruire† /detrɥir/ *v.t.* destroy.

dette /dɛt/ *n.f.* debt.

deuil /dœj/ *n.m.* mourning; (*perte*)
bereavement.

deux /dø/ *a. & n.m.* two. **∼ fois**,
twice. **tous (les) ∼**, both. **∼-
pièces** *n.m. invar.* (*vêtement*) two-
piece; (*logement*) two-room flat *or*
apartment. **∼-points** *n.m. invar.*
(*gram.*) colon. **∼-roues** *n.m.
invar.* two-wheeled vehicle.

deuxième /døzjɛm/ *a. & n.m./f.*
second. **∼ment** *adv.* secondly.

dévaloriser /devalɔrize/ *v.t.*, **se ∼**
v. pr. reduce in value.

déval|uer /devalɥe/ *v.t.*, **se ∼uer**
v. pr. devalue. **∼uation** *n.f.*
devaluation.

devancer /dəvɑ̃se/ *v.t.* be *ou* go
ahead of; (*arriver*) arrive ahead
of; (*prévenir*) anticipate.

devant /dəvɑ̃/ *prép.* in front of;
(*distance*) ahead of; (*avec mouvement*) past; (*en présence de*) before;
(*face à*) in the face of. —*adv.* in
front; (*à distance*) ahead. —*n.m.*
front. **de ∼**, front. **par ∼**, at *ou*
from the front, in front.

devanture /dəvɑ̃tyr/ *n.f.* shop front;
(*étalage*) shop-window.

développ|er /devlɔpe/ *v.t.*, **se ∼er**
v. pr. develop. **∼ement** *n.m.*
development; (*de photos*) developing.

devenir† /dəvnir/ *v.i.* (*aux. être*)
become. **qu'est-il devenu?**, what
has become of him?

déviation /devjasjɔ̃/ *n.f.* diversion.

dévier /devje/ *v.t.* divert; (*coup*)
deflect.

deviner /dvine/ *v.t.* guess;
(*apercevoir*) distinguish.

devinette /dvinɛt/ *n.f.* riddle.

devis /dvi/ *n.m.* estimate.

dévisager /devizaʒe/ *v.t.* stare at.

devise /dviz/ *n.f.* motto. **∼s**,
(*monnaie*) (foreign) currency.

dévisser /devise/ v.t. unscrew.

dévitaliser /devitalize/ v.t. (dent) kill the nerve in.

dévoiler /devwale/ v.t. reveal.

devoir¹ /dvwar/ n.m. duty; (scol.) homework; (fait en classe) exercise.

devoir†² /dvwar/ v.t. owe. —v. aux. ~ faire, (nécessité) must do, have (got) to do; (intention) be due to do. ~ être, (probabilité) must be. vous devriez, you should. il aurait dû, he should have.

dévorer /devɔre/ v.t. devour.

dévouer (se) /(sə)devwe/ v. pr. devote o.s. (à, to); (se sacrifier) sacrifice o.s. ~é a. devoted. ~ement /-vumɑ̃/ n.m. devotion.

diabète /djabɛt/ n.m. diabetes. ~étique a. & n.m./f. diabetic.

diable /djabl/ n.m. devil. ~olique a. diabolical.

diagnostic /djagnɔstik/ n.m. diagnosis. ~quer v.t. diagnose.

diagonal, ~ale (m. pl. ~aux) /djagɔnal, -o/ a. & n.f. diagonal. en ~ale, diagonally.

dialecte /djalɛkt/ n.m. dialect.

dialogue /djalɔg/ n.m. dialogue. ~er v.i. (pol.) have a dialogue.

diamant /djamɑ̃/ n.m. diamond.

diamètre /djamɛtr/ n.m. diameter.

diaphragme /djafragm/ n.m. diaphragm.

diapo /djapo/ n.f. (colour) slide.

diapositive /djapozitiv/ n.f. (colour) slide.

diarrhée /djare/ n.f. diarrhoea.

dictat|eur /diktatœr/ n.m. dictator. ~ure n.f. dictatorship.

dict|er /dikte/ v.t. dictate. ~ée n.f. dictation.

dictionnaire /diksjɔnɛr/ n.m. dictionary.

dièse /djɛz/ n.m. (mus.) sharp.

diesel /djezɛl/ n.m. & a. invar. diesel.

diététicien, ~ne /djetetisjɛ̃, -jɛn/ n.m., f. dietician.

diététique /djetetik/ n.f. dietetics. —a. produit ou aliment ~, dietary product.

dieu (pl. ~x) /djø/ n.m. god. D~, God.

diffamatoire /difamatwar/ a. defamatory.

diffam|er /difame/ v.t. slander; (par écrit) libel. ~ation n.f. slander; libel.

différé (en) /(ɑ̃)difere/ adv. (émission) recorded.

différemment /diferamɑ̃/ adv. differently.

différence /diferɑ̃s/ n.f. difference.

différent, ~e /diferɑ̃, -t/ a. different (de, from).

différer /difere/ v.i. differ (de, from).

difficile /difisil/ a. difficult. ~ment adv. with difficulty.

difficulté /difikylte/ n.f. difficulty.

difform|e /diform/ a. deformed. ~ité n.f. deformity.

diffus|er /difyze/ v.t. broadcast; (lumière, chaleur) diffuse. ~ion n.f. broadcasting; diffusion.

dig|érer /diʒere/ v.t. digest; (endurer: fam.) stomach. ~este, ~estible adjs. digestible. ~estion n.f. digestion.

digest|if, ~ve /diʒɛstif, -v/ a. digestive. —n.m. after-dinner liqueur.

digital, (m. pl. ~aux) /diʒital, -o/ a. digital.

digne /diɲ/ a. (noble) dignified; (honnête) worthy. ~ de, worthy of. ~ de foi, trustworthy.

dignité /diɲite/ n.f. dignity.

digue /dig/ n.f. dike.

dilapider /dilapide/ v.t. squander.

dilater /dilate/ v.t., se ~er v. pr. dilate.

dilemme /dilɛm/ n.m. dilemma.

diluant /dilyã/ n.m. thinner.

diluer /dilɥe/ v.t. dilute.

dimanche /dimãʃ/ n.m. Sunday.

dimension /dimãsjɔ̃/ n.f. (taille) size; (mesure) dimension.

dimin|uer /diminɥe/ v.t. reduce, decrease. —v.i. decrease. **~ution** n.f. decrease (de, in).

diminutif /diminytif/ n.m. diminutive; (surnom) pet name ou form.

dinde /dɛ̃d/ n.f. turkey.

dindon /dɛ̃dɔ̃/ n.m. turkey.

dîn|er /dine/ n.m. dinner. —v.i. have dinner.

dingue /dɛ̃g/ a. (fam.) crazy.

dinosaure /dinozɔr/ n.m. dinosaur.

diocèse /djosɛz/ n.m. diocese.

diphtérie /difteri/ n.f. diphtheria.

diphtongue /diftɔ̃g/ n.f. diphthong.

diplomate /diplɔmat/ n.m. diplomat. —a. diplomatic.

diplomat|ie /diplɔmasi/ n.f. diplomacy. **~ique** /-atik/ a. diplomatic.

diplôm|e /diplom/ n.m. certificate, diploma; (univ.) degree. **~é** a. qualified.

dire† /dir/ v.t. say; (secret, vérité, heure) tell; (penser) think. **~ que**, say that. **~ à qn. que/de**, tell s.o. that/to. **ça me/vous/etc. dit de faire**, I/you/etc. feel like doing. **on dirait que**, it would seem that, it seems that. **dis/dites donc!**, hey!

direct /dirɛkt/ a. direct. **en ~**, (émission) live. **~ement** adv. directly.

direc|teur, ~trice /dirɛktœr, -tris/ n.m., f. director; (chef de service) manager, manageress; (d'école) headmaster, headmistress.

direction /dirɛksjɔ̃/ n.f. (sens)

direction; (de société etc.) management; (auto.) steering. **en ~ de**, (going) to.

dirigeant, ~e /diriʒã, -t/ n.m., f. (pol.) leader; (comm.) manager.

diriger /diriʒe/ v.t. run, manage, direct; (véhicule) steer; (orchestre) conduct; (braquer) aim; (tourner) turn. **se ~ v. pr.** guide o.s. **se ~ vers**, make one's way to.

dis /di/ voir **dire**.

disciple /disipl/ n.m. disciple.

discipline /disiplin/ n.f. discipline.

discontinu /diskɔ̃tiny/ a. intermittent.

discothèque /diskɔtɛk/ n.f. record library; (club) disco(thèque).

discount /diskunt/ n.m. discount.

discours /diskur/ n.m. speech.

discréditer /diskredite/ v.t. discredit.

discr|et, ~ète /diskrɛ, -t/ a. discreet. **~ètement** adv. discreetly.

discrétion /diskresjɔ̃/ n.f. discretion. **à ~**, as much as one desires.

discrimination /diskriminɑsjɔ̃/ n.f. discrimination.

discriminatoire /diskriminatwar/ a. discriminatory.

discussion /diskysjɔ̃/ n.f. discussion; (querelle) argument.

discuté /diskyte/ a. controversial.

discuter /diskyte/ v.t. discuss; (contester) question. —v.i. (parler) talk; (répliquer) argue. **~ de**, discuss.

disgrâce /disgras/ n.f. disgrace.

disjoindre /disʒwɛ̃dr/ v.t. take apart. **se ~ v. pr.** come apart.

dislo|quer /disloke/ v.t. (membre) dislocate; (machine etc.) break (apart). **se ~quer v. pr.** (parti, cortège) break up; (meuble) come apart.

dispar|aître† /disparɛtr/ v.i. disappear; (mourir) die. **faire**

~aître, get rid of. ~ition *n.f.* disappearance; (*mort*) death. ~u, ~ue *a.* (*soldat etc.*) missing; *n.m., f.* missing person; (*mort*) dead person.

dispensaire /dispãser/ *n.m.* clinic.

dispense /dispãs/ *n.f.* exemption.

dispenser /dispãse/ *v.t.* exempt (**de**, from).

disponib|le /disponibl/ *a.* available. ~ilité *n.f.* availability.

dispos, ~e /dispo, -z/ *a.* **frais et** ~, fresh and alert.

disposé /dispoze/ *a.* bien/mal ~, in a good/bad mood. ~ **à**, prepared to.

disposer /dispoze/ *v.t.* arrange. ~ **à**, (*engager à*) incline to. —*v.i.* ~ **de**, have at one's disposal.

dispositif /dispozitif/ *n.m.* device; (*plan*) plan of action.

disposition /dispozisjõ/ *n.f.* arrangement; (*humeur*) mood. **à la** ~ **de**, at the disposal of.

disproportionné /disproporsjone/ *a.* disproportionate.

dispute /dispyt/ *n.f.* quarrel.

disputer /dispyte/ *v.t.* (*match*) play; (*course*) run in; (*prix*) fight for. **se** ~ *v. pr.* quarrel; (*match*) be played.

disquaire /disker/ *n.m./f.* record dealer.

disqualif|ier /diskalifje/ *v.t.* disqualify. ~**ication** *n.f.* disqualification.

disque /disk/ *n.m.* (*mus.*) record; (*sport*) discus; (*cercle*) disc, disk. ~ **dur**, hard disk.

disquette /disket/ *n.f.* (floppy) disk.

dissection /diseksjõ/ *n.f.* dissection.

disséquer /diseke/ *v.t.* dissect.

dissertation /disɛrtasjõ/ *n.f.* (*scol.*) essay.

dissiden|t, ~**te** /disidã, -t/ *a., n.m., f.* dissident. ~**ce** *n.f.* dissidence.

dissimuler /disimyle/ *v.t.* conceal (**à**, from).

dissolvant /disolvã/ *n.m.* solvent; (*pour ongles*) nail polish remover.

dissonant, ~**e** /disonã, -t/ *a.* discordant.

dissoudre† /disudr/ *v.t.*, **se** ~ *v. pr.* dissolve.

dissua|der /disɥade/ *v.t.* dissuade (**de**, from). ~**sion** /-qazjõ/ *n.f.* dissuasion. **force de** ~**sion**, deterrent force.

dissuasi|f, ~**ve** /disɥazif, -v/ *a.* dissuasive.

distance /distãs/ *n.f.* distance; (*écart*) gap. **à** ~, at ou from a distance.

distant, ~**e** /distã, -t/ *a.* distant.

distill|er /distile/ *v.t.* distil. ~**ation** *n.f.* distillation.

distillerie /distilri/ *n.f.* distillery.

distinct, ~**e** /distĕ(kt), -ĕkt/ *a.* distinct. ~**ement** /-ĕktəmã/ *adv.* distinctly.

distinction /distĕksjõ/ *n.f.* distinction.

distingué /distĕge/ *a.* distinguished.

distinguer /distĕge/ *v.t.* distinguish.

distraction /distraksjõ/ *n.f.* absent-mindedness; (*oubli*) lapse; (*passe-temps*) distraction.

distraire† /distrɛr/ *v.t.* amuse; (*rendre inattentif*) distract. **se** ~ *v. pr.* amuse o.s.

distrait, ~**e** /distrɛ, -t/ *a.* absent-minded.

distrayant, ~**e** /distrɛjã, -t/ *a.* entertaining.

distrib|uer /distribɥe/ *v.t.* hand out, distribute; (*répartir, amener*) distribute; (*courrier*) deliver. ~**uteur** *n.m.* (*auto., comm.*)

...r (auto-
district ...machine); (de
...t/ n.m. district.
dist... dit/ *voir* **dire**.
...e /djyretik/ a. & n.m.
...e.

...l /divɑ̃/ n.m. divan.
diverg|ent, ~te /diverʒɑ̃, -t/ a.
divergent. ~ce n.f. divergence.
diverger /diverʒe/ v.i. diverge.
divers, ~e /diver, -s/ a. (*varié*)
diverse; (*différent*) various.
diversifier /diversifje/ v.t. diversify.
diversité /diversite/ n.f. diversity.
divert|ir /divertir/ v.t. amuse. **se**
~**ir** v. pr. amuse o.s. ~**issement**
n.m. amusement.
dividende /dividɑ̃d/ n.m. dividend.
divis|er /divize/ v.t./i, **se** ~**er** v. pr.
divide. ~**ion** n.f. division.
divorc|e /divɔrs/ n.m. divorce. ~**é**
~**ée** a. divorced; n.m., f. divorcee.
~**er** v.i. ~**er (d'avec)**, divorce.
dix /dis/ (/di/ before consonant,
/diz/ before vowel) a. & n.m. ten.
~**ième** /dizjɛm/ a. & n.m./f.
tenth.
dix-huit /dizɥit/ a. & n.m.
eighteen. ~**ième** a. & n.m./f.
eighteenth.
dix-neu|f /diznœf/ a. & n.m.
nineteen. ~**vième** a. & n.m./f.
nineteenth.
dix-sept /disɛt/ a. & n.m. seventeen. ~**ième** a. & n.m./f. seven-
teenth.
dizaine /dizɛn/ n.f. (about) ten.
docile /dɔsil/ a. docile.
docilité /dɔsilite/ n.f. docility.
dock /dɔk/ n.m. dock.
docker /dɔkɛr/ n.m. docker.
doct|eur /dɔktœr/ n.m. doctor.
~**oresse** n.f. (*fam.*) lady doctor.
doctorat /dɔktɔra/ n.m. doctorate.

doctrine /dɔktrin/ n.f. doctrine.
document /dɔkymɑ̃/ n.m. document. ~**aire** /-tɛr/ a. & n.m.
documentary.
documentaliste /dɔkymɑ̃talist/
n.m./f. information officer.
document|er /dɔkymɑ̃te/ **se** ~**er**
v. pr. collect information. ~**ation**
n.f. information, literature. ~**é** a.
well-documented.
dodo /dodo/ n.m. **faire** ~,
(*langage enfantin*) go to byebyes.
dodu /dɔdy/ a. plump.
doigt /dwa/ n.m. finger. **un** ~ **de**, a
drop of. ~ **de pied**, toe.
dois, doit /dwa/ *voir* **devoir²**.
Dolby /dɔlbi/ n.m. & a. (P.) Dolby
(P.).
dollar /dɔlar/ n.m. dollar.
domaine /dɔmɛn/ n.m. estate,
domain; (*fig.*) domain.
dôme /dom/ n.m. dome.
domestique /dɔmɛstik/ a. domestic. —n.m./f. servant.
domicile /dɔmisil/ n.m. home. **à**
~, (*livrer*) to the home.
domicilié /dɔmisilje/ a. resident.
dominer /dɔmine/ v.t./i.
dominate; (*surplomber*) tower
over, dominate; (*équipe*) dictate
the game (to).
dommage /dɔmaʒ/ n.m. (*tort*)
harm. ~**(s)**, (*dégâts*) damage.
c'est ~, it's a pity. **quel** ~, what
a shame. ~**s-intérêts** n.m. pl.
(*jurid.*) damages.
don /dɔ̃/ n.m. (*cadeau, aptitude*)
gift.
donation /dɔnasjɔ̃/ n.f. donation.
donc /dɔ̃(k)/ conj. so, then; (*par
conséquent*) so, therefore.
donjon /dɔ̃ʒɔ̃/ n.m. (*tour*) keep.
donné /dɔne/ a. (*fixé*) given; (*pas
cher: fam.*) dirt cheap.
données /dɔne/ n.f. pl. (*de science*)
data; (*de problème*) facts.
donner /dɔne/ v.t. give; (*vieilles*

affaires) give away; (*distribuer*)
give out; (*récolte etc.*) produce;
(*film*) show; (*pièce*) put on. —*v.i.*
~ **sur**, look out on to. ~ **à**
réparer/*etc.*, take to be repaired/
etc. **se** ~ **du mal**, go to a lot of
trouble (**pour faire**, to do).

donneu|r, ~**se** /dɔnœr, -øz/
n.m., f. (*de sang*) donor.

dont /dɔ̃/ *pron. rel.* (*chose*) whose,
of which; (*personne*) whose;
(*partie d'un tout*) of whom; (*chose*)
of which; (*provenance*) from
which; (*manière*) in which. **le**
père ~ **la fille**, the father whose
daughter. **ce** ~, what. ~ **il a**
besoin, which he needs.

dopage /dɔpaʒ/ *n.m.* doping.

doré /dɔre/ *a.* (*couleur d'or*) golden;
(*avec dorure*) gold. **la bour-**
geoisie ~**e** the affluent middle
class.

dorénavant /dɔrenavɑ̃/ *adv.*
henceforth.

dormir† /dɔrmir/ *v.i.* sleep; (*être*
endormi) be asleep. **il dort**
debout, he can't keep awake.

dortoir /dɔrtwar/ *n.m.* dormitory.

dos /do/ *n.m.* back; (*de livre*) spine.
de ~, from behind.

dos|e /doz/ *n.f.* dose. ~**age** *n.m.*
(*mélange*) mixture. ~**er** *v.t.*
measure out; (*équilibrer*) balance.

dossier /dɔsje/ *n.m.* (*documents*)
file; (*de chaise*) back.

dot /dɔt/ *n.f.* dowry.

doter /dɔte/ *v.t.* ~ **de**, equip with.

douan|e /dwan/ *n.f.* customs.
~**ier**, ~**ière** *a.* customs; *n.m., f.*
customs officer.

double /dubl/ *a. & adv.* double.
—*n.m.* (*copie*) duplicate; (*sosie*)
double. **le** ~ (**de**), twice as much
ou as many (as). ~ **décimètre**,
ruler.

doubl|er /duble/ *v.t./i.* double;
(*dépasser*) overtake; (*vêtement*)

line; (*film*) dub, (*cap*) round. ~**ure**
n.f. lining.

douce /dus/ *voir* **doux**.

doucement /dusmɑ̃/ *adv.* gen[tly]

douceur /dusœr/ *n.f.* (*molle[sse]*)
softness; (*de climat*) mildness; (*de*
personne) gentleness.

douch|e /duʃ/ *n.f.* shower. ~**er** *v.t.*
give a shower to. **se** ~**er** *v. pr.*
have *ou* take a shower.

doudoune /dudun/ *n.f.* (*fam.*)
anorak.

doué /dwe/ *a.* gifted.

douille /duj/ *n.f.* (*électr.*) socket.

douillet, ~**te** /dujɛ, -t/ *a.* cosy,
comfortable; (*personne* *péj.*) soft.

doul|eur /dulœr/ *n.f.* pain;
(*chagrin*) grief. ~**oureux**,
~**oureuse** *a.* painful. **la**
~**oureuse** *n.f.* the bill.

doute /dut/ *n.m.* doubt. **sans** ~, no
doubt.

douter /dute/ *v.i.* ~ **de**, doubt. **se**
~ **de**, suspect.

douteu|x, ~**se** /dutø, -z/ *a.*
doubtful.

Douvres /duvr/ *n.m./f.* Dover.

doux, douce /du, dus/ *a.*
(*moelleux*) soft; (*sucré*) sweet;
(*clément, pas fort*) mild; (*pas*
brusque, bienveillant) gentle.

douzaine /duzɛn/ *n.f.* about
twelve; (*douze*) dozen. **une** ~
d'œufs/*etc.*, a dozen eggs/*etc.*

douz|e /duz/ *a. & n.m.* twelve.
~**ième** *a. & n.m./f.* twelfth.

doyen, ~**ne** /dwajɛ, -ɛn/ *n.m., f.*
dean; (*en âge*) most senior person.

dragée /draʒe/ *n.f.* sugared almond.

dragon /dragɔ̃/ *n.m.* dragon.

drain /drɛ̃/ *n.m.* drain.

drainer /drene/ *v.t.* drain.

dramatique /dramatik/ *a.* dra-
matic; (*tragique*) tragic. —*n.f.*
(television) drama.

drame /drɑm/ *n.m.* ...a. ~**-housse** ...heet.

dra...e /drapo/ *n.m.*
dra...e *v.t.* put up, erect;
...e; (*animal*) train; (*liste*)
...p. **se ~** *v. pr.* (*bâtiment*)
...stand; (*personne*) draw o.s.
up.

drive /drajv/ *n.m.* (*comput.*) drive.

drogue /drɔg/ *n.f.* drug. **la ~,**
drugs.

drogu|er /drɔge/ **se ~er** *v. pr.*
take drugs. ~**é, ~ée** *n.m., f.* drug
addict.

droguerie /drɔgri/ *n.f.* hardware
and chemist's shop.

droit[1] **~e** /drwa, -t/ *a.* (*non
courbe*) straight; (*loyal*) upright;
(*angle*) right. —*adv.* straight.
—*n.f.* straight line.

droit[2] **~e** /drwa, -t/ *a.* (*contraire
de gauche*) right. **à ~e,** on the
right; (*direction*) (to the) right. **la
~e,** the right (side); (*pol.*) the
right (wing). **~ier, ~ière** /-tje,
-tjɛr/ *a. & n.m., f.* right-handed
(person).

droit[3] /drwa/ *n.m.* right. **~(s),**
(*taxe*) duty; (*d'inscription*) fee(s).
le ~, (*jurid.*) law. **avoir ~ à,** be
entitled to. **avoir le ~ de,** be
allowed to. **~s d'auteur,** royal-
ties.

drôle /drol/ *a.* funny. **~ment** *adv.*
(*extrêmement: fam.*) dreadfully.

dromadaire /drɔmadɛr/ *n.m.*
dromedary.

drugstore /drœgstɔr/ *n.m.* drugstore.

du /dy/ *voir* **de.**

dû, due /dy/ *voir* **devoir**[2]. —*a.*
due. —*n.m.* due; (*argent*) dues. **du
à,** due to.

duc, duchesse /dyk, dyʃɛs/ *n.m., f.*
duke, duchess.

duel /dyɛl/ *n.m.* duel.

dune /dyn/ *n.f.* dune.

duo /dyo/ *n.m.* (*mus.*) duet.

duplex /dyplɛks/ *n.m.* split-level
apartment; (*émission*) link-up.

duquel /dykɛl/ *voir* **lequel.**

dur /dyr/ *a.* hard; (*sévère*) harsh,
hard; (*viande*) tough, hard; (*col,
brosse*) stiff. —*adv.* hard.

durable /dyrabl/ *a.* lasting.

durant /dyrɑ̃/ *prép.* during;
(*mesure de temps*) for.

durc|ir /dyrsir/ *v.t./i.,* **se ~ir** *v. pr.*
harden. **~issement** *n.m.* harden-
ing.

durée /dyre/ *n.f.* length; (*période*)
duration.

durement /dyrmɑ̃/ *adv.* harshly.

durer /dyre/ *v.i.* last.

dureté /dyrte/ *n.f.* hardness;
(*sévérité*) harshness.

duvet /dyvɛ/ *n.m.* down; (*sac*)
(down-filled) sleeping-bag.

dynami|que /dinamik/ *a.* dy-
namic. **~sme** *n.m.* dynamism.

dynamit|e /dinamit/ *n.f.* dyna-
mite. **~er** *v.t.* dynamite.

dynamo /dinamo/ *n.f.* dynamo.

dynastie /dinasti/ *n.f.* dynasty.

dysenterie /disɑ̃tri/ *n.f.* dysentery.

E

eau (*pl.* **~x**) /o/ *n.f.* water. **~
courante/dormante,** run-
ning/still water. **~ de Cologne,**
eau-de-Cologne. **~ de toilette,**
toilet water. **~ de-vie** (*pl.* **~x-
de-vie**) *n.f.* brandy. **~ douce/
salée,** fresh/salt water. **~
potable,** drinking water. **~ de
Javel,** bleach. **~ minérale,**
mineral water. **~ gazeuse,** fizzy
water. **~ plate,** still water.

ébène /ebɛn/ *n.f.* ebony.

ébéniste /ebenist/ n.m. cabinet-maker.

éblouir /ebluir/ v.t. dazzle.

éboueur /ebwœr/ n.m. dustman.

ébouillanter /ebujɑ̃te/ v.t. scald.

éboulement /ebulmɑ̃/ n.m. landslide.

ébriété /ebrijete/ n.f. intoxication.

ébullition /ebylisjɔ̃/ n.f. boiling. **en ~,** boiling.

écaille /ekaj/ n.f. (de poisson) scale; (matière) tortoiseshell.

écailler /ekaje/ v.t. (poisson) scale.

écarlate /ekarlat/ a. & n.f. scarlet.

écarquiller /ekarkije/ v.t. ~ **les yeux,** open one's eyes wide.

écart /ekar/ n.m. gap; (de prix etc.) difference; (embardée) swerve; (de conduite) lapse (de, in). **à l'~,** out of the way.

écarté /ekarte/ a. (lieu) remote. **les jambes ~es,** (with) legs apart. **les bras ~s,** with one's arms out.

écartement /ekartəmɑ̃/ n.m. gap.

écarter /ekarte/ v.t. (objets) move apart; (ouvrir) open; (éliminer) dismiss. ~ **qch. de,** move sth. away from. ~ **v. pr.** (s'éloigner) move away. **s'~ de,** stray from.

ecclésiastique /eklezjastik/ a. ecclesiastical. —n.m. clergyman.

échafaud|age /eʃafodaʒ/ n.m. scaffolding; (amas) heap. ~**er** v.t. (projets) construct.

échalote /eʃalɔt/ n.f. shallot.

échang|e /eʃɑ̃ʒ/ n.m. exchange. **en ~e (de),** in exchange (for). ~**er** v.t. exchange (**contre,** for).

échangeur /eʃɑ̃ʒœr/ n.m. (auto.) interchange.

échantillon /eʃɑ̃tijɔ̃/ n.m. sample.

échappement /eʃapmɑ̃/ n.m. exhaust.

échapper /eʃape/ v.i. ~ **à,** escape;

(en fuyant) escape (from). **s'~** v. pr. escape.

écharde /eʃard/ n.f. splinter.

écharpe /eʃarp/ n.f. scarf; (de maire) sash. **en ~, (bras)** in a sling.

échasse /eʃas/ n.f. stilt.

échassier /eʃasje/ n.m. wader.

échéance /eʃeɑ̃s/ n.f. due date (for payment); (délai) deadline; (obligation) (financial) commitment.

échéant (le cas) /(lǝkaz)eʃeɑ̃/ adv. if the occasion arises, possibly.

échec /eʃɛk/ n.m. failure. ~**s,** (jeu) chess. ~ **et mat,** checkmate.

échelle /eʃɛl/ n.f. ladder; (dimension) scale.

échelon /eʃlɔ̃/ n.m. rung; (de fonctionnaire) grade; (niveau) level.

échelonner /eʃlɔne/ v.t. spread out, space out.

échiquier /eʃikje/ n.m. chessboard.

écho /eko/ n.m. echo.

échographie /ekɔgrafi/ n.f. ultrasound (scan).

échouer¹ /eʃwe/ v.i. fail.

échouer² /eʃwe/ v.t. (bateau) ground. —v.i. **s'~** v. pr. run aground.

éclabouss|er /eklabuse/ v.t. splash. ~**ure** n.f. splash.

éclair /eklɛr/ n.m. (flash of) lightning; (gâteau) éclair.

éclairage /eklɛraʒ/ n.m. lighting.

éclaircie /eklɛrsi/ n.f. sunny interval.

éclaircir /eklɛrsir/ v.t. make lighter; (mystère) clear up.

éclairer /eklere/ v.t. light (up); (personne) give some light to.

éclaireu|r, ~se /eklɛrœr, -øz/ n.m., n.f. (boy) scout, (girl) guide.

éclat /ekla/ n.m. fragment; (de lumière) brightness; (de rire) (out)burst; (splendeur) give some light to.

éclatant, ~e /eklatã, -t/ *a.*
brilliant.

éclater /eklate/ *v.i.* burst;
(*exploser*) go off; (*verre*) shatter;
(*guerre*) break out; (*groupe*) split
up. **~ de rire**, burst out laugh-
ing.

éclipse /eklips/ *n.f.* eclipse.

éclipser /eklipse/ *v.t.* eclipse. **s'~**
v. pr. slip away.

éclore /eklɔr/ *v.i.* (*œuf*) hatch;
(*fleur*) open. **~osion** *n.f.* hatch-
ing; opening.

écluse /eklyz/ *n.f.* (*de canal*) lock.

écœurant, ~e /ekœrã, -t/ *a.*
(*gâteau*) sickly; (*fig.*) disgusting.

école /ekɔl/ *n.f.* school. **~ maternelle / primaire / secondaire**,
nursery / primary / secondary
school.

écol|ier, ~ière /ekɔlje, -jɛr/
n.m., f. schoolboy, schoolgirl.

écolo /ekɔlo/ *a. & n.m./f.* green.

écologie /ekɔlɔʒi/ *n.f.* ecology.
~ique *a.* ecological, green.

écologiste /ekɔlɔʒist/ *n.m./f.* eco-
logist.

économat /ekɔnɔma/ *n.m.* bur-
sary.

économe /ekɔnɔm/ *a.* thrifty.
—*n.m./f.* bursar.

économ|ie /ekɔnɔmi/ *n.f.* eco-
nomy. **~ies**, (*argent*) savings.
une ~ie de, (*gain*) a saving of.
~ique *a.* (*pol.*) economic; (*bon
marché*) economical. **~iser** *v.t./i.*
save. **~iste** *n.m./f.* economist.

écorce /ekɔrs/ *n.f.* bark; (*de fruit*)
peel.

écorch|er /ekɔrʃe/ **s'~er** *v. pr.*
graze o.s. **~ure** *n.f.* graze.

écossais, ~e /ekɔsɛ, -z/ *a.*
Scottish. —*n.m., f.* Scot.

Écosse /ekɔs/ *n.f.* Scotland.

écosser /ekɔse/ *v.t.* shell.

écouler[1] /ekule/ *v.t.* dispose of,
sell.

écouler² (**s'**) /(s)ekule/ *v. pr.* flow
(out), run (off); (*temps*) pass.
~ement *n.m.* flow.

écourter /ekurte/ *v.t.* shorten.

écoute /ekut/ *n.f.* listening. **à l'~
(de)**, listening in (to). **heures de
grande ~**, peak time.

écout|er /ekute/ *v.t.* listen to;
(*radio*) listen (in) to. —*v.i.* listen.
~eur *n.m.* earphones; (*de
téléphone*) receiver.

écran /ekrã/ *n.m.* screen. **~ total**,
sun-block.

écrasant, ~e /ekrazã, -t/ *a.*
overwhelming.

écraser /ekraze/ *v.t.* crush;
(*piéton*) run over. **s'~** *v. pr.* crash
(*contre*, into).

écrémé /ekreme/ *a.* **lait ~**,
skimmed milk. **lait demi-~**,
semi-skimmed milk.

écrevisse /ekrəvis/ *n.f.* crayfish.

écrin /ekrɛ̃/ *n.m.* case.

écrire[1] /ekrir/ *v.t./i.* write;
(*orthographier*) spell.

écrit /ekri/ *n.m.* document;
(*examen*) written paper. **par ~**,
in writing.

écriteau (*pl.* **~x**) /ekrito/ *n.m.*
notice.

écriture /ekrityr/ *n.f.* writing.

écrivain /ekrivɛ̃/ *n.m.* writer.

écrou /ekru/ *n.m.* nut.

écrouer /ekrue/ *v.t.* imprison.

écrouler (**s'**) /(s)ekrule/ *v. pr.*
collapse.

écru /ekry/ *a.* (*couleur*) natural;
(*tissu*) raw.

Écu /eky/ *n.m. invar.* ecu.

écueil /ekœj/ *n.m.* reef; (*fig.*)
danger.

écume /ekym/ *n.f.* foam.

écureuil /ekyrœj/ *n.m.* squirrel.

écurie /ekyri/ *n.f.* stable.

écuy|er, ~ère /ekɥije, -jɛr/ *n.m.,
f.* (horse) rider.

eczéma /ɛgzema/ *n.m.* eczema.

édifice /edifis/ n.m. building.

édit|er /edite/ v.t. publish; (*annoter*) edit. ∼**teur**, ∼**trice** n.m., f. publisher; editor.

édition /edisjɔ̃/ n.f. edition; (*industrie*) publishing.

édredon /edrədɔ̃/ n.m. eiderdown.

éducateur, ∼**trice** /edykatœr, -tris/ n.m., f. teacher.

éducati|f, ∼**ve** /edykatif, -v/ a. educational.

éducation /edykasjɔ̃/ n.f. education; (*dans la famille*) upbringing; (*manières*) manners. ∼ **physique**, physical education.

édulcorant /edylkɔrɑ̃/ n.m. & a. (*produit*) ∼, sweetener.

éduquer /edyke/ v.t. educate; (*à la maison*) bring up.

effacer /efase/ v.t. (*gommer*) rub out; (*par lavage*) wash out; (*souvenir etc.*) erase. s'∼ v. pr. fade; (*s'écarter*) step aside.

effecti|f, ∼**ve** /efɛktif, -v/ a. effective. ∼**vement** adv. effectively; (*en effet*) indeed.

effectuer /efɛktɥe/ v.t. carry out, make.

effervescen|t, ∼**te** /efɛrvesɑ̃, -t/ a. **comprimé** ∼**t**, effervescent tablet. ∼**ce** n.f. excitement.

effet /efɛ/ n.m. effect; (*impression*) impression. **en** ∼, indeed. **faire bon/mauvais** ∼, make a good/bad impression.

efficac|e /efikas/ a. effective; (*personne*) efficient. ∼**ité** n.f. effectiveness; efficiency.

effleurer /eflœre/ v.t. touch lightly; (*sujet*) touch on.

effluves /eflyv/ n.m. pl. exhalations.

effondr|er (s') /(s)efɔ̃dre/ v. pr. collapse. ∼**ement** n.m. collapse.

efforcer (s') /(s)efɔrse/ v. pr. try (hard) (**de**, to).

effort /efɔr/ n.m. effort.

effraction /efraksjɔ̃/ n.f. **entrer par** ∼, break in.

effray|er /efreje/ v.t. frighten. ∼**ant**, ∼**ante** a. frightening; (*fig.*) frightful.

effriter (s') /(s)efrite/ v. pr. crumble.

effroi /efrwa/ n.m. dread.

effronté /efrɔ̃te/ a. impudent.

effroyable /efrwajabl/ a. dreadful.

ég|al, ∼**ale** (m. pl. ∼**aux**) /egal, -o/ a. equal; (*surface, vitesse*) even. —n.m., f. equal. **ça m'est/lui est** ∼**al**, it is all the same to me/him. **sans égal**, matchless. **d'**∼ **à égal**, between equals.

également /egalmɑ̃/ adv. equally; (*aussi*) as well.

égaler /egale/ v.t. equal.

égaliser /egalize/ v.t. (*cheveux*) trim.

égalité /egalite/ n.f. equality; (*de surface, d'humeur*) evenness.

égard /egar/ n.m. regard. ∼**s**, consideration.

égarer /egare/ s'∼ v. pr. get lost; (*se tromper*) go astray.

égayer /egeje/ v.t. (*personne*) cheer up; (*pièce*) brighten up.

églantier /eglɑ̃tje/ n.m. wild rose (-bush).

églefin /egləfɛ̃/ n.m. haddock.

église /egliz/ n.f. church.

égoïs|te /egɔist/ a. selfish. —n.m./f. egoist. ∼**me** n.m. selfishness, egoism.

égorger /egɔrʒe/ v.t. slit the throat of.

égout /egu/ n.m. sewer.

égout|ter /egute/ v.t./i., **s'**∼**er** v. pr. (*vaisselle*) drain. ∼**oir** n.m. draining-board; (*panier*) dish drainer.

égratign|er /egratiɲe/ v.t. scratch. ∼**ure** n.f. scratch.

Égypte /eʒipt/ n.f. Egypt.

égyptien, ~ne /eʒipsjɛ̃, -jɛn/ *a. & n.m., f.* Egyptian.

eh /e/ *int.* hey. **eh bien,** well.

éjecter /eʒɛkte/ *v.t.* eject.

élaborer /elabɔre/ *v.t.* elaborate.

élaguer /elage/ *v.t.* prune.

élan[1] /elɑ̃/ *n.m.* (*sport*) run-up; (*vitesse*) momentum; (*fig.*) surge.

élan[2] /elɑ̃/ *n.m.* (*animal*) moose.

élancé /elɑ̃se/ *a.* slender.

élancement /elɑ̃smɑ̃/ *n.m.* twinge.

élancer (s') /(s)elɑ̃se/ *v. pr.* leap forward, dash; (*se dresser*) soar.

élargir /elarʒir/ *v.t.*, **s'~** *v. pr.* widen.

élasti|que /elastik/ *a.* elastic. —*n.m.* elastic band; (*tissu*) elastic. **~cité** *n.f.* elasticity.

élec|teur, ~trice /elɛktœr, -tris/ *n.m., f.* voter, elector.

élection /elɛksjɔ̃/ *n.f.* election.

élector|al (*m. pl. ~aux*) /elɛktɔral, -o/ *a.* (*réunion etc.*) election; (*collège*) electoral.

électorat /elɛktɔra/ *n.m.* electorate, voters.

électricien /elɛktrisjɛ̃/ *n.m.* electrician.

électricité /elɛktrisite/ *n.f.* electricity.

électrique /elɛktrik/ *a.* electric (al).

électroménager /elɛktrɔmenaʒe/ *n.m.* l'**~**, household appliances.

électron /elɛktrɔ̃/ *n.m.* electron.

électronique /elɛktrɔnik/ *a.* electronic. —*n.f.* electronics.

électrophone /elɛktrɔfɔn/ *n.m.* record-player.

élég|ant, ~ante /elegɑ̃, -t/ *a.* elegant. **~ance** *n.f.* elegance.

élément /elemɑ̃/ *n.m.* element; (*meuble*) unit. **~aire** /-tɛr/ *a.* elementary.

éléphant /elefɑ̃/ *n.m.* elephant.

élevage /elvaʒ/ *n.m.* (stock-) breeding.

élève /elɛv/ *n.m./f.* pupil.

élevé /elve/ *a.* high; (*noble*) elevated. **bien ~,** well-mannered.

élever /elve/ *v.t.* raise; (*enfants*) bring up, raise; (*animal*) breed. **s'~ à,** amount to.

éleveu|r, ~se /elvœr, -øz/ *n.m., f.* (stock-)breeder.

élimin|er /elimine/ *v.t.* eliminate. **~ation** *n.f.* elimination.

élire† /elir/ *v.t.* elect.

elle /ɛl/ *pron.* she; (*complément*) her; (*chose*) it. **~-même** *pron.* herself; itself.

elles /ɛl/ *pron.* they; (*complément*) them. **~-mêmes** *pron.* themselves.

ellipse /elips/ *n.f.* ellipse.

élocution /elɔkysjɔ̃/ *n.f.* diction.

éloge /elɔʒ/ *n.m.* praise. **faire l'~ de,** praise.

éloigné /elwaɲe/ *a.* distant. **~ de,** far away from. **parent ~,** distant relative.

éloigner /elwaɲe/ *v.t.* take away *ou* remove (**de,** from). **s'~** *v. pr.* go *ou* move away (**de,** from).

élongation /elɔ̃gasjɔ̃/ *n.f.* strained muscle.

éloquen|t, ~te /elɔkɑ̃, -t/ *a.* eloquent. **~ce** *n.f.* eloquence.

élu, ~e /ely/ *a.* elected. —*n.m., f.* (*pol.*) elected representative.

ém|ail (*pl. ~aux*) /emaj, -o/ *n.m.* enamel.

émaillé /emaje/ *a.* enamelled.

emball|er /ɑ̃bale/ *v.t.* pack, wrap; (*personne: fam.*) enthuse. **s'~er.** (*personne*) get carried away. **~age** *n.m.* package, wrapping.

embarcadère /ɑ̃barkadɛr/ *n.m.* landing-stage.

embarcation /ɑ̃barkasjɔ̃/ *n.f.* boat.

embarqu|er /ɑ̃barke/ *v.t.* embark; (*charger*) load; (*emporter: fam.*)

cart off. —*v.i.* s'**~**er *v. pr.* board, embark. **~**ement *n.m.* embarkation; loading.

embarras /ābara/ *n.m.* (*gêne*) embarrassment; (*difficulté*) difficulty.

embarrasser /ābarase/ *v.t.* (*fig.*) embarrass.

embauch|e /āboʃ/ *n.f.* hiring; (*emploi*) employment. **~**er *v.t.* hire, take on.

embauchoir /āboʃwar/ *n.m.* shoe tree.

embaumer /ābome/ *v.t./i.* (make) smell fragrant.

embellir /ābelir/ *v.t.* brighten up; (*récit*) embellish.

embêt|er /ābete/ *v.t.* (*fam.*) annoy. s'**~**er *v. pr.* (*fam.*) get bored. **~**ant, **~**ante *a.* (*fam.*) annoying. **~**ement /ābetmã/ *n.m.* (*fam.*) annoyance.

emboîter /ābwate/ *v.t.*, s'**~** *v. pr.* fit together.

embouchure /ābuʃyr/ *n.f.* (*de fleuve*) mouth.

embourber (s') /(s)āburbe/ *v. pr.* get bogged down.

embout /ābu/ *n.m.* tip.

embouteillage /ābutɛjaʒ/ *n.m.* traffic jam.

emboutir /ābutir/ *v.t.* (*heurter*) crash into.

embranchement /ābrāʃmã/ *n.m.* (*de routes*) junction.

embrasser /ābrase/ *v.t.* kiss; (*adopter, contenir*) embrace. s'**~** *v. pr.* kiss.

embray|er /ābreje/ *v.i.* let in the clutch. **~**age /ābrejaʒ/ *n.m.* clutch.

embrouiller /ābruje/ *v.t.* mix up; (*fils*) tangle. s'**~** *v. pr.* get mixed up.

embryon /ābrijɔ̃/ *n.m.* embryo. **~**naire /-jɔnɛr/ *a.* embryonic.

embûches /ābyʃ/ *n.f. pl.* traps.

éméché /emeʃe/ *a.* tipsy.

émeraude /emrod/ *n.f.* emerald.

émerger /emɛrʒe/ *v.i.* emerge; (*fig.*) stand out.

émerveill|er /emɛrveje/ *v.t.* amaze. s'**~**er de, marvel at, be amazed at. **~**ement /-vɛjmã/ *n.m.* amazement, wonder.

émett|re† /emɛtr/ *v.t.* give out; (*message*) transmit; (*timbre, billet*) issue; (*opinion*) express. **~**eur *n.m.* transmitter.

émeute /emøt/ *n.f.* riot.

émietter /emjete/ *v.t.*, s'**~** *v. pr.* crumble.

émigrant, ~e /emigrã, -t/ *n.m., f.* emigrant.

émigr|er /emigre/ *v.i.* emigrate. **~**ation *n.f.* emigration.

émincer /emɛ̃se/ *v.t.* cut into thin slices.

émin|ent, ~ente /eminã, -t/ *a.* eminent. **~**emment /-amã/ *adv.* eminently.

émissaire /emisɛr/ *n.m.* emissary.

émission /emisjɔ̃/ *n.f.* emission; (*de message*) transmission; (*de timbre*) issue; (*programme*) broadcast.

emmanchure /āmāʃyr/ *n.f.* armhole.

emmêler /āmele/ *v.t.* tangle. s'**~** *v. pr.* get mixed up.

emménager /āmenaʒe/ *v.i.* move in. **~** dans, move into.

emmener /āmne/ *v.t.* take; (*comme prisonnier*) take away.

emmerder /āmɛrde/ *v.t.* (*argot*) bother. s'**~** *v. pr.* (*argot*) get bored.

emmitoufler /āmitufle/ *v.t.*, s'**~** *v. pr.* wrap up (warmly).

émonder /emɔ̃de/ *v.t.* prune.

émoti|f, ~ve /emotif, -v/ *a.* emotional.

émotion /emosjɔ̃/ *n.f.* emotion; (*peur*) fright.

émouv|oir /emuvwar/ *v.t.* move. **~ant**, **~ante** *a.* moving.

empailler /ɑ̃paje/ *v.t.* stuff.

empaqueter /ɑ̃pakte/ *v.t.* package.

emparer (s') /(s)ɑ̃pare/ *v. pr.* **s'~ de**, seize.

empêchement /ɑ̃pɛʃmɑ̃/ *n.m.* hitch, difficulty.

empêch|er /ɑ̃peʃe/ *v.t.* prevent. **~ de faire**, prevent *ou* stop (from) doing.

empereur /ɑ̃prœr/ *n.m.* emperor.

empester /ɑ̃peste/ *v.i.* stink.

empêtrer (s') /(s)ɑ̃petre/ *v. pr.* become entangled.

emphase /ɑ̃faz/ *n.f.* pomposity.

empil|er /ɑ̃pile/ *v.t.*, **s'~** *v. pr.* pile (up).

empire /ɑ̃pir/ *n.m.* empire; (*fig.*) control.

empirer /ɑ̃pire/ *v.i.* worsen.

emplacement /ɑ̃plasmɑ̃/ *n.m.* site.

emplâtre /ɑ̃platr/ *n.m.* (*méd.*) plaster.

empl|ir /ɑ̃plir/ *v.t.*, **s'~** *v. pr.* fill.

emploi /ɑ̃plwa/ *n.m.* use; (*travail*) job. **~ du temps**, timetable. **l'~**, (*pol.*) employment.

employ|er /ɑ̃plwaje/ *v.t.* use; (*personne*) employ. **~é**, **~ée** *n.m.*, *f.* employee. **~eur**, **~euse** *n.m.*, *f.* employer.

empocher /ɑ̃pɔʃe/ *v.t.* pocket.

empoisonn|er /ɑ̃pwazɔne/ *v.t.* poison (*embêter*: *fam.*) annoy. **~ement** *n.m.* poisoning.

emport|é /ɑ̃pɔrte/ *a.* quick-tempered. **~ement** *n.m.* anger.

emporter /ɑ̃pɔrte/ *v.t.* take (away); (*entraîner*) carry away; (*prix*) carry off; (*arracher*) tear off. **s'~** *v. pr.* lose one's temper. **plat à ~**, take-away.

empreinte /ɑ̃prɛ̃t/ *n.f.* mark. **~e (digitale)**, fingerprint.

empress|er (s') /(s)ɑ̃prese/ *v. pr.* **s'~er auprès de**, be attentive to. **s'~er de**, hasten to. **~é** *a.* eager, attentive. **~ement** /ɑ̃presmɑ̃/ *n.m.* eagerness.

emprise /ɑ̃priz/ *n.f.* influence.

emprisonn|er /ɑ̃prizɔne/ *v.t.* imprison. **~ement** *n.m.* imprisonment.

emprunt /ɑ̃prœ̃/ *n.m.* loan. **faire un ~**, take out a loan.

emprunter /ɑ̃prœ̃te/ *v.t.* borrow (**à**, from); (*route*) take; (*fig.*) assume.

ému /emy/ *a.* moved; (*apeuré*) nervous; (*joyeux*) excited.

émulsion /emylsjɔ̃/ *n.f.* emulsion.

en[1] /ɑ̃/ *prép.* in; (*avec direction*) to; (*manière, état*) in, on; (*moyen de transport*) by; (*composition*) made of.

en[2] /ɑ̃/ *pron.* of it, of them; (*moyen*) with it; (*cause*) from it; (*lieu*) from there. **en avoir/vouloir/***etc.*, have/want/*etc.* some. **ne pas en avoir/vouloir/***etc.*, not have/ want/*etc.* any. **j'en ai assez**, I've had enough. **en êtes-vous sûr?**, are you sure?

encadr|er /ɑ̃kadre/ *v.t.* frame; (*entourer d'un trait*) circle; (*entourer*) surround. **~ement** *n.m.* framing; (*de porte*) frame.

encaisser /ɑ̃kese/ *v.t.* (*argent*) collect; (*chèque*) cash.

encastré /ɑ̃kastre/ *a.* built-in.

encaustique /ɑ̃kɔstik/ *n.f.* wax polish. **~er** *v.t.* wax.

enceinte[1] /ɑ̃sɛ̃t/ *a.f.* pregnant. **~ de 3 mois**, 3 months pregnant.

enceinte[2] /ɑ̃sɛ̃t/ *n.f.* enclosure. **~ (acoustique)**, loudspeaker.

encens /ɑ̃sɑ̃/ *n.m.* incense.

encercler /ɑ̃sɛrkle/ *v.t.* surround.

enchaîner /ɑ̃ʃene/ *v.t.* chain (up); (*coordonner*) link (up).

enchant|er /ɑ̃ʃɑte/ *v.t.* delight; (*ensorceler*) enchant. **~é** *a.* (*ravi*) delighted.

enchère /ɑ̃ʃɛr/ *n.f.* bid. **mettre** *ou* **vendre aux ~s**, sell by auction.

enclave /ɑklav/ *n.f.* enclave.

enclencher /ɑ̃klɑ̃ʃe/ *v.t.* engage.

enclore /ɑklɔr/ *v.t.* enclose.

enclos /ɑklo/ *n.m.* enclosure.

enclume /ɑklym/ *n.f.* anvil.

encoche /ɑkɔʃ/ *n.f.* notch.

encoignure /ɑkɔɲyr/ *n.f.* corner.

encolure /ɑkɔlyr/ *n.f.* neck.

encombr|er /ɑ̃kɔ̃bre/ *v.t.* clutter (up); (*gêner*) hamper. **~er de**, burden o.s. with. **~ant, ~ante** *a.* cumbersome. **~ement** *n.m.* (*auto*) traffic jam.

encore /ɑkɔr/ *adv.* (*toujours*) still; (*de nouveau*) again; (*de plus*) more; (*aussi*) also. **~ mieux/ plus grand**/*etc.*, even better/larger/*etc.* **~ une heure/un café**/*etc.*, another hour/coffee/ *etc.* **pas ~**, not yet.

encourag|er /ɑkuraʒe/ *v.t.* encourage. **~ement** *n.m.* encouragement.

encr|e /ɑ̃kr/ *n.f.* ink. **~er** *v.t.* ink.

encrier /ɑkrije/ *n.m.* ink-well.

encyclopéd|ie /ɑsiklɔpedi/ *n.f.* encyclopaedia. **~ique** *a.* encyclopaedic.

endetter /ɑdete/ *v.t.*, **s'~** *v. pr.* get into debt.

endive /ɑdiv/ *n.f.* chicory.

endocrinolo|gie /ɑdɔkrinɔlɔʒi/ *n.f.* endocrinology. **~gue** *n.m./f.* endocrinologist.

endommager /ɑdɔmaʒe/ *v.t.* damage.

endorm|ir /ɑdɔrmir/ *v.t.* send to sleep; (*atténuer*) allay. **s'~ir** *v. pr.* fall asleep. **~i** *a.* asleep.

endosser /ɑdose/ *v.t.* (*vêtement*) put on; (*assumer*) assume; (*comm.*) endorse.

endroit /ɑdrwa/ *n.m.* place; (*de tissu*) right side. **à l'~**, the right way round, right side out.

end|uire /ɑdɥir/ *v.t.* coat. **~uit** *n.m.* coating.

endurance /ɑdyrɑ̃s/ *n.f.* endurance.

endurcir /ɑdyrsir/ *v.t.* harden. **s'~** *v. pr.* become hard(ened).

énerg|ie /enɛrʒi/ *n.f.* energy; (*techn.*) power. **~étique** *a.* energy. **~ique** *a.* energetic.

énervant, ~e /enɛrvɑ̃, -t/ *a.* irritating, annoying.

énerver /enɛrve/ *v.t.* irritate. **s'~** *v. pr.* get worked up.

enfance /ɑfɑ̃s/ *n.f.* childhood.

enfant /ɑfɑ̃/ *n.m./f.* child. **~ine** /-tɛ̃, -tin/ *a.* childlike; (*puéril*) childish; (*jeu, langage*) children's.

enfer /ɑfɛr/ *n.m.* hell.

enfermer /ɑfɛrme/ *v.t.* shut up. **s'~** *v. pr.* shut o.s. up.

enfilade /ɑfilad/ *n.f.* string, row.

enfiler /ɑfile/ *v.t.* (*aiguille*) thread; (*vêtement*) slip on.

enfin /ɑfɛ̃/ *adv.* at last, finally; (*en dernier lieu*) finally; (*somme toute*) after all; (*résignation, conclusion*) well.

enflammer /ɑflame/ *v.t.* set fire to; (*méd.*) inflame. **s'~** *v. pr.* catch fire.

enfl|er /ɑfle/ *v.t./i.*, **s'~er** *v. pr.* swell. **~é a.* swollen.

enfoncer /ɑfɔse/ *v.t.* (*épingle etc.*) push ou drive in; (*chapeau*) push down; (*porte*) break down; (*mettre*) thrust, put. —*v.i.*, **s'~** *v. pr.* sink (**dans**, into).

enfouir /ɑfwir/ *v.t.* bury.

enfourcher /ɑfurʃe/ *v.t.* mount.

enfourner /ɑfurne/ *v.t.* put in the oven.

enfreindre /ɑfrɛdr/ *v.t.* infringe.

enfuir† (s') /(s)ɑfɥir/ *v. pr.* run off.

engagé /ãgaʒe/ *a.* committed.

engageant, ~e /ãgaʒã, -t/ *a.* attractive.

engager /ãgaʒe/ *v.t.* (*lier*) bind, commit; (*embaucher*) take on; (*commencer*) start; (*introduire*) insert; (*investir*) invest. **s'~** *v. pr.* (*promettre*) commit o.s.; (*concurrent*) enter. **s'~ à faire,** undertake to do. **s'~ dans,** (*voie*) enter.

engelure /ãʒlyr/ *n.f.* chilblain.

engendrer /ãʒɑ̃dre/ *v.t.* beget; (*causer*) generate.

engin /ãʒɛ̃/ *n.m.* machine; (*outil*) instrument; (*projectile*) missile. **~ explosif,** explosive device.

englober /ãglɔbe/ *v.t.* include.

engloutir /ãglutir/ *v.t.* swallow (up).

engouffrer /ãgufre/ *v.t.* devour. **s'~ dans,** rush into (with force).

engourdir /ãgurdir/ *v.t.* numb. **s'~** *v. pr.* go numb. **~i** *a.* numb.

engrais /ãgrɛ/ *n.m.* manure; (*chimique*) fertilizer.

engraisser /ãgrese/ *v.t.* fatten. **s'~** *v. pr.* get fat.

engrenage /ãgrənaʒ/ *n.m.* gears; (*fig.*) chain (of events).

énième /ɛnjɛm/ *a.* (*fam.*) umpteenth.

énigme /enigm/ *n.f.* riddle, enigma. **~atique** *a.* enigmatic.

enivrer /ãnivre/ *v.t.* intoxicate. **s'~** *v. pr.* get drunk.

enjamber /ãʒãbe/ *v.t.* step over; (*pont*) span. **~ée** *n.f.* stride.

enjeu (*pl.* **~x**) /ãʒø/ *n.m.* stake(s).

enjoliveur /ãʒɔlivœr/ *n.m.* hubcap.

enlacer /ãlase/ *v.t.* entwine.

enlaidir /ãledir/ *v.t.* make ugly. —*v.i.* grow ugly.

enlèvement /ãlɛvmã/ *n.m.* removal; (*rapt*) kidnapping.

enlever /ãlve/ *v.t.* (*emporter*) take (away), remove (**à,** from); (*vêtement*) take off, remove; (*tache, organe*) take out, remove; (*kidnapper*) kidnap.

enliser (s') /(s)ãlize/ *v. pr.* get bogged down.

enluminure /ãlyminyr/ *n.f.* illumination.

enneigé /ãneʒe/ *a.* snow-covered. **~ement** /ãnɛʒmã/ *n.m.* snow conditions.

ennemi /ɛnmi/ *n.m. & a.* enemy.

ennui /ãnɥi/ *n.m.* boredom; (*tracas*) trouble, worry.

ennuyer /ãnɥije/ *v.t.* bore; (*irriter*) annoy; (*préoccuper*) worry. **s'~** *v. pr.* get bored.

ennuyeu|x, ~se /ãnɥijø, -z/ *a.* boring; (*fâcheux*) annoying.

énoncé /enɔ̃se/ *n.m.* wording, text; (*gram.*) utterance.

énoncer /enɔ̃se/ *v.t.* express, state.

enorm|e /enɔrm/ *a.* enormous. **~ément** *adv.* enormously. **~ément de,** an enormous amount of.

enquêt|e /ãkɛt/ *n.f.* investigation; (*jurid.*) inquiry; (*sondage*) survey. **~er** /-ete/ *v.i.* **~er (sur),** investigate.

enraciné /ãrasine/ *a.* deep-rooted.

enrag|er /ãraʒe/ *v.i.* be furious. **faire ~er,** annoy. **~é** *a.* furious; (*chien*) mad; (*fig.*) fanatical.

enregistr|er /ãrʒistre/ *v.t.* note, record; (*mus.*) record. **(faire) ~er,** (*bagages*) register, check in. **~ement** *n.m.* recording; (*des bagages*) registration.

enrhumer (s') /(s)ãryme/ *v. pr.* catch a cold.

enrich|ir /ãriʃir/ *v.t.* enrich. **s'~ir** *v. pr.* grow rich(er). **~issement** *n.m.* enrichment.

enrou|er (s') /(s)ãrwe/ *v. pr.* become hoarse. **~é** *a.* hoarse.

enrouler /ãrule/ *v.t.,* **s'~** *v. pr.*

wind. **s'~ dans une couverture**, roll o.s. up in a blanket.
enseignant, **~e** /ɑ̃sɛɲɑ̃, -t/ *n.m.*, *f.* teacher. —*a.* teaching.
enseigne /ɑ̃sɛɲ/ *n.f.* sign.
enseignement; (*instruction*) education.
enseigner /ɑ̃sɛɲe/ *v.t./i.* teach. **~ qch. à qn.**, teach s.o. sth.
ensemble /ɑ̃sɑ̃bl/ *adv.* together. —*n.m.* unity; set; (*mus.*) ensemble; (*vêtements*) outfit. **dans l'~**, on the whole. **d'~**, (*idée etc.*) general. **l'~ de**, (*totalité*) all of, the whole of.
ensoleillé /ɑ̃sɔleje/ *a.* sunny. **~ement** /ɑ̃sɔlejmɑ̃/ *n.m.* (*period of*) sunshine.
ensommeillé /ɑ̃sɔmeje/ *a.* sleepy.
ensuite /ɑ̃sɥit/ *adv.* next, then; (*plus tard*) later.
ensuivre (s') /(s)ɑ̃sɥivr/ *v. pr.* follow. **et tout ce qui s'ensuit**, and so on.
entaille /ɑ̃taj/ *n.f.* notch; (*blessure*) gash. **~er** *v.t.* notch; gash.
entamer /ɑ̃tame/ *v.t.* start; (*inciser*) cut into.
entasser /ɑ̃tase/ *v.t.*, **s'~** *v. pr.* pile up. **(s')~ dans**, cram (together) into.
entendre /ɑ̃tɑ̃dr/ *v.t.* hear; (*comprendre*) understand; (*vouloir*) intend, mean; (*vouloir dire*) mean. **s'~** *v. pr.* (*être d'accord*) agree. **~ dire que**, hear that. **~ parler de**, hear of. **s'~** (bien), get on (avec, with).
entendu /ɑ̃tɑ̃dy/ *a.* (*convenu*) agreed; (*sourire*, *air*) knowing. **bien ~**, of course. **(c'est) ~!**, all right!
entente /ɑ̃tɑ̃t/ *n.f.* understanding. **à double ~**, with a double meaning.
entériner /ɑ̃terine/ *v.t.* ratify.

enterr|er /ɑ̃tere/ *v.t.* bury. **~ement** /ɑ̃tɛrmɑ̃/ *n.m.* burial, funeral.
en-tête /ɑ̃tɛt/ *n.m.* heading. **à ~**, headed.
entêt|é /ɑ̃tete/ *a.* stubborn. **~ement** /ɑ̃tɛtmɑ̃/ *n.m.* stubbornness.
entêter (s') /(s)ɑ̃tete/ *v. pr.* persist (à, dans, in).
enthousias|me /ɑ̃tuzjasm/ *n.m.* enthusiasm. **~mer** *v.t.* enthuse. **s'~mer pour**, enthuse over. **~te** *a.* enthusiastic.
ent|ier, **~ière** /ɑ̃tje, -jɛr/ *a.* whole; (*absolu*) absolute; (*entêté*) unyielding. —*n.m.* whole. **en ~ier**, entirely. **~ièrement** *adv.* entirely.
entonnoir /ɑ̃tɔnwar/ *n.m.* funnel.
entorse /ɑ̃tɔrs/ *n.f.* sprain. **~ à**, (*loi*) infringement of.
entortiller /ɑ̃tɔrtije/ *v.t.* wrap (up); (*enrouler*) wind, wrap.
entourage /ɑ̃turaʒ/ *n.m.* circle of family and friends.
entourer /ɑ̃ture/ *v.t.* surround (de, with). **~ de**, wrap round.
entracte /ɑ̃trakt/ *n.m.* interval.
entraide /ɑ̃trɛd/ *n.f.* mutual aid.
entraider (s') /(s)ɑ̃trɛde/ *v. pr.* help each other.
entrain /ɑ̃trɛ̃/ *n.m.* zest, spirit.
entraînant, **~e** /ɑ̃trɛnɑ̃, -t/ *a.* rousing.
entraînement /ɑ̃trɛnmɑ̃/ *n.m.* (*sport*) training.
entraîn|er /ɑ̃trene/ *v.t.* carry away ou along; (*emmener*, *influencer*) lead; (*impliquer*) entail; (*sport*) train; (*roue*) drive. **~eur** /ɑ̃trɛnœr/ *n.m.* trainer.
entre /ɑ̃tr(ə)/ *prép.* between; (*parmi*) among(st). **l'un d'~ nous/vous/eux**, one of us/you/them.
entrebâillé /ɑ̃trəbaje/ *a.* ajar.

entrechoquer (s') /(s)ātrəʃɔke/ v. pr. knock against each other.

entrecôte /ātrəkot/ n.f. rib steak.

entrecroiser (s') /(s)ātrəkrwaze/ v. pr. (routes) intersect.

entrée /ātre/ n.f. entrance; (accès) admission, entry; (billet) ticket; (culin.) first course; (de données: techn.) input. ~ **interdite,** no entry.

entrefilet /ātrəfile/ n.m. paragraph.

entrejambe /ātrəʒɑ̃b/ n.m. crotch.

entremets /ātrəmɛ/ n.m. dessert.

entremetteu|r, ~**se** /ātrəmɛtœr, -øz/ n.m., f. (péj.) go-between.

entremettre (s') /(s)ātrəmɛtr/ v. pr. intervene. ~**mise** n.f. intervention. **par l'**~**mise de,** through.

entreposer /ātrəpoze/ v.t. store.

entrepôt /ātrəpo/ n.m. warehouse.

entreprendre† /ātrəprɑ̃dr/ v.t. ~ **de faire,** undertake to do.

entrepreneur /ātrəprənœr/ n.m. ~ **(de bâtiments),** (building) contractor.

entreprise /ātrəpriz/ n.f. undertaking; (société) firm.

entrer /ātre/ v.i. (aux. être) go in, enter; (venir) come in, enter. **faire** ~, (personne) show in.

entresol /ātrəsɔl/ n.m. mezzanine.

entre-temps /ātrətɑ̃/ adv. meanwhile.

entretenir† /ātrətnir/ v.t. maintain; (faire durer) keep alive. **s'**~ v. pr. speak (**de,** about; **avec,** to).

entretien /ātrətjɛ̃/ n.m. maintenance; (discussion) discussion; (audience pour un emploi) interview.

entrevue /ātrəvy/ n.f. interview.

entrouvrir /ātruvrir/ v.t. half-open.

énumér|er /enymere/ v.t. enumerate. ~**ation** n.f. enumeration.

envah|ir /āvair/ v.t. invade, overrun; (douleur, peur) overcome. ~**isseur** n.m. invader.

enveloppe /āvlɔp/ n.f. envelope; (emballage) covering; (techn.) casing.

envelopper /āvlɔpe/ v.t. wrap (up); (fig.) envelop.

envers /āver/ prép. toward(s), to. —n.m. (de tissu) wrong side. **à l'**~, upside down; (pantalon) back to front; (chaussette) inside out.

envie /āvi/ n.f. desire, wish; (jalousie) envy. **avoir** ~ **de,** want, feel like. **avoir** ~ **de faire,** want to do, feel like doing.

envier /āvje/ v.t. envy.

envieu|x, ~**se** /āvjø, -z/ a. & n.m., f. envious (person).

environ /āvirɔ̃/ adv. (round) about. ~**s** n.m. pl. surroundings. **aux** ~**s de,** round about.

environnement /āvirɔnmɑ̃/ n.m. environment.

envoi /āvwa/ n.m. dispatch; (paquet) consignment.

envoler (s') /(s)āvɔle/ v. pr. fly away; (avion) take off; (papiers) blow away.

envoyer† /āvwaje/ v.t. send; (lancer) throw.

enzyme /āzim/ n.m. enzyme.

épagneul, ~**e** /epaɲœl/ n.m., f. spaniel.

épais, ~**se** /epɛ, -s/ a. thick. ~**seur** /-sœr/ n.f. thickness.

épaissir /epesir/ v.t./i., **s'**~ v. pr. thicken.

épanoui /epanwi/ a. (joyeux) beaming, radiant.

épanouir (s') /(s)epanwir/ v. pr. (fleur) open out; (visage) beam; (personne) blossom.

épargne /eparɲ/ *n.f.* saving; (*somme*) savings. **caisse d'~,** savings bank.

épargn|er /eparɲe/ *v.t./i.* save; (*ne pas tuer*) spare. **~ant, ~ante** *n.m., f.* saver.

épat|er /epate/ *v.t.* (*fam.*) amaze. **~ant, ~ante** *a.* (*fam.*) amazing.

épaule /epol/ *n.f.* shoulder.

épauler /epole/ *v.t.* (*arme*) raise; (*aider*) support.

épave /epav/ *n.f.* wreck.

épée /epe/ *n.f.* sword.

épeler /eple/ *v.t.* spell.

éperon /eprɔ̃/ *n.m.* spur.

épervier /epɛrvje/ *n.m.* sparrow-hawk.

éphémère /efemɛr/ *a.* ephemeral.

épi /epi/ *n.m.* (*de blé*) ear. **~ de cheveux,** tuft of hair.

épic|e /epis/ *n.f.* spice. **~é a.** spicy. **~er** *v.t.* spice.

épic|ier, ~ière /episje, -jɛr/ *n.m., f.* grocer. **~erie** *n.f.* grocery shop; (*produits*) groceries.

épidémie /epidemi/ *n.f.* epidemic.

épiderme /epidɛrm/ *n.m.* skin.

épier /epje/ *v.t.* spy on.

épilep|sie /epilɛpsi/ *n.f.* epilepsy. **~tique** *a. & n.m./f.* epileptic.

épiler /epile/ *v.t.* remove unwanted hair from; (*sourcils*) pluck.

épilogue /epilɔg/ *n.m.* epilogue; (*fig.*) outcome.

épinard /epinar/ *n.m.* (*plante*) spinach. **~s,** (*nourriture*) spinach.

épine /epin/ *n.f.* thorn, prickle.

éping|le /epɛ̃gl/ *n.f.* pin. **~e de nourrice, ~e de sûreté,** safety-pin.

épisode /epizɔd/ *n.m.* episode.

épithète /epitɛt/ *n.f.* epithet.

épluche-légumes /eplyʃlegym/ *n.m. invar.* (potato) peeler.

épluch|er /eplyʃe/ *v.t.* peel; (*examiner*; *fig.*) scrutinize. **~ures** *n.f. pl.* peelings.

épong|e /epɔ̃ʒ/ *n.f.* sponge. **~er** *v.t.* (*liquide*) sponge up; (*surface*) sponge (down); (*front*) mop.

époque /epɔk/ *n.f.* time, period. **à l'~,** at the time. **d'~,** period.

épouse /epuz/ *n.f.* wife.

épouser /epuze/ *v.t.* marry.

épouvantable /epuvɑ̃tabl/ *a.* appalling.

épouvantail /epuvɑ̃taj/ *n.m.* scarecrow.

épouvante /epuvɑ̃t/ *n.f.* terror. **~er** *v.t.* terrify.

époux /epu/ *n.m.* husband. **les ~,** the married couple.

épreuve /eprœv/ *n.f.* test; (*sport*) event; (*malheur*) ordeal; (*photo.*) print; (*d'imprimerie*) proof. **mettre à l'~,** put to the test.

éprouv|er /epruve/ *v.t.* test; (*ressentir*) experience; (*affliger*) distress. **~ant, ~ante** *a.* testing.

éprouvette /epruvɛt/ *n.f.* test-tube. **bébé-~,** test-tube baby.

épuis|er /epɥize/ *v.t.* (*fatiguer*, *user*) exhaust. **s'~er** *v. pr.* become exhausted. **~é a.** exhausted; (*livre*) out of print. **~ement** *n.m.* exhaustion.

épuisette /epɥizɛt/ *n.f.* fishing-net.

équateur /ekwatœr/ *n.m.* equator.

équation /ekwasjɔ̃/ *n.f.* equation.

équerre /ekɛr/ *n.f.* (set) square.

équilibr|e /ekilibr/ *n.m.* balance. **être** *ou* **se tenir en ~e,** (*personne*) balance; (*objet*) be balanced. **~é a.** well-balanced. **~er** *v.t.* balance.

équinoxe /ekinɔks/ *n.m.* equinox.

équipage /ekipaʒ/ *n.m.* crew.

équipe /ekip/ *n.f.* team. **~ de nuit/jour,** night/day shift.

équipé /ekipe/ *a.* **bien/mal ~,** well/poorly equipped.

équipement /ekipmɑ̃/ *n.m.*
equipment. **~s,** (*installations*)
amenities, facilities.

équiper /ekipe/ *v.t.* equip (**de,**
with). **s'~** *v. pr.* equip o.s.

équip|ier, **~ière** /ekipje, -jɛr/
n.m., f. team member.

équitation /ekitasjɔ̃/ *n.f.* (horse-)
riding.

équivalen|t, **~te** /ekivalɑ̃, -t/ *a.*
equivalent. **~ce** *n.f.* equivalence.

érable /erabl/ *n.m.* maple.

érafl|er /erafle/ *v.t.* scratch. **~ure**
n.f. scratch.

ère /ɛr/ *n.f.* era.

érection /erɛksjɔ̃/ *n.f.* erection.

ermite /ɛrmit/ *n.m.* hermit.

érosion /erozjɔ̃/ *n.f.* erosion.

éroti|que /erɔtik/ *a.* erotic. **~sme**
n.m. eroticism.

errer /ɛre/ *v.i.* wander.

erreur /erœr/ *n.f.* mistake, error.
dans l'~, mistaken. **par ~,** by
mistake. **~ judiciaire,** miscarriage of justice.

erroné /erɔne/ *a.* erroneous.

érudit, **~e** /erydi, -t/ *a.*
scholarly. **—** *n.m., f.* scholar.

éruption /erypsjɔ̃/ *n.f.* eruption;
(*méd.*) rash.

es /ɛ/ *voir* **être**.

escabeau (*pl.* **~x**) /ɛskabo/ *n.m.*
step-ladder; (*tabouret*) stool.

escadron /ɛskadrɔ̃/ *n.m.* (*mil.*)
squadron.

escalad|e /ɛskalad/ *n.f.* climbing;
(*pol., comm.*) escalation. **~er** *v.t.*
climb.

escalator /ɛskalatɔr/ *n.m.* (P.)
escalator.

escale /ɛskal/ *n.f.* (*d'avion*)
stopover; (*port*) port of call. **faire
~ à,** (*avion, passager*) stop over
at; (*navire, passager*) put in at.

escalier /ɛskalije/ *n.m.* stairs. **~
mécanique** *ou* **roulant,** escalator.

escalope /ɛskalɔp/ *n.f.* escalope.

escamotable /ɛskamɔtabl/ *a.*
(*techn.*) retractable.

escargot /ɛskargo/ *n.m.* snail.

escarpé /ɛskarpe/ *a.* steep.

escarpin /ɛskarpɛ̃/ *n.m.* pump.

esclav|e /ɛsklav/ *n.m./f.* slave.
~age *n.m.* slavery.

escompte /ɛskɔ̃t/ *n.m.* discount.

escompter /ɛskɔ̃te/ *v.t.* expect;
(*comm.*) discount.

escort|e /ɛskɔrt/ *n.f.* escort. **~er**
v.t. escort.

escrime /ɛskrim/ *n.f.* fencing.

escroc /ɛskro/ *n.m.* swindler.

escroqu|er /ɛskrɔke/ *v.t.* swindle.
~er qch. à qn., swindle s.o. out
of sth. **~erie** *n.f.* swindle.

espace /ɛspas/ *n.m.* space. **~s
verts,** gardens, parks.

espacer /ɛspase/ *v.t.* space out.
s'~ *v. pr.* become less frequent.

espadrille /ɛspadrij/ *n.f.* rope
sandals.

Espagne /ɛspaɲ/ *n.f.* Spain.

espagnol, **~e** /ɛspaɲɔl/ *a.*
Spanish. **—** *n.m.,* *f.* Spaniard.
— *n.m.* (*lang.*) Spanish.

espèce /ɛspɛs/ *n.f.* kind, sort; (*race*)
species. **~s,** (*argent*) cash.

espérance /ɛsperɑ̃s/ *n.f.* hope.

espérer /ɛspere/ *v.t.* hope for. **~
faire/que,** hope to do/that. **—** *v.i.*
hope. **~ en,** have faith in.

espiègle /ɛspjɛgl/ *a.* mischievous.

espion, **~ne** /ɛspjɔ̃, -jɔn/ *n.m., f.*
spy.

espionn|er /ɛspjɔne/ *v.t./i.* spy
(on). **~age** *n.m.* espionage,
spying.

espoir /ɛspwar/ *n.m.* hope.

esprit /ɛspri/ *n.m.* spirit; (*intellect*)
mind; (*humour*) wit. **perdre l'~,**
lose one's mind.

Esquimau, **~de** (*m. pl.* **~x**)
/ɛskimo, -d/ *n.m., f.* Eskimo.

esquisse /ɛskis/ *n.f.* sketch.

essai /esɛ/ *n.m.* testing; (*épreuve*) test, trial; (*tentative*) try; (*article*) essay. **à l'~,** on trial.

essaim /esɛ̃/ *n.m.* swarm.

essayage /esɛjaʒ/ *n.m.* (*de vêtement*) fitting. **salon d'~,** fitting room.

essayer /eseje/ *v.t./i.* try; (*vêtement*) try (on); (*voiture etc.*) try (out). **~ de faire,** to try to do.

essence[1] /esɑ̃s/ *n.f.* (*carburant*) petrol; (*Amer.*) gas.

essence[2] /esɑ̃s/ *n.f.* (*nature, extrait*) essence.

essentiel, ~le /esɑ̃sjɛl/ *a.* essential. —*n.m.* **l'~,** the main thing; (*quantité*) the main part. **~lement** *adv.* essentially.

essieu (*pl.* **~x**) /esjø/ *n.m.* axle.

essor /esɔr/ *n.m.* expansion.

essor|er /esɔre/ *v.t.* (*linge*) spin-dry; (*en tordant*) wring. **~euse** *n.f.* spin-drier.

essouffler (s') /(s)esufle/ *v.pr.* get out of breath.

ess|uyer /esɥije/ *v.t.* wipe. **s'~uyer** *v. pr.* dry *ou* wipe o.s. **~uie-glace** *n.m. invar.* windscreen wiper.

est[1] /ɛ/ *voir* **être.**

est[2] /ɛst/ *n.m.* east. —*a. invar.* east; (*partie*) eastern; (*direction*) easterly.

estampe /ɛstɑ̃p/ *n.f.* print.

esthéticienne /ɛstetisjɛn/ *n.f.* beautician.

estimable /ɛstimabl/ *a.* worthy.

estimation /ɛstimasjɔ̃/ *n.f.* valuation.

estime /ɛstim/ *n.f.* esteem.

estim|er /ɛstime/ *v.t.* (*objet*) value; (*calculer*) estimate; (*respecter*) esteem; (*considérer*) consider.

estiv|al (*m. pl.* **~aux**) /ɛstival, -o/ *a.* summer. **~ant, ~ante** *n.m., f.* summer visitor, holiday-maker.

estomac /ɛstɔma/ *n.m.* stomach.

estrade /ɛstrad/ *n.f.* platform.

estragon /ɛstragɔ̃/ *n.m.* tarragon.

estuaire /ɛstɥɛr/ *n.m.* estuary.

esturgeon /ɛstyrʒɔ̃/ *n.m.* sturgeon.

et /e/ *conj.* and. **et moi/lui/***etc.***?,** what about me/him/*etc.*?

étable /etabl/ *n.f.* cow-shed.

établi[1] /etabli/ *a.* established. **un fait bien ~,** a well-established fact.

établi[2] /etabli/ *n.m.* work-bench.

établir /etablir/ *v.t.* establish; (*liste, facture*) draw up; (*personne, camp, record*) set up. **s'~ à son compte,** set up on one's own.

établissement /etablismɑ̃/ *n.m.* (*bâtiment, institution*) establishment.

étage /etaʒ/ *n.m.* floor, storey; (*de fusée*) stage. **à l'~,** upstairs. **au premier ~,** on the first floor.

étagère /etaʒɛr/ *n.f.* shelf; (*meuble*) shelving unit.

étain /etɛ̃/ *n.m.* pewter.

étal (*pl.* **~s**) /etal/ *n.m.* stall.

étalage /etalaʒ/ *n.m.* display; (*vitrine*) shop-window.

étaler /etale/ *v.t.* spread; (*journal*) spread (out); (*vacances*) stagger; (*exposer*) display. **s'~ sur,** (*paiement*) be spread over.

étalon /etalɔ̃/ *n.m.* (*cheval*) stallion; (*modèle*) standard.

étanche /etɑ̃ʃ/ *a.* watertight; (*montre*) waterproof.

étang /etɑ̃/ *n.m.* pond.

étant /etɑ̃/ *voir* **être.**

étape /etap/ *n.f.* stage; (*lieu d'arrêt*) stopover.

état /eta/ *n.m.* state; (*liste*) statement; (*métier*) profession; (*nation*) State. **en bon/mauvais ~,** in good/bad condition. **en ~ de,** in a position to. **~ civil,** civil status. **~ des lieux,** inventory.

étatisé /etatize/ *a.* State-controlled.

États-Unis /etazyni/ *n.m. pl.* ~ **(d'Amérique),** United States (of America).

étau (*pl.* ~x) /eto/ *n.m.* vice.

été¹ /ete/ *voir* **être.**

été² /ete/ *n.m.* summer.

étein|dre† /etɛ̃dr/ *v.t.* put out, extinguish; (*lumière, radio*) turn off. **s'~dre** *v. pr.* (*feu*) go out; (*mourir*) die. ~**t,** ~**te** /etɛ̃, -t/ *a.* (*feu*) out; (*volcan*) extinct.

étendard /etɑ̃dar/ *n.m.* standard.

étendre /etɑ̃dr/ *v.t.* spread (*journal, nappe*) spread out; (*bras, jambes*) stretch (out); (*linge*) hang out. **s'~** *v. pr.* (*s'allonger*) stretch out.

étendu, ~**e** /etɑ̃dy/ *a.* extensive. —*n.f.* area; (*d'eau*) stretch; (*importance*) extent.

éternel, ~**le** /etɛrnɛl/ *a.* eternal. ~**lement** *adv.* eternally.

éternité /etɛrnite/ *n.f.* eternity.

étern|uer /etɛrnɥe/ *v.i.* sneeze. ~**uement** /-ymã/ *n.m.* sneeze.

êtes /ɛt/ *voir* **être.**

éthique /etik/ *a.* ethical. —*n.f.* ethics.

ethn|ie /ɛtni/ *n.f.* ethnic group. ~**ique** *a.* ethnic.

éthylisme /etilism/ *n.m.* alcoholism.

étinceler /etɛ̃sle/ *v.i.* sparkle.

étincelle /etɛ̃sɛl/ *n.f.* spark.

étiquette /etikɛt/ *n.f.* label; (*protocole*) etiquette.

étirer /etire/ *v.t.,* **s'~** *v. pr.* stretch.

étoffe /etɔf/ *n.f.* fabric.

étoil|e /etwal/ *n.f.* star. **à la belle** ~**e,** in the open. ~ **de mer,** starfish. ~**é** *a.* starry.

étonn|er /etɔne/ *v.t.* amaze. **s'~er** *v. pr.* be amazed (**de,** at). ~**ant,** ~**ante** *a.* amazing. ~**ement** *n.m.* amazement.

étouffée /etufe/ *n.f.* **cuire à l'~,** braise.

étouff|er /etufe/ *v.t./i.* suffocate; (*sentiment, révolte*) stifle; (*feu*) smother; (*bruit*) muffle. **on ~e,** it is stifling. **s'~er** *v. pr.* suffocate; (*en mangeant*) choke. ~**ant,** ~**ante** *a.* stifling.

étourd|i, ~**ie** /eturdi/ *a.* unthinking, scatter-brained. —*n.m., f.* scatter-brain. ~**erie** *n.f.* thoughtlessness; (*acte*) thoughtless act.

étrange /etrɑ̃ʒ/ *a.* strange.

étrang|er, ~**ère** /etrɑ̃ʒe, -ɛr/ *a.* strange, unfamiliar; (*d'un autre pays*) foreign. —*n.m., f.* foreigner; (*inconnu*) stranger. **à l'~er,** abroad. **de l'~er,** from abroad.

étrangler /etrɑ̃gle/ *v.t.* strangle; (*col*) stifle. **s'~** *v. pr.* choke.

être† /ɛtr/ *v.i.* be. —*v. aux.* (*avec aller, sortir, etc.*) have. ~ **donné/fait par,** (*passif*) be given/done by. —*n.m.* (*personne, créature*) being. ~ **humain,** human being. ~ **médecin/tailleur/***etc.,* be a doctor/a tailor/*etc.* ~ **à qn.,** be s.o.'s. **c'est à faire,** it needs to be *ou* should be done. **est-ce qu'il travaille?,** is he working?, does he work? **vous travaillez, n'est-ce pas?,** you are working, aren't you?, you work, don't you? **il est deux heures/***etc.,* it is two o'clock/*etc.* **nous sommes le six mai,** it is the sixth of May.

étrier /etrije/ *n.m.* stirrup.

étriqué /etrike/ *a.* tight; (*fig.*) small-minded.

étroit, ~**e** /etrwa, -t/ *a.* narrow; (*vêtement*) tight; (*liens, surveillance*) close. **à l'~,** cramped.

étude /etyd/ *n.f.* study; (*bureau*) office. (**salle d')**~, (*scol.*) prep room. **faire des** ~**s (de),** study.

étudiant, ~e /etydjɑ̃, -t/ *n.m., f.* student.

étudier /etydje/ *v.t./i.* study.

étui /etɥi/ *n.m.* case.

étuve /etyv/ *n.f.* steamroom. **quelle étuve!,** it's like a hothouse in here.

étuvée /etyve/ *n.f.* **cuire à l'~,** braise.

etymologie /etimɔlɔʒi/ *n.f.* etymology.

eu, eue /y/ *voir* avoir.

eucalyptus /økaliptys/ *n.m.* eucalyptus.

Europe /ørɔp/ *n.f.* Europe.

européen, ~**ne** /ørɔpeɛ̃, -ɛɛn/ *a.* & *n.m., f.* European.

eux /ø/ *pron.* they; *(complément)* them. ~**-mêmes** *pron.* themselves.

évac|uer /evakɥe/ *v.t.* evacuate. ~**uation** *n.f.* evacuation.

évad|er (s') /(s)evade/ *v. pr.* escape. ~**é,** ~**ée** *a.* escaped; *n.m., f.* escaped prisoner.

éval|uer /evalɥe/ *v.t.* assess. ~**uation** *n.f.* assessment.

évang|ile /evɑ̃ʒil/ *n.m.* gospel. **l'Évangile,** the Gospel.

évan|ouir (s') /(s)evanwir/ *v. pr.* faint; *(disparaître)* vanish. ~**ouissement** *n.m.* *(syncope)* fainting fit.

évapor|er /evapɔre/ *v.t., s'~er v. pr.* evaporate. ~**ation** *n.f.* evaporation.

évasion /evazjɔ̃/ *n.f.* escape.

éveil /evɛj/ *n.m.* awakening.

éveill|er /eveje/ *v.t.* awake(n); *(susciter)* arouse. **s'~er** *v. pr.* awake(n); be aroused. ~**é** *a.* awake; *(intelligent)* alert.

événement /evenmɑ̃/ *n.m.* event.

éventail /evɑ̃taj/ *n.m.* fan; *(gamme)* range.

éventaire /evɑ̃tɛr/ *n.m.* stall, stand.

éventé /evɑ̃te/ *a.* *(gâté)* stale.

éventualité /evɑ̃tɥalite/ *n.f.* possibility.

éventuel, ~**le** /evɑ̃tɥɛl/ *a.* possible. ~**lement** *adv.* possibly.

évêque /evɛk/ *n.m.* bishop.

évidemment /evidamɑ̃/ *adv.* obviously; *(bien sûr)* of course.

évidence /evidɑ̃s/ *n.f.* obviousness; *(fait)* obvious fact. **être en ~,** be conspicuous. **mettre en ~,** *(fait)* highlight.

évident, ~**e** /evidɑ̃, -t/ *a.* obvious, evident.

évider /evide/ *v.t.* hollow out.

évier /evje/ *n.m.* sink.

éviter /evite/ *v.t.* avoid **(de faire,** doing). ~ **à qn.,** *(dérangement etc.)* spare s.o.

évolué /evɔlɥe/ *a.* highly developed.

évolu|er /evɔlɥe/ *v.i.* develop. ~**tion** *n.f.* development; *(d'une espèce)* evolution.

évoquer /evɔke/ *v.t.* call to mind, evoke.

ex- /ɛks/ *préf.* ex-.

exact, ~**e** /egza(kt), -akt/ *a.* exact, accurate; *(correct)* correct; *(personne)* punctual. ~**ement** /-ktəmã/ *adv.* exactly.

ex aequo /egzeko/ *adv.* *(classer)* equal. **être ~,** be equally placed.

exagéré /egzaʒere/ *a.* excessive.

exagér|er /egzaʒere/ *v.t./i.* exaggerate; *(abuser)* go too far. ~**ation** *n.f.* exaggeration.

examen /egzamɛ̃/ *n.m.* examination; *(scol.)* exam(ination).

examin|er /egzamine/ *v.t.* examine. ~**ateur,** ~**atrice** *n.m., f.* examiner.

exaspér|er /ɛgzaspere/ *v.t.* exasperate. ~**ation** *n.f.* exasperation.

exaucer /egzose/ *v.t.* grant; *(personne)* grant the wish(es) of.

excavateur /ɛkskavatœr/ *n.m.* digger.

excavation /ɛkskavasjɔ̃/ *n.f.* excavation.

excédent /ɛksedɑ̃/ *n.m.* surplus. ~ **de bagages**, excess luggage. ~ **de la balance commerciale**, trade surplus. ~**aire** /-tɛr/ *a.* excess, surplus.

excéder /ɛksede/ *v.t.* (*dépasser*) exceed.

excellen|t, ~**te** /ɛkselɑ̃, -t/ *a.* excellent. ~**ce** *n.f.* excellence.

excentrique /ɛksɑ̃trik/ *a.* & *n.m./f.* eccentric.

excepté /ɛksɛpte/ *a.* & *prép.* except.

exception /ɛksɛpsjɔ̃/ *n.f.* exception. **à l'**~ **de**, except for. ~**nel**, ~**nelle** /-jɔnɛl/ *a.* exceptional. ~**nellement** /-jɔnɛlma/ *adv.* exceptionally.

excès /ɛksɛ/ *n.m.* excess. ~ **de vitesse**, speeding.

excessi|f, ~**ve** /ɛksesif, -v/ *a.* excessive. ~**vement** *adv.* excessively.

excitant /ɛksitɑ̃/ *n.m.* stimulant.

excit|er /ɛksite/ *v.t.* excite; (*encourager*) exhort (à, to); (*irriter: fam.*) annoy. ~**ation** *n.f.* excitement.

exclam|er (s') /(s)ɛksklame/ *v. pr.* exclaim. ~**ation** *n.f.* exclamation.

exclu|re† /ɛksklyr/ *v.t.* exclude; (*expulser*) expel; (*empêcher*) preclude. ~**sion** *n.f.* exclusion.

exclusi|f, ~**ve** /ɛksklyzif, -v/ *a.* exclusive. ~**vement** *adv.* exclusively. ~**vité** *n.f.* (*comm.*) exclusive rights. **en** ~**vité à**, (*film*) (showing) exclusively at.

excursion /ɛkskyrsjɔ̃/ *n.f.* excursion; (*à pied*) hike.

excuse /ɛkskyz/ *n.f.* excuse. ~**s**, apology. **faire des** ~**s**, apologize.

excuser /ɛkskyze/ *v.t.* excuse. **s'**~ *v. pr.* apologize (**de**, for). **je m'excuse**, (*fam.*) excuse me.

exécrable /ɛgzekrabl/ *a.* abominable.

exécut|er /ɛgzekyte/ *v.t.* carry out, execute; (*mus.*) perform; (*tuer*) execute.

exécuti|f, ~**ve** /ɛgzekytif, -v/ *a.* & *n.m.* (*pol.*) executive.

exemplaire /ɛgzɑ̃plɛr/ *a.* exemplary. —*n.m.* copy.

exemple /ɛgzɑ̃pl/ *n.m.* example. **par** ~, for example. **donner l'**~, set an example.

exempt, ~**e** /ɛgzɑ̃, -t/ *a.* ~ **de**, exempt from.

exempt|er /ɛgzɑ̃te/ *v.t.* exempt (**de**, from). ~**ion** /-psjɔ̃/ *n.f.* exemption.

exercer /ɛgzɛrse/ *v.t.* exercise; (*influence*, *contrôle*) exert; (*métier*) work at; (*former*) train, exercise. **s'**~ (**à**), practise.

exercice /ɛgzɛrsis/ *n.m.* exercise; (*mil.*) drill; (*de métier*) practice. **en** ~, in office; (*médecin*) in practice.

exigence /ɛgziʒɑ̃s/ *n.f.* demand.

exig|er /ɛgziʒe/ *v.t.* demand. ~**eant**, ~**eante** *a.* demanding.

exigu, ~**ë** /ɛgzigy/ *a.* tiny.

exil /ɛgzil/ *n.m.* exile. ~**é**, ~**ée** *n.m.*, *f.* exile. ~**er** *v.t.* exile. **s'**~**er** *v. pr.* go into exile.

existence /ɛgzistɑ̃s/ *n.f.* existence.

exist|er /ɛgziste/ *v.i.* exist. ~**ant**, ~**ante** *a.* existing.

exode /ɛgzɔd/ *n.m.* exodus.

exonér|er /ɛgzɔnere/ *v.t.* exempt (**de**, from). ~**ation** *n.f.* exemption.

exorbitant, ~**e** /ɛgzɔrbitɑ̃, -t/ *a.* exorbitant.

exotique /ɛgzɔtik/ *a.* exotic.

expansion /ɛkspɑ̃sjɔ̃/ *n.f.* expansion.

expatr|ier (s') /(s)ɛkspatrije/ *v. pr.* leave one's country. **~ié, ~iée** *n.m., f.* expatriate.

expéd|ier /ɛkspedje/ *v.t.* send, dispatch; (*tâche: péj.*) dispatch. **~iteur, ~itrice** *n.m., f.* sender. **~ition** *n.f.* dispatch; (*voyage*) expedition.

expérience /ɛksperjɑ̃s/ *n.f.* experience; (*scientifique*) experiment.

expérimenté /ɛksperimɑ̃te/ *a.* experienced.

expériment|er /ɛksperimɑ̃te/ *v.t.* test, experiment with. **~al** (*m. pl.* **~aux**) *a.* experimental.

expert, ~e /ɛkspɛr, -t/ *a.* expert. **—***n.m.* expert; (*d'assurances*) valuer. **~-comptable** (*pl.* **~s-comptables**) *n.m.* accountant.

expertis|e /ɛkspɛrtiz/ *n.f.* expert appraisal. **~er** *v.t.* appraise.

expir|er /ɛkspire/ *v.i.* breathe out; (*finir, mourir*) expire. **~ation** *n.f.* expiry.

explicati|f, ~ve /ɛksplikatif, -v/ *a.* explanatory.

explication /ɛksplikasjɔ̃/ *n.f.* explanation; (*fig.*) discussion; (*scol.*) commentary.

explicite /ɛksplisit/ *a.* explicit.

expliquer /ɛksplike/ *v.t.* explain. **s'~** *v. pr.* explain o.s.; (*discuter*) discuss things; (*être compréhensible*) be understandable.

exploit /ɛksplwa/ *n.m.* exploit.

exploitant /ɛksplwatɑ̃/ *n.m.* **~ (agricole),** farmer.

exploit|er /ɛksplwate/ *v.t.* (*personne*) exploit; (*ferme*) run; (*champs*) work. **~ation** *n.f.* exploitation; running; working; (*affaire*) concern.

explor|er /ɛksplɔre/ *v.t.* explore. **~ateur, ~atrice** *n.m., f.* explorer. **~ation** *n.f.* exploration.

explos|er /ɛksploze/ *v.i.* explode.

faire ~er, explode; (*bâtiment*) blow up. **~ion** *n.f.* explosion.

explosi|f, ~ve /ɛksplozif, -v/ *a.* & *n.m.* explosive.

export|er /ɛkspɔrte/ *v.t.* export. **~ateur, ~atrice** *n.m., f.* exporter; *a.* exporting. **~ation** *n.f.* export.

exposant, ~e /ɛkspozɑ̃, -t/ *n.m., f.* exhibitor.

exposé /ɛkspoze/ *n.m.* talk (**sur,** on); (*d'une action*) account.

expos|er /ɛkspoze/ *v.t.* display, show. **~é au nord**/*etc.,* facing north/*etc.*

exposition /ɛkspozisjɔ̃/ *n.f.* display; (*salon*) exhibition.

exprès[1] /ɛksprɛ/ *adv.* specially; (*délibérément*) on purpose.

exprès[2], **~esse** /ɛksprɛs/ *a.* express.

exprès[3] /ɛksprɛs/ *a. invar.* & *n.m.* **lettre ~,** express letter. **(par) ~,** sent special delivery.

express /ɛksprɛs/ *a.* & *n.m. invar.* (*café*) **~,** espresso. (*train*) **~,** fast train.

expression /ɛksprɛsjɔ̃/ *n.f.* expression.

exprimer /ɛksprime/ *v.t.* express. **s'~** *v. pr.* express o.s.

expuls|er /ɛkspylse/ *v.t.* expel; (*locataire*) evict. **~ion** *n.f.* expulsion; eviction.

extasier (s') /(s)ɛkstazje/ *v. pr.* **s'~ sur,** be ecstatic about.

extensible /ɛkstɑ̃sibl/ *a.* expandable, extendible. **tissu ~,** stretch fabric.

extension /ɛkstɑ̃sjɔ̃/ *n.f.* extension; (*expansion*) expansion.

extérieur /ɛksterjœr/ *a.* outside; (*signe, gaieté*) outward; (*politique*) foreign. **—***n.m.* outside, exterior; (*de personne*) exterior. **à l'~ (de),** outside. **~ement** *adv.* outwardly.

exterminer /ɛkstɛrmine/ v.t. exterminate.

externe /ɛkstɛrn/ a. external. —n.m./f. (scol.) day pupil.

extincteur /ɛkstɛ̃ktœr/ n.m. fire extinguisher.

extinction /ɛkstɛ̃ksjɔ̃/ n.f. extinction. ~ **de voix**, loss of voice.

extorquer /ɛkstɔrke/ v.t. extort.

extorsion /ɛkstɔrsjɔ̃/ n.f. extortion.

extra /ɛkstra/ a. invar. first-rate.

extra- /ɛkstra/ préf. extra-.

extrader /ɛkstrade/ v.t. extradite.

extr|aire† /ɛkstrɛr/ v.t. extract. **~action** n.f. extraction.

extrait /ɛkstrɛ/ n.m. extract.

extraordinaire /ɛkstraɔrdinɛr/ a. extraordinary.

extravagan|t, ~te /ɛkstravagɑ̃, -t/ a. extravagant. **~ce** n.f. extravagance.

extrême /ɛkstrɛm/ a. & n.m. extreme. **E~-Orient** n.m. Far East. **~ment** adv. extremely.

extrémiste /ɛkstremist/ n.m., f. extremist.

extrémité /ɛkstremite/ n.f. extremity, end.

exubéran|t, ~te /ɛgzyberɑ̃, -t/ a. exuberant. **~ce** n.f. exuberance.

F

F abrév. (franc, francs) franc, francs.

fabrique /fabrik/ n.f. factory.

fabri|quer /fabrike/ v.t. make; (industriellement) manufacture; (fig.) make up. **~cant** n.m., f. manufacturer. **~cation** n.f. making; manufacture.

fabuleu|x, ~se /fabylø, -z/ a. fabulous.

fac /fak/ n.f. (fam.) university.

façade /fasad/ n.f. front; (fig.) façade.

face /fas/ n.f. face; (d'un objet) side. **en ~ (de), d'en ~**, opposite. **en ~ de**, (fig.) faced with. **~ à**, facing; (fig.) faced with. **faire ~ à**, face.

fâch|er /faʃe/ v.t. anger. **se ~er** v. pr. get angry; (se brouiller) fall out. **~é** a. angry.

facile /fasil/ a. easy; (caractère) easygoing. **~ement** adv. easily. **~ité** n.f. easiness. **~ités de paiement**, easy terms.

faciliter /fasilite/ v.t. facilitate.

façon /fasɔ̃/ n.f. way; (de vêtement) cut. **~s**, (chichis) fuss. **de toute ~**, anyway.

façonner /fasɔne/ v.t. shape; (faire) make.

facteur /faktœr/ n.m. postman.

facteur² /faktœr/ n.m. (élément) factor.

factice /faktis/ a. artificial.

factur|e /faktyr/ n.f. bill; (comm.) invoice. **~er** v.t. invoice.

facultati|f, ~ve /fakyltatif, -v/ a. optional.

faculté /fakylte/ n.f. faculty; (possibilité) power; (univ.) faculty.

fade /fad/ a. insipid.

faibl|e /fɛbl/ a. weak; (espoir, quantité, écart) slight; (revenu, intensité) low. —n.m. weakling; (penchant, défaut) weakness. **~esse** n.f. weakness.

faïence /fajɑ̃s/ n.f. earthenware.

faille /faj/ n.f. (géog.) fault.

faillir /fajir/ v.i. **j'ai failli acheter**/etc., I almost bought/ etc.

faillite /fajit/ n.f. bankruptcy.

faim /fɛ̃/ n.f. hunger. **avoir ~**, be hungry.

faire† /fɛr/ v.t. make; (activité) do; (rêve, chute, etc.) have; (dire) say.

ça fait 20 F, that's 20 F. **ça fait 3 ans**, it's been 3 years. —*v.i.* do; (*paraître*) look. **se ~**, *v. pr.* (*petit etc.*) make o.s.; (*amis, argent*) make; (*illusions*) have; (*devenir*) become. **~ du rugby/du violon**/*etc.*, play rugby/the violin/*etc.* **~ construire/punir**/*etc.*, have *ou* get built/punished/*etc.*, **~ pleurer/tomber/** *etc.*, make cry/fall/*etc.* **se ~ tuer**/*etc.*, get killed/*etc.* **se ~ couper les cheveux**, have one's hair cut. **il fait beau/chaud**/*etc.*, it is fine/hot/*etc.* **~ l'idiot**, play the fool. **ça ne fait rien**, it doesn't matter. **ça se fait**, that is done. **~-part** *n.m. invar.* announcement.

fais, fait¹ /fɛ/ *voir* faire.

faisable /fəzabl/ *a.* feasible.

faisan /fəzɑ̃/ *n.m.* pheasant.

fait², **~e** /fɛ, fɛt/ *a.* done; (*fromage*) ripe. **~ pour**, made for. **c'est bien ~ pour toi**, it serves you right.

fait³ /fɛ/ *n.m.* fact; (*événement*) event. **~ divers**, (trivial) news item.

faites /fɛt/ *voir* faire.

faitout /fɛtu/ *n.m.* stew-pot.

falaise /falɛz/ *n.f.* cliff.

falloir† /falwar/ *v.i.* **il faut qch./qn.**, we, you, *etc.* need sth./so. **il lui faut du pain**, he needs bread. **il faut rester**, we, you, *etc.* have to *ou* must stay. **il faut que j'y aille**, I have to *ou* must go. **il faudrait que tu partes**, you should leave. **il aurait fallu le faire**, we, you, *etc.* should have done it. **comme il faut**, properly; *a.* proper.

falsifier /falsifje/ *v.t.* falsify.

fameu|x, **~se** /famø, -z/ *a.* famous; (*excellent*: *fam.*) first-rate.

famil|ial (*m. pl.* **~iaux**) /familjal, -jo/ *a.* family.

famil|iariser /familjarize/ *v.t.* familiarize (**avec**, with). **se ~iser** *v. pr.* familiarize o.s. **~isé** *a.* familiar. **~ité** *n.f.* familiarity.

famil|ier, **~ière** /familje, -jɛr/ *a.* familiar; (*amical*) informal. —*n.m.* regular visitor.

famille /famij/ *n.f.* family. **en ~**, with one's family.

famine /famin/ *n.f.* famine.

fanati|que /fanatik/ *a.* fanatical. —*n.m./f.* fanatic. **~sme** *n.m.* fanaticism.

faner (se) /(sə)fane/ *v. pr.* fade.

fanfare /fɑ̃far/ *n.f.* brass band; (*musique*) fanfare.

fantaisie /fɑ̃tezi/ *n.f.* imagination, fantasy; (*caprice*) whim. **(de) ~**, (*boutons etc.*) fancy.

fantasme /fɑ̃tasm/ *n.m.* fantasy.

fantastique /fɑ̃tastik/ *a.* fantastic.

fantôme /fɑ̃tom/ *n.m.* ghost. —*a.* (*péj.*) bogus.

faon /fɑ̃/ *n.m.* fawn.

farce¹ /fars/ *n.f.* (practical) joke; (*théâtre*) farce. **~eur**, **~euse** *n.m., f.* joker.

farce² /fars/ *n.f.* (*hachis*) stuffing. **~ir** *v.t.* stuff.

fard /far/ *n.m.* make-up. **piquer un ~**, blush. **~er** /-de/ *v.t.*, **se ~er** *v. pr.* make up.

fardeau (*pl.* **~x**) /fardo/ *n.m.* burden.

farfelu, **~e** /farfəly/ *a. & n.m., f.* eccentric.

farine /farin/ *n.f.* flour.

farouche /faruʃ/ *a.* shy; (*peu sociable*) unsociable; (*violent*) fierce. **~ment** *adv.* fiercely.

fascicule /fasikyl/ *n.m.* volume.

fascin|er /fasine/ *v.t.* fascinate. **~ation** *n.f.* fascination.

fasci|ste /faʃist/ *a. & n.m./f.* fascist. **~me** *n.m.* fascism.

fasse /fas/ *voir* faire.

faste /fast/ *n.m.* splendour.

fast-food /fastfud/ *n.m.* fast-food place.

fastidieu|x, **~se** /fastidjø, -z/ *a.* tedious.

fat|al (*m. pl.* **~als**) /fatal/ *a.* inevitable; (*mortel*) fatal. **~alité** *n.f.* (*destin*) fate.

fatidique /fatidik/ *a.* fateful.

fatigant, **~e** /fatigã, -t/ *a.* tiring; (*ennuyeux*) tiresome.

fatigue /fatig/ *n.f.* fatigue, tiredness.

fatigu|er /fatige/ *v.t.* tire; (*yeux, moteur*) strain. —*v.i.* (*moteur*) labour. **se ~er** *v. pr.* get tired, tire (**de**, of). **~é** *a.* tired.

faubourg /fobur/ *n.m.* suburb.

fauché /foʃe/ *a.* (*fam.*) broke.

faucille /fosij/ *n.f.* sickle.

faucon /fokɔ̃/ *n.m.* falcon, hawk.

faudra, **faudrait** /fodra, fodrɛ/ *voir* falloir.

faufiler (se) /(sə)fofile/ *v. pr.* edge one's way.

faune /fon/ *n.f.* wildlife, fauna.

faussaire /foser/ *n.m.* forger.

fausse /fos/ *voir* faux².

faussement /fosmã/ *adv.* falsely, wrongly.

faut /fo/ *voir* falloir.

faute /fot/ *n.f.* mistake; (*responsabilité*) fault; (*délit*) offence. **sans faute**, without fail.

fauteuil /fotœj/ *n.m.* armchair; (*de président*) chair; (*théâtre*) seat. **~ roulant**, wheelchair.

fauve /fov/ *a.* (*couleur*) fawn. —*n.m.* wild cat.

faux¹ /fo/ *n.f.* scythe.

faux², **fausse** /fo, fos/ *a.* false; (*falsifié*) fake, forged; (*numéro, calcul*) wrong; (*voix*) out of tune. **c'est ~!**, that is wrong! —*n.m.* (*chanter*) out of tune. —*n.m.* témoignage, perjury. —*adv.*

forgery. **fausse alerte**, false alarm. **fausse couche**, miscarriage. **~-filet** *n.m.* sirloin.

faveur /favœr/ *n.f.* favour.

favorable /favɔrabl/ *a.* favourable.

favori, **~te** /favɔri, -t/ *a.* & *n.m.*, *f.* favourite.

favoriser /favɔrize/ *v.t.* favour.

fax /faks/ *n.m.* fax. **~er** *v.t.* fax.

fécond, **~e** /fekɔ̃, -d/ *a.* fertile. **~er** /-de/ *v.t.* fertilize. **~ité** /-dite/ *n.f.* fertility.

fédér|al (*m. pl.* **~aux**) /federal, -o/ *a.* federal. **~ation** /federasjɔ̃/ *n.f.* federation.

fée /fe/ *n.f.* fairy.

fêler /fele/ *v.t.*, **se ~** *v. pr.* crack.

félicit|er /felisite/ *v.t.* congratulate (**de**, on). **~ations** *n.f. pl.* congratulations (**pour**, on).

félin, **~e** /felɛ̃, -in/ *a.* & *n.m.* feline.

femelle /fəmɛl/ *a.* & *n.f.* female.

fémin|in, **~ine** /feminɛ̃, -in/ *a.* feminine; (*sexe*) female; (*mode, équipe*) women's. —*n.m.* feminine. **~ité** *n.f.* femininity.

féministe /feminist/ *n.m./f.* feminist.

femme /fam/ *n.f.* woman; (*épouse*) wife. **~ au foyer**, housewife. **~ de chambre**, chambermaid. **~ de ménage**, cleaning lady.

fémur /femyr/ *n.m.* thigh-bone.

fendre /fãdr/ *v.t.* (*couper*) split; (*fissurer*) crack; (*foule*) push through. **se ~** *v. pr.* crack.

fenêtre /fənɛtr/ *n.f.* window.

fenouil /fənuj/ *n.m.* fennel.

fente /fãt/ *n.f.* (*ouverture*) slit, slot; (*fissure*) crack.

fer /fɛr/ *n.m.* iron. **~ (à repasser)**, iron. **~ forgé**, wrought iron.

fera, **ferait** /fəra, fərɛ/ *voir* faire.

férié /ferje/ a. jour ~, public holiday.

ferme[1] /fɛrm/ a. firm.

ferme[2] /fɛrm/ n.f. farm; (*maison*) farm(house).

fermé /fɛrme/ a. closed; (*gaz, radio, etc.*) off.

fermer /fɛrme/ v.t./i. close, shut; (*cesser d'exploiter*) close *ou* shut down; (*gaz, robinet*) turn off. **se ~** v. pr. close, shut.

fermeté /fɛrməte/ n.f. firmness.

fermeture /fɛrmətyr/ n.f. closing; (*dispositif*) catch. **~ annuelle**, annual closure. **~ éclair**, (P.) zip(-fastener); (*Amer.*) zipper.

ferm|ier, ~ière /fɛrmje, -jɛr/ n.m. farmer. —n.f. farmer's wife. —a. farm.

féroc|e /ferɔs/ a. ferocious. **~ité** n.f. ferocity.

ferroviaire /ferɔvjɛr/ a. rail(way).

ferry(-boat) /feri(bɔt)/ n.m. ferry.

fertil|e /fɛrtil/ a. fertile. **~e en**, (*fig.*) rich in. **~iser** v.t. fertilize. **~ité** n.f. fertility.

fesse /fɛs/ n.f. buttock.

fessée /fese/ n.f. spanking.

festin /fɛstɛ̃/ n.m. feast.

festival (*pl.* **~s**) /fɛstival/ n.m. festival.

festivités /fɛstivite/ n.f. pl. festivities.

fête /fɛt/ n.f. holiday; (*religieuse*) feast; (*du nom*) name-day; (*réception*) party; (*en famille*) celebration; (*foire*) fair; (*folklorique*) festival. **~ foraine**, funfair. **les ~s** (**de fin d'année**), the Christmas season.

fêter /fete/ v.t. celebrate.

fétiche /fetiʃ/ n.m. fetish; (*fig.*) mascot.

feu /fø/ (*pl.* **~x**) /fø/ n.m. fire; (*lumière*) light; (*de réchaud*) burner. **~x** (**rouges**), (traffic) lights. **à ~ doux/vif**, on a low/ high heat. **du ~**, (*pour cigarette*) a light. **au ~!**, fire! **~ d'artifice**, firework display. **~ rouge/vert/orange**, red/green/amber. **~ de position**, sidelight. **mettre le ~ à**, set fire to. **prendre ~**, catch fire.

feuille /fœj/ n.f. leaf; (*de papier, bois, etc.*) sheet; (*formulaire*) form.

feuillet /fœjɛ/ n.m. leaf.

feuilleter /fœjte/ v.t. leaf through.

feuilleton /fœjtɔ̃/ n.m. (*à suivre*) serial; (*histoire complète*) series.

feutre /føtr/ n.m. felt; (*chapeau*) felt hat; (*crayon*) felt-tip (pen).

fève /fɛv/ n.f. broad bean.

février /fevrije/ n.m. February.

fiançailles /fjɑ̃saj/ n.f. pl. engagement.

fianc|er (**se**) /(sə)fjɑ̃se/ v. pr. become engaged (**avec**, to). **~é**, **~ée** a. engaged; n.m. fiancé; n.f. fiancée.

fiasco /fjasko/ n.m. fiasco.

fibre /fibr/ n.f. fibre. **~ de verre**, fibreglass.

ficeler /fisle/ v.t. tie up.

ficelle /fisɛl/ n.f. string.

fiche /fiʃ/ n.f. (*index*) card; (*formulaire*) form, slip; (*électr.*) plug.

ficher /fiʃe/ v.t. (*faire*: *fam.*) do; (*donner*: *fam.*) give; (*mettre*: *fam.*) put. **se ~ de**, (*fam.*) make fun of. **~ le camp**, (*fam.*) clear off. **il s'en fiche**, (*fam.*) he couldn't care less.

fichier /fiʃje/ n.m. file.

fichu /fiʃy/ a. (*mauvais*: *fam.*) rotten; (*raté*: *fam.*) done for. **mal ~**, (*fam.*) terrible.

ficti|f, ~ve /fiktif, -v/ a. fictitious.

fiction /fiksjɔ̃/ n.f. fiction.

fidèle /fidɛl/ a. faithful. **~** (*client*) regular; (*relig.*) believer.

fidélité /fidelite/ *n.f.* fidelity.

fier, fière /fjɛr/ *a.* proud (**de**, of). **fièrement** *adv.* proudly. **~té** *n.f.* pride.

fièvre /fjɛvr/ *n.f.* fever.

fiévreu|x, **~se** /fjevrø, -z/ *a.* feverish.

figu|e /fig/ *n.f.* fig. **~ier** *n.m.* fig-tree.

figurant, ~e /figyrɑ̃, -t/ *n.m., f.* (*cinéma*) extra.

figure /figyr/ *n.f.* face.

figuré /figyre/ *a.* (*sens*) figurative. **au ~,** figuratively.

fil /fil/ *n.m.* thread; (*métallique, électrique*) wire; (*de couteau*) edge; (*à coudre*) cotton. **~ de fer,** wire. **au bout du ~,** on the phone.

filament /filamɑ̃/ *n.m.* filament.

filature /filatyr/ *n.f.* (*textile*) mill; (*surveillance*) shadowing.

file /fil/ *n.f.* line; (*voie: auto.*) lane. **~ (d'attente),** queue.

filer /file/ *v.t.* spin; (*suivre*) shadow. **~ qch. à qn.,** (*fam.*) slip s.o. sth. **—***v.i.* (*bas*) ladder, run; (*liquide*) run; (*aller vite: fam.*) speed along, fly by; (*partir: fam.*) dash off.

filet /filɛ/ *n.m.* net; (*d'eau*) trickle; (*de viande*) fillet. **~ (à bagages),** (luggage) rack. **~ à provisions,** string bag (*for shopping*).

fil|ial, ~iale (*m. pl.* **~iaux**) /filjal, -jo/ *a.* filial. **—***n.f.* subsidiary (*company*).

filière /filjɛr/ *n.f.* (*official*) channels; (*de trafiquants*) network.

fille /fij/ *n.f.* girl; (*opposé à fils*) daughter.

fillette /fijɛt/ *n.f.* little girl.

filleul /fijœl/ *n.m.* godson. **~e** *n.f.* god-daughter.

film /film/ *n.m.* film. **~ d'épouvante / muet / parlant,** horror/silent/talking film. **~er** *v.t.* film.

fils /fis/ *n.m.* son.

filtr|e /filtr/ *n.m.* filter. **~er** *v.t./i.* filter; (*personne*) screen.

fin¹ /fɛ̃/ *n.f.* end. **à la ~,** finally. **en ~ de compte,** all things considered. **~ de semaine,** weekend. **mettre ~ à,** put an end to. **prendre ~,** come to an end.

fin², fine /fɛ̃, fin/ *a.* fine; (*tranche, couche*) thin; (*taille*) slim; (*plat*) exquisite; (*esprit, vue*) sharp. **—***adv.* (*couper*) finely. **~es herbes,** herbs.

fin|al, ~ale (*m. pl.* **~aux** *ou* **~als**) /final, -o/ *a.* final. **—***n.f.* (*sport*) final; (*gram.*) final syllable. **—***n.m.* (*pl.* **~aux** *ou* **~als**) (*mus.*) finale. **~alement** *adv.* finally; (*somme toute*) after all.

finaliste /finalist/ *n.m./f.* finalist.

financ|e /finɑ̃s/ *n.f.* finance. **~er** *v.t.* finance. **~ier, ~ière** *a.* financial; *n.m.* financier.

finesse /finɛs/ *n.f.* fineness; (*de taille*) slimness; (*acuité*) sharpness. **~s,** (*de langue*) niceties.

fini /fini/ *a.* finished.

finir /finir/ *v.t./i.* finish, end; (*arrêter*) stop; (*manger*) finish (up).

finlandais, ~e /fɛ̃lɑ̃dɛ, -z/ *a.* Finnish. **—***n.m., f.* Finn.

Finlande /fɛ̃lɑ̃d/ *n.f.* Finland.

finnois, ~e /finwa, -z/ *a.* Finnish. **—***n.m.* (*lang.*) Finnish.

firme /firm/ *n.f.* firm.

fisc /fisk/ *n.m.* tax authorities. **~al** (*m. pl.* **~aux**) *a.* tax, fiscal. **~alité** *n.f.* tax system.

fission /fisjɔ̃/ *n.f.* fission.

fissur|e /fisyr/ *n.f.* crack. **~er** *v.t.*, **se ~er** *v. pr.* crack.

fixation /fiksasjɔ̃/ *n.f.* fixing; (*complexe*) fixation.

fixe /fiks/ *a.* fixed; (*stable*) steady. **à heure ~,** at a set time. **menu à prix ~,** set menu.

fixer /fikse/ *v.t.* fix.

flacon /flakɔ̃/ *n.m.* bottle.

flageolet /flaʒɔlɛ/ *n.m.* (*haricot*) (dwarf) kidney bean.

flagrant, ~e /flagrɑ̃, -t/ *a.* flagrant. **en ~ délit**, in the act.

flair /flɛr/ *n.m.* (sense of) smell; (*fig.*) intuition.

flamand, ~e /flamɑ̃, -d/ *a.* Flemish. —*n.m.* (*lang.*) Flemish. —*n.m.*, *f.* Fleming.

flamant /flamɑ̃/ *n.m.* flamingo.

flambé, ~e /flɑ̃be/ *a.* (*culin.*) flambé.

flambeau (*pl.* **~x**) /flɑ̃bo/ *n.m.* torch.

flamme /flam/ *n.f.* flame; (*fig.*) ardour. **en ~s**, ablaze.

flan /flɑ̃/ *n.m.* custard-pie.

flanc /flɑ̃/ *n.m.* side; (*d'animal*, *d'armée*) flank.

Flandre(s) /flɑ̃dr/ *n.f.* (*pl.*) Flanders.

flanelle /flanɛl/ *n.f.* flannel.

flân|er /flane/ *v.i.* stroll. **~erie** *n.f.* stroll.

flanquer /flɑ̃ke/ *v.t.* flank; (*jeter: fam.*) chuck; (*donner: fam.*) give. **~ à la porte**, kick out.

flaque /flak/ *n.f.* (*d'eau*) puddle; (*de sang*) pool.

flash (*pl.* **~es**) /flaʃ/ *n.m.* (*photo.*) flash; (*information*) news flash.

flatter /flate/ *v.t.* flatter.

flèche /flɛʃ/ *n.f.* arrow; (*de clocher*) spire. **monter en ~**, spiral.

fléchette /fleʃɛt/ *n.f.* dart.

flegmatique /flɛgmatik/ *a.* phlegmatic.

flemm|e /flɛm/ *n.f.* (*fam.*) laziness. **j'ai la ~e de faire**, I can't be bothered doing. **~ard, ~arde** *a.* (*fam.*) lazy; *n.m.*, *f.* (*fam.*) lazybones.

flétrir /fletrir/ *v.t.*, **se ~** *v. pr.* wither.

fleur /flœr/ *n.f.* flower. **à ~s**, flowery. **en ~s**, in flower.

fleur|ir /flœrir/ *v.i.* flower; (*arbre*) blossom; (*fig.*) flourish. —*v.t.* adorn with flowers. **~i** *a.* flowery.

fleuriste /flœrist/ *n.m./f.* florist.

fleuve /flœv/ *n.m.* river.

flexible /flɛksibl/ *a.* flexible.

flexion /flɛksjɔ̃/ *n.f.* (*anat.*) flexing.

flic /flik/ *n.m.* (*fam.*) cop.

flipper /flipœr/ *n.m.* pinball (machine).

flirter /flœrte/ *v.i.* flirt.

flocon /flɔkɔ̃/ *n.m.* flake.

flore /flɔr/ *n.f.* flora.

florissant, ~e /flɔrisɑ̃, -t/ *a.* flourishing.

flot /flo/ *n.m.* flood, stream.

flottant, ~e /flɔtɑ̃, -t/ *a.* (*vêtement*) loose; (*indécis*) indecisive.

flotte /flɔt/ *n.f.* fleet; (*pluie: fam.*) rain; (*eau: fam.*) water.

flott|er /flɔte/ *v.i.* float; (*drapeau*) flutter; (*nuage, parfum, pensées*) drift; (*pleuvoir: fam.*) rain. **~eur** *n.m.* float.

flou /flu/ *a.* out of focus; (*fig.*) vague.

fluctu|er /flyktɥe/ *v.i.* fluctuate. **~ation** *n.f.* fluctuation.

fluide /flɥid/ *a. & n.m.* fluid.

fluor /flyɔr/ *n.m.* (*pour les dents*) fluoride.

fluorescent, ~e /flyɔresɑ̃, -t/ *a.* fluorescent.

flût|e /flyt/ *n.f.* flute; (*verre*) champagne glass. **~iste** *n.m./f.* flautist.

fluv|ial (*m. pl.* **~iaux**) /flyvjal, -jo/ *a.* river.

flux /fly/ *n.m.* flow.

FM /ɛfɛm/ *abrév. f.* FM.

foc /fɔk/ *n.m.* jib.

foi /fwa/ *n.f.* faith. **être de bonne/mauvaise ~**, be acting in good/bad faith.

foie /fwa/ n.m. liver. **~ gras**, foie gras.

foin /fwɛ̃/ n.m. hay.

foire /fwar/ n.f. fair.

fois /fwa/ n.f. time. **une ~**, once. **deux ~**, twice. **à la ~**, at the same time. **des ~**, (parfois) sometimes. **une ~ pour toutes**, once and for all.

fol /fɔl/ voir **fou**.

folie /fɔli/ n.f. madness; (bêtise) foolish thing, folly.

folklor|e /fɔlklɔr/ n.m. folklore. **~ique** a. folk.

folle /fɔl/ voir **fou**.

follement /fɔlmɑ̃/ adv. madly.

fonc|er¹ /fɔ̃se/ v.t./i. darken. **~é** a. dark.

foncer² /fɔ̃se/ v.i. (fam.) dash along. **~ sur**, (fam.) charge at.

fonc|ier, ~ière /fɔ̃sje, -jɛr/ a. fundamental; (comm.) real estate.

fonction /fɔ̃ksjɔ̃/ n.f. function; (emploi) position. **en ~ de**, according to.

fonctionnaire /fɔ̃ksjɔnɛr/ n.m./f. civil servant.

fonctionnel, ~le /fɔ̃ksjɔnɛl/ a. functional.

fonctionn|er /fɔ̃ksjɔne/ v.i. work. **faire ~er**, work. **~ement** n.m. working.

fond /fɔ̃/ n.m. bottom; (de salle, magasin, etc.) back; (essentiel) basis; (plan) background. **à ~**, thoroughly. **au ~**, basically. **au ou dans le ~**, really.

fondament|al (m. pl. **~aux**) /fɔ̃damɑ̃tal, -o/ a. fundamental.

fondation /fɔ̃dasjɔ̃/ n.f. foundation.

fond|er /fɔ̃de/ v.t. found; (baser) base (sur, on). **se ~er sur**, be guided by, place one's reliance on. **~ateur, ~atrice** n.m., f. founder.

fonderie /fɔ̃dri/ n.f. foundry.

fondre /fɔ̃dr/ v.t./i. melt; (dans l'eau) dissolve; (mélanger) merge. **faire ~**, melt; dissolve. **~ en larmes**, burst into tears.

fondrière /fɔ̃drijɛr/ n.f. pot-hole.

fonds /fɔ̃/ n.m. fund. —n.m. pl. (capitaux) funds. **~ de commerce**, business.

fondu /fɔ̃dy/ a. melted.

font /fɔ̃/ voir **faire**.

fontaine /fɔ̃tɛn/ n.f. fountain; (source) spring.

fonte /fɔ̃t/ n.f. melting; (fer) cast iron. **~ des neiges**, thaw.

foot /fut/ n.m. (fam.) football.

football /futbol/ n.m. football. **~eur** n.m. footballer.

footing /futiŋ/ n.m. fast walking.

forage /fɔraʒ/ n.m. drilling.

force /fɔrs/ n.f. force; (physique) strength; (hydraulique etc.) power. **~s**, (physiques) strength. **à ~ de**, by sheer force of. **de ~**, **par la ~**, by force. **~s de l'ordre**, police (force).

forcé /fɔrse/ a. forced; (inévitable) inevitable.

forcément /fɔrsemɑ̃/ adv. necessarily; (évidemment) obviously.

forceps /fɔrsɛps/ n.m. forceps.

forcer /fɔrse/ v.t. force (**à faire**, to do). **se ~** v. pr. force o.s.

forer /fɔre/ v.t. drill.

forest|ier, ~ière /fɔrɛstje, -jɛr/ a. forest.

forêt /fɔrɛ/ n.f. forest.

forfait /fɔrfɛ/ n.m. (comm.) inclusive price. **~aire** /-tɛr/ a. (prix) inclusive.

forge /fɔrʒ/ n.f. forge.

forgeron /fɔrʒərɔ̃/ n.m. blacksmith.

formalité /fɔrmalite/ n.f. formality.

format /fɔrma/ n.m. format.

formater /fɔrmate/ v.t. (comput.) format.

formation /fɔrmasjɔ̃/ *n.f.* formation; (de médecin etc.) training; (culture) education. **∼ professionnelle**, professional training.

forme /fɔrm/ *n.f.* form; (contour) shape, form. **en ∼**, (sport) on good shape, on form. **en ∼ de**, in the shape of.

formel, **∼le** /fɔrmɛl/ *a.* formal; (catégorique) positive.

former /fɔrme/ *v.t.* form; (instruire) train. **se ∼** *v. pr.* form.

formidable /fɔrmidabl/ *a.* fantastic.

formulaire /fɔrmylɛr/ *n.m.* form.

formule /fɔrmyl/ *n.f.* formula; (expression) expression. **∼ de politesse**, polite phrase, letter ending.

fort¹, **∼e** /fɔr, -t/ *a.* strong; (grand) big; (pluie) heavy; (bruit) loud; (pente) steep; (élève) clever. —*adv.* (frapper) hard; (parler) loud; (très) very; (beaucoup) very much.

fort² /fɔr/ *n.m.* (mil.) fort.

forteresse /fɔrtərɛs/ *n.f.* fortress.

fortifiant /fɔrtifjɑ̃/ *n.m.* tonic.

fortune /fɔrtyn/ *n.f.* fortune. **de ∼**, (improvisé) makeshift. **faire ∼**, make one's fortune.

fortuné /fɔrtyne/ *a.* wealthy.

fosse /fos/ *n.f.* pit; (tombe) grave. **∼ d'orchestre**, orchestral pit. **∼ septique**, septic tank.

fossé /fose/ *n.m.* ditch; (fig.) gulf.

fossette /fosɛt/ *n.f.* dimple.

fossile /fosil/ *n.m.* fossil.

fou *ou* **fol***, **folle** /fu, fɔl/ *a.* mad; (course, regard) wild; (énorme: fam.) tremendous. **∼ de**, crazy about. —*n.m.* madman; (bouffon) jester. —*n.f.* madwoman; (fam.) gay. **le ∼ rire**, the giggles.

foudre /fudr/ *n.f.* lightning.

foudroyer /fudrwaje/ *v.t.* strike by lightning; (maladie etc.) strike down; (atterrer) stagger.

fouet /fwɛ/ *n.m.* whip; (culin.) whisk.

fouetter /fwete/ *v.t.* whip; (crème etc.) whisk.

fougère /fuʒɛr/ *n.f.* fern.

fouille /fuj/ *n.f.* search; (archéol.) excavation. **∼er** *v.t./i.* search; (creuser) dig. **∼er dans**, (tiroir) rummage through.

fouillis /fuji/ *n.m.* jumble.

fouine /fwin/ *n.f.* beech-marten.

foulard /fular/ *n.m.* scarf.

foule /ful/ *n.f.* crowd. **une ∼ de**, (fig.) a mass of.

fouler /fule/ *v.t.* press; (sol) tread. **se ∼ le poignet/le pied** sprain one's wrist/foot.

foulure /fulyr/ *n.f.* sprain.

four /fur/ *n.m.* oven; (de potier) kiln; (théâtre) flop. **∼ à microondes**, microwave oven.

fourbe /furb/ *a.* deceitful.

fourche /furʃ/ *n.f.* fork; (à foin) pitchfork.

fourchette /furʃɛt/ *n.f.* fork; (comm.) margin.

fourgon /furgɔ̃/ *n.m.* van; (wagon) wagon. **∼ mortuaire**, hearse.

fourgonnette /furgɔnɛt/ *n.f.* (small) van.

fourmi /furmi/ *n.f.* ant. **avoir des ∼s**, have pins and needles.

fourneau (*pl.* **∼x**) /furno/ *n.m.* stove.

fournée /furne/ *n.f.* batch.

fourni /furni/ *a.* (épais) thick.

fourn|ir /furnir/ *v.t.* supply; provide; (client) supply; (effort) put in. **∼ir à qn.**, supply s.o. with. **se ∼ir chez**, shop at. **∼isseur** *n.m.* supplier. **∼iture** *n.f.* supply.

fourrage /furaʒ/ *n.m.* fodder.

fourré /fure/ *a.* (vêtement) furlined; (gâteau etc.) filled (with jam, cream, etc.).

fourr|er /fure/ v.t. (mettre: fam.) stick. **∼e-tout** n.m. invar. (sac) holdall.

fourreur /furœr/ n.m. furrier.

fourrière /furjɛr/ n.f. (lieu) pound.

fourrure /furyr/ n.f. fur.

foutre /futr/ v.t. (argot) = **ficher²**.

foutu, ∼e /futy/ a. (argot) = **fichu**.

foyer /fwaje/ n.m. home; (âtre) hearth; (club) club; (d'étudiants) hostel; (théâtre) foyer; (photo.) focus; (centre) centre.

fracas /fraka/ n.m. din; (de train) roar; (d'objet qui tombe) crash.

fracasser /frakase/ v.t., **se ∼** v. pr. smash.

fraction /fraksjɔ̃/ n.f. fraction. **∼ner** /-jɔne/ v.t., **se ∼ner** v. pr. split (up).

fractur|e /fraktyr/ n.f. fracture. **∼er** v.t. (os) fracture; (porte etc.) break open.

fragil|e /fraʒil/ a. fragile. **∼ité** /-ite/ n.f. fragility.

fragment /fragmɑ̃/ n.m. bit, fragment.

fraîche /frɛʃ/ voir **frais¹**.

fraîcheur /frɛʃœr/ n.f. coolness; (nouveauté) freshness.

fraîchir /freʃir/ v.i. freshen.

frais¹, fraîche /frɛ, -ʃ/ a. fresh; (temps, accueil) cool; (peinture) wet. —n.m. **mettre au ∼**, put in a cool place. **il fait ∼**, it is cool.

frais² /frɛ/ n.m. pl. expenses; (droits) fees. **∼ généraux**, (comm.) overheads, running expenses. **∼ de scolarité**, school fees.

fraise /frɛz/ n.f. strawberry.

framboise /frɑ̃bwaz/ n.f. raspberry.

fran|c¹, ∼che /frɑ̃, -ʃ/ a. frank; (regard) open; (net) clear.

franc² /frɑ̃/ n.m. franc.

français, ∼e /frɑ̃sɛ, -z/ a. French. —n.m., f. Frenchman;

Frenchwoman. —n.m. (lang.) French.

France /frɑ̃s/ n.f. France.

franche /frɑ̃ʃ/ voir **franc¹**.

franchement /frɑ̃ʃmɑ̃/ adv. frankly; (tout à fait) really.

franchir /frɑ̃ʃir/ v.t. (obstacle) get over; (traverser) cross; (distance) cover; (limite) exceed.

franchise /frɑ̃ʃiz/ n.f. frankness; (douanière) exemption (from duties).

franco /frɑ̃ko/ adv. postage paid.

franco- /frɑ̃ko/ préf. Franco-.

francophone /frɑ̃kɔfɔn/ a. French-speaking. —n.m./f. French speaker.

frange /frɑ̃ʒ/ n.f. fringe.

frappe /frap/ n.f. (de courrier etc.) typing; (de dactylo) touch.

frappé, ∼e /frape/ a. chilled.

frapper /frape/ v.t./i. strike; (battre) hit, strike; (monnaie) mint; (à la porte) knock, bang.

fratern|el, ∼elle /fratɛrnɛl/ a. brotherly.

fraude /frod/ n.f. fraud; (à un examen) cheating.

frauder /frode/ v.t./i. cheat.

frauduleu|x, ∼se /frodylø, -z/ a. fraudulent.

fredonner /frədɔne/ v.t. hum.

free-lance /frilɑ̃s/ a. & n.m./f. freelance.

freezer /frizœr/ n.m. freezer.

frégate /fregat/ n.f. frigate.

frein /frɛ̃/ n.m. brake. **∼ à main**, hand brake.

frein|er /frene/ v.t. slow down; (modérer, enrayer) curb. —v.i. (auto.) brake. **∼age** /frenaʒ/ n.m. braking.

frêle /frɛl/ a. frail.

frelon /frəlɔ̃/ n.m. hornet.

frémir /fremir/ v.i. shudder, shake; (feuille, eau) quiver.

frêne /frɛn/ n.m. ash.

fréné|sie /frenezi/ *n.f.* frenzy. **~tique** *a.* frenzied.

fréqu|ent, ~ente /frekɑ̃, -t/ *a.* frequent. **~emment** /-amɑ̃/ *adv.* frequently. **~ence** *n.f.* frequency.

fréquenté /frekɑ̃te/ *a.* crowded.

fréquent|er /frekɑ̃te/ *v.t.* frequent; (*école*) attend; (*personne*) see. **~ations** *n.f. pl.* acquaintances.

frère /frɛr/ *n.m.* brother.

fresque /frɛsk/ *n.f.* fresco.

fret /frɛ/ *n.m.* freight.

friable /frijabl/ *a.* crumbly.

friand, ~e /frijɑ̃, -d/ *a.* **~ de**, fond of.

friandise /frijɑ̃diz/ *n.f.* sweet; (*gâteau*) cake.

fric /frik/ *n.m.* (*fam.*) money.

fricassée /frikase/ *n.f.* casserole.

friction /friksjɔ̃/ *n.f.* friction; (*massage*) rub-down. **~ner** /-jɔne/ *v.t.* rub (down).

frigidaire /friʒidɛr/ *n.m.* (P.) refrigerator.

frigo /frigo/ *n.m.* (*fam.*) fridge.

frileu|x, ~se /frilø, -z/ *a.* sensitive to cold.

fringale /frɛ̃gal/ *n.f.* (*fam.*) ravenous appetite.

fringant, ~e /frɛ̃gɑ̃, -t/ *a.* dashing.

friper /fripe/ *v.t.*, **se ~** *v. pr.* crumple.

fripouille /fripuj/ *n.f.* rogue.

frire /frir/ *v.t./i.* **faire ~**, fry.

frise /friz/ *n.f.* frieze.

fris|er /frize/ *v.t./i.* (*cheveux*) curl; (*personne*) curl the hair of. **~é** *a.* curly.

frisquet /friskɛ/ *a.m.* (*fam.*) chilly.

frisson /frisɔ̃/ *n.m.* (*de froid*) shiver; (*de peur*) shudder. **~ner** /-ɔne/ *v.i.* shiver; shudder.

frit, ~e /fri, -t/ *a.* fried. —*n.f.* chip. **avoir la ~e**, (*fam.*) feel good.

friteuse /fritøz/ *n.f.* (deep)fryer.

friture /frityr/ *n.f.* fried fish; (*huile*) (frying) oil *ou* fat.

frivol|e /frivɔl/ *a.* frivolous. **~ité** *n.f.* frivolity.

froid, ~e /frwa, -d/ *a. & n.m.* cold. **avoir/prendre ~**, be/ catch cold. **il fait ~**, it is cold.

froisser /frwase/ *v.t.* crumple; (*fig.*) offend. **se ~** *v. pr.* crumple; (*fig.*) take offence. **se ~ un muscle**, strain a muscle.

frôler /frole/ *v.t.* brush against, skim; (*fig.*) come close to.

fromage /frɔmaʒ/ *n.m.* cheese.

froment /frɔmɑ̃/ *n.m.* wheat.

froncer /frɔ̃se/ *v.t.* gather. **~ les sourcils**, frown.

front /frɔ̃/ *n.m.* forehead; (*mil., pol.*) front.

frontali|er, ère /frɔ̃talje, -ɛr/ *a.* border. **(travailleur)or ~**, commuter from across the border.

frontière /frɔ̃tjɛr/ *n.f.* border, frontier.

frott|er /frɔte/ *v.t./i.* rub; (*allumette*) strike. **~ement** *n.m.* rubbing.

frottis /frɔti/ *n.m.* **~ vaginal**, smear test.

frouss|e /frus/ *n.f.* (*fam.*) fear. **avoir la ~e**, (*fam.*) be scared. **~ard, ~arde** *n.m.*, *f.* (*fam.*) coward.

fructifier /fryktifje/ *v.i.* **faire ~**, put to work.

fructueu|x, ~se /fryktɥø, -z/ *a.* fruitful.

fruit /frɥi/ *n.m.* fruit. **des ~s**, (some) fruit. **~s de mer**, seafood.

frustr|er /frystre/ *v.t.* frustrate. **~ant, ~ante** *a.* frustrating. **~ation** *n.f.* frustration.

fuel /fjul/ *n.m.* fuel oil.

fugue /fyg/ *n.f.* (*mus.*) fugue. **faire une ~**, run away.

fuir† /fɥir/ *v.i.* flee, run away; (*eau, robinet, etc.*) leak. —*v.t.* (*éviter*) shun.

fuite /fɥit/ *n.f.* flight; (*de liquide*,

d'une nouvelle) leak. **prendre la** ∼, take (to) flight.

fumée /fyme/ *n.f.* smoke; (*vapeur*) steam.

fum|er /fyme/ *v.t./i.* smoke. ∼e-**cigarette** *n.m. invar.* cigarette-holder. ∼é *a.* (*poisson, verre*) smoked. ∼eur, ∼euse *n.m., f.* smoker.

fumet /fymɛ/ *n.m.* aroma.

fumier /fymje/ *n.m.* manure.

funambule /fynɑ̃byl/ *n.m./f.* tightrope walker.

funèbre /fynɛbr/ *a.* funeral; (*fig.*) gloomy.

funérailles /fyneraj/ *n.f. pl.* funeral.

funéraire /fynerɛr/ *a.* funeral.

funiculaire /fynikylɛr/ *n.m.* funicular.

fur /fyr/ *n.m.* **au ∼ et à mesure,** as one goes along, progressively. **au ∼ et à mesure que,** as.

furet /fyrɛ/ *n.m.* ferret.

fureur /fyrœr/ *n.f.* fury; (*passion*) passion.

furie /fyri/ *n.f.* fury; (*femme*) shrew.

furieu|x, ∼se /fyrjø, -z/ *a.* furious.

furoncle /fyrɔ̃kl/ *n.m.* boil.

fusain /fyzɛ̃/ *n.m.* (*crayon*) charcoal; (*arbre*) spindle-tree.

fuseau (*pl.* ∼x) /fyzo/ *n.m.* ski trousers; (*pour filer*) spindle. ∼ **horaire,** time zone.

fusée /fyze/ *n.f.* rocket.

fuselage /fyzlaʒ/ *n.m.* fuselage.

fusible /fyzibl/ *n.m.* fuse.

fusil /fyzi/ *n.m.* rifle, gun; (*de chasse*) shotgun.

fusill|er /fyzije/ *v.t.* shoot. ∼ade *n.f.* shooting.

fusion /fyzjɔ̃/ *n.f.* fusion; (*comm.*) merger. ∼ner /-jɔne/ *v.t./i.* merge.

fut /fy/ *voir* **être.**

fût /fy/ *n.m.* (*tonneau*) barrel.

futé /fyte/ *a.* cunning.

futil|e /fytil/ *a.* futile. ∼ité *n.f.* futility.

futur /fytyr/ *a. & n.m.* future. ∼e **femme/maman,** wife-/mother-to-be.

fuyard, ∼e /fɥijar, -d/ *n.m., f.* runaway.

G

gabardine /gabardin/ *n.f.* gabardine; raincoat.

gabarit /gabari/ *n.m.* dimension; (*patron*) template; (*fig.*) calibre.

gâcher /gɑʃe/ *v.t.* (*gâter*) spoil; (*gaspiller*) waste.

gâchette /gɑʃɛt/ *n.f.* trigger.

gâchis /gɑʃi/ *n.m.* waste.

gaff|e /gaf/ *n.f.* blunder. **faire ∼e,** (*fam.*) be careful (**à,** of). ∼er *v.i.* blunder.

gag /gag/ *n.m.* gag.

gagn|er /gaɲe/ *v.t.* (*match, prix, etc.*) win; (*argent, pain*) earn; (*temps, terrain*) gain. —*v.i.* win; (*fig.*) gain. ∼er **sa vie,** earn one's living. ∼ant, ∼ante, *a.* winning; *n.m., f.* winner. ∼e-pain *n.m. invar.* job.

gai /ge/ *a.* cheerful; (*ivre*) merry. ∼ement *adv.* cheerfully.

gaillard /gajar/ *n.m.* (*type: fam.*) fellow.

gain /gɛ̃/ *n.m.* (*salaire*) earnings; (*avantage*) gain; (*économie*) saving. ∼s, (*comm.*) profits; (*au jeu*) winnings.

gala /gala/ *n.m.* gala.

galant, ∼e /galɑ̃, -t/ *a.* courteous; (*scène, humeur*) romantic.

galb|e /galb/ *n.m.* curve. ∼é *a.* shapely.

galère /galɛr/ *n.f.* (*navire*) galley.

c'est la ~!, (*fam.*) what an ordeal!

galérer /galere/ *v.i.* (*fam.*) have a hard time.

galerie /galri/ *n.f.* gallery; (*théâtre*) circle; (*de voiture*) roof-rack.

galet /galɛ/ *n.m.* pebble.

galette /galɛt/ *n.f.* flat cake.

Galles /gal/ *n.f. pl.* **le pays de ~**, Wales.

gallois, ~e /galwa, -z/ *a.* Welsh. —*n.m., f.* Welshman, Welshwoman. —*n.m.* (*lang.*) Welsh.

galon /galɔ̃/ *n.m.* braid; (*mil.*) stripe. **prendre du ~**, be promoted.

galop /galo/ *n.m.* gallop. **~er** /-ɔpe/ *v.i.* (*cheval*) gallop; (*personne*) run.

galopade /galɔpad/ *n.f.* wild rush.

gamelle /gamɛl/ *n.f.* (*de soldat*) mess bowl *ou* tin; (*d'ouvrier*) foodbox.

gamin, ~e /gamɛ̃, -in/ *a.* playful. —*n.m., f.* (*fam.*) kid.

gamme /gam/ *n.f.* (*mus.*) scale; (*série*) range. **haut de ~**, upmarket, top of the range. **bas de ~**, down-market, bottom of the range.

ganglion /gɑ̃glijɔ̃/ *n.m.* swelling.

gangster /gɑ̃gstɛr/ *n.m.* gangster; (*escroc*) crook.

gant /gɑ̃/ *n.m.* glove. **~ de toilette**, face-flannel, face-cloth.

garag|e /garaʒ/ *n.m.* garage. **~iste** *n.m.* garage owner; (*employé*) garage mechanic.

garant|ie /garɑ̃ti/ *n.f.* guarantee; (*protection*) safeguard. **~ies**, (*de police d'assurance*) cover. **~ir** *v.t.* guarantee; (*protéger*) protect (de, from).

garçon /garsɔ̃/ *n.m.* boy; (*célibataire*) bachelor. **~ (de café)**, waiter. **~ d'honneur**, best man.

garde¹ /gard/ *n.f.* guard; (*d'en-*

fants, de bagages) care; (*service*) guard (duty). **de ~**, on duty. **mettre en ~**, warn. **prendre ~**, be careful (à, of). **(droit de) ~**, custody (de, of).

garde² /gard/ *n.m.* (*personne*) guard; (*de propriété*) warden.

gard|er /garde/ *v.t.* (*conserver, maintenir*) keep; (*vêtement*) keep on; (*surveiller*) look after; (*défendre*) guard. **se ~er** *v. pr.* (*denrée*) keep. **~er le lit**, stay in bed. **~e-boue** *n.m. invar.* mudguard. **~e-manger** *n.m. invar.* (food) safe; (*placard*) larder. **~e-robe** *n.f.* wardrobe.

garderie /gardəri/ *n.f.* crèche.

gardien, ~ne /gardjɛ̃, -jɛn/ *n.m., f.* (*de prison, réserve*) warden; (*d'immeuble*) caretaker; (*de musée*) attendant; (*garde*) guard. **~ de but**, goalkeeper. **~ de la paix**, policeman. **~ne d'enfants**, child-minder.

gare¹ /gar/ *n.f.* (*rail.*) station. **~ routière**, coach station.

gare² /gar/ *int.* **~ (à toi)**, watch out!

garer /gare/ *v.t.*, **se ~** *v. pr.* park.

gargarisme /gargarism/ *n.m.* gargle.

gargouille /garguj/ *n.f.* (water-) spout; (*sculptée*) gargoyle.

garn|ir /garnir/ *v.t.* fill; (*décorer*) decorate; (*culin.*) garnish. **~i** *a.* (*plat*) served with vegetables.

garniture /garnityr/ *n.f.* (*légumes*) vegetables; (*ornement*) trimming.

garrot /garo/ *n.m.* (*méd.*) tourniquet.

gars /ga/ *n.m.* (*fam.*) fellow.

gas-oil /gazɔjl/ *n.m.* diesel oil.

gaspill|er /gaspije/ *v.t.* waste. **~age** *n.m.* waste.

gastrique /gastrik/ *a.* gastric.

gastronom|e /gastronɔm/ *n.m./f.* gourmet. **~ie** *n.f.* gastronomy.

gâteau (*pl.* ~x) /gato/ *n.m.* cake.
~ **sec**, biscuit.

gâter /gate/ *v.t.* spoil. **se** ~ *v. pr.*
(*temps*) get worse.

gâterie /gatri/ *n.f.* little treat.

gauch|e¹ /goʃ/ *a.* left. **à** ~**e**, on the
left; (*direction*) (to the) left. **la** ~**e**,
the left (side); (*pol.*) the left
(wing). ~**er**, ~**ère** *a. & n.m., f.*
left-handed (person). ~**iste** *a. &
n.m./f.* (*pol.*) leftist.

gauche² /goʃ/ *a.* (*maladroit*)
awkward.

gaufre /gofr/ *n.f.* waffle.

gaufrette /gofrɛt/ *n.f.* wafer.

gaulois, ~**e** /golwa, -z/ *a.* Gallic;
(*fig.*) bawdy. —*n.m., f.* Gaul.

gaz /gaz/ *n.m. invar.* gas.

gaze /gaz/ *n.f.* gauze.

gazelle /gazɛl/ *n.f.* gazelle.

gazeu|x, ~**se** /gazø, -z/ *a.*
(*boisson*) fizzy.

gazoduc /gazɔdyk/ *n.m.* gas
pipeline.

gazomètre /gazɔmɛtr/ *n.m.* gaso-
meter.

gazon /gazɔ̃/ *n.m.* lawn, grass.

geai /ʒɛ/ *n.m.* jay.

géant, ~**e** /ʒeɑ̃, -t/ *a. & n.m., f.*
giant.

gel /ʒɛl/ *n.m.* frost; (*pâte*) gel.

gélatine /ʒelatin/ *n.f.* gelatine.

gel|er /ʒǝle/ *v.t./i.* freeze. **on gèle**,
it's freezing. ~**é** *a.* frozen;
(*membre abîmé*) frost-bitten. ~**ée**
n.f. frost; (*culin.*) jelly.

gélule /ʒelyl/ *n.f.* (*méd.*) capsule.

Gémeaux /ʒemo/ *n.m. pl.* Gemini.

gém|ir /ʒemir/ *v.i.* groan. ~**isse-
ment** *n.m.* groan(ing).

gênant, ~**e** /ʒɛnɑ̃, -t/ *a.* embarrassing; (*irritant*) annoying.

gencive /ʒɑ̃siv/ *n.f.* gum.

gendarme /ʒɑ̃darm/ *n.m.* policeman, gendarme. ~**rie** /-ǝri/ *n.f.*
police force; (*local*) police station.

gendre /ʒɑ̃dr/ *n.m.* son-in-law.

gène /ʒɛn/ *n.m.* gene.

gêne /ʒɛn/ *n.f.* discomfort;
(*confusion*) embarrassment.

gên|er /ʒɛne/ *v.t.* bother, disturb;
(*troubler*) embarrass; (*encombrer*) hamper; (*bloquer*) block.
~**é** *a.* embarrassed.

génér|al (*m. pl.* ~**aux**) /ʒeneral,
-o/ *a.* general. —*n.m.* (*pl.* ~**aux**)
general. **en** ~**al**, in general.
~**alement** *adv.* generally.

généralis|er /ʒeneralize/ *v.t./i.*
generalize.

généraliste /ʒeneralist/ *n.m./f.*
general practitioner, GP.

génération /ʒenerasjɔ̃/ *n.f.* generation.

généreu|x, ~**se** /ʒenerø, -z/ *a.*
generous. ~**sement** *adv.* generously.

générosité /ʒenerozite/ *n.f.* gener-
osity.

genêt /ʒǝnɛ/ *n.m.* (*plante*) broom.

génétique /ʒenetik/ *a.* genetic.
—*n.f.* genetics.

Genève /ʒǝnɛv/ *n.m./f.* Geneva.

gén|ial (*m. pl.* ~**iaux**) /ʒenjal,
-jo/ *a.* brilliant; (*fam.*) fantastic.

génie /ʒeni/ *n.m.* genius. ~ **civil**,
civil engineering.

genièvre /ʒǝnjɛvr/ *n.m.* juniper.

génit|al (*m. pl.* ~**aux**) /ʒenital,
-o/ *a.* genital.

génoise /ʒenwaz/ *n.f.* sponge
(cake).

genou (*pl.* ~**x**) /ʒnu/ *n.m.* knee. **à**
~**x**, kneeling.

genre /ʒɑ̃r/ *n.m.* sort, kind; (*gram.*)
gender.

gens /ʒɑ̃/ *n.m./f. pl.* people.

genti|l, ~**lle** /ʒɑ̃ti, -j/ *a.* kind,
nice; (*agréable*) nice; (*sage*) good.
~**llesse** /-jɛs/ *n.f.* kindness.
~**ment** *adv.* kindly.

géograph|ie /ʒeɔgrafi/ *n.f.* geo-
graphy. ~**e** *n.m./f.* geographer.
~**ique** *a.* geographical.

géolo|gie /ʒeɔlɔʒi/ *n.f.* geology. **~gique** *a.* geological.

géométr|ie /ʒeɔmetri/ *n.f.* geometry. **~ique** *a.* geometric.

géranium /ʒeranjɔm/ *n.m.* geranium.

géran|t, ~te /ʒerɑ̃, -t/ *n.m., f.* manager, manageress.

gercé /ʒerse/ *a.* chapped.

gérer /ʒere/ *v.t.* manage.

germain, ~e /ʒermɛ̃, -ɛn/ *a.* **cousin ~**, first cousin.

germanique /ʒermanik/ *a.* Germanic.

germe /ʒerm/ *n.m.* germ. **~er** *v.i.* germinate.

gésier /ʒezje/ *n.m.* gizzard.

geste /ʒɛst/ *n.m.* gesture.

gesticul|er /ʒɛstikyle/ *v.i.* gesticulate. **~ation** /-ɑsjɔ̃/ *n.f.* gesticulation.

gestion /ʒɛstjɔ̃/ *n.f.* management.

geyser /ʒezɛr/ *n.m.* geyser.

gibier /ʒibje/ *n.m.* game.

giboulée /ʒibule/ *n.f.* shower.

gifl|e /ʒifl/ *n.f.* slap (in the face). **~er** *v.t.* slap.

gigantesque /ʒigɑ̃tɛsk/ *a.* gigantic.

gigot /ʒigo/ *n.m.* leg (of lamb).

gilet /ʒile/ *n.m.* waistcoat; (*cardigan*) cardigan. **~ de sauvetage**, life-jacket.

gin /dʒin/ *n.m.* gin.

gingembre /ʒɛ̃ʒɑ̃br/ *n.m.* ginger.

gingivite /ʒɛ̃ʒivit/ *n.f.* gum infection.

girafe /ʒiraf/ *n.f.* giraffe.

giratoire /ʒiratwar/ *a.* **sens ~**, roundabout.

giroflée /ʒirɔfle/ *n.f.* wallflower.

girouette /ʒirwet/ *n.f.* weathercock, weather-vane.

gisement /ʒizmɔ̃/ *n.m.* deposit.

gitan, ~e /ʒitɑ̃, -an/ *n.m., f.* gypsy.

gîte /ʒit/ *n.m.* (*maison*) home;

(*abri*) shelter. **~ rural**, holiday cottage.

givre /ʒivr/ *n.m.* (hoar-)frost.

glace /glas/ *n.f.* ice; (*crème*) ice-cream. (*miroir*) mirror.

glac|er /glase/ *v.t.* (*gâteau, boisson*) ice; (*papier*) glaze; (*pétrifier*) chill. **~é a.** (*vent, accueil*) icy.

glac|ial (*m. pl.* **~iaux**) /glasjal, -jo/ *a.* icy.

glacier /glasje/ *n.m.* (*géog.*) glacier; (*vendeur*) ice-cream man.

glacière /glasjɛr/ *n.f.* icebox.

glaçon /glasɔ̃/ *n.m.* ice-cube.

glaïeul /glajœl/ *n.m.* gladiolus.

glaise /glɛz/ *n.f.* clay.

gland /glɑ̃/ *n.m.* acorn; (*ornement*) tassel.

glande /glɑ̃d/ *n.f.* gland.

glissant, ~e /glisɑ̃, -t/ *a.* slippery.

gliss|er /glise/ *v.i.* slide; (*sur l'eau*) glide; (*déraper*) slip; (*véhicule*) skid. **~ement de terrain**, landslide.

glissière /glisjɛr/ *n.f.* groove. **à ~**, (*porte, système*) sliding.

glob|al (*m. pl.* **~aux**) /glɔbal, -o/ *a.* (*entier, général*) overall. **~alement** *adv.* as a whole.

globe /glɔb/ *n.m.* globe. **~ oculaire**, eyeball. **~ terrestre**, globe.

globule /glɔbyl/ *n.m.* (*du sang*) corpuscle.

gloire /glwar/ *n.f.* glory.

glorieu|x, ~se /glɔrjø, -z/ *a.* glorious. **~sement** *adv.* gloriously.

glossaire /glɔsɛr/ *n.m.* glossary.

glouton, ~ne /glutɔ̃, -ɔn/ *a.* gluttonous. —*n.m., f.* glutton.

gluant, ~e /glyɑ̃, -t/ *a.* sticky.

glucose /glykoz/ *n.m.* glucose.

glycérine /gliserin/ *n.f.* glycerine.

glycine /glisin/ *n.f.* wisteria.

gnome /gnom/ *n.m.* gnome.

GO (*abrév.* grandes ondes) long wave.

goal /gol/ *n.m.* goalkeeper.

gobelet /gɔblɛ/ *n.m.* tumbler, mug.

goéland /gɔelɑ̃/ *n.m.* (sea)gull.

goélette /gɔelɛt/ *n.f.* schooner.

gogo (à) /(a)gɔgo/ *adv.* (*fam.*) galore, in abundance.

goinfr|e /gwɛ̃fr/ *n.m.* (*glouton: fam.*) pig. **se ~er** *v. pr.* (*fam.*) stuff o.s. like a pig (**de**, with).

golf /gɔlf/ *n.m.* golf; golf course.

golfe /gɔlf/ *n.m.* gulf.

gomm|e /gɔm/ *n.f.* rubber; (*Amer.*) eraser; (*résine*) gum. **~er** *v.t.* rub out.

gond /gɔ̃/ *n.m.* hinge. **sortir de ses ~s**, go mad.

gondole /gɔ̃dɔl/ *n.f.* gondola.

gonfl|er /gɔ̃fle/ *v.t./i.* swell; (*ballon, pneu*) pump up, blow up; (*exagérer*) inflate. **se ~er** *v. pr.* swell. **~é** *a.* swollen. **~ement** *n.m.* swelling.

gorge /gɔrʒ/ *n.f.* throat; (*poitrine*) breast; (*vallée*) gorge.

gorgée /gɔrʒe/ *n.f.* sip, gulp.

gorille /gɔrij/ *n.m.* gorilla; (*garde: fam.*) bodyguard.

gosier /gozje/ *n.m.* throat.

gosse /gɔs/ *n.m./f.* (*fam.*) kid.

gothique /gɔtik/ *a.* Gothic.

goudron /gudrɔ̃/ *n.m.* tar. **à faible teneur en ~**, low tar.

gouffre /gufr/ *n.m.* gulf, abyss.

goulot /gulo/ *n.m.* neck.

goulu, ~e /guly/ *a.* gluttonous. —*n.m., f.* glutton.

gourde /gurd/ *n.f.* (*à eau*) flask.

gourdin /gurdɛ̃/ *n.m.* club, cudgel.

gourmand, ~e /gurmɑ̃, -d/ *a.* greedy. —*n.m., f.* glutton. **~ise** /-diz/ *n.f.* greed; (*mets*) delicacy.

gourmet /gurmɛ/ *n.m.* gourmet.

gourmette /gurmɛt/ *n.f.* chain bracelet.

gousse /gus/ *n.f.* **~ d'ail**, clove of garlic.

goût /gu/ *n.m.* taste.

goûter /gute/ *v.t.* taste; (*apprécier*) enjoy. —*v.i.* have tea. —*n.m.* tea, snack. **~ à** *ou* **de**, taste.

goutt|e /gut/ *n.f.* drop; (*méd.*) gout. **~er** *v.i.* drip.

gouttière /gutjɛr/ *n.f.* gutter.

gouvernail /guvɛrnaj/ *n.m.* rudder; (*barre*) helm.

gouvernante /guvɛrnɑ̃t/ *n.f.* governess.

gouvernement /guvɛrnəmɑ̃/ *n.m.* government.

gouvern|er /guvɛrne/ *v.t./i.* govern. **~eur** *n.m.* governor.

grâce /gras/ *n.f.* (*charme*) grace; (*jurid.*) pardon. **~ à**, thanks to.

gracieu|x, ~se /grasjø, -z/ *a.* graceful; (*gratuit*) free. **~sement** *adv.* gracefully; free (of charge).

grade /grad/ *n.m.* rank.

gradé /grade/ *n.m.* non-commissioned officer.

gradin /gradɛ̃/ *n.m.* tier, step.

gradué /gradye/ *a.* graded, graduated.

graffiti /grafiti/ *n.m. pl.* graffiti.

grain /grɛ̃/ *n.m.* grain; (*naut.*) squall; (*de café*) bean; (*de poivre*) pepper corn. **~ de beauté**, beauty spot. **~ de raisin**, grape.

graine /grɛn/ *n.f.* seed.

graiss|e /grɛs/ *n.f.* fat; (*lubrifiant*) grease. **~er** *v.t.* grease.

gramm|aire /gramɛr/ *n.f.* grammar. **~atical** (*m. pl.* **~aticaux**) *a.* grammatical.

gramme /gram/ *n.m.* gram.

grand, ~e /grɑ̃, -d/ *a.* big, large; (*haut*) tall; (*mérite, distance, ami*) great; (*bruit*) loud; (*plus âgé*) big. —*adv.* (*ouvrir*) wide. **~ ouvert**, wide open. **voir ~**, think big. —*n.m., f.* (*adulte*) grown-up; (*enfant*) older child. **au ~ air**, in

the open air. **en ~e partie,**
largely. **~-angle,** *n.m.* wide
angle. **~e banlieue,** outer sub-
urbs. **G~e-Bretagne** *n.f.* Great
Britain. **pas ~-chose,** not much.
~es lignes, (*rail.*) main lines. **~e
magasin,** department store. **~-
mère** (*pl.* **~s-mères**) *n.f.* grand-
mother. **~s-parents** *n.m. pl.*
grandparents. **~-père** (*pl.* **~s-
pères**) *n.m.* grandfather. **~e
personne,** grown-up. **~e surface,** hypermarket. **~es
vacances,** summer holidays.

grandiose /grãdjoz/ *a.* grandiose.
grandir /grãdir/ *v.i.* grow; (*bruit*)
grow louder. **~** *v.t.* make taller.
grange /grãʒ/ *n.f.* barn.
granit /granit/ *n.m.* granite.
granulé /granyle/ *n.m.* granule.
graphique /grafik/ *a.* graphic.
—*n.m.* graph.
grappe /grap/ *n.f.* cluster. **~ de
raisin,** bunch of grapes.
gras, ~se /grɑ, -s/ *a.* fat;
(*aliment*) fatty; (*surface*) greasy;
(*épais*) thick; (*caractères*) bold.
—*n.m.* (*culin.*) fat.
gratification /gratifikasjɔ̃/ *n.f.*
bonus, satisfaction.
gratifiant~ante /gratifjã, -t/ *a.*
rewarding.
gratin /gratɛ̃/ *n.m.* baked dish
with cheese topping; (*élite: fam.*)
upper crust.
gratis /gratis/ *adv.* free.
gratitude /gratityd/ *n.f.* gratitude.
gratter /grate/ *v.t./i.* scratch; (*avec
un outil*) scrape. **se ~** *v. pr.*
scratch o.s. **ça me gratte,** (*fam.*)
it itches.
gratuit, ~e /gratɥi, -t/ *a.* free;
(*acte*) gratuitous. **~ement**
/-tmã/ *adv.* free (of charge).
grave /grav/ *a.* serious; (*solennel*)
grave; (*voix*) deep; (*accent*) grave.
~ment *adv.* seriously; gravely.

grav|er /grave/ *v.t.* engrave; (*sur
bois*) carve. **~eur** *n.m.* engraver.
gravier /gravje/ *n.m.* gravel.
gravure /gravyr/ *n.f.* engraving;
(*de tableau, photo*) print, plate.
gré /gre/ *n.m.* **bon ~ mal gré,** like
it or not.
grec, ~que /grɛk/ *a. & n.m., f.*
Greek. —*n.m.* (*lang.*) Greek.
Grèce /grɛs/ *n.f.* Greece.
greff|e /grɛf/ *n.f.* graft; (*d'organe*)
transplant. **~er** /grefe/ *v.t.* graft;
transplant.
grêle[1] /grɛl/ *a.* (*maigre*) spindly;
(*voix*) shrill.
grêl|e[2] /grɛl/ *n.f.* hail. **~er** /grele/
v.i. hail. **~on** *n.m.* hailstone.
grelot /grəlo/ *n.m.* (little) bell.
grelotter /grələte/ *v.i.* shiver.
grenade[1] /grənad/ *n.f.* (*fruit*)
pomegranate.
grenade[2] /grənad/ *n.f.* (*explosif*)
grenade.
grenat /grəna/ *a. invar.* dark red.
grenier /grənje/ *n.m.* attic.
grenouille /grənuj/ *n.f.* frog.
grès /grɛ/ *n.m.* sandstone; (*poterie*)
stoneware.
grève[1] /grɛv/ *n.f.* strike.
grève[2] /grɛv/ *n.f.* (*rivage*) shore.
gréviste /grevist/ *n.m./f.* striker.
gribouill|er /gribuje/ *v.t./i.* scrib-
ble. **~is** /-ji/ *n.m.* scribble.
grièvement /grijɛvmã/ *adv.* seriously.
griff|e /grif/ *n.f.* claw; (*de
couturier*) label. **~er** *v.t.* scratch,
claw.
griffonner /grifone/ *v.t./i.* scrawl.
grignoter /griɲote/ *v.t./i.* nibble.
gril /gril/ *n.m.* grill, grid(iron).
grillade /grijad/ *n.f.* (*viande*) grill.
grillage /grijaʒ/ *n.m.* wire netting.
grille /grij/ *n.f.* railings; (*portail*)
(metal) gate; (*de fenêtre*) bars; (*de
cheminée*) grate; (*fig.*) grid.
grill|er /grije/ *v.t./i.* burn;

(*ampoule*) blow; (*feu rouge*) go through. (**faire**) ∼**er**, (*pain*) toast; (*viande*) grill; (*café*) roast. ∼**e-pain** *n.m. invar.* toaster.

grillon /grijɔ̃/ *n.m.* cricket.

grimace /grimas/ *n.f.* (funny) face; (*de douleur, dégoût*) grimace.

grimper /grɛ̃pe/ *v.t./i.* climb.

grinc|er /grɛ̃se/ *v.i.* creak. ∼**ement** *n.m.* creak(ing).

gripp|e /grip/ *n.f.* influenza, flu. **être** ∼**é**, have (the) flu; (*mécanisme*) be seized up *ou* jammed.

gris, ∼**e** /gri, -z/ *a.* grey.

grive /griv/ *n.f.* (*oiseau*) thrush.

grog /grɔg/ *n.m.* grog.

grogn|er /grɔɲe/ *v.i.* growl; (*fig.*) grumble. ∼**ement** *n.m.* growl; grumble.

grognon, ∼**ne** /grɔɲɔ̃, -ɔn/ *a.* grumpy.

grond|er /grɔ̃de/ *v.i.* rumble; (*chien*) growl; (*conflit etc.*) be brewing. —*v.t.* scold. ∼**ement** *n.m.* rumbling; growling.

groom /grum/ *n.m.* page(-boy).

gros, ∼**se** /gro, -s/ *a.* big, large; (*gras*) (*épais*) thick. —*n.m.f.* fat man, fat woman. —*n.m.* **de** ∼, (*comm.*) wholesale. **en** ∼, roughly; (*comm.*) wholesale. ∼ **mot,** rude word. ∼ **plan,** close-up.

groseille /grozɛj/ *n.f.* (red *ou* white) currant. ∼ **à maquereau,** gooseberry.

grosse /gros/ *voir* **gros**.

grossesse /grosɛs/ *n.f.* pregnancy.

grosseur /grosœr/ *n.f.* (*volume*) size; (*enflure*) lump.

gross|ier, ∼**ière** /grosje, -jɛr/ *a.* coarse, rough; (*imitation, instrument*) crude; (*vulgaire*) coarse; (*insolent*) rude; (*erreur*) gross. ∼**ièreté** *n.f.* rudeness; (*mot*) rude word.

grossir /grosir/ *v.t./i.* swell; (*personne*) put on weight; (*au microscope*) magnify; (*augmenter*) grow; (*exagérer*) magnify.

grossiste /grosist/ *n.m./f.* wholesaler.

grotesque /grɔtɛsk/ *a.* grotesque; (*ridicule*) ludicrous.

grotte /grɔt/ *n.f.* cave, grotto.

groupe /grup/ *n.m.* group; (*mus.*) band. ∼ **électrogène,** generating set.

group|er /grupe/ *v.t.,* **se** ∼**er** *v. pr.* group (together). ∼**ement** *n.m.* grouping.

grue /gry/ *n.f.* crane.

grumeau (*pl.* ∼**x**) /grymo/ *n.m.* lump.

gruyère /gryjɛr/ *n.m.* gruyère (cheese).

guenon /gənɔ̃/ *n.f.* female monkey.

guépard /gepar/ *n.m.* cheetah.

guêp|e /gɛp/ *n.f.* wasp. ∼**ier** /gepje/ *n.m.* wasp's nest; (*fig.*) trap.

guère /gɛr/ *adv.* (**ne**) ∼, hardly. **il n'y a** ∼ **d'espoir,** there is no hope.

guéridon /geridɔ̃/ *n.m.* pedestal table.

guér|ir /gerir/ *v.t.* (*personne, maladie, mal*) cure (**de,** of); (*plaie, membre*) heal. —*v.i.* get better; (*blessure*) heal.

guerre /gɛr/ *n.f.* war.

guerr|ier, ∼**ière** /gɛrje, -jɛr/ *a.* warlike. —*n.m., f.* warrior.

guetter /gete/ *v.t.* watch; (*attendre*) watch out for.

gueule /gœl/ *n.f.* mouth; (*figure: fam.*) face. **ta** ∼!, (*fam.*) shut up!

gueuler /gœle/ *v.i.* (*fam.*) bawl.

gueuleton /gœltɔ̃/ *n.m.* (*repas: fam.*) blow-out, slap-up meal.

gui /gi/ *n.m.* mistletoe.

guichet /giʃɛ/ *n.m.* window,

counter; *(de gare)* ticket-office (window); *(de théâtre)* box-office (window).

guide /gid/ *n.m.* guide. —*n.f.* *(fille scout)* girl guide. ∼s *n.f. pl.* *(rênes)* reins.

guider /gide/ *v.t.* guide.

guidon /gidɔ̃/ *n.m.* handlebars.

guignol /giɲɔl/ *n.m.* puppet; *(personne)* clown; *(spectacle)* puppet-show.

guillemets /gijmɛ/ *n.m. pl.* quotation marks, inverted commas. **entre** ∼, in inverted commas.

guimauve /gimov/ *n.f.* marshmallow.

guirlande /girlãd/ *n.f.* garland.

guitar|e /gitar/ *n.f.* guitar. ∼iste *n.m./f.* guitarist.

gym /ʒim/ *n.f.* gym.

gymnas|e /ʒimnaz/ *n.m.* gym(nasium). ∼tique /-astik/ *n.f.* gymnastics.

gynécolo|gie /ʒinekɔlɔʒi/ *n.f.* gynaecology. ∼gue /-gɡ/ *n.m./f.* gynaecologist.

gypse /ʒips/ *n.m.* gypsum.

H

habile /abil/ *a.* skilful, clever. ∼té *n.f.* skill.

habilité /abilite/ *a.* ∼ à faire, entitled to do.

habill|er /abije/ *v.t.* dress **(de,** in). **s'**∼**er** *v. pr.* dress (o.s.), get dressed. ∼é *a.* *(costume)* dressy. ∼ement *n.m.* clothing.

habit /abi/ *n.m.* dress, outfit; *(de cérémonie)* tails. ∼s, clothes.

habitant, ∼**e** /abitã, -t/ *n.m., f.* *(de maison)* occupant; *(de pays)* inhabitant.

habitation /abitasjɔ̃/ *n.f.* living; *(logement)* house.

habit|er /abite/ *v.i.* live. —*v.t.* live in; *(planète, zone)* inhabit. ∼é *a.* *(terre)* inhabited.

habitude /abityd/ *n.f.* habit. **avoir l'**∼ **de faire,** be used to doing. **d'**∼, usually. **comme d'**∼, as usual.

habitué, ∼**e** /abitye/ *n.m., f.* regular visitor; *(client)* regular.

habituel, ∼**le** /abityɛl/ *a.* usual. ∼**lement** *adv.* usually.

habituer /abitye/ *v.t.* ∼ **à,** accustom to. **s'**∼ **à,** get used to.

hache /aʃ/ *n.f.* axe.

haché /aʃe/ *a.* *(viande)* minced.

hacher /aʃe/ *v.t.* mince; *(au couteau)* chop.

hachis /aʃi/ *n.f.* minced meat.

haie /ɛ/ *n.f.* hedge; *(rangée)* row. **course de** ∼s, hurdle race.

haillon /ajɔ̃/ *n.m.* rag.

hain|e /ɛn/ *n.f.* hatred. ∼**eux,** ∼**euse** *a.* full of hatred.

haïr /air/ *v.t.* hate.

hâl|e /ɑl/ *n.m.* (sun-)tan. ∼é *a.* (sun-)tanned.

haleine /alɛn/ *n.f.* breath. **hors d'**∼, out of breath.

hal|er /ale/ *v.t.* tow. ∼**age** *n.m.* towing.

hall /ol/ *n.m.* hall; *(de gare)* concourse.

halle /al/ *n.f.* (covered) market. ∼**s,** (main) food market.

halt|e /alt/ *n.f.* stop; *(repos)* break; *(escale)* stopping place. —*int.* stop; *(mil.)* halt. **faire** ∼, stop.

hamac /amak/ *n.m.* hammock.

hamburger /ãburɡœr/ *n.m.* hamburger.

hameau *(pl.* ∼**x)** /amo/ *n.m.* hamlet.

hameçon /amsɔ̃/ *n.m.* (fish-)hook.

hanche /ɑ̃ʃ/ *n.f.* hip.

hand-ball /ɑ̃dbal/ *n.m.* handball.

handicap /ɑ̃dikap/ *n.m.* handicap. ∼é, ∼ée *a.* & *n.m., f.*

handicapped (person). **∼er** *v.t.* handicap.

hangar /'ᾶgɑr/ *n.m.* shed; (*pour avions*) hangar.

hanneton /'antɔ̃/ *n.m.* May-bug.

hanter /'ᾶte/ *v.t.* haunt.

haras /'arɑ/ *n.m.* stud-farm.

harcèlement /arsɛlmᾶ/ *n.m.* ∼ **sexuel,** sexual harassment.

harceler /'arsəle/ *v.t.* harass.

hareng /'arᾶ/ *n.m.* herring.

haricot /'ariko/ *n.m.* bean. ∼ **vert,** French *ou* string bean.

harmonica /armɔnika/ *n.m.* harmonica.

harmon|ie /armɔni/ *n.f.* harmony. ∼**ieux,** ∼**ieuse** *a.* harmonious.

harnais /'arnɛ/ *n.m.* harness.

harp|e /'arp/ *n.f.* harp. ∼**iste** *n.m./f.* harpist.

hasard /'azar/ *n.m.* chance; (*coïncidence*) coincidence. ∼**s** (*risques*) hazards. **au** ∼, (*choisir etc.*) at random; (*flâner*) aimlessly. ∼**eux,** ∼**euse** /-dø, -z/ *a.* risky.

hâte /'ɑt/ *n.f.* haste. **à la** ∼, **en** ∼, hurriedly. **avoir** ∼ **de,** be eager to.

hâter /'ɑte/ *v.t.* hasten. **se** ∼ *v. pr.* hurry (**de,** to).

hauss|e /'os/ *n.f.* rise (**de,** in). ∼ **e des prix,** price rises. **en** ∼**e,** rising. ∼**er** *v.t.* raise; (*épaules*) shrug.

haut, ∼**e** /'o, 'ot/ *a.* high; (*de taille*) tall. —*adv.* high; (*parler*) loud(ly); (*lire*) aloud. —*n.m.* top. **à** ∼ **voix,** aloud. **des** ∼**s et des bas,** ups and downs. **en** ∼, (*regarder, jeter*) up; (*dans une maison*) upstairs. **en** ∼ (**de**), at the top (of). **plus** ∼, further up, higher up; (*dans un texte*) above. ∼**parleur** *n.m.* loudspeaker.

hautain, ∼**e** /'otɛ̃, -ɛn/ *a.* haughty.

hautbois /'obwɑ/ *n.m.* oboe.

hautement /'otmᾶ/ *adv.* highly.

hauteur /'otœr/ *n.f.* height; (*colline*) hill; (*arrogance*) haughtiness. **à la** ∼, (*fam.*) up to it.

Haye (La) /'lɑ'ɛ/ *n.f.* The Hague.

hayon /'ɛjɔ̃/ *n.m.* (*auto.*) rear opening, tail-gate.

hebdo /ɛbdo/ *n.m.* (*fam.*) weekly.

hebdomadaire /ɛbdɔmadɛr/ *a. & n.m.* weekly.

héberg|er /ebɛrʒe/ *v.t.* accommodate, take in. ∼**ement** *n.m.* accommodation.

hébraïque /ebraik/ *a.* Hebrew.

hébreu (*pl.* ∼**x**) /ebrø/ *a.m.* Hebrew. —*n.m.* (*lang.*) Hebrew.

hectare /ɛktar/ *n.m.* hectare (= *10,000 square metres*).

hein /'ɛ̃/ *int.* (*fam.*) eh.

hélas /'elɑs/ *int.* alas. —*adv.* sadly.

hélice /elis/ *n.f.* propeller.

hélicoptère /elikɔptɛr/ *n.m.* helicopter.

helvétique /ɛlvetik/ *a.* Swiss.

hématome /ematɔm/ *n.m.* bruise.

hémisphère /emisfɛr/ *n.m.* hemisphere.

hémorragie /emɔraʒi/ *n.f.* haemorrhage

hémorroïdes /emɔrɔid/ *n.f. pl.* piles, haemorrhoids.

hépatite /epatit/ *n.f.* hepatitis.

herbe /ɛrb/ *n.f.* grass; (*méd., culin.*) herb.

herbicide /ɛrbisid/ *n.m.* weed-killer.

hérédit|é /eredite/ *n.f.* heredity. ∼**aire** *a.* hereditary.

héré|sie /erezi/ *n.f.* heresy. ∼**tique** *a.* heretical; *n.m./f.* heretic.

hérisson /'erisɔ̃/ *n.m.* hedgehog.

héritage /eritaʒ/ *n.m.* inheritance; (*spirituel etc.*) heritage.

hérit|er /erite/ *v.t./i.* inherit (**de,** from). ∼**er de qch.,** inherit sth.

~ier, ~ière *n.m., f.* heir, heiress.

hermétique /ɛrmetik/ *a.* airtight.

hermine /ɛrmin/ *n.f.* ermine.

hernie /'ɛrni/ *n.f.* hernia.

héroïne /eroin/ *n.f.* (*femme*) heroine.

héroï|que /eroik/ *a.* heroic. **~sme** *n.m.* heroism.

héron /'erɔ̃/ *n.m.* heron.

héros /'ero/ *n.m.* hero.

hésit|er /ezite/ *v.i.* hesitate (à, to). **en ~ant,** hesitantly. **~ant, ~ante** *a.* hesitant. **~ation** *n.f.* hesitation.

hétérosexuel, ~le /eterɔseksɥɛl/ *n.m., f. & a.* heterosexual.

hêtre /'ɛtr/ *n.m.* beech.

heure /œr/ *n.f.* time; (*mesure de durée*) hour; (*scol.*) period. **quelle ~ est-il?**, what time is it? **il est dix**/*etc.* **~s,** it is ten/*etc.* o'clock. **à l'~,** (*venir, être*) on time. **d'affluence, ~ de pointe,** rush-hour.

heureusement /œrøzmã/ *adv.* fortunately, luckily.

heureu|x, ~se /œrø, -z/ *a.* happy; (*chanceux*) lucky, fortunate.

heurter /'œrte/ *v.t.* (*cogner*) hit; (*mur etc.*) bump into, hit. **se ~ à,** bump into, hit.

hexagone /ɛgzagon/ *n.m.* hexagon. **l'~,** France.

hibou (*pl.* **~x**) /'ibu/ *n.m.* owl.

hier /jɛr/ *adv.* yesterday. **~ soir,** last night, yesterday evening.

hiérarch|ie /jerarʃi/ *n.f.* hierarchy. **~ique** *a.* hierarchical.

hi-fi /'ifi/ *a. invar. & n.f.* (*fam.*) hi-fi.

hindou, ~e /ɛ̃du/ *a. & n.m., f.* Hindu.

hippi|que /ipik/ *a.* horse, equestrian. **~sme** *n.m.* horse-riding.

hippodrome /ipodrom/ *n.m.* racecourse.

hippopotame /ipopotam/ *n.m.* hippopotamus.

hirondelle /irɔ̃dɛl/ *n.f.* swallow.

hisser /'ise/ *v.t.* hoist, haul.

histoire /istwar/ *n.f.* (*récit, mensonge*) story; (*étude*) history; (*affaire*) business. **~(s),** (*chichis*) fuss. **~s,** (*ennuis*) trouble.

historique /istorik/ *a.* historical.

hiver /iver/ *n.m.* winter. **~nal** (*m. pl.* **~naux**) *a.* winter; (*glacial*) wintry. **~ner** *v.i.* winter.

H.L.M. /'aʃɛlɛm/ *n.m./f.* (= *habitation à loyer modéré*) block of council flats.

hocher /'ɔʃe/ *v.t.* ~ **la tête,** (*pour dire oui*) nod; (*pour dire non*) shake one's head.

hochet /'ɔʃɛ/ *n.m.* rattle.

hockey /'ɔkɛ/ *n.m.* hockey.

hollandais, ~e /'ɔlɑ̃dɛ, -z/ *a.* Dutch. **~,** *n.m., f.* Dutchman, Dutchwoman. **—n.m.** (*lang.*) Dutch.

Hollande /'ɔlɑ̃d/ *n.f.* Holland.

hologramme /ɔlɔgram/ *n.m.* hologram.

homard /'ɔmar/ *n.m.* lobster.

homéopathie /ɔmeopati/ *n.f.* homoeopathy.

homicide /ɔmisid/ *n.m.* homicide.

hommage /ɔmaʒ/ *n.m.* tribute. **~s,** (*salutations*) respects.

homme /ɔm/ *n.m.* man; (*espèce*) man(kind). **~ d'affaires,** businessman.

homologue /ɔmɔlɔg/ *n.m./f.* counterpart.

homologué /ɔmɔlɔge/ *a.* (*record*) officially recognized; (*tarif*) official.

homonyme /ɔmɔnim/ *n.m.* (*personne*) namesake.

homosex|uel, ~uelle /ɔmɔsɛk-sɥɛl/ *a. & n.m., f.* homosexual. **~ualité** *n.f.* homosexuality.

Hongrie /'ɔ̃gri/ *n.f.* Hungary.

hongrois, **~e** /'ɔ̃grwa, -z/ a. &
n.m., f. Hungarian.
honnête /ɔnɛt/ a. honest; (satisfaisant) fair. **~ment** adv.
honestly; fairly. **~té** n.f.
honesty.
honneur /ɔnœr/ n.m. honour;
(mérite) credit. **d'~**, (invité,
place) of honour; (membre)
honorary. **en l'~ de**, in honour
of.
honorable /ɔnɔrabl/ a. honour-
able; (convenable) respectable.
honoraire /ɔnɔrɛr/ a. honorary.
~s n.m. pl. fees.
honorer /ɔnɔre/ v.t. honour; (faire
honneur à) do credit to.
hont|e /'ɔ̃t/ n.f. shame. **avoir ~e**,
be ashamed (de, of). **~eux,
~euse** a. (personne) ashamed
(de, of); (action) shameful.
hôpit|al (pl. **~aux**) /ɔpital, -o/
n.m. hospital.
hoquet /'ɔkɛ/ n.m. hiccup. **le ~**,
(the) hiccups.
horaire /ɔrɛr/ a. hourly. **—** n.m.
timetable. **~ flexible**, flexi-
time.
horizon /ɔrizɔ̃/ n.m. horizon.
horizont|al (m. pl. **~aux**)
/ɔrizɔtal, -o/ a. horizontal.
horloge /ɔrlɔʒ/ n.f. clock.
horlog|er, ~ère /ɔrlɔʒe, -ɛr/
n.m., f. watchmaker.
hormon|al (m. pl. **~aux**)
/ɔrmɔnal, -no/ a. hormonal, hormone.
hormone /ɔrmɔn/ n.f. hormone.
horoscope /ɔrɔskɔp/ n.m. horoscope.
horreur /ɔrœr/ n.f. horror. **avoir
~ de**, detest.
horrible /ɔribl/ a. horrible.
hors /'ɔr/ prép. **~ de**, out of; (à
l'extérieur de) outside. **~-bord**
n.m. invar. speedboat. **~-
d'œuvre** n.m. invar. hors-

d'œuvre. **~ de prix**, exorbitant.
~-taxe a. invar. duty-free.
hortensia /ɔrtɑ̃sja/ n.m. hydrangea.
horticulture /ɔrtikyltyr/ n.f. horticulture.
hospice /ɔspis/ n.m. home.
hospital|ier, ~ière[1] /ɔspitalje,
-jɛr/ a. hospitable. **~ité** n.f.
hospitality.
hospital|ier, ~ière[2] /ɔspitalje,
-jɛr/ a. (méd.) hospital.
hostie /ɔsti/ n.f. (relig.) host.
hostil|e /ɔstil/ a. hostile. **~ité** n.f.
hostility.
hôte /ot/ n.m. (maître) host;
(invite) guest.
hôtel /otɛl/ n.m. hotel. **~ (particulier)**, (private) mansion. **~
de ville**, town hall. **~ier, ~ière**
/otalje, -jɛr/ a. hotel; n.m., f.
hotelier. **~lerie** n.f. hotel business; (auberge) country hotel.
hôtesse /otɛs/ n.f. hostess. **~ de
l'air**, air hostess.
hotte /'ɔt/ n.f. basket; (de
cuisinière) hood.
houblon /'ublɔ̃/ n.m. **le ~**,
hops.
houille /'uj/ n.f. coal.
hourra /'ura/ n.m. & int. hurrah.
housse /'us/ n.f. dust-cover.
houx /'u/ n.m. holly.
hublot /'yblo/ n.m. porthole.
huer /'ɥe/ v.t. boo. **huées** n.f. pl.
boos.
huile /ɥil/ n.f. oil.
huissier /ɥisje/ n.m. (appariteur)
usher; (jurid.) bailiff.
huit /'ɥi(t)/ a. eight. **—**n.m. eight.
~ jours, a week. **lundi en ~**,
a week on Monday. **~ième**
/'ɥitjɛm/ a. & n.m./f. eighth.
huître /ɥitr/ n.f. oyster.
humain, **~e** /ymɛ̃, ymɛn/ a.
human; (compatissant) humane.

humanitaire /ymanitɛr/ *a.* humanitarian.

humanité /ymanite/ *n.f.* humanity.

humble /œbl/ *a.* humble.

humeur /ymœr/ *n.f.* mood; (*tempérament*) temper. **de bonne/mauvaise ~**, in a good/bad mood.

humid|e /ymid/ *a.* damp; (*chaleur*, *climat*) humid; (*lèvres*, *yeux*) moist. **~ité** *n.f.* humidity.

humili|er /ymilje/ *v.t.* humiliate. **~ation** *n.f.* humiliation.

humilité /ymilite/ *n.f.* humility.

humorist|e /ymɔrist/ *n.m./f.* humorist. **~ique** *a.* humorous.

humour /ymur/ *n.m.* humour; (*sens*) sense of humour.

hurl|er /'yrle/ *v.t./i.* howl. **~ement** *n.m.* howl(ing).

hydratant, ~e /idratɑ̃, -t/ *a.* (*lotion*) moisturizing.

hydrate /idrat/ *n.m.* **~ de carbone**, carbohydrate.

hydraulique /idrolik/ *a.* hydraulic.

hydravion /idravjɔ̃/ *n.m.* seaplane.

hydro-electrique /idrɔelɛktrik/ *a.* hydroelectric.

hydrogène /idrɔʒɛn/ *n.m.* hydrogen.

hyène /jɛn/ *n.f.* hyena.

hygiène /iʒjɛn/ *n.f.* hygiene.

hymne /imn/ *n.m.* hymn. **~ national**, national anthem.

hyper- /ipɛr/ *préf.* hyper-.

hypermarché /ipɛrmarʃe/ *n.m.* (*supermarché*) hypermarket.

hypermétrope /ipɛrmetrɔp/ *a.* long-sighted.

hypertension /ipɛrtɑ̃sjɔ̃/ *n.f.* high blood-pressure.

hypnose /ipnoz/ *n.f.* hypnosis.

hypocrisie /ipokrizi/ *n.f.* hypocrisy.

hypocrite /ipokrit/ *a.* hypocritical. **~n.m./f.** hypocrite.

hypoth|èque /ipotɛk/ *n.f.* mortgage. **~équer** *v.t.* mortgage.

hypoth|èse /ipotɛz/ *n.f.* hypothesis. **~étique** *a.* hypothetical.

I

iceberg /isbɛrg/ *n.m.* iceberg.

ici /isi/ *adv.* (*espace*) here; (*temps*) now. **d'~ peu**, shortly.

icône /ikon/ *n.f.* icon.

idé|al (*m. pl.* **~aux**) /ideal/ *a.* ideal, -o/ *a.* ideal. **—n.m.** (*pl.* **~aux**) ideal. *ideal*.

idéaliste /idealist/ *a.* idealistic. **—n.m./f.** idealist.

idée /ide/ *n.f.* idea; (*esprit*) mind.

identif|ier /idɑ̃tifje/ *v.t.*, **s'~ier** *v. pr.* identify (**à**, with). **~ication** *n.f.* identification.

identique /idɑ̃tik/ *a.* identical.

identité /idɑ̃tite/ *n.f.* identity.

idéolog|ie /ideɔlɔʒi/ *n.f.* ideology. **~ique** *a.* ideological.

idiom|e /idjom/ *n.m.* idiom. **~atique** /idjɔmatik/ *a.* idiomatic.

idiot, ~e /idjo, idjɔt/ *a.* idiotic. **—n.m., f.** idiot. **~ie** /idjɔsi/ *n.f.* idiocy; (*acte, parole*) idiotic thing.

idole /idol/ *n.f.* idol.

if /if/ *n.m.* (*arbre*) yew.

igloo /iglu/ *n.m.* igloo.

ignifugé /iɲifyʒe/ *a.* fireproof.

ignoble /iɲɔbl/ *a.* vile.

ignoran|t, ~te /iɲɔrɑ̃, -t/ *a.* ignorant. **—n.m., f.** ignoramus. **~ce** *n.f.* ignorance.

ignorer /iɲɔre/ *v.t.* not know; (*personne*) ignore.

il /il/ *pron.* he; (*chose*) it. **il neige/pleut/etc.**, it is snowing/raining/*etc.* **il y a**, there is; (*pluriel*) there are; (*temps*) ago; (*durée*) for. **il y a 2 ans**, 2 years ago. **il y a plus d'une heure que j'attends**, I've been waiting for over an hour.

île /il/ *n.f.* island. **~ déserte**, desert island. **~ anglo-normandes**, Channel Islands. **~s Britanniques**, British Isles.

illégalal (*m. pl.* **~aux**) /ilegal, -o/ *a.* illegal. **~alité** *n.f.* illegality.

illicite /ilisit/ *a.* illicit.

illisible /ilizibl/ *a.* illegible; (*livre*) unreadable.

illogique /iloʒik/ *a.* illogical.

illumin|er /ilymine/ *v.t.*, s'**~er** *v. pr.* light up. **~ation** *n.f.* illumination. **~é é** *a.* (*monument*) floodlit.

illusion /ilyzjɔ̃/ *n.f.* illusion.

illustre /ilystr/ *a.* illustrious.

illustr|er /ilystre/ *v.t.* illustrate. **~ation** *n.f.* illustration. **~é é** *a.* illustrated; *n.m.* illustrated magazine.

ils /il/ *pron.* they.

imag|e /imaʒ/ *n.f.* picture; (*métaphore*) image; (*reflet*) reflection. **~é é** *a.* full of imagery.

imaginaire /imaʒinɛr/ *a.* imaginary.

imagin|er /imaʒine/ *v.t.* imagine; (*inventer*) think up. s'**~er** *v. pr.* imagine (**que**, that). **~ation** *n.f.* imagination.

imbattable /ɛ̃batabl/ *a.* unbeatable.

imbécile /ɛ̃besil/ *a.* idiotic. —*n.m./f.* idiot.

imbuvable /ɛ̃byvabl/ *a.* undrinkable; (*personne: fam.*) insufferable.

imit|er /imite/ *v.t.* imitate; (*personnage*) impersonate; (*faire comme*) do the same as; (*document*) copy. **~ateur, ~atrice** *n.m., f.* imitator; impersonator. **~ation** *n.f.* imitation; impersonation.

immaculé /imakyle/ *a.* spotless.

immangeable /ɛ̃mɑ̃ʒabl/ *a.* inedible.

immatricul|er /imatrikyle/ *v.t.* register. **(se) faire ~er**, register. **~ation** *n.f.* registration.

immature /imatyr/ *a.* immature.

immédiat, **~e** /imedja, -t/ *a.* immediate. —*n.m.* **dans l'~**, for the moment. **~ement** /-tmɑ̃/ *adv.* immediately.

immens|e /imɑ̃s/ *a.* immense. **~ément** *adv.* immensely.

immeuble /imœbl/ *n.m.* block of flats, building. **~ (de bureaux)**, (office) building *ou* block.

immigr|er /imigre/ *v.i.* immigrate. **~ant, ~ante** *a. & n.m., f.* immigrant. **~ation** *n.f.* immigration. **~é, ~ée** *a. & n.m., f.* immigrant.

imminen|t, **~te** /iminɑ̃, -t/ *a.* imminent. **~ce** *n.f.* imminence.

immobil|e /imɔbil/ *a.* still, motionless. **~ité** *n.f.* stillness; (*inaction*) immobility.

immobil|ier, **~ière** /imɔbilje, -jɛr/ *a.* property. **agence ~ière**, estate agent's office **agent ~ier**, estate agent. **l'~ier**, property.

immobilis|er /imɔbilize/ *v.t.* immobilize; (*stopper*) stop. s'**~er** *v. pr.* stop. **~ation** *n.f.* immobilization.

immonde /imɔ̃d/ *a.* filthy.

immondices /imɔ̃dis/ *n.f. pl.* refuse.

immor|al (*m. pl.* **~aux**) /imɔral, -o/ *a.* immoral. **~alité** *n.f.* immorality.

immort|el, **~elle** /imɔrtɛl/ *a.* immortal. **~alité** *n.f.* immortality.

immunis|er /imynize/ *v.t.* immunize. **~é contre**, (*à l'abri de*) immune to.

immunité /imynite/ *n.f.* immunity.

impact /ɛ̃pakt/ *n.m.* impact.

impair /ɛ̃pɛr/ *a.* (*numéro*) odd.

impardonnable /ɛ̃pardɔnabl/ *a.* unforgivable.

imparfait, **~e** /ɛ̃parfɛ, -t/ *a. & n.m.* imperfect.

impartial (*m. pl.* **~iaux**) /ɛ̃parsjal, -jo/ *a.* impartial.

impasse /ɛ̃pas/ *n.f.* (*rue*) dead end; (*situation*) deadlock.

impat|ient, **~iente** /ɛ̃pasjã, -t/ *a.* impatient. **~iemment** /-jamã/ *adv.* impatiently. **~ience** *n.f.* impatience.

impatienter /ɛ̃pasjãte/ *v.t.* annoy. **s'~** *v. pr.* lose patience (**contre**, with).

impayé /ɛ̃peje/ *a.* unpaid.

impeccable /ɛ̃pekabl/ *a.* impeccable.

impensable /ɛ̃pãsabl/ *a.* unthinkable.

impérati|f, **~ve** /ɛ̃peratif, -v/ *a.* imperative. —*n.m.* requirement; (*gram.*) imperative.

impératrice /ɛ̃peratris/ *n.f.* empress.

imperceptible /ɛ̃pɛrsɛptibl/ *a.* imperceptible.

imperfection /ɛ̃pɛrfɛksjɔ̃/ *n.f.* imperfection.

impér|ial (*m. pl.* **~iaux**) /ɛ̃perjal, -jo/ *a.* imperial. **~ialisme** *n.m.* imperialism.

impériale /ɛ̃perjal/ *n.f.* upper deck.

imperméable /ɛ̃pɛrmeabl/ *a.* impervious (**à**, to); (*manteau, tissu*) waterproof. —*n.m.* raincoat.

impertinen|t, **~te** /ɛ̃pɛrtinã, -t/ *a.* impertinent. **~ce** *n.f.* impertinence.

imperturbable /ɛ̃pɛrtyrbabl/ *a.* unshakeable.

impitoyable /ɛ̃pitwajabl/ *a.* merciless.

implacable /ɛ̃plakabl/ *a.* implacable.

implant|er /ɛ̃plãte/ *v.t.* establish. **s'~er** *v. pr.* become established.

implication /ɛ̃plikasjɔ̃/ *n.f.* implication.

impliquer /ɛ̃plike/ *v.t.* imply (**que**, that). **~ dans**, implicate in.

impoli /ɛ̃poli/ *a.* impolite. **~tesse** *n.f.* impoliteness; (*remarque*) impolite remark.

impopulaire /ɛ̃popylɛr/ *a.* unpopular.

importance /ɛ̃portãs/ *n.f.* importance; (*taille*) size; (*ampleur*) extent. **sans ~**, unimportant.

important, **~e** /ɛ̃portã, -t/ *a.* important; (*en quantité*) considerable, sizeable, big. —*n.m.* l'**~**, the important thing.

import|er¹ /ɛ̃porte/ *v.t.* (*comm.*) import. **~ateur**, **~atrice** *n.m., f.* importer; *a.* importing. **~ation** *n.f.* import.

import|er² /ɛ̃porte/ *v.i.* matter, be important (**à**, to). **n'~e où**, anywhere. **n'~e qui**, anybody. **n'~e quoi**, anything.

imposant, **~e** /ɛ̃pozã, -t/ *a.* imposing.

imposer /ɛ̃poze/ *v.t.* impose (**à**, on); (*taxer*) tax.

imposition /ɛ̃pozisjɔ̃/ *n.f.* taxation.

impossibilité /ɛ̃posibilite/ *n.f.* impossibility. **dans l'~ de**, unable to.

impossible /ɛ̃posibl/ *a. & n.m.* impossible. **faire l'~**, do the impossible.

impost|eur /ɛ̃pɔstœr/ *n.m.* impostor. **~ure** *n.f.* imposture.

impôt /ɛ̃po/ *n.m.* tax. **~s**, (*contributions*) tax(ation), taxes. **~ sur le revenu**, income tax.

impraticable /ɛ̃pratikabl/ *a.* (*route*) impassable.

imprécis, ~e /ɛ̃presi, -z/ *a.* imprecise. ~ion /-zjɔ̃/ *n.f.* imprecision.

impression /ɛ̃presjɔ̃/ *n.f.* impression; (*de livre*) printing.

impressionn|er /ɛ̃presjone/ *v.t.* impress. ~ant, ~ante *a.* impressive.

imprévisible /ɛ̃previzibl/ *a.* unpredictable.

imprévoyant, ~e /ɛ̃prevwajã, -t/ *a.* improvident.

imprévu /ɛ̃prevy/ *a.* unexpected. —*n.m.* unexpected incident.

imprim|er /ɛ̃prime/ *v.t.* print; (*marquer*) imprint; (*transmettre*) impart. ~ante *n.f.* (*d'un ordinateur*) printer. ~é *a.* printed; *n.m.* (*formulaire*) printed form. ~erie *n.f.* printing works. ~eur *n.m.* printer.

improbable /ɛ̃prɔbabl/ *a.* unlikely, improbable.

impropre /ɛ̃prɔpr/ *a.* incorrect.

improvis|er /ɛ̃prɔvize/ *v.t./i.* improvise. ~ation *n.f.* improvisation.

improviste (à l') /(al)ɛ̃prɔvist/ *adv.* unexpectedly.

imprud|ent, ~ente /ɛ̃prydã, -t/ *a.* careless. **il est ~ent de**, it is unwise to. ~emment /-amã/ *adv.* carelessly. ~ence *n.f.* carelessness; (*acte*) careless action.

impuissan|t, ~te /ɛ̃pɥisã, -t/ *a.* helpless; (*méd.*) impotent. ~t à, powerless to. ~ce *n.f.* helplessness; (*méd.*) impotence.

impuls|if, ~ve /ɛ̃pylsif, -v/ *a.* impulsive.

impunément /ɛ̃pynemã/ *adv.* with impunity.

impur /ɛ̃pyr/ *a.* impure. ~eté *n.f.* impurity.

inabordable /inabɔrdabl/ *a.* (*prix*) prohibitive.

inacceptable /inaksɛptabl/ *a.* un-

acceptable; (*scandaleux*) outrageous.

inaccessible /inaksesibl/ *a.* inaccessible.

inachevé /inaʃve/ *a.* unfinished.

inacti|f, ~ve /inaktif, -v/ *a.* inactive.

inaction /inaksjɔ̃/ *n.f.* inactivity.

inadapté, ~e /inadapte/ *a.*, *n.m.*, *f.* (*psych.*) maladjusted person.

inadmissible /inadmisibl/ *a.* unacceptable.

inaltérable /inalterabl/ *a.* stable, that does not deteriorate.

inanimé /inanime/ *a.* (*évanoui*) unconscious; (*mort*) lifeless.

inaperçu /inapɛrsy/ *a.* unnoticed.

inappréciable /inapresjabl/ *a.* invaluable.

inapte /inapt/ *a.* unsuited (à, to).

inattendu /inatãdy/ *a.* unexpected.

inattenti|f, ~ve /inatãtif, -v/ *a.* inattentive (à, to).

inattention /inatãsjɔ̃/ *n.f.* inattention.

inaugur|er /inɔgyre/ *v.t.* inaugurate. ~ation *n.f.* inauguration.

inaugur|al (*m. pl.* ~aux) /inɔgyral, -o/ *a.* inaugural.

incalculable /ɛ̃kalkylabl/ *a.* incalculable.

incapable /ɛ̃kapabl/ *a.* incapable (**de qch.**, of sth.). ~ **de faire**, unable to do, incapable of doing. —*n.m./f.* incompetent.

incapacité /ɛ̃kapasite/ *n.f.* incapacity. **dans l'~ de**, unable to.

incarcérer /ɛ̃karsere/ *v.t.* incarcerate.

incarn|er /ɛ̃karne/ *v.t.* embody. ~é *a.* (*ongle*) ingrowing.

incassable /ɛ̃kasabl/ *a.* unbreakable.

incend|ie /ɛ̃sãdi/ *n.m.* fire. ~ie

criminel, arson. **~ier** v.t. set fire to.

incert|ain, **~aine** /ɛ̃sɛrtɛ̃, -ɛn/ a. uncertain; (contour) vague. **~itude** n.f. uncertainty.

incessamment /ɛ̃sɛsamɑ̃/ adv. shortly.

incessant, **~e** /ɛ̃sɛsɑ̃, -t/ a. incessant.

inchangé /ɛ̃ʃɑ̃ʒe/ a. unchanged.

incidence /ɛ̃sidɑ̃s/ n.f. effect.

incident /ɛ̃sidɑ̃/ n.m. incident. **~ technique,** technical hitch.

incinér|er /ɛ̃sinere/ v.t. incinerate; (mort) cremate. **~ateur** n.m. incinerator.

inciser /ɛ̃size/ v.t. (abcès etc.) lance.

incit|er /ɛ̃site/ v.t. incite (à, to). **~ation** n.f. incitement.

inclinaison /ɛ̃klinɛzɔ̃/ n.f. incline; (de la tête) tilt.

inclin|er /ɛ̃kline/ v.t. tilt, lean; (courber) bend. **~ la tête,** (approuver) nod; (révérence) bow.

incl|ure /ɛ̃klyr/ v.t. include; (enfermer) enclose. **jusqu'au lundi ~us,** up to and including Monday.

incohéren|t, **~te** /ɛ̃kɔerɑ̃, -t/ a. incoherent. **~ce** n.f. incoherence.

incollable /ɛ̃kɔlabl/ a. il est **~,** he can't be stumped.

incolore /ɛ̃kɔlɔr/ a. colourless; (crème, verre) clear.

incombustible /ɛ̃kɔ̃bystibl/ a. incombustible.

incomparable /ɛ̃kɔ̃parabl/ a. incomparable.

incompatib|le /ɛ̃kɔ̃patibl/ a. incompatible. **~ilité** n.f. incompatibility.

incompéten|t, **~te** /ɛ̃kɔ̃petɑ̃, -t/ a. incompetent. **~ce** n.f. incompetence.

incompl|et, **~ète** /ɛ̃kɔ̃plɛ, -t/ a. incomplete.

incompréhensible /ɛ̃kɔ̃preɑ̃sibl/ a. incomprehensible.

incompréhension /ɛ̃kɔ̃preɑ̃sjɔ̃/ n.f. lack of understanding.

inconcevable /ɛ̃kɔ̃svabl/ a. inconceivable.

inconditionnel, **~le** /ɛ̃kɔ̃disjɔnɛl/ a. unconditional.

inconduite /ɛ̃kɔ̃dμit/ n.f. loose behaviour.

inconfort /ɛ̃kɔ̃fɔr/ n.m. discomfort. **~able** /-tabl/ a. uncomfortable.

inconnu, **~e** /ɛ̃kɔny/ a. unknown (à, to). —n.m., f. stranger. —n.m. **l'~,** the unknown. —n.f. unknown (quantity).

inconscient, **~iente** /ɛ̃kɔ̃sjɑ̃, -t/ a. unconscious (de, of); (fou) mad. —n.m. (psych.) subconscious.

inconsolable /ɛ̃kɔ̃sɔlabl/ a. inconsolable.

incontestable /ɛ̃kɔ̃tɛstabl/ a. indisputable. **~é** a. undisputed.

incontinen|t, **~te** /ɛ̃kɔ̃tinɑ̃, -t/ a. incontinent. **~ce** n.f. incontinence.

incontrôlable /ɛ̃kɔ̃trolabl/ a. unverifiable.

inconvenan|t, **~te** /ɛ̃kɔ̃vnɑ̃, -t/ a. improper. **~ce** n.f. impropriety.

inconvénient /ɛ̃kɔ̃venjɑ̃/ n.m. disadvantage; (risque) risk; (objection) objection.

incorpor|er /ɛ̃kɔrpore/ v.t. incorporate; (mil.) enlist.

incorrect /ɛ̃kɔrɛkt/ a. (faux) incorrect; (malséant) improper; (impoli) impolite.

incorrigible /ɛ̃kɔriʒibl/ a. incorrigible.

increvable /ɛ̃krəvabl/ a. (fam.) tireless.

incriminer /ɛ̃krimine/ *v.t.* incriminate.

incroyable /ɛ̃krwajabl/ *a.* incredible.

incrust|er /ɛ̃kryste/ *v.t. (décorer)* inlay (**de**, with). **s'~er** *(invité: péj.)* take root. **~ation** *n.f.* inlay.

incubateur /ɛ̃kybatœr/ *n.m.* incubator.

inculp|er /ɛ̃kylpe/ *v.t.* charge (**de**, with). **~ation** *n.f.* charge. **~é, ~ée** *n.m., f.* accused.

inculquer /ɛ̃kylke/ *v.t.* instil (**à**, into).

inculte /ɛ̃kylt/ *a.* uncultivated; *(personne)* uneducated.

incurable /ɛ̃kyrabl/ *a.* incurable.

Inde /ɛ̃d/ *n.f.* India.

indécen|t /ɛ̃desɑ̃, -t/ *a.* indecent. **~ce** *n.f.* indecency.

indéchiffrable /ɛ̃deʃifrabl/ *a.* indecipherable.

indécis, ~e /ɛ̃desi, -z/ *a.* indecisive; *(qui n'a pas encore pris de décision)* undecided. **~ion** /-izjɔ̃/ *n.f.* indecision.

indéfini /ɛ̃defini/ *a.* indefinite; *(vague)* undefined. **~ment** *adv.* indefinitely.

indélébile /ɛ̃delebil/ *a.* indelible.

indemne /ɛ̃dɛmn/ *a.* unharmed.

indemniser /ɛ̃dɛmnize/ *v.t.* compensate (**de**, for).

indemnité /ɛ̃dɛmnite/ *n.f.* indemnity; *(allocation)* allowance.

indéniable /ɛ̃denjabl/ *a.* undeniable.

indépend|ant, ~ante /ɛ̃depɑ̃dɑ̃, -t/ *a.* independent. **~amment** *adv.* independently. **~amment de**, apart from. **~ance** *n.f.* independence.

indescriptible /ɛ̃dɛskriptibl/ *a.* indescribable.

indestructible /ɛ̃dɛstryktibl/ *a.* indestructible.

indéterminé /ɛ̃detɛrmine/ *a.* unspecified.

index /ɛ̃dɛks/ *n.m.* forefinger; *(liste)* index. **~er** *v.t.* index.

indicateur /ɛ̃dikatœr/ *n.m. (livre)* guide; *(techn.)* indicator. **~ des chemins de fer**, railway timetable. **~ des rues**, street directory.

indicatif /ɛ̃dikatif/ *n.m. (radio)* signature tune; *(téléphonique)* dialling code; *(gram.)* indicative.

indication /ɛ̃dikasjɔ̃/ *n.f.* indication; *(renseignement)* information; *(directive)* instruction.

indice /ɛ̃dis/ *n.m.* sign; *(dans une enquête)* clue; *(des prix)* index; *(de salaire)* rating.

indien, ~ne /ɛ̃djɛ̃, -jɛn/ *a. & n.m., f.* Indian.

indifféremment /ɛ̃diferamɑ̃/ *adv.* equally.

indifféren|t, ~te /ɛ̃diferɑ̃, -t/ *a.* indifferent (**à**, to). **~ce** *n.f.* indifference.

indigène /ɛ̃diʒɛn/ *a. & n.m./f.* native.

indigest|e /ɛ̃diʒɛst/ *a.* indigestible. **~ion** *n.f.* indigestion.

indignation /ɛ̃diɲasjɔ̃/ *n.f.* indignation.

indigne /ɛ̃diɲ/ *a.* unworthy (**de**, of); *(acte)* vile.

indigner /ɛ̃diɲe/ **s'~** *v. pr.* become indignant (**de**, at).

indiquer /ɛ̃dike/ *v.t.* show, indicate; *(renseigner sur)* point out, tell; *(déterminer)* give, state, appoint. **~ du doigt**, point to *ou* out *ou* at.

indirect /ɛ̃dirɛkt/ *a.* indirect.

indiscipliné /ɛ̃disipline/ *a.* unruly.

indiscr|et, ~ète /ɛ̃diskrɛ, -t/ *a.* inquisitive. **~étion** *n.f.* indiscretion; inquisitiveness.

indiscutable /ɛ̃diskytabl/ *a.* unquestionable.

indispensable /ɛ̃dispɑ̃sabl/ *a.* indispensable.

individ|u /ɛ̃dividy/ *n.m.* individual. **~ualiste** /-ualist/ *a./f.* individualist.

individuel, ~le /ɛ̃dividɥɛl/ *a.* individual; (*opinion*) personal. **chambre ~le,** single room.

indivisible /ɛ̃divizibl/ *a.* indivisible.

indolore /ɛ̃dɔlɔr/ *a.* painless.

Indonésie /ɛ̃dɔnezi/ *n.f.* Indonesia.

Indonésien, ~ne /ɛ̃dɔnezjɛ̃, -jɛn/ *a. & n.m., f.* Indonesian.

indu, ~e /ɛ̃dy/ *a.* **à une heure ~e,** at some ungodly hour.

induire /ɛ̃dɥir/ *v.t.* infer (**de,** from). **~ en erreur,** mislead.

indulgen|t, ~te /ɛ̃dylʒɑ̃, -t/ *a.* indulgent; (*clément*) lenient. **~ce** *n.f.* indulgence; leniency.

industr|ie /ɛ̃dystri/ *n.f.* industry. **~ialisé** *a.* industrialized.

industriel, ~le /ɛ̃dystrijɛl/ *a.* industrial. **—***n.m.* industrialist. **~lement** *adv.* industrially.

inébranlable /inebrɑ̃labl/ *a.* unshakeable.

inédit, ~e /inedi, -t/ *a.* unpublished; (*fig.*) original.

inefficace /inefikas/ *a.* ineffective.

inég|al (*m. pl.* **~aux**) /inegal, -o/ *a.* unequal; (*irrégulier*) uneven. **~alité** *n.f.* (*injustice*) inequality; (*différence*) difference (**de,** between).

inéluctable /inelyktabl/ *a.* inescapable.

inépuisable /inepɥizabl/ *a.* inexhaustible.

inespéré /inɛspere/ *a.* unhoped for.

inestimable /inɛstimabl/ *a.* priceless.

inévitable /inevitabl/ *a.* inevitable.

inexact, ~e /inɛgza(kt), -akt/ *a.*

(*imprécis*) inaccurate; (*incorrect*) incorrect.

inexcusable /inɛkskyzabl/ *a.* unforgivable.

inexistant, ~e /inɛgzistɑ̃, -t/ *a.* non-existent.

inexpérience /inɛksperjɑ̃s/ *n.f.* inexperience.

inexpli|cable /inɛksplikabl/ *a.* inexplicable. **~qué** *a.* unexplained.

infaillible /ɛ̃fajibl/ *a.* infallible.

infantile /ɛ̃fɑ̃til/ *a.* infantile.

infarctus /ɛ̃farktys/ *n.m.* coronary (thrombosis).

infatigable /ɛ̃fatigabl/ *a.* tireless.

infect /ɛ̃fɛkt/ *a.* revolting.

infect|er /ɛ̃fɛkte/ *v.t.* infect. **s'~er** *v. pr.* become infected. **~ion** /-ksjɔ̃/ *n.f.* infection.

infectieu|x, ~se /ɛ̃fɛksjø, -z/ *a.* infectious.

inférieur, ~e /ɛ̃ferjœr/ *a.* (*plus bas*) lower; (*moins bon*) inferior (**à,** to). **—***n.m., f.* inferior. **~ à,** (*plus petit que*) smaller than.

infériorité /ɛ̃ferjɔrite/ *n.f.* inferiority.

infern|al (*m. pl.* **~aux**) /ɛ̃fɛrnal, -o/ *a.* infernal.

infid|èle /ɛ̃fidɛl/ *a.* unfaithful. **~élité** *n.f.* unfaithfulness; (*acte*) infidelity.

infiltr|er (s') /(s)ɛ̃filtre/ *v. pr.* **s'~er (dans),** (*personnes, idées, etc.*) infiltrate; (*liquide*) percolate. **~ation** *n.f.* infiltration.

infime /ɛ̃fim/ *a.* tiny, minute.

infini, ~e /ɛ̃fini/ *a.* infinite. **—***n.m.* infinity. **à l'~,** endlessly. **~ment** *adv.* infinitely.

infinité /ɛ̃finite/ *n.f.* **une ~ de,** an infinite amount of.

infinitif /ɛ̃finitif/ *n.m.* infinitive.

infirm|e /ɛ̃firm/ *a. & n.m./f.* disabled (person). **~ité** *n.f.* disability.

infirm|erie /ɛ̃firmɔri/ *n.f.* sickbay;

infirmary. **~ier** *n.m.* (male) nurse. **~ière** *n.f.* nurse.

inflammable /ɛ̃flamabl/ *a.* (in)flammable.

inflammation /ɛ̃flamɑsjɔ̃/ *n.f.* inflammation.

inflation /ɛ̃flɑsjɔ̃/ *n.f.* inflation.

influen|ce /ɛ̃flyɑ̃s/ *n.f.* influence. **~çable** *a.* easily influenced. **~cer** *v.t.* influence.

influent, **~e** /ɛ̃flyɑ̃, -t/ *a.* influential.

info /ɛ̃fo/ *n.f.* (some) news. **les ~s**, the news.

informaticien, **~ne** /ɛ̃fɔrmatisjɛ̃, -jɛn/ *n.m., f.* computer scientist.

information /ɛ̃fɔrmɑsjɔ̃/ *n.f.* information; (*jurid.*) inquiry. **une ~**, (some) information; (*nouvelle*) (some) news. **les ~s**, the news.

informatique /ɛ̃fɔrmatik/ *n.f.* computer science; (*techniques*) data processing.

informer /ɛ̃fɔrme/ *v.t.* inform (de, about, of). **s'~** *v. pr.* enquire (de, about).

infraction /ɛ̃fraksjɔ̃/ *n.f.* offence. **~ à**, breach of.

infranchissable /ɛ̃frɑ̃ʃisabl/ *a.* impassable; (*fig.*) insuperable.

infrarouge /ɛ̃fraruʒ/ *a.* infra-red.

infrastructure /ɛ̃frastryktyr/ *n.f.* infrastructure.

infus|er /ɛ̃fyze/ *v.t./i.* infuse, brew. **~ion** *n.f.* herb-tea, infusion.

ingénieur /ɛ̃ʒenjœr/ *n.m.* engineer.

ingén|ieux, **~ieuse** /ɛ̃ʒenjø, -z/ *a.* ingenious. **~iosité** *n.f.* ingenuity.

ingér|er (s') /(s)ɛ̃ʒere/ *v. pr.* **s'~er dans**, interfere in. **~ence** *n.f.* interference.

ingrat, **~e** /ɛ̃gra, -t/ *a.* ungrateful; (*pénible*) thankless; (*disgracieux*) unattractive. **~itude** /-tityd/ *n.f.* ingratitude.

ingrédient /ɛ̃gredjɑ̃/ *n.m.* ingredient.

inhabité /inabite/ *a.* uninhabited.

inhabituel, **~le** /inabityɛl/ *a.* unusual.

inhalation /inalɑsjɔ̃/ *n.f.* inhaling.

inhospital|ier, **~ière** /inɔspitalje, -jɛr/ *a.* inhospitable.

inhumain, **~e** /inymɛ̃, -ɛn/ *a.* inhuman.

inhum|er /inyme/ *v.t.* bury. **~ation** *n.f.* burial.

inimaginable /inimaʒinabl/ *a.* unimaginable.

ininterrompu /inɛ̃tɛrɔ̃py/ *a.* continuous, uninterrupted.

initiale /inisjal/ *n.f.* initial.

initialis|er /inisjalize/ (*comput.*) format. **~ation** *n.f.* formatting.

initiative /inisjativ/ *n.f.* initiative.

initier /inisje/ *v.t.* initiate (à, into). **s'~** *v. pr.* become initiated (à, into).

inject|er /ɛ̃ʒɛkte/ *v.t.* inject. **~ion** /-ksjɔ̃/ *n.f.* injection.

injur|e /ɛ̃ʒyr/ *n.f.* insult. **~ier** *v.t.* insult.

injust|e /ɛ̃ʒyst/ *a.* unjust, unfair. **~ice** *n.f.* injustice.

innocent, **~e** /inɔsɑ̃, -t/ *a. & n.m., f.* innocent. **~ce** *n.f.* innocence.

innombrable /inɔ̃brabl/ *a.* countless.

inoccupé /inɔkype/ *a.* unoccupied.

inoculer /inɔkyle/ *v.t.* inoculate.

inodore /inɔdɔr/ *a.* odourless.

inoffensi|f, **~ve** /inɔfɑ̃sif, -v/ *a.* harmless.

inond|er /inɔ̃de/ *v.t.* flood; (*mouiller*) soak; (*envahir*) inundate (de, with). **~ation** *n.f.* flood; (*action*) flooding.

inoubliable /inublijabl/ *a.* unforgettable.

inouï /inwi/ *a.* incredible.

inox /inɔks/ *n.m.* (P.) stainless steel.

inoxydable /inɔksidabl/ *a.* **acier** ~, stainless steel.

inqui|et, ~iète /ɛ̃kjɛ, -ɛkjɛt/ *a.* worried. —*n.m., f.* worrier.

inquiét|er /ɛ̃kjete/ *v.t.* worry. **s'~er** worry (de, about). ~**ant**, ~**ante** *a.* worrying.

inquiétude /ɛ̃kjetyd/ *n.f.* anxiety, worry.

insalubre /ɛ̃salybr/ *a.* unhealthy.

insatiable /ɛ̃sasjabl/ *a.* insatiable.

insatisfaisant, ~e /ɛ̃satisfəzɑ̃, -t/ *a.* unsatisfactory.

insatisfait, ~e /ɛ̃satisfɛ, -t/ *a.* (*mécontent*) dissatisfied; (*frustré*) unfulfilled.

inscription /ɛ̃skripsjɔ̃/ *n.f.* inscription; (*immatriculation*) enrolment.

inscrire† /ɛ̃skrir/ *v.t.* write (down); (*graver, tracer*) inscribe; (*personne*) enrol; (*sur une liste*) put down. **s'~** *v. pr.* put one's name down. **s'~ à**, (*école*) enrol at; (*club, parti*) join; (*examen*) enter for.

insecte /ɛ̃sɛkt/ *n.m.* insect.

insecticide /ɛ̃sɛktisid/ *n.m.* insecticide.

insécurité /ɛ̃sekyrite/ *n.f.* insecurity.

insensé /ɛ̃sɑ̃se/ *a.* mad.

insensib|le /ɛ̃sɑ̃sibl/ *a.* insensitive (à, to); (*graduel*) imperceptible.

insérer /ɛ̃sere/ *v.t.* insert.

insigne /ɛ̃siɲ/ *n.m.* badge.

insignifian|t, ~te /ɛ̃siɲifjɑ̃, -t/ *a.* insignificant. ~**ce** *n.f.* insignificance.

insinuer /ɛ̃sinɥe/ *v.t.* insinuate.

insipide /ɛ̃sipid/ *a.* insipid.

insistan|t, ~te /ɛ̃sistɑ̃, -t/ *a.* insistent. ~**ce** *n.f.* insistence.

insist|er /ɛ̃siste/ *v.i.* insist (**pour faire**, on doing). ~ **sur**, stress.

insolation /ɛ̃sɔlasjɔ̃/ *n.f.* (*méd.*) sunstroke.

insolen|t, ~te /ɛ̃sɔlɑ̃, -t/ *a.* insolent. ~**ce** *n.f.* insolence.

insolite /ɛ̃sɔlit/ *a.* unusual.

insomnie /ɛ̃sɔmni/ *n.f.* insomnia.

insonoriser /ɛ̃sɔnɔrize/ *v.t.* soundproof.

insoucian|t, ~te /ɛ̃susjɑ̃, -t/ *a.* carefree. ~**ce** *n.f.* unconcern.

insoutenable /ɛ̃sutnabl/ *a.* unbearable; (*argument*) untenable.

inspec|ter /ɛ̃spɛkte/ *v.t.* inspect. ~**teur, ~trice** *n.m., f.* inspector. ~**tion** /-ksjɔ̃/ *n.f.* inspection.

inspir|er /ɛ̃spire/ *v.t.* inspire. —*v.i.* breathe in. ~**ation** *n.f.* inspiration; (*respiration*) breath.

instable /ɛ̃stabl/ *a.* unstable; (*temps*) unsettled; (*meuble, équilibre*) unsteady.

install|er /ɛ̃stale/ *v.t.* install; (*gaz, meuble*) put in; (*étagère*) put up; (*équiper*) fit out. **s'~er** *v. pr.* settle (down); (*emménager*) settle in. ~**ation** *n.f.* installation; (*de local*) fitting out; (*de locataire*) settling in. ~**ations** *n.f. pl.* (*appareils*) fittings.

instant /ɛ̃stɑ̃/ *n.m.* moment, instant. **à l'~**, this instant.

instantané /ɛ̃stɑ̃tane/ *a.* instantaneous; (*café*) instant.

instinct /ɛ̃stɛ̃/ *n.m.* instinct. **d'~**, instinctively.

instincti|f, ~ve /ɛ̃stɛ̃ktif, -v/ *a.* instinctive. ~**vement** *adv.* instinctively.

instit /ɛ̃stit/ *n.m./f.* (*fam.*) teacher.

instituer /ɛ̃stitɥe/ *v.t.* establish.

institut /ɛ̃stity/ *n.m.* institute. ~ **de beauté**, beauty parlour.

institu|teur, ~trice /ɛ̃stitytœr, -tris/ *n.m., f.* primary-school teacher.

institution /ɛ̃stitysjɔ̃/ n.f. institution; (école) private school.

instructif, **∼ve** /ɛ̃stryktif, -v/ a. instructive.

instruction /ɛ̃stryksjɔ̃/ n.f. education; (document) directive. **∼s**, (ordres, mode d'emploi) instructions.

instruire† /ɛ̃strɥir/ v.t. teach, educate. **∼ de**, inform of. **s'∼** v. pr. educate o.s.

instruit, **∼e** /ɛ̃strɥi, -t/ a. educated.

instrument /ɛ̃strymɑ̃/ n.m. instrument; (outil) implement.

insuffisant, **∼te** /ɛ̃syfizɑ̃, -t/ a. inadequate; (en nombre) insufficient. **∼ce** n.f. inadequacy.

insulaire /ɛ̃syler/ a. island. —n.m./f. islander.

insuline /ɛ̃sylin/ n.f. insulin.

insulte| /ɛ̃sylt/ n.f. insult. **∼er** v.t insult.

insupportable /ɛ̃syportabl/ a. unbearable.

insurmontable /ɛ̃syrmɔ̃tabl/ a. insurmountable.

insurrection /ɛ̃syreksjɔ̃/ n.f. insurrection.

intact /ɛ̃takt/ a. intact.

intégral, **∼aux** /ɛ̃tegral, -o/ a. complete; (édition) unabridged. **∼alement** adv. in full.

intègre /ɛ̃tegr/ a. upright.

intégrer /ɛ̃tegre/ v.t., **s'∼** v. pr. integrate.

intégri|**ste** /ɛ̃tegrist/ a. fundamentalist. **∼sme** /-sm/ n.m. fundamentalism.

intégrité /ɛ̃tegrite/ n.f. integrity.

intellect /ɛ̃telekt/ n.m. intellect. **∼uel**, **∼uelle** /-ɥel/ a. & n.m., f. intellectual.

intelligence /ɛ̃teliʒɑ̃s/ n.f. intelligence; (compréhension) understanding; (complicité) complicity.

intelligent, **∼ente** /ɛ̃teliʒɑ̃, -t/

a. intelligent. **∼emment** /-amɑ̃/ adv. intelligently.

intelligible /ɛ̃teliʒibl/ a. intelligible.

intempéries /ɛ̃tɑ̃peri/ n.f. pl. severe weather.

intenable /ɛ̃tnabl/ a. unbearable; (enfant) impossible.

intens|**e** /ɛ̃tɑ̃s/ a. intense; (circulation) heavy. **∼ément** adv. intensely. **∼ité** n.f. intensity.

intensif, **∼ve** /ɛ̃tɑ̃sif, -v/ a. intensive.

intenter /ɛ̃tɑ̃te/ v.t. **∼ un procès ou une action**, institute proceedings (à, contre, against).

intention /ɛ̃tɑ̃sjɔ̃/ n.f. intention (de faire, of doing). **à l'∼ de qn.**, for s.o. **∼né** /-jone/ a. **bien/mal ∼né**, well-/ill-intentioned.

inter- /ɛ̃ter/ préf. inter-.

intercaler /ɛ̃terkale/ v.t. insert.

intercéder /ɛ̃tersede/ v.i. intercede (**en faveur de**, on behalf of).

intercepter /ɛ̃tersɛpte/ v.t. intercept.

interchangeable /ɛ̃terʃɑ̃ʒabl/ a. interchangeable.

interdiction /ɛ̃terdiksjɔ̃/ n.f. ban. **∼ de fumer**, no smoking.

interdire† /ɛ̃terdir/ v.t. forbid; (officiellement) ban, prohibit. **∼ à qn. de faire**, forbid s.o. to do.

intéressant, **∼e** /ɛ̃teresɑ̃, -t/ a. interesting; (avantageux) attractive.

intéressé, **∼e** /ɛ̃terese/ a. (en cause) concerned; (pour profiter) self-interested. —n.m., f. person concerned.

intéresser /ɛ̃terese/ v.t. interest; (concerner) concern. **s'∼ à**, be interested in.

intérêt /ɛ̃terɛ/ n.m. interest; (égoïsme) self-interest. **∼(s)**, (comm.) interest. **vous avez ∼ à**, it is in your interest to.

interférence /ɛtɛrferɑ̃s/ n.f. interference.

intérieur /ɛ̃terjœr/ a. inner, inside; (vol, politique) domestic; (vie, calme) inner. —n.m. interior; (de boîte, tiroir) inside. **à l'~ (de)**, inside; (fig.) within.

intérim /ɛ̃terim/ n.m. interim. **faire de l'~**, temp. **~aire** a. temporary, interim.

interjection /ɛ̃tɛrʒɛksjɔ̃/ n.f. interjection.

interlocu|teur, ~trice /ɛ̃tɛrlɔkytœr, -tris/ n.m., f. **son ~teur**, the person one is speaking to.

intermédiaire /ɛ̃tɛrmedjɛr/ a. intermediate. —n.m./f. intermediary.

interminable /ɛ̃tɛrminabl/ a. endless.

internat /ɛ̃tɛrna/ n.m. boarding-school.

internation|al (m. pl. **~aux**) /ɛ̃tɛrnasjɔnal, -o/ a. international.

interne /ɛ̃tɛrn/ a. internal. —n.m./f. (scol.) boarder.

interner /ɛ̃tɛrne/ v.t. (pol.) intern; (méd.) confine.

interpeller /ɛ̃tɛrpəle/ v.t. shout to; (apostropher) shout at; (interroger) question.

interphone /ɛ̃tɛrfɔn/ n.m. intercom.

interposer (s') /(s)ɛ̃tɛrpoze/ v. pr. intervene.

interpr|ète /ɛ̃tɛrprɛt/ n.m./f. interpreter; (artiste) performer.

interprét|er /ɛ̃tɛrprete/ v.t. interpret; (jouer) play; (chanter) sing. **~ation** n.f. interpretation; (d'artiste) performance.

interrogat|if, ~ve /ɛ̃terɔgatif, -v/ a. interrogative.

interrogatoire /ɛ̃terɔgatwar/ n.m. interrogation.

interro|ger /ɛ̃terɔʒe/ v.t. question; (élève) test. **~gation** n.f. question; (action) questioning; (épreuve) test.

interr|ompre† /ɛ̃terɔ̃pr/ v.t. break off, interrupt. **~upteur** n.m. switch. **~uption** n.f. interruption; (arrêt) break.

intersection /ɛ̃tɛrsɛksjɔ̃/ n.f. intersection.

intervalle /ɛ̃tɛrval/ n.m. space; (temps) interval.

interven|ir† /ɛ̃tɛrvənir/ v.i. intervene; (survenir) occur; (méd.) operate. **~tion** /-vɑ̃sjɔ̃/ n.f. intervention; (méd.) operation.

interview /ɛ̃tɛrvju/ n.f. interview. **~er** /-ve/ v.t. interview.

intestin /ɛ̃tɛstɛ̃/ n.m. intestine.

intim|e /ɛ̃tim/ a. intimate; (fête, vie) private; (dîner) quiet. —n.m./f. intimate friend. **~ement** adv. intimately. **~ité** n.f. intimacy; (vie privée) privacy.

intolérable /ɛ̃tɔlerabl/ a. intolerable.

intoléran|t, ~te /ɛ̃tɔlerɑ̃, -t/ a. intolerant. **~ce** n.f. intolerance.

intonation /ɛ̃tɔnasjɔ̃/ n.f. intonation.

intoxi|quer /ɛ̃tɔksike/ v.t. poison. **~cation** n.f. poisoning.

intraduisible /ɛ̃tradɥizibl/ a. untranslatable.

intransigean|t, ~te /ɛ̃trɑ̃siʒɑ̃, -t/ a. intransigent. **~ce** n.f. intransigence.

intransiti|f, ~ve /ɛ̃trɑ̃zitif, -v/ a. intransitive.

intraveineu|x, ~se /ɛ̃travɛno, -z/ a. intravenous.

intrigu|e /ɛ̃trig/ n.f. intrigue; (théâtre) plot. **~er** v.t./i. intrigue.

introduction /ɛ̃trɔdyksjɔ̃/ n.f. introduction.

introduire† /ɛ̃trɔdɥir/ v.t. introduce, bring in; (insérer) put in.

insert. ~ **qn.**, show s.o. in. **s'~ dans**, get into, enter.

introuvable /ɛ̃truvabl/ a. that cannot be found.

intrus, ~e /ɛ̃try, -z/ n.m., f. intruder. ~**ion** /-zjɔ̃/ n.f. intrusion.

intuition /ɛ̃tɥisjɔ̃/ n.f. intuition.

inusable /inyzabl/ a. hard-wearing.

inutil|e /inytil/ a. useless; (vain) needless. ~**ement** adv. needlessly. ~**ité** n.f. uselessness.

inutilisable /inytilizabl/ a. unusable.

invalide /ɛ̃valid/ a. & n.m./f. disabled (person).

invariable /ɛ̃varjabl/ a. invariable.

invasion /ɛ̃vazjɔ̃/ n.f. invasion.

inventaire /ɛ̃vɑ̃tɛr/ n.m. inventory. **faire l'~ de**, take stock of.

invent|er /ɛ̃vɑ̃te/ v.t. invent. ~**eur** n.m. inventor. ~**ion** /ɛ̃vɑ̃sjɔ̃/ n.f. invention.

inverse /ɛ̃vɛrs/ a. opposite; (ordre) reverse. —n.m. reverse. ~**ment** /-əmɑ̃/ adv. conversely.

invers|er /ɛ̃vɛrse/ v.t. reverse, invert. ~**ion** n.f. inversion.

invest|ir /ɛ̃vɛstir/ v.t. invest. ~**issement** n.m. (comm.) investment.

investiture /ɛ̃vɛstityr/ n.f. nomination.

invincible /ɛ̃vɛ̃sibl/ a. invincible.

invisible /ɛ̃vizibl/ a. invisible.

invit|er /ɛ̃vite/ v.t. invite (à, to). ~**ation** n.f. invitation. **s'~é**, ~**ée** n.m., f. guest.

involontaire /ɛ̃vɔlɔ̃tɛr/ a. involuntary.

invraisembl|able /ɛ̃vrɛsɑ̃blabl/ a. improbable; (incroyable) incredible.

iode /jɔd/ n.m. iodine.

ion /jɔ̃/ n.m. ion.

ira, irait /ira, irɛ/ voir aller[1].

Irak /irak/ n.m. Iraq. ~**ien**, ~**ienne** a. & n.m., f. Iraqi.

Iran /irɑ̃/ n.m. Iran. ~**ien**, ~**ienne** /iranjɛ̃, -jɛn/ a. & n.m., f. Iranian.

iris /iris/ n.m. iris.

irlandais, ~e /irlɑ̃dɛ, -z/ a. Irish. —n.m., f. Irishman, Irishwoman.

Irlande /irlɑ̃d/ n.f. Ireland.

iron|ie /irɔni/ n.f. irony. ~**ique** a. ironic(al).

irrationnel, ~**le** /irasjɔnɛl/ a. irrational.

irréalisable /irealizabl/ a. (projet) unworkable.

irrégul|ier, ~**ière** /iregylje, -jɛr/ a. irregular. ~**arité** n.f. irregularity.

irremplaçable /irɑ̃plasabl/ a. irreplaceable.

irréparable /ireparabl/ a. beyond repair.

irréprochable /ireprɔʃabl/ a. flawless.

irrésistible /irezistibl/ a. irresistible; (drôle) hilarious.

irrespirable /irɛspirabl/ a. stifling.

irresponsable /irɛspɔ̃sabl/ a. irresponsible.

irréversible /irevɛrsibl/ a. irreversible.

irrigation /irigasjɔ̃/ n.f. irrigation.

irriguer /irige/ v.t. irrigate.

irrit|er /irite/ v.t. irritate. **s'~er de**, be annoyed at. ~**able** a. irritable. ~**ation** n.f. irritation.

Islam /islam/ n.m. Islam.

islamique /islamik/ a. Islamic.

islandais, ~e /islɑ̃dɛ, -z/ a. Icelandic. —n.m., f. Icelander. —n.m. (lang.) Icelandic.

Islande /islɑ̃d/ n.f. Iceland.

isolé /izole/ a. isolated.

isol|er /izole/ v.t. isolate; (électr.) insulate. **s'~er** v. pr. isolate o.s. **~ant** n.m. insulating material. **~ation** n.f. insulation. **~ement** n.m. isolation.

isotope /izɔtɔp/ n.m. isotope.

Israël /israɛl/ n.m. Israel.

israélien, ~ne /israeljɛ̃, -jɛn/ a. & n.m., f. Israeli.

israélite /israelit/ a. Jewish. —n.m./f. Jew, Jewess.

issue /isy/ n.f. exit; (résultat) outcome; (fig.) solution. **rue ou voie sans ~**, dead end.

Italie /itali/ n.f. Italy.

italien, ~ne /italjɛ̃, -jɛn/ a. & n.m., f. Italian. —n.m. (lang.) Italian.

italique /italik/ n.m. italics.

itinéraire /itinerɛr/ n.m. itinerary, route.

I.U.T. /iyte/ n.m. (abrév.) polytechnic.

I.V.G. /iveʒe/ n.f. (abrév.) abortion.

ivoire /ivwar/ n.m. ivory.

ivr|e /ivr/ a. drunk. **~esse** n.f. drunkenness. **~ogne** n.m. drunk(ard).

J

j' /ʒ/ voir je.

jacinthe /ʒasɛ̃t/ n.f. hyacinth.

jade /ʒad/ n.m. jade.

jaillir /ʒajir/ v.i. (liquide) spurt (out); (lumière) stream out; (apparaître, fuser) burst forth.

jalou|x, ~se /ʒalu, -z/ a. jealous. **~sie** n.f. jealousy.

jamais /ʒamɛ/ adv. ever. (ne) **~**, never.

jambe /ʒɑ̃b/ n.f. leg.

jambon /ʒɑ̃bɔ̃/ n.m. ham.

jante /ʒɑ̃t/ n.f. rim.

janvier /ʒɑ̃vje/ n.m. January.

Japon /ʒapɔ̃/ n.m. Japan.

japonais, ~e /ʒapɔnɛ, -z/ a. & n.m., f. Japanese. —n.m. (lang.) Japanese.

jaquette /ʒakɛt/ n.f. (de livre, femme) jacket; (d'homme) morning coat.

jardin /ʒardɛ̃/ n.m. garden. **~ d'enfants**, nursery (school). **~ public**, public park.

jardin|er /ʒardine/ v.i. garden. **~age** n.m. gardening. **~ier, ~ière** n.m., f. gardener; n.f. (meuble) plant-stand. **~ière de légumes**, mixed vegetables.

jarret /ʒarɛ/ n.m. back of the knee.

jasmin /ʒasmɛ̃/ n.m. jasmine.

jatte /ʒat/ n.f. bowl.

jauge /ʒoʒ/ n.f. gauge.

jaun|e /ʒon/ a. & n.m. yellow; (péj.) scab. **~e d'œuf**, (egg) yolk. **~ir** v.t./i. turn yellow.

jaunisse /ʒonis/ n.f. jaundice.

javelot /ʒavlo/ n.m. javelin.

jazz /dʒaz/ n.m. jazz.

J.C. /ʒezykri/ n.m. (abrév.) **500 avant/après ~**, 500 B.C./A.D.

je, j'* /ʒə, ʒ/ pron. I.

jean /dʒin/ n.m. jeans.

jeep /(d)ʒip/ n.f. jeep.

jerrycan /(d)ʒerikan/ n.m. jerrycan.

jersey /ʒɛrze/ n.m. jersey.

Jersey /ʒɛrze/ n.f. Jersey.

Jésus /ʒezy/ n.m. Jesus.

jet[1] /ʒɛ/ n.m. throw; (de liquide, vapeur) jet. **~ d'eau**, fountain.

jet[2] /dʒɛt/ n.m. (avion) jet.

jetable /ʒətabl/ a. disposable.

jetée /ʒte/ n.f. pier.

jeter /ʒte/ v.t. throw; (au rebut) throw away; (regard, ancre, lumière) cast; (cri) utter; (bases) lay. **~ un coup d'œil**, have ou take a look (**à**, at). **se ~ contre**, (*heurter*) bash into. **se ~ sur**, (*se ruer sur*) rush at.

jeu /ʒø/ (*pl.* **~x**) *n.m.* game; (*amusement*) play; (*au casino etc.*) gambling; (*théâtre*) acting; (*série*) set; (*de lumière, ressort*) play. **~ de cartes**, (*paquet*) pack of cards. **~ d'échecs**, (*boîte*) chess set.

jeudi /ʒødi/ *n.m.* Thursday.

jeun (à) /a/(ʒœ̃/ *adv.* **être/rester à ~**, be/stay without food.

jeune /ʒœn/ *a.* young. —*n.m./f.* young person. **~ fille**, girl. **~s mariés**, newlyweds. **les ~s**, young people.

jeunesse /ʒœnɛs/ *n.f.* youth; (*apparence*) youthfulness. **la ~**, (*jeunes*) the young.

joaill|ier, **~ière** /ʒɔaje, -jɛr/ *n.m.*, *f.* jeweller.

job /dʒɔb/ *n.m.* (*fam.*) job.

jockey /ʒɔkɛ/ *n.m.* jockey.

joie /ʒwa/ *n.f.* joy.

joindre† /ʒwɛ̃dr/ *v.t.* join (**à**, to); (*contacter*) contact; (*dans une enveloppe*) enclose.

joint, **~e** /ʒwɛ̃, -t/ *a.* (*efforts*) joint; (*pieds*) together. —*n.m.* joint; (*ligne*) join; (*de robinet*) washer.

joker /ʒɔkɛr/ *n.m.* (*carte*) joker.

joli /ʒɔli/ *a.* pretty, nice; (*somme, profit*) nice. **c'est du ~!**, (*ironique*) charming!

jonc /ʒɔ̃/ *n.m.* (bul)rush.

jonction /ʒɔ̃ksjɔ̃/ *n.f.* junction.

jongl|er /ʒɔ̃gle/ *v.i.* juggle. **~eur**, **~euse** *n.m.*, *f.* juggler.

jonquille /ʒɔ̃kij/ *n.f.* daffodil.

Jordanie /ʒɔrdani/ *n.f.* Jordan.

joue /ʒu/ *n.f.* cheek.

jou|er /ʒwe/ *v.t./i.* play; (*théâtre*) act; (*au casino etc.*) gamble. **~er à**, play. **~er la comédie**, put on an act. **bien ~é!**, well done!

jouet /ʒwɛ/ *n.m.* toy.

joueu|r, **~se** /ʒwœr, -øz/ *n.m.*, *f.* player; (*parieur*) gambler.

joufflu /ʒufly/ *a.* chubby-cheeked; (*visage*) chubby.

jouir /ʒwir/ *v.i.* (*sexe*) come.

joujou (*pl.* **~x**) /ʒuʒu/ *n.m.* (*fam.*) toy.

jour /ʒur/ *n.m.* day; (*opposé à nuit*) day(time); (*lumière*) daylight. **de nos ~**, nowadays. **du ~ au lendemain**, overnight. **il fait ~**, it is (day)light. **~ chômé** *ou* **férié**, public holiday. **~ de fête**, holiday. **~ ouvrable**, **~ de travail**, working day.

journ|al (*pl.* **~aux**) /ʒurnal, -o/ *n.m.* (news)paper; (*spécialisé*) journal; (*intime*) diary; (*radio*) news. **~al de bord**, log-book.

journalis|te /ʒurnalist/ *n.m./f.* journalist. **~me** *n.m.* journalism.

journée /ʒurne/ *n.f.* day.

joyeu|x, **~se** /ʒwajø, -z/ *a.* merry, joyful. **~x anniversaire**, happy birthday.

judiciaire /ʒydisjɛr/ *a.* judicial.

judicieu|x, **~se** /ʒydisjø, -z/ *a.* judicious.

judo /ʒydo/ *n.m.* judo.

juge /ʒyʒ/ *n.m.* judge; (*arbitre*) referee. **~ de paix**, Justice of the Peace. **~ de touche**, linesman.

jugement /ʒyʒmã/ *n.m.* judgement; (*criminel*) sentence.

juger /ʒyʒe/ *v.t./i.* judge; (*estimer*) consider (**que**, that). **~ de**, judge.

jui|f, **~ve** /ʒɥif, -v/ *a.* Jewish. —*n.m.*, *f.* Jew, Jewess.

juillet /ʒɥijɛ/ *n.m.* July.

juin /ʒɥɛ̃/ *n.m.* June.

jules /ʒyl/ *n.m.* (*fam.*) guy.

jum|eau, **~elle** (*m. pl.* **~eaux**) /ʒymo, -ɛl/ *a. & n.m.*, *f.* twin. **~elage** *n.m.* twinning. **~eler** *v.t.* (*villes*) twin.

jumelles /ʒymɛl/ *n.f. pl.* binoculars.

jument /ʒymã/ n.f. mare.

jungle /ʒœgl/ n.f. jungle.

junior /ʒynjɔr/ n.m./f. & a. junior.

jupe /ʒyp/ n.f. skirt.

jupon /ʒypɔ̃/ n.m. slip, petticoat.

juré, **~e** /ʒyre/ n.m., f. juror.

jurer /ʒyre/ v.t. swear (**que**, that). —v.i. (pester) swear.

juridiction /ʒyridiksjɔ̃/ n.f. jurisdiction; (tribunal) court of law.

juridique /ʒyridik/ a. legal.

juriste /ʒyrist/ n.m./f. legal expert.

juron /ʒyrɔ̃/ n.m. swear-word.

jury /ʒyri/ n.m. jury.

jus /ʒy/ n.m. juice; (de viande) gravy. **~ de fruit**, fruit juice.

jusque /ʒysk(ə)/ prép. **jusqu'à**, (up to, as far as; (temps) until, till; (limite) up to; (y compris) even. **jusqu'à ce que**, until **jusqu'à présent**, until now **jusqu'en**, until. **jusqu'ou'**, how far?

juste /ʒyst/ a. fair, just; (légitime) just; (correct, exact) right; (vrai) true; (vêtement) tight; (quantité) on the short side. **le ~ milieu**, the happy medium. —adv. rightly, correctly; (chanter) in tune; (seulement, exactement) just. **(un peu) ~**, (calculer, mesurer) a bit fine ou close.

justement /ʒystəmã/ adv. just; (avec justice ou justesse) justly.

justice /ʒystis/ n.f. justice; (autorités) law; (tribunal) court.

justif|ier /ʒystifje/ v.t. justify. —v.i. to defend, de prove. **se ~ier** v. pr. justify o.s.

juteu|x, **~se** /ʒytø, -z/ a. juicy.

K

kaki /kaki/ a. invar. & n.m. khaki.

kangourou /kãguru/ n.m. kangaroo.

karaté /karate/ n.m. karate.

kascher /kaʃɛr/ a. invar. kosher.

képi /kepi/ n.m. kepi.

kermesse /kɛrmɛs/ n.f. fair; (de charité) fête.

kérosène /kerozɛn/ n.m. kerosene, aviation fuel.

kidnapper /kidnape/ v.t. kidnap.

kilo /kilo/ n.m. kilo.

kilogramme /kilɔgram/ n.m. kilogram.

kilohertz /kilɔɛrts/ n.m. kilohertz.

kilom|ètre /kilɔmɛtr/ n.m. kilometre. **~étrage** n.m. (approx.) mileage.

kilowatt /kilɔwat/ n.m. kilowatt.

kinésithérapie /kineziterapi/ n.f. physiotherapy.

kiosque /kjɔsk/ n.m. kiosk. **~ à musique**, bandstand.

kit /kit/ n.m. **meubles en ~**, flat-pack furniture.

kiwi /kiwi/ n.m. kiwi (fruit, bird).

klaxon /klaksɔn/ n.m. (P.) (auto.) horn. **~ner** /-e/ v.i. sound one's horn.

ko /kao/ n.m. (comput.) k.

K.O. /kao/ a. invar. (knocked) out.

kyste /kist/ n.m. cyst.

L

l', **la** /l, la/ voir le.

là /la/ adv. there; (ici) here; (chez soi) in; (temps) then. **c'est là que**, this is where. **là où**, where. **là-bas** adv. over there. **là-dedans** adv. inside, in there. **là-dessous** adv. underneath, under there. **là-dessus** adv. on there, in there. **là-haut** adv. up there; (à l'étage) upstairs.

-là /la/ (après un nom précédé de ce, cette, etc.) **cet homme-là**, that man. **ces maisons-là**, those houses.

laboratoire /labɔratwar/ n.m. laboratory.

labour /labur/ n.m. ploughing. **~er** v.t./i. plough.

labyrinthe /labirɛ̃t/ n.m. maze.

lac /lak/ n.m. lake.

lacer /lase/ v.t. lace up.

lacérer /lasere/ v.t. tear (up).

lacet /lasɛ/ n.m. (shoe-)lace; (de route) sharp bend, zigzag.

lâche /lɑʃ/ a. cowardly; (détendu) loose. —n.m./f. coward.

lâcher /lɑʃe/ v.t. let go of; (abandonner) give up; (laisser) leave; (libérer) release; (parole) utter; (desserrer) loosen. —v.i. give way. **~ prise**, let go.

lâcheté /lɑʃte/ n.f. cowardice.

lacrymogène /lakrimɔʒɛn/ a. **gaz ~**, tear gas. **grenade ~**, tear gas grenade.

lacté /lakte/ a. milk.

laid, ~e /lɛ, lɛd/ a. ugly; (action) vile. **~eur** /lɛdœr/ n.f. ugliness.

lain|e /lɛn/ n.f. wool. **de ~e**, woollen. **~age** n.m. woollen garment.

laïque /laik/ a. secular; (habit, personne) lay.

laisse /lɛs/ n.f. lead, leash.

laisser /lese/ v.t. leave. **~ qn. faire**, let s.o. do. **~ qch.**, let s.o. have sth., leave s.o. sth. **~ tomber**, drop. **laissez-passer** n.m. invar. pass.

lait /lɛ/ n.m. milk. **~age** n.m. milk product.

lait|ier, ~ière /letje, letjɛr/ a. dairy. —n.m. (livreur) milkman. **~erie** /lɛtri/ n.f. dairy.

laiton /lɛtɔ̃/ n.m. brass.

laitue /lety/ n.f. lettuce.

lama /lama/ n.m. llama.

lambeau (pl. **~x**) /lɑ̃bo/ n.m. shred. **en ~x**, in shreds.

lambris /lɑ̃bri/ n.m. panelling.

lame /lam/ n.f. blade; (lamelle) strip; (vague) wave.

lamelle /lamɛl/ n.f. (thin) strip.

lamentable /lamɑ̃tabl/ a. deplorable.

lamenter (se) /(sə)lamɑ̃te/ v. pr. moan.

lampadaire /lɑ̃pader/ n.m. standard lamp; (de rue) street lamp.

lampe /lɑ̃p/ n.f. lamp. **~ (de poche)**, torch. **~ de chevet**, bedside lamp.

lance /lɑ̃s/ n.f. spear; (de tournoi) lance; (tuyau) hose. **~ d'incendie**, fire hose.

lanc|er /lɑ̃se/ v.t. throw; (avec force) hurl; (navire, idée, personne) launch. **se ~er dans**, launch into. —n.m. throw; (action) throwing. **~ement** n.m. throwing; (de navire) launching.

landau /lɑ̃do/ n.m. pram; (Amer.) baby carriage.

lande /lɑ̃d/ n.f. heath, moor.

langage /lɑ̃gaʒ/ n.m. language.

langoust|e /lɑ̃gust/ n.f. (spiny) lobster. **~ine** /-in/ n.f. (Norway) lobster.

langue /lɑ̃g/ n.f. tongue; (idiome) language. **de ~ anglaise/française**, English-/French-speaking. **~ maternelle**, mother tongue.

languette /lɑ̃gɛt/ n.f. tongue.

lanière /lanjɛr/ n.f. strap.

lanterne /lɑ̃tɛrn/ n.f. lantern; (électrique) lamp.

laper /lape/ v.t./i. lap.

lapin /lapɛ̃/ n.m. rabbit. **poser un ~ à qn.**, stand s.o. up.

laque /lak/ n.f. lacquer. **~er** v.t. lacquer.

laquelle /lakɛl/ voir **lequel**.

lard /lar/ n.m. (pig's) fat; (viande) bacon.

large /larʒ/ a. wide, broad; (grand) large; (non borné) broad;

(généreux) generous. —*n.m.* de ~, *(mesure)* wide. **au ~ de**, *(en face de: naut.)* off. **~ d'esprit**, broad-minded. **~ment** /-ɔmɑ̃/ *adv.* widely; *(ouvrir)* wide; *(amplement)* amply; *(généreusement)* generously; *(au moins)* easily.

largeur /larʒœr/ *n.f.* width, breadth; *(fig.)* breadth.

larguer /large/ *v.t.* drop. **~ les amarres**, cast off.

larme /larm/ *n.f.* tear.

larve /larv/ *n.f.* larva.

laryngite /larɛ̃ʒit/ *n.f.* laryngitis.

larynx /larɛ̃ks/ *n.m.* larynx.

las, ~se /lɑ, lɑs/ *a.* weary.

lasagnes /lazaɲ/ *n.f. pl.* lasagne.

laser /lazer/ *n.m.* laser.

lasse /lɑs/ *voir* **las**.

lasser /lɑse/ *v.t.* weary. **se ~** *v. pr.* weary **(de,** of).

lassitude /lɑsityd/ *n.f.* weariness.

latent, ~e /latɑ̃, -t/ *a.* latent.

latér|al *(m. pl.* **~aux)** /lateral, -o/ *a.* lateral.

latex /latɛks/ *n.m.* latex.

latin, ~e /latɛ̃, -in/ *a.* & *n.m., f.* Latin. —*n.m. (lang.)* Latin.

latitude /latityd/ *n.f.* latitude.

latte /lat/ *n.f.* lath; *(de plancher)* board.

lauréat, ~e /lɔrea, -t/ *a.* prize-winning. —*n.m., f.* prize-winner.

laurier /lɔrje/ *n.m.* laurel; *(culin.)* bay-leaves.

lavable /lavabl/ *a.* washable.

lavabo /lavabo/ *n.m.* wash-basin. **~s**, toilet(s).

lavage /lavaʒ/ *n.m.* washing. **~ de cerveau**, brainwashing.

lavande /lavɑ̃d/ *n.f.* lavender.

lave /lav/ *n.f.* lava.

lav|er /lave/ *v.t.* wash; *(injure etc.)* avenge. **se ~er** *v. pr.* wash (o.s.). **~e-vaisselle** *n.m. invar.* dishwasher.

laverie /lavri/ *n.f.* ~ **(automatique)**, launderette.

laxati|f, ~ve /laksatif, -v/ *a.* & *n.m.* laxative.

layette /lɛjɛt/ *n.f.* baby clothes.

le ou **l'*** , **la** ou **l'*** /lə, l/, /la, le/ *article* the; *(mesure)* a, per. —*pron. (homme)* him; *(femme)* her; *(chose, animal)* it. **les** *pron.* them. **aimer le thé/la France**, like tea/France. **le matin**, in the morning. **il sort le mardi**, he goes out on Tuesdays. **levez le bras**, raise your arm.

lécher /leʃe/ *v.t.* lick.

lèche-vitrines /lɛʃvitrin/ *n.m.* **faire du ~**, go window-shopping.

leçon /ləsɔ̃/ *n.f.* lesson.

lec|teur, ~trice /lɛktœr, -tris/ *n.m., f.* reader; *(univ.)* foreign language assistant. **~teur de cassettes**, cassette player. **~teur de disquettes**, (disk) drive.

lecture /lɛktyr/ *n.f.* reading.

lég|al *(m. pl.* **~aux)** /legal, -o/ *a.* legal. **~alement** *adv.* legally. **~aliser** *v.t.* legalize. **~alité** *n.f.* legality; *(loi)* law.

légende /leʒɑ̃d/ *n.f.* legend.

léger, ~ère /leʒe, -ɛr/ *a.* light; *(bruit, faute, maladie)* slight; *(café, argument)* weak. **~èrement** /-ɛrmɑ̃/ *adv.* lightly; *(un peu)* slightly. **~èreté** /-ɛrte/ *n.f.* lightness; thoughtlessness.

législati|f, ~ve /leʒislatif, -v/ *a.* legislative.

législation /leʒislasjɔ̃/ *n.f.* legislation.

législature /leʒislatyr/ *n.f.* term of office.

légitim|e /leʒitim/ *a.* legitimate. **en état de ~e défense**, acting in self-defence. **~ité** *n.f.* legitimacy.

léguer /lege/ *v.t.* bequeath.

légume /legym/ *n.m.* vegetable.

lendemain /lɑ̃dmɛ̃/ n.m. le ~, the next day, the day after; (fig.) the future. le ~ de, the day after. le ~ matin/soir, the next morning/evening.

lent, ~e /lɑ̃, lɑ̃t/ a. slow. ~ement /lɑ̃tmɑ̃/ adv. slowly. ~eur /lɑ̃tœr/ n.f. slowness.

lentille[1] /lɑ̃tij/ n.f. (plante) lentil.

lentille[2] /lɑ̃tij/ n.f. (verre) lens; ~s de contact, (contact) lenses.

léopard /leɔpar/ n.m. leopard.

lequel, **laquelle** (pl. lesquel(le)s) /ləkɛl, lakɛl, lekɛl/ pron. (à + lequel = auquel, à + lesquel(le)s = auxquel(le)s; de + lequel = duquel, de + lesquel(le)s = desquel(le)s) which; (interrogatif) which (one); (personne) who; (complément indirect) whom.

les /le/ voir le.

lésiner /lezine/ v.i. ne pas ~ sur, not stint on.

lésion /lezjɔ̃/ n.f. lesion.

lesquels, **lesquelles** /lekɛl/ voir lequel.

lessive /lesiv/ n.f. washing-powder; (linge, action) washing.

lettre /lɛtr/ n.f. letter. ~ exprès, express letter. les ~s, (univ.) (the) arts.

leucémie /løsemi/ n.f. leukaemia.

leur /lœr/ a. (f. invar.) their. —pron. (to) them. le ~, la ~, les ~s, theirs.

levain /ləvɛ̃/ n.m. leaven.

levé /ləve/ a. (debout) up.

levée /ləve/ n.f. (de courrier) collection.

lever /ləve/ v.t. lift (up), raise; (interdiction) lift; (séance) close; (armée, impôts) levy. —v.i. (pâte) rise. se ~ v. pr. get up (soleil, rideau) rise; (jour) break. ~ n.m. ~ du rideau, (théâtre) curtain (up). ~ du soleil, sunrise.

levier /ləvje/ n.m. lever.

lèvre /lɛvr/ n.f. lip.

lévrier /levrije/ n.m. greyhound.

levure /ləvyr/ n.f. yeast. ~ alsacienne ou chimique, baking powder.

lexicographie /lɛksikɔgrafi/ n.f. lexicography.

lexique /lɛksik/ n.m. vocabulary; (glossaire) lexicon.

lézard /lezar/ n.m. lizard.

liaison /ljɛzɔ̃/ n.f. connection; (transport) link; (gram., mil.) liaison; (amoureuse) affair.

liane /ljan/ n.f. creeper.

liasse /ljas/ n.f. bundle, wad.

Liban /libã/ n.m. Lebanon.

libanais, ~e /libanɛ, -z/ a. & n.m., f. Lebanese.

libeller /libele/ v.t. (chèque) write; (lettre) draw up. ~é à l'ordre de, made out to.

libellule /libelyl/ n.f. dragonfly.

libér|al (m. pl. ~aux) /liberal, -o/ a. liberal. les professions ~ales the professions.

libér|er /libere/ v.t. (personne) free, release; (pays) liberate, free. se ~er v. pr. free o.s. ~ateur, ~atrice a. liberating; n.m., f. liberator. ~ation n.f. release; (de pays) liberation.

liberté /liberte/ n.f. freedom, liberty; (loisir) free time. être/mettre en ~, be/set free.

librair|e /librɛr/ n.m./f. bookseller. ~ie /-eri/ n.f. bookshop.

libre /libr/ a. free; (place, pièce) vacant, free; (passage) clear. ~ de faire, free to do. ~-échange n.m. free trade. ~ment /-əmã/ adv. freely. ~-service (pl. ~s-services) n.m. self-service.

Libye /libi/ n.f. Libya.

libyen, ~ne /libjɛ̃, -jɛn/ a. & n.m., f. Libyan.

licence /lisɑ̃s/ n.f. licence; (univ.) degree.

licencié, **~e** /lisãsje/ *n.m.*, *f.* **~ ès lettres/sciences**, Bachelor of Arts/Science.

licenc|ier /lisãsje/ *v.t.* make redundant, (*pour faute*) dismiss. **~iements** *n.m. pl.* redundancies.

lichen /likɛn/ *n.m.* lichen.

licite /lisit/ *a.* lawful.

licorne /likɔrn/ *n.f.* unicorn.

liège /ljɛʒ/ *n.m.* cork.

lien /ljɛ̃/ *n.m.* (*rapport*) link; (*attache*) bond, tie; (*corde*) rope.

lier /lje/ *v.t.* tie (up), bind; (*relier*) link; (*engager*, *unir*) bind. **ils sont très liés**, they are very close.

lierre /ljɛr/ *n.m.* ivy.

lieu (*pl.* **~x**) /ljø/ *n.m.* place. **~x**, (*locaux*) premises; (*d'un accident*) scene. **au ~ de**, instead of.

lieutenant /ljøtnã/ *n.m.* lieutenant.

lièvre /ljɛvr/ *n.m.* hare.

ligament /ligamã/ *n.m.* ligament.

ligne /liɲ/ *n.f.* line; (*trajet*) route; (*formes*) lines; (*de femme*) figure. **en ~**, (*personne au téléphone*) on the phone.

ligue /lig/ *n.f.* league.

lilas /lila/ *n.m.* & *a. invar.* lilac.

limace /limas/ *n.f.* slug.

limande /limãd/ *n.f.* (*poisson*) dab.

lim|e /lim/ *n.f.* file. **~e à ongles**, nail file. **~er** *v.t.* file.

limitation /limitasjɔ̃/ *n.f.* limitation. **~ de vitesse**, speed limit.

limit|e /limit/ *n.f.* limit; (*de jardin*, *champ*) boundary. *—a.* (*vitesse*, *âge*) maximum. **date ~e**, deadline. **~er** *v.t.* limit; (*délimiter*) form the border of.

limon /limɔ̃/ *n.m.* silt.

limonade /limɔnad/ *n.f.* lemonade.

limpide /lɛ̃pid/ *a.* limpid, clear.

lin /lɛ̃/ *n.m.* (*tissu*) linen.

linceul /lɛ̃sœl/ *n.m.* shroud.

linéaire /lineɛr/ *a.* linear.

linge /lɛ̃ʒ/ *n.m.* linen; (*lessive*) washing; (*torchon*) cloth. **~rie** *n.f.* underwear.

linguiste /lɛ̃gɥist/ *n.m./f.* linguist.

linguistique /lɛ̃gɥistik/ *a.* linguistic. *—n.f.* linguistics.

lion, **~ne** /ljɔ̃, ljɔn/ *n.m.*, *f.* lion, lioness. **le L~**, leo.

lionceau (*pl.* **~x**) /ljɔ̃so/ *n.m.* lion cub.

liqueur /likœr/ *n.f.* liqueur.

liquide /likid/ *a.* & *n.m.* liquid. (*argent*) **~**, ready money. **payer en ~**, pay cash.

liquid|er /likide/ *v.t.* liquidate; (*vendre*) sell. **~ation** *n.f.* liquidation; (*vente*) (clearance) sale.

lire¹ /lir/ *v.t./i.* read.

lire² /lir/ *n.f.* lira.

lis¹ /li/ *voir* **lire¹**.

lis² /lis/ *n.m.* (*fleur*) lily.

lisible /lizibl/ *a.* legible; (*roman etc.*) readable.

lisse /lis/ *a.* smooth..

liste /list/ *n.f.* list. **~ électorale**, register of voters.

listing /listiŋ/ *n.m.* printout.

lit¹ /li/ *voir* **lire¹**.

lit² /li/ *n.m.* (*de personne*, *fleuve*) bed. **se mettre au ~**, get into bed. **~ de camp**, camp-bed. **~ d'enfant**, cot.

litchi /litʃi/ *n.m.* litchi.

literie /litri/ *n.f.* bedding.

litige /litiʒ/ *n.m.* dispute.

litre /litr/ *n.m.* litre.

littéraire /literɛr/ *a.* literary.

littérature /literatyr/ *n.f.* literature.

littor|al (*pl.* **~aux**) /litɔral, -o/ *n.m.* coast.

liturgie /lityrʒi/ *n.f.* liturgy.

livraison /livrɛzɔ̃/ *n.f.* delivery.

livre¹ /livr/ *n.m.* book. **~ de bord**, log-book. **~ de compte**, books. **~ de poche**, paperback.

livre² /livr/ *n.f.* (*monnaie, poids*) pound.

livrer /livre/ *v.t.* deliver; (*abandonner*) give over (**à**, to); (*secret*) give away.

livret /livrɛ/ *n.m.* book; (*mus.*) libretto. **~ scolaire**, school report (book).

livreu|r /livrœr, -øz/ *n.m.*, *f.* delivery boy *ou* girl.

lobe /lɔb/ *n.m.* lobe.

loc|al¹ (*m. pl.* **~aux**) /lɔkal, -o/ *a.* local. **~alement** *adv.* locally.

loc|al² (*pl.* **~aux**) /lɔkal, -o/ *n.m.* premises. **~aux**, premises.

localisé /lɔkalize/ *a.* localized.

localité /lɔkalite/ *n.f.* locality.

locataire /lɔkatɛr/ *n.m./f.* tenant; (*de chambre, d'hôtel*) lodger.

location /lɔkasjɔ̃/ *n.f.* (*de maison*) renting; (*de voiture*) hiring, renting; (*de place*) booking, reservation; (*guichet*) booking office; (*théâtre*) box office; (*par propriétaire*) renting out; hiring out. **en ~**, (*voiture*) on hire, rented.

locomotion /lɔkɔmosjɔ̃/ *n.f.* locomotion.

locomotive /lɔkɔmɔtiv/ *n.f.* engine, locomotive.

loge /lɔʒ/ *n.f.* (*de concierge*) lodge; (*d'acteur*) dressing-room; (*de spectateur*) box.

logement /lɔʒmɑ̃/ *n.m.* accommodation; (*appartement*) flat; (*habitat*) housing.

log|er /lɔʒe/ *v.t.* accommodate. **—v.i.**, **se ~er** *v. pr.* live. **trouver à se ~er**, find accommodation. **être ~é**, live.

logeu|r /lɔʒœr, -øz/ *n.m.*, *f.* landlord, landlady.

logiciel /lɔʒisjɛl/ *n.m.* software.

logique /lɔʒik/ *a.* logical. **—n.f.** logic. **~ment** *adv.* logically.

logistique /lɔʒistik/ *n.f.* logistics.

logo /lɔgo/ *n.m.* logo.

loi /lwa/ *n.f.* law.

loin /lwɛ̃/ *adv.* far (away). **au ~**, far away. **de ~**, from far away; (*de beaucoup*) by far. **~ de là**, far from it. **plus ~**, further. **il revient de ~**, (*fig.*) he had a close shave.

lointain, **~e** /lwɛ̃tɛ̃, -ɛn/ *a.* distant. **—n.m.** distance.

loir /lwar/ *n.m.* dormouse.

loisir /lwazir/ *n.m.* (spare) time. **~s**, spare time; (*distractions*) spare time activities.

londonien, **~ne** /lɔ̃dɔnjɛ̃, -jɛn/ *a.* London. **—n.m.**, *f.* Londoner.

Londres /lɔ̃dr/ *n.m./f.* London.

long, **~ue** /lɔ̃, lɔ̃g/ *a.* long. **—n.m.** **de ~**, (*mesure*) along. **(tout) le ~ de**, (all) along.

longer /lɔ̃ʒe/ *v.t.* go along.

longitude /lɔ̃ʒityd/ *n.f.* longitude.

longtemps /lɔ̃tɑ̃/ *adv.* a long time. **avant ~**, before long. **trop ~**, too long. **ça prendra ~**, it will take a long time.

longue /lɔ̃g/ *voir* **long**.

longuement /lɔ̃gmɑ̃/ *adv.* at length.

longueur /lɔ̃gœr/ *n.f.* length. **~ d'onde**, wavelength.

longue-vue /lɔ̃gvy/ *n.f.* telescope.

look /luk/ *n.m.* (*fam.*) look, image.

lopin /lɔpɛ̃/ *n.m.* **~ de terre**, patch of land.

loquet /lɔkɛ/ *n.m.* latch.

lors de /lɔrdə/ *prép.* at the time of.

lorsque /lɔrsk(ə)/ *conj.* when.

losange /lɔzɑ̃ʒ/ *n.m.* diamond.

lot /lo/ *n.m.* prize; (*portion, destin*) lot.

loterie /lɔtri/ *n.f.* lottery.

lotion /lɔsjɔ̃/ *n.f.* lotion.

lotissement /lɔtismɑ̃/ *n.m.* (*à construire*) building plot; (*construit*) (housing) development.

louange /lwɑ̃ʒ/ *n.f.* praise.

louche /luʃ/ *a.* shady, dubious.

loucher /luʃe/ v.i. squint.

louer /lwe/ v.t. (maison) rent; (voiture) hire, rent; (place) book, reserve; (propriétaire) rent out; hire out. **à ~**, to let.

loup /lu/ n.m. wolf.

loupe /lup/ n.f. magnifying glass.

lourd, ~e /lur, -d/ a. heavy; (chaleur) close; (faute) gross.

loutre /lutr/ n.f. otter.

louve /luv/ n.f. she-wolf.

louveteau (pl. ~x) /luvto/ n.m. wolf cub; (scout) Cub (Scout).

louvoyer /luvwaje/ v.i. (fig.) sidestep the issue; (naut.) tack.

loy|al (m. pl. ~aux) /lwajal, -o/ a. loyal; (honnête) fair. **~alement** adv. loyally; fairly. **~auté** n.f. loyalty; fairness.

loyer /lwaje/ n.m. rent.

lu /ly/ voir **lire**[1].

lubrif|ier /lybrifje/ v.t. lubricate. **~iant** n.m. lubricant.

lucarne /lykarn/ n.f. skylight.

lucid|e /lysid/ a. lucid. **~ité** n.f. lucidity.

lucrati|f, ~ve /lykratif, -v/ a. lucrative. **à but non ~f**, nonprofit-making.

lueur /lqœr/ n.f. (faint) light, glimmer; (fig.) glimmer, gleam.

luge /lyʒ/ n.f. toboggan.

lugubre /lygybr/ a. gloomy.

lui /lqi/ pron. him; (sujet) he; (chose) it; (objet indirect) (to) him; (femme) her; (chose) (to) it. **~-même** pron. himself; itself.

lumbago /lɔ̃bago/ n.m. lumbago.

lumière /lymjɛr/ n.f. light.

luminaire /lyminɛr/ n.m. lamp.

lumineu|x, ~se /lyminø, -z/ a. luminous; (éclairé) illuminated; (source, rayon) (of) light; (vif) bright.

lunaire /lynɛr/ a. lunar.

lunatique /lynatik/ a. temperamental.

lunch /lœntʃ/ n.m. buffet lunch.

lundi /lœdi/ n.m. Monday.

lune /lyn/ n.f. moon. **~ de miel**, honeymoon.

lunette /lynɛt/ n.f. **~s**, glasses; (de protection) goggles. **~ arrière**, (auto.) rear window. **~s de soleil**, sun-glasses.

lustre /lystr/ n.m. (éclat) lustre; (objet) chandelier.

luth /lyt/ n.m. lute.

lutin /lytɛ̃/ n.m. goblin.

lutt|e /lyt/ n.f. fight, struggle; (sport) wrestling. **~er** v.i. fight, struggle; (sport) wrestle.

luxe /lyks/ n.m. luxury. **de ~**, luxury; (produit) de luxe.

Luxembourg /lyksãbur/ n.m. Luxemburg.

lux|er /lykse/ v.t. **se ~er le genou**, dislocate one's knee. **~ation** n.f. dislocation.

luxueu|x, ~se /lyksyø, -z/ a. luxurious.

luzerne /lyzɛrn/ n.f. (plante) lucerne, alfalfa.

lycée /lise/ n.m. (secondary) school. **~n, ~nne** /-ɛ̃, -ɛn/ n.m., f. pupil (at secondary school).

lynx /lɛ̃ks/ n.m. lynx.

lyophilis|er /ljɔfilize/ v.t. freezedry. **~é** a. freeze-dried.

lyre /lir/ n.f. lyre.

lyri|que /lirik/ a. (poésie) lyric; (passionné) lyrical. **artiste ~que**, opera singer/-house. **~sme** n.m. lyricism.

lys /lis/ n.m. lily.

M

m' /m/ voir **me**.

ma /ma/ voir **mon**.

maboul /mabul/ *a.* (*fam.*) mad.

macabre /makabr/ *a.* gruesome, macabre.

macadam /makadam/ *n.m.* (*goudronné*) Tarmac (P.).

macaron /makarɔ̃/ *n.m.* (*gâteau*) macaroon; (*insigne*) badge.

macaronis /makarɔni/ *n.m. pl.* macaroni.

macédoine /masedwan/ *n.f.* mixed vegetables. **~ de fruits,** fruit salad.

macérer /masere/ *v.t./i.* soak; (*dans du vinaigre*) pickle.

mâcher /maʃe/ *v.t.* chew.

machin /maʃɛ̃/ *n.m.* (*chose: fam.*) thing; (*personne: fam.*) what's-his-name.

machin|al (*m. pl.* **~aux**) /maʃinal, -o/ *a.* automatic. **~alement** *adv.* automatically.

machine /maʃin/ *n.f.* machine; (*d'un train, navire*) engine. **~ à écrire,** typewriter. **~ à laver/ coudre,** washing-/sewing- machine. **~ à sous,** fruit machine.

machiniste /maʃinist/ *n.m.* (*théâtre*) stage-hand; (*conducteur*) driver.

mâchoire /maʃwar/ *n.f.* jaw.

maçon /masɔ̃/ *n.m.* builder; (*poseur de briques*) bricklayer.

macrobiotique /makrɔbjɔtik/ *a.* macrobiotic.

Madagascar /madagaskar/ *n.f.* Madagascar.

madame (*pl.* **mesdames**)/ madam, medam/ *n.f.* madam. **M~** *ou* **Mme Dupont,** Mrs Dupont. **bonsoir, mesdames,** good evening, ladies.

madeleine /madlɛn/ *n.f.* madeleine (*small shell-shaped sponge-cake*).

mademoiselle (*pl.* **mesdemoiselles**) /madmwazɛl, medmwazɛl/

n.f. miss. **M~** *ou* **Mlle Dupont,** Miss Dupont. **bonsoir, mesdemoiselles,** good evening, ladies.

madère /madɛr/ *n.m.* (*vin*) Madeira.

maf(f)ia /mafja/ *n.f.* Mafia.

magasin /magazɛ̃/ *n.m.* shop, store; (*entrepôt*) warehouse.

magazine /magazin/ *n.m.* magazine; (*émission*) programme.

Maghreb /magrɛb/ *n.m.* North Africa. **~in, ~ine** *a.* & *n.m., f.* North African.

magicien, ~ne /maʒisjɛ̃, -jɛn/ *n.m., f.* magician.

magie /maʒi/ *n.f.* magic.

magique /maʒik/ *a.* magic; (*mystérieux*) magical.

magistr|al (*m. pl.* **~aux**) /maʒistral, -o/ *a.* masterly; (*grand: hum.*) colossal.

magistrat /maʒistra/ *n.m.* magistrate.

magistrature /maʒistratyr/ *n.f.* judiciary.

magnésie /maɲezi/ *n.f.* magnesia.

magnéti|que /maɲetik/ *a.* magnetic. **~ser** *v.t.* magnetize. **~sme** *n.m.* magnetism.

magnétophone /maɲetɔfɔn/ *n.m.* tape recorder. **~ à cassettes,** cassette recorder.

magnétoscope /maɲetɔskɔp/ *n.m.* video-recorder.

magnifique /maɲifik/ *a.* magnificent.

magnolia /maɲɔlja/ *n.m.* magnolia.

magret /magrɛ/ *n.m.* **~ de canard,** steaklet of duck.

mai /mɛ/ *n.m.* May.

maigr|e /mɛgr/ *a.* thin; (*viande*) lean; (*yaourt*) low-fat; (*fig.*) poor, meagre. **~eur** *n.f.* thinness; leanness.

maigrir /megrir/ *v.i.* get thin(ner); (*en suivant un régime*) slim.

maille /maj/ *n.f.* stitch; (*de filet*) mesh. ∿ **filée**, ladder, run.

maillet /majɛ/ *n.m.* mallet.

maillon /majɔ̃/ *n.m.* link.

maillot /majo/ *n.m.* (*de sport*) jersey. ∿ **(de corps)**, vest. ∿ **(de bain)**, (swimming) costume.

main /mɛ̃/ *n.f.* hand. **donner la** ∿ **à qn.**, hold s.o.'s hand. **en** ∿**s propres**, in person. **en bonnes** ∿, in good hands. ∿**-d'œuvre** (*pl.* ∿**s-d'œuvre**) *n.f.* labour; (*ensemble d'ouvriers*) labour force.

maintenant /mɛ̃tnɑ̃/ *adv.* now; (*de nos jours*) nowadays.

maintenir† /mɛ̃tnir/ *v.t.* keep, maintain; (*soutenir*) hold up; (*affirmer*) maintain. **se** ∿ *v.* pr. (*continuer*) persist; (*rester*) remain.

maintien /mɛ̃tjɛ̃/ *n.m.* (*attitude*) bearing; (*conservation*) maintenance.

maire /mɛr/ *n.m.* mayor.

mairie /meri/ *n.f.* town hall; (*administration*) town council.

mais /mɛ/ *conj.* but. ∿ **oui**, ∿ **si**, of course. ∿ **non**, definitely not.

maïs /mais/ *n.m.* (*à cultiver*) maize; (*culin.*) sweet corn.

maison /mɛzɔ̃/ *n.f.* house; (*foyer*) home; (*immeuble*) building. ∿ **(de commerce)**, firm. —*a. invar.* (*culin.*) home-made. **à la** ∿, **-**mate, at home. **rentrer** *ou* **aller à la** ∿, go home. ∿ **des jeunes**, youth centre. ∿ **de retraite**, old people's home. ∿ **mère**, parent company.

maître /mɛtr/ *n.m.* master. ∿ **(d'école)**, schoolmaster. ∿ **de**, in control of. ∿ **d'hôtel**, head waiter. ∿ **nageur**, swimming instructor.

maîtresse /mɛtrɛs/ *n.f.* mistress. ∿ **(d'école)**, schoolmistress. ∿ **de**, in control of.

maîtris|e /metriz/ *n.f.* mastery; (*univ.*) master's degree. ∿**e (de soi)**, self-control. ∿**er** *v.t.* master; (*incendie*) control; (*personne*) subdue. **se** ∿**er** *v. pr.* control o.s.

maïzena /maizena/ *n.f.* (P.) cornflour.

majesté /maʒɛste/ *n.f.* majesty.

majestueu|x, ∿**se** /maʒɛstɥø, -z/ *a.* majestic. ∿**sement** *adv.* majestically.

majeur /maʒœr/ *a.* major; (*jurid.*) of age. —*n.m.* middle finger. **en** ∿**e partie**, mostly. **la** ∿**e partie de**, most of.

major|er /maʒɔre/ *v.t.* increase. ∿**ation** *n.f.* increase (**de**, in).

majorit|é /maʒɔrite/ *n.f.* majority. **en** ∿**é**, chiefly. ∿**aire** *a.* majority. **être** ∿**aire**, be in the majority.

Majorque /maʒɔrk/ *n.f.* Majorca.

majuscule /maʒyskyl/ *a.* capital. —*n.f.* capital letter.

mal[1] /mal/ *adv.* badly; (*incorrectement*) wrong(ly). ∿ **(à l'aise)**, uncomfortable. **aller** ∿, (*malade*) be bad. **c'est** ∿ **de**, it is wrong *ou* bad to. ∿ **entendre/comprendre**, not hear/understand properly. **pas** ∿, not bad; quite a lot.

mal[2] (*pl.* **maux**) /mal, mo/ *n.m.* evil; (*douleur*) pain, ache; (*effort*) trouble; (*dommage*) harm. **avoir** ∿ **à la tête/aux dents/à la gorge**, have a headache/a toothache/a sore throat. **avoir le** ∿ **de mer/du pays**, be seasick/homesick. **faire du** ∿ **à**, hurt, harm. **se donner du** ∿ **pour faire qch.**, go to a lot of trouble to do sth.

malade /malad/ *a.* sick, ill; (*bras,*

maladie 142 **mandarine**

gorge) bad. —*n.m./f.* sick person; (*d'un médecin*) patient.
maladie /maladi/ *n.f.* illness, disease.
maladresse /maladrɛs/ *n.f.* clumsiness; (*erreur*) blunder.
maladroit, ~e /maladrwa, -t/ *a. & n.m., f.* clumsy (person).
malais, ~e[1] /malɛ, -z/ *a. & n.m., f.* Malay.
malaise[2] /malɛz/ *n.m.* feeling of faintness *ou* dizziness; (*fig.*) uneasiness, malaise.
malaria /malarja/ *n.f.* malaria.
Malaysia /malɛzja/ *n.f.* Malaysia.
malaxer /malakse/ *v.t.* (*pétrir*) knead; (*mêler*) mix.
malchance /malʃɑ̃s/ *n.f.* misfortune. **~eux, ~euse** *a.* unlucky.
mâle /mɑl/ *a.* male; (*viril*) manly. —*n.m.* male.
malédiction /malediksjɔ̃/ *n.f.* curse.
malencontreux|x, ~se /malɑ̃kɔ̃trø, -z/ *a.* unfortunate.
malentendant, ~e *a. & n.m., f.* hard of hearing.
malentendu /malɑ̃tɑ̃dy/ *n.m.* misunderstanding.
malfaçon /malfasɔ̃/ *n.f.* fault.
malfaiteur /malfɛtœr/ *n.m.* criminal.
malformation /malfɔrmasjɔ̃/ *n.f.* malformation.
malgache /malgaʃ/ *a. & n.m./f.* Malagasy.
malgré /malgre/ *prép.* in spite of, despite. **~ tout**, after all.
malheur /malœr/ *n.m.* misfortune; (*accident*) accident. **faire un ~**, be a big hit.
malheureu|x, ~se /malœrø, -z/ *a.* unhappy; (*regrettable*) unfortunate; (*sans succès*) unlucky; (*insignifiant*) wretched. —*n.m., f.* (*poor*) wretch. **~sement** *adv.* unfortunately.

malhonnête /malɔnɛt/ *a.* dishonest. **~té** *n.f.* dishonesty; (*action*) dishonest action.
mal|in, ~igne /malɛ̃, -iɲ/ *a.* clever, smart; (*méchant*) malicious; (*tumeur*) malignant; (*difficile: fam.*) difficult.
malle /mal/ *n.f.* (*valise*) trunk; (*auto.*) boot.
mallette /malɛt/ *n.f.* (small) suitcase.
malmener /malmǝne/ *v.t.* manhandle, handle roughly.
malnutrition /malnytrisjɔ̃/ *n.f.* malnutrition.
malodorant, ~e /malɔdɔrɑ̃, -t/ *a.* smelly, foul-smelling.
malpoli /malpɔli/ *a.* impolite.
malpropre /malprɔpr/ *a.* dirty. **~té** /-ǝte/ *n.f.* dirtiness.
malsain, ~e /malsɛ̃, -ɛn/ *a.* unhealthy.
malt /malt/ *n.m.* malt.
maltais, ~e /maltɛ, -z/ *a. & n.m., f.* Maltese.
Malte /malt/ *n.f.* Malta.
maltraiter /maltrete/ *v.t.* ill-treat.
maman /mamɑ̃/ *n.f.* mum(my), mother.
mamelle /mamɛl/ *n.f.* teat.
mamie /mami/ *n.f.* (*fam.*) granny.
mammifère /mamifɛr/ *n.m.* mammal.
mammouth /mamut/ *n.m.* mammoth.
manche[1] /mɑ̃ʃ/ *n.f.* sleeve; (*sport, pol.*) round. **la M~**, the Channel.
manche[2] /mɑ̃ʃ/ *n.m.* (*d'un instrument*) handle.
manchette /mɑ̃ʃɛt/ *n.f.* cuff; (*de journal*) headline.
manchot /mɑ̃ʃo/ *n.m.* (*oiseau*) penguin.
mandarin /mɑ̃darɛ̃/ *n.m.* (*fonctionnaire*) mandarin.
mandarine /mɑ̃darin/ *n.f.* tangerine, mandarin (orange).

mandat /mɑ̃da/ n.m. (postal) money order; (pol.) mandate; (procuration) proxy; (de police) warrant.

manège /manɛʒ/ n.m. riding-school; (à la foire) merry-go-round; (manœuvre) wiles, ploy.

manette /manɛt/ n.f. lever; (comput.) joystick.

mangeable /mɑ̃ʒabl/ a. edible.

mang|er /mɑ̃ʒe/ v.t./i. eat; (fortune) go through; (ronger) eat into. —n.m. food. donner à ~ à, feed. ~eur, ~euse n.m., f. eater.

mangue /mɑ̃g/ n.f. mango.

maniable /manjabl/ a. easy to handle.

maniaque /manjak/ a. fussy. —n.m./f. fuss-pot; (fou) maniac.

manie /mani/ n.f. habit; obsession.

man|ier /manje/ v.t. handle. ~iement n.m. handling.

manière /manjɛr/ n.f. way, manner. ~s, (politesse) manners; (chichis) fuss. de cette ~, in this way. de ~ à, so as to. de toute ~, anyway, in any case.

maniéré /manjere/ a. affected.

manifestant, ~e /manifɛstɑ̃, -t/ n.m., f. demonstrator.

manifester[1] /manifɛste/ v.t. show, manifest. se ~ v. pr. (sentiment) show itself; (apparaître) appear.

manifest|er[2] /manifɛste/ v.i. (pol.) demonstrate. ~ation n.f. (pol.) demonstration; (événement) event.

manipul|er /manipyle/ v.t. handle; (péj.) manipulate. ~ation n.f. handling; (péj.) manipulation.

manivelle /manivɛl/ n.f. crank.

mannequin /mankɛ̃/ n.m. (personne) model; (statue) dummy.

manœuvre[1] /manœvr/ n.f. manœuvre. ~er v.t./i. manœuvre; (machine) operate.

manœuvre[2] /manœvr/ n.m. (ouvrier) labourer.

manoir /manwar/ n.m. manor.

manque /mɑ̃k/ n.m. lack (de, of); (vide) gap. ~s, (défauts) faults.

manqué /mɑ̃ke/ a. (écrivain etc.) failed. garçon ~, tomboy.

manqu|er /mɑ̃ke/ v.t. miss; (gâcher) spoil; (examen) fail. —v.i. be short ou lacking; (absent) be absent; (en moins, disparu) be missing; (échouer) fail. ~ à, (devoir) fail in. ~ de, be short of, lack. il/ça lui manque, he misses him/it.

manteau (pl. ~x) /mɑ̃to/ n.m. coat.

manucur|e /manykyr/ n.m./f. manicurist. ~er v.t. manicure.

manuel, ~le /manɥɛl/ a. manual. —n.m. (livre) manual.

manufactur|e /manyfaktyr/ n.f. factory. ~é a. manufactured.

manuscrit, ~e /manyskri, -t/ a. handwritten. —n.m. manuscript.

manutention /manytɑ̃sjɔ̃/ n.f. handling.

maquereau (pl. ~x) /makro/ n.m. (poisson) mackerel.

maquette /makɛt/ n.f. (scale) model; (mise en page) paste-up.

maquill|er /makije/ v.t. make up; (truquer) fake. se ~er v. pr. make (o.s.) up. ~age n.m. make-up.

maraîch|er, ~ère /mareʃe, -ɛʃɛr/ n.m., f. market gardener. cultures ~ères, market gardening.

marais /marɛ/ n.m. marsh.

marbre /marbr/ n.m. marble.

mare /mar/ n.m. (eau-de-vie) marc.

marchand, ~e /marʃɑ̃, -d/ n.m., f. trader; (de charbon, vins) merchant. —a. (valeur) market. ~ de journaux, newsagent. ~ de

légumes, greengrocer. ～ **de poissons,** fishmonger.

marchander /marʃɑ̃de/ *v.t.* haggle over. —*v.i.* haggle.

marchandise /marʃɑ̃diz/ *n.f.* goods.

marche /marʃ/ *n.f.* (*démarche, trajet*) walk; (*rythme*) pace; (*mil., mus.*) march; (*d'escalier*) step; (*sport*) walking; (*de machine*) working; (*de véhicule*) running. **en ～,** (*train etc.*) moving. **faire ～ arrière,** (*véhicule*) reverse. **mettre en ～,** start (up).

marché /marʃe/ *n.m.* market; (*contrat*) deal. **faire son ～,** do one's shopping. **～ aux puces,** flea market. **M～ commûn,** Common Market. **～ noir,** black market.

march|er /marʃe/ *v.i.* walk; (*aller*) go; (*fonctionner*) work, run; (*prospérer*) go well. **～eur,** **～euse** *n.m., f.* walker.

mardi /mardi/ *n.m.* Tuesday. **M～ gras,** Shrove Tuesday.

mare /mar/ *n.f.* (*étang*) pond; (*flaque*) pool.

marécag|e /marekaʒ/ *n.m.* marsh. **～eux, ～euse** *a.* marshy.

marée /mare/ *n.f.* tide; (*poissons*) fresh fish. **～ haute/basse,** high/low tide. **～ noire,** oil-slick.

margarine /margarin/ *n.f.* margarine.

marge /marʒ/ *n.f.* margin. **～ bénéficiaire,** profit margin.

margin|al, ～ale (*m. pl.* **～aux**) /marʒinal, -o/ *a.* marginal. —*n.m., f.* drop-out.

marguerite /margərit/ *n.f.* daisy.

mari /mari/ *n.m.* husband.

mariage /marjaʒ/ *n.m.* marriage; (*cérémonie*) wedding.

marié, ～e /marje/ *a.* married. —*n.m.* (bride)groom. —*n.f.* bride. **les ～s,** the bride and groom.

marier /marje/ *v.t.* marry. **se ～,** marry, get married (**avec,** to).

marin, ～e /marɛ̃, -in/ *a.* sea. —*n.m.* sailor. —*n.f.* navy.

mariner /marine/ *v.t./i.* marinate.

marionnette /marjɔnɛt/ *n.f.* puppet; (*à fils*) marionette.

maritime /maritim/ *a.* maritime, coastal; (*droit, agent*) shipping.

mark /mark/ *n.m.* mark.

marmelade /marməlad/ *n.f.* **～ (d'oranges),** marmelade.

marmite /marmit/ *n.f.* (cooking-) pot.

marmonner /marmɔne/ *v.t./i.* mumble.

Maroc /marɔk/ *n.m.* Morocco.

marocain, ～e /marɔkɛ̃, -ɛn/ *a. & n.m., f.* Moroccan.

maroquinerie /marɔkinri/ *n.f.* (*magasin*) leather goods shop.

marquant, ～e /markɑ̃, -t/ *a.* (*remarquable*) outstanding; (*qu'on n'oublie pas*) significant.

marque /mark/ *n.f.* mark; (*de produits*) brand, make. **de ～,** (*comm.*) brand-name; (*fig.*) important. **～ déposée,** registered trade mark.

marquer /marke/ *v.t.* mark; (*indiquer*) show; (*écrire*) note down; (*point, but*) score. —*v.i.* (*trace*) leave a mark; (*événement*) stand out.

marraine /marɛn/ *n.f.* godmother.

marrant, ～e /marɑ̃, -t/ *a.* (*fam.*) funny.

marre /mar/ *adv.* **en avoir ～,** (*fam.*) be fed up (**de,** with).

marrer (se) /(sə)mare/ *v. pr.* (*fam.*) laugh, have a (good) laugh.

marron /marɔ̃/ *n.m.* chestnut; (*couleur*) brown —*a. invar.* brown.

mars /mars/ *n.m.* March.

marsouin /marswɛ̃/ *n.m.* porpoise.

marteau (*pl.* ∼x) /marto/ *n.m.*
hammer. ∼ **piqueur** pneumatic
drill.

martien, ∼ne /marsjɛ̃, -jɛn/ *a.* &
n.m., f. Martian.

martyr, ∼e /martir/ *n.m., f.*
martyr. —*a.* martyred. ∼**iser** *v.t.*
martyr; (*fig.*) batter.

marxis|te /marksist/ *a.* & *n.m./f.*
Marxist. ∼**me** *n.m.* Marxism.

mascara /maskara/ *n.m.* mascara.

masculin, ∼e /maskylɛ̃, -in/ *a.*
masculine; (*sexe*) male; (*mode,
équipe*) men's. —*n.m.* masculine.
∼**ité** /-inite/ *n.f.* masculinity.

masochis|te /mazɔʃist/ *n.m./f.*
masochist. —*a.* masochistic.
∼**me** *n.m.* masochism.

masqu|e /mask/ *n.m.* mask. ∼**er**
v.t. (*cacher*) hide, conceal (**à**,
from); (*lumière*) block (off).

massacr|e /masakr/ *n.m.* mas-
sacre. ∼**er** *v.t.* massacre;
(*abîmer: fam.*) spoil.

massage /masaʒ/ *n.m.* massage.

masse /mas/ *n.f.* (*volume*) mass;
(*gros morceau*) lump, mass;
(*outil*) sledge-hammer. **en** ∼,
(*vendre*) in bulk; (*venir*) in force;
(*production*) mass. **la** ∼, (*foule*)
the masses. **une** ∼ **de**, (*fam.*)
masses of.

mass|er /mase/ *v.t.* (*pétrir*) mas-
sage. ∼**eur, ∼euse** *n.m., f.*
masseur, masseuse.

massi|f, ∼ve /masif, -v/ *a.* mas-
sive; (*or, argent*) solid. —*n.m.* (*de
fleurs*) clump; (*géog.*) massif.

massue /masy/ *n.f.* club, bludgeon.

mastiquer /mastike/ *v.t.* (*mâcher*)
chew.

mat /mat/ *a.* (*couleur*) matt; (*bruit*)
dull. **être** ∼, (*aux échecs*) be
checkmate.

mât /mɑ/ *n.m.* mast; (*pylône*) pole.

match /matʃ/ *n.m.* match; (*Amer.*)
game. (**faire**) ∼ **nul**, tie, draw. ∼

aller, first leg. ∼ **retour**, return
match.

matelas /matla/ *n.m.* mattress. ∼
pneumatique, air mattress.

matelassé /matlase/ *a.* padded;
(*tissu*) quilted.

matelot /matlo/ *n.m.* sailor.

matérialiste /materjalist/ *a.*
materialistic. —*n.m./f.* material-
ist.

matériaux /materjo/ *n.m. pl.*
materials.

matériel, ∼le /materjɛl/ *a.*
material.

maternel, ∼le /maternɛl/ *a.*
motherly, maternal; (*rapport de
parenté*) maternal. —*n.f.* nursery
school.

maternité /maternite/ *n.f.* maternity hospital; (*état de mère*)
motherhood.

mathémati|que /matematik/ *a.*
mathematical. —*n.f. pl.* mathematics. ∼**cien, ∼cienne** *n.m., f.*
mathematician.

maths /mat/ *n.f. pl.* (*fam.*) maths.

matière /matjɛr/ *n.f.* matter;
(*produit*) material; (*sujet*) subject.
∼ **plastique**, plastic. ∼**s
grasses**, fat. **à 0% de** ∼**s
grasses**, fat free. ∼**s premières**,
raw materials.

matin /matɛ̃/ *n.m.* morning. **de
bon** ∼, early in the morning.

matin|al (*m. pl.* ∼**aux**) /matinal,
-o/ *a.* morning; (*de bonne heure*)
early. **être** ∼, be up early.

matinée /matine/ *n.f.* morning;
(*spectacle*) matinée.

matrimon|ial (*m. pl.* ∼**iaux**)
/matrimɔnjal, -jo/ *a.* matri-
monial.

maturité /matyrite/ *n.f.* maturity.

maudit, ∼e /modi, -t/ *a.* (*fam.*)
damned.

maussade /mosad/ *a.* gloomy.

mauvais, ∼e /mɔvɛ, -z/ *a.* def-

(erroné) wrong; *(malveillant)* evil; *(désagréable)* nasty, bad; *(mer)* rough. —*n.m.* il fait ~, the weather is bad. le ~ moment, the wrong time.

mauve /mov/ *a.* & *n.m.* mauve.

maux /mo/ *voir* **mal²**.

maxim|al *(m. pl.* ~**aux**) /maksimal, -o/ *a.* maximal.

maximum /maksimɔm/ *a.* & *n.m.* maximum. **au** ~, as much as possible; *(tout au plus)* at most.

mayonnaise /majɔnɛz/ *n.f.* mayonnaise.

mazout /mazut/ *n.m.* (fuel) oil.

me, m'* /mə, m/ *pron.* me; *(indirect)* (to) me; *(réfléchi)* myself.

mec /mɛk/ *n.m.* *(fam.)* bloke, guy.

mécanicien /mekanisjɛ̃/ *n.m.* mechanic; *(rail.)* train driver.

mécanique /mekanik/ *a.* mechanical; *(jouet)* clockwork. **problème** ~, engine trouble. —*n.f.* mechanics; *(mécanisme)* mechanism.

mécanisme /mekanism/ *n.m.* mechanism.

méch|ant, ~ante /meʃɑ̃, -t/ *a.* *(cruel)* wicked; *(désagréable)* nasty; *(enfant)* naughty; *(chien)* vicious; *(sensationnel: fam.)* terrific. —*n.m., f.* *(enfant)* naughty child. **~amment** *adv.* wickedly. **~anceté** *n.f.* wickedness; *(action)* wicked action.

mèche /mɛʃ/ *n.f.* *(de cheveux)* lock; *(de bougie)* wick; *(d'explosif)* fuse.

méconnu /mekɔny/ *a.* unrecognized.

mécontent, ~e /mekɔ̃tɑ̃, -t/ *a.* dissatisfied *(de,* with); *(irrité)* annoyed *(de,* at, with). **~ement** /-tmɑ̃/ *n.m.* dissatisfaction; annoyance.

médaill|e /medaj/ *n.f.* medal; *(insigne)* badge; *(bijou)* medallion.

médaillon /medajɔ̃/ *n.m.* medallion; *(bijou)* locket.

médecin /medsɛ̃/ *n.m.* doctor.

médecine /medsin/ *n.f.* medicine.

média /medja/ *n.m.* medium. **les** ~**s,** the media.

média|teur, ~trice /medjatœr, -tris/ *n.m., f.* mediator.

médiation /medjasjɔ̃/ *n.f.* mediation.

médiatique /medjatik/ *a.* **événement/personnalité** ~, media event/personality.

médic|al *(m. pl.* ~**aux**) /medikal, -o/ *a.* medical.

médicament /medikamɑ̃/ *n.m.* medicine.

médiév|al *(m. pl.* ~**aux**) /medjeval, -o/ *a.* medieval.

médiocr|e /medjɔkr/ *a.* mediocre, poor. **~ement** *adv.* *(peu)* not very; *(mal)* in a mediocre way. **~ité** *n.f.* mediocrity.

Méditerranée /mediterane/ *n.f.* **la** ~, the Mediterranean.

méditerranéen, ~ne /mediteraneɛ̃, -ɛn/ *a.* Mediterranean.

médium /medjɔm/ *n.m.* *(personne)* medium.

méduse /medyz/ *n.f.* jellyfish.

meeting /mitiŋ/ *n.m.* meeting.

méfait /mefɛ/ *n.m.* misdeed.

méfian|t, ~te /mefjɑ̃, -t/ *a.* distrustful. **~ce** *n.f.* distrust.

méfier (se) /(sə)mefje/ *v. pr.* be wary *ou* careful. **se** ~ **de,** distrust, be wary of.

mégarde (par) /(par)megard/ *adv.* by accident, accidentally.

mégot /mego/ *n.m.* *(fam.)* cigarette-end.

meilleur, ~e /mɛjœr/ *a.* & *adv.* better *(que,* than). **le** ~ **livre**/*etc.,* the best book/*etc.* **mon** ~ **ami**/*etc.,* my best friend/*etc.* ~ **marché,** cheaper. —*n.m., f.* **le** ~/**la** ~**e,** the best (one).

mélancolie /melɑ̃kɔli/ *n.f.* melancholy. ~**ique** *a.* melancholy.

mélange /melɑ̃ʒ/ *n.m.* mixture, blend. ~**er** *v.t.* mix (à, with). se ~**er** *v. pr.* mix, blend; (*embrouiller*) mix up.

mêler /mele/ *v.t.* mix (à, with). se ~ **à**, (*se joindre à*) join. se ~ **de**, meddle in. **mêle-toi de ce qui te regarde**, mind your own business.

mélo /melo/ (*fam.*) *n.m.* melodrama. —*a. invar.* melodramatic.

mélodie /melɔdi/ *n.f.* melody. ~**ieux**, ~**ieuse** *a.* melodious. ~**ique** *a.* melodic.

mélodrame /melɔdram/ *n.m.* melodrama.

mélomane /melɔman/ *n.m./f.* music lover.

melon /ml̃ɔ/ *n.m.* melon.

membrane /mɑ̃bran/ *n.f.* membrane.

membre[1] /mɑ̃br/ *n.m.* limb.

membre[2] /mɑ̃br/ *n.m.* member.

même /mɛm/ *a.* same. —*pron.* le ~/**la** ~, the same (one). de ~, (*aussi*) too; (*de la même façon*) likewise. de ~ **que**, just as. en ~ **temps**, at the same time.

mémé /meme/ *n.f.* (*fam.*) granny.

mémoire /memwar/ *n.f.* memory. —*n.m.* (*requête*) memorandum; (*univ.*) dissertation. ~**s**, (*souvenirs écrits*) memoirs. à la ~ **de**, to the memory of. de ~, from memory. ~ **morte/vive**, (*comput.*) ROM/RAM.

menace /mənas/ *n.f.* threat. ~**er** *v.t.* threaten (**de faire**, to do).

ménage /menaʒ/ *n.m.* (married) couple; (*travail*) housework. se **mettre en** ~, set up house. **scène de** ~, scene. **dépenses du** ~, household expenditure.

ménagement /menaʒmɑ̃/ *n.m.* care and consideration.

ménag|er[1], ~**ère** /menaʒe, -ɛr/ *a.* household, domestic. **travaux** ~**ers**, housework.

ménager[2] /menaʒe/ *v.t.* treat with tact; (*utiliser*) be sparing in the use of.

mendiant, ~**e** /mɑ̃djɑ̃, -t/ *n.m.*, *f.* beggar.

mendier /mɑ̃dje/ *v.t.* beg for. —*v.i.* beg.

mener /məne/ *v.t.* lead; (*entreprise, pays*) run. —*v.i.* lead. ~ **à**, (*accompagner à*) take to.

méningite /menɛ̃ʒit/ *n.f.* meningitis.

ménopause /menɔpoz/ *n.f.* menopause.

mensonge /mɑ̃sɔ̃ʒ/ *n.m.* lie.

menstruation /mɑ̃stryasjɔ̃/ *n.f.* menstruation.

mensualité /mɑ̃sɥalite/ *n.f.* monthly payment.

mensuel, ~**le** /mɑ̃sɥel/ *a.* & *n.m.* monthly. ~**lement** *adv.* monthly.

mensurations /mɑ̃syrasjɔ̃/ *n.f. pl.* measurements.

ment|al (*m. pl.* ~**aux**) /mɑ̃tal, -o/ *a.* mental.

mentalité /mɑ̃talite/ *n.f.* mentality.

menteu|r, ~**se** /mɑ̃tœr, -øz/ *n.m.*, *f.* liar. —*a.* untruthful.

menthe /mɑ̃t/ *n.f.* mint.

mention /mɑ̃sjɔ̃/ *n.f.* mention; (*annotation*) note; (*scol.*) grade. ~**ner** /-jɔne/ *v.t.* mention.

mentir† /mɑ̃tir/ *v.i.* lie.

menton /mɑ̃tɔ̃/ *n.m.* chin.

menu[1] /məny/ *n.m.* (*carte*) menu; (*repas*) meal.

menu[2] /məny/ *a.* (*petit*) tiny; (*fin*) fine; (*insignifiant*) minor. —*adv.* (*couper*) fine.

menuis|ier /mənɥizje/ *n.m.* carpenter, joiner. ~**erie** *n.f.* carpentry, joinery.

mépris /mepri/ *n.m.* contempt, scorn (**de**, for).

méprisable /meprizabl/ *a.* despicable.

méprisjer /meprize/ *v.t.* scorn, despise. ∼**ant**, ∼**ante** *a.* scornful.

mer /mɛr/ *n.f.* sea; (**marée**) tide.

merci /mɛrsi/ *int.* thank you, thanks (**de**, **pour**, for). —*n.f.* mercy. ∼ **beaucoup**, ∼ **bien**, thank you very much.

mercredi /mɛrkrədi/ *n.m.* Wednesday.

mercure /mɛrkyr/ *n.m.* mercury.

merde /mɛrd/ *n.f.* (*fam.*) shit. **être dans la** ∼, be in a mess.

mère /mɛr/ *n.f.* mother. ∼ **de famille**, mother.

méridien /meridjɛ̃/ *n.m.* meridian.

méridionjal, ∼**ale** (*m. pl.* ∼**aux**) /meridjɔnal, -o/ *a.* southern. —*n.m.*, *f.* southerner.

meringue /mərɛ̃g/ *n.f.* meringue.

mérite /merit/ *n.m.* merit.

mériter /merite/ *v.t.* deserve.

merlan /mɛrlɑ̃/ *n.m.* whiting.

merle /mɛrl/ *n.m.* blackbird.

merveille /mɛrvɛj/ *n.f.* wonder, marvel. **à** ∼, wonderfully.

merveilleu|x, ∼**se** /mɛrvɛjø, -z/ *a.* wonderful, marvellous.

mes /me/ *voir* **mon**.

mésange /mezɑ̃ʒ/ *n.f.* tit(mouse).

mésaventure /mezavɑ̃tyr/ *n.f.* misadventure.

mesdames /medam/ *voir* **madame**.

mesdemoiselles /medmwazɛl/ *voir* **mademoiselle**.

mésentente /mezɑ̃tɑ̃t/ *n.f.* disagreement.

mesquin, ∼**e** /mɛskɛ̃, -in/ *a.* mean.

messagje /mesaʒ/ *n.m.* message. ∼**er**, ∼**ère** *n.m.*, *f.* messenger.

messe /mɛs/ *n.f.* (*relig.*) mass.

Messie /mesi/ *n.m.* Messiah.

messieurs /mesjø/ *voir* **monsieur**.

mesure /məzyr/ *n.f.* measurement; (*quantité*, *étalon*) measure; (*disposition*) measure, step; (*cadence*) time; (*modération*) moderation. **dans la** ∼ **où**, in so far as.

mesurer /məzyre/ *v.t.* measure; (*argent*, *temps*) ration.

met /mɛ/ *voir* **mettre**.

métabolisme /metabɔlism/ *n.m.* metabolism.

métjal (*pl.* ∼**aux**) /metal, -o/ *n.m.* metal; (*objet*) metal; (*éclat etc.*) metallic.

métallurgjie /metalyrʒi/ *n.f.* (*industrie*) steel *ou* metal industry. ∼**iste** *n.m.* steel *ou* metal worker.

métamorphosje /metamɔrfoz/ *n.f.* metamorphosis. ∼**er** *v.t.*, **se** ∼**er** *v. pr.* transform.

météo /meteo/ *n.f.* (*bulletin*) weather forecast.

météore /meteɔr/ *n.m.* meteor.

météorologjie /meteɔrɔlɔʒi/ *n.f.* meteorology; (*service*) weather bureau. ∼**ique** *a.* weather; (*études etc.*) meteorological.

méthodje /metɔd/ *n.f.* method; (*ouvrage*) course, manual. ∼**ique** *a.* methodical.

méticuleu|x, ∼**se** /metikylø, -z/ *a.* meticulous.

métier /metje/ *n.m.* job; (*manuel*) trade; (*intellectuel*) profession; (*expérience*) skill. ∼ (**à tisser**), loom.

métrage /metraʒ/ *n.m.* length. **court** ∼, short film. **long** ∼, full-length film.

mètre /mɛtr/ *n.m.* metre; (*règle*) rule. ∼ **ruban**, tape-measure.

métrique /metrik/ *a.* metric.

métro /metro/ *n.m.* underground; (*à Paris*) Métro.

métropole /metrɔpɔl/ *n.f.* metropolis; (*pays*) mother country.

mets[1] /mɛ/ *n.m.* dish.

mets[2] /mɛ/ *voir* **mettre**.

mettable /metabl/ *a.* wearable.

metteur /metœr/ *n.m.* ~ **en scène**, (*théâtre*) producer; (*cinéma*) director.

mettre† /metr/ *v.t.* put; (*vêtement*) put on; (*radio, chauffage, etc.*) put ou switch on; (*table*) lay; (*temps*) take; (*installer*) put in. **se** ~ *v. pr.* put o.s.; (*objet*) go; (*porter*) wear. ~ **en colère**, make angry. **se** ~ **à faire**, start doing. **se** ~ **à l'aise**, make o.s. comfortable. **se** ~ **à table**, sit down at the table. **se** ~ **au travail**, set to work. **se** ~ **dans tous ses états**, get into a state.

meuble /mœbl/ *n.m.* piece of furniture. ~**s**, furniture.

meublé /mœble/ *n.m.* furnished flatlet.

meubler /mœble/ *v.t.* furnish; (*fig.*) fill. **se** ~ *v. pr.* buy furniture.

meule /møl/ *n.f.* (*de foin*) haystack; (*à moudre*) millstone.

meurs, meurt /mœr/ *voir* **mourir**.

meurtr|e /mœrtr/ *n.m.* murder. ~**ier**, ~**ière** *a.* deadly; *n.m.* murderer; *n.f.* murderess.

mexicain, ~**e** /mɛksikɛ̃, -ɛn/ *a. & n.m., f.* Mexican.

Mexique /mɛksik/ *n.m.* Mexico.

mi- /mi/ *préf.* mid-, half-. **à mi-chemin**, half-way. **la mi-juin**/*etc.*, mid-June/*etc.*

miaou /mjau/ *n.m.* mew.

miauler /mjole/ *v.i.* mew.

miche /miʃ/ *n.f.* round loaf.

micro /mikro/ *n.m.* microphone, mike; (*comput.*) micro.

micro- /mikro/ *préf.* micro-.

microbe /mikrɔb/ *n.m.* germ.

micro-onde /mikrɔõd/ *n.f.* microwave. **un** (**four à**) ~**s**, microwave (oven).

microphone /mikrɔfɔn/ *n.m.* microphone.

microprocesseur /mikroprɔsesœr/ *n.m.* microprocess.

microscop|e /mikrɔskɔp/ *n.m.* microscope. ~**ique** *a.* microscopic.

midi /midi/ *n.m.* twelve o'clock, midday, noon; (*déjeuner*) lunchtime; (*sud*) south. **le M**~, the South of France.

mie /mi/ *n.f.* soft part of the loaf. **un pain de** ~, a sandwich loaf.

miel /mjɛl/ *n.m.* honey.

mien, ~**ne** /mjɛ̃, mjɛn/ *pron.* **le** ~, **la** ~**ne**, **les** ~(**ne**)**s**, mine.

miette /mjɛt/ *n.f.* crumb.

mieux /mjø/ *adv. & a. invar.* better (**que**, than). **le** *ou* **la** *ou* **les** ~, (the) best. —*n.m.* best; (*progrès*) improvement. **faire de son** ~, do one's best. **tu ferais** ~ **de faire**, you would be better off doing.

mignon, ~**ne** /miɲɔ̃, -ɔn/ *a.* pretty.

migraine /migrɛn/ *n.f.* headache.

migration /migrɑsjɔ̃/ *n.f.* migration.

mijoter /miʒɔte/ *v.t./i.* simmer.

milieu (*pl.* ~**x**) /miljø/ *n.m.* middle; (*environnement*) environment; (*groupe*) circle. **au** ~ **de**, in the middle of.

militaire /militɛr/ *a.* military. —*n.m.* soldier.

milk-shake /milkʃɛk/ *n.m.* milk shake.

mille[1] /mil/ *a. & n.m. invar.* a thousand. **deux** ~, two thousand. **dans le** ~, bang on target.

mille[2] /mil/ *n.m.* ~ (**marin**), (nautical) mile.

millénaire /milenɛr/ *n.m.* millennium.

mille-pattes /milpat/ *n.m. invar.* centipede.

millésime /milezim/ *n.m.* year.

millésimé /milezime/ *a.* **vin** ~, vintage wine.

milliard /miljar/ *n.m.* thousand million, billion. ~**aire** /-dɛr/ *n.m./f.* multimillionaire.

millier /milje/ *n.m.* thousand. **un** ~ **(de)**, about a thousand.

millimètre /milimɛtr/ *n.m.* millimetre.

million /miljɔ̃/ *n.m.* million. **deux** ~**s (de)**, two million. ~**naire** /-jɔnɛr/ *n.m./f.* millionaire.

mimosa /mimoza/ *n.m.* mimosa.

minable /minabl/ *a.* shabby.

minaret /minarɛ/ *n.m.* minaret.

minc|e /mɛ̃s/ *a.* thin; (*svelte, insignifiant*) slim. —*int.* dash (it). ~**ir** *v.i.* get slimmer. **ça te** ~**it**, it makes you look slimmer. ~**eur** *n.f.* thinness; slimness.

mine[1] /min/ *n.f.* expression; (*allure*) appearance. **avoir bonne** ~, look well.

mine[2] /min/ *n.f.* (*exploitation, explosif*) mine; (*de crayon*) lead.

minerai /minrɛ/ *n.m.* ore.

minér|al (*m. pl.* ~**aux**) /mineral, -o/ *a.* mineral. —*n.m.* (*pl.* ~**aux**) mineral.

minéralogique /mineralɔʒik/ *a.* **plaque** ~, number/license (*Amer.*) plate.

mineur[1], ~**e** /minœr/ *a.* minor; (*jurid.*) under age. —*n.m.*, *f.* (*jurid.*) minor.

mineur[2] /minœr/ *n.m.* (*ouvrier*) miner.

mini- /mini/ *préf.* mini-.

miniature /minjatyr/ *n.f. & a.* miniature.

minibus /minibys/ *n.m.* minibus.

minim|al (*m. pl.* ~**aux**) /minimal, -o/ *a.* minimum.

minimum /minimɔm/ *a. & n.m.* minimum. **au** ~, (*pour le moins*) at the very least.

mini-ordinateur /miniɔrdinatœr/ *n.m.* minicomputer.

minist|ère /minister/ *n.m.* ministry; (*gouvernement*) government. ~**ère de l'Intérieur**, Home Office. ~**ériel**, ~**érielle** *a.* ministerial, government.

ministre /ministr/ *n.m.* minister. ~ **de l'Intérieur**, Home Secretary.

Minitel /minitɛl/ *n.m.* (P.) Minitel (*telephone videotext system*).

minorit|é /minɔrite/ *n.f.* minority. **être** ~**aire**, be in the minority.

minuit /minɥi/ *n.m.* midnight.

minuscule /minyskyl/ *a.* minute. —*n.f.* (*lettre*) ~, small letter.

minute /minyt/ *n.f.* minute.

minuterie /minytri/ *n.f.* time-switch.

minutieu|x, ~**se** /minysjø, -z/ *a.* meticulous. ~**sement** *adv.* meticulously.

mirabelle /mirabɛl/ *n.f.* (mirabelle) plum.

miracle /mirakl/ *n.m.* miracle.

miraculeu|x, ~**se** /mirakylø, -z/ *a.* miraculous.

mirage /miraʒ/ *n.m.* mirage.

mire /mir/ *n.f.* (*fig.*) centre of attraction; (TV) test card.

miroir /mirwar/ *n.m.* mirror.

mis, ~**e**[1] /mi, miz/ *voir* **mettre**. —*a.* **bien** ~, well-dressed.

mise[2] /miz/ *n.f.* (*argent*) stake; (*tenue*) attire. ~ **au point**, adjustment; (*fig.*) clarification. ~ **en scène**, (*théâtre*) production; (*cinéma*) direction.

miser /mize/ *v.t.* (*argent*) bet, stake (**sur**, on).

misérable /mizerabl/ *a.* miserable, wretched; (*indigent*) poverty-stricken;   (*minable*) seedy. /mizɛr/ n.*f.* wretch.

misère /mizɛr/ n.*f.* (grinding) poverty; (*malheur*) misery.

miséricorde /mizerikɔrd/ n.*f.* mercy.

missel /misɛl/ n.*m.* missal.

missile /misil/ n.*m.* missile.

mission /misjɔ̃/ n.*m.* mission.

mistral /mistral/ n.*m. invar.* (*vent*) mistral.

mite /mit/ n.*f.* (clothes-)moth.

mi-temps /mitɑ̃/ n.*f. invar.* (*repos: sport*) half-time; (*période: sport*) half. ∼, part time.

mitonner /mitɔne/ v.*t.* cook slowly with care; (*fig.*) cook up.

mitoyen, ∼ne /mitwajɛ̃, -ɛn/ a. mur ∼, party wall.

mitraillette /mitrajɛt/ n.*f.* sub-machine-gun. ∼euse n.*f.* machine-gun.

mixeur /miksœr/ n.*m.* liquidizer, blender.

mixte /mikst/ a. mixed; (*usage*) dual; (*tribunal*) joint; (*école*) co-educational.

mobile /mɔbil/ a. mobile; (*pièce*) moving; (*feuillet*) loose. —n.*m.* (*art*) mobile.

mobilier /mɔbilje/ n.*m.* furniture.

mobilis|er /mɔbilize/ v.*t.* mobilize. ∼ation n.*f.* mobilization.

mobilité /mɔbilite/ n.*f.* mobility.

mobylette /mɔbilɛt/ n.*f.* (P.) moped.

mocassin /mɔkasɛ̃/ n.*m.* mocassin.

moche /mɔʃ/ a. (*laid: fam.*) ugly; (*mauvais: fam.*) lousy.

modalité /mɔdalite/ n.*f.* mode.

mode[1] /mɔd/ n.*f.* fashion; (*coutume*) custom. à la ∼, fashionable.

mode[2] /mɔd/ n.*m.* method, mode; (*genre*) way. ∼ d'emploi, directions (for use).

modèle /mɔdɛl/ n.*m. & a.* model.

modem /mɔdɛm/ n.*m.* modem.

modéré, ∼e /mɔdere/ a. & n.*m., f.* moderate. ∼ment adv. moderately.

modér|er /mɔdere/ v.*t.* moderate. ∼ation n.*f.* moderation.

modern|e /mɔdɛrn/ a. modern. —n.*m.* modern style. ∼iser v.*t.* modernize.

modest|e /mɔdɛst/ a. modest. ∼ement adv. modestly. ∼ie n.*f.* modesty.

modif|ier /mɔdifje/ v.*t.* modify. se ∼ier v. pr. alter. ∼ication n.*f.* modification.

moelle /mwal/ n.*f.* marrow. ∼ épinière, spinal cord.

moelleu|x, ∼se /mwalø, -z/ a. soft; (*onctueux*) smooth.

mœurs /mœr(s)/ n.*f. pl.* (*morale*) morals; (*habitudes*) customs; (*manières*) ways.

moi /mwa/ pron. me; (*indirect*) (to) me; (*sujet*) I. —n.*m.* self. ∼-même pron. myself.

moindre /mwɛ̃dr/ a. (*moins grand*) less(er). le ou la ∼, les ∼s, the slightest, the least.

moine /mwan/ n.*m.* monk.

moineau (pl. ∼x) /mwano/ n.*m.* sparrow.

moins /mwɛ̃/ adv. less (*que*, than). —prép. (*soustraction*) minus. ∼ de, (*quantité*) less, not so much (*que*, as); (*objets, personnes*) fewer, not so many (*que*, as). ∼ de dix francs/d'une livre/*etc.*, less than ten francs/one pound/ *etc.* le ou la ou les ∼, the least. le ∼ grand/haut, the smallest/lowest. au ∼, du ∼, at least. de ∼, less. en ∼, less; (*manquant*) missing. une heure ∼ dix, ten to one. à ∼ que, unless. de ∼ en moins, less and less.

mois /mwa/ *n.m.* month.

moïse /mɔiz/ *n.m.* moses basket.

mois|i /mwazi/ *a.* mouldy. —*n.m.* mould. **de ~i,** (*odeur, goût*) musty. **~ir** *v.i.* go mouldy. **~issure** *n.f.* mould.

moisson /mwasɔ̃/ *n.f.* harvest.

moissonn|er /mwasɔne/ *v.t.* harvest, reap. **~euse-batteuse** (*pl.* **~euses-batteuses**) *n.f.* combine harvester.

moit|e /mwat/ *a.* sticky, clammy. **~eur** *n.f.* stickiness.

moitié /mwatje/ *n.f.* half; (*milieu*) half-way mark. **à ~,** half-way. **à ~ vide/fermé**/*etc.,* half empty/ closed/*etc.* **à ~ prix,** (at) half-price. **la ~ de,** half (of). **~ moitié,** half-and-half.

moka /mɔka/ *n.m.* (*gâteau*) coffee cream cake.

mol /mɔl/ *voir* **mou**.

molaire /mɔlɛr/ *n.f.* molar.

molécule /mɔlekyl/ *n.f.* molecule.

molle /mɔl/ *voir* **mou**.

mollement /mɔlmɑ̃/ *adv.* softly; (*faiblement*) feebly.

mollet /mɔlɛ/ *n.m.* (*de jambe*) calf.

molletonné /mɔltɔne/ *a.* (fleece)-lined.

mollusque /mɔlysk/ *n.m.* mollusc.

môme /mom/ *n.m./f.* (*fam.*) kid.

moment /mɔmɑ̃/ *n.m.* moment; (*période*) time. (**petit**) **~,** short while. **au ~ où,** when. **en ce ~,** at the moment.

momentané /mɔmɑ̃tane/ *a.* momentary. **~ment** *adv.* momentarily; (*en ce moment*) at present.

mon, ma *ou* **mon*** (*pl.* **mes**) /mɔ̃, ma, mɔ̃n, me/ *a.* my.

Monaco /mɔnako/ *n.f.* Monaco.

monarchie /mɔnarʃi/ *n.f.* monarchy.

monastère /mɔnastɛr/ *n.m.* monastery.

mondain, ~e /mɔ̃dɛ̃, -ɛn/ *a.* society, social.

monde /mɔ̃d/ *n.m.* world. **du ~,** (a lot of) people; (*quelqu'un*) somebody.

mond|ial (*m. pl.* **~iaux**) /mɔ̃djal, -jo/ *a.* world; (*influence*) worldwide. **~ialement** *adv.* the world over.

monégasque /mɔnegask/ *a.* & *n.m./f.* Monegasque.

monétaire /mɔnetɛr/ *a.* monetary.

moni|teur, ~trice /mɔnitœr, -tris/ *n.m., f.* instructor, instructress; (*de colonie de vacances*) supervisor; (*Amer.*) (camp) counselor.

monnaie /mɔnɛ/ *n.f.* currency; (*pièce*) coin; (*appoint*) change. **faire la ~ de,** get change for. **faire à qn. la ~ de,** give s.o. change for. **menue** *ou* **petite ~,** small change.

mono /mɔno/ *a. invar.* mono.

monopol|e /mɔnɔpɔl/ *n.m.* monopoly. **~iser** *v.t.* monopolize.

monoton|e /mɔnɔtɔn/ *a.* monotonous. **~ie** *n.f.* monotony.

monseigneur /mɔ̃sɛɲœr/ *n.m.* Your *ou* His Grace.

monsieur (*pl.* **messieurs**) /məsjø, mesjø/ *n.m.* gentleman. **M~** *ou* **M. Dupont,** Mr Dupont. **Messieurs** *ou* **MM. Dupont,** Messrs Dupont. **oui ~,** yes; (*avec déférence*) yes, sir.

monstre /mɔ̃str/ *n.m.* monster. —*a.* (*fam.*) colossal.

monstr|ueux, ~ueuse /mɔ̃stryø, -z/ *a.* monstrous.

mont /mɔ̃/ *n.m.* mount.

montage /mɔ̃taʒ/ *n.m.* (*assemblage*) assembly; (*cinéma*) editing.

montagn|e /mɔ̃taɲ/ *n.f.* mountain; (*région*) mountains. **~es russes,** roller-coaster. **~ard, ~arde**

n.m., f. mountain dweller. **~eux,**
~euse *a.* mountainous.

montant¹, ~e /mõtã, -t/ *a.*
rising; (*col*) high-necked.

montant² /mõtã/ *n.m.* amount;
(*pièce de bois*) upright.

monte-charge /mõtʃarʒ/ *n.m.* invar. service lift.

montée /mõte/ *n.f.* ascent, climb;
(*de prix*) rise; (*côte*) hill.

monter /mõte/ *v.i.* (*aux. être*) go ou
come up; (*grimper*) climb; (*prix,*
mer) rise. **~ à,** (*cheval*) mount. **~**
dans, (*train, avion*) get on to;
(*voiture*) get into. **~ sur,** (*colline*)
climb up; (*trône*) ascend. —*v.t.*
(*aux. avoir*) go ou come up; (*objet*)
take ou bring up; (*cheval, garde*)
mount; (*société*) start up. **~ à**
cheval, (*sport*) ride.

monteu|r, ~se /mõtœr, -øz/
n.m., f. (*techn.*) fitter; (*cinéma*)
editor.

montre /mõtr/ *n.f.* watch.

montrer /mõtre/ *v.t.* show (**à,** to).
~ du doigt, point to.

monture /mõtyr/ *n.f.* (*cheval*)
mount; (*de lunettes*) frame.

monument /mõnymã/ *n.m.* monument. **~ aux morts,** war
memorial.

moqu|er (se) /(sə)mɔke/ *v. pr.* se
~er de, make fun of.

moquette /mɔkɛt/ *n.f.* fitted carpet.

mor|al, ~ale (*m. pl.* **~aux**)
/mɔral, -o/ *a.* moral. —*n.m.* (*pl.*
~aux) morale. —*n.f.* moral code;
(*mœurs*) morals; (*de fable*) moral.
avoir le ~al, be on form.

morceau (*pl.* **~x**) /mɔrso/ *n.m.*
piece, bit; (*de sucre*) lump; (*de*
viande) cut; (*passage*) passage.
manger un ~, have a bite to eat.

mordre /mɔrdr/ *v.t./i.* bite. **~ sur,**
overlap into. **~ à l'hameçon,**
bite.

morgue /mɔrg/ *n.f.* morgue, mortuary.

morne /mɔrn/ *a.* dull.

morose /mɔroz/ *a.* morose.

morphine /mɔrfin/ *n.f.* morphine.

mors /mɔr/ *n.m.* (*de cheval*) bit.

morse¹ /mɔrs/ *n.m.* walrus.

morse² /mɔrs/ *n.m.* (*code*) Morse
code.

morsure /mɔrsyr/ *n.f.* bite.

mort¹ /mɔr/ *n.f.* death.

mort², ~e /mɔr, -t/ *a.* dead.
—*n.m., f.* dead man, dead woman.
les ~s, the dead. **~ de fatigue,**
dead tired. **~-né** *a.* stillborn.

mortadelle /mɔrtadɛl/ *n.f.* mor-
tadella.

mortalité /mɔrtalite/ *n.f.* death
rate.

mortel, ~le /mɔrtɛl/ *a.* mortal;
(*accident*) fatal; (*poison, silence*)
deadly. —*n.m., f.* mortal.

mortier /mɔrtje/ *n.m.* mortar.

morue /mɔry/ *n.f.* cod.

mosaïque /mozaik/ *n.f.* mosaic.

Moscou /mɔsku/ *n.m./f.* Moscow.

mosquée /mɔske/ *n.f.* mosque.

mot /mo/ *n.m.* word; (*lettre,*
message) line, note. **~s croisés,**
crossword (puzzle).

motard /mɔtar/ *n.m.* biker;
(*policier*) police motorcyclist.

motel /mɔtɛl/ *n.m.* motel.

moteur¹ /mɔtœr/ *n.m.* engine,
motor; **barque à ~,** motor
launch.

mo|teur², ~trice /mɔtœr, -tris/
a. (*nerf*) motor; (*force*) driving. **à**
4 roues motrices, 4-wheel drive.

motif /mɔtif/ *n.m.* reason; (*jurid.*)
motive; (*dessin*) pattern.

motiv|er /mɔtive/ *v.t.* motivate;
(*justifier*) justify. **~ation** *n.f.*
motivation.

moto /mɔto/ *n.f.* motor cycle.
~cycliste *n.m./f.* motorcyclist.

motorisé /mɔtorize/ *a.* motorized.

motrice /mɔtris/ *voir* **moteur**².

motte /mɔt/ *n.f.* lump; (*de beurre*) slab; (*de terre*) clod.

mou *ou* **mol*** , **molle** /mu, mɔl/ *a.* soft; (*péj.*) flabby; (*faible, indolent*) feeble.

mouche /muʃ/ *n.f.* fly.

moucher (se) /(sə)muʃe/ *v. pr.* blow one's nose.

moucheron /muʃrɔ̃/ *n.m.* midge.

mouchoir /muʃwar/ *n.m.* hanky; handkerchief; (*en papier*) tissue.

moudre /mudr/ *v.t.* grind.

moue /mu/ *n.f.* long face. **faire la ~**, pull a long face.

mouette /mwɛt/ *n.f.* (sea)gull.

moufle /mufl/ *n.f.* (*gant*) mitten.

mouiller /muje/ *v.t.* wet, make wet. **se ~er** *v. pr.* get (o.s.) wet. **~er (l'ancre)**, anchor.

moulage /mulaʒ/ *n.m.* cast.

moule¹ /mul/ *n.m.* mould. **~er** *v.t.* mould; (*statue*) cast. **~e à gâteau**, cake tin. **~e à tarte**, flan dish.

moule² /mul/ *n.f.* (*coquillage*) mussel.

moulin /mulɛ̃/ *n.m.* mill. **~ à vent**, windmill.

moulinet /mulinɛ/ *n.m.* (*de canne à pêche*) reel.

mourir† /murir/ *v.i.* (*aux. être*) die. **~ d'envie de**, be dying to. **~ de faim**, be starving. **~ d'ennui**, be dead bored.

mousquetaire /muskətɛr/ *n.m.* musketeer.

mousse /mus/ *n.f.* moss; (*écume*) froth, foam; (*de savon*) lather; (*dessert*) mousse. **~ à raser**, shaving cream.

mousseline /muslin/ *n.f.* muslin; (*de soie*) chiffon.

mousser /muse/ *v.i.* froth, foam; (*savon*) lather.

mousseu|x, **~se** /musø, -z/ *a.* frothy. —*n.m.* sparkling wine.

moustach|e /mustaʃ/ *n.f.* moustache. **~es**, (*d'animal*) whiskers. **~u** *a.* wearing a moustache.

moustiquaire /mustikɛr/ *n.f.* mosquito-net.

moustique /mustik/ *n.m.* mosquito.

moutarde /mutard/ *n.f.* mustard.

mouton /mutɔ̃/ *n.m.* sheep; (*peau*) sheepskin; (*viande*) mutton.

mouvement /muvmɑ̃/ *n.m.* movement; (*agitation*) bustle; (*en gymnastique*) exercise. **en ~**, in motion.

mouvementé /muvmɑ̃te/ *a.* eventful.

moyen¹, **~ne** /mwajɛ̃, -jɛn/ *a.* average; (*médiocre*) poor. —*n.f.* average; (*scol.*) pass-mark. **de taille ~ne**, medium-sized. **~ âge**, Middle Ages. **M~-Orient** *n.m.* Middle East.

moyen² /mwajɛ̃/ *n.m.* means, way. **~s**, means; (*dons*) abilities. **il n'y a pas de ~ de**, it is not possible to.

moyeu /mwajø/ *n.m.* (*pl.* **~x**) hub.

mucoviscidose /mykɔvisidoz/ *n.f.* cystic fibrosis.

mue /my/ *n.f.* moulting; (*de voix*) breaking of the voice.

muer /mɥe/ *v.i.* moult; (*voix*) break. **se ~ en**, change into.

muesli /mysli/ *n.m.* muesli.

muet, **~te** /mɥɛ, -t/ *a.* (*personne*) dumb; (*fig.*) speechless (**de**, with); (*silencieux*) silent. —*n.m.*, *f.* dumb person.

mufle /myfl/ *n.m.* nose, muzzle.

muguet /mygɛ/ *n.m.* lily of the valley.

mule /myl/ *n.f.* (she-)mule; (*pantoufle*) mule.

mulet /mylɛ/ *n.m.* (he-)mule.

multi- /mylti/ *préf.* multi-.

multicolore /myltikɔlɔr/ *a.* multicoloured.

multination|al, **~ale** (*m. pl.*

~aux /myltinasjɔnal, -o/ a. &
n.f. multinational.

multiple /myltipl/ a. & n.m.
multiple.

multipl|ier /myltiplije/ v.t., se
~ier v. pr. multiply. **~ication**
n.f. multiplication.

municip|al (m. pl. **~aux**)
/mynisipal, -o/ a. municipal;
(conseil) town. **~alité** n.f. (ville)
municipality; (conseil) town
council.

munir /mynir/ v.t. **~ de**, provide
with. se **~ de**, provide o.s. with.

mur /myr/ n.m. wall.

mûr /myr/ a. ripe; (personne)
mature.

muraille /myrɑj/ n.f. (high) wall.

mûre /myr/ n.f. blackberry.

mûrir /myrir/ v.t./i. ripen;
(personne, projet) mature.

murmur|e /myrmyr/ n.m. mur-
mur. **~er** v.t./i. murmur.

muscade /myskad/ n.f. **noix (de)**
~, nutmeg.

muscl|e /myskl/ n.m. muscle. **~é**
a. muscular, brawny.

muscul|aire /myskylɛr/ a. mus-
cular. **~ature** n.f. muscles.

museau (pl. **~x**) /myzo/ n.m.
muzzle; (de porc) snout.

musée /myze/ n.m. museum; (de
peinture) art gallery.

museler /myzle/ v.t. muzzle.

muselière /myzəljɛr/ n.f. muzzle.

muséum /myzeɔm/ n.m. (natural
history) museum.

music|al (m. pl. **~aux**) /myzikal,
-o/ a. musical.

music-hall /myzikol/ n.m. variety
theatre.

musicien, ~ne /myzisjɛ̃, -jɛn/ a.
musical. —n.m., f. musician.

musique /myzik/ n.f. music;
(orchestre) band.

musulman, ~e /myzylmã, -an/
a. & n.m., f. Muslim.

mutation /mytasjɔ̃/ n.f. change;
(biologique) mutation.

muter /myte/ v.t. transfer.

mutuel, ~le /mytɥɛl/ a. mutual.
—n.f. Friendly Society; (Amer.)
benefit society. **~lement** adv.
mutually; (l'un l'autre) each
other.

myop|e /mjɔp/ a. short-sighted.
~ie n.f. short-sightedness.

myosotis /mjɔzɔtis/ n.m. forget-
me-not.

myrtille /mirtij/ n.f. bilberry.

mystère /mistɛr/ n.m. mystery.

mystérieu|x, ~se /misterjø, -z/
a. mysterious.

mystif|ier /mistifje/ v.t. deceive,
hoax. **~ication** n.f. hoax.

mystique /mistik/ a. mystic(al).
—n.m./f. mystic.

mythe /mit/ n.m. myth.

mytholog|ie /mitɔlɔʒi/ n.f. mytho-
logy. **~ique** a. mythological.

N

n' /n/ voir ne.

nacr|e /nakr/ n.f. mother-of-pearl.
~é a. pearly.

nage /naʒ/ n.f. swimming;
(manière) (swimming) stroke. à
la **~**, by swimming. **traverser à**
la ~, swim across. **en ~**,
sweating.

nageoire /naʒwar/ n.f. fin.

nag|er /naʒe/ v.t./i. swim. **~eur,**
~euse n.m., f. swimmer.

naïf, ~ve /naif, -v/ a. naïve.

nain, ~e /nɛ̃, nɛn/ n.m., f. & a.
dwarf.

naissance /nɛsãs/ n.f. birth.

naître /nɛtr/ v.i. be born;
(résulter) arise (de, from). **faire**
~, (susciter) give rise to.

naïveté /naivte/ n.f. naïvety.

nana /nana/ *n.f.* (*fam.*) girl.

naphtaline /naftalin/ *n.f.* moth-balls.

nappe /nap/ *n.f.* table-cloth; (*de pétrole, gaz*) layer.

napperon /napr3/ *n.m.* (cloth) table-mat.

narcotique /narkɔtik/ *a. & n.m.* narcotic.

narine /narin/ *n.f.* nostril.

naseau (*pl.* ∼x) /nazo/ *n.m.* nostril.

nat|al (*m. pl.* ∼als) /natal/ *a.* native.

natalité /natalite/ *n.f.* birth rate.

natation /natasjɔ̃/ *n.f.* swimming.

nati|f, ∼ve /natif, -v/ *a.* native.

nation /nasjɔ̃/ *n.f.* nation.

nation|al, ∼ale (*m. pl.* ∼aux) /nasjɔnal, -o/ *a.* national. —*n.f.* road. ∼aliser *v.t.* nationalize. ∼alisme *n.m.* nationalism.

nationalité /nasjɔnalite/ *n.f.* nationality.

Nativité /nativite/ *n.f.* **la** ∼, the Nativity.

natte /nat/ *n.f.* (*de cheveux*) plait; (*tapis de paille*) mat.

naturaliser /natyralize/ *v.t.* naturalize.

nature /natyr/ *n.f.* nature. —*a. invar.* (*eau, omelette, etc.*) plain.

naturel, ∼le /natyrɛl/ *a.* natural. —*n.m.* nature; (*simplicité*) naturalness. ∼lement *adv.* naturally.

naufrage /nofraʒ/ *n.m.* (ship)wreck. **faire** ∼, be shipwrecked; (*bateau*) be wrecked.

nausée /noze/ *n.f.* nausea.

nautique /notik/ *a.* nautical; (*sports*) aquatic.

naval (*n pl.* ∼s) /naval/ *a.* naval.

navet /navɛ/ *n.m.* turnip; (*film, tableau*) dud.

navette /navɛt/ *n.f.* shuttle.

navigable /navigabl/ *a.* navigable.

navig|uer /navige/ *v.i.* sail; (*piloter*) navigate. ∼ateur *n.m.* seafarer; (*d'avion*) navigator. ∼ation *n.f.* navigation; (*trafic*) shipping.

navire /navir/ *n.m.* ship.

navré /navre/ *a.* sorry (**de**, to).

ne, n'* /nə, n/ *adv.* **ne pas**, not. **ne jamais**, never. **ne plus**, (*temps*) no longer, not any more. **ne que**, only.

né, née /ne/ *voir* **naître**. —*a. & n.m., f.* born. **il est né**, he was born.

néanmoins /neɑ̃mwɛ̃/ *adv.* nevertheless.

néant /neɑ̃/ *n.m.* nothingness; (*aucun*) none.

nécessaire /neseser/ *a.* necessary. —*n.m.* (*sac*) bag; (*trousse*) kit. **le** ∼, (*l'indispensable*) the necessities. **faire le** ∼, do what is necessary.

nécessiter /nesesite/ *v.t.* necessitate.

néerlandais, ∼e /neɛrlɑ̃dɛ, -z/ *a.* Dutch. —*n.m., f.* Dutchman, Dutchwoman. —*n.m.* (*lang.*) Dutch.

nef /nɛf/ *n.f.* nave.

négati|f, ∼ve /negatif, -v/ *a. & n.m., f.* negative.

négation /negasjɔ̃/ *n.f.* negation.

négligeable /negliʒabl/ *a.* negligible, insignificant.

néglig|ent, ∼te /negliʒɑ̃, -t/ *a.* careless, negligent. ∼ce *n.f.* carelessness, negligence; (*erreur*) omission.

négliger /negliʒe/ *v.t.* neglect; (*ne pas tenir compte de*) disregard. **se** ∼ *v. pr.* neglect o.s.

négoc|e /negɔs/ *n.m.* business. ∼iant, ∼iante *n.m., f.* merchant.

négoc|ier /negɔsje/ *v.t./i.* negotiate. ∼iable *a.* negotiable.

~iateur, ~iatrice *n.m., f.* negotiator. **~iation** *n.f.* negotiation.

nègre /nɛgr/ *a.* Negro.

neig|e /nɛʒ/ *n.f.* snow. **~eux, ~euse** *a.* snowy.

neiger /neʒe/ *v.i.* snow.

nénuphar /nenyfar/ *n.m.* water-lily.

néon /neɔ̃/ *n.m.* neon.

néo-zélandais, ~e /neɔzelɑ̃dɛ, -z/ *a.* New Zealand. —*n.m., f.* New Zealander.

nerf /nɛr/ *n.m.* nerve.

nerv|eux, ~euse /nɛrvø, -z/ *a.* nervous; (*irritable*) nervy; (*centre, cellule*) nervous; (*voiture*) responsive. **~osité** *n.f.* (*irritabilité*) touchiness.

net, ~te /nɛt/ *a.* (*clair, distinct*) clear; (*propre*) clean; (*soigné*) neat; (*prix, poi..s*) net. —*adv.* (*s'arrêter*) dead; (*refuser*) flatly.

nettoy|er /netwaje/ *v.t.* clean. **~age** *n.m.* cleaning. **~age à sec,** dry-cleaning.

neuf¹ /nœf/ (/nœv/ *before heures, ans*) *a. & n.m.* nine.

neu|f², ~ve /nœf, -v/ *a. & n.m.* new.

neutr|e /nøtr/ *a.* neutral; (*gram.*) neuter. —*n.m.* (*gram.*) neuter. **~alité** *n.f.* neutrality.

neutron /nøtrɔ̃/ *n.m.* neutron.

neuve /nœv/ *voir* **neuf².**

neuvième /nœvjɛm/ *a. & n.m./f.* ninth.

neveu (*pl.* **~x**) /nəvø/ *n.m.* nephew.

nez /ne/ *n.m.* nose.

ni /ni/ *conj.* neither, nor. **ni grand ni petit,** neither big nor small. **ni l'un ni l'autre ne fument,** neither (one nor the other) smokes.

niche /niʃ/ *n.f.* (*de chien*) kennel; (*cavité*) niche; (*farce*) trick.

nicher /niʃe/ *v.i.* nest. **se ~** *v. pr.* nest; (*se cacher*) hide.

nickel /nikɛl/ *n.m.* nickel.

nicotine /nikɔtin/ *n.f.* nicotine.

nid /ni/ *n.m.* nest.

nièce /njɛs/ *n.f.* niece.

nier /nje/ *v.t.* deny.

nippon, ~e /nipɔ̃, -ɔn/ *a. & n.m., f.* Japanese.

niveau (*pl.* **~x**) /nivo/ *n.m.* level; (*compétence*) standard. **~ de vie,** standard of living.

nivel|er /nivle/ *v.t.* level. **~lement** /-ɛlmɑ̃/ *n.m.* levelling.

noble /nɔbl/ *a.* noble. —*n.m./f.* nobleman, noblewoman.

noblesse /nɔblɛs/ *n.f.* nobility.

noce /nɔs/ *n.f.* wedding. **faire la ~,** (*fam.*) make merry.

noci|f, ~ve /nɔsif, -v/ *a.* harmful.

noctambule /nɔktɑ̃byl/ *n.m./f.* night-owl, late-night reveller.

nocturne /nɔktyrn/ *a.* nocturnal.

Noël /nɔɛl/ *n.m.* Christmas.

nœud¹ /nø/ *n.m.* knot; (*ornemental*) bow. **~s,** (*fig.*) ties. **~ papillon,** bow-tie.

nœud² /nø/ *n.m.* (*naut.*) knot.

noir, ~e /nwar/ *a.* black; (*obscur, sombre*) dark; (*triste*) gloomy. —*n.m.* black; (*obscurité*) dark. **travail au ~,** moonlighting. —*n.m., f.* (*personne*) Black. —*n.f.* (*mus.*) crotchet.

nois|ette /nwazɛt/ *n.f.* hazel-nut; (*de beurre*) knob. **~etier** *n.m.* hazel tree.

noix /nwa/ *n.f.* nut; (*du noyer*) walnut; (*de beurre*) knob. **~ de cajou,** cashew nut. **~ de coco,** coconut. **à la ~,** (*fam.*) useless.

nom /nɔ̃/ *n.m.* name; (*gram.*) noun. **au ~ de,** on behalf of. **~ de famille,** surname. **~ de jeune fille,** maiden name. **~ propre,** proper noun.

nomade /nɔmad/ *a.* nomadic.
—*n.m./f.* nomad.

nombre /nɔ̃br/ *n.m.* number. **en
(grand) ∼,** in large numbers.

nombreu|x, ∼**se** /nɔ̃brø -z/ *a.*
numerous; (*important*) large.

nombril /nɔ̃bri/ *n.m.* navel.

nomination /nɔminɑsjɔ̃/ *n.f.* appointment.

nommer /nɔme/ *v.t.* name; (*élire*)
appoint. **se** ∼ *v. pr.* (*s'appeler*) be
called.

non /nɔ̃/ *adv.* no; (*pas*) not. —*n.m.
invar.* no. **moi** ∼ **plus,** neither
am, do, can, *etc.* I.

non- /nɔ̃/ *préf.* non-. ∼**-fumeur,**
non-smoker.

nonante /nɔnɑ̃t/ *a. & n.m.* ninety.

non-sens /nɔ̃sɑ̃s/ *n.m.* absurdity.

nord /nɔr/ *n.m.* north. —*a. invar.*
north; (*partie*) northern;
(*direction*) northerly. **au** ∼ **de,** to
the north of. ∼**-africain,** ∼**-
africaine** *a. & n.m., f.* North
African. ∼**-est** *n.m.* north-east.
∼**-ouest** *n.m.* north-west.

nordique /nɔrdik/ *a. & n.m./f.*
Scandinavian.

norm|al, ∼**ale** (*m. pl.* ∼**aux**)
/nɔrmal, -o/ *a.* normal. —*n.f.*
normality; (*norme*) norm;
(*moyenne*) average. ∼**alement**
adv. normally.

normand, ∼**e** /nɔrmɑ̃, -d/ *a. &
n.m., f.* Norman.

Normandie /nɔrmɑ̃di/ *n.f.* Nor-
mandy.

norme /nɔrm/ *n.f.* norm; (*de
production*) standard.

Norvège /nɔrvɛʒ/ *n.f.* Norway.

norvégien, ∼**ne** /nɔrveʒjɛ̃, -jɛn/
a. & n.m., f. Norwegian.

nos /no/ *voir* **notre.**

nostalgie /nɔstalʒi/ *n.f.* nostalgia.

notaire /nɔtɛr/ *n.m.* notary.

notamment /nɔtamɑ̃/ *adv.* notably.

note /nɔt/ *n.f.* (*remarque*) note;
(*chiffrée*) mark; (*facture*) bill;
(*mus.*) note.

noter /nɔte/ *v.t.* note, notice;
(*écrire*) note (down); (*devoir*)
mark.

notice /nɔtis/ *n.f.* note; (*mode
d'emploi*) directions.

notion /nɔsjɔ̃/ *n.f.* notion.

notoire /nɔtwar/ *a.* well-known;
(*criminel*) notorious.

notre (*pl.* **nos**) /nɔtr, no/ *a.* our.

nôtre /notr/ *pron.* **le** *ou* **la** ∼**, les**
∼**s,** ours.

nouer /nwe/ *v.t.* tie, knot;
(*relations*) strike up.

nougat /nuga/ *n.m.* nougat.

nouilles /nuj/ *n.f. pl.* noodles.

nounours /nunurs/ *n.m.* teddy
bear.

nourri /nuri/ *a.* (*fig.*) intense. **logé**
∼**,** bed and board.

nourrice /nuris/ *n.f.* child-minder.

nourr|ir /nurir/ *v.t.* feed. **se** ∼**ir** *v.
pr.* eat. ∼**issant,** ∼**issante** *a.*
nourishing.

nourrisson /nurisɔ̃/ *n.m.* infant.

nourriture /nurityr/ *n.f.* food.

nous /nu/ *pron.* we; (*complément*)
us; (*indirect*) (to) us; (*réfléchi*)
ourselves; (*l'un l'autre*) each
other. ∼**-mêmes** *pron.* ourselves.

nouveau *ou* **nouvel*, **nouvelle¹**
(*m. pl.* ∼**x**) /nuvo, nuvɛl/ *a. & n.m.*
new. —*n.m., f.* (*élève*) new boy,
new girl. **de** ∼**, à** ∼**,** again. **du** ∼**,**
(*fait nouveau*) some new develop-
ment. **nouvel an,** new year. ∼**x
mariés,** newly-weds. ∼**-né,** ∼**-
née** *a. new-born; n.m., f.* newborn
baby. **Nouvelle Zélande,** New
Zealand.

nouveauté /nuvote/ *n.f.* novelty;
(*chose*) new thing.

nouvelle² /nuvɛl/ *n.f.* (piece of)
news; (*récit*) short story. ∼**s,**
news.

novembre /nɔvɑ̃br/ *n.m.* November.

noyade /nwajad/ *n.f.* drowning.

noyau (*pl.* **~x**) /nwajo/ *n.m.* (*de fruit*) stone; (*de cellule*) nucleus; (*groupe*) group; (*centre: fig.*) core.

noyer[1] /nwaje/ *v.t.* drown; (*inonder*) flood. **se ~** *v. pr.* drown; (*volontairement*) drown o.s.

noyer[2] /nwaje/ *n.m.* (*arbre*) walnut-tree.

nu /ny/ *a.* naked; (*mains, mur, fil*) bare. —*n.m.* nude. **nu-pieds** *adv.* barefoot. **nu-tête** *adv.* bareheaded. **à l'oeil nu**, to the naked eye.

nuage /nɥaʒ/ *n.m.* cloud. **~eux, ~euse** *a.* cloudy.

nuance /nɥɑ̃s/ *n.f.* shade; (*de sens*) nuance; (*différence*) difference.

nuancer /nɥɑ̃se/ *v.t.* (*opinion*) qualify.

nucléaire /nykleɛr/ *a.* nuclear.

nudis|te /nydist/ *n.m./f.* nudist. **~me** *n.m.* nudism.

nudité /nydite/ *n.f.* (*de personne*) nudity; (*de chambre etc.*) bareness.

nuire† /nɥir/ *v.i.* **~ à**, harm.

nuisible /nɥizibl/ *a.* harmful.

nuit /nɥi/ *n.f.* night. **cette ~**, tonight; (*hier*) last night. **il fait ~**, it is dark. **~ blanche**, sleepless night. **la ~, de ~**, at night. **~ de noces**, wedding night.

nul, ~le /nyl/ *a.* (*aucun*) no; (*zéro*) nil; (*qui ne vaut rien*) useless; (*non valable*) null. **match ~**, draw. **~ en**, no good at.

numérique /nymerik/ *a.* numerical; (*montre, horloge*) digital.

numéro /nymero/ *n.m.* number; (*de journal*) issue; (*spectacle*) act. **~ter** /-ɔte/ *v.t.* number.

nuque /nyk/ *n.f.* nape (of the neck).

nurse /nœrs/ *n.f.* (children's) nurse.

nutriti|f, ~ve /nytritif, -v/ *a.* nutritious; (*valeur*) nutritional.

nutrition /nytrisjɔ̃/ *n.f.* nutrition.

nylon /nilɔ̃/ *n.m.* nylon.

O

oasis /ɔazis/ *n.f.* oasis.

obéir /ɔbeir/ *v.i.* obey. **~ à**, obey.

obéissan|t, ~te /ɔbeisɑ̃, -t/ *a.* obedient. **~ce** *n.f.* obedience.

obèse /ɔbɛz/ *a.* obese.

obésité /ɔbezite/ *n.f.* obesity.

object|er /ɔbʒɛkte/ *v.t.* put forward (as an excuse). **~er que**, object that. **~ion** /-ksjɔ̃/ *n.f.* objection.

objecti|f, ~ve /ɔbʒɛktif, -v/ *a.* objective. —*n.m.* objective; (*photo.*) lens. **~vement** *adv.* objectively. **~vité** *n.f.* objectivity.

objet /ɔbʒɛ/ *n.m.* object; (*sujet*) subject. **~ d'art**, objet d'art. **~s trouvés**, lost property.

obligation /ɔbligɑsjɔ̃/ *n.f.* obligation; (*comm.*) bond. **être dans l'~ de**, be under obligation to.

obligatoire /ɔbligatwar/ *a.* compulsory. **~ment** *adv.* of necessity; (*fam.*) inevitably.

oblig|er /ɔbliʒe/ *v.t.* compel, oblige (**à faire**, to do); (*aider*) oblige. **être ~é de**, have to.

oblique /ɔblik/ *a.* oblique.

obliquer /ɔblike/ *v.i.* turn off (**vers**, towards).

oblitérer /ɔblitere/ *v.t.* (*timbre*) cancel.

obscène /ɔpsɛn/ *a.* obscene. **~énité** /-enite/ *n.f.* obscenity.

obscur /ɔpskyr/ *a.* dark; (*confus, humble*) obscure.

obscurité /ɔpskyrite/ *n.f.* dark (-ness); (*passage, situation*) obscurity.

obséd|er /ɔpsede/ *v.t.* obsess. **~ant**, **~ante** *a.* obsessive. **~é**, **~ée** *n.m.*, *f.* maniac.

obsèques /ɔpsɛk/ *n.f. pl.* funeral.

observation /ɔpsɛrvasjɔ̃/ *n.f.* observation; (*reproche*) criticism; (*obéissance*) observance. **en ~**, under observation.

observatoire /ɔpsɛrvatwar/ *n.m.* observatory.

observ|er /ɔpsɛrve/ *v.t.* observe; (*surveiller*) watch, observe. **faire ~er qch.**, point sth. out (à, to). **~ateur**, **~atrice** *a.* observant; *n.m.*, *f.* observer.

obsession /ɔpsesjɔ̃/ *n.f.* obsession.

obstacle /ɔpstakl/ *n.m.* obstacle; (*cheval*) jump; (*athlète*) hurdle. **faire ~ à**, stand in the way of.

obstin|é /ɔpstine/ *a.* obstinate. **~ation** *n.f.* obstinacy.

obstiner (s') /(s)ɔpstine/ *v. pr.* persist (à, in).

obstruction /ɔpstryksjɔ̃/ *n.f.* obstruction.

obtenir† /ɔptənir/ *v.t.* get, obtain.

obturateur /ɔptyratœr/ *n.m.* (*photo.*) shutter.

obus /ɔby/ *n.m.* shell.

occasion /ɔkazjɔ̃/ *n.f.* opportunity (**de faire**, of doing); (*circonstance*) occasion; (*achat*) bargain; (*article non neuf*) second-hand buy. **d'~**, second-hand.

occasionner /ɔkazjɔne/ *v.t.* cause.

occident /ɔksidã/ *n.m.* west. **~al**, **~ale** (*m. pl.* **~aux**) /-tal, -to/ *a.* western. **—*n.m.*, *f.* westerner.

occupant, **~e** /ɔkypã, -t/ *n.m.*, *f.* occupant. **—*n.m.* (*mil.*) forces of occupation.

occupation /ɔkypasjɔ̃/ *n.f.* occupation.

occupé /ɔkype/ *a.* busy; (*place*, *pays*) occupied; (*téléphone*) engaged.

occuper /ɔkype/ *v.t.* occupy;

(*poste*) hold. **s'~ de**, (*personne*, *problème*) take care of; (*bureau*, *firme*) be in charge of.

océan /ɔseã/ *n.m.* ocean.

ocre /ɔkr/ *a. invar.* ochre.

octante /ɔktãt/ *a.* (*régional*) eighty.

octave /ɔktav/ *n.f.* (*mus.*) octave.

octet /ɔktɛ/ *n.m.* byte.

octobre /ɔktɔbr/ *n.m.* October.

octogone /ɔktɔgɔn/ *n.m.* octagon.

octroyer /ɔktrwaje/ *v.t.* grant.

oculiste /ɔkylist/ *n.m./f.* eye-specialist.

odeur /ɔdœr/ *n.f.* smell.

odieu|x, **~se** /ɔdjø, -z/ *a.* odious.

odorat /ɔdɔra/ *n.m.* (sense of) smell.

œcuménique /ekymenik/ *a.* ecumenical.

œil (*pl.* **yeux**) /œj, jø/ *n.m.* eye. **à l'~**, (*fam.*) free. **à mes yeux**, in my view. **ouvrir l'~**, keep one's eye open. **fermer l'~**, shut one's eyes.

œillet /œjɛ/ *n.m.* (*plante*) carnation; (*trou*) eyelet.

œuf (*pl.* **~s**) /œf, ø/ *n.m.* egg. **~ à la coque/dur/sur le plat**, boiled/hard-boiled/fried egg.

œuvre /œvr/ *n.f.* (*ouvrage*, *travail*) work. **~ d'art**, work of art. **~ (de bienfaisance)**, charity.

offense /ɔfãs/ *n.f.* insult.

offenser /ɔfãse/ *v.t.* offend.

offert, **~e** /ɔfɛr, -t/ *voir* **offrir**.

office /ɔfis/ *n.m.* office; (*relig.*) service; (*de cuisine*) pantry. **d'~**, automatically.

officiel, **~le** /ɔfisjɛl/ *a. & n.m.*, *f.* official. **~lement** *adv.* officially.

officier /ɔfisje/ *n.m.* officer.

officieu|x, **~se** /ɔfisjø, -z/ *a.* unofficial. **~sement** *adv.* unofficially.

offrant /ɔfrã/ *n.m.* **au plus ~**, to the highest bidder.

offre /ɔfr/ *n.f.* offer; (*aux enchères*) bid. **l'~ et la demande,** supply and demand. **~s d'emploi,** jobs advertised, (*rubrique*) situations vacant.

offrir† /ɔfrir/ *v.t.* offer (**de faire,** to do); (*cadeau*) give; (*acheter*) buy. **s'~** *v. pr.* offer o.s. (**comme,** as); (*spectacle*) present itself; (*s'acheter*) treat o.s. to. **~ à boire à,** (*chez soi*) give a drink to; (*au café*) buy a drink for.

oh /o/ *int.* oh.

oie /wa/ *n.f.* goose.

oignon /ɔɲɔ̃/ *n.m.* (*légume*) onion; (*de tulipe etc.*) bulb.

oiseau (*pl.* **~x**) /wazo/ *n.m.* bird.

O.K. /ɔke/ *int.* O.K.

oléoduc /ɔleɔdyk/ *n.m.* oil pipeline.

oliv|e /ɔliv/ *n.f. & a. invar.* olive. **~ier** *n.m.* olive-tree.

olympique /ɔlɛ̃pik/ *a.* Olympic.

ombre /ɔ̃br/ *n.f.* (*pénombre* shade; (*contour*) shadow; (*soupçon: fig.*) hint, shadow.

omelette /ɔmlɛt/ *n.f.* omelette.

omettre† /ɔmɛtr/ *v.t.* omit.

omission /ɔmisjɔ̃/ *n.f.* omission.

omnibus /ɔmnibys/ *n.m.* stopping train.

omoplate /ɔmɔplat/ *n.f.* shoulder-blade.

on /ɔ̃/ *pron.* we, you, one; (*les gens*) people, they; (*quelqu'un*) someone. **on dit,** people say, they say, it is said (**que,** that).

once /ɔ̃s/ *n.f.* ounce.

oncle /ɔ̃kl/ *n.m.* uncle.

onctueu|x, **~se** /ɔktɥø, -z/ *a.* smooth.

onde /ɔ̃d/ *n.f.* wave. **~s courtes/longues,** short/long wave. **sur les ~s,** on the radio.

ondul|er /ɔ̃dyle/ *v.i.* undulate; (*cheveux*) be wavy. **~é a.** (*chevelure*) wavy.

ongle /ɔ̃gl/ *n.m.* (finger-)nail.

ont /ɔ̃/ *voir* **avoir.**

ONU *abrév.* (*Organisation des nations unies*) UN.

onz|e /ɔ̃z/ *a.* & *n.m.* eleven. **~ième** *a.* & *n.m./f.* eleventh.

opale /ɔpal/ *n.f.* opal.

open /ɔpɛn/ *n.m.* open (championship).

opéra /ɔpera/ *n.m.* opera; (*édifice*) opera-house. **~-comique** (*pl.* **~s-comiques**) *n.m.* light opera.

opérateur /ɔperatœr/ *n.m.* (*caméraman*) cameraman.

opération /ɔperasjɔ̃/ *n.f.* operation; (*comm.*) deal.

opérationnel, **~le** /ɔperasjɔnɛl/ *a.* operational.

opératoire /ɔperatwar/ *a.* (*méd.*) surgical. **bloc ~,** operating suite.

opérer /ɔpere/ *v.t.* (*personne*) operate on; (*kyste etc.*) remove. **se faire ~,** have an operation. —*v.i.* (*méd.*) operate.

opérette /ɔperɛt/ *n.f.* operetta.

opinion /ɔpinjɔ̃/ *n.f.* opinion.

opium /ɔpjɔm/ *n.m.* opium.

opportun, **~e** /ɔpɔrtœ̃, -yn/ *a.* opportune. **~ité** /-ynite/ *n.f.* opportuneness.

opposant, **~e** /ɔpozɑ̃, -t/ *n.m., f.* opponent.

opposé /ɔpoze/ *a.* (*sens, angle, etc.*) opposite; (*factions*) opposing; (*intérêts*) conflicting. —*n.m.* opposite. **être ~ à,** be opposed to.

opposer /ɔpoze/ *v.t.* (*personnes*) oppose; (*contraster*) contrast; (*résistance, argument*) put up. **s'~** *v. pr.* (*personnes*) confront each other; (*styles*) contrast. **s'~ à,** oppose.

opposition /ɔpozisjɔ̃/ *n.f.* opposition. **faire ~ à un chèque,** stop a cheque.

opticien, **~ne** /ɔptisjɛ̃, -jɛn/ *n.m., f.* optician.

optimis|te /ɔptimist/ *n.m./f.* optimist. —*a.* optimistic. ~**me** *n.m.* optimism.

option /ɔpsjɔ̃/ *n.f.* option.

optique /ɔptik/ *a.* (*verre*) optical. —*n.f.* (*perspective*) perspective.

or[1] /ɔr/ *n.m.* gold. **d'~**, golden. **en or**, gold; (*occasion*) golden.

or[2] /ɔr/ *conj.* now, well.

orage /ɔraʒ/ *n.m.* (thunder)storm. ~**eux**, ~**euse** *a.* stormy.

or|al (*m. pl.* ~**aux**) /ɔral, -o/ *a.* oral. —*n.m.* (*pl.* ~**aux**) oral.

orang|e /ɔrɑ̃ʒ/ *n.f. & a. invar.* orange. ~**é** *a.* orange-coloured. ~**er** *n.m.* orange-tree.

orangeade /ɔrɑ̃ʒad/ *n.f.* orangeade.

orateur /ɔratœr/ *n.m.* speaker.

orchestre /ɔrkɛstr/ *n.m.* orchestra; (*de jazz*) band; (*parterre*) stalls. ~**r** *v.t.* orchestrate.

orchidée /ɔrkide/ *n.f.* orchid.

ordinaire /ɔrdinɛr/ *a.* ordinary; (*habituel*) usual; (*qualité*) standard. —*n.m.* **l'~**, the ordinary; (*nourriture*) the standard fare. **d'~**, **à l'~**, usually.

ordinateur /ɔrdinatœr/ *n.m.* computer.

ordonnance /ɔrdɔnɑ̃s/ *n.f.* (*de médecin*) prescription.

ordonné /ɔrdɔne/ *a.* tidy.

ordonner /ɔrdɔne/ *v.t.* order (**à qn. de**, s.o. to); (*agencer*) arrange; (*méd.*) prescribe; (*prêtre*) ordain.

ordre /ɔrdr/ *n.m.* order; (*propreté*) tidiness. **de premier ~**, first-rate. **mettre en ~**, tidy (up). **de premier ~**, first rate. **jusqu'à nouvel ~**, until further notice.

ordure /ɔrdyr/ *n.f.* filth. ~**s**, (*détritus*) rubbish. ~**s ménagères**, household refuse.

oreille /ɔrɛj/ *n.f.* ear.

oreiller /ɔreje/ *n.m.* pillow.

oreillons /ɔrejɔ̃/ *n.m. pl.* mumps.

orfèvr|e /ɔrfɛvr/ *n.m.* goldsmith, silversmith. ~**erie** *n.f.* goldsmith's *ou* silversmith's trade.

organe /ɔrgan/ *n.m.* organ.

organigramme /ɔrganigram/ *n.m.* flow chart.

organique /ɔrganik/ *a.* organic.

organisation /ɔrganizasjɔ̃/ *n.f.* organization.

organis|er /ɔrganize/ *v.t.* organize. **s'~er** *v. pr.* organize o.s. ~**ateur**, ~**atrice** *n.m.*, *f.* organizer.

organisme /ɔrganism/ *n.m.* body, organism.

organiste /ɔrganist/ *n.m./f.* organist.

orge /ɔrʒ/ *n.f.* barley.

orgelet /ɔrʒəlɛ/ *n.m.* (*furoncle*) sty.

orgue /ɔrg/ *n.m.* organ. ~**s** *n.f. pl.* organ.

orgueil /ɔrgœj/ *n.m.* pride.

orgueilleu|x, ~**se** /ɔrgœjø, -z/ *a.* proud.

Orient /ɔrjɑ̃/ *n.m.* **l'~**, the Orient.

orientable /ɔrjɑ̃tabl/ *a.* adjustable.

orient|al, ~**ale** (*m. pl.* ~**aux**) /ɔrjɑ̃tal, -o/ *a.* eastern; (*de l'Orient*) oriental. —*n.m.*, *f.* Oriental.

orientation /ɔrjɑ̃tasjɔ̃/ *n.f.* direction; (*de maison*) aspect.

orienter /ɔrjɑ̃te/ *v.t.* position; (*personne*) direct. **s'~** *v. pr.* (*se repérer*) find one's bearings. **s'~ vers**, turn towards.

orifice /ɔrifis/ *n.m.* orifice.

origan /ɔrigɑ̃/ *n.m.* oregano.

originaire /ɔriʒinɛr/ *a.* **être ~ de**, be a native of.

origin|al, ~**ale** (*m. pl.* ~**aux**) /ɔriʒinal, -o/ *a.* original; (*curieux*) eccentric. —*n.m.* original. —*n.m.*, *f.* eccentric. ~**alité** *n.f.* originality; eccentricity.

origine /ɔriʒin/ *n.f.* origin. **à l'~**, originally. **d'~**, (*pièce, pneu*) original.

orme /ɔrm/ *n.m.* elm.

ornement /ɔrnəmɑ̃/ *n.m.* ornament.

orner /ɔrne/ *v.t.* decorate.

ornière /ɔrnjɛr/ *n.f.* rut.

orphelin, ~e /ɔrfəlɛ̃, -in/ *n.m., f.* orphan. —*a.* orphaned. **~at** /-ina/ *n.m.* orphanage.

orteil /ɔrtɛj/ *n.m.* toe.

orthodoxe /ɔrtɔdɔks/ *a.* orthodox.

orthographe /ɔrtɔgraf/ *n.f.* spelling. **~ier** *v.t.* spell.

orthopédique /ɔrtɔpedik/ *a.* orthopaedic.

ortie /ɔrti/ *n.f.* nettle.

os (*pl.* **os**) /ɔs, o/ *n.m.* bone.

OS *abrév. voir* **ouvrier spécialisé**.

oscar /ɔskar/ *n.m.* award; (*au cinéma*) oscar.

oseille /ozɛj/ *n.f.* (*plante*) sorrel.

os|er /oze/ *v.t./i.* dare. **~é** *a.* daring.

osier /ozje/ *n.m.* wicker.

ostéopathe /ɔsteɔpat/ *n.m./f.* osteopath.

otage /ɔtaʒ/ *n.m.* hostage.

otarie /ɔtari/ *n.f.* sea-lion.

ôter /ote/ *v.t.* remove (**à qn.**, from s.o.); (*déduire*) take away.

otite /ɔtit/ *n.f.* ear infection.

ou /u/ *conj.* or. **ou bien,** or else. **vous ou moi,** either you or me.

où /u/ *adv. & pron.* where; (*dans lequel*) in which; (*sur lequel*) on which; (*auquel*) at which; (*d'où,* from which; (*pour cette raison*) hence. **d'où?**, from where? **par où,** through which. **par où?**, which way? **au prix où c'est,** at those prices. **le jour où,** the day when.

ouate /wat/ *n.f.* cotton wool.

oubli /ubli/ *n.m.* forgetfulness;

(*trou de mémoire*) lapse of memory; (*négligence*) oversight.

oublier /ublije/ *v.t.* forget.

ouest /wɛst/ *n.m.* west. —*a. invar.* west; (*partie*) western; (*direction*) westerly.

ouf /uf/ *int.* phew.

oui /wi/ *int.* yes.

ouïe /wi/ *n.f.* hearing.

ouïes /wi/ *n.f. pl.* gills.

ouille /uj/ *int.* ouch.

ouragan /uragɑ̃/ *n.m.* hurricane.

ourlet /urlɛ/ *n.m.* hem.

ours /urs/ *n.m.* bear. **~ en peluche,** teddy bear.

ouste /ust/ *int.* (*fam.*) scram.

outil /uti/ *n.m.* tool.

outillage /utijaʒ/ *n.m.* tools; (*d'une usine*) equipment.

outre /utr/ *prép.* besides. **en ~**, besides. **~-mer** *adv.* overseas.

outsider /awtsajdœr/ *n.m.* outsider.

ouvert, ~e /uvɛr, -t/ *a.* open; (*gaz, radio, etc.*) on. **~ement** /-təmɑ̃/ *adv.* openly.

ouvrir —*a.* open; (*gaz, radio, etc.*) on. **~ement** /-təmɑ̃/ *adv.* openly.

ouverture /uvɛrtyr/ *n.f.* opening; (*mus.*) overture; (*photo.*) aperture. **~s,** (*offres*) overtures. **~ d'esprit,** open-mindedness.

ouvrable /uvrabl/ *a.* **jour ~,** working day.

ouvrag|e /uvraʒ/ *n.m.* (*travail, livre*) work; (*couture*) needle-work. **~é** *a.* finely worked.

ouvreuse /uvrøz/ *n.f.* usherette.

ouvr|ier, ~ière /uvrije, -jɛr/ *n.m., f.* worker. —*a.* working-class; (*conflit*) industrial; (*syndicat*) workers'.

ouvr|ir† /uvrir/ *v.t.* open (up); (*gaz, robinet, etc.*) turn *ou* switch on. —*v.i.* open (up). **s'~ir** *v. pr.* open (up). **~e-boîte(s)** *n.m.* tin-opener. **~e-bouteille(s)** *n.m.* bottle-opener.

ovaire /ɔvɛr/ *n.m.* ovary.

ovale /ɔval/ *a. & n.m.* oval.

ovule /ɔvyl/ *n.f. (à féconder)* egg; *(gynécologique)* pessary.

oxyder (s') /(s)ɔkside/ *v. pr.* become oxidized.

oxygène /ɔksiʒɛn/ *n.m.* oxygen.

ozone /ozon/ *n.f.* ozone. **la couche d'~,** the ozone layer.

P

pacemaker /pesmekœr/ *n.m.* pacemaker.

pacifique /pasifik/ *a.* peaceful; *(personne)* peaceable; *(géog.)* Pacific.

pacotille /pakotij/ *n.f.* trash.

pacte /pakt/ *n.m.* pact.

pagaille /pagaj/ *n.f.* mess, shambles.

page /paʒ/ *n.f.* page.

paie /pɛ/ *n.f.* pay.

paiement /pɛmɑ̃/ *n.m.* payment.

paillasson /pajasɔ̃/ *n.m.* doormat.

paille /paj/ *n.f.* straw.

paillette /pajɛt/ *n.f. (sur robe)* sequin; *(de savon)* flake.

pain /pɛ̃/ *n.m.* bread: *(unité)* loaf (of bread); *(de savon etc.)* bar. **~ d'épice,** gingerbread. **~ grillé,** toast.

pair[1] /pɛr/ *a. (nombre)* even.

pair[2] /pɛr/ *n.m. (personne)* peer. **au ~,** *(jeune fille etc.)* au pair.

paire /pɛr/ *n.f.* pair.

paisible /pezibl/ *a.* peaceful.

paître /pɛtr/ *v.i. (brouter)* graze.

paix /pɛ/ *n.f.* peace; *(papier)* peace treaty.

Pakistan /pakistɑ̃/ *n.m.* Pakistan.

pakistanais, ~e /pakistanɛ, -z/ *a. & n.m., f.* Pakistani.

palace /palas/ *n.m.* luxury hotel.

palais[1] /palɛ/ *n.m.* palace. **P~ de**

Justice, Law Courts. ~ des sports, sports stadium.

palais[2] /palɛ/ *n.m. (anat.)* palate.

pâle /pal/ *a.* pale.

Palestine /palɛstin/ *n.f.* Palestine.

palestinien, ~ne /palɛstinjɛ̃, -jɛn/ *a. & n.m., f.* Palestinian.

palet /palɛ/ *n.m. (hockey)* puck.

palette /palɛt/ *n.f.* palette.

pâleur /palœr/ *n.f.* paleness.

palier /palje/ *n.m. (d'escalier)* landing; *(étape)* stage.

pâlir /palir/ *v.t./i.* (turn) pale.

palissade /palisad/ *n.f.* fence.

palmarès /palmarɛs/ *n.m.* list of prize-winners.

palme /palm/ *n.f.* palm leaf; *(symbole)* palm; *(de nageur)* flipper. **~ier** *n.m.* palm(-tree).

pâlot, ~te /palo, -ɔt/ *a.* pale.

palourde /palurd/ *n.f.* clam.

palper /palpe/ *v.t.* feel.

palpiter /palpite/ *v.i. (battre)* pound, palpitate; *(frémir)* quiver. **~ations** *n.f. pl.* palpitations.

paludisme /palydism/ *n.m.* malaria.

pamplemousse /pɑ̃pləmus/ *n.m.* grapefruit.

pan /pɑ̃/ *int.* bang.

panaché /panaʃe/ *a. (bariolé, mélangé)* motley. **glace ~e,** mixed-flavour ice cream. —*n.m.* shandy. **bière ~e, demi ~,** shandy.

pancarte /pɑ̃kart/ *n.f.* sign; *(de manifestant)* placard.

pancréas /pɑ̃kreas/ *n.m.* pancreas.

pané /pane/ *a.* breaded.

panier /panje/ *n.m.* basket. **~ à provisions,** shopping basket.

panique /panik/ *n.f.* panic. *(fam.)* **~er** *v.i.* panic.

panne /pan/ *n.f.* breakdown. **être en ~,** have broken down. **être en ~ sèche,** have run out of petrol.

~ **d'électricité** *ou* **de courant**, power failure.

panneau (*pl.* ~**x**) /pano/ *n.m.* sign; (*publicitaire*) hoarding; (*de porte etc.*) panel. ~ **(d'affichage)**, notice-board. ~ **(de signalisation)**, road sign.

pans|er /pɑ̃se/ *v.t.* (*plaie*) dress. ~**ement** *n.m.* dressing. ~**ement adhésif**, sticking-plaster.

pantalon /pɑ̃talɔ̃/ *n.m.* (pair of) trousers. ~**s**, trousers.

panthère /pɑ̃tɛr/ *n.f.* panther.

pantin /pɑ̃tɛ̃/ *n.m.* puppet.

pantomime /pɑ̃tɔmim/ *n.f.* mime; (*spectacle*) mime show.

pantoufle /pɑ̃tufl/ *n.f.* slipper.

paon /pɑ̃/ *n.m.* peacock.

papa /papa/ *n.m.* dad(dy).

pape /pap/ *n.m.* pope.

paperass|e /papras/ *n.f.* ~**e(s)**, (*péj.*) papers. ~**erie** *n.f.* (*péj.*) papers; (*tracasserie*) red tape.

papeterie /papetri/ *n.f.* (*magasin*) stationer's shop.

papier /papje/ *n.m.* paper; (*formulaire*) form. ~**s (d'identité)**, (identity) papers. ~ **à lettres**, writing-paper. ~ **aluminium**, tin foil. ~ **de verre**, sandpaper. ~ **hygiénique**, toilet-paper. ~ **journal**, newspaper. ~ **peint**, wallpaper.

papillon /papijɔ̃/ *n.m.* butterfly; (*contravention*) parking-ticket. ~ **(de nuit)**, moth.

paprika /paprika/ *n.m.* paprika.

Pâque /pɑk/ *n.f.* Passover.

paquebot /pakbo/ *n.m.* liner.

pâquerette /pakrɛt/ *n.f.* daisy.

Pâques /pɑk/ *n.f. pl. & n.m.* Easter.

paquet /pakɛ/ *n.m.* packet; (*de cartes*) pack; (*colis*) parcel.

par /par/ *prép.* by; (*à travers*) through; (*motif*) out of, from; (*provenance*) from. **commencer** ~

finir ~ **qch.**, begin/end with sth. **commencer/finir** ~ **faire**, begin by/end up (by) doing. ~ **an/mois/etc.**, a *ou* per year/ month/*etc.* ~ **avion**, (*lettre*) (by) airmail. ~ **hasard**, by chance. ~ **contre**, on the other hand. ~ **hasard**, by chance. ~ **ici/là**, this/that way. ~ **l'intermédiaire de**, through. ~ **jour**, a day. ~ **moments**, at times. ~ **opposition à**, as opposed to. ~ **personne**, each, per person.

paracétamol /parasetamɔl/ *n.m.* paracetamol.

parachut|e /paraʃyt/ *n.m.* parachute. ~**er** *v.t.* parachute. ~**iste** *n.m./f.* parachutist; (*mil.*) paratrooper.

parade /parad/ *n.f.* parade.

paradis /paradi/ *n.m.* paradise. ~ **fiscal**, tax haven.

paraffine /parafin/ *n.f.* paraffin wax.

paragraphe /paragraf/ *n.m.* paragraph.

paraître† /parɛtr/ *v.i.* appear; (*sembler*) seem, appear; (*ouvrage*) be published, come out. **faire** ~, (*ouvrage*) bring out.

parallèle /paralɛl/ *a.* parallel. —*n.m.* parallel. **faire le** ~, make a connection. —*n.f.* parallel (line). ~**ment** *adv.* parallel (**à**, to).

paraly|ser /paralize/ *v.t.* paralyse. ~**sie** *n.f.* paralysis.

paramètre /parametr/ *n.m.* parameter.

parapet /parapɛ/ *n.m.* parapet.

parapluie /paraplɥi/ *n.m.* umbrella.

parasite /parazit/ *n.m.* parasite. ~**s**, (*radio*) interference.

parasol /parasɔl/ *n.m.* sunshade.

paratonnerre /paratɔnɛr/ *n.m.* lightning-conductor *ou* -rod.

paravent /paravɑ̃/ *n.m.* screen.

parc /park/ *n.m.* park; (*de bébé*) play-pen. **~ de stationnement,** car-park.

parcelle /parsɛl/ *n.f.* fragment; (*de terre*) plot.

parce que /parsk(ə)/ *conj.* because.

parcmètre /parkmɛtr/ *n.m.* parking-meter.

parcourir† /parkurir/ *v.t.* travel *ou* go through; (*distance*) travel; (*des yeux*) glance at *ou* over.

parcours /parkur/ *n.m.* route; (*voyage*) journey.

par-delà /pardəla/ *prép. & adv.* beyond.

par-derrière /pardɛrjɛr/ *prép. & adv.* behind, at the back *ou* rear (of).

par-dessous /pardsu/ *prép. & adv.* under(neath).

pardessus /pardəsy/ *n.m.* overcoat.

par-dessus /pardəsy/ *prép. & adv.* over. **~ bord,** overboard. **~ le marché,** into the bargain.

par-devant /pardvã/ *adv.* at *ou* from the front, in front.

pardon /pardɔ̃/ *n.m.* forgiveness. (**je vous demande) ~!,** (I am sorry)!; (*pour demander qch.*) excuse me!

pardonn|er /pardone/ *v.t.* forgive. **~er qch. à qn.,** forgive s.o. for sth. **~able** *a.* forgivable.

pare-brise /parbriz/ *n.m. invar.* windscreen; (*Amer.*) windshield.

pare-chocs /parʃɔk/ *n.m. invar.* bumper.

pareil, ~le /parɛj/ *a.* similar (à to); (*tel*) such (a). —*n.m., f.* equal. —*adv.* (*fam.*) the same. **c'est ~,** it is the same.

parent, ~e /parã, -t/ *a.* related (**de,** to). —*n.m., f.* relative, relation. **~s** (*père et mère*) *n.m. pl.* parents. **~ seul,** single parent.

parenthèse /parãtɛz/ *n.f.* bracket, parenthesis; (*fig.*) digression.

paress|e /parɛs/ *n.f.* laziness. **~er** /-ese/ *v.i.* laze (about). **~eux, ~euse** *a.* lazy; *n.m., f.* lazybones.

parfait, ~e /parfɛ, -t/ *a.* perfect. **~ement** /-tmã/ *adv.* perfectly; (*bien sûr*) certainly.

parfois /parfwa/ *adv.* sometimes.

parfum /parfœ̃/ *n.m.* scent; (*substance*) perfume, scent; (*goût*) flavour.

parfum|er /parfyme/ *v.t.* perfume; (*gâteau*) flavour. **se ~er** *v. pr.* put on one's perfume. **~é** *a.* fragrant; (*savon*) scented. **~erie** *n.f.* (*produits*) perfumes; (*boutique*) perfume shop.

pari /pari/ *n.m.* bet.

par|ier /parje/ *v.t.* bet. **~ieur, ~ieuse** *n.m., f.* punter, better.

Paris /pari/ *n.m./f.* Paris.

parisien, ~ne /parizjɛ̃, -jɛn/ *a.* Paris, Parisian. —*n.m., f.* Parisian.

parit|é /parite/ *n.f.* parity. **~aire** *a.* (*commission*) joint.

parking /parkiŋ/ *n.m.* car-park; (*stationnement*) parking.

parlement /parləmã/ *n.m.* parliament.

parl|er /parle/ *v.i.* talk, speak (à, to). —*v.t.* (*langue*) speak; (*politique, affaires, etc.*) talk. **se ~er** *v. pr.* (*langue*) be spoken. —*n.m.* speech; (*dialecte*) dialect.

parmi /parmi/ *prép.* among(st).

paroi /parwa/ *n.f.* wall; (*cloison*) partition (wall). **~ rocheuse,** rock face.

paroisse /parwas/ *n.f.* parish.

parole /parɔl/ *n.f.* (*mot, promesse*) word; (*langage*) speech. **demander la ~,** ask to speak. **prendre la ~,** (begin to) speak.

paroxysme /parɔksism/ *n.m.* height, highest point.

parquer /parke/ *v.t.,* **se ~** *v. pr.* (*auto.*) park.

parquet /parkɛ/ n.m. floor; (jurid.) public prosecutor's department.

parrain /parɛ̃/ n.m. godfather; (fig.) sponsor. **∼er** /-ene/ v.t. sponsor.

pars, part[1] /par/ voir **partir**.

part[2] /par/ n.f. share, part. **à ∼**, (de côté) aside; (séparément) apart; (excepté) apart from. **d'autre ∼**, on the other hand; (de plus) moreover. **de la ∼ de**, from. **d'une ∼**, on the one hand. **prendre ∼ à**, take part in; (joie, douleur) share.

partag|e /partaʒ/ n.m. dividing; sharing out; (part) share. **∼er** v.t. divide; (distribuer) share out; (avoir en commun) share. **se ∼er** qch., share sth.

partance (en) /(ɑ̃)partɑ̃s/ adv. about to depart.

partant /partɑ̃/ n.m. (sport) starter.

partenaire /partənɛr/ n.m./f. partner.

parterre /partɛr/ n.m. flower-bed; (théâtre) stalls.

parti /parti/ n.m. (pol.) party; (en mariage) match; (décision) decision. **∼ pris**, prejudice. **prendre ∼ pour**, side with.

part|ial (m. pl. **∼iaux**) /parsjal, -jo/ a. biased. **∼ialité** n.f. bias.

participe /partisip/ n.m. (gram.) participle.

particip|er /partisipe/ v.i. **∼er à**, take part in, participate in; (profits, frais) share; (spectacle) appear in. **∼ant, ∼ante** n.m., f. participant (à, in); (à un concours) entrant. **∼ation** n.f. participation; sharing; (comm.) interest.

particularité /partikylarite/ n.f. particularity.

particule /partikyl/ n.f. particle.

particul|ier, ∼ière /partikylje, -jɛr/ a. (spécifique) particular;

(bizarre) peculiar; (privé) private. **∼**, n.m. private individual. **en ∼ier**, in particular; (en privé) in private. **∼ièrement** adv. particularly.

partie /parti/ n.f. part; (cartes, sport) game; (jurid.) party; (sortie) outing, party. **une ∼ de pêche**, a fishing trip. **en ∼**, partly. **faire ∼ de**, be part of; (adhérer à) belong to. **en grande ∼**, largely.

partir† /partir/ v.i. (aux. être) go; (quitter un lieu) leave, go; (tache) come out; (bouton) come off. **à ∼ de**, from.

partisan, ∼e /partizɑ̃, -an/ n.m., f. supporter. —n.m. (mil.) partisan. **être ∼ de**, be in favour of.

partition /partisjɔ̃/ n.f. (mus.) score.

partout /partu/ adv. everywhere. **∼ où**, wherever.

paru /pary/ voir **paraître**.

parure /paryr/ n.f. adornment; (bijoux) jewellery; (de draps) set.

parution /parysjɔ̃/ n.f. publication.

parvenir† /parvənir/ v.i. (aux. être) **∼ à**, reach; (résultat) achieve. **∼ à faire**, manage to do. **faire ∼**, send.

parvis /parvi/ n.m. (place) square.

pas[1] /pa/ adv. not. (ne) **∼**, not. **je ne sais ∼**, I do not know. **∼ de sucre/livres/etc.**, no sugar/books/etc. **∼ du tout**, not at all. **∼ encore**, not yet. **∼ mal**, not bad; (beaucoup) quite a lot (de, of). **∼ vrai?**, (fam.) isn't that so?

pas[2] /pa/ n.m. step; (bruit) footstep; (trace) footprint; (vitesse) pace; (de vis) thread. **à deux ∼ (de)**, close by. **au ∼**, at a walking pace; (véhicule) very slowly.

passable /pɑsabl/ a. tolerable.

passage /pasaʒ/ *n.m.* passing, passage; (*traversée*) crossing; (*visite*) visit; (*chemin*) way, passage; (*d'une œuvre*) passage. de ∼, (*voyageur*) visiting; (*amant*) casual. ∼ à niveau, level crossing. ∼ clouté, pedestrian crossing. ∼ interdit, (*panneau*) no thoroughfare. ∼ souterrain, subway.

passag|er, ∼ère /pasaʒe, -ɛr/ *a.* temporary. —*n.m.*, *f.* passenger.

passant, ∼e /pasã, -t/ *a.* (*rue*) busy. —*n.m.*, *f.* passer-by.

passe /pas/ *n.f.* pass. ∼**-partout** *n.m. invar.* master-key; (*a. invar.* for all occasions). ∼**-temps** *n.m. invar.* pastime.

passé /pase/ *a.* (*révolu*) past; (*dernier*) last; (*fini*) over; (*fané*) faded. —*prép.* after. —*n.m.* past. ∼ **de mode**, out of fashion.

passeport /paspɔr/ *n.m.* passport.

passer /pase/ *v.i.* (*aux. être ou avoir*) pass; (*aller*) go; (*venir*) come; (*temps*) pass (by), go by; (*film*) be shown; (*couleur*) fade. —*v.t.* (*aux. avoir*) pass, cross; (*donner*) pass, hand; (*mettre*) put; (*oublier*) overlook; (*enfiler*) slip on; (*dépasser*) go beyond; (*temps*) spend, pass; (*film*) show; (*examen*) take; (*commande*) place; (*soupe*) strain. **se ∼** *v. pr.* happen, take place. **laisser ∼**, let through; (*occasion*) miss. ∼ **devant**, (*édifice*) go past. ∼ **par**, go through. ∼ **pour**, (*riche etc.*) be taken to be. ∼ **sur**, (*détail*) pass over. ∼ **l'aspirateur**, hoover, vacuum. ∼ **un coup de fil à qn.**, give s.o. a ring. **je vous passe Mme X**, (*par le standard*) I'm putting you through to Mrs X; (*en donnant l'appareil*) I'll hand you over to Mrs X. **se ∼ de**, go ou do without.

passerelle /pasrɛl/ *n.f.* footbridge; (*pour accéder à un avion, à un navire*) gangway.

passible /pasibl/ *a.* ∼ **de**, liable to.

passi|f, ∼ve /pasif, -v/ *a.* passive. —*n.m.* (*comm.*) liabilities. ∼**vité** *n.f.* passiveness.

passion /pasjɔ̃/ *n.f.* passion.

passionn|er /pasjɔne/ *v.t.* fascinate. ∼**é a.** passionate. **être ∼é de**, have a passion for. ∼**ément** *adv.* passionately.

passoire /paswar/ *n.f.* (*à thé*) strainer; (*à légumes*) colander.

pastel /pastɛl/ *n.m. & a. invar.* pastel.

pastèque /pastɛk/ *n.f.* watermelon.

pasteur /pastœr/ *n.m.* (*relig.*) minister.

pasteurisé /pastœrize/ *a.* pasteurized.

pastille /pastij/ *n.f.* (*bonbon*) pastille, lozenge.

pastis /pastis/ *n.m.* aniseed liqueur.

patate /patat/ *n.f.* (*fam.*) potato. ∼ (**douce**), sweet potato.

patauger /patoʒe/ *v.i.* splash about.

pâte /pat/ *n.f.* paste; (*farine*) dough; (*à tarte*) pastry; (*à frire*) batter. ∼**s** (**alimentaires**), pasta. ∼ **à modeler**, Plasticine (P.). ∼ **dentifrice**, toothpaste.

pâté /pate/ *n.m.* (*culin.*) pâté; (*d'encre*) ink-blot. ∼ **de maisons**, block of houses; (*de sable*) sand-pie. ∼ **en croûte**, meat pie.

pâtée /pate/ *n.f.* feed, mash.

patelin /patlɛ̃/ *n.m.* (*fam.*) village.

patent|e /patɑ̃t/ *n.f.* trade licence. ∼**é a.** licensed.

patern|el, ∼elle /patɛrnɛl/ *a.* paternal. ∼**ité** *n.f.* paternity.

pâteu|x, ~se /pɑtø, -z/ a. pasty.

pathétique /patetik/ a. moving.

patholog|ie /patɔlɔʒi/ n.f. pathology. **~ique** a. pathological.

pat|ient, ~iente /pasjɑ̃, -t/ a. & n.m., f. patient. **~iemment** /-jamɑ̃/ adv. patiently. **~ience** n.f. patience.

patienter /pasjɑ̃te/ v.i. wait.

patin /patɛ̃/ n.m. skate. **~ à roulettes,** roller-skate.

patin|er /patine/ v.i. skate; (voiture) spin. **~age** n.m. skating. **~eur, ~euse** n.m., f. skater.

patinoire /patinwar/ n.f. skating-rink.

pâtiss|ier, ~ière /patisje, -jɛr/ n.m., f. pastry-cook. **~erie** n.f. cake shop; (gâteau) pastry.

patois /patwa/ n.m. patois.

patrie /patri/ n.f. homeland.

patrimoine /patrimwan/ n.m. heritage.

patron[1]**, ~ne** /patrɔ̃, -ɔn/ n.m., f. employer, boss; (propriétaire) owner, boss; (saint) patron saint. **~al** (m. pl. **~aux**) /-ɔnal, -o/ a. employers'. **~at** /-ɔna/ n.m. employers.

patron[2] /patrɔ̃/ n.m. (couture) pattern.

patrouill|e /patruj/ n.f. patrol. **~er** v.i. patrol.

patte /pat/ n.f. leg; (pied) foot; (de chat) paw.

pâturage /patyraʒ/ n.m. pasture.

paume /pom/ n.f. (de main) palm.

paupière /popjɛr/ n.f. eyelid.

pause /poz/ n.f. pause; (halte) break.

pauvre /povr/ a. poor. —n.m./f. poor man, poor woman. **~ment** /-əma/ adv. poorly. **~té** /-ɔte/ n.f. poverty.

pavé /pave/ n.m. paving-stone; cobble(-stone).

pavillon[1] /pavijɔ̃/ n.m. house.

pavillon[2] /pavijɔ̃/ n.m. (drapeau) flag.

payant, ~e /pejɑ̃, -t/ a. (billet) for which a charge is made; (spectateur) (fee-)paying; (rentable) profitable.

payer /peje/ v.t./i. pay; (service, travail, etc.) pay for; (acheter) buy (à, for). **se ~** v. pr. (s'acheter) buy o.s. **faire ~ à qn.,** (cent francs etc.) charge s.o. (**pour,** for).

pays /pei/ n.m. country; (région) region; (village) village. **du ~,** local. **les P~-Bas,** the Netherlands. **le ~ de Galles,** Wales.

paysage /peizaʒ/ n.m. landscape.

paysan, ~ne /peizɑ̃, -an/ n.m., f. farmer, country person; (péj.) peasant. —a. (agricole) farming; (rural) country.

PCV (en) /(ɑ̃)peseve/ adv. **appeler** ou **téléphoner en ~,** reverse the charges.

PDG abrév. voir **président directeur général.**

péage /peaʒ/ n.m. toll; (lieu) toll-gate.

peau (pl. **~x**) /po/ n.f. skin; (cuir) hide. **être bien/mal dans sa ~,** be/not be at ease with oneself.

pêche[1] /pɛʃ/ n.f. peach.

pêche[2] /pɛʃ/ n.f. (activité) fishing; (poissons) catch. **~ à la ligne,** angling.

péché /peʃe/ n.m. sin.

pêch|er /peʃe/ v.t. (poisson) catch; (dénicher: fam.) dig up. —v.i. fish. **~eur** n.m. fisherman; (à la ligne) angler.

pédagog|ie /pedagɔʒi/ n.f. education. **~gique** a. educational.

pédal|e /pedal/ n.f. pedal. **~er** v.i. pedal.

pédalo /pedalo/ n.m. pedal boat.

pédant, ~e /pedɑ̃, -t/ a. pedantic.

pédestre /pedɛstr/ a. **faire de la**

randonnée ~, go walking *ou* hiking.

pédiatre /pedjatr/ *n.m./f.* paediatrician.

pédicure /pedikyr/ *n.m./f.* chiropodist.

pedigree /pedigri/ *n.m.* pedigree.

peign|e /pɛɲ/ *n.m.* comb. ~**er** /pɛɲe/ *v.t.* comb; (*personne*) comb the hair of. se ~**er** *v. pr.* comb one's hair.

peignoir /pɛɲwar/ *n.m.* dressing-gown.

peindre† /pɛ̃dr/ *v.t.* paint.

peine /pɛn/ *n.f.* sadness, sorrow; (*effort, difficulté*) trouble; (*punition*) punishment; (*jurid.*) sentence. avoir de la ~, feel sad. faire de la ~ à, hurt. ce n'est pas la ~ de faire, it is not worth (while) doing.

peine (à) /(a)pɛn/ *adv.* hardly.

peintre /pɛ̃tr/ *n.m.* painter. ~ **en bâtiment,** house painter.

peinture /pɛ̃tyr/ *n.f.* painting; (*matière*) paint. ~ **à l'huile,** oil-painting.

péjorati|f, ~**ve** /peʒɔratif, -v/ *a.* pejorative.

pelage /pɔlaʒ/ *n.m.* coat, fur.

peler /pɔle/ *v.t./i.* peel.

pèlerin /pɛlrɛ̃/ *n.m.* pilgrim. ~**age** /-inaʒ/ *n.m.* pilgrimage.

pélican /pelikã/ *n.m.* pelican.

pelle /pɛl/ *n.f.* shovel; (*d'enfant*) spade. ~**tée** *n.f.* shovelful.

pellicule /pelikyl/ *n.f.* film. ~**s,** (*cheveux*) dandruff.

pelote /pɔlɔt/ *n.f.* ball; (*d'épingles*) pincushion.

peloton /plɔtɔ̃/ *n.m.* troop, squad; (*sport*) pack.

pelouse /pluz/ *n.f.* lawn.

peluche /plyʃ/ *n.f.* (*tissu*) plush; (*jouet*) cuddly toy. en ~, (*lapin, chien*) fluffy, furry.

pén|al (*m. pl.* ~**aux**) /penal, -o/

a. penal. ~**aliser** *v.t.* penalize. ~**alité** *n.f.* penalty.

penalt|y (*pl.* ~**ies**) /penalti/ *n.m.* penalty (kick).

penchant /pɑ̃ʃɑ̃/ *n.m.* inclination; (*goût*) liking (pour, for).

pencher /pɑ̃ʃe/ *v.t.* tilt. —*v.i.* lean (over), tilt. se ~ *v. pr.* lean (forward).

pendant /pɑ̃dɑ̃/ *prép.* (*au cours de*) during; (*durée*) for. ~ **que,** while.

pendentif /pɑ̃dɑ̃tif/ *n.m.* pendant.

penderie /pɑ̃dri/ *n.f.* wardrobe.

pend|re /pɑ̃dr/ *v.t./i.* hang. se ~**re** *v. pr.* hang (à, from); (*se tuer*) hang o.s. ~**re la crémaillère,** have a house-warming. ~**u,** ~**ue** *a.* hanging (à, from); *n.m., f.* hanged man, hanged woman.

pendul|e /pɑ̃dyl/ *n.f.* clock. —*n.m.* pendulum. ~**ette** *n.f.* (travelling) clock.

pénétr|er /penetre/ *v.i.* ~**er** (**dans**), enter. —*v.t.* penetrate. ~**ant,** ~**ante** *a.* penetrating.

pénible /penibl/ *a.* difficult; (*douloureux*) painful; (*fatigant*) tiresome. ~**ment** /-əmɑ̃/ *adv.* with difficulty; (*cruellement*) painfully.

péniche /peniʃ/ *n.f.* barge.

pénicilline /penisilin/ *n.f.* penicillin.

péninsule /penɛ̃syl/ *n.f.* peninsula.

pénis /penis/ *n.m.* penis.

pensée[1] /pɑ̃se/ *n.f.* thought.

pensée[2] /pɑ̃se/ *n.f.* (*fleur*) pansy.

pens|er /pɑ̃se/ *v.t./i.* think. ~**er à,** (*réfléchir à*) think about; (*se souvenir de, prévoir*) think of. ~**er faire,** think of doing. **faire** ~**er à,** remind one of.

pensi|f, ~**ve** /pɑ̃sif, -v/ *a.* pensive.

pension /pɑ̃sjɔ̃/ *n.f.* (*scol.*) boarding-school; (*repas, somme*) board; (*allocation*) pension. ~-

(de famille), guest-house. ~
alimentaire, (*jurid.*) alimony.
~**naire** /-jɔnɛr/ *n.m./f.* boarder;
(*d'hôtel*) guest. ~**nat** /-jɔna/ *n.m.*
boarding-school.

pente /pɑ̃t/ *n.f.* slope. **en** ~,
sloping.

Pentecôte /pɑ̃tkot/ *n.f.* **la** ~,
Whitsun.

pénurie /penyri/ *n.f.* shortage.

pépin /pepɛ̃/ *n.m.* (*graine*) pip;
(*ennui: fam.*) hitch; (*parapluie:
fam.*) brolly.

perce-neige /pɛrsənɛʒ/ *n.m./f.* in-
var. snowdrop.

percepteur /pɛrsɛptœr/ *n.m.* tax-
collector.

perceptible /pɛrsɛptibl/ *a.* perceptible.

perception /pɛrsɛpsjɔ̃/ *n.f.* perception; (*d'impôts*) collection.

percer /pɛrse/ *v.t.* pierce; (*avec
perceuse*) drill.

perceuse /pɛrsøz/ *n.f.* drill.

percevoir† /pɛrsəvwar/ *v.t.* perceive; (*impôt*) collect.

perche /pɛrʃ/ *n.f.* (*bâton*) pole.

perch|er /pɛrʃe/ *v.t.*, **se** ~**er** *v. pr.*
perch. ~**oir** *n.m.* perch.

percolateur /pɛrkɔlatœr/ *n.m.* percolator.

percussion /pɛrkysjɔ̃/ *n.f.* percussion.

percuter /pɛrkyte/ *v.t.* strike;
(*véhicule*) crash into.

perd|re /pɛrdr/ *v.t./i.* lose;
(*gaspiller*) waste; (*ruiner*) ruin.
se ~**re** *v. pr.* get lost; (*rester
inutilisé*) go to waste. ~**ant**,
~**ante** *a.* losing; *n.m., f.* loser.
~**u** *a.* (*endroit*) isolated;
(*moments*) spare.

perdreau (*pl.* ~**x**) /pɛrdro/ *n.m.*
(young) partridge.

perdrix /pɛrdri/ *n.f.* partridge.

père /pɛr/ *n.m.* father. ~ **de
famille**, father, family man. **le** ~

Noël, Father Christmas, Santa
Claus.

perfection /pɛrfɛksjɔ̃/ *n.f.* perfection.

perfectionn|er /pɛrfɛksjɔne/ *v.t.*
improve. **se** ~**er en anglais**/*etc.*,
improve one's English/*etc.* ~**é** *a.*
sophisticated. ~**ement** *n.m.* improvement.

perfectionniste /pɛrfɛksjɔnist/
n.m./f. perfectionist.

perforer /pɛrfɔre/ *v.t.* perforate;
(*billet, bande*) punch.

performance /pɛrfɔrmɑ̃s/ *n.f.* performance.

perfusion /pɛrfyzjɔ̃/ *n.f.* drip.
mettre qn. sous ~, put s.o. on a
drip.

péridural /peridyral/ *a.*
(**anesthésie**) ~**e**, epidural.

péril /peril/ *n.m.* peril.

périlleu|x, ~**se** /perijø, -z/ *a.*
perilous.

périmé /perime/ *a.* expired;
(*désuet*) outdated.

périmètre /perimɛtr/ *n.m.* perimeter.

périod|e /perjɔd/ *n.f.* period.
~**ique** *a.* periodic(al); *n.m.*
(*journal*) periodical.

périphér|ie /periferi/ *n.f.* peri-
phery; (*banlieue*) outskirts.
~**ique** *a.* peripheral; *n.m.*
(**boulevard**) ~**ique**, ring road.

perle /pɛrl/ *n.f.* (*bijou*) pearl;
(*boule, de sueur*) bead.

permanence /pɛrmanɑ̃s/ *n.f.* permanence; (*bureau*) duty office. **en**
~, permanently. **assurer une**
~, keep the office open.

permanent, ~**e** /pɛrmanɑ̃, -t/ *a.*
permanent; (*spectacle*) continuous; (*comité*) standing. —*n.f.*
(*coiffure*) perm.

perméable /pɛrmeabl/ *a.* perme-
able.

permettre† /pɛrmɛtr/ *v.t.* allow,

permit. **~ à qn. de,** allow ou permit s.o. to.

permis /permi, -z/ a. allowed. —*n.m.* licence, permit. **~ (de conduire),** driving-licence.

permission /permisjɔ̃/ *n.f.* permission. **en ~,** (*mil.*) on leave.

Pérou /peru/ *n.m.* Peru.

perpendiculaire /pɛrpɑ̃dikylɛr/ a. & *n.f.* perpendicular.

perpétuel, ~le /pɛrpetɥɛl/ a. perpetual.

perpétuité (à) /(a)pɛrpetɥite/ adv. for life.

perron /perɔ̃/ *n.m.* (front) steps.

perroquet /pɛrɔkɛ/ *n.m.* parrot.

perruche /peryʃ/ *n.f.* budgerigar.

perruque /peryk/ *n.f.* wig.

persan, ~e /pɛrsɑ̃, -an/ a. & *n.m.* (*lang.*) Persian.

persécut|er /pɛrsekyte/ v.t. persecute. **~ion** /-ysjɔ̃/ *n.f.* persecution.

persévér|er /pɛrsevere/ v.i. persevere. **~ance** /-ɑ̃s/ *n.f.* perseverance.

persienne /pɛrsjɛn/ *n.f.* (outside) shutter.

persil /pɛrsi/ *n.m.* parsley.

persister /pɛrsiste/ v.i. persist (**à faire,** in doing).

personnage /pɛrsɔnaʒ/ *n.m.* character; (*important*) personality.

personnalité /pɛrsɔnalite/ *n.f.* personality.

personne /pɛrsɔn/ *n.f.* person. **~s,** people. —*pron.* (*quelqu'un*) anybody. **(ne) ~,** nobody.

personnel, ~le /pɛrsɔnɛl/ a. personal; (*égoïste*) selfish. —*n.m.* staff. **~lement** adv. personally.

perspective /pɛrspɛktiv/ *n.f.* (*art*) perspective; (*vue*) view; (*possibilité*) prospect; (*point de vue*) viewpoint, perspective.

persuader /pɛrsɥade/ v.t. persuade (**de faire,** to do).

perte /pɛrt/ *n.f.* loss; (*ruine*) ruin.

~ de, (*temps, argent*) waste of. **~s,** (*méd.*) discharge.

perturber /pɛrtyrbe/ v.t. disrupt; (*personne*) perturb.

pervenche /pɛrvɑ̃ʃ/ *n.f.* periwinkle; (*fam.*) traffic warden.

pervers, ~e /pɛrvɛr, -s/ a. perverse; (*dépravé*) perverted.

pes|ant, ~ante /pəzɑ̃, -t/ a. heavy. **la ~anteur,** gravity.

pèse-personne /pɛzpɛrsɔn/ *n.m.* (bathroom) scales.

peser /pəze/ v.t./i. weigh.

peseta /pezeta/ *n.f.* peseta.

pessimis|te /pesimist/ a. pessimistic. —*n.m.* pessimist. **~me** *n.m.* pessimism.

peste /pɛst/ *n.f.* plague; (*personne*) pest.

pester /pɛste/ v.i. **~ (contre),** curse.

pétale /petal/ *n.m.* petal.

pétanque /petɑ̃k/ *n.f.* bowls.

pétard /petar/ *n.m.* banger.

péter /pete/ v.i. fart; (*fam.*) go bang; (*casser: fam.*) snap.

pétill|er /petije/ v.i. crackle; (*champagne, yeux*) sparkle. **~ant, ~ante** a. (*gazeux*) fizzy.

petit, ~e /pti, -t/ a. small; (*avec nuance affective*) little; (*jeune*) young, small; (*faible*) slight; (*mesquin*) petty. —*n.m., -f.* little child. **~ ami,** boy-friend. **~e amie,** girl-friend. **~ à petit,** little by little. **~es annonces,** small ads. **~e cuiller,** teaspoon. **~ déjeuner,** breakfast. **le ~ écran,** the small screen, television. **~-enfant** (*pl.* **~s-enfants**) *n.m.* grandchild. **~e-fille** (*pl.* **~es-filles**) *n.f.* granddaughter. **~-fils** (*pl.* **~s-fils**) *n.m.* grandson. **~ pain,** roll. **~-pois** (*pl.* **~s-pois**) *n.m.* garden pea.

pétition /petisjɔ̃/ *n.f.* petition.

pétrir /petrir/ v.t. knead.

pétrol|e /petʀɔl/ *n.m.* (*brut*) oil; (*pour lampe etc.*) paraffin. **lampe à ~e,** oil lamp. **~ier, ~ière** *a.* oil; *n.m.* (*navire*) oil-tanker.

peu /pø/ *adv.* **~ (de),** (*quantité*) little, not much; (*nombre*) few, not many. **~ intéressant**/*etc.*, not very interesting/*etc.* **—pron.** few. **—n.m.** little. **un ~ (de),** a little. **à ~ près,** more or less. **~ après/avant,** shortly after/before. **~ de chose,** not much. **~ nombreux,** few. **~ souvent,** seldom.

peuple /pœpl/ *n.m.* people.

peupler /pœple/ *v.t.* populate.

peuplier /pøplije/ *n.m.* poplar.

peur /pœʀ/ *n.f.* fear. **avoir ~,** be afraid (**de,** of). **de ~ de/que,** for fear of. **faire ~ à,** frighten. **~eux,~euse** *a.* fearful, timid.

peut /pø/ *voir* **pouvoir**[1].

peut-être /pøtɛtʀ/ *adv.* perhaps, maybe. **~ que,** perhaps, maybe.

peux /pø/ *voir* **pouvoir**[1].

phare /faʀ/ *n.m.* (*tour*) lighthouse; (*de véhicule*) headlight. **~ anti-brouillard,** fog lamp.

pharmaceutique /faʀmasøtik/ *a.* pharmaceutical.

pharmac|ie /faʀmasi/ *n.f.* (*magasin*) chemist's (shop); (*armoire*) medicine cabinet. **~ien, ~ienne** *n.m., f.* chemist, pharmacist.

pharyngite /faʀɛ̃ʒit/ *n.f.* pharyngitis.

phénomène /fenɔmɛn/ *n.m.* phenomenon; (*original: fam.*) eccentric.

Philippines /filipin/ *n.f. pl.* **les ~,** the Philippines.

philosoph|e /filozɔf/ *n.m./f.* philosopher. *—a.* philosophical. **~ie** *n.f.* philosophy. **~ique** *a.* philosophical.

phonétique /fɔnetik/ *a.* phonetic.

phoque /fɔk/ *n.m.* (*animal*) seal.

phosphate /fɔsfat/ *n.m.* phosphate.

phosphore /fɔsfɔʀ/ *n.m.* phosphorus.

photo /fɔto/ *n.f.* photo; (*art*) photography. **prendre en ~,** take a photo of. **~ d'identité,** passport photograph.

photocop|ie /fɔtɔkɔpi/ *n.f.* photocopy. **~ier** *v.t.* photocopy. **~ieuse** *n.f.* photocopier.

photograph|e /fɔtɔgʀaf/ *n.m./f.* photographer. **~ie** *n.f.* photograph. **~ier** *v.t.* take a photo of.

phrase /fʀaz/ *n.f.* sentence.

physicien, ~ne /fizisjɛ̃, -jɛn/ *n.m., f.* physicist.

physiologie /fizjɔlɔʒi/ *n.f.* physiology.

physique[1] /fizik/ *a.* physical. **—n.m.** physique. **au ~,** physically. **~ment** *adv.* physically.

physique[2] /fizik/ *n.f.* physics.

pian|o /pjano/ *n.m.* piano. **~iste** *n.m./f.* pianist.

pic /pik/ *n.m.* (*outil*) pickaxe; (*sommet*) peak; (*oiseau*) woodpecker. **à ~,** (*verticalement*) sheer; (*couler*) straight to the bottom; (*arriver*) just at the right time.

pichet /piʃɛ/ *n.m.* jug.

pickpocket /pikpɔkɛt/ *n.m.* pickpocket.

pick-up /pikœp/ *n.m. invar.* record-player.

picot|er /pikɔte/ *v.t.* prick; (*yeux*) make smart. **~ement** *n.m.* pricking; smarting.

pie /pi/ *n.f.* magpie.

pièce /pjɛs/ *n.f.* piece; (*chambre*) room; (*écrit*) document. **~ (de monnaie),** coin. **~ (de théâtre),** play. **dix francs/*etc.* (la) ~,** ten francs/*etc.* each. **~ de rechange,** spare part. **~ détachée,** part. **~**

d'identité, identity paper. **~s justificatives,** supporting documents. **deux/trois** *etc.* **~,** two-/three-/*etc.* room flat.

pied /pje/ *n.m.* foot; (*de meuble*) leg; (*de lampe*) base; (*de salade*) base. **à ~,** on foot. **avoir ~,** have a footing. **mettre les ~s dans le plat,** put one's foot in it. **c'est le ~!,** (*fam.*) it's great!

piège /pjɛʒ/ *n.m.* trap.

piég|er /pjeʒe/ *v.t.* trap; (*avec explosifs*) booby-trap. **lettre/voiture ~ée,** letter-/car-bomb.

pierre /pjɛr/ *n.f.* stone.

piétiner /pjetine/ *v.i.* stamp one's feet; (*ne pas avancer: fig.*) mark time. —*v.t.* trample on.

piéton /pjetɔ̃/ *n.m.* pedestrian. **~nier,** **~nière** /-ɔnje, -jɛr/ *a.* pedestrian.

pieuvre /pjœvr/ *n.f.* octopus.

pif /pif/ *n.m.* (*fam.*) nose.

pigeon /piʒɔ̃/ *n.m.* pigeon.

piger /piʒe/ *v.t./i.* (*fam.*) understand, get (it).

pigment /pigmɑ̃/ *n.m.* pigment.

pile /pil/ *n.f.* (*tas, pilier*) pile; (*électr.*) battery; (*atomique*) pile. —*adv.* (*s'arrêter. fam.*) dead. **à dix heures ~,** (*fam.*) at ten on the dot. **~ ou face?,** heads or tails?

pilier /pilje/ *n.m.* pillar.

pilot|e /pilɔt/ *n.m.* pilot; (*auto.*) driver. —*a.* pilot. **~er** *v.t.* (*aviat., naut.*) pilot; (*auto.*) drive.

pilule /pilyl/ *n.f.* pill. **la ~,** the pill.

piment /pimɑ̃/ *n.m.* pepper, pimento; (*fig.*) spice. **~é** /-te/ *a.* spicy.

pin /pɛ̃/ *n.m.* pine.

pinard /pinar/ *n.m.* (*vin: fam.*) plonk, cheap wine.

pince /pɛ̃s/ *n.f.* (*outil*) pliers; (*levier*) crowbar; (*de crabe*) pincer. **~ (à épiler),** tweezers. **~ (à linge),** (clothes-) peg.

pinceau (*pl.* **~x**) /pɛ̃so/ *n.m.* paintbrush.

pinc|er /pɛ̃se/ *v.t.* pinch. **se ~er le doigt,** catch one's finger. **~ée** *n.f.* pinch (**de,** of).

pinède /pinɛd/ *n.f.* pine forest.

pingouin /pɛ̃gwɛ̃/ *n.m.* penguin.

ping-pong /piŋpɔ̃g/ *n.m.* table tennis, ping-pong.

pingre /pɛ̃gr/ *a.* miserly.

pinson /pɛ̃sɔ̃/ *n.m.* chaffinch.

pintade /pɛ̃tad/ *n.f.* guinea-fowl.

pioche /pjɔʃ/ *n.f.* pick(axe).

pion /pjɔ̃/ *n.m.* (*de jeu*) piece; (*échecs*) pawn; (*scol., fam.*) supervisor.

pionnier /pjɔnje/ *n.m.* pioneer.

pipe /pip/ *n.f.* pipe.

pipe-line /piplin/ *n.m.* pipeline.

piquant, ~e /pikɑ̃, -t/ *a.* (*barbe etc.*) prickly; (*goût*) pungent; (*détail etc.*) spicy. —*n.m.* prickle; (*de hérisson*) spine, prickle.

pique /pik/ *n.m.* (*cartes*) spades.

pique-nique /piknik/ *n.m.* picnic. **~er** *v.i.* picnic.

piquer /pike/ *v.t.* prick; (*langue*) burn, sting; (*abeille etc.*) sting; (*serpent etc.*) bite; (*enfoncer*) stick; (*coudre*) (machine-)stitch; (*curiosité*) excite; (*crise*) have; (*voler: fam.*) pinch. —*v.i.* (*avion*) dive; (*goût*) be hot.

piquet /pikɛ/ *n.m.* stake; (*de tente*) peg. **au ~,** (*scol.*) in the corner.

piqûre /pikyr/ *n.f.* prick; (*d'abeille etc.*) sting; (*de serpent etc.*) bite; (*point*) stitch; (*méd.*) injection.

pirate /pirat/ *n.m.* pirate. **~ de l'air,** hijacker. **~rie** *n.f.* piracy.

pire /pir/ *a.* worse (**que,** than). **le ~ livre/etc.,** the worst book/etc. —*n.m.* **le ~,** the worst (thing). **au ~,** at worst.

pis¹ /pi/ *n.m.* (*de vache*) udder.

pis² /pi/ *a. invar. & adv.* worse.

aller de mal en ~, go from bad to worse.

piscine /pisin/ *n.f.* swimming-pool. ~ **couverte**, indoor swimming-pool.

pissenlit /pisɑ̃li/ *n.m.* dandelion.

pistache /pistaʃ/ *n.f.* pistachio.

piste /pist/ *n.f.* track; (*de personne, d'animal*) track, trail; (*aviat.*) runway; (*de cirque*) ring; (*de ski*) run; (*de patinage*) rink; (*de danse*) floor; (*sport*) race-track. ~ **cyclable**, cycle-track; (*Amer.*) bicycle path.

pistolet /pistɔlɛ/ *n.m.* gun, pistol.

piston /pistɔ̃/ *n.m.* (*techn.*) piston.

pitié /pitje/ *n.f.* pity. **il me fait ~**, **j'ai ~ de lui**, I pity him.

piton /pitɔ̃/ *n.m.* (*à crochet*) hook; (*sommet pointu*) peak.

pitoyable /pitwajabl/ *a.* pitiful.

pitre /pitr/ *n.m.* clown. **faire le ~**, clown around.

pittoresque /pitɔrɛsk/ *a.* picturesque.

pivot /pivo/ *n.m.* pivot.

pizza /pidza/ *n.f.* pizza.

placard /plakar/ *n.m.* cupboard; (*affiche*) poster. ~**er** /-de/ *v.t.* (*affiche*) post up; (*mur*) cover with posters.

place /plas/ *n.f.* place; (*espace libre*) room, space; (*siège*) seat, place; (*prix d'un trajet*) fare; (*esplanade*) square; (*emploi*) post; (*de parking*) space. **à la ~ de**, instead of. **en ~, à sa ~**, in its place. **sur ~**, on the spot. **ça prend de la ~**, it takes up a lot of room. **se mettre à la ~ de qn.** put oneself in s.o.'s shoes *ou* place.

plac|er /plase/ *v.t.* (*invité, spectateur*) seat; (*argent*) invest. **se ~er** *v. pr.* (*personne*) take up a position; (*troisième etc.*: *sport*) come (in); (*à un endroit*) to go and stand (à, in). ~**é a.** (*sport*) placed.

bien ~é pour, in a position to. ~**ement** *n.m.* (*d'argent*) investment.

placide /plasid/ *a.* placid.

plafond /plafɔ̃/ *n.m.* ceiling.

plage /plaʒ/ *n.f.* beach; (*station*) (seaside) resort; (*aire*) area.

plaider /plede/ *v.t./i.* plead.

plaie /plɛ/ *n.f.* wound; (*personne*: *fam.*) nuisance.

plaignant, ~e /plɛɲɑ̃, -t/ *n.m., f.* plaintiff.

plaindre† /plɛ̃dr/ *v.t.* pity. **se ~** *v. pr.* complain (**de**, about). **se ~ de**, (*souffrir de*) complain of.

plaine /plɛn/ *n.f.* plain.

plainte /plɛ̃t/ *n.f.* complaint; (*gémissement*) groan. ~**if, ~ive** *a.* plaintive.

plaire† /plɛr/ *v.i.* ~ **à**, please. **ça lui plaît**, he likes it. **elle lui plaît**, he likes her. **s'il vous plaît**, please.

plaisance /plɛzɑ̃s/ *n.f.* **la** (**navigation de**) ~, yachting.

plaisant, ~e /plɛzɑ̃, -t/ *a.* pleasant; (*drôle*) amusing.

plaisant|er /plɛzɑ̃te/ *v.i.* joke. ~**erie** *n.f.* joke. ~**in** *n.m.* joker.

plaisir /plɛzir/ *n.m.* pleasure. **faire ~ à**, please. **pour le ~**, for fun *ou* pleasure.

plan /plɑ̃/ *n.m.* plan; (*de ville*) map; (*surface, niveau*) plane.

planche /plɑ̃ʃ/ *n.f.* board, plank. ~ **à repasser**, ironing-board. ~ **à voile**, sailboard; (*sport*) windsurfing.

plancher /plɑ̃ʃe/ *n.m.* floor.

plan|er /plane/ *v.i.* glide. ~**eur** *n.m.* (*avion*) glider.

planète /planɛt/ *n.f.* planet.

planif|ier /planifje/ *v.t.* plan. ~**ication** *n.f.* planning.

plante /plɑ̃t/ *n.f.* plant. ~ **des pieds**, sole (of the foot).

plant|er /plɑ̃te/ *v.t.* (*plante etc.*)

plant; (*enfoncer*) drive in. **~ation** *n.f.* planting; (*de tabac etc.*) plantation.

plaque /plak/ *n.f.* plate; (*de marbre*) slab; (*insigne*) badge; (*commémorative*) plaque. **~ chauffante**, hotplate. **~ minéralogique**, number-plate.

plaquer /plake/ *v.t.* (*bois*) veneer; (*aplatir*) flatten; (*rugby*) tackle; (*abandonner: fam.*) ditch.

plasma /plasma/ *n.m.* plasma.

plastique /plastik/ *a. & n.m.* plastic. **en ~**, plastic.

plat¹, **~e** /pla, -t/ *a.* flat. —*n.m.* (*de la main*) flat. **à ~** *adv.* (*poser*) flat; *a.* (*batterie, pneu*) flat. **à ~ ventre**, flat on one's face.

plat² /pla/ *n.m.* (*culin.*) dish; (*partie de repas*) course.

platane /platan/ *n.m.* plane(-tree).

plateau (*pl.* **~x**) /plato/ *n.m.* tray; (*d'électrophone*) turntable, deck; (*de balance*) pan; (*géog.*) plateau. **~ de fromages**, cheeseboard.

plateau-repas (*pl.* **plateaux-repas**) *n.m.* tray meal.

plate-bande (*pl.* **plates-bandes**) /platbãd/ *n.f.* flower-bed.

plate-forme (*pl.* **plates-formes**) /platform/ *n.f.* platform.

platine¹ /platin/ *n.m.* platinum.

platine² /platin/ *n.f.* (*de tourne-disque*) turntable.

plâtr|e /platr/ *n.m.* plaster; (*méd.*) (plaster) cast. **~er** *v.t.* plaster; (*membre*) put in plaster.

plein, **~e** /plẽ, plɛn/ *a.* full (**de**, of); (*total*) complete. —*n.m.* faire le **~ (d'essence)**, fill up (the tank). **à ~**, to the full. **à ~ temps**, full-time. **en ~ air**, in the open air. **en ~ milieu/visage**, right in the middle/the face. **en ~ nuit/etc.**, in the middle of the night/*etc.*

pleurer /plœre/ *v.i.* cry, weep (**sur**, over); (*yeux*) water. —*v.t.* mourn.

pleurésie /plœrezi/ *n.f.* pleurisy.

pleurs (en) /(ã)plœr/ *adv.* in tears.

pleuvoir† /plœvwar/ *v.i.* rain. **il pleut**, it is raining.

pli /pli/ *n.m.* fold; (*de jupe*) pleat; (*de pantalon*) crease; (*enveloppe*) cover; (*habitude*) habit. **(faux) ~**, crease.

pliant, **~e** /plijã, -t/ *a.* folding; (*parapluie*) telescopic. —*n.m.* folding stool, camp-stool.

plier /plije/ *v.t.* fold; (*courber*) bend. —*v.i.* bend. **se ~** *v. pr.* fold.

plomb /plõ/ *n.m.* lead; (*fusible*) fuse. **~s**, (*de chasse*) lead shot. **de ou en ~**, lead. **de ~**, (*ciel*) leaden.

plomb|er /plõbe/ *v.t.* (*dent*) fill. **~age** *n.m.* filling.

plomb|ier /plõbje/ *n.m.* plumber. **~erie** *n.f.* plumbing.

plongeant, **~e** /plõʒã, -t/ *a.* (*vue*) from above; (*décolleté*) plunging.

plongeoir /plõʒwar/ *n.m.* diving-board.

plongeon /plõʒõ/ *n.m.* dive.

plong|er /plõʒe/ *v.i.* dive; (*route*) plunge. —*v.t.* plunge. **se ~er** *v. pr.* plunge (dans, into). **~é dans**, (*lecture*) immersed in. **~ée** *n.f.* diving. **en ~ée** (*sous-marin*) submerged.

plouf /pluf/ *n.m. & int.* splash.

ploy /plwa/ *voir* **plaire**, **pleuvoir**.

pluie /plɥi/ *n.f.* rain; (*averse*) shower.

plume /plym/ *n.f.* feather; (*stylo*) pen; (*pointe*) nib.

plupart /plypar/ *n.f.* most. **la ~ des**, (*gens, cas, etc.*) most. **la ~ du temps**, most of the time.

pluriel, **~le** /plyrjɛl/ *a. & n.m.* plural. **au ~**, (*nom*) plural.

plus¹ /ply/ *adv.* de négation. **(ne) ~**, (*temps*) no longer, not any more. **(ne) ~ de**, (*quantité*) no more. **je n'y vais ~**, I do not go there any longer or any more. **(il**

n'y a) ~ **de pain,** (there is) no
more bread.

plus² /ply/ (/plyz/ *before vowel,*
/plys/ *in final position) adv.* more
(que, than). ~ **âgé/tard/**etc.,
older/later/etc. ~ **beau/**etc.,
more beautiful/etc. **le** ~, the
most. **le** ~ **beau/**etc., the most
beautiful; (*de deux*) the more
beautiful. **le** ~ **de,** (*gens etc.*)
most. ~ **de,** (*pain etc.*) more; (*dix
jours etc.*) more than. **il est** ~ **de
huit heures/**etc. it is after
eight/etc. o'clock. **de** ~, more
(que, than); (*en outre*) moreover.
(âgés) de ~ **de** (*huit ans etc.*)
over, more than. **de** ~ **en plus,**
more and more. **en** ~, extra. **en
~ de,** in addition to. ~ **ou
moins,** more or less.

plus³ /plys/ *conj.* plus.

plusieurs /plyzjœr/ *a. & pron.*
several.

plus-value /plyvaly/ *n.f.* (*bénéfice*)
profit.

plutôt /plyto/ *adv.* rather **(que,**
than).

pluvieu|x, ~**se** /plyvjø, -z/ *a.*
rainy.

pneu (*pl.* ~**s**) /pnø/ *n.m.* tyre;
(*lettre*) express letter. ~**matique**
a. inflatable.

pneumonie /pnømɔni/ *n.f.* pneumonia.

poche /pɔʃ/ *n.f.* pocket; (*sac*) bag.
~**s,** (*sous les yeux*) bags.

pocher /pɔʃe/ *v.t.* (*œuf*) poach.

pochette /pɔʃɛt/ *n.f.* pack(et),
envelope; (*sac*) bag, pouch;
(*d'allumettes*) book; (*de disque*)
sleeve; (*mouchoir*) pocket handkerchief. ~ **surprise,** lucky
bag.

podium /pɔdjɔm/ *n.m.* rostrum.

poêle¹ /pwal/ *n.f.* ~ **(à frire),**
frying-pan.

poêle² /pwal/ *n.m.* stove.

poème /pɔɛm/ *n.m.* poem.

poésie /pɔezi/ *n.f.* poetry; (*poème*)
poem.

poète /pɔɛt/ *n.m.* poet.

poétique /pɔetik/ *a.* poetic.

poids /pwa/ *n.m.* weight. ~**lourd,**
(*camion*) lorry, juggernaut.

poignard /pwaɲar/ *n.m.* dagger.

poignée /pwaɲe/ *n.f.* handle;
(*quantité*) handful. ~ **de main,**
handshake.

poignet /pwaɲɛ/ *n.m.* wrist; (*de
chemise*) cuff.

poil /pwal/ *n.m.* hair; (*pelage*) fur;
(*de brosse*) bristle. ~**s,** (*de tapis*)
pile. **à** ~, (*fam.*) naked. ~**u** *a.*
hairy.

poinçon /pwɛ̃sɔ̃/ *n.m.* awl;
(*marque*) hallmark. ~**ner** /-ɔne/
v.t. (*billet*) punch.

poing /pwɛ̃/ *n.m.* fist.

point¹ /pwɛ̃/ *n.m.* point; (*note:
scol.*) mark; (*tache*) spot, dot; (*de
couture*) stitch. ~ **(final),** full
stop, period. **à** ~, (*culin.*)
medium; (*arriver*) at the right
time. **mettre au** ~, (*photo.*)
focus. **deux** ~**s,** colon. ~**s de
suspension,** suspension points.
~ **de suture,** (*méd.*) stitch. ~
de vente, retail outlet. ~ **de
vue,** point of view. ~
**d'interrogation / d'exclama-
tion,** question/exclamation-
mark. ~ **mort,** (*auto.*) neutral. ~
virgule, semicolon.

point² /pwɛ̃/ *adv.* (**ne**) ~, not.

pointe /pwɛ̃t/ *n.f.* point, tip; (*clou*)
tack; (*de grille*) spike; (*fig.*) touch
(**de,** of). **de** ~, (*industrie*) highly
advanced. **en** ~, pointed. **heure
de** ~, peak hour. **sur la** ~ **des
pieds,** on tiptoe.

pointillé /pwɛ̃tije/ *n.m.* dotted
line. —*a.* dotted.

pointu /pwɛ̃ty/ *a.* pointed;
(*aiguisé*) sharp.

pointure /pwɛ̃tyr/ n.f. size.

poire /pwar/ n.f. pear.

poireau (pl. ∼x) /pwaro/ n.m. leek.

poirier /pwarje/ n.m. pear-tree.

pois /pwa/ n.m. pea; (dessin) dot.

poison /pwazɔ̃/ n.m. poison.

poisseu|x, ∼se /pwasø, -z/ a. sticky.

poisson /pwasɔ̃/ n.m. fish. ∼ rouge, goldfish. ∼ d'avril, April fool. les P∼s, Pisces.

poissonn|ier, ∼ière /pwasɔnje, -jer/ n.m., f. fishmonger. ∼erie n.f. fish shop.

poitrine /pwatrin/ n.f. chest; (seins) bosom; (culin.) breast.

poivr|e /pwavr/ n.m. pepper. ∼é a. peppery. ∼ière n.f. pepper-pot.

poivron /pwavrɔ̃/ n.m. pepper, capsicum.

poker /poker/ n.m. poker.

polaire /poler/ a. polar.

polaroïd /polaroid/ n.m. (P.) Polaroid (P.).

pôle /pol/ n.m. pole.

polémique /polemik/ n.f. argument. —a. controversial.

poli /poli/ a. (personne) polite. ∼ment adv. politely.

polic|e[1] /polis/ n.f. police; (discipline) (law and) order. ∼ier, ∼ière a. police; (roman) detective; n.m. policeman.

police[2] /polis/ n.f. (d'assurance) policy.

polio(myélite) /poljo(mjelit)/ n.f. polio(myelitis).

polir /polir/ v.t. polish.

politesse /polites/ n.f. politeness.

politique /politik/ a. political. —n.f. politics.

pollen /polɛn/ n.m. pollen.

poll|uer /polɥe/ v.t. pollute. ∼ution n.f. pollution.

polo /polo/ n.m. polo; (vêtement) sports shirt, tennis shirt.

Pologne /poloɲ/ n.f. Poland.

polonais, ∼e /polonɛ, -z/ a. Polish. —n.m., f. Pole. —n.m. (lang.) Polish.

polycopier /polikopje/ v.t. duplicate, stencil.

polyglotte /poliglot/ n.m./f. polyglot.

pommade /pomad/ n.f. ointment.

pomme /pom/ n.f. apple; (d'arrosoir) rose. ∼ d'Adam, Adam's apple. ∼ de pin, pine cone. ∼ de terre, potato. ∼s frites, chips.

pommier /pomje/ n.m. apple-tree.

pompe /pɔ̃p/ n.f. pump; (splendeur) pomp. ∼ à incendie, fireengine. ∼s funèbres, undertaker's.

pomper /pɔ̃pe/ v.t. pump.

pompier /pɔ̃pje/ n.m. fireman.

pompiste /pɔ̃pist/ n.m./f. petrol pump attendant.

poncer /pɔ̃se/ v.t. rub down.

ponctuation /pɔ̃ktɥasjɔ̃/ n.f. punctuation.

ponct|uel, ∼uelle /pɔ̃ktɥel/ a. punctual. ∼ualité n.f. punctuality.

ponctuer /pɔ̃ktɥe/ v.t. punctuate.

pondre /pɔ̃dr/ v.t./i. lay.

poney /ponɛ/ n.m. pony.

pont /pɔ̃/ n.m. bridge; (de navire) deck; (de graissage) ramp. faire le ∼, take the extra day(s) off (between holidays). ∼ aérien, airlift.

pop /pop/ n.m. & a. invar. (mus.) pop.

popul|aire /popyler/ a. popular; (expression) colloquial; (quartier, origine) working-class. ∼arité n.f. popularity.

population /popylasjɔ̃/ n.f. population.

porc /por/ n.m. pig; (viande) pork.

porcelaine /porsələn/ n.f. china, porcelain.

porc-épic (*pl.* **porcs-épics**) /pɔrkepik/ *n.m.* porcupine.

porche /pɔrʃ/ *n.m.* porch.

porcherie /pɔrʃri/ *n.f.* pigsty.

por|e /pɔr/ *n.m.* pore. **~eux**, **~euse** *a.* porous.

pornograph|ie /pɔrnɔgrafi/ *n.f.* pornography. **~ique** *a.* pornographic.

port[1] /pɔr/ *n.m.* port, harbour. **à bon ~**, safely. **~ maritime**, seaport.

port[2] /pɔr/ *n.m.* (*transport*) carriage; (*d'armes*) carrying.

portail /pɔrtaj/ *n.m.* portal.

portant, **~e** /pɔrtɑ̃, -t/ *a.* **bien/mal ~**, in good/bad health.

portati|f, **~ve** /pɔrtatif, -v/ *a.* portable.

porte /pɔrt/ *n.f.* door; (*passage*) doorway; (*de jardin, d'embarquement*) gate. **mettre à la ~**, throw out. **~ d'entrée**, front door.

portée /pɔrte/ *n.f.* (*d'animaux*) litter; (*impact*) significance; (*mus.*) stave. **à ~ de**, within reach of. **à ~ de (la) main**, within (arm's) reach. **à la ~ de qn.** at s.o.'s level.

portefeuille /pɔrtəfœj/ *n.m.* wallet; (*de ministre*) portfolio.

portemanteau (*pl.* **~x**) /pɔrtmɑ̃to/ *n.m.* coat ou hat stand.

port|er /pɔrte/ *v.t.* carry; (*vêtement, bague*) wear; (*fruits, responsabilité, nom*) bear; (*coup*) strike; (*amener*) bring. —*v.i.* (*bruit*) carry; (*coup*) hit home. **se ~er bien**, be *ou* feel well. **~e-bagages** *n.m. invar.* luggage rack. **~e-bonheur** *n.m. invar.* (*objet*) charm. **~e-clefs** *n.m. invar.* key-ring. **~e-documents** *n.m. invar.* attaché case, document wallet. **~e-monnaie** *n.m. invar.* purse.

porteu|r, **~se** /pɔrtœr, -øz/ *n.m.,*

f. (*méd.*) carrier. —*n.m.* (*rail.*) porter.

portier /pɔrtje/ *n.m.* door-man.

portière /pɔrtjɛr/ *n.f.* door.

portillon /pɔrtijɔ̃/ *n.m.* gate.

portion /pɔrsjɔ̃/ *n.f.* portion.

porto /pɔrto/ *n.m.* port (wine).

portrait /pɔrtrɛ/ *n.m.* portrait. **~robot** (*pl.* **~s-robots**) *n.m.* identikit, photofit.

portuaire /pɔrtɥɛr/ *a.* port.

portugais, **~e** /pɔrtygɛ, -z/ *a.* & *n.m.,* *f.* Portuguese. —*n.m.* (*lang.*) Portuguese.

Portugal /pɔrtygal/ *n.m.* Portugal.

pose /poz/ *n.f.* installation; (*attitude*) pose; (*photo.*) exposure.

poser /poze/ *v.t.* put (down); (*installer*) install, put in; (*fondations*) lay; (*question*) ask; (*problème*) pose. —*v.i.* (*modèle*) pose. **se ~** *v. pr.* (*avion, oiseau*) land; (*regard*) alight.

positi|f, **~ve** /pozitif, -v/ *a.* positive.

position /pozisjɔ̃/ *n.f.* position; (*banque*) balance (of account).

posologie /pozɔlɔʒi/ *n.f.* directions for use.

poss|éder /pɔsede/ *v.t.* possess; (*propriété*) own, possess. **~esseur** *n.m.* possessor; owner.

possession /pɔsesjɔ̃/ *n.f.* possession.

possibilité /pɔsibilite/ *n.f.* possibility.

possibl|e /pɔsibl/ *a.* possible. **dès que ~**, as soon as possible. **faire son ~**, do one's utmost. **le plus tard/etc. ~**, as late/etc. as possible. **pas ~**, impossible; (*int.*) really!

post- /pɔst/ *préf.* post-.

post|al (*m. pl.* **~aux**) /pɔstal, -o/ *a.* postal.

poste[1] /pɔst/ *n.f.* (*service*) post; (*bureau*) post office. **~ aérienne**, airmail. **mettre à la** ~, post. ~ **restante**, poste restante.

poste² /pɔst/ *n.m.* (*lieu, emploi*) post; (*de radio, télévision*) set; (*téléphone*) extension (number). ~ **d'essence**, petrol station. ~ **d'incendie**, fire point. ~ **de police**, police station. ~ **de secours**, first-aid post.

poster¹ /pɔste/ *v.t.* (*lettre, personne*) post.

poster² /pɔstɛr/ *n.m.* poster.

postérieur /pɔsterjœr/ *a.* later; (*partie*) back. ~ **à**, after.

postiche /pɔstiʃ/ *a.* false.

post|ier, ~**ière** /pɔstje, -jɛr/ *n.m., f.* postal worker.

post-scriptum /pɔstskriptɔm/ *n.m. invar.* postscript.

postuler /pɔstyle/ *v.t./i.* apply (à *ou* pour, for).

posture /pɔstyr/ *n.f.* posture.

pot /po/ *n.m.* pot; (*en carton*) carton; (*en verre*) jar; (*chance: fam.*) luck; (*boisson: fam.*) drink. ~**-au-feu** /pɔtofø/ *n.m. invar.* (*plat*) stew. ~ **d'échappement**, exhaust-pipe.

potable /pɔtabl/ *a.* drinkable. **eau** ~, drinking water.

potage /pɔtaʒ/ *n.m.* soup.

potag|er, ~**ère** /pɔtaʒe, -ɛr/ *a.* vegetable. —*n.m.* vegetable garden.

poteau (*pl.* ~**x**) /pɔto/ *n.m.* post; (*télégraphique*) pole. ~ **indicateur**, signpost.

pot|erie /pɔtri/ *n.f.* pottery; (*objet*) piece of pottery. ~**ier** *n.m.* potter.

potiron /pɔtirɔ̃/ *n.m.* pumpkin.

pou (*pl.* ~**x**) /pu/ *n.m.* louse.

poubelle /pubɛl/ *n.f.* dustbin.

pouce /pus/ *n.m.* thumb; (*de pied*) big toe; (*mesure*) inch.

poudr|e /pudr/ *n.f.* powder. **en** ~**e**, (*lait*) powdered; (*chocolat*) drinking. ~**er** *v.t.* powder.

poudrier /pudrije/ *n.m.* (powder) compact.

pouf /puf/ *n.m.* pouffe.

poulailler /pulaje/ *n.m.* (hen-) coop.

poulain /pulɛ̃/ *n.m.* foal; (*protégé*) protégé.

poule /pul/ *n.f.* hen; (*culin.*) fowl.

poulet /pulɛ/ *n.m.* chicken.

pouliche /puliʃ/ *n.f.* filly.

poulie /puli/ *n.f.* pulley.

pouls /pu/ *n.m.* pulse.

poumon /pumɔ̃/ *n.m.* lung.

poupée /pupe/ *n.f.* doll.

poupon /pupɔ̃/ *n.m.* baby. ~**nière** /-ɔnjɛr/ *n.f.* crèche, day nursery.

pour /pur/ *prép.* for; (*envers*) to; (*à la place de*) on behalf of; (*comme*) as. ~ **cela**, for that reason. ~ **cent**, per cent. ~ **de bon**, for good. ~ **faire**, (in order) to do. ~ **que**, so that. **le** ~ **et le contre**, the pros and cons.

pourboire /purbwar/ *n.m.* tip.

pourcentage /pursɑ̃taʒ/ *n.m.* percentage.

pourchasser /purʃase/ *v.t.* pursue.

pourpre /purpr/ *a. & n.m.* crimson; (*violet*) purple.

pourquoi /purkwa/ *conj. & adv.* why. —*n.m. invar.* reason.

pourra, **pourrait** /pura, purɛ/ *voir* **pouvoir¹**.

pourr|ir /purir/ *v.t./i.* rot. ~**i a** rotten. ~**iture** *n.f.* rot.

poursuite /pursɥit/ *n.f.* pursuit (**de**, of). ~**s**, (*jurid.*) legal action.

poursuiv|re† /pursɥivr/ *v.t.* pursue; (*continuer*) continue (with). ~**re** (**en justice**), (*au criminel*) prosecute; (*au civil*) sue. —*v.i.*, **se** ~**re** *v. pr.* continue. ~**ant**, ~**ante**, *n.m., f.* pursuer.

pourtant /purtɑ̃/ *adv.* yet.

pourvu que /purvyk(ə)/ *conj.* (*condition*) provided (that); (*souhait*) let us hope (that). **pourvu**

qu'il ne soit rien arrivé, I hope nothing's happened.

pousse /pus/ *n.f.* growth; (*bourgeon*) shoot.

poussé /puse/ *a.* (*études*) advanced.

pousser /puse/ *v.t.* push; (*du coude*) nudge; (*faire*) let out; (*soupir*) heave; (*continuer*) continue; (*exhorter*) urge (à, to); (*forcer*) force (à, to); (*amener*) bring (à, to). —*v.i.* push; (*grandir*) grow. **faire ~**, (*cheveux*) let grow; (*plante*) grow. **se ~** *v. pr.* move over *ou* up.

poussette /puset/ *n.f.* push-chair.

pouss|ière /pusjɛr/ *n.f.* dust. **~iéreux**, **~iéreuse** *a.* dusty.

poussin /pusɛ̃/ *n.m.* chick.

poutre /putr/ *n.f.* beam.

pouvoir[1]† /puvwar/ *v. aux.* (*possibilité*) can, be able; (*permission, éventualité*) may, can. **il peut/pouvait/pourrait venir**, he can/could/might come. **je n'ai pas pu**, I could not. **j'ai pu faire**, (*réussi à*) I managed to do. **je n'en peux plus**, I am exhausted.

pouvoir[2] /puvwar/ *n.m.* power; (*gouvernement*) government.

prairie /preri/ *n.f.* meadow.

praline /pralin/ *n.f.* sugared almond.

praticable /pratikabl/ *a.* practicable.

praticien, **~ne** /pratisjɛ̃, -jɛn/ *n.m.*, *f.* practitioner.

pratique /pratik/ *a.* practical. —*n.f.* practice; (*expérience*) experience. **la ~ du cheval**, riding. **~ment** *adv.* in practice; (*presque*) practically.

pratiquer /pratike/ *v.t./i.* practise; (*sport*) play; (*faire*) make.

pré /pre/ *n.m.* meadow.

pré- /pre/ *préf.* pre-.

préalable /prealabl/ *a.* preliminary. **au ~**, first.

préavis /preavi/ *n.m.* (advance) notice.

précaution /prekosjɔ̃/ *n.f.* (*mesure*) precaution; (*prudence*) caution.

précéd|ent, **~ente** /presedɑ̃, -t/ *a.* previous. —*n.m.* precedent.

précéder /presede/ *v.t./i.* precede.

précepte /presɛpt/ *n.m.* precept.

précep|teur, **~trice** /preseptœr, -tris/ *n.m.*, *f.* tutor.

prêcher /preʃe/ *v.t./i.* preach.

précieu|x, **~se** /presjø, -z/ *a.* precious.

précipice /presipis/ *n.m.* abyss, chasm.

précipité /presipite/ *a.* hasty.

précipiter /presipite/ *v.t.* throw, precipitate; (*hâter*) hasten. **se ~** *v. pr.* rush (**sur**, at on to); (*se jeter*) throw o.s; (*s'accélérer*) speed up.

précis, **~e** /presi, -z/ *a.* precise; (*mécanisme*) accurate. **dix heures ~es**, ten o'clock sharp.

préciser /presize/ *v.t./i.* specify; (*pensée*) be more specific about.

précision /presizjɔ̃/ *n.f.* precision; (*détail*) detail.

précoce /prekɔs/ *a.* early; (*enfant*) precocious.

prédécesseur /predesesœr/ *n.m.* predecessor.

prédire† /predir/ *v.t.* predict.

préfabriqué /prefabrike/ *a.* prefabricated.

préface /prefas/ *n.f.* preface.

préfecture /prefɛktyr/ *n.f.* prefecture. **~ de police**, police headquarters.

préférence /preferɑ̃s/ *n.f.* preference. **de ~**, preferably.

préférentiel, **~le** /preferɑ̃sjɛl/ *a.* preferential.

préfér|er /prefere/ *v.t.* prefer (à, to). **je ne préfère pas**, I'd rather not. **~er faire**, prefer to do. **~é**, **~ée** *a. & n.m.*, *f.* favourite.

préfet /prefɛ/ n.m. prefect. **~ de police**, prefect ou chief of police.

préfixe /prefiks/ n.m. prefix.

préhistorique /preistɔrik/ a. prehistoric.

préjudic|e /preʒydis/ n.m. harm, prejudice. **porter ~e à**, harm.

préjugé /preʒyʒe/ n.m. prejudice. **avoir un ~ contre**, be prejudiced against. **sans ~s**, without prejudices.

prél|ever /prelve/ v.t. deduct (**sur**, from); take (*sang*) take. **~èvement** n.m. deduction. **~èvement de sang**, blood sample.

préliminaire /preliminɛr/ a. & n.m. preliminary. **~s**, (*sexuels*) foreplay.

prélude /prelyd/ n.m. prelude.

prématuré /prematyre/ a. premature. —n.m. premature baby.

prémédit|er /premedite/ v.t. premeditate. **~ation** n.f. premeditation.

prem|ier, **~ière** /prəmje, -jɛr/ a. first; (*rang*) front, first; (*nécessité, souci*) prime; (*qualité*) top, prime; (*état*) primary. —n.m., f. first (one). —n.m. (*date*) first; (*étage*) first floor. —n.f. (*rail.*) first class; (*exploit jamais vu*) first; (*cinéma, théâtre*) première. **de ~ier ordre**, first-rate. **en ~ier**, first. **~ier ministre**, Prime Minister.

premièrement /prəmjɛrmã/ adv. firstly.

prémunir /premynir/ v.t. protect (**contre**, against).

prénatal (m. pl. **~s**) /prenatal/ a. antenatal.

prendre† /prãdr/ v.t. take; (*attraper*) catch, get; (*acheter*) get; (*repas*) have; (*engager, adopter*) take on; (*poids*) put on; (*chercher*) pick up. —v.i. (*liquide*) set; (*feu*) catch; (*vaccin*) take. **se ~ pour**, think one is. **s'y ~**, set about (it).

prénom /prenɔ̃/ n.m. first name. **~mer** /-ɔme/ v.t. call. **se ~mer** v. pr. be called.

préoccup|er /preɔkype/ v.t. worry; (*absorber*) preoccupy. **~ation** n.f. worry.

préparatifs /preparatif/ n.m. pl. preparations.

préparatoire /preparatwar/ a. preparatory.

prépar|er /prepare/ v.t. prepare; (*repas, café*) make. **se ~er** v. pr. prepare o.s.; (*être proche*) be brewing. **~er à qn.**, (*surprise*) have (got) in store for s.o. **~ation** n.f. preparation.

préposé, ~ée /prepoze/ n.m., f. employee; (*des postes*) postman, postwoman.

préposition /prepozisjɔ̃/ n.f. preposition.

près /prɛ/ adv. near, close. **~ de**, near (to), close to; (*presque*) nearly. **de ~**, closely.

presbyte /prɛsbit/ a. long-sighted, far-sighted.

presbytère /prɛsbitɛr/ n.m. presbytery.

prescr|ire† /prɛskrir/ v.t. prescribe. **~iption** n.f. prescription.

présence /prezãs/ n.f. presence; (*scol.*) attendance.

présent, ~e /prezã, -t/ a. present. —n.m. (*temps, cadeau*) present. **à ~**, now.

présent|er /prezãte/ v.t. present; (*personne*) introduce (**à**, to); (*montrer*) show. **se ~er** v. pr. introduce o.s. (**à**, to); (*aller*) go; (*apparaître*) appear; (*candidat*) come forward; (*occasion etc.*) arise. **se ~er à**, (*examen*) sit for; (*élection*) stand for. **~able a**. presentable. **~ateur, ~atrice** n.m., f. presenter. **~ation** n.f. presentation; introduction.

préservatif /prezɛrvatif/ n.m. condom.

présiden|t, **~te** /prezidã, -t/ n.m., f. president; (de firme, comité) chairman, chairwoman. **~t directeur général**, managing director.

présidentiel, **~le** /prezidãsjɛl/ a. presidential.

presque /prɛsk(ə)/ adv. almost, nearly. **~ jamais**, hardly ever. **~ rien**, hardly anything. **~ pas (de)**, hardly any.

presqu'île /prɛskil/ n.f. peninsula.

presse /prɛs/ n.f. (journaux, appareil) press.

pressent|ir /presãtir/ v.t. sense. **~iment** n.m. presentiment.

press|er /prese/ v.t. squeeze, press; (appuyer sur, harceler) press; (hâter) hasten; (inciter) urge (de, to). — v.i. (temps) press; (affaire) be pressing. **se ~er** v. pr. (se hâter) hurry; (se grouper) crowd. **~é** a. in a hurry; (orange, citron) freshly squeezed. **~e-papiers** n.m. invar. paperweight.

pressing /presiŋ/ n.m. (magasin) dry-cleaner's.

pression /presjõ/ n.f. pressure. **—n.m./f.** (bouton) press-stud.

prestation /prɛstasjõ/ n.f. allowance; (d'artiste etc.) performance.

prestig|e /prɛstiʒ/ n.m. prestige. **~ieux**, **~ieuse** a. prestigious.

présumer /prezyme/ v.t. presume.

prêt¹, **~e** /prɛ, -t/ a. ready (à qch., for sth., à faire, to do). **~-à-porter** /ɛ/(t)aporte/ n.m. invar. ready-to-wear clothes.

prêt² /prɛ/ n.m. loan.

prétend|re /pretãdr/ v.t. claim (que, that); (vouloir) intend. **~re qn. riche**/etc., claim that s.o. is rich/etc. **~u** a. so-called.

prétentieux, **~ieuse** /pretãsjø, -z/ a. pretentious.

prêter /prete/ v.t. lend (à, to); (attribuer) attribute. —v.i. **~er à**, lead to. **~er attention**, pay attention.

prétext|e /pretɛkst/ n.m. pretext, excuse. **~er** v.t. plead.

prêtre /prɛtr/ n.m. priest.

preuve /prœv/ n.f. proof.

prévaloir /prevalwar/ v.i. prevail.

prévenant, **~e** /prevnã, -t/ a. thoughtful.

prévenir† /prevnir/ v.t. (menacer) warn; (informer) tell.

préventi|f, **~ve** /prevãtif, -v/ a. preventive.

prévention /prevãsjõ/ n.f. prevention; (préjugé) prejudice. **~ routière**, road safety.

prévenu, **~e** /prevny/ n.m., f. defendant.

prév|oir† /prevwar/ v.t. foresee; (temps) forecast; (organiser) plan (for), provide for; (envisager) allow (for). **~u que** (jouet etc.) designed for. **~isible** a. foreseeable. **~ision** n.f. prediction; (météorologique) forecast.

prévoyant, **~e** /prevwajã, -t/ a. showing foresight.

prier /prije/ v.i. pray. —v.t. pray to; (implorer) beg (de, to); (demander à) ask (de, to). **je vous en prie**, please; (il n'y a pas de quoi) don't mention it.

prière /prijɛr/ n.f. prayer; (demande) request. **~ de**, (vous êtes prié de) will you please.

primaire /primɛr/ a. primary.

prime /prim/ n.f. free gift; (d'employé) bonus; (subvention) subsidy; (d'assurance) premium.

primé /prime/ a. prize-winning.

primeurs /primœr/ n.f. pl. early fruit and vegetables.

primevère /primvɛr/ n.f. primrose.

primiti|f, **~ve** /primitif, -v/ a. primitive; (originel) original.

primordial (*m. pl.* ~**iaux**) /primɔrdjal, -jo/ *a.* essential.

princ|e /prɛ̃s/ *n.m.* prince. ~**esse** *n.f.* princess.

princip|al (*m. pl.* ~**aux**) /prɛ̃sipal, -o/ *a.* main, principal. —*n.m.* (*pl.* ~**aux**) headmaster; (*chose*) main thing. ~**alement** *adv.* mainly.

principauté /prɛ̃sipote/ *n.f.* principality.

principe /prɛ̃sip/ *n.m.* principle. **en** ~, theoretically; (*d'habitude*) as a rule.

printemps /prɛ̃tɑ̃/ *n.m.* spring.

priorit|é /prijorite/ *n.f.* priority; (*auto.*) right of way. ~**aire** *a.* priority. **être** ~**aire**, have priority.

pris, ~**e**[1] /pri, -z/ *voir* **prendre**. —*a.* (*place*) taken; (*personne, journée*) busy; (*gorge*) infected.

prise[2] /priz/ *n.f.* hold, grip; (*animal etc. attrapé*) catch; (*mil.*) capture. ~ (**de courant**), (*mâle*) plug; (*femelle*) socket. ~ **de sang**, blood test.

prison /prizɔ̃/ *n.f.* prison, gaol, jail; (*réclusion*) imprisonment. ~**nier**, ~**nière** /-ɔnje, -jɛr/ *n.m.*, *f.* prisoner.

privé /prive/ *a.* private. —*n.m.* (*comm.*) private sector. **en** ~, **dans le** ~, in private.

priv|er /prive/ *v.t.* ~**er de**, deprive of. **se** ~**er de**, go without.

privilège /privilɛʒ/ *n.m.* privilege. ~**égié**, ~**égiée** *a.* & *n.m.*, *f.* privileged (person).

prix /pri/ *n.m.* price; (*récompense*) prize. **à tout** ~, at all costs. ~ **coûtant**, ~ **de revient**, cost price. **à** ~ **fixe**, set price.

pro- /pro/ *préf.* pro-.

probab|le /prɔbabl/ *a.* probable, likely. ~**ilité** *n.f.* probability. ~**lement** *adv.* probably.

problème /prɔblɛm/ *n.m.* problem.

procédure /prɔsedyr/ *n.f.* procedure.

procès /prɔsɛ/ *n.m.* (*criminel*) trial; (*civil*) lawsuit, proceedings. ~**verbal** (*pl.* ~**verbaux**) *n.m.* report; (*contravention*) ticket.

procession /prɔsesjɔ̃/ *n.f.* procession.

processus /prɔsesys/ *n.m.* process.

prochain, ~**e** /prɔʃɛ̃, -ɛn/ *a.* (*suivant*) next; (*proche*) imminent; (*avenir*) near. **je descends à la** ~**e**, I'm getting off at the next stop. —*n.m.* fellow. ~**ement** /-ɛnmɑ̃/ *adv.* soon.

proche /prɔʃ/ *a.* near, close; (*avoisinant*) neighbouring; (*parent, ami*) close. ~ **de**, close *ou* near to. **être** ~, (*imminent*) be approaching. ~**s** *n.m. pl.* close relations. **P**~**-Orient** *n.m.* Near East.

proclam|er /prɔklame/ *v.t.* declare, proclaim. ~**ation** *n.f.* declaration, proclamation.

procuration /prɔkyrasjɔ̃/ *n.f.* proxy.

procurer /prɔkyre/ *v.t.* bring (**à**, to). **se** ~ *v. pr.* obtain.

procureur /prɔkyrœr/ *n.m.* public prosecutor.

prodige /prɔdiʒ/ *n.m.* marvel; (*personne*) prodigy.

producti|f, ~**ve** /prɔdyktif, -v/ *a.* productive. ~**vité** *n.f.* productivity.

prod|uire† /prɔdɥir/ *v.t.* produce. **se** ~**uire** *v. pr.* (*survenir*) happen; (*acteur*) perform. ~**ucteur**, ~**uctrice** *a.* producing; *n.m.*, *f.* producer. ~**uction** *n.f.* production; (*produit*) product.

produit /prɔdɥi/ *n.m.* product. ~**s**, (*de la terre*) produce. ~ **chimique**, chemical. ~**s alimentaires**, foodstuffs. ~ **de**

consommation, consumer goods. **∿ national brut,** gross national product.

prof /prɔf/ *n.m.* (*fam.*) teacher.

professeur /prɔfesœr/ *n.m.* teacher; (*univ.*) lecturer; (*avec chaire*) professor.

profession /prɔfesjɔ̃/ *n.f.* occupation; (*intellectuelle*) profession. **∿nel, ∿nelle** /-jɔnel/ *a.* professional; (*école*) vocational; *n.m., f.* professional.

profil /prɔfil/ *n.m.* profile.

profit /prɔfi/ *n.m.* profit. **au ∿ de,** in aid of. **∿able** /-tabl/ *a.* profitable.

profiter /prɔfite/ *v.i.* **∿ à,** benefit. **∿ de,** take advantage of.

profond, ∿e /prɔfɔ̃, -d/ *a.* deep; (*sentiment, intérêt*) profound; (*causes*) underlying. **∿ément** /-demã/ *adv.* deeply; (*différent, triste*) profoundly; (*dormir*) soundly. **∿eur** /-dœr/ *n.f.* depth.

programmation /prɔgramasjɔ̃/ *n.f.* programming.

programm|e /prɔgram/ *n.m.* programme; (*matières: scol.*) syllabus; (*informatique*) program. **∿e d'études),** curriculum. **∿er** *v.t.* (*ordinateur, appareil*) program; (*émission*) schedule. **∿eur, ∿euse** *n.m., f.* computer programmer.

progrès /prɔgrɛ/ *n.m. & n.m. pl.* progress. **faire des ∿,** make progress.

progress|er /prɔgrese/ *v.i.* progress. **∿ion** /-esjɔ̃/ *n.f.* progression.

progressi|f, ∿ve /prɔgresif, -v/ *a.* progressive. **∿vement** *adv.* progressively.

prohib|er /prɔibe/ *v.t.* prohibit. **∿ition** *n.f.* prohibition.

prohibiti|f, ∿ve /prɔibitif, -v/ *a.* prohibitive.

projecteur /prɔʒɛktœr/ *n.m.* floodlight; (*cinéma*) projector.

projection /prɔʒɛksjɔ̃/ *n.f.* projection; (*séance*) show.

projet /prɔʒɛ/ *n.m.* plan; (*ébauche*) draft. **∿ de loi,** bill.

projeter /prɔʒte/ *v.t.* plan (**de,** to); (*film*) project, show; (*jeter*) hurl, project.

prologue /prɔlɔg/ *n.m.* prologue.

prolongation /prɔlɔ̃gasjɔ̃/ *n.f.* extension; (*football*) extra time.

prolong|er /prɔlɔ̃ʒe/ *v.t.* prolong. **se ∿er** *v. pr.* continue, extend. **∿é** *a.* prolonged. **∿ement** *n.m.* extension.

promenade /prɔmnad/ *n.f.* walk; (*à bicyclette, à cheval*) ride; (*en auto*) drive, ride. **faire une ∿,** go for a walk.

promen|er /prɔmne/ *v.t.* take for a walk. **se ∿er** *v. pr.* walk. (**aller**) **se ∿er,** go for a walk. **∿eur, ∿euse** *n.m., f.* walker.

promesse /prɔmɛs/ *n.f.* promise.

promett|re† /prɔmɛtr/ *v.t./i.* promise. **∿eur, ∿euse** *a.* promising.

promoteur /prɔmɔtœr/ *n.m.* (*immobilier*) property developer.

prom|ouvoir /prɔmuvwar/ *v.t.* promote. **être ∿u,** be promoted. **∿otion** *n.f.* promotion; (*comm.*) special offer.

pronom /prɔnɔ̃/ *n.m.* pronoun. **∿inal** (*m. pl.* **∿inaux**) /-ɔminal, -o/ *a.* pronominal.

prononc|er /prɔnɔ̃se/ *v.t.* pronounce; (*discours*) make. **se ∿er** *v. pr.* (*mot*) be pronounced. **∿iation** *n.f.* pronunciation.

pronostic /prɔnɔstik/ *n.m.* forecast; (*méd.*) prognosis.

propagande /prɔpagɑ̃d/ *n.f.* propaganda.

propager /prɔpaʒe/ *v.t.*, **se ~er** *v. pr.* spread.

prophète /prɔfɛt/ *n.m.* prophet.

proportion /prɔpɔrsjɔ̃/ *n.f.* proportion; (*en mathématiques*) ratio. **~né** -jɔne/ *a.* proportionate (**à**, to). **~nel, ~nelle** -jɔnɛl/ *a.* proportional. **~ner** -jɔne/ *v.t.* proportion.

propos /prɔpo/ *n.m.* intention; (*sujet*) subject. — *n.m. pl.* (*paroles*) remarks. **à ~**, at the right time; (*dans un dialogue*) by the way. **à ~ de**, about. **à tout ~**, at every possible occasion.

propos|er /prɔpoze/ *v.t.* propose; (*offrir*) offer. **se ~er** *v. pr.* volunteer (**pour,** to); (*but*) set o.s. **~ition** *n.f.* proposal; (*affirmation*) proposition; (*gram.*) clause.

propre[1] /prɔpr/ *a.* clean; (*soigné*) neat; (*honnête*) decent. **mettre au ~**, write out again neatly. **c'est du ~!** (*ironique*) well done!

propre[2] /prɔpr/ *a.* (*à soi*) own; (*sens*) literal. **~ à**, (*qui convient*) suited to; (*spécifique*) peculiar to.

propreté /prɔprəte/ *n.f.* cleanliness; (*netteté*) neatness.

propriétaire /prɔprijetɛr/ *n.m./f.* owner; (*comm.*) proprietor; (*qui loue*) landlord, landlady.

propriété /prɔprijete/ *n.f.* property; (*droit*) ownership.

proroger /prɔrɔʒe/ *v.t.* (*contrat*) defer; (*passeport*) extend.

proscrire /prɔskrir/ *v.t.* proscribe. **~it, ~ite** *a.* proscribed; *n.m., f.* (*exilé*) exile.

prose /proz/ *n.f.* prose.

prospec|ter /prɔspɛkte/ *v.t.* prospect. **~teur, ~trice** *n.m., f.* prospector. **~tion** -ksjɔ̃/ *n.f.* prospecting.

prospectus /prɔspɛktys/ *n.m.* leaflet.

prospère /prɔsper/ *a.* flourishing, thriving, prosperous. **~érer** *v.i.* thrive, prosper. **~érité** *n.f.* prosperity.

prostitu|ée /prɔstitɥe/ *n.f.* prostitute. **~ution** *n.f.* prostitution.

protec|teur, ~trice /prɔtɛktœr, -tris/ *n.m., f.* protector. — *a.* protective.

protection /prɔtɛksjɔ̃/ *n.f.* protection; (*fig.*) patronage.

protég|er /prɔteʒe/ *v.t.* protect; (*fig.*) patronize. **se ~er** *v. pr.* protect o.s.

protéine /prɔtein/ *n.f.* protein.

protestant, ~e /prɔtɛstɑ̃, -t/ *a.* & *n.m., f.* Protestant.

protest|er /prɔtɛste/ *v.t./i.* protest. **~ation** *n.f.* protest.

prouver /pruve/ *v.t.* prove.

provenance /prɔvnɑ̃s/ *n.f.* origin. **en ~ de**, from.

provençal, ~ale (*m. pl.* **~aux**) /prɔvɑ̃sal, -o/ *a.* & *n.m., f.* Provençal.

Provence /prɔvɑ̃s/ *n.f.* Provence.

provenir† /prɔvnir/ *v.i.* **~ de**, come from.

proverbe /prɔvɛrb/ *n.m.* proverb.

providence /prɔvidɑ̃s/ *n.f.* providence.

provinc|e /prɔvɛ̃s/ *n.f.* province. **de ~e**, provincial. **la ~e**, the provinces. **~ial, ~iale** (*m. pl.* **~iaux**) *a.* & *n.m., f.* provincial.

proviseur /prɔvizœr/ *n.m.* headmaster, principal.

provision /prɔvizjɔ̃/ *n.f.* supply, store; (*dans un compte*) funds; (*acompte*) deposit. **~s**, (*vivres*) provisions.

provisoire /prɔvizwar/ *a.* temporary. **~ment** *adv.* temporarily.

provo|quer /prɔvɔke/ *v.t.* cause; (*exciter*) arouse; (*défier*) provoke. **~cation** *n.f.* provocation.

proximité /prɔksimite/ n.f. proximity. **à ~ de**, close to.

prud|ent, **~ente** /prydɑ̃, -t/ a. cautious; (sage) wise. **soyez ~ent**, be careful. **~emment** /-amɑ̃/ adv. cautiously; wisely. **~ence** n.f. caution; wisdom.

prune /pryn/ n.f. plum.

pruneau (pl. **~x**) /pryno/ n.m. prune.

pseudo- /psødo/ préf. pseudo-.

pseudonyme /psødɔnim/ n.m. pseudonym.

psychanalys|e /psikanaliz/ n.f. psychoanalysis. **~er** v.t. psychoanalyse. **~te** /-st/ n.m./f. psychoanalyst.

psychiatre /psikjatr/ n.m./f. psychiatrist.

psychique /psiʃik/ a. mental, psychological.

psycholog|ie /psikɔlɔʒi/ n.f. psychology. **~gique** a. psychological. **~gue** n.m./f. psychologist.

PTT abrév. (Postes, Télécommunications et Télédiffusion) Post Office.

pu /py/ voir **pouvoir¹**.

puant, **~e** /pɥɑ̃, -t/ a. stinking.

pub /pyb/ n.f. **la ~**, advertising. **une ~**, an advert.

publi|c, **~que** /pyblik/ a. public. —n.m. public; (assistance) audience. **en ~c**, in public.

publicit|é /pyblisite/ n.f. publicity, advertising; (annonce) advertisement. **~aire** a. publicity.

publi|er /pyblije/ v.t. publish. **~cation** n.f. publication.

publiquement /pyblikmɑ̃/ adv. publicly.

puce¹ /pys/ n.f. flea. **marché aux ~s**, flea market.

puce² /pys/ n.f. (électronique) chip.

pud|eur /pydœr/ n.f. modesty. **~ique** a. modest.

puer /pɥe/ v.i. stink. —v.t. stink of.

puis /pɥi/ adv. then.

puisque /pɥisk(ə)/ conj. since, as.

puissance /pɥisɑ̃s/ n.f. power.

puiss|ant, **~ante** /pɥisɑ̃, -t/ a. powerful. **~amment** adv. powerfully.

puits /pɥi/ n.m. well; (de mine) shaft.

pull(-over) /pyl(ɔvɛr)/ n.m. pullover, jumper.

pulpe /pylp/ n.f. pulp.

pulsation /pylsasjɔ̃/ n.f. (heart)beat.

pulvéris|er /pylverize/ v.t. pulverize; (liquide) spray. **~ateur** n.m. spray.

punaise /pynɛz/ n.f. (insecte) bug; (clou) drawing-pin.

punch /pɔ̃ʃ/ n.m. punch.

pun|ir /pynir/ v.t. punish. **~ition** n.f. punishment.

punk /pœ̃k/ a. invar. punk.

pupille /pypij/ n.f. (de l'œil) pupil.

pur /pyr/ a. pure; (whisky) neat. **~ement** adv. purely. **~eté** n.f. purity. **~sang** n.m. invar. (cheval) thoroughbred.

purée /pyre/ n.f. purée; (de pommes de terre) mashed potatoes.

purif|ier /pyrifje/ v.t. purify. **~ication** n.f. purification.

puritain, **~e** /pyritɛ̃, -ɛn/ n.m., f. puritan. —a. puritanical.

pus /py/ n.m. pus.

putain /pytɛ̃/ n.f. (fam.) whore.

putsch /putʃ/ n.m. putsch.

puzzle /pœzl/ n.m. jigsaw (puzzle).

P-V abrév. (procès-verbal) ticket, traffic fine.

pyjama /piʒama/ n.m. pyjamas. **un ~**, a pair of pyjamas.

pylône /pilon/ n.m. pylon.

pyramide /piramid/ n.f. pyramid.

Pyrénées /pirene/ n.f. pl. **les ~**, the Pyrenees.

Q

QG abrév. (quartier général) HQ.

QI abrév. (quotient intellectuel) IQ.

qu' /k/ voir que.

quadrupl|e /kadrypl/ a. & n.m. quadruple. **~er** v.t./i. quadruple.

quai /ke/ n.m. (de gare) platform; (de port) quay; (de rivière) embankment.

qualificatif /kalifikatif/ n.m. (épithète) term.

qualifi|er /kalifje/ v.t. qualify; (décrire) describe (**de,** as). **se ~ier** v. pr. qualify (**pour,** for).

qualité /kalite/ n.f. quality; (titre) occupation.

quand /kã/ conj. & adv. when. **~ même,** all the same. **~ (bien) même,** even if.

quant (à) /kãt(a)/ prép. as for.

quantité /kãtite/ n.f. quantity. **une ~ de,** a lot of. **des ~s,** masses.

quarantaine /karãtɛn/ n.f. (méd.) quarantine. **une ~ (de),** about forty.

quarant|e /karãt/ a. & n.m. forty. **~ième** a. & n.m./f. fortieth.

quart /kar/ n.m. quarter; (naut.) watch. **~ (de litre),** quarter litre. **~ de finale,** quarter-final. **~ d'heure,** quarter of an hour.

quartier /kartje/ n.m. neighbourhood, district; (de lune, bœuf) quarter; (de fruit) segment. **de ~, du ~,** local.

quasi- /kazi/ préf. quasi-.

quatorz|e /katorz/ a. & n.m. fourteen. **~ième** a. & n.m./f. fourteenth.

quatre /katr(ə)/ a. & n.m. four. **~-vingt(s)** a. & n.m. eighty. **~-vingt-dix** a. & n.m. ninety.

quatrième /katrijɛm/ a. & n.m./f. fourth. **~ment** adv. fourthly.

quatuor /kwatɥɔr/ n.m. quartet.

que, qu'* /kə, k/ conj. that; (comparaison) than. **qu'il vienne,** let him come. **qu'il vienne ou non,** whether he comes or not. **ne faire ~ demander**/etc., only ask/etc. **—adv. (ce) ~ tu es bête, qu'est-ce ~ tu es bête,** how silly you are. **~ de,** what a lot of. —pron. rel. (personne) that, whom; (chose) that, which; (temps, moment) when; (interrogatif) what. **un jour**/etc. **~,** one day/etc. when. **~ faites-vous?, qu'est-ce ~ vous faites?,** what are you doing?

Québec /kebɛk/ n.m. Quebec.

quel, ~le /kɛl/ a. what; (interrogatif) which, what; (qui) who. —pron. which. **~ dommage,** what a pity. **~ qu'il soit,** (chose) whatever ou whichever it may be; (personne) whoever he may be.

quelconque /kɛlkõk/ a. (banal) ordinary; (médiocre) poor.

quelque /kɛlkə/ a. some. **~s,** a few, some. —adv. (environ) some. **et ~,** (fam.) and a bit. **~ chose,** something; (interrogation) anything. **~ part,** somewhere. **~ peu,** somewhat.

quelquefois /kɛlkəfwa/ adv. sometimes.

quelques|-uns, ~-unes /kɛlkəzœ̃, -yn/ pron. some, a few.

quelqu'un /kɛlkœ̃/ pron. someone, somebody; (interrogation) anyone, anybody.

quereller (se) /(sə)kərele/ v. pr. quarrel.

question /kɛstjõ/ n.f. question; (affaire) matter, question. **en ~,** in question; (en jeu) at stake. **il est**

~ de, (cela concerne) it is about; (on parle de) there is talk of. Il n'en est pas ~, it is out of the question. ~ner /-jɔne/ v.t. question.

questionnaire /kɛstjɔnɛr/ n.m. questionnaire.

quête /kɛt/ n.f. (relig.) collection.

quetsche /kwɛtʃ/ n.f. (sort of dark red) plum.

queue /kø/ n.f. tail; (de poêle) handle; (file) queue; (de train) rear. **faire la** ~, queue (up). ~ **de cheval**, pony-tail.

qui /ki/ pron. rel. (personne) who; (chose) which, that; (interrogatif) who; (après prép.) whom; (quiconque) whoever. **à** ~ **est ce stylo/etc.?**, whose pen/etc. is this? **qu'est-ce** ~?, what? ~ **est-ce qui?**, who?

quiche /kiʃ/ n.f. quiche.

quiconque /kikɔ̃k/ pron. whoever; (n'importe qui) anyone.

quint|al (pl. ~**aux**) /kɛ̃tal, -o/ n.m. quintal (= 100 kg.).

quinte /kɛ̃t/ n.f. ~ **de toux**, coughing fit.

quintette /kɛ̃tɛt/ n.m. quintet.

quintupl|e /kɛ̃typl/ a. fivefold. —n.m. quintuple. ~**er** v.t./i. increase fivefold.

quinzaine /kɛ̃zɛn/ n.f. **une** ~ (**de**), about fifteen.

quinz|e /kɛ̃z/ a. & n.m. fifteen. ~**e jours**, two weeks. ~**ième** a. & n.m./f. fifteenth.

quiproquo /kiprɔko/ n.m. misunderstanding.

quittance /kitãs/ n.f. receipt.

quitte /kit/ a. quits (**envers**, with).

quitter /kite/ v.t. leave; (vêtement) take off. **se** ~ v. pr. part.

quoi /kwa/ pron. what; (après prép.) which. **de** ~ **vivre/manger/etc.**, (assez) enough to

live on/to eat/etc. **de** ~ **écrire**, sth. to write with, what is necessary to write with. ~ **que**, whatever. ~ **que ce soit**, anything.

quoique /kwak(ə)/ conj. (al)though.

quota /kɔta/ n.m. quota.

quotidien, ~**ne** /kɔtidjɛ̃, -jɛn/ a. daily; (banal) everyday. —n.m. daily (paper). ~**nement** /-jɛnmã/ adv. daily.

R

rabais /rabɛ/ n.m. (price) reduction.

rabaisser /rabese/ v.t. (déprécier) belittle; (réduire) reduce.

rabat /raba/ n.m. flap. ~**-joie** n.m. invar. killjoy.

rabattre /rabatr/ v.t. pull ou put down; (déduire) take off. **se** ~ v. pr. (se refermer) close; (véhicule) cut in, turn sharply.

rabbin /rabɛ̃/ n.m. rabbi.

rabot /rabo/ n.m. plane. ~**er** /-ɔte/ v.t. plane.

raccommoder /rakɔmɔde/ v.t. mend; (personnes: fam.) reconcile.

raccompagner /rakɔ̃paɲe/ v.t. see ou take back (home).

raccord /rakɔr/ n.m. link; (de papier peint) join. ~ (**de peinture**), touch-up.

raccord|er /rakɔrde/ v.t. connect, join. ~**ement** n.m. connection.

raccourci /rakursi/ n.m. short cut. **en** ~, in brief.

raccourcir /rakursir/ v.t. shorten. —v.i. get shorter.

raccrocher /rakrɔʃe/ v.t. hang back up; (personne) grab hold of;

(relier) connect. **~ (le récepteur)**, hang up.

rac|e /ras/ *n.f.* race; *(animale)* breed. **de ~e**, pure-bred. **~ial** *(m. pl. ~iaux)* *a.* racial.

rachat /raʃa/ *n.m.* buying (back).

racheter /raʃte/ *v.t.* buy (back); *(davantage)* buy more; *(nouvel objet)* buy another.

racine /rasin/ *n.f.* root. **~ carrée/cubique**, square/cube root.

racis|te /rasist/ *a. & n.m./f.* racist. **~me** *n.m.* racism.

racler /rɑkle/ *v.t.* scrape. **se ~ la gorge**, clear one's throat.

raconter /rakɔ̃te/ *v.t.* *(histoire)* tell, relate; *(vacances etc.)* tell about. **~ à qn. que**, tell s.o. that, say to s.o. that.

radar /radar/ *n.m.* radar.

rade /rad/ *n.f.* harbour.

radeau *(pl. ~x)* /rado/ *n.m.* raft.

radiateur /radjatœr/ *n.m.* radiator; *(électrique)* heater.

radiation /radjasjɔ̃/ *n.f.* *(énergie)* radiation.

radic|al *(m. pl. ~aux)* /radikal, -o/ *a.* radical. —*n.m.* *(pl. ~aux)* radical.

radin, **~e** /radɛ̃, -in/ *a.* *(fam.)* stingy.

radio /radjo/ *n.f.* radio; *(radiographie)* X-ray.

radioacti|f, **~ve** /radjoaktif, -v/ *a.* radioactive. **~vité** *n.f.* radioactivity.

radiocassette /radjokasɛt/ *n.f.* radiocassette-player.

radiograph|ie /radjografi/ *n.f.* *(photographie)* X-ray. **~ier** *v.t.* X-ray. **~ique** *a.* X-ray.

radiologue /radjolɔg/ *n.m./f.* radiographer.

radiophonique /radjofonik/ *a.* radio.

radis /radi/ *n.m.* radish.

radoucir (se) /(sə)radusir/ *v. pr.* calm down; *(temps)* become milder.

rafale /rafal/ *n.f.* *(de vent)* gust; *(tir)* burst of gunfire.

raffiné /rafine/ *a.* refined.

raffin|er /rafine/ *v.t.* refine. **~age** *n.m.* refining. **~erie** *n.f.* refinery.

raffoler /rafole/ *v.i.* **~ de**, be extremely fond of.

rafle /rafl/ *n.f.* *(police)* raid.

rafraîch|ir /rafreʃir/ *v.t.* cool (down); *(raviver)* brighten up; *(personne, mémoire)* refresh. **se ~ir** *v. pr.* *(se laver)* freshen up; *(boire)* refresh o.s.; *(temps)* get cooler. **~issant**, **~issante** *a.* refreshing.

rafraîchissement /rafreʃismɑ̃/ *n.m.* *(boisson)* cold drink. **~s**, *(fruits etc.)* refreshments.

rage /raʒ/ *n.f.* rage; *(maladie)* rabies. **faire ~**, rage. **~ de dents**, raging toothache.

ragot(s) /rago/ *n.m. (pl.)* *(fam.)* gossip.

ragoût /ragu/ *n.m.* stew.

raide /rɛd/ *a.* stiff; *(côte)* steep; *(corde)* tight; *(cheveux)* straight. —*adv.* *(en pente)* steeply.

raie[1] /rɛ/ *n.f.* line; *(bande)* strip; *(de cheveux)* parting.

raie[2] /rɛ/ *n.f.* *(poisson)* skate.

raifort /rɛfɔr/ *n.m.* horse-radish.

rail /raj/ *n.m.* *(barre)* rail. **le ~**, *(transport)* rail.

rainure /renyr/ *n.f.* groove.

raisin /rezɛ̃/ *n.m.* **~(s)**, grapes. **~ sec**, raisin.

raison /rezɔ̃/ *n.f.* reason. **avec ~**, rightly. **avoir ~**, be right *(de faire*, to do*)*. **donner ~ à**, prove right. **en ~ de**, *(cause)* because of. **~ de plus**, all the more reason. **perdre la ~**, lose one's mind.

raisonnable /rɛzɔnabl/ a. reasonable, sensible.

raisonn|er /rɛzɔne/ v.i. reason. —v.t. (personne) reason with. **~ement** n.m. reasoning; (propositions) argument.

rajeunir /raʒœnir/ v.t. make (look) younger.

rajout /raʒu/ n.m. addition. **~er** /-te/ v.t. add.

ralent|ir /ralɑ̃tir/ v.t./i., **se ~ir** v. pr. slow down. **~i** a. slow; n.m. (cinéma) slow motion. **être au tourner au ~i**, tick over, idle.

rall|ier /ralje/ v.t. rally; (rejoindre) rejoin. **se ~ier** v. pr. rally.

rallonge /ralɔ̃ʒ/ n.f. (de table) extension.

rallonger /ralɔ̃ʒe/ v.t. lengthen.

rallumer /ralyme/ v.t. light (up) again; (lampe) switch on again; (ranimer; fig.) revive.

rallye /rali/ n.m. rally.

ramadan /ramadɑ̃/ n.m. Ramadan.

ramass|er /ramase/ v.t. pick up; (récolter) gather; (recueillir) collect. **~age** n.m. (cueillette) gathering. **~age scolaire**, school bus service.

rambarde /rɑ̃bard/ n.f. guardrail.

rame /ram/ n.f. (aviron) oar; (train) train; (perche) stake.

rameau (pl. **~x**) /ramo/ n.m. branch.

ramener /ramne/ v.t. bring back.

ram|er /rame/ v.i. row. **~eur, ~euse** n.m., f. rower.

ramollir /ramɔlir/ v.t./i., **se ~** v. pr. soften.

ramon|er /ramɔne/ v.t. sweep. **~eur** n.m. (chimney-)sweep.

rampe /rɑ̃p/ n.f. banisters; (pente) ramp.

ramper /rɑ̃pe/ v.i. crawl.

ranc|e /rɑ̃s/ a. rancid.

rançon /rɑ̃sɔ̃/ n.f. ransom.

rancun|e /rɑ̃kyn/ n.f. grudge. **sans ~!**, no hard feelings. **~ier, ~ière** a. vindictive.

randonnée /rɑ̃dɔne/ n.f. walk; (en auto, vélo) ride.

rang /rɑ̃/ n.m. row; (hiérarchie, condition) rank. **se mettre en ~**, line up. **au premier ~**, in the first row; (fig.) at the forefront. **de second ~**, (péj.) second-rate.

rangée /rɑ̃ʒe/ n.f. row.

rang|er /rɑ̃ʒe/ v.t. put away; (chambre etc.) tidy (up); (disposer) place; (véhicule) park. **~ement** n.m. (de chambre) tidying (up); (espace) storage space.

ranimer /ranime/ v.t./i., **se ~** v. pr. revive.

rapace /rapas/ n.m. bird of prey.

rapatr|ier /rapatrije/ v.t. repatriate. **~iement** n.m. repatriation.

râp|e /rɑp/ n.f. (culin.) grater; (lime) rasp. **~er** v.t. grate; (bois) rasp.

rapid|e /rapid/ a. fast, rapid. —n.m. (train) express (train); (cours d'eau) rapids pl. **~ement** adv. fast, rapidly. **~ité** n.f. speed.

rappel /rapɛl/ n.m. recall; (deuxième avis) reminder; (de salaire) back pay; (méd.) booster.

rappeler /raple/ v.t. call back; (diplomate, réserviste) recall; (évoquer) remind, recall. **~ qch. à qn.**, (redire) remind s.o. of sth. **se ~** v. pr. remember, recall.

rapport /rapɔr/ n.m. connection; (compte rendu) report; (profit) yield. **~s**, (relations) relations. **par ~ à**, in relation to. **~s (sexuels)**, intercourse.

rapport|er /rapɔrte/ v.t. bring back; (profit) bring in; (dire, répéter) report. —v.i. (comm.) bring in a good return;

(*mouchard: fam.*) tell. **se ⁓er à**, relate to; **⁓eur**, **⁓euse** *n.m., f.* tell-tale.

rapprocher /raprɔʃe/ *v.t.* bring closer (**de**, to); (*réconcilier*) bring together; (*comparer*) compare. **se ⁓** *v. pr.* get ou come closer (**de**, to); (*personnes*, *pays*) come together; (*s'apparenter*) be close (**de**, to).

rapt /rapt/ *n.m.* abduction.

raquette /rakɛt/ *n.f.* (*de tennis*) racket; (*de ping-pong*) bat.

rare /rar/ *a.* rare; (*insuffisant*) scarce. **⁓ment** *adv.* rarely, seldom.

ras, **⁓e** /ra, raz/ *a.* (*herbe, poil*) short. **à ⁓ de**, very close to. **pull ⁓ du cou**, round-neck pull-over. **en avoir ⁓ le bol**, be fed-up.

ras|er /raze/ *v.t.* shave; (*cheveux, barbe*) shave off; (*frôler*) skim; (*abattre*) raze; (*ennuyer: fam.*) bore. **se ⁓er** *v. pr.* shave.

rasoir /razwar/ *n.m.* razor.

rassembl|er /rasãble/ *v.t.* gather; (*courage*) muster. **se ⁓er** *v. pr.* gather. **⁓ement** *n.m.* gathering.

rasseoir (se) /(sə)raswar/ *v. pr.* sit down again.

rass|is, **⁓ise** ou **⁓ie** /rasi, -z/ *a.* (*pain*) stale.

rassurer /rasyre/ *v.t.* reassure.

rat /ra/ *n.m.* rat.

rate /rat/ *n.f.* spleen.

râteau (*pl.* **⁓x**) /rato/ *n.m.* rake.

râtelier /ratəlje/ *n.m.*; (*fam.*) dentures.

rat|er /rate/ *v.t./i.* miss; (*gâcher*) spoil; (*échouer*) fail. **c'est ⁓é**, that's right out. **⁓é**, **⁓ée** *n.m., f.* (*personne*) failure. **avoir des ⁓és**, (*auto.*) backfire.

ratio /rasjo/ *n.f.* ratio.

ration /rasjɔ̃/ *n.f.* ration.

rationnel, **⁓le** /rasjɔnɛl/ *a.* rational.

rattacher /rataʃe/ *v.t.* tie up again; (*relier*) link; (*incorporer*) join.

rattraper /ratrape/ *v.t.* catch; (*rejoindre*) catch up with (*retard, erreur*) make up for. **se ⁓** *v. pr.* catch up; (*se dédommager*) make up for it. **se ⁓ à**, catch hold of.

rauque /rok/ *a.* raucous, harsh.

ravi /ravi/ *a.* delighted (**que**, that).

ravier /ravje/ *n.m.* hors-d'œuvre dish.

ravin /ravɛ̃/ *n.m.* ravine.

ravioli /ravjɔli/ *n.m. pl.* ravioli.

ravissant, **⁓e** /ravisã, -t/ *a.* beautiful.

ravisseu|r, **⁓se** /ravisœr, -øz/ *n.m., f.* kidnapper.

ravitaill|er /ravitaje/ *v.t.* provide with supplies; (*avion*) refuel. **se ⁓er** *v. pr.* stock up. **⁓ement** *n.m.* provision of supplies (**de**, to), refuelling; (*denrées*) supplies.

rayé /reje/ *a.* striped.

rayer /reje/ *v.t.* scratch; (*biffer*) cross out.

rayon /rɛjɔ̃/ *n.m.* ray; (*planche*) shelf; (*de magasin*) department; (*de roue*) spoke; (*de cercle*) radius.

rayonner /rɛjɔne/ *v.i.* radiate; (*de joie*) beam; (*se déplacer*) tour around (*from a central point*).

rayure /rajyr/ *n.f.* scratch; (*dessin*) stripe. **à ⁓s**, striped.

raz-de-marée /radmare/ *n.m. invar.* tidal wave.

re- /rə/ *préf.* re-.

ré- /re/ *préf.* re-.

réacteur /reaktœr/ *n.m.* jet engine; (*nucléaire*) reactor.

réaction /reaksjɔ̃/ *n.f.* reaction. **⁓naire** /-jɔnɛr/ *a.* & *n.m./f.* reactionary.

réaffirmer /reafirme/ *v.t.* reaffirm.

réagir /reaʒir/ *v.i.* react.

réalis|er /realize/ *v.t.* carry out; (*rêve*) fulfil; (*film*) produce,

direct; (se rendre compte de)
realize. se ~er v. pr. materialize.
~ateur, ~atrice n.m., f.
(cinéma) director; (TV) producer.
~ation n.f. realization; (œuvre)
achievement.

réalis|te /realist/ a. realistic.
—n.m./f. realist. ~me n.m.
realism.

réalité /realite/ n.f. reality.

réanim|er /reanime/ v.t. resus-
citate. ~ation n.f. resuscitation.
service de ~ation, intensive
care.

réapparaître /reaparɛtr/ v.i. reappear.

rebelle /rǝbɛl/ a. rebellious;
(soldat) rebel. —n.m./f. rebel.

rebeller (se) /(sǝ)rǝbele/ v. pr.
rebel, hit back defiantly.

rébellion /rebeljɔ̃/ n.f. rebellion.

rebond /rǝbɔ̃/ n.m. bounce; (par
ricochet) rebound. ~ir /-dir/ v.i.
bounce; rebound.

rebondissement /rǝbɔ̃dismɑ̃/
n.m. (new) development.

rebord /rǝbɔr/ n.m. edge. ~ de la
fenêtre, window-ledge.

rebours (à) /(a)rǝbur/ adv. the
wrong way.

rebrousser /rǝbruse/ v.t. ~
chemin, turn back.

rébus /rebys/ n.m. rebus.

rebut|er /rǝbyte/ v.t. put off.
~ant, ~ante a. off-putting.

récalcitrant, ~e /rekalsitrɑ̃, -t/
a. stubborn.

récapitul|er /rekapityle/ v.t./i.
recapitulate. ~ation n.f.
recapitulation.

récemment /resamɑ̃/ adv.
recently.

récent, ~e /resɑ̃, -t/ a. recent.

récépissé /resepise/ n.m. receipt.

récepteur /resɛptœr/ n.m. receiver.

réception /resɛpsjɔ̃/ n.f. reception.

~ de, (lettre etc.) receipt of.
~niste /-ʒɔnist/ n.m./f. recep-
tionist.

récession /resesjɔ̃/ n.f. recession.

recette /rǝsɛt/ n.f. (culin.) recipe;
(argent) takings. ~s, (comm.)
receipts.

receveu|r, ~se /rǝsvœr, -øz/
n.m., f. (des impôts) tax collector.

recevoir† /rǝsvwar/ v.t. receive;
(client, malade) see; (obtenir) get,
receive. être reçu (à), pass. —v.i.
(médecin) receive patients. se ~
v. pr. (tomber) land.

rechange (de) /(dǝ)rǝʃɑ̃ʒ/ a. (roue,
vêtements, etc.) spare.

recharge /rǝʃarʒ/ n.f. (de stylo)
refill. ~er v.t. refill; (batterie)
recharge.

réchaud /reʃo/ n.m. stove.

réchauff|er /reʃofe/ v.t. warm up.
se ~er v. pr. warm o.s. up;
(temps) get warmer.

rêche /rɛʃ/ a. rough.

recherche /rǝʃɛrʃ/ n.f. search (de,
for); (raffinement) elegance. ~s,
(enquête) investigations.

recherch|er /rǝʃɛrʃe/ v.t. search
for. ~é a. in great demand;
(élégant) elegant.

rechut|e /rǝʃyt/ n.f. (méd.) relapse.
~er v.i. relapse.

récif /resif/ n.m. reef.

récipient /resipjɑ̃/ n.m. container.

réciproque /resiprɔk/ a. mutual,
reciprocal. ~ment adv. each
other; (inversement) conversely.

récit /resi/ n.m. (compte rendu)
account, story; (histoire) story.

récital (pl. ~s) /resital/ n.m.
recital.

récit|er /resite/ v.t. recite. ~ation
n.f. recitation.

réclame /reklam/ n.f. faire de la
~, advertise. en ~, on offer.

réclam|er /reklame/ v.t. call for,
demand; (revendiquer) claim.

—*v.i.* complain. **∼ation** *n.f.* complaint.

récolt|e /rekɔlt/ *n.f.* (*action*) harvest; (*produits*) crop, harvest; (*fig.*) crop. **∼er** *v.t.* harvest, gather; (*fig.*) collect.

recommand|er /rəkɔmɑ̃de/ *v.t.* recommend; (*lettre*) register. **envoyer en ∼é,** send registered. **∼ation** *n.f.* recommendation.

recommence|r /rəkɔmɑ̃se/ *v.t./i.* (*reprendre*) begin *ou* start again; (*refaire*) repeat. **ne ∼ pas,** don't do it again.

récompens|e /rekɔ̃pɑ̃s/ *n.f.* reward; (*prix*) award. **∼er** *v.t.* reward (**de,** for).

réconcil|ier /rekɔ̃silje/ *v.t.* reconcile. **se ∼ier** *v. pr.* become reconciled (**avec,** with). **∼iation** *n.f.* reconciliation.

reconduire† /rəkɔ̃dųir/ *v.t.* see home; (*à la porte*) show out; (*renouveler*) renew.

réconfort /rekɔ̃fɔr/ *n.m.* comfort. **∼er** /-te/ *v.t.* comfort.

reconnaissable /rəkɔnɛsabl/ *a.* recognizable.

reconnaissan|t, ∼te /rəkɔnɛsɑ̃, -t/ *a.* grateful (**de,** for). **∼ce** *n.f.* gratitude.

reconnaître† /rəkɔnɛtr/ *v.t.* recognize; (*admettre*) admit (**que,** that); (*enfant, tort*) acknowledge.

reconstituant /rəkɔ̃stitɥɑ̃/ *n.m.* tonic.

reconstituer /rəkɔ̃stitɥe/ *v.t.* reconstitute; (*crime*) reconstruct.

reconstr|uire† /rəkɔ̃strɥir/ *v.t.* rebuild. **∼uction** *n.f.* rebuilding.

reconversion /rəkɔ̃vɛrsjɔ̃/ *n.f.* (*de main-d'œuvre*) redeployment.

recopier /rəkɔpje/ *v.t.* copy out.

record /rəkɔr/ *n.m. & a. invar.* record.

recours /rəkur/ *n.m.* resort. **avoir ∼ à,** have recourse to, resort to.

recouvrer /rəkuvre/ *v.t.* recover.

recouvrir† /rəkuvrir/ *v.t.* cover.

récréation /rekreasjɔ̃/ *n.f.* recreation; (*scol.*) playtime.

récrimination /rekriminɑsjɔ̃/ *n.f.* recrimination.

recrut|er /rəkryte/ *v.t.* recruit. **∼ement** *n.m.* recruitment.

rectang|le /rɛktɑ̃gl/ *n.m.* rectangle. **∼ulaire** *a.* rectangular.

rectif|ier /rɛktifje/ *v.t.* correct, rectify. **∼ication** *n.f.* correction.

recto /rɛkto/ *n.m.* front of the page.

reçu /rəsy/ *voir* **recevoir.** —*n.m.* receipt.

recueil /rəkœj/ *n.m.* collection.

recueill|ir† /rəkœjir/ *v.t.* collect; (*prendre chez soi*) take in.

recul /rəkyl/ *n.m.* retreat; (*éloignement*) distance; (*déclin*) decline.

reculé /rəkyle/ *a.* (*région*) remote.

reculer /rəkyle/ *v.t./i.* move back; (*véhicule*) reverse; (*diminuer*) decline; (*différer*) postpone. **∼ devant,** (*fig.*) shrink from.

reculons (à) /(a)rəkylɔ̃/ *adv.* backwards.

récupér|er /rekypere/ *v.t./i.* recover; (*vieux objets*) salvage. **∼ation** *n.f.* recovery; salvage.

récurer /rekyre/ *v.t.* scour. **poudre à ∼,** scouring powder.

recycl|er /rəsikle/ *v.t.* (*personne*) retrain; (*chose*) recycle. **se ∼er** *v. pr.* retrain. **∼age** *n.m.* retraining; recycling.

rédac|teur, ∼trice /redaktœr, -tris/ *n.m., f.* writer, editor. **le ∼teur en chef,** the editor (in chief).

rédaction /redaksjɔ̃/ *n.f.* writing; (*scol.*) composition; (*personnel*) editorial staff.

redemander /rədmɑ̃de/ *v.t.* ask again for; ask for more of.

redevance /rədvɑ̃s/ n.f. (de télévision) licence fee.

rédiger /rediʒe/ v.t. write; (contrat) draw up.

redire† /rədir/ v.t. repeat.

redonner /rədɔne/ v.t. give back; (davantage) give more.

redoubler /rəduble/ v.t./i. increase; (classe: scol.) repeat.

redouter /rədute/ v.t. dread. ~**able** a. formidable.

redoux /rədu/ n.m. milder weather.

redress|er /rədrese/ v.t. straighten (out ou up); (situation) right, redress. se ~**er** v. pr. (personne) straighten (o.s.) up; (se remettre debout) stand up; (pays, économie) recover. ~**ement** /rədrɛsmɑ̃/ n.m. (relèvement) recovery.

réduction /redyksjɔ̃/ n.f. reduction.

réduire† /redɥir/ v.t. reduce (à, to). se ~**à**, (revenir à) come down to.

réduit, -te /redɥi, -t/ a. (objet) small-scale; (limité) limited.

réel, ~le /reɛl/ a. real. —n.m. reality. ~**lement** adv. really.

réexpédier /reɛkspedje/ v.t. forward; (retourner) send back.

refaire† /rəfɛr/ v.t. do again; (erreur, voyage) make again; (réparer) do up, redo.

réfectoire /refɛktwar/ n.m. refectory.

référence /referɑ̃s/ n.f. reference.

référendum /referɛ̃dɔm/ n.m. referendum.

référer /refere/ v.i. en ~ **à**, refer the matter to. se ~ **à**, refer to.

refermer /rəfɛrme/ v.t., se ~, v. pr. close (again).

réfléch|ir /refleʃir/ v.i. think (à, about). —v.t. reflect. se ~**ir** v. pr. be reflected

réfl|et /reflɛ/ n.m. reflection; (lumière) light. ~**éter** /-ete/ v.t. reflect. se ~**éter** v. pr. be reflected.

réflexe /reflɛks/ a. & n.m. reflex.

réflexion /reflɛksjɔ̃/ n.f. reflection; (pensée) thought, reflection.

reflux /rəfly/ n.m. (de marée) ebb.

réforme /refɔrm/ n.f. reform.

refouler /rəfule/ v.t. (larmes) force back; (désir) repress.

refrain /rəfrɛ̃/ n.m. chorus. le même ~, the same old story.

réfrigér|er /refriʒere/ v.t. refrigerate. ~**ateur** n.m. refrigerator.

refroid|ir /rəfrwadir/ v.t./i. cool (down). se ~**ir** v. pr. (personne, temps) get cold; (ardeur) cool (off). ~**issement** n.m. cooling; (rhume) chill.

refuge /rəfyʒ/ n.m. refuge; (chalet) mountain hut.

réfugi|er (se) /(sə)refyʒje/ v. pr. take refuge. ~**ié, ~iée** n.m., f. refugee.

refus /rəfy/ n.m. refusal. ce n'est pas de ~, I wouldn't say no. ~**er** /-ze/ v.t. refuse (de, to); (recaler) fail. se ~**er à**, (évidence etc.) reject.

régal (pl. ~**s**) /regal/ n.m. treat. ~**er** v.t. treat (de, to). se ~**er** v. pr. treat o.s. (de, to).

regard /rəgar/ n.m. (expression, coup d'œil) look; (fixe) stare.

regarder /rəgarde/ v.t. look at; (observer) watch; (considérer) consider; (concerner) concern. ~ (fixement), stare at. —v.i. look. se ~ v. pr. (personnes) look at each other.

régates /regat/ n.f. pl. regatta.

régen|t, ~te /reʒɑ̃, -t/ n.m., f. regent. ~**ce** n.f. regency.

régie /reʒi/ n.f. (entreprise) public corporation; (radio, TV) control room; (*cinéma, théâtre*) production.

régime /reʒim/ *n.m.* (*pol.*) regime; (*méd.*) diet; (*de moteur*) speed; (*de bananes*) bunch. **se mettre au ～,** go on a diet.

régiment /reʒimɑ̃/ *n.m.* regiment.

région /reʒjɔ̃/ *n.f.* region. **～al** (*m. pl.* **～aux**) /-jɔnal, -o/ *a.* regional.

registre /rəʒistr/ *n.m.* register.

réglage /reglaʒ/ *n.m.* adjustment.

règle /rɛgl/ *n.f.* rule; (*instrument*) ruler. **～s,** (*de femme*) period. **en ～,** in order.

réglé /regle/ *a.* (*vie*) ordered; (*arrangé*) settled.

règlement /rɛgləmɑ̃/ *n.m.* regulation; (*règles*) regulations; (*solution, paiement*) settlement.

réglement|er /regləmɑ̃te/ *v.t.* regulate. **～ation** *n.f.* regulation.

régler /regle/ *v.t.* settle; (*machine*) adjust; (*programmer*) set; (*facture*) settle; (*personne*) settle up with; (*papier*) rule.

réglisse /reglis/ *n.f.* liquorice.

règne /rɛɲ/ *n.m.* reign; (*végétal, animal, minéral*) kingdom.

régner /rene/ *v.i.* reign.

regret /rəgrɛ/ *n.m.* regret.

regrett|er /rəgrete/ *v.t.* regret; (*personne*) miss. **～able** *a.* regrettable.

regrouper /rəgrupe/ *v.t.*, group together. **se ～** *v. pr.* gather (together).

régulariser /regylarize/ *v.t.* regularize.

régulation /regylasjɔ̃/ *n.f.* regulation.

régul|ier, -ière /regylje, -jɛr/ *a.* regular; (*qualité, vitesse*) steady, even; (*ligne, paysage*) even; (*légal*) legal; (*honnête*) honest. **～ièrement** *adv.* regularly; (*d'ordinaire*) normally.

rein /rɛ̃/ *n.m.* kidney. **～s,** (*dos*) back.

reine /rɛn/ *n.f.* queen. **～-claude** *n.f.* greengage.

réintégrer /reɛ̃tegre/ *v.t.* (*lieu*) return to; (*jurid.*) reinstate.

rejet /rəʒɛ/ *n.m.* rejection.

rejeter /rəʒte/ *v.t.* throw back; (*refuser*) reject; (*vomir*) bring up; (*déverser*) discharge.

rejoindre† /rəʒwɛ̃dr/ *v.t.* go back to, rejoin; (*rattraper*) catch up with; (*rencontrer*) join, meet. **se ～** *v. pr.* (*personnes*) meet; (*routes*) join, meet.

réjoui /reʒwi/ *a.* joyful.

réjou|ir /reʒwir/ *v.t.* delight. **se ～ir** *v. pr.* be delighted (*de qch.*, at sth.). **～issances** *n.f. pl.* festivities.

relâche /rəlaʃ/ *n.m.* (*repos*) respite. **faire ～,** (*théâtre*) close.

relâch|er /rəlaʃe/ *v.t.* slacken; (*personne*) release; (*discipline*) relax. **se ～er** *v. pr.* slacken. **～ement** *n.m.* slackening.

relais /rəlɛ/ *n.m.* relay. **～ (routier),** roadside café.

relanc|e /rəlɑ̃s/ *n.f.* boost. **～er** *v.t.* boost, revive; (*renvoyer*) throw back.

relati|f, -ve /rəlatif, -v/ *a.* relative.

relation /rəlasjɔ̃/ *n.f.* relation(ship); (*ami*) acquaintance. **～s,** relation.

relativement /rəlativmɑ̃/ *adv.* relatively. **～ à,** in relation to.

relax|er (se) /(sə)rəlakse/ *v. pr.* relax. **～ation** *n.f.* relaxation. **～e** *a.* (*fam.*) laid-back.

relevé /rəlve/ *n.m.* list; (*de compte*) statement; (*de compteur*) reading. **—a.** spicy.

relever /rəlve/ *v.t.* pick up; (*personne tombée*) help up; (*remonter*) raise; (*col*) turn up;

(*manches*) roll up; (*sauce*) season; (*goût*) bring out; (*compteur*) read; (*défi*) accept; (*relayer*) relieve; (*remarquer, noter*) note; (*rebâtir*) rebuild.

relief /rəljɛf/ n.m. relief. **mettre en ~,** highlight.

relier /rəlje/ v.t. link (à, to); (*ensemble*) link together; (*livre*) bind.

religieu|x, ~se /rəliʒjø, -z/ a. religious. —n.m. monk. —n.f. nun; (*culin.*) choux bun.

religion /rəliʒjɔ̃/ n.f. religion.

relique /rəlik/ n.f. relic.

reliure /rəljyr/ n.f. binding.

reman|ier /rəmanje/ v.t. revise; (*ministère*) reshuffle. **~iement** n.m. revision; reshuffle.

remarier (se) /(sə)rəmarje/ v. pr. remarry.

remarquable /rəmarkabl/ a. remarkable.

remarque /rəmark/ n.f. remark; (*par écrit*) note.

remarquer /rəmarke/ v.t. notice; (*dire*) say. **faire ~,** point out (à, to). **se faire ~,** attract attention. **remarque(z),** mind you.

rembours|er /rɑ̃burse/ v.t. repay; (*billet, frais*) refund. **~ement** n.m. repayment; refund.

remède /rəmɛd/ n.m. remedy; (*médicament*) medicine.

remerc|ier /rəmɛrsje/ v.t. thank (**de,** for); (*licencier*) dismiss. **~iements** n.m. pl. thanks.

remettre† /rəmɛtr/ v.t. put back; (*vêtement*) put back on; (*donner*) hand (over); (*devoir, démission*) hand in; (*restituer*) give back; (*différer*) put off; (*ajouter*) add. **se ~ à,** go back to. **se ~ à faire,** start doing again.

remise¹ /rəmiz/ n.f. (*abri*) shed.

remise² /rəmiz/ n.f. (*rabais*) discount; (*livraison*) delivery; (*ajournement*) postponement.

rémission /remisjɔ̃/ n.f. remission.

remontant /rəmɔ̃tɑ̃/ n.m. tonic.

remontée /rəmɔ̃te/ n.f. **~ mécanique,** ski-lift.

remont|er /rəmɔ̃te/ v.i. go *ou* come (back) up; (*prix, niveau*) rise (again); (*revenir*) go back. —v.t. (*rue etc.*) go *ou* come (back) up; (*relever*) raise; (*montre*) wind up; (*objet démonté*) put together again; (*personne*) buck up. **~e-pente** n.m. ski-lift.

remords /rəmɔr/ n.m. remorse.

remorqu|e /rəmɔrk/ n.f. (*véhicule*) trailer. **~er** v.t. tow.

remorqueur /rəmɔrkœr/ n.m. tug.

rempart /rɑ̃par/ n.m. rampart.

remplaç|ant, ~e /rɑ̃plasɑ̃, -t/ n.m., f. replacement; (*joueur*) reserve.

remplac|er /rɑ̃plase/ v.t. replace. **~ement** n.m. replacement.

rempli /rɑ̃pli/ a. full (**de,** of).

remplir /rɑ̃plir/ v.t. fill (up); (*formulaire*) fill in *ou* out); **se ~** v. pr. fill (up).

remporter /rɑ̃pɔrte/ v.t. take back; (*victoire*) win.

remuer /rəmɥe/ v.t./i. move; (*thé, café*) stir; (*gigoter*) fidget.

rémunér|er /remynere/ v.t. pay. **~ation** n.f. payment.

renaître /rənɛtr/ v.i. be reborn; (*sentiment*) be revived.

renard /rənar/ n.m. fox.

rencontr|e /rɑ̃kɔ̃tr/ n.f. meeting; (*de routes*) junction; (*match*) match. **~er** v.t. meet; (*trouver*) find. **se ~er** v. pr. meet.

rendement /rɑ̃dmɑ̃/ n.m. yield; (*travail*) output.

rendez-vous /rɑ̃devu/ n.m. appointment; (*d'amoureux*) date; (*lieu*) meeting-place. **prendre ~ (avec),** make an appointment (with).

rendormir (se) /(sə)rɑ̃dɔrmir/ *v. pr.* go back to sleep.

rendre /rɑ̃dr/ *v.t.* give back, return; (*donner en retour*) return; (*monnaie*) give; (*hommage*) pay. **∼ heureux/possible/***etc.*, make happy/possible/*etc.* —*v.i.* (*terres*) yield; (*vomir*) vomit. **se ∼ v. pr.** (*capituler*) surrender; (*aller*) go (**à,** to); (*ridicule, utile, etc.*) make o.s. **∼ service (à),** help. **∼ visite à,** visit. **se ∼ compte de,** realize.

rêne /rɛn/ *n.f.* rein.

renfermer /rɑ̃fɛrme/ *v.t.* contain.

renfl|é /rɑ̃fle/ *a.* bulging. **∼ement** *n.m.* bulge.

renforcer /rɑ̃fɔrse/ *v.t.* reinforce.

renfort /rɑ̃fɔr/ *n.m.* reinforcement. **à grand ∼ de,** with a great deal of.

renier /rənje/ *v.t.* (*personne, pays*) disown, deny; (*foi*) renounce.

renifler /rənifle/ *v.t./i.* sniff.

renne /rɛn/ *n.m.* reindeer.

renom /rənɔ̃/ *n.m.* renown; (*réputation*) reputation. **∼mé** /-ɔme/ *a.* famous. **∼mée** /-ɔme/ *n.f.* fame; reputation.

renoncer /rənɔ̃se/ *v.i.* **∼ à,** (*habitude, ami, etc.*) give up, renounce. **∼ à faire,** give up (all thought of) doing.

renouer /rənwe/ *v.t.* tie up (again); (*reprendre*) renew. —*v.i.* **∼ avec,** start up again with.

renouveler /rənuvle/ *v.t.* renew; (*réitérer*) repeat. **se ∼ v. pr.** be renewed; be repeated.

rénov|er /renɔve/ *v.t.* (*édifice*) renovate; (*institution*) reform. **∼ation** *n.f.* renovation; reform.

renseignement /rɑ̃sɛɲmɑ̃/ *n.m.* **∼(s),** information. **(bureau des) ∼s,** information desk.

renseigner /rɑ̃seɲe/ *v.t.* inform, give information to. **se ∼ v. pr.** enquire, make enquiries, find out.

rentab|le /rɑ̃tabl/ *a.* profitable. **∼ilité** *n.f.* profitability.

rent|e /rɑ̃t/ *n.f.* (private) income; (*pension*) pension, annuity.

rentrée /rɑ̃tre/ *n.f.* return; **la ∼ parlementaire,** the reopening of Parliament; (*scol.*) start of the new year.

rentrer /rɑ̃tre/ (*aux. être*) *v.i.* go ou come back home, return home; (*entrer*) go in; (*entrer à nouveau*) go ou come back in; (*revenu*) come in; (*élèves*) go back. **∼ dans,** (*heurter*) smash into. —*v.t.* (*aux. avoir*) bring in.

renverser /rɑ̃vɛrse/ *v.t.* knock over ou down; (*piéton*) knock down; (*liquide*) upset, spill; (*mettre à l'envers*) turn upside down; (*gouvernement*) overturn; (*inverser*) reverse. **se ∼ v. pr.** (*véhicule*) overturn; (*verre, vase*) fall over.

renv|oi /rɑ̃vwa/ *n.m.* return; dismissal; expulsion; postponement; reference; (*rot*) belch. **∼oyer†** *v.t.* send back, return; (*employé*) dismiss; (*élève*) expel; (*ajourner*) postpone; (*référer*) refer; (*réfléchir*) reflect.

réorganiser /reɔrganize/ *v.t.* reorganize.

réouverture /reuvɛrtyr/ *n.f.* re-opening.

repaire /rəpɛr/ *n.m.* den.

répandre /repɑ̃dr/ *v.t.* (*liquide*) spill; (*étendre, diffuser*) spread; (*lumière, sang*) shed; (*odeur*) give off. **se ∼ v. pr.** spread; (*liquide*) spill.

répandu /repɑ̃dy/ *a.* (*courant*) widespread.

réparer /repare/ *v.t.* repair, mend.

repartir† /rəpartir/ *v.i.* set off (up) again; (*voyageur*) set off again; (*s'en retourner*) go back.

répart|ir /repartir/ *v.t.* distribute;

(*partager*) share out; (*étaler*) spread. **~ition** *n.f.* distribution.

repas /rəpɑ/ *n.m.* meal.

repass|er /rəpɑse/ *v.i.* come ou go back. —*v.t.* (*linge*) iron; (*film*) show again. **~age** *n.m.* ironing.

repère /rəpɛr/ *n.m.* mark; (*jalon*) marker; (*fig.*) landmark.

repérer /rəpere/ *v.t.* locate, spot. se **~** *v. pr.* find one's bearings.

répert|oire /repɛrtwar/ *n.m.* index; (*artistique*) repertoire. **~orier** *v.t.* index.

répéter /repete/ *v.t.* repeat. —*v.t./i.* (*théâtre*) rehearse. se **~** *v. pr.* be repeated; (*personne*) repeat o.s.

répétition /repetisjɔ̃/ *n.f.* repetition; (*théâtre*) rehearsal.

replacer /rəplase/ *v.t.* replace.

repl|i /rəpli/ *n.m.* fold; (*retrait*) withdrawal. **~ier** *v.t.* fold (up); (*ailes, jambes*) tuck in. se **~ier** *v. pr.* withdraw (**sur soi-même**, into o.s.).

réplicqu|e /replik/ *n.f.* reply; (*riposte*) retort; (*discussion*) objection; (*théâtre*) line(s); (*copie*) replica. **~er** *v.t./i.* reply; (*riposter*) retort; (*objecter*) answer back.

répondeur /repɔ̃dœr/ *n.m.* answering machine.

répondre /repɔ̃dr/ *v.t.* **~ que**, answer ou reply that. —*v.i.* answer, reply. **~ à**, answer. **~ de**, answer for.

réponse /repɔ̃s/ *n.f.* answer, reply; (*fig.*) response.

report /rəpɔr/ *n.m.* (*transcription*) transfer; (*renvoi*) postponement.

reportage /rəpɔrtaʒ/ *n.m.* report; (*en direct*) commentary; (*par écrit*) article.

reporter /rəpɔrte/ *v.t.* take back; (*ajourner*) put off; (*transcrire*) transfer. se **~ à**, refer to.

repos /rəpo/ *n.m.* rest; (*paix*) peace; (*tranquillité*) peace and quiet; (*moral*) peace of mind.

repos|er /rəpoze/ *v.t.* put down again; (*délasser*) rest. —*v.i.* rest (**sur**, on). se **~er** *v. pr.* rest. **~ant, ~ante** *a.* restful. **laisser ~er**, (*pâte*) leave to stand.

repousser /rəpuse/ *v.t.* push back; (*écarter*) push away; (*dégoûter*) repel; (*décliner*) reject; (*ajourner*) put back. —*v.i.* grow again.

reprendre† /rəprɑ̃dr/ *v.t.* take back; (*retrouver*) regain; (*souffle*) get back; (*recommencer*) resume; (*redire*) repeat. **~ du pain/***etc.*, take some more bread/*etc.* —*v.i.* (*recommencer*) resume; (*affaires*) pick up.

représent|er /rəprezɑ̃te/ *v.t.* represent; (*théâtre*) perform. **~ant, ~ante** *n.m.,* *f.* representative. **~ation** *n.f.* representation; (*théâtre*) performance.

réprimand|e /reprimɑ̃d/ *n.f.* reprimand. **~er** *v.t.* reprimand.

réprimer /reprime/ *v.t.* (*peuple*) repress; (*sentiment*) suppress. **~ession** *n.f.* repression.

reprise /rəpriz/ *n.f.* resumption; (*théâtre*) revival; (*télévision*) repeat; (*de tissu*) darn, mend; (*essor*) recovery; (*comm.*) part-exchange, trade-in. **à plusieurs ~s**, on several occasions.

reproch|e /rəprɔʃ/ *n.m.* reproach, blame. **~er** *v.t.* **~er qch. à qn.**, reproach ou blame s.o. for sth.

reproduire† /rəprɔdɥir/ *v.t.* reproduce. se **~** *v. pr.* reproduce; (*arriver*) recur.

reptile /reptil/ *n.m.* reptile.

république /repyblik/ *n.f.* republic.

réputation /repytasjɔ̃/ *n.f.* reputation.

réputé /repyte/ *a.* renowned

(*pour*, for). ~ **pour être**, reputed to be.

requérir /rəkerir/ *v.t.* require, demand.

requête /rɔkɛt/ *n.f.* request; (*jurid.*) petition.

requin /rɔkɛ̃/ *n.m.* shark.

requis, ~e /rɔki, -z/ *a.* required.

rescapé, ~e /rɛskape/ *n.m.*, *f.* survivor. —*a.* surviving.

réseau (*pl.* ~x) /rezo/ *n.m.* network.

réservation /rezervasjɔ̃/ *n.f.* reservation. **bureau de** ~, booking office.

réserve /rezɛrv/ *n.f.* reserve; (*restriction*) reservation, reserve; (*indienne*) reservation; (*entrepôt*) store-room. **en** ~, in reserve.

réserv|er /rezɛrve/ *v.t.* reserve; (*place*) book, reserve. ~é *a.* (*personne, place*) reserved.

réservoir /rezɛrvwar/ *n.m.* tank; (*lac*) reservoir.

résidence /rezidɑ̃s/ *n.f.* residence.

résident, ~e /rezidɑ̃, -t/ *n.m.*, *f.* resident foreigner. ~**iel**, ~**ielle** /-sjɛl/ *a.* residential.

résid|er /rezide/ *v.i.* reside.

résidu /rezidy/ *n.m.* residue.

résigner (se) /(sə)reziɲe/ *v. pr.* **se** ~ **à faire**, resign o.s. to doing.

résilier /rezilje/ *v.t.* terminate.

résine /rezin/ *n.f.* resin.

résistance /rezistɑ̃s/ *n.f.* resistance; (*fil électrique*) element.

résistant, ~e /rezistɑ̃, -t/ *a.* tough.

résister /reziste/ *v.i.* resist. ~ **à**, resist; (*examen, chaleur*) stand up to.

résolution /rezɔlysjɔ̃/ *n.f.* (*fermeté*) resolution; (*d'un problème*) solving.

résonance /rezɔnɑ̃s/ *n.f.* resonance.

résonner /rezɔne/ *v.i.* resound.

résoudre† /rezudr/ *v.t.* solve; (*décider*) decide on.

respect /rɛspɛ/ *n.m.* respect.

respectab|le /rɛspɛktabl/ *a.* respectable. ~**ilité** *n.f.* respectability.

respecter /rɛspɛkte/ *v.t.* respect. **faire** ~, (*loi, décision*) enforce.

respecti|f, ~**ve** /rɛspɛktif, -v/ *a.* respective. ~**vement** *adv.* respectively.

respectueu|x, ~**se** /rɛspɛktɥø, -z/ *a.* respectful.

respir|er /rɛspire/ *v.i.* breathe; (*se reposer*) get one's breath. —*v.t.* breathe; (*exprimer*) radiate. ~**ation** *n.f.* breathing; (*haleine*) breath. ~**atoire** *a.* breathing.

resplend|ir /rɛsplɑ̃dir/ *v.i.* shine (*de*, with). ~**issant**, ~**issante** *a.* radiant.

responsabilité /rɛspɔ̃sabilite/ *n.f.* responsibility; (*légale*) liability.

responsable /rɛspɔ̃sabl/ *a.* responsible (*de*, for). ~ **de**, (*chargé de*) in charge of. —*n.m./f.* person in charge; (*coupable*) person responsible.

ressembl|er /rɔsɑ̃ble/ *v.i.* ~**er à**, resemble, look like. **se** ~**er** *v. pr.* look alike. ~**ance** *n.f.* resemblance. ~**ant**, ~**ante** *a.* (*portrait*) true to life; (*pareil*) alike.

ressemeler /rɔsəmle/ *v.t.* sole.

ressentir /rɔsɑ̃tir/ *v.t.* feel.

resserre /rɔsɛr/ *n.f.* shed.

resserrer /rɔsere/ *v.t.* tighten; (*contracter*) contract. **se** ~ *v. pr.* tighten; contract; (*route etc.*) narrow.

resservir /rɔsɛrvir/ *v.i.* come in useful (again).

ressort /rɔsɔr/ *n.m.* (*objet*) spring; (*fig.*) energy.

ressortir† /rɔsɔrtir/ *v.i.* go ou come back out; (*se voir*) stand out. **faire** ~, bring out.

ressortissant, ~e /rəsɔrtisɑ̃, -t/
n.m./f. national.

ressource /rəsurs/ *n.f.* resource.

ressusciter /resysite/ *v.i.* come
back to life.

restant, ~e /rɛstɑ̃, -t/ *a.* remain-
ing. —*n.m.* remainder.

restaur|ant /rɛstɔrɑ̃/ *n.m.* res-
taurant. ~**ateur,** ~**atrice** *n.m.,*
f. restaurant owner.

restaur|er /rɛstɔre/ *v.t.* restore. **se**
~**er** *v. pr.* eat. ~**ation** *n.f.*
restoration; (*hôtellerie*) catering.

reste /rɛst/ *n.m.* rest; (*d'une
soustraction*) remainder. ~**s,**
remains (**de,** of); (*nourriture*)
leftovers.

rest|er /rɛste/ *v.i.* (*aux. être*) stay,
remain; (*subsister*) be left,
remain. **il** ~**e du pain**/*etc.* there
is some bread/*etc.* left (over).

restit|uer /rɛstitɥe/ *v.t.* (*rendre*)
return, restore; (*son*) reproduce.
~**ution** *n.f.* return.

restreindre† /rɛstrɛ̃dr/ *v.t.* restrict. **se** ~ *v. pr.* (*dans les
dépenses*) cut down.

restricti|f, ~**ve** /rɛstriktif, -v/ *a.*
restrictive.

restriction /rɛstriksjɔ̃/ *n.f.* restriction.

résultat /rezylta/ *n.m.* result.

résulter /rezylte/ *v.i.* ~ **de,** result
from.

résum|er /rezyme/ *v.t.,* **se** ~**er** *v.
pr.* summarize. ~**é** *n.m.* sum-
mary. **en** ~**é,** in short.

rétabl|ir /retablir/ *v.t.* restore;
(*personne*) restore to health. **se**
~**ir** *v. pr.* be restored; (*guérir*)
recover. ~**issement** *n.m.* restor-
ing; (*méd.*) recovery.

retaper /rətape/ *v.t.* (*maison etc.*)
do up.

retard /rətar/ *n.m.* lateness; (*sur
un programme*) delay. **avoir du**
~, be late; (*montre*) be slow. **en**

~, late. **en** ~ **sur,** behind.

rattraper *ou* **combler son** ~,
catch up.

retardataire /rətardatɛr/ *n.m./f.*
latecomer. —*a.* (*arrivant*) late.

retardement (à) /(a)rətardəmɑ̃/ *a.*
(*bombe etc.*) delayed-action.

retarder /rətarde/ *v.t.* delay; (*sur
un programme*) set back; (*montre*)
put back. —*v.i.* (*montre*) be slow.

retenir† /rətnir/ *v.t.* hold back;
(*souffle, attention, prisonnier*)
hold; (*eau, chaleur*) retain, hold;
(*larmes*) hold back; (*garder*) keep;
(*retarder*) detain; (*réserver*) book;
(*se rappeler*) remember; (*déduire*)
deduct.

rétention /retɑ̃sjɔ̃/ *n.f.* retention.

retenue /rətny/ *n.f.* restraint;
(*somme*) deduction; (*scol.*) detention.

rétine /retin/ *n.f.* retina.

retiré /rətire/ *a.* (*vie*) secluded;
(*lieu*) remote.

retirer /rətire/ *v.t.* (*ôter*) take off;
(*argent*) withdraw. ~ **à qn.,** take
away from s.o. **se** ~ *v. pr.*
withdraw, retire.

retomber /rətɔ̃be/ *v.i.* fall; (*à
nouveau*) fall again. ~ **dans,**
(*erreur etc.*) fall back into.

retour /rətur/ *n.m.* return. **être de**
~, be back (**de,** from). **par** ~ **du
courrier,** by return of post. **en**
~, in return.

retourner /rəturne/ *v.t.* (*aux.
avoir*) turn over; (*lettre*) return.
—*v.i.* (*aux. être*) go back, return.
se ~ *v. pr.* turn round; (*dans son
lit*) twist and turn.

retrait /rətrɛ/ *n.m.* withdrawal.

retraite /rətrɛt/ *n.f.* retirement;
(*pension*) (retirement) pension.
prendre sa ~, retire.

retraité, ~e /rətrete/ *a.* retired.
—*n.m., f.* (old-age) pensioner,
senior citizen.

retransm|ettre /rətrɑ̃smɛtr/ v.t. broadcast. **~ission** n.f. broadcast.

rétrécir /retresir/ v.t. narrow; (vêtement) take in. —v.i. (tissu) shrink. **se ~,** (rue) narrow.

rétroactif, -ve /retrɔaktif, -v/ a. retrospective.

rétrospective /retrɔspɛktivmɑ̃/ adv. in retrospect.

retrousser /rətruse/ v.t. pull up.

retrouvailles /rətruvaj/ n.f. pl. reunion.

retrouver /rətruve/ v.t. find (again); (rejoindre) meet (again); (forces, calme) regain; (se rappeler) remember. **se ~** v. pr. find o.s. (back); (se réunir) meet (again). **s'y ~,** (s'orienter, comprendre) find one's way.

rétroviseur /retrɔvizœr/ n.m. (auto.) (rear-view) mirror.

réunion /reynjɔ̃/ n.f. meeting.

réunir /reynir/ v.t. gather, collect; (rapprocher) bring together; (convoquer) call together; (raccorder) join; (qualités) combine. **se ~** v. pr. meet.

réussi† /reysi/ a. successful.

réussir /reysir/ v.i. succeed, be successful (à faire, in doing). —v.t. make a success of.

réussite /reysit/ n.f. success; (jeu) patience.

revanche /rəvɑ̃ʃ/ n.f. revenge; (sport) return ou revenge match. **en ~,** on the other hand.

rêve /rɛv/ n.m. dream. **faire un ~,** have a dream.

réveil /revɛj/ n.m. waking up, (pendule) alarm-clock.

réveill|er /reveje/ v.t., **se ~er** v. pr. wake (up); (fig.) awaken. **~é** a. awake. **~e-matin** n.m. invar. alarm-clock.

réveillon /revɛjɔ̃/ n.m. (Noël) Christmas Eve; (nouvel an) New Year's Eve. **~ner** /-jɔne/ v.i. celebrate the réveillon.

révéler /revele/ v.t. reveal.

revendi|quer /rəvɑ̃dike/ v.t. claim. **~cation** n.f. claim; (action) claiming.

revend|re /rəvɑ̃dr/ v.t. sell (again). **~eur, ~euse** n.m., f. dealer.

revenir† /rəvnir/ v.i. (aux. être) come back, return (à, to). **~ à,** (coûter) cost. **faire ~,** (culin.) brown. **ça me revient,** it comes back to me.

revente /rəvɑ̃t/ n.f. resale.

revenu /rəvny/ n.m. income; (d'un état) revenue.

rêver /reve/ v.t./i. dream (à ou de, of).

réverbération /reverberasjɔ̃/ n.f. reflection, reverberation.

réverbère /reverbɛr/ n.m. street lamp.

révérence /reverɑ̃s/ n.f. reverence; (salut d'homme) bow; (salut de femme) curtsy.

revers /rəvɛr/ n.m. (d'étoffe) wrong side; (de veste) lapel; (tennis) backhand; (fig.) set-back.

réversible /reversibl/ a. reversible.

revêtement /rəvɛtmɑ̃/ n.m. covering; (de route) surface.

rêveu|r, ~se /revœr, -øz/ a. dreamy. —n.m., f. dreamer.

révis|er /revize/ v.t. revise; (véhicule) overhaul. **~ion** n.f. revision; overhaul.

revivre† /rəvivr/ v.i. live again. —v.t. relive (again). **faire ~,** revive.

revoir† /rəvwar/ v.t. see (again); (réviser) revise. **au ~,** goodbye.

révolte /revɔlt/ n.f. revolt.

révolter /revɔlte/ v.t., **se ~er** v. pr. revolt.

révolution /revɔlysjɔ̃/ n.f. revolution. **~ner** /-jɔne/ v.t. revolutionize.

revolver /revɔlvr/ *n.m.* revolver, gun.

revue /rəvy/ *n.f.* (*examen, défilé*) review; (*magazine*) magazine; (*spectacle*) variety show.

rez-de-chaussée /redʃose/ *n.m. invar.* ground floor.

RF *abrév.* (*République Française*) French Republic.

rhabiller (se) /(s)abije/ *v. pr.* get dressed (again), dress (again).

rhinocéros /rinɔserɔs/ *n.m.* rhinoceros.

rhubarbe /rybarb/ *n.f.* rhubarb.

rhum /rɔm/ *n.m.* rum.

rhumatisme /rymatism/ *n.m.* rheumatism.

rhume /rym/ *n.m.* cold. **∼ des foins,** hay fever.

ri /ri/ *voir* **rire**.

riche /riʃ/ *a.* rich (**en,** in). —*n.m./f.* rich person. **∼ment** *adv.* richly.

richesse /riʃɛs/ *n.f.* wealth; (*de sol, décor*) richness. **∼s,** wealth.

ride /rid/ *n.f.* wrinkle.

rideau (*pl.* **∼x**) /rido/ *n.m.* curtain; (*métallique*) shutter.

ridicule /ridikyl/ *a.* ridiculous. —*n.m.* absurdity. **le ∼,** ridicule.

rien /rjɛ̃/ *pron.* (**ne**) **∼,** nothing. —*n.m.* trifle. **de ∼!,** don't mention it! **∼ d'autre/de plus,** nothing else/more. **∼ du tout,** nothing at all. **trois fois ∼,** next to nothing. **il n'y est pour ∼,** he has nothing to do with it. **∼ à faire,** it's no good!

rigide /riʒid/ *a.* rigid; (*muscle*) stiff. **∼ité** *n.f.* rigidity; stiffness.

rigoler /rigɔle/ *v.i.* laugh; (*s'amuser*) have some fun; (*plaisanter*) joke. **∼ade** *n.f.* fun.

rigolo, ∼te /rigɔlo, -ɔt/ *a.* (*fam.*) funny. —*n.m., f.* (*fam.*) joker.

rigoureu|x /riguro, -z/ *a.* rigorous; (*hiver*) harsh. **∼sement** *adv.* rigorously.

rigueur /rigœr/ *n.f.* rigour. **à la ∼,** at a pinch.

rim|e /rim/ *n.f.* rhyme. **∼er** *v.i.* rhyme (**avec,** with).

rin|cer /rɛ̃se/ *v.t.* rinse. **∼çage** *n.m.* rinse; (*action*) rinsing.

ring /riŋ/ *n.m.* boxing ring.

rire /rir/ *v.i.* laugh (**de,** at); (*plaisanter*) joke; (*s'amuser*) have fun. **c'était pour ∼,** it was a joke. —*n.m.* laugh. **∼s, le ∼,** laughter.

risible /rizibl/ *a.* laughable.

risqu|e /risk/ *n.m.* risk. **∼é** *a.* risky; (*osé*) daring. **∼er** *v.t.* risk. **∼er de faire,** stand a good chance of doing.

rissoler /risɔle/ *v.t./i.* brown. **(faire) ∼,** brown.

ristourne /risturn/ *n.f.* discount.

rivage /rivaʒ/ *n.m.* shore.

riv|al, ∼ale (*m. pl.* **∼aux**) /rival, -o/ *n.m., f.* rival. —*a.* rival. **∼aliser** *v.i.* compete (**avec,** with). **∼alité** *n.f.* rivalry.

rive /riv/ *n.f.* (*de fleuve*) bank; (*de lac*) shore.

riverain, ∼e /rivrɛ̃, -ɛn/ *a.* riverside. —*n.m., f.* riverside resident; (*d'une rue*) resident.

rivière /rivjɛr/ *n.f.* river.

riz /ri/ *n.m.* rice.

robe /rɔb/ *n.f.* (*de femme*) dress. **∼ de chambre,** dressing-gown.

robinet /rɔbinɛ/ *n.m.* tap.

robot /rɔbo/ *n.m.* robot.

robuste /rɔbyst/ *a.* robust.

roc /rɔk/ *n.m.* rock.

rocaille /rɔkɑj/ *n.f.* rocky ground; (*de jardin*) rockery. **∼eux, ∼euse** *a.* (*terrain*) rocky.

roch|e /rɔʃ/ *n.f.* rock. **∼eux, ∼euse** *a.* rocky.

rocher /rɔʃe/ *n.m.* rock.

rock /rɔk/ *n.m.* (*mus.*) rock.

rod|er /rɔde/ *v.t.* (*auto.*) run in. **être ∼é,** (*personne*) be broken in. **∼age** *n.m.* running in.

rognon /rɔɲɔ̃/ *n.m.* (*culin.*) kidney.

roi /rwa/ *n.m.* king. **les Rois mages**, the Magi. **la fête des Rois**, Twelfth Night.

rôle /rol/ *n.m.* role, part.

romain, **~e** /rɔmɛ̃, -ɛn/ *a.* & *n.m.,f.* Roman. —*n.f.* (*laitue*) cos.

roman /rɔmɑ̃/ *n.m.* novel.

romanesque /rɔmanɛsk/ *a.* romantic; (*fantastique*) fantastic.

romanti|que /rɔmɑ̃tik/ *a.* & *n.m./f.* romantic. **~sme** *n.m.* romanticism.

rompre† /rɔ̃pr/ *v.t./i.* break; (*relations*) break off. (*fiançés*) break it off. **se ~** *v. pr.* break.

ronces /rɔ̃s/ *n.f. pl.* brambles.

rond, **~e¹** /rɔ̃, rɔ̃d/ *a.* round; (*gras*) plump; (*ivre: fam.*) tight. —*n.m.* (*cercle*) ring; (*tranche*) slice. **il n'a pas un ~**, (*fam.*) he hasn't got a penny. **~-point** (*pl.* **~s-points**) *n.m.* roundabout.

ronde² /rɔ̃d/ *n.f.* round(s); (*de policier*) beat; (*mus.*) semibreve.

rondelle /rɔ̃dɛl/ *n.f.* (*techn.*) washer; (*tranche*) slice.

ronfl|er /rɔ̃fle/ *v.i.* snore; (*moteur*) hum. **~ement(s)** *n.m.* (*pl.*) snoring; humming.

rong|er /rɔ̃ʒe/ *v.t.* gnaw (at); (*vers*) eat into. **se ~er les ongles**, bite one's nails. **~eur** *n.m.* rodent.

ronronn|er /rɔ̃rɔne/ *v.i.* purr. **~ement** *n.m.* purr(ing).

rosace /rɔzas/ *n.f.* (*d'église*) rose window.

rosbif /rɔsbif/ *n.m.* roast beef.

rose /roz/ *n.f.* rose. —*a.* pink; (*situation, teint*) rosy. —*n.m.* pink.

rosé /roze/ *a.* pinkish; (*vin*) rosé. —*n.m.* rosé.

roseau (*pl.* **~x**) /rozo/ *n.m.* reed.

rosée /roze/ *n.f.* dew.

rosier /rozje/ *n.m.* rose-bush, rose tree.

rossignol /rɔsiɲɔl/ *n.m.* nightingale.

rot /ro/ *n.m.* (*fam.*) burp.

rotation /rɔtasjɔ̃/ *n.f.* rotation.

roter /rɔte/ *v.i.* (*fam.*) burp.

rotin /rɔtɛ̃/ *n.m.* (rattan) cane.

rôt|ir /rotir/ *v.t./i.*, roast. **~i** *n.m.* roasting meat; (*cuit*) roast. **~i de porc**, roast pork.

rotule /rɔtyl/ *n.f.* kneecap.

rouage /rwaʒ/ *n.m.* (*techn.*) (working) part.

roue /ru/ *n.f.* wheel. **~ (dentée)**, cog(-wheel). **~ de secours**, spare wheel.

rouge /ruʒ/ *a.* red; (*fer*) red-hot. —*n.m.* red. (*fard*) rouge. **~ (à lèvres)**, lipstick. **~-gorge** (*pl.* **~s-gorges**) *n.m.* robin.

rougeole /ruʒɔl/ *n.f.* measles.

rouget /ruʒɛ/ *n.m.* red mullet.

rougeur /ruʒœr/ *n.f.* redness; (*tache*) red blotch; (*gêne, honte*) red face.

rougir /ruʒir/ *v.t./i.* turn red; (*de honte*) blush.

rouill|e /ruj/ *n.f.* rust. **~é,a** rusty.

roulant, **~e** /rulã, -t/ *a.* (*meuble*) on wheels; (*escalier*) moving.

rouleau (*pl.* **~x**) /rulo/ *n.m.* roll; (*outil, vague*) roller. **~ à pâtisserie**, rolling-pin. **~ compresseur**, steamroller.

roulement /rulmã/ *n.m.* rotation; (*bruit*) rumble; (*succession de personnes*) turnover; (*de tambour*) roll. **~ à billes**, ball-bearing. **par ~**, in rotation.

rouler /rule/ *v.t./i.* roll; (*manches*) roll up; (*duper: fam.*) cheat; (*véhicule, train*) go, travel; (*conducteur*) drive.

roulette /rulɛt/ *n.f.* (*de meuble*) castor; (*de dentiste*) drill; (*jeu*) roulette. **comme sur des ~s**, very smoothly.

roulis /ruli/ *n.m.* rolling.

roulotte /rulɔt/ *n.f.* caravan.

roumain /rumɛ̃, -ɛn/ *a.* & *n.m.*, *f.* Romanian.

Roumanie /rumani/ *n.f.* Romania.

rousse /rus/ *voir* **roux.**

roussir /rusir/ *v.t.* scorch. —*v.i.* turn brown.

route /rut/ *n.f.* road; (*naut.*, *aviat.*) route; (*direction*) way; (*voyage*) journey. **en ~,** on the way. **en ~!,** let's go! **mettre en ~,** start. **~ nationale,** trunk road, main road. **se mettre en ~,** set out.

routine /rutin/ *n.f.* routine.

rouvrir /ruvrir/ *v.t.,* **se ~ir** *v. pr.* reopen, open again.

rou|x, ~sse /ru, rus/ *a.* red, reddish-brown; (*personne*) red-haired. —*n.m., f.* redhead.

roy|al (*m. pl.* **~aux**) /rwajal, -jo/ *a.* royal; (*total: fam.*) thorough.

royaume /rwajom/ *n.m.* kingdom. **R~-Uni** *n.m.* United Kingdom.

ruban /rybɑ̃/ *n.m.* ribbon; (*de magnétophone*) tape; (*de chapeau*) band. **~ adhésif,** sticky tape.

rubéole /rybeɔl/ *n.f.* German measles.

rubis /rybi/ *n.m.* ruby; (*de montre*) jewel.

rubrique /rybrik/ *n.f.* heading; (*article*) column.

ruche /ryʃ/ *n.f.* beehive.

rude /ryd/ *a.* rough; (*pénible*) tough; (*grossier*) crude; (*fameux: fam.*) tremendous. **~ment** *adv.* (*frapper etc.*) hard; (*traiter*) harshly; (*très: fam.*) awfully.

rue /ry/ *n.f.* street.

ruelle /rɥɛl/ *n.f.* alley.

ruer /rɥe/ *v.i.* (*cheval*) kick. **se ~ dans/vers,** rush into/towards.

rugby /rygbi/ *n.m.* Rugby.

rug|ir /ryʒir/ *v.i.* roar. **~issement** *n.m.* roar.

rugueu|x, ~se /rygø, -z/ *a.* rough.

ruin|e /rɥin/ *n.f.* ruin. **en ~e(s),** in ruins. **~er** *v.t.* ruin.

ruineu|x, ~se /rɥinø, -z/ *a.* ruinous.

ruisseau (*pl.* **~x**) /rɥiso/ *n.m.* stream; (*rigole*) gutter.

ruisseler /rɥisle/ *v.i.* stream.

rumeur /rymœr/ *n.f.* rumour.

ruminer /rymine/ *v.t./i.* (*herbe*) ruminate; (*méditer*) meditate.

rupture /ryptyr/ *n.f.* break; (*action*) breaking; (*de contrat*) breach; (*de pourparlers*) breakdown.

rur|al (*m. pl.* **~aux**) /ryral, -o/ *a.* rural.

rus|e /ryz/ *n.f.* **une ~e,** a trick, a ruse. **~é** *a.* cunning.

russe /rys/ *a.* & *n.m./f.* Russian. —*n.m.* (*lang.*) Russian.

Russie /rysi/ *n.f.* Russia.

rustique /rystik/ *a.* rustic.

rythm|e /ritm/ *n.m.* rhythm; (*vitesse*) rate; (*de la vie*) pace.

S

s' /s/ *voir* **se.**

sa /sa/ *voir* **son[1].**

SA *abrév.* (*société anonyme*) PLC.

sabbat /saba/ *n.m.* sabbath.

sabl|e /sabl/ *n.m.* sand. **~es mouvants,** quicksands. **~er le champagne,** drink champagne.

sablier /sablije/ *n.m.* (*culin.*) egg-timer.

sabot /sabo/ *n.m.* (*de cheval etc.*) hoof; (*chaussure*) clog; (*de frein*) shoe. **~ de Denver,** (*wheel*) clamp.

sabot|er /sabɔte/ *v.t.* sabotage; (*bâcler*) botch. **~age** *n.m.* sabotage; (*acte*) act of sabotage.

sabre /sɑbr/ *n.m.* sabre.

sac /sak/ *n.m.* bag; (*grand, en toile*) sack. **~ à dos,** rucksack. **~ à main,** handbag. **~ de couchage,** sleeping-bag.

saccager /sakaʒe/ *v.t.* (*ville, pays*) sack; (*maison*) ransack; (*ravager*) wreck.

saccharine /sakarin/ *n.f.* saccharin.

sachet /saʃɛ/ *n.m.* (small) bag; (*de médicament etc.*) sachet. **~ de thé,** tea-bag.

sacoche /sakɔʃ/ *n.f.* bag; (*d'élève*) satchel; (*de moto*) saddle-bag.

sacquer /sake/ *v.t.* (*fam.*) sack.

sacré /sakre/ *a.* sacred; (*maudit: fam.*) damned.

sacrifice /sakrifis/ *n.m.* sacrifice.

sacrifier /sakrifje/ *v.t.* sacrifice. **~ à,** conform to. **se ~** *v. pr.* sacrifice o.s.

sacrilège /sakrilɛʒ/ *n.m.* sacrilege.
　—a. sacrilegious.

sacristie /sakristi/ *n.f.* (*protestante*) vestry; (*catholique*) sacristy.

sadi|que /sadik/ *a.* sadistic.
　—n.m./f. sadist. **~sme** *n.m.* sadism.

safari /safari/ *n.m.* safari.

sage /saʒ/ *a.* wise; (*docile*) good.
　—n.m. wise man. **~-femme** (*pl.* **~s-femmes**) *n.f.* midwife. **~ment** *adv.* wisely; (*docilement*) quietly. **~sse** /-ɛs/ *n.f.* wisdom.

Sagittaire /saʒitɛr/ *n.m.* **le ~,** Sagittarius.

Sahara /saara/ *n.m.* **le ~,** the Sahara (desert).

saignant, ~e /sɛɲɑ̃, -t/ *a.* (*culin.*) rare.

saign|er /seɲe/ *v.t./i.* bleed. **~er du nez,** have a nosebleed. **~ement** *n.m.* bleeding.

sain, ~e /sɛ̃, sɛn/ *a.* healthy; (*moralement*) sane. **~ et sauf,**

safe and sound. **~ement** /sɛnmɑ̃/ *adv.* healthily; (*juger*) sanely.

saindoux /sɛdu/ *n.m.* lard.

saint, ~e /sɛ̃, sɛ̃t/ *a.* holy; (*bon*) saintly. *—n.m., f.* saint. **S~-Esprit** *n.m.* Holy Spirit. **S~-Sylvestre** *n.f.* New Year's Eve. **S~e Vierge,** Blessed Virgin.

sais /sɛ/ *voir* **savoir**.

saisie /sezi/ *n.f.* (*jurid.*) seizure; (*comput.*) keyboarding. **~ de données,** data capture.

sais|ir /sezir/ *v.t.* grab (hold of), seize; (*occasion, biens*) seize; (*comprendre*) grasp; (*comput.*) keyboard, capture.

saison /sɛzɔ̃/ *n.f.* season. **la morte ~,** the off season. **~nier, ~nière** /-ɔnje, -jɛr/ *a.* seasonal.

sait /sɛ/ *voir* **savoir**.

salad|e /salad/ *n.f.* salad; (*laitue*) lettuce; (*désordre: fam.*) mess. **~ier** *n.m.* salad bowl.

salaire /salɛr/ *n.m.* wages, salary.

salami /salami/ *n.m.* salami.

salarié, ~e /salarje/ *a.* wage-earning. *—n.m., f.* wage-earner.

salaud /salo/ *n.m.* (*argot*) bastard.

sale /sal/ *a.* dirty, filthy; (*mauvais*) nasty.

sal|er /sale/ *v.t.* salt. **~é a.** (*goût*) salty; (*plat*) salted; (*viande, poisson*) salt; (*grivois: fam.*) spicy.

saleté /salte/ *n.f.* (*crasse*) dirt; (*action*) dirty trick. **~s,** (*détritus*) mess.

salière /saljɛr/ *n.f.* salt-cellar.

sal|ir /salir/ *v.t.* (make) dirty; (*réputation*) tarnish. **se ~ir** *v. pr.* get dirty. **~issant, ~issante** *a.* dirty; (*étoffe*) easily dirtied.

salive /saliv/ *n.f.* saliva.

salle /sal/ *n.f.* room; (*grande, publique*) hall; (*d'hôpital*) ward; (*théâtre, cinéma*) auditorium. **~ à manger,** dining-room. **~ d'attente,** waiting-room. **~ de**

bains, bathroom. ⟋ **de séjour**, living-room. ⟋ **de classe**, class-room. ⟋ **d'embarquement**, departure lounge. ⟋ **d'opération**, operating theatre. ⟋ **des ventes**, saleroom.

salon /salɔ̃/ n.m. lounge; (de coiffure, beauté) salon; (exposition) show. ⟋ **de thé**, tea-room.

salope /salɔp/ n.f. (argot) bitch.

saloperie /salɔpri/ n.f. (fam.) (action) dirty trick; (chose de mauvaise qualité) rubbish.

salopette /salɔpɛt/ n.f. dungarees; (d'ouvrier) overalls.

salsifis /salsifi/ n.m. salsify.

saluer /salɥe/ v.t. greet; (en partant) take one's leave of; (de la tête) nod to; (de la main) wave to.

salut /saly/ n.m. greeting; (de la tête) nod; (de la main) wave; (mil.) salute; (sauvegarde, rachat) salvation. —int. (bonjour. fam.) hallo; (au revoir. fam.) bye-bye.

salutation /salytasjɔ̃/ n.f. greeting. **veuillez agréer, Monsieur, mes** ⟋**s distingués**, yours faithfully.

samedi /samdi/ n.m. Saturday.

sanction /sɑ̃ksjɔ̃/ n.f. sanction.

sandale /sɑ̃dal/ n.f. sandal.

sandwich /sɑ̃dwitʃ/ n.m. sandwich.

sang /sɑ̃/ n.m. blood. ⟋**-froid** n.m. invar. calm, self-control.

sangl|e /sɑ̃gl/ n.f. strap. ⟋**er** v.t. strap.

sanglier /sɑ̃glije/ n.m. wild boar.

sanglot /sɑ̃glo/ n.m. sob.

sangsue /sɑ̃sy/ n.f. leech.

sanguin, ⟋**e** /sɑ̃gɛ̃, -in/ a. (groupe etc.) blood; (caractère) fiery.

sanitaire /sanitɛr/ a. health; (conditions) sanitary; (appareils, installations) bathroom, sanitary. ⟋**s** n.m. pl. bathroom.

sans /sɑ̃/ prép. without. ⟋ **que vous le sachiez**, without your knowing. ⟋**-abri** /sɑ̃zabri/ n.m./f. invar. homeless person. ⟋ **ça**, ⟋ **quoi**, otherwise. ⟋ **arrêt**, nonstop. ⟋ **encombre/faute/tarder**, without incident/fail/delay. ⟋ **fin/goût/limite**, endless/tasteless/limitless. ⟋**-gêne** a. invar. inconsiderate, thoughtless; n.m. invar. thoughtlessness. ⟋ **importance / pareil / précédent / travail**, unimportant / unparalleled / unprecedented / unemployed.

santé /sɑ̃te/ n.f. health. **à ta** ou **votre santé**, cheers!

saoul, ⟋**e** /su, sul/ voir **soûl**.

sapeur /sapœr/ n.m. (mil.) sapper. ⟋**-pompier** (pl. ⟋**s-pompiers**) n.m. fireman.

saphir /safir/ n.m. sapphire.

sapin /sapɛ̃/ n.m. fir-(tree). ⟋ **de Noël**, Christmas tree.

sardine /sardin/ n.f. sardine.

satellite /satelit/ n.m. satellite.

satin /satɛ̃/ n.m. satin.

satir|e /satir/ n.f. satire. ⟋**ique** a. satirical.

satisfaction /satisfaksjɔ̃/ n.f. satisfaction.

satis|faire† /satisfɛr/ v.t. satisfy. —v.i. ⟋ **faire à**, satisfy. ⟋**faisant**, ⟋**faisante** a. (acceptable) satisfactory. ⟋**fait**, ⟋**faite** a. satisfied (**de**, with).

sauc|e /sos/ n.f. sauce; (jus de viande) gravy. ⟋**er** v.t. (plat) wipe. ⟋**e tartare**, tartar sauce. ⟋**ière** n.f. sauce-boat.

saucisse /sosis/ n.f. sausage.

saucisson /sosisɔ̃/ n.m. (slicing) sausage.

sauf[1] /sof/ prép. except. ⟋ **erreur/imprévu**, barring error/the unforeseen.

sau|f², **~ve** /sof, sov/ *a.* safe,
unharmed.

sauge /soʒ/ *n.f.* (*culin.*) sage.

saule /sol/ *n.m.* willow. **~
pleureur**, weeping willow.

saumon /somɔ̃/ *n.m.* salmon. —*a.
invar.* salmon-pink.

saumure /somyr/ *n.f.* brine.

sauna /sona/ *n.m.* sauna.

saupoudrer /sopudre/ *v.t.*
sprinkle (**de**, with).

saut /so/ *n.m.* jump, leap. **faire un
~ chez qn.**, pop round to s.o.'s
(place). **le ~**, (*sport*) jumping. **~
en hauteur/longueur**, high/
long jump.

sauté /sote/ *a. & n.m.* (*culin.*)
sauté.

sauter /sote/ *v.i.* jump, leap;
(*exploser*) hear. (*fusible*) blow;
(*se détacher*) come off. —*v.t.* jump
(over); (*page*, *classe*) skip. **faire
~**, (*détruire*) blow up; (*fusible*)
blow; (*casser*) break; (*culin.*)
sauté. **~ à la corde**, skip. **~ sur
une occasion**, jump at an
opportunity.

sauterelle /sotrɛl/ *n.f.* grasshopper.

sautiller /sotije/ *v.i.* hop.

sauvage /sovaʒ/ *a.* wild; (*primitif,
cruel*) savage; (*farouche*) unsociable; (*illégal*) unauthorized.
—*n.m./f.* unsociable person;
(*brute*) savage.

sauve /sov/ *voir* **sauf²**.

sauvegard|e /sovgard/ *n.f.* safe-
guard; (*comput.*) backup. **~er** *v.t.*
safeguard; (*comput.*) save.

sauv|er /sove/ *v.t.* save; (*d'un
danger*) rescue, save; (*matériel*)
salvage. **se ~er** *v. pr.* (*fuir*) run
away; (*partir. fam.*) be off.
~etage *n.m.* rescue; salvage.
~eteur *n.m.* rescuer.

savan|t, **~e** /savã, -t/ *a.* learned;
(*habile*) skilful. —*n.m.* scientist.

saveur /savœr/ *n.f.* flavour; (*fig.*)
savour.

savoir† /savwar/ *v.t.* know;
(*apprendre*) hear. **elle sait con-
duire/nager**, she can drive/
swim. —*n.m.* learning. **faire ~ à
qn. que**, inform s.o. that.

savon /savɔ̃/ *n.m.* soap. **~ner**
/-ɔne/ *v.t.* soap. **~nette** /-ɔnɛt/ *n.f.*
bar of soap.

saveur|er /savure/ *v.t.* savour.
~eux, **~euse** *a.* tasty; (*fig.*)
spicy.

saxo(phone) /saksɔ(fɔn)/ *n.m.*
sax(ophone).

scandal|e /skãdal/ *n.m.* scandal;
(*tapage*) uproar; (*en public*) noisy
scene. **faire ~e**, shock people.
faire un ~e, make a scene.
~eux, **~euse** *a.* scandalous.

scandinave /skãdinav/ *a. &
n.m./f.* Scandinavian.

Scandinavie /skãdinavi/ *n.f.* Scandinavia.

scarabée /skarabe/ *n.m.* beetle.

scarlatine /skarlatin/ *n.f.* scarlet
fever.

scarole /skarɔl/ *n.f.* endive.

sceau (*pl.* **~x**) /so/ *n.m.* seal.

scell|er /sele/ *v.t.* seal; (*fixer*)
cement. **~és** *n.m. pl.* seals.

scénario /senarjo/ *n.m.* scenario.

scène /sɛn/ *n.f.* scene; (*estrade, art
dramatique*) stage. **mettre en ~**,
(*pièce*) stage. **~. de ménage**,
domestic scene.

scepti|que /sɛptik/ *a.* sceptical.
—*n.m./f.* sceptic. **~cisme** *n.m.*
scepticism.

schéma /ʃema/ *n.m.* diagram.

sciatique /sjatik/ *n.f.* sciatica.

scie /si/ *n.f.* saw.

scien|ce /sjãs/ *n.f.* science; (*savoir*)
knowledge. **~ce-fiction** *n.f.*
science fiction. **~tifique** *a.* scien-
tific; *n.m./f.* scientist.

scier /sje/ *v.t.* saw.

scintiller /sɛ̃tije/ *v.i.* glitter; (*étoile*) twinkle.

scission /sisjɔ̃/ *n.f.* split.

sciure /sjyr/ *n.f.* sawdust.

sclérose /skleroz/ *n.f.* sclerosis. **∼ en plaques,** multiple sclerosis.

scol|aire /skolɛr/ *a.* school. **∼arisation** *n.f.,* **∼arité** *n.f.* schooling.

scorbut /skɔrbyt/ *n.m.* scurvy.

score /skɔr/ *n.m.* score.

scorpion /skɔrpjɔ̃/ *n.m.* scorpion. **le S∼,** Scorpio.

scotch[1] /skɔtʃ/ *n.m.* (*boisson*) Scotch (whisky).

scotch[2] /skɔtʃ/ *n.m.* (P.) Sellotape (P.); (*Amer.*) Scotch (tape) (P.).

scout, ∼e /skut/ *n.m. & a.* scout.

script /skript/ *n.m.* (*cinéma*) script; (*écriture*) printing.

scrupule /skrypyl/ *n.m.* scruple.

scrutin /skrytɛ̃/ *n.m.* (*vote*) ballot; (*opération électorale*) poll.

sculpt|er /skylte/ *v.t.* sculpture; (*bois*) carve (**dans,** out of). **∼eur** *n.m.* sculptor. **∼ure** *n.f.* sculpture.

se, s'[*] /sə, s/ *pron.* himself; (*femelle*) herself; (*indéfini*) oneself; (*non humain*) itself; (*pl.*) themselves; (*réciproque*) each other, one another. **se faire,** (*soi-même*) talk to o.s.; (*réciproque*) talk to each other. **se faire,** (*passif*) be done. **se laver les mains,** (*possessif*) wash one's hands.

séance /seɑ̃s/ *n.f.* session; (*cinéma, théâtre*) show.

seau (*pl.* **∼x**) /so/ *n.m.* bucket, pail.

sec, sèche /sɛk, sɛʃ/ *a.* dry; (*fruits*) dried; (*coup, bruit*) sharp; (*whisky*) neat. —*n.m.* **à ∼,** (*sans eau*) dry; (*sans argent*) broke.

sécateur /sekatœr/ *n.m.* (*pour les haies*) shears; (*petit*) secateurs.

sèche /sɛʃ/ *voir* sec. **∼ment** *adv.* drily.

sèche-cheveux /sɛʃʃəvø/ *n.m. invar.* hair-drier.

sécher /seʃe/ *v.t./i.* dry. **se ∼** *v. pr.* dry o.s.

sécheresse /seʃrɛs/ *n.f.* dryness; (*temps sec*) drought.

séchoir /seʃwar/ *n.m.* drier.

second, ∼e[1] /sgɔ̃, -d/ *a. & n.m., f.* second. —*n.m.* (*adjoint*) second in command; (*étage*) second floor. —*n.f.* second class.

seconde[2] /sgɔ̃d/ *n.f.* (*instant*) second.

secouer /skwe/ *v.t.* shake; (*poussière, torpeur*) shake off. **se ∼,** (*fam.*) (*se dépêcher*) get a move on; (*réagir*) shake o.s. up.

secour|ir /skurir/ *v.t.* assist, help. **∼iste** *n.m./f.* first-aid worker.

secours /skur/ *n.m.* assistance, help. —*n.m. pl.* (*méd.*) first aid. **au ∼!,** help! **de ∼,** emergency; (*équipe, opération*) rescue.

secousse /skus/ *n.f.* jolt, jerk; (*électrique*) shock; (*séisme*) tremor.

secr|et, ∼ète /səkrɛ, -t/ *a.* secret. —*n.m.* secret; (*discrétion*) secrecy. **en ∼,** in secret, secretly.

secrétaire /skretɛr/ *n.m./f.* secretary. —*n.m.* (*meuble*) writing-desk. **∼ d'État,** junior minister.

secrétariat /skretarja/ *n.m.* (*bureau*) secretary's office.

secte /sɛkt/ *n.f.* sect.

secteur /sɛktœr/ *n.m.* area; (*comm.*) sector; (*électr.*) mains.

section /sɛksjɔ̃/ *n.f.* section; (*transports publics*) fare stage.

sécu /seky/ *n.f.* (*fam.*) **la ∼,** the social security services.

sécuriser /sekyrize/ *v.t.* reassure.

sécurité /sekyrite/ *n.f.* security;

(*absence de danger*) safety. **en ~**, safe, secure. **S~ sociale**, social services, social security services.

sédatif /sedatif/ *n.m.* sedative.

séduire† /seduir/ *v.t.* charm; (*plaire à*) appeal to; (*abuser de*) seduce. **~ucteur, ~uctrice** *a.* seductive; *n.m., f.* seducer. **~uisant, ~uisante** *a.* attractive.

segment /sɛgmã/ *n.m.* segment.

ségrégation /segregasjɔ̃/ *n.f.* segregation.

seigle /sɛgl/ *n.m.* rye.

seigneur /sɛɲœr/ *n.m.* lord. **le S~**, the Lord.

sein /sɛ̃/ *n.m.* breast; (*fig.*) bosom.

Seine /sɛn/ *n.f.* Seine.

séisme /seism/ *n.m.* earthquake.

seiz|e /sɛz/ *a. & n.m.* sixteen. **~ième** *a. & n.m./f.* sixteenth.

séjour /seʒur/ *n.m.* stay; (*pièce*) living-room. **~ner** *v.i.* stay.

sel /sɛl/ *n.m.* salt; (*piquant*) spice.

sélection /selɛksjɔ̃/ *n.f.* selection. **~ner** /-jɔne/ *v.t.* select.

self(-service) /sɛlf(sɛrvis)/ *n.m.* self-service.

selle /sɛl/ *n.f.* saddle.

selon /slɔ̃/ *prép.* according to (**que**, whether).

semaine /səmɛn/ *n.f.* week. **en ~**, in the week.

semblable /sãblabl/ *a.* similar (**à**, to). —*n.m.* fellow (creature).

semblant /sãblã/ *n.m.* **faire ~ de**, pretend to.

sembl|er /sãble/ *v.i.* seem (**à**, to; **que**, that). **il me ~e que**, it seems to me that.

semelle /səmɛl/ *n.f.* sole.

sem|er /səme/ *v.t.* sow; (*jeter, parsemer*) strew; (*répandre*) spread; (*personne: fam.*) lose.

semestre /səmɛstr/ *n.m.* half-year; (*univ.*) semester.

semi- /səmi/ *préf.* semi-.

séminaire /seminɛr/ *n.m.* (*relig.*) seminary; (*univ.*) seminar.

semi-remorque /səmirəmɔrk/ *n.m.* articulated lorry; (*Amer.*) semi(-trailer).

semoule /səmul/ *n.f.* semolina.

sénat /sena/ *n.m.* senate. **~eur** /-tœr/ *n.m.* senator.

sénile /senil/ *a.* senile.

sens /sãs/ *n.m.* sense; (*signification*) meaning, sense; (*direction*) direction. **à ~ unique**, (*rue etc.*) one-way. **ça n'a pas de ~**, that does not make sense. **~ giratoire**, roundabout. **~ interdit**, no entry; (*rue*) one-way street.

sensation /sãsasjɔ̃/ *n.f.* feeling, sensation.

sensé /sãse/ *a.* sensible.

sensibiliser /sãsibilize/ *v.t.* **~ à**, make sensitive to.

sensib|le /sãsibl/ *a.* sensitive (**à**, to); (*appréciable*) noticeable. **~ilité** *n.f.* sensitivity.

sens|uel, ~uelle /sãsɥɛl/ *a.* sensuous; (*sexuel*) sensual. **~ualité** *n.f.* sensuousness; sensuality.

senteur /sãtœr/ *n.f.* scent.

sentier /sãtje/ *n.m.* path.

sentiment /sãtimã/ *n.m.* feeling.

sentiment|al (*m. pl.* **~aux**) /sãtimãtal, -o/ *a.* sentimental.

sentinelle /sãtinɛl/ *n.f.* sentry.

sentir† /sãtir/ *v.t.* feel; (*odeur*) smell; (*goût*) taste; (*pressentir*) sense. **~ la lavande**/*etc.*, smell of lavender/*etc.* **se ~ fier/mieux**/*etc.*, feel proud/better/*etc.*

séparé /separe/ *a.* separate; (*conjoints*) separated. **~ment** *adv.* separately.

sépar|er /separe/ *v.t.* separate; (*en deux*) split. **se ~er** *v. pr.* separate, part (**de**, from); (*se détacher*) split.

se ~er de, (se défaire de) part with. ~ation n.f. separation.

sept /sɛt/ a. & n.m. seven.

septante /sɛptɑ̃t/ a. & n.m. (en Belgique, Suisse) seventy.

septembre /sɛptɑ̃br/ n.m. September.

septième /sɛtjɛm/ a. & n.m./f. seventh.

séquence /sekɑ̃s/ n.f. sequence.

sera, serait /sra, srɛ/ voir être.

serein, ~e /sərɛ̃, -ɛn/ a. serene.

sérénité /serenite/ n.f. serenity.

sergent /sɛrʒɑ̃/ n.m. sergeant.

série /seri/ n.f. series; (d'objets) set. de ~, (véhicule etc.) standard. fabrication ou production en ~, mass production.

sérieu|x, ~se /serjø, -z/ a. serious; (digne de foi) reliable; (chances, raison) good. —n.m. seriousness. garder/perdre son ~x, keep/be unable to keep a straight face. prendre au ~x, take seriously. ~sement adv. seriously.

seringue /sərɛ̃g/ n.f. syringe.

serment /sɛrmɑ̃/ n.m. oath; (promesse) pledge.

sermon /sɛrmɔ̃/ n.m. sermon.

séropositi|f, ~ve /seropozitif, -v/ a. HIV-positive.

serpent /sɛrpɑ̃/ n.m. snake.

serpillière /sɛrpijɛr/ n.f. floorcloth.

serre[1] /sɛr/ n.f. (local) greenhouse.

serre[2] /sɛr/ n.f. (griffe) claw.

serré /sere/ a. (habit, nœud, programme) tight; (personnes) packed, crowded; (lutte, mailles) close; (cœur) heavy.

serrer /sere/ v.t. (saisir) grip; (presser) squeeze; (vis, corde, ceinture) tighten; (poing, dents) clench; (pieds) pinch. ~ qn. dans ses bras, hug. ~ qn., (vêtement) be tight on s.o. —v.i. ~ à droite,

keep over to the right. se ~ v. pr. (se rapprocher) squeeze (up) (contre, against). ~ la main à, shake hands with.

serrur|e /seryr/ n.f. lock. ~ier n.m. locksmith.

sérum /serɔm/ n.m. serum.

servante /sɛrvɑ̃t/ n.f. (maid)servant.

serveu|r, ~se /sɛrvœr, -øz/ n.m., f. waiter, waitress; (au bar) barman, barmaid.

serviable /sɛrvjabl/ a. helpful.

service /sɛrvis/ n.m. service; (fonction, temps de travail) duty; (pourboire) service (charge). ~ (non) compris, service (not) included. être de ~, be on duty. rendre un ~ à qn., do s.o. a favour. ~ d'ordre, (policiers) police. ~ après-vente, after-sales service. ~ militaire, military service.

serviette /sɛrvjɛt/ n.f. (de toilette) towel; (sac) briefcase. ~ (de table), serviette. ~ hygiénique, sanitary towel.

servir† /sɛrvir/ v.t./i. serve; (être utile) be of use, serve. ~ qn. (à table), wait on s.o. ça sert à, (outil, récipient) it is used for. ça me sert à/de, I use it for/as. ~ de, serve as, be used as. se ~ v. pr. (à table) help o.s. (de, to). se ~ de, use.

serviteur /sɛrvitœr/ n.m. servant.

ses /se/ voir son[1].

session /sesjɔ̃/ n.f. session.

seuil /sœj/ n.m. doorstep; (entrée) doorway; (fig.) threshold.

seul, ~e /sœl/ a. alone, on one's own; (unique) only. un ~ travail/etc., only one job/etc. pas un ~ ami/etc., not a single friend/etc. parler tout ~, talk to o.s. faire qch. tout ~, do sth. on one's own. —n.m., f. le ~, la ~e, the only one. **un ~, une ~e**, only one. **pas un ~**, not (a single) one.

seulement /sœlmɑ̃/ *adv.* only.

sève /sɛv/ *n.f.* sap.

sévère /sevɛr/ *a.* severe.

sevrer /səvre/ *v.t.* wean.

sexe /sɛks/ *n.m.* sex; (*organes*) sex organs.

sex|uel, ~uelle /sɛksɥɛl/ *a.* sexual. **~ualité** *n.f.* sexuality.

seyant, ~e /sɛjɑ̃, -t/ *a.* becoming.

shampooing /ʃɑ̃pwɛ̃/ *n.m.* shampoo.

short /ʃɔrt/ *n.m.* (pair of) shorts.

si[1] (**s'** before **il, ils**) /si, s/ *conj.* if; (*interrogation indirecte*) if, whether. **si on partait?**, (*suggestion*) what about going? **s'il vous ou te plaît**, please. **si oui**, if so.

si[2] /si/ *adv.* (*tellement*) so; (*oui*) yes. **un si bon repas**, such a good meal. **pas si riche que**, not as rich as.

Sicile /sisil/ *n.f.* Sicily.

sida /sida/ *n.m.* (*méd.*) AIDS.

sidérurgie /sideryrʒi/ *n.f.* iron and steel industry.

siècle /sjɛkl/ *n.m.* century; (*époque*) age.

siège /sjɛʒ/ *n.m.* seat. **~ social**, head office, headquarters.

siéger /sjeʒe/ *v.i.* (*assemblée*) sit.

sien, ~ne /sjɛ̃, sjɛn/ *pron.* **le ~, la ~ne, les ~(ne)s**, his; (*femme*) hers; (*chose*) its.

sieste /sjɛst/ *n.f.* nap. **faire la ~**, have an afternoon nap.

siffl|er /sifle/ *v.i.* whistle; (*avec un sifflet*) blow one's whistle; (*serpent, gaz*) hiss. —*v.t.* (*air*) whistle; (*chien*) whistle to ou for. **~et** /siflɛ/ *n.m.* whistle.

sifflet /siflɛ/ *n.m.* whistle.

sigle /sigl/ *n.m.* abbreviation, acronym.

sign|al (*pl.* **~aux**) /siɲal, -o/ *n.m.* signal.

signaler /siɲale/ *v.t.* indicate; (*par une sonnerie, un écriteau*) signal; (*dénoncer, mentionner*) report; (*faire remarquer*) point out.

signalisation /siɲalizasjɔ̃/ *n.f.* signalling, signposting; (*signaux*) signals.

signature /siɲatyr/ *n.f.* signature; (*action*) signing.

signe /siɲ/ *n.m.* sign; (*de ponctuation*) mark. **faire ~ à**, beckon (**de**, to); (*contacter*) contact.

signer /siɲe/ *v.t.* sign.

signification /siɲifikasjɔ̃/ *n.f.* meaning.

signifier /siɲifje/ *v.t.* mean, signify.

silenc|e /silɑ̃s/ *n.m.* silence; (*mus.*) rest. **~ieux, ~ieuse** *a.* silent.

silhouette /silwɛt/ *n.f.* outline, silhouette.

silicium /silisjɔm/ *n.m.* silicon.

sillon /sijɔ̃/ *n.m.* furrow; (*de disque*) groove.

sillonner /sijɔne/ *v.t.* criss-cross.

silo /silo/ *n.m.* silo.

simil|aire /similɛr/ *a.* similar. **~itude** *n.f.* similarity.

simple /sɛ̃pl/ *a.* simple; (*non double*) single. —*n.m.* (*tennis*) singles. **~ment** /-əmɑ̃/ *adv.* simply.

simplicité /sɛ̃plisite/ *n.f.* simplicity; (*naïveté*) simpleness.

simplif|ier /sɛ̃plifje/ *v.t.* simplify. **~ication** *n.f.* simplification.

simultané /simyltane/ *a.* simultaneous. **~ment** *adv.* simultaneously.

sincère /sɛ̃sɛr/ *a.* sincere. **~rement** *adv.* sincerely. **~érité** *n.f.* sincerity.

singe /sɛ̃ʒ/ *n.m.* monkey, ape.

singer /sɛ̃ʒe/ *v.t.* mimic, ape.

singul|ier, ~ière /sɛ̃gylje, -jɛr/ *a.* peculiar, remarkable; (*gram.*) singular. —*n.m.* (*gram.*) singular.

sinistre[1] /sinistr/ a. sinister.

sinistr|e[2] /sinistr/ n.m. disaster; (*incendie*) blaze; (*dommages*) damage. —**é** a. disaster-stricken; n.m., f. disaster victim.

sinon /sinɔ̃/ conj. (*autrement*) otherwise; (*sauf*) except (**que**, that); (*si ce n'est*) if not.

sinus /sinys/ n.m. (*anat.*) sinus.

sionisme /sjɔnism/ n.m. Zionism.

siphon /sifɔ̃/ n.m. siphon; (*de WC*) U-bend.

sirène[1] /siʀɛn/ n.f. (*appareil*) siren.

sirène[2] /siʀɛn/ n.f. (*femme*) mermaid.

sirop /siʀo/ n.m. syrup; (*boisson*) cordial.

site /sit/ n.m. setting; (*pittoresque*) beauty spot; (*emplacement*) site; (*monument etc.*) place of interest.

sitôt /sito/ adv. ~ **entré** etc., immediately after coming in/*etc.* **pas de** ~, not for a while.

situation /situasjɔ̃/ n.f. situation, position. ~ **de famille**, marital status.

situ|er /situe/ v.t. situate, locate. **se** ~**er** v. pr. (*se trouver*) be situated. ~**é** a. situated.

six /sis/ (/si/ before consonant, /siz/ before vowel) a. & n.m. six. ~**ième** /sizjɛm/ a. & n.m./f. sixth.

sketch (pl. ~**es**) /skɛtʃ/ n.m. (*théâtre*) sketch.

ski /ski/ n.m. (*patin*) ski; (*sport*) skiing. **faire du** ~, ski. ~ **de fond**, cross-country skiing. ~ **nautique**, water-skiing.

skj|ier /skje/ v.i. ski. ~**ieur** /-jœʀ/, ~**ieuse** n.m., f. skier.

slalom /slalɔm/ n.m. slalom.

slave /slav/ a. Slav. (*lang.*) Slavonic. —n.m./f. Slav.

slip /slip/ n.m. (*d'homme*) (under-)pants; (*de femme*) knickers. ~ **de bain**, (swimming) trunks. briefs.

smoking /smokiŋ/ n.m. evening *ou* dinner suit, dinner-jacket.

snack(-bar) /snak(baʀ)/ n.m. snack-bar.

snob /snɔb/ n.m./f. snob. —a. snobbish. ~**isme** n.m. snobbery.

sociable /sɔsjabl/ a. sociable.

soc|ial (m. pl. ~**iaux**) /sɔsjal, -jo/ a. social.

socialis|te /sɔsjalist/ n.m./f. socialist. ~**me** n.m. socialism.

société /sɔsjete/ n.f. society; (*compagnie, firme*) company.

sociolo|gie /sɔsjɔlɔʒi/ n.f. sociology. ~**gique** a. sociological.

socle /sɔkl/ n.m. (*de colonne, statue*) plinth; (*de lampe*) base.

socquette /sɔkɛt/ n.f. ankle sock.

soda /sɔda/ n.m. (fizzy) drink.

sodium /sɔdjɔm/ n.m. sodium.

sœur /sœʀ/ n.f. sister.

sofa /sɔfa/ n.m. sofa.

soi /swa/ pron. oneself. ~**-disant** a. invar. so-called. adv. supposedly.

soie /swa/ n.f. silk.

soif /swaf/ n.f. thirst. **avoir** ~, be thirsty. **donner** ~ **à**, make thirsty.

soigné /swaɲe/ a. tidy, neat; (*bien fait*) careful.

soigner /swaɲe/ v.t. look after, take care of; (*tenue, style*) take care over; (*maladie*) treat. **se** ~ v. pr. look after o.s.

soigneu|x, ~**se** /swaɲø, -z/ a. careful (**de**, about); (*ordonné*) tidy. ~**sement** adv. carefully.

soi-même /swamɛm/ pron. oneself.

soin /swɛ̃/ n.m. care; (*ordre*) tidiness. ~**s**, care; (*méd.*) treatment. **premiers** ~**s**, first aid.

soir /swaʀ/ n.m. evening.

soirée /swaʀe/ n.f. evening;

(*réception*) party. ～ **dansante,** dance.

soit /swa/ *voir* **être.** —*conj.* (*à savoir*) that is to say. ～ **. . . soit,** either &ddd. or.

soixantaine /swasɑ̃tɛn/ *n.f.* **une** ～ **(de),** about sixty.

soixant|e /swasɑ̃t/ *a. & n.m.* sixty. ～**e-dix** *a. & n.m.* seventy. ～**e-dixième** *a. & n.m./f.* seventieth. ～**ième** *a. & n.m./f.* sixtieth.

soja /sɔʒa/ *n.m.* (*graines*) soya beans; (*plante*) soya.

sol /sɔl/ *n.m.* ground; (*de maison*) floor; (*terrain agricole*) soil.

solaire /sɔlɛr/ *a.* solar; (*huile, filtre*) sun. **les rayons** ～**s,** the sun's rays.

soldat /sɔlda/ *n.m.* soldier.

solde¹ /sɔld/ *n.m.* (*comm.*) balance. ～**s,** (*articles*) sale goods. **en** ～ (*acheter etc.*) at sale price. **les** ～**s,** the sales.

solde² /sɔlde/ *v.t.* reduce; (*liquider*) sell off. at sale price; (*compte*) settle.

sole /sɔl/ *n.f.* (*poisson*) sole.

soleil /sɔlɛj/ *n.m.* sun; (*chaleur*) sunshine. **il y a du** ～, it is sunny.

solex /sɔlɛks/ *n.m.* (P.) moped.

solfège /sɔlfɛʒ/ *n.m.* elementary musical theory.

solid|aire /sɔlidɛr/ *a.* (*couple*) (mutually) supportive; (*ouvriers*) who show solidarity. ～**arité** *n.f.* solidarity.

solid|e /sɔlid/ *a.* solid. ～**ité** *n.f.* solidity.

soliste /sɔlist/ *n.m./f.* soloist.

solitaire /sɔlitɛr/ *a.* solitary. —*n.m./f.* (*personne*) loner.

solitude /sɔlityd/ *n.f.* solitude.

solliciter /sɔlisite/ *v.t.* request.

solo /sɔlo/ *n.m. & a. invar.* (*mus.*) solo.

solstice /sɔlstis/ *n.m.* solstice.

soluble /sɔlybl/ *a.* soluble.

solution /sɔlysjɔ̃/ *n.f.* solution.

solvable /sɔlvabl/ *a.* solvent.

solvant /sɔlvã/ *n.m.* solvent.

sombre /sɔ̃br/ *a.* dark; (*triste*) sombre.

sommaire /sɔmɛr/ *a.* summary. —*n.m.* summary.

somme¹ /sɔm/ *n.f.* sum. **en** ～, ～ **toute,** in short. **faire la** ～ **de,** add (up), total (up).

somme² /sɔm/ *n.m.* (*sommeil*) nap.

sommeil /sɔmɛj/ *n.m.* sleep; (*besoin de dormir*) drowsiness. **avoir** ～, be *ou* feel sleepy.

sommelier /sɔmǝlje/ *n.m.* wine waiter.

sommes /sɔm/ *voir* **être.**

sommet /sɔmɛ/ *n.m.* top; (*de montagne*) summit; (*de triangle*) apex; (*gloire*) height.

sommier /sɔmje/ *n.m.* base (of bed).

somnambule /sɔmnãbyl/ *n.m.* sleep-walker.

somnifère /sɔmnifɛr/ *n.m.* sleeping-pill.

somnolen|t, ～**te** /sɔmnɔlɑ̃, -t/ *a.* drowsy. ～**ce** *n.f.* drowsiness.

somnoler /sɔmnɔle/ *v.i.* doze.

sompt|ueux, ～**ueuse** /sɔ̃ptɥø, -z/ *a.* sumptuous.

son¹, sa *ou* **son*** (*pl.* **ses**) /sɔ̃, sa, se/ *a.* his; (*femme*) her; (*chose*) its; (*indéfini*) one's.

son² /sɔ̃/ *n.m.* (*bruit*) sound.

son³ /sɔ̃/ *n.m.* (*de blé*) bran.

sonate /sɔnat/ *n.f.* sonata.

sonde /sɔ̃d/ *n.f.* (*pour les forages*) drill; (*méd.*) probe.

sond|er /sɔ̃de/ *v.t.* sound; (*terrain*) drill; (*personne*) sound out. ～**age** *n.m.* ～ **(d'opinion),** (opinion) poll.

song|e /sɔ̃ʒ/ *n.m.* dream. ～**er** *v.i.* dream; *v.t.* ～**er que,** think that. ～**er à,** think about. ～**eur,** ～**euse** *a.* pensive.

sonnantes /sɔnɑ̃t/ *a.f.pl.* **à six/etc. heures** ∿, on the stroke of six/etc.

sonné ∿ *a.* (*fam.*) crazy; (*fatigué*) knocked out.

sonn|er /sɔne/ *v.t./i.* ring; (*clairon, glas*) sound; (*heure*) strike; (*domestique*) ring for. **midi** ∿**é,** well past noon. ∿**er de,** (*clairon etc.*) sound, blow.

sonnerie /sɔnri/ *n.f.* ringing; (*de clairon*) sound; (*mécanisme*) bell.

sonnette /sɔnɛt/ *n.f.* bell.

sonor|e /sɔnɔr/ *a.* resonant; (*onde, effets, etc.*) sound. ∿**ité** *n.f.* resonance; (*d'un instrument*) tone.

sonoris|er /sɔnɔrize/ *v.t.* (*salle*) wire for sound. ∿**ation** *n.f.* (*matériel*) sound equipment.

sont /sɔ̃/ *voir* **être.**

sophistiqué /sɔfistike/ *a.* sophisticated.

sorbet /sɔrbɛ/ *n.m.* sorbet.

sorc|ier /sɔrsje/ *n.m.* sorcerer. ∿**ière** *n.f.* witch.

sordide /sɔrdid/ *a.* sordid; (*lieu*) squalid.

sort /sɔr/ *n.m.* (*destin, hasard*) fate; (*condition*) lot; (*maléfice*) spell. **tirer (qch.) au** ∿, draw lots (for sth.).

sorte /sɔrt/ *n.f.* sort, kind. **faire en** ∿ **que,** see to it that.

sortie /sɔrti/ *n.f.* departure, exit; (*porte*) exit; (*promenade, dîner*) outing; (*invective*) outburst; (*parution*) appearance; (*de disque, gaz*) release; (*d'un ordinateur*) output. ∿**s,** (*argent*) outgoings.

sortir† /sɔrtir/ *v.i.* (*aux. être*) go out, leave; (*venir*) come out; (*aller au spectacle etc.*) go out; (*livre, film*) come out. ∿ **de,** (*pièce*) leave. —*v.t.* (*aux. avoir*) take out; (*livre, modèle*) bring out; (*dire:*

fam.) come out with. **(s')en** ∿, get out of an awkward situation.

sot, ∿**te** /so, sɔt/ *a.* foolish.

sottise /sɔtiz/ *n.f.* foolishness; (*action, remarque*) foolish thing.

sou /su/ *n.m.* ∿**s,** money. **pas un** ∿, not a penny.

souche /suʃ/ *n.f.* (*d'arbre*) stump; (*de famille, vigne*) stock; (*de carnet*) counterfoil.

souci¹ /susi/ *n.m.* (*inquiétude*) worry; (*préoccupation*) concern. **se faire du** ∿, worry.

souci² /susi/ *n.m.* (*plante*) marigold.

soucieu|x, ∿**se** /susjø, -z/ *a.* concerned (**de,** about).

soucoupe /sukup/ *n.f.* saucer. ∿ **volante,** flying saucer.

soudain, ∿**e** /sudɛ̃, -ɛn/ *a.* sudden. —*adv.* suddenly.

soude /sud/ *n.f.* soda.

souder /sude/ *v.t.* solder, (*à la flamme*) weld.

souffle /sufl/ *n.m.* blow, puff; (*haleine*) breath; (*respiration*) breathing; (*explosion*) blast; (*vent*) breath of air.

soufflé /sufle/ *n.m.* (*culin.*) soufflé.

souffl|er /sufle/ *v.i.* blow; (*haleter*) puff. —*v.t.* (*bougie*) blow out; (*poussière, fumée*) blow; (*par explosion*) destroy.

souffrance /sufrɑ̃s/ *n.f.* suffering.

souffrir† /sufrir/ *v.i.* suffer (**de,** from). —*v.t.* (*endurer*) suffer.

soufre /sufr/ *n.m.* sulphur.

souhait /swɛ/ *n.m.* wish. **nos** ∿**s de,** (*vœux*) good wishes for. **à vos** ∿**s!,** bless you!

souhait|er /swɛte/ *v.t.* (*bonheur etc.*) wish for. ∿**er qch. à qn.,** wish s.o. sth. ∿**er que/faire,** hope that/to do. ∿**able** /swɛtabl/ *a.* desirable.

souiller /suje/ *v.t.* soil.

soûl, ∿**e** /su, sul/ *a.* drunk.

soulag|er /sulaʒe/ v.t. relieve. **~ement** n.m. relief.

soûler /sule/ v.t. make drunk. **se ~** v. pr. get drunk.

soulèvement /sulɛvmɑ̃/ n.m. uprising.

soulever /sulve/ v.t. lift, raise. **se ~** v. pr. lift ou raise o.s. up; (se révolter) rise up.

soulier /sulje/ n.m. shoe.

souligner /suliɲe/ v.t. underline; (taille, yeux) emphasize.

soumettre† /sumɛtr/ v.t. (dompter, assujettir) subject (à, to); (présenter) submit (à, to). **se ~** v. pr. submit (à, to).

soupape /supap/ n.f. valve.

soupçon /supsɔ̃/ n.m. suspicion. **un ~ de,** (fig.) a touch of. **~ner** /-ɔne/ v.t. suspect. **~neux** /-ɔnø, -z/ a. suspicious.

soupe /sup/ n.f. soup.

souper /supe/ n.m. supper. —v.i. have supper.

soupière /supjɛr/ n.f. (soup) tureen.

soupir /supir/ n.m. sigh. **pousser un ~,** heave a sigh. **~er** v.i. sigh.

souple /supl/ a. supple; (règlement, caractère) flexible. **~sse** /-ɛs/ n.f. suppleness; flexibility.

source /surs/ n.f. source; (eau) spring. **~ thermale,** hot spring.

sourcil /sursi/ n.m. eyebrow.

sourd, ~e /sur, -d/ a. deaf; (bruit, douleur) dull; (inquiétude, conflit) silent, hidden. —n.m., f. deaf person.

sourire /surir/ n.m. smile. —v.i. smile (à, at).

souris /suri/ n.f. mouse.

sournoi, ~e /surnwa, -z/ a. sly, underhand.

sous /su/ prép. under, beneath. **~ la main,** handy. **~ la pluie,** in the rain. **~ peu,** shortly. **~ terre,** underground.

sous- /su/ préf. (subordination) sub-; (insuffisance) under-.

souscri|re /suskrir/ v.i. **~ire à,** subscribe to. **~iption** n.f. subscription.

sous-direct|eur, ~rice /sudirɛktœr, -ris/ n.m., f. assistant manager.

sous-entend|re /suzɑ̃tɑ̃dr/ v.t. imply. **~u** n.m. insinuation.

sous-estimer /suzɛstime/ v.t. underestimate.

sous-jacent, ~e /suʒasɑ̃, -t/ a. underlying.

sous-marin, ~e /sumarɛ̃, -in/ a. underwater. —n.m. submarine.

sous-préfecture /suprefɛktyr/ n.f. sub-prefecture.

sous-produit /suprɔdɥi/ n.m. by-product.

soussigné, ~e /susiɲe/ a. & n.m., f. undersigned.

sous-sol /susɔl/ n.m. (cave) basement.

sous-titr|e /sutitr/ n.m. subtitle. **~er** v.t. subtitle.

soustrai|re† /sustrɛr/ v.t. remove; (déduire) subtract. **~action** n.f. (déduction) subtraction.

sous-trait|er /sutrete/ v.t. subcontract. **~ant** n.m. subcontractor.

sous-vêtement /suvɛtmɑ̃/ n.m. undergarment. **~s,** underwear.

soute /sut/ n.f. (de bateau) hold. **~ à charbon,** coal-bunker.

soutenir† /sutnir/ v.t. support; (fortifier, faire durer) sustain; (résister à) withstand.

souterrain, ~e /sutɛrɛ̃, -ɛn/ a. underground. —n.m. underground passage, subway.

soutien /sutjɛ̃/ n.m. support. **~gorge** (pl. **~s-gorge**) n.m. bra.

soutirer /sutire/ v.t. **~ à qn.,** extract from s.o.

souvenir[1] /suvnir/ n.m. memory, recollection; (*objet*) memento; (*cadeau*) souvenir. **en ~ de,** in memory of.

souvenir[2]† (se) /(sə)suvnir/ v. pr. **se ~ de,** remember. **se ~ que,** remember that.

souvent /suvã/ adv. often.

souverain, ~e /suvrɛ̃, -ɛn/ —n.m., f. sovereign. **~eté** /-ɛnte/ n.f. sovereignty.

soviétique /sɔvjetik/ a. Soviet. —n.m./f. Soviet citizen.

soyeu|x, ~se /swajø, -z/ a. silky.

spacieu|x, ~se /spasjø, -z/ a. spacious.

spaghetti /spageti/ n.m. pl. spaghetti.

sparadrap /sparadra/ n.m. sticking-plaster.

spat|ial (m. pl. **~iaux**) /spasjal, -jo/ a. space.

spatule /spatyl/ n.f. spatula.

speaker, ~ine /spikœr, -rin/ n.m., f. announcer.

spéc|ial (m. pl. **~iaux**) /spesjal, -jo/ a. special; (*singulier*) peculiar. **~ialement** adv. especially; (*exprès*) specially.

spécialis|er (se) /(sə)spesjalize/ v. pr. specialize (**dans,** in). **~ation** n.f. specialization.

spécialiste /spesjalist/ n.m./f. specialist.

spécialité /spesjalite/ n.f. speciality.

spécifier /spesifje/ v.t. specify. **~ication** n.f. specification.

spécifique /spesifik/ a. specific.

spécimen /spesimen/ n.m. specimen.

spectacle /spɛktakl/ n.m. sight, spectacle; (*représentation*) show.

spectaculaire /spɛktakylɛr/ a. spectacular.

specta|teur, ~trice /spɛktatœr, -tris/ n.m., f. onlooker; (*sport*)

spectator. **les ~teurs,** (*théâtre*) the audience.

spectre /spɛktr/ n.m. (*revenant*) spectre; (*images*) spectrum.

spécul|er /spekyle/ v.i. speculate. **~ateur, ~atrice** n.m., f. speculator. **~ation** n.f. speculation.

spéléologie /speleɔlɔʒi/ n.f. cave exploration, pot-holing.

sperme /spɛrm/ n.m. sperm.

sph|ère /sfɛr/ n.f. sphere. **~érique** a. spherical.

sphinx /sfɛ̃ks/ n.m. sphinx.

spirale /spiral/ n.f. spiral.

spirituel, ~le /spirityɛl/ a. spiritual; (*amusant*) witty.

spiritueux /spirityø/ n.m. (*alcool*) spirit.

splend|ide /splãdid/ a. splendid. **~eur** n.f. splendour.

sponsor /spɔ̃sɔr/ n.m. sponsor. **~iser** v.t. sponsor.

spontané ~ /spɔ̃tane/ a. spontaneous. **~ité** n.f. spontaneity. **~ment** adv. spontaneously.

sport /spɔr/ n.m. sport. —a. invar. (*vêtements*) casual.

sporti|f, ~ve /spɔrtif, -v/ a. sporting; (*physique*) athletic; (*résultats*) sports. —n.m. sportsman. —n.f. sportswoman.

spot /spɔt/ n.m. spotlight; (*publicitaire*) ad.

spray /sprɛ/ n.m. spray; (*méd.*) inhaler.

square /skwar/ n.m. (public) garden.

squash /skwaʃ/ n.m. squash.

squelette /skəlɛt/ n.m. skeleton.

stabiliser /stabilize/ v.t. stabilize.

stab|le /stabl/ a. stable. **~ilité** n.f. stability.

stade[1] /stad/ n.m. (*sport*) stadium.

stade[2] /stad/ n.m. (*phase*) stage.

stag|e /staʒ/ n.m. course. **~iaire**

a. & n.m./f. course member; (*apprenti*) trainee.

stand /stɑ̃d/ *n.m.* stand, stall.

standard[1] /stɑ̃dar/ *n.m.* switchboard. **~iste** /-dist/ *n.m./f.* switchboard operator.

standard[2] /stɑ̃dar/ *a. invar.* standard.

standing /stɑ̃diŋ/ *n.m.* status, standing. **de ~,** (*hôtel etc.*) luxury.

star /star/ *n.f.* (*actrice*) star.

starter /starter/ *n.m.* (*auto.*) choke.

station /stasjɔ̃/ *n.f.* station; (*halte*) stop. **~ balnéaire,** seaside resort. **~ de taxis,** taxi rank. **~-service** (*pl.* **~s-service**) *n.f.* service station. **~ thermale,** spa.

stationn|er /stasjɔne/ *v.i.* park. **~ement** *n.m.* parking.

statistique /statistik/ *n.f.* statistic; (*science*) statistics. —*a.* statistical.

statue /staty/ *n.f.* statue.

statut /staty/ *n.m.* status. **~s,** (*règles*) statutes.

steak /stɛk/ *n.m.* steak.

sténo /steno/ *n.f.* (*personne*) stenographer; (*sténographie*) shorthand.

stéréo /stereo/ *n.f. & a. invar.* stereo.

stéril|e /steril/ *a.* sterile. **~ité** *n.f.* sterility.

stérilet /sterilɛ/ *n.m.* coil, IUD.

stérilis|er /sterilize/ *v.t.* sterilize. **~ation** *n.f.* sterilization.

stéroïde /steroid/ *a. & n.m.* steroid.

stimul|er /stimyle/ *v.t.* stimulate. **~ant** *n.m.* stimulus; (*médicament*) stimulant. **~ateur cardiaque,** pacemaker.

stock /stɔk/ *n.m.* stock. **~er** *v.t.* stock. **~iste** *n.m.* stockist; (*Amer.*) dealer.

stop /stɔp/ *int.* stop. —*n.m.* stop sign; (*feu arrière*) brake light. **faire du ~,** (*fam.*) hitch-hike.

stopper /stɔpe/ *v.t./i.* stop.

store /stɔr/ *n.m.* blind.

strapontin /strapɔ̃tɛ̃/ *n.m.* folding seat, jump seat.

stratég|ie /strateʒi/ *n.f.* strategy. **~ique** *a.* strategic.

stress /stres/ *n.* stress, stress. **~ant** *a.* stressful. **~er** *v.t.* put under stress.

strict /strikt/ *a.* strict; (*tenue, vérité*) plain. **le ~ minimum,** the absolute minimum. **~ement** *adv.* strictly.

strip-tease /striptiz/ *n.m.* striptease.

strophe /strɔf/ *n.f.* stanza, verse.

structur|e /stryktyr/ *n.f.* structure. **~er** *v.t.* structure.

studieu|x /stydjø/ a. (*~se* /stydjø, -z/ *a.*) studious.

studio /stydjo/ *n.m.* (*d'artiste, de télévision, etc.*) studio; (*logement*) studio flat, bed-sitter.

stupéf|ait, **~aite** /stypefɛ, -t/ *a.* amazed. **~action** *n.f.* amazement.

stupid|e /stypid/ *a.* stupid. **~ité** *n.f.* stupidity.

style /stil/ *n.m.* style.

styliste /stilist/ *n.m./f.* fashion designer.

stylo /stilo/ *n.m.* pen. **~ (à) bille,** ball-point pen. **~ (à) encre,** fountain-pen.

su /sy/ *voir* **savoir.**

subconscient, **~e** /sypkɔ̃sjɑ̃, -t/ *a. & n.m.* subconscious.

subir /sybir/ *v.t.* suffer; (*traitement, expériences*) undergo.

subit, **~e** /sybi, -t/ *a.* sudden. **~ement** /-tmɑ̃/ *adv.* suddenly.

subjecti|f, **~ve** /sybʒɛktif, -v/ *a.* subjective. **~vité** *n.f.* subjectivity.

subjonctif /sybʒɔ̃ktif/ *a. & n.m.* subjunctive.

sublime /syblim/ *a.* sublime.

submerger /sybmɛrʒe/ *v.t.* submerge; *(fig.)* overwhelm.

subside /sybzid/ *n.m.* grant.

subsist|er /sybziste/ *v.i.* subsist; *(durer, persister)* exist. ∼ance *n.f.* subsistence.

substance /sypstɑ̃s/ *n.f.* substance.

substantif /sypstɑ̃tif/ *n.m.* noun.

substit|uer /sypstitɥe/ *v.t.* substitute (à, for). se ∼uer à, *(remplacer)* substitute for; *(évincer)* take over from. ∼ution *n.f.* substitution.

subtil /syptil/ *a.* subtle. ∼ité *n.f.* subtlety.

subvenir /sybvənir/ *v.i.* ∼ à, provide for.

subvention /sybvɑ̃sjɔ̃/ *n.f.* subsidy. ∼ner /-jɔne/ *v.t.* subsidize.

subversi|f, ∼ve /sybvɛrsif, -v/ *a.* subversive.

subversion /sybvɛrsjɔ̃/ *n.f.* subversion.

succéder /syksede/ *v.i.* ∼ à, succeed. se ∼ *v. pr.* succeed one another.

succès /syksɛ/ *n.m.* success. avoir du ∼, be a success.

successeur /syksesœr/ *n.m.* successor.

successi|f, ∼ve /syksesif, -v/ *a.* successive. ∼vement *adv.* successively.

succession /syksesjɔ̃/ *n.f.* succession; *(jurid.)* inheritance.

succulent, ∼e /sykylɑ̃, -t/ *a.* succulent.

succursale /sykyrsal/ *n.f.* (*comm.*) branch.

sucer /syse/ *v.t.* suck.

sucette /sysɛt/ *n.f.* (*bonbon*) lollipop; (*tétine*) dummy.

sucr|e /sykr/ *n.m.* sugar. ∼ier *n.m.* (*récipient*) sugar-bowl.

sucr|er /sykre/ *v.t.* sugar, sweeten. ∼é *a.* sweet; (*additionné de sucre*) sweetened.

sucreries /sykrəri/ *n.f. pl.* sweets.

sud /syd/ *n.m.* south. —*a. invar.* south; (*partie*) southern; (*direction*) southerly. ∼-africain, ∼-africaine *a. & n.m., f.* South African. ∼-est *n.m.* south-east. ∼-ouest *n.m.* south-west.

Suède /sɥɛd/ *n.f.* Sweden.

suédois, ∼e /sɥedwa, -z/ *a.* Swedish. —*n.m., f.* Swede. —*n.m.* (*lang.*) Swedish.

sueur /sɥœr/ *n.f.* sweat. en ∼, sweating.

suff|ire† /syfir/ *v.i.* be enough (à **qn.**, for s.o.). il ∼it de faire, one only has to do. ∼ire à, (*besoin*) satisfy.

suffis|ant, ∼ante /syfizɑ̃, -t/ *a.* sufficient; (*vaniteux*) conceited. ∼amment *adv.* sufficiently. ∼ance *n.f.* sufficient.

suffixe /syfiks/ *n.m.* suffix.

suffoquer /syfɔke/ *v.t./i.* choke, suffocate.

suffrage /syfraʒ/ *n.m.* (*voix: pol.*) vote; (*modalité*) suffrage.

sugg|érer /sygʒere/ *v.t.* suggest. ∼estion /-ʒɛstjɔ̃/ *n.f.* suggestion.

suicide /sɥisid/ *n.m.* suicide.

suicider (se) /(sə)sɥiside/ *v. pr.* commit suicide.

suis /sɥi/ *voir* être, suivre.

Suisse /sɥis/ *n.f.* Switzerland.

suisse /sɥis/ *a. & n.m.* Swiss. ∼sse /-ɛs/ *n.f.* Swiss (woman).

suite /sɥit/ *n.f.* continuation, rest; (*d'un film*) sequel; (*série*) series; (*appartement, escorte*) suite; (*résultat*) consequence. ∼s, (*de maladie*) after-effects. à la ∼, de ∼, (*successivement*) in succession. faire ∼ (à), follow. par la

∼, afterwards. **∼ à votre lettre du,** further to your letter of the.

suivant[1], **∼e** /sɥivã, -t/ *a.* following, next. —*n.m., f.* following *ou* next person.

suivant[2] /sɥivã/ *prép.* (*selon*) according to.

suivi /sɥivi/ *a.* steady, sustained; (*cohérent*) consistent. **peu/très ∼,** (*cours*) poorly-/well-attended.

suivre† /sɥivr/ *v.t./i.* follow; (*comprendre*) keep up (with), follow. **se ∼** *v. pr.* follow each other. **faire ∼** (*courrier etc.*) forward.

sujet /sɥʒɛ/ *n.m.* (*matière, individu*) subject; (*motif*) cause; (*gram.*) subject. **au ∼ de,** about.

sulfurique /sylfyrik/ *a.* sulphuric.

super /sypɛr/ *n.m.* (*essence*) four-star. —*a. invar.* (*fam.*) great. —*adv.* (*fam.*) ultra, fantastically.

superbe /sypɛrb/ *a.* superb.

supérette /sypɛrɛt/ *n.f.* mini-market.

superficie /sypɛrfisi/ *n.f.* area.

superficiel, ∼le /sypɛrfisjɛl/ *a.* superficial.

superflu /sypɛrfly/ *a.* superfluous. —*n.m.* (*excédent*) surplus.

supérieur, ∼e /sypɛrjœr/ *a.* (*plus haut*) upper; (*quantité, nombre*) greater (**à,** than); (*études, principe*) higher (**à,** than); (*meilleur, hautain*) superior (**à,** to). —*n.m., f.* superior.

supériorité /sypɛrjɔrite/ *n.f.* superiority.

supermarché /sypɛrmarʃe/ *n.m.* supermarket.

superposer /sypɛrpoze/ *v.t.* superimpose.

superproduction /sypɛrprɔdyksjɔ̃/ *n.f.* (*film*) spectacular.

superstition /sypɛrstisjɔ̃/ *n.f.* superstition. **∼ieux, ∼ieuse** *a.* superstitious.

superviser /sypɛrvize/ *v.t.* supervise.

suppléer /syplee/ *v.t.* (*remplacer*) replace; (*ajouter*) supply. —*v.i.* **∼ à,** (*compenser*) make up for.

supplément /syplemã/ *n.m.* (*argent*) extra charge; (*de frites, légumes*) extra portion. **en ∼,** extra. **un ∼ de,** (*travail etc.*) extra. **payer pour un ∼ de bagages,** pay extra for excess luggage. **∼aire** /-tɛr/ *a.* extra, additional.

supplice /syplis/ *n.m.* torture.

supplier /syplije/ *v.t.* beg, beseech (**de,** to).

support /sypɔr/ *n.m.* support.

supporter[1] /sypɔrte/ *v.t.* (*endurer*) bear; (*subir*) suffer; (*soutenir*) support; (*résister à*) withstand. **∼able** *a.* bearable.

supporter[2] /sypɔrtɛr/ *n.m.* (*sport*) supporter.

supposer /sypoze/ *v.t.* suppose; (*impliquer*) imply. **∼ition** *n.f.* supposition.

suppositoire /sypozitwar/ *n.m.* suppository.

suppr|imer /syprime/ *v.t.* get rid of, remove; (*annuler*) cancel; (*mot*) delete.

suprême /syprɛm/ *a.* supreme.

sur /syr/ *prép.* on, upon; (*pardessus*) over; (*au sujet de*) about, on; (*proportion*) out of; (*mesure*) by. **aller/tourner/etc. ∼,** go/turn/etc. towards. **mettre/jeter/etc. ∼,** put/throw/etc. on to. **∼-le-champ** *adv.* immediately. **∼ mesure,** made to measure. **∼ place,** on the spot. **∼ce,** hereupon.

sur- /syr/ *préf.* over-.

sûr /syr/ *a.* certain, sure; (*sans danger*) safe; (*digne de confiance*) reliable; (*main*) steady; (*jugement*) sound.

surcharge /syrʃarʒ/ *n.f.* overloading; (*poids*) extra load.

sureau (*pl.* ~x) /syro/ *n.m.* (*arbre*) elder.

sûrement /syrmɑ̃/ *adv.* certainly; (*sans danger*) safely.

surestimer /syrɛstime/ *v.t.* overestimate.

sûreté /syrte/ *n.f.* safety; (*garantie*) surety; (*d'un geste*) steadiness. **être en ~**, be safe. **S~ (nationale)**, division of French Ministère de l'Intérieur in charge of police.

surexcité /syrɛksite/ *a.* very excited.

surf /syrf/ *n.m.* surfing.

surface /syrfas/ *n.f.* surface. **en ~**, (*fig.*) superficially.

surgelé /syrʒəle/ *a.* (deep-)frozen. **(aliments) ~s**, frozen food.

surgir /syrʒir/ *v.i.* appear (suddenly); (*difficulté*) arise.

surlendemain /syrlɑ̃dmɛ̃/ *n.m.* le **~**, two days later. le **~ de**, two days after.

surligneur /syrliɲœr/ *n.m.* highlighter (pen).

surmen|er /syrmane/ *v.t.*, **se ~er** *v. pr.* overwork. **~age** *n.m.* overworking; (*méd.*) overwork.

surmonter /syrmɔ̃te/ *v.t.* (*vaincre*) overcome, surmount; (*être au-dessus de*) surmount, top.

surnager /syrnaʒe/ *v.i.* float.

surnaturel, ~le /syrnatyrɛl/ *a.* supernatural.

surnom /syrnɔ̃/ *n.m.* nickname.

surplomb /syrplɔ̃/ *n.m.* en **~**, overhanging. **~er** /-be/ *v.t./i.* overhang.

surplus /syrply/ *n.m.* surplus.

surpr|endre /syrprɑ̃dr/ *v.t.* (*étonner*) surprise; (*prendre au dépourvu*) catch, surprise; (*entendre*) overhear. **~enant,**

~enante *a.* surprising. **~is, ~ise** *a.* surprised (**de**, at).

surprise /syrpriz/ *n.f.* surprise. **~-partie** (*pl.* **~s-parties**) *n.f.* party.

surréalisme /syrrealism/ *n.m.* surrealism.

sursaut /syrso/ *n.m.* start, jump. **~er** /-te/ *v.i.* start, jump.

sursis /syrsi/ *n.m.* reprieve. **deux ans (de prison) avec ~**, a two-year suspended sentence.

surtaxe /syrtaks/ *n.f.* surcharge.

surtout /syrtu/ *adv.* especially, mainly; (*avant tout*) above all. **~ pas**, certainly not.

surveillant, ~e /syrvejɑ̃, -t/ *n.m., f.* (*de prison*) warder; (*au lycée*) supervisor (in charge of discipline).

surveill|er /syrveje/ *v.t.* watch; (*travaux, élèves*) supervise. **~ance** *n.f.* watch; supervision; (*de la police*) surveillance.

survenir /syrvanir/ *v.i.* occur, come about; (*personne*) turn up; (*événement*) take place.

survêtement /syrvɛtmɑ̃/ *n.m.* (*sport*) track suit.

surviv|re /syrvivr/ *v.i.* survive. **~re à**, (*conflit etc.*) survive; (*personne*) outlive. **~ant, ~ante** *a.* surviving; *n.m., f.* survivor.

survoler /syrvɔle/ *v.t.* fly over.

susceptible /sysɛptibl/ *a.* touchy. **~ilité** *n.f.* susceptibility.

susciter /syiste/ *v.t.* (*éveiller*) arouse; (*occasionner*) create.

suspect, ~e /syspɛ, -ɛkt/ *a.* (*témoignage*) suspect; (*individu*) suspicious. **~ de**, suspected of. **—n.m., f.** suspect. **~er** /-ɛkte/ *v.t.* suspect.

suspendre /syspɑ̃dr/ *v.t.* (*arrêter*) suspend; (*accrocher*) hang (up).

suspense /syspɑ̃s/ *n.m.* suspense.

suspicion /syspisjɔ̃/ *n.f.* suspicion.

suture /sytyr/ *n.f.* **point de ～**, stitch.

svelte /svɛlt/ *a.* slender.

S.V.P. *abrév. voir* **s'il vous plaît.**

sweat-shirt /switʃœrt/ *n.m.* sweat-shirt.

syllabe /silab/ *n.f.* syllable.

symbol|e /sɛbɔl/ *n.m.* symbol. **～ique** *a.* symbolic(al).

symétr|ie /simetri/ *n.f.* symmetry. **～ique** *a.* symmetrical.

sympa /sɛpa/ *a. invar.* (*fam.*) nice. **sois ～**, be a pal.

sympath|ie /sɛpati/ *n.f.* (*goût*) liking; (*affinité*) affinity; (*condoléances*) sympathy. **～ique** *a.* nice, pleasant.

symphon|ie /sɛfɔni/ *n.f.* symphony. **～ique** *a.* symphonic; (*orchestre*) symphony.

symptôme /sɛptom/ *n.m.* symptom.

synagogue /sinagɔg/ *n.f.* synagogue.

syncope /sɛkɔp/ *n.f.* (*méd.*) blackout.

syndic /sɛdik/ *n.m.* **～ (d'immeuble),** managing agent.

syndic|at /sɛdika/ *n.m.* (trade) union. **～at d'initiative,** tourist office. **～al** (*m. pl.* **～aux**) *a.* (trade-)union. **～aliste** *n.m./f.* trade-unionist; *a.* (trade-)union.

syndiqué, ～e /sɛdike/ *n.m., f.* (trade-)union member.

synonyme /sinɔnim/ *a.* synonymous. **—***n.m.* synonym.

synthétique /sɛtetik/ *a.* synthetic.

synthé(tiseur) /sɛte(tizœr)/ *n.m.* synthesizer.

syphilis /sifilis/ *n.f.* syphilis.

Syrie /siri/ *n.f.* Syria.

syrien, ～ne /sirjɛ̃, -jɛn/ *a. & n.m., f.* Syrian.

systématique /sistematik/ *a.* systematic.

système /sistɛm/ *n.m.* system.

T

t' /t/ *voir* **te.**

ta /ta/ *voir* **ton**[1].

tabac /taba/ *n.m.* tobacco; (*magasin*) tobacconist's shop.

table /tabl/ *n.f.* table. **à ～!,** come and eat! **～ de nuit,** bedside table. **～ des matières,** table of contents. **～ roulante,** (tea-)trolley.

tableau (*pl.* **～x**) /tablo/ *n.m.* picture; (*peinture*) painting; (*panneau*) board; (*graphique*) chart; (*liste*) list. **～ (noir),** blackboard. **～ d'affichage,** notice-board. **～ de bord,** dashboard.

tablette /tablɛt/ *n.f.* shelf. **～ de chocolat,** bar of chocolate.

tablier /tablije/ *n.m.* apron.

tabouret /tabure/ *n.m.* stool.

tabulateur /tabylatœr/ *n.m.* tabulator.

tache /taʃ/ *n.f.* mark, spot; (*salissure*) stain. **faire ～ d'huile,** spread. **～ de rousseur,** freckle.

tâche /taʃ/ *n.f.* task, job.

tacher /taʃe/ *v.t.* stain. **se ～** *v. pr.* (*personne*) get stains on one's clothes.

tâcher /taʃe/ *v.i.* **～ de faire,** try to do.

tact /takt/ *n.m.* tact.

tactique /taktik/ *a.* tactical. **—***n.f.* tactics. **une ～,** a tactic.

taie /tɛ/ *n.f.* **～ d'oreiller,** pillowcase.

taille[1] /taj/ *n.f.* (*milieu du corps*) waist; (*hauteur*) height; (*grandeur*) size. **de ～,** sizeable.

taill|e[2] /taj/ *n.f.* cutting; pruning; (*forme*) cut. **～er** *v.t.* cut; (*arbre*) prune; (*crayon*) sharpen; (*vêtement*) cut out. **~e-crayon(s)** *n.m. invar.* pencil-sharpener.

tailleur /tɑjœr/ *n.m.* tailor; (*costume*) lady's suit. **en ~**, cross-legged.

taillis /tɑji/ *n.m.* copse.

taire† /tɛr/ *v.t.* say nothing about. **se ~** *v. pr.* be silent *ou* quiet; (*devenir silencieux*) fall silent. **faire ~**, silence.

talc /talk/ *n.m.* talcum powder.

talent /talɑ̃/ *n.m.* talent.

talon /talɔ̃/ *n.m.* heel; (*de chèque*) stub.

talus /taly/ *n.m.* embankment.

tambour /tɑ̃bur/ *n.m.* drum; (*personne*) drummer; (*porte*) revolving door.

tamis /tami/ *n.m.* sieve. **~er** /-ze/ *v.t.* sieve.

Tamise /tamiz/ *n.f.* Thames.

tampon /tɑ̃pɔ̃/ *n.m.* (*pour boucher*) plug; (*ouate*) wad, pad; (*timbre*) stamp; (*de train*) buffer. **~ (hygiénique)**, tampon.

tamponner /tɑ̃pɔne/ *v.t.* (*timbrer*) stamp; (*plaie*) dab.

tandem /tɑ̃dɛm/ *n.m.* (*bicyclette*) tandem; (*personnes: fig.*) duo.

tandis que /tɑ̃dik(ə)/ *conj.* while.

tanguer /tɑ̃ge/ *v.i.* pitch.

tank /tɑ̃k/ *n.m.* tank.

tann|er /tane/ *v.t.* tan. **~é** *a.* (*visage*) tanned, weather-beaten.

tant /tɑ̃/ *adv.* (*travailler, manger, etc.*) so much. **~ (de)**, (*quantité*) so much; (*nombre*) so many. **~ que**, as long as **~ mieux!**, fine!, all the better! **~ pis!**, too bad!

tante /tɑ̃t/ *n.f.* aunt.

tantôt /tɑ̃to/ *adv.* sometimes; (*cet après-midi*) this afternoon.

tapage /tapaʒ/ *n.m.* din.

tapant, **~e** /tapɑ̃, -t/ *a.* **à deux/trois/etc. heures ~es** at exactly two/three/etc. o'clock.

tape /tap/ *n.f.* slap.

taper /tape/ *v.t.* bang; (*enfant*) slap; (*emprunter: fam.*) touch for money. **~ (à la machine)**, type. —*v.i.* (*cogner*) bang; (*soleil*) beat down.

tapis /tapi/ *n.m.* carpet; (*petit*) rug; (*aux cartes*) baize. **~ de bain**, bath mat. **~ roulant**, (*pour objets*) conveyor belt.

tapiss|er /tapise/ *v.t.* (*wall*)paper; (*fig.*) cover (**de**, with). **~erie** *n.f.* tapestry; (*papier peint*) wallpaper.

tapoter /tapɔte/ *v.t.* tap, pat.

taquin, **~e** /takɛ̃, -in/ *a.* fond of teasing. —*n.m.*, *f.* tease(r). **~er** /-ine/ *v.t.* tease.

tard /tar/ *adv.* late. **au plus ~**, at the latest. **plus ~**, later.

tard|er /tarde/ *v.i.* be a long time coming. **~ (à faire)**, take a long time (doing), delay (doing). **sans (plus) ~er**, without (further) delay.

tardi|f, **~ve** /tardif, -v/ *a.* late; (*regrets*) belated.

tare /tar/ *n.f.* (*défaut*) defect.

targette /tarʒɛt/ *n.f.* bolt.

tarif /tarif/ *n.m.* tariff; (*de train, taxi*) fare. **~s postaux**, postage *ou* postal rates. **~aire** *a.* tariff.

tarir /tarir/ *v.t./i.*, **se ~** *v. pr.* dry up.

tartare /tartar/ *a.* (*culin.*) tartar.

tarte /tart/ *n.f.* tart.

tartin|e /tartin/ *n.f.* slice of bread. **~e beurrée**, slice of bread and butter. **~er** *v.t.* spread.

tartre /tartr/ *n.m.* (*bouilloire*) fur, calcium deposit; (*dents*) tartar.

tas /tɑ/ *n.m.* pile, heap. **un** *ou* **des ~ de**, (*fam.*) lots of.

tasse /tɑs/ *n.f.* cup. **~ à thé**, teacup.

tasser /tɑse/ *v.t.* pack, squeeze; (*terre*) pack (down).

tâter /tate/ v.t. feel; (fig.) sound out. —v.i. ～ **de**, try out.

tátonn|er /tatɔne/ v.i. grope about. **～ements** n.m. pl. (essais) trial and error.

tâtons (à) /(a)tatɔ̃/ adv. **avancer ou marcher à ～**, grope one's way along.

tatou|er /tatwe/ v.t. tattoo. **～age** n.m. (dessin) tattoo.

taudis /todi/ n.m. hovel.

taule /tol/ n.f. (fam.) prison.

taupe /top/ n.f. mole.

taureau (pl. **～x**) /tɔro/ n.m. bull. **le T～**, Taurus.

taux /to/ n.m. rate.

taverne /tavɛrn/ n.f. tavern.

tax|e /taks/ n.f. tax. **～e sur la valeur ajoutée**, value added tax. **～er** v.t. tax; (produit) fix the price of.

taxi /taksi/ n.m. taxi(-cab); (personne: fam.) taxi-driver.

taxiphone /taksifɔn/ n.m. pay phone.

Tchécoslovaquie /tʃekɔslɔvaki/ n.f. Czechoslovakia.

tchèque /tʃɛk/ a. & n.m./f. Czech.

te, t'* /tə, t/ pron. you; (indirect) (to) you; (réfléchi) yourself.

technicien, ～ne /tɛknisjɛ̃, -jɛn/ n.m., f. technician.

technique /tɛknik/ a. technical. —n.f. technique. **～ment** adv. technically.

technolog|ie /tɛknɔlɔʒi/ n.f. technology. **～ique** a. technological.

teck /tɛk/ n.m. teak.

tee-shirt /tiʃœrt/ n.m. tee-shirt.

teindre† /tɛ̃dr/ v.t. dye. **se ～ les cheveux** v. pr. dye one's hair.

teint /tɛ̃/ n.m. complexion.

teinte /tɛ̃t/ n.f. shade, tint.

teintur|e /tɛ̃tyr/ n.f. dyeing; (produit) dye. **～erie** n.f. (boutique) dry-cleaner's.

tel, ～le /tɛl/ a. such. **～ quel**, (just) as it is.

télé /tele/ n.f. (fam.) TV.

télécommande /telekɔmɑ̃d/ n.f. remote control.

télécommunications /telekɔmynikasjɔ̃/ n.f. pl. telecommunications.

télécopi|e /telekɔpi/ n.f. tele(fax). **～eur** n.m. fax machine.

téléfilm /telefilm/ n.m. (tele)film.

télégramme /telegram/ n.m. telegram.

télégraph|e /telegraf/ n.m. telegraph. **～ier** v.t./i. **～ier (à)**, cable. **～ique** a. telegraphic; (fil, poteau) telegraph.

téléguid|er /telegide/ v.t. control by radio. **～é** a. radio-controlled.

téléphérique /teleferik/ n.m. cable-car.

téléphon|e /telefɔn/ n.m. (tele)phone. **～er** v.t./i. **～er (à)**, (tele)phone. **～ique** a. (tele)phone. **～iste** n.m./f. operator.

télésiège /telesjɛʒ/ n.m. chair-lift.

téléski /teleski/ n.m. ski tow.

téléspecta|teur, ～trice /telespɛktatœr, -tris/ n.m., f. (television) viewer.

télévente /televɑ̃t/ n.f. telesales.

télévis|é /televize/ a. **émission ～ée**, television programme. **～eur** n.m. television set.

télévision /televizjɔ̃/ n.f. television.

télex /telɛks/ n.m. telex.

télexer /telɛkse/ v.t. telex.

telle /tɛl/ voir **tel**.

tellement /tɛlmɑ̃/ adv. (tant) so much; (si) so. **～ de**, (quantité) so much; (nombre) so many.

témoignage /temwaɲaʒ/ n.m. testimony, evidence; (récit) account. **～ de**, (sentiment) token of.

témoigner /temwaɲe/ v.i. testify (**de**, to).

témoin /temwɛ̃/ *n.m.* witness.

tempéramant /tãperamã/ *n.m.* temperament; *(physique)* constitution. **à ~,** *(acheter)* on hire-purchase.

température /tãperatyr/ *n.f.* temperature.

tempête /tãpɛt/ *n.f.* storm.

temple /tãpl/ *n.m.* temple; *(protestant)* church.

temporaire /tãporɛr/ *a.* temporary. **~ment** *adv.* temporarily.

temps[1] /tã/ *n.m.* time; *(gram.)* tense; *(étape)* stage. **à ~** partiel/plein, part-/full-time. **ces derniers ~,** lately. **dans quelque ~,** in a while. **de ~ en temps,** from time to time.

temps[2] /tã/ *n.m.* weather. **quel ~ fait-il?,** what's the weather like?

tenace /tənas/ *a.* stubborn.

tendance /tãdãs/ *n.f.* tendency; *(opinions)* leanings; *(évolution)* trend. **avoir ~ à,** have a tendency to, tend to.

tendon /tãdɔ̃/ *n.m.* tendon.

tendre[1] /tãdr/ *v.t.* stretch; *(piège)* set; *(bras)* stretch out; *(main)* hold out; *(cou)* crane; *(tapisserie)* hang. **~ à qn.,** hold out to s.o.

tendre[2] /tãdr/ *a.* tender; *(couleur, bois)* soft. **~ment** /-əmã/ *adv.* tenderly. **~sse** /-ɛs/ *n.f.* tenderness.

tendu /tãdy/ *a.* *(corde)* tight; *(personne, situation)* tense.

teneur /tənœr/ *n.f.* content.

tenir† /tənir/ *v.t.* hold; *(pari, promesse, hôtel)* keep; *(place)* take up; *(propos)* utter; *(rôle)* play. **~ propre/ chaud/***etc.*,** keep clean/warm/ *etc.* —*v.i.* hold. **~ à,** be attached to. **~ à faire,** be anxious to do. **~ dans,** fit into. **se ~ v. pr.** *(rester)* remain; *(debout)* stand; *(avoir lieu)* be held. **se ~ à,**

hold on to. **se ~ bien,** behave o.s. **~ compte de,** take into account. **tiens!,** *(surprise)* hey!

tennis /tenis/ *n.m.* tennis; *(terrain)* tennis-court. —*n.m. pl.* *(chaussures)* sneakers. **~ de table,** table tennis.

ténor /tenor/ *n.m.* tenor.

tension /tãsjɔ̃/ *n.f.* tension. **avoir de la ~,** have high blood-pressure.

tentative /tãtativ/ *n.f.* attempt.

tente /tãt/ *n.f.* tent.

tenter[1] /tãte/ *v.t.* try **(de faire,** to do).

tent|er[2] /tãte/ *v.t.* *(allécher)* tempt. **~é de,** tempted to. **~ation** *n.f.* temptation.

tenture /tãtyr/ *n.f.* (wall) hanging. **~s,** drapery.

tenu /təny/ *voir* **tenir.** —*a.* **bien ~,** well-kept. **~ de,** obliged to.

tenue /təny/ *n.f.* *(habillement)* dress; *(de sport)* clothes; *(de maison)* upkeep; *(conduite)* (good) behaviour; *(maintien)* posture. **~ de soirée,** evening dress.

ter /tɛr/ *a. invar.* *(numéro)* B, b.

terme /tɛrm/ *n.m.* *(mot)* term; *(date limite)* time-limit; *(fin)* end; *(date de loyer)* term.

termin|al, ~ale *(m. pl.* **~aux)** /tɛrminal, -o/ *a.* terminal. **(classe) ~ale,** sixth form.

termin|er /tɛrmine/ *v.t./i.* finish; *(soirée, débat)* end, finish. **se ~er** *v. pr.* end *(par,* with). **~aison** *n.f.* *(gram.)* ending.

terminus /tɛrminys/ *n.m.* terminus.

terne /tɛrn/ *a.* dull, drab.

terrain /tɛrɛ̃/ *n.m.* ground; *(parcelle)* piece of land; *(à bâtir)* plot. **~ de camping,** campsite. **~ de golf,** golf-course. **~ de jeu,** playground. **~ vague,** waste ground.

terrasse /tɛras/ *n.f.* terrace; (*de café*) pavement area.

terre /tɛr/ *n.f.* (*planète, matière*) earth; (*étendue, pays*) land; ground; (*domaine*) estate. **à ~,** (*naut.*) ashore. **par ~,** (*tomber, jeter*) to the ground; (*s'asseoir, poser*) on the ground. **~ (cuite)**, terracotta.

terreau /tɛro/ *n.m. invar.* compost.

terrestre /tɛrɛstr/ *a.* land; (*de notre planète*) earth's; (*fig.*) earthly.

terreur /tɛrœr/ *n.f.* terror.

terrible /tɛribl/ *a.* terrible; (*formidable: fam.*) terrific.

terrier /tɛrje/ *n.m.* (*trou de lapin etc.*) burrow; (*chien*) terrier.

terrifier /tɛrifje/ *v.t.* terrify.

terrine /tɛrin/ *n.f.* (*culin.*) terrine.

territoire /tɛritwar/ *n.m.* territory.

terroir /tɛrwar/ *n.m.* (*sol*) soil; (*région*) region. **du ~,** country.

terroriser /tɛrɔrize/ *v.t.* terrorize.

terroris|te /tɛrɔrist/ *n.m./f.* terrorist. **~me** /-sm/ *n.m.* terrorism.

tes /te/ *voir* **ton**[1].

test /tɛst/ *n.m.* test. **~er** *v.t.* test.

testament /tɛstamɑ̃/ *n.m.* (*jurid.*) will; (*politique, artistique*) testament. **Ancien/Nouveau T~,** Old/New Testament.

testicule /tɛstikyl/ *n.m.* testicle.

tétanos /tetanos/ *n.m.* tetanus.

têtard /tetar/ *n.m.* tadpole.

tête /tɛt/ *n.f.* head; (*figure*) face; (*cheveux*) hair; (*cerveau*) brain. **à la ~ de,** at the head of. **de ~,** (*calculer*) in one's head. **en ~,** (*sport*) in the lead. **faire la ~,** sulk. **tenir ~ à qn.,** stand up to s.o. **une forte ~,** a rebel. **de la aux pieds,** from head to toe. **~-à-queue** *n.m. invar.* (*auto.*) spin. **en ~-à-tête,** in private.

tétée /tete/ *n.f.* feed.

téter /tete/ *v.t./i.* suck.

tétine /tetin/ *n.f.* (*de biberon*) teat; (*sucette*) dummy.

têtu /tety/ *a.* stubborn.

texte /tɛkst/ *n.m.* text; (*de leçon*) subject; (*morceau choisi*) passage.

textile /tɛkstil/ *n.m. & a.* textile.

texture /tɛkstyr/ *n.f.* texture.

thaïlandais, ~e /tailɑ̃dɛ, -z/ *a. & n.m., f.* Thai.

Thaïlande /tailɑ̃d/ *n.f.* Thailand.

thé /te/ *n.m.* tea.

théâtr|al (*m. pl.* **~aux**) /teatral, -o/ *a.* theatrical.

théâtre /teatr/ *n.m.* theatre; (*jeu forcé*) play-acting; (*d'un crime*) scene. **faire du ~,** act.

théière /tejɛr/ *n.f.* teapot.

thème /tɛm/ *n.m.* theme; (*traduction: scol.*) prose.

théologie /teɔlɔʒi/ *n.f.* theology.

théorème /teɔrɛm/ *n.m.* theorem.

théorie /teɔri/ *n.f.* theory.

thérapie /terapi/ *n.f.* therapy.

thermique /tɛrmik/ *a.* thermal.

thermomètre /tɛrmɔmɛtr/ *n.m.* thermometer.

thermos /tɛrmos/ *n.m./f.* (P.) Thermos (P.) (flask).

thermostat /tɛrmɔsta/ *n.m.* thermostat.

thèse /tɛz/ *n.f.* thesis.

thon /tɔ̃/ *n.m.* (*poisson*) tuna.

thrombose /trɔ̃boz/ *n.f.* thrombosis.

thym /tɛ̃/ *n.m.* thyme.

thyroïde /tiroid/ *n.f.* thyroid.

tibia /tibja/ *n.m.* shin-bone.

tic /tik/ *n.m.* (*contraction*) twitch; (*manie*) mannerism.

ticket /tikɛ/ *n.m.* ticket.

tic-tac /tiktak/ *n.m. invar.* (*de pendule*) ticking. **faire ~,** go tick tock.

tiède /tjɛd/ *a.* lukewarm.

tien /tjɛ̃/, **~ne** /tjɛn/ *pron.* le **~**, la **~ne**, les **~(ne)s**, yours. à la **~ ne!**, cheers!

tiens, tient /tjɛ̃/ *voir* tenir.

tiercé /tjɛrse/ *n.m.* place-betting.

tier|s, **~ce** /tjɛr, -s/ *a.* third. —*n.m.* (*fraction*) third; (*personne*) third party. **T~s-Monde** *n.m.* Third World.

tige /tiʒ/ *n.f.* (*bot.*) stem, stalk; (*en métal*) shaft.

tigre /tigr/ *n.m.* tiger.

tigré /tigre/ *a.* (*rayé*) striped; (*chat*) tabby.

tilleul /tijœl/ *n.m.* lime(-tree), linden(-tree); (*infusion*) lime tea.

timbale /tɛ̃bal/ *n.f.* (*gobelet*) (metal) tumbler.

timbr|e /tɛ̃br/ *n.m.* stamp; (*sonnette*) bell; (*de voix*) tone. **~e-poste** (*pl.* **~es-poste**) *n.m.* postage stamp. **~er** *v.t.* stamp.

timid|e /timid/ *a.* timid. **~ité** *n.f.* timidity.

tint|er /tɛ̃te/ *v.i.* ring; (*clefs*) jingle. **~ement** *n.m.* ringing; jingling.

tique /tik/ *n.f.* (*insecte*) tick.

tir /tir/ *n.m.* (*sport*) shooting; (*action de tirer*) firing; (*feu, rafale*) fire.

tirage /tiraʒ/ *n.m.* (*de photo*) printing; (*de loterie*) draw. **~ au sort**, drawing lots.

tire-bouchon /tirbuʃõ/ *n.m.* corkscrew.

tire-lait /tirlɛ/ *n.m.* breastpump.

tirelire /tirlir/ *n.f.* money-box.

tirer /tire/ *v.t.* pull; (*navire*) tow, tug; (*langue*) stick out; (*conclusion, trait, rideaux*) draw; (*coup de feu*) fire; (*gibier*) shoot; (*photo*) print. **~ de**, (*sortir*) take ou get out of; (*extraire*) extract from. —*v.i.* shoot, fire (**sur**, at). **~ au** (*couleur*) verge on; (*corde*) pull at. **se ~ v. pr.** (*fam.*) clear off. **se ~ de**, get out of. **s'en ~**, (*en*

réchapper*) pull through; (*réussir: fam.*) cope. **~ au sort, draw lots (for).

tiret /tire/ *n.m.* dash.

tireur /tirœr/ *n.m.* gunman.

tiroir /tirwar/ *n.m.* drawer. **~-caisse** (*pl.* **~s-caisses**) *n.m.* till.

tisane /tizan/ *n.f.* herb-tea.

tisonnier /tizonje/ *n.m.* poker.

tiss|er /tise/ *v.t.* weave.

tissu /tisy/ *n.m.* fabric, material; (*biologique*) tissue.

titr|e /titr/ *n.m.* title; (*diplôme*) qualification; (*comm.*) bond. **~s**, (*droits*) claims. (**gros**) **~s**, headlines. **~ de propriété**, title-deed.

titré /titre/ *a.* titled.

tituber /titybe/ *v.i.* stagger.

titulaire /tityler/ *a.* être **~**, have tenure. être **~ de**, hold. —*n.m./f.* (*de permis etc.*) holder.

toast /tost/ *n.m.* piece of toast; (*allocution*) toast.

toboggan /tɔbɔgɑ̃/ *n.m.* slide.

toc /tɔk/ *int.* **~ toc!** knock knock!

toi /twa/ *pron.* you; (*réfléchi*) yourself. **lève-~**, stand up.

toile /twal/ *n.f.* cloth; (*sac, tableau*) canvas; (*coton*) cotton. **~ d'araignée**, (spider's) web; (*délabrée*) cobweb.

toilette /twalɛt/ *n.f.* washing; (*habillement*) clothes, dress. **~s**, (*cabinets*) toilet(s). **de ~**, (*articles, savon, etc.*) toilet. **faire sa ~**, wash and get ready.

toi-même /twamɛm/ *pron.* yourself.

toison /twazõ/ *n.f.* (*laine*) fleece.

toit /twa/ *n.m.* roof. **~ ouvrant**, (*auto.*) sun-roof.

tôle /tol/ *n.f.* (*plaque*) iron sheet. **~ ondulée**, corrugated iron.

toléran|t, **~te** /tɔlerɑ̃, -t/ *a.* tolerant. **~ce** *n.f.* tolerance.

tolérer /tɔlere/ *v.t.* tolerate; (*importations: comm.*) allow.

tomate /tɔmat/ *n.f.* tomato.

tombe /tɔ̃b/ *n.f.* grave; (*avec monument*) tomb.

tombeau (*pl.* ∼x) /tɔ̃bo/ *n.m.* tomb.

tombée /tɔ̃be/ *n.f.* ∼ **de la nuit**, nightfall.

tomber /tɔ̃be/ *v.i.* (*aux. être*) fall; (*fièvre, vent*) drop; (*enthousiasme*) die down. **faire** ∼, knock over; (*gouvernement*) bring down. **laisser** ∼, drop; (*abandonner*) let down. **laisse** ∼!, forget it! ∼ **en panne**, break down. ∼ **sur**, (*trouver*) run across.

tombola /tɔ̃bɔla/ *n.f.* tombola.

tome /tɔm/ *n.m.* volume.

ton[1], **ta** *ou* **ton*** (*pl.* **tes**) /tɔ̃, ta, tɔ̃, te/ *a.* your.

ton[2] /tɔ̃/ *n.m.* tone; (*gamme: mus.*) key; (*hauteur de la voix*) pitch.

tonalité /tɔnalite/ *n.f.* tone; (*téléphone*) dialling tone.

tond|**re** /tɔ̃dr/ *v.t.* (*herbe*) mow; (*mouton*) shear; (*cheveux*) clip. ∼**euse** *n.f.* shears; clippers. ∼**euse (à gazon)**, (lawn-)mower.

tonifier /tɔnifje/ *v.t.* tone up.

tonique /tɔnik/ *a. & n.m.* tonic.

tonne /tɔn/ *n.f.* ton(ne).

tonneau (*pl.* ∼x) /tɔno/ *n.m.* (*récipient*) barrel; (*naut.*) ton; (*culbute*) somersault.

tonnerre /tɔnɛr/ *n.m.* thunder.

tonton /tɔ̃tɔ̃/ *n.m.* (*fam.*) uncle.

tonus /tɔnys/ *n.m.* energy.

top /tɔp/ *n.m.* (*signal pour marquer un instant précis*) stroke.

toque /tɔk/ *n.f.* (*fur*) hat; (*de jockey*) cap; (*de cuisinier*) hat.

torche /tɔrʃ/ *n.f.* torch.

torchon /tɔrʃɔ̃/ *n.m.* cloth, duster; (*pour la vaisselle*) tea-towel.

tordre /tɔrdr/ *v.t.* twist; (*linge*) wring. **se** ∼ *v. pr.* twist, bend; (*de douleur*) writhe. **se** ∼ **(de rire)**, split one's sides.

tordu /tɔrdy/ *a.* twisted, bent; (*esprit*) warped.

tornade /tɔrnad/ *n.f.* tornado.

torpeur /tɔrpœr/ *n.f.* lethargy.

torréfier /tɔrefje/ *v.t.* roast.

torrent /tɔrɑ̃/ *n.m.* torrent.

torride /tɔrid/ *a.* torrid.

torsade /tɔrsad/ *n.f.* twist.

torse /tɔrs/ *n.m.* chest; (*sculpture*) torso.

tort /tɔr/ *n.m.* wrong. **à** ∼, wrongly. **à** ∼ **et à travers**, without thinking. **avoir** ∼, be wrong (**de faire**, to do).

torticolis /tɔrtikɔli/ *n.m.* stiff neck. **le plus** ∼.

tortiller /tɔrtije/ *v.t.* twist, twirl. **se** ∼ *v. pr.* wriggle, wiggle.

tortue /tɔrty/ *n.f.* tortoise; (*de mer*) turtle.

tortueu|**x**, ∼**se** /tɔrtɥø, -z/ *a.* (*explication*) tortuous; (*chemin*) twisting.

tortur|**e(s)** /tɔrtyr/ *n.f.* (*pl.*) torture. ∼**er** *v.t.* torture.

tôt /to/ *adv.* early. **plus** ∼, earlier. **au plus** ∼, at the earliest. **le plus** ∼ **possible**, as soon as possible. ∼ **ou tard**, sooner or later.

tot|**al** (*m. pl.* ∼**aux**) /tɔtal, -o/ *a.* total. —*n.m.* (*pl.* ∼**aux**) total. —*adv.* (*fam.*) to conclude, in short. **au** ∼**al**, all in all. ∼**alement** *adv.* totally. ∼**aliser** *v.t.* total.

totalitaire /tɔtalitɛr/ *a.* totalitarian.

totalité /tɔtalite/ *n.f.* entirety. **la** ∼ **de**, all of.

toubib /tubib/ *n.m.* (*fam.*) doctor.

touchant, ∼**e** /tuʃɑ̃, -t/ *a.* (*émouvant*) touching.

touche /tuʃ/ *n.f.* (*de piano*) key; (*de peintre*) touch. **(ligne de)** ∼, touch-line. **une** ∼ **de**, a touch of.

toucher /tuʃe/ *v.t.* touch; (*émouvoir*) move, touch; (*contacter*) get in touch with; (*cible*) hit; (*argent*) draw; (*chèque*) cash; (*concerner*) affect. —*v.i.* ~ **à,** touch; (*question*) touch on; (*fin, but*) approach. **je vais lui en** ~ **un mot,** I'll talk to him about it. **se** ~ *v. pr.* (*lignes*) touch.

touffe /tuf/ *n.f.* (*de poils, d'herbe*) tuft; (*de plantes*) clump.

touffu /tufy/ *a.* thick, bushy; (*fig.*) complex.

toujours /tuʒur/ *adv.* always; (*encore*) still; (*en tout cas*) anyhow. **pour** ~ **,** for ever.

toupet /tupɛ/ *n.m.* (*culot: fam.*) cheek, nerve.

toupie /tupi/ *n.f.* (*jouet*) top.

tour[1] /tur/ *n.f.* tower; (*immeuble*) tower block; (*échecs*) rook.

tour[2] /'tur/ *n.m.* (*mouvement, succession, tournure*) turn; (*excursion*) trip; (*à pied*) walk; (*en auto*) drive; (*artifice*) trick; (*circonférence*) circumference; (*techn.*) lathe. ~ **(de piste),** lap. **à** ~ **de rôle,** in turn. **à mon**/*etc.* ~ **,** when it is my/*etc.* turn. **c'est mon**/*etc.* ~ **de,** it is my/*etc.* turn to. **faire le** ~ **de,** go round. ~ **de contrôle,** control tower. ~ **de taille,** waist measurement; (*ligne*) waistline.

tourbe /turb/ *n.f.* peat.

tourbillon /turbijɔ̃/ *n.m.* whirlwind; (*d'eau*) whirlpool; (*fig.*) whirl, swirl.

tourelle /turɛl/ *n.f.* turret.

tourisme /turism/ *n.m.* tourism. **faire du** ~ **,** do some sightseeing.

tourist|e /turist/ *n.m./f.* tourist. ~**ique** *a.* touristic; (*route*) scenic.

tourment /turmɑ̃/ *n.m.* torment. ~**er** /-te/ *v.t.* torment. **se** ~**er** *v. pr.* worry.

tournage /turnaʒ/ *n.m.* (*cinéma*) shooting.

tournant[1], ~**e** /turnɑ̃, -t/ *a.* (*qui pivote*) revolving.

tournant[2] /turnɑ̃/ *n.m.* bend; (*fig.*) turning-point.

tourne-disque /turnədisk/ *n.m.* record-player.

tournée /turne/ *n.f.* (*voyage, consommations*) round; (*théâtre*) tour. **je paye** *ou* **j'offre la** ~ **,** I'll buy this round.

tourner /turne/ *v.t.* turn; (*film*) shoot, make. —*v.i.* turn; (*toupie, tête*) spin; (*moteur, usine*) run. **se** ~ *v. pr.* turn. ~ **autour de,** go round; (*personne, maison*) hang around; (*terre*) revolve round; (*question*) centre on. ~ **en ridicule,** ridicule. ~ **le dos à,** turn one's back on.

tournesol /turnəsɔl/ *n.m.* sunflower.

tournevis /turnəvis/ *n.m.* screwdriver.

tourniquet /turnikɛ/ *n.m.* (*barrière*) turnstile.

tournoi /turnwa/ *n.m.* tournament.

tournoyer /turnwaje/ *v.i.* whirl.

tournure /turnyr/ *n.f.* turn; (*locution*) turn of phrase.

tourte /turt/ *n.f.* pie.

tourterelle /turtərɛl/ *n.f.* turtledove.

Toussaint /tusɛ̃/ *n.f.* **la** ~ **,** All Saints' Day.

tousser /tuse/ *v.i.* cough.

tout[1], ~**e** (*pl.* **tous, toutes** /tu, tut/ *a. all;* (*n'importe quel*) any; (*tout à fait*) entirely. ~ **le pays**/*etc.,* the whole country/*etc.,* all the country/*etc.* ~ **e la nuit**/**journée,** the whole night/day. ~ **un paquet,** a whole pack. **tous les jours**/**mois**/*etc.,* every day/month/*etc.* —*pron.* everything, all. **tous** /tus/ /tus/, **toutes,** take everything. **prendre** ~ **,** take everything, take it all. ~ **ce que,** all that. ~ **le monde,** everyone. **tous les**

deux, toutes les deux, both of them. **tous les trois,** all three (of them). —*adv.* (*très*) very; (*tout à fait*) quite. **~ au bout/début/***etc.*, right at the end/beginning/*etc.* **le ~ premier,** the very first. **~ en chantant/marchant/***etc.*, while singing/walking/*etc.* **à coup,** all of a sudden. **~ à fait,** quite, completely. **~ à l'heure,** in a moment; (*passé*) a moment ago. **~ au** *ou* **le long de,** throughout. **~ de même,** all the same. **~ de suite,** straight away. **~ entier,** whole, brand-new. **~ nu,** stark naked. **~ près,** nearby. **~ seul,** alone. **~ terrain** *a. invar.* all terrain.

tout² /tu/ *n.m.* (*ensemble*) whole. **en ~,** in all. **pas du ~!,** not at all! **tout-à-l'égout** /tutalegu/ *n.m.* main drainage.

toutefois /tutfwa/ *adv.* however.

toux /tu/ *n.f.* cough.

toxicomane /tɔksikɔman/ *n.m./f.* drug addict.

toxine /tɔksin/ *n.f.* toxin.

toxique /tɔksik/ *a.* toxic.

trac /trak/ *n.m.* **le ~,** nerves; (*théâtre*) stage fright.

tracas /traka/ *n.m.* worry.

trace /tras/ *n.f.* trace; mark; (*d'animal, de pneu*) tracks; (*vestige*) trace. **~s de pas,** footprints.

tracé /trase/ *n.m.* (*ligne*) line; (*plan*) layout.

tracer /trase/ *v.t.* draw, trace; (*écrire*) write; (*route*) mark out.

trachée-(artère) /traʃe(artɛr)/ *n.f.* windpipe.

tracteur /traktœr/ *n.m.* tractor.

tradition /tradisjɔ̃/ *n.f.* tradition. **~nel, ~nelle** /-jɔnɛl/ *a.* traditional.

trad|uiret /tradɥir/ *v.t.* translate; (*sentiment*) express. **~uire en**

justice, take to court. **~ucteur, ~uctrice** *n.m., f.* translator. **~uction** *n.f.* translation.

trafic /trafik/ *n.m.* (*commerce, circulation*) traffic.

trafiqu|er /trafike/ *v.i.* traffic. —*v.t.* (*fam.*) (*vin*) doctor; (*moteur*) fiddle with. **~ant, ~ante** *n.m., f.* trafficker; (*d'armes, de drogues*) dealer.

tragédie /traʒedi/ *n.f.* tragedy.

tragique /traʒik/ *a.* tragic. **~ment** *adv.* tragically.

trah|ir /trair/ *v.t.* betray. **~ison** *n.f.* betrayal; (*crime*) treason.

train /trɛ̃/ *n.m.* (*rail.*) train; (*allure*) pace. **en ~ de faire,** (busy) doing. **~ d'atterrissage,** undercarriage. **~ électrique,** (*jouet*) electric train set. **~ de vie,** lifestyle.

traîneau (*pl.* **~x**) /treno/ *n.m.* sledge.

traînée /trene/ *n.f.* (*trace*) trail; (*bande*) streak; (*femme, péj.*) slut.

traîner /trene/ *v.t.* drag (along); (*véhicule*) pull. —*v.i.* (*pendre*) trail; (*rester en arrière*) trail behind; (*flâner*) hang about; (*papiers, affaires*) lie around. **~ (en longueur),** drag on.

traire† /trɛr/ *v.t.* milk.

trait /trɛ/ *n.m.* line; (*en dessinant*) stroke; (*caractéristique*) feature. trait. **~s,** (*du visage*) features. **~ d'union,** hyphen.

traite /trɛt/ *n.f.* (*de vache*) milking; (*comm.*) draft. **d'une (seule) ~,** in one go, at a stretch.

traitement /trɛtmɑ̃/ *n.m.* treatment; (*salaire*) salary. **~ de données,** data processing. **~ de texte,** word processing.

traiter /trɛte/ *v.t.* treat; (*affaire*) deal with; (*données, produit*) process. **~ qn. de lâche/***etc.*, call s.o. a coward/*etc.* —*v.i.* deal (avec, with). **~ de**, (sujet) deal with.

traiteur /tretœr/ n.m. caterer; (boutique) delicatessen.

traître, **~sse** /trɛtr, -ɛs/ a. treacherous. —n.m./f. traitor.

trajectoire /traʒɛktwar/ n.f. path.

trajet /traʒɛ/ n.m. (à parcourir) distance; (voyage) journey; (itinéraire) route.

trame /tram/ n.f. (de tissu) weft; (de récit etc.) framework.

tramway /tramwɛ/ n.m. tram.

tranche /trɑ̃ʃ/ n.f. (rondelle) slice; (partie) portion.

tranch|er[1] /trɑ̃ʃe/ v.t. cut; (question) decide. —v.i. (décider) decide. **~é** a. (net) clear-cut.

trancher[2] /trɑ̃ʃe/ v.i. (contraster) contrast (sur, with).

tranquill|e /trɑ̃kil/ a. quiet; (esprit) at rest; (conscience) clear. **être/laisser ~e**, be/leave in peace. **~ement** adv. quietly.

tranquillisant /trɑ̃kilizɑ̃/ n.m. tranquillizer.

tranquilliser /trɑ̃kilize/ v.t. reassure.

transaction /trɑ̃zaksjɔ̃/ n.f. transaction.

transat /trɑ̃zat/ n.m. (fam.) deckchair.

transatlantique /trɑ̃zatlɑ̃tik/ n.m. transatlantic liner.

transcr|ire /trɑ̃skrir/ v.t. transcribe. **~iption** n.f. transcription; (copie) transcript.

transférer /trɑ̃sfere/ v.t. transfer.

transfert /trɑ̃sfɛr/ n.m. transfer.

transform|er /trɑ̃sfɔrme/ v.t. change; (radicalement) transform; (vêtement) alter. **se ~er** v. pr. change; be transformed. (se) **~er en**, turn into. **~ateur** n.m. transformer. **~ation** n.f. change; transformation.

transfuge /trɑ̃sfyʒ/ n.m./f. renegade.

transfusion /trɑ̃sfyzjɔ̃/ n.f. transfusion.

transgresser /trɑ̃sgrese/ v.t. disobey.

transistor /trɑ̃zistɔr/ n.m. (dispositif, poste de radio) transistor.

transit /trɑ̃zit/ n.m. transit. **~er** v.t./i. pass in transit.

transiti|f, **~ve** /trɑ̃zitif, -v/ a. transitive.

transition /trɑ̃zisjɔ̃/ n.f. transition.

transm|ettre† /trɑ̃smɛtr/ v.t. pass on; (techn.) transmit; (radio) broadcast. **~ission** n.f. transmission; (radio) broadcasting.

transparen|t, **~te** /trɑ̃sparɑ̃, -t/ a. transparent. **~ce** n.f. transparency.

transpercer /trɑ̃spɛrse/ v.t. pierce.

transpir|er /trɑ̃spire/ v.i. perspire. **~ation** n.f. perspiration.

transplant|er /trɑ̃splɑ̃te/ v.t. (bot., méd.) transplant. **~ation** n.f. (bot.) transplantation; (méd.) transplant.

transport /trɑ̃spɔr/ n.m. transport(ation). **les ~s en commun**, public transport.

transport|er /trɑ̃spɔrte/ v.t. transport; (à la main) carry.

transposer /trɑ̃spoze/ v.t. transpose.

transvers|al (m. pl. **~aux**) /trɑ̃vɛrsal, -o/ a. cross, transverse.

trappe /trap/ n.f. trapdoor.

trapu /trapy/ a. stocky.

traquer /trake/ v.t. track down.

traumatis|me /tromatism/ n.m. trauma. **~ant**, **~ante** /-zɑ̃, -t/ a. traumatic.

trav|ail (pl. **~aux**) /travaj, -o/ n.m. work; (emploi, poste) job; (façonnage) working. **~aux**, work. **en ~ail**, (femme) in labour. **~ail à la chaîne**, production line work. **~ail au

noir, (*fam.*) moonlighting. **~aux ménagers,** housework.

travailler /travaje/ *v.i.* work. —*v.t.* (*façonner*) work; (*étudier*) work at *ou* on; (*tourmenter*) worry. **~eur, ~euse** *n.m., f.* worker; *a.* hardworking.

travailliste /travajist/ *a.* Labour. —*n.m./f.* Labour party member.

travers /traver/ *n.m.* à **~,** through. de **~,** (*chapeau, nez*) crooked; (*mal*) badly, the wrong way; (*regarder*) askance. en **~ (de),** across.

traversée /traverse/ *n.f.* crossing.

traverser /traverse/ *v.t.* cross; (*transpercer*) go (right) through; (*période, forêt*) go *ou* pass through.

traversin /traversẽ/ *n.m.* bolster.

travesti /travesti/ *n.m.* transvestite.

trébucher /trebyʃe/ *v.i.* stumble, trip (over). **faire ~,** trip (up).

trèfle /trefl/ *n.m.* (*plante*) clover; (*cartes*) clubs.

treillis /treji/ *n.m.* trellis; (*en métal*) wire mesh.

treiz|e /trɛz/ *a.* & *n.m.* thirteen. **~ième** *a.* & *n.m./f.* thirteenth.

tréma /trema/ *n.m.* diaeresis.

trembl|er /trɑ̃ble/ *v.i.* shake, tremble; (*lumière, voix*) quiver. **~ement** *n.m.* shaking; (*frisson*) shiver. **~ement de terre,** earthquake.

tremper /trɑ̃pe/ *v.t./i.* soak; (*plonger*) dip; (*acier*) temper. **mettre à ~ ou faire ~,** soak. se **~** *v. pr.* (*se baigner*) have a dip.

trempette /trɑ̃pɛt/ *n.f.* **faire ~,** have a little dip.

tremplin /trɑ̃plẽ/ *n.m.* springboard.

trentaine /trɑ̃tɛn/ *n.f.* **une ~ (de),** about thirty. **il a la ~,** he's about thirty.

trent|e /trɑ̃t/ *a.* & *n.m.* thirty. **~ième** *a.* & *n.m./f.* thirtieth.

trépied /trepje/ *n.m.* tripod.

très /trɛ/ (/trɛz/ *before vowel*) *adv.* very. **~ aimé/estimé,** much liked/esteemed.

trésor /trezɔr/ *n.m.* treasure; (*ressources: comm.*) finances. **le T~,** the revenue department.

trésorerie /trezɔrri/ *n.f.* (*bureaux*) accounts department; (*du Trésor*) revenue office; (*argent*) finances; (*gestion*) accounts.

trésor|ier, ~ière /trezɔrje, -jɛr/ *n.m., f.* treasurer.

tressaillir /tresajir/ *v.i.* shake, quiver; (*sursauter*) start.

tressauter /tresote/ *v.i.* (*sursauter*) start, jump.

tresse /trɛs/ *n.f.* braid, plait.

tresser /trese/ *v.t.* braid, plait.

tréteau (*pl.* **~x**) /treto/ *n.m.* trestle. **~x,** (*théâtre*) stage.

treuil /trœj/ *n.m.* winch.

trêve /trɛv/ *n.f.* truce; (*fig.*) respite. **~ de plaisanteries,** enough of this joking.

tri /tri/ *n.m.* (*classement*) sorting; (*sélection*) selection. **faire le ~ de,** sort; select.

triang|le /trijɑ̃gl/ *n.m.* triangle. **~ulaire** *a.* triangular.

tribord /tribɔr/ *n.m.* starboard.

tribu /triby/ *n.f.* tribe.

tribun|al (*m. pl.* **~aux**) /tribynal, -o/ *n.m.* court.

tribune /tribyn/ *n.f.* (*public*) gallery; (*dans un stade*) grandstand; (*d'orateur*) rostrum; (*débat*) forum.

trich|er /triʃe/ *v.i.* cheat. **~erie** *n.f.* cheating. **une ~erie,** piece of trickery. **~eur, ~euse** *n.m., f.* cheat.

tricolore /trikɔlɔr/ *a.* three-coloured; (*français*) red, white and blue; (*français: fig.*) French.

tricot /triko/ *n.m.* knitting; (*pull*) sweater. **en ～**, knitted. **～er** /-ɔte/ *v.t./i.* knit.

trictrac /triktrak/ *n.m.* backgammon.

tricycle /trisikl/ *n.m.* tricycle.

trier /trije/ *v.t.* (*classer*) sort; (*choisir*) select.

trimestr|e /trimɛstr/ *n.m.* quarter; (*scol.*) term. **～iel**, **～ielle** *a.* quarterly; (*bulletin*) end-of-term.

tringle /trɛ̃gl/ *n.f.* rod.

Trinité /trinite/ *n.f.* **la ～**, (*dogme*) the Trinity; (*fête*) Trinity.

trinquer /trɛ̃ke/ *v.i.* clink glasses.

trio /trijo/ *n.m.* trio.

triomph|e /trijɔ̃f/ *n.m.* triumph. **～al** (*m. pl.* **～aux**) *a.* triumphant.

triomph|er /trijɔ̃fe/ *v.i.* triumph (**de**, over); (*jubiler*) be triumphant. **～ant**, **～ante** *a.* triumphant.

tripes /trip/ *n.f. pl.* (*mets*) tripe.

triple /tripl/ *a.* triple, treble. *—n.m.* **le ～**, three times as much (**de**, as).

tripler /triple/ *v.t./i.* triple, treble.

trisomique /trizɔmik/ *a.* **enfant ～**, Down's (syndrome) child.

triste /trist/ *a.* sad; (*rue, temps, couleur*) gloomy; (*lamentable*) wretched, dreadful. **～ment** /-əmɑ̃/ *adv.* sadly. **～sse** /-ɛs/ *n.f.* sadness; gloominess.

triv|ial (*m. pl.* **～iaux**) /trivjal, -jo/ *a.* coarse. **～ialité** *n.f.* coarseness.

troc /trɔk/ *n.m.* exchange; (*comm.*) barter.

trognon /trɔɲɔ̃/ *n.m.* core.

trois /trwa/ *a. & n.m.* three. **hôtel ～étoiles**, three-star hotel. **～ième** *a. & n.m./f.* third. **～ièmement** /-zjɛmmɑ̃/ *adv.* thirdly.

trombe /trɔ̃b/ *n.f.* **～ d'eau**, downpour.

trombone /trɔ̃bɔn/ *n.m.* (*mus.*) trombone; (*agrafe*) paper-clip.

trompe /trɔ̃p/ *n.f.* (*d'éléphant*) trunk; (*mus.*) horn.

tromp|er /trɔ̃pe/ *v.t.* deceive, mislead; (*déjouer*) elude. **se ～er** *v. pr.* be mistaken. **se ～er de route/train/***etc.***, take the wrong road/train/***etc.*

trompette /trɔ̃pɛt/ *n.f.* trumpet.

tronc /trɔ̃/ *n.m.* trunk; (*boîte*) collection box.

tronçon /trɔ̃sɔ̃/ *n.m.* section. **～ner** /-ɔne/ *v.t.* cut into sections.

trône /tron/ *n.m.* throne.

tronquer /trɔ̃ke/ *v.t.* truncate.

trop /tro/ *adv.* (*grand, loin, etc.*) too; (*boire, marcher, etc.*) too much. **～ (de)**, (*quantité*) too much; (*nombre*) too many. **c'est ～ chauffé**, it's overheated. **de ～, en ～**, too much; too many.

trophée /trofe/ *n.m.* trophy.

tropic|al (*m. pl.* **～aux**) /trɔpikal, -o/ *a.* tropical.

tropique /trɔpik/ *n.m.* tropic. **～s**, tropics.

troquer /trɔke/ *v.t.* exchange; (*comm.*) barter (**contre**, for).

trot /tro/ *n.m.* trot.

trotter /trɔte/ *v.i.* trot.

trotteuse /trɔtøz/ *n.f.* (*aiguille de montre*) second hand.

trottinette /trɔtinɛt/ *n.f.* (*jouet*) scooter.

trottoir /trɔtwar/ *n.m.* pavement.

trou /tru/ *n.m.* hole; (*moment*) gap; (*lieu: péj.*) dump. **～ (de mémoire)**, lapse of memory. **～ de la serrure**, keyhole.

trouble /trubl/ *a.* (*eau, image*) unclear; (*louche*) shady. **～n.m.** agitation. **～s**, (*pol.*) disturbances; (*méd.*) trouble.

troubl|er /truble/ *v.t.* disturb.

(*eau*) make cloudy; (*inquiéter*) trouble. **~ant**, **~ante** *a.* disturbing.

trouer /true/ *v.t.* make a hole *ou* holes in.

trouille /truj/ *n.f.* **avoir la ~**, (*fam.*) be scared.

troupe /trup/ *n.f.* troop; (*d'acteurs*) troupe. **~s**, (*mil.*) troops.

troupeau (*pl.* **~x**) /trupo/ *n.m.* herd; (*de moutons*) flock.

trousse /trus/ *n.f.* case, bag; (*de réparations*) kit. **~ de toilette**, toilet bag.

trousseau (*pl.* **~x**) /truso/ *n.m.* (*de clefs*) bunch; (*de mariée*) trousseau.

trouver /truve/ *v.t.* find; (*penser*) think. **se ~** *v. pr.* find o.s.; (*être*) be; (*se sentir*) feel.

truc /tryk/ *n.m.* (*moyen*) way; (*artifice*) trick; (*chose. fam.*) thing. **~age** *n.m.* = **truquage**.

truelle /tryɛl/ *n.f.* trowel.

truffe /tryf/ *n.f.* (*champignon, chocolat*) truffle; (*nez*) nose.

truffer /tryfe/ *v.t.* (*fam.*) fill, pack (**de**, with).

truie /trɥi/ *n.f.* (*animal*) sow.

truite /trɥit/ *n.f.* trout.

truqu|er /tryke/ *v.t.* fix, rig; (*photo, texte*) fake. **~age** *n.m.* fixing; faking; (*cinéma*) special effect.

trust /trœst/ *n.m.* (*comm.*) trust.

tsigane /tsigan/ *a.* & *n.m./f.* (Hungarian) gypsy.

tu[1] /ty/ *pron.* (*parent, ami, enfant, etc.*) you.

tu[2] /ty/ *voir* **taire**.

tuba /tyba/ *n.m.* (*mus.*) tuba; (*sport*) snorkel.

tube /tyb/ *n.m.* tube.

tubercul|eux, **~euse** /tybɛrkylø, -z/ *a.* **être ~eux**, have tuberculosis. **~ose** *n.f.* tuberculosis.

tuer /tɥe/ *v.t.* kill; (*d'une balle*) shoot, kill; (*épuiser*) exhaust. **se**

~ *v. pr.* kill o.s.; (*accident*) be killed.

tuile /tɥil/ *n.f.* tile; (*malchance: fam.*) (stroke of) bad luck.

tulipe /tylip/ *n.f.* tulip.

tumeur /tymœr/ *n.f.* tumour.

tumulte /tymylt/ *n.m.* commotion; (*désordre*) turmoil.

tunique /tynik/ *n.f.* tunic.

Tunisie /tynizi/ *n.f.* Tunisia.

tunisien, **~ne** /tynizjɛ̃, -jɛn/ *a.* & *n.m.*, *f.* Tunisian.

tunnel /tynɛl/ *n.m.* tunnel.

turban /tyrbɑ̃/ *n.m.* turban.

turbine /tyrbin/ *n.f.* turbine.

turbo /tyrbo/ *a.* turbo. *n.f.* (*voiture*) turbo.

turbulen|t, **~te** /tyrbylɑ̃, -t/ *a.* boisterous, turbulent. **~ce** *n.f.* turbulence.

tur|c, **~que** /tyrk/ *a.* Turkish. —*n.m.*, *f.* Turk. —*n.m.* (*lang.*) Turkish.

turf /tyrf/ *n.m.* **le ~**, the turf. **~iste** *n.m./f.* racegoer.

Turquie /tyrki/ *n.f.* Turkey.

turquoise /tyrkwaz/ *a. invar.* turquoise.

tutelle /tytɛl/ *n.f.* (*jurid.*) guardianship; (*fig.*) protection.

tu|teur, **~trice** /tytœr, -tris/ *n.m.*, *f.* (*jurid.*) guardian. —*n.m.* (*bâton*) stake.

tut|oyer /tytwaje/ *v.t.* address familiarly (using *tu*). **~oiement** *n.m.* use of (familiar) *tu*.

tuyau (*pl.* **~x**) /tɥijo/ *n.m.* pipe; (*conseil: fam.*) tip. **~ d'arrosage**, hose-pipe. **~terie** *n.f.* piping.

TVA *abrév.* (*taxe sur la valeur ajoutée*) VAT.

tympan /tɛ̃pɑ̃/ *n.m.* ear-drum.

type /tip/ *n.m.* (*modèle*) type; (*traits*) features; (*individu: fam.*) bloke, guy. —*a. invar.* typical.

typhoïde /tifɔid/ *n.f.* typhoid (fever).

typhon /tifɔ̃/ n.m. typhoon.

typhus /tifys/ n.m. typhus.

typique /tipik/ a. typical. **~ment** adv. typically.

tyran /tirã/ n.m. tyrant.

tyrann|ie /tirani/ n.f. tyranny. **~ique** a. tyrannical.

U

ulcère /ylsɛr/ n.m. ulcer.

ULM abrév. m. (ultraléger motorisé) microlight.

ultérieur /ylterjœr/ a., **~ement** adv. later.

ultimatum /yltimatɔm/ n.m. ultimatum.

ultra /yltra/ n.m./f. hardliner.

ultra- /yltra/ préf. ultra-.

un, une /œ̃, yn/ a. one; (indéfini) a, an. **un enfant**, (/œ̃nãfã/) a child. —pron. & n.m., f. one. **l'un**, one. **les uns**, some. **l'un et l'autre**, both. **l'un l'autre, les uns les autres**, each other. **l'un ou l'autre**, either. **la une**, (de journal) front page. **un autre**, another. **un par un**, one by one.

unanim|e /ynanim/ a. unanimous. **~ité** n.f. unanimity. **à l'~ité**, unanimously.

uni /yni/ a. united; (couple) close; (surface) smooth; (sans dessins) plain.

unième /ynjɛm/ a. -first. **vingt et ~**, twenty-first. **cent ~**, one hundred and first.

uniforme /yniform/ n.m. uniform. —a. uniform.

unilatér|al (m. pl. **~aux**) /ynilateral, -o/ a. unilateral.

union /ynjɔ̃/ n.f. union. **l'U~ soviétique**, the Soviet Union.

unique /ynik/ a. (seul) only; (prix, voie) one; (incomparable) unique.

enfant ~, only child. **sens ~**, one-way street. **~ment** adv. only, solely.

unir /ynir/ v.t., **s'~** v. pr. unite, join.

unité /ynite/ n.f. unit; (harmonie) unity.

univers /yniver/ n.m. universe.

universel, ~le /ynivɛrsɛl/ a. universal.

université /ynivɛrsite/ n.f. university.

uranium /yranjɔm/ n.m. uranium.

urbain, ~e /yrbɛ̃, -ɛn/ a. urban.

urgence /yrʒãs/ n.f. (cas) emergency; (de situation, tâche, etc.) urgency. **d'~** a. emergency; adv. urgently.

urgent, ~e /yrʒã, -t/ a. urgent.

urin|e /yrin/ n.f. urine. **~er** v.i. urinate.

urinoir /yrinwar/ n.m. urinal.

urne /yrn/ n.f. (électorale) ballot-box; (vase) urn. **aller aux ~s**, go to the polls.

urticaire /yrtikɛr/ n.f. une **crise d'~**, nettle rash.

usage /yzaʒ/ n.m. use; (coutume) custom; (de langage) usage.

usagé /yzaʒe/ a. worn.

usager /yzaʒe/ n.m. user.

usé /yze/ a. worn (out).

user /yze/ v.t. wear (out); (consommer) use (up). —v.i. ~ **de**, use. **s'~** v. pr. (tissu etc.) wear (out).

usine /yzin/ n.f. factory; (de métallurgie) works.

ustensile /ystãsil/ n.m. utensil.

usufruit /yzyfrɥi/ n.m. usufruct.

usure /yzyr/ n.f. (détérioration) wear (and tear).

utérus /yterys/ n.m. womb, uterus.

utile /ytil/ a. useful. **~ment** adv. usefully.

utilis|er /ytilize/ v.t. use. **~able** a. usable. **~ation** n.f. use.

utilitaire /ytilitɛr/ *a.* utilitarian.

utilité /ytilite/ *n.f.* use(fulness).

UV *abrév. f.* (*unité de valeur*) (*scol.*) credit.

V

va /va/ *voir* **aller**[1].

vacance /vakɑ̃s/ *n.f.* (*poste*) vacancy. **~es**, holiday(s). en **~es**, on holiday. **~ier**, **~ière** *n.m.*, *f.* holiday-maker.

vacant, **~e** /vakɑ̃, -t/ *a.* vacant.

vacarme /vakarm/ *n.m.* uproar.

vaccin /vaksɛ̃/ *n.m.* vaccine; (*inoculation*) vaccination.

vaccin|er /vaksine/ *v.t.* vaccinate. **~ation** *n.f.* vaccination.

vache /vaʃ/ *n.f.* cow. —*a.* (*méchant: fam.*) nasty. **~ment** *adv.* (*très: fam.*) damned; (*pleuvoir, manger, etc.: fam.*) a hell of a lot.

va-et-vient /vaevjɛ̃/ *n.m. invar.* to and fro (motion); (*de personnes*) comings and goings.

vagabond, **~e** /vagabɔ̃, -d/ *n.m.*, *f.* (*péj.*) vagrant, vagabond.

vagin /vaʒɛ̃/ *n.m.* vagina.

vague[1] /vag/ *a.* vague. —*n.m.* vagueness. **~ment** *adv.* vaguely.

vague[2] /vag/ *n.f.* wave. **~ de froid**, cold spell. **~ de chaleur**, hot spell.

vaille /vaj/ *voir* **valoir**.

vain, **~e** /vɛ̃, vɛn/ *a.* vain. en **~**, in vain. **~ement** /vɛnmɑ̃/ *adv.* vainly.

vain|cre† /vɛ̃kr/ *v.t.* defeat; (*surmonter*) overcome. **~cu**, **~cue** *n.m.*, *f.* (*sport*) loser. **~queur** *n.m.* victor; (*sport*) winner.

vais /vɛ/ *voir* **aller**[1].

vaisseau (*pl.* **~x**) /vɛso/ *n.m.* ship;

(*veine*) vessel. **~ spatial**, spaceship.

vaisselle /vɛsɛl/ *n.f.* crockery; (*à laver*) dishes. **faire la ~**, do the washing-up, wash the dishes. **produit pour la ~**, washing-up liquid.

val (*pl.* **~s** *ou* **vaux**) /val, vo/ *n.m.* valley.

valable /valabl/ *a.* valid; (*de qualité*) worthwhile.

valet /valɛ/ *n.m.* (*cartes*) jack.

valeur /valœr/ *n.f.* value; (*mérite*) worth, value. **~s**, (*comm.*) stocks and shares. **avoir de la ~**, be valuable.

valid|e /valid/ *a.* (*personne*) fit; (*billet*) valid. **~er** *v.t.* validate.

valise /valiz/ *n.f.* (suit)case. **faire ses ~s**, pack (one's bags).

vallée /vale/ *n.f.* valley.

vallon /valɔ̃/ *n.m.* (small) valley.

valoir† /valwar/ *v.i.* be worth; (*s'appliquer*) apply. **~ qch.**, be worth sth.; (*être aussi bon que*) be as good as sth. **se ~** *v. pr.* (*être équivalents*) be as good as each other. **~ la peine**, **~ le coup**, be worth it. **ça ne vaut rien**, it is no good. **il vaudrait mieux faire**, we'd better do.

vals|e /vals/ *n.f.* waltz. **~er** *v.i.* waltz.

valve /valv/ *n.f.* valve.

van /vɑ̃/ *n.m.* van.

vanille /vanij/ *n.f.* vanilla.

vanit|é /vanite/ *n.f.* vanity. **~eux**, **~euse** *a.* vain, conceited.

vanne /van/ *n.f.* (*d'écluse*) sluice (-gate); (*fam.*) joke.

vantard, **~e** /vɑ̃tar, -d/ *a.* boastful; *n.m.*, *f.* boaster.

vanter /vɑ̃te/ *v.t.* praise. **se ~** *v. pr.* boast (**de**, about).

vapeur /vapœr/ *n.f.* (*eau*) steam; (*brume, émanation*) vapour.

vaporis|er /vapoɾize/ *v.t.* spray. **∼ateur** *n.m.* spray.

varappe /vaɾap/ *n.f.* rock climbing.

variable /vaɾjabl/ *a.* variable; (*temps*) changeable.

variante /vaɾjɑ̃t/ *n.f.* variant.

varicelle /vaɾisɛl/ *n.f.* chickenpox.

varices /vaɾis/ *n.f. pl.* varicose veins.

var|ier /vaɾje/ *v.t./i.* vary. **∼iation** *n.f.* variation. **∼ié** *a.* (*non monotone, étendu*) varied; (*divers*) various.

variété /vaɾjete/ *n.f.* variety. **∼s**, (*spectacle*) variety.

variole /vaɾjɔl/ *n.f.* smallpox.

vase¹ /vɑz/ *n.m.* vase.

vase² /vɑz/ *n.f.* (*boue*) silt, mud.

vaste /vast/ *a.* vast, huge.

vaudeville /vodvil/ *n.m.* vaudeville, light comedy.

vautour /votuɾ/ *n.m.* vulture.

veau (*pl.* **∼x**) /vo/ *n.m.* calf; (*viande*) veal; (*cuir*) calfskin.

vécu /veky/ *voir* **vivre**. —*a.* (*réel*) true, real.

vedette¹ /vədɛt/ *n.f.* (*artiste*) star.

vedette² /vədɛt/ *n.f.* (*bateau*) launch.

végét|al (*m. pl.* **∼aux**) /veʒetal, -o/ *a.* plant. —*n.m.* (*pl.* **∼aux**) plant.

végétalien, **∼ne** /veʒetaljɛ̃, -jɛn/ *n.m., f. & a.* vegan.

végétarien, **∼ne** /veʒetaɾjɛ̃, -jɛn/ *a. & n.m., f.* vegetarian.

végétation /veʒetasjɔ̃/ *n.f.* vegetation. **∼s**, (*méd.*) adenoids.

véhicule /veikyl/ *n.m.* vehicle.

veille¹ /vɛj/ *n.f.* **la ∼** (**de**), the day before. **la ∼ de Noël**, Christmas Eve. **à la ∼ de**, on the eve of.

veille² /vɛj/ *n.f.* (*état*) wakefulness.

veillée /veje/ *n.f.* evening (gathering); (*mortuaire*) vigil, wake.

veiller /veje/ *v.i.* stay up *ou* awake. **∼ à**, attend to. **∼ sur**, watch over. —*v.t.* (*malade*) watch over.

veilleur /vejœɾ/ *n.m.* **∼ de nuit**, night-watchman.

veilleuse /vejøz/ *n.f.* night-light; (*de véhicule*) sidelight; (*de réchaud*) pilot-light.

veinard, **∼e** /vɛnaɾ, -d/ *n.m., f.* (*fam.*) lucky devil.

veine¹ /vɛn/ *n.f.* (*anat.*) vein; (*nervure, filon*) vein.

veine² /vɛn/ *n.f.* (*chance: fam.*) luck. **avoir de la ∼**, (*fam.*) be lucky.

velcro /vɛlkɾo/ *n.m.* (P.) velcro.

véliplanchiste /veliplɑ̃ʃist/ *n.m./f.* windsurfer.

vélo /velo/ *n.m.* bicycle, bike; (*activité*) cycling.

vélomoteur /velomɔtœɾ/ *n.m.* moped.

velours /vluɾ/ *n.m.* velvet. **∼ côtelé**, **∼ à côtes**, corduroy.

velu /vəly/ *a.* hairy.

venaison /vənɛzɔ̃/ *n.f.* venison.

vendanges /vɑ̃dɑ̃ʒ/ *n.f. pl.* grape harvest.

vendeu|r, **∼se** /vɑ̃dœɾ, -øz/ *n.m., f.* shop assistant; (*marchand*) salesman, saleswoman.

vendre /vɑ̃dɾ/ *v.t.*, **se ∼** *v. pr.* sell. **à ∼**, for sale.

vendredi /vɑ̃dɾədi/ *n.m.* Friday. **V∼ saint**, Good Friday.

vénéneu|x, **∼se** /veneno, -z/ *a.* poisonous.

vénérien, **∼ne** /veneɾjɛ̃, -jɛn/ *a.* venereal.

vengeance /vɑ̃ʒɑ̃s/ *n.f.* revenge, vengeance.

venger /vɑ̃ʒe/ *v.t.* avenge. **se ∼** *v. pr.* take (one's) revenge (**de**, for).

ven|in /vənɛ̃/ *n.m.* venom. **∼imeux**, **∼imeuse** *a.* poisonous, venomous.

venir† /vənir/ *v.i.* (*aux. être*) come (de, from). **~ faire,** come to do. **~ de faire,** to have just done. **il vient/venait d'arriver,** he has/had just arrived. **faire ~,** send for.

vent /vɑ̃/ *n.m.* wind.

vente /vɑ̃t/ *n.f.* sale. **~ (aux enchères),** auction. **en ~,** on *ou* for sale. **~ de charité,** (charity) bazaar.

ventil|er /vɑ̃tile/ *v.t.* ventilate. **~ateur** *n.m.* fan, ventilator. **~ation** *n.f.* ventilation.

ventouse /vɑ̃tuz/ *n.f.* (*dispositif*) suction pad; (*pour déboucher l'évier etc.*) plunger.

ventre /vɑ̃tr/ *n.m.* belly, stomach; (*utérus*) womb.

ventru /vɑ̃try/ *a.* pot-bellied.

venu /vəny/ *voir* venir.

venue /vəny/ *n.f.* coming.

vêpres /vɛpr/ *n.f. pl.* vespers.

ver /vɛr/ *n.m.* worm; (*des fruits, de la viande*) maggot; (*du bois*) woodworm. **~ à soie,** silkworm. **~ solitaire,** tapeworm. **~ de terre,** earthworm.

véranda /verɑ̃da/ *n.f.* veranda.

verb|e /vɛrb/ *n.m.* (*gram.*) verb. **~al** (*m. pl.* **~aux**) *a.* verbal.

verdâtre /vɛrdatr/ *a.* greenish.

verdict /vɛrdikt/ *n.m.* verdict.

verdure /vɛrdyr/ *n.f.* greenery.

verger /vɛrʒe/ *n.m.* orchard.

vergla|s /vɛrɡla/ *n.m.* (black) ice. **~cé** *a.* icy.

vérifi|er /verifje/ *v.t.* check, verify; (*compte*) audit; (*confirmer*) confirm. **~ication** *n.f.* check(ing), verification.

véritable /veritabl/ *a.* true, real; (*authentique*) real. **~ment** /-əmɑ̃/ *adv.* really.

vérité /verite/ *n.f.* truth. **en ~,** in fact.

vermicelle(s) /vɛrmisɛl/ *n.m.* (*pl.*) vermicelli.

vermouth /vɛrmut/ *n.m.* (*apéritif*) vermouth.

verni /vɛrni/ *a.* (*fam.*) lucky. **chaussures ~es,** patent (leather) shoes.

vernir /vɛrnir/ *v.t.* varnish.

vernis /vɛrni/ *n.m.* varnish; (*de poterie*) glaze. **~ à ongles,** nail polish *ou* varnish.

vernissage /vɛrnisaʒ/ *n.m.* (*exposition*) preview.

vernisser /vɛrnise/ *v.t.* glaze.

verra, verrait /vɛra, vɛrɛ/ *voir* voir.

verre /vɛr/ *n.m.* glass. **prendre** *ou* **boire un ~,** have a drink. **~ de contact,** contact lens.

verrou /vɛru/ *n.m.* bolt.

verrouiller /vɛruje/ *v.t.* bolt.

verrue /vɛry/ *n.f.* wart.

vers¹ /vɛr/ *prép.* towards; (*temps*) about.

vers² /vɛr/ *n.m.* (*ligne*) line. **les ~,** (*poésie*) verse.

versant /vɛrsɑ̃/ *n.m.* slope, side.

verse (à) /(a)vɛrs/ *adv.* in torrents.

Verseau /vɛrso/ *n.m.* le ~, Aquarius.

vers|er /vɛrse/ *v.t./i.* pour; (*payer*) pay. **~ement** *n.m.* payment.

verset /vɛrsɛ/ *n.m.* (*relig.*) verse.

version /vɛrsjɔ̃/ *n.f.* version; (*traduction*) translation.

verso /vɛrso/ *n.m.* back (of the page).

vert, ~e /vɛr, -t/ *a.* green. —*n.m.* green.

vertèbre /vɛrtɛbr/ *n.f.* vertebra.

vertic|al, ~ale (*m. pl.* **~aux**) /vɛrtikal, -o/ *a. & n.f.* vertical. **~alement** *adv.* vertically.

vertige /vɛrtiʒ/ *n.m.* dizziness. **avoir le ~,** feel dizzy.

vertu /vɛrty/ *n.f.* virtue. **en ~ de,** by virtue of.

verveine /vɛrvɛn/ *n.f.* verbena.

vésicule /vezikyl/ *n.f.* ~ **biliaire,** gall-bladder.

vessie /vesi/ *n.f.* bladder.

veste /vɛst/ *n.f.* jacket.

vestiaire /vɛstjɛr/ *n.m.* cloakroom; (*sport*) changing-room.

vestibule /vɛstibyl/ *n.m.* hall.

vestige /vɛstiʒ/ *n.m.* (*objet*) relic; (*trace*) vestige.

veston /vɛstɔ̃/ *n.m.* jacket.

vêtement /vɛtmɑ̃/ *n.m.* article of clothing. ~**s,** clothes.

vétéran /veterɑ̃/ *n.m.* veteran.

vétérinaire /veterinɛr/ *n.m./f.* vet, veterinary surgeon.

vêt|ir /vetir/ *v.t.* **se** ~**ir** *v. pr.* dress. ~**u** *a.* dressed (**de,** in).

veto /veto/ *n.m. invar.* veto.

vétuste /vetyst/ *a.* dilapidated.

veu|f, ~**ve** /vœf, -v/ *a.* widowed. —*n.m.* widower. —*n.f.* widow.

veuille /vœj/ *voir* **vouloir.**

veut, veux /vø/ *voir* **vouloir.**

vex|er, ~**ante** /vɛkse/ *v.t.* upset, hurt. se ~**er** *v. pr.* be upset, be hurt. ~**ant,** ~**ante** *a.* upsetting.

via /vja/ *prép.* via.

viaduc /vjadyk/ *n.m.* viaduct.

viande /vjɑ̃d/ *n.f.* meat.

vibr|er /vibre/ *v.i.* vibrate; (*être ému*) thrill. ~**ation** *n.f.* vibration.

vicaire /vikɛr/ *n.m.* curate.

vice /vis/ *n.m.* (*moral*) vice; (*défectuosité*) defect.

vice- /vis/ *préf.* vice-.

vice versa /vis(e)vɛrsa/ *adv.* vice versa.

vicieu|x, ~**se** /visjø, -z/ *a.* depraved. —*n.m., f.* pervert.

victime /viktim/ *n.f.* victim; (*d'un accident*) casualty.

vict|oire /viktwar/ *n.f.* victory; (*sport*) win. ~**orieux,** ~**orieuse** *a.* victorious; (*équipe*) winning.

victuailles /viktɥaj/ *n.f. pl.* provisions.

vidang|e /vidɑ̃ʒ/ *n.f.* emptying; (*auto.*) oil change; (*dispositif*) waste pipe. ~**er** *v.t.* empty.

vide /vid/ *a.* empty. —*n.m.* emptiness, void; (*trou, manque*) gap; (*espace sans air*) vacuum.

vidéo /video/ *a. invar.* video. **jeu** ~, video game. ~**cassette** *n.f.* video(tape). ~**thèque** *n.f.* video library.

vide-ordures /vidɔrdyr/ *n.m. invar.* (rubbish) chute.

vider /vide/ *v.t.* empty; (*poisson*) gut; (*expulser: fam.*) throw out.

videur /vidœr/ *n.m.* bouncer.

vie /vi/ *n.f.* life; (*durée*) lifetime. **en** ~, alive.

vieil /vjɛj/ *voir* **vieux.**

vieillard /vjɛjar/ *n.m.* old man.

vieille /vjɛj/ *voir* **vieux.**

vieillesse /vjɛjɛs/ *n.f.* old age.

vieill|ir /vjɛjir/ *v.i.* grow old, age; (*mot, idée*) become old-fashioned. —*v.t.* age. ~**issement** *n.m.* ageing.

viens, vient /vjɛ̃/ *voir* **venir.**

vierge /vjɛrʒ/ *n.f.* virgin. **la V**~, Virgo. —*a.* virgin; (*feuille, film*) blank.

vieux ou vieil*, vieille (*m. pl.* **vieux**) /vjø, vjɛj/ *a.* old. —*n.m.* old man. —*n.f.* old woman. **mon** ~, (*fam.*) old man ou boy. **ma vieille,** (*fam.*) old girl, dear. **vieille fille,** (*péj.*) spinster. ~ **garçon,** bachelor.

vif, vive /vif, viv/ *a.* lively; (*émotion, vent*) keen; (*froid*) biting; (*lumière*) bright; (*douleur, parole*) sharp; (*souvenir, style, teint*) vivid; (*succès, impatience*) great.

vigilan|t, ~**te** /viʒilɑ̃, -t/ *a.* vigilant. ~**ce** *n.f.* vigilance.

vigne /viɲ/ *n.f.* (*plante*) vine; (*vignoble*) vineyard.

vigneron, ~ne /viɲrɔ̃, -ɔn/ *n.m., f.* wine-grower.

vignette /viɲɛt/ *n.f.* (*étiquette*) label; (*auto.*) road tax sticker.

vignoble /viɲɔbl/ *n.m.* vineyard.

vigoureu|x, ~se /viguərø, -z/ *a.* vigorous, sturdy.

vigueur /vigœr/ *n.f.* vigour. **être/entrer en ~,** (*loi*) be/come into force. **en ~,** (*terme*) in use.

VIH *abrév.* (*virus d'immunodéficiencehumaine*) HIV.

vilain, ~e /vilɛ̃, -ɛn/ *a.* (*mauvais*) nasty; (*laid*) ugly.

villa /villa/ *n.f.* (detached) house.

village /vilaʒ/ *n.m.* village.

villageois, ~e /vilaʒwa, -z/ *a.* village. —*n.m., f.* villager.

ville /vil/ *n.f.* town; (*importante*) city. **~ d'eaux,** spa.

vin /vɛ̃/ *n.m.* wine.

vinaigre /vinɛgr/ *n.m.* vinegar.

vinaigrette /vinɛgrɛt/ *n.f.* oil and vinegar dressing, vinaigrette.

vindicati|f, ~ve /vɛ̃dikatif, -v/ *a.* vindictive.

vingt /vɛ̃/ (/vɛ̃t/ *before vowel and in numbers* 22–29) *a.* & *n.m.* twenty. **~ième** *a.* & *n.m./f.* twentieth. **~aine** /vɛ̃tɛn/ *n.f.* **une ~ (de),** about twenty.

vinicole /vinikɔl/ *a.* wine(-growing).

vinyle /vinil/ *n.m.* vinyl.

viol /vjɔl/ *n.m.* (*de femme*) rape; (*de lieu, loi*) violation.

viol|ent, ~ente /vjɔlɑ̃, -t/ *a.* violent. **~emment** /-amɑ̃/ *adv.* violently. **~ence** *n.f.* violence; (*acte*) act of violence.

viol|er /vjɔle/ *v.t.* rape; (*lieu, loi*) viol..ce. **~ation** *n.f.* violation.

violet, ~te /vjɔlɛ, -t/ *a.* & *n.m.* purple. —*n.f.* violet.

violon /vjɔlɔ̃/ *n.m.* violin. **~iste**

/-ɔnist/ *n.m./f.* violinist. **~ d'Ingres,** hobby.

violoncelle /vjɔlɔ̃sɛl/ *n.m.* cello.

vipère /vipɛr/ *n.f.* viper, adder.

virage /viraʒ/ *n.m.* bend; (*de véhicule*) turn.

vir|er /vire/ *v.i.* turn. —*v.t.* (*argent*) transfer; (*expulser: fam.*) throw out. **~ement** *n.m.* (*comm.*) (credit) transfer.

virginité /virʒinite/ *n.f.* virginity.

virgule /virgyl/ *n.f.* comma; (*dans un nombre*) (decimal) point.

viril /viril/ *a.* manly, virile.

virus /virys/ *n.m.* virus.

vis¹ /vi/ *voir* **vivre, voir.**

vis² /vis/ *n.f.* screw.

visa /viza/ *n.m.* visa.

visage /vizaʒ/ *n.m.* face.

vis-à-vis /vizavi/ *adv.* face to face, opposite. **~ de,** opposite; (*à l'égard de*) with respect to.

viscères /visɛr/ *n.m. pl.* intestines.

viser /vize/ *v.t.* aim at; (*concerner*) be aimed at; (*timbrer*) stamp.

visib|le /vizibl/ *a.* visible. **~ilité** *n.f.* visibility.

visière /vizjɛr/ *n.f.* (*de casquette*) peak; (*de casque*) visor.

vision /vizjɔ̃/ *n.f.* vision.

vision|ner /vizjɔne/ *v.t.* view. **~euse** *n.f.* (*appareil*) viewer.

visite /vizit/ *n.f.* visit; (*examen*) examination; (*personne*) visitor. **heures de ~,** visiting hours. **~ guidée,** guided tour. **rendre ~ à,** visit.

visit|er /vizite/ *v.t.* visit. **~eur, ~euse** *n.m., f.* visitor.

vison /vizɔ̃/ *n.m.* mink.

visqueu|x, ~se /viskø, -z/ *a.* viscous.

visser /vise/ *v.t.* screw (on).

visuel, ~le /vizɥɛl/ *a.* visual.

vit /vi/ *voir* **vivre, voir.**

vit|al (*m. pl.* **~aux**) /vital, -o/ *a.* vital. **~alité** *n.f.* vitality.

vitamine /vitamin/ *n.f.* vitamin.

vite /vit/ *adv.* fast, quickly; (*tôt*) soon. ∼!, quick! **faire** ∼, be quick.

vitesse /vites/ *n.f.* speed; (*régime: auto.*) gear. **à toute** ∼, at top speed. **en** ∼, in a hurry, quickly.

viticole /vitikɔl/ *a.* wine. ∼ulteur /-yltœr/ *n.m.* wine-grower. ∼ulture *n.f.* wine-growing.

vitrage /vitraʒ/ *n.m.* (*vitres*) windows. **double-**∼, double glazing.

vitr|ail (*pl.* ∼**aux**) /vitraj, -o/ *n.m.* stained-glass window.

vitr|e /vitr/ *n.f.* (window) pane; (*de véhicule*) window. ∼**é** *a.* glass, glazed. ∼**er** *v.t.* glaze.

vitrine /vitrin/ *n.f.* (shop) window.

vivant, ∼**e** /vivɑ̃, -t/ *a.* (*doué de vie, en usage*) living; (*en vie*) alive, living; (*actif, vif*) lively. —*n.m.* **un bon** ∼, a bon viveur.

vive[1] /viv/ *voir* **vif**.

vive[2] /viv/ *int.* ∼ **le roi/prési-dent/***etc.*!, long live the king/ president/*etc.*!

vivier /vivje/ *n.m.* fish-pond.

vivisection /vivisɛksjɔ̃/ *n.f.* vivisection.

vivre† /vivr/ *v.i.* live. ∼ **de**, (*nourriture*) live on. —*v.t.* (*vie*) live; (*période, aventure*) live through. ∼**s** *n.m. pl.* supplies. **faire** ∼, (*famille etc.*) support.

vlan /vlɑ̃/ *int.* bang.

vocabulaire /vɔkabylɛr/ *n.m.* vocabulary.

vocation /vɔkasjɔ̃/ *n.f.* vocation.

vodka /vɔdka/ *n.f.* vodka.

vœu (*pl.* ∼**x**) /vø/ *n.m.* (*souhait*) wish; (*promesse*) vow.

voici /vwasi/ *prép.* here is, this is; (*au pluriel*) here are, these are.

voie /vwa/ *n.f.* (*route*) road; (*chemin*) way; (*moyen*) means, way; (*partie de route*) lane; (*rails*) track; (*quai*) platform. **en** ∼ **de**,

in the process of. **en** ∼ **de développement**, (*pays*) developing. ∼ **ferrée**, railway. ∼ **lactée**, Milky Way. ∼ **navig-able**, waterway. ∼ **publique**, public highway. ∼ **sans issue**, cul-de-sac dead end.

voilà /vwala/ *prép.* there is, that is; (*au pluriel*) there are, those are; (*voici*) here is; here are. **le** ∼, there he is. ∼!, right!; (*en offrant qch.*) there you are!

voilage /vwalaʒ/ *n.m.* net curtain.

voile[1] /vwal/ *n.f.* (*de bateau*) sail; (*sport*) sailing.

voile[2] /vwal/ *n.m.* veil; (*tissu léger et fin*) net.

voiler /vwale/ *v.t.* veil. ∼**é** *a.* (*terme, femme*) veiled; (*flou*) hazy.

voilier /vwalje/ *n.m.* sailing-ship.

voir† /vwar/ *v.t./i.* see. ∼ **v.** *pr.* (*être visible*) show; (*se produire*) be seen; (*se trouver*) find o.s.; (*se fréquenter*) see each other. **ça n'a rien à** ∼ **avec**, that has nothing to do with. **faire** ∼, **laisser** ∼, show. **je ne peux pas le** ∼, (*fam.*) I cannot stand him. **voyons!**, (*irritation*) come on!

voirie /vwari/ *n.f.* (*service*) highway maintenance. **travaux de** ∼, road-works.

voisin, ∼**e** /vwazɛ̃, -in/ *a.* (*proche*) neighbouring; (*adjacent*) next (**de**, to); (*semblable*) similar (**de**, to). —*n.m.*, *f.* neighbour. **le** ∼, the man next door.

voisinage /vwazinaʒ/ *n.m.* neigh-bourhood; (*proximité*) proximity.

voiture /vwatyr/ *n.f.* (motor) car; (*wagon*) coach, carriage. **en** ∼!, all aboard! ∼ **de course**, racing-car. ∼ **d'enfant**, pram. ∼ **de tourisme**, private car.

voix /vwa/ *n.f.* voice; (*suffrage*) vote.

vol[1] /vɔl/ *n.m.* (*d'avion, d'oiseau*)

flight; (groupe d'oiseaux etc.) flock, flight.

vol² /vɔl/ n.m. (délit) theft; (hold-up) robbery.

volaille /vɔlɑj/ n.f. **la ~**, (poules etc.) poultry. **une ~**, a fowl.

volant /vɔlɑ̃/ n.m. (steering-) wheel; (de jupe) flounce.

volcan /vɔlkɑ̃/ n.m. volcano.

volée /vɔle/ n.f. flight; (oiseaux) flight, flock; (de coups, d'obus) volley.

voler¹ /vɔle/ v.i. (oiseau etc.) fly.

vol|er² /vɔle/ v.t./i. steal (à, from). **il ne l'a pas ~é**, he deserved it. **~er qn.**, rob s.o. **~eur, ~euse** n.m., f. thief; a. thieving.

volet /vɔle/ n.m. (de fenêtre) shutter; (de document) (folded ou tear-off) section.

volontaire /vɔlɔ̃tɛr/ a. voluntary; (personne) determined. —n.m./f. volunteer. **~ment** adv. voluntarily; (exprès) intentionally.

volonté /vɔlɔ̃te/ n.f. (faculté, intention) will; (souhait) wish; (énergie) will-power. **à ~**, (à son gré) at will. **bonne ~**, goodwill. **mauvaise ~**, ill will.

volontiers /vɔlɔ̃tje/ adv. (de bon gré) willingly, gladly.

volt /vɔlt/ n.m. volt. **~age** n.m. voltage.

volume /vɔlym/ n.m. volume.

volumineu|x, ~se /vɔlyminø, -z/ a. bulky.

vom|ir /vɔmir/ v.t./i. vomit. **~i** n.m. vomit. **~issement(s)** n.m. (pl.) vomiting.

vont /vɔ̃/ voir **aller¹**.

vorace /vɔras/ a. voracious.

vos /vo/ voir **votre**.

vote /vɔt/ n.m. (action) voting; (d'une loi) passing; (suffrage) vote.

voter /vɔte/ v.i. vote. —v.t. vote for; (adopter) pass; (crédits) vote.

votre (pl. **vos**) /vɔtr, vo/ a. your.

vôtre /votr/ pron. **le ou la ~**, **les ~s**, yours.

vouloir† /vulwar/ v.t. want (faire, to do). **ça ne veut pas bouger/etc.**, it will not move/etc. **je voudrais/voudrais bien venir/etc.**, I should ou would like/really like to come/etc. **je veux bien venir/etc.**, I am happy to come/etc. **voulez-vous attendre/etc.?**, will you wait/etc.? **veuillez attendre/etc.**, kindly wait/etc. **~ absolument faire**, insist on doing. **comme ou si vous voulez**, if you like ou wish. **en ~ à qn.**, have a grudge against s.o.; (être en colère contre) be annoyed with s.o. **qu'est ce qu'il me veut?**, what does he want with me? **ne pas ~ de qch./qn.**, not want sth./s.o. **~ dire**, mean. **~ du bien à**, wish well.

voulu /vuly/ a. (délibéré) intentional; (requis) required.

vous /vu/ pron. (sujet, complément) you; (indirect) (to) you; (réfléchi) yourself; (pl.) yourselves; (l'un l'autre) each other. **~-même** pron. yourself. **~-mêmes** pron. yourselves.

voûte /vut/ n.f. (plafond) vault; (porche) archway.

voûté /vute/ a. bent, stooped.

vouv|oyer /vuvwaje/ v.t. address politely (using vous). **~oiement** n.m. use of (polite) vous.

voyage /vwajaʒ/ n.m. journey, trip; (par mer) voyage. **~(s)**, (action) travelling. **~ d'affaires**, business trip. **~ de noces**, honeymoon. **~ organisé**, (package) tour.

voyag|er /vwajaʒe/ v.i. travel. **~eur, ~euse** n.m., f. traveller.

voyant /vwajɑ̃/ n.m. (signal) (warning) light.

voyelle /vwajɛl/ *n.f.* vowel.

voyou /vwaju/ *n.m.* hooligan.

vrac (en) /(ɑ̃)vrak/ *adv.* in disorder; (*sans emballage, au poids*) loose, in bulk.

vrai /vrɛ/ *a.* true; (*réel*) real.

vraiment /vrɛmɑ̃/ *adv.* really.

vraisemblable /vrɛsɑ̃blabl/ *a.* likely.

VRP *abrév. m.* (*voyageur représentant placier*) rep.

vu /vy/ *voir* **voir**. ~ **que**, seeing that.

vue /vy/ *n.f.* (*spectacle*) sight; (*sens*) (eye)sight; (*panorama, idée*) view.

vulg|aire /vylgɛr/ *a.* (*grossier*) vulgar; (*ordinaire*) common. ~**arité** *n.f.* vulgarity.

vulnérable /vylnerabl/ *a.* vulnerable.

vulve /vylv/ *n.f.* vulva.

W

wagon /vagɔ̃/ *n.m.* (*de voyageurs*) carriage; (*de marchandises*) wagon. ~**-lit** (*pl.* ~**s-lits**) *n.m.* sleeping-car, sleeper. ~**-restaurant** (*pl.* ~**s-restaurants**) *n.m.* dining-car.

walkman /wɔkman/ *n.m.* (P.) walkman.

wallon, ~**ne** /walɔ̃, -ɔn/ *a. & n.m., f.* Walloon.

waters /watɛr/ *n.m. pl.* toilet.

watt /wat/ *n.m.* watt.

w.-c. /(dubləl)vese/ *n.m. pl.* toilet.

week-end /wikɛnd/ *n.m.* weekend.

western /wɛstɛrn/ *n.m.* western.

whisk|y (*pl.* ~**ies**) /wiski/ *n.m.* whisky.

X

xérès /kseres/ *n.m.* sherry.

xylophone /ksilɔfɔn/ *n.m.* xylophone.

Y

y /i/ *adv. & pron.* there; (*dessus*) on it; (*pl.*) on them; (*dedans*) in it; (*pl.*) in them. **s'y habituer**, (*à cela*) get used to it. **s'y attendre**, expect it. **y penser**, think of it. **il y entra**, (*dans cela*) he entered it. **j'y vais**, I'm on my way. **ça y est**, that is it.

yacht /jɔt/ *n.m.* yacht.

yaourt /jaur(t)/ *n.m.* yoghurt.

yeux /jø/ *voir* **œil**.

yiddish /(j)idiʃ/ *n.m.* Yiddish.

yoga /jɔga/ *n.m.* yoga.

yougoslave /jugɔslav/ *a. & n.m./f.* Yugoslav.

Yougoslavie /jugɔslavi/ *n.f.* Yugoslavia.

Z

zèbre /zɛbr/ *n.m.* zebra.

zèle /zɛl/ *n.m.* zeal.

zéro /zero/ *n.m.* nought; zero; (*température*) zero; (*dans un numéro*) 0; (*football*) nil. **(re)partir de** ~, start from scratch.

zeste /zɛst/ *n.m.* peel. **un** ~ **de**, (*fig.*) a pinch of.

zigzag /zigzag/ *n.m.* zigzag.

zinc /zɛ̃g/ *n.m.* (*métal*) zinc; (*comptoir. fam.*) bar.

zodiaque /zɔdjak/ *n.m.* zodiac.

zona /zona/ *n.m.* (*méd.*) shingles.

zone /zon/ *n.f.* zone, area; (*faubourgs*) shanty town. **~ bleue,** restricted parking zone.

zoo /zo(o)/ *n.m.* zoo.

zoom /zum/ *n.m.* zoom lens.

zut /zyt/ *int.* blast (it), (oh) hell.

ANGLAIS–FRANÇAIS
ENGLISH–FRENCH

A

a *a.* (*before vowel* **an**) un(e). **I'm a painter,** je suis peintre. **ten pence a kilo,** dix pence le kilo. **once a year,** une fois par an.

abandon *v.t.* abandonner. —*n.* désinvolture *f.* ~**ed** *a.* (*behaviour*) débauché.

abate *v.i.* se calmer. —*v.t.* diminuer. ~**ment** *n.* diminution *f.*

abattoir *n.* abattoir *m.*

abbey *n.* abbaye *f.*

abbot *n.* abbé *m.*

abbreviat|e *v.t.* abréger. ~**ion** *n.* abréviation *f.*

abdicat|e *v.t./i.* abdiquer. ~**ion** *n.* abdication *f.*

abdom|en *n.* abdomen *m.* ~**inal** *a.* abdominal.

abduct *v.t.* enlever. ~**ion** *n.* rapt *m.* ~**or** *n.* ravisseur|r, -se *m., f.*

aberration *n.* aberration *f.*

abet *v.t.* (*jurid.*) encourager.

abhor *v.t.* (*p.t.* **abhorred**) exécrer. ~**rence** *n.* horreur *f.* ~**rent** *a.* exécrable.

ability *n.* aptitude *f.* (**to do,** à faire); (*talent*) talent *m.*

abject *a.* abject.

able *a.* capable (**to,** de). **be** ~**e,** pouvoir; (*know how to*) savoir.

abnormal *a.* anormal. ~**ity** *n.* anomalie *f.*

aboard *adv.* à bord. —*prep.* à bord de.

aboli|sh *v.t.* supprimer, abolir. ~**tion** *n.* suppression *f.*, abolition *f.*

abominable *a.* abominable.

aboriginal *a. & n.* aborigène (*m.*).

aborigines *n. pl.* aborigènes *m. pl.*

abort *v.t.* faire avorter. —*v.i.* avorter. ~**ive** *a.* (*attempt etc.*) manqué.

abortion *n.* avortement *m.* **have an** ~, se faire avorter.

about *adv.* (*approximately*) environ; (*here and there*) çà et là; (*all round*) partout, autour; (*nearby*) dans les parages; (*of rumour*) en circulation. —*prep.* au sujet de; (*round*) autour de; (*somewhere in*) dans. ~**-face,** ~**-turn** *ns.* (*fig.*) volteface *f. invar.* ~ **here,** par ici. **be** ~ **to do,** être sur le point de faire. **how** *or* **what** ~ **leaving,** si on partait. **what's the film** ~?, quel est le sujet du film? **talk** ~, parler de.

above *adv.* au-dessus; (*on page*) ci-dessus. —*prep.* au-dessus de. **he is not** ~ **lying,** il n'est pas incapable de mentir. ~ **all,** par-dessus tout. ~**-mentioned** *a.* mentionné ci-dessus.

abrasive *a.* abrasif; (*manner*) brusque. —*n.* abrasif *m.*

abreast *adv.* de front. **keep** ~ **of,** se tenir au courant de.

abroad adv. à l'étranger; (far and wide) de tous côtés.

abrupt a. (sudden, curt) brusque; (steep) abrupt. **∿ly** adv. (suddenly) brusquement; (curtly, rudely) avec brusquerie. **∿ness** n. brusquerie f.

abscess n. abcès m.

abseil v.i. descendre en rappel.

absen|t[1] a. absent; (look etc.) distrait. **∿ce** n. absence f.; (lack) manque m. **in the ∿ce of**, à défaut de. **∿t-minded** a. distrait. **∿t-mindedness** n. distraction f.

absent[2] v. pr. **∿ o.s.**, s'absenter.

absentee n. absent(e) m. (f.). **∿ism** n. absentéisme m.

absolute a. absolu; (coward etc.: fam.) véritable. **∿ly** adv. absolument.

absolution n. absolution f.

absor|b v.t. absorber. **∿ption** n. absorption f.

absorbent a. absorbant.

abst|ain v.i. s'abstenir (from, de). **∿ention** n. abstention f.

abstinence n. abstinence f.

abstract a. abstrait. —n. (quality) abstrait m.; (summary) résumé m.

absurd a. absurde. **∿ity** n. absurdité f.

abundan|t a. abondant. **∿ce** n. abondance f.

abuse[1] v.t. (misuse) abuser de; (ill-treat) maltraiter; (insult) injurier.

abus|e[2] n. (misuse) abus m. (of, de); (insults) injures f.pl. **∿ive** a. injurieux. **get ∿ive**, devenir grossier.

abyss n. abîme m.

academic a. universitaire; (scholarly) intellectuel; (pej.) théorique. —n. universitaire m./f. **∿ally** adv. intellectuellement.

academy n. (school) école f. **A∿**, (society) Académie f.

accelerat|e v.t. accélérer. —v.i. (speed up) s'accélérer; (auto.) accélérer. **∿ion** n. accélération f.

accelerator n. accélérateur m.

accent n. accent m.

accept v.t. accepter. **∿able** a. acceptable. **∿ance** n. acceptation f.; (approval, favour) approbation f.

access n. accès m. **(to sth.**, à qch.; **to s.o.**, auprès de qn.). **∿ible** a. accessible. **∿ road**, route d'accès f.

accession n. accession f.; (thing added) nouvelle acquisition f.

accessory a. accessoire. —n. accessoire m.; (person: jurid.) complice m./f.

accident n. accident m.; (chance) hasard m. **∿al** a. accidentel, fortuit. **∿ally** adv. involontairement.

acclaim v.t. acclamer. —n. acclamation(s) f. (pl.).

acclimatiz|e v.t./i. (s')acclimater. **∿ation** n. acclimatation f.

accommodat|e v.t. loger, avoir de la place pour; (adapt) adapter; (supply) fournir; (oblige) obliger. **∿ing** a. obligeant. **∿ion** n. (living premises) logement m.; (rented rooms) chambres f. pl.

accompan|y v.t. accompagner. **∿iment** n. accompagnement m. **∿ist** n. accompagna|teur, -trice m., f.

accomplice n. complice m./f.

accomplish v.t. (perform) accomplir; (achieve) réaliser. **∿ed** a. accompli. **∿ment** n. accomplissement m. **∿ments** n. pl. (abilities) talents m. pl.

accord v.i. concorder. —v.t. accorder. —n. accord m. **of one's own ∿**, de sa propre initiative. **∿ance** n. **in ∿ance with**, conformément à.

according adv. ~ to, selon, suivant. ~ly adv. en conséquence.

accordion n. accordéon m.

account n. (comm.) compte m.; (description) compte rendu m.; (importance) importance f. —v.t. considérer. ~ for, rendre compte de, expliquer. **on ~ of**, à cause de. **on no ~**, en aucun cas. **take into ~**, tenir compte de. ~**able** a. responsable (**for**, de; **to**, envers). ~**ability** n. responsabilité f.

accountan|t n. comptable m./f., expert-comptable m. ~**cy** n. comptabilité f.

accredited a. accrédité.

accumulat|e v.t./i. (s')accumuler. ~**ion** n. accumulation f.

accumulator n. (battery) accumulateur m.

accura|te a. exact, précis. ~**cy** n. exactitude f., précision f. ~**tely** adv. exactement, avec précision.

accus|e v.t. accuser. the ~**ed**, l'accusé(e) m.(f.). ~**ation** n. accusation f.

accustom v.t. accoutumer. ~**ed** a. **become** ~**ed to**, s'accoutumer à.

ace n. (card, person) as m.

ache n. douleur f., mal m. —v.i. faire mal. **my leg** ~**s**, ma jambe me fait mal.

achieve v.t. réaliser, accomplir; (success) obtenir. ~**ment** n. réalisation f. (**of**, de); (feat) exploit m., réussite f.

acid a. & n. acide (m.). ~**ity** n. acidité f. ~ **rain**, pluies acides f. pl.

acknowledge v.t. reconnaître. ~**ment** n. reconnaissance f.; accusé de réception m.

acne n. acné f.

acorn n. (bot.) gland m.

acoustic a. acoustique. ~**s** n. pl. acoustique f.

acquaint v.t. ~ s.o. with sth., mettre qn. au courant de qch. **be** ~**ed with**, (person) connaître; (fact) savoir. ~**ance** n. connaissance f.

acquiesce v.i. consentir. ~**nce** n. consentement m.

acqui|re v.t. acquérir; (habit) prendre. ~**sition** n. acquisition f.

acquit v.t. acquitter. ~**tal** n. acquittement m.

acre n. (approx.) demi-hectare m. ~**age** n. superficie f.

acrid a. âcre.

acrobat n. acrobate m./f. ~**ic** a. acrobatique. ~**ics** n. pl. acrobatie f.

acronym n. sigle m.

across adv. & prep. (side to side) d'un côté à l'autre (de); (on other side) de l'autre côté (**from**, de); (crosswise) en travers (de), à travers. **go** or **walk** ~, traverser.

acrylic a. & n. acrylique (m.).

act n. (deed, theatre) acte m.; (in variety show) numéro m.; (decree) loi f. —v.i. agir; (theatre) jouer; (function) marcher; (pretend) jouer la comédie. —v.t. (part, role) jouer. ~ **as**, servir de. ~**ing** a. (temporary) intérimaire; n. (theatre) jeu m.

action n. action f.; (mil.) combat m. **out of** ~, hors de service. **take** ~, agir.

activate v.t. (machine) actionner; (reaction) activer.

activ|e a. actif; (interest) vif; (volcano) en activité. ~**ism** n. activisme m. ~**ist** n. activiste m./f. ~**ity** n. activité f.

ac|tor n. acteur m. ~**tress** n. actrice f.

actual a. réel; (example) concret. **the** ~ **pen which**, le stylo même que. **in the** ~ **house**, (the house itself) dans la maison elle-même. **no ~ promise,** pas de promesse en tant que telle. **~ly** adv. (in fact) en réalité, réellement.

acumen n. perspicacité f.

acupuncture n. acupuncture f. **~ist** n. acupuncteur m.

acute a. aigu; (mind) pénétrant; (emotion) intense, vif; (shortage) grave. **~ly** adv. vivement.

ad n. (fam.) annonce f.

AD abbr. après J.-C.

adamant a. inflexible.

Adam's apple /ˈædəmzˈæpl/ n. pomme d'Adam f.

adapt v.t./i. (s')adapter. **~ation** n. adaptation f. **~or** n. (electr.) adaptateur m.; (for two plugs) prise multiple f.

adaptab|le a. souple; (techn.) adaptable. **~ility** n. souplesse f.

add v.t./i. ajouter. **~ (up),** (total) additionner. **~ up to,** (total) s'élever à.

adder n. vipère f.

addict n. intoxiqué(e) m. (f.); (fig.) fanatique m./f.

addict|ed a. **~ed to,** (drink) adonné à. **be ~ed to,** (fig.) être un fanatique de. **~ion** n. (med.) dépendance f.; (fig.) manie f. **~ive** a. (drug etc.) qui crée une dépendance.

addition n. addition f. **in ~,** en outre. **~al** a. supplémentaire.

additive n. additif m.

address n. adresse f.; (speech) allocution f. —v.t. adresser; (speak to) s'adresser à.

adenoids n. pl. végétations (adénoïdes) f. pl.

adept a. & n. expert (at, en) (m.).

adequa|te a. suffisant; (satisfactory) satisfaisant. **~cy** n. quantité suffisante f.; (competence) compétence f. **~tely** adv. suffisamment.

adhere v.i. adhérer (to, à). **~ to,** (fig.) respecter. **~nce** n. adhésion f.

adhesion n. (grip) adhérence f.; (support: fig.) adhésion f.

adhesive a. & n. adhésif (m.).

adjacent a. contigu (to, à).

adjective n. adjectif m.

adjoin v.t. être contigu à.

adjourn v.t. ajourner. —v.t./i. **~ (the meeting),** suspendre la séance.

adjust v.t. (machine) régler; (prices) (r)ajuster; (arrange) rajuster, arranger. —v.t./i. **~ (o.s.) to,** s'adapter à. **~able** a. réglable. **~ment** n. (techn.) réglage m.; (of person) adaptation f.

administer v.t. administrer.

administration n. administration f.

administrative a. administratif.

administrator n. administra|teur, -trice m., f.

admirable a. admirable.

admiral n. amiral m.

admir|e v.t. admirer. **~ation** n. admiration f. **~er** n. admira|teur, -trice m., f.

admissible a. admissible.

admission n. admission f.; (to museum, theatre, etc.) entrée f.; (confession) aveu m.

admit v.t. (p.t. admitted) laisser entrer; (acknowledge) reconnaître, admettre. **~ to,** avouer. **~tance** n. entrée f. **~tedly** adv. il est vrai (que).

admonish v.t. réprimander.

adolescen|t n. & a. adolescent(e) (m. (f.)). **~ce** n. adolescence f.

adopt v.t. adopter. **~ed** a. (child) adoptif. **~ion** n. adoption f.

adoptive a. adoptif.

ador|e v.t. adorer. **~able** a. adorable. **~ation** n. adoration f.

adorn v.t. orner.

adult a. & n. adulte (m./f.).

adultery n. adultère m.

advance v.t. avancer. —v.i. (s')avancer; (progress) avancer. —n. avance f. —a. (payment) anticipé. **in** ~, à l'avance. **~d** a. avancé; (studies) supérieur.

advantage n. avantage m. **take** ~ **of**, profiter de; (person) exploiter.

Advent n. Avent m.

adventur|e n. aventure f. **~er** n. explora|teur, -trice m., f.; (pej.) aventur|ier, -ière m., f. **~ous** a. aventureux.

adverb n. adverbe m.

adversary n. adversaire m./f.

advers|e a. défavorable. **~ity** n. adversité f.

advert n. (fam.) annonce f.; (TV) pub f., publicité f. **~isement** n. publicité f.; (in paper etc.) annonce f.

advertis|e v.t./i. faire de la publicité (pour); (sell) mettre une annonce (pour vendre). ~ **for**, (seek) chercher (par voie d'annonce). **~ing** n. publicité f.

advice n. conseil(s) m. (pl.); (comm.) avis m. **some** ~, **a piece of** ~, un conseil.

advis|e v.t. conseiller; (inform) aviser. **~able** a. conseillé, prudent (**to**, de). **~er** n. conseil|ler, -ère m., f.

advocate[1] n. (jurid.) avocat m. **~s of**, les défenseurs de.

advocate[2] v.t. recommander.

aerial a. aérien. —n. antenne f.

aerobatics n. pl. acrobatie aérienne f.

aerobics n. aérobic m.

aerodynamic a. aérodynamique.

aeroplane n. avion m.

aerosol n. atomiseur m.

aesthetic a. esthétique.

afar adv. from ~, de loin.

affable a. affable.

affair n. (matter) affaire f.; (romance) liaison f.

affect v.t. affecter. **~ation** n. affectation f. **~ed** a. affecté.

affection n. affection f.

affectionate a. affectueux.

affirm v.t. affirmer. **~ation** n. affirmation f.

affirmative a. affirmatif. —n. affirmative f.

affix v.t. apposer.

afflict v.t. affliger. **~ion** n. affliction f., détresse f.

affluen|t a. riche. **~ce** n. richesse f.

afford v.t. avoir les moyens d'acheter; (provide) fournir. ~ **to do**, avoir les moyens de faire; (be able) se permettre de faire.

affront n. affront m. —v.t. insulter.

afloat adv. à flot.

afoot adv. sth. is ~, il se trame or se prépare qch.

afraid a. be ~, avoir peur (**of**, **to**, de; **that**, que); (be sorry) regretter. **I am** ~ **that**, (regret to say) je regrette de dire que.

afresh adv. de nouveau.

Africa n. Afrique f. **~n** a. & n. africain(e) (m. (f.)).

after adv. & prep. après. —conj. après que. ~ **doing**, après avoir fait. ~ **all** après tout. **~-effect** n. suite f. **~-sales service**, service après-vente m.

afternoon n. après-midi m./f. invar.

aftershave n. lotion après-rasage f.

afterwards adv. après, par la suite.

again adv. de nouveau, encore une fois; (besides) en outre. **do** ~, ~/etc., refaire, revoir/etc.

against *prep.* contre. ∼ **the law,** illégal.

age *n.* âge *m.* —*v.t./i.* (*pres. p.* **ageing**) vieillir. ∼ **group,** tranche d'âge *f.* ∼ **limit,** limite d'âge *m.* **for** ∼**s,** (*fam.*) une éternité. **of** ∼, (*jurid.*) majeur.

aged[1] *a.* ∼ **six,** âgé de six ans.

aged[2] *a.* âgé, vieux.

agen|cy *n.* agence *f.*; (*means*) entremise *f.* ∼**t** *n.* agent *m.*

agenda /ə'dʒendə/ *n.* ordre du jour *m.*

aggravate *v.t.* (*make worse*) aggraver; (*annoy. fam.*) exaspérer.

aggregate *a.* & *n.* total (*m.*).

aggress|ive *a.* agressif. ∼**ion** *n.* agression *f.* ∼**iveness** *n.* agressivité *f.*

aghast /ə'gɑːst/ *a.* horrifié.

agil|e *a.* agile. ∼**ity** *n.* agilité *f.*

agitat|e *v.t.* agiter. ∼**ion** *n.* agitation *f.* ∼**or** *n.* agita|teur, -trice *m., f.*

agnostic *a.* & *n.* agnostique (*m./f.*).

ago /ə'gəʊ/ *adv.* il y a. **a month** ∼, il y a un mois. **long** ∼, il y a longtemps. **how long** ∼?, il y a combien de temps?

agon|y *n.* grande souffrance *f.*; (*mental*) angoisse *f.* ∼**izing** *a.* angoissant.

agree *v.i.* être *or* se mettre d'accord (**on,** sur); (*of figures*) concorder. —*v.t.* (*date*) convenir de. ∼ **that,** reconnaître que. ∼ **to do,** accepter de faire. ∼ **to sth.,** accepter qch. **onions don't** ∼ **with me,** je ne digère pas les oignons. ∼**d** *a.* (*time, place*) convenu. **be** ∼**d,** être d'accord.

agreeable *a.* agréable.

agreement *n.* accord *m.* **in** ∼, d'accord.

agricultur|e *n.* agriculture *f.* ∼**al** *a.* agricole.

aground *adv.* **run** ∼, (*of ship*) (s')échouer.

ahead *adv.* (*in front*) en avant, devant; (*in advance*) à l'avance. ∼ **of s.o.,** devant qn.; en avance sur qn. ∼ **of time,** en avance. **straight** ∼, tout droit.

aid *v.t.* aider. —*n.* aide *f.* **in** ∼ **of,** au profit de.

AIDS *n.* (*med.*) sida *m.*

aim *v.t.* diriger; (*gun*) braquer (**at,** sur); (*remark*) destiner. —*v.i.* viser. —*n.* but *m.* ∼ **at,** viser. ∼ **to,** avoir l'intention de. **take** ∼, viser. ∼**less** *a.,* ∼**lessly** *adv.* sans but.

air *n.* air *m.* —*v.t.* aérer; (*views*) exposer librement. —*a.* (*base etc.*) aérien. ∼**-bed** *n.* matelas pneumatique *m.* ∼**-conditioned** *a.* climatisé. ∼**-conditioning** *n.* climatisation *f.* ∼ **force/hostess,** armée/hôtesse de l'air *f.* ∼ **letter,** aérogramme *m.* ∼**mail,** poste aérienne *f.* **by** ∼**mail,** par avion. **by** ∼, par avion. **in the** ∼, (*rumour*) répandu; (*plan*) incertain. **on the** ∼, sur l'antenne.

aircraft *n. invar.* avion *m.* ∼**-carrier** *n.* porte-avions *m. invar.*

airfield *n.* terrain d'aviation *m.*

airgun *n.* carabine à air comprimé *f.*

airlift *n.* pont aérien *m.* —*v.t.* transporter par pont aérien.

airline *n.* ligne aérienne *f.* ∼**r** *n.* avion de ligne *m.*

airman *n.* aviateur *m.*

airplane *n.* (*Amer.*) avion *m.*

airport *n.* aéroport *m.*

airsickness *n.* mal de l'air *m.*

airtight *a.* hermétique.

airways *n. pl.* compagnie d'aviation *f.*

airworthy *a.* en état de navigation.

airy *a.* bien aéré.

aisle n. (of church) nef latérale f.; (gangway) couloir m.

ajar adv. & a. entr'ouvert.

akin a. ~ **to,** apparenté à.

à la carte adv. & a. (culin.) à la carte.

alacrity n. empressement m.

alarm n. alarme f. —v.t. alarmer. ~-**clock** n. réveil.

albatross n. albatros m.

album n. album m.

alcohol n. alcool m. ~**ic** a. alcoolique; (drink) alcoolisé; n. alcoolique m./f. ~**ism** n. alcoolisme m.

alcove n. alcôve f.

ale n. bière f.

alert a. (lively) vif; (watchful) vigilant. —n. alerte f. —v.t. alerter. ~ **s.o. to,** prévenir qn de. **on the** ~, sur le qui-vive. ~**ness** n. vivacité f.; vigilance f.

A-level n. baccalauréat m.

algebra n. algèbre f.

Algeria /ælˈdʒɪərɪə/ n. Algérie f. ~**n** a. & n. algérien(ne) (m. (f.)).

algorithm n. algorithme m.

alibi /ˈælɪbaɪ/ n. (pl. -**is**) alibi m.

alien n. & a. étrang|er, -ère (m., f.) (to, à).

alight[1] v.i. (person) descendre; (bird) se poser.

alight[2] a. en feu, allumé.

align v.t. aligner. ~**ment** n. alignement m.

alike a. semblable. —adv. de la même façon. **look** or **be** ~, se ressembler.

alimony n. pension alimentaire f.

alive a. vivant.

alkali n. (pl. -**is**) alcali m.

all a. tout(e), tous, toutes. —pron. tous, toutes; (everything) tout. —adv. tout. ~ **(the) men,** tous les hommes. ~ **of it,** (le) tout. ~ **of us,** nous tous. ~ **for sth.,** à fond pour qch. ~ **in,** (exhausted)

épuisé. ~-**in** a. tout compris. ~ **out,** à fond. ~-**out** a. (effort) maximum. ~ **over,** partout (sur or dans); (finished) fini. ~ **right,** bien; (agreeing) bon! ~ **round,** dans tous les domaines; (for all) pour tous. ~-**round** a. général. ~ **the same,** tout de même.

allegation n. allégation f.

allege v.t. prétendre. ~**dly** adv. d'après ce qu'on dit.

allerg|y n. allergie f. ~**ic** a. allergique (**to,** à).

alley n. (street) ruelle f.

alliance n. alliance f.

allied a. allié.

alligator n. alligator m.

allocat|e v.t. (assign) attribuer; (share out) distribuer. ~**ion** n. allocation f.

allot v.t. attribuer. ~**ment** n. (land) parcelle de terre f.

allow v.t. permettre; (grant) accorder; (reckon on) prévoir; (agree) reconnaître. ~ **s.o. to,** permettre à qn de. ~ **for,** tenir compte de.

allowance n. allocation f., indemnité f. **make** ~**s for,** être indulgent envers; (take into account) tenir compte de.

alloy n. alliage m.

allude v.i. ~ **to,** faire allusion à.

allusion n. allusion f.

ally[1] n. allié(e) m. (f.).

ally[2] v.t. allier. ~ **o.s. with,** s'allier à or avec.

almond n. amande f.

almost adv. presque.

alone a. & adv. seul.

along prep. le long de. —adv. **come** ~, venir. **go** or **walk** ~, passer. **all** ~, (time) tout le temps, depuis le début. ~ **with,** avec.

alongside adv. (naut.) bord à bord. **come** ~, accoster. —prep. le long de.

aloof adv. à l'écart. —a. distant. ~**ness** n. réserve f.

aloud adv. à haute voix.

alphabet n. alphabet m. ~**ical** a. alphabétique.

alpine a. (landscape) alpestre; (climate) alpin.

Alp:ne a. des Alpes.

Alps n. pl. the ~, les Alpes f. pl.

already adv. déjà.

alright a. & adv. = **all right**.

Alsatian n. (dog) berger allemand m.

also adv. aussi.

altar n. autel m.

alter v.t./i. changer. ~**ation** n. changement m.; (to garment) retouche f.

alternate[1] a. alterné, alternatif; (Amer.) = **alternative. on** ~ **days**/etc., (first one then the other) tous les deux jours/etc. ~**ly** adv. tour à tour.

alternate[2] v.i. alterner. —v.t. faire alterner.

alternative a. autre; (policy) de rechange. —n. alternative f., choix m. ~**ly** adv. comme alternative. **or** ~**ly**, ou alors.

alternator n. alternateur m.

although conj. bien que.

altitude n. altitude f.

altogether adv. (completely) tout à fait; (on the whole) à tout prendre.

aluminium n. aluminium n.

always adv. toujours.

a.m. adv. du matin.

amalgamate v.t./i. (s')amalgamer; (comm.) fusionner.

amass v.t. amasser.

amateur n. amateur m. —a. (musician etc.) amateur.

amaz|e v.t. étonner. ~**ed** a. étonné. ~**ement** n. étonnement m. ~**ingly** adv. étonnamment.

ambassador n. ambassadeur m.

amber n. ambre m.; (auto.) feu orange m.

ambiguous a. ambigu.

ambiti|on n. ambition f. ~**ous** a. ambitieux.

amble v.i. marcher sans se presser, s'avancer lentement.

ambulance n. ambulance f.

amend v.t. modifier, corriger. ~**ment** n. (to rule) amendement m.

amends n. pl. **make** ~, réparer son erreur.

amenities n. pl. (pleasant features) attraits m. pl.; (facilities) aménagements m. pl.

America n. Amérique f. ~**n** a. & n. américain(e) (m. (f.)).

amiable a. aimable.

amicable a. amical.

amid(st) prep. au milieu de.

amiss a. & adv. mal. **sth.** ~, qch. qui ne va pas.

ammonia n. (gas) ammoniac m.; (water) ammoniaque f.

ammunition n. munitions f. pl.

amnesia n. amnésie f.

amnesty n. amnistie f.

among(st) prep. parmi, entre. ~ **the crowd,** (in the middle of) parmi la foule. ~ **the English**/ etc., (race, group) chez les Anglais/ etc. ~ **ourselves**/etc., entre nous/etc.

amoral a. amoral.

amorphous a. amorphe.

amount n. quantité f.; (total) montant m.; (sum of money) somme f. —v.i. ~ **to,** (add up to) s'élever à; (be equivalent to) revenir à.

amp n. (fam.) ampère m.

ample a. (enough) (bien) assez de; (large, roomy) ample. ~**y** adv. amplement.

amplif|y v.t. amplifier. ~**ier** n. amplificateur m.

amputat|e v.t. amputer. ~**ion** n. amputation f.

amuse *v.t.* amuser. **~ment** *n.* amusement *m.*, divertissement *m.* **~ment arcade,** salle de jeux *f.*

anachronism *n.* anachronisme *m.*

anaem|ia *n.* anémie *f.* **~ic** *a.* anémique.

anaesthetic *n.* anesthésique *m.* **give an ~,** faire une anesthésie (**to,** à).

analogue, analog *a.* analogique.

analogy *n.* analogie *f.*

analys|e *v.t.* analyser. **~t** *n.* analyste *m./f.*

analysis *n.* analyse *f.*

analytic(al) *a.* analytique.

anarch|y *n.* anarchie *f.* **~ist** *n.* anarchiste *m./f.*

anatom|y *n.* anatomie *f.* **~ical** *a.* anatomique.

ancestor *n.* ancêtre *m.*

anchor *n.* ancre *f.* —*v.t.* mettre à l'ancre. —*v.i.* jeter l'ancre.

anchovy *n.* anchois *m.*

ancient *a.* ancien.

ancillary *a.* auxiliaire.

and *conj.* et. **go ~ see him,** allez le voir.

anecdote *n.* anecdote *f.*

angel *n.* ange *m.*

anger *n.* colère *f.* —*v.t.* mettre en colère, fâcher.

angle *n.* angle *m.*

angler *n.* pêcheu|r, -se *m.*, *f.*

Anglican *a.* & *n.* anglican(e) (*m.* (*f.*)).

angr|y *a.* fâché, en colère. **get ~y,** se fâcher, se mettre en colère (**with,** contre). **make s.o. ~y,** mettre qn. en colère. **~ily** *adv.* en colère.

anguish *n.* angoisse *f.*

animal *n.* & *a.* animal (*m.*).

animat|e *v.t.* animer. **~ion** *n.* animation *f.*

animosity *n.* animosité *f.*

aniseed *n.* anis *m.*

ankle *n.* cheville *f.* **~ sock,** socquette *f.*

annexe *n.* annexe *f.*

annihilate *v.t.* anéantir.

anniversary *n.* anniversaire *m.*

announce *v.t.* annoncer. **~ment** *n.* annonce *f.* **~r** *n.* (*radio, TV*) speaker(ine) *m.* (*f.*).

annoy *v.t.* agacer, ennuyer. **~ance** *n.* contrariété *f.* **~ed** *a.* fâché (**with,** contre). **get ~ed,** se fâcher. **~ing** *a.* ennuyeux.

annual *a.* annuel. —*n.* publication annuelle *f.* **~ly** *adv.* annuellement.

annul *v.t.* annuler. **~ment** *n.* annulation *f.*

anomal|y *n.* anomalie *f.* **~ous** *a.* anormal.

anonymous *a.* anonyme.

anorak *n.* anorak *m.*

another *a.* & *pron.* un(e) autre. **~ coffee,** (*one more*) encore un café.

answer *n.* réponse *f.*; (*solution*) solution *f.* —*v.t.* répondre à; (*prayer*) exaucer. —*v.i.* répondre. **~ the door,** ouvrir la porte. **~ing machine,** répondeur *m.*

ant *n.* fourmi *f.*

antagonism *n.* antagonisme *m.*

antagonize *v.t.* provoquer l'hostilité de.

Antarctic *a.* & *n.* antarctique (*m.*).

antelope *n.* antilope *f.*

antenatal *a.* prénatal.

antenna /æn'tenə/ *n.* (*of insect*) antenne *f.*; (*aerial*) antenne *f.*

anti- *pref.* anti-. **~aircraft** *a.* antiaérien.

antibiotic *n.* antibiotique *m.*

antibody *n.* anticorps *m.*

anticipat|e *v.t.* (*foresee, expect*) prévoir, s'attendre à; (*forestall*) devancer. **~ion** *n.* attente *f.*

anticlimax *n.* (*let-down*) déception *f.*

anticlockwise *adv.* & *a.* dans le

sens inverse des aiguilles d'une montre.

anticyclone n. anticyclone m.

antidote n. antidote m.

antifreeze n. antigel m.

antihistamine n. antihistaminique m.

antipathy n. antipathie f.

antique a. objet ancien m., antiquité f. ~ **dealer**, antiquaire m./f. ~ **shop**, magasin d'antiquités m.

anti-Semit|ic a. antisémite. ~**sm** n. antisémitisme m.

antiseptic a. & n. antiseptique (m.).

antisocial a. asocial, antisocial; (unsociable) insociable.

antlers n. pl. bois m. pl.

anus n. anus m.

anxiety n. (worry) anxiété f.; (eagerness) impatience f.

anxious a. (troubled) anxieux; (eager) impatient (**to**, de). ~**ly** adv. anxieusement; impatiemment.

any a. (some) du, de l', de la, des; (after negative) de, d'; (every) tout; (no matter which) n'importe quel. **at** ~ **moment**, à tout moment. **have you** ~ **water?**, avez-vous de l'eau? —pron. (no matter which one) n'importe lequel; (someone) quelqu'un; (any amount of it or them) en. **I do not have** ~, je n'en ai pas. **did you see** ~ **of them?**, en avez-vous vu? —adv. (a little) un peu. **do you have** ~ **more?**, en avez-vous encore? **do you have** ~ **more tea?**, avez-vous encore du thé? **not** ~, nullement. **I do not do it** ~ **more**, je ne le fais plus.

anybody pron. n'importe qui; (somebody) quelqu'un; (after negative) personne. **he did not see** ~, il n'a vu personne.

anyhow adv. de toute façon; (badly) n'importe comment.

anyone pron. = anybody.

anything pron. n'importe quoi; (something) quelque chose; (after negative) rien. **he did not see** ~, il n'a rien vu.

anyway adv. de toute façon.

anywhere adv. n'importe où; (somewhere) quelque part; (after negative) nulle part. **he does not go** ~, il ne va nulle part. ~ **you go**, partout où tu vas, où que tu ailles.

apart adv. (on or to one side) à part; (separated) séparé; (into pieces) en pièces. ~ **from**, à part, excepté. **ten metres** ~, (distant) à dix mètres l'un de l'autre.

apartment n. (Amer.) appartement m. ~**s**, logement m.

apathy n. apathie f. ~**etic** a. apathique.

ape n. singe m. —v.t. singer.

aperitif n. apéritif m.

aperture n. ouverture f.

apex n. sommet m.

apiece adv. chacun.

apologetic a. (tone etc.) d'excuse. **be** ~, s'excuser.

apologize v.i. s'excuser (**for**, de; **to**, auprès de).

apology n. excuses f. pl.

Apostle n. apôtre m.

apostrophe n. apostrophe f.

appal v.t. épouvanter. ~**ling** a. épouvantable.

apparatus n. appareil m.

apparent a. apparent. ~**ly** adv. apparemment.

appeal n. appel m.; (attractiveness) attrait m., charme m. —v.i. (jurid.) faire appel. ~ **to s.o.**, (beg) faire appel à qn.; (attract) plaire à qn. ~ **to s.o. for sth.**, demander qch. à qn. ~**ing** a. (attractive) attirant.

appear v.i. apparaître; (arrive) se présenter; (seem, be published) paraître; (theatre) jouer. **~ance** n. apparition f.; (aspect) apparence f.

appease v.t. apaiser.

appendicitis n. appendicite f.

appendix n. appendice m.

appetite n. appétit m.

appetizing a. appétissant.

applau|d v.t./i. applaudir; (decision) applaudir à. **~se** n. applaudissements m. pl.

apple n. pomme f. **~-tree** n. pommier m.

appliance n. appareil m.

applicable a. applicable.

applicant n. candidat(e) m. (f.) (for, à).

application /æplɪ'keɪʃn/ n. application f.; (request, form) demande f.; (for job) candidature f.

apply v.t. appliquer. —v.i. for, (job) postuler pour; (grant) demander. **applied** a. appliqué.

appoint v.t. (to post) nommer; (fix) désigner. **~ment** n. nomination f.; (meeting) rendez-vous m. invar.; (job) poste m. **make an ~ment**, prendre rendez-vous (with, avec).

apprais|e v.t. évaluer. **~al** n. évaluation f.

appreciable a. appréciable.

appreciat|e v.t. (like) apprécier; (understand) comprendre; (be grateful for) être reconnaissant de. —v.i. prendre de la valeur. **~ion** n. appréciation f.; (gratitude) reconnaissance f.; (rise) augmentation f.

apprehensive a. inquiet.

apprentice n. apprenti m. **~ship** n. apprentissage m.

approach v.t. (s')approcher de; (accost) aborder; (with request)

s'adresser à. —v.i. (s')approcher. —n. approche f. **~ an ~ to**, (problem) une façon d'aborder; (person) une démarche auprès de. **~able** a. accessible; (person) abordable.

appropriate a. approprié, propre. **~ly** adv. à propos.

approval n. approbation f. **on ~**, à or sous condition.

approve v.t./i. approuver. **~ of**, approuver.

approximate a. approximatif. **~ly** adv. approximativement.

apricot n. abricot m.

April n. avril m. **make an ~ fool of**, faire un poisson d'avril à.

apron n. tablier m.

apt a. (suitable) approprié; (pupil) doué. **be ~ to**, avoir tendance à. **~ly** adv. à propos.

aptitude n. aptitude f.

aqualung n. scaphandre autonome m.

aquarium n. aquarium m.

Aquarius n. le Verseau.

Arab n. & a. arabe (m./f.). **~ic** a. & n. (lang.) arabe (m.).

Arabian a. arabe.

arbitrary a. arbitraire.

arbitrat|e v.i. arbitrer. **~ion** /-'treɪʃn/ n. arbitrage m.

arc n. arc m.

arcade n. (shops) galerie f.; (arches) arcades f. pl.

arch n. arche f.; (in church etc.) arc m.; (of foot) voûte plantaire f. —v.t./i. (s')arquer.

archaeolog|y n. archéologie f. **~ical** a. archéologique. **~ist** n. archéologue m./f.

archaic a. archaïque.

archbishop n. archevêque m.

archer n. archer m. **~y** n. tir à l'arc m.

architect n. architecte m.

architecture n. architecture f.

archives n. pl. archives f. pl. ~**ist** n. archiviste m./f.

archway n. voûte f.

Arctic a. & n. arctique (m.). **arctic** a. glacial.

ardent a. ardent. ~**ly** adv. ardemment.

ardour n. ardeur f.

arduous a. ardu.

area n. (surface) superficie f.; (region) région f.; (district) quartier m.; (fig.) domaine m.

parking/picnic ~ aire de parking/de pique-nique f.

arena n. arène f.

Argentin|a n. Argentine f. ~**e**, ~**ian** a. & n. argentin(e) (m. (f.)).

argue v.i. (quarrel) se disputer; (reason) argumenter. —v.t. (debate) discuter. ~**e** that, on allèguer que. ~**ably** adv. selon certains.

argument n. dispute f.; (reasoning) argument m.; (discussion) débat m. ~**ative** a. raisonneur, contrariant.

arid a. aride.

Aries n. le Bélier.

arise v.i. se présenter; (old use) se lever. ~ **from**, résulter de.

aristocracy n. aristocratie f.

aristocrat n. aristocrate m./f. ~**ic** a. aristocratique.

arithmetic n. arithmétique f.

ark n. (relig.) arche f.

arm[1] n. bras m. ~ **in arm**, bras dessus bras dessous. ~**band** n. brassard m.

arm[2] v.t. armer. ~**ed robbery**, vol à main armée m.

armament n. armement m.

armchair n. fauteuil m.

armour n. armure f.; (on tanks etc.) blindage m.

armpit n. aisselle f.

arms n. pl. (weapons) armes f. pl. ~ **dealer**, trafiquant d'armes m.

army n. armée f.

aroma n. arôme m.

around adv. (tout) autour; (here and there) çà et là. —prep. autour de. ~ **here**, par ici.

arouse v.t. (awaken, cause) éveiller; (excite) exciter.

arrange v.t. arranger; (time, date) fixer. ~ **to**, s'arranger pour. ~**ment** n. arrangement m. **make** ~**ments**, prendre des dispositions.

array n. **an** ~ **of**, (display) un étalage impressionnant de.

arrears n. pl. arriéré m. **in** ~, (rent) arriéré. **he is in** ~, il a des paiements en retard.

arrest v.t. arrêter; (attention) retenir. —n. arrestation f. **under** ~, en état d'arrestation.

arrival n. arrivée f. **new** ~, nouveau venu m., nouvelle venue f.

arrive v.i. arriver.

arrogan|t a. arrogant. ~**ce** n. arrogance f. ~**tly** adv. avec arrogance.

arrow n. flèche f.

arson n. incendie criminel m. ~**ist** n. incendiaire m./f.

art n. art m.; (fine arts) beaux-arts m. pl. ~**s**, (univ.) lettres f. pl. ~ **gallery**, (public) musée (d'art) m.; (private) galerie (d'art) f.

artefact n. objet fabriqué m.

artery n. artère f.

artful a. astucieux, rusé. ~**ness** n. astuce f.

arthriti|s n. arthrite f. ~**c** /-ɪtɪk/ a. arthritique.

artichoke n. artichaut m.

article n. article m. ~ **of clothing**, vêtement m.

articulate a. (person) capable de s'exprimer clairement; (speech) distinct.

articulated lorry semi-remorque *m.*

artificial *a.* artificiel.

artillery *n.* artillerie *f.*

artisan *n.* artisan *m.*

artist *n.* artiste *m./f.* ～**ic** *a.* artistique.

artwork *n.* (*of book*) illustrations *f. pl.*

as *adv. & conj.* comme; (*while*) pendant que. **as you get older,** en vieillissant. **as she came in,** en entrant. **as a mother,** en tant que mère. **as a gift,** en cadeau. **as from Monday,** à partir de lundi. **as tall as,** aussi grand que. ～ **for, as to,** quant à ～ **if,** comme si. **you look as if you're tired,** vous avez l'air (d'être) fatigué. **as much, as many,** autant (as, que). **as soon as,** aussitôt que. **as well,** aussi (as, bien que). **as wide as possible,** aussi large que possible.

asbestos *n.* amiante *f.*

ascend *v.t.* gravir; (*throne*) monter sur. —*v.i.* monter.

ascent *n.* (*climbing*) ascension *f.*

ascertain *v.t.* s'assurer de. ～ **that,** s'assurer que.

ash[1] *n.* ～(**-tree**) frêne *m.*

ash[2] *n.* cendre *f.*

ashamed *a.* be ～, avoir honte (of, de).

ashore *adv.* à terre.

ashtray *n.* cendrier *m.*

Asia *n.* Asie *f.* ～**n** *a. & n.* asiatique (*m./f.*). **the** ～**n community,** la communauté indo-pakistanaise.

aside *adv.* de côté. —*n.* aparté *m.* ～ **from,** à part.

ask *v.t./i.* demander; (*a question*) poser; (*invite*) inviter. ～ **s.o. sth.,** demander qch. à qn. ～ **s.o. to do,** demander à qn. de faire. ～ **about,** (*thing*) se renseigner sur;

(*person*) demander des nouvelles de. ～ **for,** demander.

askew *adv. & a.* de travers.

asleep *a.* endormi; (*numb*) engourdi. —*adv.* **fall** ～, s'endormir.

asparagus *n.* (*plant*) asperge *f.*; (*culin.*) asperges *f. pl.*

aspect *n.* aspect *m.*; (*direction*) orientation *f.*

asphalt *n.* asphalte *m.* —*v.t.* asphalter.

asphyxiat|e *v.t./i.* (s')asphyxier. ～**ion** *n.* asphyxie *f.*

aspir|e /əsˈpaɪə(r)/ *v.i.* ～**e to,** aspirer à. ～**ation** /æspəˈreɪʃn/ *n.* aspiration *f.*

aspirin *n.* aspirine *f.*

ass *n.* âne *m.*; (*person: fam.*) idiot(e) *m.* (*f.*).

assail *v.t.* assaillir. ～**ant** *n.* agresseur *m.*

assassin *n.* assassin *m.*

assassinat|e *v.t.* assassiner. ～**ion** *n.* assassinat *m.*

assault *n.* (*mil.*) assaut *m.*; (*jurid.*) agression *f.* —*v.t.* (*person: jurid.*) agresser.

assemble *v.t.* (*things*) assembler; (*people*) rassembler. —*v.i.* s'assembler, se rassembler.

assembly *n.* assemblée *f.* ～ **line,** chaîne de montage *f.*

assent *n.* assentiment *m.* —*v.i.* consentir.

assert *v.t.* affirmer; (*one's rights*) revendiquer. ～**ion** /-ʃn/ *n.* affirmation *f.* ～**ive** *a.* affirmatif, péremptoire.

assess *v.t.* évaluer; (*payment*) déterminer le montant de. ～**ment** *n.* évaluation *f.* ～**or** *n.* (*valuer*) expert *m.*

asset *n.* (*advantage*) atout *m.* ～**s,** (*comm.*) actif *m.*

assign *v.t.* (*allot*) assigner. ～ **s.o. to,** (*appoint*) affecter qn. à.

assignment n. (*task*) mission f., tâche f.; (*schol.*) rapport m.

assimilat|e v.t./i. (s')assimiler. **~ion** n. assimilation f.

assist v.t./i. aider. **~ance** n. aide f.

assistant n. aide m./f.; (*in shop*) vendeu|r, -se m., f. —a. (*manager etc.*) adjoint.

associat|e¹ v.t. associer. —v.i. **~e with,** fréquenter. **~ion** n. association f.

associate² n. & a. associé(e) m. (f.)).

assort|ed a. divers; (*foods*) assortis. **~ment** n. assortiment m.

assume v.t. supposer, présumer, (*power, attitude*) prendre; (*role, burden*) assumer.

assumption n. (*sth. supposed*) supposition f.

assurance n. assurance f.

assure v.t. assurer. **~d** a. assuré.

asterisk n. astérisque m.

asthma n. asthme m. **~tic** a. & n. asthmatique (m./f.).

astonish v.t. étonner. **~ment** n. étonnement m.

astound v.t. stupéfier.

astray adv. & a. go **~,** s'égarer. **lead ~,** égarer.

astride adv. & prep. à califourchon (sur).

astrolog|y n. astrologie f. **~er** n. astrologue m.

astronaut n. astronaute m./f.

astronom|y n. astronomie f. **~er** n. astronome m. **~ical** /æstrə'nɒmɪkl/ a. astronomique.

astute a. astucieux.

asylum n. asile m.

at prep. à. **at the doctor's/***etc.*, chez le médecin/*etc.*, **not at all,** pas du tout. **no wind/***etc.* **at all,** (*of any kind*) pas le moindre vent/*etc.* **at night,** la nuit. **at once,** tout de suite; (*simul-*

taneously) à la fois. **~ sea,** en mer. **at times,** parfois.

atheis|m n./*m.f.* **~m** n. athéisme m.

atheist n. athée m./f. **~ic** a. athéistique.

athlet|e n. athlète m./f. **~ic** a. athlétique. **~ics** n. pl. athlétisme m.

Atlantic a. atlantique. —n. **~** (**Ocean**), Atlantique m.

atlas n. atlas m.

atmospher|e n. atmosphère f. **~ic** a. atmosphérique.

atoll n. atoll m.

atom n. atome m. **~ic** a. atomique. **~(ic) bomb,** bombe atomique f.

atrocious a. atroce.

atrocity n. atrocité f.

attach v.t. attacher; (*letter*) joindre (**to,** à). **~ed a. be ~ed to,** (*like*) être attaché à. **~ment** n. (*accessory*) accessoire m.; (*affection*) attachement m.

attaché n. (*pol.*) attaché(e) m. (f.). **~ case,** mallette f.

attack n. attaque f.; (*med.*) crise f. —v.t. attaquer. **~er** n. agresseur m., attaquant(e) m. (f.).

attain v.t. atteindre (à); (*gain*) acquérir. **~able** a. accessible. **~ment** n. acquisition f. (**of,** de). **~ments,** réussites f. pl.

attempt v.t. tenter. —n. tentative f. **an ~ on s.o.'s life,** un attentat contre qn.

attend v.t. assister à; (*class*) suivre; (*school, church*) aller à; (*escort*) accompagner. —v.i. assister. **~ (to),** (*look after*) s'occuper de. **~ance** n. présence f.; (*people*) assistance f.

attendant n. employé(e) m. (f.); (*servant*) serviteur m.

attention n. attention f. **pay ~,** faire *or* prêter attention (**to,** à).

attentive a. attentif; (*considerate*) attentionné.

attic n. grenier m.

attitude n. attitude f.

attorney n. mandataire m.; (*Amer.*) avocat m.

attract v.t. attirer. **∼ion** n. attraction f.; (*charm*) attrait m.

attractive a. attrayant, séduisant. **∼ly** adv. agréablement. **∼ness** n. attrait m., beauté f.

attribute[1] v.t. **∼ to**, attribuer à.

attribute[2] n. attribut m.

aubergine n. aubergine f.

auburn a. châtain roux invar.

auction n. vente aux enchères f. —v.t. vendre aux enchères.

audacious a. audacieux. **∼ty** n. audace f.

audible a. audible.

audience n. auditoire m.; (*theatre, radio*) public m.; (*interview*) audience f.

audio typist n. audiotypiste m./f.

audio-visual a. audio-visuel.

audit n. vérification des comptes f. —v.t. vérifier.

audition n. audition f. —v.t./i. auditionner.

auditor n. commissaire aux comptes m.

auditorium n. (*of theatre etc.*) salle f.

August n. août m.

aunt n. tante f.

au pair n. jeune fille au pair f.

auster|e a. austère. **∼ity** n. austérité f.

Australia n. Australie f. **∼n** a. & n. australien(ne) (m. (f.)).

Austria n. Autriche f. **∼n** a. & n. autrichien(ne) (m. (f.)).

authentic a. authentique. **∼ity** n. authenticité f.

author n. auteur m.

authoritarian a. autoritaire.

authority n. autorité f.; (*permission*) autorisation f.

authoriz|e v.t. autoriser. **∼ation** n. autorisation f.

autistic a. autistique.

autobiography n. autobiographie f.

autograph n. autographe m. —v.t. signer, dédicacer.

auto-immune a. auto-immune.

automat|e v.t. automatiser. **∼ion** n. automatisation f.

automatic a. automatique. —n. (*auto.*) voiture automatique f. **∼ally** adv. automatiquement.

autonom|y n. autonomie f. **∼ous** a. autonome.

autumn n. automne m.

auxiliary a. & n. auxiliaire (m./f.).

availab|le a. disponible. **∼ility** n. disponibilité f.

avalanche n. avalanche f.

avaric|e n. avarice f. **∼ious** a. avare.

avenge v.t. venger. **∼ o.s.**, se venger (on, de).

avenue n. avenue f.

average n. moyenne f. —a. moyen. **on ∼**, en moyenne.

avers|e a. **be ∼e to**, répugner à. **∼ion** n. aversion f.

avert v.t. (*turn away*) détourner; (*ward off*) éviter.

aviation n. aviation f.

avid a. avide.

avocado n. avocat m.

avoid v.t. éviter. **∼able** a. évitable.

await v.t. attendre.

awake v.t./i. (s')éveiller. —a. **be ∼**, ne pas dormir, être (r)éveillé.

awaken v.t./i. (s')éveiller.

award v.t. attribuer. —n. récompense f., prix m.; (*scholarship*) bourse f. **pay ∼**, augmentation (salariale) f.

aware a. averti. **be ∼ of**, (*danger*) être conscient de; (*fact*) savoir. **become ∼ of**, prendre conscience de. **∼ness** n. conscience f.

awash a. inondé (**with**, de).

away adv. (far) (au) loin; (absent) absent, parti; (persistently) sans arrêt; (entirely) complètement. **~ from**, loin de. **move ~**, s'écarter; (to new home) déménager. **six kilometres ~**, à six kilomètres (de distance). **take ~**, emporter. **—a. & n. ~** (**match**), match à l'extérieur m.

awe n. crainte (révérencielle) f. **~-inspiring**, **~some** adjs. terrifiant; (sight) imposant.

awful a. affreux. **~ly** adv. (badly) affreusement; (very: fam.) rudement.

awkward a. difficile; (inconvenient) inopportun; (clumsy) maladroit; (embarrassing) gênant; (embarrassed) gêné. **~ly** adv. maladroitement; avec gêne. **~ness** n. maladresse f.

awning n. auvent m.; (of shop) store m.

axe, n. hache f. —v.t. (pres. p. **axing**) réduire; (eliminate) supprimer; (employee) renvoyer.

axis n. axe m.

axle n. essieu m.

B

babble v.i. babiller; (stream) gazouiller. —n. babillage m.

baboon n. babouin m.

baby n. bébé m. **~-sitter** n. baby-sitter m./f.

bachelor n. célibataire m. **B~ of Arts/Science**, licencié(e) ès lettres/sciences m. (f.).

back n. (of person, hand, page, etc.) dos m.; (of house) derrière m.; (of vehicle) arrière m.; (of room) fond m.; (of chair) dossier m.; (football) arrière m. —a. de derrière,

arrière invar.; (taxes) arriéré —adv. en arrière; (returned) de retour, rentré. —v.t. (support) appuyer; (bet on) miser sur; (vehicle) faire reculer. —v.i. (of person, vehicle) reculer. **at the ~ of the book**, à la fin du livre. **come ~**, revenir. **give ~**, rendre. **take ~**, reprendre. **I want it ~**, je veux le récupérer. **~ down**, abandonner, se dégonfler. **~ out**, se dégager, se dégonfler; (auto.) sortir en reculant. **~ up**, (support) appuyer. **~-up** n. appui m.; (comput.) sauvegarde f.; a. de réserve; (comput.) de sauvegarde.

backache n. mal de reins m., mal aux reins m.

backbone n. colonne vertébrale f.

backdate v.t. antidater; (arrangement) rendre rétroactif.

backer n. partisan m.; (comm.) bailleur de fonds m.

backfire v.i. (auto.) pétarader; (fig.) mal tourner.

backgammon n. trictrac m.

background n. fond m., arrière-plan m.; (context) contexte m.; (environment) milieu m.; (experience) formation f. —a. (music, noise) de fond.

backhand n. revers m. **~ed a.** équivoque. **~ed stroke**, revers m.

backing n. appui m.

backlash n. choc en retour m., répercussions f. pl.

backlog n. accumulation (de travail) n.

backpack n. sac à dos m.

backside n. (buttocks: fam.) derrière m.

backstage a. & adv. dans les coulisses.

backstroke n. dos crawlé m.

backtrack v.i. rebrousser chemin; (*change one's opinion*) faire marche arrière.

backward a. (*step etc.*) en arrière; (*retarded*) arriéré.

backwards adv. en arrière; (*walk*) à reculons; (*read*) à l'envers; (*fall*) à la renverse. **go ~ and forwards**, aller et venir.

bacon n. lard m.; (*in rashers*) bacon m.

bacteria n. pl. bactéries f. pl.

bad a. mauvais; (*wicked*) méchant; (*ill*) malade; (*accident*) grave; (*food*) gâté. **feel ~**, se sentir mal. **go ~**, se gâter. **~ language**, gros mots m. pl. **~-tempered** a. grincheux. **~ly** adv. mal; (*hurt*) grièvement. **too ~!**, tant pis; (*I'm sorry*) dommage!

badge n. insigne m.; (*of identity*) plaque f.

badger n. blaireau m. —v.t. harceler.

badminton n. badminton m.

baffle v.t. déconcerter.

bag n. sac m. **~s**, (*luggage*) bagages m.pl. —v.t. mettre en sac; (*take: fam.*) s'adjuger.

baggage n. bagages m. pl. **~ reclaim**, livraison des bagages f.

baggy a. trop grand.

Bahamas n. pl. the **~**, les Bahamas f. pl.

bail[1] n. caution f. **on ~**, sous caution. —v.t. mettre en liberté (provisoire) sous caution. **~ out**, (*fig.*) sortir d'affaire.

bail[2] n. (*cricket*) bâtonnet m.

bail[3] v.t. (*naut.*) écoper.

bailiff n. huissier m.

bait n. appât m. —v.t. appâter; (*fig.*) tourmenter.

bak|e v.t. (*bread*) cuire (au four). —v.i. cuire (au four); (*person*) faire du pain or des gâteaux. **~ed beans**, haricots blancs à la

tomate m.pl. **~ed potato**, pomme de terre en robe de champs f. **~er** n. boulang|er, -ère m., f. **~ing** n. cuisson f. **~ing-powder** n. levure f.

bakery n. boulangerie f.

balance n. équilibre m.; (*scales*) balance f.; (*outstanding sum: comm.*) solde m.; (*of payments, of trade*) balance f.; (*remainder*) reste m.; (*money in account*) position f. —v.t. tenir en équilibre; (*weigh up & comm.*) balancer; (*budget*) équilibrer; (*to compensate*) contrebalancer. —v. i. être en équilibre. **~d** a. équilibré.

balcony n. balcon m.

bald a. chauve; (*tyre*) lisse; (*fig.*) simple. **~ness** n. calvitie f.

bale[1] n. (*of cotton*) balle f.; (*of straw*) botte f.

bale[2] v.i. **~ out**, sauter en parachute.

ball[1] n. (*golf, tennis, etc.*) balle f.; (*football*) ballon m.; (*croquet, billiards, etc.*) boule f.; (*of wool*) pelote f.; (*sphere*) boule f. **~-bearing** n. roulement à billes m. **~-cock** n. robinet à flotteur m. **~-point** n. stylo à bille m.

ball[2] n. (*dance*) bal m.

ballet n. ballet m.

balloon n. ballon m.

ballot n. scrutin m. **~-box** n. urne f. —v.i. (*p.t.* **balloted**) (*pol.*) voter. —v.t. (*members*) consulter par voie de scrutin.

ballroom n. salle de bal f.

bamboo n. bambou m.

ban v.t. interdire. **~ from**, exclure de. —n. interdiction f.

banal a. banal. **~ity** n. banalité f.

banana n. banane f.

band n. (*strip, group of people*) bande f.; (*mus.*) orchestre m.; (*pop*

group) groupe *m.* (*mil.*) fanfare *f.*
—*v.i.* ~ **together**, se liguer.
bandage *n.* pansement *m.* —*v.t.*
bander, panser.
bandit *n.* bandit *m.*
bang *n.* (*blow, noise*) coup (violent)
m.; (*explosion*) détonation *f.*; (*of
door*) claquement *m.* —*v.t./i.*
frapper; (*door*) claquer. —*int.*
vlan. —*adv.* (*fam.*) exactement.
~ **one's head**, se cogner la tête.
~**s**, frange *f.*
banger *n.* (*firework*) pétard *m.*;
(*culin., sl.*) saucisse *f.* (**old**) ~,
(*car: sl.*) guimbarde *f.*
bangle *n.* bracelet *m.*
banish *v.t.* bannir.
banisters *n. pl.* rampe (d'escalier)
f.
banjo *n.* banjo *m.*
bank[1] *n.* (*of river*) rive *f.*; (*of earth*)
talus *m.*; (*of sand*) banc *m.* —*v.t.*
(*earth*) amonceler; (*fire*) couvrir.
—*v.i.* (*aviat.*) virer.
bank[2] *n.* banque *f.* —*v.t.* mettre en
banque. —*v.i.* ~ **with**, avoir un
compte à. ~ **account**, compte en
banque *m.* ~ **card**, carte bancaire *f.* ~ **holiday**, jour férié *m.*
~ **on**, compter sur. ~ **statement**, relevé de compte *m.*
bankrupt *a.* be ~, être en faillite.
go ~, faire faillite. —*n.* failli(e)
m. (*f.*). —*v.t.* mettre en faillite.
~**cy** *n.* faillite *f.*
banner *n.* bannière *f.*
banquet *n.* banquet *m.*
banter *n.* plaisanterie *f.* —*v.i.*
plaisanter.
bap *n.* petit pain *m.*
baptism *n.* baptême *m.*
Baptist *n.* baptiste *m./f.*
baptize *v.t.* baptiser.
bar *n.* (*of metal*) barre *f.*; (*on
window & jurid.*) barreau *m.*; (*of
chocolate*) tablette *f.*; (*pub*) bar *m.*;
(*counter*) comptoir *m.*, bar *m.*;

(*division: mus.*) mesure *f.*; (*fig.*)
obstacle *m.* —*v.t.* (*obstruct*) barrer; (*prohibit*) interdire; (*exclude*)
exclure. —*prep.* sauf. ~ **code**,
code-barres *m. invar.* ~ **of soap**,
savonnette *f.*
barbarian *n.* barbare *m./f.*
barbaric *a.* barbare.
barbarous *a.* barbare.
barbecue *n.* barbecue *m.* —*v.t.*
griller, rôtir (au barbecue).
barbed ~ **wire**, fil de fer
barbelé *m.*
barber *n.* coiffeur *m.* (*pour
hommes*)
barbiturate *n.* barbiturique *m.*
bare *a.* (*not covered or adorned*)
nu; (*cupboard*) vide; (*mere*)
simple. —*v.t.* mettre à nu.
barefaced *a.* éhonté.
barefoot *a.* nu-pieds *invar.*, pieds
nus.
barely *adv.* à peine.
bargain *n.* (*deal*) marché *m.*;
(*cheap thing*) occasion *f.* —*v.i.*
négocier; (*haggle*) marchander.
not ~ **for**, ne pas s'attendre à.
barge *n.* chaland *m.* —*v.i.* ~ **in**, interrompre; (*into room*) faire irruption.
baritone *n.* baryton *m.*
bark[1] *n.* (*of tree*) écorce *f.*
bark[2] *n.* (*of dog*) aboiement *m.*
—*v.i.* aboyer.
barley *n.* orge *f.* ~ **sugar**, sucre
d'orge *m.*
barmaid *n.* serveuse *f.*
barman *n.* barman *m.*
barn *n.* grange *f.*
barometer *n.* baromètre *m.*
baroque *a.* & *n.* baroque (*m.*).
barracks *n. pl.* caserne *f.*
barrage *n.* (*barrier*) barrage *m.*;
(*mil.*) tir de barrage *m.*; (*of
complaints*) série *f.*
barrel *n.* tonneau *m.*; (*of oil*) baril
m.; (*of gun*) canon *m.*

barren a. stérile.

barricade n. barricade f. —v.t. barricader.

barrier n. barrière f.

barring prep. sauf.

barrister n. avocat m.

barrow n. charrette à bras f.; (wheelbarrow) brouette f.

bartender n. (Amer.) barman m.

barter n. troc m., échange m. —v.t. troquer, échanger (**for,** contre).

base n. base f. —v.t. baser (**on,** sur; **in,** à). —a. bas, ignoble.

baseball n. base-ball m.

basement n. sous-sol m.

bash v.t. cogner. —n. coup (violent) m. **~ed in,** enfoncé.

basic a. fondamental, élémentaire. **the ~s,** les élements de base m. pl. **~ally** adv. au fond.

basil n. basilic m.

basin n. (for liquids) cuvette f.; (for food) bol m.; (for washing) lavabo m.; (of river) bassin m.

basis n. base f.

bask v.i. se chauffer.

basket n. corbeille f.; (with handle) panier m.

basketball n. basket(-ball) m.

Basque a. & n. basque (m./f.).

bass[1] a. (mus.) bas, grave. —n. basse f.

bass[2] n. invar. (freshwater fish) perche f.; (sea) bar m.

bassoon n. basson m.

baste[1] v.t. (sew) bâtir.

baste[2] v.t. (culin.) arroser.

bat[1] n. (cricket etc.) batte f.; (table tennis) raquette f. —v.t. (ball) frapper.

bat[2] n. (animal) chauve-souris f.

batch n. (of papers) paquet m.; (of goods) lot m.

bath n. bain m.; (tub) baignoire f. (swimming) **~s,** piscine f. —v.t. donner un bain à —a. de bain. **have a ~,** prendre un bain.

bathe v.t. baigner. —v.i. se baigner; (Amer.) prendre un bain. —n. bain (de mer) m. **~r** n. baigneur, -se m., f.

bathing n. baignade f. **~-costume** n. maillot de bain m.

bathroom n. salle de bains f.

baton n. (mil.) bâton m.; (mus.) baguette f.

battalion n. bataillon m.

batter v.t. (strike) battre; (ill-treat) maltraiter. —n. (culin.) pâte (à frire) f. **~ed** a. (pan, car) cabossé; (face) meurtri.

battery n. (mil., auto.) batterie f.; (of torch, radio) pile f.

battle n. bataille f.; (fig.) lutte f. —v.i. se battre.

baulk v.t./i. = **balk.**

bawl v.t./i. brailler.

bay[1] n. (bot.) laurier m. **~-leaf** n. feuille de laurier f.

bay[2] n. (geog., archit.) baie f.; (area) aire f. **~ window,** fenêtre en saillie f.

bay[3] n. (bark) aboiement m. —v.i. aboyer. **keep** or **hold at ~,** tenir à distance.

bayonet n. baïonnette f.

bazaar n. (shop, market) bazar m.; (sale) vente f.

BC abbr. (before Christ) avant J.-C.

be v.i. être. **be hot/right**/etc., avoir chaud/raison/etc. **he is** 30, (age) il a 30 ans. **it is fine/cold**/etc., (weather) il fait beau/froid/etc. **how are you?,** (health) comment allez-vous? **how much is it?,** (cost) ça fait or c'est combien? **be reading/walking/**etc., (aux.) lire/marcher/etc. **have been to,** avoir été à, être allé à.

beach n. plage f.

beacon n. (lighthouse) phare m.; (marker) balise f.

bead n. perle f.

beak n. bec m.

beaker n. gobelet m.

beam n. (timber) poutre f.; (of light) rayon m.; (of torch) faisceau m. —v.i. (radiate) rayonner. —v.t. (broadcast) diffuser. ~ing a. radieux.

bean n. haricot m.; (of coffee) grain m.

bear¹ n. ours m.

bear² v.t. (carry, show, feel) porter; (endure, sustain) supporter; (child) mettre au monde. —v.i. ~ left/etc., (go) prendre à gauche/ etc. ~ in mind, tenir compte de. ~able a. supportable. ~er n. porteur, -se m., f.

beard n. barbe f.

bearing n. (behaviour) maintien m.; (relevance) rapport m. get one's ~s, s'orienter.

beast n. bête f.; (person) brute f.

beastly a. (fam.) détestable.

beat v.t./i. battre. —n. (of drum, heart) battement m.; (mus.) mesure f.; (of policeman) ronde f. ~ it!, dégage! ~ s.o. down, faire baisser son prix à qn. ~ up, tabasser. it ~s me, (fam.) ça me dépasse. ~ing n. raclée f.

beautician n. esthéticien(ne) m. (f.).

beautiful a. beau. ~ly adv. merveilleusement.

beauty n. beauté f. ~ spot, grain de beauté m.; (fig.) site pittoresque m.

beaver n. castor m.

because conj. parce que. ~ of, à cause de.

beckon v.t./i. ~ (to), faire signe à.

become v.t./i. devenir.

bed n. lit m.; (layer) couche f.; (of sea) fond m.; (of flowers) parterre m. go to ~, (aller) se coucher.

bedbug n. punaise f.

bedclothes n. pl. couvertures f. pl. et draps m. pl.

bedraggled a. (untidy) débraillé.

bedroom n. chambre (à coucher) f.

bedside n. chevet m.

bedsit, bedsitter ns. (fam.) n. chambre meublée f., studio m.

bedspread n. dessus-de-lit m. invar.

bedtime n. heure du coucher f.

bee n. abeille f. make a ~-line for, aller tout droit vers.

beech n. hêtre m.

beef n. bœuf m.

beefburger n. hamburger m.

beehive n. ruche f.

beer n. bière f.

beet n. (plant) betterave f.

beetle n. scarabée m.

beetroot n. invar. (culin.) betterave f.

before prep. (time) avant; (place) devant. —adv. avant; (already) déjà. —conj. ~ leaving, avant de partir. ~ he leaves, avant qu'il (ne) parte. **the day ~**, la veille. **two days ~**, deux jours avant.

beforehand adv. à l'avance, avant.

beg v.t. (entreat) supplier (to do, de faire). ~ (for), (money, food) mendier; (request) solliciter, demander. —v.i. ~ (for alms), mendier. it is going ~ging, personne n'en veut.

beggar n. mendiant(e) m. (f.); (sl.) individu m.

begin v.t./i. commencer (to do, à faire). ~ner n. débutant(e) m. (f.). ~ning n. commencement m., début m.

begrudge v.t. (envy) envier; (give unwillingly) donner à contrecœur. ~ doing, faire à contrecœur.

behalf /bɪˈhɑːf/ *n.* on ~ of, pour; (*as representative*) au nom de, pour (le compte de).

behave *v.i.* se conduire. ~ (o.s.), se conduire bien.

behaviour *n.* conduite *f.*, comportement *m.*

behind *prep.* derrière; (*in time*) en retard sur. —*adv.* derrière; (*late*) en retard. —*n.* (*buttocks*) derrière *m.* **leave** ~, oublier.

behold *v.t.* (*old use*) voir.

beige *a.* & *n.* beige (*m.*).

being *n.* (*person*) être *m.* **bring into** ~, créer. **come into** ~, prendre naissance.

belch *v.i.* faire un renvoi. —*v.t.* ~ **out**, (*smoke*) vomir. —*n.* renvoi *m.*

Belgi|um *n.* Belgique *f.* ~**an** *a.* & *n.* belge (*m./f.*).

belief *n.* croyance *f.*; (*trust*) confiance *f.*; (*faith: relig.*) foi *f.*

believ|e *v.t./i.* croire. ~**e in**, croire à; (*deity*) croire en. ~**able** *a.* croyable. ~**er** *n.* croyant(e) *m.* (*f.*).

bell *n.* cloche *f.*; (*small*) clochette *f.*; (*on door*) sonnette *f.*; (*of phone*) sonnerie *f.*

bellow *v.t./i.* beugler.

belly *n.* ventre *m.* ~**ache** *n.* mal au ventre *m.*

belong *v.i.* ~ **to**, appartenir à; (*club*) être membre de.

belongings *n. pl.* affaires *f. pl.*

below *prep.* au-dessous de; (*fig.*) indigne de. —*adv.* en dessous; (*on page*) ci-dessous.

belt *n.* ceinture *f.*; (*techn.*) courroie *f.*; (*fig.*) région *f.* —*v.t.* (*hit: sl.*) rosser.

beltway *n.* (*Amer.*) périphérique *m.*

bemused *a.* (*confused*) stupéfié; (*thoughtful*) pensif.

bench *n.* banc *m.*; (*working-table*) établi *m.* **the** ~, (*jurid.*) la magistrature (assise).

bend *v.t./i.* (se) courber; (*arm, leg*) plier. —*n.* courbe *f.*; (*in road*) virage *m.*; (*of arm, knee*) pli *m.* ~ **down** or **over**, se pencher.

beneath *prep.* sous, au-dessous de; (*fig.*) indigne de. —*adv.* (au-)dessous.

beneficial *a.* avantageux, favorable.

benefit *n.* avantage *m.*; (*allowance*) allocation *f.* —*v.t.* (*be useful to*) profiter à; (*do good to*) faire du bien à. ~ **from**, tirer profit de.

benign *a.* (*kindly*) bienveillant; (*med.*) bénin.

bent *n.* (*talent*) aptitude *f.*; (*inclination*) penchant *m.* —*a.* tordu; (*sl.*) corrompu. ~ **on doing**, décidé à faire.

bequeath *v.t.* léguer.

bequest *n.* legs *m.*

beret *n.* béret *m.*

Bermuda *n.* Bermudes *f. pl.*

berry *n.* baie *f.*

berserk *a.* **go** ~, devenir fou furieux.

berth *n.* (*in train, ship*) couchette *f.*; (*anchorage*) mouillage *m.* —*v.i.* mouiller.

beseech *v.t.* supplier.

beside *prep.* à côté de. ~ **o.s.**, hors de soi. ~ **the point**, sans rapport.

besides *prep.* en plus de; (*except*) excepté. —*adv.* en plus.

besiege *v.t.* assiéger.

best *a.* meilleur. **the** ~ **book**/*etc.*, le meilleur livre/*etc.* —*adv.* (**the**) ~, (*sing etc.*) le mieux. —*n.* **the** ~ (**one**), le meilleur, la meilleure. ~ **man**, garçon d'honneur *m.* **the** ~ **part of**, la plus grande partie de.

best-seller *n.* best-seller *m.*, succès de librairie *m.*

bet n. pari m. —v.t./i. parier.

betray v.t. trahir.

better a. meilleur. —adv. mieux. —v.t. (improve) améliorer; (do better than) surpasser. **be ~ off,** (financially) avoir plus d'argent. **-he's ~ off at home,** il est mieux chez lui. **I had ~ go,** je ferais mieux de partir. **get ~,** s'améliorer; (recover) se remettre. **get the ~ of,** l'emporter sur. **so much the ~,** tant mieux.

betting-shop n. bureau de P.M.U. m.

between prep. entre. —adv. **in ~,** au milieu.

beware v.i. prendre garde (of, à).

bewilder v.t. désorienter, embarrasser. **~ment** n. désorientation f.

beyond prep. au-delà de; (doubt, reach) hors de; (besides) excepté. —adv. au-delà. **it is ~ me,** ça me dépasse.

bias n. (inclination) penchant m. **~ed** a. partial.

bib n. bavoir m.

Bible n. Bible f.

biblical a. biblique.

bicarbonate n. bicarbonate m.

biceps n. biceps m.

bicker v.i. se chamailler.

bicycle n. bicyclette f.

bid n. (at auction) offre f., enchère f.; (attempt) tentative f. —v.t./i. (offer) faire une offre or une enchère (de).

biennial a. biennal.

bifocals n. pl. lunettes bifocales f. pl.

big a. grand; (in bulk) gros; (generous: sl.) généreux. —adv. (fam.) en grand; (earn: fam.) gros. **~-headed** a. prétentieux. **~ shot,** (sl.) huile f. **think ~,** (fam.) voir grand.

bigamy n. bigamie f.

bigot n. fanatique m./f. **~ed** a. fanatique.

bike n. (fam.) vélo m.

bikini n. bikini m.

bilberry n. myrtille f.

bile n. bile f.

bill[1] n. (invoice) facture f.; (in hotel, for gas, etc.) note f.; (in restaurant) addition f.; (of sale) acte m.; (pol.) projet de loi m.; (banknote: Amer.) billet de banque m. —v.t. (person: comm.) envoyer la facture à. (theatre) **on the ~,** à l'affiche.

bill[2] n. (of bird) bec m.

billboard n. panneau d'affichage m.

billfold n. (Amer.) portefeuille m.

billiards n. billard m.

billion n. billion m.; (Amer.) milliard m.

billy-goat n. bouc m.

bin n. (for rubbish, litter) boîte (à ordures) f., poubelle f.

binary a. binaire.

bind v.t. lier; (book) relier; (jurid.) obliger. —n. (bore: sl.) plaie f.

binge n. **go on a ~,** (spree: sl.) faire la bringue.

bingo n. loto m.

binoculars n. pl. jumelles f. pl.

biodegradable a. biodégradable.

biography n. biographie f.

biolog|y n. biologie f. **~ical** a. biologique.

biorhythm n. biorythme m.

birch n. (tree) bouleau m.; (whip) verge f., fouet m.

bird n. oiseau m.; (fam.) individu m.; (girl: sl.) poule f.

Biro n. (P.) stylo à bille m., Bic m. (P.).

birth n. naissance f. **give ~,** accoucher. **~-control** n. contrôle des naissances m.

birthday n. anniversaire m.

birthmark n. tache de vin f.

biscuit n. biscuit m.

bishop n. évêque m.

bit[1] n. morceau m.; (of horse) mors m.; (of tool) mèche f. **a ~**, (a little) un peu.

bit[2] n. (comput.) bit m., élément binaire m.

bitch n. chienne f.; (woman: fam.) garce f. —v.i. (grumble: fam.) râler. **~y a.** (fam.) vache.

bite v.t./i. mordre. —n. morsure f.; (by insect) piqûre f.; (mouthful) bouchée f. **have a ~**, manger un morceau.

bitter a. amer; (weather) glacial, âpre. —n. bière anglaise f. **~ness** n. amertume f.

bizarre a. bizarre.

blab v.i. jaser.

black a. noir. —n. (colour) noir m. B**~**, (person) Noir(e) m. (f.). —v.t. noircir; (goods) boycotter. **~ eye**, œil poché m. **~ ice**, verglas m. **~ list**, liste noire f. **~ market**, marché noir m. **~ spot**, point noir m.

blackberry n. mûre f.

blackbird n. merle m.

blackboard n. tableau noir m.

blackcurrant n. cassis m.

blacken v.t./i. noircir.

blackhead n. point noir m.

blackleg n. jaune m.

blacklist v.t. mettre sur la liste noire or à l'index.

blackmail n. chantage m. —v.t. faire chanter. **~er** n. maîtrechanteur m.

blackout n. panne d'électricité f.; (med.) syncope f.

bladder n. vessie f.

blade n. (of knife etc.) lame f.; (of propeller, oar) pale f. **~ of grass**, brin d'herbe m.

blame v.t. accuser. —n. faute f. **~ s.o. for sth.**, reprocher qch. à qn.

he is to ~, il est responsable (for, de).

bland a. (gentle) doux; (insipid) fade.

blank a. blanc; (look) vide; (cheque) en blanc. —n. blanc m. **~ (cartridge)**, cartouche à blanc f.

blanket n. couverture f.; (layer: fig.) couche f.

blare v.t./i. beugler. —n. vacarme m., beuglement m.

blasé a. blasé.

blast n. explosion f.; (wave of air) souffle m.; (of wind) rafale f.; (noise from siren etc.) coup m. —v.t. (blow up) faire sauter. **~ed** a. (fam.) maudit, fichu. **~ off**, être mis à feu. **~-off** n. mise à feu f.

blatant a. (obvious) flagrant; (shameless) éhonté.

blaze n. flamme f.; (conflagration) incendie m.; (fig.) éclat m. —v.i. (fire) flamber; (sky, eyes, etc.) flamboyer.

blazer n. blazer m.

bleach n. décolorant m.; (for domestic use) eau de Javel f. —v.t./i. blanchir; (hair) décolorer.

bleak a. morne.

bleary a. (eyes) voilé.

bleat n. bêlement m. —v.i. bêler.

bleed v.t./i. saigner.

bleep n. bip m. **~er** n. bip m.

blemish n. tare f., défaut m.; (on reputation) tache f. —v.t. entacher.

blend v.t./i. (se) mélanger. —n. mélange m. **~er** n. mixer m.

bless v.t. bénir. **~ing** n. bénédiction f.; (benefit) avantage m.; (stroke of luck) chance f.

blight n. (disease: bot.) rouille f.; (fig.) fléau m.

blind a. aveugle. —v.t. aveugler. —n. (on window) store m.;

(*deception*) feinte *f.* **~ corner,** virage sans visibilité *m.* **~ man,** aveugle *m.* **~ spot,** (*auto.*) angle mort *m.* **~ly** *adv.* aveuglément. **~ness** *n.* cécité *f.*

blindfold *n. & adv.* les yeux bandés. —*n.* bandeau *m.* —*v.t.* bander les yeux à.

blink *v.i.* cligner des yeux; (*of light*) clignoter.

blinkers *n. pl.* œillères *f. pl.*

bliss *n.* félicité *f.* **~ful** *a.* bienheureux.

blister *n.* ampoule *f.* (*on paint*) cloque *f.* —*v.i.* se couvrir d'ampoules; cloquer.

blizzard *n.* tempête de neige *f.*

bloated *a.* gonflé.

bloater *n.* hareng saur *m.*

blob *n.* (*drop*) (grosse) goutte *f.*; (*stain*) tache *f.*

bloc *n.* bloc *m.*

block *n.* bloc *m.*; (*buildings*) pâté de maisons *m.*; (*in pipe*) obstruction *f.* **~ (of flats),** immeuble *m.* —*v.t.* bloquer. **~ letters,** majuscules *f. pl.* **~age** *n.* obstruction *f.*

blockade *n.* blocus *m.* —*v.t.* bloquer.

bloke *n.* (*fam.*) type *m.*

blond *a. & n.* blond (*m.*).

blonde *a. & n.* blonde (*f.*).

blood *n.* sang *m.* —*a.* (*donor, bath, etc.*) de sang; (*bank, poisoning, etc.*) du sang; (*group, vessel*) sanguin. **~-pressure** *n.* tension artérielle *f.* **~test,** prise de sang *f.*

bloodhound *n.* limier *m.*

bloodshed *n.* effusion de sang *f.*

bloodstream *n.* sang *m.*

bloody *a.* sanglant; (*sl.*) sacrée. —*adv.* (*sl.*) vachement.

bloom *n.* fleur *f.* —*v.i.* fleurir; (*fig.*) s'épanouir.

blossom *n.* fleur(s) *f.* (*pl.*). —*v.i.* fleurir; (*person; fig.*) s'épanouir.

blot *n.* tache *f.* —*v.t.* tacher; (*dry*) sécher. **~ out,** effacer.

blotch *n.* tache *f.* **~y** *a.* couvert de taches.

blouse *n.* chemisier *m.*

blow[1] *v.t./i.* souffler; (*fuse*) (faire) sauter; (*squander: sl.*) claquer; (*opportunity*) rater. **~ one's nose,** se moucher. **~ a whistle,** siffler. **~ away** *or* **off,** emporter. **~-dry** *v.t.* sécher; (*hair*) brushing *m.* **~-out** *n.* (*of tyre*) éclatement *m.* **~ over,** passer. **~ up,** (faire) sauter; (*tyre*) gonfler; (*photo.*) aggrandir.

blow[2] *n.* coup *m.*

blowlamp *n.* chalumeau *m.*

blue *a.* bleu; (*film*) porno. —*n.* bleu *m.* **come out of the ~,** être inattendu.

bluebell *n.* jacinthe des bois *f.*

bluebottle *n.* mouche à viande *f.*

blueprint *n.* plan *m.*

bluff *v.t./i.* bluffer. —*n.* bluff *m.* **call. s.o.'s ~,** dire chiche à qn.

blunder *v.i.* faire une gaffe; (*move*) avancer à tâtons. —*n.* gaffe *f.*

blunt *a.* (*knife*) émoussé; (*person*) brusque. —*v.t.* émousser. **~ly** *adv.* carrément.

blur *n.* tache floue *f.* —*v.t.* rendre flou.

blurt *v.t.* **~ out,** lâcher, dire.

blush *v.i.* rougir. —*n.* rougeur *f.* **~er** *n.* blush *m.*

bluster *v.i.* (*wind*) faire rage; (*swagger*) fanfaronner. **~y** *a.* bourrasques.

boar *n.* sanglier *m.*

board *n.* planche *f.*; (*for notices*) tableau *m.*; (*food*) pension *f.*; (*committee*) conseil *m.* —*v.t./i.* (*bus, train*) monter dans; (*naut.*) monter à bord (de). **~ of directors,** conseil d'administration *m.* **go by the ~,** passer à l'as. **full ~,** pension complète *f.* **half**

~, demi-pension f. **on** ~, à bord.
~ing-house n. pension (de famille) f. **~ing-school** n. pensionnat m., pension f.

boast v.i. se vanter (**about**, de). —v.t. s'enorgueillir de. —n. vantardise f. **~ful** a. vantard.

boat n. bateau m.; (small) canot m.

boatswain n. maitre d'équipage m.

bob v.i. ~ **up and down**, monter et descendre.

bobby n. (fam.) flic m.

bobsleigh n. bob- (sleigh) m.

body n. corps m.; (mass) masse f.; (organization) organisme m. ~(**work**), (auto.) carrosserie f.

bodyguard n. garde du corps m.

bog n. marécage m. —v.t. **get ~ged down**, s'embourber.

bogus a. faux.

boil¹ n. furoncle m.

boil² v.t./i. (faire) bouillir. **bring to the** ~, porter à ébullition. ~ **down to**, se ramener à. ~ed (egg) à la coque; (potatoes) à l'eau.

boiler n. chaudière f.

boisterous a. tapageur.

bold a. hardi; (cheeky) effronté; (type) gras. **~ness** n. hardiesse f.

Bolivia n. Bolivie f. **~n** a. & n. bolivien(ne) (m. (f.)).

bollard n. (on road) borne f.

bolster n. traversin m. —v.t. soutenir.

bolt n. verrou m.; (for nut) boulon m.; (lightning) éclair m. —v.t. (door etc.) verrouiller; (food) engouffrer. —v.i. se sauver.

bomb n. bombe f. —v.t. bombarder. ~ **scare**, alerte à la bombe f. **~er** n. (aircraft) bombardier m.; (person) plastiqueur m.

bombard v.t. bombarder.

bombshell n. **be a** ~, tomber comme une bombe.

bond n. (agreement) engagement

m.; (link) lien m.; (comm.) obligation f., bon m.

bone n. os m.; (of fish) arête f. —v.t. désosser. **~-dry** a. tout à fait sec.

bonfire n. feu m.; (for celebration) feu de joie m.

bonnet n. (hat) bonnet m.; (of vehicle) capot m.

bonny a. prime f.

bonus n. prime f.

bony a. (thin) osseux; (meat) plein d'os; (fish) plein d'arêtes.

boo int. hou. —v.t./i. huer.

booby-trap n. engin piégé m. —v.t. piéger.

book n. livre m.; (of tickets etc.) carnet m. ~**s**, (comm.) comptes m. pl. —v.t. (reserve) réserver; (driver) faire un P.V. à; (player) prendre le nom de; (write down) inscrire. —v.i. retenir des places. **~ing office**, guichet m.

bookcase n. bibliothèque f.

bookkeeping n. comptabilité f.

booklet n. brochure f.

bookmaker n. bookmaker m.

bookseller n. libraire m./f.

bookshop n. librairie f.

boom v.i. (gun, wind, etc.) gronder; (trade) prospérer. —n. grondement m.; (comm.) boom m.

boon n. (benefit) aubaine f.

boost v.t. stimuler; (morale) remonter; (price) augmenter; (publicize) faire de la réclame pour. —n. **give a** ~ **to**, = **boost**.

boot n. (knee-length) botte f.; (ankle-length) chaussure (montante) f.; (for walking) chaussure de marche f.; (sport) chaussure de sport f.; (of vehicle) coffre m. —v.t./i. ~ **up**, (comput.) démarrer, lancer (le programme).

booth n. (for telephone) cabine f.; (at fair) baraque f.

booty n. butin m.

booze v.i. (fam.) boire (beaucoup). —n. (fam.) alcool m.

border n. (edge) bord m.; (frontier) frontière f.; (in garden) bordure f. —v.i. ~ **on**, être voisin de, avoisiner.

borderline n. ligne de démarcation f. ~ **case**, cas limite m.

bore v.t./i. (techn.) forer.

bore v.t. ennuyer. —n. raseu(se m., f.; (thing) ennui m. **be** ~**d**, s'ennuyer. ~**dom** ennui m.

boring a. ennuyeux.

born a. né. **be** ~, naître.

borrow v.t. emprunter (from, à). ~**ing** n. emprunt m.

bosom n. sein m. ~ **friend**, ami(e) intime m. (f.).

boss n. (fam.) patron(ne) m. (f.). —v.t. ~ (about), (fam.) donner des ordres à, régenter.

bossy a. autoritaire.

botan|y n. botanique f. ~**ical** a. botanique.

botch v.t. bâcler, saboter.

both a. les deux. —pron. tous or toutes (les) deux, l'un(e) et l'autre. —adv. à la fois. ~ **the books**, les deux livres. **we** ~ **agree**, nous sommes tous les deux d'accord. **I bought** ~ (of them), j'ai acheté les deux. **I saw** ~ **of you**, je vous ai vus tous les deux. ~ **Paul and Anne**, (et) Paul et Anne.

bother v.t. (annoy, worry) ennuyer; (disturb) déranger. —v.i. se déranger. —n. ennui m.; (effort) peine f. **don't** ~ (calling), ce n'est pas la peine (d'appeler). **don't** ~ **about us**, ne t'inquiète pas pour nous. **I can't be** ~**ed**, j'ai la flemme.

bottle n. bouteille f.; (for baby) biberon m. —v.t. mettre en bouteille(s). ~ **bank**, collecteur (de verre usagé) m. ~**opener** n. ouvre-bouteille(s) m.

bottleneck n. (traffic jam) bouchon m.

bottom n. fond m.; (of hill, page, etc.) bas m.; (buttocks) derrière m. —a. inférieur, du bas.

bough n. rameau m.

boulder n. rocher m.

boulevard n. boulevard m.

bounce v.i. rebondir; (person) faire des bonds, bondir; (cheques sl.) être refusé. —v.t. faire rebondir. ~ n. rebond m.

bouncer n. videur m.

bound[1] v.i. (leap) bondir. —n. bond m.

bound[2] a. **be** ~ **for**, être en route pour, aller, vers. ~ **to**, (obliged) obligé de; (certain) sûr de.

boundary n. limite f.

bound|s n. pl. limites f. pl. **out of** ~**s**, interdit. ~**ed by**, limité par.

bouquet n. bouquet m.

bout n. période f.; (med.) accès m.; (boxing) combat m.

bow[1] n. (weapon) arc m.; (mus.) archet m.; (knot) nœud m. ~**tie** n. nœud papillon m.

bow[2] n. (with head) salut m.; (with body) révérence f. —v.t./i. (s')incliner.

bow[3] n. (naut.) proue f.

bowels n. pl. intestins m. pl.

bowl[1] n. cuvette f.; (for food) bol m.; (for soup etc.) assiette creuse f.

bowl[2] n. (ball) boule f. —v.t./i. (cricket) lancer. ~**ing** n. jeu de boules m.

bowler[1] n. (cricket) lanceur m.

bowler[2] n. ~ (hat), (chapeau) melon m.

box[1] n. boîte f.; (cardboard) carton m. —v.t. mettre en boîte. **the** ~, (fam.) la télé. ~**office** n. bureau de location m. **Boxing Day**, le lendemain de Noël.

box[2] v.t./i. (sport) boxer. ~**ing** n. boxe f.; a. de boxe.

boy n. garçon m. ~**friend** n. (petit) ami m.

boycott *v.t.* boycotter. —*n.* boycottage *m.*

bra *n.* soutien-gorge *m.*

brace *n.* (*fastener*) attache *f.*; (*dental*) appareil *m.*; (*for bit*) vilbrequin *m.* ~**s**, (*for trousers*) bretelles *f. pl.* —*v.t.* soutenir. ~ **o.s.**, rassembler ses forces.

bracelet *n.* bracelet *m.*

bracken *n.* fougère *f.*

bracket *n.* (*for lamp etc.*) tasseau *m.*; support *m.*; (*group*) tranche *f.* (**round**) ~, (*printing sign*) parenthèse *f.*

brag *v.i.* se vanter.

braid *n.* (*trimming*) galon *m.*; (*of hair*) tresse *f.*

Braille *n.* braille *m.*

brain *n.* cerveau *m.* ~**s**, (*fig.*) intelligence *f.*

brainwash *v.t.* faire un lavage de cerveau à.

brainwave *n.* idée géniale *f.*

brainy *a.* intelligent.

braise *v.t.* braiser.

brake *n.* frein *m.* —*v.t./i.* freiner. ~ **fluid**, liquide de frein *m.* ~ **light**, feu de stop *m.* ~ **lining**, garniture de frein *f.*

bramble *n.* ronce *f.*

bran *n.* (*husks*) son *m.*

branch *n.* branche *f.*; (*of road*) embranchement *m.*; (*comm.*) succursale *f.*; (*of bank*) agence *f.* —*v.i.* ~ (**off**), bifurquer.

brand *n.* marque *f.* —*v.t.* ~ **s.o. as**, donner à qn. la réputation de. ~-**new** *a.* tout neuf.

brandish *v.t.* brandir.

brandy *n.* cognac *m.*

brash *a.* effronté.

brass *n.* cuivre *m.* **the** ~, (*mus.*) les cuivres *m. pl.*

brassière *n.* soutien-gorge *m.*

brat *n.* (*child: pej.*) môme *m./f.*; (*ill-behaved*) garnement *m.*

bravado *n.* bravade *f.*

brave *a.* courageux, brave. —*v.t.* braver. ~**ry** *n.* courage *m.*

bravo *int.* bravo.

brawl *n.* bagarre *f.* —*v.i.* se bagarrer.

bray *n.* braiment *m.* —*v.i.* braire.

Brazil *n.* Brésil *m.* ~**ian** *a. & n.* brésilien(ne) (*m. (f.)*).

breach *n.* violation *f.*; (*of contract*) rupture *f.*; (*gap*) brèche *f.* —*v.t.* ouvrir une brèche dans.

bread *n.* pain *m.* ~ **and butter**, tartine *f.* ~-**bin**, (*Amer.*) ~-**box** *ns.* boîte à pain *f.*

breadcrumbs *n. pl.* (*culin.*) chapelure *f.*

breadth *n.* largeur *f.*

break *v.t.* casser; (*smash into pieces*) briser; (*vow, silence, rank, etc.*) rompre; (*law*) violer; (*a record*) battre; (*news*) révéler; (*journey*) interrompre; (*heart, strike, ice*) briser. —*v.i.* (se) casser; se briser. —*n.* cassure *f.*, rupture *f.*; (*in relationship, continuity*) rupture *f.*; (*interval*) interruption *f.*; (*at school*) récréation *f.*, récré *f.*; (*for coffee*) pause *f.*; (*luck: fam.*) chance *f.* ~ **one's arm**, se casser le bras. ~ **down** *v.i.* (*collapse*) s'effondrer; (*fail*) échouer; (*machine*) tomber en panne; *v.t.* (*door*) enfoncer; (*analyse*) analyser. ~-**in** *n.* cambriolage *m.* ~ **into**, cambrioler. ~ **off**, (se) détacher; (*suspend*) rompre; (*stop talking*) s'interrompre. ~ **out**, (*fire, war, etc.*) éclater. ~ **up**, (*end*) (faire) cesser; (*couple*) rompre; (*marriage*) (se) briser; (*crowd*) (se) disperser; (*schools*) entrer en vacances. ~**able** *a.* cassable. ~**age** *n.* casse *f.*

breakdown *n.* (*techn.*) panne *f.*; (*med.*) dépression *f.*; (*of figures*) analyse *f.*

breakfast n. petit déjeuner m.

breakthrough n. percée f.

breast n. sein m.; (chest) poitrine f. **~-feed** v.t. allaiter. **~-stroke** n. brasse f.

breath n. souffle m., haleine f. **out of ~,** essoufflé.

breathalyser n. alcootest m.

breath|e v.t./i. respirer. **~ in,** inspirer. **~ out,** expirer. **~ing** n. respiration f.

breather n. moment de repos m.

breathtaking a. à vous couper le souffle.

breed v.t. élever; (give rise to) engendrer. —v.i. se reproduire. —n. race f.

breez|e n. brise f. **~y** a. (weather) frais; (cheerful) jovial.

Breton a. & n. breton(ne) (m. (f.)).

brew v.t. (beer) brasser; (tea) faire infuser. —v.i. fermenter; infuser; (fig.) se préparer. —n. décoction f. **~ery** n. brasserie f.

bribe n. pot-de-vin m. —v.t. soudoyer. **~ry** n. corruption f.

brick n. brique f.

bricklayer n. maçon m.

bridal a. nuptial.

bride n. mariée f.

bridegroom n. marié m.

bridesmaid n. demoiselle d'honneur f.

bridge[1] n. pont m.; (naut.) passerelle f.; (of nose) arête f.

bridge[2] n. (cards) bridge m.

bridle n. bride f. —v.t. brider. **~-path** n. allée cavalière f.

brief[1] a. bref. **~ly** adv. brièvement.

brief[2] n. instructions f. pl.; (jurid.) dossier m. —v.t. donner des instructions à. **~ing** n. briefing m.

briefcase n. serviette f.

briefs n. pl. slip m.

brigad|e n. brigade f. **~ier** n. général de brigade m.

bright a. brillant, vif; (day, room) clair; (cheerful) gai; (clever) intelligent. **~ness** n. éclat m.

brighten v.t. égayer. —v.i. (weather) s'éclaircir; (of face) s'éclairer.

brilliant a. brillant; (light) éclatant; (very good: fam.) super.

brim n. bord m.

brine n. saumure f.

bring v.t. (thing) apporter; (person, vehicle) amener. **~ back,** rapporter; ramener. **~ down,** faire tomber; (shoot down, knock down) abattre. **~ forward,** avancer. **~ off,** réussir. **~ up,** élever; (med.) vomir; (question) soulever.

brink n. bord m.

brisk a. vif.

bristle n. poil m. —v.i. se hérisser.

Britain n. Grande-Bretagne f.

British a. britannique. **the ~,** les Britanniques m. pl.

Brittany n. Bretagne f.

brittle a. fragile.

broad a. large; (daylight, outline) grand. **~ bean,** fève f. **~-minded** a. large d'esprit.

broadcast v.t./i. diffuser; (person) parler à la télévision or à la radio. —n. émission f.

broaden v.t./i. (s')élargir.

broccoli n. invar. brocoli m.

brochure n. brochure f.

broke a. (penniless: sl.) fauché.

broker n. courtier m.

bronchitis n. bronchite f.

bronze n. bronze m.

brooch n. broche f.

brood n. nichée f., couvée f. —v.i. couver; (fig.) méditer tristement. **~y** a. mélancolique.

brook n. ruisseau m.

broom n. balai m.

broomstick n. manche à balai m.

broth n. bouillon m.

brothel 273 bullfight

brothel n. maison close f.
brother n. frère m. **~-in-law** n. beau-frère m.
brow n. front m.; (of hill) sommet m.
browbeat v.t. intimider.
brown a. marron (invar.); (cheveux) brun. —n. marron m.; brun m. —v.t./i. brunir; (culin.) (faire) dorer. **~ bread**, pain bis m. **~ sugar**, cassonade f.
Brownie n. jeannette f.
browse v.i. feuilleter.
bruise n. bleu m. —v.t. (hurt) faire un bleu à; (fruit) abîmer. **~d** a. couvert de bleus.
brunch n. petit déjeuner copieux m. (pris comme déjeuner)
brunette n. brunette f.
brunt n. **the ~ of**, le plus fort de.
brush n. brosse f.; (bushes) broussailles f. pl. —v.t. brosser. **~ aside**, écarter. **give s.o. the ~-off**, (reject: fam.) envoyer promener qn.
Brussels n. Bruxelles m./f. **~ sprouts**, choux de Bruxelles m. pl.
brutal a. brutal. **~ity** n. brutalité f.
brute n. brute f. **by ~ force**, par la force.
bubble n. bulle f. —v.i. bouillonner. **~ bath**, bain moussant m.
buck¹ n. mâle m. —v.i. ruer. **~** (sl.) prendre courage; (hurry: sl.) se grouiller.
buck² n. (Amer., sl.) dollar m.
buck³ n. **pass the ~**, rejeter la responsabilité (to, sur).
bucket n. seau m.
buckle n. boucle f. —v.t./i. (fasten) (se) boucler; (bend) voiler.
bud n. bourgeon m. —v.i. bourgeonner.
Buddhis|t a. & n. bouddhiste (m./f.) **~m** n. bouddhisme m.

buddy n. (fam.) copain m.
budge v.t./i. (faire) bouger.
budgerigar n. perruche f.
budget n. budget m. —v.i. **~ for**, prévoir (dans son budget).
buff n. (colour) chamois m.; (fam.) fanatique m./f.
buffalo n. buffle m.; (Amer.) bison m.
buffer n. tampon m. **~ zone**, zone tampon f.
buffet n. (meal, counter) buffet m. **~ car**, buffet m.
buffoon n. bouffon m.
bug n. (insect) punaise f.; (any small insect) bestiole f.; (germ: sl.) microbe m.; (device: sl.) micro m.; (defect: sl.) défaut m. —v.t. mettre des micros dans; (Amer., sl.) embêter.
buggy n. (child's) poussette f.
bugle n. clairon m.
build v.t./i. bâtir, construire. —n. carrure f. **~ up**, (increase) augmenter, monter; (accumulate) (s')accumuler. **~-up** n. accumulation f.; (fig.) publicité f. **~er** n. entrepreneur m.; (workman) ouvrier m.
building n. bâtiment m.; (dwelling) immeuble m.
bulb n. oignon m.; (electr.) ampoule f.
bulg|e n. renflement m. —v.i. se renfler, être renflé. **be ~ing with**, être gonflé ou bourré de.
bulimia n. boulimie f.
bulk n. grosseur f. **in ~**, en gros; (loose) en vrac. **~y** a. gros.
bull n. taureau m.
bulldog n. bouledogue m.
bulldozer n. bulldozer m.
bullet n. balle f. **~-proof** a. pare-balles invar.; (vehicle) blindé.
bulletin n. bulletin m.
bullfight n. corrida f. **~er** n. torero m.

bullion *n.* or *or* argent en lingots *m.*

bullring *n.* arène *f.*

bully *n.* brute *f.*; tyran *m.* —*v.t.* (*treat badly*) brutaliser; (*persecute*) tyranniser; (*coerce*) forcer (**into,** à).

bum¹ *n.* (*sl.*) derrière *m.*

bum² *n.* (*Amer.*, *sl.*) vagabond(e) *m.* (*f.*).

bumble-bee *n.* bourdon *m.*

bump *n.* choc *m.*; (*swelling*) bosse *f.* —*v.t./i.* cogner, heurter. **~ into,** (*hit*) rentrer dans; (*meet*) tomber sur. **~y** *a.* cahoteux.

bumper *n.* pare-chocs *m. invar.* —*a.* exceptionnel.

bun *n.* (*cake*) petit pain au lait *m.*; (*hair*) chignon *m.*

bunch *n.* (*of flowers*) bouquet *m.*; (*of keys*) trousseau *m.*; (*of people*) groupe *m.*; (*of bananas*) régime *m.* **~ of grapes,** grappe de raisin *f.*

bundle *n.* paquet *m.* —*v.t.* mettre en paquet; (*push*) pousser.

bung *n.* bonde *f.* —*v.t.* boucher; (*throw: sl.*) flanquer.

bungalow *n.* bungalow *m.*

bungle *v.t.* gâcher.

bunion *n.* (*med.*) oignon *m.*

bunk *n.* couchette *f.* **~-beds** *m. pl.* lits superposés *m. pl.*

bunker *n.* (*mil.*) bunker *m.*

buoy *n.* bouée *f.* —*v.t.* **~ up,** (*hearten*) soutenir, encourager.

burden *n.* fardeau *m.* —*v.t.* accabler.

bureau *n.* bureau *m.*

bureaucracy *n.* bureaucratie *f.*

bureaucrat *n.* bureaucrate *m./f.* **~ic** *a.* bureaucratique.

burglar *n.* cambrioleur *m.* **~ize** *v.t.* (*Amer.*) cambrioler. **~ alarm,** alarme *f.* **~y** *n.* cambriolage *m.*

burgle *v.t.* cambrioler.

Burgundy *n.* (*wine*) bourgogne *m.*

burial *n.* enterrement *m.*

burly *a.* costaud.

Burm|a *n.* Birmanie *f.* **~ese** *a.* & *n.* birman(e) (*m.* (*f.*)).

burn *v.t./i.* brûler. —*n.* brûlure *f.* **~er** *n.* brûleur *m.* **~ing** *a.* (*fig.*) brûlant.

burp *n.* (*fam.*) rot *m.* —*v.i.* (*fam.*) roter.

burrow *n.* terrier *m.* —*v.t.* creuser.

burst *v.t./i.* crever, (faire) éclater. —*n.* explosion *f.*; (*of laughter*) éclat *m.*; (*surge*) élan *m.* **be ~ing with,** déborder de. **~ into,** faire irruption dans.

bury *v.t.* (*person etc.*) enterrer; (*hide, cover*) enfouir; (*engross, thrust*) plonger.

bus *n.* (auto)bus *m.* **~-stop** *n.* arrêt d'autobus *m.*

bush *n.* buisson *m.*; (*land*) brousse *f.* **~y** *a.* broussailleux.

business *n.* (*task, concern*) affaire *f.*; (*commerce*) affaires *f. pl.*; (*line of work*) métier *m.*; (*shop*) commerce *m.* **that's none of your ~!,** ça ne vous regarde pas! **~man,** homme d'affaires *m.*

businesslike *a.* sérieux.

busker *n.* musicien(ne) des rues *m.* (*f.*).

bust¹ *n.* buste *m.*; (*bosom*) poitrine *f.*

bust² *v.t./i.* (*burst: sl.*) crever; (*break: sl.*) (se) casser. —*a.* (*broken, finished: sl.*) fichu. **~-up** *n.* (*sl.*) engueulade *f.*

bustl|e *v.i.* s'affairer. —*n.* remue-ménage *m.* **~ing** *a.* (*place*) bruyant, animé.

bus|y *a.* occupé; (*street*) animé; (*day*) chargé. **~ily** *adv.* activement.

but *conj.* mais. —*prep.* sauf. —*adv.* (*only*) seulement.

butane *n.* butane *m.*

butcher *n.* boucher *m.* —*v.t.* massacrer.

butler *n.* maître d'hôtel *m.*

butt *n.* (*of gun*) crosse *f.*; (*of cigarette*) mégot *m.*; (*target*) cible *f.*; (*barrel*) tonneau; (*Amer., fam.*) derrière *m.* —*v.i.* **~ in**, interrompre.

butter *n.* beurre *m.* —*v.t.* beurrer. **~-bean** *n.* haricot blanc *m.*

buttercup *n.* bouton-d'or *m.*

butterfly *n.* papillon *m.*

buttock *n.* fesse *f.*

button *n.* bouton *m.*

buttonhole *n.* boutonnière *f.* —*v.t.* accrocher.

buy *v.t.* acheter (**from**, à); (*believe: sl.*) croire, avaler; **~** achat *m.* **~er** *n.* acheteu|r, -se *m., f.*

buzz *n.* bourdonnement *m.* —*v.i.* bourdonner. **~er** *n.* sonnerie *f.*

by *prep.* par, de; (*near*) à côté de; (*before*) avant; (*means*) en à, par. **by bike**, à vélo. **by car**, en auto. **by day**, de jour. **by the kilo**, au kilo. **by running**/*etc.*, en courant/*etc.* **by sea**, par mer. **by that time**, à ce moment-là. **~ the way**, à propos. —*adv.* (*near*) tout près. **by-law** *n.* arrêté *m.*; (*of club etc.*) statut *m.* **by o.s.**, tout seul. **~-product** *n.* sousproduit *m.*; (*fig.*) conséquence.

bye(-bye) *int.* (*fam.*) au revoir.

bypass *n.* (*auto.*) route qui contourne *f.*; (*med.*) pontage *m.* —*v.t.* contourner.

bystander *n.* specta|teur, -trice *m., f.*

byte *n.* octet *m.*

C

cab *n.* taxi *m.*; (*of lorry, train*) cabine *f.*

cabaret *n.* spectacle (de cabaret) *m.*

cabbage *n.* chou *m.*

cabin *n.* (*hut*) cabane *f.*; (*in ship, aircraft*) cabine *f.*

cabinet *n.* (*petite*) armoire *f.*; (*for filing*) classeur *m.* **C~**, (*pol.*) cabinet *m.*

cable *n.* câble *m.* —*v.t.* câbler. **~car** *n.* téléphérique *m.* **~ railway**, funiculaire *m.*

cache *n.* (*place*) cachette *f.* **a ~ of arms**, des armes cachées.

cactus *n.* cactus *m.*

caddie *n.* (*golf*) caddie *m.*

caddy *n.* boite à thé *f.*

cadet *n.* élève officier *m.*

cadge *v.t.* se faire payer, écornifler. —*v.i.* quémander. **~ money from**, taper. **~r** *n.* écornifleu|r, -se *m., f.*

Caesarean *a.* **~ (section)**, césarienne *f.*

café *n.* café(-restaurant) *m.*

cafeteria *n.* cafétéria *f.*

caffeine *n.* caféine *f.*

cage *n.* cage *f.*

cagey *a.* peu communicatif.

cagoule *n.* K-way *m.* (P.).

cajole *v.t.* **~ s.o. into doing**, faire l'enjoleur pour que qn. fasse.

cake *n.* gâteau *m.*

calamity *n.* calamité *f.*

calcium *n.* calcium *m.*

calculat|**e** *v.t./i.* calculer. **~ed** *a.* (*action*) délibéré. **~ion** *n.* calcul *m.* **~or** *n.* calculatrice *f.*

calendar *n.* calendrier *m.*

calf[1] *n.* (*young cow or bull*) veau *m.*

calf[2] *n.* (*of leg*) mollet *m.*

calibre *n.* calibre *m.*

calico *n.* calicot *m.*

call *v.t./i.* appeler. **~ (in or round)**, (*visit*) passer. **~** *n.* appel *m.*; (*of bird*) cri *m.*; visite *f.* **be ~ed**, (*named*) s'appeler. **~ back**, rappeler; (*visit*) repasser.

~-box n. cabine téléphonique f.
~ for, (require) demander;
(fetch) passer prendre. **~ off,**
annuler. **~ on,** (visit) passer
chez; (appeal to) faire appel à.
~er n. visiteu|r, -se m., f.; (on
phone) personne qui appelle m.
~ing n. vocation f.

callous a., **~ly** adv. sans pitié.

calm a. calme. —n. calme m.
—v.t./i. **~ (down),** (se) calmer.
~ness n. calme m.

calorie n. calorie f.

camber n. (of road) bombement m.

camcorder n. caméscope m.

camel n. chameau m.

cameo n. camée m.

camera n. appareil (-photo) m.;
(for moving pictures) caméra f.
~man n. caméraman m.

camouflage n. camouflage m.
—v.t. camoufler.

camp n. camp m. —v.i. camper. **~-
bed** n. lit de camp m. **~er** n.
campeu|r, -se m., f. **~er (-van),**
camping-car m. **~ing** n. camping
m.

campaign n. campagne f. —v.i.
faire campagne.

campsite n. (for holiday-makers)
camping m.

campus n. campus m.

can¹ n. bidon m.; (sealed container
for food) boîte f. —v.t. mettre en
boîte. **~-opener** n. ouvre-boîte(s)
m.

can² v. aux. (be able to) pouvoir;
(know how to) savoir.

Canad|a n. Canada m. **~ian** a. &
n. canadien(ne) (m. (f.)).

canal n. canal m.

canary n. canari m.

cancel v.t./i. (call off, revoke) annuler; (cross out) barrer. **~lation**
n. annulation f.; oblitération f.

cancer n. cancer m.

Cancer n. le Cancer.

candid a. franc.

candidate n. candidat(e) m. (f.).

candle n. bougie f., chandelle f.;
(in church) cierge m.

candlestick n. chandelier m.

candour n. franchise f.

candy n. (Amer.) bonbon(s) m.
(pl.). **~-floss** n. barbe à papa f.

cane n. canne f.; (for baskets) rotin
m.; (for punishment: schol.)
baguette f., bâton m.

canister n. boîte f.

cannabis n. cannabis m.

cannibal n. cannibale m./f.

cannon n. canon m.

canny a. rusé, madré.

canoe n. (sport) canoë m., kayak
m. —v.i. faire du canoë or du
kayak. **~ist** n. canoëiste m./f.

canon n. (clergyman) chanoine m.;
(rule) canon m.

canopy n. dais m.; (over doorway)
marquise f.

canteen n. (restaurant) cantine f.;
(flask) bidon m.

canter n. petit galop m. —v.i. aller
au petit galop.

canvas n. toile f.

canvass v.t./i. (comm., pol.) solliciter des commandes or des voix
(de).

canyon n. cañon m.

cap n. (hat) casquette f.; (of bottle,
tube) bouchon m.; (of beer or milk
bottle) capsule f.; (of pen)
capuchon m.; (for toy gun) amorce
f.

capab|le a. (person) capable (of,
de), compétent. **be ~le of,** (of
situation, text, etc.) être susceptible de. **~ility** n. capacité f.

capacity n. capacité f.

cape¹ n. (cloak) cape f.

cape² n. (geog.) cap m.

caper¹ v.i. gambader. —n. (prank)
farce f.; (activity: sl.) affaire f.

caper² n. (culin.) câpre f.

capital a. capital. —n. (town) capitale f.; (money) capital m. ~ (letter), majuscule f.

capitalis|t a. & n. capitaliste (m./f.). ~m n. capitalisme m.

capitalize v.i. ~ on, tirer profit de.

Capricorn n. le Capricorne.

capsize v.t./i. (faire) chavirer.

capsule n. capsule f.

captain n. capitaine m.

caption n. (for illustration) légende f.; (heading) sous-titre m.

captivate v.t. captiver.

captive a. & n. capti|f, -ve (m., f.). ~ity n. captivité f.

capture v.t. (person, animal) prendre, capturer; (attention) retenir. —n. capture f.

car n. voiture f. ~ ferry, ferry m. ~-park, parking m. ~-phone, téléphone de voiture m. ~-wash n. station de lavage f.

carafe n. carafe f.

caramel n. caramel m.

carat n. carat m.

caravan n. caravane f.

carbohydrate n. hydrate de carbone m.

carbon n. carbone m. ~ copy, ~ paper, carbone m.

carburettor, n. carburateur m.

carcass n. carcasse f.

card n. carte f.

cardboard n. carton m.

cardiac a. cardiaque.

cardigan n. cardigan m.

cardinal a. cardinal. —n. (relig.) cardinal m.

care n. (attention) soin m., attention f.; (worry) souci m.; (protection) garde f. —v.i. ~ about, s'intéresser à. ~ for, s'occuper de; (invalid) soigner. ~ to or for, aimer, vouloir. I don't ~, ça m'est égal. take ~ of, s'occuper de. take ~ to do sth., faire bien attention à faire qch.

career n. carrière f.

carefree a. insouciant.

careful a. soigneux; (cautious) prudent. ~ (be) !, (fais) attention! ~ly adv. avec soin.

careless a. négligent; (work) peu soigné. ~ about, peu soucieux de.

caress n. caresse f. —v.t. caresser.

caretaker n. gardien(ne) m. (f.).

cargo n. cargaison f.

Caribbean a. caraïbe. —n. the ~, (sea) la mer des Caraïbes; (islands) les Antilles f. pl.

caring a. (mother, son, etc.) aimant. —n. affection f.

carnation n. œillet m.

carnival n. carnaval m.

carol n. chant (de Noël) m.

carp[1] n. invar. carpe f.

carp[2] v.i. ~ (at), critiquer.

carpent|er n. charpentier m.; (for light woodwork, furniture) menuisier m. ~ry n. charpenterie f.; menuiserie f.

carpet n. tapis m. —v.t. recouvrir d'un tapis.

carriage n. (rail & horse-drawn) voiture f.; (of goods) transport m.; (cost) port m.

carriageway n. chaussée f.

carrier n. transporteur m.; (med.) porteu|r, -se m., f. ~ (bag), sac en plastique m.

carrot n. carotte f.

carry v.t./i. porter; (goods) transporter; (involve) comporter; (motion) voter. ~-cot n. porte-bébé m. ~ off, enlever; (prize) remporter. ~ on, continuer; (behave: fam.) se conduire (mal). ~ out, (an order, plan) exécuter; (duty) accomplir; (task) effectuer.

cart n. charrette f. —v.t. transporter; (heavy object: sl.) trimballer.

cartilage n. cartilage m.

carton n. (*box*) carton m.; (*of yoghurt, cream*) pot m.; (*of cigarettes*) cartouche f.

cartoon n. dessin (humoristique) m.; (*cinema*) dessin animé m., f.

cartridge n. cartouche f.

carve v.t. tailler; (*meat*) découper.

cascade n. cascade f. —v.i. tomber en cascade.

case[1] n. cas m.; (*jurid.*) affaire f.; (*phil.*) arguments m. pl. **in ～ he comes**, au cas où il viendrait. **in that ～**, à ce moment-là.

case[2] n. (*crate*) caisse f.; (*for camera, cigarettes, spectacles, etc.*) étui m.; (*suitcase*) valise f.

cash n. argent m.; (*price etc.*) (au) comptant. —v.t. encaisser. **～ a cheque**, (*person*) encaisser un chèque; (*bank*) payer un chèque. **pay ～**, payer comptant. **in ～**, en espèces. **～ desk**, caisse f. **～ dispenser**, distributeur de billets m.f.

cashew n. noix de cajou f.

cashier n. caiss|ier, -ière m.f.

cashmere n. cachemire m.

casino n. casino m.

cask n. tonneau m.

casket n. (*box*) coffret m.; (*coffin: Amer.*) cercueil m.

casserole n. (*utensil*) cocotte f.; (*stew*) daube f.

cassette n. cassette f.

cast v.t. jeter; (*glance, look*) jeter; (*shadow*) projeter; (*vote*) donner; (*metal*) couler. —n. (*theatre*) distribution f.; (*of dice*) coup m.; (*mould*) moule m.; (*med.*) plâtre m. **～-iron**, fonte f. **～-iron** a. de fonte; (*fig.*) solide.

castle n. château m.; (*chess*) tour f.

castor n. (*wheel*) roulette f. **～ sugar**, sucre en poudre m.

casual a. (*remark*) fait au hasard; (*meeting*) fortuit; (*attitude*) désinvolte; (*work*) temporaire; (*clothes*) sport invar.

casualty n. (*dead*) mort(e) m. (f.); (*injured*) blessé(e) m. (f.); (*accident victim*) accidenté(e) m. (f.).

cat n. chat m. **C～'s-eyes** n. pl. (P.) catadioptres m. pl.

catalogue n. catalogue m. —v.t. cataloguer.

catalyst n. catalyseur m.

catapult n. lance-pierres m. invar. —v.t. catapulter.

cataract n. (*waterfall & med.*) cataracte f.

catarrh n. rhume m., catarrhe m.

catastroph|e n. catastrophe f. **～ic** a. catastrophique.

catch v.t. attraper; (*grab*) prendre, saisir; (*catch unawares*) surprendre; (*jam, trap*) prendre; (*understand*) saisir. —v.i. prendre; (*get stuck*) se prendre (**in**, dans). —n. capture f., prise f.; (*on door*) loquet m.; (*fig.*) piège m. **～ s.o.'s eye**, attirer l'attention de qn. **～ up**, se rattraper. **～ up (with)**, rattraper.

catching a. contagieux.

categorical a. catégorique.

category n. catégorie f.

cater v.i. s'occuper de la nourriture. **～ for**, (*pander to*) satisfaire; (*of magazine etc.*) s'adresser à. **～er** n. traiteur m.

caterpillar n. chenille f.

cathedral n. cathédrale f.

catholic a. universel. **C～** a. & n. catholique (m./f.).

cattle n. pl. bétail m.

cauliflower n. chou-fleur m.

cause n. cause f.; (*reason*) raison f., motif m. —v.t. causer. **～ sth. to grow/move/etc.**, faire pousser/bouger/etc. qch.

causeway n. chaussée f.

cauti|on n. prudence f.; (*warning*) avertissement m. —v.t. avertir. **~ous** a. prudent.

cavalry n. cavalerie f.

cave n. caverne f., grotte f. —v.i. **~ in**, s'effondrer; (*agree*) céder.

cavern n. caverne f.

caviare, n. caviar m.

cavity n. cavité f.

CD n. compact disc m.

cease v.t./i. cesser. **~-fire** n. cessez-le-feu m. invar.

cedar n. cèdre m.

cede v.t. céder.

cedilla n. cédille f.

ceiling n. plafond m.

celebrate v.t. (*perform, glorify*) célébrer. **~ion** n. fête f.

celebrity n. célébrité f.

celery n. céleri m.

cell n. cellule f.; (*electr.*) élément m.

cellar n. cave f.

cell|o n. violoncelle m. **~ist** n. violoncelliste m./f.

Cellophane n. (P.) cellophane f. (P.).

Celt n. Celte m./f. **~ic** a. celtique, celte.

cement n. ciment m. **~-mixer** n. bétonnière f.

cemetery n. cimetière m.

censor n. censeur m. —v.t. censurer.

census n. recensement m.

cent n. (*coin*) cent m.

centenary n. centenaire m.

centigrade a. centigrade.

centilitre n. centilitre m.

centimetre n. centimètre m.

centipede n. millepattes m. invar.

central a. central. **~ heating**, chauffage central m.

centre n. centre m.

century n. siècle m.

ceramic a. (*art*) céramiq~ (*object*) en céramique.

cereal n. céréale f.

ceremonial a. de cérémonie. —n. cérémonial m.

ceremony n. cérémonie f.

certain a. certain. **for ~**, avec certitude. **make ~ of**, s'assurer de. **~ly** adv. certainement. **~ty** n. certitude f.

certificate n. certificat m.

certify v.t. certifier.

cervical a. cervical.

cessation n. cessation f.

chafe v.t. frotter (contre).

chaffinch n. pinson m.

chain n. chaîne f. —v.t. enchaîner. **~ store**, magasin à succursales multiples m.

chair n. chaise f.; (*armchair*) fauteuil m.; (*univ.*) chaire f. —v.t. (*preside over*) présider.

chairman n. président(e) m. (f.).

chalet n. chalet m.

chalk n. craie f.

challeng|e n. défi m.; (*task*) gageure f. —v.t. (*summon*) défier (**to do**, de faire); (*question truth of*) contester. **~er** n. (*sport*) challenger m.

chamber n. (*old use*) chambre f. **~ music**, musique de chambre f.

chambermaid n. femme de chambre f.

chamois n. **~(-leather)**, peau de chamois f.

champagne n. champagne m.

champion n. champion(ne) m. (f.). —v.t. défendre. **~~p** n. championnat m.

chance n. (*luck*) ~ (*opportunity*) ~ ~ *hood*) chan~~

m. —a

pren~

(*exchange*) échanger (**for**, contre); (*money*) changer. ∼ **trains/one's dress/***etc.*, (*by substitution*) changer de train/de robe/*etc.* —*v.i.* changer; (*change clothes*) se changer. —*n.* changement *m.*; (*money*) monnaie *f.* **a ∼ for the better**, une amélioration. **∼ into**, se transformer en; (*clothes*) mettre. **a ∼ of clothes**, des vêtements de rechange. **∼ one's mind**, changer d'avis. **for a ∼**, pour changer. **∼-over** *n.* passage *m.* **∼able** *a.* changeant; (*weather*) variable. **∼ing** *a.* changeant. **∼ing room**, (*in shop*) cabine d'essayage; (*sport.*) vestiaire *m.*

channel *n.* chenal *m.*; (*TV*) chaîne *f.*; (*medium, agency*) canal *m.*; (*groove*) rainure *f.* **the (English) C∼**, la Manche. **the C∼ Islands**, les îles anglo-normandes *f. pl.*

chant *n.* (*relig.*) psalmodie *f.*; (*of demonstrators*) chant (scandé) *m.* —*v.t./i.* psalmodier; scander (des slogans).

chao|s *n.* chaos *m.* **∼tic** *a.* chaotique.

chap *n.* (*man: fam.*) type *m.*

chapel *n.* chapelle *f.*

chaperon *n.* chaperon *m.* —*v.t.* chaperonner.

chaplain *n.* aumônier *m.*

chapped *a.* gercé.

chapter *n.* chapitre *m.*

char[1] *n.* (*fam.*) femme de ménage *f.*

char[2] *v.t.* carboniser.

character *n.* caractère *m.*; (*in novel, play*) personnage *m.*

characteristic *a.* & *n.* caractéristique (*f.*).

de n. charade *f.*

bon (de bois) *m.*

i.l charge *f.*;

tion

f.; (*task, custody*) charge *f.* **∼s**, frais *m. pl.* —*v.t.* faire payer; (*ask*) demander (**for**, pour); (*enemy, gun*) charger; (*jurid.*) inculper, accuser (**with**, de). **∼ se précipiter. ∼ card**, carte d'achat *f.* **in ∼ of**, responsable de. **take ∼ of**, se charger de. **∼able to**, (*comm.*) aux frais de.

charisma *n.* magnétisme *m.* **∼tic** *a.* charismatique.

charity *n.* charité *f.*; (*society*) fondation charitable *f.*

charm *n.* charme *m.*; (*trinket*) amulette *f.* —*v.t.* charmer. **∼ing** *a.* charmant.

chart *n.* (*naut.*) carte (marine) *f.*; (*table*) tableau *m.*, graphique *m.*

charter *n.* charte *f.*; (*flight*) charter *m.* —*v.t.* affréter. **∼ed accountant**, expert-comptable *m.*

chase *v.t.* poursuivre. —*v.i.* courir (**after**, après). —*n.* chasse *f.* **∼ away** or **off**, chasser.

chasm *n.* abîme *m.*

chassis *n.* châssis *m.*

chastity *n.* chasteté *f.*

chat *n.* causette *f.* —*v.i.* bavarder. **have a ∼**, bavarder. **∼ show**, talk-show *m.* **∼ up**, (*fam.*) draguer.

chatter *n.* bavardage *m.* —*v.i.* bavarder.

chauffeur *n.* chauffeur (de particulier) *m.*

chauvinis|t *n.* chauvin(e) *m.* (*f.*). **male ∼t**, (*pej.*) phallocrate *m.* **∼m** *n.* chauvinisme *m.*

cheap *a.* bon marché *invar.*; (*fare, rate*) réduit; (*worthless*) sans valeur. **∼er**, meilleur marché *invar.* **∼(ly)** *adv.* à bon marché.

cheat *v.i.* tricher; (*by fraud*) frauder. —*v.t.* (*defraud*) frauder; (*deceive*) tromper. —*n.* escroc *m.*

check[1] *v.t./i.* vérifier; (*tickets*)

contrôler; (*stop*) enrayer, arrêter; (*restrain*) contenir; (*rebuke*) réprimander; (*tick off: Amer.*) cocher. —*n.* vérification *f.*; contrôle *m.*; (*curb*) frein *m.*; (*chess*) échec *m.*; (*bill: Amer.*) addition *f.*; (*cheque: Amer.*) chèque *m.* ~ **in,** signer le registre; (*at airport*) passer à l'enregistrement. ~**-in** *n.* en registrement *m.* ~**-out** *n.* caisse *f.* ~ **up,** vérifier. ~ **up on,** (*detail*) vérifier; ~ (*situation*) s'informer sur. ~**-up** *n.* examen médical *m.*

check² *n.* (*pattern*) carreaux *m. pl.* ~**ed** *a.* à carreaux.

checkmate *n.* échec et mat *m.*

cheek *n.* joue *f.*; (*impudence*) culot *m.* ~**y** *a.* effronté.

cheer *n.* gaieté *f.* ~**s,** acclamations *f. pl.*; (*when drinking*) à votre santé. —*v.t.* acclamer, applaudir. ~ **up,** prendre courage. ~**ful** *a.* gai.

cheese *n.* fromage *m.*

cheetah *n.* guépard *m.*

chef *n.* (*cook*) chef *m.*

chemical *a.* chimique. —*n.* produit chimique *m.*

chemist *n.* pharmacien(ne) *m.* (*f.*); (*scientist*) chimiste *m./f.* ~**'s shop,** pharmacie *f.* ~**ry** *n.* chimie *f.*

cheque *n.* chèque *m.* ~**-book** *n.* chéquier *m.* ~ **card,** carte bancaire *f.*

cherish *v.t.* chérir; (*hope*) nourrir, caresser.

cherry *n.* cerise *f.*

chess *n.* échecs *m. pl.* ~**-board** *n.* échiquier *m.*

chest *n.* (*anat.*) poitrine *f.*; (*box*) coffre *m.*

chestnut *n.* châtaigne *f.*; (*edible*) marron *m.*, châtaigne *f.*

chew *v.t.* mâcher. ~**ing-gum** *n.* chewing-gum *m.*

chic *a.* chic *invar.*

chick *n.* poussin *m.*

chicken *n.* poulet *m.* —*a.* (*sl.*) froussard. ~**-pox** *n.* varicelle *f.*

chick-pea *n.* pois chiche *m.*

chicory *n.* (*for salad*) endive *f.*; (*in coffee*) chicorée *f.*

chief *n.* chef *m.* —*a.* principal.

chilblain *n.* engelure *f.*

child *n.* enfant *m./f.* ~**hood** *n.* enfance *f.* ~**ish** *a.* enfantin. ~**minder** *n.* nourrice *f.*

Chile *n.* Chili *m.* ~**an** *a.* & *n.* chilien(ne) (*m.* (*f.*)).

chill *n.* froid *m.*; (*med.*) refroidissement *m.* —*a.* froid. —*v.t.* (*wine*) rafraîchir; (*food*) mettre au frais. ~**y** *a.* froid; (*sensitive to cold*) frileux. **be** or **feel** ~**y,** avoir froid.

chilli *n.* piment *m.*

chime *n.* carillon *m.* —*v.t./i.* carillonner.

chimney *n.* cheminée *f.*

chimpanzee *n.* chimpanzé *m.*

chin *n.* menton *m.*

china *n.* porcelaine *f.*

China *n.* Chine *f.* ~**se** *a.* & *n.* chinois(e) (*m.* (*f.*)).

chink¹ *n.* (*slit*) fente *f.*

chink² *n.* tintement *m.* —*v.t./i.* (faire) tinter.

chip *n.* (*on plate etc.*) ébréchure *f.*; (*piece*) éclat *m.*; (*of wood*) copeau *m.*; (*culin.*) frite *f.*; (*microchip*) puce *f.* —*v.t./i.* (s')ébrécher. (**potato**) ~**s,** (*Amer.*) chips *m.*

chipboard *n.* aggloméré *m.*

chiropodist *n.* pédicure *m.*

chirp *n.* pépiement *m.* —*v.i.* pépier.

chisel *n.* cisea[u…]

chit *n.* note[…]

chit-ch[…]

chi[…]

chocolate n. chocolat m.

choice n. choix m. —a. de choix.

choir n. chœur m.

choirboy n. jeune choriste m.

choke v.t./i. (s')étrangler. —n. starter m.

cholera n. choléra m.

cholesterol n. cholestérol m.

choose v.t./i. choisir. **~ to do,** décider de faire.

choosy a. (fam.) exigeant.

chop v.t./i. (wood) couper (à la hache); (food) hacher. —n. (meat) côtelette f. **~ down,** abattre.

choppy a. (sea) agité.

chopstick n. baguette f.

choral a. choral.

chord n. (mus.) accord m.

chore n. travail (routinier) m.; (unpleasant task) corvée f.

chortle n. gloussement m. —v.i. glousser.

chorus n. chœur m.; (of song) refrain m.

Christ n. le Christ m.

christen v.t. baptiser. **~ing** n. baptême m.

Christian a. & n. chrétien(ne) (m. (f.)). **~ name,** prénom m. **~ity** n. christianisme m.

Christmas n. Noël m. —a. (card, tree, etc.) de Noël.

chrome n. chrome m.

chromium n. chrome m.

chromosome n. chromosome m.

chronic a. (situation, disease) chronique; (bad: fam.) affreux.

chronicle n. chronique f.

chronolog|y n. chronologie f. **~ical** a. chronologique.

chrysanthemum n. chrysanthème m.

chubby a. dodu, potelé.

chuck v.t. (fam.) lancer. **~ away** (fam.) balancer.

m. —v.i.

chum n. cop|ain, -ine m., f.

chunk n. (gros) morceau m.

chunky a. trapu.

church n. église f.

churchyard n. cimetière m.

churn n. baratte f.; (milk-can) bidon m. —v.t. baratter. **~ out,** produire (en série).

chute n. glissière f.; (for rubbish) vide-ordures m. invar.

chutney n. condiment (de fruits) m.

cider n. cidre m.

cigar n. cigare m.

cigarette n. cigarette f.

cinder n. cendre f.

cine-camera n. caméra f.

cinema n. cinéma m.

cinnamon n. cannelle f.

cipher n. (numeral, code) chiffre m.; (person) nullité f.

circle n. cercle m.; (theatre) balcon m. —v.t. (go round) faire le tour de; (word, error, etc.) entourer d'un cercle. —v.i. décrire des cercles.

circuit n. circuit m. **~-breaker** n. disjoncteur m.

circular a. & n. circulaire (f.).

circulate v.t./i. (faire) circuler.

circumference n. circonférence f.

circumflex n. circonflexe f.

circumstance n. circonstance f. **~s,** (financial) situation financière f.

circus n. cirque m.

cistern n. réservoir m.

cit|e v.t. citer. **~ation** n. citation f.

citizen n. citoyen(ne) m. (f.); (of town) habitant(e) m. (f.).

citrus a. **~ fruit(s),** agrumes m. pl.

city n. (grande) ville f.

civic a. civique. **~ centre,** centre administratif m.

civil a. civil; (rights) civique;

(defence) passif. ∼ **engineer,** ingénieur civil *m.* **C∼ Servant,** fonctionnaire *m./f.* ∼ **war,** guerre civile *f.*

civilian *a. & n.* civil(e) *(m. (f.)).*

civiliz|e *v.t.* civiliser. ∼**ation** *n.* civilisation *f.*

clad *a.* ∼ **in,** vêtu de.

claim *v.t.* revendiquer, réclamer; *(assert)* prétendre. —*n.* revendication *f.*; prétention *f.*; *(assertion)* affirmation *f.*; *(for insurance)* réclamation *f.*; *(right)* droit *m.*

claimant *n. (of social benefits)* demandeur *m.*

clairvoyant *n.* voyant(e) *m. (f.).*

clam *n.* palourde *f.*

clamber *v.i.* grimper.

clammy *a.* moite.

clamour *n.* clameur *f.*, cris *m. pl.* —*v.i.* ∼ **for,** demander à grands cris.

clamp *n.* agrafe *f.*; *(large)* crampon *m.*; *(for carpentry)* serrejoint(s) *m.*; *(for car)* sabot de Denver *m.* —*v.t.* serrer; *(car)* mettre un sabot de Denver à. ∼ **down on,** sévir contre.

clan *n.* clan *m.*

clandestine *a.* clandestin.

clang *n.* son métallique *m.*

clap *v.t./i.* applaudir. —*n.* applaudissement *m.*

claret *n.* bordeaux rouge *m.*

clarif|y *v.t./i.* (se) clarifier. ∼**ication** *n.* clarification *f.*

clarinet *n.* clarinette *f.*

clarity *n.* clarté *f.*

clash *n.* choc *m.*; *(fig.)* conflit *m.* —*v.i. (metal objects)* s'entrechoquer; *(fig.)* se heurter.

clasp *n. (fastener)* fermoir *m.*, agrafe *f.* —*v.t.* serrer.

class *n.* classe *f.* —*v.t.* classer.

classic *a. & n.* classique *(m.). pl.* ∼**al** *a.* classique.

classif|y *v.t.* classifier. ∼**ication** *n.* classification *f.*; *(information etc.)* secret. ∼**ied advertisement,** petite annonce *f.*

classroom *n.* salle de classe *f.*

classy *a. (sl.)* chic *invar.*

clatter *n.* cliquetis *m.* —*v.i.* cliqueter.

clause *n.* clause *f.*; *(gram.)* proposition *f.*

claustrophob|ia *n.* claustrophobie *f.* ∼**ic** *a. & n.* claustrophobe *(m./f.).*

claw *n. (of animal, small bird)* griffe *f.*; *(of bird of prey)* serre *f.*; *(of lobster)* pince *f.* —*v.t.* griffer.

clay *n.* argile *f.*

clean *a.* propre, net; *(shape, stroke, etc.)* net. —*adv.* complètement. —*v.t.* nettoyer. —*v.i.* ∼ **up,** faire le nettoyage. ∼ **one's teeth,** se brosser les dents. ∼**er** *n. (at home)* femme de ménage *f.*; *(industrial)* agent de nettoyage *m./f.*; *(of clothes)* teinturl|ier, -ière *m., f.*

cleans|e *v.t.* nettoyer; *(fig.)* purifier. ∼**ing cream,** crème démaquillante *f.*

clear *a.* clair; *(glass)* transparent; *(road)* dégagé. —*adv.* complètement. —*v.t. (free)* dégager (of, de); *(table)* débarrasser; *(building)* évacuer; *(cheque)* encaisser; *(jump over)* franchir; *(debt)* liquider; *(jurid.)* disculper. —*v.i. (fog)* se dissiper. ∼ **off** *or* **out,** *(sl.)* décamper. ∼ **out,** *(clean)* nettoyer. ∼ **up,** *(tidy)* ranger; *(mystery)* éclaircir; *(of weather)* s'éclaircir. **make sth.** ∼ être très clair sur qch. ∼**ly** *adv.* clairement.

clearance *n. (permission)* autorisation *f.*; *(space)* dégagement

clearing n. clairière f.

clearway n. route à stationnement interdit m.

cleavage n. clivage m.; (breasts) décolleté m.

clef n. (mus.) clé f.

cleft n. fissure f.

clench v.t. serrer.

clergy n. clergé m. **~man** n. ecclésiastique m.

clerk n. employé(e) de bureau m. (f.).

clever a. intelligent; (skilful) habile. **~ly** adv. intelligemment, habilement.

cliché n. cliché m.

click n. déclic m. —v.i. faire un déclic; (people: sl.) s'entendre, se plaire. —v.t. (heels, tongue) faire claquer.

client n. client(e) m. (f.).

clientele n. clientèle f.

cliff n. falaise f.

climate n. climat m.

climax n. point culminant m.

climb v.t. (stairs) monter; (tree, ladder) monter or grimper à; (mountain) faire l'ascension de. —v.i. monter, grimper. —n. montée f. **~-down**, n. recul m. **~er** n. (sport) alpiniste m./f.

clinch v.t. (a deal) conclure.

cling v.i. (p.t. **clung**) se cramponner (to, à); (stick) coller. **~-film** n. (P.) film adhésif.

clinic n. centre médical m.

clinical a. clinique.

clink n. tintement m. —v.t./i. (faire) tinter.

clip[1] n. (for paper) trombone m.; (for hair) barrette f.; (for tube) collier m. —v.t. attacher (to, à).

clip[2] v.t. (cut) couper. —n. coupe f.; (of film) extrait m.

clippers n. pl. tondeuse f.; (for nails) coupe-ongles m.

cloak n. (grande) cape f.

cloakroom n. vestiaire m.; (toilet) toilettes f. pl.

clock n. pendule f.; (large) horloge f. —v.i. **~ in** or **out**, pointer.

clockwise a. & adv. dans le sens des aiguilles d'une montre.

clockwork n. mécanisme m. —a. mécanique.

clog n. sabot m. —v.t./i. (se) boucher.

cloister n. cloître m.

close[1] a. (near) proche (to, de); (link, collaboration) étroit; (examination) attentif; (friend) intime; (weather) lourd. **~ together**, (crowded) serrés. —adv. (tout) près. —n. (street) impasse f. **~ by**, tout près. **~-up** n. gros plan m. **~ly** adv. (follow) de près.

close[2] v.t. fermer. —v.i. se fermer; (of shop etc.) fermer; (end) (se) terminer. —n. fin f.

closet n. (Amer.) placard m.

closure n. fermeture f.

clot n. (of blood) caillot m. —v.t./i. (se) coaguler.

cloth n. tissu m.; (duster) linge m.; (table-cloth) nappe f.

clothes n. pl. vêtements m. pl., habits m. pl. **~-hanger** n. cintre m. **~-line** n. corde à linge f.

clothing n. vêtements m. pl.

cloud n. nuage m. **~y** a. (sky) couvert; (liquid) trouble.

clout n. (blow) coup de poing m.; (power: fam.) pouvoir effectif m. —v.t. frapper.

clove n. clou de girofle m. **~ of garlic**, gousse d'ail f.

clover n. trèfle m.

clown n. clown m. —v.i. faire le clown.

club n. (group) club m.; (weapon) massue f. **~s**, (cards) trèfle m. —v.t./i. matraquer. (golf) **~**, club (de golf) m. **~ together**, (share costs) se cotiser.

cluck v.i. glousser.

clue n. indice m.; (in crossword) définition f.

clump n. massif m.

clumsy a. maladroit; (tool) peu commode.

cluster n. (petit) groupe m. —v.i. se grouper.

clutch v.t. (hold) serrer fort; (grasp) saisir. —v.i. ~ **at**, (try to grasp) essayer de saisir. —n. étreinte f.; (auto.) embrayage m.

clutter n. désordre m., fouillis m. —v.t. encombrer.

coach n. autocar m.; (of train) wagon m.; (horse-drawn) carrosse m.; (sport) entraîneu|r, -se m., f. —v.t. donner des leçons (particulières) à; (sport) entraîner.

coagulate v.t./i. (se) coaguler.

coal n. charbon m.

coalition n. coalition f.

coarse a. grossier.

coast n. côte f. —v.i. (car, bicycle) descendre en roue libre. ~**al** a. côtier.

coastguard n. gardecôte m.

coastline n. littoral m.

coat n. manteau m.; (of animal) pelage m.; (of paint) couche f. —v.t. enduire, couvrir; (with chocolate) enrober (with, de). ~**hanger** n. cintre m. ~**ing** n. couche f.

coax v.t. amadouer.

cob n. (of corn) épi m.

cobble n. pavé m. ~**-stone** n. pavé m.

cobweb n. toile d'araignée f.

cocaine n. cocaïne f.

cock n. (oiseau) mâle m.; (rooster) coq m. —v.t. (gun) armer; (ears) dresser. ~**-up** n. (sl.) pagaille f.

cockerel n. jeune coq m.

cockle n. (culin.) coque f.

cockpit n. poste de pilotage m.

cockroach n. cafard m.

cocktail n. cocktail m. ~ **party**, cocktail m. **fruit** ~, macédoine (de fruits) f.

cocky a. arrogant.

cocoa n. cacao m.

coconut n. noix de coco f.

cocoon n. cocon m.

COD abbr. (cash on delivery) paiement à la livraison m.

cod n. invar. morue f.

code n. code m. —v.t. coder.

coerce v.t. contraindre. ~**ion** n. contrainte f.

coexist v.i. coexister. ~**ence** n. coexistence f.

coffee n. café m. ~ **bar**, café m., cafétéria f. ~**-pot** n. cafetière f.

coffin n. cercueil m.

cog n. dent f.; (fig.) rouage m.

coherent a. cohérent.

coil v.t./i. (s')enrouler. —n. rouleau m.; (one ring) spire f.; (contraceptive) stérilet m.

coin n. pièce de monnaie f. —v.t. (word) inventer. ~**-box** n. téléphone public m.

coincide v.i. coïncider.

coinciden|ce n. coïncidence f. ~**tal** a. dû à une coïncidence.

coke n. coke m.

colander n. passoire f.

cold a. froid. **be** or **feel** ~, avoir froid. **it is** ~, il fait froid. —n. froid m.; (med.) rhume m. ~ **cream**, crème de beauté f. ~ **sore**, bouton de fièvre m. ~**ness** n. froideur f.

coleslaw n. salade de chou cru f.

colic n. coliques f. pl.

collaborat|e v.i. collaborer. ~**or** n. collabora|teur, -trice m., f.

collapse v.i. s'effondrer; (med.) avoir un malaise. —n. effondrement m.

collapsible a. pliant.

collar n. col m.; (of dog) collier m.

collateral   286   command

—*v.t.* (*take: sl.*) piquer. **~-bone** n. clavicule *f.*

collateral n. nantissement m.

colleague n. collègue m./f.

collect v.t. rassembler; (*pick up*) ramasser; (*call for*) passer prendre; (*money, rent*) encaisser; (*taxes*) percevoir; (*as hobby*) collectionner. —*adv.* **call ~**, (*Amer.*) téléphoner en PCV. **~ion** n. collection *f.*; (*in church*) quête *f.*; (*of mail*) levée *f.* **~or** n. (*as hobby*) collectionneu|r, -se m., *f.*

collective a. collectif.

college n. (*for higher education*) institut m., école *f.*; (*within university*) collège m.

collide v.i. entrer en collision (**with**, avec).

colliery n. houillère *f.*

collision n. collision *f.*

collusion n. collusion *f.*

colon n. (*gram.*) deux-points m. invar.; (*anat.*) côlon m.

colonel n. colonel m.

colonize v.t. coloniser.

colon|y n. colonie *f.* **~ial** a. & n. colonial(e) (m. (*f.*)).

colossal a. colossal.

colour n. couleur *f.* —a. (*photo etc.*) en couleur, (*TV set*) couleur invar. —v.t. colorer; (*with crayon*) colorier. **~-blind** a. daltonien. **~-fast** a. grand teint. invar. **~ful** a. coloré; (*person*) haut en couleur. **~ing** n. (*of skin*) teint m.; (*in food*) colorant m.

coloured a. (*person, pencil*) de couleur. —n. personne de couleur *f.*

colt n. poulain m.

column n. colonne *f.*

coma n. coma m.

comb n. peigne m. —v.t. peigner; (*search*) ratisser.

combat n. combat m. —v.t. combattre.

combination n. combinaison *f.*

combine v.t./i. (se) combiner, (s')unir.

combine² n. (*comm.*) trust m., cartel m. **~ harvester**, moissonneuse-batteuse *f.*

combustion n. combustion *f.*

come v.i. venir; (*occur*) arriver; (*sexually*) jouir. **~ across**, rencontrer *or* trouver par hasard. **~ back**, revenir. **~ by**, obtenir. **~ down**, descendre; (*price*) baisser. **~ from**, être de. **~ in**, entrer. **~ into**, (*money*) hériter de. **~ on**, (*actor*) entrer en scène; (*light*) s'allumer; (*improve*) faire des progrès. **~ on!**, allez! **~ out**, sortir. **~ through**, s'en tirer (indemne de). **~ to**, (*amount*) revenir à; (*decision, conclusion*) arriver à. **~ up**, monter; (*fig.*) se présenter. **~ up with**, (*find*) trouver; (*produce*) produire.

comedian n. comique m.

comedy n. comédie *f.*

comet n. comète *f.*

comfort n. confort m.; (*consolation*) réconfort m. —v.t. consoler. **~able** a. (*chair, car, etc.*) confortable; (*person*) à l'aise, bien; (*wealthy*) aisé.

comfy a. (*fam.*) = **comfortable**.

comic a. comique. —n. (*person*) comique m.; (*periodical*) comic m. **~ strip**, bande dessinée *f.*

coming n. arrivée *f.* —a. à venir. **~s and goings**, allées et venues *f. pl.*

comma n. virgule *f.*

command n. (*authority*) commandement m.; (*order*) ordre m.; (*mastery*) maîtrise *f.* —v.t. commander (**s.o. to**, à qn. de); (*be able to use*) disposer de; (*require*) nécessiter; (*respect*) inspirer. **~er** n. commandant m. **~ing** a. imposant.

commandeer v.t. réquisitionner.
commandment n. commandement m.
commando n. commando m.
commemorat|e v.t. commémorer. **~ion** n. commémoration f.
commence v.t./i. commencer. **~ment** n. commencement m.
commend v.t. (praise) louer; (entrust) confier.
comment n. commentaire m. —v.i. faire des commentaires. **~ on,** commenter.
commentary n. commentaire m.; (radio, TV) reportage m.
commentat|e v.i. faire un reportage. **~or** n. commenta|teur, -trice m., f.
commerce n. commerce m.
commercial a. commercial; (traveller) de commerce. —n. publicité f.
commiserate v.i. compatir (with, avec).
commission n. commission f.; (order for work) commande f. —v.t. (order) commander; (mil.) nommer officier. **out of ~,** hors service. **~er** n. préfet (de police) m.; (in E.C.) commissaire m.
commissionaire n. commissionnaire m.
commit v.t. commettre; (entrust) confier. **~ o.s.,** s'engager. **~ suicide,** se suicider. **~ment** n. engagement m.
committee n. comité m.
commodity n. produit m.
common a. (shared by all) commun; (usual) courant, commun; (vulgar) vulgaire, commun. —n. terrain communal m. **C~ Market,** Marché Commun m. **~ sense,** bon sens m. **in ~,** en commun.
commotion n. agitation f.

communal a. (shared) commun; (life) collectif.
commune n. (group) communauté f.
communicat|e v.t./i. communiquer. **~ion** n. communication f.
communion n. communion f.
communiqué n. communiqué m.
Communis|t a. & n. communiste (m./f.). **~m** n. communisme m.
community n. communauté f.
commuter n. banlieusard(e) m. (f.).
compact[1] a. compact. **~ disc,** (disque) compact m.
compact[2] n. (lady's case) poudrier m.
companion n. comp|agnon, -agne m., f.
company n. (companionship, firm) compagnie f.; (guests) invité(e)s m. (f.) pl.
comparable a. comparable.
compar|e v.t. comparer (with, to, à). **~ed with** or **to,** en comparaison de. —v.i. être comparable. **~ative** a. (study, form) comparatif; (comfort etc.) relatif. **~atively** adv. relativement.
comparison n. comparaison f.
compartment n. compartiment m.
compass n. (for direction) boussole f.; (scope) portée f. **~(es),** (for drawing) compas m.
compassion n. compassion f.
compatib|le a. compatible. **~ility** n. compatibilité f.
compatriot n. compatriote m./f.
compel v.t. contraindre.
compensat|e v.t./i. (financially) dédommager (for, de). **~e for sth.,** compenser qch. **~ion** n. compensation f.; (financial) dédommagement m.
compete v.i. concourir. **~ with,** rivaliser avec.

competen|t *a.* compétent. **~ce** *n.* compétence *f.*

competition *n.* (*contest*) concours *m.*; (*sport*) compétition *f.*; (*comm.*) concurrence *f.*

competitive *a.* (*prices*) concurrentiel, compétitif.

competitor *n.* concurrent(e) *m.* (*f.*).

compile *v.t.* (*list*) dresser; (*book*) rédiger. **~r** *n.* rédac|teur, -trice *m.*, *f.*

complacen|t *a.* content de soi. **~cy** contentement de soi *m.*

complain *v.i.* se plaindre (**about, of**, de).

complaint *n.* plainte *f.*; (*in shop etc.*) réclamation *f.*; (*illness*) maladie *f.*

complement *n.* complément *m.* —*v.t.* compléter. **~ary** *a.* complémentaire.

complet|e *a.* complet; (*finished*) achevé; (*downright*) parfait. —*v.t.* achever; (*a form*) remplir. **~ely** *adv.* complètement. **~ion** *n.* achèvement *m.*

complex *a.* complexe. —*n.* (*psych.*, *archit.*) complexe *m.* **~ity** *n.* complexité *f.*

complexion *n.* (*of face*) teint *n.*

compliance *n.* (*agreement*) conformité *f.*

complicat|e *v.t.* compliquer. **~ed** *a.* compliqué. **~ion** *n.* complication *f.*

complicity *n.* complicité *f.*

compliment *n.* compliment *m.* —*v.t.* complimenter.

complimentary *a.* (*offert*) à titre gracieux; (*praising*) flatteur.

comply *v.i.* **~ with**, se conformer à, obéir à.

component *n.* (*of machine etc.*) pièce *f.*; (*chemical substance*) composant *m.*; (*element: fig.*) composante *f.* —*a.* constituant.

compose *v.t.* composer. **~ o.s.**, se calmer. **~r** *n.* (*mus.*) compositeur *m.*

composition *n.* composition *f.*

compost *n.* compost *m.*

composure *n.* calme *m.*

compound *n.* (*substance*, *word*) composé *m.*; (*enclosure*) enclos *m.* —*a.* composé.

comprehen|d *v.t.* comprendre. **~sion** *n.* compréhension *f.*

comprehensive *a.* étendu, complet; (*insurance*) tous-risques *invar.* **~ school**, collège d'enseignement secondaire *m.*

compress *v.t.* comprimer. **~ion** *n.* compression *f.*

comprise *v.t.* comprendre.

compromise *n.* compromis *m.* —*v.t.* compromettre. —*v.i.* transiger, trouver un compromis. **not ~ on**, ne pas transiger sur.

compulsion *n.* contrainte *f.*

compulsive *a.* (*psych.*) compulsif; (*liar*, *smoker*) invétéré.

compulsory *a.* obligatoire.

computer *n.* ordinateur *m.* **~ science**, informatique *f.* **~ize** *v.t.* informatiser.

comrade *n.* camarade *m./f.*

con[1] *v.t.* (*sl.*) rouler, escroquer (**out of**, de). —*n.* (*sl.*) escroquerie *f.* **~ s.o. into doing**, arnaquer qn. en lui faisant faire. **~ man**, (*sl.*) escroc *m.*

con[2] *see* **pro**.

concave *a.* concave.

conceal *v.t.* dissimuler.

concede *v.t.* concéder.

conceited *a.* suffisant.

conceivable *a.* concevable.

conceive *v.t./i.* concevoir. **~ of**, concevoir.

concentrat|e *v.t./i.* (se) concentrer. **~ion** *n.* concentration *f.*

concept *n.* concept *m.*

conception *n.* conception *f.*

concern n. (*interest, business*) affaire f.; (*worry*) inquiétude f.; (*firm*: *comm.*) affaire f. —v.t. concerner. **be ⁓ed with,** s'occuper de. **⁓ing** *prep.* en ce qui concerne.

concerned a. inquiet.

concert n. concert m.

concertina n. concertina m.

concerto n. concerto m.

concession n. concession f.

conciliation n. conciliation f.

concise a. concis. **⁓ly** adv. avec concision.

conclu|de v.t. conclure. —v.i. se terminer. **⁓sion** n. conclusion f.

conclusive a. concluant. **⁓ly** adv. de manière concluante.

concoct v.t. confectionner; (*invent*: *fig.*) fabriquer. **⁓ion** n. mélange m.

concourse n. (*rail.*) hall m.

concrete n. béton m. —a. concret. —v.t. bétonner. **⁓-mixer** n. bétonnière f.

concur v.i. être d'accord.

concussion n. commotion (cérébrale) f.

condemn v.t. condamner. **⁓ation** n. condamnation f.

condens|e v.t./i. (se) condenser. **⁓ation** n. condensation f.; (*mist*) buée f.

condescend v.i. condescendre.

condiment n. condiment m.

condition n. condition f. **on ⁓ that,** à condition que. **⁓al** a. conditionnel. **⁓er** n. après-shampooing m.

condom n. préservatif m.

condone v.t. pardonner, fermer les yeux sur.

conduct[1] v.t. conduire; (*orchestra*) diriger.

conduct[2] n. conduite f.

conductor n. chef d'orchestre m.; (*of bus*) receveur m.; (*on train*:

Amer.) chef de train m.; (*electr.*) conducteur m.

cone n. cône m.; (*of ice-cream*) cornet m.

confectioner n. confiserie f.

confederation n. confédération f.

confer v.t./i. conférer.

conference n. conférence f.

confess v.t./i. avouer; (*relig.*) (se) confesser. **⁓ion** n. confession f.; (*of crime*) aveu m.

confide v.t. confier. —v.i. **⁓ in,** se confier à.

confiden|t a. sûr. **⁓ce** n. (*trust*) confiance f.; (*boldness*) confiance en soi f.; (*secret*) confidence f.

confidential a. confidentiel.

configure v.t. (*comput.*) configurer.

confine v.t. enfermer; (*limit*) limiter. **⁓d space,** espace réduit. **⁓d to,** limité à.

confines n. pl. confins m. pl.

confirm v.t. confirmer. **⁓ation** n. confirmation f.

confiscate v.t. confisquer.

conflict[1] n. conflit m.

conflict[2] v.i. (*statements, views*) être en contradiction (**with,** avec); (*appointments*) tomber en même temps (**with,** que). **⁓ing** a. contradictoire.

conform v.t./i. (se) conformer.

confound v.t. confondre.

confront v.t. affronter. **⁓ with,** confronter avec. **⁓ation** n. confrontation f.

confus|e v.t. embrouiller; (*mistake, confound*) confondre. **become ⁓ed,** s'embrouiller. **⁓ing** a. déroutant. **⁓ion** n. confusion f.

congeal v.t./i. (se) figer.

congenial a. sympathique.

congenital a. congénital.

congest|ed a. encombré; (*med.*) congestionné. **⁓ion** n. (*traffic*) encombrement(s) m. (pl.); (med.) congestion f.

conglomerate n. (comm.) conglomérat m.

congratulat|e v.t. féliciter (**on**, de). **~ions** n. pl. félicitations f. pl.

congregation n. assemblée f.

congress n. congrès m. **C~**, (Amer.) le Congrès.

conic(al) a. conique.

conifer n. conifère m.

conjecture n. conjecture f. —v.t./i. conjecturer.

conjugat|e v.t. conjuguer. **~ion** n. conjugaison f.

conjunction n. conjonction f. **in ~ with**, conjointement avec.

conjunctivitis n. conjonctivite f.

conjur|e v.t. **~e up**, faire apparaître. **~or** n. prestidigita|teur, -trice m., f.

conk v.i. **~ out**, (sl.) tomber en panne.

connect v.t./i. (se) relier; (in mind) faire le rapport entre; (install, wire up to mains) brancher. **~ed** a. lié.

connection n. rapport m.; (rail.) correspondance f.; (phone call) communication f.; (electr.) contact m.; (joining piece) raccord m. **~s**, (comm.) relations f. pl.

connive v.i. **~e at**, se faire le complice de.

connoisseur n. connaisseur m.

connotation n. connotation f.

conquer v.t. vaincre; (country) conquérir. **~or** n. conquérant m.

conquest n. conquête f.

conscience n. conscience f.

conscientious a. consciencieux.

conscious a. conscient; (deliberate) voulu. **~ly** adv. consciemment. **~ness** n. conscience f.; (med.) connaissance f.

conscript[1] v.t. recruter par conscription. **~ion** n. conscription f.

conscript[2] n. conscrit m.

consecrate v.t. consacrer.

consecutive a. consécutif. **~ly** adv. consécutivement.

consensus n. consensus m.

consent v.i. consentir (**to**, à). —n. consentement m.

consequence n. conséquence f.

consequent a. résultant. **~ly** adv. par conséquent.

conservation n. préservation f. **~ area**, zone classée f.

conservationist n. défenseur de l'environnement m.

conservative a. conservateur; (estimate) modeste. **C~** a. & n. conserva|teur, -trice (m. (f.)).

conservatory n. (greenhouse) serre f.; (room) véranda f.

conserve v.t. conserver; (energy) économiser.

consider v.t. considérer; (allow for) tenir compte de; (possibility) envisager (**doing**, de faire). **~ation** n. considération f.; (respect) égard(s) m. (pl.). **~ing** prep. compte tenu de.

considerabl|e a. considérable; (much) beaucoup de. **~y** adv. beaucoup de, considérablement.

considerate a. attentionné.

consist v.i. consister (**of**, en; **in doing**, à faire).

consistent a. cohérent.

consol|e v.t. consoler. **~ation** n. consolation f.

consolidat|e v.t./i. (se) consolider. **~ion** n. consolidation f.

consonant n. consonne f.

conspicuous a. (easily seen) en évidence; (showy) voyant.

conspiracy n. complot m.

conspire v.i. (person) comploter (**to do**, de faire).

constable n. agent de police m.

constant a. incessant; (un-

changing) constant. **~ly** adv. constamment.

constellation n. constellation f.

consternation n. consternation f.

constipation n. constipation f.

constitut|e v.t. constituer. **~ion** n. constitution f.

constraint n. contrainte f.

constrict v.t. resserrer; (*movement*) gêner. **~ion** n. resserrement m.

construct v.t. construire. **~ion** n. construction f.

constructive a. constructif.

consul n. consul m. **~ar** a. consulaire.

consulate n. consulat m.

consult v.t. consulter. —v.i. **~ with**, conférer avec. **~ation** n. consultation f.

consultant n. conseill|er, -ère m., f.; (*med.*) spécialiste m./f.

consume v.t. consommer; (*destroy*) consumer. **~r** n. consomma|teur, -trice m., f.

consumption n. consommation f.; (*med.*) phtisie f.

contact n. contact m.; (*person*) relation f. —v.t. contacter. **~ lenses**, lentilles (de contact) f. pl.

contagious a. contagieux.

contain v.t. contenir. **~ o.s.**, se contenir. **~er** n. récipient m.; (*for transport*) container m.

contaminat|e v.t. contaminer. **~ion** n. contamination f.

contemplat|e v.t. (*gaze at*) contempler; (*think about*) envisager. **~ion** n. contemplation f.

contemporary a. & n. contemporain(e) (m. (f.)).

contempt n. mépris m. **~ible** a. méprisable.

contend v.t. soutenir. —v.i. **~ with**, (*compete*) rivaliser avec; (*face*) faire face à. **~er** n. adversaire m./f.

content[1] a. satisfait. —v.t. contenter. **~ed** a. satisfait.

content[2] n. (*of letter*) contenu m.; (*amount*) teneur f. **~s**, contenu m.

contention n. dispute f.; (*claim*) affirmation f.

contest[1] n. (*competition*) concours m.; (*fight*) combat m.

contest[2] v.t. contester; (*compete for or in*) disputer. **~ant** n. concurrent(e) m. (f.).

context n. contexte m.

continent n. continent m. **~al** a. continental. **~al quilt**, couette f.

continual a. continuel. **~ly** adv. continuellement.

continu|e v.t./i. continuer; (*resume*) reprendre. **~ation** n. continuation f. **~ed** a. continu.

continuous a. continu. **~ stationery**, papier continu m. **~ly** adv. sans interruption.

contort v.t. tordre. **~ o.s.**, se contorsionner. **~ion** n. torsion f.; contorsion f.

contour n. contour m.

contraband n. contrebande f.

contraception n. contraception f.

contraceptive a. & n. contraceptif (m.).

contract[1] n. contrat m.

contract[2] v.t./i. (se) contracter. **~ion** n. contraction f.

contractor n. entrepreneur m.

contradict v.t. contredire. **~ion** n. contradiction f.

contralto n. contralto m.

contraption n. (*fam.*) engin m.

contrary a. contraire (**to**, à). **on the ~**, au contraire.

contrast[1] n. contraste m.

contrast[2] v.t./i. contraster. **~ing** a. contrasté.

contravene v.t. enfreindre.

contribut|e v.t. donner. —v.i. **~e to**, contribuer à; (*take part*)

participer à; (*newspaper*) collaborer à. **~ion** *n.* contribution *f.* **~or** *n.* collabora|teur, -trice *m., f.*
contrive *v.t.* imaginer. **~ to do,** trouver moyen de faire. **~d** *a.* tortueux.
control *v.t.* (*a firm etc.*) diriger; (*check*) contrôler; (*restrain*) maîtriser. **—n.** contrôle *m.*; (*mastery*) maîtrise *f.* **~s,** commandes *f. pl.*; (*knobs*) boutons *m. pl.* **have under ~,** (*event*) avoir en main. **in ~ of,** maître de.
controversial *a.* discutable, discuté.
controversy *n.* controverse *f.*
convalesce *v.i.* être en convalescence. **~nce** *n.* convalescence *f.*
convector *n.* radiateur à convection *m.*
convene *v.t.* convoquer. **—v.i.** se réunir.
convenience *n.* commodité *f.* **~s,** toilettes *f. pl.* **~ foods,** plats tout préparés *m. pl.*
convenient *a.* commode, pratique; (*time*) bien choisi. **be ~ for,** convenir à. **~ly** *adv.* (*arrive*) à propos. **~ly situated,** bien situé.
convent /ˈkɒnvənt/ *n.* couvent *m.*
convention *n.* (*assembly, agreement*) convention *f.*; (*custom*) usage *m.* **~al** *a.* conventionnel.
converge *v.i.* converger.
conversation *n.* conversation *f.*
converse[1] *v.i.* s'entretenir, converser (**with,** avec).
converse[2] *a. & n.* inverse (*m.*). **~ly** *adv.* inversement.
conver|t[1] *v.t.* convertir; (*house*) aménager. **—v.i.** **~t into,** se transformer en. **~sion** *n.* conversion *f.* **~tible** *a.* convertible. **—n.** (*car*) décapotable *f.*
convert[2] *n.* converti(e) *m.* (*f.*).

convex *a.* convexe.
convey *v.t.* (*wishes, order*) transmettre; (*goods, people*) transporter; (*idea, feeling*) communiquer. **~or belt,** tapis roulant *m.*
convict[1] *v.t.* déclarer coupable. **~ion** *n.* condamnation *f.*; (*opinion*) conviction *f.*
convict[2] *n.* prisonn|ier, ère *m., f.*
convinc|e *v.t.* convaincre. **~ing** *a.* convaincant.
convoy *n.* convoi *m.*
convulsion *n.* convulsion *f.*
coo *v.i.* roucouler.
cook *v.t./i.* (faire) cuire; (*of person*) faire la cuisine. **—n.** cuisin|ier, -ière *m., f.* **~ up,** (*fam.*) fabriquer. **~ing** *n.* cuisine *f.*; *a.* de cuisine.
cooker *n.* (*stove*) cuisinière *f.*; (*apple*) pomme à cuire *f.*
cookery *n.* cuisine *f.* **~ book,** livre de cuisine *m.*
cookie *n.* (*Amer.*) biscuit *m.*
cool *a.* frais; (*calm*) calme; (*unfriendly*) froid. **—n.** fraîcheur *f.*; (*calmness: sl.*) sang-froid *m.* **—v.t./i.** rafraîchir. **in the ~,** au frais. **~ box,** glacière *f.* **~er** *n.* (*for food*) glacière *f.*; **~ly** *adv.* calmement; froidement. **~ness** *n.* fraîcheur *f.*; froideur *f.*
coop *n.* poulailler *m.* **—v.t. ~ up,** enfermer.
co-operat|e *v.i.* coopérer. **~ion** *n.* coopération *f.*
co-operative *a.* coopératif. **—n.** coopérative *f.*
co-ordinat|e *v.t.* coordonner. **~ion** *n.* coordination *f.*
cop *v.t.* (*sl.*) piquer. **—n.** (*policeman: sl.*) flic *m.* **~ out,** (*sl.*) dérobade *f.*
cope *v.i.* assurer. **~ with,** s'en sortir avec.
copious *a.* copieux.

copper[1] n. cuivre m.; (coin) sou m.
—a. de cuivre.

copper[2] n. (sl.) flic m.

coppice, copse ns. taillis m.

copy n. copie f.; (of book, newspaper) exemplaire m.; (print: photo.) épreuve f. —v.t./i. copier.

copyright n. copyright m.

coral n. corail m.

cord n. (petite) corde f.; (of curtain, pyjamas, etc.) cordon m.; (electr.) cordon électrique m.; (fabric) velours côtelé m.

cordial a. cordial. —n. (fruit-flavoured drink) sirop m.

cordon n. cordon m. —v.t. ∼ off, mettre un cordon autour de.

corduroy n. velours côtelé m.

core n. (of apple) trognon m.; (of problem) cœur m.; (techn.) noyau m. —v.t. vider.

cork n. liège m.; (for bottle) bouchon m. —v.t. boucher.

corkscrew n. tire-bouchon m.

corn[1] n. blé m.; (maize: Amer.) maïs m.; (seed) grain m. ∼-cob n. épi de maïs m.

corn[2] n. (hard skin) cor m.

cornea n. cornée f.

corned a. ∼ beef, corned-beef m.

corner n. coin m.; (bend in road) virage m.; (football) corner m. —v.t. coincer, acculer; (market) accaparer. —v.i. prendre un virage.

cornet n. cornet m.

cornflakes n. pl. corn flakes m. pl.

cornflour n. farine de maïs f.

Corn|wall n. Cornouailles f. ∼ish a. de Cornouailles.

corny a. (trite: fam.) rebattu; (mawkish: fam.) à l'eau de rose.

corollary n. corollaire m.

coronary n. infarctus m.

coronation n. couronnement m.

coroner n. coroner m.

corporal[1] n. caporal m.

corporal[2] a. ∼ punishment, châtiment corporel m.

corporate a. en commun; (body) constitué.

corporation n. (comm.) société f.; (of town) municipalité f.

corps n. corps m.

corpse n. cadavre m.

corpuscle n. globule m.

correct a. (right) exact, juste, correct; (proper) correct. **you are** ∼, vous avez raison. —v.t. corriger. ∼ion n. correction f.

correlat|e v.t./i. (faire) correspondre. ∼ion n. corrélation f.

correspond v.i. correspondre. ∼ence n. correspondance f. ∼ent n. correspondant(e) m. (f.).

corridor n. couloir m.

corroborate v.t. corroborer.

corro|de v.t./i. (se) corroder. ∼sion n. corrosion f.

corrugated a. ondulé. ∼ iron, tôle ondulée f.

corrupt a. corrompu. —v.t. corrompre. ∼ion n. corruption f.

corset n. (boned) corset m.; (elasticated) gaine f.

Corsica n. Corse f.

cortisone n. cortisone f.

cosh n. matraque f. —v.t. matraquer.

cosmetic n. produit de beauté m.

cosmic a. cosmique.

cosmonaut n. cosmonaute m./f.

cosmopolitan a. & n. cosmopolite (m./f.).

cosmos n. cosmos m.

cosset v.t. dorloter.

cost v.t. (be priced at) coûter; (ask price of) établir le prix de. —n. coût m. ∼s, (jurid.) dépens m. pl. **at all** ∼s, à tout prix. ∼ **effective** a. rentable. ∼-**effectiveness** n. rentabilité f. ∼ **of living,** coût de la vie.

co-star n. partenaire m./f.

costly a. coûteux; (*valuable*) précieux.

costume n. costume m.; (*for swimming*) maillot m. **~ jewellery**, bijoux de fantaisie m. pl.

cosy a. confortable, intime. —n. couvrethéière m.

cot n. lit d'enfant m.; (*camp-bed: Amer.*) lit de camp m.

cottage n. petite maison de campagne f.; (*thatched*) chaumière f. **~ cheese**, fromage blanc (maigre) m.

cotton n. coton m.; (*for sewing*) fil (à coudre) m. —v.i. **~ on**, (sl.) piger. **~ wool**, coton hydrophile m.

couch n. divan m.

couchette n. couchette f.

cough v.i. tousser. —n. toux f. **~ up**, (sl.) cracher, payer.

council n. conseil m. **~ house**, (*approx.*) H.L.M. m./f.

councillor n. conseill|er, -ère municipal(e) m., f.

counsel n. conseil m. —n. invar. (*jurid.*) avocat(e) m. (f.). **~lor** n. conseill|er, -ère m., f.

count[1] v.t./i. compter. —n. compte m. **~ on**, compter sur.

count[2] n. (*nobleman*) comte m.

countdown n. compte à rebours m.

countenance n. mine f. —v.t. admettre, approuver.

counter[1] n. comptoir m.; (*in bank etc.*) guichet m.; (*token*) jeton m.

counter[2] adv. **~ to**, à l'encontre de. —a. opposé. —v.t. opposer; (*blow*) parer. —v.i. riposter.

counter- pref. contre-.

counteract v.t. neutraliser.

counter-attack n. contre-attaque f. —v.t./i. contre-attaquer.

counterbalance n. contrepoids m. —v.t. contre-balancer.

counter-clockwise a. & adv. (*Amer.*) dans le sens inverse des aiguilles d'une montre.

counterfeit a. & n. faux (m.). —v.t. contrefaire.

counterfoil n. souche f.

countermand v.t. annuler.

counterpart n. équivalent m.; (*person*) homologue m./f.

counter-productive a. (*measure*) qui produit l'effet contraire.

counter-tenor n. haute-contre m.

countess n. comtesse f.

countless a. innombrable.

country n. (*land, region*) pays m.; (*homeland*) patrie f.; (*countryside*) campagne f.

countryman n. campagnard m.; (*fellow citizen*) compatriote m.

countryside n. campagne f.

county n. comté m.

coup n. (*achievement*) joli coup m.; (*pol.*) coup d'état m.

couple n. (*people, animals*) couple m. **a ~ (of)**, (*two or three*) deux ou trois.

coupon n. coupon m.; (*for shopping*) bon ou coupon de réduction m.

courage n. courage m. **~ous** a. courageux.

courgette n. courgette f.

courier n. messag|er, -ère m., f.; (*for tourists*) guide m.

course n. cours m.; (*for training*) stage m.; (*series*) série f.; (*culin.*) plat m.; (*for golf*) terrain m.; (*at sea*) itinéraire m. **change ~**, changer de cap. **~ (of action)**, façon de faire f. **of ~**, bien sûr.

court n. cour f.; (*tennis*) court m. —v.t. faire la cour à; (*danger*) rechercher. **~-house** n. (*Amer.*) palais de justice m. **~ shoe**, escarpin m. **go to ~**, aller devant les tribunaux.

courteous a. courtois.

courtesy n. courtoisie f. **by ~ of**, avec la permission de.

courtroom n. salle de tribunal f.

courtyard n. cour f.

cousin n. cousin(e) m. (f.).

cove n. anse f., crique f.

covenant n. convention f.

cover v.t. couvrir. —n. (for bed, book, etc.) couverture f.; (lid) couvercle m.; (for furniture) housse f.; (shelter) abri m. ~ **charge,** couvert m. ~ **up,** cacher; (crime) couvrir. ~ **up for,** couvrir. ~**-up** n. tentative pour cacher la vérité f. ~**ing letter,** lettre f. (jointe à un document).

coverage n. reportage m.

covert a. (activity) secret; (threat) voilé (look) dérobé.

covet v.t. convoiter.

cow n. vache f.

coward n. lâche m./f. ~**ly** a. lâche.

cowardice n. lâcheté f.

cowboy n. cow-boy m.

cower v.i. se recroqueviller (sous l'effet de la peur).

cox n. barreur m. —v.t. barrer.

coy a. (faussement) timide.

crab n. crabe m. ~**-apple** n. pomme sauvage f.

crack n. fente f.; (in glass) fêlure f.; (noise) craquement m.; (joke: sl.) plaisanterie f. —a. (fam.) d'élite, —v.t./i. (break partially) (se) fêler; (split) (se) fendre; (nut) casser; (joke) raconter; (problem) résoudre. ~ **down on,** (fam.) sévir contre. ~ **up,** (fam.) craquer. **get** ~**ing,** (fam.) s'y mettre.

cracker n. pétard m.; (culin.) biscuit (salé) m.

crackers a. (sl.) cinglé.

crackle v.i. crépiter. —n. crépitement m.

cradle n. berceau m. —v.t. bercer.

craft[1] n. métier artisanal m.;

(technique) art m.; (cunning) ruse f.

craft[2] n. invar. (boat) bateau m.

craftsman n. artisan m. ~**ship** n. art m.

crafty a. rusé.

crag n. rocher à pic m. ~**gy** a. à pic; (face) rude.

cram v.t./i. ~ **into,** (pack) (s')entasser dans. ~ **with,** (fill) bourrer de.

cramp n. crampe f.

cramped a. à l'étroit.

cranberry n. canneberge f.

crane n. grue f. —v.t. (neck) tendre.

crank[1] n. (techn.) manivelle f.

crank[2] n. excentrique m./f. ~**y** a. excentrique; (Amer.) grincheux.

cranny n. fissure f.

crash n. accident m.; (noise) fracas m.; (of thunder) coup m.; (of firm) faillite f. —v.t./i. avoir un accident (avec); (of plane) s'écraser; (two vehicles) se percuter. —a. (course) intensif. ~**-helmet** n. casque (anti-choc) m. ~ **into,** rentrer dans.

crass a. grossier.

crate n. cageot m.

crater n. cratère m.

cravat n. foulard m.

crav|e v.t./i. ~**e (for),** désirer ardemment. ~**ing** n. envie irrésistible f.

crawl v.i. ramper; (vehicle) se traîner. —n. (pace) pas m.; (swimming) crawl m. **be** ~**ing with,** grouiller de.

crayfish n. invar. écrevisse f.

crayon n. crayon m.

craze n. engouement m.

crazy a. fou. ~ **about,** (person) fou de.

creak n. grincement m. —v.i. grincer. ~**y** a. grinçant.

cream n. crème f. —a. crème

invar. —*v.t.* écrémer. ~ **cheese,** fromage frais m. —*v.* ~**y** a. crémeux.

crease n. pli m. —*v.t./i.* (se) froisser.

creat|e *v.t.* créer. ~**ion** n. création f. ~**ive** a. créateur. ~**or** n. créa|teur, -trice m., f.

creature n. créature f.

crèche n. garderie f.

credence n. **give** ~ **to,** ajouter foi à.

credentials n. pl. (*identity*) pièces d'identité f. pl.; (*competence*) références f. pl.

credib|le a. (*excuse etc.*) croyable. ~**ility** n. crédibilité f.

credit n. crédit m.; (*honour*) honneur m. □ n., créditeur. ~**s,** (*cinema*) générique m. —a. (*balance*) créditeur. —*v.t.* croire; (*comm.*) créditer. ~ **card,** carte de crédit f. ~ **note,** avoir m. ~ **s.o. with,** attribuer à qn. ~**worthy** a. solvable. ~**or** n. créan|cier, -ière m., f.

creditable a. honorable.

credulous a. crédule.

creed n. credo m.

creek n. crique f.; (*Amer.*) ruisseau m.

creep *v.i.* ramper; (*fig.*) se glisser. —n. (*person: sl.*) pauvre type m. ~**er** n. liane f. ~**y** a. qui fait frissonner.

Creole n. créole m./f.

crêpe n. crêpe m. ~ **paper,** papier crépon m.

crescendo n. crescendo m.

crescent n. croissant m.; (*fig.*) rue en demi-lune f.

cress n. cresson m.

crest n. crête f.; (*coat of arms*) armoiries f. pl.

Crete n. Crète f.

cretin n. crétin(e) m. (f.).

crevasse n. crevasse f.

crevice n. fente f.

crew n. équipage m.; (*gang*) équipe f. ~ **cut,** coupe en brosse f. ~ **neck,** (col) ras du cou m.

crib[1] n. lit d'enfant m.

crib[2] *v.t./i.* copier. —n. (*schol., fam.*) traduction f., aide-mémoire m. *invar.*

crick n. (*in neck*) torticolis m.

cricket[1] n. (*sport*) cricket m. ~**er** n. joueur de cricket m.

cricket[2] n. (*insect*) grillon m.

crime n. crime m.; (*minor*) délit m.; (*acts*) criminalité f.

criminal a. & n. criminel(le) (m. (f.)).

crimp *v.t.* (*hair*) friser.

crimson a. & n. cramoisi (m.).

cring|e *v.i.* reculer; (*fig.*) s'humilier. ~**ing** a. servile.

crinkle *v.t./i.* (se) froisser. —n. pli m.

cripple n. infirme m./f. —*v.t.* estropier; (*fig.*) paralyser.

crisis n. crise f.

crisp a. (*culin.*) croquant; (*air, reply*) vif. ~**s** n. pl. chips m. pl.

criss-cross a. entrecroisé. —*v.t./i.* (s')entrecroiser.

criterion n. critère m.

critic n. critique m. ~**al** a. critique. ~**ally** adv. d'une manière critique; (*ill*) gravement.

criticism n. critique f.

criticize *v.t./i.* critiquer.

croak n. (*bird*) croassement; (*frog*) coassement m. —*v.i.* croasser; coasser.

crochet n. crochet m. —*v.t.* faire au crochet.

crockery n. vaisselle f.

crocodile n. crocodile m.

crocus n. crocus m.

crook n. (*criminal: fam.*) escroc m.; (*stick*) houlette f.

crooked a. tordu; (*winding*) tortueux; (*askew*) de travers; (*dishonest: fig.*) malhonnête.

croon v.t./i. chantonner.

crop n. récolte f.; (fig.) quantité f. —v.i. ~ **up**, se présenter.

croquet n. croquet m.

croquette n. croquette f.

cross n. croix f.; (hybrid) hybride m. —v.t./i. traverser; (legs, animals) croiser; (cheque) barrer; (paths) se croiser. —a. en colère, fâché (**with**, contre). ~**check** v.t. vérifier (pour confirmer). ~**country (running)**, cross m. ~ **off** or **out**, rayer. ~ **s.o.'s mind**, venir à l'esprit de qn.

crossbar n. barre transversale f.

cross-examine v.t. faire subir un examen contradictoire à.

cross-eyed a. be ~, loucher.

crossfire n. feux croisés m. pl.

crossing n. (by boat) traversée f.; (on road) passage clouté m.

cross-reference n. renvoi m.

crossroads n. carrefour m.

cross-section n. coupe transversale f.; (sample: fig.) échantillon m.

crosswise adv. en travers.

crossword n. mots croisés m. pl.

crotch n. (of garment) entre-jambes m. invar.

crotchet n. (mus.) noire f.

crouch v.i. s'accroupir.

crow n. corbeau m. —v.i. (of cock) chanter; (fig.) jubiler. ~**'s feet**, pattes d'oie f. pl.

crowbar n. pied-de-biche m.

crowd n. foule f. —v.i. affluer. —v.t. remplir. ~ **into**, (s')entasser dans. ~**ed** a. plein.

crown n. couronne f.; (top part) sommet m. —v.t. couronner.

crucial a. crucial.

crude a. (raw) brut; (rough, vulgar) grossier.

cruel a. cruel. ~**ty** n. cruauté f.

cruet n. huilier m.

cruis|e n. croisière f. —v.i. (ship) croiser; (tourists) faire une croisière; (vehicle) rouler. ~**er** n. croiseur m. ~**ing speed**, vitesse de croisière f.

crumb n. miette f.

crumble v.t./i. (s')effriter; (bread) (s')émietter; (collapse) s'écrouler.

crummy a. (sl.) minable.

crumpet n. (culin.) petite crêpe (grillée) f.

crumple v.t./i. (se) froisser.

crunch v.t. croquer. —n. (event) moment critique m.

crusade n. croisade f.

crush v.t. écraser; (clothes) froisser. —n. (crowd) presse f. **a ~ on**, (sl.) le béguin pour.

crust n. croûte f. ~**y** a. croustillant.

crutch n. béquille f.; (crotch) entre-jambes m. invar.

cry n. cri m.; (weep) pleurer; (call out) crier. ~ **off**, abandonner.

crypt n. crypte f.

cryptic a. énigmatique.

crystal n. cristal m. ~**-clear** a. parfaitement clair. ~**lize** v.t./i. (se) cristalliser.

cub n. petit m. **Cub (Scout)**, louveteau m.

Cuba n. Cuba m. ~**n** a. & n. cubain(e) (m. (f.)).

cubby-hole n. cagibi m.

cub|e n. cube m. ~**ic** a. cubique; (metre etc.) cube.

cubicle n. (in room, hospital, etc.) box m.; (at swimming-pool) cabine f.

cuckoo n. coucou m.

cucumber n. concombre m.

cuddl|e v.t. câliner. —v.i. (kiss and) ~**e**, s'embrasser. —n. caresse f. ~**y** a. câlin.

cue[1] n. signal m.; (theatre) réplique f.

cue[2] n. (billiards) queue f.

cuff n. manchette f.; (Amer.) revers m. —v.t. gifler. **~-link** n. bouton de manchette m.

cul-de-sac n. impasse f.

culinary a. culinaire.

cull v.t. (select) choisir; (kill) abattre sélectivement.

culminat|e v.i. **~e in,** se terminer par. **~ion** n. point culminant m.

culprit n. coupable m./f.

cult n. culte m.

cultivat|e v.t. cultiver. **~ion** n. culture f.

cultural a. culturel.

culture n. culture f.

cunning a. rusé. —n. ruse f.

cup n. tasse f.; (prize) coupe f.

cupboard n. placard m.

curator n. (of museum) conservateur m.

curb[1] n. (restraint) frein m. —v.t. (desires etc.) refréner; (price increase etc.) freiner.

curb[2] n. bord du trottoir m.

curdle v.t./i. (se) cailler.

cure[1] v.t. guérir; (fig.) éliminer. —n. (recovery) guérison f.; (remedy) remède m.

cure[2] v.t. (culin.) fumer; (in brine) saler.

curio n. bibelot m.

curi|ous a. curieux. **~osity** n. curiosité f.

curl v.t./i. (hair) boucler. —n. boucle f. **~ up,** se pelotonner; (shrivel) se racornir.

curler n. bigoudi m.

curly a. bouclé.

currant n. raisin de Corinthe m.; (berry) groseille f.

currency n. (money) monnaie f.; (acceptance) cours m. **foreign ~,** devises étrangères f. pl.

current a. (common) courant; (topical) actuel; (year etc.) en cours. —n. courant m. **~ account,** compte courant m.

curry n. curry m., cari m.

curse n. malédiction f.; (oath) juron m. —v.t. maudire. —v.i. (swear) jurer.

cursor n. curseur m.

curt a. brusque.

curtain n. rideau m.

curve n. courbe f. —v.t./i. (se) courber; (of road) tourner.

cushion n. coussin m. —v.t. (a blow) amortir; (fig.) protéger.

custard n. crème anglaise f.; (set) crème renversée f.

custody n. garde f.; (jurid.) détention préventive f.

custom n. coutume f.; (patronage: comm.) clientèle f. **~-built, ~-made** adjs. fait etc. sur commande. **~ary** a. d'usage.

customer n. client(e) m. (f.); (fam.) **an odd/a difficult ~,** un individu curieux/difficile.

customize v.t. personnaliser.

customs n. pl. douane f. **~ officer,** douanier m.

cut v.t./i. couper; (hedge, jewel) tailler; (prices etc.) réduire. —n. coupure f.; (of clothes) coupe f.; (piece) morceau m.; réduction f. **~ back** or **down (on),** réduire. **~-back** n. réduction f. **~ off,** couper; (fig.) isoler. **~ out,** découper; (leave out) supprimer. **~-price** a. à prix réduit.

cute a. (fam.) astucieux; (Amer.) mignon.

cuticle n. petites peaux f. pl. (de l'ongle).

cutlery n. couverts m. pl.

cutlet n. côtelette f.

cutting a. cinglant. —n. (from newspaper) coupure f.; (plant) bouture f. **~ edge,** tranchant m.

cycl|e n. cycle m.; (bicycle) vélo m. —v.i. aller à vélo. **~ing** n. cyclisme m. **~ist** n. cycliste m./f.

cyclic(al) a. cyclique.

cyclone n. cyclone m.

cylinder n. cylindre m.

cymbal n. cymbale f.

cynic n. cynique m./f. ∼al a. cynique. ∼ism n. cynisme m.

cypress n. cyprès m.

Cypr|us n. Chypre f. ∼iot a. & n. cypriote (m./f.).

cyst n. kyste m. ∼ic fibrosis, mucoviscidose f.

cystitis n. cystite f.

Czech a. & n. tchèque (m./f.).

D

dab v.t. tamponner. —n. a ∼ of, un petit coup de; ∼ sth. on, appliquer qch. à petits coups sur.

dabble v.i. ∼ in, se mêler un peu de.

dad n. (fam.) papa m. ∼dy n. (children's use) papa m.

daffodil n. jonquille f.

daft a. idiot.

dagger n. poignard m.

dahlia n. dahlia m.

daily a. quotidien. —adv. tous les jours.

dainty a. délicat.

dairy n. (on farm) laiterie f.; (shop) crémerie f. —a. laitier.

daisy n. pâquerette f. ∼ wheel, marguerite f.

dale n. vallée f.

dam n. barrage m. —v.t. endiguer.

damag|e n. dégâts m. pl., dommages m. pl.; (harm: fig.) préjudice m. ∼es, (jurid.) dommages et intérêts m. pl. —v.t. abîmer. (fig.) nuire à.

damn v.t. (relig.) damner; (condemn: fig.) condamner. —int. zut, merde. —n. **not care a** ∼ s'en foutre. —a. sacré. —adv. rudement.

damp n. humidité f. —a. humide.

dance v.t./i. danser. —n. danse f.; (gathering) bal m. ∼r n. danseu|r, -se m., f.

dandelion n. pissenlit m.

dandruff n. pellicules f. pl.

dandy n. dandy m.

Dane n. Danois(e) m. (f.).

danger n. danger m.; (risk) risque m. **be in** ∼ **of**, risquer de. ∼ous a. dangereux.

dangle v.t./i. (se) balancer, (laisser) pendre. ∼ sth. **in front of** s.o., (fig.) faire miroiter qch. à qn.

Danish a. danois. —n. (lang.) danois m.

dare v.t./i. ∼ (**to**) **do**, oser faire. ∼ s.o. **to do**, défier qn. de faire. —n. défi m.

daring a. audacieux.

dark a. obscur, sombre, noir; (colour) foncé, sombre; (skin) brun, foncé; (gloomy) sombre. —n. noir m.; (nightfall) tombée de la nuit f. ∼ness n. obscurité f.

darken v.t./i. (s')assombrir.

darling a. & n. chéri(e) (m. (f.)).

darn v.t. repriser.

dart n. fléchette f. ∼s, (game) fléchettes f. pl. —v.i. s'élancer.

dartboard n. cible f.

dash v.i. (hurry) se dépêcher; (forward etc.) se précipiter. —v.t. jeter (avec violence); (hopes) briser. —n. ruée f.; (stroke) tiret m. ∼ **off**, (leave) partir en vitesse.

dashboard n. tableau de bord m.

data n. pl. données f. pl. ∼ **processing**, traitement des données m.

database n. base de données f.

date[1] n. date f.; (meeting: fam.) rendez-vous m. —v.t./i. dater; (go out with: fam.) sortir avec. **out of** ∼, (old-fashioned) démodé; (passport) périmé. **up to** ∼, (modern)

moderne; (list) à jour. **~d** a.
démodé.

date² n. (fruit) datte f.

daub v.t. barbouiller.

daughter n. fille f. **~-in-law** n.
belle-fille f.

dawdle v.i. lambiner.

dawn n. aube f. —v.i. poindre;
(fig.) naître. **it ~ed on me,** je
m'en suis rendu compte.

day n. jour m.; (whole day) journée
f.; (period) époque f. **~-dream** n.
rêverie f.; v.i. rêvasser. **the ~
before,** la veille. **the next ~,** le
lendemain.

daylight n. jour m.

daytime n. jour m., journée f.

daze v.t. étourdir; (with drugs)
hébéter. —n. **in a ~,** étourdi;
hébété.

dazzle v.t. éblouir.

deacon n. diacre m.

dead a. mort; (numb) engourdi.
—adv. complètement. —n. **the
~,** les morts. **~ end,** impasse f.
~-end job, travail sans avenir
m. **stop ~,** s'arrêter net. **the race
was a ~ heat,** ils ont été classés
ex aequo.

deaden v.t. (sound, blow) amortir;
(pain) calmer.

deadline n. date limite f.

deadlock n. impasse f.

deadly a. mortel; (weapon)
meurtrier.

deaf a. sourd. **the ~ and dumb,**
les sourds-muets. **~-aid** n. appareil acoustique m. **~ness** n.
surdité f.

deafen v.t. assourdir.

deal v.t. donner; (a blow) porter.
—v.i. (trade) commercer. —n.
affaire f.; (cards) donne f. **a good
~,** beaucoup (of, de). **~ in,** faire
le commerce de. **~ with,** (handle,
manage) s'occuper de; (be about)
traiter de. **~er** n. marchand(e) m.

(f.); (agent) concessionnaire
m./f.

dealings n. pl. relations f. pl.

dean n. doyen m.

dear a. cher. —adv. cher. —int. **oh
~!,** oh mon Dieu!

death n. mort f.

debar v.t. exclure.

debase v.t. avilir.

debate|e n. discussion f., débat m.
—v.t. discuter. **~e whether,** se
demander si. **~able** a. discutable.

debilitate v.t. débiliter.

debility n. débilité f.

debit n. débit m. **in ~,** débiteur.
—a. (balance) débiteur. —v.t.
débiter.

debris n. débris m. pl.

debt n. dette f. **in ~,** endetté. **~or**
n. débi|teur, -trice m., f.

debunk v.t. (fam.) démythifier.

decade n. décennie f.

decaden|t a. décadent. **~ce** n.
décadence f.

decaffeinated a. décaféiné.

decanter n. carafe f.

decay v.i. se gâter, pourrir; (fig.)
décliner. —n. pourriture f.; (of
tooth) carie f.; (fig.) déclin m.

deceased a. décédé. —n. défunt(e)
m. (f.).

deceit n. tromperie f. **~ful** a.
trompeur.

deceive v.t. tromper.

December n. décembre m.

decen|t a. décent, convenable;
(good: fam.) (assez) bon; (kind:
fam.) gentil. **~cy** n. décence f.

decentralize v.t. décentraliser.

decept|ive a. trompeur. **~ion** n.
tromperie f.

decide v.t./i. décider; (question)
régler. **~ on,** se décider pour. **~
to do,** décider de faire.

deciduous a. à feuillage caduc.

decimal a. décimal. —n. décimale
f. **~ point,** virgule f.

decimate v.t. décimer.

decipher v.t. déchiffrer.

decision n. décision f.

decisive a. (conclusive) décisif; (firm) décidé.

deck n. pont m.; (of cards: Amer.) jeu m. ~-**chair** n. chaise longue f. **top** ~, (of bus) impériale f.

declar|e v.t. déclarer. ~**ation** n. déclaration f.

decline v.t./i. refuser (poliment); (deteriorate) décliner; (fall) baisser. —n. déclin m.; baisse f.

decode v.t. décoder.

decompos|e v.t./i. (se) décomposer. ~**ition** n. décomposition f.

décor n. décor m.

decorat|e v.t. décorer; (room) peindre or tapisser. ~**ion** n. décoration f. ~**ive** a. décoratif.

decorator n. peintre en bâtiment m.

decorum n. décorum m.

decoy[1] n. (bird) appeau m.; (trap) piège m., leurre m.

decoy[2] v.t. attirer, appâter.

decrease v.t./i. diminuer. —n. diminution f.

decree n. (pol., relig.) décret m.; (jurid.) jugement m. —v.t. décréter.

decrepit a. (building) délabré; (person) décrépit.

decry v.t. dénigrer.

dedicat|e v.t. dédier. ~**e o.s. to**, se consacrer à. ~**ed** a. dévoué. ~**ion** n. dévouement m.; (in book) dédicace f.

deduce v.t. déduire.

deduct v.t. déduire; (from wages) retenir. ~**ion** n. déduction f.; retenue f.

deed n. acte m.

deep a. profond. —adv. profondément. ~-**freeze** n. congélateur m.; v.t. congeler. ~-**fry**, frire. ~**ly** adv. profondément.

deepen v.t. approfondir. —v.i. devenir plus profond; (mystery, night) s'épaissir.

deer n. invar. cerf m.; (doe) biche f.

deface v.t. dégrader.

defamation n. diffamation f.

default v.i. (jurid.) faire défaut. —n. by ~, (jurid.) par défaut. **win by** ~, gagner par forfait. —a. (comput.) par défaut.

defeat v.t. vaincre; (thwart) faire échouer. —n. défaite f.; (of plan etc.) échec m.

defect[1] n. défaut m. ~**ive** a. défectueux.

defect[2] v.i. faire défection. ~ **to**, passer à. ~**or** n. transfuge m./f.

defence n. défense f.

defend v.t. défendre. ~**ant** n. (jurid.) accusé(e) m. (f.).

defensive a. défensif.

defer[2] v.t. remettre.

deference n. déférence f.

defian|ce n. défi m. **in** ~**ce of**, au mépris de. ~**t** a. de défi.

deficien|t a. insuffisant. **be** ~**t in**, manquer de. ~**cy** n. insuffisance f.; (fault) défaut m.

deficit n. déficit m.

define v.t. définir.

definite a. précis; (obvious) net; (firm) catégorique; (certain) certain. ~**ly** adv. certainement; (clearly) nettement.

definition n. définition f.

definitive a. définitif.

deflat|e v.t. dégonfler. ~**ion** n. dégonflement m.; (comm.) déflation f.

deflect v.t./i. (faire) dévier.

deforestation n. déforestation f.

deform v.t. déformer. ~**ed** a. difforme. ~**ity** n. difformité f.

defraud v.t. (state, customs) frauder. ~ **s.o. of sth.**, escroquer qch. à qn.

defray v.t. payer.

defrost *v.t.* dégivrer.

deft *a.* adroit.

defuse *v.t.* désamorcer.

defy *v.t.* défier; (*attempts*) résister à.

degenerate[1] *v.i.* dégénérer (**into**, en).

degenerate[2] *a. & n.* dégénéré(e) (*m. (f.)*).

degrad|e *v.t.* dégrader. **~ation** *n.* dégradation *f.*; (*state*) déchéance *f.*

degree *n.* degré *m.*; (*univ.*) diplôme universitaire *m.*; (*Bachelor's degree*) licence *f.*

dehydrate *v.t./i.* (se) déshydrater.

de-ice *v.t.* dégivrer.

deign *v.t.* **~ to do**, daigner faire.

deject|ed *a.* abattu. **~ion** *n.* abattement *m.*

delay *v.t.* retarder. —*v.i.* tarder. —*n.* (*lateness, time overdue*) retard *m.*; (*waiting*) délai *m.* **~ doing**, attendre pour faire.

delegate[1] *n.* délégué(e) *m. (f.)*.

delegat|e[2] *v.t.* déléguer. **~ion** *n.* délégation *f.*

delet|e *v.t.* effacer; (*with line*) barrer. **~ion** *n.* suppression *f.*

deliberate[1] *a.* délibéré. **~ly** *adv.* exprès, délibérément.

deliberat|e[2] *v.i.* délibérer. —*v.t.* considérer. **~ion** *n.* délibération *f.*

delica|te *a.* délicat. **~cy** *n.* délicatesse *f.*; (*food*) mets délicat *or* raffiné *m.*

delicatessen *n.* épicerie fine *f.*

delicious *a.* délicieux.

delight *n.* grand plaisir *m.*, joie *f.*; (*thing*) délice *m.* (*f. in pl.*). —*v.t.* réjouir. **~ed** *a.* ravi. **~ful** *a.* charmant.

delinquen|t *a. & n.* délinquant(e) (*m. (f.)*) **~cy** *n.* délinquance *f.*

delirious *a.* **be ~ous**, délirer.

deliver *v.t.* (*message*) remettre; (*goods*) livrer; (*letters*) distribuer;

(*free*) délivrer; (*utter*) prononcer; (*med.*) accoucher; (*a blow*) porter. **~y** *n.* livraison *f.*; distribution *f.*; accouchement *m.*

delta *n.* delta *m.*

delu|de *v.t.* tromper. **~de o.s.**, se faire des illusions. **~sion** *n.* illusion *f.*

deluge *n.* déluge *m.* —*v.t.* inonder (**with**, de).

de luxe *a.* de luxe.

demand *v.t.* exiger; (*in negotiations*) réclamer. —*n.* exigence *f.*; (*claim*) revendication *f.*; (*comm.*) demande *f.* **~ing** *a.* exigeant.

demarcation *n.* démarcation *f.*

demean *v.t.* **~ o.s.**, s'abaisser, s'avilir.

demeanour *n.* comportement *m.*

demerara *n.* (*brown sugar*) cassonade *f.*

demobilize *v.t.* démobiliser.

democracy *n.* démocratie *f.*

democrat *n.* démocrate *m./f.* **~ic** *a.* démocratique.

demoli|sh *v.t.* démolir. **~tion** *n.* démolition *f.*

demon *n.* démon *m.*

demonstrat|e *v.t.* démontrer. —*v.i.* (*pol.*) manifester. **~ion** *n.* démonstration *f.*; (*pol.*) manifestation *f.* **~or** *n.* manifestant(e) *m. (f.)*.

demonstrative *a.* démonstratif.

demoralize *v.t.* démoraliser.

demote *v.t.* rétrograder.

demure *a.* modeste.

den *n.* antre *m.*

denial *n.* dénégation *f.*; (*statement*) démenti *m.*

denigrate *v.t.* dénigrer.

denim *n.* toile de coton *f.*; (*jeans*) blue-jeans *m. pl.* **~s**,

Denmark *n.* Danemark *m.*

denomination *n.* (*relig.*) confession *f.*; (*money*) valeur *f.*

denote *v.t.* dénoter.

denounce *v.t.* dénoncer.

dens|e *a.* dense; (*person*) obtus. **~ity** *n.* densité *f.*

dent *n.* bosse *f.* —*v.t.* cabosser.

dental *a.* dentaire. **~ floss,** fil dentaire *m.* **~ surgeon,** dentiste *m./f.*

dentist *n.* dentiste *m./f.*

dentures *n. pl.* dentier *m.*

denude *v.t.* dénuder.

denunciation *n.* dénonciation *f.*

deny *v.t.* nier (**that, que**); (*rumour*) démentir; (*disown*) renier; (*refuse*) refuser.

deodorant *n. & a.* déodorant (*m.*).

depart *v.i.* partir. **~ from,** (*deviate*) s'écarter de.

department *n.* département *m.*; (*in shop*) rayon *m.*; (*in office*) service *m.* **~ store,** grand magasin *m.*

departure *n.* départ *m.*

depend *v.i.* dépendre (**on,** de). **~ on,** (*rely on*) compter sur. **~ing on the weather,** selon le temps qu'il fera. **~able** *a.* sûr. **~ence** *n.* dépendance *f.* **~ent** *a.* dépendant.

dependant *n.* personne à charge *f.*

depict *v.t.* (*describe*) dépeindre; (*in picture*) représenter.

deplor|e *v.t.* déplorer. **~able** *a.* déplorable.

deploy *v.t.* déployer.

deport *v.t.* expulser.

deposit *v.t.* déposer. —*n.* dépôt *m.*; (*of payment*) acompte *m.*; (*to reserve*) arrhes *f. pl.*; (*against damage*) caution *f.*; (*on bottle etc.*) consigne *f.*; (*of mineral*) gisement *m.* **~ account,** compte dépôt *m.* **~or** *n.* (*comm.*) déposant(e) *m.* (*f.*), épargnant(e) *m.* (*f.*).

depot *n.* dépôt *m.*; (*Amer.*) gare (*routière*) *f.*

depreciat|e *v.t./i.* (se) déprécier. **~ion** *n.* dépréciation *f.*

depress *v.t.* (*sadden*) déprimer; (*push down*) appuyer sur. **become ~ed,** déprimer. **~ing** *a.* déprimant. **~ion** *n.* dépression *f.*

deprivation *n.* privation *f.*

deprive *v.t.* **~ of,** priver de. **~d** *a.* (*child etc.*) déshérité.

depth *n.* profondeur *f.*

deputation *n.* députation *f.*

deputize *v.i.* assurer l'intérim (**for,** de).

deputy *n.* suppléant(e) *m.* (*f.*) —*a.* adjoint.

derail *v.t.* faire dérailler. **be ~ed,** dérailler. **~ment** *n.* déraillement *m.*

deranged *a.* (*mind*) dérangé.

derelict *a.* abandonné.

deri|de *v.t.* railler. **~sion** *n.* dérision *f.*

derisory *a.* (*scoffing*) railleur; (*offer etc.*) dérisoire.

derogatory *a.* (*word*) péjoratif; (*remark*) désobligeant.

derv *n.* gas-oil *m.*, gazole *m.*

descend *v.t./i.* descendre. **be ~ed from,** descendre de. **~ant** *n.* descendant(e) *m.* (*f.*).

descent *n.* descente *f.*; (*lineage*) origine *f.*

descri|be *v.t.* décrire. **~ption** *n.* description *f.* **~ptive** *a.* descriptif.

desert[1] *n.* désert *m.* **~ island,** île déserte *f.*

desert[2] *v.t./i.* déserter. **~ed** *a.* désert. **~er** *n.* déserteur *m.* **~ion** *n.* désertion *f.*

deserve *v.t.* mériter (**to,** de).

design *n.* (*sketch*) dessin *m.*, plan *m.*; (*construction*) conception *f.*; (*pattern*) motif *m.*; (*style of dress*) modèle *m.*; (*aim*) dessein *m.* —*v.t.* concevoir. **~er** *n.* dessina|teur, -trice *m.*; (*of fashion*) styliste *m./f.*

designat|e v.t. désigner. **~ion** n. désignation f.

desir|e n. désir m. —v.t. désirer. **~able** a. désirable.

desk n. bureau m.; (of pupil) pupitre m.; (in hotel) réception f.; (in bank) caisse f.

desolat|e a. (place) désolé; (bleak: fig.) morne. **~ion** n. désolation f.

despair n. désespoir m. —v.i. désespérer (of, de).

despatch v.t. = **dispatch**.

desperate a. désespéré; (criminal) prêt à tout. **be ~ for**, avoir une envie folle de; **~ly** adv. désespérément; (worried) terriblement; (ill) gravement.

desperation n. désespoir m.

despicable a. méprisable.

despise v.t. mépriser.

despite prep. malgré.

despondent a. découragé.

despot n. despote m.

dessert n. dessert m. **~spoon** n. cuiller à dessert f.

destination n. destination f.

destine v.t. destiner.

destiny n. destin m.

destitute a. indigent.

destr|oy v.t. détruire; (animal) abattre. **~uction** n. destruction f. **~uctive** a. destructeur.

destroyer n. (warship) contretorpilleur m.

detach v.t. détacher. **~able** a. détachable. **~ed** a. détaché. **~ed house**, maison individuelle f.

detachment n. détachement m.

detail n. détail m. —v.t. exposer en détail; (troops) détacher. **go into ~**, entrer dans le détail. **~ed** a. détaillé.

detain v.t. retenir; (in prison) détenir. **~ee** n. détenu(e) m. (f.).

detect v.t. découvrir; (perceive) distinguer; (tumour) dépister;

(mine) détecter. **~ion** n. découverte f.; dépistage m.; détection f. **~or** n. détecteur m.

detective n. policier m.; (private) détective m.

detention n. détention f.; (schol.) retenue f.

deter v.t. dissuader (from, de).

detergent a. & n. détergent (m.).

deteriorat|e v.i. se détériorer. **~ion** n. détérioration f.

determin|e v.t. déterminer. **~e to do**, décider de faire. **~ation** n. détermination f. **~ed** a. déterminé. **~ed to do**, décidé à faire.

deterrent n. force de dissuasion f.

detest v.t. détester.

detonat|e v.t./i. (faire) détoner. **~ion** n. détonation f.

detour n. détour m.

detract v.i. **~ from**, diminuer.

detriment n. détriment m. **~al** a. préjudiciable (to, à).

devalu|e v.t. dévaluer. **~ation** n. dévaluation f.

devastat|e v.t. dévaster. (overwhelm: fig.) accabler. **~ing** a. accablant.

develop v.t./i. (se) développer; (contract) contracter; (build on, transform) exploiter, aménager; (change) évoluer; (appear) se manifester. **~ into**, devenir. **~ing country**, pays en voie de développement m. **~ment** n. développement m. (housing) **~**, lotissement m.

deviant a. anormal. —n. (psych.) déviant m.

deviat|e v.i. dévier. **~e from**, (norm) s'écarter de. **~ion** n. déviation f.

device n. appareil m.; (scheme) procédé m.

devil n. diable m.

devious a. tortueux. **he is ~**, il a l'esprit tortueux.

devise v.t. inventer; (plan, means) combiner, imaginer.

devoid a. ~ of, dénué de.

devolution n. décentralisation f.; (of authority, power) délégation f. (to, à).

devot|e v.t. consacrer. ~**ed** a. dévoué. ~**ion** n. dévouement m.; (relig.) dévotion f.

devotee n. ~ of, passionné(e) de m. (f.).

devour v.t. dévorer.

devout a. fervent.

dew n. rosée f.

dexterity n. dextérité f.

dexterous a. dextérité f.

diabet|es n. diabète m. ~**ic** a. & n. diabétique (m./f.).

diabolical a. diabolique; (bad: fam.) atroce.

diagnose v.t. diagnostiquer.

diagnosis n. diagnostic m.

diagonal a. diagonal. —n. diagonale f. ~**ly** adv. en diagonale.

diagram n. schéma m.

dial n. cadran m. —v.t. (number) faire; (person) appeler. ~**ling code**, indicatif m. ~**ling tone**, tonalité f.

dialect n. dialecte m.

dialogue n. dialogue m.

diameter n. diamètre m.

diamond n. diamant m.; (shape) losange m.; (baseball) terrain m. ~**s**, (cards) carreau m.

diaper n. (Amer.) couche f.

diaphragm n. diaphragme m.

diarrhoea n. diarrhée f.

diary n. (for appointments etc.) agenda m.; (appointments) emploi du temps m. (for private thoughts) journal intime m.

dice n. invar. dé m. —v.t. (food) couper en dés.

dicey a. (fam.) risqué.

dictat|e v.t./i. dicter. ~**ion** n. dictée f.

dictator n. dictateur m.

dictatorial a. dictatorial.

diction n. diction f.

dictionary n. dictionnaire m.

diddle v.t. (sl.) escroquer.

die[1] v.i. mourir. ~ **out**, disparaître. **be dying to do/for**, mourir d'envie de faire/de.

die[2] n. (metal mould) matrice f.

diesel n. diesel m.

diet n. (habitual food) alimentation f.; (restricted) régime m. —v.i. suivre un régime.

diet|etic a. diététique. ~**ician** n. diététicien(ne) m. (f.).

differ v.i. différer (**from**, de); (disagree) ne pas être d'accord.

differen|t a. différent. ~**ce** n. différence f.; (disagreement) différend m.

differentiate v.t. différencier. —v.i. faire la différence (**between**, entre).

difficult a. difficile. ~**y** n. difficulté f.

diffiden|t a. qui manque d'assurance. ~**ce** n. manque d'assurance m.

diffuse[1] a. diffus.

diffus|e[2] v.t. diffuser. ~**ion** n. diffusion f.

dig v.t./i. creuser; (thrust) enfoncer. —n. (poke) coup de coude m.; (remark) coup de patte m.; (archaeol.) fouilles f. pl. ~**s**, (lodgings: fam.) chambre meublée f. ~ **up**, déterrer.

digest[1] v.t./i. digérer. ~**ion** n. digestion f.

digest[2] n. sommaire m.

digestive a. digestif.

digger n. (techn.) pelleteuse f.

digit n. chiffre m.

digital a. numérique.

dignif|y v.t. donner de la dignité à. ~**ied** a. digne.

dignity n. dignité f.

digress v.i. faire une digression. **~ from**, s'écarter de. **~ion** n. digression f.

dike n. digue f.

dilapidated a. délabré.

dilat|e v.t./i. (se) dilater. **~ion** n. dilatation f.

dilemma n. dilemme m.

dilettante n. dilettante m./f.

diligen|t a. assidu. **~ce** n. assiduité f.

dilute v.t. diluer.

dim a. (weak) faible; (dark) sombre; (indistinct) vague; (fam.) stupide. —v.t./i. (light) (s')atténuer. **~mer** n. variateur d'intensité m. (switch).

dime n. pièce de dix cents f.

dimension n. dimension f.

diminish v.t./i. diminuer.

diminutive a. minuscule. —n. diminutif m.

dimple n. fossette f.

din n. vacarme m.

dine v.i. dîner. **~r** n. dîneu|r, -se m., f.; (rail.) wagon-restaurant m.; (Amer.) restaurant à service rapide m.

dinghy n. canot m.; (inflatable) canot pneumatique m.

ding|y a. minable.

dining-room n. salle à manger f.

dinner n. (evening meal) dîner m.; (lunch) déjeuner m. **~-jacket** n. smoking m.

dinosaur n. dinosaure m.

dint n. by **~ of**, à force de.

diocese n. diocèse m.

dip v.t./i. plonger. —n. (slope) déclivité f.; (in sea) bain rapide m. **~ one's headlights**, se mettre en code.

diphtheria n. diphtérie f.

diphthong n. diphtongue f.

diploma n. diplôme m.

diplomacy n. diplomatie f.

diplomat n. diplomate m./f. **~ic** a. (pol.) diplomatique; (tactful) diplomate.

dire a. affreux; (need, poverty) extrême.

direct a. direct. —adv. directement. —v.t. diriger; (letter, remark) adresser; (a play) mettre en scène. **~ness** n. franchise f.

direction n. direction f.; (theatre) mise en scène f. **~s**, indications f. pl. **ask ~s**, demander le chemin. **~s for use**, mode d'emploi m.

directly adv. directement; (at once) tout de suite. —conj. dès que.

director n. direc|teur, -trice m., f.; (theatre) metteur en scène m.

directory n. (phone book) annuaire m.

dirt n. saleté f.; (earth) terre f.

dirty a. sale; (word) grossier. **get ~**, se salir.

disability n. handicap m.

disabled a. handicapé.

disadvantage n. désavantage m. **~d** a. déshérité.

disagree v.i. ne pas être d'accord (with, avec). **~ with** s.o., (food, climate) ne pas convenir à qn. **~ment** n. désaccord m.; (quarrel) différend m.

disagreeable a. désagréable.

disappear v.i. disparaître. **~ance** n. disparition f.

disappoint v.t. décevoir. **~ing** a. décevant. **~ed** a. déçu. **~ment** n. déception f.

disapprov|e v.i. **~e (of)**, désapprouver. **~al** n. désapprobation f.

disarm v.t./i. désarmer. **~ament** n. désarmement m.

disarray n. désordre m.

disast|er n. désastre m. **~rous** a. désastreux.

disband *v.t./i.* (se) disperser.

disbelief *n.* incrédulité *f.*

disc *n.* disque *m.*; (*comput.*) = **disk.** **~ brake,** frein à disque *m.* **~ jockey,** disc-jockey *m.*

discard *v.t.* se débarrasser de; (*beliefs etc.*) abandonner.

discern *v.t.* discerner. **~ible** *a.* perceptible. **~ing** *a.* perspicace.

discharge[1] *v.t.* (*unload*) décharger; (*liquid*) déverser; (*duty*) remplir; (*dismiss*) renvoyer; (*prisoner*) libérer. —*v.i.* (*of pus*) s'écouler.

discharge[2] *n.* (*med.*) écoulement *m.*; (*dismissal*) renvoi *m.*; (*electr.*) décharge *m.*

disciple *n.* disciple *m.*

disciplin|e *n.* discipline *f.* —*v.t.* discipliner; (*punish*) punir. **~ary** *a.* disciplinaire.

disclaim *v.t.* désavouer. **~er** *n.* correctif *m.*

disclos|e *v.t.* révéler. **~ure** *n.* révélation *f.*

disco *n.* disco *m.*

discomfort *n.* gêne *f.*

disconcert *v.t.* déconcerter.

disconnect *v.t.* détacher; (*unplug*) débrancher; (*cut off*) couper.

discontent *n.* mécontentement *m.* **~ed** *a.* mécontent.

discord *n.* discorde *f.*; (*mus.*) dissonance *f.* **~ant** *a.* discordant.

discothèque *n.* discothèque *f.*

discount[1] *n.* rabais *m.*

discount[2] *v.t.* ne pas tenir compte de.

discourage *v.t.* décourager.

discourse *n.* discours *m.*

discover *v.t.* découvrir. **~y** *n.* découverte *f.*

discredit *v.t.* discréditer. —*n.* discrédit *m.*

discreet *a.* discret. **~ly** *adv.* discrètement.

discrepancy *n.* incohérence *f.*

discretion *n.* discrétion *f.*

discriminat|e *v.t./i.* distinguer. **~e against,** faire de la discrimination contre. **~ing** *a.* (*person*) qui a du discernement. **~ion** *n.* discernement *m.*; (*bias*) discrimination *f.*

discus *n.* disque *m.*

discuss *v.t.* (*talk about*) discuter de; (*argue about, examine critically*) discuter. **~ion** *n.* discussion *f.*

disdain *n.* dédain *m.*

disease *n.* maladie *f.* **~d** *a.* malade.

disembark *v.t./i.* débarquer.

disengage *v.t.* dégager; (*mil.*) retirer. —*v.i.* (*mil.*) retirer; (*auto.*) débrayer. **~ment** *n.* dégagement *m.*

disentangle *v.t.* démêler.

disfavour *n.* défaveur *f.*

disfigure *v.t.* défigurer.

disgrace *n.* (*shame*) honte *f.*; (*disfavour*) disgrâce *f.* —*v.t.* déshonorer. **~ful** *a.* honteux.

disgruntled *a.* mécontent.

disguise *v.t.* déguiser. —*n.* déguisement *m.* **in ~,** déguisé.

disgust *n.* dégoût *m.* —*v.t.* dégoûter. **~ing** *a.* dégoûtant.

dish *n.* plat *m.* —*v.t.* **~ out,** (*fam.*) distribuer. **the ~es,** (*crockery*) la vaisselle.

dishcloth *n.* lavette *f.*; (*for drying*) torchon *m.*

dishonest *a.* malhonnête. **~y** *n.* malhonnêteté *f.*

dishonour *n.* déshonneur *m.* —*v.t.* déshonorer. **~able** *a.* déshonorant.

dishwasher *n.* lave-vaisselle *m.* invar.

disillusion *v.t.* désillusionner. **~ment** *n.* désillusion *f.*

disincentive *n.* be a ∼ to, décourager.

disinclined *a.* ∼ to, peu disposé à.

disinfect *v.t.* désinfecter. ∼ant *n.* désinfectant *m.*

disinherit *v.t.* déshériter.

disintegrate *v.t./i.* (se) désintégrer.

disinterested *a.* désintéressé.

disjointed *a.* (*talk*) décousu.

disk *n.* (*Amer.*) = **disc**; (*comput.*) disque *m.* ∼ **drive**, drive *m.*, lecteur de disquettes *m.*

diskette *n.* disquette *f.*

dislike *n.* aversion *f.* —*v.t.* ne pas aimer.

dislocate *v.t.* (*limb*) disloquer.

dislodge *v.t.* (*move*) déplacer; (*drive out*) déloger.

disloyal *a.* déloyal. ∼**ty** *f.* déloyauté *f.*

dismal *a.* morne, triste.

dismantle *v.t.* démonter, défaire.

dismay *n.* consternation *f.* —*v.t.* consterner.

dismiss *v.t.* renvoyer; (*appeal*) rejeter; (*from mind*) écarter. ∼**al** *n.* renvoi *m.*

dismount *v.i.* descendre.

disobedien|t *a.* désobéissant. ∼**ce** *n.* désobéissance *f.*

disobey *v.t.* désobéir à —*v.i.* désobéir.

disorder *n.* désordre *m.*; (*ailment*) trouble(s) *m.* (*pl.*). ∼**ly** *a.* désordonné.

disorganize *v.t.* désorganiser.

disorientate *v.t.* désorienter.

disparaging *a.* désobligeant.

disparity *n.* disparité *f.*, écart *m.*

dispatch *v.t.* (*send, complete*) expédier; (*troops*) envoyer. —*n.* expédition *f.*; envoi *m.*; (*report*) dépêche *f.*

dispel *v.t.* dissiper.

dispense *v.t.* distribuer; (*medicine*) préparer. —*v.i.* ∼ **with**, se passer de. ∼**r** *n.* (*container*) distributeur *m.*

dispers|e *v.t./i.* (se) disperser. ∼**al** *n.* dispersion *f.*

dispirited *a.* abattu.

displace *v.t.* déplacer.

display *v.t.* montrer, exposer; (*feelings*) manifester. —*n.* exposition *f.*; manifestation *f.*; (*comm.*) étalage *m.*; (*of computer*) visuel *m.*

disposable *a.* à jeter.

dispos|e *v.t.* disposer. —*v.i.* ∼**e of**, se débarrasser de. ∼**al** *n.* (*of waste*) évacuation *f.* **at s.o.'s** ∼**al**, à la disposition de qn.

disposition *n.* disposition *f.*; (*character*) naturel *m.*

disprove *v.t.* réfuter.

dispute *v.t.* contester. —*n.* discussion *f.*; (*pol.*) conflit *m.* **in** ∼, contesté.

disqualif|y *v.t.* rendre inapte; (*sport*) disqualifier. ∼**y from driving**, retirer le permis à. ∼**ication** *n.* disqualification *f.*

disregard *v.t.* ne pas tenir compte de. —*n.* indifférence *f.* (**for**, à).

disrepair *n.* mauvais état *m.*

disreputable *a.* peu recommendable.

disrespect *n.* manque de respect *m.* ∼**ful** *a.* irrespectueux.

disrupt *v.t.* (*disturb, break up*) perturber; (*plans*) déranger. ∼**ion** *n.* perturbation *f.* ∼**ive** *a.* perturbateur.

dissatisf|ied *a.* mécontent. ∼**action** *n.* mécontentement *m.*

dissect *v.t.* disséquer.

disseminate *v.t.* disséminer.

dissent *v.i.* différer (**from**, de). —*n.* dissentiment *m.*

dissertation *n.* (*univ.*) mémoire *m.*

disservice *n.* mauvais service *m.*

dissident *a.* & *n.* dissident(e) (*m.* (*f.*)).

dissimilar *a.* dissemblable, différent.

dissipate *v.t./i.* (se) dissiper; (*efforts*) gaspiller.

dissociate *v.t.* dissocier. **∼ o.s. from,** se désolidariser de.

dissolute *a.* dissolu.

dissolve *v.t./i.* (se) dissoudre.

dissuade *v.t.* dissuader.

distance *n.* distance *f.* **from a ∼,** de loin. **in the ∼,** au loin.

distant *a.* éloigné, lointain; (*relative*) éloigné; (*aloof*) distant.

distaste *n.* dégoût *m.* **∼ful** *a.* désagréable.

distemper *n.* (*paint*) badigeon *m.*; (*animal disease*) maladie *f.* —*v.t.* badigeonner.

distend *v.t./i.* (se) distendre.

distil *v.t.* distiller. **∼lation** *n.* distillation *f.*

distillery *n.* distillerie *f.*

distinct *a.* distinct; (*marked*) net. **as ∼ from,** par opposition à. **∼ion** *n.* distinction *f.* **∼ive** *a.* distinctif. **∼ly** *adv.* (*see*) distinctement; (*forbid*) expressément; (*markedly*) nettement.

distinguish *v.t./i.* distinguer. **∼ed** *a.* distingué.

distort *v.t.* déformer. **∼ion** *n.* distorsion *f.*; (*of facts*) déformation *f.*

distract *v.t.* distraire. **∼ed** *a.* (*distraught*) éperdu. **∼ing** *a.* gênant. **∼ion** *n.* distraction *f.*

distraught *a.* éperdu.

distress *n.* douleur *f.*; (*poverty, danger*) détresse *f.* —*v.t.* peiner. **∼ing** *a.* pénible.

distribut|**e** *v.t.* distribuer. **∼ion** *n.* distribution *f.* **∼or** *n.* distributeur *m.*

district *n.* région *f.*; (*of town*) quartier *m.*

distrust *n.* méfiance *f.* —*v.t.* se méfier de.

disturb *v.t.* déranger; (*alarm, worry*) troubler. **∼ance** *n.* dérangement *m.* (**of,** de); (*noise*) tapage *m.* **∼ed** *a.* troublé; (*psychologically*) perturbé. **∼ing** *a.* troublant.

disused *a.* désaffecté.

ditch *n.* fossé *m.* —*v.t.* (*sl.*) abandonner.

dither *v.i.* hésiter.

ditto *adv.* idem.

divan *n.* divan *m.*

div|**e** *v.i.* plonger; (*rush*) se précipiter. —*n.* plongeon *m.*; (*of plane*) piqué *m.*; (*place:* *sl.*) bouge *m.* **∼er** *n.* plongeur, -se *m.*, *f.* **∼ing-board** *n.* plongeoir *m.*

diverge *v.i.* diverger.

diverse *a.* divers.

diversify *v.t.* diversifier.

diversity *n.* diversité *f.*

diver|**t** *v.t.* détourner; (*traffic*) dévier. **∼sion** *n.* (*of traffic*) déviation *f.*

divide *v.t./i.* (se) diviser.

dividend *n.* dividende *m.*

division *n.* division *f.*

divorce *n.* divorce *m.* (**from,** d'avec). —*v.t./i.* divorcer (d'avec). **∼d** *a.* divorcé.

divorcee *n.* divorcé(e) *m.* (*f.*).

DIY *abbr. see* **do-it-yourself.**

dizz|**y** *a.* (**-ier, -iest**) vertigineux. **be or feel ∼y,** avoir le vertige. **∼iness** *n.* vertige *m.*

do *v.t./i.* faire; (*progress, be suitable*) aller; (*be enough*) suffire; (*swindle: sl.*) avoir. **do well/badly,** se débrouiller bien/mal. **do the house,** peindre ou nettoyer *etc.* la maison. **well done!,** bravo! **well done,** (*culin.*) bien cuit. —*v. aux.* **do you see?,** voyez-vous? **do you live here?—I do,** est-ce que vous habitez ici?—oui. **I do live here,** si, j'habite ici. **I do not smoke,** je ne fume pas. **don't you?, doesn't he?,** *etc.*, n'est-ce pas? —*n.* (*pl.* **dos** *or* **do's**) soirée *f.*; fête *f.* **do-it-yourself** *n.* bricolage *m.* **do up,** (*fasten*) fermer; (*house*) refaire. **it's to ~ with the house,** c'est à propos de la maison. **it's nothing to do with me,** ça n'a rien à voir avec moi. **I could do with a holiday,** j'aurais bien besoin de vacances. **~ without,** se passer de.

docile *a.* docile.

dock[1] *n.* dock *m.* —*v.t./i.* (se) mettre à quai. **~er** *n.* docker *m.*

dock[2] *n.* (*jurid.*) banc des accusés *m.*

dock[3] *v.t.* (*money*) retrancher.

doctor *n.* médecin *m.*, docteur *m.*; (*univ.*) docteur *m.*

doctrine *n.* doctrine *f.*

document *n.* document *m.* **~ary** *a.* & *n.* documentaire (*m.*). **~ation** *n.* documentation *f.*

dodge *v.t.* esquiver. —*v.i.* faire un saut de côté. —*n.* (*fam.*) truc *m.*

dodgems *n. pl.* autos tamponneuses *f. pl.*

dodgy *a.* (*fam.:* *difficult*) épineux, délicat; (*dangerous*) douteux.

doe *n.* (*deer*) biche *f.*

dog *n.* chien *m.* —*v.t.* poursuivre. *n.*

dogged *a.* obstiné.

doings *n. pl.* (*fam.*) activités *f. pl.*, occupations *f. pl.*

dole *v.t.* **~ out,** distribuer. —*n.* (*fam.*) indemnité de chômage *f.* **on the ~,** (*fam.*) au chômage.

doll *n.* poupée *f.* —*v.t.* **~ up,** (*fam.*) bichonner.

dollar *n.* dollar *m.*

dollop *n.* (*of food etc.:* *fam.*) gros morceau *m.*

dolphin *n.* dauphin *m.*

domain *n.* domaine *m.*

dome *n.* dôme *m.*

domestic *a.* familial; (*trade, flights, etc.*) intérieur; (*animal*) domestique.

dominant *a.* dominant.

dominate *v.t./i.* dominer. **~ion** *n.* domination *f.*

domineering *a.* autoritaire.

domino *n.* dominos *m. pl.*

donate *v.t.* faire don de. **~ion** *n.* don *m.*

donkey *n.* âne *m.*

donor *n.* dona|teur, -trice *m.*, *f.*; (*of blood*) donneu|r, -se *m.*, *f.*

doodle *v.i.* griffonner.

doom *n.* (*ruin*) ruine *f.*; (*fate*) destin *m.* —*v.t.* **be ~ed to,** être destiné *or* condamné à. **~ed (to failure),** voué à l'échec.

door *n.* porte *f.*; (*of vehicle*) portière *f.*, porte *f.*

doorbell *n.* sonnette *f.*

doorman *n.* portier *m.*

doormat *n.* paillasson *m.*

doorstep *n.* seuil *m.*

doorway *n.* porte *f.*

dope *n.* (*fam.*) drogue *f.*; (*idiot:* *sl.*) imbécile *m./f.* —*v.t.* doper. **~y** *a.* (*foolish:* *sl.*) imbécile.

dormant *a.* en sommeil.

dormitory *n.* dortoir *m.*; (*univ.*, *Amer.*) résidence *f.*

dormouse *n.* loir *m.*

dos|e *n.* dose *f.* **~age** *n.* dose *f.*; (*on label*) posologie *f.*

doss *v.i.* (*sl.*) roupiller. **~-house** *n.* asile de nuit *m.*

dossier *n.* dossier *m.*

dot *n.* point *m.* **on the ~,** (*fam.*) à l'heure pile. **~-matrix** *a.* (*printer*) matriciel.

dotted *a.* (*fabric*) à pois. **~ line,** ligne en pointillés *f.* **~ with,** parsemé de.

double *a.* double; (*room, bed*) pour deux personnes. —*adv.* deux fois.

—n. double m.; (stuntman)
doublure f. ~,s, (tennis) double m.
—v.t./i. doubler; (fold) plier en
deux. ~ **the size,** deux fois plus
grand: **pay** ~, payer le double.
~**-bass** n. (mus.) contrebasse f.
~**-breasted** a. croisé. ~**-check**
v.t. revérifier. ~**-cross** v.t.
tromper. ~**-dealing** n. double jeu
m. ~**-decker** n. autobus m.
à impériale m.

doubly adv. doublement.

doubt n. doute m. —v.t. douter de.
~ **if** or **that,** douter que. ~**ful** a.
incertain, douteux; (person) qui a
des doutes.

dough n. pâte f.; (money: sl.) fric m.

doughnut n. beignet m.

douse v.t. arroser; (light, fire)
éteindre.

dove n. colombe f.

Dover n. Douvres m./f.

dovetail v.t./i. (s')ajuster.

dowdy a. (clothes) sans chic,
monotone.

down[1] n. (fluff) duvet m.

down[2] adv. en bas; (of sun) couché;
(lower) plus bas. —prep. en bas
de; (along) le long de. —v.t. (knock
down, shoot down) abattre;
(drink) vider. **come** or **go** ~,
descendre. **go** ~ **to the post
office,** aller à la poste. ~**-
hearted** a. découragé. ~ **payment,** acompte m. ~**-to-earth** a.
terre-à-terre invar.

downcast a. démoralisé.

downfall n. chute f.

downgrade v.t. déclasser.

downhill adv. **go** ~, descendre;
(pej.) baisser.

downpour n. grosse averse f.

downright a. (utter) véritable;
(honest) franc. —adv. carrément.

downstairs adv. en bas. —a. d'en
bas.

downstream adv. en aval.

downtown a. (Amer.) du centre de
la ville. ~ **Boston**/etc., le centre
de Boston/etc.

downward a. & adv. ~**s** adv. vers
le bas.

doze v.i. sommeiller. ~ **off,**
s'assoupir. —n. somme m.

dozen n. douzaine f. **a** ~ **eggs,** une
douzaine d'œufs. ~**s of,** (fam.)
des dizaines de.

drab a. terne.

draft[1] n. (outline) brouillon m.;
(comm.) traite f. —v.t. faire le
brouillon de; (draw up) rédiger.
the ~, (mil., Amer.) la conscription. **a** ~ **treaty,** un projet de
traité.

draft[2] n. (Amer.) = **draught.**

drag v.t./i. traîner; (river)
draguer; (pull away) arracher.
—n. (task: fam.) corvée f.;
(person: fam.) raseu|r, -se m., f.

dragon n. dragon m.

dragon-fly n. libellule f.

drain v.t. (land) drainer;
(vegetables) égoutter; (tank,
glass) vider; (use up) épuiser. ~
(off), (liquid) faire écouler. —v.i.
~ (off), (of liquid) s'écouler. —n.
(sewer) égout m. ~**-(pipe),** tuyau
d'écoulement m.

drama n. art dramatique m.,
théâtre m.; (play, event) drame m.
~**tic** a. (situation) dramatique;
(increase) spectaculaire.

drape v.t. draper. ~**s** n. pl. (Amer.)
rideaux m. pl.

drastic a. sévère.

draught n. courant d'air m. ~**s,**
(game) dames f. pl. ~ **beer,** bière
(à la) pression f. ~**y** a. plein de
courants d'air.

draughtsman n. dessina|teur,
-trice industriel(le) m., f.

draw v.t. passer; (picture)
dessiner; (line) tracer. —v.i. dessiner; (sport) faire match nul;

(*come, move*) venir. —*n.* (*sport*)
match nul *m.*; (*in lottery*) tirage au
sort *m.* ~ **up** *v.i.* (*stop*) s'arrêter;
v.t. (*document*) dresser; (*chair*)
approcher.

drawback *n.* inconvénient *m.*

drawer *n.* tiroir *m.*

drawing *n.* dessin *m.* ~-**board** *n.*
planche *f.* dessin *f.* ~-**pin** *n.*
punaise *f.* ~-**room** *n.* salon *m.*

drawl *n.* voix traînante *f.*

dread *n.* terreur *f.*, crainte *f.* —*v.t.*
redouter.

dreadful *a.* épouvantable, affreux.
~**ly** *adv.* terriblement.

dream *n.* rêve *m.* —*v.t./i.* rêver. ~
up, imaginer. ~**er** *n.* rêveu|r, -se
m., f.

drear|y *a.* triste; (*boring*)
monotone. ~**iness** *n.* tristesse *f.*,
monotonie *f.*

dredge *n.* drague *f.* —*v.t./i.*
draguer. ~**r** *n.* dragueur *m.*

dregs *n. pl.* lie *f.*

drench *v.t.* tremper.

dress *n.* robe *f.*; (*clothing*) tenue *f.*
—*v.t./i.* (s')habiller; (*food*) assaisonner; (*wound*) panser. ~
circle, premier balcon *m.* ~ **up**
as, se déguiser en. **get** ~**ed**,
s'habiller.

dresser *n.* buffet *m.*; (*actor's*)
habilleu|r, -se *m., f.*

dressing *n.* (*sauce*) assaisonnement *m.*; (*bandage*) pansement *m.*
~-**gown** *n.* robe de chambre *f.* ~-
room *n.* (*sport*) vestiaire *m.*;
(*theatre*) loge *f.* ~-**table** *n.*
coiffeuse *f.*

dressmaker *n.* couturière *f.*

dribble *v.i.* couler goutte à goutte;
(*person*) baver.

dried *a.* (*fruit etc.*) sec.

drier *n.* séchoir *m.*

drift *v.i.* aller à la dérive; (*pile up*)
s'amonceler. —*n.* dérive *f.*; amon-
cellement *m.*; (*of events*) tournure

f.; (*meaning*) sens *m.* ~ **towards**,
glisser vers. ~**er** *n.* personne
sans but dans la vie *f.*

drill *n.* (*tool*) perceuse *f.*; (*for
teeth*) roulette *f.*; (*training*) exercice *m.*; (*procedure: fam.*) marche
à suivre *f.* (*pneumatic*) ~,
marteau piqueur *m.* —*v.t.* percer;
(*train*) entraîner. —*v.i.* être à
l'exercice.

drily *adv.* sèchement.

drink *v.t./i.* boire. —*n.* (*liquid*)
boisson *f.*; (*glass of alcohol*) verre
m. **a** ~ **of water**, un verre d'eau.
~**er** *n.* buveu|r, -se *m., f.* ~**ing**
water, eau potable *f.*

drip *v.i.* (dé)goutter. (*washing*)
s'égoutter. —*n.* goutte *f.*; (*person:
sl.*) lavette *f.* ~-**dry** *v.t.* laisser
égoutter; *a.* sans repassage.

dripping *n.* graisse de rôti *f.*

drive *v.t.* chasser, pousser;
(*vehicle*) conduire; (*machine*) actionner. —*v.i.* conduire. —*n.*
promenade en voiture *f.*; (*private
road*) allée *f.*; (*fig.*) énergie *f.*;
(*psych.*) instinct *m.*; (*pol.*) campagne *f.*; (*auto.*) traction; (*golf,
comput.*) drive *m.* ~ **at**, en venir
à. ~ **away**, (*of car*) partir. ~
mad, rendre fou. **left-hand** ~,
conduite à gauche *f.*

drivel *n.* radotage *m.*

driver *n.* conduc|teur, -trice *m., f.*,
chauffeur *m.*

driving *n.* conduite *f.* ~ **licence**,
permis de conduire *m.*

drizzle *n.* bruine *f.* —*v.i.* bruiner.

dromedary *n.* dromadaire *m.*

drone *n.* (*noise*) bourdonnement
m.; (*bee*) faux bourdon *m.* —*v.i.*
bourdonner; (*fig.*) parler d'une
voix monotone.

drool *v.i.* baver (**over**, sur).

droop *v.i.* pencher, tomber.

drop *n.* goutte *f.*; (*fall, lowering*)
chute *f.* —*v.t./i.* (laisser) tomber;

(*decrease, lower*) baisser. **~ (off),** (*person from car*) déposer. **~ in,** passer (**on, chez**). **~ off,** (*doze*) s'assoupir.

droppings n. pl. crottes f. pl.

drought n. sécheresse f.

droves n. pl. foule(s) f. (pl.).

drown v.t./i. (se) noyer.

drowsy a. somnolent. **be or feel ~,** avoir envie de dormir.

drudge n. esclave du travail m. **~ry** n. travail pénible et ingrat m.

drug n. drogue f.; (*med.*) médicament m. —v.t. droguer. **~ addict,** drogué(e) m. (f.).

drugstore n. (*Amer.*) drug-store(ne) m. (f.).

drum n. tambour m.; (*for oil*) bidon m. **~s,** batterie f. —v.t. **into s.o.,** répéter sans cesse à qn. **~ up,** (*support*) susciter; (*business*) créer. **~mer** n. tambour m.; (*in pop group*) batteur m.

drumstick n. baguette de tambour f.; (*of chicken*) pilon m.

drunk —a. ivre. **get ~,** s'enivrer. —n. (*d.*) (day).

dry a. sec; (*day*) sans pluie. —v.t./i. (faire) sécher. **~-clean** v.t. nettoyer à sec. **~-cleaner** n. teinturier m. **~ up,** (*dry dishes*) essuyer la vaisselle; (*of supplies*) (se) tarir; (*be silent: fam.*) se taire. **~ness** n. sécheresse f.

dual a. double. **~ carriageway,** route à quatre voies f.

dub v.t. (*film*) doubler; (*nickname*) surnommer.

dubious a. (*pej.*) douteux. **be ~ about sth.,** (*person*) avoir des doutes sur qch.

duchess n. duchesse f.

duck n. canard m. —v.i. se baisser subitement. —v.t. (*head*) baisser; (*person*) plonger dans l'eau.

duct n. conduit m.

dud a. (*tool etc.: sl.*) mal fichu; (*coin: sl.*) faux; (*cheque: sl.*) provision.

due a. (*owing*) dû; (*expected*) attendu; (*proper*) qui convient. —adv. **~ east/etc.,** droit vers l'est/etc. —n. dû m. **~s,** droits m. pl.; (*of club*) cotisation f. **~ to,** à cause de; (*caused by*) dû à. **she's ~ to leave now,** c'est prévu qu'elle parte maintenant.

duel n. duel m.

duet n. duo m.

duffle a. **~ bag,** sac de marin m. **~ coat,** duffel-coat m.

duke n. duc m.

dull a. ennuyeux; (*colour*) terne; (*weather*) morne; (*sound*) sourd; (*stupid*) bête; (*blunt*) émoussé. —v.t. (*pain*) amortir; (*mind*) engourdir.

dumb a. muet; (*stupid: fam.*) bête.

dumbfound v.t. sidérer.

dummy n. (*comm.*) article factice m.; (*of tailor*) mannequin m.; (*of baby*) sucette f. —a. factice.

dump v.t. déposer; (*abandon: fam.*) se débarrasser de; (*comm.*) dumper. —n. tas d'ordures m.; (*refuse tip*) décharge f.; (*mil.*) dépôt m.; (*dull place: fam.*) trou m.

dumpling n. boulette de pâte f.

dumpy a. boulot.

dunce n. cancre m., âne m.

dune n. dune f.

dung n. (*excrement*) bouse f., crotte f.; (*manure*) fumier m.

dungarees n. pl. salopette f.

dungeon n. cachot m.

dunk v.t. tremper.

dupe v.t. duper. —n. dupe f.

duplex n. duplex m.

duplicate[1] n. double m.

duplicat|e[2] v.t. faire un double de; (*on machine*) polycopier. **~or** n. duplicateur m.

duplicity n. duplicité f.

durable *a.* (*tough*) résistant; (*enduring*) durable.

duration *n.* durée *f.*

during *prep.* pendant.

dusk *n.* crépuscule *m.*

dusky *a.* foncé.

dust *n.* poussière *f.* —*v.t.* épousseter; (*sprinkle*) saupoudrer (with, de).

dustbin *n.* poubelle *f.*

duster *n.* chiffon *m.*

dustman *n.* éboueur *m.*

dustpan *n.* pelle à poussière *f.*

dusty *a.* poussiéreux.

Dutch *a.* hollandais. —*n.* (*lang.*) hollandais *m.* **~man** *n.* Hollandais *m.* **~woman** *n.* Hollandaise *f.*

dutiful *a.* obéissant.

dut|**y** *n.* devoir *m.*; (*tax*) droit *m.* **~y-free** *a.* hors-taxe. **on ~y,** de service.

duvet *n.* couette *f.*

dwarf *n.* nain(e) *m.* (*f.*).

dwell *v.i.* demeurer. **~ on,** s'étendre sur.

dwindle *v.i.* diminuer.

dye *v.t.* teindre. —*n.* teinture *f.*

dying *a.* mourant; (*art*) qui se perd.

dynamic *a.* dynamique.

dynamism *n.* dynamisme *m.*

dynamite *n.* dynamite *f.*

dynamo *n.* dynamo *f.*

dynasty *n.* dynastie *f.*

dysentery *n.* dysenterie *f.*

dyslexi|**a** *n.* dyslexie *f.* **~c** *a.* & *n.* dyslexique (*m.*/*f.*).

E

each *a.* chaque. —*pron.* chacun(e). **~ one,** chacun(e). **~ other,** l'un(e) l'autre, les un(e)s les autres. **know ~ other,** se

connaître. **love ~ other,** s'aimer.

eager *a.* impatient (**to,** de); (*supporter, desire*) ardent. **be ~ to,** (*want*) avoir envie de. **~ly** *adv.* avec impatience *or* ardeur.

eagle *n.* aigle *m.*

ear[1] /ɪə(r)/ *n.* oreille *f.* **~-ring** *n.* boucle d'oreille *f.*

ear[2] *n.* (*of corn*) épi *m.*

earache *n.* mal à l'oreille *m.*, mal d'oreille *m.*

earl *n.* comte *m.*

earlier *a.* (*in series*) précédent; (*in history*) plus ancien, antérieur; (*in future*) plus avancé. —*adv.* précédemment; antérieurement; avant.

early *adv.* tôt, de bonne heure; (*ahead of time*) en avance. —*a.* premier; (*hour*) matinal; (*fruit*) précoce; (*retirement*) anticipé.

earmark *v.t.* destiner, réserver (**for,** à).

earn *v.t.* gagner; (*interest: comm.*) rapporter.

earnest *a.* sérieux. **in ~,** sérieusement.

earnings *n. pl.* salaire *m.*; (*profits*) bénéfices *m. pl.*

earphone *n.* écouteur *m.*

earshot *n.* **within ~,** à portée de voix.

earth *n.* terre *f.* —*v.t.* (*electr.*) mettre à la terre.

earthenware *n.* faïence *f.*

earthquake *n.* tremblement de terre *m.*

earthy *a.* (*of earth*) terreux; (*coarse*) grossier.

earwig *n.* perce-oreille *m.*

ease *n.* aisance *f.*, facilité *f.*; (*comfort*) bien-être *m.* —*v.t./i.* (se) calmer; (*relax*) (se) détendre; (*slow down*) ralentir; (*slide*) glisser. **at ~,** à l'aise; (*mil.*) au repos.

easel n. chevalet m.

east n. est m. —a. d'est. —adv. vers l'est. **the E~,** (Orient) l'Orient m. **~erly** a. d'est. **~ern** a. de l'est, oriental.

Easter n. Pâques f. pl. (or m. sing.). **~ egg,** œuf de Pâques m.

easy a. facile; (relaxed) aisé. **~ chair,** fauteuil m. **easily** adv. facilement.

easygoing a. (with people) accommodant; (relaxed) décontracté.

eat v.t./i. manger. **~ into,** ronger.

eau-de-Cologne n. eau de Cologne f.

eaves n. pl. avant-toit m.

eavesdrop v.i. **~ (on),** écouter en cachette.

ebb n. reflux m. —v.i. refluer; (fig.) décliner.

ebony n. ébène f.

EC abbr. (European Community) CE.

eccentric a. & n. excentrique (m./f.). **~ity** n. excentricité f.

ecclesiastical a. ecclésiastique.

echo n. écho m. —v.t./i. (se) répercuter; (fig.) répéter.

eclipse n. éclipse f. —v.t. éclipser.

ecology n. écologie f. **~ical** a. écologique.

economic a. économique; (profitable) rentable. **~al** a. économique; (person) économe. **~s** n. économie politique f.

economist n. économiste m./f.

econom|y n. économie f. **~ize** v.i. **~ (on),** économiser.

ECU n. ÉCU m.

eczema n. eczéma m.

eddy n. tourbillon m.

edge n. bord m.; (of town) abords m. pl.; (of knife) tranchant m. —v.i. (move) se glisser. **on ~,** énervé.

edgeways adv. de côte. **I can't get**

a word in **~,** je ne peux pas placer un mot.

edgy /'edʒɪ/ a. énervé.

edible a. mangeable; (not poisonous) comestible.

edify v.t. édifier.

edit v.t. (newspaper) diriger; (prepare text of) mettre au point, préparer; (write) rédiger; (cut) couper.

edition n. édition f.

editor n. (writer) rédac|teur, -trice m., f.; (annotator) édi|teur, -trice m., f. the **~ (in chief),** le rédacteur en chef.

educat|e v.t. instruire; (mind, public) éduquer. **~ed** a. instruit. **~ion** n. éducation f.; (schooling) enseignement m.

EEC abbr. (European Economic Community) CEE f.

eel n. anguille f.

effect n. effet m. —v.t. effectuer.

effective a. efficace; (striking) frappant; (actual) effectif.

effervescent a. effervescent.

efficien|t a. efficace; (person) compétent. **~cy** n. efficacité f.; compétence f. **~tly** adv. efficacement.

effort n. effort m. **~less** a. facile.

e.g. abbr. par exemple.

egalitarian a. égalitaire.

egg¹ n. œuf m. **~-cup** n. coquetier m.

egg² v.t. **~ on,** (fam.) inciter.

eggshell n. coquille d'œuf f.

ego n. moi m.

Egypt n. Égypte f. **~ian** a. & n. égyptien(ne) m. (f.)).

eh int. (fam.) hein.

eiderdown n. édredon m.

eight a. & n. huit (m.). **eighth** a. & n. huitième (m./f.).

eighteen a. & n. dix-huit (m.). **~th** a. & n. dix-huitième (m./f.).

eight|y a. & n. quatre-vingts (m.)

~ieth a. & n. quatre-vingtième (m./f.).

either a. & pron. l'un(e) ou l'autre; (with negative) ni l'un(e) ni l'autre; (each) chaque. —adv. non plus. —conj. ~ . . or, ou (bien) . . . ou (bien); (with negative) ni . . . ni.

eject v.t. éjecter.

eke v.t. ~ out, faire durer; (living) gagner difficilement.

elaborate[1] a. compliqué

elaborate[2] v.t. élaborer.

elapse v.i. s'écouler.

elastic a. & n. élastique (m.). ~ band, élastique m.

elated a. fou de joie.

elbow n. coude m.

elder[1] a. & n. aîné(e) (m. (f.)).

elder[2] n. (tree) sureau m.

elderly a. (assez) âgé.

eldest a. & n. aîné(e) (m. (f.)).

elect v.t. élire. —a. (president etc.) futur. ~ion n. élection f.

elector n. élec|teur, -trice m., f. ~al a. électoral.

electric a. électrique. ~ blanket, couverture chauffante f. ~al a. électrique.

electrician n. électricien m.

electricity n. électricité f.

electrify v.t. électrifier; (excite) électriser.

electron n. électron m.

electronic a. électronique. ~s n. électronique f.

elegan|t a. élégant. ~ce n. élégance f.

element n. élément m.; (of heater etc.) résistance f. ~ary a. élémentaire.

elephant n. éléphant m.

elevator n. (Amer.) ascenseur m.

eleven a. & n. onze (m.). ~th a. & n. onzième (m./f.).

elf (pl. elves) lutin m.

elicit v.t. obtenir (**from**, de).

eligible a. be ~ for, avoir droit à.

eliminat|e v.t. éliminer. ~ion n. élimination f.

ellipse n. ellipse f.

elm n. orme m.

elocution n. élocution f.

elongate v.t. allonger.

eloquen|t a. éloquent. ~ce n. éloquence f. ~tly adv. avec éloquence.

else adv. d'autre. **everybody** ~, tous les autres. **nobody** ~, personne d'autre. **nothing** ~, rien d'autre. **or** ~, ou bien. **somewhere** ~, autre part. ~ **where** adv. ailleurs.

elucidate v.t. élucider.

elude v.t. échapper à; (question) éluder.

emaciated a. émacié.

emanate v.i. émaner.

emancipat|e v.t. émanciper. ~ion n. émancipation f.

embalm v.t. embaumer.

embankment n. (of river) quai m.; (of railway) remblai m.

embark v.t./i. (s')embarquer. ~ on, (business etc.) se lancer dans; (journey) commencer.

embarrass v.t. embarrasser, gêner. ~ment n. embarras m.

embassy n. ambassade f.

embed v.t. encastrer.

embellish v.t. embellir. ~ment n. enjolivement m.

embers n. pl. braise f.

embezzle v.t. détourner. ~ment n. détournement de fonds m. ~r n. escroc m.

embod|y v.t. incarner, exprimer; (include) contenir. ~iment n. incarnation f.

emboss v.t. (metal) repousser; (paper) gaufrer.

embrace v.t./i. (s')embrasser. —n. étreinte f.

embroider v.t. broder. ~y n. broderie f.

embroil v.t. mêler (**in**, à).

embryo n. embryon m.

emerald n. émeraude f.

emerge v.i. apparaître. ~**nce** n. apparition f.

emergency n. (crisis) crise f.; (urgent case: med.) urgence f. —a. d'urgence. ~ **exit**, sortie de secours f.

emigrant n. émigrant(e) m. (f.).

emigrat|e v.i. émigrer. ~**ion** n. émigration f.

eminen|t a. éminent. f. ~**tly** adv. éminemment.

emi|t v.t. émettre. ~**ssion** n. émission f.

emotion n. émotion f. ~**al** a. (person, shock) émotif; (speech, scene) émouvant.

emotive a. émotif.

emperor n. empereur m.

emphasis n. (on word) accent m. **lay** ~ **on**, mettre l'accent sur.

emphasize v.t. souligner; (syllable) insister sur.

emphatic a. catégorique; (manner) énergique.

empire n. empire m.

employ v.t. employer. ~**er** n. employeu|r, -se m., f. ~**ment** n. emploi m. ~**ment agency**, agence de placement f.

employee n. employé(e) m. (f.).

empower v.t. autoriser (**to do**, à faire).

empress n. impératrice f.

empt|y a. vide; (promise) vain. —v.t./i. (se) vider.

emulate v.t. imiter.

emulsion n. émulsion f. ~ (**paint**), peinture-émulsion f.

enable v.t. ~ **s.o. to**, permettre à qn. de.

enact v.t. (law) promulguer; (scene) représenter.

enamel n. émail m. —v.t. émailler.

encase v.t. (cover) recouvrir (**in**, de); (enclose) enfermer (**in**, dans).

enchant v.t. enchanter. ~**ing** a. enchanteur.

encircle v.t. encercler.

enclave n. enclave f.

enclose v.t. (land) clôturer; (with letter) joindre. ~**d** a. (space) clos; (market) couvert; (with letter) ci-joint.

enclosure n. enceinte f.; (comm.) pièce jointe f.

encore int. & n. bis (m.).

encounter v.t. rencontrer. —n. rencontre f.

encourage v.t. encourager. ~**ment** n. encouragement m.

encroach v.i. ~ **upon**, empiéter sur.

encumber v.t. encombrer.

encyclopaed|ia, encyclped|ia n. encyclopédie f. ~**ic** a. encyclopédique.

end n. fin f.; (farthest part) bout m. —v.t./i. (se) terminer. ~ **up doing**, finir par faire. **in the** ~, finalement. **put an** ~ **to**, mettre fin à.

endanger v.t. mettre en danger.

endearing a. attachant.

endeavour n. effort m. —v.i. s'efforcer (**to**, de).

ending n. fin f.

endive n. chicorée f.

endless a. interminable; (times) innombrable; (patience) infini.

endorse v.t. (document) endosser; (action) approuver. ~**ment** n. (auto.) contravention f.

endow v.t. doter. ~**ed with**, doté de.

endur|e v.t. supporter. —v.i. durer. ~**able** a. supportable. ~**ance** n. endurance f.

enemy n. & a. ennemi(e) (m. (f.)).

energetic a. énergique.

energy n. énergie f.

enforce v.t. appliquer, faire respecter; (*impose*) imposer (**on**, à). **~d** a. forcé.

engage v.t. engager. —v.i. **~ in**, prendre part à. **~d** a. fiancé; (*busy*) occupé. **~ment** n. fiançailles f. pl.; (*meeting*) rendezvous m.; (*undertaking*) engagement m.

engender v.t. engendrer.

engine n. moteur m.; (*of train*) locomotive f.; (*of ship*) machine f.

engineer n. ingénieur m.; (*appliance repairman*) dépanneur m. —v.t. (*contrive; fam.*) machiner. **~ing** n. (*mechanical*) mécanique f.; (*road-building etc.*) génie m.

England n. Angleterre f.

English a. anglais. —n. (*lang.*) anglais m. **~-speaking** a. anglophone. **the ~**, les Anglais m. pl. **~man** n. Anglais m. **~woman** n. Anglaise f.

engrav|e v.t. graver. **~ing** n. gravure f.

enhance v.t. rehausser; (*price, value*) augmenter.

enigma n. énigme f. **~tic** a. énigmatique.

enjoy v.t. aimer (*doing*, faire); (*benefit from*) jouir de. **~ o.s.**, s'amuser. **~able** a. agréable. **~ment** n. plaisir m.

enlarge v.t./i. (s')agrandir. **~ment** n. agrandissement m.

enlighten v.t. éclairer. **~ment** n. édification f.

enlist v.t. (*person*) recruter; (*fig.*) obtenir. —v.i. s'engager.

enliven v.t. animer.

enmity n. inimitié f.

enormity n. énormité f.

enormous a. énorme. **~ly** adv. énormément.

enough adv. & n. assez. —a. assez de. **~ glasses/time/**etc., assez de

verres/de temps/etc. **have ~ of**, en avoir assez de.

enquir|e v.t./i. demander. **~e about**, se renseigner sur. **~y** n. demande de renseignements f.

enrage v.t. mettre en rage.

enrol v.t./i.(s')inscrire. **~ment** n. inscription f.

ensemble n. (*clothing & mus.*) ensemble m.

enslave v.t. asservir.

ensue v.i. s'ensuivre.

ensure v.t. assurer. **~ that**, (*ascertain*) s'assurer que.

entail v.t. entraîner.

entangle v.t. emmêler.

enter v.t. (*room, club, race, etc.*) entrer dans; (*note down, register*) inscrire; (*data*) entrer, saisir. —v.i. entrer (**into**, dans). **~ for**, s'inscrire à.

enterprise n. entreprise f.; (*boldness*) initiative f.

enterprising a. entreprenant.

entertain v.t. amuser, divertir; (*guests*) recevoir; (*ideas*) considérer. **~er** n. artiste m./f. **~ing** a. divertissant. **~ment** n. amusement m.; divertissement m.; (*performance*) spectacle m.

enthral v.t. captiver.

enthusiasm n. enthousiasme m.

enthusiast n. fervent(e) m. (f.), passionné(e) m. (f.) (**for**, de). **~ic** a. (*supporter*) enthousiaste. **be ~ic about**, être enthousiasmé par. **~ically** adv. adv. avec enthousiasme.

entice v.t. attirer. **~ to do**, entraîner à faire. **~ment** n. (*attraction*) attrait m.

entire a. entier. **~ly** adv. entièrement.

entitle v.t. donner droit à (**to sth.**, à qch.; **to do**, de faire). **~d** a. (*book*) intitulé. **be ~d to sth.**, avoir droit à qch.

entity n. entité f.

entrance[1] n. (*entering, way in*) entrée f. (**to**, de); (*right to enter*) admission f. —a. (*charge, exam*) d'entrée.

entrance[2] v.t. transporter.

entrant n. (*sport*) concurrent(e) m. (f.); (*in exam*) candidat(e) m. (f.).

entrepreneur n. entrepreneur m.

entrust v.t. confier.

entry n. (*entrance*) entrée f.; (*word on list*) mot inscrit m. ~ **form**, feuille d'inscription f.

envelope n. enveloppe f.

enviable a. enviable.

envious a. envieux (**of sth.**, de qch.). ~**of s.o.**, jaloux/de qn. ~**ly** adv. avec envie.

environment n. milieu m.; (*ecological*) environnement m. ~**al** a. du milieu; de l'environnement. ~**alist** n. spécialiste de l'environnement m./f.

envisage v.t. envisager.

envoy n. envoyé(e) m. (f.).

envy n. envie f. —v.t. envier.

enzyme n. enzyme m.

epidemic n. épidémie f.

epilep|sy n. épilepsie f. ~**tic** a. & n. épileptique (m./f.).

episode n. épisode m.

epitom|e n. (*embodiment*) modèle m.; (*summary*) résumé m. ~**ize** v.t. incarner.

epoch n. époque f.

equal a. & n. égal(e) (m.f.). —v.t. égaler. ~ **to**, (*task*) à la hauteur de. ~**ity** n. égalité f. ~**ly** adv. également; (*just as*) tout aussi.

equalize v.t./i. égaliser. ~**r** n. (*goal*) but égalisateur m.

equanimity n. égalité d'humeur f., calme m.

equate v.t. assimiler, égaler (**with**, à).

equation n. équation f.

equator n. équateur m.

equilibrium n. équilibre m.

equinox n. équinoxe m.

equip v.t. équiper (**with**, de). ~**ment** n. équipement m.

equitable a. équitable.

equity n. équité f.

equivalent a. & n. équivalent (m.).

equivocal a. équivoque.

era n. ère f., époque f.

eradicate v.t. supprimer.

erase v.t. effacer. ~**r** n. (*rubber*) gomme f.

erect a. droit. —v.t. ériger. ~**ion** n. érection f.

ermine n. hermine f.

ero|de v.t. ronger. ~**sion** n. érosion f.

erotic a. érotique.

err v.i. (*be mistaken*) se tromper; (*sin*) pécher.

errand n. course f.

erratic a. (*uneven*) irrégulier; (*person*) capricieux.

erroneous a. erroné.

error n. erreur f.

erudit|e a. érudit. ~**ion** n. érudition f.

erupt v.i. (*volcano*) entrer en éruption; (*fig.*) éclater. ~**ion** n. éruption f.

escalat|e v.t./i. (s')intensifier; (*of prices*) monter en flèche. ~**ion** n. escalade f.

escalator n. escalier mécanique m., escalator m.

escape v.i. s'échapper (**from a place**, d'un lieu); (*prisoner*) s'évader. —v.t. échapper à. —n. fuite f., évasion f.; (*of gas etc.*) fuite f. ~ **from s.o.**, échapper à qn.

escort[1] n. (*guard*) escorte f.; (*of lady*) cavalier m.

escort[2] v.t. escorter.

Eskimo n. Esquimau(de) m. (f.).

especial a. particulier. **~ly** adv. particulièrement.

espionage n. espionnage m.

espresso n. (café) express m.

essay n. essai m.; (schol.) rédacton f.; (univ.) dissertation f.

essence n. essence f.; (main point) essentiel m.

essential a. essentiel. —n. pl. the **~s**, l'essentiel m. **~ly** adv. essentiellement.

establish v.t. établir; (business, state) fonder. **~ment** n. établissement m.; fondation f.

estate n. (land) propriété f.; (possessions) biens m. pl.; (inheritance) succession f.; (district) cité f. **~ agent**, agent immobilier m. **~ car**, break m.

esteem v.t. estimer. —n. estime f.

estimate[1] n. (calculation) estimation f.; (comm.) devis m.

estimate[2] v.t. estimer. **~ion** n. jugement m.; (high regard) estime f.

estuary n. estuaire m.

etc. adv. etc.

etching n. eau-forte f.

eternal a. éternel.

eternity n. éternité f.

ether n. éther m.

ethic n. éthique f. **~s**, moralité f. **~al** a. éthique.

ethnic a. ethnique.

etiquette n. étiquette f.

etymology n. étymologie f.

eucalyptus n. eucalyptus m.

eurocheque n. eurochèque m.

Europe n. Europe f. **~an** a. & n. européen(ne) (m. (f.)). **E~an Community**, Communauté Européenne f.

evacuate v.t. évacuer. **~ion** n. évacuation f.

evade v.t. esquiver. **~ tax**, frauder le fisc.

evaluate v.t. évaluer.

evangelist n. évangéliste m.

evaporate v.i. s'évaporer. **~ion** n. évaporation f.

evasion n. fuite f. (of, devant); (excuse) subterfuge m. **tax ~**, fraude fiscale.

eve n. veille f. (of, de).

even a. régulier; (surface) uni; (equal, unvarying) égal; (number) pair. —v.t./i. **~ (out** or **up)**, (s')égaliser. —adv. même. **~ better/etc.**, (still) encore mieux/ etc. **get ~ with**, se venger de.

evening n. soir m.; (whole evening, event) soirée f.

event n. événement m.; (sport) épreuve f.

eventual a. final, définitif. **~ly** adv. en fin de compte; (in future) un jour ou l'autre.

ever adv. jamais; (at all times) toujours. **~ since** prep. & adv. depuis (ce moment-là); conj. depuis que.

evergreen a. à feuilles persistantes. —n. arbre à feuilles persistantes m.

everlasting a. éternel.

every a. chaque. **~ one**, chacun(e).

everybody pron. tout le monde.

everyday a. quotidien.

everyone pron. tout le monde.

everything pron. tout.

everywhere adv. partout.

evict v.t. expulser. **~ion** n. expulsion f.

evidence n. (proof) preuve(s) f. (pl.); (certainty) évidence f.; (signs) signes m. pl.; (testimony) témoignage m. **give ~**, témoigner. **in ~**, en vue.

evident a. évident. **~ly** adv. de toute évidence.

evil a. mauvais. —n. mal m.

evoke v.t. évoquer.

evolution n. évolution f.

evolve v.i. se développer, évoluer. —v.t. développer.

ewe n. brebis f.

ex- pref. ex-, ancien.

exacerbate v.t. exacerber.

exact[1] a. exact. **~ly** adv. exactement.

exact[2] v.t. exiger (**from**, de). **~ing** a. exigeant.

exaggerat|e v.t./i. exagérer. **~ion** n. exagération f.

exalted a. (in rank) de haut rang; (ideal) élevé.

exam n. (fam.) examen m.

examination n. examen m.

examine v.t. examiner; (witness etc.) interroger.

example n. exemple m. **for ~**, par exemple.

exasperat|e v.t. exaspérer. **~ion** n. exaspération f.

excavat|e v.t. creuser; (uncover) déterrer. **~ions** n. pl. (archaeol.) fouilles f. pl.

exceed v.t. dépasser. **~ingly** adv. extrêmement.

excellen|t a. excellent. **~ce** n. excellence f.

except prep. sauf, excepté. —v.t. excepter. **~ for**, à part. **~ing** prep. sauf, excepté.

exception n. exception f.

exceptional a. exceptionnel. **~ly** adv. exceptionnellement.

excerpt n. extrait m.

excess[1] n. excès m.

excess[2] a. excédentaire. **~ fare**, supplément m. **~ luggage**, excédent de bagages m.

excessive a. excessif. **~ly** adv. excessivement.

exchange v.t. échanger. —n. échange m.; (between currencies) change m. **~ rate**, taux

d'échange m. (**telephone**) **~**, central (téléphonique) m.

excit|e v.t. exciter; (enthuse) enthousiasmer. **~able** a. excitable. **~ed** a. excité. **~ement** n. excitation f. **~ing** a. passionnant.

exclaim v.t./i. s'écrier.

exclamation n. exclamation f. **~ mark** or **point** (Amer.), point d'exclamation m.

exclu|de v.t. exclure. **~sion** n. exclusion f.

exclusive a. (rights etc.) exclusif; (club etc.) sélect; (news item) en exclusivité. **~ly** adv. exclusivement.

excruciating a. atroce.

excursion n. excursion f.

excuse[1] v.t. excuser. **~ me!**, excusez-moi; pardon!

excuse[2] n. excuse f.

execute v.t. exécuter.

execution n. exécution f. **~er** n. bourreau m.

executive n. (pouvoir) exécutif m.; (person) cadre m. —a. exécutif.

exemplary a. exemplaire.

exemplify v.t. illustrer.

exempt a. exempt (**from**, de). —v.t. exempter. **~ion** n. exemption f.

exercise n. exercice m. —v.t. exercer; (restraint, patience) faire preuve de. —v.i. prendre de l'exercice. **~ book**, cahier m.

exert v.t. exercer. **~ o.s.**, faire des efforts.' **~ion** n. effort m.

exhaust v.t. épuiser. —n. (auto.) (pot d')échappement m. **~ed** a. épuisé. **~ion** n. épuisement m.

exhibit v.t. exposer; (fig.) faire preuve de. —n. objet exposé m. **~or** n. exposant(e) m. (f.).

exhibition n. exposition f.

exhilarating a. euphorisant.

exile n. exil m.; (person) exilé(e) m. (f.). —v.t. exiler.

exist v.i. exister. ∿ence n. existence f. **be in** ∿ence, exister. ∿ing a. actuel.

exit n. sortie f. —v.t./i. (comput.) sortir (de).

exodus n. exode m.

exonerate v.t. disculper.

exotic a. exotique.

expand v.t./i. (develop) (se) développer; (extend) (s')étendre; (metal, liquid) (se) dilater. ∿sion n. développement m.; dilatation f.

expanse n. étendue f.

expatriate a. & n. expatrié(e) (m. (f.)).

expect v.t. attendre, s'attendre à; (suppose) supposer; (demand) exiger; (baby) attendre. ∿ to do, compter faire. ∿ation n. attente f.

expectant a. ∿ look, air d'attente m. ∿ mother, future maman f.

expedient a. opportun. —n. expédient m.

expedition n. expédition f.

expel v.t. expulser; (from school) renvoyer.

expendable a. remplaçable.

expenditure n. dépense(s) f. (pl.).

expense n. dépense f.; frais m. pl. **at s.o.'s** ∿, aux dépens de qn.

expensive a. cher, coûteux; (tastes, habits) de luxe. ∿ly adv. coûteusement.

experience n. expérience f.; (adventure) aventure f. —v.t. (undergo) connaître; (feel) éprouver. ∿d a. expérimenté.

experiment n. expérience f. —v.i. faire une expérience. ∿al a. expérimental.

expert n. expert(e) m. (f.). —a. expert. ∿ly adv. habilement.

expertise n. compétence f. (in, en).

expire v.i. expirer. ∿ed a. périmé. ∿y n. expiration f.

explain v.t. expliquer. ∿anation n. explication f.

explicit a. explicite.

explode v.t./i. (faire) exploser. ∿sion n. explosion f. ∿sive a. & n. explosif (m.).

exploit[1] n. exploit m.

exploit[2] v.t. exploiter. ∿ation n. exploitation f.

explore v.t. explorer; (fig.) examiner. ∿ation n. exploration f. ∿er n. explora|teur, -trice m., f.

export[1] v.t. exporter. ∿er n. exportateur m.

export[2] n. exportation f.

expose /ık'spəʊz/ v.t. exposer; (disclose) dévoiler. ∿ure n. exposition f.; (photo.) pose f.

express[1] a. formel, exprès; (letter) exprès invar. —adv. (by express post) (par) exprès. —n. (train) rapide m.; (less fast) express m.

express[2] v.t. exprimer. ∿ion n. expression f.

expressway n. voie express f.

expulsion n. expulsion f.; (from school) renvoi m.

extend v.t. (increase) étendre, agrandir; (arm, leg) étendre; (prolong) prolonger; (house) agrandir; (grant) offrir. —v.i. (stretch) s'étendre; (in time) se prolonger. ∿sion n. (of line, road) prolongement m.; (in time) prolongation f.; (building) annexe f.; (of phone) appareil supplémentaire m.; (phone number) poste m.; (cable, hose, etc.) rallonge f.

extensive a. vaste; (study) profond; (damage etc.) important. ∿ly adv. (much) beaucoup; (very) très.

extent n. (size, scope) étendue f.; (degree) mesure f. **to some** ∿, dans une certaine mesure.

exterior *a. & n.* extérieur (*m.*).

exterminate *v.t.* exterminer.

external *a.* extérieur; (*cause, medical use*) externe. **~ly** *adv.* extérieurement.

extinct *a.* (*species*) disparu; (*volcano, passion*) éteint. **~ion** *n.* extinction *f.*

extinguish *v.t.* éteindre. **~er** *n.* extincteur *m.*

extol *v.t.* exalter, chanter les louanges de.

extort *v.t.* extorquer (**from,** à).

extra *a.* de plus, supplémentaire. **—adv.** plus (que d'habitude). **—n.** (*additional thing*) supplément *m.*; (*cinema*) figurant(e) *m. (f.).* **~ charge,** supplément *m.*

extra- *pref.* extra-.

extract[1] *v.t.* extraire; (*promise, tooth*) arracher; (*fig.*) obtenir. **~ion** *n.* extraction *f.*

extract[2] *n.* extrait *m.*

extradite *v.t.* extrader.

extraordinary *a.* extraordinaire.

extravagan|t *a.* extravagant; (*wasteful*) prodigue. **~ce** *n.* extravagance *f.*; prodigalité *f.*

extrem|e *a. & n.* extrême (*m.*). **~ely** *adv.* extrêmement. **~ist** *n.* extrémiste *m./f.*

extremity *n.* extrémité *f.*

extricate *v.t.* dégager.

exuberan|t *a.* exubérant. **~ce** *n.* exubérance *f.*

exude *v.t.* (*charm etc.*) dégager.

exult *v.i.* exulter.

eye *n.* œil *m.* (*pl.* yeux). **—v.t.** regarder. **keep an ~ on,** surveiller. **~-shadow** *n.* ombre à paupières *f.*

eyeball *n.* globe oculaire *m.*

eyebrow *n.* sourcil *m.*

eyeful *n.* **get an ~,** (*fam.*) se rincer l'œil.

eyelash *n.* cil *m.*

eyelid *n.* paupière *f.*

eyesight *n.* vue *f.*

eyesore *n.* horreur *f.*

eyewitness *n.* témoin oculaire *m.*

F

fabric *n.* (*cloth*) tissu *m.*

fabrication *n.* (*invention*) invention *f.*

fabulous *a.* fabuleux; (*marvellous: fam.*) formidable.

façade *n.* façade *f.*

face *n.* visage *m.*, figure *f.*; (*aspect*) face *f.*; (*of clock*) cadran *m.* **—v.t.** être en face de; (*risk*) devoir affronter; (*confront*) faire face à, affronter. **—v.i.** se tourner; (*of house*) être exposé. **~ to face,** face à face. **~ up/down,** tourné vers le haut/bas. **~ up to,** faire face à. **in the ~ of, ~d with,** face à.

facet *n.* facette *f.*

facetious *a.* facétieux.

facial *a.* de la face, facial. **—n.** soin du visage *m.*

facile *a.* facile, superficiel.

facilitate *v.t.* faciliter.

facilit|y *n.* facilité *f.* **~ies,** (*equipment*) équipements *m. pl.*

facing *n.* parement *m.* **—prep.** en face de. **—a.** en face.

facsimile *n.* facsimilé *m.* **~ transmission,** télécopie *m.*

fact *n.* fait *m.* **in ~,** en fait.

faction *n.* faction *f.*

factor *n.* facteur *m.*

factory *n.* usine *f.*

factual *a.* basé sur les faits.

faculty *n.* faculté *f.*

fad *n.* manie *f.*, folie *f.*

fade *v.i.* (*sound*) s'affaiblir; (*memory*) s'évanouir; (*flower*) se faner; (*material*) déteindre; (*colour*) passer.

fag n. (*chore: fam.*) corvée f.; (*cigarette: sl.*) sèche f.

fail v.i. échouer; (*grow weak*) (s'af)faiblir; (*run short*) manquer; (*engine etc.*) tomber en panne. —v.t. (*exam*) échouer à; (*candidate*) refuser, recaler; (*disappoint*) décevoir. **~ to do**, (*not do*) ne pas faire; (*not be able*) ne pas réussir à faire. **without ~**, à coup sûr.

failing n. défaut m. —*prep.* à défaut de.

failure n. échec m.; (*person*) raté(e) m. (f.); (*breakdown*) panne f.

faint a. léger, faible. —v.i. s'évanouir. —n. évanouissement m. **feel ~**, (*ill*) se trouver mal. **~ly** adv. (*weakly*) faiblement; (*slightly*) légèrement.

fair[1] n. foire f. **~-ground** n. champ de foire m.

fair[2] a. (*hair, person*) blond; (*skin etc.*) clair; (*just*) juste, équitable; (*weather*) beau; (*amount, quality*) raisonnable. —*adv.* (*play*) loyalement. **~ly** adv. (*justly*) équitablement; (*rather*) assez. **~ness** n. justice f.

fairy n. fée f. **~ story**, **~-tale** n. conte de fées m.

faith n. foi f.

faithful a. fidèle. **~ly** adv. fidèlement.

fake n. (*forgery*) faux m.; (*person*) imposteur m. —a. faux. —v.t. (*copy*) faire un faux de; (*alter*) falsifier, truquer; (*illness*) simuler.

falcon n. faucon m.

fall v.i. tomber. —n. chute f.; (*autumn: Amer.*) automne m. **~ back on**, se rabattre sur. **~ behind**, prendre du retard. **~ down** or **off**, tomber. **~ off**, (*decrease*) diminuer. **~ out**, se brouiller (**with**, avec). **~-out** n.

retombées f. pl. **~ over**, tomber (par terre). **~ through**, (*plans*) tomber à l'eau.

fallacy n. erreur f.

fallible a. faillible.

false a. faux. **~ly** adv. faussement.

falsetto n. fausset m.

falsify v.t. falsifier.

falter v.i. vaciller; (*nerve*) faire défaut.

fame n. renommée f.

familiar a. familier. **be ~ with**, connaître. **~ity** n. familiarité f. **~ize** v.t. familiariser.

family n. famille f.

famine n. famine f.

famished a. affamé.

famous a. célèbre.

fan[1] n. ventilateur m.; (*hand-held*) éventail m. —v.t. éventer; (*fig.*) attiser. **~ belt**, courroie de ventilateur f.

fan[2] n. (*of person*) fan m./f.; admirateur, -trice m., f.; (*enthusiast*) fervent(e) m. (f.), passionné(e) m. (f.).

fanatic n. fanatique m./f. **~al** a. fanatique.

fanciful a. fantaisiste.

fancy n. (*whim, fantasy*) fantaisie f.; (*liking*) goût m. —a. (*buttons etc.*) fantaisie invar.; (*prices*) extravagant; (*impressive*) impressionnant. —v.t. s'imaginer; (*want: fam.*) avoir envie de; (*like: fam.*) aimer. **~ dress**, déguisement m.

fanfare n. fanfare f.

fang n. (*of dog etc.*) croc m.; (*of snake*) crochet m.

fanlight n. imposte f.

fantastic a. fantastique.

fantasy n. fantaisie f.; (*daydream*) fantasme m.

far adv. loin; (*much*) beaucoup; (*very*) très. —a. lointain; (*end,* *side)* autre. **~ away**, **~ off**, au loin. **as ~ as**, *(up to)* jusqu'à. **~away** *a.* lointain. **by ~**, de loin. **~ from**, loin de. **the Far East**, l'Extrême-Orient *m.* **~-fetched** *a.* bizarre, exagéré.

farce *n.* farce *f.*

fare *n.* (prix du) billet *m.*; *(food)* nourriture *f.* —*v.i. (progress)* aller; *(manage)* se débrouiller.

farewell *int.* & *n.* adieu *(m.).*

farm *n.* ferme *f.* —*v.t.* cultiver. —*v.i.* être fermier. **~ worker**, ouvrier, -ère agricole *m.*, *f.* **~er** *n.* fermier *m.* **~ing** *n.* agriculture *f.*

farmhouse *n.* ferme *f.*

farmyard *n.* basse-cour *f.*

fart *v.i.* péter. —*n.* pet *m.*

farth|er *adv.* plus loin. —*a.* plus éloigné. **~est** *adv.* le plus loin; *a.* le plus éloigné.

fascinat|e *v.t.* fasciner. **~ion** *n.* fascination *f.*

Fascis|t *n.* fasciste *m./f.* **~m** *n.* fascisme *m.*

fashion *n. (current style)* mode *f.*; *(manner)* façon *f.* **~ designer**, styliste *m./f.* **in ~**, à la mode. **out of ~**, démodé.

fast[1] *a.* rapide; *(colour)* grand teint *invar.*, fixe; *(firm)* fixe; solide. —*adv.* vite; *(firmly)* ferme. **be ~**, *(clock etc.)* avancer.

fast[2] *v.i. (go without food)* jeûner. —*n.* jeûne *m.*

fasten *v.t./i.* (s')attacher. **~er** *n.* fermeture *f.*

fastidious *a.* difficile.

fat *n.* graisse *f.*; *(on meat)* gras *m.* —*a.* gros, gras; *(meat)* gras; *(sum, volume, fig.)* gros.

fatal *a.* mortel; *(fateful, disastrous)* fatal. **~ity** *n.* mort *m.* **~ly** *adv.* mortellement.

fate *n. (controlling power)* destin *m.*, sort *m.*; *(one's lot)* sort *m.*

father *n.* père *m.* **~-in-law** *n.* beau-père *m.*

fathom *n.* brasse *f.* —*v.t.* **~ (out)**, comprendre.

fatigue *n.* fatigue *f.* —*v.t.* fatiguer.

fatten *v.t./i.* engraisser. **~ing** *a.* qui fait grossir.

fatty *a.* gras; *(tissue)* adipeux.

fatuous *a.* stupide.

fault *n. (defect, failing)* défaut *m.*; *(blame)* faute *f.*; *(geol.)* faille *f.* **at ~**, fautif. **find ~ with**, critiquer. **~y** *a.* défectueux.

fauna *n.* faune *f.*

favour *n.* faveur *f.* —*v.t.* favoriser; *(support)* être en faveur de; *(prefer)* préférer. **do s.o. a ~**, rendre service à qn. **in ~ of**, pour. **~able** *a.* favorable. **~ably** *adv.* favorablement.

favourite *a.* & *n.* favori(te) *(m. (f.)).*

fawn[1] *n.* faon *m.* —*a.* fauve.

fawn[2] *v.i.* **~ on**, flatter bassement, flagorner.

fax *n.* fax *m.*, télécopie *f.* —*v.t.* faxer, envoyer par télécopie. **~ machine**, télécopieur *m.*

fear *n.* crainte *f.*, peur *f.*; *(fig.)* risque *m.* —*v.t.* craindre. **~ful** *a. (terrible)* affreux; *(timid)* craintif. **~less** *a.* intrépide.

fearsome *a.* redoutable.

feasib|le *a.* faisable; *(likely)* plausible. **~ility** *n.* possibilité *f.*; plausibilité *f.*

feast *n.* festin *m.*; *(relig.)* fête *f.*

feat *n.* exploit *m.*

feather *n.* plume *f.*

feature *n.* caractéristique *f.*; *(of person, face)* trait *m.*; *(film)* long métrage *m.*; *(article)* article vedette *m.* —*v.t.* représenter; *(give prominence to)* mettre en vedette. —*v.i.* figurer **(in**, dans).

February *n.* février *m.*

feckless *a.* inepte.

fed *a.* be ~ up, (*fam.*) en avoir marre (with, de).

federal *a.* fédéral. ~**tion** *n.* fédération *f.*

fee *n.* (*for entrance*) prix *m.* ~(**s**), (*of doctor etc.*) honoraires *m. pl.*; (*of actor, artist*) cachet *m.*; (*for tuition*) frais *m. pl.*; (*for enrolment*) droits *m. pl.*

feeble *a.* faible.

feed *v.t.* (*p.t.* fed) nourrir, donner à manger à; (*suckle*) allaiter; (*supply*) alimenter. —*v.i.* se nourrir (on, de). —*n.* nourriture *f.*; (*of baby*) tétée *f.* ~ **in information**, rentrer des données. ~**er** *n.* alimentation. *f.*

feedback *n.* réaction(s) *f.* (*pl.*); (*med., techn.*) feed-back *m.*

feel *v.t.* (*touch*) tâter; (*be conscious of*) sentir; (*emotion*) ressentir; (*experience*) éprouver; (*think*) estimer. —*v.i.* (*tired, lonely, etc.*) se sentir. ~ hot/thirsty/*etc.*, avoir chaud/ soif/*etc.* ~ as if, avoir l'impression que. ~ awful, (*ill*) se sentir malade. ~ like, (*want: fam.*) avoir envie de.

feeler *n.* antenne *f.* put out a ~, lancer un ballon d'essai.

feeling *n.* sentiment *m.*; (*physical*) sensation *f.*

feign *v.t.* feindre.

feint *n.* feinte *f.*

feline *a.* félin.

fell *v.t.* (*cut down*) abattre.

fellow *n.* compagnon *m.*, camarade *m.*; (*man: fam.*) type *m.* ~**-countryman** *n.* compatriote *m.* ~**-traveller** *n.* compagnon de voyage *m.*

felony *n.* crime *m.*

felt *n.* feutre *m.* ~**-tip** *n.* feutre *m.*

female *a.* (*animal etc.*) femelle; (*voice, sex, etc.*) féminin. —*n.* femme *f.*; (*animal*) femelle *f.*

feminine *a. & n.* féminin (*m.*).

feminist *n.* féministe *m./f.*

fenc|e *n.* barrière *f.*; (*person: jurid.*) receleu|r, -se *m.*, *f.* —*v.t.* ~**e** (**in**), clôturer. —*v.i.* (*sport*) faire de l'escrime. ~**er** *n.* escrimeu|r, -se *m.*, *f.* ~**ing** *n.* escrime *f.*

fend *v.i.* ~ for o.s., se débrouiller tout seul. —*v.t.* ~ off, (*blow, attack*) parer.

fender *n.* (*for fireplace*) garde-feu *m. invar.*; (*mudguard: Amer.*) garde-boue *m. invar.*

fennel *n.* (*culin.*) fenouil *m.*

ferment¹ *v.t./i.* (faire) fermenter. ~**ation** *n.* fermentation *f.*

ferment² *n.* ferment *m.*; (*excitement: fig.*) agitation *f.*

fern *n.* fougère *f.*

feroc|ious *a.* féroce. ~**ity** *n.* férocité *f.*

ferret *n.* (*animal*) furet *m.* —*v.i.* (*p.t.* ferreted) fureter. —*v.t.* ~ **out**, dénicher.

ferry *n.* ferry *m.*, bac *m.* —*v.t.* transporter.

fertil|e *a.* fertile; (*person, animal*) fécond. ~**ity** /fə'tılıtı/ *n.* fertilité *f.*; fécondité *f.*

fertilizer *n.* engrais *m.*

fervent *a.* fervent.

fervour *n.* ferveur *f.*

festival *n.* festival *m.*; (*relig.*) fête *f.*

festiv|e *a.* de fête, gai. ~**ity** *n.* réjouissances *f. pl.*

fetch *v.t.* (*go for*) aller chercher; (*bring person*) amener; (*bring thing*) apporter; (*be sold for*) rapporter.

fête *n.* fête *f.* —*v.t.* fêter.

fetid *a.* fétide.

fetish *n.* (*object*) fétiche *m.*; (*psych.*) obsession *f.*

feud *n.* querelle *f.*

feudal *a.* féodal.

fever *n.* fièvre *f.* ~**ish** *a.* fiévreux.

few a. & n. peu (de). ~ **books,** peu de livres. **a** ~ a. quelques; n. quelques-un(e)s. **quite a** ~, (fam.) bon nombre (de). ~**er** a. & n. moins (de). **be** ~**er,** être moins nombreux (**than,** que). ~**est** a. & n. le moins (de).

fiancé n. fiancé m.

fiancée n. fiancée f.

fiasco n. fiasco m.

fib n. mensonge m. ~**ber** n. menteu|r, -se m., f.

fibre n. fibre f. ~ **optics,** fibres optiques.

fibreglass, n. fibre de verre f.

fickle a. inconstant.

fiction n. fiction f. (**works of**) ~, romans m. pl. ~**al** a. fictif.

fictitious a. fictif.

fiddle n. (fam.) violon m.; (swindle: sl.) combine f. —v.i. (sl.) frauder. —v.t. (sl.) falsifier. ~ **with,** (fam.) tripoter. ~**r** n. (fam.) violoniste m./f.

fidelity n. fidélité f.

fidget v.i. remuer sans cesse. —n. **be a** ~, être remuant. ~ **with,** tripoter. ~**y** a. remuant.

field n. champ m.; (sport) terrain m.; (fig.) domaine m. —v.t. (ball: cricket) bloquer.

fieldwork n. travaux pratiques m. pl.

fiend n. démon m.

fierce a. féroce; (storm, attack) violent. ~**ness** n. férocité f.; violence f.

fiery a. (hot) ardent; (spirited) fougueux.

fiesta n. fiesta f.

fifteen a. & n. quinze (m.). ~**th** a. & n. quinzième (m./f.).

fifth a. & n. cinquième (m./f.).

fift|y a. & n. cinquante (m.). ~**ieth** a. & n. cinquantième (m./f.). **a** ~**y-fifty chance,** (equal) une chance sur deux.

fig n. figue f.

fight v.i. se battre; (struggle: fig.) lutter; (quarrel) se disputer. —v.t. se battre avec; (evil etc.: fig.) lutter contre. —n. (struggle) lutte f.; (quarrel) dispute f.; (brawl) bagarre f.; (mil.) combat m. ~ **over sth.,** se disputer qch. ~**er** n. (brawler, soldier) combattant m.; (fig.) battant m.; (aircraft) chasseur m. ~**ing** n. combats m. pl.

figment n. invention f.

figure n. (number) chiffre m.; (diagram) figure f.; (shape) forme f.; (body) ligne f. —v.t. s'imaginer. —v.i. (appear) figurer. ~ **out,** comprendre.

filament n. filament m.

filch v.t. voler, piquer.

file[1] n. (tool) lime f. —v.t. limer.

file[2] n. dossier m., classeur m.; (comput.) fichier m.; (row) file f. —v.t. (papers) classer; (jurid.) déposer. —v.i. ~ **in,** entrer en file. ~**ing cabinet,** classeur m.

fill v.t./i.(se) remplir. ~ **in** or **up,** (form) remplir. ~ **out,** (get fat) grossir. ~ **up,** (auto.) faire le plein (d'essence).

fillet n. filet m. —v.t. découper en filets.

filling n. (of tooth) plombage m.; (of sandwich) garniture f. ~ **station,** station-service f.

filly n. pouliche f.

film n. film m.; (photo.) pellicule f. —v.t. filmer. ~ **star,** vedette de cinéma f.

filter n. filtre m.; (traffic signal) flèche f. —v.t./i. filtrer; (of traffic) suivre la flèche. ~ **coffee,** café-filtre m. ~**tip** n. bout filtre m.

filth n. saleté f. ~**iness** n. saleté f. ~**y** a. sale.

fin n. (of fish, seal) nageoire f.; (of shark) aileron m.

final a. dernier; (conclusive)

définitif. —*n.* (*sport*) finale *f.*
~**ist** *n.* finaliste *m./f.* ~**ly** *adv.*
(*lastly, at last*) enfin, finalement;
(*once and for all*) définitivement.

finale *n.* (*mus.*) final(e) *m.*

finalize *v.t.* mettre au point.

finance *n.* finance *f.* —*a.* financier.
—*v.t.* financer.

financial *a.* financier. ~**ly** *adv.*
financièrement.

find *v.t.* trouver; (*sth. lost*)
retrouver. —*n.* trouvaille *f.* ~
out *v.t.* découvrir; *v.i.* se renseigner (*about, sur*). ~**ings** *n. pl.*
conclusions *f. pl.*

fine[1] *n.* amende *f.* —*v.t.* condamner à une amende.

fine[2] *a.* fin; (*excellent*) beau. —*adv.*
(*très*) bien; (*small*) fin. ~**ly** *adv.*
(*admirably*) magnifiquement;
(*cut*) fin.

finesse *n.* finesse *f.*

finger *n.* doigt *m.* —*v.t.* palper. ~
nail *n.* ongle *m.*

fingerprint *n.* empreinte digitale
f.

fingertip *n.* bout du doigt *m.*

finish *v.t./i.* finir. —*n.* fin *f.*; (*of
race*) arrivée *f.*; (*appearance*)
finition *f.* ~ **doing,** finir de faire.
~ **up doing,** finir par faire. ~ **up
in,** (*land up in*) se retrouver à.

finite *a.* fini.

Fin|land *n.* finlande *f.* ~**n** *n.*
finlandais(e) *m.* (*f.*). ~**nish** *a.*
finlandais; *n.* (*lang.*) finnois *m.*

fir *n.* sapin *m.*

fire *n.* feu *m.*; (*conflagration*)
incendie *m.*; (*heater*) radiateur *m.*
—*v.t.* (*bullet etc.*) tirer; (*dismiss*)
renvoyer. —*v.i.* tirer (**at,** sur). ~
a gun, tirer un coup de revolver
or de fusil. **set ~ to,** mettre le feu
à. ~ **alarm,** avertisseur
d'incendie *m.* ~ **brigade,** pompiers *m. pl.* ~**-engine** *n.* voiture
de pompiers *f.* ~**-escape** *n.*

escalier de secours *m.* ~ **extinguisher,** extincteur d'incendie
m.

fireman *n.* pompier *m.*

fireplace *n.* cheminée *f.*

firewood *n.* bois de chauffage *m.*

firework *n.* feu d'artifice *m.*

firm[1] *n.* firme *f.*, société *f.*

firm[2] *a.* ferme; (*belief*) solide. ~**ly**
adv. fermement. ~**ness** *n.* fermeté *f.*

first *a.* premier. —*n.* prem|ier,
-ière *m.*, *f.* —*adv.* d'abord,
premièrement; (*arrive etc.*) le
premier, la première. **at ~,**
d'abord. ~ **aid,** premiers soins *m.*
pl. ~**-class** *a.* de première classe.
~ (**gear**), première (vitesse) *f.* ~
name, prénom *m.* ~ **of all,** tout
d'abord. ~**-rate** *a.* de premier
ordre. ~**ly** *adv.* premièrement.

fiscal *a.* fiscal.

fish *n.* (*usually invar.*) poisson *m.*
—*v.i.* pêcher. ~ **for,** (*cod etc.*)
pêcher. ~ **out,** (*from water*)
repêcher; (*take out: fam.*) sortir.
~ **shop,** poissonnerie *f.* ~**ing** *n.*
pêche *f.* **go** ~**ing,** aller à la pêche.
~**ing rod,** canne à pêche *f.*

fisherman *n.* pêcheur *m.*

fishmonger *n.* poisson|ier, -ière
m., *f.*

fission *n.* fission *f.*

fist *n.* poing *m.*

fit[1] *n.* (*bout*) accès *m.*, crise *f.*

fit[2] *a.* en bonne santé; (*proper*)
convenable; (*good enough*) bon;
(*able*) capable. —*v.t./i.* (*clothes*)
aller (à); (*match*) s'accorder
(avec); (*put or go in or on*)
(s')adapter (**to,** à); (*into space*)
aller; (*install*) poser. ~ **in,** *v.t.*
caser; *v.i.* (*newcomer*) s'intégrer.
~ **out,** ~ **up,** équiper. ~**ness** *n.*
santé *f.*

fitful *a.* irrégulier.

fitment *n.* meuble fixe *m.*

fitted a. (*wardrobe*) encastré. **~ carpet**, moquette f.

fitting a. approprié. **~ room**, cabine d'essayage f.

fittings n. pl. (*in house*) installations f. pl.

five a. & n. cinq (m.).

fiver n. (*fam.*) billet de cinq livres m.

fix v.t. (*make firm, attach, decide*) fixer; (*mend*) réparer; (*deal with*) arranger. **~ s.o. up with sth.**, trouver qch. à qn. **~ed** a. fixe.

fixation n. fixation f.

fixture n. (*sport*) match m. **~s**, (*in house*) installations f. pl.

fizz v.i. pétiller. —n. pétillement m. **~y** a. gazeux.

fizzle v.i. **~ out**, (*plan etc.*) finir en queue de poisson.

flab n. (*fam.*) corpulence f. **~by** a. flasque.

flabbergast v.t. sidérer.

flag[1] n. drapeau m.; (*naut.*) pavillon m. **~-pole** n. mât m.

flag[2] v.i. (*weaken*) faiblir; (*sick person*) s'affaiblir; (*droop*) dépérir.

flagrant a. flagrant.

flagstone n. dalle f.

flair n. flair m.

flak n. (*fam.*) critiques f. pl.

flake n. flocon m.; (*of paint, metal*) écaille f. —v.i. s'écailler. **~y** a. (*paint*) écailleux.

flamboyant a. (*colour*) éclatant; (*manner*) extravagant.

flame n. flamme f. —v.i. flamber.

flamingo n. flamant (rose) m.

flammable a. inflammable.

flan n. tarte f.; (*custard tart*) flan m.

flank n. flanc m. —v.t. flanquer.

flannel n. flannelle f.; (*for face*) gant de toilette m.

flannelette n. pilou m.

flap v.i. battre. —v.t. **~ its wings**, battre des ailes. —n. (*of pocket*) rabat m.; (*of table*) abattant m.

flare v.i. **~ up**, s'enflammer, flamber; (*fighting*) éclater; (*person*) s'emporter. —n. flamboiement m.; (*mil.*) fusée éclairante f.; (*in skirt*) évasement m. **~d** a. (*skirt*) évasé.

flash v.i. briller; (*on and off*) clignoter. —v.t. faire briller; (*aim torch*) diriger (**at**, sur); (*flaunt*) étaler. —n. éclair m., éclat m.; (*of news, camera*) flash m. **in a ~**, en un éclair. **~ one's headlights**, faire un appel de phares.

flashback n. retour en arrière m.

flashlight n. (*torch*) lampe électrique f.

flashy a. voyant.

flask n. flacon m.; (*vacuum flask*) thermos m./f. invar. (P.).

flat a. plat; (*tyre*) à plat; (*refusal*) catégorique; (*fare, rate*) fixe. —adv. (*say*) carrément. —n. (*rooms*) appartement m.; (*tyre: fam.*) crevaison f.; (*mus.*) bémol m.

flatten v.t./i. (s')aplatir.

flatter v.t. flatter. **~er** n. flatteu|r, -se m., f. **~ing** a. flatteur. **~y** n. flatterie f.

flatulence n. flatulence f.

flaunt v.t. étaler, afficher.

flavour n. goût m.; (*of ice-cream etc.*) parfum m. —v.t. parfumer, assaisonner. **~ing** n. arôme synthétique m.

flaw n. défaut m. **~ed** a. imparfait. **~less** a. parfait.

flax n. lin m. **~en** a. de lin.

flea n. puce f.

fleck n. petite tache f.

flee v.i. s'enfuir. —v.t. s'enfuir de; (*danger*) fuir.

fleece n. toison f. —v.t. voler.

fleet n. (*naut., aviat.*) flotte f. **a ~ of vehicles**, un parc automobile.

Flemish *a.* flamand. —*n.* (*lang.*) flamand *m.*

flesh *n.* chair *f.*

flex[1] *v.t.* (*knee etc.*) fléchir; (*muscle*) faire jouer.

flex[2] *n.* (*electr.*) fil souple *m.*

flexib|le *a.* flexible. **~ility** *f.* flexibilité *f.*

flick *n.* petit coup *m.* —*v.t.* donner un petit coup à.

flicker *v.i.* vaciller. —*n.* vacillement *m.*; (*light*) lueur *f.*

flies *n. pl.* (*on trousers: fam.*) braguette *f.*

flight *n.* (*of bird, plane, etc.*) vol *m.* **~ of stairs,** escalier *m.*

flimsy *a.* (*pej.*) peu solide.

flinch *v.i.* (*wince*) broncher; (*draw back*) reculer.

fling *v.t.* jeter. —*n.* **have a ~,** faire la fête.

flint *n.* silex *m.*; (*for lighter*) pierre *f.*

flip *v.t.* donner un petit coup à. **~ through,** chiquenaude *f.* **~ through,** feuilleter. **~ flops** *n. pl.* tongs *f. pl.*

flipper *n.* (*of seal etc.*) nageoire *f.*; (*of swimmer*) palme *f.*

flirt *v.i.* flirter. —*n.* flirteu|r, -se *m.*, *f.* **~ation** *f.* flirt *m.*

float *v.t./i.* (faire) flotter. —*n.* flotteur *m.*; (*cart*) char *m.*

flock *n.* (*of sheep etc.*) troupeau *m.*; (*of people*) foule *f.*

flog *v.t.* (*beat*) fouetter; (*sell: sl.*) vendre.

flood *n.* inondation *f.*; (*fig.*) flot *m.* —*v.t.* inonder. —*v.i.* (*building etc.*) être inondé; (*river*) déborder; (*people: fig.*) affluer.

floodlight *n.* projecteur *m.*

floor *n.* sol *m.*, plancher *m.*; (*storey*) étage *m.* —*v.t.* (*knock down*) terrasser.

flop *v.i.* (*drop*) s'affaler; (*fail: sl.*) échouer. —*n.* (*sl.*) échec *m.*, fiasco

m. **~py** *a.* lâche, flasque. **~py (disk),** disquette *f.*

flora *n.* flore *f.*

floral *a.* floral.

florist *n.* fleuriste *m./f.*

flounce *n.* volant *m.*

flounder *v.i.* patauger (avec difficulté).

flour *n.* farine *f.* **~y** *a.* farineux.

flourish *v.i.* prospérer. —*v.t.* brandir. —*n.* geste élégant *m.*; (*curve*) floriture *f.*

flout *v.t.* faire fi de.

flow *v.i.* couler; (*circulate*) circuler; (*traffic*) s'écouler; (*hang loosely*) flotter. —*n.* (*of liquid, traffic*) écoulement *m.*; (*of tide*) flux *m.*; (*of orders, words: fig.*) flot *m.* **~ chart,** organigramme *m.*

flower *n.* fleur *f.* —*v.i.* fleurir. **~-bed** *n.* plate-bande *f.* **~ed** *a.* à fleurs. **~y** *a.* fleuri.

flu *n.* (*fam.*) grippe *f.*

fluctuat|e *v.i.* varier. **~ion** *n.* variation *f.*

flue *n.* (*duct*) tuyau *m.*

fluent *a.* (*style*) aisé. **be ~ (in a language),** parler (une langue) couramment; (*lang.*) avec facilité. **~ly** *adv.* couramment.

fluff *n.* peluche(s) *f.* (*pl.*); (*down*) duvet *m.* **~y** *a.* pelucheux.

fluid *a.* & *n.* fluide (*m.*).

fluke *n.* coup de chance *m.*

fluorescent *a.* fluorescent.

fluoride *n.* (*in toothpaste, water*) fluor *m.*

flurry *n.* (*squall*) rafale *f.*; (*fig.*) agitation *f.*

flush[1] *v.i.* rougir. —*v.t.* nettoyer à grande eau. —*n.* (*blush*) rougeur *f.*; (*fig.*) excitation *f.* —*a.* **~ with,** (*level with*) au ras de. **~ the toilet,** tirer la chasse d'eau.

flush[2] *v.t.* **~ out,** chasser.

fluster *v.t.* énerver.

flute *n.* flûte *f.*

flutter *v.i.* voleter; *(of wings)* battre. —*n.* *(of wings)* battement *m.*; *(fig.)* agitation *f.*; *(bet: fam.)* pari *m.*

fly[1] *n.* mouche *f.*

fly[2] *v.i.* voler; *(of passengers)* voyager en avion; *(of flag)* flotter; *(rush)* filer. —*v.t.* *(aircraft)* piloter; *(passengers, goods)* transporter par avion; *(flag)* arborer. ~ *off* *(of trousers)* braguette *f.* ~ **off,** s'envoler.

flying *a.* *(saucer etc.)* volant. —*n.* *(activity)* aviation *f.*

flyover *n.* *(road)* toboggan *m.*

foal *n.* poulain *m.*

foam *n.* écume *f.*, mousse *f.* —*v.i.* écumer, mousser. ~ **(rubber)** *n.* caoutchouc mousse *m.*

fob *v.t.* ~ **off on (to) s.o.,** *(palm off)* refiler à qn. ~ **s.o. off with,** forcer qn. à se contenter de.

focal *a.* focal.

focus *n.* foyer *m.*; *(fig.)* centre *m.* —*v.t./i.* (faire) converger; *(instrument)* mettre au point; *(with camera)* faire la mise au point **(on,** sur); *(fig.)* (se) concentrer. **be in/out of** ~, être/ne pas être au point.

fodder *n.* fourrage *m.*

foe *n.* ennemi(e) *m.(f.).*

foetus *n.* fœtus *m.*

fog *n.* brouillard *m.* —*v.t./i.* *(window etc.)* (s')embuer. *f.* ~**gy** *a.* brumeux. **it is** ~**gy,** il fait du brouillard.

foil *n.* *(tin foil)* papier d'aluminium *m.*; *(fig.)* repoussoir *m.*

foist *v.t.* imposer **(on,** à).

fold *v.t./i.* (se) plier; *(arms)* croiser; *(fail)* s'effondrer. —*n.* pli *m.* ~**er** *n.* *(file)* chemise *f.*; *(leaflet)* dépliant *m.* ~**ing** *a.* pliant.

foliage *n.* feuillage *m.*

folk *n.* gens *m. pl.* —*a.* folklorique.

folklore *n.* folklore *m.*

follow *v.t./i.* suivre. ~**er** *n.* partisan *m.*

folly *n.* sottise *f.*

fond *a.* *(loving)* affectueux; *(hope)* cher. **be** ~ **of,** aimer.

fondle *v.t.* caresser.

food *n.* nourriture *f.* —*a.* alimentaire. **French** ~, la cuisine française. ~ **processor,** robot (ménager) *m.*

fool *n.* idiot(e) *m.* (*f.*). —*v.t.* duper.

foolish *a.* idiot.

foot *n.* pied *m.*; *(measure)* pied *m.*; *(of stairs, page)* bas *m.* —*v.t.* *(bill)* payer. **on** ~, à pied.

football *n.* *(ball)* ballon *m.*; *(game)* football *m.* ~ **pools,** paris sur les matchs de football *m. pl.* ~**er** *n.* footballeur *m.*

footing *n.* prise *(de pied)* *f.*, équilibre *m.* **on an equal** ~, sur un pied d'égalité.

footpath *n.* sentier *m.*; *(at the side of the road)* chemin *m.*

footprint *n.* empreinte *(de pied)* *f.*

footstep *n.* pas *m.*

for *prep.* pour; *(during)* pendant; *(before)* avant. —*conj.* car. **he has been away** ~, il est absent depuis. **he stopped** ~ **ten minutes,** il s'est arrêté (pendant) dix minutes. **it continues** ~ **ten kilometres,** ça continue pendant dix kilomètres. ~ **ever,** pour toujours. ~ **good,** pour de bon.

forbid *v.t.* interdire, défendre **(s.o. to do,** à qn. de faire). ~ **s.o. sth.,** interdire *or* défendre qch. à qn. **you are** ~**den to leave,** il vous est interdit de partir.

force *n.* force *f.* —*v.t.* forcer. ~ **into,** faire entrer de force. ~ **on,** imposer à. **come into** ~, entrer en vigueur. ~**ful** *a.* énergique.

forcible *a.*, ~**y** *adv.* de force.

ford n. gué m. —v.t. passer à gué.

fore a. antérieur. —n. **to the ~,** en évidence.

foreboding n. pressentiment m.

forecast v.t. (p.t.) prévoir. —n. prévision f.

forecourt n. (of garage) devant m.; (of station) cour f.

forefinger n. index m.

forefront n. premier rang m.

foreground n. premier plan m.

forehead n. front m.

foreign a. étranger; (trade) extérieur; (travel) à l'étranger. **~er** n. étranger, -ère m., f.

foreman n. contremaître m.

forename n. prénom m.

foreplay n. préliminaires m. pl.

forerunner n. précurseur m.

foresee v.t. prévoir. **~able** a. prévisible.

foreshadow v.t. présager.

foresight n. prévoyance f.

forest n. forêt f.

forestall v.t. devancer.

forestry n. sylviculture f.

foretaste n. avant-goût m.

foretell v.t. prédire.

forever adv. toujours.

foreword n. avant-propos m. invar.

forfeit n. (penalty) peine f.; (in game) gage m. —v.t. perdre.

forge[1] v.i. **~ ahead,** avancer.

forge[2] n. forge f. —v.t. (metal, friendship) forger; (copy) contrefaire, falsifier. **~r** n. faussaire m. **~ry** n. faux m., contrefaçon f.

forget v.t./i. oublier. **~-me-not** n. myosotis m. **~ful** a. distrait.

forgive v.t. pardonner (**s.o. for sth.,** qch. à qn.). **~ness** n. pardon m.

forgo v.t. renoncer à.

fork n. fourchette f.; (for digging

etc.) fourche f.; (in road) bifurcation f. —v.i. (road) bifurquer. **~-lift truck,** chariot élévateur m. **~ out,** (sl.) payer.

form n. forme f.; (document) formulaire m.; (schol.) classe f. —v.t./i. (se) former.

formal a. officiel, en bonne et due forme; (person) compassé, cérémonieux; (dress) de cérémonie; (denial, grammar) formel; (language) soutenu. **~ity** n. cérémonial m.; (requirement) formalité f. **~ly** adv. officiellement.

format n. format m. —v.t. (disk) initialiser, formater.

formation n. formation f.

formative a. formateur.

former a. ancien; (first of two) premier. —n. **the ~,** celui-ci, celle-là. **~ly** adv. autrefois.

formidable a. redoutable.

formula n. formule f.

formulate v.t. formuler.

fort n. (mil.) fort m.

forte n. (talent) fort m.

forth adv. en avant. **and so ~,** et ainsi de suite. **go back and ~,** aller et venir.

forthcoming a. à venir, prochain; (sociable: fam.) communicatif.

forthright a. direct.

fortify v.t. fortifier.

fortnight n. quinze jours m. pl. **~ly** a. bimensuel; adv. tous les quinze jours.

fortress n. forteresse f.

fortunate a. heureux. **be ~,** avoir de la chance. **~ly** adv. heureusement.

fortune n. fortune f. **~-teller** n. diseuse de bonne aventure f.

fort[y] a. quarante (m.). **~ieth** a. & n. quarantième (m./f.).

forum n. forum m.

forward a. en avant; (advanced) précoce; (pert) effronté. —n.

sl.) monter un coup contre. **~ of mind**, humeur *f.*

(sport) avant *m.* —*adv.* en avant. —*v.t. (letter)* faire suivre; *(goods)* expédier; *(fig.)* favoriser. **come ~**, se présenter. **go ~**, avancer.

forwards *adv.* en avant.

fossil *n.* & *a.* fossile *(m.).*

foster *v.t. (promote)* encourager; *(child)* élever. **~-child** *n.* enfant adoptif *m.* **~-mother** *n.* mère adoptive *f.*

foul *a. (smell, weather, etc.)* infect; *(place, action)* immonde; *(language)* ordurier; *(football)* faute *f.* —*v.t.* souiller, encrasser. **~ up**, *(sl.)* gâcher.

found *v.t.* fonder. **~ation** *n.* fondation *f.; (basis)* fondement *m.; (make-up)* fond de teint *m.* **~er¹** *n.* fonda|teur, -trice *m.*, *f.*

founder² *v.i.* sombrer.

foundry *n.* fonderie *f.*

fountain *n.* fontaine *f.* **~-pen** *n.* stylo à encre *m.*

four *a.* & *n.* quatre *(m.).* **~th** *a.* & *n.* quatrième *(m./f.).* **~-wheel drive**, quatre roues motrices; *(car)* quatre-quatre *f.*

fourteen *a.* & *n.* quatorze *(m.).* **~th** *a.* & *n.* quatorzième *(m./f.).*

fowl *n.* volaille *f.*

fox *n.* renard *m.* —*v.t. (baffle)* mystifier; *(deceive)* tromper.

foyer *n. (hall)* foyer *m.*

fraction *n.* fraction *f.*

fracture *n.* fracture *f.* —*v.t./i.* (se) fracturer.

fragile *a.* fragile.

fragment *n.* fragment *m.*

fragran|t *a.* parfumé. **~ce** *n.* parfum *m.*

frail *a.* frêle.

frame *n.* charpente *f.; (of picture)* cadre *m.; (of window)* châssis *m.; (of spectacles)* monture *f.* —*v.t.* encadrer; *(fig.)* formuler; *(jurid.,*

framework *n.* structure *f.; (context)* cadre *m.*

franc *n.* franc *m.*

France *n.* France *f.*

franchise *n. (pol.)* droit de vote *m.; (comm.)* franchise *f.*

frank¹ *a.* franc. **~ly** *adv.* franchement. **~ness** *n.* franchise *f.*

frank² *v.t.* affranchir.

frantic *a.* frénétique.

fraud *n. (deception)* fraude *f.; (person)* imposteur *m.* **~ulent** *a.* frauduleux.

fraught *a. (tense)* tendu. **~ with**, chargé de.

fray¹ *n.* rixe *f.*

fray² *v.t./i.* (s')effilocher.

freak *n.* phénomène *m.* —*a.* anormal. **~ish** *a.* anormal.

freckle *n.* tache de rousseur *f.* **~d** *a.* couvert de taches de rousseur.

free *a.* libre; *(gratis)* gratuit; *(lavish)* généreux. —*v.t.* libérer; *(clear)* dégager. **~ enterprise**, la libre entreprise. **~ kick**, coup franc *m.* **~lance** *a.* & *n.* free-lance *(m./f.)*, indépendant(e) *m., f.* **~ (of charge)**, gratuit(ement). **~ly** *adv.* librement.

freedom /ˈfriːdəm/ *n.* liberté *f.*

freeway *n. (Amer.)* autoroute *f.*

freeze *v.t./i.* geler; *(culin.)* (se) congeler; *(wages etc.)* bloquer. —*n.* gel *m.; (wages etc.)* blocage *m.* **~er** *n.* congélateur *m.* **~ing** *a.* glacial.

freight *n.* fret *m.*

French *a.* français. —*n. (lang.)* français *m.* **~ bean**, haricot vert *m.* **~ fries**, frites *f. pl.* **~ window** *n.* porte-fenêtre *f.* **the ~**, les Français *m. pl.* **~man** *n.* Français *m.* **~woman** *n.* Française *f.*

frenz|y *n.* frénésie *f.* **~ied** *a.* frénétique.

frequen|t¹ *a.* fréquent. **~cy** *n.* fréquence *f.* **~tly** *adv.* fréquemment.

frequent² *v.t.* fréquenter.

fresco *n.* fresque *f.*

fresh *a.* frais; (*different, additional*) nouveau; (*cheeky: fam.*) culotté. **~ly** *adv.* nouvellement. **~ness** *n.* fraîcheur *f.*

freshen *v.i.* **~** up, (*person*) se rafraîchir.

fret *v.i.* se tracasser. **~ful** *a.* insatisfait.

friction *n.* friction *f.*

Friday *n.* vendredi *m.*

fridge *n.* frigo *m.*

fried *a.* frit. **~** eggs, œufs sur le plat *m. pl.*

friend *n.* ami(e) *m.* (*f.*). **~ship** *n.* amitié *f.*

friend|ly *a.* amical, gentil. **~iness** *n.* gentillesse *f.*

frieze *n.* frise *f.*

frigate *n.* frégate *f.*

fright *n.* peur *f.*; (*person, thing*) horreur *f.* **~ful** *a.* affreux. **~fully** *adv.* affreusement.

frighten *v.t.* effrayer. **~** off, faire fuir. **~ed** *a.* effrayé. **be ~ed**, avoir peur (**of**, de). **~ing** *a.* effrayant.

frill *n.* (*trimming*) fanfreluche *f.*

fringe *n.* (*edging, hair*) frange *f.*; (*of area*) bordure *f.*; (*of society*) marge *f.* **~ benefits**, avantages sociaux *m. pl.*

frisk *v.t.* (*search*) fouiller.

frisky *a.* frétillant.

fritter¹ *n.* beignet *m.*

fritter² *v.t.* **~** away, gaspiller.

frivol|ous *a.* frivole. **~ity** *n.* frivolité *f.*

frock *n.* robe *f.*

frog *n.* grenouille *f.*

frogman *n.* homme-grenouille *m.*

frolic *v.i.* s'ébattre. —*n.* ébats *m. pl.*

from *prep.* de; (*with time, prices, etc.*) à partir de; (*habit, conviction, etc.*) par; (*according to*) d'après. **take ~ s.o.**, prendre à qn. **take ~ one's pocket**, prendre dans sa poche.

front *n.* (*of car, train, etc.*) avant *m.*; (*of garment, building*) devant *m.*; (*mil., pol.*) front *m.*; (*of book, pamphlet, etc.*) début *m.*; (*appearance: fig.*) façade *f.* —*a.* de devant, avant *invar.*; (*first*) premier. **~ door**, porte d'entrée *f.* **~-wheel drive**, traction avant *f.* **in ~ (of)**, devant.

frontier *n.* frontière *f.*

frost *n.* gel *m.*, gelée *f.*; (*on glass etc.*) givre *m.* —*v.t./i.* (se) givrer.

froth *n.* mousse *f.*, écume *f.* —*v.i.* mousser, écumer. **~y** *a.* mousseux.

frown *v.i.* froncer les sourcils. —*n.* froncement de sourcils *m.*

frozen *a.* congelé.

frugal *a.* (*person*) économe; (*meal, life*) frugal. **~ly** *adv.* (*live*) simplement.

fruit *n.* fruit *m.*; (*collectively*) fruits *m. pl.* **~ machine**, machine à sous *f.* **~ salad**, salade de fruits *f.* **~y** *a.* (*taste*) fruité.

fruit|ful *a.* (*discussions*) fructueux. **~less** *a.* stérile.

frustrat|e *v.t.* (*plan*) faire échouer; (*person: psych.*) frustrer; (*upset: fam.*) exaspérer. **~ion** *n.* (*psych.*) frustration *f.*; (*disappointment*) déception *f.*

fry *v.t./i.* (faire) frire. **~ing-pan** *n.* poêle (à frire) *f.*

fudge *n.* (sorte de) caramel mou *m.* —*v.t.* se dérober à.

fuel *n.* combustible *m.*; (*for car engine*) carburant *m.* —*v.t.* alimenter en combustible.

fugitive *n.* & *a.* fugitif, -ve (*m.*, *f.*).

fugue *n.* (*mus.*) fugue *f.*

fulfil v.t. accomplir, réaliser; (condition) remplir. ∼ o.s., s'épanouir. ∼ment n. réalisation f.; épanouissement m.

full a. plein (of, de); (bus, hotel) complet; (name) complet; (skirt) ample. —n. **in** ∼, intégral(ement). ∼ **back**, (sport) arrière m. ∼ **moon**, pleine lune f. ∼**scale** a. (drawing etc.) grandeur nature invar.; (fig.) de grande envergure. **at** ∼ **speed**, à toute vitesse. ∼ **stop**, point m. ∼**time** a. & adv. à plein temps. ∼**y** adv. complètement.

fumble v.i. tâtonner, fouiller. ∼ **with**, tripoter.

fume v.i. rager. ∼**s** n. pl. exhalaisons f. pl., vapeurs f. pl.

fumigate v.t. désinfecter.

fun n. amusement m. **be** ∼, être chouette. **for** ∼, pour rire. ∼**fair** n. fête foraine f. **make** ∼ **of**, se moquer de.

function n. (purpose, duty) fonction f.; (event) réception f. —v.i. fonctionner. ∼**al** a. fonctionnel.

fund n. fonds m. —v.t. fournir les fonds pour.

fundamental a. fondamental.

funeral n. enterrement m., funérailles f. pl. —a. funèbre.

fungus n. (plant) champignon m.; (mould) moisissure f.

funnel n. (for pouring) entonnoir m.; (of ship) cheminée f.

funny a. drôle; (odd) bizarre.

fur n. fourrure f.; (in kettle) tartre m.

furious a. furieux. ∼**ly** adv. furieusement.

furnace n. fourneau m.

furnish v.t. (with furniture) meubler; (supply) fournir. ∼**ings** n. pl. ameublement n.

furniture n. meubles m. pl.

furrow n. sillon m.

furry a. (animal) à fourrure; (toy) en peluche.

further a. plus éloigné; (additional) supplémentaire. —adv. plus loin; (more) davantage. —v.t. avancer. ∼**er education**, formation continue f. ∼**est** a. le plus éloigné; adv. le plus loin.

furthermore adv. de plus.

furtive a. furtif.

fury n. fureur f.

fuse[1] v.t./i. (melt) fondre; (unite: fig.) fusionner. —n. fusible m., plomb m. ∼ **the lights** etc., faire sauter les plombs.

fuse[2] n. (of bomb) amorce f.

fuselage n. fuselage m.

fusion n. fusion f.

fuss n. (when upset) histoire(s) f. (pl.); (when excited) agitation f. —v.i. s'agiter. **make a** ∼, faire des histoires; s'agiter; (about food) faire des chichis. **make a** ∼ **of**, faire grand cas de. ∼**y** a. (finicky) tatillon; (hard to please) difficile.

futile a. futile, vain.

future a. futur. —n. avenir m.; (gram.) futur m. **in** ∼, à l'avenir.

G

gabardine n. gabardine f.

gabble v.t./i. bredouiller.

gable n. pignon m.

gadget n. gadget m.

Gaelic n. gaélique m.

gaffe n. (blunder) gaffe f.

gag n. bâillon m.; (joke) gag m. —v.t. bâillonner.

gaiety n. gaieté f.

gaily adv. gaiement.

gain v.t. gagner; (speed, weight) prendre. —v.i. (of clock) avancer. —n. acquisition f.; (profit) gain m.

gait n. démarche f.

gala n. (festive occasion) gala m.; (sport) concours m.

gale n. tempête f.

gall n. bile f.; (fig.) fiel m.; (impudence) sl.) culot m. **~-bladder** n. vésicule biliaire f.

gallant a. (brave) courageux; (chivalrous) galant. **~ry** n. courage m.

gallery n. galerie f. **(art) ~**, (public) musée m.

galley n. (ship) galère f.; (kitchen) cambuse f.

Gallic a. française.

gallon n. gallon m.

gallop n. galop m. —v.i. galoper.

gallows n. potence f.

galvanize v.t. galvaniser.

gambit n. (opening) **~**, (move) première démarche f.; (ploy) stratagème m.

gambl|e v.t./i. jouer. —n. (venture) entreprise risquée f.; (bet) pari m.; (risk) risque m. **~e on**, miser sur. **~er** n. joueu|r, -se m., f. **~ing** n. le jeu.

game¹ n. jeu m.; (football) match m.; (tennis) partie f.; (animals, birds) gibier m. —a. (brave) brave. **~ for**, prêt à.

game² a. (lame) estropié.

gammon n. jambon fumé m.

gamut n. gamme f.

gamy a. faisandé.

gang n. bande f.; (of workmen) équipe f. —v.i. **~ up**, se liguer (on, against, contre).

gangrene n. gangrène f.

gangster n. gangster m.

gangway n. passage m.; (aisle) allée f.; (of ship) passerelle f.

gap n. trou m., vide m.; (in time) intervalle m.; (in education) lacune f.; (difference) écart m.

gap|e v.i. rester bouche bée. **~ing** a. béant.

garage n. garage m. —v.t. mettre au garage.

garb n. costume m.

garbage n. ordures f. pl.

garble v.t. déformer.

garden n. jardin m. —v.i. jardiner. **~er** n. jardin|ier, -ière m., f. **~ing** n. jardinage m.

gargle v.i. se gargariser. —n. gargarisme m.

garland n. guirlande f.

garlic n. ail m.

garment n. vêtement m.

garnish v.t. garnir (with, de). —n. garniture f.

garter n. jarretière f. **~-belt** n. porte-jarretelles n.m. invar.

gas n. gaz m.; (med.) anesthésique m.; (petrol: Amer., fam.) essence f. —a. (mask, pipe) à gaz. —v.t. asphyxier; (mil.) gazer. —v.i. (fam.) bavarder.

gash n. entaille f. —v.t. entailler.

gasket n. (auto.) joint de culasse m.; (for pressure cooker) rondelle f.

gasoline n. (petrol: Amer.) essence f.

gasp v.i. haleter; (in surprise: fig.) avoir le souffle coupé. —n. halètement m.

gassy a. gazeux.

gastric a. gastrique.

gastronomy n. gastronomie f.

gate n. porte f.; (of metal) grille f.; (barrier) barrière f.

gather v.t. (people, objects) rassembler; (pick up) ramasser; (flowers) cueillir; (fig.) comprendre; (sewing) froncer. —v.i. (people) se rassembler; (crowd) se former; (pile up) s'accumuler. **~ing** n. rassemblement m.

gaudy a. voyant, criard.

gauge n. jauge f., indicateur m. —v.t. jauger, évaluer.

gaunt *a.* (*lean*) émacié; (*grim*) lugubre.

gauze *n.* gaze *f.*

gawky *a.* gauche, maladroit.

gawp (*or* **gawk**) *v.i.* ∼ (**at**), regarder bouche bée.

gay *a.* (*joyful*) gai; (*fam.*) gay *invar.* —*n.* gay *m./f.*

gaze *v.i.* ∼ (**at**), regarder (fixement). —*n.* regard (fixe) *m.*

gazelle *n.* gazelle *f.*

gazette *n.* journal (officiel) *m.*

gear *n.* équipement *m.*; (*techn.*) engrenage *m.*; (*auto.*) vitesse *f.* —*v.t.* adapter. ∼-**lever**, (*Amer.*) ∼-**shift** *ns.* levier de vitesse *m.* **in** ∼, en prise.

gearbox *n.* (*auto.*) boîte de vitesses *f.*

gel *n.* gelée *f.*; (*for hair*) gel *m.*

gelatine *n.* gélatine *f.*

gelignite *n.* nitroglycérine *f.*

gem *n.* pierre précieuse *f.*

Gemini *n.* les Gémeaux *m. pl.*

gender *n.* genre *m.*

gene *n.* gène *m.*

general *a.* général. —*n.* général *m.* ∼ **practitioner**, (*med.*) généraliste *m.* **in** ∼, en général. ∼**ly** *adv.* généralement.

generaliz|e *v.t./i.* généraliser. ∼**ation** *n.* généralisation *f.*

generate *v.t.* produire.

generation *n.* génération *f.*

generator *n.* (*electr.*) groupe électrogène *m.*

gener|ous *a.* généreux, (*plentiful*) copieux. ∼**osity** *n.* générosité *f.*

genetic *a.* génétique. ∼**s** *n.* génétique *f.*

genial *a.* affable, sympathique, (*climate*) doux.

genital *a.* génital. ∼**s** *n. pl.* organes génitaux *m. pl.*

genius *n.* (*pl. -uses*) génie *m.*

genteel *a.* distingué.

gentl|e *a.* (*mild, kind*) doux; (*slight*) léger; (*hint*) discret. ∼**eness** *n.* douceur *f.* ∼**y** *adv.* doucement.

gentleman *n.* (*man*) monsieur *m.*; (*wellbred*) gentleman *m.*

genuine *a.* (*true*) véritable; (*person, belief*) sincère.

geograph|y *n.* géographie *f.* ∼**ical** *a.* géographique.

geolog|y *n.* géologie *f.* ∼**ical** *a.* géologique.

geometr|y *n.* géométrie *f.* ∼**ic(al)** *a.* géométrique.

geranium *n.* géranium *m.*

geriatric *a.* gériatrique.

germ *n.* (*rudiment, seed*) germe *m.*; (*med.*) microbe *m.*

German *a. & n.* allemand(e) (*m. (f.)*); (*lang.*) allemand *m.* ∼ **measles**, rubéole *f.* ∼**y** *n.* Allemagne *f.*

germinate *v.t./i.* (faire) germer.

gestation *n.* gestation *f.*

gesticulate *v.i.* gesticuler.

gesture *n.* geste *m.*

get *v.t.* avoir, obtenir, recevoir; (*catch*) prendre; (*buy*) acheter, prendre; (*find*) trouver; (*fetch*) aller chercher; (*understand: sl.*) comprendre. ∼ **s.o. to do sth.**, faire faire qch. à qn. ∼ **sth. done**, faire faire qch. —*v.i.* aller, arriver (**to, à**); (*become*) devenir; (*start*) se mettre (**to, à**); (*manage*) parvenir (**to, à**). ∼ **married/ ready**/*etc.*, se marier/se préparer/*etc.* ∼ **promoted/hurt**/*etc.*, être promu/blessé/ *etc.* ∼ **arrested/ robbed**/*etc.*, se faire arrêter/voler/*etc.* ∼ **across**, (*cross*) traverser. ∼ **along** *or* **by**, (*manage*) se débrouiller. ∼ **along** *or* **on**, (*progress*) avancer. ∼ **along** *or* **on with**, s'entendre avec. ∼ **at**, (*reach*) parvenir à. ∼ **away**, partir; (*escape*) s'échapper. ~ **back** v.i. revenir; v.t. (recover) récupérer. ~ **by** or **through,** (pass) passer. ~ **down** v.t./i. descendre; (depress) déprimer. ~ **in,** entrer, arriver. ~ **into,** (car) monter dans; (dress) mettre. ~ **into trouble,** avoir des ennuis. ~ **off** v.i. (from bus etc.) descendre; (leave) partir; (jurid.) être acquitté; v.t. (remove) enlever. ~ **on,** (on train etc.) monter; (succeed) réussir. ~ **on with,** (job) attaquer; (person) s'entendre avec. ~ **out,** sortir. ~ **round,** (rule) contourner; (person) entortiller. ~ **through,** (finish) finir. ~ **up** v.i. se lever; v.t. (climb, bring) monter.

Ghana n. Ghana m.

ghastly a. affreux.

gherkin n. cornichon m.

ghetto n. ghetto m.

ghost n. fantôme m.

giant n. & a. géant (m.).

gibe n. raillerie f.

giblets n. pl. abattis m. pl., abats m. pl.

gidd|y a. vertigineux. **be** or **feel** ~**y,** avoir le vertige. ~**iness** n. vertige m.

gift n. cadeau m.; (ability) don m. ~**-wrap** v.t. faire un paquet-cadeau de.

gifted a. doué.

gig n. (fam.) concert m.

gigantic a. gigantesque.

giggle v.i. ricaner (sottement), glousser. —n. ricanement m.

gild v.t. dorer.

gill n. (approx.) décilitre m.

gills n. pl. ouïes f. pl.

gilt a. doré. —n. dorure f.

gimmick n. truc m.

gin n. gin m.

ginger n. gingembre m. —a. roux. ~ **ale,** ~ **beer,** boisson gazeuse au gingembre f.

gingerbread n. pain d'épice m.

gipsy n. = **gypsy.**

giraffe n. girafe f.

girder n. poutre f.

girdle n. (belt) ceinture f.; (corset) gaine f.

girl n. (petite) fille f.; (young woman) (jeune) fille f. ~**-friend** n. amie f.; (of boy) petite amie f.

giro n. virement bancaire m.; (cheque: fam.) mandat m.

girth n. circonférence f.

gist n. essentiel m.

give /gɪv/ v.t. donner; (gesture) faire; (laugh, sigh, etc.) pousser. ~ **s.o. sth.,** donner qch. à qn. —v.i. donner; (yield) céder; (stretch) se détendre. —n. élasticité f. ~ **away,** donner; (secret) trahir. ~ **back,** rendre. ~ **in,** (yield) se rendre. ~ **up** v.t./i. (renounce) renoncer (à); (yield) céder. ~ **o.s. up,** se rendre. ~ **way,** céder; (collapse) s'effondrer.

glacier n. glacier m.

glad a. content. ~**ly** adv. avec plaisir.

gladiolus n. glaïeul m.

glam|our n. enchantement m., séduction f. ~**orous** a. séduisant, ensorcelant.

glance n. coup d'œil m. —v.i. ~ **at,** jeter un coup d'œil à.

gland n. glande f.

glare v.i. briller très fort. —n. éclat (aveuglant) m.; (stare: fig.) regard furieux m. ~ **at,** regarder d'un air furieux.

glass n. verre m.; (mirror) miroir m. ~**es,** (spectacles) lunettes f. pl. ~**y** a. vitreux.

glaze v.t. (door etc.) vitrer; (pottery) vernisser. —n. vernis m.

gleam n. lueur f. —v.i. luire.

glen n. vallon m.

glib a. (person: pej.) qui a la parole facile or du bagou; (reply, excuse) désinvolte, spécieux. **～ly** *adv.* avec désinvolture.

glide *v.i.* glisser; (*of plane*) planer. **～r** *n.* planeur *m.*

glimmer *n.* lueur *f.* —*v.i.* luire.

glimpse *n.* aperçu *m.* **catch a ～ of,** entrevoir.

glint *n.* éclair *m.* —*v.i.* étinceler.

glitter *v.i.* scintiller. —*n.* scintillement *m.*

gloat *v.i.* jubiler **(over,** à l'idée de).

global *a.* (*world-wide*) mondial; (*all-embracing*) global.

globe *n.* globe *m.*

gloom *n.* obscurité *f.*; (*sadness*: *fig.*) tristesse *f.* **～y** *a.* triste; (*pessimistic*) pessimiste.

glorious *a.* splendide; (*deed, hero, etc.*) glorieux.

glory *n.* gloire *f.*

gloss *n.* lustre *m.*, brillant *m.* —*a.* brillant. **～y** *a.* brillant.

glove *n.* gant *m.* **～ compartment,** (*auto.*) vide-poches *m. invar.*

glow *v.i.* rougeoyer; (*person, eyes*) rayonner. —*n.* rougeoiement *m.*, éclat *m.*

glucose *n.* glucose *m.*

glue *n.* colle *f.* —*v.t.* coller.

glum *a.* triste, morne.

glut *n.* surabondance *f.*

glutton *n.* glouton(ne) *m. (f.).*

glycerine *n.* glycérine *f.*

gnash *v.t.* **～ one's teeth,** grincer des dents.

gnat *n.* (*fly*) cousin *m.*

gnaw *v.t./i.* ronger.

gnome *n.* gnome *m.*

go *v.i.* aller; (*leave*) partir; (*work*) marcher; (*become*) devenir; (*be sold*) se vendre; (*vanish*) disparaître. **～ by car/on foot,** aller en voiture/à pied. **～ for a walk/ride,** aller se promener/ faire un tour en voiture. **go red/dry/**etc., rougir/tarir/ etc. **～**

riding/shopping/ *etc.*, faire du cheval/les courses/ *etc.* —*n.* (*try*) coup *m.*; (*success*) réussite *f.*; (*turn*) tour *m.*; (*energy*) dynamisme *m.* **have a ～,** essayer. **be ～ing to do,** aller faire. **～ across,** traverser. **～ ahead!,** allez-y! **～ away,** s'en aller. **～ back,** retourner; (*go home*) rentrer. **～ by,** (*pass*) passer. **～ down,** descendre; (*sun*) se coucher. **～ for,** aller chercher; (*like*) aimer; (*attack*: *sl.*) attaquer. **～ in,** (r)entrer. **～ in for,** (*exam*) se présenter à. **～ into,** entrer dans; (*subject*) examiner. **～ off,** partir; (*explode*) sauter; (*ring*) sonner; (*take place*) se dérouler; (*dislike*) revenir de. **～ on,** continuer; (*happen*) se passer. **～ out,** sortir; (*light, fire*) s'éteindre. **～ over,** (*cross*) traverser; (*pass*) passer. **～ over or through,** (*check*) vérifier; (*search*) fouiller. **～ round,** (*be enough*) suffire. **～ through,** (*suffer*) subir. **～ up,** monter. **～ without,** se passer de. **on the ～,** actif.

goal *n.* but *m.* **～-post** *n.* poteau de but *m.*

goalkeeper *n.* gardien de but *m.*

goat *n.* chèvre *f.*

gobble *v.t.* engouffrer.

goblin *n.* lutin *m.*

God *n.* Dieu *m.* **～-forsaken** *a.* perdu.

god *n.* dieu *m.* **～dess** *n.* déesse *f.* **～ly** *a.* dévot.

god|child *n.* filleul(e) *m. (f.).* **～daughter** *n.* filleule *f.* **～father** *n.* parrain *m.* **～mother** *n.* marraine *f.* **～son** *n.* filleul *m.*

godsend *n.* aubaine *f.*

goggle *v.i.* **～ (at),** regarder avec de gros yeux.

goggles *n. pl.* lunettes (protectrices) *f. pl.*

going *n.* it is slow/hard ～, c'est lent/difficile. —*a.* (*price, rate*) actuel.

gold *n.* or *m.* —*a.* en or, d'or.

golden *a.* d'or; (*in colour*) doré; (*opportunity*) unique.

goldfish *n. invar.* poisson rouge *m.*

gold-plated *a.* plaqué or.

goldsmith *n.* orfèvre *m.*

golf *n.* golf *m.* ～ **ball,** balle de golf *f.;* (*on typewriter*) boule *f.* ～ **course** *n.* terrain de golf *m.* ～**er** *n.* joueu|r, -se de golf *m., f.*

gong *n.* gong *m.*

good *a.* bon; (*weather*) beau; (*well-behaved*) sage. —*n.* bien *m.* **as ～ as,** (*almost*) pratiquement. **to ～,** faire du bien. **feel ～,** se sentir bien. ～**-for-nothing** *a.* & *n.* propre à rien (*m./f.*). ～**-afternoon,** ～**-morning** *ints.* bonjour. ～**-evening** *int.* bonsoir. ～**looking** *a.* beau. ～**-night** *int.* bonsoir, bonne nuit. **it is ～ for you,** ça vous fait du bien. **is it any ～?,** est-ce que c'est bien? **it's no ～,** ça ne vaut rien. **it is no ～ shouting/***etc.,* ça ne sert à rien de crier/*etc.* **for ～,** pour toujours. ～**ness** *n.* bonté *f.* **my ～ness!,** mon Dieu!

goodbye *int.* & *n.* au revoir (*m. invar.*).

goods *n. pl.* marchandises *f. pl.*

goose *n.* oie *f.* ～**-pimples** *ns.* chair de poule *f.*

gooseberry *n.* groseille à maquereau *f.*

gore *n.* (*blood*) sang *m.*

gorge *n.* (*geog.*) gorge *f.* —*v.t.* **o.s.,** se gorger.

gorgeous *a.* magnifique.

gorilla *n.* gorille *m.*

gorse *n. invar.* ajoncs *m. (pl.).*

gory *a.* sanglant; (*horrific: fig.*) horrible.

gosh *int.* mince (alors).

gospel *n.* évangile *m.*

gossip *n.* commérage(s) *m. (pl.);* (*person*) bavard(e) *m. (f.).* —*v.i.* bavarder.

got *in v.* **have ～,** avoir. **have ～ to do,** devoir faire.

Gothic *a.* gothique.

gouge *v.t.* ～ **out,** arracher.

gourmet *n.* gourmet *m.*

gout *n.* (*med.*) goutte *f.*

govern *v.t./i.* gouverner. ～**or** *n.* gouverneur *m.*

government *n.* gouvernement *m.*

gown *n.* robe *f.;* (*of judge, teacher*) toge *f.*

GP *abbr. see* **general practitioner.**

grab *v.t.* saisir.

grace *n.* grâce *f.* —*v.t.* (*honour*) honorer; (*adorn*) orner. ～**ful** *a.* gracieux.

gracious *a.* (*kind*) bienveillant; (*elegant*) élégant.

gradation *n.* gradation *f.*

grade *n.* catégorie *f.;* (*of goods*) qualité *f.;* (*on scale*) grade *m.;* (*school mark*) note *f.;* (*class: Amer.*) classe *f.* —*v.t.* classer; (*school work*) noter.

gradient *n.* (*slope*) inclinaison *f.*

gradual *a.* progressif, graduel. ～**ly** *adv.* progressivement.

graduate[^1] *n.* (*univ.*) diplômé(e) *m. (f.).*

graduat|e[^2] *v.i.* obtenir son diplôme. —*v.t.* graduer. ～**ion** *n.* remise de diplômes *f.*

graffiti *n. pl.* graffiti *m. pl.*

graft[^1] *n.* (*med., bot.*) greffe *f.* (*work*) boulot. —*v.t.* greffer; (*work*) trimer.

graft[^2] *n.* (*bribery: fam.*) corruption *f.*

grain *n.* (*seed, quantity, texture*) grain *m.;* (*in wood*) fibre *f.*

gram *n.* gramme *m.*

gramm|ar *n.* grammaire *f.* **∼atical** *a.* grammatical.

grand *a.* magnifique; (*duke, chorus*) grand. **∼ piano,** piano à queue *m.*

grandad *n.* (*fam.*) papy *m.*

grand|child *n.* petit(e)-enfant *m.* (*f.*). **∼daughter** *n.* petite-fille *f.* **∼father** *n.* grand-père *m.* **∼ mother** *n.* grand-mère *f.* **∼ parents** *n. pl.* grands-parents *m. pl.* **∼son** *n.* petit-fils *m.*

grandeur *n.* grandeur *f.*

grandiose *a.* grandiose.

grandma *n.* = **granny.**

grandstand *n.* tribune *f.*

granite *n.* granit *m.*

granny *n.* mamie *f.*

grant *v.t.* (*give*) accorder; (*request*) accéder à; (*admit*) admettre (**that,** que). —*n.* subvention *f.*; (*univ.*) bourse *f.* **take sth. for ∼ed,** considérer qch. comme une chose acquise.

granule *n.* granule *m.*

grape *n.* grain de raisin *m.* **∼s,** raisin(s) *m.* (*pl.*).

grapefruit *n. invar.* pamplemousse *m.*

graph *n.* graphique *m.*

graphic *a.* (*arts etc.*) graphique; (*fig.*) vivant, explicite. **∼s** *n. pl.* (*comput.*) graphiques *m. pl.*

grapple *v.i.* **∼ with,** affronter, être aux prises avec.

grasp *v.t.* saisir. —*n.* (*hold*) prise *f.*; (*strength of hand*) poigne *f.*; (*reach*) portée *f.*; (*fig.*) compréhension *f.*

grasping *a.* rapace.

grass *n.* herbe *f.*

grasshopper *n.* sauterelle *f.*

grate¹ *n.* (*fireplace*) foyer *m.*; (*frame*) grille *f.*

grate² *v.t.* râper. —*v.i.* grincer. **∼r** *n.* râpe *f.*

grateful *a.* reconnaissant.

gratitude *n.* gratitude *f.*

gratuitous *a.* gratuit.

grave¹ *n.* tombe *f.* **∼-digger** *n.* fossoyeur *m.*

grave² *a.* (*serious*) grave. **∼ly** *adv.* gravement.

grave³ *a.* **∼ accent,** accent grave *m.*

gravel *n.* gravier *m.*

gravestone *n.* pierre tombale *f.*

graveyard *n.* cimetière *m.*

gravity *n.* (*seriousness*) gravité *f.*; (*force*) pesanteur *f.*

gravy *n.* jus (de viande) *m.*

gray *a.* & *n.* = **grey.**

graze¹ *v.t./i.* (*eat*) paître.

graze² *v.t.* (*touch*) frôler; (*scrape*) écorcher. —*n.* écorchure *f.*

grease|e *n.* graisse *f.* —*v.t.* graisser. **∼-proof paper,** papier sulfurisé *m.* **∼y** *a.* graisseux.

great *a.* grand; (*very good: fam.*) magnifique. **∼ Britain,** Grande-Bretagne *f.* **∼ly** *adv.* (*very*) très; (*much*) beaucoup. **∼ness** *n.* grandeur *f.*

Greece *n.* Grèce *f.*

greed *n.* avidité *f.*; (*for food*) gourmandise *f.* **∼y** *a.* avide; gourmand.

Greek *a.* & *n.* grec(que) (*m.* (*f.*)); (*lang.*) grec *m.*

green *a.* vert; (*fig.*) naïf. —*n.* vert *m.*; (*grass*) pelouse *f.*; (*golf*) green *m.*

greengage *n.* (*plum*) reine-claude *f.*

greengrocer *n.* marchand(e) de fruits et légumes *m.* (*f.*).

greenhouse *n.* serre *f.*

greet *v.t.* (*receive*) accueillir; (*address politely*) saluer. **∼ing** *n.* accueil *m.*; salut *m.* **∼ings card,** carte de vœux *f.*

grenade *n.* grenade *f.*

grey *a.* gris; (*fig.*) triste. —*n.* gris *m.*

greyhound n. lévrier m.

grid n. grille f.; (network: electr.) réseau m.; (culin.) gril m.

grief n. chagrin m.

grievance n. grief m.

grieve v.t./i. (s')affliger. **∼ for**, pleurer.

grill n. (cooking device) gril m.; (food) grillade f.; (auto.) calandre f. —v.t./i. griller; (interrogate) cuisiner.

grille n. grille f.

grim a. sinistre.

grimace n. grimace f. —v.i. grimacer.

grim|e n. crasse f. **∼y** a. crasseux.

grin v.i. sourire. —n. (large) sourire m.

grind v.t. écraser; (coffee) moudre; (sharpen) aiguiser. —n. corvée f.

grip v.t. saisir; (interest) passionner. —n. prise f.; (strength of hand) poigne f.; (bag) sac de voyage m.

grisly a. horrible.

gristle n. cartilage m.

grit n. gravillon m., sable m.; (fig.) courage m. —v.t. (road) sabler; (teeth) serrer.

grizzle v.i. (cry) pleurnicher.

groan v.i. gémir. —n. gémissement m.

grocer n. épic|ier, -ière m., f. **∼ies** n. pl. (goods) épicerie f. **∼y** n. (shop) épicerie f.

grog n. grog m.

groggy a. (weak) faible; (unsteady) chancelant; (ill) mal fichu.

groin n. aine f.

groom n. marié m.; (for horses) valet d'écurie m. —v.t. (horse) panser; (fig.) préparer.

groove n. (for door etc.) rainure f.; (in record) sillon m.

grope v.i. tâtonner. **∼ for**, chercher à tâtons.

gross a. (coarse) grossier; (comm.) brut. —n. invar. grosse f.

grotesque a. grotesque.

grotto n. grotte f.

ground n. terre f., sol m.; (area) terrain m.; (reason) raison f. **∼s**, terres f. pl., parc m.; (of coffee) marc m. —v.t./i. (naut.) échouer; (aircraft) retenir au sol. **on the ∼**, par terre. **lose ∼**, perdre du terrain. **∼ floor**, rez-de-chaussée m. invar. **∼less** a. sans fondement.

groundsheet n. tapis de sol m.

groundwork n. travail préparatoire m.

group n. groupe m. —v.t./i. (se) grouper.

grouse[1] n. invar. (bird) coq de bruyère m., grouse f.

grouse[2] v.i. (grumble: fam.) rouspéter, râler.

grove n. bocage m.

grovel v.i. ramper.

grow v.i. grandir; (of plant) pousser; (become) devenir. —v.t. cultiver. **∼ up**, devenir adulte, grandir. **∼er** n. cultiva|teur, -trice m., f. **∼ing** a. grandissant.

growl v.i. grogner. —n. grognement m.

grown-up a. & n. adulte (m./f.).

growth n. croissance f.; (in numbers) accroissement m.; (of hair, tooth) pousse f.; (med.) tumeur f.

grub n. (larva) larve f.; (food: sl.) bouffe f.

grubby a. sale.

grudge n. rancune f. **have a ∼ against**, en vouloir à. **grudgingly** adv. à contrecœur.

gruesome a. macabre.

gruff a. bourru.

grumble v.i. ronchonner, grogner (at, après).

grumpy a. grincheux.

grunt *v.i.* grogner. —*n.* grognement *m.*

guarantee *n.* garantie *f.* —*v.t.* garantir.

guard *v.t.* protéger; (*watch*) surveiller. —*n.* (*vigilance, mil., group*) garde *f.*; (*person*) garde *m.*; (*on train*) chef de train *m.* **~ian** *n.* gardien(ne) *m.* (*f.*); (*of orphan*) tu|teur, -trice *m., f.*

guarded *a.* prudent.

guerrilla *n.* guérillero *m.* **~ warfare**, guérilla *f.*

guess *v.t./i.* deviner; (*suppose*) penser. —*n.* conjecture *f.*

guesswork *n.* conjectures *f. pl.*

guest *n.* invité(e) *m.* (*f.*); (*in hotel*) client(e) *m.* (*f.*).

guffaw *n.* gros rire *m.* —*v.i.* s'esclaffer, rire bruyamment.

guidance *n.* (*advice*) conseils *m. pl.*; (*information*) information *f.*

guide *n.* (*person, book*) guide *m.* —*v.t.* guider. **~d a. ~d missile**, missile téléguidé *m.* **~-lines** *n. pl.* grandes lignes *f. pl.*

Guide *n.* (*girl*) guide *f.*

guidebook *n.* guide *m.*

guile *n.* ruse *f.*

guilt *n.* culpabilité *f.* **~y** *a.* coupable.

guinea-pig *n.* cobaye *m.*

guinea-fowl *n.* pintade *f.*

guitar *n.* guitare *f.* **~ist** *n.* guitariste *m./f.*

gulf *n.* (*part of sea*) golfe *m.*; (*hollow*) gouffre *m.*

gull *n.* mouette *f.*, goéland *m.*

gullet *n.* gosier *m.*

gullible *a.* crédule.

gully *n.* (*ravine*) ravine *f.*; (*drain*) rigole *f.*

gulp *v.t.* **~ (down)**, avaler en vitesse. —*v.i.* (*from fear etc.*) avoir un serrement de gorge. —*n.* gorgée *f.*

gum[1] *n.* (*anat.*) gencive *f.*

gum[2] *n.* (*from tree*) gomme *f.*; (*glue*) colle *f.*; (*for chewing*) chewing-gum *m.* —*v.t.* gommer.

gun *n.* (*pistol*) revolver *m.*; (*rifle*) fusil *m.*; (*large*) canon *m.*

gunpowder *n.* poudre à canon *f.*

gunshot *n.* coup de feu *m.*

gurgle *n.* glouglou *m.* —*v.i.* glouglouter.

gush *v.i.* **~ (out)**, jaillir.

gust *n.* rafale *f.*; (*of smoke*) bouffée *f.* **~y** *a.* venteux.

gusto *n.* enthousiasme *m.*

gut *n.* boyau *m.* **~s**, boyaux *m. pl.*, ventre *m.*; (*courage: fam.*) cran *m.*

gutter *n.* (*on roof*) gouttière *f.*; (*in street*) caniveau *m.*

guy *n.* (*man: fam.*) type *m.*

gym *n.* (*fam.*) gymnase *m.*; (*fam.*) gym(nastique) *f.* **~-slip** *n.* tunique *f.* **~nasium** *n.* gymnase *m.*

gymnast *n.* gymnaste *m./f.* **~ics** *n. pl.* gymnastique *f.*

gynaecolog|**y** *n.* gynécologie *f.* **~ist** *n.* gynécologue *m./f.*

gypsy *n.* bohémien(ne) *m.* (*f.*).

gyrate *v.i.* tournoyer.

H

habit *n.* habitude *f.*; (*costume: relig.*) habit *m.* **be in/get into the ~ of**, avoir/prendre l'habitude de.

habitual *a.* (*usual*) habituel; (*smoker, liar*) invétéré. **~ly** *adv.* habituellement.

hack[1] *n.* (*old horse*) haridelle *f.*; (*writer*) nègre *m.*, écrivailleu|r, -se *m., f.*

hack[2] *v.t.* hacher, tailler.

haddock *n. invar.* églefin *m.* **smoked ~**, haddock *m.*

haemorrhage *n.* hémorragie *f.*

haemorrhoids n. pl. hémorroïdes f. pl.

haggle v.i. marchander. ～ **over**, (object) marchander; (price) discuter.

hail[1] v.t. (greet) saluer; (taxi) héler. —v.i. ～ **from**, venir de.

hail[2] n. grêle f. —v.i. grêler.

hailstone n. grêlon m.

hair n. (on head) cheveux m. pl.; (on body, of animal) poils m. pl.; (single strand on head) cheveu m.; (on body) poil m. ～**do** n. (pl.) coiffure f. ～**drier** n. séchoir (à cheveux) m. ～**grip** n. pince à cheveux f. ～**style** n. coiffure f.

hairbrush n. brosse à cheveux f.

haircut n. coupe de cheveux f. **have a** ～, se faire couper les cheveux.

hairdresser n. coiffeu|r, -se f, m.

hairpin n. épingle à cheveux f.

hake n. invar. colin m.

half n. moitié f., demi(e) m. (f.). —a. demi. —adv. à moitié. ～ **a dozen**, une demi-douzaine. ～ **an hour**, une demi-heure. **four and a** ～, quatre et demi(e). ～ **and half**, moitié moitié. **in** ～, en deux. ～**back** n. (sport) demi m. ～ **price**, moitié prix. ～**time** n. mi-temps f. ～**way** adv. à mi-chemin.

halibut n. invar. (fish) flétan m.

hall n. (room) salle f.; (entrance) vestibule m.; (mansion) manoir m.; (corridor) couloir m.

hallmark n. (on gold etc.) poinçon m.; (fig.) sceau m.

hallo int. & n. bonjour (m.). ～!, (on telephone) allô!; (in surprise) tiens!

hallucination n. hallucination f.

halo n. auréole f.

halt n. halte f. —v.t./i. (s')arrêter.

halve v.t. diviser en deux; (time etc.) réduire de moitié.

ham n. jambon m.; (theatre: sl.) cabotin(e) m. (f.).

hamburger n. hamburger m.

hammer n. marteau m. —v.t./i. marteler, frapper; (defeat) battre à plate couture. ～ **out**, (differences) arranger; (agreement) arriver à.

hammock n. hamac m.

hamper[1] n. panier m.

hamper[2] v.t. gêner.

hamster n. hamster m.

hand n. main f.; (of clock) aiguille f.; (writing) écriture f.; (worker) ouvr|ier, -ière m. f.; (cards) jeu m. —v.t. donner. **at** ～, proche. ～**baggage** n. bagages à main m. pl. **give s.o. a** ～, donner un coup de main à qn. ～ **in** or **over**, remettre. ～ **out**, distribuer.

handbag n. sac à main m.

handbook n. manuel m.

handbrake n. frein à main m.

handcuffs n. pl. menottes f. pl.

handful n. poignée f.

handicap n. handicap m. ～**ped** n. handicapé.

handkerchief n. mouchoir m.

handle n. (of door etc.) poignée f.; (of implement) manche m.; (of cup etc.) anse f.; (of pan etc.) queue f.; (for turning) manivelle f. —v.t. manier; (deal with) s'occuper de; (touch) toucher à.

handlebar n. guidon m.

handshake n. poignée de main f.

handsome a. (goodlooking) beau; (generous) généreux; (large) considérable.

handwriting n. écriture f.

handy a. (useful) commode, utile; (person) adroit; (near) accessible.

handyman n. bricoleur m.; (servant) homme à tout faire m.

hang v.t. suspendre, accrocher; (criminal) pendre. ～ **about**, traîner. ～**gliding** n. vol libre m.

~ **on,** (*hold out*) tenir bon; (*wait: sl.*) attendre. ~ **out** *v.i.* pendre; (*live: sl.*) crécher; (*spend time: sl.*) passer son temps; (*washing*) étendre. ~ **up,** (*telephone*) raccrocher. ~**-up** *n.* (*sl.*) complexe *m.*

hangar *n.* hangar *m.*

hanger *n.* (*for clothes*) cintre *m.*

hangover *n.* (*after drinking*) gueule de bois *f.*

hanker *v.i.* ~ **after,** avoir envie de.

haphazard *a.*, ~**ly** *adv.* au petit bonheur, au hasard.

happen *v.i.* arriver, se passer. **it so** ~**s that,** il se trouve que. **he** ~**s to know that,** il se trouve qu'il sait que.

happ|**y** *a.* heureux. **I'm not** ~ **about the idea,** je n'aime pas trop l'idée. ~ **with sth.,** satisfait de qch. ~**ily** *adv.* joyeusement; (*fortunately*) heureusement. ~**iness** *n.* bonheur *m.*

harass *v.t.* harceler. ~**ment** *n.* harcèlement *m.*

harbour, *n.* port *m.* —*v.t.* (*shelter*) héberger.

hard *a.* dur; (*difficult*) difficile, dur. —*adv.* dur; (*think*) sérieusement; (*pull*) fort. ~**-boiled egg,** œuf dur *m.* ~ **disk,** disque dur *m.* ~**-headed** *a.* réaliste. **the** ~ **of hearing,** les malentendants *m. pl.* ~**-line** *a.* pur et dur. ~ **shoulder,** accotement stabilisé *m.* ~ **up,** (*fam.*) fauché. ~**ness** *n.* dureté *f.*

hardboard *n.* Isorel *m.* (P.).

harden *v.t./i.* durcir.

hardly *adv.* à peine. ~ **ever,** presque jamais.

hardship *n.* ~(**s**), épreuves *f. pl.*

hardware *n.* (*metal goods*) quincaillerie *f.*; (*machinery, of computer*) matériel *m.*

hardy *a.* résistant.

hare *n.* lièvre *m.*

hark *v.i.* écouter. ~ **back to,** revenir sur.

harm *n.* (*hurt*) mal *m.*; (*wrong*) tort *m.* —*v.t.* (*hurt*) faire du mal à; (*wrong*) faire du tort à; (*object*) endommager. **there is no** ~ **in,** il n'y a pas de mal à. ~**ful** *a.* nuisible. ~**less** *a.* inoffensif.

harmonica *n.* harmonica *m.*

harmony *n.* harmonie *f.*

harness *n.* harnais *m.* —*v.t.* (*horse*) harnacher; (*control*) maîtriser; (*use*) exploiter.

harp *n.* harpe *f.* ~**ist** *n.* harpiste *m./f.*

harpoon *n.* harpon *m.*

harpsichord *n.* clavecin *m.*

harrowing *a.* déchirant.

harsh *a.* dur, rude; (*taste*) âpre; (*sound*) rude, âpre. ~**ly** *adv.* durement; (*ness*) dureté *f.*

harvest *n.* moisson *f.*, récolte *f.* —*v.t.* moissonner, récolter.

hash *n.* (*culin.*) hachis *m.*; (*fig.*) gâchis *m.* **make a** ~ **of,** (*bungle: sl.*) saboter.

hashish *n.* ha(s)chisch *m.*

hassle *n.* (*fam.*) difficulté(s) *f. (pl.)*; (*bother, effort: fam.*) mal *m.*, peine *f.*; (*quarrel: fam.*) chamaillerie *f.* —*v.t.* (*harass: fam.*) harceler.

haste *n.* hâte *f.* **in** ~, à la hâte.

hast|**y** *a.* précipité. ~**ily** *adv.* à la hâte.

hat *n.* chapeau *m.*

hatch[1] *n.* (*for food*) passeplat *m.*; (*naut.*) écoutille *f.*

hatch[2] *v.t./i.* (faire) éclore.

hatchback *n.* voiture avec hayon arrière *f.*

hatchet *n.* hachette *f.*

hate *n.* haine *f.* —*v.t.* haïr.

hatred *n.* haine *f.*

haughty *a.* hautain.

haul v.t. traîner, tirer. —n. (of thieves) butin m.; (catch) prise f.; (journey) voyage m.

haunch n. on one's ∼es, accroupi.

haunt v.t. hanter.

have v.t. avoir; (meal, bath, etc.) prendre; (walk, dream, etc.) faire. —v. aux. avoir; (with aller, partir, etc. & pronominal verbs) être. ∼ just done, venir de faire. ∼ sth. done, faire faire qch. ∼ to do, devoir faire.

haven n. havre m., abri m.

havoc n. ravages m. pl.

hawk[1] n. faucon m.

hawk[2] v.t. colporter. ∼er n. colporteu|r, -se m., f.

hawthorn n. aubépine f.

hay n. foin m. ∼ fever, rhume des foins m.

haywire a. go ∼, (plans) se désorganiser; (machine) se détraquer.

hazard n. risque m. —v.t. risquer, hasarder. ∼ warning lights, feux de détresse m. pl. ∼ous a. hasardeux, risqué.

haze n. brume f.

hazel n. (bush) noisetier m. ∼-nut n. noisette f.

hazy a. (misty) brumeux; (fig.) flou, vague.

he pron. il; (emphatic) lui. —n. mâle m.

head n. tête f.; (leader) chef m.; (of beer) mousse f. —a. principal. —v.t. être à la tête de. —v.i. ∼ for, se diriger vers. ∼s or tails?, pile ou face? ∼ office, siège m. ∼ rest, appui-tête m. ∼er n. (football) tête f.

headache n. mal de tête m.

heading n. titre m.; (subject category) rubrique f.

headlamp n. phare m.

headland n. cap m.

headlight n. phare m.

headline n. titre m.

headlong adv. (in a rush) à toute allure.

head|master n. (of school) directeur m. ∼mistress n. directrice f.

headphone n. écouteur m. ∼s, casque (à écouteurs) m.

headquarters n. pl. siège m., bureau central m.; (mil.) quartier général m.

headstrong a. têtu.

headway n. progrès m. (pl.) make ∼, faire des progrès.

heady a. (wine) capiteux; (exciting) grisant.

heal v.t./i. guérir.

health n. santé f. ∼ centre, dispensaire m. ∼ foods, aliments diététiques m. pl. ∼y a. sain; (person) en bonne santé.

heap n. tas m. —v.t. entasser. ∼s of, (fam.) des tas de.

hear v.t./i. entendre. ∼ about, entendre parler de. ∼ing n. ouïe f.; (of witness) audition f.; (of case) audience f. ∼ing-aid n. appareil acoustique m.

hearsay n. ouï-dire m. invar. from ∼, par ouï-dire.

heart n. cœur m. ∼s, (cards) cœur m. by ∼, par cœur. ∼ attack, crise cardiaque f. be ∼-broken, avoir le cœur brisé.

heartache n. chagrin m.

heartburn n. brûlures d'estomac f. pl.

hearten v.t. encourager.

hearth n. foyer m.

heartless a. cruel.

heart|y a. (sincere) chaleureux; (meal) gros. ∼ily adv. (eat) avec appétit.

heat n. chaleur f.; (excitement: fig.) feu m.; (contest) éliminatoire f. —v.t./i. chauffer. ∼ stroke, insolation f. **∼ up**, (food) réchauffer. **∼ wave**, vague de chaleur f. **∼er** n. radiateur m. **∼ing** n. chauffage m.

heath n. (area) lande f.

heather n. bruyère f.

heave v.t./i. (lift) (se) soulever; (a sigh) pousser; (throw: fam.) lancer; (retch) avoir des nausées.

heaven n. ciel m. **∼ly** a. céleste; (pleasing: fam.) divin.

heav|y a. lourd; (cold, work, etc.) gros; (traffic) dense. **∼y goods vehicle**, poids lourd m. **∼ily** adv. lourdement; (smoke, drink) beaucoup.

heavyweight n. poids lourd m.

Hebrew n. hébreu m. (m. only), hébraïque. —n. (lang.) hébreu m.

heckle v.t. interpeller.

hectic a. agité.

hedge n. haie f. —v.t. entourer. —v.i. (in answering) répondre évasivement.

hedgehog n. hérisson m.

heed v.t. faire attention à.

heel n. talon m.; (man: sl.) salaud m.

hefty a. gros, lourd.

heifer n. génisse f.

height n. hauteur f.; (of person) taille f.; (of plane, mountain) altitude f.; (of fame, glory) apogée m.; (of joy, folly, pain) comble m.

heighten v.t. (raise) rehausser; (fig.) augmenter.

heir n. héritier m. **∼ess** n. héritière f.

heirloom n. bijou (meuble, tableau, etc.) de famille m.

helicopter n. hélicoptère m.

heliport n. héliport m.

hell n. enfer m.

hello int. & n. = **hallo**.

helm n. (of ship) barre f.

helmet n. casque m.

help v.t./i. aider. —n. aide f.; (employees) personnel m.; (charwoman) femme de ménage f. **∼ o.s. to**, se servir de. **∼** n. aide m./f. **∼ful** a. utile; (person) serviable. **∼less** a. impuissant.

helping n. portion f.

hem n. ourlet m. —v.t. ourler. **∼ in**, enfermer.

hemisphere n. hémisphère m.

hen n. poule f.

hence adv. (for this reason) d'où; (from now) d'ici. **∼forth** adv. désormais.

henchman n. acolyte m., homme de main m.

hepatitis n. hépatite f.

her pron. la, l'*; (after prep.) elle. **(to) ∼**, lui. **I know ∼**, je la connais. —a. son, sa, pl. ses.

herald v.t. annoncer.

herb n. herbe f. **∼s**, (culin.) fines herbes f. pl.

herd n. troupeau m.

here adv. ici. **∼!**, (take this) tenez! **∼ is, ∼ are**, voici.

hereby adv. par le présent acte; (in letter) par la présente.

hereditary a. héréditaire.

heredity n. hérédité f.

here|sy n. hérésie f. **∼tic** n. hérétique m./f.

herewith adv. (comm.), ci-joint.

heritage n. héritage m.

hermit n. ermite m.

hernia n. hernie f.

hero n. héros m. **∼ine** n. héroïne f. **∼ism** n. héroïsme m.

heroic a. héroïque.

heroin n. héroïne f.

heron n. héron m.

herpes n. herpès m.

herring n. hareng m.

hers poss. pron. le sien, la sienne, les sien(ne)s. **it is ∼**, c'est à elle ou le sien.

herself *pron.* elle-même; *(reflexive)* se; *(after prep.)* elle.

hesitant *a.* hésitant.

hesitate *v.i.* hésiter. **~ion** *n.* hésitation *f.*

heterosexual *a.* & *n.* hétérosexuel(le) *(m. (f.)).*

hexagon *n.* hexagone *m.*

hey *int.* dites donc.

heyday *n.* apogée *f.*

HGV *abbr. see* heavy goods vehicle.

hi *int.* salut.

hibernate *v.i.* hiberner. **~ion** *n.* hibernation *f.*

hiccup *n.* hoquet *m.* —*v.i.* hoqueter. **(the) ~s,** le hoquet.

hide[1] *v.t.* cacher **(from,** à). —*v.i.* se cacher **(from,** de). **go into hiding,** se cacher. **~-out** *n.* *(fam.)* cachette *f.*

hide[2] *n.* *(skin)* peau *f.*

hideous *a.* *(dreadful)* atroce; *(ugly)* hideux.

hiding *n.* *(thrashing: fam.)* correction *f.*

hierarchy *n.* hiérarchie *f.*

hi-fi *a.* & *n.* hi-fi *a.* & *f. invar.;* *(machine)* chaîne hi-fi *f.*

high *a.* haut; *(price, number)* élevé; *(priest, speed)* grand; *(voice)* aigu. —*adv.* haut. **~ chair,** chaise haute *f.* **~-jump,** saut en hauteur *m.* **~-level** *a.* de haut niveau. **~ school,** lycée *m.* **~-speed** *a.* ultra-rapide. **~ spot,** *(fam.)* point culminant *m.* **~ street,** grand-rue *f.*

highbrow *a.* & *n.* intellectuel(le) *(m. (f.)).*

highlight *n.* *(vivid moment)* moment fort *m.* **~s,** *(in hair)* balayage *m.* **recorded ~s,** extraits enregistrés *m. pl.* —*v.t.* *(emphasize)* souligner.

highly *adv.* extrêmement; *(paid)* très bien. **~-strung** *a.* nerveux.

speak/think ~ of, dire/penser du bien de.

highway *n.* route nationale *f.* **~ code,** code de la route *m.*

hijack *v.t.* détourner. —*n.* détournement *m.* **~er** *n.* pirate (de l'air) *m.*

hike *n.* randonnée *f.* —*v.i.* faire de la randonnée. **price ~,** hausse de prix *f.* **~r** *n.* randonneu|r, -se *m., f.*

hilarious *a.* *(funny)* désopilant.

hill *n.* colline *f.;* *(slope)* côte *f.* **~y** *a.* accidenté.

hillside *n.* coteau *m.*

hilt *n.* *(of sword)* garde *f.* **to the ~,** tout à fait, au maximum.

him *pron.* le, l'*; *(after prep.)* lui. **(to) ~,** lui.

himself *pron.* lui-même; *(reflexive)* se; *(after prep.)* lui.

hinder *v.t.* *(hamper)* gêner; *(prevent)* empêcher.

hindsight *n.* **with ~,** rétrospectivement.

Hindu *a.* & *n.* hindou(e) *(m. (f.)).* **~ism** *n.* hindouisme *m.*

hinge *n.* charnière *f.* —*v.i.* **~ on,** *(depend on)* dépendre de.

hint *n.* allusion *f.;* *(advice)* conseil *m.* —*v.t.* laisser entendre. —*v.i.* **~ at,** faire allusion à.

hip *n.* hanche *f.*

hippopotamus *n.* hippopotame *m.*

hire *v.t.* *(thing)* louer; *(person)* engager. —*n.* location *f.* **~-car** *n.* voiture de location *f.* **~-purchase** *n.* achat à crédit *m.*

his *a.* son, sa, *pl.* ses. —*poss. pron.* le sien, la sienne, les sien(ne)s. **it is ~,** c'est à lui or le sien.

hiss *n.* sifflement *m.* —*v.t./i.* siffler.

historian *n.* historien(ne) *m. (f.).*

histor|y *n.* histoire *f.* **~ic(al)** *a.* historique.

hit v.t. frapper; (*knock against, collide with*) heurter; (*find*) trouver; (*affect, reach*) toucher. —n. ⟨*blow*⟩ coup m.; (*fig.*) succès m.; (*song*) tube m.

hitch v.t. (*fasten*) accrocher. —n. (*snag*) anicroche f. ~ **a lift**, ~**-hike** v.i. faire de l'auto-stop. ~**-hiker** n. auto-stoppeur|r, -se m., f.

hi-tech a. & n. high-tech (m.) invar.

HIV abbr. HIV. ~**-positive** a. séropositif.

hive n. ruche f. —v.t. ~ **off**, séparer; (*industry*) vendre.

hoard v.t. amasser. —n. réserve(s) f. (pl.); (*of money*) magot m., trésor m.

hoarding n. panneau d'affichage m.

hoarse a. enroué.

hoax n. canular m.

hob n. plaque chauffante f.

hobble v.i. clopiner.

hobby n. passe-temps m. invar. ~**-horse** n. (*fig.*) dada m.

hockey n. hockey m.

hoe n. binette f. —v.t. biner.

hog n. cochon m. —v.t. (*fam.*) accaparer.

hoist v.t. hisser. —n. palan m.

hold[1] v.t. (*p.t.* **held**) tenir; (*contain*) contenir; (*interest, breath, etc.*) retenir; (*possess*) avoir; (*believe*) maintenir. —v.i. (*of rope, weather, etc.*) tenir. —n. prise f. **get** ~ **of**, saisir; (*fig.*) trouver. ~ **down**, (*job*) garder; (*in struggle*) retenir. ~ **on**, (*stand firm*) tenir bon; (*wait*) attendre. ~ **on to**, (*keep*) garder; (*cling to*) se cramponner à. ~ **out** v.t. (*offer*) offrir; v.i. (*resist*) tenir le coup. ~ (**the line**), **please**, ne quittez pas. ~ **up**, (*support*) soutenir; (*delay*) retarder; (*rob*)

attaquer. ~**-up** n. retard m.; (*of traffic*) bouchon m.; (*robbery*) hold-up m. invar.

hold[2] n. (*of ship*) cale f.

holdall n. (*bag*) fourre-tout m. invar.

holding n. (*possession, land*) possession f. ~ **company**, holding m.

hole n. trou m. —v.t. trouer.

holiday n. vacances f. pl.; (*public*) jour férié m.; (*day off*) congé m. —v.i. passer ses vacances. —a. de vacances. ~**-maker** n. vacanc|ier, -ière m., f.

holistic a. holistique.

Holland n. Hollande f.

hollow a. creux; (*fig.*) faux. —n. creux m. —v.t. creuser.

holly n. houx m.

holster n. étui de revolver m.

holy a. saint, sacré; (*water*) bénit. H~ **Spirit**, Saint-Esprit m.

homage n. hommage m.

home n. maison f., foyer m.; (*institution*) maison f.; (*for soldiers, workers*) foyer·m.; (*country*) pays natal m. —a. de la maison, du foyer; (*of family*) de famille; (*pol.*) national, intérieur; (*match, visit*) à domicile. —adv. (**at**) ~, à la maison, chez soi. **come** or **go** ~, rentrer; (*from abroad*) rentrer dans son pays. ~**-made** a. (*food*) fait maison; (*clothes*) fait à la maison. ~**less** a. sans abri.

homeland n. patrie f.

homesick a. **be** ~, avoir le mal du pays.

homework n. devoirs m. pl.

homicide n. homicide m.

homœopath|y n. homéopathie f. ~**ic** a. homéopathique.

homogeneous a. homogène.

homosexual a. & n. homosexuel(le) (m. (f.)).

honest a. honnête; (*frank*) franc.
~**ly** adv. honnêtement; franchement. ~**y** n. honnêteté f.

honey n. miel m.; (*person: fam.*)
chéri(e) m. (f.).

honeymoon n. lune de miel f.

honk v.i. klaxonner.

honorary a. (*person*) honoraire;
(*duties*) honorifique.

honour n. honneur m. —v.t.
honorer. ~**able** a. honorable.

hood n. capuchon m.; (*car roof*)
capote f.

hoof n. sabot m.

hook n. crochet m.; (*on garment*)
agrafe f.; (*for fishing*) hameçon m.
—v.t./i. (s')accrocher; (*garment*)
(s')agrafer.

hooligan n. houligan m.

hoop n. (*toy etc.*) cerceau m.

hooray int. & n. = **hurrah**.

hoot n. (h)ululement m.; (*of car*)
coup de klaxon m.; huée f. —v.i. (*owl*)
(h)ululer; (*of car*) klaxonner;
(*jeer*) huer. ~**er** n. klaxon m. (P.);
(*of factory*) sirène f.

Hoover n. (P.) aspirateur m. —v.t.
passer à l'aspirateur.

hop[1] v.i. sauter (à cloche-pied).
—n. saut m.; (*flight*) étape f.

hop[2] n. ~(**s**), houblon m.

hope n. espoir m. —v.t./i. espérer.
~ **for**, espérer (avoir). I ~ **so**, je
l'espère. ~**ful** a. encourageant.
be ~**ful (that)**, avoir bon espoir
(que). ~**fully** adv. avec espoir; (*it
is hoped*) on l'espère. ~**less** a.
sans espoir; (*useless: fig.*) nul.

horde n. horde f., foule f.

horizon n. horizon m.

horizontal a. horizontal.

hormone n. hormone f.

horn n. corne f.; (*of car*) klaxon m.
(P.); (*mus.*) cor m.

hornet n. frelon m.

horoscope n. horoscope m.

horrible a. horrible.

horrid a. horrible.

horrific a. horrifiant.

horr|or n. horreur f. —a. (*film
etc.*) d'épouvante. ~**ify** v.t. hor-
rifier.

hors-d'œuvre n. hors d'œuvre m.
invar.

horse n. cheval m.

horsepower n. (*unit*) cheval
(vapeur) m.

horseshoe n. fer à cheval m.

horticultur|e n. horticulture f.
~**al** a. horticole.

hose n. (*tube*) tuyau m. —v.t.
arroser. ~-**pipe** n. tuyau m.

hosiery n. bonneterie f.

hospice n. hospice m.

hospit|able a. hospitalier. ~**ably**
adv. avec hospitalité. ~**ality** n.
hospitalité f.

hospital n. hôpital m.

host[1] n. (*to guests*) hôte m.; (*on TV*)
animateur m. ~**ess** n. hôtesse f.

host[2] n. **a** ~ **of**, une foule de.

host[3] n. (*relig.*) hostie f.

hostage n. otage m.

hostel n. foyer m. (**youth**) ~,
auberge (de jeunesse) f.

hostil|e a. hostile. ~**ity** n. hos-
tilité f.

hot a. chaud; (*culin.*) épicé; (*news*)
récent. be or feel ~, avoir chaud.
it is ~, il fait chaud. ~ **dog**, hot-
dog m. ~-**water bottle**, bouillotte f.

hotchpotch n. fatras m.

hotel n. hôtel m.

hotplate n. plaque chauffante f.

hound n. chien courant m. —v.t.
poursuivre.

hour n. heure f. ~**ly** a. & adv.
toutes les heures. ~**ly rate**, tarif
horaire m.

house[1] n. maison f.; (*theatre*)
salle f.; (*pol.*) chambre f.

house[2] v.t. loger; (*of building*)
abriter; (*keep*) garder.

housebreaking n. cambriolage m.

housecoat n. blouse f., tablier m.

household n. (*house, family*) ménage m. —a. ménager. **~er** n. occupant(e) m. (f.); (*owner*) propriétaire m./f.

housekeeper n. gouvernante f.

housewife n. ménagère f.

housework n. ménage m. travaux de ménage m. pl.

housing n. logement m. **~ development**, cité f.

hover v.i. (*bird, threat, etc.*) planer; (*loiter*) rôder.

hovercraft n. aéroglisseur m.

how adv. comment. **~ long/tall is** . . .?, quelle est la longueur/hauteur de . . .? **~ pretty!**, comme or que c'est joli! **~ are you?**, comment allez-vous? **~ do you do?**, (*introduction*) enchanté. **~ many?, ~ much?**, combien?

however adv. de quelque manière que; (*nevertheless*) cependant. **~ small/delicate/etc.** it may be, quelque petit/délicat/ etc. que ce soit.

howl n. hurlement m. —v.i. hurler.

HP abbr. see **hire-purchase**.

hp abbr. see **horsepower**.

HQ abbr. see **headquarters**.

hub n. moyeu m.; (*fig.*) centre m. **~-cap** n. enjoliveur m.

huddle /'hʌdl/ v.i. se blottir.

hue n. (*colour*) teinte f.

hug v.t. serrer dans ses bras; (*keep close to*) serrer. —n. étreinte f.

huge a. énorme.

hulk n. (*of ship*) épave f.; (*person*) mastodonte m.

hull n. (*of ship*) coque f.

hum v.t./i. (*person*) fredonner; (*insect*) bourdonner; (*engine*) vrombir. —n. bourdonnement m.;

vrombissement m. **~ and haw**, hésiter.

human a. humain. —n. être humain m. **~itarian** a. humanitaire.

humane a. humain.

humanity n. humanité f.

humbl|e a. humble. —v.t. humilier. **~y** adv. humblement.

humid a. humide. **~ity** n. humidité f.

humiliat|e v.t. humilier. **~ion** n. humiliation f.

humility n. humilité f.

hum|our n. humour m.; (*mood*) humeur f. —v.t. ménager. **~orous** a. humoristique; (*person*) plein d'humour.

hump n. bosse f. —v.t. voûter.

hunch[1] v.t. voûter.

hunch[2] n. petite idée f.

hundred a. & n. cent (m.). **~s of,** des centaines de. **~fold** a. centuple; adv. au centuple. **~th** a. & n. centième (m./f.).

hundredweight n. 50.8 kg.; (*Amer.*) 45.36 kg.

Hungar|y n. Hongrie f. **~ian** a. & n. hongrois(e) (m. (f.)).

hunger n. faim f. —v.i. **~ for,** avoir faim de.

hungr|y a. affamé. **be ~y,** avoir faim.

hunt v.t./i. chasser. —n. chasse f. **~ for,** chercher. **~er** n. chasseur m. **~ing** n. chasse f.

hurdle n. (*sport*) haie f.; (*fig.*) obstacle m.

hurl v.t. lancer.

hurrah, hurray int. & n. hourra (m.).

hurricane n. ouragan m.

hurried a. précipité.

hurry v.i. se dépêcher, se presser. —v.t. presser, activer. —n. hâte f. **in a ~,** pressé.

hurt v.t./i. faire mal (à); (*injure,*

offend) blesser. —*a.* blessé. —*n.* mal *m.*

hurtle *v.i.* **~ along,** avancer à toute vitesse.

husband *n.* mari *m.*

hush *v.t.* faire taire. —*n.* silence *m.* **~ up,** (*news etc.*) étouffer.

husk *n.* (*of grain*) enveloppe *f.*

husky *a.* (*hoarse*) rauque; (*burly*) costaud. —*n.* chien de traîneau *m.*

hustle *v.t.* (*push, rush*) bousculer. —*v.i.* (*work busily: Amer.*) se démener. —*n.* bousculade *f.* **~ and bustle,** agitation *f.*

hut *n.* cabane *f.*

hutch *n.* clapier *m.*

hyacinth *n.* jacinthe *f.*

hybrid *a. & n.* hybride (*m.*).

hydrangea *n.* hortensia *m.*

hydrant *n.* (*fire*) **~,** bouche d'incendie *f.*

hydraulic *a.* hydraulique.

hydroelectric *a.* hydro-électrique.

hydrofoil *n.* hydroptère *m.*

hydrogen *n.* hydrogène *m.*

hyena *n.* hyène *f.*

hygiene *n.* hygiène *f.*

hygienic *a.* hygiénique.

hymn *n.* cantique *m.*, hymne *m.*

hype *n.* tapage publicitaire *m.* —*v.t.* faire du tapage autour de.

hyper- *pref.* hyper-.

hypermarket *n.* hypermarché *m.*

hyphen *n.* trait d'union *m.* **~ate** *v.t.* mettre un trait d'union à.

hypno|sis *n.* hypnose *f.* **~tic** *a.* hypnotique.

hypnot|ize *v.t.* hypnotiser. **~ism** *n.* hypnotisme *m.*

hypochondriac *n.* malade imaginaire *m./f.*

hypocrisy *n.* hypocrisie *f.*

hypocrit|e *n.* hypocrite *m./f.* **~ical** *a.* hypocrite.

hypodermic *a.* hypodermique. —*n.* seringue hypodermique *f.*

hypothe|sis *n.* hypothèse *f.* **~tical** *a.* hypothétique.

hyster|ia *n.* hystérie *f.* **~ical** *a.* hystérique; (*person*) surexcité.

hysterics *n. pl.* crise de nerfs *or* de rire *f.*

I

I *pron.* je, j'*; (*stressed*) moi.

ice *n.* glace *f.*; (*on road*) verglas *m.* —*v.t.* (*cake*) glacer. —*v.i.* **~ (up),** (*window*) se givrer; (*river*) geler. **~-cream** *n.* glace *f.* **~-cube** *n.* glaçon *m.* **~ hockey,** hockey sur glace *m.* **~ lolly,** glace (*sur bâtonnet*) *f.* **~ rink,** patinoire *f.* **~ skate,** patin à glace *m.*

iceberg *n.* iceberg *m.*

Iceland *n.* Islande *f.* **~er** *n.* Islandais(e) *m.* (*f.*). **~ic** *a.* islandais; *n.* (*lang.*) islandais *m.*

icicle *n.* glaçon *m.*

icing *n.* (*sugar*) glace *f.*

icon *n.* icône *f.*

icy *a.* (*hands, wind*) glacé; (*road*) verglacé; (*manner, welcome*) glacial.

idea *n.* idée *f.*

ideal *a.* idéal. —*n.* idéal *m.* **~ly** *adv.* idéalement.

idealis|t *n.* idéaliste *m./f.* **~m** *n.* idéalisme *m.*

identical *a.* identique.

identif|y *v.t.* identifier. **~ication** *n.* identification *f.*; (*papers*) une pièce d'identité.

identity *n.* identité *f.*

ideolog|y *n.* idéologi *f.* **~ical** *a.* idéologique.

idiom *n.* expression idiomatique

f.; (*language*) idiome *m.* ~atic *a.*
idiomatique.

idiot *n.* idiot(e)*n.* (*f.*). ~ic *a.* idiot.

idle *a.* désœuvré, oisif; (*lazy*)
paresseux; (*unemployed*) sans
travail; (*machine*) au repos; (*fig.*)
vain. —*v.i.* (*engine*) tourner au
ralenti. —*v.t.* ~ away, gaspiller.
~ness *n.* oisiveté *f.*

idol *n.* idole *f.* ~ize *v.t.* idolâtrer.

idyllic *a.* idyllique.

i.e. *abbr.* c'est-à-dire.

if *conj.* si.

igloo *n.* igloo *m.*

ignite *v.t./i.* (s')enflammer.

ignition *n.* (*auto.*) allumage *m.* ~
key, clé de contact. ~ (switch),
contact *m.*

ignoran|t *a.* ignorant (of, de).
~ce *n.* ignorance *f.*

ignore *v.t.* ne faire *or* prêter
aucune attention à; (*person in
street etc.*) faire semblant de ne
pas voir; (*facts*) ne pas tenir
compte de.

ill *a.* malade; (*bad*) mauvais.
—*adv.* mal. —*n.* mal *m.*

illegal *a.* illégal.

illegible *a.* illisible.

illness *n.* maladie *f.*

illogical *a.* illogique.

illuminat|e *v.t.* éclairer; (*decorate
with lights*) illuminer. ~ion *n.*
éclairage *m.*; illumination *f.*

illusion *n.* illusion *f.*

illusory *a.* illusoire.

illustrat|e *v.t.* illustrer. ~ion *n.*
illustration *f.* ~ive *a.* qui illustre.

illustrious *a.* illustre.

image *n.* image *f.* (public) ~, (*of
firm, person*) image de marque *f.*
~ry *n.* images *f. pl.*

imaginary *a.* imaginaire.

imaginat|ion *n.* imagination *f.*
~ive *a.* plein d'imagination.

imagin|e *v.t.* (*picture to o.s.*)

(s')imaginer; (*suppose*) imaginer.
~able *a.* imaginable.

imbalance *n.* déséquilibre *m.*

imbecile *n.* & *a.* imbécile (*m./f.*).

imitat|e *v.t.* imiter. ~ion *n.*
imitation *f.* ~or *n.* imita|teur,
-trice *m.*, *f.*

immaterial *a.* sans importance
(to, pour; that, que).

immature *a.* pas mûr; (*person*)
immature.

immediate *a.* immédiat. ~ly *adv.*
immédiatement; *conj.* dès que.

immense *a.* immense.

immers|e *v.t.* plonger, immerger.
~ion *n.* immersion *f.* ~ion
heater, chauffe-eau (électrique)
m. invar.

immigr|ate *v.i.* immigrer. ~ant
n. & *a.* immigré(e) (*m.* (*f.*));
(*newly-arrived*) immigrant(e) (*m.*
(*f.*)). ~ation *n.* immigration *f.*

imminen|t *a.* imminent. ~ce *n.*
imminence *f.*

immobil|e *a.* immobile. ~ize *v.t.*
immobiliser.

immoral *a.* immoral. ~ity *n.*
immoralité *f.*

immortal *a.* immortel. ~ity *n.*
immortalité *f.*

immun|e *a.* immunisé (from, to,
contre). ~ity *n.* immunité *f.*

immuniz|e *v.t.* immuniser.
~ation *n.* immunisation *f.*

imp *n.* lutin *m.*

impact *n.* impact *m.*

impair *v.t.* détériorer.

impartial *a.* impartial.

impassable *a.* (*barrier etc.*) infranchissable; (*road*) impraticable.

impasse *n.* impasse *f.*

impassive *a.* impassible.

impatien|t *a.* impatient. get ~t,
s'impatienter. ~ce *n.* impatience
f. ~tly *adv.* impatiemment.

impeccable *a.* impeccable.

impede v.t. gêner.

impel v.t. pousser (**to do**, à faire).

impending a. imminent.

impenetrable a. impénétrable.

imperative a. nécessaire; (*need etc.*) impérieux. —n. (*gram.*) impératif m.

imperceptible a. imperceptible.

imperfect a. imparfait; (*faulty*) défectueux.

imperial a. impérial; (*measure*) légal (au Royaume-Uni).

imperil v.t. mettre en péril.

impersonal a. impersonnel.

impersonat|e v.t. se faire passer pour; (*mimic*) imiter. ~**ion** n. imitation f. ~**or** n. imita|teur, -trice m., f.

impertinen|t a. impertinent. ~**ce** n. impertinence f.

impetuous a. impétueux.

impetus n. impulsion f.

impinge v.i. ~ **on**, affecter; (*encroach*) empiéter sur.

implacable a. implacable.

implant v.t. implanter. —n. implant m.

implement[1] n. (*tool*) outil m.; (*utensil*) ustensile m.

implement[2] v.t. exécuter.

implicat|e v.t. impliquer. ~**ion** n. implication f.

implicit a. (*implied*) implicite; (*unquestioning*) absolu.

implore v.t. implorer.

impl|y v.t. (*assume, mean*) impliquer; (*insinuate*) laisser entendre. ~**ied** a. implicite.

impolite a. impoli.

import[1] v.t. importer. f. ~**er** n. importa|teur, -trice m., f.

import[2] n. (*article*) importation f.; (*meaning*) sens m.

importan|t a. important. ~**ce** n. importance f.

impose v.t. imposer.

imposing a. imposant.

impossible a. impossible.

impostor n. imposteur m.

impoten|t a. impuissant. ~**ce** n. impuissance f.

impound v.t. confisquer.

impoverish v.t. appauvrir.

impracticable a. impraticable.

impractical a. peu pratique.

impresario n. impresario m.

impress v.t. impressionner; (*imprint*) imprimer.

impression n. impression f. ~**able** a. impressionnable.

impressive a. impressionnant.

imprint[1] n. empreinte f.

imprint[2] v.t. imprimer.

imprison v.t. emprisonner. ~**ment** n. emprisonnement m.

improbable a. (*not likely*) improbable; (*incredible*) invraisemblable.

impromptu a. & adv. impromptu.

improper a. inconvenant, indécent; (*wrong*) incorrect.

improve v.t./i. (s')améliorer. ~**ment** n. amélioration f.

improvis|e v.t./i. improviser. ~**ation** n. improvisation f.

impuden|t a. impudent. ~**ce** n. impudence f.

impulse n. impulsion f. **on** ~, sur un coup de tête.

impulsive a. impulsif.

impunity n. impunité f. **with** ~, impunément.

impur|e a. impur. ~**ity** n. impureté f.

in prep. dans, à, en. —adv. (*inside*) dedans; (*at home*) là, à la maison; (*in fashion*) à la mode. **in the box/garden**, dans la boîte/le jardin. **in Paris/school**, à Paris/l'école. **in town**, en ville. **in the country**, à la campagne. **in winter/English**, en hiver/anglais. **in India**, en Inde. **in Japan**, au Japon. **in blue**, en bleu. **in ink**, à l'encre. **in uniform**, en uniforme. **in a skirt**, en jupe. **in winter**, en hiver. **in spring**, au printemps. **in an hour**, (at end of) au bout d'une heure. **in an hour('s time)**, dans une heure. **in (the space of) an hour**, en une heure. **in the evening**, le soir. **one in ten**, un sur dix. **in-laws** n. pl. (fam.) beaux-parents m. pl. ∿**patient** a. malade hospitalisé(e) m.(f.).

inability n. incapacité f. **(to do**, de faire).

inaccessible a. inaccessible.

inaccurate a. inexact.

inaction n. inaction f.

inactiv|e a. inactif. ∿**ity** n. inaction f.

inadequa|te a. insuffisant. ∿**cy** n. insuffisance f.

inadvertently adv. par mégarde.

inane a. inepte.

inanimate a. inanimé.

inappropriate a. inopportun; (term) inapproprié.

inarticulate a. qui a du mal à s'exprimer.

inaudible a. inaudible.

inaugural a. inaugural.

inaugurat|e v.t. (open, begin) inaugurer; (person) investir. ∿**ion** n. inauguration f.; investiture f.

inborn a. inné.

inbred a. (inborn) inné.

inc. abbr. (incorporated) S.A.

incalculable a. incalculable.

incapable a. incapable.

incapacit|y n. incapacité f. ∿**ate** v.t. rendre incapable (de travailler etc.).

incarnat|e a. incarné. ∿**ion** n. incarnation f.

incendiary a. incendiaire. —n. (bomb) bombe incendiaire f.

incense[1] n. encens m.

incense[2] v.t. mettre en fureur.

incentive n. motivation f.; (payment) prime (d'encouragement) f.

inception n. début m.

incessant a. incessant. ∿**ly** adv. sans cesse.

incest n. inceste m.

inch n. pouce m. (= 2.54 cm.).

incidence n. fréquence f.

incident n. incident m.; (in play, film, etc.) épisode m.

incidental a. accessoire. ∿**ly** adv. accessoirement; (by the way) à propos.

incinerat|e v.t. incinérer. ∿**or** n. incinérateur m.

incision n. incision f.

incite v.t. inciter, pousser. ∿**ment** n. incitation f.

inclination n. (propensity, bowing) inclination f.

incline[1] v.t./i. incliner. **be** ∿**d to**, avoir tendance à.

incline[2] n. pente f.

inclu|de v.t. comprendre, inclure. ∿**ding** prep. (y) compris. ∿**sion** n. inclusion f.

inclusive a. & adv. inclus, compris. **be** ∿ **of**, comprendre.

incoherent a. incohérent.

income n. revenu m. ∿ **tax**, impôt sur le revenu m.

incoming a. (tide) montant; (tenant etc.) nouveau.

incomparable a. incomparable.

incompatible a. incompatible.

incompeten|t a. incompétent. ∿**ce** n. incompétence f.

incomplete a. incomplet.

incomprehensible a. incompréhensible.

inconceivable a. inconcevable.

incongruous a. déplacé, incongru.

inconsiderate *a.* (*person*) qui ne se soucie pas des autres; (*act*) irréfléchi.

inconsisten|t *a.* (*treatment*) sans cohérence, inconséquent; (*argument*) contradictoire; (*performance*) irrégulier. **~t with**, incompatible avec. **~cy** *n.* inconséquence *f.* contradiction *f.*; irrégularité *f.*

inconspicuous *a.* peu en évidence.

inconvenien|t *a.* incommode, peu pratique; (*time*) mal choisi. **be ~t for**, ne pas convenir à. **~ce** *n.* dérangement *m.*; (*drawback*) inconvénient *m.*; *v.t.* déranger.

incorporate *v.t.* incorporer; (*include*) contenir.

incorrect *a.* inexact.

incorrigible *a.* incorrigible.

increase[1] *v.t./i.* augmenter. **~ing** *a.* croissant. **~ingly** *adv.* de plus en plus.

increase[2] *n.* augmentation *f.* (**in**, **of**, de). **be on the ~**, augmenter.

incredible *a.* incroyable.

increment *n.* augmentation *f.*

incriminat|e *v.t.* incriminer. **~ing** *a.* compromettant.

incubat|e *v.t.* (*eggs*) couver. **~ion** *n.* incubation *f.* **~or** *n.* couveuse *f.*

inculcate *v.t.* inculquer.

incur *v.t.* encourir; (*debts*) contracter; (*anger*) s'exposer à.

incurable *a.* incurable.

incursion *n.* incursion *f.*

indebted *a.* **~ to s.o.**, redevable à qn. (**for**, de).

indecen|t *a.* indécent. **~cy** *n.* indécence *f.*

indecision *n.* indécision *f.*

indecisive *a.* indécis; (*ending*) peu concluant.

indeed *adv.* en effet, vraiment.

indefensible *a.* indéfendable.

indefinable *a.* indéfinissable.

indefinite *a.* indéfini; (*time*) déterminé. **~ly** *adv.* indéfiniment.

indelible *a.* indélébile.

indemnity *n.* (*money*) indemnité *f.*; (*guarantee*) garantie *f.*

indent *v.t.* (*text*) renfoncer.

independen|t *a.* indépendant. **~ce** *n.* indépendance *f.* **~tly** *adv.* de façon indépendante. **~tly of**, indépendamment de.

indescribable *a.* indescriptible.

indestructible *a.* indestructible.

indeterminate *a.* indéterminé.

index *n.* (*figure*) indice *m.*; (*in book*) index *m.*; (*in library*) catalogue *m.* *—v.t.* classer. **~ card**, fiche *f.* **~ finger** index *m.* **~-linked** *a.* indexé.

India *n.* Inde *f.* **~n** *a.* & *n.* indien(ne) (*m. (f.)*).

indicat|e *v.t.* indiquer. **~ion** *n.* indication *f.* **~or** *n.* (*device*) indicateur *m.*; (*on vehicle*) clignotant *m.*; (*board*) tableau *m.*

indict *v.t.* accuser. **~ment** *n.* accusation *f.*

indifferen|t *a.* indifférent; (*not good*) médiocre. **~ce** *n.* indifférence *f.*

indigenous *a.* indigène.

indigest|ion *n.* indigestion *f.* **~ible** *a.* indigeste.

indign|ant *a.* indigné. **~ation** *n.* indignation *f.*

indigo *n.* indigo *m.*

indirect *a.* indirect. **~ly** *adv.* indirectement.

indiscr|eet *a.* indiscret; (*not wary*) imprudent. **~etion** *n.* indiscrétion *f.*

indiscriminate *a.* qui manque de discernement; (*random*) fait au hasard. **~ly** *adv.* sans discernement; au hasard.

indispensable *a.* indispensable.

indispos|ed *a.* indisposé, souffrant. **~ition** *n.* indisposition *f.*

indisputable *a.* incontestable.

indistinguishable *a.* indifférenciable.

individual *a.* individuel. —*n.* individu *m.* **~ity** *n.* individualité *f.* **~ly** *adv.* individuellement.

indivisible *a.* indivisible.

Indonesia *n.* Indonésie *f.* **~n** *a.* & *n.* indonésien(ne) (*m.* (*f.*)).

indoor *a.* (*clothes etc.*) d'intérieur; (*under cover*) couvert. **~s** *adv.* à l'intérieur.

induce *v.t.* (*influence*) persuader; (*cause*) provoquer. **~ment** *n.* encouragement *m.*

indulge *v.t.* (*desires*) satisfaire; (*person*) se montrer indulgent pour, gâter. —*v.i.* **~ in**, se livrer à, s'offrir.

indulgen|t *a.* indulgent. **~ce** *n.* indulgence *f.*; (*treat*) gâterie *f.*

industrial *a.* industriel; (*unrest etc.*) ouvrier; (*action*) revendicatif; (*accident*) du travail. **~ist** *n.* industriel(le) *m.*(*f.*). **~ized** *a.* industrialisé.

industrious *a.* travailleur.

industry *n.* industrie *f.*; (*zeal*) application *f.*

inedible *a.* (*food*) immangeable.

ineffective *a.* inefficace; (*person*) incapable.

ineffectual *a.* inefficace; (*person*) incapable.

inefficien|t *a.* inefficace; (*person*) incompétent. **~cy** *n.* inefficacité *f.*; incompétence *f.*

ineligible *a.* inéligible. **be ~ for**, ne pas avoir droit à.

inept *a.* (*absurd*) inepte; (*out of place*) mal à propos.

inequality *n.* inégalité *f.*

inert *a.* inerte.

inertia *n.* inertie *f.*

inescapable *a.* inéluctable.

inevitabl|e *a.* inévitable. **~y** *adv.* inévitablement.

inexact *a.* inexact.

inexcusable *a.* inexcusable.

inexhaustible *a.* inépuisable.

inexpensive *a.* bon marché *invar.*, pas cher.

inexplicable *a.* inexplicable.

infallib|le *a.* infaillible. **~ility** *n.* infaillibilité *f.*

infam|ous *a.* infâme. **~y** *n.* infamie *f.*

infant *n.* (*baby*) nourrisson *m.*; (*at school*) petit(e) enfant *m.*(*f.*).

infantry *n.* infanterie *f.*

infatuat|ed *a.* **~ed with**, engoué de. **~ion** *n.* engouement *m.*, béguin *m.*

infect *v.t.* infecter. **~ s.o. with**, communiquer à qn. **~ion** *n.* infection *f.*

infectious *a.* (*med.*) infectieux; (*fig.*) contagieux.

infer *v.t.* déduire. **~ence** *n.* déduction *f.*

inferior *a.* inférieur (**to**, à); (*work, product*) de qualité inférieure. —*n.* inférieur(e) *m.* (*f.*). **~ity** *n.* infériorité *f.*

infernal *a.* infernal.

inferno *n.* (*hell*) enfer *m.*; (*blaze*) incendie *m.*

infertil|e *a.* infertile. **~ity** *n.* infertilité *f.*

infest *v.t.* infester.

infidelity *n.* infidélité *f.*

infiltrat|e *v.t./i.* s'infiltrer (dans). **~ion** *n.* infiltration *f.*

infinite *a.* infini. **~ly** *adv.* infiniment.

infinitive *n.* infinitif *m.*

infinity *n.* infinité *f.*

infirm *a.* infirme. **~ity** *n.* infirmité *f.*

infirmary *n.* hôpital *m.*; (*sick-bay*) infirmerie *f.*

inflam|e *v.t.* enflammer. **~mable**

a. inflammable. **∼mation** *n.* inflammation *f.*

inflat|e *v.t.* (*balloon, prices, etc.*) gonfler. **∼able** *a.* gonflable.

inflation *n.* inflation *f.*

inflict *v.t.* infliger (**on,** à).

influence *n.* influence *f.* —*v.t.* influencer.

influential *a.* influent.

influenza *n.* grippe *f.*

influx *n.* afflux *m.*

inform *v.t.* informer (**of,** de). **keep ∼ed,** tenir au courant. **∼er** *n.* indica|teur, -trice *m., f.*

informal *a.* (*simple*) simple, sans cérémonie; (*unofficial*) officieux; (*colloquial*) familier. **∼ity** *n.* simplicité *f.* **∼ly** *adv.* sans cérémonie.

information *n.* renseignements *m.* (*pl.*), information(s) *f.* (*pl.*). **some ∼,** un renseignement. **∼ technology,** informatique *f.*

informative *a.* instructif.

infra-red *a.* infrarouge.

infrastructure *n.* infrastructure *f.*

infringe *v.t.* contrevenir à. **∼ on,** empiéter sur. **∼ment** *n.* infraction *f.*

infuriate *v.t.* rendre furieux.

infus|e *v.t.* infuser. **∼ion** *n.* infusion *f.*

ingen|ious *a.* ingénieux. **∼uity** *n.* ingéniosité *f.*

ingenuous *a.* ingénu.

ingot *n.* lingot *m.*

ingrained *a.* enraciné.

ingratitude *n.* ingratitude *f.*

ingredient *n.* ingrédient *m.*

inhabit *v.t.* habiter. **∼able** *a.* habitable. **∼ant** *n.* habitant(e) *m.* (*f.*).

inhale *v.t.* inhaler; (*tobacco smoke*) avaler. **∼r** *n.* spray *m.*

inherent *a.* inhérent. **∼ly** *adv.* en soi, intrinsèquement.

inherit *v.t.* hériter (de). **∼ance** *n.* héritage *m.*

inhibit *v.t.* (*hinder*) gêner; (*prevent*) empêcher. **be ∼ed,** avoir des inhibitions. **∼ion** *n.* inhibition *f.*

inhospitable *a.* inhospitalier.

inhuman *a.* (*brutal, not human*) inhumain. **∼ity** *n.* inhumanité *f.*

inhumane *a.* inhumain.

inimitable *a.* inimitable.

iniquit|ous *a.* inique. **∼y** *n.* iniquité *f.*

initial *n.* initiale *f.* —*v.t.* parapher. —*a.* initial.

initiat|e *v.t.* (*begin*) amorcer; (*scheme*) lancer; (*person*) initier (**into,** à). **∼ion** *n.* initiation *f.*; (*start*) amorce *f.*

initiative *n.* initiative *f.*

inject *v.t.* injecter; (*new element, fig.*) insuffler. **∼ion** *n.* piqûre *f.*

injunction *n.* (*court order*) ordonnance *f.*

injure *v.t.* blesser; (*do wrong to*) nuire à.

injury *n.* (*physical*) blessure *f.*

injustice *n.* injustice *f.*

ink *n.* encre *f.*

inkling *n.* petite idée *f.*

inland *a.* l'intérieur. —*adv.* à l'intérieur. **I∼ Revenue,** fisc *m.*

in-laws *n. pl.* (*parents*) beaux-parents; (*family*) belle-famille *f.*

inlay¹ *v.t.* incruster.

inlay² *n.* incrustation *f.*

inlet *n.* bras de mer *m.*; (*techn.*) arrivée *f.*

inmate *n.* (*of asylum*) interné(e) *m.* (*f.*); (*of prison*) détenu(e) *m.* (*f.*).

inn *n.* auberge *f.*

innate *a.* inné.

inner *a.* intérieur, interne; (*fig.*) profond, intime. **∼ city,** quartiers défavorisés *m. pl.* **∼ tube,** chambre à air *f.*

innings n. invar. tour de batte m.; (fig.) tour m.

innocen|t a. & n. innocent(e) (m. (f.)). **~ce** n. innocence f.

innocuous a. inoffensif.

innovat|e v.i. innover. **~ion** n. innovation f. **~or** n. innova|teur, -trice m., f.

innuendo n. insinuation f.

innumerable a. innombrable.

inoculat|e v.t. inoculer. **~ion** n. inoculation f.

inoffensive a. inoffensif.

inoperative a. inopérant.

inopportune a. inopportun.

inordinate a. excessif. **~ly** adv. excessivement.

input n. (data) données f. pl.; (computer process) entrée f.; (power: electr.) énergie f.

inquest n. enquête f.

inquire v.t./i. = enquire.

inquiry n. enquête f.

inquisition n. inquisition f.

inquisitive a. curieux; (prying) indiscret.

insan|e a. fou. **~ity** n. folie f.

insatiable a. insatiable.

inscri|be v.t. inscrire; (book) dédicacer. **~ption** n. inscription f.; dédicace f.

insect n. insecte m.

insecticide n. insecticide m.

insecur|e a. (not firm) peu solide; (unsafe) peu sûr; (worried) anxieux. **~ity** n. insécurité f.

insemination n. insémination f.

insensible a. insensible; (unconscious) inconscient.

insensitive a. insensible.

inseparable a. inséparable.

insert[1] v.t. insérer. **~ion** n. insertion f.

insert[2] n. insertion f.; (advertising) encart m.

in-service a. (training) continu.

inshore a. côtier.

inside n. intérieur m. —a. intérieur. —adv. à l'intérieur, dedans. —prep. à l'intérieur de; (of time) en moins de. **~ out**, à l'envers; (thoroughly) à fond.

insidious a. insidieux.

insight n. (perception) perspicacité f.; (idea) aperçu m.

insignificant a. insignifiant.

insincer|e a. peu sincère. **~ity** n. manque de sincérité m.

insinuat|e v.t. insinuer. **~ion** n. insinuation f.

insipid a. insipide.

insist v.t./i. insister. **~ on**, affirmer; (demand) exiger. **~ on doing**, insister pour faire.

insisten|t a. insistant. **~ce** n. insistance f. **~tly** adv. avec insistance.

insole n. (separate) semelle f.

insolen|t a. insolent. **~ce** n. insolence f.

insoluble a. insoluble.

insolvent a. insolvable.

insomnia n. insomnie f. **~c** n. insomniaque m./f.

inspect v.t. inspecter; (tickets) contrôler. **~ion** n. inspection f.; contrôle m. **~or** n. inspec|teur, -trice m., f.; (on train, bus) contrôleu|r, -se m., f.

inspir|e v.t. inspirer. **~ation** n. inspiration f.

instability n. instabilité f.

install v.t. installer. **~ation** n. installation f.

instalment n. (payment) acompte m., versement m.; (of serial) épisode m.

instance n. exemple m.; (case) cas m. **for ~**, par exemple. **in the first ~**, en premier lieu.

instant a. immédiat; (food) instantané. —n. instant m. **~ly** adv. immédiatement.

instantaneous a. instantané.

instead adv. plutôt. ～ of doing, au lieu de faire. ～ of s.o., à la place de qn.

instigat|e v.t. provoquer. ～ion n. instigation f.

instil v.t. inculquer; (inspire) insuffler.

instinct n. instinct m. ～ive a. instinctif.

institut|e n. institut m. —v.t. instituer; (inquiry etc.) entamer. ～ion n. institution f.; (school, hospital) établissement m.

instruct v.t. instruire; (order) ordonner. ～ s.o. in sth., enseigner qch. à qn. ～ s.o. to do, ordonner à qn. de faire. ～ion n. instruction f. ～ions n. pl. (for use) mode d'emploi m. ～ive a. instructif. ～or n. professeur m.; (skiing, driving) moni|teur, -trice m., f.

instrument n. instrument m. ～ panel, tableau de bord m.

instrumental a. instrumental. be ～ in, contribuer à. ～ist n. instrumentaliste m./f.

insufferable a. intolérable.

insufficien|t a. insuffisant. ～ly adv. insuffisamment.

insular a. insulaire; (mind, person: fig.) borné.

insulat|e v.t. (room, wire, etc.) isoler. ～ion n. isolation f.

insulin n. insuline f.

insult[1] v.t. insulter.

insult[2] n. insulte f.

insuperable a. insurmontable.

insur|e v.t. assurer. ～ance n. assurance f.

insurmountable a. insurmontable.

insurrection n. insurrection f.

intact a. intact.

intake n. admission(s) f. (pl.); (techn.) prise f.

intangible a. intangible.

integral a. intégral. be an ～ part of, faire partie intégrante de.

integrat|e v.t./i. (s')intégrer. ～ion n. intégration f.

integrity n. intégrité f.

intellect n. intelligence f. ～ual a. & n. intellectuel(le) (m. (f.)).

intelligen|t a. intelligent. ～ce n. intelligence f.; (mil.) renseignements m. pl. ～tly adv. intelligemment.

intelligible a. intelligible.

intend v.t. destiner. ～ to do, avoir l'intention de faire. ～ed a. (deliberate) intentionnel; (planned) prévu.

intens|e a. intense; (person) passionné. ～ely adv. (to live etc.) intensément; (very) extrêmement. ～ity n. intensité f.

intensify v.t. intensifier. ～ication n. intensification f.

intensive a. intensif. in ～ care, en réanimation.

intent n. intention f. —a. attentif. ～ on, absorbé par. ～ on doing, résolu à faire. ～ly adv. attentivement.

intention n. intention f. ～al a. intentionnel.

inter v.t. enterrer.

inter- pref. inter-.

interact v.i. avoir une action réciproque. ～ion n. interaction f.

intercede v.i. intercéder.

intercept v.t. intercepter. ～ion n. interception f.

interchange n. échangeur m.

interchangeable a. interchangeable.

intercom n. interphone m.

interconnected a. lié.

intercourse n. (sexual, social) rapports m. pl.

interest n. intérêt m.; (stake) intérêts m. pl. —v.t. intéresser. ～

rates, taux d'intérêt *m. pl.* ~ed *a.*
intéressé. **be ~ed in,** s'intéresser
à. ~ing *a.* intéressant.

interface *n.* (*comput.*) interface *f.*;
(*fig.*) zone de rencontre *f.*

interfer|e *v.i.* se mêler des affaires
des autres. ~e in, s'ingérer dans.
~e with, (*plans*) créer un
contretemps avec; (*work*)
s'immiscer dans; (*radio*) faire des
interférences avec; (*lock*) toucher
à. ~ence *n.* ingérence *f.*; (*radio*)
parasites *m. pl.*

interim *n.* intérim *m.* —*a.* intérimaire.

interior *n.* intérieur *m.* —*a.*
intérieur.

interjection *n.* interjection *f.*

interlinked *a.* lié.

interlock *v.t./i.* (*techn.*)
(s')emboîter, (s')enclencher.

interlude *n.* intervalle *m.*;
(*theatre, mus.*) intermède *m.*

intermediary *a. & n.* intermédiaire (*m./f.*).

intermediate *a.* intermédiaire;
(*exam etc.*) moyen.

interminable *a.* interminable.

intermission *n.* pause *f.*; (*theatre
etc.*) entracte *m.*

intern *v.t.* interner. ~ment *n.*
internement *m.*

internal *a.* interne; (*domestic,
pol.*) intérieur. ~ly *adv.* intérieurement.

international *a. & n.* international (*m.*).

interpolate *v.t.* interpoler.

interpret *v.t.* interpréter. —*v.i.*
faire l'interprète. ~ation *n.* interprétation *f.* ~er *n.* interprète
m./f.

interrelated *a.* lié.

interrogat|e *v.t.* interroger. ~ion
n. interrogation *f.* (*of,* de);
(*session of questions*) interrogatoire *m.*

interrogative *a. & n.* interrogatif
(*m.*).

interrupt *v.t.* interrompre. ~ion
n. interruption *f.*

intersect *v.t./i.* (*lines, roads*) (se)
couper. ~ion *n.* intersection *f.*;
(*crossroads*) croisement *m.*

interspersed *a.* (*scattered*) dis-
persé.

interval *n.* intervalle *m.*; (*theatre*)
entracte *m.* **at ~s,** par inter-
valles.

interven|e *v.i.* intervenir; (*of
time*) s'écouler (*between,* entre);
(*happen*) survenir. ~tion *n.*
intervention *f.*

interview *n.* (*with reporter*) interview *f.*; (*for job etc.*) entrevue *f.*
—*v.t.* interviewer. ~er *n.* interviewer *m.*

intestin|e *n.* intestin *m.* ~al *a.*
intestinal.

intima|te[1] *a.* intime; (*detailed*)
profond. ~cy *n.* intimité *f.* ~tely
adv. intimement.

intimate[2] *v.t.* (*state*) annoncer;
(*imply*) suggérer.

intimidat|e *v.t.* intimider. ~ion
n. intimidation *f.*

into *prep.* (*put, go, etc.*) dans;
(*divide, translate, etc.*) en.

intolerable *a.* intolérable.

intoleran|t *a.* intolérant. ~ce *n.*
intolérance *f.*

intonation *n.* intonation *f.*

intoxicat|e *v.t.* enivrer. ~ed *a.*
ivre. ~ion *n.* ivresse *f.*

intra- *pref.* intra-.

intransigent *a.* intransigeant.

intransitive *a.* (*verb*) intrans-
itif.

intravenous *a.* (*med.*) intra-
veineux.

intrepid *a.* intrépide.

intrica|te *a.* complexe. ~cy *n.*
complexité *f.*

intrigu|e *v.t./i.* intriguer.

intrigue *f.* ∼ing *a.* très intéressant; (*curious*) curieux.

intrinsic *a.* intrinsèque. ∼ally *adv.* intrinsèquement.

introduce *v.t.* (*bring in, insert*) introduire; (*programme, question*) présenter. ∼ **s.o. to,** (*person*) présenter qn. à; (*subject*) faire connaître à qn.

introduct|ion *n.* introduction *f.*; (*to person*) présentation *f.* ∼ory *a.* (*letter, words*) d'introduction.

introspective *a.* introspectif.

intru|de *v.i.* (*person*) s'imposer (**on s.o.,** à qn.), déranger. ∼der *n.* intrus(e) *m.* (*f.*). ∼sion *n.* intrusion *f.*

intuit|ion *n.* intuition *f.* ∼ive *a.* intuitif.

inundat|e *v.t.* inonder (**with,** de). ∼ion *n.* inondation *f.*

invade *v.t.* envahir. ∼r *n.* envahisseu|r, ∼se *m., f.*

invalid[1] *n.* malade *m./f.*; (*disabled*) infirme *m./f.*

invalid[2] *a.* non valable. ∼ate *v.t.* invalider.

invaluable *a.* inestimable.

invariab|le *a.* invariable. ∼y *adv.* invariablement.

invasion *n.* invasion *f.*

invent *v.t.* inventer. ∼ion *n.* invention *f.* ∼ive *a.* inventif. ∼or *n.* inven|teur, -trice *m., f.*

inventory *n.* inventaire *m.*

inverse *a. & n.* inverse (*m.*). ∼ly *adv.* inversement.

inver|t *v.t.* intervertir. ∼ted commas, guillemets *m. pl.* ∼sion *n.* inversion *f.*

invest *v.t.* investir; (*time, effort; fig.*) consacrer. —*v.i.* faire un investissement. ∼ **in,** (*buy: fam.*) se payer. ∼ment *n.* investissement *m.* ∼or *n.* actionnaire *m./f.*; (*saver*) épargnant(e) *m.* (*f.*).

investigat|e *v.t.* étudier; (*crime etc.*) enquêter sur. ∼ion *n.*

investigation *f.* ∼or *n.* (*police*) enquêteur|r, -se *m., f.*

inveterate *a.* invétéré.

invigorate *v.t.* vivifier; (*encourage*) stimuler.

invincible *a.* invincible.

invisible *a.* invisible.

invit|e *v.t.* inviter; (*ask for*) demander. ∼ation *n.* invitation *f.* ∼ing *a.* (*meal, smile, etc.*) engageant.

invoice *n.* facture *f.* —*v.t.* facturer.

invoke *v.t.* invoquer.

involuntary *a.* involontaire.

involve *v.t.* entraîner; (*people*) faire participer. ∼d *a.* (*complex*) compliqué; (*at stake*) en jeu. be ∼d in, (*work*) participer à; (*crime*) être mêlé à. ∼ment *n.* participation *f.* (**in,** à).

inward *a. & adv.* vers l'intérieur; (*feeling etc.*) intérieur. ∼ly *adv.* intérieurement. ∼s *adv.* vers l'intérieur.

iodine *n.* iode *m.*; (*antiseptic*) teinture d'iode *f.*

iota *n.* (*amount*) brin *m.*

IOU *abbr.* (*I owe you*) reconnaissance de dette *f.*

IQ *abbr.* (*intelligence quotient*) QI *m.*

Iran *n.* Iran *m.* ∼ian *a. & n.* iranien(ne) (*m.* (*f.*)).

Iraq *n.* Irak *m.* ∼i *a. & n.* irakien(ne) (*m.* (*f.*)).

irascible *a.* irascible.

irate *a.* en colère, furieux.

Ireland *n.* Irlande *f.*

iris *n.* (*anat., bot.*) iris *m.*

Irish *a.* irlandais. —*n.* (*lang.*) irlandais *m.* ∼man *n.* Irlandais *m.* ∼woman *n.* Irlandaise *f.*

iron *n.* fer *m.*; (*appliance*) fer (à repasser) *m.* —*a.* de fer. —*v.t.* repasser. ∼ing-board *n.* planche à repasser *f.*

ironic(al) a. ironique.
ironmonger n. quincaillier m.
~y n. quincaillerie f.
irony n. ironie f.
irrational a. irrationnel; (*person*) pas rationnel.
irreconcilable a. irréconciliable; (*incompatible*) inconciliable.
irregular a. irrégulier. ~ity n. irrégularité f.
irrelevan|t a. sans rapport (**to**, avec). ~ce n. manque de rapport m.
irreparable a. irréparable.
irreplaceable a. irremplaçable.
irrepressible a. irrépressible.
irresistible a. irrésistible.
irresolute a. irrésolu.
irrespective a. ~ **of**, sans tenir compte de.
irresponsible a. irresponsable.
irretrievable a. irréparable.
irreverent a. irrévérencieux.
irreversible a. irréversible; (*decision*) irrévocable.
irrigat|e v.t. irriguer. ~ion n. irrigation f.
irritable a. irritable.
irritat|e v.t. irriter. **be** ~**ed by**, être énervé par. ~**ing** a. énervant. ~**ion** n. irritation f.
Islam n. Islam m. ~**ic** a. islamique.
island n. île f.
isle n. île f.
isolat|e v.t. isoler. ~**ion** n. isolement m.
Israel n. Israël m. ~**i** a. & n. israélien(ne) (m. (f.)).
issue n. question f.; (*outcome*) résultat m.; (*of magazine etc.*) numéro m. —v.t. distribuer, donner; (*stamps etc.*) émettre; (*book*) publier; (*order*) donner. **at** ~, en cause. **take** ~, engager une controverse.
isthmus n. isthme m.

it pron. (*subject*) il, elle; (*object*) le, la, l'*; (*impersonal subject*) il; (*non-specific*) ce, c'*, cela, ça. **it is**, (*quiet, my book, etc.*) c'est. **it is/cold/warm/late/** *etc.*, il fait froid/chaud/tard/*etc.* **that's it**, c'est ça. **who is it?**, qui est-ce? **of it, from it**, en. **in it, at it, to it**, y.
IT abbr. *see* **information technology**.
italic a. italique. ~**s** n. pl. italique m.
Ital|y n. Italie f. ~**ian** a. & n. italien(ne) (m. (f.)); (*lang.*) italien m.
itch n. démangeaison f. —v.i. démanger. **my arm** ~**es**, mon bras me démange. ~**y** a. qui démange.
item n. article m., chose f.; (*on agenda*) question f. **news** ~, nouvelle f. ~**ize** v.t. détailler.
itinerant a. itinérant; (*musician, actor*) ambulant.
itinerary n. itinéraire m.
its a. son, sa, pl. ses.
itself pron. lui-même, elle-même; (*reflexive*) se.
IUD abbr. (*intrauterine device*) stérilet m.
ivory n. ivoire m.
ivy n. lierre m.

J

jab v.t. (*thrust*) enfoncer; (*prick*) piquer. —n. coup m.; (*injection*) piqûre f.
jack n. (*techn.*) cric m.; (*cards*) valet m.; (*plug*) fiche f. —v.t. ~ **up**, soulever (avec un cric).
jackal n. chacal m.
jacket n. veste f., veston m.; (*of book*) jaquette f.

jack-knife n. couteau pliant m.
—v.i. (lorry) faire un tête-à-queue.
jackpot n. gros lot m. **hit the ~**,
gagner le gros lot.
jade n. (stone) jade m.
jaded a. las; (appetite) blasé.
jagged a. dentelé.
jail n. prison f. —v.t. mettre en
prison. **~er** n. geôlier m.
jam¹ n. confiture f.
jam² v.t./i. (wedge, become wedged)
(se) coincer; (cram) (s')entasser;
(street etc.) encombrer; (thrust)
enfoncer; (radio) brouiller. —n.
foule f.; (of traffic) embouteillage
m.; (situation: fam.) pétrin m. **~-
packed** a. (fam.) bourré.
Jamaica n. Jamaïque f.
jangle n. cliquetis m. —v.t./i.
(faire) cliqueter.
janitor n. concierge m.
January n. janvier m.
Japan n. Japon m. **~ese** a. & n.
japonais(e) (m. (f.)); (lang.)
japonais m.
jar¹ n. pot m., bocal m.
jar² v.i. grincer; (of colours etc.)
détonner. —v.t. ébranler. —n. son
discordant m.
jargon n. jargon m.
jasmine n. jasmin m.
jaundice n. jaunisse f.
jaunt n. (trip) balade f.
jaunty a. allègre.
javelin n. javelot m.
jaw n. mâchoire f. jacasser.
jay n. geai m.
jazz n. jazz m.
jealous a. jaloux. **~y** n. jalousie f.
jeans n. pl. (blue-)jean m.
jeep n. jeep f.
jeer v.t./i. **~ (at)**, railler; (boo)
huer. —n. raillerie f.; huée f.
jelly n. gelée f.
jellyfish n. méduse f.
jeopardy n. péril m. **~ize** v.t.
mettre en péril.

jerk n. secousse f.; (fool: sl.) idiot
m.; (creep: sl.) salaud m. —v.t.
donner une secousse à.
jersey n. (garment) chandail m.,
tricot m.; (fabric) jersey m.
jest n. plaisanterie f. —v.i.
plaisanter. **~er** n. bouffon m.
Jesus n. Jésus m.
jet¹ n. (mineral) jais m.
jet² n. (stream) jet m.; (plane)
avion à réaction m., jet m.
jettison v.t. jeter à la mer; (aviat.)
larguer; (fig.) abandonner.
jetty n. (breakwater) jetée f.
Jew n. Juif m. **~ess** n. Juive f.
jewel n. bijou m. **~ler** n.
bijou|tier, -ière m., f. **~lery** n.
bijoux m. pl.
Jewish a. juif.
jib v.i. regimber (at, devant).
jibe n. = **gibe**.
jig n. (dance) gigue f.
jigsaw n. puzzle m.
jingle v.t./i. (faire) tinter. —n.
tintement m.; (advertising) jingle
m., sonal m.
jinx n. (person: fam.) porte-
malheur m. invar.; (spell: fig.)
mauvais sort m.
jitter|s n. pl. **the ~s**, (fam.) la
frousse f. **~y** a. **be ~y**, (fam.)
avoir la frousse.
job n. travail m.; (post) poste m.
jockey n. jockey m. —v.i.
(manœuvre) manœuvrer.
jocular a. jovial.
jog v.t. pousser; (memory)
rafraîchir. —v.i. faire du jogging.
~ging n. jogging m.
join v.t. joindre, unir; (club)
devenir membre de; (political
group) adhérer à; (army)
s'engager dans. —n. (in
activity) se joindre à qn.; (meet)
rejoindre qn. —v.i. (roads etc.) se
rejoindre. **~ joint** m. **~ in**,
participer (à).

joiner n. menuisier m.

joint a. (account, venture) commun. —n. (join) joint m.; (anat.) articulation f.; (culin.) rôti m.

joist n. solive f.

jok|e n. plaisanterie f.; (trick) farce f. —v.i. plaisanter. **~er** n. blagueu|r, -se m., f.; (pej.) petit malin m.; (cards) joker m.

joll|y a. gai. —adv. (fam.) rudement.

jolt v.t./i. (vehicle, passenger) cahoter; (shake) secouer. —n. cahot m.; secousse f.

Jordan n. Jordanie f.

jostle v.t./i. (push) bousculer; (push each other) se bousculer.

jot n. brin m. —v.t. (p.t. jotted) **~ down**, noter. **~ter** n. (pad) bloc-notes m.

journal n. journal m. **~ism** n. journalisme m. **~ist** n. journaliste m./f.

journey n. voyage m.; (distance) trajet m. —v.i. voyager.

jovial a. jovial.

joy n. joie f.

joystick n. (comput.) manette f.

Judaism n. judaïsme m.

judder v.i. vibrer. —n. vibration f.

judge n. juge m. —v.t. juger. **~ment** n. jugement m.

judic|iary n. magistrature f. **~ial** a. judiciaire.

judicious a. judicieux.

judo n. judo m.

jug n. cruche f., pichet m.

juggernaut n. (lorry) poids lourd m., mastodonte m.

juggle v.t./i. jongler (avec). **~r** n. jongleu|r, -se m., f.

juic|e n. jus m. **~y** a. juteux; (details etc.: fam.) croustillant.

juke-box n. juke-box m.

July n. juillet m.

jumble v.t. mélanger. —n. (muddle) fouillis m. **~ sale**, vente (de charité) f.

jumbo a. **~ jet**, avion géant m., jumbo-jet m.

jump v.t./i. sauter; (start) sursauter; (of price etc.) faire un bond. —n. saut m.; sursaut m.; (increase) hausse f. **~ at**, sauter sur. **~-leads** n. pl. câbles de démarrage m. pl.

jumper n. pull(-over) m.

junction n. jonction f.; (of roads etc.) embranchement m.

June n. juin m.

jungle n. jungle f.

junior a. (in age) plus jeune (to, que); (in rank) subalterne; (school) élémentaire; (executive, doctor) jeune. —n. cadet(te) m. (f.); (schol.) petit(e) élève m. (f.); (sport) junior m./f.

junk n. bric-à-brac m. invar.; (poor material) camelote f. —v.t. (Amer., sl.) balancer.

junkie n. (sl.) drogué(e) m. (f.).

junta n. junte f.

jurisdiction n. juridiction f.

juror n. juré m.

jury n. jury m.

just a. (fair) juste. —adv. juste, exactement; (only, slightly) juste; (simply) tout simplement. **he has/had ~ left/etc.**, il vient/venait de partir/etc. **have ~ missed**, avoir manqué de peu. **it's ~ a cold**, ce n'est qu'un rhume. **~ly** adv. avec justice.

justice n. justice f.

justifiabl|e a. justifiable.

justify v.t. justifier. **~ication** n. justification f.

jut v.i. **~ out**, dépasser.

juvenile a. (youthful) juvénile; (childish) puéril; (delinquent) jeune; (court) pour enfants. —n. jeune m./f.

K

kangaroo n. kangourou m.

karate n. karaté m.

kebab n. brochette f.

keel n. (of ship) quille f. —v.i. ~ over, chavirer.

keen a. (interest, wind, feeling, etc.) vif; (mind, analysis) pénétrant; (edge, appetite) aiguisé; (eager) enthousiaste. **be ~ on,** (person, thing: fam.) aimer beaucoup. **be ~ to do or on doing,** tenir beaucoup à faire. m.

keep v.t. garder; (promise, shop, diary, etc.) tenir; (family) entretenir; (animals) élever; (rule etc.) respecter; (celebrate) célébrer; (delay) retenir; (prevent) empêcher; (conceal) cacher. —v.i. (food) se garder; (remain) rester. ~ (on), continuer (doing, à faire). ~ back v.t. retenir; v.i. ne pas s'approcher. ~ s.o. from doing, empêcher qn. de faire. ~ in/out, empêcher d'entrer/de sortir. ~ up, (se) maintenir. ~ up (with), suivre. ~-fit n. exercices physiques m. pl.

keg n. tonnelet m.

kennel n. niche f.

Kenya n. Kenya m.

kerb n. bord du trottoir m.

kernel n. amande f.

kerosene n. (aviation fuel) kérosène m.; (paraffin) pétrole (lampant) m.

ketchup n. ketchup m.

kettle n. bouilloire f.

key n. clef f.; (of piano etc.) touche f. —a. clef (f. invar.). ~-ring n. porte-clefs m. invar. —v.t. ~ in, (comput.) saisir.

keyboard n. clavier m.

keyhole n. trou de la serrure m.

khaki a. kaki invar.

kick v.t./i. donner un coup de pied (à); (of horse) ruer. —n. coup de pied m.; ruade f.; (of gun) recul m.; (thrill: fam.) (malin) plaisir m. ~ **off** n. coup d'envoi m. ~ **out,** (fam.) flanquer dehors.

kid n. (goat, leather) chevreau m.; (child: sl.) gosse m./f. —v.t./i. blaguer.

kidnap v.t. enlever, kidnapper. ~**ping** n. enlèvement m.

kidney n. rein m.; (culin.) rognon m.

kill v.t. tuer; (fig.) mettre fin à. —n. mise à mort f. ~**er** n. tueu|r, -se m., f. ~**ing** n. massacre m.; meurtre m.; a. (funny: fam.) tordant; (tiring: fam.) tuant.

kiln n. four m.

kilo n. kilo m.

kilobyte /ˈkɪləbaɪt/ n. kilo-octet m.

kilogram n. kilogramme m.

kilohertz n. kilohertz m.

kilometre n. kilomètre m.

kilowatt n. kilowatt m.

kilt n. kilt m.

kin n. parents m. pl.

kind[1] n. genre m., sorte f., espèce f. **in ~,** en nature f.

kind[2] a. gentil, bon. ~**ness** n. bonté f.

kindle v.t./i. (s')allumer.

kindly a. bienveillant. —adv. avec bonté. ~ **wait**/etc., voulez-vous avoir la bonté d'attendre/etc.

king n. roi m. ~**-size(d)** a. géant.

kingdom n. royaume m.; (bot.) règne m.

kingfisher n. martin-pêcheur m.

kink n. (in rope) entortillement m.; déformation f.; (fig.) perversion f.

kiosk n. kiosque m. **telephone ~,** cabine téléphonique f.

kip n. (sl.) roupillon m. —v.i. (sl.) roupiller.

kipper n. hareng fumé m.

kirby-grip n. pince à cheveux f.

kiss n. baiser m. —v.t./i. (s')embrasser.

kit n. équipement m.; (clothing) affaires f. pl.; (set of tools etc.) trousse f.; (for assembly) kit m. —v.t. ~ out, équiper.

kitchen n. cuisine f.

kite n. (toy) cerf-volant m.

kitten n. chaton m.

kitty n. (fund) cagnotte f.

knack n. truc m., chic m.

knead v.t. pétrir.

knee n. genou m.

kneecap n. rotule f.

kneel v.i. ~ (down), s'agenouiller.

knickers n. pl. (woman's undergarment) culotte f., slip m.

knife n. couteau m. —v.t. poignarder.

knight n. chevalier m.; (chess) cavalier m. —v.t. faire or armer chevalier.

knit v.t./i. tricoter; (bones etc.) (se) souder. —**ting** n. tricot m.

knitwear n. tricots m. pl.

knob n. bouton m.

knock v.t./i. frapper, cogner; (criticize: sl.) critiquer. —n. coup m. ~ down, (chair, pedestrian) renverser; (demolish) abattre; (reduce) baisser. ~ off v.t. faire tomber; (fam.) expédier; v.i. (fam.) s'arrêter de travailler. ~ out, (by blow) assommer; (tire) épuiser. ~out n. (boxing) knockout m. ~ over, renverser. ~ up, (meal etc.) préparer en vitesse. ~er n. heurtoir m.

knot n. nœud m. —v.t. nouer.

know v.t./i. savoir (that, que); (person, place) connaître. ~ how to do, savoir comment faire. ~ about, (cars etc.) s'y connaître en.

knowledge n. connaissance f.; (learning) connaissances f. pl.

knuckle n. articulation du doigt f.

Koran n. Coran m.

Korea n. Corée f.

kosher a. kascher invar.

Kurd a. & n. kurde m./f.

L

lab n. (fam.) labo m.

label n. étiquette f. —v.t. étiqueter.

laboratory n. laboratoire m.

laborious a. laborieux.

labour n. travail m.; (workers) main-d'œuvre f. —v.i. peiner. —v.t. trop insister sur. in ~, en train d'accoucher, en couches. **Labour** n. le parti travailliste m. —a. travailliste.

labourer n. manœuvre m.; (on farm) ouvrier agricole m.

labyrinth n. labyrinthe m.

lace n. dentelle f.; (of shoe) lacet m. —v.t. (fasten) lacer; (drink) arroser. ~-ups n. pl. chaussures à lacets f. pl.

lack n. manque m. —v.t. manquer de, être ~ing, manquer (in, de). for ~ of, faute de.

laconic a. laconique.

lacquer n. laque f.

lad n. garçon m., gars m.

ladder n. échelle f.; (in stocking) maille filée f. —v.t./i. (stocking) filer.

ladle n. louche f.

lady n. dame f.

ladybird n. coccinelle f.

lag[1] v.i. traîner. —n. (interval) décalage m.

lag[2] v.t. (pipes) calorifuger.

lager n. bière blonde f.

lagoon n. lagune f.

lake n. lac m.

lamb n. agneau m.

lambswool n. laine d'agneau f.

lame a. boiteux; (*excuse*) faible.

lament n. lamentation f. —v.t./i. se lamenter (sur).

laminated a. laminé.

lamp n. lampe f.

lamppost n. réverbère m.

lampshade n. abat-jour m. invar.

lance n. lance f. —v.t. (*med.*) inciser.

land n. terre f.; (*plot*) terrain m.; (*country*) pays m. —a. terrestre; (*policy, reform*) agraire. —v.t./i. débarquer; (*aircraft*) (se) poser, (faire) atterrir; (*fall*) tomber; (*obtain*) décrocher; (*put*) mettre; (*a blow*) porter. ~ **up**, se retrouver.

landing n. débarquement m.; (*aviat.*) atterrissage m.; (*top of stairs*) palier m. ~**stage** m. débarcadère m. ~**strip**, piste d'atterrissage f.

land|lady n. propriétaire f.; (*of inn*) patronne f. ~**lord** n. propriétaire m.; patron m.

landmark n. (point de) repère m.

landscape n. paysage m.

landslide n. glissement de terrain m.; (*pol.*) raz-de-marée (électoral) m. invar.

lane n. (*path, road*) chemin m.; (*strip of road*) voie f.; (*of traffic*) file f.; (*aviat.*) couloir m.

language n. langue f.; (*speech, style*) langage m.

languid a. languissant.

languish v.i. languir.

lank a. grand et maigre.

lanky a. grand et maigre.

lanolin n. lanoline f.

lantern n. lanterne f.

lap[1] n. genoux m. pl.; (*sport*) tour (de piste) m.

lap[2] v.t. ~ **up**, laper. —v.i. (*waves*) clapoter.

lapel n. revers m.

lapse v.i. (*decline*) se dégrader; (*expire*) se périmer. —n. défaillance f., erreur f.; (*of time*) intervalle m. ~ **into**, retomber dans.

lard n. saindoux m.

larder n. garde-manger m. invar.

large a. grand, gros. **by and** ~, en général. ~**ly** adv. en grande mesure.

lark[1] n. (*bird*) alouette f.

lark[2] n. (*bit of fun. fam.*) rigolade f. —v.i. (*fam.*) rigoler.

larva n. larve f.

laryngitis n. laryngite f.

larynx n. larynx m.

laser n. laser m. ~ **printer**, imprimante laser f.

lash v.t. fouetter. —n. coup de fouet m.; (*eyelash*) cil m.

lashings n. pl. ~ **of**, (*cream etc. sl.*) des masses de.

lass n. jeune fille f.

lasso n. lasso m.

last[1] a. dernier. —adv. en dernier; (*most recently*) la dernière fois. —n. dernier, -ière m., f.; (*remainder*) reste m. **at** ~, enfin. ~**-minute** a. de dernière minute. ~ **night**, hier soir. ~**ly** adv. en dernier lieu.

last[2] v.i. durer. ~**ing** a. durable.

latch n. loquet m.

late a. (*not on time*) en retard; (*recent*) récent; (*former*) ancien; (*hour, fruit, etc.*) tardif; (*deceased*) défunt. ~**st** (*last*) dernier. —adv. (*not early*) tard; (*not on time*) en retard. **in** ~ **July**, fin juillet.

latecomer n. retardataire m./f.

lately adv. dernièrement.

latent a. latent.

lateral a. latéral.

lathe n. tour m.

lather n. mousse f. —v.t. savonner. —v.i. mousser.

Latin n. (lang.) latin m. —a. latin. **~ America,** Amérique latine f.

latitude n. latitude f.

latrine n. latrines f. pl.

latter a. dernier. —n. **the ~,** celui-ci, celle-ci.

lattice n. treillage m.

laugh v.i. rire (**at,** de). —n. rire m. **~able** a. ridicule.

laughter n. (act) rire m.; (sound of laughs) rires m. pl.

launch[1] v.t. lancer. —n. lancement m. **~ing pad,** aire de lancement f.

launch[2] n. (boat) vedette f.

launderette n. laverie automatique f.

laundry n. (place) blanchisserie f.; (clothes) linge m.

laurel n. laurier m.

lava n. lave f.

lavatory n. cabinets m. pl.

lavender n. lavande f.

lavish a. (person) prodigue; (plentiful) copieux; (lush) somptueux. —v.t. prodiguer (**on,** à). **~ly** adv. copieusement.

law n. loi f.; (profession, subject of study) droit m.

lawcourt n. tribunal m.

lawn n. pelouse f., gazon m. **~mower** n. tondeuse à gazon f. **~ tennis,** tennis (sur gazon) m.

lawsuit n. procès m.

lawyer n. avocat m.

lax a. négligent; (morals etc.) relâché.

laxative n. laxatif m.

lay[1] a. (non-clerical) laïque; (opinion etc.) d'un profane.

lay[2] v.t. poser, mettre; (trap) tendre; (table) mettre; (plan) former; (eggs) pondre. —v.i. pondre. **~ down,** (dé)poser; (condition) (im)poser. **~ off** v.t. (worker) licencier; v.i. (fam.) arrêter. **~off** n. licenciement m.

~ on, (provide) fournir. **~ out,** (design) disposer; (display) disposer; (money) dépenser.

lay-by n. petite aire de stationnement f.

layer n. couche f.

layman n. profane m.

layout n. disposition f.

laze v.i. paresser.

laz|y a. paresseux. **~iness** n. paresse f.

lead[1] v.t./i. (p.t. **led**) mener; (team etc.) diriger; (life) mener; (induce) amener. **~ to,** conduire à, mener à. —n. avance f.; (clue) indice m.; (leash) laisse f.; (theatre) premier rôle m.; (wire) fil m.; (example) exemple m. **~ up to,** (come to) en venir à; (precede) précéder.

lead[2] n. plomb m.; (of pencil) mine f.

leader n. chef m.; (of country, club, etc.) dirigeant(e) m. (f.); (leading article) éditorial m. **~ship** n. direction f.

leading a. principal.

leaf n. feuille f.; (of table) rallonge f.

leaflet n. prospectus m.

league n. ligue f.; (sport) championnat m.

leak n. fuite f. —v.i. fuir; (news: fig.) s'ébruiter. —v.t. répandre; (fig.) divulguer. **~age** n. fuite f. **~y** a. qui a une fuite.

lean[1] a. maigre. —n. (of meat) maigre m.

lean[2] v.t./i. (rest) (s')appuyer; (slope) pencher. **~ out,** se pencher à l'extérieur.

leaning a. penché —n. tendance f.

leap v.i. bondir. —n. bond m. **~-frog** n. saute-mouton m. jouer.

learn v.t./i. apprendre (**to do,** à faire). **~er** n. débutant(e) m. (f.).

learned a. érudit.

lease n. bail m. —v.t. louer à bail.

leaseback n. cession-bail f.

leash n. laisse f.

least a. the **~**, (smallest amount of) le moins de; (slightest) le or la moindre. —n. le moins. —adv. le moins; (with adjective) le or la moins. **at ~**, au moins.

leather n. cuir m.

leave v.t. laisser; (depart from) quitter. —n. (holiday) congé m.; (consent) permission f. **be left (over)**, rester. **~ behind**, laisser. **~ out**, omettre.

Leban|on n. Liban m. **~ese** a. & n. libanais(e) (m. (f.)).

lecture n. cours m., conférence f.; (rebuke) réprimande f. —v.t./i. faire un cours or une conférence (à); (rebuke) réprimander. **~r** n. conférenc|ier, -ière m., f., (univ.) enseignant(e) m. (f.).

ledge n. (window) rebord m.; (rock) saillie f.

ledger n. grand livre m.

leek n. poireau m.

leer v.i. **~ (at)**, lorgner. —n. regard sournois m.

leeway n. (naut.) dérive f.; (fig.) liberté d'action f. **make up ~**, rattraper le retard.

left[1] **~ luggage (office)**, consigne f. **~overs** n. pl. restes m. pl.

left[2] a. gauche; (pol.) à gauche. —n. gauche f. **~-hand** a. à or de gauche. **~-handed** a. gaucher. **~-wing** a. (pol.) de gauche.

leg n. jambe f.; (of animal) patte f.; (of table) pied m.; (of chicken) cuisse f.; (of lamb) gigot m.; (of journey) étape f.

legacy n. legs m.

legal a. légal; (affairs etc.) juridique. **~ly** adv. légalement.

legend n. légende f. **~ary** a. légendaire.

leggings n. pl. collant sans pieds m.

legib|le a. lisible. **~ility** n. lisibilité f.

legion n. légion f.

legislat|e v.i. légiférer. **~ion** n. (body of laws) législation f.; (law) loi f.

legitimate a. légitime.

leisure n. loisir(s) m. (pl.). **~ centre**, centre de loisirs m. **~ly** a. lent; adv. sans se presser.

lemon n. citron m.

lemonade n. (fizzy) limonade f.; (still) citronnade f.

lend v.t. prêter; (contribute) donner. **~er** n. prêteu|r, -se m., f.

length n. longueur f.; (in time) durée f.; (section) morceau m. **at ~**, (at last) enfin. **in (great) ~**, longuement. **~y** a. long.

lengthen v.t./i. (s')allonger.

lengthways adv. dans le sens de la longueur.

lenien|t a. indulgent. **~cy** n. indulgence f. **~tly** adv. avec indulgence.

lens n. lentille f.; (of spectacles) verre m.; (photo.) objectif m.

Lent n. Carême m.

lentil n. (bean) lentille f.

Leo n. le Lion.

leopard n. léopard m.

leotard n. body m.

leper n. lépreu|x, -se m., f.

leprosy n. lèpre f.

lesbian n. lesbienne f. —a. lesbien.

lesion n. lésion f.

less a. (in quantity etc.) moins de (than, que). —adv., n. & prep. moins. **~ than**, (with numbers) moins de; **work**/etc. **~ than**, travailler/etc. moins que. **ten pounds**/etc. **~**, dix livres/etc. de moins.

lessen v.t./i. diminuer.

lesson n. leçon f.

lest conj. de peur que or de.

let v.t. laisser; (*lease*) louer. —n. location f. **~ down,** baisser; (*deflate*) dégonfler; (*fig.*) décevoir. **~-down** n. déception f. **go** v.t. lâcher; v.i. lâcher prise. **~ sb. in/out,** laisser or faire entrer/sortir qn. **~ off,** (*explode, fire*) faire éclater or partir; (*excuse*) dispenser; (*not punish*) ne pas punir.

lethal a. mortel; (*weapon*) meurtrier.

letharg|y n. léthargie f. **~ic** a. léthargique.

letter n. lettre f. **~-box** n. boite f or aux lettres f.

lettuce n. laitue f., salade f.

leukaemia n. leucémie f.

level a. plat, uni; (*on surface*) horizontal; (*in height*) au même niveau (**with,** que); (*in score*) à égalité. —n. niveau m. (*spirit*) **~,** niveau à bulle m. —v.t. niveler; (*aim*) diriger. **~ crossing,** passage à niveau m.

lever n. levier m. —v.t. soulever au moyen d'un levier.

levy v.t. (*tax*) (pré)lever. —n. impôt m.

liable a. be **~ to do,** avoir tendance à faire, pouvoir faire. **~ to,** (*illness etc.*) sujet à; (*fine*) passible de. **~ for,** responsable de.

liability n. responsabilité f.; (*fam.*) handicap m.

liais|e v.i. (*fam.*) faire la liaison. **~on** n. liaison f.

liar n. menteu|r, -se m., f.

libel n. diffamation f. —v.t. diffamer.

liberal a. libéral; (*generous*) généreux, libéral.

Liberal a. & n. (*pol.*) libéral(e) (m. (f.)).

liberat|e v.t. libérer. **~ion** n. libération f.

liberty n. liberté f.

Libra n. la Balance.

librar|y n. bibliothèque f. **~ian** n. bibliothécaire m. f.

libretto n. (*mus.*) livret m.

Libya n. Libye f. **~n** a. & n. libyen(ne) (m. (f.)).

licence n. permis m.; (*for television*) redevance f.; (*comm.*) licence f.; (*liberty: fig.*) licence f.

license v.t. accorder un permis à, autoriser.

lichen n. lichen m.

lick v.t. lécher; (*defeat: sl.*) rosser. —n. coup de langue m.

lid n. couvercle m.

lie[1] n. mensonge m. —v.i. (*tell lies*) mentir.

lie[2] v.i. s'allonger; (*remain*) rester; (*be*) se trouver, être; (*in grave*) reposer. **be lying,** être allongé. **~ down,** s'allonger.

lieutenant n. lieutenant m.

life n. vie f. **~-guard** n. sauveteur m. **~ insurance,** assurance-vie f. **~-jacket** n. gilet de sauvetage m. **~-size(d)** a. grandeur nature invar. **~-style** n. style de vie m.

lifebelt n. bouée de sauvetage f.

lifeboat n. canot de sauvetage m.

lifebuoy n. bouée de sauvetage f.

lifelike a. très ressemblant.

lifetime n. vie f.

lift v.t. lever; (*steal: fam.*) voler. —v.i. (*of fog*) se lever. —n. (*in building*) ascenseur m. **give a ~ to,** emmener (en voiture).

ligament n. ligament m.

light[1] n. lumière f.; (*lamp*) lampe f.; (*for fire, on vehicle, etc.*) feu m.; (*headlight*) phare m. —a. (*not dark*) clair. —v.t. allumer; (*room etc.*) éclairer; (*match*) frotter. **~ bulb,** ampoule f. **~ pen,** crayon optique m. **~ up** v.i. s'allumer; v.t. (*room*) éclairer. **~-year** n. année lumière f.

light² *a.* (*not heavy*) léger. **~-
hearted** *a.* gai. **~ly** *adv.* légèrement. **~ness** *n.* légèreté *f.*

lighten¹ *v.t.* (*give light to*) éclairer; (*make brighter*) éclaircir.

lighten² *v.t.* (*make less heavy*) alléger.

lighter *n.* briquet *m.*

lighthouse *n.* phare *m.*

lighting *n.* éclairage *m.* **~ technician,** éclairagiste *m./f.*

lightning *n.* éclair(s) *m.* (pl.), foudre *f.* —*a.* éclair *invar.*

lightweight *a.* léger. —*n.* (*boxing*) poids léger *m.*

like¹ *a.* semblable, pareil. —*prep.*
comme. —*conj.* (*fam.*) comme. —*n.* pareil *m.*

like² *v.t.* aimer (bien). **~s** *n. pl.*
goûts *m. pl.* **I should ~,** je voudrais, j'aimerais. **would you
~?,** voulez-vous? **~able** *a.* sympathique.

likel|y *a.* probable. —*adv.*
probablement. **he is ~y to do,** il fera probablement. **~ihood** *n.*
probabilité *f.*

liken *v.t.* comparer.

likewise *adv.* de même.

liking *n.* (*for thing*) penchant *m.*; (*for person*) affection *f.*

lilac *n.* lilas *m.* —*a.* lilas *invar.*

lily *n.* lis *m.*, lys *m.* **~ of the
valley,** muguet *m.*

limb *n.* membre *m.*

limber *v.i.* **~ up,** faire des exercices d'assouplissement.

lime¹ *n.* chaux *f.*

lime² *n.* (*fruit*) citron vert *m.*

lime³ *n.* **~(-tree),** tilleul *m.*

limit *n.* limite *f.* —*v.t.* limiter. **~ed company,** société anonyme *f.* **~ation** *n.* limitation *f.*

limousine *n.* (*car*) limousine *f.*

limp¹ *v.i.* boiter. —*n.* **have a ~,** boiter.

limp² *a.* mou.

limpid *a.* limpide.

line¹ *n.* ligne *f.*; (*track*) voie *f.*; (*wrinkle*) ride *f.*; (*row*) rangée *f.*, file *f.*; (*of poem*) vers *m.*; (*rope*) corde *f.*; (*of goods*) gamme *f.*; (*queue: Amer.*) queue *f.* —*v.t.* (*paper*) régler; (*streets etc.*) border. **in ~ with,** en accord avec. **~ up,** (s')aligner; (*in queue*) faire la queue. **~ sth. up,** prévoir qch.

line² *v.t.* (*garment*) doubler; (*fill*) remplir, garnir.

linear *a.* linéaire.

linen *n.* (*sheets etc.*) linge *m.*; (*material*) lin *m.*, toile de lin *f.*

liner *n.* paquebot *m.*

linesman *n.* (*football*) juge de touche *m.*

linger *v.i.* s'attarder; (*smells etc.*) persister.

lingerie *n.* lingerie *f.*

linguist *n.* linguiste *m./f.*

linguistic *a.* linguistique. **~s** *n.*
linguistique *f.*

lining *n.* doublure *f.*

link *n.* lien *m.*; (*of chain*) maillon *m.* —*v.t.* relier; (*relate*) (re)lier. **~
up,** (*of roads*) se rejoindre. **~age**
n. lien *m.* **~-up** *n.* liaison *f.*

lino *n.* lino *m.*

linoleum *n.* linoléum *m.*

lint *n.* (*med.*) tissu ouaté *m.*; (*fluff*) peluche(s) *f.* (pl.).

lion *n.* lion *m.*

lip *n.* lèvre *f.*; (*edge*) rebord *m.* **~-
read** *v.t./i.* lire sur les lèvres.

lipstick *n.* rouge (à lèvres) *m.*

liqueur *n.* liqueur *f.*

liquid *n. & a.* liquide (*m.*). **~ize**
v.t. passer au mixeur. **~izer** *n.*
mixeur *m.*

liquidat|e *v.t.* liquider. **~ion** *n.*
liquidation *f.* **go into ~ion,**
déposer son bilan.

liquor *n.* alcool *m.*

liquorice *n.* réglisse *f.*

lisp *n.* zézaiement *m.* —*v.i.* zézayer.

list *n.* liste *f.* —*v.t.* dresser la liste de.

listen *v.i.* écouter. **~ to** écouter. **~er** *n.* audi|teur, -trice *m./f.*

literal *a.* littéral; (*person*) prosaïque. **~ly** *adv.* littéralement.

literary *a.* littéraire.

litera|te *a.* qui sait lire et écrire. **~cy** *n.* capacité de lire et écrire *f.*

literature *n.* littérature *f.*; (*fig.*) documentation *f.*

litigation *n.* litige *m.*

litre *n.* litre *m.*

litter *n.* détritus *m. pl.*, papiers *m. pl.*; (*animals*) portée *f.* —*v.t.* éparpiller; (*make untidy*) laisser des détritus dans. **~-bin** *n.* poubelle *f.* **~ed with**, jonché de.

little *a.* petit; (*not much*) peu de. —*n.* peu *m.* —*adv.* peu. **a ~**, un peu (de).

liturgy *n.* liturgie *f.*

live[1] *a.* vivant; (*wire*) sous tension; (*broadcast*) en direct.

live[2] *v.t./i.* vivre; (*reside*) habiter, vivre. **~ on**, (*feed o.s. on*) vivre de; (*continue*) survivre.

livelihood *n.* moyens d'existence *m. pl.*

lively *a.* vif, vivant.

liven *v.t./i.* **~ up**, (s')animer; (*cheer up*) (s')égayer.

liver *n.* foie *m.*

livestock *n.* bétail *m.*

livid *a.* livide; (*angry: fam.*) furieux.

living *a.* vivant. —*n.* vie *f.* **make a ~**, gagner sa vie. **~ conditions**, conditions de vie *f. pl.* **~-room** *n.* salle de séjour *f.*

lizard *n.* lézard *m.*

llama *n.* lama *m.*

load *n.* charge *f.*; (*loaded goods*) chargement *m.*, charge *f.*; (*weight,*

strain) poids *m.* **~s of**, (*fam.*) des masses de. —*v.t.* charger.

loaf[1] *n.* pain *m.*

loaf[2] *v.i.* **~ (about)**, fainéanter.

loam *n.* terreau *m.*

loan *n.* prêt *m.*; (*money borrowed*) emprunt *m.* —*v.t.* (*lend: fam.*) prêter.

loathe *v.t.* détester. **~ing** *n.* dégoût *m.*

lobby *n.* entrée *f.*, vestibule *m.*; (*pol.*) lobby *m.*, groupe de pression *m.* —*v.t.* faire pression sur.

lobe *n.* lobe *m.*

lobster *n.* homard *m.*

local *a.* local; (*shops etc.*) du quartier. —*n.* personne du coin *f.*; (*pub: fam.*) pub du coin *m.* **~ly** *adv.* localement; (*nearby*) dans les environs.

locat|e *v.t.* (*situate*) situer; (*find*) repérer. **~ion** *n.* emplacement *m.*

lock[1] *n.* mèche (de cheveux) *f.*

lock[2] *n.* (*of door etc.*) serrure *f.*; (*on canal*) écluse *f.* —*v.t./i.* fermer à clef; (*wheels: auto.*) (se) bloquer. **~ in** or **up**, (*person*) enfermer. **~ out**, (*by mistake*) enfermer dehors. **~-out** *n.* lockout *m.* invar.

locker *n.* casier *m.*

locket *n.* médaillon *m.*

locomotion *n.* locomotion *f.*

locomotive *n.* locomotive *f.*

locum *n.* (*doctor etc.*) remplaçant(e) *m.* (*f.*).

locust *n.* criquet *m.*

lodge *n.* (*house*) pavillon (de gardien *or* de chasse) *m.*; (*of porter*) loge *f.* —*v.t.* loger; (*money, complaint*) déposer. —*v.i.* être logé (*with*, chez); (*become fixed*) se loger. **~r** *n.* locataire *m./f.*, pensionnaire *m./f.*

lodgings *n.* chambre (meublée) *f.*; (*flat*) logement *m.*

loft *n.* grenier *m.*

lofty a. (tall, noble) élevé; (haughty) hautain.

log n. (of wood) bûche f. ~(-book), (naut.) journal de bord m.; (auto.) (équivalent de la) carte grise f. —v.t. noter; (distance) parcourir. ~ on, entrer. ~ off, sortir.

logarithm n. logarithme m.

logic a. logique. ~al a. logique. ~ally adv. logiquement.

logistics n. logistique f.

logo n. (fam.) emblème m.

loin n. (culin.) filet m.

loiter v.i. traîner.

loll v.i. se prélasser.

loll|ipop n. sucette f. ~y n. (fam.) sucette f.; (sl.) fric m.

London n. Londres m./f.

lone a. solitaire.

lonely a. solitaire; (person) seul, solitaire.

long[1] a. long. —adv. longtemps. how ~ is?, quelle est la longueur de?; (in time) quelle est la durée de? how ~?, combien de temps? he will not be ~, il n'en a pas pour longtemps. a ~ time, longtemps. as or so ~ as, pourvu que. before ~, avant peu. I no ~er do, je ne fais plus. ~-distance a. (flight) sur long parcours; (phone call) interurbain. ~ jump, saut en longueur m. ~-term a. à long terme. ~ wave, grandes ondes f. pl. ~-winded a. (speaker etc.) verbeux.

long[2] v.i. avoir bien or très envie (for, to, de). ~ for s.o., (pine for) languir après qn. ~ing n. envie f.; (nostalgia) nostalgie f.

longevity n. longévité f.

longitude n. longitude f.

loo n. (fam.) toilettes f. pl.

look v.t./i. regarder; (seem) avoir l'air. —n. regard m.; (appearance) air m., aspect m. (good) ~s, beauté f. ~ after, s'occuper de,

soigner. ~ at, regarder. ~ for, chercher. ~ forward to, attendre avec impatience. ~ into, examiner. ~ like, ressembler à, avoir l'air de. ~ out, faire attention. ~ out for, chercher; (watch) guetter. ~ round, se retourner. ~ up, (word) chercher; (visit) passer voir. ~ up to, respecter.

loom[1] n. métier à tisser m.

loom[2] v.i. surgir; (event etc.: fig.) paraître imminent.

loop n. boucle f. —v.t. boucler.

loophole n. (in rule) échappatoire f.

loose a. (knot etc.) desserré; (page etc.) détaché; (clothes) ample, lâche; (tooth) qui bouge; (lax) relâché; (not packed) en vrac; (inexact) vague; (pej.) immoral. ~ly adv. sans serrer; (roughly) vaguement.

loosen v.t. (slacken) desserrer; (untie) défaire.

loot n. butin m. —v.t. piller.

lop v.t. ~ off, couper.

lop-sided a. de travers.

lord n. seigneur m.; (British title) lord m. the L~, le Seigneur.

lore n. traditions f. pl.

lorry n. camion m.

lose v.t./i. perdre. get lost, se perdre. ~r n. perdant(e) m. (f.).

loss n. perte f. be at a ~, être perplexe.

lost a. perdu. ~ property objets trouvés m. pl.

lot[1] n. (fate) sort m.; (at auction) lot m.; (land) lotissement m.

lot[2] n. the ~, (le) tout m.; (people) tous m. pl., toutes f. pl. a ~ (of), ~s (of), (fam.) beaucoup (de).

lotion n. lotion f.

lottery n. loterie f.

loud a. bruyant, fort. —adv. fort. ~ly adv. fort.

loudspeaker n. haut-parleur m.

lounge v.i. paresser. —n. salon m.

louse n. pou m.

lousy a. pouilleux; (bad: sl.) infect.

lout n. rustre m.

lovable a. adorable.

love n. amour m.; (tennis) zéro m. —v.t. aimer; (like greatly) aimer (beaucoup) (**to do**, faire). **in ~**, amoureux (**with**, de). **make ~**, faire l'amour.

lovely a. joli; (delightful: fam.) très agréable.

lover n. amant m.; (devotee) amateur m. (**of**, de).

loving a. affectueux.

low a. & adv. bas. —n. (low pressure) dépression f. **~ in sth.**, à faible teneur en qch. **~-calorie** a. basses-calories.

lower v.t. baisser. **~ o.s.**, s'abaisser.

loyal a. loyal. **~ly** adv. loyalement. **~ty** n. loyauté f.

lozenge n. (shape) losange m.; (tablet) pastille f.

Ltd. abbr. (Limited) SA.

lubric|ate v.t. graisser, lubrifier. **~ant** n. lubrifiant m. **~ation** n. graissage m.

lucid a. lucide.

luck n. chance f. **bad ~**, malchance f. **good ~!**, bonne chance!

luck|y a. qui a de la chance, heureux; (event) heureux; (number) qui porte bonheur. **~ily** adv. heureusement.

lucrative a. lucratif.

ludicrous a. ridicule.

lug v.t. traîner.

luggage n. bagages m. pl. **~-rack** n. porte-bagages m. invar.

lukewarm a. tiède.

lull v.t. (soothe, send to sleep) endormir. —n. accalmie f.

lullaby n. berceuse f.

lumbago n. lumbago m.

lumber n. bric-à-brac m. invar.; (wood) bois de charpente m.

lumberjack n. (Amer.) bûcheron m.

luminous a. lumineux.

lump n. morceau m.; (swelling on body) grosseur f.; (in liquid) grumeau m. **~y** a. (sauce) grumeleux; (bumpy) bosselé.

lunar a. lunaire.

lunatic n. fou, folle m., f.

lunch n. déjeuner m. —v.i. déjeuner. **~ box**, cantine f.

lung n. poumon m.

lunge n. mouvement brusque en avant m. —v.i. s'élancer (**at**, sur).

lurch[1] **leave in the ~**, planter là, laisser en plan.

lurch[2] v.i. (person) tituber.

lure v.t. appâter, attirer. —n. (attraction) attrait m., appât m.

lurid a. choquant, affreux; (gaudy) voyant.

lurk v.i. se cacher; (in ambush) s'embusquer; (prowl) rôder.

luscious a. appétissant.

lush a. luxuriant.

lust n. luxure f.; (fig.) convoitise f. —v.i. **~ after**, convoiter.

lustre n. lustre m.

lusty a. robuste.

lute n. (mus.) luth m.

Luxemburg n. Luxembourg m.

luxuriant a. luxuriant.

luxurious a. luxueux.

luxury n. luxe m. —a. de luxe.

lynch v.t. lyncher.

lynx n. lynx m.

lyric a. lyrique. **~s** n. pl. paroles f. pl. **~al** a. lyrique.

M

mac n. (fam.) imper m.

macaroni n. macaronis m. pl.

macaroon n. macaron m.

machine n. machine f. —v.t. (sew) coudre à la machine; (techn.) usiner. **~-gun** n. mitrailleuse f. mitrailler. **~ tool,** machine-outil f.

machinery n. machinerie f.; (working parts & fig.) mécanisme(s) m. (pl.).

machinist n. (operator) opéra|teur, -trice sur machine m., f.; (on sewing-machine) piqueu|r, -se m., f.

macho n. macho m. —a. macho invar.

mackerel n. invar. (fish) maquereau m.

mackintosh n. imperméable m.

macrobiotic a. macrobiotique.

mad a. fou; (foolish) insensé (dog etc.) enragé; (angry: fam.) furieux. **be ~ about,** se passionner pour; (person) être fou de. **drive s.o. ~,** exaspérer qn. **~ly** adv. (interested, in love, etc.) follement; (frantically) comme un fou. **~ness** n. folie f.

madam n. madame f.; (unmarried) mademoiselle f.

madden v.t. exaspérer.

made ~ to measure, fait sur mesure.

madman n. fou m.

madrigal n. madrigal m.

magazine n. revue f., magazine m.; (of gun) magasin m.

magenta a. magenta (invar.).

maggot n. ver m., asticot m. **~y** a. véreux.

magic n. magie f. —a. magique. **~al** a. magique.

magician n. magicien(ne) m. (f.).

magistrate n. magistrat m.

magnanim|ous a. magnanime. **~ity** n. magnanimité f.

magnate n. magnat m.

magnesia n. magnésie f.

magnet n. aimant m. **~ic** a. magnétique. **~ism** n. magnétisme m. **~ize** v.t. magnétiser.

magneto n. magnéto f.

magnificen|t a. magnifique. **~ce** n. magnificence f.

magnif|y v.t. grossir; (sound) amplifier; (fig.) exagérer. **~ication** n. grossissement m.; amplification f. **~ying glass,** loupe f.

magnolia n. magnolia m.

magpie n. pie f.

mahogany n. acajou m.

maid n. (servant) bonne f.

maiden n. (old use) jeune fille f. —a. (aunt) célibataire; (voyage) premier. **~ name,** nom de jeune fille m.

mail[1] n. poste f.; (letters) courrier m. —a. (bag, van) postal. —v.t. envoyer par la poste. **mail box,** boîte à lettres f. **~ing list,** liste d'adresses f. **~ order,** vente par correspondance f.

mail[2] /meɪl/ n. (armour) cotte de mailles f.

maim v.t. mutiler.

main[1] a. principal. **~ line,** grande ligne f. **a ~ road,** une grande route. **~ly** adv. principalement, surtout.

main[2] n. (water/gas) ~, conduite d'eau/de gaz f. **the ~s,** (electr.) le secteur.

mainframe n. unité centrale f.

mainland n. continent m.

maintain v.t. (continue, keep, assert) maintenir; (house, machine, family) entretenir; (rights) soutenir.

maintenance n. (care) entretien m.; (continuation) maintien m.;

(allowance) pension alimentaire f.

maisonette n. duplex m.

maize n. maïs m.

majestic a. majestueux.

majesty n. majesté f.

major a. majeur. —n. commandant m. ∼ **road**, route à priorité f.

Majorca n. Majorque f.

majority n. majorité f. —a. majoritaire. **the** ∼ **of people**, la plupart des gens.

make v.t./i. *(p.t. made)* faire; *(manufacture)* fabriquer; *(friends)* se faire; *(money)* gagner, se faire; *(decision)* prendre; *(destination)* arriver à; *(cause to be)* rendre. ∼ **s.o. do sth.**, faire faire qch. à qn.; *(force)* obliger qn. à faire qch. —n. fabrication f.; *(brand)* marque f. **be made of**, être fait de. ∼ **s.o. happy**, rendre qn. heureux. **I cannot** ∼ **anything of it**, je n'y comprends rien. ∼ **believe**, faire semblant. ∼**believe**, a. feint, illusoire; n. fantaisie f. ∼ **do**, *(manage)* se débrouiller (**with**, avec). ∼ **do with**, *(content o.s.)* se contenter de. ∼ **off**, filer (**with**, avec). ∼ **out** v.t. distinguer; *(understand)* comprendre; *(draw up)* faire; *(assert)* prétendre; v.i. *(fam.)* se débrouiller. ∼ **over**, céder (**to**, à); *(convert)* transformer. ∼ **up** v.t. faire, former; *(story)* inventer; *(deficit)* combler; v.i. se réconcilier. ∼ **up** *(one's face)*, se maquiller. ∼**up** n. maquillage m.; *(of object)* constitution f.; *(psych.)* caractère m. ∼ **up for**, compenser; *(time)* rattraper. ∼ **up one's mind**, se décider.

maker n. fabricant m.

makeshift n. expédient m. —a. provisoire.

malaria n. malaria f.

Malay a. & n. malais(e) (m. (f.)).

∼**sia** n. Malaysia f.

Malaya n. Malaisie f.

male a. *(voice, sex)* masculin; *(bot., techn.)* mâle. —n. mâle m.

malformation n. malformation f. ∼**ed** a. difforme.

malfunction n. mauvais fonctionnement m. —v.i. mal fonctionner.

malice n. méchanceté f.

malicious a. méchant. ∼**ly** adv. méchamment.

malign a. pernicieux. —v.t. calomnier.

malignan|t a. malveillant; *(tumour)* malin. ∼**cy** n. malveillance f.; malignité f.

mall n. *(shopping)* ∼, centre commercial m.

malleable a. malléable.

mallet n. maillet m.

malnutrition n. sous-alimentation f.

malt n. malt m.

Malt|a n. Malte f. ∼**ese** a. & n. maltais(e) (m. (f.)).

maltreat v.t. maltraiter. ∼**ment** n. mauvais traitement m.

mammal n. mammifère m.

mammoth n. mammouth m. —a. monstre.

man n. homme m.; *(in sports team)* joueur m.; *(chess)* pièce f. —v.t. pourvoir en hommes; *(ship)* armer; *(guns)* servir; *(be on duty at)* être de service à. ∼**-made** a. artificiel. ∼**ned space flight**, vol spatial habité m.

manage v.t. diriger; *(shop, affairs)* gérer; *(handle)* manier. —v.i. se débrouiller. ∼ **to do**, réussir à faire. ∼**able** a. *(tool, size, person, etc.)* maniable; *(job)* faisable. ∼**ment** n. direction f.; *(of shop)* gestion f. **managing director**, directeur général m.

manager n. direc|teur, -trice m./f.; (of shop) gérant(e) m.(f.); (of actor) impresario m. **~ess** n. directrice f.; gérante f. **~ial** a. directorial.

mandarin n. mandarin m.; (orange) mandarine f.

mandate n. mandat m.

mandatory a. obligatoire.

mane n. crinière f.

manganese n. manganèse m.

mangetout n. mange-tout m. invar.

mangle v.t. mutiler.

mango n. mangue f.

manhandle v.t. maltraiter, malmener.

manhole n. trou d'homme m.

mania n. manie f. **~c** n. maniaque m./f., fou m., folle f.

manic-depressive a & n. maniaco-dépressif(-ive) (m. (f.)).

manicur|e n. soin des mains m. —v.t. soigner, manucurer. **~ist** n. manucure m./f.

manifest a. manifeste. —v.t. manifester. **~ation** n. manifestation f.

manifesto n. manifeste m.

manifold a. multiple. —n. (auto.) collecteur m.

manipulat|e v.t. (tool, person) manipuler. **~ion** n. manipulation f.

mankind n. genre humain m.

manly a. viril.

manner n. manière f.; (attitude) attitude f.; (kind) sorte f. **~s**, (social behaviour) manières f. pl. **~ed** a. maniéré.

manœuvre n. manœuvre f. —v.t./i. manœuvrer.

manor n. manoir m.

manpower n. main-d'œuvre f.

mansion n. château m.

manslaughter n. homicide involontaire m.

mantelpiece n. (shelf) cheminée f.

manual a. manuel. —n. (handbook) manuel m.

manufacture v.t. fabriquer. —n. fabrication f. **~r** n. fabricant m.

manure n. fumier m.; (artificial) engrais m.

manuscript n. manuscrit m.

many a. & n. beaucoup (de). **a great** or **good ~**, un grand nombre (de). **~ a**, bien des.

Maori a. maori. —n. Maori(e) m. (f.).

map n. carte f.; (of streets etc.) plan m. —v.t. faire la carte de. **~ out**, (route) tracer; (arrange) organiser.

maple n. érable m.

mar v.t. gâter; (spoil beauty of) déparer.

marathon n. marathon m.

marble n. marbre m.; (for game) bille f.

March n. mars m.

march v.i. (mil.) marcher (au pas). —v.t. **~ off**, (lead away) emmener. —n. marche f. **~-past** n. défilé m.

mare n. jument f.

margarine n. margarine f.

margin n. marge f. **~al** a. marginal; (increase etc.) léger, faible. **~alize** v.t. marginaliser. **~ally** adv. très légèrement.

marigold n. souci m.

marijuana n. marijuana f.

marina n. marina f.

marinate v.t. mariner.

marine a. marin. —n. (shipping) marine f.; (sailor) fusilier marin m.

marionette n. marionnette f.

marital a. conjugal. **~ status**, situation de famille f.

maritime a. maritime.

marjoram n. marjolaine f.

mark[1] n. (currency) mark m.

mark^2 n. marque f.; (*trace*) trace f., marque f.; (*school.*) note f.; (*target*) but m. —v.t. marquer; (*exam*) corriger.

marked a. marqué.

market n. marché m. —v.t. (*sell*) vendre; (*launch*) commercialiser. **~ research**, étude de marché f. **~ value**, valeur marchande f. **on the ~**, en vente. **~ing** n. marketing m.

marksman n. tireur d'élite m.

marmalade n. confiture d'oranges f.

maroon n. bordeaux m. *invar*. —a. bordeaux *invar*.

marquee n. grande tente f.; (*awning: Amer.*) marquise f.

marriage n. mariage m.

marrow n. (*of bone*) moelle f.; (*vegetable*) courge f.

marr|y v.t. épouser; (*give or unite in marriage*) marier. —v.i. se marier. **~ied** a. marié; (*life*) conjugal. **get ~ied**, se marier (**to**, avec).

Mars n. (*planet*) Mars f.

marsh n. marais m.

marshal n. maréchal m.; (*at event*) membre du service d'ordre m. —v.t. rassembler.

marshmallow n. guimauve f.

martial a. martial. **~ law**, loi martiale f.

martyr n. martyr(e) m. (f.). —v.t. martyriser.

marvel n. merveille f. —v.i. s'émerveiller (**at**, de).

marvellous a. merveilleux.

Marxis|t a. & n. marxiste (m./f.). **~m** n. marxisme m.

marzipan n. pâte d'amandes f.

mascara n. mascara m.

mascot n. mascotte f.

masculin|e a. & n. masculin (m.). **~ity** n. masculinité f.

mash n. pâtée f.; (*potatoes: fam.*) purée f. —v.t. écraser. **~ed potatoes**, purée (de pommes de terre) f.

mask n. masque m. —v.t. masquer.

masochis|t n. masochiste m./f. **~m** n. masochisme m.

mason n. (*builder*) maçon m. **~ry** n. maçonnerie f.

masquerade n. mascarade f. —v.i. **~ as**, se faire passer pour.

mass^1 n. (*relig.*) messe f.

mass^2 n. masse f. —v.t./i. (se) masser. **~-produce** v.t. fabriquer en série. **the ~ media**, les media m.pl.

massacre n. massacre m. —v.t. massacrer.

massage n. massage m. —v.t. masser.

masseu|r n. masseur m. **~se** n. masseuse f.

massive a. (*large*) énorme; (*heavy*) massif.

mast n. mât m.; (*for radio, TV*) pylône m.

master n. maître m.; (*in secondary school*) professeur m. —v.t. maîtriser. **~y** n. maîtrise f.

masterpiece n. chef-d'œuvre m.

mastiff n. dogue m.

masturbat|e v.i. se masturber. **~ion** n. masturbation f.

mat n. (*petit*) tapis m., natte f.; (*at door*) paillasson m.

match^1 n. allumette f.

match^2 n. (*sport*) match m.; (*equal*) égal(e) m. (f.); (*marriage*) mariage m.; (*s.o. to marry*) parti m. —v.t. opposer; (*go with*) aller avec; (*cups etc.*) assortir; (*equal*) égaler. —v.i. (*be alike*) être assorti. **~ing** a. assorti.

matchbox n. boîte à allumettes f.

mate^1 n. camarade m./f.; (*of

animal) compagnon *m.*, compagne *f.*; (*assistant*) aide *m./f.* —*v.t./i.* (s')accoupler (**with**, avec).

mate² *n.* (*chess*) mat *m.*

material *n.* matière *f.*; (*fabric*) tissu *m.*; (*documents, for building*) matériau(x) *m.* (*pl.*). **~s**, (*equipment*) matériel *m.* —*a.* matériel; (*fig.*) important.

maternal *a.* maternel.

maternity *n.* maternité *f.* —*a.* (*clothes*) de grossesse. **~ hospital**, maternité *f.* **~ leave**, congé maternité *m.*

mathematic|s *n. & n. pl.* mathématiques *f. pl.* **~ian** *n.* mathématicien(ne) *m.* (*f.*). **~al** *a.* mathématique.

maths *n. pl.* (*fam.*) maths *f. pl.*

matinée *n.* matinée *f.*

mating *n.* accouplement *m.* **~ season**, saison des amours *f.*

matrimon|y *n.* mariage *m.* **~ial** *a.* matrimonial.

matrix *n.* matrice *f.*

matron *n.* (*married, elderly*) dame âgée *f.*; (*in hospital: former use*) infirmière-major *f.*

matt *a.* mat.

matted *a.* (*hair*) emmêlé.

matter *n.* (*substance*) matière *f.*; (*affair*) affaire *f.*; (*pus*) pus *m.* —*v.i.* importer. **as a ~ of fact**, en fait. **it does not ~**, ça ne fait rien. **no ~ what happens**, quoi qu'il arrive. **what is the ~?**, qu'est-ce qu'il y a?

mattress *n.* matelas *m.*

matur|e *a.* mûr. —*v.t./i.* (se) mûrir. **~ity** *n.* maturité *f.*

mauve *a. & n.* mauve (*m.*).

maverick *n.* non-conformiste.

maxim *n.* maxime *f.*

maxim|um *a. & n.* maximum (*m.*).

may *v. aux.* pouvoir. **he ~/might come**, il peut/pourrait venir.

you might have, vous auriez pu. **you ~ leave**, vous pouvez partir. **~ I smoke?**, puis-je fumer? **I ~ or might as well stay**, je ferais aussi bien de rester.

May *n.* mai *m.* **~ Day**, le Premier Mai.

maybe *adv.* peut-être.

mayhem *n.* (*havoc*) ravages *m. pl.*

mayonnaise *n.* mayonnaise *f.*

mayor *n.* maire *m.* **~ess** *n.* (*wife*) femme du maire *f.*

maze *n.* labyrinthe *m.*

me *pron.* me, m'*; (*after prep.*) moi. (**to**) **~**, me, m'*. **he knows ~**, il me connaît.

meadow *n.* pré *m.*

meagre *a.* maigre.

meal¹ *n.* repas *m.*

meal² *n.* (*grain*) farine *f.*

mean¹ *a.* (*poor*) misérable; (*miserly*) avare; (*unkind*) méchant. **~ness** *n.* avarice *f.*; méchanceté *f.*

mean² *a.* moyen. —*n.* milieu *m.*; (*average*) moyenne *f.* **in the ~ time**, en attendant.

mean³ *v.t.* vouloir dire, signifier; (*involve*) entraîner. **I ~ that!**, je suis sérieux. **be meant for**, être destiné à. **~ to do**, avoir l'intention de faire.

meander *v.i.* faire des méandres.

meaning *n.* sens *m.*, signification *f.* **~less** *a.* denué de sens.

means *n.* moyen(s) *m.* (*pl.*). **by ~ of sth.**, au moyen de qch. —*n. pl.* (*wealth*) moyens financiers *m. pl.*

mean|time ~while *advs.* en attendant.

measles *n.* rougeole *f.*

measly *a.* (*sl.*) minable.

measurable *a.* mesurable.

measure *n.* mesure *f.*; (*ruler*) règle *f.* —*v.t./i.* mesurer. **~d** *a.* mesuré. **~ment** *n.* mesure *f.*

meat *n.* viande *f.*

mechanic a. mécanicien(ne) m. (f.).

mechanic|al d. mécanique. **~s** n. (science) mécanique f.; n. pl. mécanisme m.

mechan|ism n. mécanisme m. **~ize** v.t. mécaniser.

medal n. médaille f. **~list** n. médaillé(e) m. (f.). **be a gold ~list**, être médaillé d'or.

medallion n. (medal, portrait, etc.) médaillon m.

meddle v.i. (interfere) se mêler (in, de); (tinker) toucher (with, à).

media n. pl. **the ~**, les media m. pl. **talk to the ~**, parler à la presse.

median a. médian. —n. médiane f.

mediat|e v.i. servir d'intermédiaire. **~ion** n. médiation f. **~or** n. média|teur, -trice m. f.

medical a. médical. —n. (fam.) visite médicale.

medicat|ed a. médical. **~ion** n. médicaments m. pl.

medicine n. (science) médecine f.; (substance) médicament m.

medieval a. médiéval.

mediocr|e a. médiocre. **~ity** n. médiocrité f.

meditat|e v.t./i. méditer. **~ion** n. méditation f.

Mediterranean a. méditerranéen. —n. **the ~**, la Méditerranée f.

medium n. milieu m.; (for transmitting data etc.) support m.; (person) médium m. —a. moyen.

medley n. mélange m.; (mus.) potpourri m.

meek a. doux.

meet v.t. rencontrer; (see again) retrouver; (fetch) (aller) chercher; (be introduced to) faire la connaissance de; (face) faire face à; (requirement) satisfaire. —v.i. se rencontrer; (see each other

again) se retrouver; (in session) se réunir.

meeting n. réunion f.; (between two people) rencontre f.

megaphone n. portevoix m. invar.

melamine n. mélamine f.

melanchol|y n. mélancolie f. —a. mélancolique. **~ic** a. mélancolique.

mellow a. (fruit) mûr; (sound, colour) moelleux, doux; (person) mûri. —v.t./i. (mature) mûrir; (soften) (s')adoucir.

melodious a. mélodieux.

melodrama n. mélodrame m. **~tic** a. mélodramatique.

melod|y n. mélodie f. **~ic** a. mélodique.

melon n. melon m.

melt v.t./i. (faire) fondre.

member n. membre m. **M~ of Parliament**, député m. **~ship** n. adhésion f.; (members) membres m. pl.; (fee) cotisation f.

membrane n. membrane f.

memento n. (object) souvenir m.

memo n. (fam.) note f.

memoir n. (record, essay) mémoire m.

memorable a. mémorable.

memorandum n. note f.

memorial n. monument m. —a. commémoratif.

memorize v.t. apprendre par cœur.

memory n. (mind, in computer) mémoire f.; (thing remembered) souvenir m. **from ~**, de mémoire. **in ~ of**, à la mémoire de.

menac|e n. menace f.; (nuisance) peste f. —v.t. menacer. **~ing** a. menaçant.

mend v.t. réparer; (darn) raccommoder.

menial a. servile.

meningitis n. méningite f.

menopause n. ménopause f.

menstruation n. menstruation f.

mental a. mental; (hospital) psychiatrique.

mentality n. mentalité f.

menthol n. menthol m. —a. mentholé.

mention v.t. mentionner. —n. mention f. **don't ~ it!**, il n'y a pas de quoi!, je vous en prie!

mentor n. mentor m.

menu n. (food, on computer) menu m.; (list) carte f.

MEP (abbr.) (member of the European Parliament) député européen m.

mercenary a. & n. mercenaire (m.).

merchandise n. marchandises f. pl.

merchant n. marchand m. —a. (ship, navy) marchand. **~ bank**, banque de commerce f.

merciful a. miséricordieux.

merciless a. impitoyable.

mercury n. mercure m.

mercy n. pitié f. **at the ~ of**, à la merci de.

mere a. simple. **~ly** adv. simplement.

merest a. moindre.

merge v.t./i. (se) mêler (with, à); (companies; comm.) fusionner. **~r** n. fusion f.

meridian n. méridien m.

meringue n. meringue f.

merit n. mérite m. —v.t. mériter.

mermaid n. sirène f.

merry a. gai. **make ~**, faire la fête. **~-go-round** n. manège m. **merrily** adv. gaiement.

mesh n. maille f.; (fabric) tissu à mailles m.; (network) réseau m.

mesmerize v.t. hypnotiser.

mess n. désordre m., gâchis m.; (dirt) saleté f.; (mil.) mess m. —v.t. **~ up**, gâcher. —v.i. **~**

about, s'amuser; (dawdle) traîner. **~ with**, (tinker with) tripoter. **make a ~ of**, gâcher.

message n. message m.

messenger n. messager m.

messy a. en désordre; (dirty) sale.

metabolism n. métabolisme m.

metal n. métal m. —a. de métal. **~lic** a. métallique; (paint, colour) métallisé.

metallurgy n. métallurgie f.

metamorphosis n. métamorphose f.

meteor n. météore m.

meteorite n. météorite m.

meteorolog|y n. météorologie f. **~ical** a. météorologique.

meter n. compteur m.

method n. méthode f.

methodical a. méthodique.

Methodist n. & a. méthodiste (m./f.).

methodology n. méthodologie f.

methylated a. **~ spirit**, alcool à brûler m.

meticulous a. méticuleux.

metre n. mètre m.

metric a. métrique.

metropolis n. (city) métropole f.

mew n. miaulement m. —v.i. miauler.

mews n. pl. (dwellings) appartements chic aménagés dans des anciennes écuries m. pl.

Mexic|o n. Mexique m. **~an** a. & n. mexicain(e) (m. (f.)).

miaow n. & v.i. = **mew.**

micro- pref. micro-.

microbe n. microbe m.

microchip n. microplaquette f., puce f.

microclimate n. microclimat m.

microcomputer n. micro(-ordinateur) m.

microcosm n. microcosme m.

microfilm n. microfilm m.

microlight n. U.L.M. m.

microphone n. microphone m.

microprocessor n. microprocesseur m.

microscop|e n. microscope m. ~**ic** a. microscopique.

microwave n. micro-onde f. ~ **oven**, four à micro-ondes m.

midday n. midi m.

middle a. du milieu; (quality) moyen. —n. milieu m. **in the** ~ **of**, au milieu de. ~**-aged** a. d'un certain âge. ~ **class**, classe moyenne f. ~**-class** a. bourgeois. **M**~ **East**, Proche-Orient m.

middleman n. intermédiaire m.

middling a. moyen.

midge n. moucheron m.

midget n. nain(e) m. (f.). —a. minuscule.

Midlands n. pl. région du centre de l'Angleterre f.

midnight n. minuit m.

midriff n. ventre m.

midst n. **in the** ~ **of**, au milieu de. **in our** ~, parmi nous.

midway adv. à mi-chemin.

midwife n. sage-femme f.

mighty a. puissant; (very great: fam.) très grand; adv. (fam.) rudement.

migraine n. migraine f.

migrant a. & n. (bird) migrateur (m.); (worker) migrant(e) (m. (f.)).

migrat|e v.i. émigrer. ~**ion** n. migration f.

mike n. (fam.) micro m.

mild a. doux; (illness) bénin. ~**ly** adv. doucement.

mildew n. moisissure f.

mile n. mille m. (= 1.6 km.). ~**age** n. (loosely) kilométrage m.

milestone n. borne f.; (event, stage: fig.) jalon m.

military a. militaire.

milk n. lait m. —a. (product) laitier. —v.t. (cow etc.) traire; (fig.) exploiter.

milkman laitier m.

mill n. moulin m.; (factory) usine f. —v.t. moudre. —v.i. ~ **around**, tourner en rond; (crowd) grouiller.

millennium n. millénaire m.

millet n. millet m.

milli- pref. milli-.

millimetre n. millimètre m.

milliner n. modiste f.

million n. million m. **a** ~ **pounds**, un million de livres. ~**aire** n. millionnaire m.

milometer n. compteur kilométrique m.

mime n. (actor) mime m./f.; (art) mime du) m. —v.t./i. mimer.

mimic v.t. imiter. —n. imita|teur, -trice m., f. ~**ry** n. imitation f.

mince v.t. hacher. —n. viande hachée f. ~ **pie**, tarte aux fruits confits f.

mincemeat n. hachis de fruits confits m.

mind n. esprit m.; (sanity) raison f.; (opinion) avis m. —v.t. (have charge of) s'occuper de; (heed) faire attention à. **be on so.'s** ~, préoccuper qn. **change one's** ~, changer d'avis. **make up one's** ~, se décider (**to**, à). **I do not** ~ **the noise**/etc., le bruit/etc. ne me dérange pas. **I do not** ~, ça m'est égal. ~**less** a. irréfléchi.

minder n. (for child) gardien(ne) m. (f.); (for protection) ange gardien m.

mine[1] poss. pron. le mien, la mienne, les mien(ne)s. **it is** ~, c'est à moi or le mien.

min|e[2] n. mine f. —v.t. extraire; (mil.) miner. ~**er** n. mineur m. ~**ing** n. exploitation minière f.; a. minier.

minefield n. champ de mines m.

mineral n. & a. minéral (m.). ~ **(water)**, (fizzy soft drink) boisson gazeuse *f.* ⁓ **water,** (*natural*) eau minérale *f.*

minesweeper *n.* (*ship*) dragueur de mines *m.*

mingle *v.t./i.* (se) mêler (**with,** à).

mini- *pref.* mini-.

miniatur|e *a. & n.* miniature (*f.*). ⁓**ize** *v.t.* miniaturiser.

minibus *n.* minibus *m.*

minicab *n.* taxi *m.*

minim *n.* blanche *f.*

minim|um *a. & n.* minimum (*m.*). ⁓**al** *a.* minimal. ⁓**ize** *v.t.* minimiser.

minist|er *n.* ministre *m.* ⁓**ry** *n.* ministère *m.*

mink *n.* vison *m.*

minor *a.* petit, mineur. —*n.* (*jurid.*) mineur(e) *m.* (*f.*).

minority *n.* minorité *f.* —*a.* minoritaire.

mint¹ *n.* **the M⁓,** l'Hôtel de la Monnaie *m.* **a ⁓,** une fortune. —*v.t.* frapper.

mint² *n.* (*plant*) menthe *f.*; (*sweet*) pastille de menthe *f.*

minus *prep.* moins; (*without: fam.*) sans. —*n.* (*sign*) moins *m.* ⁓ **sign,** moins *m.*

minute¹ *n.* minute *f.* ⁓**s,** (*of meeting*) procès-verbal *m.*

minute² *a.* (*tiny*) minuscule; (*detailed*) minutieux.

mirac|le *n.* miracle *m.* ⁓**ulous** *a.* miraculeux.

mirage *n.* mirage *m.*

mire *n.* fange *f.*

mirror *n.* miroir *m.*, glace *f.* —*v.t.* refléter.

misadventure *n.* mésaventure *f.*

misbehav|e *v.i.* se conduire mal. ⁓**iour** *n.* mauvaise conduite *f.*

miscalculat|e *v.t.* mal calculer. —*v.i.* se tromper. ⁓**ion** *n.* erreur de calcul *f.*

miscarr|y *v.i.* faire une fausse couche. ⁓**iage** *n.* fausse couche *f.*

⁓**iage of justice,** erreur judiciaire *f.*

miscellaneous *a.* divers.

mischief *n.* (*foolish conduct*) espièglerie *f.*; (*harm*) mal *m.* **get into ⁓,** faire des sottises.

mischievous *a.* espiègle; (*malicious*) méchant.

misconception *n.* idée fausse *f.*

misconduct *n.* mauvaise conduite *f.*

misdemeanour *n.* (*jurid.*) délit *m.*

miser *n.* avare *m./f.* ⁓**ly** *a.* avare.

miserable *a.* (*sad*) malheureux; (*wretched*) misérable; (*unpleasant*) affreux.

misery *n.* (*unhappiness*) malheur *m.*; (*pain*) souffrances *f. pl.*; (*poverty*) misère *f.*; (*person: fam.*) grincheu|x, -se *m., f.*

misfire *v.i.* (*plan etc.*) rater; (*engine*) avoir des ratés.

misfit *n.* inadapté(e) *m.* (*f.*).

misfortune *n.* malheur *m.*

misgiving *n.* (*doubt*) doute *m.*; (*apprehension*) crainte *f.*

misguided *a.* (*foolish*) imprudent; (*mistaken*) erroné. **be ⁓,** (*person*) se tromper.

mishap *n.* mésaventure *f.*, contretemps *m.*

misinform *v.t.* mal renseigner.

misinterpret *v.t.* mal interpréter.

misjudge *v.t.* mal juger.

mislay *v.t.* égarer.

mislead *v.t.* tromper. ⁓**ing** *a.* trompeur.

misplace *v.t.* mal placer; (*lose*) égarer.

misprint *n.* coquille *f.*

misread *v.t.* mal lire; (*intentions*) mal comprendre.

misrepresent *v.t.* présenter sous un faux jour.

miss¹ *v.t./i.* manquer; (*deceased person etc.*) regretter. **he ⁓es her/Paris/***etc.*, elle/Paris/*etc.* lui manque. **I ~ you,** tu me manques. **~ coup** manqué *m.* **I was a near ~,** on l'a échappé belle *or* de peu. **~ out,** omettre. **~ out on sth,** rater qch.

miss² *n.* mademoiselle *f.* (*pl.* mesdemoiselles).

misshapen *a.* difforme.

missile *n.* (*mil.*) missile *m.*; (*object thrown*) projectile *m.*

missing *a.* (*person*) disparu; (*thing*) qui manque. **something's ~,** il manque quelque chose.

mission *n.* mission *f.*

missionary *n.* missionnaire *m./f.*

misspell *v.t.* mal écrire.

mist *n.* brume *f.*; (*on window*) buée *f.* —*v.t./i.* (s')embuer.

mistake *n.* erreur *f.* —*v.t.* mal comprendre; (*choose wrongly*) se tromper de **by ~,** par erreur. **make a ~,** faire une erreur. **~ for,** prendre pour. **~n** *a.* erroné. **be ~n,** se tromper.

mistletoe *n.* gui *m.*

mistreat *v.t.* maltraiter.

mistress *n.* maîtresse *f.*

mistrust *v.t.* se méfier de. —*n.* méfiance *f.*

misty *a.* brumeux; (*window*) embué.

misunderstand *v.t.* mal comprendre. **~ing** *n.* malentendu *m.*

misuse¹ *v.t.* mal employer; (*power etc.*) abuser de.

misuse² *n.* mauvais emploi *m.*; (*unfair use*) abus *m.*

mitten *n.* moufle *f.*

mix *v.t./i.* (se) mélanger. —*n.* mélange *m.* **~ up,** mélanger; (*bewilder*) embrouiller; (*mistake, confuse*) confondre (**with,** avec). **~-up** *n.* confusion *f.* **~ with,** (*people*) fréquenter. **~er** *n.* (*culin.*) mélangeur *m.* **be a good ~er,** être sociable.

mixed *a.* (*school etc.*) mixte; (*assorted*) assorti.

mixture *n.* mélange *m.*

moan *n.* gémissement *m.* —*v.i.* gémir; (*complain*) grogner. **~er** *n.* (*grumbler*) grognon *m.*

mob *n.* (*crowd*) cohue *f.*; (*gang: sl.*) bande *f.* —*v.t.* assiéger.

mobile *a.* mobile. **~e home,** caravane *f.* —*n.* mobile *m.* **~ity** *n.* mobilité *f.*

mobilize *v.t./i.* mobiliser. **~ation** *n.* mobilisation *f.*

moccasin *n.* mocassin *m.*

mock *v.t./i.* se moquer (de). —*a.* faux. **~-up** *n.* maquette *f.*

mockery *n.* moquerie *f.*

mode *n.* (*way, method*) mode *m.*; (*fashion*) mode *f.*

model *n.* modèle *m.*; (*of toy*) modèle réduit *m.*; (*artist's*) modèle *m.*; (*for fashion*) mannequin *m.* —*a.* modèle; (*car etc.*) modèle réduit *invar.* —*v.t.* modeler; (*clothes*) présenter.

modem *n.* modem *m.*

moderate¹ *a. & n.* modéré(e) (*m. (f.)*). **~ly** *adv.* (*in moderation*) modérément; (*fairly*) moyennement.

moderate² *v.t./i.* (se) modérer. **~ion** *n.* modération *f.* **in ~ion,** avec modération.

modern *a.* moderne. *pl.* **~ize** *v.t.* moderniser.

modest *a.* modeste. **~y** *n.* modestie *f.*

modify *v.t.* modifier. **~ication** *n.* modification *f.*

modular *a.* modulaire.

modulate *v.t./i.* moduler. **~ion** *n.* modulation *f.*

module *n.* module *m.*

mohair *n.* mohair *m.*

moist *a.* humide, moite. **~ure** *n.* humidité *f.* **~urizer** *n.* produit hydratant.

moisten *v.t.* humecter.

molar *n.* molaire *f.*

molasses *n.* mélasse *f.*

mole[1] /məʊl/ *n.* grain de beauté *m.*

mole[2] *n.* (*animal*) taupe *f.*

molecule *n.* molécule *f.*

molest *v.t.* (*pester*) importuner; (*ill-treat*) molester.

mollusc *n.* mollusque *m.*

molten *a.* en fusion.

moment *n.* moment *m.*

momentar|y *a.* momentané. **∼ily** *adv.* momentanément.

momentous *a.* important.

momentum *n.* élan *m.*

Monaco *n.* Monaco *f.*

monarch *n.* monarque *m.*

monast|ery *n.* monastère *m.* **∼ic** *a.* monastique.

Monday *n.* lundi *m.*

monetary *a.* monétaire.

money *n.* argent *m.* **∼s,** sommes d'argent *f. pl.* **∼-box** *n.* tirelire *f.* **∼ order,** mandat *m.*

mongrel *n.* (chien) bâtard *m.*

monitor *n.* (*pupil*) chef de classe *m.*; (*techn.*) moniteur *m.* —*v.t.* contrôler; (*a broadcast*) écouter.

monk *n.* moine *m.*

monkey *n.* singe *m.* **∼-nut** *n.* cacahuète *f.* **∼-wrench** *n.* clef à molette *f.*

mono *n.* mono *f.* —*a.* mono *invar.*

monochrome *a. & n.* (en) noir et blanc (*m.*).

monogram *n.* monogramme *m.*

monologue *n.* monologue *m.*

monopol|y *n.* monopole *f.* **∼ize** *v.t.* monopoliser.

monoton|ous *a.* monotone. **∼y** *n.* monotonie *f.*

monsoon *n.* mousson *f.*

monst|er *n.* monstre *m.* **∼rous** *a.* monstrueux.

monstrosity *n.* monstruosité *f.*

month *n.* mois *m.*

monthly *a.* mensuel. —*adv.* mensuellement. —*n.* (*periodical*) mensuel *m.*

monument *n.* monument *m.* **∼al** *a.* monumental.

moo *n.* meuglement *m.* —*v.i.* meugler.

mood *n.* humeur *f.* **in a good/bad ∼,** de bonne/mauvaise humeur. **∼y** *a.* d'humeur changeante; (*sullen*) maussade.

moon *n.* lune *f.*

moon|light *n.* clair de lune *m.* **∼lit** *a.* éclairé par la lune.

moonlighting *n.* (*fam.*) travail au noir *m.*

moor[1] *n.* lande *f.*

moor[2] *v.t.* amarrer. **∼ings** *n. pl.* (*chains etc.*) amarres *f. pl.*; (*place*) mouillage *m.*

moose *n. invar.* élan *m.*

moot *a.* discutable. —*v.t.* (*question*) soulever.

mop *n.* balai à franges *m.* —*v.t.* **∼ (up),** éponger.

mope *v.i.* se morfondre.

moped *n.* cyclomoteur *m.*

moral *a.* moral. —*n.* morale *f.* **∼s,** moralité *f.* **∼ize** *v.i.* moraliser. **∼ly** *adv.* moralement.

morale *n.* moral *m.*

morality *n.* moralité *f.*

morbid *a.* morbide.

more *a.* (*a greater amount of*) plus de (**than,** que). —*n. & adv.* plus (**than,** que). (**some**) **∼** tea/pens/*etc.*, (*additional*) encore du thé/des stylos/*etc.* **no ∼ bread/** *etc.*, plus de pain/*etc.*

moreover *adv.* de plus.

morgue /mɔːg/ *n.* morgue *f.*

morning *n.* matin *m.*; (*whole morning*) matinée *f.*

Morocc|o *n.* Maroc *m.* **∼an** *a. & n.* marocain(e) (*m.* (*f.*)).

moron *n.* crétin(e) *m.* (*f.*).

morose *a.* morose.

morphine n. morphine f.

Morse n. ～ **(code)**, morse m.

mortal a. & n. mortel(le) (m.(f.)). ～**ity** n. mortalité f.

mortar n. mortier m.

mortgage n. crédit immobilier m. —v.t. hypothéquer.

mortise n. ～ **lock** serrure encastrée f.

mortuary n. morgue f.

mosaic n. mosaïque f.

Moscow n. Moscou m./f.

Moses a. ～ **basket**, moïse m.

mosque n. mosquée f.

mosquito n. moustique m.

moss n. mousse f.

most a. (the greatest amount of) le plus de; (the majority of) la plupart de. —n. le plus. —adv. (le) plus; (very) fort. ～ **of**, la plus grande partie de; (majority) la plupart de ～, tout au plus. ～**ly** adv. surtout.

motel n. motel m.

moth n. papillon de nuit m.; (in cloth) mite f. ～**ball** n. boule de naphtaline f.

mother n. mère f. —v.t. entourer de soins maternels, materner. ～**in-law** n. belle-mère f.

motif n. motif m.

motion n. mouvement m.; (proposal) motion f.

motivat|e v.t. motiver. ～**ion** n. motivation f.

motive n. motif m.

motley a. bigarré.

motor n. moteur m.; (car) auto f. —a. (anat.) moteur; (boat) à moteur. —v.i. aller en auto. ～ **bike**, (fam.) moto f. ～ **car**, auto f. ～ **cycle**, motocyclette f. ～**cyclist** n. motocycliste m./f. ～**ized** a. motorisé

motorist n. automobiliste m./f.

motorway n. auto- route f.

mottled a. tacheté.

motto n. devise f.

mould[1] n. moule m. —v.t. mouler; (influence) former. ～**ing** n. (on wall etc.) moulure f.

mould[2] n. (fungus, rot) moisissure f. ～**y** a. moisi.

moult v.i. muer.

mound n. monticule m., tertre m.; (pile: fig.) tas m.

mount[1] n. (hill) mont m.

mount[2] v.t./i. monter. —n. monture f. ～ **up**, s'accumuler; (add up) chiffrer (to, à).

mountain n. montagne f. ～ **bike**, (vélo) tout terrain m., vtt m. ～**ous** a. montagneux.

mountaineer n. alpiniste m./f. ～**ing** n. alpinisme m.

mourn v.t./i. ～ **(for)**, pleurer. ～**er** n. personne qui suit le cortège funèbre f. ～**ing** n. deuil m.

mournful a. triste.

mouse n. souris f.

mousetrap n. souricière f.

mousse n. mousse f.

moustache n. moustache f.

mouth n. bouche f.; (of dog, cat, etc.) gueule f. ～**organ** n. harmonica m.

mouthful n. bouchée f.

mouthpiece n. (mus.) embouchure f.; (person: fig.) porte-parole m. invar.

mouthwash n. eau dentifrice f.

mouthwatering a. qui fait venir l'eau à la bouche.

movable a. mobile.

move v.t./i. remuer, (se) déplacer, bouger; (incite) pousser; (emotionally) émouvoir; (propose) proposer; (depart) partir; (act) agir. ～ **(out)**, déménager. —n. mouvement m.; (change of house) déménagement m.; (player's turn) tour m.; (procedure: fig.) démarche f.; (house change) déménagement m.

$\sim$ **back,** (faire) reculer. $\sim$ **in,** emménager. $\sim$ **over,** se pousser.

movement *n.* mouvement *m.*

movie *n.* film *m.* **the $\sim$s,** le cinéma.

moving *a.* en mouvement; *(touching)* émouvant.

mow *v.t.* *(corn etc.)* faucher; *(lawn)* tondre. $\sim$ **down,** faucher. $\sim$ **er** *n.* *(for lawn)* tondeuse *f.*

MP *abbr. see* **Member of Parliament**.

Mr *n.* $\sim$ **Smith,** Monsieur *or* M. Smith.

Mrs *n.* $\sim$ **Smith,** Madame *or* Mme Smith.

Ms *n.* $\sim$ **Smith,** Madame *or* Mme Smith.

much *a.* beaucoup de. —*adv. & n.* beaucoup.

muck *n.* fumier *m.*; *(dirt: fam.)* saleté *f.* —*v.i.* $\sim$ **about,** *(sl.)* s'amuser. $\sim$ **about with,** *(sl.)* tripoter. —*v.t.* $\sim$ **up,** *(sl.)* gâcher. $\sim$ **y** *a.* sale.

mucus *n.* mucus *m.*

mud *n.* boue *f.* $\sim$ **dy** *a.* couvert de boue.

muddle *v.t.* embrouiller. —*v.i.* $\sim$ **through,** se débrouiller. —*n.* désordre *m.*, confusion *f.*; *(mix-up)* confusion *f.*

mudguard *n.* garde-boue *m. invar.*

muff *n.* manchon *f.*

muffin *n.* muffin *m.*

muffle *v.t.* emmitoufler; *(sound)* assourdir. $\sim$ **r** *n.* *(scarf)* cache-nez *m. invar.*

mug *n.* tasse *f.*; *(in plastic, metal)* gobelet *m.*; *(for beer)* chope *f.*; *(face: sl.)* gueule *f.*; *(fool: sl.)* idiot(e) *m.* *(f.)* —*v.t.* agresser. $\sim$ **ger** *n.* agresseur *m.* $\sim$ **ging** *n.* agression *f.*

mule *n.* *(male)* mulet *m.*; *(female)* mule *f.*

multi- *pref.* multi-.

multicoloured *a.* multicolore.

multinational *a. & n.* multinational(e) *(f.)*.

multiple *a. & n.* multiple *(m.)*. $\sim$ **sclerosis,** sclérose en plaques *f.*

multipl|y *v.t./i.* (se) multiplier. $\sim$ **ication** *n.* multiplication *f.*

multistorey *a.* *(car park)* à étages.

multitude *n.* multitude *f.*

mum *n.* *(fam.)* maman *f.*

mumble *v.t./i.* marmotter.

mummy[1] *n.* *(embalmed body)* momie *f.*

mummy[2] *n.* *(mother: fam.)* maman *f.*

mumps *n.* oreillons *m. pl.*

munch *v.t./i.* mastiquer.

mundane *a.* banal.

municipal *a.* municipal.

munitions *n. pl.* munitions *f. pl.*

mural *a.* mural. —*n.* peinture murale *f.*

murder *n.* meurtre *m.* —*v.t.* assassiner; *(ruin: fam.)* massacrer. $\sim$ **er** *n.* assassin *m.*

murky *a.* *(night, plans, etc.)* sombre, ténébreux; *(liquid)* épais, sale.

murmur *n.* murmure *m.* —*v.t./i.* murmurer.

muscle *n.* muscle *m.*

muscular *a.* musculaire; *(brawny)* musclé.

muse *v.i.* méditer.

museum *n.* musée *m.*

mush *n.* *(pulp, soft food)* bouillie *f.* $\sim$ **y** *a.* mou.

mushroom *n.* champignon *m.*

music *n.* musique *f.* $\sim$ **al** *a.* musical; *(instrument)* de musique; *(talented)* doué pour la musique; *n.* comédie musicale *f.*

musician *n.* musicien(ne) *m.* *(f.)*.

musk *n.* musc *m.*

Muslim *a. & n.* musulman(e) *(m. (f.))*.

muslin *n.* mousseline *f.*

mussel n. moule f.

must v. aux. devoir. **you ~ go,** vous devez partir, il faut que vous partiez. **he ~ be old,** il doit être vieux.

mustard n. moutarde f.

muster v.t./i. (se) rassembler.

musty a. (room, etc.) qui sent le moisi; (smell, taste) de moisi.

mutation n. mutation f.

mute a. & n. muet(te) (m. (f.)). **~d** a. (colour, sound) sourd, atténué; (criticism) voilé.

mutilat|e v.t. mutiler. **~ion** n. mutilation f.

mutiny n. mutinerie f. —v.i. se mutiner.

mutter v.t./i. marmonner.

mutton n. mouton m.

mutual a. mutuel; (common to two or more: fam.) commun. **~ly** adv. mutuellement.

muzzle n. (snout) museau m.; (device) muselière f.; (of gun) gueule f. —v.t. museler.

my a. mon, ma, pl. mes.

myopic a. myope.

myself pron. moi-même; (reflexive) me, m'*; (after prep.) moi.

mysterious a. mystérieux.

mystery n. mystère m.

mystify v.t. laisser perplexe.

myth n. mythe m. **~ical** a. mythique.

mythology n. mythologie f.

N

nab v.t. (arrest: sl.) épingler, attraper.

nag v.t./i. critiquer; (pester) harceler.

nail n. clou m.; (of finger, toe) ongle m. —v.t. clouer. **~-brush** n. brosse à ongles f. **~-file** n. lime à ongles f. **~ polish,** vernis à ongles m.

naïve a. naïf.

naked a. nu.

name n. nom m.; (fig.) réputation f. —v.t. nommer; (fix) fixer.

namely adv. à savoir.

namesake n. (person) homonyme m.

nanny n. nounou f. **~-goat** n. chèvre f.

nap n. somme m.

nape n. nuque f.

napkin n. (at meals) serviette f.; (for baby) couche f.

nappy n. couche f.

narcotic a. & n. narcotique (m.).

narrat|e v.t. raconter. **~ion** n. narration f. **~or** n. narra|teur, -trice m., f.

narrative n. récit m.

narrow a. étroit. —v.t./i. (se) rétrécir; (limit) (se) limiter. **~ down the choices,** limiter les choix. **~ly** adv. étroitement; (just) de justesse. **~-minded** a. à l'esprit étroit; (ideas etc.) étroit.

nasal a. nasal.

nasty a. mauvais, désagréable; (malicious) méchant. f.

nation n. nation f. **~-wide** a. dans l'ensemble du pays.

national a. national. **~ism** n. nationalisme m. **~ize** v.t. nationaliser.

nationality n. nationalité f.

native n. (local inhabitant) autochtone m./f.; (non-European) indigène m./f. —a. indigène; (country) natal; (inborn) inné.

natter v.i. bavarder.

natural a. naturel. **~ist** n. naturaliste m./f. **~ly** adv. (normally, of course) naturellement; (by nature) de nature.

naturaliz|e v.t. naturaliser. **~ation** n. naturalisation f.

nature n. nature f.

naughty a. vilain, méchant; (indecent) grivois.

nause|a n. nausée f. **~ous** a. nauséabond.

nauseate v.t. écœurer.

nautical a. nautique.

naval a. (battle etc.) naval; (officer) de marine.

nave n. (of church) nef f.

navel n. nombril m.

navigable a. navigable.

navigat|e v.t. (sea etc.) naviguer sur; (ship) piloter. —v.i. naviguer. **~ion** n. navigation f. **~or** n. navigateur m.

navvy n. terrassier m.

navy n. marine f. **~ (blue)**, bleu marine invar.

near adv. près. —prep. près de. —a. proche. —v.t. approcher de. **~ by** adv. tout près. **~ to**, près de.

nearby a. proche.

nearly adv. presque. **I ~ forgot**, j'ai failli oublier.

nearside n. (auto.) du côté du passager.

neat a. soigné, net; (room etc.) bien rangé; (clever) habile; (whisky, brandy, etc.) sec.

necessar|y a. nécessaire. **~ily** adv. nécessairement.

necessitate v.t. nécessiter.

necessity n. nécessité f.; (thing) chose indispensable f.

neck n. cou m.; (of dress) encolure f.

necklace n. collier m.

neckline n. encolure f.

nectarine n. nectarine f.

need n. besoin m. —v.t. avoir besoin de; (demand) demander. **you ~ not come**, vous n'êtes pas obligé de venir. **~less** a. inutile.

needle n. aiguille f. —v.t. (annoy: fam.) asticoter, agacer.

needlework n. couture f.; (object) ouvrage (à l'aiguille) m.

negation n. négation f.

negative a. négatif. —n. (of photograph) négatif m.; (word: gram.) négation f.

neglect v.t. négliger, laisser à l'abandon. n. manque de soins m. **(state of) ~**, abandon m.

negligen|t a. négligent. **~ce** n. négligence f.

negligible a. négligeable.

negotiable a. négociable.

negotiat|e v.t./i. négocier. **~ion** n. négociation f. **~or** n. négocia|teur, -trice m., f.

Negr|o n. Noir m. —a. noir; (art, music) nègre. **~ess** n. Noire f.

neigh n. hennissement m. —v.i. hennir.

neighbour n. voisin(e) m. (f.). **~hood** n. voisinage m., quartier m. **~ing** a. voisin.

neither a. & pron. aucun(e) des deux, ni l'un(e) ni l'autre. —adv. ni. —conj. (ne) non plus. **~ big nor small**, ni grand ni petit.

neon n. néon m. —a. (lamp etc.) au néon.

nephew n. neveu m.

nerve n. nerf m.; (courage) courage m.; (calm) sang-froid m.; (impudence: fam.) culot m. **~s**, (before exams etc.) le trac m.

nervous a. nerveux. **be or feel ~**, (afraid) avoir peur. **~ break-down**, dépression nerveuse f. **~ly** adv. (tensely) nerveusement; (timidly) craintivement. **~ness** n. nervosité f.; (fear) crainte f.

nest n. nid m. —v.i. nicher.

nestle v.i. se blottir.

net¹ n. filet m. **~ting** n. (nets) filets m. pl.; (wire) treillis m.; (fabric) voile m.

net² a. (weight etc.) net.

netball n. netball m.

Netherlands *n. pl.* the ∼, les Pays-Bas *m. pl.*

nettle *n.* ortie *f.*

network *n.* réseau *m.*

neuralgia *n.* névralgie *f.*

neuro|sis *n.* névrose *f.* ∼**tic** *a.* & *n.* névrosé(e) (*m.* (*f.*)).

neuter *a.* & *n.* neutre (*m.*). —*v.t.* (*castrate*) castrer.

neutral *a.* neutre. ∼ (**gear**), (*auto.*) point mort *m.* ∼**ity** *n.* neutralité *f.*

never *adv.* ne (*m.*) jamais; (*not: fam.*) (ne) pas. **I** ∼ **saw him,** (*fam.*) je ne l'ai pas vu. ∼ **again,** plus jamais. ∼ **mind,** (*don't worry*) ne vous en faites pas; (*it doesn't matter*) peu importe.

nevertheless *adv.* toutefois.

new *a.* nouveau; (*brand-new*) neuf. ∼**-laid egg,** œuf frais *m.* ∼ **year,** nouvel an *m.* **New Year's Day,** le jour de l'an. **New Year's Eve,** la Saint-Sylvestre. **New Zealand,** Nouvelle-Zélande *f.* **New Zealander,** Néo-Zélandais(e) *m.* (*f.*).

newcomer *n.* nouveau venu *m.*, nouvelle venue *f.*

newly *adv.* nouvellement. ∼**weds** *n. pl.* nouveaux mariés *m. pl.*

news *n.* nouvelle(s) *f.* (*pl.*); (*radio, press*) informations *f. pl.*; (*TV*) actualités *f. pl.*, informations *f. pl.* ∼ **agency,** agence de presse *f.*

newsagent *n.* marchand(e) de journaux *m.* (*f.*).

newsletter *n.* bulletin *m.*

newspaper *n.* journal *m.*

newt *n.* triton *m.*

next *a.* prochain; (*adjoining*) voisin; (*following*) suivant. —*adv.* la prochaine fois; (*afterwards*) ensuite. ∼ **door,** à côté (**to,** de). ∼ **of kin,** parent le plus proche *m.* ∼ **to,** à côté de.

nib *n.* bec *m.*, plume *f.*

nibble *v.t./i.* grignoter.

nice *a.* agréable, bon; (*kind*) gentil; (*pretty*) joli; (*respectable*) bien *invar.*; (*subtle*) délicat.

niche *n.* (*recess*) niche *f.*; (*fig.*) place *f.*, situation *f.*

nick *n.* petite entaille *f.* —*v.t.* (*steal, arrest: sl.*) piquer.

nickel *n.* nickel *m.*

nickname *n.* surnom *m.*; (*short form*) diminutif *m.* —*v.t.* surnommer.

nicotine *n.* nicotine *f.*

niece *n.* nièce *f.*

Nigeria *n.* Nigéria *m.* / *f.* ∼**n** *a.* & *n.* nigérian(e) (*m.* (*f.*)).

niggardly *a.* chiche.

niggling *a.* (*person*) tatillon; (*detail*) insignifiant.

night *n.* nuit *f.*; (*evening*) soir *m.* —*a.* de nuit. ∼**-club** *n.* boîte de nuit *f.* ∼**-dress,** ∼**ie** *ns.* chemise de nuit *f.* ∼**-time** *n.* nuit *f.*

nightingale *n.* rossignol *m.*

nightly *a.* & *adv.* (de) chaque nuit or soir.

nightmare *n.* cauchemar *m.*

nil *n.* rien *m.*; (*sport*) zéro *m.* —*a.* (*chances, risk, etc.*) nul.

nimble *a.* agile.

nin|e *a.* & *n.* neuf (*m.*). ∼**th** *a.* & *n.* neuvième (*m.* / *f.*).

nineteen *a.* & *n.* dix-neuf (*m.*). ∼**th** *a.* & *n.* dix-neuvième (*m.* / *f.*).

ninet|y *a.* & *n.* quatre-vingt-dix (*m.*). ∼**ieth** *a.* & *n.* quatre-vingt-dixième (*m.* / *f.*).

nip *v.t./i.* (*pinch*) pincer; (*rush: sl.*) courir. ∼ **out/back/***etc.***,** sortir/rentrer/ *etc.* rapidement. —*n.* pincement *m.*; (*cold*) fraîcheur *f.*

nipple *n.* bout de sein *m.*; (*of baby's bottle*) tétine *f.*

nippy *a.* (*fam.*) alerte; (*chilly: fam.*) frais.

nitrogen *n.* azote *m.*

no *a.* aucun(e); pas de. —*adv.* non. —*n.* non *m. invar.* **no man**/*etc.* aucun homme/*etc.* **no money/time**/*etc.*, pas d'argent/de temps/ *etc.* **no one = nobody. no smoking/entry**, défense de fumer/ d'entrer.

noble *a.* noble.

nobody *pron.* (ne) personne. —*n.* nullité *f.* **he knows** ∼, il ne connaît personne. ∼ **is there**, personne n'est là.

nocturnal *a.* nocturne.

nod *v.t./i.* ∼ (**one's head**), faire un signe de tête. ∼ **off**, s'endormir. —*n.* signe de tête *m.*

noise *n.* bruit *m.*

nois|y *a.* bruyant. ∼**ily** *adv.* bruyamment.

nomad *n.* nomade *m./f.* ∼**ic** *a.* nomade.

nominal *a.* symbolique, nominal; (*value*) nominal. ∼**ly** *adv.* nominalement.

nominat|e *v.t.* nommer; (*put forward*) proposer. ∼**ion** *n.* nomination *f.*

non-*pref.* non-. ∼**-iron** *a.* qui ne se repasse pas. ∼**-skid** *a.* antidérapant. ∼**-stick** *a.* à revêtement antiadhésif.

nondescript *a.* indéfinissable.

none *pron.* aucun(e). ∼ **of us**, aucun de nous. **I have** ∼, je n'en ai pas.

non-existent *a.* inexistant.

nonsens|e *n.* absurdités *f. pl.* ∼**ical** *a.* absurde.

non-smoker *n.* non-fumeur *m.*

non-stop *a.* (*train, flight*) direct. —*adv.* sans arrêt.

noodles *n. pl.* nouilles *f. pl.*

nook *n.* (re)coin *m.*

noon *n.* midi *m.*

noose *n.* nœud coulant *m.*

nor *adv.* ni. —*conj.* (ne) non plus.

norm *n.* norme *f.*

normal *a.* normal. ∼**ity** *n.* normalité *f.* ∼**ly** *adv.* normalement.

Norman *a. & n.* normand(e) (*m.(f.)*). ∼**dy** *n.* Normandie *f.*

north *n.* nord *m.* —*a.* nord *invar.*, du nord. —*adv.* vers le nord. **N**∼ **America**, Amérique du Nord *f.* **N**∼ **American** *a. & n.* nord-américain(e) (*m. (f.)*). ∼**-east** *n.* nord-est *m.* ∼**wards** *adv.* vers le nord. ∼**-west** *n.* nord-ouest *m.*

northern *a.* du nord. ∼**er** *n.* habitant(e) du Nord (*m. (f.)*).

Norw|ay *n.* Norvège *f.* ∼**egian** *a. & n.* norvégien(ne) (*m. (f.)*).

nose *n.* nez *m.* —*v.i.* ∼ **about**, fouiner.

nosebleed *n.* saignement de nez *m.*

nosedive *n.* piqué *m.* —*v.i.* descendre en piqué.

nostalg|ia *n.* nostalgie *f.* ∼**ic** *a.* nostalgique.

nostril *n.* narine *f.*

nosy *a.* (*fam.*) indiscret.

not *adv.* (ne) pas. **I do** ∼ **know**, je ne sais pas. ∼ **at all**, pas du tout. ∼ **yet**, pas encore.

notable *a.* notable.

notably *adv.* notamment.

notary *n.* notaire *m.*

notation *n.* notation *f.*

notch *n.* entaille *f.*

note *n.* note *f.*; (*banknote*) billet *m.*; (*short letter*) mot *m.* —*v.t.* noter; (*notice*) remarquer.

notebook *n.* carnet *m.*

noted *a.* connu (**for**, pour).

notepaper *n.* papier à lettres *m.*

noteworthy *a.* remarquable.

nothing *pron.* (ne) rien. —*n.* rien *m.*; (*person*) nullité *f.* —*adv.* nullement. ∼ **much**, pas grand-chose. **for** ∼, pour rien, gratis.

notice n. avis m., annonce f.; (poster) affiche f. **at short ∼,** dans des délais très brefs. —v.t. remarquer, observer. **∼-board** n. tableau d'affichage m. **take ∼,** faire attention (**of,** à).

noticeabl|e a. visible. **∼y** adv. visiblement.

notif|y v.t. (inform) aviser; (make known) notifier. **∼ication** n. avis m.

notion n. idée, notion f.

notor|ious a. (tristement) célèbre. **∼iety** n. notoriété f. **∼iously** adv. notoirement.

notwithstanding prep. malgré. —adv. néanmoins.

nougat n. nougat m.

nought n. zéro m.

noun n. nom m.

nourish v.t. nourrir. **∼ing** a. nourrissant.

novel n. roman m. —a. nouveau. **∼ist** n. romanc|ier, -ière m., f. **∼ty** n. nouveauté f.

November n. novembre m.

novice n. novice m./f.

now adv. maintenant. —conj. maintenant que. **∼ and again,** **∼ and then,** de temps à autre.

nowadays adv. de nos jours.

nowhere adv. nulle part.

nozzle n. (tip) embout m.; (of hose) lance f.

nuance n. nuance f.

nuclear a. nucléaire.

nucleus n. noyau m.

nud|e a. nu. —n. nu m. **in the ∼e,** tout nu. **∼ity** n. nudité f.

nudge v.t. pousser du coude. —n. coup de coude m.

nudist n. nudiste m./f.

nuisance n. (thing, event) ennui m.; (person) peste f. **be a ∼,** être embêtant.

null a. nul.

numb a. engourdi. —v.t. engourdir.

number n. nombre m.; (of ticket, house, page, etc.) numéro m. —v.t. numéroter; (count, include) compter. **a ∼ of people,** plusieurs personnes. **∼-plate** n. plaque d'immatriculation f.

numeral n. chiffre m.

numerical a. numérique.

numerous a. nombreux.

nun n. religieuse f.

nurs|e n. infirmière f., infirmier m. —v.t. soigner. **∼ing home,** clinique f.

nursery n. chambre d'enfants f.; (for plants) pépinière f. **(day) ∼,** crèche f. **∼ school,** (école) maternelle f.

nurture v.t. élever.

nut n. (walnut, Brazil nut, etc.) noix f.; (hazelnut) noisette f.; (peanut) cacahuète f.; (techn.) écrou m.; (sl.) idiot(e) m. (f.).

nutcrackers n. pl. casse-noix m. invar.

nutmeg n. muscade f.

nutrit|ion n. nutrition f. **∼ious** a. nutritif.

nylon n. nylon m. **∼s,** bas nylon m. pl.

O

oaf n. lourdaud(e) m. (f.).

oak n. chêne m.

OAP abbr. (old-age pensioner) retraité(e) m. (f.), personne âgée f.

oar n. aviron m., rame f.

oasis n. oasis f.

oath n. (promise) serment m.; (swear-word) juron m.

oatmeal n. farine d'avoine f., flocons d'avoine m. pl.

oats n. pl. avoine f.

obedien|t a. obéissant. **~ce** n. obéissance f. **~tly** adv. docilement, avec soumission.

obes|e a. obèse. **~ity** n. obésité f.

obey v.t./i. obéir (à).

obituary n. nécrologie f.

object¹ n. (thing) objet m.; (aim) but m., objet m.; (gram.) complément (d'objet) m. **money/etc. is no ~,** l'argent/etc. ne pose pas de problèmes.

object² v.i. protester. **—v.t. ~ that,** objecter que. **~ to,** (behaviour) désapprouver; (plan) protester contre. **~ion** n. objection f.; (drawback) inconvénient m.

objective a. objectif. **—n.** objectif m.

obligation n. obligation f.

obligatory a. obligatoire.

oblig|e v.t. obliger. **~e to do,** obliger à faire. **~ed** a. obligé (to, de).

oblique a. oblique; (reference etc.: fig.) indirect.

oblivious a. (unaware) inconscient (to, of, de).

oblong a. oblong. **—n.** rectangle m.

obnoxious a. odieux.

oboe n. hautbois m.

obscen|e a. obscène. **~ity** n. obscénité f.

obscur|e a. obscur. **—v.t.** obscurcir; (conceal) cacher. **~ity** n. obscurité f.

observan|t a. observateur. **~ce** n. observance f.

observatory n. observatoire m.

observ|e v.t. observer; (remark) remarquer. **~ation** n. observation f.; **~er** n. observa|teur, -trice m., f.

obsess v.t. obséder. **~ion** n. obsession f.

obsolete a. dépassé.

obstacle n. obstacle m.

obstetric|s n. obstétrique f. **~ian** n. médecin accoucheur m.

obstina|te a. obstiné. **~cy** n. obstination f. **~tely** adv. obstinément.

obstruct v.t. (block) boucher; (congest) encombrer; (hinder) entraver. **~ion** n. (act) obstruction f.; (thing) obstacle m.; (traffic jam) encombrement m.

obtain v.t. obtenir. **—v.i.** avoir cours.

obtrusive a. importun; (thing) trop en évidence.

obvious a. évident, manifeste. **~ly** adv. manifestement.

occasion n. occasion f.; (big event) événement m. **—v.t.** occasionner. **on ~,** à l'occasion.

occasional a. fait, pris, etc. de temps en temps; (visitor etc.) qui vient de temps en temps. **~ly** adv. de temps en temps.

occult a. occulte.

occupation n. (activity, occupying) occupation f.; (job) métier m., profession f. **~al** a. professionnel, du métier.

occup|y v.t. occuper. **~ant, ~ier** ns. occupant(e) m. (f.).

occur v.i. se produire; (arise) se présenter. **~ to s.o.,** venir à l'esprit de qn.

occurrence n. événement m.

ocean n. océan m.

o'clock adv. **it is six ~/etc.,** il est six heures/etc.

octagon n. octogone m.

octane n. octane m.

octave n. octave f.

October n. octobre m.

octopus n. pieuvre f.

odd a. bizarre; (number) impair; (left over) qui reste; (not of set) dépareillé; (occasional) fait, pris, *etc.* de temps en temps. **∼ jobs,** menus travaux *m. pl.* **∼ly** *adv.* bizarrement.

oddment *n.* fin de série *f.*

odds *n. pl.* chances *f. pl.*; (*in betting*) cote *f.* (**on,** de). at **∼,** en désaccord. **∼ and ends,** des petites choses.

ode *n.* ode *f.*

odious *a.* odieux.

odour *n.* odeur *f.*

of *prep.* de. **of the,** du, de la, *pl.* des. **of it, of them,** en. **a friend of mine,** un de mes amis. **six of them,** six d'entre eux. **the fifth of June/***etc.*, le cinq juin/*etc.* **a litre of water,** un litre d'eau. **made of steel,** en acier.

off *adv.* parti, absent; (*switched off*) éteint; (*tap*) fermé; (*taken off*) enlevé, détaché; (*cancelled*) annulé. —*prep.* de; (*distant from*) éloigné de. **go ∼,** (*leave*) partir; (*milk*) tourner; (*food*) s'abîmer. **20% ∼,** une réduction de 20%. **take sth. ∼,** (*a surface*) prendre qch. sur. **∼-licence** *n.* débit de vins *m.* **∼-line** *a.* autonome; (*switched off*) déconnecté. **∼-load** *v.t.* décharger. **∼-peak** *a.* (*hours*) creux; (*rate*) des heures creuses. **∼-putting** *a.* (*fam.*) rebutant. **∼-stage** *a. & adv.* dans les coulisses. **∼-white** *a.* blanc cassé *invar.*

offal *n.* abats *m. pl.*

offence *n.* délit *m.* **give ∼ to,** offenser. **take ∼,** s'offenser (**at,** de).

offend *v.t.* offenser; (*fig.*) choquer. **be ∼ed,** s'offenser (**at,** de). **∼er** *n.* délinquant(e) *m. (f.).*

offensive *a.* offensant; (*disgusting*) dégoûtant; (*weapon*) offensif. —*n.* offensive *f.*

offer *v.t.* offrir. —*n.* offre *f.* **on ∼,** en promotion.

offhand *a.* désinvolte. —*adv.* à l'improviste.

office *n.* bureau *m.*; (*duty*) fonction *f.* —*a.* de bureau. **in ∼,** au pouvoir. **∼ building,** immeuble de bureaux *m.*

officer *n.* (*army etc.*) officier *m.*; (*policeman*) agent *m.*

official *a.* officiel. —*n.* officiel *m.*; (*civil servant*) fonctionnaire *m./f.* **∼ly** *adv.* officiellement.

officious *a.* trop zélé.

offset *v.t.* compenser.

offshoot *n.* (*bot.*) rejeton *m.*; (*fig.*) ramification *f.*

offshore *a.* (*waters*) côtier; (*exploration*) en mer; (*banking*) dans les paladis fiscaux.

offside *a.* (*sport*) hors jeu *invar.*; (*auto.*) du côté du conducteur.

offspring *n. invar.* progéniture *f.*

often *adv.* souvent. **how ∼?,** combien de fois? **every so ∼,** de temps en temps.

ogle *v.t.* lorgner.

oh *int.* oh, ah.

oil *n.* huile *f.*; (*petroleum*) pétrole *m.*; (*for heating*) mazout *m.* —*v.t.* graisser. **∼-tanker** *n.* pétrolier *m.* **∼y** *a.* graisseux.

oilfield *n.* gisement pétrolifère *m.*

ointment *n.* pommade *f.*

OK *a. & adv.* (*fam.*) bien.

old *a.* vieux; (*person*) vieux, âgé; (*former*) ancien. **how ∼ is he?,** quel âge a-t-il? **he is eight years ∼,** il a huit ans. **of ∼,** jadis. **∼ age,** vieillesse *f.* **old-age pensioner,** retraité(e) *m. (f.).* **∼er, ∼est,** (*son etc.*) aîné. **∼-fashioned** *a.* démodé; (*person*) vieux jeu *invar.* **∼ man,** vieillard *m.*, vieux *m.* **∼ woman,** vieille *f.*

olive *n.* olive *f.* —*a.* olive *invar.* **∼ oil,** huile d'olive *f.*

Olympic *a.* olympique. **∼s** *n. pl.*, **∼ Games,** Jeux olympiques *m. pl.*

omelette n. omelette f.

omen n. augure m.

ominous a. de mauvais augure; (fig.) menaçant.

omi|t v.t. omettre. **~ssion** n. omission f.

on prep. sur. —adv. en avant; (switched on) allumé; (tap) ouvert; (machine) en marche; (put on) mis. **on Tuesday**, mardi. **walk/etc. on**, continuer à marcher/etc. **be on**, (of film) passer. **on and off**, de temps en temps.

once adv. une fois; (formerly) autrefois. —conj. une fois que. **all at ~**, tout à coup. **~-over** n. (fam.) coup d'œil rapide m.

oncoming a. (vehicle etc.) qui approche.

one a. & n. un(e) (m. (f.)). —pron. un(e) m. (f.); (impersonal) on. **a big/red/etc.~**, un(e) grand(e)/rouge/etc. **this/that ~**, celui-ci/-là, celle-ci/-là. **~ another**, l'un(e) l'autre. **~-sided** a. (biased) partial; (unequal) inégal. **~-way** a. (street) à sens unique; (ticket) simple.

oneself pron. soi-même; (reflexive) se.

ongoing a. qui continue à évoluer.

onion n. oignon m.

onlooker n. spectateur, -trice m., f.

only a. seul. —adv. & conj. seulement. **he ~ has six**, il n'en a que six, il en a six seulement.

onset n. début m.

onslaught n. attaque f.

onward(s) adv. en avant.

ooze v.i. suinter.

opal n. opale f.

opaque a. opaque.

open a. ouvert; (view) dégagé; (free to all) public; (undisguised) manifeste; (question) en attente. —v.t./i. (s')ouvrir; (of shop, play)

ouvrir. **in the ~ air**, en plein air. **~ out** or **up**, (s')ouvrir. **~-minded** a. à l'esprit ouvert.

opener n. ouvre-boîte(s) m.; ouvre-bouteille(s) m.

opening n. ouverture f.; (job) débouché m., poste vacant m.

openly adv. ouvertement.

opera n. opéra m. **~tic** a. d'opéra.

operate v.t./i. opérer; (techn.) (faire) fonctionner. **~e on**, (med.) opérer. **~ing theatre**, salle d'opération f. **~tion** n. opération f. **have an ~tion**, se faire opérer. **in ~tion**, en vigueur; (techn.) en service. **~or** n. opérateur, -trice m., f.; (telephonist) standardiste m./f.

operational a. opérationnel.

operetta n. opérette f.

opinion n. opinion f., avis m.

opium n. opium m.

opponent n. adversaire m./f.

opportune a. opportun.

opportunist n. opportuniste m./f.

opportunity n. occasion f. (to do, de faire).

oppos|e v.t. s'opposer à. **~ed to**, opposé à. **~ing** a. opposé.

opposite a. opposé. —n. contraire m., opposé m. —adv. en face. —prep. **~ (to)**, en face de.

opposition n. opposition f.; (mil.) résistance f.

oppress v.t. opprimer. **~ion** n. oppression f. **~ive** a. (cruel) oppressif; (heat) oppressant. **~or** n. oppresseur m.

opt v.i. **~ for**, opter pour. **~ out**, refuser de participer (of, à).

optical a. optique.

optician n. opticien(ne) m. (f.).

optimis|t n. optimiste m./f. **~m** n. optimisme m. **~tic** a. optimiste. **~tically** adv. avec optimisme.

optimum a. & n. optimum (m.).

option n. choix m., option f.

optional a. facultatif.

opulent a. opulent.

or conj. ou; (with negative) ni.

oracle n. oracle m.

oral a. oral. —n. (examination; fam.) oral m.

orange n. (fruit) orange f. —a. (colour) orange invar.

oratorio n. oratorio m.

orbit n. orbite f. —v.t. graviter autour de, orbiter.

orchard n. verger m.

orchestra n. orchestre m.

orchestrate v.t. orchestrer.

orchid n. orchidée f.

ordain v.t. décréter (that, que); (relig.) ordonner.

ordeal n. épreuve f.

order n. ordre m.; (comm.) commande f. —v.t. ordonner; (goods etc.) commander. **in ~,** (tidy) en ordre; (document) en règle; (fitting) de règle. **in ~ that,** pour que. **in ~ to,** pour. **~ s.o. to,** ordonner à qn. de.

orderly a. (tidy) ordonné; (not unruly) discipliné.

ordinary a. (usual) ordinaire; (average) moyen.

ore n. mineral m.

organ n. organe m.; (mus.) orgue m. **~ist** n. organiste m./f.

organic a. organique.

organism n. organisme m.

organize v.t. organiser. **~ation** n. organisation f. **~er** n. organisa|teur, -trice m., f.

orgasm n. orgasme m.

orgy n. orgie f.

oriental a. oriental.

orient(ate) v.t. orienter. **~ion** n. orientation f.

orifice n. orifice m.

origin n. origine f.

original a. (first) originel; (not copied) original. **~ity** n.

originalité f. **~ly** adv. (at the outset) à l'origine; (write etc.) originalement.

originat|e v.i. (plan) prendre naissance. —v.t. être l'auteur de. **~e from,** provenir de; (person) venir de. **~or** n. auteur m.

ornament n. (decoration) ornement m.; (object) objet décoratif m. **~al** a. ornemental.

ornate a. richement orné.

ornithology n. ornithologie f.

orphan n. orphelin(e) m. (f.). —v.t. rendre orphelin.

orthodox a. orthodoxe.

orthopaedic a. orthopédique.

oscillate v.i. osciller.

ostentati|on n. ostentation f. **~ous** a. prétentieux.

osteopath n. ostéopathe m./f.

ostrich n. autruche f.

other a. autre. —n. & pron. autre m./f. —adv. **~ than,** autrement que; (except) à part. (some) **~s,** d'autres. **the ~ one,** l'autre m./f.

otherwise adv. autrement.

otter n. loutre f.

ouch int. aïe!

ought v. aux. devoir. **you ~ to stay,** vous devriez rester. **he ~ to succeed,** il devrait réussir. **I ~ to have done it,** j'aurais dû le faire.

ounce n. once f. (= 28.35 g.)

our a. notre, pl. nos.

ours poss. le or la nôtre, les nôtres.

ourselves pron. nous-mêmes; (reflexive & after prep.) nous.

oust v.t. évincer.

out adv. dehors; (sun) levé. **be ~,** (person, book) être sorti; (light) être éteint; (flower) être épanoui; (tide) être bas; (secret) se savoir; (wrong) se tromper. **be ~ to do,** être résolu à faire. **run**/etc. **~,** sortir en courant/etc. **~ of,** hors de; (without) sans, à court de. **~**

of pity/*etc.*, par pitié/*etc.* **made ~ of**, fait ou de. **take ~ of**, prendre dans. **5 ~ of 6**, 5 sur 6. **~ of date**, démodé; (*not valid*) périmé. **~ of doors**, dehors. **~ of order**, (*broken*) en panne. **~ of place**, (*object, remark*) déplacé. **get ~ of the way!** écarte-toi! **~ of work**, sans travail. **~-patient** *n.* malade en consultation externe *m./f.*

outboard *a.* (*motor*) hors-bord *invar.*

outbreak *n.* (*of war etc.*) début *m.*; (*of violence, boils*) éruption *f.*

outburst *n.* explosion *f.*

outcast *n.* paria *m.*

outclass *v.t.* surclasser.

outcome *n.* résultat *m.*

outcrop *n.* affleurement *m.*

outcry *n.* tollé *m.*

outdated *a.* démodé.

outdo *v.t.* surpasser.

outdoor *a.* de *or* en plein air. **~s** *adv.* dehors.

outer *a.* extérieur. **~ space**, espace (cosmique) *m.*

outfit *n.* (*articles*) équipement *m.*; (*clothes*) tenue *f.*; (*group: fam.*) équipe *f.*

outgoing *a.* (*minister, tenant*) sortant; (*sociable*) ouvert. **~s** *n. pl.* dépenses *f. pl.*

outgrow *v.t.* (*clothes*) devenir trop grand pour; (*habit*) dépasser.

outhouse *n.* appentis *m.*; (*of mansion*) dépendance *f.*

outing *n.* sortie *f.*

outlandish *a.* bizarre.

outlaw *n.* hors-la-loi *m. invar.* —*v.t.* proscrire.

outlay *n.* dépenses *f. pl.*

outlet *n.* (*for water, gases*) sortie *f.*; (*for goods*) débouché *m.*; (*for feelings*) exutoire *m.*

outline *n.* contour *m.*; (*summary*) esquisse *f.* —*v.t.* tracer le contour

de; (*summarize*) exposer sommairement.

outlook *n.* perspective *f.*

outlying *a.* écarté.

outmoded *a.* démodé.

outnumber *v.t.* surpasser en nombre.

outpost *n.* avant-poste *m.*

output *n.* rendement *m.*; (*comput.*) sortie *f.* —*v.t./i.* (*comput.*) sortir.

outrage *n.* atrocité *f.*; (*scandal*) scandale *m.* —*v.t.* (*morals*) outrager; (*person*) scandaliser.

outrageous *a.* scandaleux.

outright *adv.* complètement; (*at once*) sur le coup; (*frankly*) carrément. —*a.* complet; (*refusal*) net.

outset *n.* début *m.*

outside[1] *n.* extérieur *m.* —*adv.* (au) dehors. —*prep.* en dehors de; (*in front of*) devant.

outside[2] *a.* extérieur.

outsider *n.* étrang|er, -ère *m., f.*; (*sport*) outsider *m.*

outsize *a.* grande taille *invar.*

outskirts *n. pl.* banlieue *f.*

outspoken *a.* franc.

outstanding *a.* exceptionnel; (*not settled*) en suspens.

outward *a. & adv.* vers l'extérieur; (*sign etc.*) extérieur; (*journey*) d'aller. **~ly** *adv.* extérieurement. **~s** *adv.* vers l'extérieur.

outweigh *v.t.* (*exceed in importance*) l'emporter sur.

outwit *v.t.* duper.

oval *n. & a.* ovale (*m.*).

ovary *n.* ovaire *m.*

oven *n.* four *m.*

over *prep.* sur, au-dessus de; (*across*) de l'autre côté de; (*during*) pendant; (*more than*) plus de. —*adv.* (par-)dessus; (*ended*) fini; (*past*) passé; (*too*) trop; (*more*) plus. **jump/etc. ~**, sauter/*etc.* par-dessus. **~ the radio,** à la radio. **ask ~,** inviter chez soi. **he has some ~,** il lui en reste. **all ~ (the table),** partout (sur la table). **~ and above,** en plus de. **~ here,** par ici. **~ there,** là-bas.

over- *pref.* sur-, trop.

overall[1] *n.* blouse *f.* **~s,** bleu(s) de travail *m.* (*pl.*).

overall[2] *a.* global, d'ensemble; (*length, width*) total. —*adv.* globalement.

overbalance *v.t./i.* (faire) basculer.

overbearing *a.* autoritaire.

overboard *adv.* pardessus bord.

overcast *a.* couvert.

overcharge *v.t.* **~ s.o. (for),** faire payer trop cher à qn.

overcoat *n.* pardessus *m.*

overcome *v.t.* triompher de; (*difficulty*) surmonter, triompher de. **~ by,** accablé de.

overcrowded *a.* bondé.

overdo *v.t.* exagérer; (*culin.*) trop cuire.

overdose *n.* overdose *f.*

overdraft *n.* découvert *m.*

overdrawn *a.* à découvert.

overdrive *n.* surmultipliée *f.*

overdue *a.* en retard; (*belated*) tardif; (*bill*) impayé.

overestimate *v.t.* surestimer.

overexposed *a.* surexposé.

overflow[1] *v.i./débor der.*

overflow[2] *n.* (*outlet*) trop-plein *m.*

overgrown *a.* (*garden etc.*) envahi par la végétation.

overhaul[1] *v.t.* réviser.

overhaul[2] *n.* révision *f.*

overhead[1] *adv.* audessus; (*in sky*) dans le ciel.

overhead[2] *a.* aérien. **~s** *n. pl.* frais généraux *m. pl.* **~ projector,** rétroprojecteur *m.*

overhear *v.t.* entendre.

overjoyed *a.* ravi.

overland *a./adv.* par voie de terre.

overlap *v.t./i.* (se) chevaucher.

overleaf *adv.* au verso.

overload *v.t.* surcharger.

overlook *v.t.* oublier, négliger; (*of window, house*) donner sur; (*of tower*) dominer.

overnight *adv.* (pendant) la nuit; (*instantly; fig.*) du jour au lendemain. —*a.* (*train etc.*) de nuit; (*stay etc.*) d'une nuit; (*fig.*) soudain.

overpower *v.t.* subjuguer; (*opponent*) maitriser; (*fig.*) accabler. **~ing** *a.* irrésistible; (*heat, smell*) accablant.

overreact *v.i.* réagir excessivement.

overrid|e *v.t.* passer outre à. **~ing** *a.* prépondérant; (*importance*) majeur.

overrule *v.t.* rejeter.

overrun *v.t.* envahir; (*a limit*) aller au-delà de. —*v.i.* (*meeting*) durer plus longtemps que prévu.

overseas *a.* d'outre-mer, étranger. —*adv.* outre-mer, à l'étranger.

oversee *v.t.* surveiller. **~r** *n.* contremaître *m.*

overshadow *v.t.* (*darken*) assombrir; (*fig.*) éclipser.

overshoot *v.t.* dépasser.

oversight *n.* omission *f.*

oversleep *v.i.* se réveiller trop tard.

overt *a.* manifeste.

overtake *v.t./i.* dépasser; (*vehicle*) doubler, dépasser; (*surprise*) surprendre.

overtax *v.t.* (*strain*) fatiguer; (*taxpayer*) surimposer.

overthrow *v.t.* renverser.

overtime *n.* heures supplémentaires *f. pl.*

overtone *n.* nuance *f.*

overture *n.* ouverture *f.*

overturn v.t./i. (se) renverser.
overweight a. be ~, peser trop.
overwhelm v.t. accabler; (defeat) écraser; (amaze) bouleverser. ~ing a. accablant; (victory) écrasant; (urge) irrésistible.
overwork v.t./i. (se) surmener. —n. surmenage m.
ow|e v.t. devoir. ~ing a. dû. ~ing to, à cause de.
owl n. hibou m.
own[1] a. propre. **a house/etc. of one's ~**, sa propre maison/etc., une maison/etc. à soi. **on one's ~**, tout seul.
own[2] v.t. posséder. ~ **up (to)**, (fam.) avouer. ~er n. propriétaire m./f. ~ership n. possession f. (**of**, de); (right) propriété f.
ox n. bœuf m.
oxygen n. oxygène m.
oyster n. huître f.
ozone n. ozone m. ~ **layer**, couche d'ozone m.

P

pace n. pas m.; (speed) allure f. —v.i. ~ **(up and down)**, faire les cent pas. **keep ~ with**, suivre.
pacemaker n. (med.) stimulateur cardiaque m.
Pacific a. pacifique. —n. ~ **(Ocean)**, Pacifique m.
pacifist n. pacifiste m./f.
pacify v.t. (country) pacifier; (person) apaiser.
pack n. paquet m.; (mil.) sac m.; (of hounds) meute f. —v.t. emballer; (suitcase) faire; (box, room) remplir; (press down) tasser. —v.i. (one's bags), faire ses valises. ~ **into**, (cram) (s')entasser dans. ~ed a.

(crowded) bondé. ~ed lunch, repas froid m. ~ing n. (action, material) emballage m. ~ing case, caisse f.
package n. paquet m. —v.t. empaqueter. ~ **deal**, forfait m. ~ **tour**, voyage organisé m.
packet n. paquet m.
pact n. pacte m.
pad n. bloc(-notes) m.; (for ink) tampon m. —v.t. rembourrer. ~ding n. rembourrage m.
paddle[1] n. pagaie f. —v.t. ~ **a canoe**, pagayer.
paddle[2] v.i. barboter, se mouiller les pieds. ~ing pool, pataugeoire f.
paddock n. paddock m.
padlock n. cadenas m. —v.t. cadenasser.
paediatrician n. pédiatre m./f.
page[1] n. (of book etc.) page f.
page[2] n. (in hotel) chasseur m. (at wedding) page m. —v.t. (faire) appeler.
pageant n. spectacle (historique) m. ~ry n. pompe f.
pail n. seau m.
pain n. douleur f. ~s, efforts m. pl. —v.t. (grieve) peiner. **be in ~**, souffrir. ~-killer n. analgésique m. ~less a. indolore.
painful a. douloureux; (laborious) pénible.
painstaking a. appliqué.
paint n. peinture f. ~s, (in tube, box) couleurs f. pl. —v.t./i. peindre. ~er n. peintre m. ~ing n. peinture f.
paintbrush n. pinceau m.
paintwork n. peintures f. pl.
pair n. paire f.; (of people) couple m. **a ~ of trousers**, un pantalon.
Pakistan n. Pakistan. ~i a. & n. pakistanais(e) (m. (f.)).
pal n. (fam.) copain, -ine m., f.
palace n. palais m.

palate n. (of mouth) palais m.

pale a. pâle. —v.i. pâlir. **~ness** n. pâleur f.

Palestin|e n. Palestine f. **~ian** a. & n. palestinien(ne) (m. (f.)).

palette n. palette f.

pallet n. palette f.

pallid a. pâle.

palm n. (of hand) paume f.; (tree) palmier m.; (symbol) ~ m. —v.t. ~ **off**, (thing) refiler, coller (on, à); (person) coller.

palpable a. manifeste.

palpitat|e v.i. palpiter. **~ion** n. palpitation f.

paltry a. dérisoire.

pamper v.t. dorloter.

pamphlet n. brochure f.

pan n. casserole f.; (for frying) poêle f.; (of lavatory) cuvette f. —v.t. (fam.) critiquer.

pancake n. crêpe f.

pancreas n. pancréas m.

panda n. panda m.

pander v.i. ~ **to**, (person, taste) flatter bassement.

pane n. carreau m., vitre f.

panel n. (of door etc.) panneau m.; (jury) jury m.; (speakers: TV) invités m. pl. (instrument) ~, tableau de bord m. ~ **of experts**, groupe d'experts m. **~led** a. lambrissé. **~ling** n. lambrissage m.

pang n. pincement au cœur m., (of hunger, death) affres f. pl.

panic n. panique f. —v.t./ i. paniquer. **~-stricken** a. affolé.

panorama n. panorama m.

pansy n. (bot.) pensée f.

pant v.i. haleter.

panther n. panthère f.

panties n. pl. (fam.) slip m., culotte f. (de femme).

pantomime n. (show) spectacle de Noël m.; (mime) pantomime f.

pantry n. office m.

pants n. pl. (underwear: fam.) slip m.; (trousers: fam. & Amer.) pantalon m.

paper n. papier m.; (newspaper) journal m.; (exam) épreuve f.; (essay) exposé m.; (wallpaper) papier peint m. (identity) **~s** papiers (d'identité) m. pl. —v.t. (room) tapisser. **on ~**, par écrit. **~-clip** n. trombone m.

paperback a. & n. ~ (book), livre broché m.

paperweight n. presse-papiers m. invar.

paperwork n. paperasserie f.

paprika n. paprika m.

par n. be below ~, ne pas être en forme. **on a ~ with**, à égalité avec.

parable n. parabole f.

parachut|e n. parachute m. —v.i. descendre en parachute. **~ist** n. parachutiste m./f.

parade n. (procession) défilé m.; (ceremony, display) parade f.; (street) avenue f. —v.i. défiler. —v.t. faire parade de.

paradise n. paradis m.

paradox n. paradoxe m. **~ical** a. paradoxal.

paraffin n. pétrole (lampant) m.; (wax) paraffine f.

paragon n. modèle m.

paragraph n. paragraphe m.

parallel a. parallèle. —n. (line) parallèle f.; (comparison & geog.) parallèle m. —v.t. être semblable à; (match) égaler.

paralyse v.t. paralyser.

paralysis n. paralysie f.

paramedic n. auxiliaire médical(e) m. (f.).

parameter n. paramètre m.

paramount a. primordial.

paranoi|a n. paranoïa f. **~d** a. paranoïaque; (fam.) parano invar.

parapet n. parapet m.

paraphernalia n. attirail m.

paraphrase n. paraphrase f. —v.t. paraphraser.

parasite n. parasite m.

parasol n. ombrelle f.; (on table, at beach) parasol m.

paratrooper n. (mil.) parachutiste m/f.

parcel n. colis m., paquet m.

parch v.t. dessécher. **be ~ed**, (person) avoir très soif.

parchment n. parchemin m.

pardon n. pardon m.; (jurid.) grâce m. —v.t. pardonner (s.o. for sth., qch. à qn.); gracier. **I beg your ~**, pardon.

pare v.t. (clip) rogner; (peel) éplucher.

parent n. père m., mère f. **~s**, parents m. pl. **~al** a. des parents.

parenthesis n. parenthèse f.

Paris n. Paris m./f. **~ian** a. & n. parisien(ne) (m. (f.)).

parish n. (relig.) paroisse f.; (municipal) commune f. **~ioner** n. paroissien(ne) m. (f.).

parity n. parité f.

park n. parc m. —v.t./i. (se) garer; (remain parked) stationner. **~ing-meter** n. parcmètre m. **~ing ticket**, procès-verbal m.

parka n. parka m./f.

parliament n. parlement m. **~ary** a. parlementaire.

parlour n. salon m.

parody n. parodie f. —v.t. parodier.

parole n. **on ~**, en liberté conditionnelle.

parrot n. perroquet m.

parry v.t. (sport) parer; (question etc.) esquiver. —n. parade f.

parsley n. persil m.

parsnip n. panais m.

parson n. pasteur m.

part n. partie f.; (of serial) épisode

m.; (of machine) pièce f.; (theatre) rôle m.; (side in dispute) parti m. —a. partiel. —adv. en partie. —v.t./i. (separate) (se) séparer. **in ~**, en partie. **on the ~ of**, de la part de. **~-exchange** n. reprise f. **~-time** a. & adv. à temps partiel. **~ with**, se séparer de. **take ~**, participer à.

partial a. partiel; (biased) partial. **be ~ to**, avoir une prédilection pour.

particip|ate v.i. participer (in, à). **~ant** n. participant(e) m. (f.). **~ation** n. participation f.

participle n. participe m.

particle n. particule f.

particular a. particulier; (fussy) difficile; (careful) méticuleux. **that ~ man**, cet homme-là en particulier. **~s** n. pl. détails m. pl. **in ~**, en particulier. **~ly** adv. particulièrement.

parting n. séparation f.; (in hair) raie f. —a. d'adieu.

partisan n. partisan(e) m. (f.).

partition n. (of room) cloison f.; (pol.) partage m., partition f. —v.t. (room) cloisonner; (country) partager.

partly adv. en partie.

partner n. associé(e) m. (f.); (sport) partenaire m./f. **~ship** n. association f.

partridge n. perdrix f.

party n. fête f.; (formal) réception f.; (for young people) boum f.; (group) groupe m., équipe f.; (pol.) parti m.

pass v.t./i. passer; (overtake) dépasser; (in exam) être reçu (à); (approve) accepter, autoriser; (law, bill) voter. **~ (by)**, (building) passer devant; (person) croiser. —n. (permit) laissez-passer m. invar.; (ticket) carte d'abonnement f.; (geog.) col m.;

(*sport*) passe *f*. **~** (**mark**), (*in exam*) moyenne *f*. **~ out** or **round**, distribuer. **~ up**, (*forego: fam.*) laisser passer.

passable *a*. (*adequate*) passable; (*road*) praticable.

passage *n*. (*way through, text, etc.*) passage *m*.; (*voyage*) traversée *f*.; (*corridor*) couloir *m*.

passenger *n*. passager|e, -ère *m*.; (*in train*) voyageur|r, -se *m*., *f*.

passer-by *n*. passant(e) *m*. (*f*.).

passing *n*. (*fleeting*) passager.

passion *n*. passion *f*. **~ate** *a*. passionné. **~ately** *adv*. passionnément.

passive *a*. passif.

Passover *n*. Pâque *f*.

passport *n*. passeport *m*.

password *n*. mot de passe *m*.

past *a*. passé; (*former*) ancien. —*n*. passé *m*. —*prep*. au-delà de; (*in front of*) devant. —*adv*. devant. **~ midnight**, minuit passé. **10 ~ 6**, six heures dix.

pasta *n*. pâtes *f. pl*.

paste *n*. (*glue*) colle *f*.; (*dough*) pâte *f*.; (*of fish, meat*) pâté *m*.; (*jewellery*) strass *m*. —*v.t*. coller.

pastel *n*. pastel *m*. —*a*. pastel invar.

pasteurize *v.t*. pasteuriser.

pastiche *n*. pastiche *m*.

pastime *n*. passetemps *m. invar*.

pastoral *a*. pastoral.

pastry *n*. (*dough*) pâte *f*.; (*tart*) pâtisserie *f*.

pasture *n*. pâturage *m*.

pat *v.t*. tapoter. —*n*. petite tape *f*. —*adv*. & *a*. à propos; (*ready*) tout prêt.

patch *n*. pièce *f*.; (*over eye*) bandeau *m*.; (*spot*) tache *f*.; (*of vegetables*) carré *m*. —*v.t*. **~ up**, rapiécer; (*fig.*) régler. **~y** *a*. inégal.

patchwork *n*. patchwork *m*.

patent *a*. patent. —*n*. brevet (d'invention) *m*. —*v.t*. breveter. **~ leather**, cuir verni *m*.

paternal *a*. paternel.

path *n*. sentier *m*., chemin *m*.; (*in park*) allée *f*.; (*of rocket*) trajectoire *f*.

pathetic *a*. pitoyable; (*bad: fam.*) minable.

pathology *n*. pathologie *f*.

patience *n*. patience *f*.

patient *a*. patient. —*n*. malade *m./f*., patient(e) *m*. (*f*.). **~ly** *adv*. patiemment.

patio *n*. patio *m*.

patriotic *a*. patriotique; (*person*) patriote.

patrol *n*. patrouille *f*. —*v.t./i*. patrouiller (dans). **~ car**, voiture de police *f*.

patron *n*. (*of the arts*) mécène *m*.; (*customer*) client(e) *m*. (*f*.) **~ize** *v.t*. être client de; (*fig.*) traiter avec condescendance.

patter[1] *n*. (*of steps*) bruit *m*.; (*of rain*) crépitement *m*.

patter[2] *n*. (*speech*) baratin *m*.

pattern *n*. motif *m*., dessin *m*.; (*for sewing*) patron *m*.; (*procedure, type*) schéma *m*.; (*example*) exemple *m*.

paunch *n*. panse *f*.

pause *n*. pause *f*. —*v.i*. faire une pause; (*hesitate*) hésiter.

pave *v.t*. paver. **~ the way**, ouvrir la voie (**for**, à).

pavement *n*. trottoir *m*.

pavilion *n*. pavillon *m*.

paw *n*. patte *f*.

pawn[1] *n*. (*chess & fig.*) pion *m*.

pawn[2] *v.t*. mettre en gage. —*n*. in **~**, en gage. **~-shop** *n*. mont-de-piété *m*.

pawnbroker *n*. prêteur sur gages *m*.

pay *v.t./i*. payer; (*yield: comm.*) rapporter; (*compliment, visit*) faire. —*n.* salaire *m.*, paie *f.* **∼ attention,** faire attention (**to,** à). **∼ back,** rembourser. **∼ for,** payer. **∼ out,** payer, verser.

payable *a.* payable.

payment *n.* paiement *m.*; (*regular*) versement *m.* (*reward*) récompense *f.*

payroll *n.* be on the **∼** of, être membre du personnel de.

pea *n.* (petit) pois *m.*

peace *n.* paix *f.* **∼ of mind,** tranquillité d'esprit *f.*

peaceful *a.* paisible; (*intention, measure*) pacifique.

peacemaker *n.* concilia|teur, -trice *m.*, *f.*

peach *n.* pêche *f.*

peacock *n.* paon *m.*

peak *n.* sommet *m.*; (*of mountain*) pic *m.*; (*maximum*) maximum *m.* **∼ hours,** heures de pointe *f. pl.*

peal *n.* (*of bells*) carillon *m.*; (*of laughter*) éclat *m.*

peanut *n.* cacahuète *f.*

pear *n.* poire *f.*

pearl *n.* perle *f.* **∼y** *a.* nacré.

peasant *n.* paysan(ne) *m.* (*f.*).

peat *n.* tourbe *f.*

pebble *n.* caillou *m.*; (*on beach*) galet *m.*

peck *v.t./i.* (*food etc.*) picorer; (*attack*) donner des coups de bec (à). —*n.* coup de bec *m.*

peculiar *a.* (*odd*) bizarre; (*special*) particulier (**to,** à).

pedal *n.* pédale *f.* —*v.i.* pédaler.

peddle *v.t.* colporter; (*drugs*) revendre.

pedestal *n.* piédestal *m.*

pedestrian *n.* piéton *m.* —*a.* (*precinct, street*) piétonnier; (*fig.*) prosaïque. **∼ crossing,** passage piétons *m.*

pedigree *n.* (*of person*) ascendance

f.; (*of animal*) pedigree *m.* —*a.* (*cattle etc.*) de race.

pee *v.i.* (*fam.*) faire pipi.

peek *v.i. & n.* = **peep**[1].

peel *n.* épluchure(s) *f.* (*pl.*); (*of orange*) écorce *f.* —*v.t.* (*fruit, vegetables*) éplucher. —*v.i.* (*of skin*) peler; (*of paint*) s'écailler. **∼ings** *n. pl.* épluchures *f. pl.*

peep[1] *v.i.* jeter un coup d'œil (*furtif*) (**at,** à). —*n.* coup d'œil (*furtif*) *m.*

peep[2] *v.i.* (*chirp*) pépier.

peer[1] *v.t.* **∼ (at),** scruter.

peer[2] *n.* (*equal, noble*) pair *m.*

peg *n.* cheville *f.*; (*for clothes*) pince à linge *f.*; (*to hang coats etc.*) patère *f.*; (*for tent*) piquet *m.* —*v.t.* (*prices*) stabiliser. **buy off the ∼,** acheter en prêt-à-porter.

pelican *n.* pélican *m.*

pellet *n.* (*round mass*) boulette *f.*; (*for gun*) plomb *m.*

pelt[1] *n.* (*skin*) peau *f.*

pelt[2] *v.t.* bombarder (**with,** de). —*v.i.* pleuvoir à torrents.

pelvis *n.* (*anat.*) bassin *m.*

pen[1] *n.* (*for sheep etc.*) enclos *m.*; (*for baby, cattle*) parc *m.*

pen[2] *n.* stylo *m.*; (*to be dipped in ink*) plume *f.* —*v.t.* écrire. **∼friend** *n.* correspondant(e) *m.* (*f.*).

penal *a.* pénal. **∼ize** *v.t.* pénaliser; (*fig.*) handicaper.

penalty *n.* peine *f.*; (*fine*) amende *f.*; (*sport*) pénalité *f.*

penance *n.* pénitence *f.*

pencil *n.* crayon *m.* —*v.t.* **∼ in,** noter provisoirement. **∼-sharpener** *n.* taille-crayon(s) *m.*

pendant *n.* pendentif *m.*

pending *a.* en suspens. —*prep.* (*until*) en attendant.

pendulum *n.* pendule *m.*; (*of clock*) balancier *m.*

penetrat|e v.t. (enter) pénétrer dans; (understand, permeate) pénétrer. —v.i. pénétrer. **~ing** a. pénétrant. **~ion** n. pénétration f.

penguin n. manchot m., pingouin m.

penicillin n. pénicilline f.

peninsula n. péninsule f.

penis n. pénis m.

penknife n. canif m.

pennant n. flamme f.

penny n. penny m.; (fig.) sou m.

pension n. pension f.; (for retirement) retraite f. —v.t. **~ off,** mettre à la retraite. **~ scheme,** caisse de retraite f. **~er** n. (old-age) **~er,** retraité(e) m. (f.), personne âgée f.

pensive a. pensif.

penthouse n. appartement de luxe m.

pent-up a. refoulé.

penultimate a. avant-dernier.

people n. pl. gens m. pl., personnes f. pl. —n. peuple m. —v.t. peupler. **English**/etc. **~,** les Anglais/ etc. m. pl. **~ say,** on dit.

pep n. entrain m. —v.t. **~ up,** donner de l'entrain à. **~ talk,** discours d'encouragement m.

pepper n. poivre m.; (vegetable) poivron m. —v.t. (culin.) poivrer. **~y** a. poivré.

peppermint n. (plant) menthe poivrée f.; (sweet) bonbon à la menthe m.

per prep. par. **~ annum,** par an. **~ cent,** pour cent. **~ kilo**/etc. le kilo/etc. **ten km. ~ hour,** dix km à l'heure.

perceive v.t. percevoir; (notice) s'apercevoir de.

percentage n. pourcentage m.

perch n. (of bird) perchoir m. —v.i. (se) percher.

percolator n. cafetière f.

percussion n. percussion f.

perfect[1] a. parfait. **~ly** adv. parfaitement.

perfect[2] v.t. parfaire, mettre au point. **~ion** n. perfection f. **to ~ion,** à la perfection.

perforat|e v.t. perforer. **~ion** n. perforation f.; (line of holes) pointillé m.

perform v.t. exécuter, faire; (a function) remplir; (mus., theatre) interpréter, jouer. —v.i. jouer; (behave, function) se comporter. **~ance** n. exécution f.; interprétation f.; (of car, engine) performance f.; (show) représentation f.; séance f.; (fuss) histoire f. **~er** n. artiste m./f.

perfume n. parfum m.

perhaps adv. peut-être.

peril n. péril m. **~ous** a. périlleux.

perimeter n. périmètre m.

period n. période f., époque f.; (era) époque f.; (lesson) cours m.; (gram.) point m.; (med.) règles f. pl. —a. d'époque. **~ic** a. périodique.

periodical n. périodique m.

peripher|y n. périphérie f. **~al** a. périphérique; (of lesser importance:fig.) accessoire; n. (comput.) périphérique m.

periscope n. périscope m.

perish v.i. périr; (rot) se détériorer. **~able** a. périssable.

perjury n. parjure m.

perk[1] v.t./i. **~ up,** (fam.) (se) remonter. **~y** a. (fam.) gai.

perk[2] n. (fam.) avantage m.

perm n. permanente f. —v.t. **have one's hair ~ed,** se faire faire une permanente.

permanen|t a. permanent. **~ce** n. permanence f. **~tly** adv. à titre permanent.

permissible a. permis.

permission n. permission f.

permit[1] *v.t.* permettre (**s.o. to,** à qn. de), autoriser (**s.o. to,** qn. à).

permit[2] *n.* permis *m.*; (*pass*) laissez-passer *m. invar.*

perpendicular *a. & n.* perpendiculaire (*f.*).

perpetrat|e *v.t.* perpétrer. ∼**or** *n.* auteur *m.*

perpetual *a.* perpétuel.

perpetuate *v.t.* perpétuer.

perplex *v.t.* rendre perplexe. ∼**ed** *a.* perplexe. ∼**ing** *a.* déroutant.

persecut|e *v.t.* persécuter. ∼**ion** *n.* persécution *f.*

persever|e *v.i.* persévérer. ∼**ance** *n.* persévérance *f.*

Persian *a. & n.* (*lang.*) persan (*m.*). ∼ **Gulf,** golfe persique *m.*

persist *v.i.* persister (**in doing,** à faire). ∼**ence** *n.* persistance *f.* ∼**ent** *a.* (*cough, snow, etc.*) persistant; (*obstinate*) obstiné; (*continual*) continuel. ∼**ently** *adv.* avec persistance.

person *n.* personne *f.*

personal *a.* personnel; (*hygiene, habits*) intime; (*secretary*) particulier. ∼**ly** *adv.* personnellement. ∼ **stereo,** baladeur *m.*

personality *n.* personnalité *f.*; (*on TV*) vedette *f.*

personify *v.t.* personnifier.

personnel *n.* personnel *m.*

perspective *n.* perspective *f.*

Perspex *n.* (P.) plexiglas *m.* (P.).

perspir|e *v.i.* transpirer. ∼**ation** *n.* transpiration *f.*

persua|de *v.t.* persuader (**to,** de). ∼**sion** *n.* persuasion *f.*

persuasive *a.* (*person, speech, etc.*) persuasif.

Peru *n.* Pérou *m.* ∼**vian** *a. & n.* péruvien(ne) (*m.* (*f.*)).

perva|de *v.t.* imprégner, envahir.

∼**sive** *a.* (*mood, dust*) envahissant.

pervers|e *a.* (*stubborn*) entêté; (*wicked*) pervers. ∼**ity** *n.* perversité *f.*

pervert[1] *v.t.* pervertir. ∼**sion** *n.* perversion *f.*

pervert[2] *n.* perverti(e) *m.* (*f.*)

peseta *n.* peseta *f.*

pessimis|t *n.* pessimiste *m./f.* ∼**m** *n.* pessimisme *m.* ∼**tic** *a.* pessimiste.

pest *n.* insecte *or* animal nuisible *m.*; (*person: fam.*) enqui-quineu|r, -se *m., f.*

pester *v.t.* harceler.

pesticide *n.* pesticide *m.*

pet *n.* animal (domestique) *m.*; (*favourite*) chouchou(te) *m.* (*f.*). —*a.* (*tame*) apprivoisé. —*v.t.* caresser; (*sexually*) peloter.

petal *n.* pétale *m.*

peter *v.i.* ∼ **out,** (*supplies*) s'épuiser; (*road*) finir.

petite *a.* (*woman*) menue.

petition *n.* pétition *f.* —*v.t.* adresser une pétition à.

petrify *v.t.* pétrifier; (*scare: fig.*) pétrifier de peur.

petrol *n.* essence *f.* ∼ **station,** station-service *f.* ∼ **tank,** réservoir d'essence.

petroleum *n.* pétrole *m.*

petticoat *n.* jupon *m.*

petty *a.* (*minor*) petit; (*mean*) mesquin. ∼ **cash,** petite caisse *f.*

petulan|t *a.* irritable. ∼**ce** *n.* irritabilité *f.*

pew *n.* banc (d'église) *m.*

pewter *n.* étain *m.*

phantom *n.* fantôme *m.*

pharmaceutical *a.* pharmaceutique.

pharmac|y *n.* pharmacie *f.* ∼**ist** *n.* pharmacien(ne) *m.* (*f.*).

pharyngitis *n.* pharyngite *f.*

phase *n.* phase *f.* —*v.t.* ∼ **in/out,**

introduire/retirer progressivement.

pheasant n. faisan m.

phenomen|on n. (pl. **-ena**)
phénomène m. **~al** a.
phénoménal.

Philippines n. pl. the **~**, les
Philippines f. pl.

philistine n. philistin m.

philosoph|y n. philosophie f. **~er**
n. philosophe m./f. **~ical** a.
philosophique; (resigned) philosophe.

phlegm n. (med.) mucosité f.

phlegmatic a. flegmatique.

phobia n. phobie f.

phone n. téléphone m. **—**v.t.
(person) téléphoner à; (message)
téléphoner. **—**v.i. téléphoner. **~**
back, rappeler. **~ book**, annuaire m. **~ box**, **~ booth**,
cabine téléphonique f. **~ call**,
coup de fil m.

phonecard n. télécarte f.

phonetic a. phonétique.

phoney a. (sl.) faux. **—**n. (person:
sl.) charlatan m.

phosphate n. phosphate m.

phosphorus n. phosphore m.

photo n. photo f.

photocop|y n. photocopie f. **—**v.t.
photocopier. **~ier** n. photo-
copieuse f.

photogenic a. photogénique.

photograph n. photographie f.
—v.t. photographier. **~er** n.
photographe m./f. **~ic** a.
photographique. **~y** n. (activity)
photographie f.

phrase n. expression f.; (idiom &
gram.) locution f. **—**v.t. exprimer,
formuler. **~-book** n. guide de
conversation m.

physical a. physique. **~ly** adv.
physiquement.

physicist n. physicien(ne) m. (f.).

physics n. physique f.

physiotherap|y n. kinésithérapie
f. **~ist** n. kinésithérapeute m./f.

physique n. constitution f.;
(appearance) physique m.

pian|o n. piano m. **~ist** n. pianiste
m./f.

pick[1] (tool) n. pioche f.

pick[2] v.t. choisir; (flower etc.)
cueillir; (lock) crocheter; (nose) se
curer; (pockets) faire. **~ (off)**,
enlever. **—**n. choix m.; (best)
meilleur(e) m. (f.). **~ off**, (mil.)
abattre un à un. **~ on**, harceler.
~ out, choisir; (identify) distinguer. **~ up** v.t. ramasser; (sth.
fallen) relever; (weight) soulever;
(habit, passenger, speed, etc.)
prendre; (learn) apprendre; v.i.
s'améliorer. **~-up** n. partenaire
de rencontre m./f.; (truck, stylus-
holder) pick-up m.

pickaxe n. pioche f.

picket n. (single striker) gréviste
m./f.; (stake) piquet m. **~ (line)**,
piquet de grève m. **—**v.t. mettre
un piquet de grève devant.

pickle n. vinaigre m.; (brine)
saumure f. **~s**, pickles m. pl.
—v.t. conserver dans du vinaigre
or de la saumure.

pickpocket n. (thief) pickpocket
m.

picnic n. pique-nique m. **—**v.i. pi-
queniquer.

pictorial a. illustré.

picture n. image f.; (painting)
tableau m.; (photograph) photo f.;
(drawing) dessin m.; (film) film
m.; (fig.) description f., tableau m.
—v.t. s'imaginer; (describe)
dépeindre. the **~s**, (cinema) le
cinéma.

picturesque a. pittoresque.

pie n. tarte f.; (of meat) pâté en
croûte m. **~ chart**, camembert
m.

piece n. morceau m.; (of currency,

machine, etc.) pièce *f.* **a ~ of advice/furniture/** *etc.*, un conseil/meuble/ *etc.*

piecemeal *a.* par bribes.

pier *n.* (*promenade*) jetée *f.*

pierc|e *v.t.* percer. **~ing** *a.* perçant; (*cold*) glacial.

pig *n.* cochon *m.* **~-headed** *a.* entêté.

pigeon *n.* pigeon *m.* **~-hole** *n.* casier *m.*; *v.t.* classer.

pigment *n.* pigment *m.* **~ation** *n.* pigmentation *f.*

pigtail *n.* natte *f.*

pike *n.* invar. (*fish*) brochet *m.*

pilchard *n.* pilchard *m.*

pile *n.* pile *f.*, tas *m.*; (*of carpet*) poils *m.pl.* —*v.t.* **~ (up)**, (*stack*) empiler. —*v.i.* **~ into**, s'empiler dans. **~ up**, (*accumulate*) (s')accumuler. **a ~ of**, (*fam.*) un tas de. **~-up** *n.* (*auto.*) carambolage *m.*

piles *n. pl.* (*fam.*) hémorroïdes *f. pl.*

pilfer *v.t.* chaparder.

pilgrim *n.* pèlerin *m.* **~age** *n.* pèlerinage *m.*

pill *n.* pilule *f.*

pillar *n.* pilier *m.* **~-box** *n.* boîte à or aux lettres *f.*

pillion *n.* siège arrière *m.* **ride ~**, monter derrière.

pillow *n.* oreiller *m.*

pillowcase *n.* taie d'oreiller *f.*

pilot *n.* pilote *m.* —*a.* pilote. —*v.t.* piloter. **~-light** *n.* veilleuse *f.*

pimento *n.* piment *m.*

pimp *n.* souteneur *m.*

pimpl|e *n.* bouton *m.* **~y** *a.* boutonneux.

pin *n.* épingle *f.*; (*techn.*) goupille *f.* —*v.t.* épingler, attacher; (*hold down*) clouer. **have ~s and needles,** avoir des fourmis. **~-point** *v.t.* repérer, définir.

pinafore *n.* tablier *m.*

pincers *n.pl.* tenailles *f. pl.*

pinch *v.t.* pincer; (*steal: sl.*) piquer. —*v.i.* (*be too tight*) serrer. —*n.* (*mark*) pinçon *m.*; (*of salt*) pincée *f.* **at a ~**, au besoin.

pine[1] *n.* (*tree*) pin *m.* **~-cone** *n.* pomme de pin *f.*

pine[2] *v.i.* **~ away**, dépérir. **~ for**, languir après.

pineapple *n.* ananas *m.*

ping *n.* bruit métallique *m.*

ping-pong *n.* ping-pong *m.*

pink *a. & n.* rose (*m.*).

pint *n.* pinte *f.*

pioneer *n.* pionnier *m.* —*v.t.* être le premier à faire, utiliser, étudier, *etc.*

pip[1] *n.* (*seed*) pépin *m.*

pip[2] *n.* (*sound*) top *m.*

pipe *n.* tuyau *m.*; (*of smoker*) pipe *f.*; (*mus.*) pipeau *m.* —*v.t.* transporter par tuyau.

pipeline *n.* pipeline *m.* **in the ~**, en route.

piping *n.* tuyau(x) *m.* (*pl.*). **~ hot**, très chaud.

pirate *n.* pirate *m.* —*v.t.* pirater.

Pisces *n.* les Poissons *m. pl.*

pistachio *n.* pistache *f.*

pistol *n.* pistolet *m.*

piston *n.* piston *m.*

pit *n.* fosse *f.*, trou *m.*; (*mine*) puits *m.*; (*quarry*) carrière *f.*; (*for orchestra*) fosse *f.*; (*of stomach*) creux *m.* —*v.t.* trouer; (*fig.*) opposer. **~ o.s. against**, se mesurer à.

pitch[1] *n.* (*tar*) poix *f.* **~-black** *a.* d'un noir d'ébène.

pitch[2] *v.t.* lancer; (*tent*) dresser. —*n.* degré *m.*; (*of voice*) hauteur *f.*; (*mus.*) ton *m.*; (*sport*) terrain *m.*

pitcher *n.* cruche *f.*

pitfall *n.* piège *m.*

pith n. (of orange) peau blanche f.; (essence: fig.) moelle f.

pithy a. concis.

pitiful a. pitoyable.

pittance n. revenu or salaire dérisoire m.

pity n. pitié f.; (regrettable fact) dommage m. —v.t. plaindre. **what a ~**, quel dommage. **it's a ~**, c'est dommage.

pivot n. pivot m. —v.i. pivoter.

pizza n. pizza f.

placard n. affiche f.

placate v.t. calmer.

place n. endroit m., lieu m.; (house) maison f.; (seat, rank, etc.) place f. —v.t. placer; (an order) passer; (remember) situer. **at** or **to my ~**, chez moi. **in the first ~**, d'abord. **out of ~**, déplacé. **take ~**, avoir lieu. **~-mat** n. set m.

placenta n. placenta m.

placid a. placide.

plague n. peste f.; (nuisance: fam.) fléau m. —v.t. harceler.

plaice n. invar. carrelet m.

plaid n. tissu écossais m.

plain a. clair; (candid) franc; (simple) simple; (not pretty) sans beauté; (not patterned) uni. —adv. franchement. —n. plaine f. **~ chocolate**, chocolat noir. **in ~ clothes**, en civil.

plaintiff n. plaignant(e) m. (f.).

plait v.t. tresser. —n. tresse f.

plan n. projet m., plan m.; (diagram) plan m. —v.t. prévoir, projeter; (arrange) organiser; (design) concevoir; (economy, work) planifier. —v.i. faire des projets. **~ to do**, avoir l'intention de faire.

plane[1] n. (tree) platane m.

plane[2] n. (level) plan m.; (aeroplane) avion m. —a. plan.

plane[3] n. (tool) rabot m. —v.t. raboter.

planet n. planète f.

plank n. planche f.

planning n. (pol., comm.) planification f. **family ~**, planning familial m.

plant n. plante f.; (techn.) matériel m.; (factory) usine f. —v.t. planter; (bomb) (dé)poser. **~ation** n. plantation f.

plaque n. plaque f.

plasma n. plasma m.

plaster n. plâtre m.; (adhesive) sparadrap m. —v.t. plâtrer; (cover) tapisser (**with**, de). **in ~**, dans le plâtre.

plastic a. en plastique; (art, substance) plastique. —n. plastique m. **~ surgery**, chirurgie esthétique f.

Plasticine n. (P.) pâte à modeler f.

plate n. assiette f.; (of metal) plaque f.

plateau n. plateau m.

platform n. (in classroom, hall, etc.) estrade f.; (for speaking) tribune f.; (rail.) quai m.

platinum n. platine m.

platoon n. (mil.) section f.

plausible a. plausible.

play v.t./i. jouer; (instrument) jouer de; (record) passer; (game) jouer à; (opponent) jouer contre; (match) disputer. —n. jeu m.; (theatre) pièce f. **~ down**, minimiser. **~-group** n. garderie f. **~-off** n. (sport) belle f. **~ on**, (take advantage of) jouer sur. **~-pen** n. parc m. **~-er** n. joueu|r, -se m., f.

playful a. enjoué; (child) joueur.

playground n. cour de récréation f.

playing n. jeu m. **~-card** n. carte à jouer f. **~-field** n. terrain de sport m.

plc abbr. (public limited company) SA.

plea n. (*entreaty*) supplication f.; (*reason*) excuse f.

plead v.t./i. (*jurid.*) plaider; (*as excuse*) alléguer. **~ for,** (*beg for*) implorer. **~ with,** (*beg*) implorer.

pleasant a. agréable.

please v.t./i. plaire (à), faire plaisir (à). —adv. s'il vous or te plaît. **~d** a. content (**with,** de).

pleasure n. plaisir m.

pleat n. pli m. —v.t. plisser.

pledge n. (*token*) gage m.; (*fig.*) promesse f. —v.t. promettre.

plentiful a. abondant.

plenty n. abondance f. **~ (of),** (*a great deal*) beaucoup (de); (*enough*) assez (de).

pliable a. souple.

pliers n. pl. pince(s) f. (pl.).

plight n. triste situation f.

plimsoll n. chaussure de gym f.

plinth n. socle m.

plod v.i. avancer péniblement or d'un pas lent; (*work*) bûcher.

plot n. complot m.; (*of novel etc.*) intrigue f. **~ (of land),** terrain m. —v.t./i. comploter; (*mark out*) tracer.

plough n. charrue f. —v.t./i. labourer. **~ back,** réinvestir. **~ into,** rentrer dans.

ploy n. (*fam.*) stratagème m.

pluck v.t. cueillir; (*bird*) plumer; (*eyebrows*) épiler; (*strings: mus.*) pincer. —n. courage m.

plug n. (*of cloth, paper, etc.*) tampon m.; (*for sink etc.*) bonde f.; (*electr.*) fiche f., prise f. —v.t. (*hole*) boucher; (*publicize: fam.*) faire du battage autour de. **~ in,** brancher. **~hole** n. vidange f.

plum n. prune f.

plumb|er n. plombier m. **~ing** n. plomberie f.

plum|e n. plume(s) f. (pl.). **~age** n. plumage m.

plummet v.i. plonger.

plump a. potelé, dodu. —v.i. **~ for,** choisir.

plunder v.t. piller. —n. (*act*) pillage m.; (*goods*) butin m.

plunge v.t./i. (*dive, thrust*) plonger; (*fall*) tomber. —n. plongeon m.; (*fall*) tomber f.

plunger n. (*for sink*) ventouse f.

plural n. pluriel; (*noun*) au pluriel. —n. pluriel m.

plus prep. plus. —a. (*electr. & fig.*) positif. —n. signe plus m.; (*fig.*) atout m. **ten ~,** plus de dix.

plush(y) a. somptueux.

ply v.t. (*tool*) manier; (*trade*) exercer. —v.i. faire la navette.

plywood n. contreplaqué m.

p.m. adv. de l'après-midi or du soir.

pneumatic a. pneumatique. **~ drill,** marteau-piqueur m.

pneumonia n. pneumonie f.

PO abbr. see Post Office.

poach v.t./i. (*game*) braconner; (*staff*) débaucher; (*culin.*) pocher. **~er** n. braconnier m.

pocket n. poche f. —a. de poche. —v.t. empocher. **~-book** n. (*notebook*) carnet m. **~-money** n. argent de poche m.

pod n. (*peas etc.*) cosse f.; (*vanilla*) gousse f.

poem n. poème m.

poet n. poète m. **~ic** a. poétique.

poetry n. poésie f.

poignant a. poignant.

point n. point m.; (*tip*) pointe f.; (*decimal point*) virgule f.; (*meaning*) sens m., intérêt m.; (*remark*) remarque f. **~s,** (*rail.*) aiguillage m. —v.t. (*aim*) braquer; (*show*) indiquer. —v.i. indiquer du doigt (*at* or *to s.o.,* qn.). **~ out that,** faire remarquer que. **good ~s,** qualités f. pl. **on the ~ of,** sur le point de. **~-blank** a. adv.

à bout portant. ∼ **of view,** point de vue m. ∼ **out,** signaler. **what is the ∼?,** à quoi bon?

pointed a. pointu; (*remark*) lourd de sens.

pointer n. (*indicator*) index m.; (*dog*) chien d'arrêt m.; (*advice: fam.*) tuyau m.

pointless a. inutile.

poise n. équilibre m.; (*carriage*) maintien m.; (*fig.*) assurance f. ∼**d** a. en équilibre; (*confident*) assuré. ∼**d for,** prêt à.

poison n. poison m. —v.t. empoisonner. ∼**ous** a. (*substance etc.*) toxique; (*plant*) vénéneux; (*snake*) venimeux.

poke v.t./i. (*push*) pousser; (*fire*) tisonner; (*thrust*) fourrer. —n. (petit) coup m. ∼ **about,** fureter. ∼ **fun at,** se moquer de.

poker[1] n. tisonnier m.

poker[2] n. (*cards*) poker m.

poky a. (*small*) exigu.

Poland n. Pologne f.

polar a. polaire. ∼ **bear,** ours blanc m.

polarize v.t. polariser.

Polaroid n. (P.) polaroïd (P.) m.

pole[1] n. (*fixed*) poteau m.; (*rod*) perche f.; (*for flag*) mât m. ∼**vault** n. saut à la perche m.

pole[2] n. (*geog.*) pôle m.

Pole n. Polonais(e)m (f.).

police n. police f. —v.t. faire la police dans. ∼ **station,** commissariat de police m.

police|man n. agent de police m. ∼**woman** femme-agent f.

policy[1] n. politique f.

policy[2] n. (*insurance*) police (d'assurance) f.

polio(myelitis) n. polio(myélite) f.

polish v.t. polir; (*shoes, floor*) cirer. —n. (*for shoes*) cirage m.; (*for floor*) encaustique f.; (*for*

nails) vernis m.; (*shine*) poli m.; (*fig.*) raffinement m.

Polish a. polonais. —n. (*lang.*) polonais m.

polite a. poli. ∼**ly** adv. poliment. ∼**ness** n. politesse f.

political a. politique.

politician n. homme politique m., femme politique f.

politics n. politique f.

poll n. scrutin m.; (*survey*) sondage m. —v.t. (*votes*) obtenir. ∼**ing-booth** n. isoloir m. ∼**ing station,** bureau de vote m.

pollen n. pollen m.

pollute v.t. polluer. ∼**ion** n. pollution f.

polo n. polo m. ∼ **neck,** col roulé m. ∼ **shirt,** polo m.

polyester n. polyester m.

polytechnic n. institut universitaire de technologie m.

polythene n. polythène m.

pomegranate n. grenade f.

pomp n. pompe f.

pompon n. pompon m.

pomp|ous a. pompeux. ∼**osity** n. solennité f.

pond n. étang m.; (*artificial*) bassin m.; (*stagnant*) mare f.

ponder v.t./i. méditer (sur).

pony n. poney m. ∼**-tail** n. queue de cheval f.

poodle n. caniche m.

pool[1] n. (*puddle*) flaque f.; (*pond*) étang m.; (*of blood*) mare f.; (*for swimming*) piscine f.

pool[2] n. (*fund*) fonds commun m.; (*of ideas*) réservoir m.; (*of typists*) pool m.; (*snooker*) billard américain m. ∼**s,** pari mutuel sur le football m. —v.t. mettre en commun.

poor a. pauvre; (*not good*) médiocre, mauvais. ∼**ly** adv. mal; a. malade.

pop[1] n. (*noise*) bruit sec m. —v.t./i.

(*burst*) crever; (*put*) mettre. ∼ in/out/off, entrer/sortir/partir. ∼ up, surgir.

pop² *n.* (*mus.*) musique pop *f.* —*a.* pop *invar.*

popcorn *n.* pop-corn *m.*

pope *n.* pape *m.*

poplar *n.* peuplier *m.*

poppy *n.* pavot *m.*; (*wild*) coquelicot *m.*

popular *a.* populaire; (*in fashion*) en vogue. be ∼ with, plaire à. ∼ity *n.* popularité *f.*

population *n.* population *f.*

porcelain *n.* porcelaine *f.*

porch *n.* porche *m.*

porcupine *n.* porc-épic *m.*

pore¹ *n.* pore *m.*

pore² *v.i.* ∼ over, étudier minutieusement.

pork *n.* (*food*) porc *m.*

pornography *n.* pornographie *f.*

porous *a.* poreux.

porpoise *n.* marsouin *m.*

porridge *n.* porridge *m.*

port¹ *n.* (*harbour*) port *m.*

port² *n.* (*left: naut.*) bâbord *m.*

port³ *n.* (*wine*) porto *m.*

portable *a.* portatif.

portal *n.* portail *m.*

porter¹ *n.* (*carrier*) porteur *m.*

porter² *n.* (*door-keeper*) portier *m.*

portfolio *n.* portefeuille *m.*

porthole *n.* hublot *m.*

portion *n.* (*share, helping*) portion *f.*; (*part*) partie *f.*

portrait *n.* portrait *m.*

portray *v.t.* représenter. ∼al *n.* portrait *m.*, peinture *f.*

Portugal|al *n.* Portugal *m.* ∼uese *a. & n. invar.* portugais(e) (*m.* (*f.*)).

pose *v.t./i.* poser. —*n.* pose *f.* ∼ as, (*expert etc.*) se poser en.

poser *n.* colle *f.*

posh *a.* (*sl.*) chic *invar.*

position *n.* position *f.*; (*job, state*) situation *f.* —*v.t.* placer.

positive *a.* (*test, help, etc.*) positif; (*sure*) sûr, certain; (*real*) réel, vrai. ∼ly *adv.* positivement; (*absolutely*) complètement.

possess *v.t.* posséder. ∼ion *n.* possession *f.*

possessive *a.* possessif.

possib|le *a.* possible. ∼ility *n.* possibilité *f.*

possibly *adv.* peut-être.

post¹ *n.* (*pole*) poteau *m.* —*v.t.* ∼ (up), (*a notice*) afficher.

post² *n.* (*station, duty*) poste *m.* —*v.t.* poster; (*appoint*) affecter.

post³ *n.* (*mail service*) poste *f.*; (*letters*) courrier *m.* —*a.* postal. —*v.t.* (*put in box*) poster; (*send*) envoyer (par la poste). keep∼ed, tenir au courant. ∼box *n.* boîte à or aux lettres *f.* ∼ code *n.* code postal *m.* P∼ Office, postes *f. pl.*; (*in France*) Postes et Télécommunications *f. pl.* ∼ office, bureau de poste *m.*, poste *f.*

post- *pref.* post-.

postage *n.* tarif postal *m.*

postal *a.* postal. ∼ order, mandat *m.*

postcard *n.* carte postale *f.*

poster *n.* affiche *f.*; (*for decoration*) poster *m.*

posterity *n.* postérité *f.*

postgraduate *n.* étudiant(e) de troisième cycle *m.* (*f.*).

postman *n.* facteur *m.*

postmark *n.* cachet de la poste *m.*

post-mortem *n.* autopsie *f.*

postpone *v.t.* remettre. ∼ment *n.* ajournement *m.*

postscript *n.* (*to letter*) postscriptum *m. invar.*

posture *n.* posture *f.* —*v.i.* (*affectedly*) prendre des poses.

pot *n.* pot *m.*; (*for cooking*) marmite *f.*; (*drug: sl.*) marie-jeanne *f.* —*v.t.* (*plants*) mettre en pot.

potato n. pomme de terre f.

potential a. & n. potentiel (m.). **~ly** adv. potentiellement.

pot-hol|e n. (in rock) caverne f.; (in road) nid de poule m. **~ing** n. spéléologie f.

potion n. potion f.

potted a. (plant etc.) en pot; (preserved) en conserve; (abridged) condensé.

potter[1] n. potier m. **~y** n. (art) poterie f.; (objects) poteries f.pl.

potter[2] v.i. bricoler.

potty n. pot m.

pouch n. poche f.; (for tobacco) blague f.

pouffe n. pouf m.

poultry n. volaille f.

pounce v.i. bondir (**on**, sur). —n. bond m.

pound[1] n. (weight) livre f. (= 454 g.); (money) livre f.

pound[2] n. (for dogs, cars) fourrière f.

pound[3] v.t. (crush) piler; (bombard) pilonner. —v.i. frapper fort; (of heart) battre fort; (walk) marcher à pas lourds.

pour v.t. verser. —v.i. couler, ruisseler (**from**, de); (rain) pleuvoir à torrents. **~ in/out**, (people) arriver/sortir en masse. **~ off or out**, vider.

pout v.t./i. **~ (one's lips)**, faire la moue. —n. moue f.

poverty n. misère f., pauvreté f.

powder n. poudre f. —v.t. poudrer. **~ed** a. en poudre. **~y** a. poudreux.

power n. puissance f.; (ability, authority) pouvoir m.; (energy) énergie f.; (electr.) courant m. **~ cut**, coupure de courant f. **~ point**, prise de courant f. **~ station** n. centrale électrique f.

powerful a. puissant. **~ly** adv. puissamment.

practicable a. praticable.

practical a. pratique. **~ity** n. sens or aspect pratique m. **~ joke**, farce f.

practically adv. pratiquement.

practice n. pratique f.; (of profession) exercice m.; (sport) entraînement m.; (clients) clientèle f. **in ~**, (in fact) en pratique. **put into ~**, mettre en pratique.

practise v.t./i. (musician, typist, etc.) s'exercer (à); (sport) s'entraîner (à); (put into practice) pratiquer; (profession) exercer. **~d** a. expérimenté.

practitioner n. praticien(ne) m. (f.).

pragmatic a. pragmatique.

prairie n. prairie f.

praise v.t. louer. —n. éloge(s) m. (pl.), louange(s) f. (pl.).

pram n. landau m.

prance v.i. caracoler.

prank n. farce f.

prawn n. crevette rose f.

pray v.i. prier.

prayer n. prière f.

pre- pref. pré-.

preach v.t./i. prêcher. **~ at or to**, prêcher. **~er** n. prédicateur m.

preamble n. préambule m.

pre-arrange v.t. fixer à l'avance.

precarious a. précaire.

precaution n. précaution f.

preced|e v.t. précéder. **~ing** a. précédent.

precedence n. priorité f.; (in rank) préséance f.

precedent n. précédent m.

precinct n. enceinte f.; (pedestrian area) zone f.

precious a. précieux. —adv. (very; fam.) très.

precipice n. (geog.) à-pic m. invar.; (fig.) précipice m.

precipitat|e v.t. (person, event, chemical) précipiter. —a.

précipité. **∿ion** n. précipitation f.

précis n. invar. précis m.

precis|e a. précis; (careful) méticuleux. **∿ely** adv. précisément. **∿ion** n. précision f.

preclude v.t. (prevent) empêcher; (rule out) exclure.

precocious a. précoce.

preconc|eived a. préconçu. **∿eption** n. préconception f.

pre-condition n. condition requise f.

predator n. prédateur m.

predecessor n. prédécesseur m.

predicament n. mauvaise situation or passe f.

predict v.t. prédire. **∿able** a. prévisible. **∿ion** n. prédiction f.

predispose v.t. prédisposer (to do, à faire).

predominant a. prédominant. **∿ly** adv. pour la plupart.

predominate v.i. prédominer.

pre-empt v.t. (buy) acquérir d'avance; (stop) prévenir. **∿ive** a. preventif.

preen v.t. (bird) lisser. **∿** o.s., (person) se bichonner.

prefab n. (fam.) bâtiment préfabriqué m. **∿ricated** a. préfabriqué.

preface n. préface f.

prefer v.t. préférer (to do, faire). **∿able** /'prefrəbl/ a. préférable. **∿ably** adv. de préférence.

preferen|ce n. préférence f. **∿tial** a. préférentiel.

prefix n. préfixe m.

pregnan|t a. (woman) enceinte; (animal) pleine. **∿cy** n. (of woman) grossesse f.

prehistoric a. préhistorique.

prejudice n. préjugé(s) m. (pl.); (harm) préjudice m. —v.t. (claim) porter préjudice à; (person) prévenir. **∿d** a. partial; (person) qui a des préjugés.

preliminar|y a. préliminaire. **∿ies** n. pl. préliminaires m. pl.

prelude n. prélude m.

premature a. prématuré.

premeditated a. prémédité.

premier a. premier. —n. premier ministre m.

première n. première f.

premises n. pl. locaux m. pl. on the **∿**, sur les lieux.

premiss n. prémisse f.

premium n. prime f. be at a **∿**, faire prime.

premonition n. prémonition f., pressentiment m.

preoccup|ation n. préoccupation f. **∿ied** a. préoccupé.

preparation n. préparation f. **∿s**, préparatifs m. pl.

preparatory a. préparatoire.

prepare v.t./i. (se) préparer (for, à). be **∿d for**, (expect) s'attendre à **∿d to**, prêt à.

preposition n. préposition f.

preposterous a. ridicule.

prerequisite n. condition préalable f.

prerogative n. prérogative f.

Presbyterian a. & n. presbytérien(ne) (m. (f.)).

prescri|be v.t. prescrire. **∿ption** n. prescription f.; (med.) ordonnance f.

presence n. présence f.

present[1] a. présent. —n. présent m. at **∿**, à présent. for the **∿**, pour le moment.

present[2] n. (gift) cadeau m.

present[3] v.t. présenter; (film, concert, etc.) donner. **∿ s.o. with**, offrir à qn. **∿ation** n. présentation f. **∿er** n. présenta|teur, -trice m., f.

presently adv. bientôt; (now, Amer.) en ce moment.

preservative n. (culin.) agent de conservation m.

preserve v.t. préserver; (*maintain & culin.*) conserver. —n. réserve f.; (*fig.*) domaine m.; (*jam*) confiture f. **~ation** n. conservation f.

preside v.i. présider. **~ over**, présider.

presiden|t n. président(e) m. (f.). **~cy** n. présidence f. **~tial** a. présidentiel.

press v.t./i. (*button etc.*) appuyer (sur); (*squeeze*) presser; (*iron*) repasser; (*pursue*) poursuivre. —n. (*newspapers, machine*) presse f.; (*for wine*) pressoir m. **~ for sth.**, faire pression pour avoir qch. **~ s.o. to do sth.**, pousser qn. à faire qch. **~ conference** conférence de presse f. **~ on**, continuer (**with sth.**, qch.). **~ stud** n. bouton-pression m. **~-up** n. traction f.

pressure n. pression f. —v.t. faire pression sur. **~ cooker** n. cocotte-minute f. **~ group**, groupe de pression m.

pressurize v.t. (*cabin etc.*) pressuriser; (*person*) faire pression sur.

prestige n. prestige m.

prestigious a. prestigieux.

presumably adv. vraisemblablement.

presum|e v.t. (*suppose*) présumer. **~ption** n. présomption f.

presumptuous a. présomptueux.

pretence n. feinte f., simulation f.; (*claim*) prétention f.; (*pretext*) prétexte m.

pretend v.t./i. faire semblant (**to do**, de faire).

pretentious a. prétentieux.

pretext n. prétexte m.

pretty a. joli. —adv. assez. **~ much**, presque.

prevail v.i. prédominer; (*win*) prévaloir. **~ on**, persuader (**to**

do, de faire). **~ing** a. actuel; (*wind*) dominant.

prevalent a. répandu.

prevent v.t. empêcher (**from doing**, de faire). **~ion** n. prévention f. **~ive** a. préventif.

preview n. avant- première f.; (*fig.*) aperçu m.

previous a. précédent, antérieur. **~ly** adv. auparavant.

prey n. proie f. —v.i. **~ on**, faire sa proie de; (*worry*) préoccuper. **bird of ~**, rapace m.

price n. prix m. —v.t. fixer le prix de. **~less** a. inestimable; (*amusing: sl.*) impayable.

prick v.t. (*with pin etc.*) piquer. —n. piqûre f.

prick|le n. piquant m.; (*sensation*) picotement m. **~y** a. piquant; (*person*) irritable.

pride n. orgueil m.; (*satisfaction*) fierté f.

priest n. prêtre m.

primary a. (*school, elections, etc.*) primaire; (*chief, basic*) premier, fondamental. —n. (*pol.: Amer.*) primaire m.

prime[1] a. principal, premier; (*first-rate*) excellent. **P~ Minister**, Premier Ministre m.

prime[2] v.t. (*pump, gun*) amorcer; (*surface*) apprêter. **~r** n. (*paint etc.*) apprêt m.

primeval a. primitif.

primitive a. primitif.

primrose n. primevère (jaune) f.

prince n. prince m.

princess n. princesse f.

principal a. principal. —n. (*of school etc.*) direc|teur, -trice m., f. **~ly** adv. principalement.

principle n. principe m. **in/on ~**, en/par principe.

print /prɪnt/ v.t. imprimer; (*write in capitals*) écrire en majuscules.

—n. (of foot etc.) empreinte f.; (letters) caractères m. pl.; (photograph) épreuve f.; (engraving) gravure f. ~-out n. listage m. ~ed matter, imprimés m. pl.

print|er n. (person) imprimeur m.; (comput.) imprimante f. ~ing n. impression f.

prior a. précédent. ~ to, prep. avant (de).

priority n. priorité f. take ~, avoir la priorité (over, sur).

prise v.t. forcer. ~ open, ouvrir en forçant.

prism n. prisme m.

prison n. prison f. ~er n. prisonn|ier, -ière m., f.

pristine a. primitif; (condition) parfait.

privacy n. intimité f., solitude f.

private a. privé; (confidential) personnel; (lessons, house, etc.) particulier; (ceremony) intime. —n. (soldier) simple soldat m. in ~, en privé; (of ceremony) dans l'intimité.

privation n. privation f.

privet n. (bot.) troène m.

privilege n. privilège m. ~d a. privilégié. be ~d to, avoir le privilège de.

prize n. prix m. —a. (entry etc.) primé; (fool etc.) parfait. —v.t (value) priser. ~-winner n. lauréat(e) m. (f.); (in lottery etc.) gagnant(e) m. (f.).

pro n. the ~s and cons, le pour et le contre.

pro- pref. pro-.

probab|le a. probable. ~ility n. probabilité f. ~ly adv. probablement.

probation n. (testing) essai m.; (jurid.) liberté surveillée f. ~ary a. d'essai.

probe n. (device) sonde f.; (fig.)

enquête f. —v.t. sonder. —v.i. ~ into, sonder.

problem n. problème m. —a. difficile. ~atic a. problématique.

procedure n. procédure f.; (way of doing sth.) démarche à suivre f.

proceed v.i. (go) aller, avancer; (pass) passer (to, à); (act) procéder. ~ (with), continuer. ~ to do, se mettre à faire.

proceedings n. pl. (jurid.) poursuites f. pl.

proceeds n. pl. bénéfices m. pl.

process n. processus m.; (method) procédé m. —v.t. (material, data) traiter. in the ~ of doing, en train de faire.

procession n. défilé m.

proclaim v.t. proclamer.

procure v.t. obtenir.

prod v.t./i. pousser. —n. poussée f., coup m.

prodigious a. prodigieux.

prodigy n. prodige m.

produce¹ v.t./i. produire; (bring out) sortir; (show) présenter; (cause) provoquer; (theatre, TV) mettre en scène; (radio) réaliser; (cinema) produire. ~r n. metteur en scène m.; réalisateur m.; producteur m. ~tion n. production f.; mise en scène f.; réalisation f.

produce² n. (food etc.) produits m. pl.

product n. produit m.

productiv|e a. productif. ~ity n. productivité f.

profession n. profession f. ~al a. professionnel; (of high quality) de professionnel; (person) qui exerce une profession libérale. n. professionnel(le) m. (f.).

professor n. professeur (titulaire d'une chaire) m.

profile n. profil m.

profit n. profit m., bénéfice m.

profound a. profond. **~ly** adv. profondément.

profuse a. abondant.

program n. (computer) **~**, programme m. **—**v.t. programmer. **~mer** n. programmeu|r, -se m., f. **~ming** n. (on computer) programmation f.

programme n. programme m.; (broadcast) émission f.

progress[1] n. progrès m. (pl.). **in ~**; en cours. **make ~**, faire des progrès. **~ report**, compte-rendu m.

progress[2] v.i. (advance, improve) progresser. **~ion** n. progression f.

progressive a. progressif; (reforming) progressiste. **~ly** adv. progressivement.

prohibit v.t. interdire (**s.o. from doing**, à qn. de faire).

project[1] v.t. projeter. **—**v.i. (jut out) être en saillie. **~ion** n. projection f.; saillie f.

project[2] n. (plan) projet m.; (undertaking) entreprise f.; (schol.) dossier m.

projector n. projecteur m.

proliferat|e v.i. proliférer. **~ion** n. prolifération f.

prolific a. prolifique.

prologue n. prologue m.

prolong v.t. prolonger.

promenade n. promenade f.

prominen|t a. (projecting) proéminent; (conspicuous) bien en vue; (fig.) important. **~ce** n. proéminence f.; importance f. **~tly** adv. bien en vue.

promiscu|ous a. qui a plusieurs partenaires. (pej.) de mœurs faciles. **~ity** n. les partenaires multiples; (pej.) liberté de mœurs f.

promis|e n. promesse f. **—**v.t./i.

promettre. ~ing a. prometteur; (person) qui promet.

promot|e v.t. promouvoir; (advertise) faire la promotion de. **~ion** n. (of person, sales, etc.) promotion f.

prompt a. rapide; (punctual) à l'heure, ponctuel. **—**adv. (on the dot) pile. **—**v.t. inciter; (cause) provoquer; (theatre) souffler (son rôle) à. **~er** n. souffleu|r, -se m., f. **~ly** adv. rapidement; ponctuellement.

prone a. **~ to**, prédisposé à.

prong n. (of fork) dent f.

pronoun n. pronom m.

pron|ounce v.t. prononcer. **~ouncement** n. déclaration f. **~unciation** n. prononciation f.

pronounced a. (noticeable) prononcé.

proof n. (evidence) preuve f.; (test, trial copy) épreuve f.; (of liquor) teneur en alcool f. **—**a. **~ against**, à l'épreuve de.

prop[1] n. support m. **—**v.t. **~ (up)**, (support) étayer; (lean) appuyer.

prop[2] n. (theatre, fam.) accessoire m.

propaganda n. propagande f.

propagat|e v.t./i. (se) propager. **~ion** n. propagation f.

propane n. propane m.

propel v.t. propulser. **~ling pencil**, porte-mine m. invar.

propeller n. hélice f.

proper a. correct, bon; (seemly) convenable; (real) vrai; (thorough: fam.) parfait. **~ noun**, nom propre m. **~ly** adv. correctement, comme il faut; (rightly) avec raison.

property n. propriété f.; (things owned) biens m. pl., propriété f. **—**a. immobilier, foncier.

prophecy n. prophétie f.

prophet n. prophète m. ∼**ic** a. prophétique.

proportion n. (ratio, dimension) proportion f.; (amount) partie f. ∼**al**, ∼**ate** adjs. proportionnel.

proposal n. proposition f.; (of marriage) demande en mariage f.

propos|e v.t. proposer. —v.i. ∼**e to**, faire une demande en mariage à. ∼**e to do**, se proposer de faire. ∼**ition** n. proposition f.; (matter: fam.) affaire f.; v.t. (fam.) faire des propositions malhonnêtes à.

proprietor n. propriétaire m./f.

propriety n. (correct behaviour) bienséance f.

propulsion n. propulsion f.

prosaic a. prosaïque.

prose n. prose f.; (translation) thème m.

prosecut|e v.t. poursuivre. ∼**ion** n. poursuites f. pl. ∼**or** n. procureur m.

prospect n. perspective f.; (chance) espoir m.

prospective a. (future) futur; (possible) éventuel.

prospectus n. prospectus m.; (univ.) guide m.

prosper v.i. prospérer.

prosper|ous a. prospère. ∼**ity** n. prospérité f.

prostate n. prostate f.

prostitut|e n. prostituée f. ∼**ion** n. prostitution f.

protect v.t. protéger. ∼**ion** n. protection f. ∼**or** n. protec|teur, -trice m., f.

protective a. protecteur; (clothes) de protection.

protégé n. protégé m. ∼**e** n. protégée f.

protein n. protéine f.

protest[1] n. protestation f. **under** ∼, en protestant.

protest[2] v.t./i. protester. ∼**er** n. (pol.) manifestant(e) m. (f.).

Protestant a. & n. protestant(e) (m. (f.)).

protocol n. protocole m.

prototype n. prototype m.

protract v.t. prolonger, faire traîner. ∼**ed** a. prolongé.

protractor n. (for measuring) rapporteur m.

protrude v.i. dépasser.

proud a. fier, orgueilleux. ∼**ly** adv. fièrement.

prove v.t. prouver. —v.i. ∼ **(to be) easy**/etc., se révéler facile/etc. ∼ **o.s.**, faire ses preuves. ∼**n** a. prouvé.

proverb n. proverbe m. ∼**ial** a. proverbial.

provide v.t. fournir (s.o. with sth., qch. à qn.). —v.i. ∼ **for**, (allow for) prévoir; (guard against) parer à; (person) pourvoir aux besoins de.

provided conj. ∼ **that**, à condition que.

providence n. providence f.

providing conj. = **provided**.

provinc|e n. province f.; (fig.) compétence f. ∼**ial** a. & n. provincial(e) (m. (f.)).

provision n. (stock) provision f.; (supplying) fourniture f.; (stipulation) disposition f. ∼**s**, (food) provisions f. pl.

provisional a. provisoire. ∼**ly** adv. provisoirement.

proviso n. condition f.

provo|ke v.t. provoquer. ∼**cation** n. provocation f. ∼**cative** a. provocant.

prow n. proue f.

prowess n. prouesse f.

prowl v.i. rôder. ∼**er** n. rôdeu|r, -se m., f.

proxy n. **by** ∼, par procuration.

prud|e n. prude f. ∼**ish** a. prude.

pruden|t a. prudent. ∼**ce** n.

prudence *f.* **~tly** *adv.* prudemment.

prune[1] *n.* pruneau *m.*

prune[2] *v.t.* (*cut*) tailler.

pry *v.i.* être indiscret. **~ into,** fourrer son nez dans.

psalm *n.* psaume *m.*

pseudo- *pref.* pseudo-.

pseudonym *n.* pseudonyme *m.*

psoriasis *n.* psoriasis *m.*

psyche *n.* psyché *f.*

psychiatr|y *n.* psychiatrie *f.* **~ic** *a.* psychiatrique. **~ist** *n.* psychiatre *m./f.*

psychic *a.* (*phenomenon etc.*) métapsychique; (*person*) doué de télépathie.

psychoanalys|e *v.t.* psychanalyser. **~t** *n.* psychanalyste *m./f.*

psychoanalysis *n.* psychanalyse *f.*

psycholog|y *n.* psychologie *f.* **~ical** *a.* psychologique. **~ist** *n.* psychologue *m./f.*

psychosomatic *a.* psychosomatique.

psychotherap|y *n.* psychothérapie *f.* **~ist** *n.* psychothérapeute *m./f.*

pub *n.* pub *m.*

puberty *n.* puberté *f.*

public *a.* public; (*library etc.*) municipal. **in ~,** en public. **~ address system,** sonorisation *f.* (*dans un lieu public*). **~ relations,** relations publiques *f. pl.* **~ transport,** transports en commun *m. pl.* **~ly** *adv.* publiquement.

publication *n.* publication *f.*

publicity *n.* publicité *f.*

publicize *v.t.* faire connaître au public.

publish *v.t.* publier. **~er** *n.* éditeur *m.* **~ing** *n.* édition *f.*

puck *n.* (*ice hockey*) palet *m.*

pucker *v.t./i.* (se) plisser.

pudding *n.* dessert *m.;* (*steamed*) pudding *m.* **black ~,** boudin *m.* **rice ~,** riz au lait *m.*

puddle *n.* flaque d'eau *f.*

puff *n.* bouffée *f.* —*v.t./i.* souffler. **~ at,** (*cigar*) tirer sur. **~ out,** (*swell*) (se) gonfler.

pull *v.t./i.* tirer; (*muscle*) se froisser. —*n.* traction *f.;* (*fig.*) attraction *f.;* (*influence*) influence *f.* **give a ~,** tirer. **~ apart,** mettre en morceaux. **~ away,** (*auto.*) démarrer. **~ back** or **out,** (*withdraw*) (se) retirer. **~ down,** (*building*) démolir. **~ in,** (*enter*) entrer; (*stop*) s'arrêter. **~ off,** enlever; (*fig.*) réussir. **~ out,** (*from bag etc.*) sortir; (*extract*) arracher; (*auto.*) déboîter. **~ over,** (*auto.*) se ranger. **~ up,** remonter; (*uproot*) déraciner; (*auto.*) (s')arrêter.

pulley *n.* poulie *f.*

pullover *n.* pull(-over) *m.*

pulp *n.* (*of fruit*) pulpe *f.;* (*for paper*) pâte à papier *f.*

pulpit *n.* chaire *f.*

pulsate *v.i.* battre.

pulse *n.* (*med.*) pouls *m.*

pulverize *v.t.* pulvériser.

pump[1] *n.* pompe *f.* —*v.t./i.* pomper; (*person*) soutirer des renseignements à. **~ up,** gonfler.

pump[2] *n.* (*plimsoll*) tennis *m.*

pumpkin *n.* potiron *m.*

pun *n.* jeu de mots *m.*

punch[1] *v.t.* donner un coup de poing à; (*perforate*) poinçonner; (*a hole*) faire. —*n.* coup de poing *m.;* (*vigour: sl.*) punch *m.;* (*device*) poinçonneuse *f.*

punch[2] *n.* (*drink*) punch *m.*

punctual *a.* à l'heure; (*habitually*) ponctuel. **~ity** *n.* ponctualité *f.* **~ly** *adv.* à l'heure; ponctuellement.

punctuation n. ponctuation f.

puncture n. (in tyre) crevaison f. —v.t./i. crever.

pundit n. expert m.

pungent a. âcre.

punish v.t. punir (**for sth.,** de qch.). **~ment** n. punition f.

punk n. (music, fan) punk m.

puny a. chétif.

pup(py) n. chiot m.

pupil n. (person) élève m./f.; (of eye) pupille f.

puppet n. marionnette f.

purchase v.t. acheter (**from s.o., à** qn.). —n. achat m. **~r** n. acheteu|r, -se m., f.

pur|e a. pur. **~ely** adv. purement. **~ity** n. pureté f.

purgatory n. purgatoire m.

purge v.t. purger (**of,** de). —n. purge f.

purif|y v.t. purifier. **~ication** n. purification f.

purist n. puriste m./f.

puritan n. puritain(e) m. (f.).

purple a. & n. violet (m.).

purpose n. but m.; (fig.) résolution f. **on ~,** exprès.

purr n. ronronnement m. —v.i. ronronner.

purse n. porte-monnaie m. invar.; (handbag: Amer.) sac à main m. —v.t. (lips) pincer.

pursue v.t. poursuivre. **~r** n. poursuivant(e) m. (f.).

pursuit n. poursuite f.; (fig.) activité f., occupation f.

pus n. pus m.

push v.t./i. pousser; (button) appuyer sur; (thrust) enfoncer; (recommend: fam.) proposer avec insistance. —n. poussée f.; (effort) gros effort m.; (drive) dynamisme m. **~ back,** repousser. **~chair** n. poussette f. **~ off,** (sl.) filer. **~ on,** continuer. **~over** n. jeu d'enfant m. **~ up,** (lift) relever;

(prices) faire monter. f. **~y** a. (fam.) autoritaire.

put v.t./i. mettre, placer, poser; (question) poser. **~sth. tactfully,** dire qch. avec tact. **~ across,** communiquer. **~ away,** ranger; (fig.) enfermer. **~ back,** remettre; (delay) retarder. **~ by,** mettre de côté. **~ down,** (dé)poser; (write) inscrire; (pay) verser; (suppress) réprimer. **~ forward,** (plan) soumettre. **~ in,** (insert) introduire; (fix) installer; (submit) soumettre. **~ off,** (postpone) renvoyer à plus tard; (discomfit) déconcerter; (displease) rebuter. **~ s.o. off sth.,** dégoûter qn. de qch. **~ on,** (clothes, radio) mettre; (light) allumer; (speed, accent, weight) prendre. **~ out,** sortir; (stretch) (é)tendre; (extinguish) éteindre; (disconcert) déconcerter; (inconvenience) déranger. **~ up,** lever, remonter; (building) construire; (notice) mettre; (price) augmenter; (guest) héberger; (offer) offrir. **~ up with,** supporter.

putt n. (golf) putt m.

putty n. mastic m.

puzzle n. énigme f.; (game) cassetête m. invar.; (jigsaw) puzzle m. —v.t. rendre perplexe.

pygmy n. pygmée m.

pyjamas n. pl. pyjama m.

pylon n. pylône m.

pyramid n. pyramide f.

python n. python m.

Q

quadruple a. & n. quadruple (m.). —v.t./i. quadrupler. **~ts** n. pl. quadruplé(e)s m. (f.) pl.

quail n. (bird) caille f.

quaint a. pittoresque; (old) vieillot; (odd) bizarre. **∼ness** n. pittoresque m.

quake v.i. trembler. —n. (fam.) tremblement de terre m.

Quaker n. quaker(esse) m. (f.).

qualification n. diplôme m.; (ability) compétence f.; (fig.) réserve f., restriction f.

qualif|y v.t. qualifier; (modify, fig.) mettre des réserves à; (statement) nuancer. —v.i. obtenir son diplôme (as, de); (sport) se qualifier; (fig.) remplir les conditions requises. **∼ied** a. diplômé; (able) qualifié (to do, pour faire); (fig.) conditionnel; (success) modéré.

quality n. qualité f.

qualm n. scrupule m.

quandary n. dilemme m.

quantity n. quantité f.

quarantine n. quarantaine f.

quarrel n. dispute f., querelle f. —v.i. se disputer. **∼some** a. querelleur.

quarry[1] n. (prey) proie f.

quarry[2] n. (excavation) carrière f. —v.t. extraire.

quart n. (approx.) litre m.

quarter n. quart m.; (of year) trimestre m.; (25 cents: Amer.) quart de dollar m.; (district) quartier m. **∼s**, logement(s) m. (pl.). —v.t. diviser en quatre; (mil.) cantonner.

quartet n. quatuor m.

quartz n. quartz m. —a. (watch etc.) à quartz.

quash v.t. (suppress) étouffer; (jurid.) annuler.

quasi- pref. quasi-.

quaver v.i. trembler, chevroter. —n. (mus.) croche f.

quay n. (naut.) quai m.

queasy a. (stomach) délicat. feel **∼**, avoir mal au cœur.

queen n. reine f.; (cards) dame f.

queer a. étrange; (dubious) louche; (ill) patraque. —n. (sl.) homosexuel m.

quell v.t. réprimer.

quench v.t. éteindre; (thirst) étancher; (desire) étouffer.

query n. question f. —v.t. mettre en question.

quest n. recherche f.

question n. question f. —v.t. interroger; (doubt) mettre en question, douter de. **in ∼**, en question. **out of the ∼**, hors de question. **∼ mark**, point d'interrogation m.

questionable a. discutable.

questionnaire n. questionnaire m.

queue n. queue f. —v.i. faire la queue.

quibble v.i. ergoter.

quick a. rapide. —adv. vite. **be ∼**, (hurry) se dépêcher. **∼ly** adv. rapidement, vite. **∼-witted** a. vif.

quicken v.t./i. (s')accélérer.

quicksand n. **∼(s)**, sables mouvants m. pl.

quid n. invar. (sl.) livre f.

quiet a. (calm, still) tranquille; (silent) silencieux; (gentle) doux; (discreet) discret. —n. tranquillité f. **keep ∼**, se taire. **∼ly** adv. tranquillement; silencieusement; doucement; discrètement.

quieten v.t./i. (se) calmer.

quilt n. édredon m. **(continental) ∼**, couette f. —v.t. matelasser.

quinine n. quinine f.

quintet n. quintette m.

quintuplets n. pl. quintuplé(e)s m. (f.) pl.

quip n. mot piquant m.

quirk n. bizarrerie f.

quit v.t. quitter. —v.i. abandonner; (resign) démissionner.

quite adv. tout à fait, vraiment;

(*rather*) assez. **~ a few,** un assez grand nombre (de).

quits *a.* quitte (**with,** envers). **call it ~,** en rester là.

quiz *n.* test *m.*; (*game*) jeu-concours *m.* —*v.t.* questionner.

quorum *n.* quorum *m.*

quota *n.* quota *m.*

quotation *n.* citation *f.*; (*price*) devis *m.*; (*stock exchange*) cotation *f.* **~ marks,** guillemets *m. pl.*

quote *v.t.* citer; (*reference: comm.*) rappeler; (*price*) indiquer; (*share price*) coter. —*v.i.* **~ for,** faire un devis pour. **~ from,** citer. —*n.* (*estimate*) devis; (*fam.*) = **quotation.**

quotient *n.* quotient *m.*

R

rabbi *n.* rabbin *m.*

rabbit *n.* lapin *m.*

rabble *n.* (*crowd*) cohue *f.*

rabid *a.* enragé.

rabies *n.* (*disease*) rage *f.*

race[1] *n.* course *f.* —*v.t.* (*horse*) faire courir; (*engine*) emballer. **~ (against),** faire la course à. —*v.i.* courir; (*rush*) foncer.

race[2] *n.* (*group*) race *f.* —*a.* racial; (*relations*) entre les races.

racecourse *n.* champ de courses *m.*

racehorse *n.* cheval de course *m.*

racial *a.* racial.

racing *n.* courses *f. pl.* **~ car,** voiture de course *f.*

racis|t *a. & n.* raciste (*m./f.*). **~m** *n.* racisme *m.*

rack *n.* (*shelf*) étagère *f.*; (*pigeon-holes*) casier *m.*; (*for luggage*) porte-bagages *m. invar.*; (*for dishes*) égouttoir *m.*; (*on car roof*) galerie *f.*

racket[1] *n.* raquette *f.*

racket[2] *n.* (*din*) tapage *m.*; (*dealings*) combine *f.*; (*crime*) racket *m.*

radar *n.* radar *m.* —*a.* (*system etc.*) radar *invar.*

radial *a.* (*tyre*) à carcasse radiale.

radiant *a.* rayonnant.

radiat|e *v.t.* dégager. —*v.i.* rayonner (**from,** de). **~ion** *n.* (*radioactivity*) radiation *f.*

radiator *n.* radiateur *m.*

radical *a.* radical. —*n.* (*person: pol.*) radical(e) *m.* (*f.*).

radio *n.* radio *f.* —*v.t.* (*message*) envoyer par radio; (*person*) appeler par radio.

radioactiv|e *a.* radioactif. **~ity** *n.* radioactivité *f.*

radish *n.* radis *m.*

radius *n.* rayon *m.*

raffle *n.* tombola *f.*

raft *n.* radeau *m.*

rafter *n.* chevron *m.*

rag *n.* lambeau *m.*, loque *f.*; (*for wiping*) chiffon *m.*; (*newspaper*) torchon *m.* **in ~s,** (*person*) en haillons; (*clothes*) en lambeaux.

rage *n.* rage *f.*, fureur *f.* —*v.i.* rager; (*storm, battle*) faire rage.

ragged *a.* (*clothes, person*) loqueteux; (*edge*) déchiqueté.

raging *a.* (*storm etc.*) violent.

raid *n.* (*mil.*) raid *m.*; (*by police*) rafle *f.*; (*by criminals*) hold-up *m. invar.* —*v.t.* faire un raid *ou* une rafle *ou* un hold-up dans. **~er** *n.* (*person*) bandit *m.*, pillard *m.* **~ers** *n. pl.* (*mil.*) commando *m.*

rail *n.* (*on balcony*) balustrade *f.*; (*stairs*) main courante *f.*, rampe *f.*; (*for train*) rail *m.*; (*for curtain*) tringle *f.*

railing *n.* **~s,** grille *f.*

railway *n.* chemin de fer *m.* **~**

line, voie ferrée f. **~man** n. (pl. **-men**) cheminot m. **~ station,** gare f.

rain n. pluie f. —v.i. pleuvoir. **~ forest,** forêt (humide) tropicale f.

rainbow n. arc-en-ciel m.

raincoat n. imperméable m.

rainfall n. précipitation f.

rainy a. pluvieux.

raise v.t. lever; (breed, build) élever; (question etc.) soulever; (price etc.) relever; (money etc.) obtenir; (voice) élever.

raisin n. raisin sec m.

rake n. râteau m. —v.t. (garden) ratisser; (search) fouiller dans.

rally v.t./i. (se) rallier; (strength) reprendre; (after illness) aller mieux. —n. rassemblement m.; (auto.) rallye m.; (tennis) échange m. **~ round,** venir en aide.

ram n. bélier m. —v.t. (thrust) enfoncer; (crash into) emboutir, percuter.

RAM abbr. (random access memory) mémoire vive f.

rambl|e n.*randonnée f. —v.i. faire une randonnée. **~ on,** parler (sans cesse). divaguer. **~er** n. randonneu|r, -se, m., f.

ramp n. (slope) rampe f.; (in garage) pont de graissage m.

rampage v.i. se déchaîner.

rampant a. **be ~,** (disease etc.) sévir, être répandu.

rampart n. rempart m.

ramshackle a. délabré.

ranch n. ranch m.

rancid a. rance.

rancour n. rancœur f.

random a. fait, pris, etc. au hasard, aléatoire (techn.). —n. **at ~,** au hasard.

randy a. (fam.) excité.

range n. (distance) portée f.; (of aircraft etc.) rayon d'action m.; (series) gamme f.; (scale) échelle

f.; (choice) choix m.; (domain) champ m.; (of mountains) chaîne f.; (stove) cuisinière f. —v.i. s'étendre; (vary) varier.

ranger n. garde forestier m.

rank n. rang m.; (grade: mil.) grade m., rang m. —v.t./i. **~ among,** compter parmi. **the ~ and file,** les gens ordinaires.

rankle v.i. **~ with s.o.,** rester sur le cœur à qn.

ransack v.t. (search) fouiller; (pillage) saccager.

ransom n. rançon f. —v.t. rançonner; (redeem) racheter. **hold to ~,** rançonner.

rant v.i. tempêter.

rap n. petit coup sec m. —v.t./i. frapper.

rape v.t. violer. —n. viol m.

rapid a. rapide.

rapist n. violeur m.

rapport n. rapport m.

raptur|e n. extase f. **~ous** a. (person) en extase; (welcome etc.) frénétique.

rar|e[1] a. rare. **~ely** adv. rarement. **~ity** n. rareté f.

rare[2] a. (culin.) saignant.

rarefied a. raréfié.

raring a. **~ to,** (fam.) impatient de.

rascal n. coquin(e) m. (f.).

rash[1] n. (med.) éruption f.

rash[2] a. imprudent. **~ly** adv. imprudemment. **~ness** n. imprudence f.

rasher n. tranche (de lard) f.

raspberry n. framboise f.

rasping a. grinçant.

rat n. rat m.

rate n. (ratio, level) taux m.; (speed) allure f.; (price) tarif m. **~s,** (taxes) impôts locaux m. pl. —v.t. évaluer; (consider) considérer. —v.i. **~ as,** être considéré comme. **at any ~,** en tout cas.

ratepayer n. contribuable m./f.

rather adv. (by preference) plutôt; (fairly) assez, plutôt; (a little) un peu. **I would ~ go**, j'aimerais mieux partir.

ratif|y v.t. ratifier. **~ication** n. ratification f.

rating n. classement m.; (sailor) matelot m.; (number) indice m. **the ~s**, (TV) l'audimat (P.).

ratio n. proportion f.

ration n. ration f. —v.t. rationner.

rational a. rationnel m.; (person) raisonnable.

rationalize v.t. tenter de justifier; (organize) rationaliser.

rattle v.i. faire du bruit; (of bottles) cliqueter. —v.t. secouer; (sl.) agacer. —n. bruit (de ferraille) m.; cliquetis m.; (toy) hochet m.

raucous a. rauque.

ravage v.t. ravager. **~s** n. pl. ravages m. pl.

rave v.i. divaguer; (in anger) tempêter. **~e about**, s'extasier sur.

raven n. corbeau m.

ravine n. ravin m.

ravioli n. ravioli m. pl.

ravish v.t. (rape) ravir. **~ing** a. (enchanting) ravissant.

raw a. cru; (not processed) brut; (wound) à vif; (immature) inexpérimenté. **~ materials**, matières premières f. pl.

ray n. (of light etc.) rayon m.

raze v.t. (destroy) raser.

razor n. rasoir m. **~-blade** n. lame de rasoir f.

re prep. concernant.

re- pref. re-, ré-, r-.

reach v.t. atteindre, arriver à; (contact) joindre; (hand over) passer. —v.i. s'étendre. —n. portée f. **~ for**, tendre la main pour prendre.

react v.i. réagir.

reaction n. réaction f. **~ary** a. & n. réactionnaire (m./f.).

reactor n. réacteur m.

read v.t./i. lire; (fig.) comprendre; (study) étudier; (of instrument) indiquer. —n. (fam.) lecture f. **~ out**, lire à haute voix. **~able** a. agréable or facile à lire. **~ing** n. lecture f.; indication f. **~ing-glasses** n. pl. lunettes pour lire f. pl.

reader n. lec|teur, -trice m., f.

readily adv. (willingly) volontiers; (easily) facilement.

readjust v.t. rajuster. —v.i. se réadapter (**to**, à).

ready a. prêt; (quick) prompt. **~made** a. tout fait.

real a. vrai, véritable, réel. —adv. (Amer., fam.) vraiment. **~ estate**, biens fonciers m. pl.

realis|t n. réaliste m./f. **~m** n. réalisme m. **~tic** a. réaliste.

reality n. réalité f.

realiz|e v.t. se rendre compte de, comprendre; (fulfil) réaliser. **~ation** n. prise de conscience f.; réalisation f.

really adv. vraiment.

realm n. royaume m.

reap v.t. (crop, field) moissonner; (fig.) récolter.

reappear v.i. réapparaître.

reappraisal n. réévaluation f.

rear¹ n. arrière m., derrière m. —a. arrière invar., de derrière. **~-view mirror**, rétroviseur m.

rear² v.t. (bring up, breed) élever. —v.i. (horse) se cabrer. **~ one's head**, dresser la tête.

rearguard n. (mil.) arrière-garde f.

rearm v.t./i. réarmer.

rearrange v.t. réarranger.

reason n. raison f. —v.i. raisonner. **~ with,** raisonner. **everything within ~,** tout dans les limites normales. **~ing** n. raisonnement m.

reasonable a. raisonnable.

reassure v.t. rassurer. **~ance** n. réconfort m.

rebate n. remboursement (partiel) m.; (discount) rabais m.

rebel[1] n. & a. rebelle (m./f.).

rebel[2] v.i. se rebeller. **~lion** n. rébellion f. **~lious** a. rebelle.

rebound v.i. rebondir. **~ on,** (backfire) se retourner contre. —n. n. rebond m.

rebuff v.t. repousser. —n. rebuffade f.

rebuild v.t. reconstruire.

rebuke v.t. réprimander. —n. réprimande f., reproche m.

recall v.t. (to s.o., call back) rappeler; (remember) se rappeler. —n. rappel m.

recap v.t./i. (fam.) récapituler. —n. (fam.) récapitulation f.

recapture v.t. reprendre; (recall) recréer.

recede v.i. s'éloigner.

receipt n. (written) reçu m.; (of letter) réception f. **~s,** (money: comm.) recettes f. pl.

receive v.t. recevoir. **~r** n. (of stolen goods) receleu|r, -se m., f.; (telephone) combiné m.

recent a. récent. **~ly** adv. récemment.

receptacle n. récipient m.

reception n. réception f. **give s.o. a warm ~,** donner un accueil chaleureux à qn. **~ist** n. réceptionniste m./f.

receptive a. réceptif.

recess n. (alcove) renfoncement m.; (nook) recoin m.; (holiday) vacances f. pl.

recession n. récession f.

recharge v.t. recharger.

recipe n. recette f.

reciprocal a. réciproque.

reciprocate v.t. offrir en retour. —v.i. en faire autant.

recital n. récital m.

recite v.t. (poem, lesson, etc.) réciter; (list) énumérer.

reckless a. imprudent. **~ly** adv. imprudemment.

reckon v.t./i. calculer; (judge) considérer; (think) penser. **~ on/with,** compter sur/avec. **~ing** n. calcul(s) m. (pl.).

reclaim v.t. (seek return of) réclamer; (flooded land) défricher; (flooded land) assécher.

recline v.i. être étendu. **~ing** a. (person) étendu; (seat) à dossier réglable.

recluse n. reclus(e) m. (f.), ermite m.

recognition n. reconnaissance f. **beyond ~,** méconnaissable. **gain ~,** être reconnu.

recognize v.t. reconnaître.

recoil v.i. reculer (from, devant).

recollect v.t. se souvenir de, se rappeler. **~ion** n. souvenir m.

recommend v.t. recommander. **~ation** n. recommandation f.

recompense v.t. (ré)compenser. —n. récompense f.

reconcil|e v.t. (people) réconcilier; (facts) concilier. **~iation** n. réconciliation f.

recondition v.t. réviser.

reconn|oitre v.t. (mil.) reconnaître. **~aissance** n. reconnaissance f.

reconsider v.t. reconsidérer. —v.i. se déjuger.

reconstruct v.t. reconstruire; (crime) reconstituer.

record[1] v.t./i. (in register, on tape, etc.) enregistrer; (in diary) noter. **~ that,** rapporter que. **~ing** n. enregistrement m.

record² n. (report) rapport m.; (register) registre m.; (mention) mention f.; (file) dossier m.; (fig.) résultats m. pl.; (mus.) disque m.; (sport) record m. **(criminal)** ~, casier judiciaire m. —a. record invar.

recorder n. (mus.) flûte à bec f.

recount v.t. raconter.

re-count v.t. recompter.

recoup v.t. récupérer.

recourse n. recours m. **have ~ to**, avoir recours à.

recover v.t. récupérer. —v.i. se remettre; (med.) se rétablir; (economy) se redresser. **~y** n. récupération f.; (med.) rétablissement m.

recreation n. récréation f. **~al** a. de récréation.

recrimination n. contre-accusation f.

recruit n. recrue f. —v.t. recruter. **~ment** n. recrutement m.

rectangle n. rectangle m. **~ular** a. rectangulaire.

rectify v.t. rectifier. **~ication** n. rectification f.

recuperate v.i. (med.) se rétablir.

recur v.i. se répéter.

recurren|t a. fréquent. **~ce** n. répétition f.

recycle v.t. recycler.

red a. rouge; (hair) roux. —n. rouge m. **in the ~**, en déficit. **~-handed** a. en flagrant délit. **~-hot** a. brûlant. **the ~ light**, le feu rouge m.

redcurrant n. groseille f.

redden v.t./i. rougir.

reddish a. rougeâtre.

redecorate v.t. refaire.

redeem v.t. racheter.

redemption n. rachat m.

redeploy v.t. réorganiser; (troops) répartir.

redirect v.t. (letter) faire suivre.

redness n. rougeur f.

redo v.t. refaire.

redolent a. ~ **of**, qui évoque.

redress v.t. (wrong etc.) redresser. —n. réparation f.

reduc|e v.t. réduire; (temperature etc.) faire baisser. **~tion** n. réduction f.

redundan|t a. superflu; (worker) licencié. **make ~**, licencier. **~cy** n. licenciement m.; (word, phrase) pléonasme m.

reed n. (plant) roseau m.; (mus.) anche f.

reef n. récif m., écueil m.

reek n. puanteur f. —v.i. ~ **(of)**, puer.

reel n. (of thread) bobine f.; (of film) bande f.; (winding device) dévidoir m. —v.i. chanceler.

refectory n. réfectoire m.

refer v.t./i. ~ **to**, (allude to) faire allusion à; (concern) s'appliquer à; (consult) consulter; (submit) soumettre à; (direct) renvoyer à.

referee n. arbitre m. —v.t. arbitrer.

reference n. référence f.; (mention) allusion f.; (person) répondant(e) m. (f.). **in** or **with ~ to**, en ce qui concerne; (comm.) suite à. **~ book**, ouvrage de référence m.

referendum n. référendum m.

refill¹ v.t. remplir (à nouveau); (pen etc.) recharger.

refill² n. (of pen, lighter, lipstick) recharge f.

refin|e v.t. raffiner. **~d** a. raffiné. **~ment** n. raffinement m.; (techn.) raffinage m. **~ry** n. raffinerie f.

reflect v.t. refléter; (of mirror) réfléchir, refléter. —v.i. réfléchir **(on, à)**. **~ion** n. réflexion f.;

(*image*) reflet *m.* ~**or** *n.* réflecteur *m.*

reflective *a.* réfléchissant.

reflex *a. & n.* réflexe (*m.*).

reflexive *a.* (*gram.*) réfléchi.

reform *v.t.* réformer. —*v.i.* (*person*) s'amender. —*n.* réforme *f.* ~**er** *n.* réforma|teur, -trice *m.*, *f.*

refrain[1] *n.* refrain *m.*

refrain[2] *v.i.* s'abstenir (**from**, de).

refresh *v.t.* rafraîchir; (*of rest etc.*) ragaillardir, délasser. ~**ing** *a.* (*drink*) rafraîchissant; (*sleep*) réparateur. ~**ments** *n. pl.* rafraîchissements *m. pl.*

refrigerator *n.* réfrigérateur *m.*

refuel *v.t./i.* (se) ravitailler.

refuge *n.* refuge *m.* **take** ~, se réfugier.

refugee *n.* réfugié(e) *m.* (*f.*).

refund *v.t.* rembourser. —*n.* remboursement *m.*

refuse[1] *v.t./i.* refuser. ~**al** *n.* refus *m.*

refuse[2] *n.* ordures *f. pl.*

refute *v.t.* réfuter.

regain *v.t.* retrouver; (*lost ground*) regagner.

regal *a.* royal, majestueux.

regard *v.t.* considérer. —*n.* considération *f.*, estime *f.* ~**s**, amitiés *f. pl.* **as** ~**s**, ~**ing** *prep.* en ce qui concerne.

regardless *adv.* quand même. ~ **of**, sans tenir compte de.

regatta *n.* régates *f. pl.*

regenerat|e *v.t.* régénérer. ~**ion** *n.* régénération *f.*

regime *n.* régime *m.*

regiment *n.* régiment *m.*

region *n.* région *f.* **in the** ~ **of**, environ. ~**al** *a.* régional.

regist|er *n.* registre *m.* —*v.t.* enregistrer; (*vehicle*) immatriculer; (*birth*) déclarer; (*letter*) recommander; (*indicate*)

indiquer; (*express*) exprimer. —*v.i.* (*enrol*) s'inscrire; (*fig.*) être compris. ~**er office**, bureau d'état civil *m.* ~**ration** *n.* enregistrement *m.*; inscription *f.*; (*vehicle document*) carte grise *f.* ~**ration (number**), (*auto.*) numéro d'immatriculation *m.*

regret *n.* regret *m.* —*v.t.* regretter (**to do**, de faire). ~**fully** *adv.* à regret.

regroup *v.t./i.* (se) regrouper.

regular *a.* régulier; (*usual*) habituel; (*thorough: fam.*) vrai. —*n.* (*fam.*) habitué(e) *m.* (*f.*). ~**ity** *n.* régularité *f.* ~**ly** *adv.* régulièrement.

regulate *v.t.* régler. ~**ion** *n.* (*rule*) règlement *m.*

rehabilitat|e *v.t.* réadapter; (*in public esteem*) réhabiliter. ~**ion** *n.* réadaptation *f.*; réhabilitation *f.*

rehash[1] *v.t.* remanier.

rehash[2] *n.* réchauffé *m.*

rehears|e *v.t.* (*theatre*) répéter. ~**al** *n.* répétition *f.*

re-heat *v.t.* réchauffer.

reign *n.* règne *m.* —*v.i.* régner (**over**, sur).

reimburse *v.t.* rembourser.

rein *n.* rêne *f.*

reindeer *n. invar.* renne *m.*

reinforce *v.t.* renforcer. ~**ment** *n.* renforcement *m.* ~**ments** *n. pl.* renforts *m. pl.* ~**d concrete**, béton armé *m.*

reinstate *v.t.* réintégrer.

reiterate *v.t.* réitérer.

reject[1] *v.t.* (*offer, plea, etc.*) rejeter; (*book, goods, etc.*) refuser. ~**ion** *n.* rejet *m.*; refus *m.*

reject[2] *n.* (article de) rebut *m.*

rejoice *v.i.* se réjouir.

relapse *n.* rechute *f.* —*v.i.* rechuter. ~ **into**, retomber dans.

relate *v.t.* raconter; (*associate*)

rapprocher. —*v.i.* ~ **to,** se
rapporter à; (*get on with*)
s'entendre avec. ~**d** *a.* (*ideas etc.*)
lié. ~**d to s.o.,** parent(e) de qn.

relation *n.* rapport *m.*; (*person*)
parent(e) *m.* (*f.*). ~**ship** *n.* lien de
parenté *m.*; (*link*) rapport *m.*;
(*affair*) liaison *f.*

relative *n.* parent(e) *m.* (*f.*). —*a.*
relatif; (*respective*) respectif. ~**ly**
adv. relativement.

relax *v.t./i.* (*less tense*) (se)
relâcher; (*for pleasure*) (se)
détendre. ~**ation** *n.* relâchement
m.; détente *f.*

relay[1] *n.* relais *m.* ~ **race,** course
de relais *f.*

relay[2] *v.t.* relayer.

release *v.t.* libérer; (*bomb*) lâcher;
(*film*) sortir; (*news*) publier;
(*smoke*) dégager; (*spring*)
déclencher. —*n.* libération *f.*;
sortie *f.*; (*record*) nouveau disque
m. (*of pollution*) émission *f.*

relegate *v.t.* reléguer.

relent *v.i.* se laisser fléchir. ~**less**
a. impitoyable.

relevan|t *a.* pertinent. **be** ~**t to,**
avoir rapport à. ~**ce** *n.* per-
tinence *f.*, rapport *m.*

reliab|le *a.* sérieux, sûr;
(*machine*) fiable. ~**ility** *n.*
sérieux *m.*; fiabilité *f.*

reliance *n.* dépendance *f.*; (*trust*)
confiance *f.*

relic *n.* relique *f.*

relief *n.* soulagement *m.* (**from,** *à*);
(*assistance*) secours *m.*; (*outline,
design*) relief *m.*

relieve *v.t.* soulager; (*help*)
secourir; (*take over from*) relayer.

religion *n.* religion *f.*

religious *a.* religieux.

relinquish *v.t.* abandonner.

relish *n.* plaisir *m.*, goût *m.*;
(*culin.*) assaisonnement *m.* —*v.t.*
savourer; (*idea etc.*) aimer.

relocate *v.t.* (*company*) déplacer;
(*employee*) muter. —*v.i.* se
déplacer, déménager.

reluctan|t *a.* fait, donné, *etc.* à
contrecœur. ~**t to,** peu disposé à.
~**ce** *n.* répugnance *f.* ~**tly** *adv.* à
contrecœur.

rely *v.i.* ~ **on,** compter sur;
(*financially*) dépendre de.

remain *v.i.* rester. ~**s** *n. pl.* restes
m. pl.

remainder *n.* reste *m.*

remand *v.t.* mettre en détention
préventive. —*n.* **on** ~, en détention préventive.

remark *n.* remarque *f.* —*v.t.*
remarquer. —*v.i.* ~ **on,** faire des
commentaires sur. ~**able** *a.*
remarquable.

remarry *v.i.* se remarier.

remed|y *n.* remède *m.* —*v.t.*
remédier à. ~**ial** *a.* (*class etc.*) de
rattrapage; (*treatment: med.*)
curatif.

remember *v.t.* se souvenir de, se
rappeler. ~ **to do,** ne pas oublier
de faire.

remind *v.t.* rappeler (**s.o. of sth.,**
qch. à qn.). ~ **s.o. to do,** rappeler
à qn. qu'il doit faire. ~**er** *n.*
(*letter, signal*) rappel *m.*

reminisce *v.i.* évoquer ses
souvenirs. ~**nces** *n. pl.* réminis-
cences *f. pl.*

reminiscent *a.* ~ **of,** qui évoque.

remission *n.* rémission *f.*; (*jurid.*)
remise (de peine) *f.*

remitance *n.* paiement *m.*

remnant *n.* reste *m.*, débris *m.*;
(*trace*) vestige *m.*; (*of cloth*)
coupon *m.*

remorse *n.* remords *m.* (*pl.*). ~**ful**
a. plein de remords.

remote *a.* (*place, time*) lointain;
(*person*) distant; (*slight*) vague.
~ **control,** télécommande *f.*

removable *a.* amovible.

remov|e v.t. enlever; (lead away) emmener; (dismiss) renvoyer; (do away with) supprimer. **~al** n. enlèvement m.; renvoi m.; suppression f.; (from house) déménagement m. **~al men,** déménageurs m. pl.

remuneration n. rémunération f.

rename v.t. rebaptiser.

render v.t. (give, make) rendre.

rendezvous n. rendez-vous n. invar.

renew v.t. renouveler; (resume) reprendre. **~able** a. renouvelable. **~al** n. renouvellement m.; reprise f.

renounce v.t. renoncer à.

renovat|e v.t. rénover. **~ion** n. rénovation f.

rent n. loyer m. —v.t. louer. **for ~,** à louer. **~al** n. prix de location m.

renunciation n. renonciation f.

reopen v.t./i. rouvrir. **~ing** n. réouverture f.

reorganize v.t. réorganiser.

rep n. (comm., fam.) représentant(e) m. (f.).

repair v.t. réparer. —n. réparation f. **in good/bad ~,** en bon/mauvais état. **~er** n. réparateur m.

repartee n. repartie f.

repay v.t. rembourser; (reward) récompenser. **~ment** n. remboursement m.; récompense f. **monthly ~ments,** mensualités f. pl.

repeal v.t. abroger, annuler. —n. abrogation f.

repeat v.t./i. répéter; (renew) renouveler. —n. répétition f.; (broadcast) reprise f.

repel v.t. repousser. **~lent** a. repoussant.

repent v.i. se repentir (of, de). **~ance** n. repentir m.

repercussion n. répercussion f.

repertoire n. répertoire m.

repertory n. répertoire m.

repetit|ion n. répétition f. **~ive** adj. plein de répétitions.

replace v.t. remettre; (take the place of) remplacer. **~ment** n. remplacement m. (of, de); (person) remplaçant(e) n. (f.); (new part) pièce de rechange f.

replay n. (sport) match rejoué m.; (recording) répétition immédiate f.

replenish v.t. (refill) remplir.

replica n. copie exacte f.

reply v.t./i. répondre. —n. réponse f.

report v.t. rapporter, annoncer (that, que); (notify) signaler; (denounce) dénoncer. —v.i. faire un rapport. **~ (on),** (news item) faire un reportage sur. —n. rapport m.; (in press) reportage m.; (schol.) bulletin m.; (sound) détonation f.

reporter n. reporter m.

repossess v.t. reprendre.

represent v.t. représenter. **~ation** n. représentation f.

representative a. représentatif, typique (of, de). —n. représentant(e) n. (f.).

repress v.t. réprimer. **~ion** n. répression f. a. répressif.

reprieve n. (delay) sursis m.; (pardon) grâce f. —v.t. accorder un sursis à; gracier.

reprimand v.t. réprimander. —n. réprimande f.

reprisals n. pl. représailles f. pl.

reproach v.t. reprocher (s.o. for sth., qch. à qn.). —n. reproche m.

reproduc|e v.t./i. (se) reproduire. **~tion** n. reproduction f. **~tive** a. reproducteur.

reptile n. reptile m.

republic n. république f. **~an** a. & n. républicain(e) (m. (f.)).

repugnan|t *a.* répugnant. **~ce** *n.* répugnance *f.*

repuls|e *v.t.* repousser. **~ion** *n.* répulsion *f.* **~ive** *a.* repoussant.

reputable *a.* honorable.

reputation *n.* réputation *f.*

request *n.* demande *f.* —*v.t.* demander (**of, from,** à).

requiem *n.* requiem *m.*

require *v.t.* (*of thing*) demander; (*of person*) avoir besoin de; (*demand, order*) exiger. **~d** *a.* requis. **~ment** *n.* exigence *f.*; (*condition*) condition (requise) *f.*

requisition *n.* réquisition *f.* —*v.t.* réquisitionner.

resale *n.* revente *f.*

rescue *v.t.* sauver. —*n.* sauvetage *m.* (**of,** de); (*help*) secours *m.* **~r** *n.* sauveteur *m.*

research *n.* recherche(s) *f.(pl.).* —*v.t./i.* faire des recherches (sur). **~er** *n.* chercheu|r, -se *m., f.*

resembl|e *v.t.* ressembler à. **~ance** *n.* ressemblance *f.*

resent *v.t.* être indigné de, s'offenser de. **~ment** *n.* ressentiment *m.*

reservation *n.* réserve *f.*; (*booking*) réservation *f.*

reserve *v.t.* réserver. —*n.* (*reticence, stock, land*) réserve *f.*; (*sport*) remplaçant·e (*m.* (*f.*). **in ~,** en réserve. **~d** *a.* (*person, room*) réservé.

reservoir *n.* réservoir *m.*

reshape *v.t.* remodeler.

reshuffle *v.t.* (*pol.*) remanier. —*n.* (*pol.*) remaniement (ministériel) *m.*

reside *v.i.* résider.

residen|t *a.* résidant. —*n.* habitant·e *m.* (*f.*). **~ce** *n.* résidence *f.*; (*of students*) foyer *m.*

residential *a.* résidentiel.

residue *n.* résidu *m.*

resign *v.t.* abandonner; (*job*)

démissionner de. —*v.i.* démissionner. **~ation** *n.* résignation *f.*; (*from job*) démission *f.* **~ed** *a.* résigné.

resilient *a.* (*person*) qui a du ressort. *n.*

resin *n.* résine *f.*

resist *v.t./i.* résister (à). **~ance** *n.* résistance *f.* **~ant** *a.* (*med.*) rebelle; (*metal*) résistant.

resolut|e *a.* résolu. **~ion** *n.* résolution *f.*

resolve *v.t.* résoudre (**to do,** de faire). —*n.* résolution *f.*

resonan|t *a.* résonnant. **~ce** *n.* résonance *f.*

resort *v.i.* **~ to,** avoir recours à. —*n.* (*recourse*) recours *m.*; (*place*) station *f.* **in the last ~,** en dernier ressort.

resounding *a.* retentissant.

resource *n.* (*expedient*) ressource *f.* **~s,** (*wealth etc.*) ressources *f. pl.* **~ful** *a.* ingénieux. **~fulness** *n.* ingéniosité *f.*

respect *n.* respect *m.*; (*aspect*) égard *m.* —*v.t.* respecter. **with ~ to,** à l'égard de.

respectab|le *a.* respectable. **~ility** *n.* respectabilité *f.*

respective *a.* respectif. **~ly** *adv.* respectivement.

respiration *n.* respiration *f.*

respite *n.* répit *m.*

respond *v.i.* répondre (**to,** à) **~ to,** (*react to*) réagir à.

response *n.* réponse *f.*

responsib|le *a.* responsable; (*job*) qui comporte des responsabilités. **~ility** *n.* responsabilité *f.*

rest[1] *v.t./i.* (se) reposer; (*lean*) (s')appuyer (**on, sur**); (*be buried, lie*) reposer. —*n.* (*repose*) repos *m.*; (*support*) support *m.* **have a ~,** se reposer; (*at work*) prendre une pause.

rest[2] *v.i.* (*remain*) demeurer. —*n.*

(remainder) reste *m.* (of, de). **the ～ (of the)**, *(others, other)* les autres.

restaurant *n.* restaurant *m.*

restful *a.* reposant.

restive *a.* rétif.

restless *a.* agité. **～ly** *adv.* avec agitation, fébrilement.

restor|e *v.t.* contenir. ～ rétablir; *(building)* restaurer. **～e sth. to s.o.**, restituer qch. à qn. **～ation** *n.* rétablissement *m.*; restauration *f.* **～er** *n.* (*art*) restaura|teur, -trice *m., f.*

restrain *v.t.* contenir. **～ s.o. from**, retenir qn. de. **～ed** *a.* *(moderate)* mesuré; *(in control of self)* maître de soi. **～t** *n.* contrainte *f.*; *(moderation)* retenue *f.*

restrict *v.t.* restreindre. **～ion** *n.* restriction *f.*

result *n.* résultat *m.* —*v.i.* résulter. **～ in**, aboutir à.

resum|e *v.t./i.* reprendre. **～ption** *n.* reprise *f.*

resurgence *n.* réapparition *f.*

resurrect *v.t.* ressusciter. **～ion** *n.* résurrection *f.*

resuscitate *v.t.* réanimer.

retail *n.* détail *m.* —*a. & adv.* au détail. —*v.t./i.* (se) vendre (au détail). **～er** *n.* détaillant(e) *m.* (*f.*).

retain *v.t.* *(hold back, remember)* retenir; *(keep)* conserver.

retaliat|e *v.i.* riposter. **～ion** *n.* représailles *f. pl.*

retch *v.i.* avoir un haut-le-cœur.

reticen|t *a.* réticent. **～ce** *n.* réticence *f.*

retina *n.* rétine *f.*

retire *v.i.* *(from work)* prendre sa retraite; *(withdraw)* se retirer; *(go to bed)* se coucher. —*v.t.* mettre à la retraite. **～d** *a.* retraité. **～ment** *n.* retraite *f.*

retiring *a.* réservé.

retort *v.t./i.* répliquer. —*n.* réplique *f.*

retract *v.t./i.* (se) rétracter.

retrain *v.t./i.* (se) recycler.

retread *n.* pneu rechapé *m.*

retreat *v.i.* (*mil.*) battre en retraite. —*n.* retraite *f.*

retribution *n.* châtiment *m.*; *(vengeance)* vengeance *f.*

retriev|e *v.t.* *(recover)* récupérer; *(restore)* rétablir; *(put right)* réparer. **～er** *n.* (*dog*) chien d'arrêt *m.*

retrospect *n.* **in ～**, rétrospectivement.

return *v.i.* *(come back)* revenir; *(go back)* retourner; *(go home)* rentrer. —*v.t.* *(give back)* rendre; *(bring back)* rapporter; *(send back)* renvoyer; *(put back)* remettre. —*n.* retour *m.*; *(yield)* rapport *m.* **in ～ for**, en échange de. **～ ticket**, aller-retour *m.*

reunion *n.* réunion *f.*

reunite *v.t.* réunir.

rev *n.* *(auto., fam.)* tour *m.* —*v.t./i.* **～ (up)**, *(engine: fam.)* (s')emballer.

revamp *v.t.* rénover.

reveal *v.t.* révéler; *(allow to appear)* laisser ～ voir. **～ing** *a.* révélateur.

revel *v.i.* faire bombance. **～ in**, se délecter de.

revelation *n.* révélation *f.*

revenge *n.* vengeance *f.*; *(sport)* revanche *f.* —*v.t.* venger.

revenue *n.* revenu *m.*

reverberate *v.i.* se répercuter.

rever|e *v.t.* révérer. **～nce** *n.* vénération *f.*

reverend *a.* révérend.

revers|e *a.* contraire, inverse. —*n.* contraire *m.*; *(back)* revers *m.*, envers *m.*; *(gear)* marche arrière *f.* —*v.t.* *(situation)* renverser;

(*order*) inverser; (*decision*) annuler. —*v.i.* faire marche arrière. **∿al** *n.* renversement *m.*; (*of view*) revirement *m.*

review *n.* (*inspection, magazine*) revue *f.*; (*of book etc.*) critique *f.* —*v.t.* passer en revue; (*situation*) réexaminer; faire la critique de. **∿er** *n.* critique *m.*

revis|e *v.t.* (*se*) réviser; (*text*) revoir. **∿ion** *n.* révision *f.*

revive *v.t./i.* (*person, hopes*) ranimer; (*play*) reprendre; (*custom*) rétablir. —*v.i.* se ranimer.

revolt *v.t./i.* (*se*) révolter. —*n.* révolte *f.* **∿ing** *a.* dégoûtant.

revolution *n.* révolution *f.* **∿ary** *a. & n.* révolutionnaire (*m./f.*).

revolve *v.i.* tourner.

revolver *n.* revolver *m.*

revulsion *n.* dégoût *m.*

reward *n.* récompense *f.* —*v.t.* récompenser (**for**, de).

rewind *v.t.* (*tape, film*) rembobiner.

rheumatism *n.* rhumatisme *m.*

rhinoceros *n.* rhinocéros *m.*

rhubarb *n.* rhubarbe *f.*

rhyme *n.* rime *f.*; (*poem*) vers *m. pl.* —*v.t./i.* (faire) rimer.

rhythm *n.* rythme *m.*

rib *n.* côte *f.*

ribbon *n.* ruban *m.*

rice *n.* riz *m.*

rich *a.* riche.

ricochet *n.* ricochet *m.* —*v.i.* ricocher.

rid *v.t.* débarrasser (**of**, de). **get ∿ of**, se débarrasser de.

riddle *n.* énigme *f.*

ride *v.i.* aller (à bicyclette, à cheval, *etc.*); (*in car*) rouler. **∿ (a horse)**, (*go riding as sport*) monter (à cheval). —*v.t.* (*a particular horse*) monter; (*distance*) parcourir. —*n.* promenade *f.*, tour *m.*; (*distance*) trajet *m.* **∿r**

n. caval|ier, -ière *m., f.*; (*in horse race*) jockey *m.*; (*cyclist*) cycliste *m./f.*; (*motorcyclist*) motocycliste *m./f.*; (*in document*) annexe *f.*

ridge *n.* arête *f.*, crête *f.*

ridicule *v.t.* ridiculiser.

ridiculous *a.* ridicule.

riding *n.* équitation *f.*

rifle *n.* fusil *m.* —*v.t.* (*rob*) dévaliser.

rift *n.* (*crack*) fissure *f.*; (*between people*) désaccord *m.*

rig[1] *v.t.* (*equip*) équiper. —*n.* (*for oil*) derrick *m.*

rig[2] *v.t.* (*election*) truquer.

right *a.* (*morally*) bon; (*fair*) juste; (*best*) bon, qu'il faut; (*not left*) droit. **be ∿**, (*person*) avoir raison (**to**, de); (*calculation, watch*) être exact. —*n.* (*entitlement*) droit *m.*; (*not left*) droite *f.*; (*not evil*) le bien. —*v.t.* (*a wrong, sth. fallen, etc.*) redresser. —*adv.* (*not left*) à droite; (*directly*) tout droit; (*exactly*) bien, juste; (*completely*) tout (à fait). **on the ∿**, à droite. **put ∿**, arranger. **∿ away**, tout de suite. **∿-hand** *a.* à or de droite. **∿ now**, (*at once*) tout de suite; (*at present*) en ce moment. **∿-wing** *a.* (*pol.*) de droite.

rightly *adv.* correctement; (*with reason*) à juste titre.

rigid *a.* rigide. **∿ity** *n.* rigidité *f.*

rig|our *n.* rigueur *f.* **∿orous** *a.* rigoureux.

rim *n.* bord *m.*; (*of wheel*) jante *f.* **∿med** *a.* bordé.

rind *n.* (*on cheese*) croûte *f.*; (*on bacon*) couenne *f.*; (*on fruit*) écorce *f.*

ring[1] *n.* anneau *m.*; (*with stone*) bague *f.*; (*circle*) cercle *m.*; (*boxing*) ring *m.*; (*arena*) piste *f.* —*v.t.* entourer; (*word in text etc.*) entourer d'un cercle. (**wedding**) **∿**, alliance *f.* **∿ road**, périphérique *m.*

ring[2] v.t./i. sonner; (of words etc.) retentir; (of bell) sonnerie f. **give s.o. a ~**, donner un coup de fil à qn. **~ back**, rappeler. **~ up**, téléphoner (à).

rink n. patinoire f.

rinse v.t. rincer. **~ out**, rincer. **—**n. rinçage m.

riot n. émeute f.; (of colours) orgie f. **—**v.i. faire une émeute. **run ~**, se déchaîner. **~er** n. émeut|ier, -ière m., f.

rip v.t./i. (se) déchirer. **—**n. déchirure f. **~ off**, (sl.) rouler. **~-off** n. (sl.) vol m.

ripe a. mûr.

ripen v.t./i. mûrir.

ripple n. ride f., ondulation f.; (sound) murmure m. **—**v.t./i. (water) (se) rider.

rise v.i. (go upwards, increase) monter, s'élever; (stand up, get up from bed) se lever; (rebel) se soulever; (sun, curtain) se lever; (water) monter. **—**n. (slope) pente f.; (of curtain) lever m.; (increase) hausse f.; (in pay) augmentation f.; (progress, boom) essor m. **give ~ to**, donner lieu à.

rising n. (revolt) soulèvement m. **—**a. (increasing) croissant; (price) qui monte; (tide) montant; (sun) levant.

risk n. risque m. **—**v.t risquer. **at ~**, menacé. **~ doing**, (venture) se risquer à faire. **~y** a. risqué.

rissole n. croquette f.

rite n. rite m.

ritual a. & n. rituel (m.).

rival n. rival(e) m. (f.). **—**a. rival; (claim) opposé. **—**v.t. rivaliser avec. **~ry** n. rivalité f.

river n. rivière f.; (flowing into sea & fig.) fleuve m..

rivet n. (bolt) rivet m. **—**v.t. riveter. **~ing** a. fascinant.

road n. route f.; (in town) rue f.;

(small) chemin m. **—**a. (sign, safety) routier. **~-block** n. barrage routier m. **~-map** n. carte routière f. **~-works** n. pl. travaux m. pl.

roadway n. chaussée f.

roam v.i. errer. **—**v.t. (streets, seas, etc.) parcourir.

roar n. hurlement m.; rugissement m.; grondement m. **—**v.t./i. hurler; (of lion, wind) rugir; (of lorry, thunder) gronder.

roast v.t./i. rôtir. **—**n. (roast or roasting meat) rôti m. **—**a. rôti. **~ beef**, rôti de bœuf m.

rob v.t. voler (s.o. of sth., qch. à qn.); (bank, house) dévaliser; (deprive) priver (of, de). **~ber** n. voleu|r, -se m., f. **~bery** n. vol m.

robe n. (of judge etc.) robe f.; (dressing-gown) peignoir m.

robin n. rouge-gorge m.

robot n. robot m.

robust a. robuste.

rock[1] n. roche f.; (rock face, boulder) rocher m.; (hurled stone) pierre f.; (sweet) sucre d'orge m. **~-climbing** n. varappe f.

rock[2] v.t./i. (se) balancer; (shake) (faire) trembler; (child) bercer. **—**n. (mus.) rock m. **~ing-chair** n. fauteuil à bascule m.

rocket n. fusée f.

rocky a. (ground) rocailleux; (hill) rocheux; (shaky: fig.) branlant.

rod n. (metal) tige f.; (for curtain) tringle f.; (wooden) baguette f.; (for fishing) canne à pêche f.

rodent n. rongeur m.

roe[1] n. œufs de poisson m. pl.

roe[2] n. (deer) chevreuil m.

rogue n. (mischievous) coquin(e) m. (f.).

role n. rôle m.

roll v.t./i. rouler. **~ (about)**, (child, dog) se rouler. **—**n. rouleau m.; (list) liste f.; (bread) petit pain m.; (of drum, thunder) roulement m.; (of ship) roulis m. **~-bar** n. arceau de sécurité m. **~ing-pin** n. rouleau à pâtisserie m. **~ over**, (turn over) se retourner.

roller n. rouleau m. **~-blind** n. store m. **~-skate** n. patin à roulettes m.

ROM (abbr.) (read-only memory) mémoire morte f.

Roman n. & a. romain(e) (m. (f.)). **~ Catholic** a. & n. catholique (m./f.). **~ numerals**, chiffres romains m. pl.

romance n. roman d'amour m.; (love) amour m.; (affair) idylle f.; (fig.) poésie f.

Romania n. Roumanie f. **~n** a. & n. roumain(e) (m. (f.)).

romantic a. (of love etc.) romantique; (of the imagination) romanesque.

romp v.i. s'ébattre; (fig.) réussir. —n. **have a ~**, s'ébattre.

roof n. toit m.; (of tunnel) plafond m.; (of mouth) palais m. —v.t. recouvrir. **~-rack** n. galerie f.

rook[1] n. (bird) corneille f.

rook[2] n. (chess) tour f.

room n. pièce f.; (bedroom) chambre f.; (large hall) salle f.; (space) place f.

roost n. perchoir m. —v.i. percher. **~er** n. coq m.

root[1] n. racine f.; (source) origine f. —v.t./i. (s')enraciner. **~out**, extirper.

root[2] v.i. about, fouiller. **~ for**, (Amer., fam.) encourager.

rope n. corde f.

rosary n. chapelet m.

rose n. (flower) rose f.; (colour) rose m.; (nozzle) pomme f.

roster n. liste de service f.

rostrum n. tribune f.; (sport) podium m.

rosy a. rose; (hopeful) plein d'espoir.

rot v.t./i. pourrir. —n. pourriture f.

rota n. liste (de service) f.

rotary a. rotatif.

rotate v.t./i. (faire) tourner; (change round) alterner. **~ing** a. tournant. **~ion** n. rotation f.

rotten a. pourri; (tooth) gâté; (bad: fam.) mauvais, sale.

rouge n. rouge (à joues) m.

rough a. (manners) rude; (to touch) rugueux; (ground) accidenté; (violent) brutal; (bad) mauvais; (estimate etc.) approximatif; (diamond) brut. —v.t. **~ it**, vivre à la dure. **~-and-ready** a. (solution etc.) grossier (mais efficace). **~-and-tumble** n. mêlée f. **~ out**, ébaucher. **~ly** adv. rudement; (approximately) à peu près. **~ness** n. rudesse f.; brutalité f.

roughage n. fibres (alimentaires) f. pl.

roulette n. roulette f.

round a. rond. —n. (circle) rond m.; (slice) tranche f.; (of visits, drinks) tournée f.; (mil.) ronde f.; (competition) partie f., manche f.; (boxing) round m.; (of talks) série f. —prep. autour de. —adv. autour. —v.t. (object) arrondir; (corner) tourner. **~ about**, (near by) par ici; (fig.) à peu près. **~ off**, terminer. **~ trip**, voyage aller-retour m. **~ up**, rassembler. **~-up** n. rassemblement m.; (of suspects) rafle f.

roundabout n. manège m.; (for traffic) rond-point (à sens giratoire) m. —a. indirect.

rouse v.t. (awaken; wake up) réveiller. **be ~ed**, (angry) être en colère. **~ing** a. (speech, music) excitant; (cheers) frénétique.

rout n. (defeat) déroute f. —v.t. mettre en déroute.

route n. itinéraire m.; parcours m.; (naut., aviat.) route f.

routine n. routine f. —a. de routine.

rov|e v.t./i. errer (dans). ~**ing** a. (life) vagabond.

row[1] n. rangée f., rang m. **in a** ~, (consecutive) consécutif.

row[2] v.i. ramer; (sport) faire de l'aviron. —v.t. faire aller à la rame. ~**ing** n. aviron m. ~(**ing**)-**boat** n. bateau à rames m.

row[3] n. (noise: fam.) tapage m.; (quarrel; fam.) engueulade f.

rowdy a. tapageur.

royal a. royal.

royalt|y n. famille royale f. ~**ies**, droits d'auteur m. pl.

rub v.t./i. frotter. —n. friction f. ~ **out**, (s')effacer.

rubber n. caoutchouc m.; (eraser) gomme f. ~ **band**, élastique m. ~ **stamp**, tampon m. ~-**stamp** v.t. approuver. ~**y** a. caoutchouteux.

rubbish n. (refuse) ordures f. pl.; (junk) saletés f. pl.; (fig.) bétises f. pl. ~**y** a. sans valeur.

rubble n. décombres m. pl.

ruby n. rubis m.

rucksack n. sac à dos m.

rudder n. gouvernail m.

ruddy a. coloré, rougeâtre; (damned: sl.) fichu.

rude a. impoli, grossier; (improper) indécent; (shock, blow) brutal. ~**ly** adv. impoliment. ~**ness** n. impolitesse f.; indécence f.; brutalité f.

ruffian n. voyou m.

ruffle v.t. (hair) ébouriffer; (clothes) froisser; (person) contrarier. —n. (frill) ruche f.

rug n. petit tapis m.

Rugby n. ~ (**football**), rugby m.

rugged a. (surface) rude, rugueux; (ground) accidenté; (character, features) rude.

ruin n. ruine f. —v.t. (destroy) ruiner; (damage) abimer; (spoil) gâter.

rule n. règle f.; (regulation) règlement m.; (pol.) gouvernement m. —v.t. gouverner; (master) dominer; (decide) décider. —v.i. régner. **as a** ~, en règle générale. ~ **out**, exclure. ~ **r** n. dirigeant(e) m. (f.), gouvernant m.; (measure) règle f.

ruling a. (class) dirigeant; (party) au pouvoir. —n. décision f.

rum n. rhum m.

rumble v.i. gronder; (stomach) gargouiller. —n. grondement m.; gargouillement m.

rummage v.i. fouiller.

rumour n. bruit m., rumeur f.

rump n. (of horse etc.) croupe f.; (of fowl) croupion m.; (steak) romsteck m.

run v.i. courir; (flow) couler; (pass) passer; (function) marcher; (melt) fondre; (extend) s'étendre; (of bus etc.) circuler; (of play) se jouer; (last) durer; (of colour in washing) déteindre; (in election) être candidat. —v.t. (manage) diriger; (event) organiser; (risk, race) courir; (house) tenir; (blockade) forcer; (temperature, errand) faire; (comput.) exécuter. —n. course f.; (journey) parcours m.; (outing) promenade f.; (rush) ruée f.; (series) série f.; (in cricket) point m. ~ **across**, rencontrer par hasard. ~ **away**, s'enfuir. ~ **down**, descendre en courant; (of vehicle) renverser; (production) réduire progressivement; (belittle) dénigrer. ~ **in**, (vehicle) roder. ~ **into**, (hit) heurter. ~ **out**, (be used up) s'épuiser; (of lease) expirer. ~ **out of**, manquer de. ~ **over**, (of vehicle) écraser; (details) revoir. ~ **through sth.**, regarder qch. rapidement. ~ **up**, (bill) accumuler. **the ~-up to**, la période qui précède.

runaway n. fugitif|f, -ve m., f. —a. fugitif; (horse, vehicle) fou; (inflation) galopant.

rung n. (of ladder) barreau m.

runner n. coureu|r, -se m., f. ~ **bean**, haricot (grimpant) m. ~ **up** n. second(e) m. (f.).

running n. course f.; (of business) gestion f.; (of machine) marche f. —a. (commentary) suivi; (water) courant. **four days/etc. ~**, quatre jours/etc. de suite.

runny a. (nose) qui coule.

runt n. avorton m.

runway n. piste f.

rupture n. (breaking, breach) rupture f.; (med.) hernie f.

rural a. rural.

ruse n. (trick) ruse f.

rush[1] n. (plant) jonc m.

rush[2] v.i.a. (move) se précipiter; (be in a hurry) se dépêcher. —v.t. faire, envoyer, etc. en vitesse; (person) bousculer; (mil.) prendre d'assaut. —n. ruée f.; (haste) bousculade f. **in a ~**, pressé. ~ **hour** n. heure de pointe f.

rusk n. biscotte f.

Russia n. Russie f. ~**n** a. & n. russe (m./f.); (lang.) russe m.

rust n. rouille f. —v.t./i. rouiller. ~**-proof** a. inoxydable. ~**y** a. (tool, person, etc.) rouillé.

rustic a. rustique.

rustle v.t./i. (leaves) (faire) bruire. ~ **up**, (food etc.: fam.) préparer.

rut n. ornière f. **be in a ~**, rester dans l'ornière.

ruthless a. impitoyable. ~**ness** n. cruauté f.

rye n. seigle m.

S

sabbath n. (Jewish) sabbat m.; (Christian) dimanche m.

sabot|age n. sabotage m. —v.t. saboter. ~**eur** n. saboteu|r, -se m., f.

saccharin n. saccharine f.

sachet n. sachet m.

sack[1] n. (bag) sac m. —v.t. (fam.) renvoyer. **get the ~**, (fam.) être renvoyé.

sack[2] v.t. (plunder) saccager.

sacrament n. sacrement m.

sacred a. sacré.

sacrifice n. sacrifice m. —v.t. sacrifier.

sad a. triste. ~**ly** adv. tristement; (unfortunately) malheureusement.

sadden v.t. attrister.

saddle n. selle f. —v.t. (horse) seller. ~ **s.o. with**, (task, person) coller à qn.

sadis|t n. sadique m./f. ~**m** n. sadisme m. ~**tic** a. sadique.

safari n. safari m.

safe a. (not dangerous) sans danger; (reliable) sûr; (out of danger) en sécurité; (after accident) sain et sauf; (wise: fig.) prudent. —n. coffre-fort m. **to be on the ~ side**, pour être sûr. ~ **from**, à l'abri de. ~**ly** adv. sans danger; (in safe place) en sûreté.

safeguard n. sauvegarde f. —v.t. sauvegarder.

safety n. sécurité f. ~**-belt** n. ceinture de sécurité f. ~**-pin** n. épingle de sûreté f. ~**-valve** n. soupape de sûreté f.

saffron n. safran m.

sag v.i. s'affaisser.

saga n. saga f.

sage n. (herb) sauge f.

Sagittarius n. le Sagittaire.

sail n. voile f.; (journey) tour en bateau m. —v.i. naviguer; (leave) partir; (sport) faire de la voile; (glide) glisser. —v.t. (boat) piloter.

sailor n. marin m.

saint n. saint(e) m. (f.).

sake n. for the ～ of, pour, pour l'amour de.

salad n. salade f. ～-**dressing** n. vinaigrette f.

salami n. salami m.

salary n. salaire m.

sale n. vente f. ～s, (at reduced prices) soldes m. pl. ～s assistant, vendeu|r, -se m., f. for ～, à vendre.

sales|man n. (in shop) vendeur m.; (traveller) représentant m. ～**woman** n. vendeuse f.

saline a. salin. —n. sérum physiologique m.

saliva n. salive f.

sallow a. jaunâtre.

salmon n. invar. saumon m.

salon n. salon m.

saloon n. (on ship) salon m.; (bar: Amer.) bar m., saloon m. ～ (**car**), berline f.

salt n. sel m. —a. (culin.) salé; (water) de mer. —v.t. saler. ～**cellar** n. salière f. ～y a. salé.

salute n. (mil.) salut m. —v.t. saluer. —v.i. faire un salut.

salvage n. sauvetage m.; (of waste) récupération f.; (goods) objets sauvés m. pl. —v.t. sauver; (for reuse) récupérer.

salvation n. salut m.

same a. même (**as**, que). —pron. the ～, le or la même, les mêmes. **at the ～ time**, en même temps. **the ～ (thing)**, la même chose.

sample n. échantillon m.; (of blood) prélèvement m. —v.t. essayer; (food) goûter.

sanction n. sanction f. —v.t. sanctionner.

sanctuary n. (relig.) sanctuaire m.; (for animals) réserve f.; (refuge) asile m.

sand n. sable m. ～s, (beach) plage f. —v.t. sabler. ～-**castle** n. château de sable m. ～-**pit** n. bac à sable m.

sandal n. sandale f.

sandpaper n. papier de verre m. —v.t. poncer.

sandstone n. grès m.

sandwich n. sandwich m. —v.t. ～ed between, pris en sandwich entre. ～ **course**, stage de formation continue à mi-temps m.

sandy a. sablonneux, de sable; (hair) blond roux invar.

sane a. (view etc.) sain; (person) sain d'esprit.

sanitary a. (clean) hygiénique; (system etc.) sanitaire. ～ **towel**, serviette hygiénique f.

sanitation n. hygiène (publique) f.; (drainage etc.) système sanitaire m.

sanity n. santé mentale f.; (good sense: fig.) bon sens m.

sap n. (of plants) sève f. —v.t. (undermine) saper.

sapphire n. saphir m.

sarcas|m n. sarcasme m. ～**tic** a. sarcastique.

sardine n. sardine f.

Sardinia n. Sardaigne f.

sash n. (on uniform) écharpe f.; (on dress) ceinture f. ～-**window** n. fenêtre à guillotine f.

satchel n. cartable m.

satellite n. & a. satellite (m.). ～ **dish**, antenne parabolique f.

satin n. satin m.

satir|e n. satire f. ～**ical** a. satirique.

satisfactor|y a. satisfaisant.

satisf|y v.t. satisfaire; (convince) convaincre. **~action** n. satisfaction f. **~ying** a. satisfaisant.

satsuma n. mandarine f.

saturat|e v.t. saturer; (wet) trempé. **~ion** n. saturation f.

Saturday n. samedi m.

sauce n. sauce f.

saucepan n. casserole f.

saucer n. soucoupe f.

saucy a. impertinent; (boldly smart) coquin.

Saudi Arabia n. Arabie Séoudite f.

sauna n. sauna m.

saunter v.i. flâner.

sausage n. saucisse f.; (precooked) saucisson m.

savage a. (fierce) féroce; (wild) sauvage. —n. sauvage m./f.

sav|e v.t. sauver; (money) économiser; (time) (faire) gagner; (keep) garder; (prevent) éviter (from, de). —n. (football) arrêt m. **~ings** n. pl. économies f.

saviour n. sauveur m.

savour n. saveur f. —v.t. savourer. **~y** a. (tasty) savoureux; (culin.) salé.

saw n. scie f. —v.t. scier.

sawdust n. sciure f.

saxophone n. saxophone m.

say v.t./i. dire; (prayer) faire.

saying n. proverbe m.

scab n. (on sore) croûte f.; (blackleg: fam.) jaune m.

scaffold n. (gallows) échafaud m. **~ing** n. (for workmen) échafaudage m.

scald v.t. (injure, cleanse) ébouillanter. —n. brûlure f.

scale[1] n. (of fish) écaille f.

scale[2] n. (for measuring, size, etc.) échelle f.; (mus.) gamme f.; (of salaries, charges) barème m. **on a**

small/etc. **~**, sur une petite etc. échelle. —v.t. (climb) escalader. **~ down**, réduire (proportionnellement).

scales n. pl. balance f.

scallop n. coquille Saint-Jacques f.

scalp n. cuir chevelu m.

scalpel n. scalpel m.

scamper v.i. trotter.

scampi n. pl. gambas f. pl.

scan v.t. scruter; (quickly) parcourir; (poetry) scander; (of radar) balayer. —n. (ultrasound) échographie f.

scandal n. (disgrace, outrage) scandale m.; (gossip) cancans m. pl. **~ous** a. scandaleux.

scandalize v.t. scandaliser.

Scandinavia n. Scandinavie f. **~n** a. & n. scandinave (m./f.).

scant a. insuffisant.

scant|y a. insuffisant; (clothing) sommaire. **~ily dressed**, à peine vêtu.

scapegoat n. bouc émissaire m.

scar n. cicatrice f. —v.t. marquer d'une cicatrice; (fig.) marquer.

scarc|e a. rare. **~ity** n. rareté f., pénurie f.

scarcely adv. à peine.

scare v.t. faire peur à. —n. peur f. **be ~d**, avoir peur.

scarecrow n. épouvantail m.

scarf n. écharpe f.; (over head) foulard m.

scarlet a. écarlate. **~ fever**, scarlatine f.

scary a. (fam.) effrayant.

scathing a. cinglant.

scatter v.t. (throw) éparpiller, répandre; (disperse) disperser. —v.i. se disperser.

scavenge v.i. fouiller (dans les ordures).

scenario n. scénario m.

scene n. scène f.; (of accident,

scenery *crime* lieu(x) *m.* (*pl.*); (*sight*) spectacle *m.*; (*incident*) incident *m.*

scenery *n.* paysage *m.*; (*theatre*) décor(s) *m.* (*pl.*).

scenic *a.* pittoresque.

scent *n.* (*perfume*) parfum *m.*; (*trail*) piste *f.* —*v.t.* flairer; (*make fragrant*) parfumer.

sceptic *n.* sceptique *m./f.* ~**al** *a.* sceptique. ~**ism** *n.* scepticisme *m.*

schedule *n.* horaire *m.*; (*for job*) planning *m.* —*v.t.* prévoir. **behind** ~, en retard. **on** ~, (*train*) à l'heure; (*work*) dans les temps. ~**d flight,** vol régulier *m.*

scheme *n.* plan *m.*; (*dishonest*) combine *f.*; (*fig.*) arrangement *m.* —*v.i.* intriguer. **pension** ~, caisse de retraite *f.*

schizophrenic *a.* & *n.* schizophrène (*m./f.*).

scholar *n.* érudit(e) *m.* (*f.*) ~**ship** *n.* érudition *f.*; (*grant*) bourse *f.*

school *n.* école *f.*; (*secondary*) lycée *m.* —*a.* (*age, year, holidays*) scolaire.

school|boy *n.* écolier *m.* ~**girl** *n.* écolière *f.*

school|master ~**mistress, ~teacher** *ns.* (*primary*) institu|teur, -trice *m.*, *f.*; (*secondary*) professeur *m.*

sciatica *n.* sciatique *f.*

scien|ce *n.* science *f.* ~**ce fiction,** science-fiction *f.* ~**tific** *a.* scientifique.

scientist *n.* scientifique *m./f.*

scissors *n. pl.* ciseaux *m. pl.*

scold *v.t.* réprimander. ~**ing** *n.* réprimande *f.*

scoop *n.* (*for grain, sugar*) pelle (à main) *f.*; (*for food*) cuiller *f.*; (*ice cream*) boule *f.*; (*news*) exclusivité *f.* ~ **out,** creuser. ~ **up,** ramasser.

scooter *n.* (*child's*) trottinette *f.*; (*motor cycle*) scooter *m.*

scope *n.* étendue *f.*; (*competence*) compétence *f.*; (*opportunity*) possibilité(s) *f.* (*pl.*).

scorch *v.t.* brûler, roussir. ~**ing** *a.* brûlant, très chaud.

score *n.* score *m.*; (*mus.*) partition *f.* —*v.t.* marquer; (*success*) remporter. —*v.i.* marquer un point; (*football*) marquer un but; (*keep score*) compter les points. **a** ~ (**of**), (*twenty*) vingt. ~**-board** *n.* tableau *m.*

scorn *n.* mépris *m.* —*v.t.* mépriser. ~**ful** *a.* méprisant.

Scorpio *n.* le Scorpion.

scorpion *n.* scorpion *m.*

Scot *n.* Écossais(e) *m.* (*f.*). ~**tish** *a.* écossais.

Scotch *a.* écossais. —*n.* whisky *m.*, scotch *m.*

scotch *v.t.* mettre fin à.

Scotland *n.* Écosse *f.*

Scots *a.* écossais. ~**man** *n.* Écossais *m.* ~**woman** *n.* Écossaise *f.*

scour[1] *v.t.* (*pan*) récurer. ~**er** *n.* tampon à récurer *m.*

scour[2] *v.t.* (*search*) parcourir.

scourge *n.* fléau *m.*

scout *n.* (*mil.*) éclaireur *m.* —*v.i.* ~ **around (for),** chercher.

Scout *n.* (*boy*) scout *m.*

scowl *n.* air renfrogné *m.* —*v.i.* faire la tête (**at,** à).

scraggy *a.* efflanqué.

scram *v.i.* (*sl.*) se tirer.

scramble *v.i.* (*clamber*) grimper. —*v.t.* (*eggs*) brouiller. —*n.* bousculade *f.*, ruée *f.* ~ **for,** se bousculer pour avoir.

scrap[1] *n.* petit morceau *m.* ~**s,** (*of metal, fabric, etc.*) déchets *m. pl.*; (*of food*) restes *m. pl.* —*v.t.* mettre au rebut; (*plan etc.*) abandonner. ~**-paper** *n.* brouillon *m.* ~**py** *a.* fragmentaire.

scrap² n. (fight: fam.) bagarre f.

scrape v.t. racler, gratter; (graze) érafler. —v.i. (rub) frotter. —n. raclement m.; éraflure f. ~ **through**, réussir de justesse.

scratch v.t./i. (se) gratter; (with claw, nail) griffer; (graze) érafler; (mark) rayer. —n. éra flure f. **start from** ~, partir de zéro.

scrawl n. gribouillage m. —v.t./i. gribouiller.

scrawny a. décharné.

scream v.t./i. crier, hurler. —n. cri (perçant) m.

scree n. éboulis m.

screech v.i. (scream) hurler; (of brakes) grincer. —n. hurlement m.; grincement m.

screen n. écran m.; (folding) paravent m. —v.t. masquer; (protect) protéger; (film) projeter; (candidates) filtrer; (med.) faire subir un test de dépistage. ~ing n. projection f.

screw n. vis f. —v.t. visser.

screwdriver n. tournevis m.

scribble v.t./i. griffonner.

scribe n. scribe m.

script n. écriture f.; (of film) scénario m.; (of play) texte m. ~writer n. scénariste m./f.

Scriptures n. pl. the ~, l'Écriture (sainte) f.

scroll n. rouleau m. —v.t./i. (comput.) (faire) défiler.

scrounge v.t. (meal) se faire payer; (steal) chiper. —v.i. (beg) quémander. ~ **money from**, taper. ~r n. parasite m.; (of money) tapeu|r, -se m., f.

scrub¹ n. (land) broussailles f. pl.

scrub² v.t. nettoyer (à la brosse)

scruffy a. (fam.) sale.

scrum n. (Rugby) mêlée f.

scruple n. scrupule m.

scrupulous a. scrupuleux. ~**ly clean**, impeccable.

scrutin|y n. examen minutieux m. ~**ize** v.t. scruter.

scuba-diving n. plongée sousmarine f.

scuffle n. bagarre f.

sculpt v.t./i. sculpter. ~**or** n. sculpteur m. ~**ure** n. sculpture f.; v.t./i. sculpter.

scum n. (on liquid) écume f.; (people: pej.) racaille f.

scurf n. pellicules f. pl.

scythe n. faux f.

sea n. mer f. —a. de (la) mer, marin. **at** ~, en mer. **by** ~, par mer. ~**-level** n. niveau de la mer m. ~**shore** n. rivage m.

seafood n. fruits de mer m. pl.

seagull n. mouette f.

seal¹ n. (animal) phoque m.

seal² n. sceau m.; (with wax) cachet m. —v.t. sceller; cacheter; (stick down) coller. ~**wax** n. cire à cacheter f. ~ **off**, (area) boucler.

seam n. (in cloth etc.) couture f.; (of coal) veine f.

seaman n. marin m.

seance n. séance de spiritisme f.

search v.t./i. fouiller; (study) examiner. —n. fouille f.; (quest) recherche(s) f. (pl.). **in** ~ **of**, à la recherche de. ~ **for**, chercher. ~**ing** a. (piercing) pénétrant.

searchlight n. projecteur m.

seasick a. **be** ~, avoir le mal de mer.

seaside n. bord de la mer m.

season n. saison f. —v.t. assaisonner. **in** ~, de saison. ~**ing** n. assaisonnement m. ~**ticket** n. carte d'abonnement f.

seasoned a. expérimenté.

seat n. siège m.; (place) place f.; (of trousers) fond m. —v.t. (put) placer; (have seats for) avoir des places assises pour. **take a** ~, s'asseoir. **~-belt** n. ceinture de sécurité f.

seaweed n. algues f. pl.

secateurs n. pl. sécateur m.

seclu|de v.t. isoler. **~ded** a. isolé. **~sion** n. solitude f.

second[1] a. deuxième, second. —n. deuxième m./f., second(e) m. (f.); (unit of time) seconde f. **~-class** a. de deuxième classe. **at ~-hand**, de seconde main. **~-hand** a. & adv. d'occasion; n. (on clock) trotteuse f. **~-rate** a. médiocre.

second[2] v.t. (transfer) détacher (to, à).

secondary a. secondaire. **~ school**, lycée m.

secrecy n. secret m.

secret a. secret. —n. secret m. **in ~**, en secret. **~ly** adv. en secret, secrètement.

secretary n. secrétaire m./f. **S~y of State**, ministre m.; (Amer.) ministre des Affaires étrangères m.

secret|e v.t. (med.) sécréter. **~ion** n. sécrétion f.

secretive a. cachottier.

sect n. secte f. **~arian** a. sectaire.

section n. section f.; (of country, town) partie f.; (in store) rayon m.; (newspaper column) rubrique f.

sector n. secteur m.

secular a. (school etc.) laïque; (art, music, etc.) profane.

secure a. (safe) en sûreté; (in mind) tranquille; (psychologically) sécurisé; (firm) solide; (against attack) sûr; (window etc.) bien fermé. —v.t. attacher; (obtain) s'assurer; (ensure) assurer. **~ly** adv. solidement; (safely) en sûreté.

security n. (safety) sécurité f.; (for loan) caution f. **~ guard**, vigile m.

sedate[1] a. calme.

sedate[2] v.t. donner un sédatif à. **~ion** n. sédation f.

sedative n. sédatif m.

sediment n. sédiment m.

seduce v.t. séduire. **~r** n. séduc|teur, -trice m., f.

seduct|ion n. séduction f. **~ive** a. séduisant.

see[1] v.t./i. voir; (escort) (r)accompagner. **~ about** or **to**, s'occuper de. **see you (soon)!**, à bientôt! **~ing that**, vu que.

seed n. graine f.; (collectively) graines f. pl.; (origin: fig.) germe m.; (tennis) tête de série f.

seedy a. miteux.

seek v.t. chercher. **~ out**, aller chercher.

seem v.i. sembler.

seep v.i. (ooze) suinter. **~ into**, s'infiltrer dans.

see-saw n. balançoire f., tape-cul m. —v.t. osciller.

seethe v.i. **~ with**, (anger) bouillir de; (people) grouiller de.

segment n. segment m.; (of orange) quartier m.

segregat|e v.t. séparer. **~ion** n. ségrégation f.

seize v.t. saisir; (take possession of) s'emparer de. —v.i. **~ on**, (chance etc.) saisir.

seizure n. (med.) crise f.

seldom adv. rarement.

select v.t. choisir, sélectionner. —a. choisi; (exclusive) sélect. **~ion** n. sélection f.

selective a. sélectif.

self n. (on cheque) moi-même. **the ~**, le moi m. invar.

self- pref. **~-assurance** n. assurance f. **~-assured** a. sûr de soi. **~-catering** a. où l'on fait la cuisine soi-même. **~-centred** a. égocentrique. **~-coloured** a. uni. **~-confidence** n. confiance en soi f. **~-confident** a. sûr de soi. **~-conscious** a. gêné, timide. **~-contained** a. (flat) indépendant. **~-control** n. maîtrise de soi f. **~-defence** n. autodéfense f.; (jurid.) légitime défense f.; **~-respect** n. respect de soi m., dignité f. **~-service** n. & a. libre-service (m.). **~-sufficient** a. indépendant.

selfish a. égoïste; (motive) intéressé. **~ness** n. égoïsme m.

sell v.t./i. (se) vendre. **~ by date,** date limite de vente f. **be sold out of,** n'avoir plus de. **~er** n. vendeu|r, -se m., f.

Sellotape n. (P.) scotch m. (P.).

semantic a. sémantique. **~s** n. sémantique f.

semen n. sperme m.

semi- pref. semi-, demi-.

semibreve n. (mus.) ronde f.

semicirc|le n. demi-cercle m. **~ular** a. en demi-cercle.

semicolon n. point-virgule m.

semiconductor n. semi-conducteur n.

semi-detached **~ house,** maison jumelle f.

semifinal n. demi-finale f.

seminar n. séminaire m.

seminary n. séminaire m.

semiquaver n. (mus.) double croche f.

semolina n. semoule f.

senat|e n. sénat m. **~or** n. sénateur m.

send v.t./i. envoyer. **~ away,** (dismiss) renvoyer. **~ back,** renvoyer. **~ for,** (person, help) envoyer chercher. **~er** n. expédi|teur, -trice m., f.

senil|e a. sénile. **~ity** n. sénilité f.

senior a. plus âgé (to, que); (in rank) supérieur; (teacher, partner) principal. **~** n. aîné(e) m. (f.); (schol.) grand(e) m. (f.). **~ citizen,** personne âgée f.

sensation n. sensation f. **~al** a. (event) qui fait sensation; (wonderful) sensationnel.

sense n. sens m.; (sensation) sensation f.; (mental impression) sentiment m.; (common sense) bon sens m. **~s,** (mind) raison f. —v.t. (pres)sentir. **make ~,** avoir du sens.

sensibilit|y n. sensibilité f. **~ies,** susceptibilité f.

sensible a. raisonnable, sensé; (clothing) fonctionnel.

sensitiv|e a. sensible (to, à); (touchy) susceptible. **~ity** n. sensibilité f.

sensual a. sensuel. **~ity** n. sensualité f.

sensuous a. sensuel.

sentence n. phrase f.; (decision: jurid.) jugement m., condamnation f.; (punishment) peine f. —v.t. **~ to,** condamner à.

sentiment n. sentiment m.

sentimental a. sentimental.

sentry n. sentinelle f.

separate¹ a. séparé, différent; (independent) indépendant. **~s** n. pl. coordonnés m. pl. **~ly** adv. séparément.

separat|e² v.t./i. (se) séparer. **~ion** n. séparation f.

September n. septembre m.

septic a. (wound) infecté. **~ tank,** fosse septique f.

sequel n. suite f.

sequence n. (order) ordre m.; (series) suite f.; (of film) séquence f.

sequin n. paillette f.

serene a. serein.

sergeant n. (mil.) sergent m.; (policeman) brigadier m.

serial n. (story) feuilleton m. —a. (number) de série.

series n. invar. série f.

serious a. sérieux; (very bad)

critical) grave, sérieux. **~ly** *adv.* sérieusement, gravement.

sermon *n.* sermon *m.*

serpent *n.* serpent *m.*

serrated *a.* (*edge*) en dents de scie.

serum *n.* sérum *m.*

servant *n.* domestique *m./f.*; (*of God etc.*) serviteur *m.*

serve *v.t./i.* (*undergo, carry out*) faire; (*of transport*) desservir. —*n.* (*tennis*) service *m.*

service *n.* service *m.*; (*maintenance*) révision *f.*; (*relig.*) office *m.* **~s**, (*mil.*) forces armées *f. pl.* —*v.t.* (*car etc.*) réviser. **of ~ to**, utile à. **~ area**, (*auto.*) aire de services *f.* **~ charge**, service *m.* **~ station**, station-service *f.*

serviceable *a.* (*usable*) utilisable; (*useful*) commode; (*durable*) solide.

serviceman *n.* militaire *m.*

serviette *n.* serviette *f.*

servile *a.* servile.

session *n.* séance *f.*; (*univ.*) année (universitaire) *f.*

set *v.t.* mettre; (*put down*) poser, mettre; (*limit etc.*) fixer; (*watch, clock*) régler; (*example, task*) donner; (*for printing*) composer; (*in plaster*) plâtrer. —*v.i.* (*of sun*) se coucher; (*of jelly*) prendre. —*n.* (*of chairs, stamps, etc.*) série *f.*; (*of knives, keys, etc.*) jeu *m.*; (*of people*) groupe *m.*; (*TV, radio*) poste *m.*; (*style of hair*) mise en plis *f.*; (*theatre*) décor *m.*; (*tennis*) set *m.*; (*mathematics*) ensemble *m.* —*a.* fixe; (*in habits*) régulier; (*meal*) à prix fixe; (*book*) au programme. **~ against sth.**, opposé à. **~ about** *or* **to**, se mettre à. **~back** *n.* revers *m.* **~ in**, (*take hold*) s'installer, commencer. **~ off** *or* **out**, partir. **~ off**, (*mechanism, activity*) déclencher; (*bomb*) faire éclater.

~ out, (*state*) exposer; (*arrange*) disposer. **~ out to do sth.**, entreprendre de faire qch. **~ up**, (*establish*) lancer. **~-up** *n.* (*fam.*) affaire *f.*

settee *n.* canapé *m.*

setting *n.* cadre *m.*

settle *v.t.* (*arrange, pay*) régler; (*date*) fixer; (*nerves*) calmer. —*v.i.* (*come to rest*) se poser; (*live*) s'installer. **~ down**, se calmer; (*become orderly*) se ranger. **~ for**, accepter. **~ in**, s'installer. **~ up (with)**, régler. **~r** *n.* colon *m.*

settlement *n.* règlement *m.* (**of**, de); (*agreement*) accord *m.*; (*place*) colonie *f.*

seven *a. & n.* sept (*m.*). **~th** *a. & n.* septième (*m./f.*).

seventeen *a. & n.* dix-sept (*m.*). **~th** *a. & n.* dix-septième (*m./f.*).

sevent|**y** *a. & n.* soixante-dix (*m.*). **~ieth** *a. & n.* soixante-dixième (*m./f.*).

sever *v.t.* (*cut*) couper; (*relations*) rompre.

several *a. & pron.* plusieurs.

severe *a.* sévère; (*violent*) violent; (*serious*) grave. **~ly** *adv.* sévèrement; gravement.

sew *v.t./i.* coudre. **~ing-machine** *n.* machine à coudre *f.*

sewage *n.* eaux d'égout *f. pl.*

sewer *n.* égout *m.*

sex *n.* sexe *m.* —*a.* sexuel. **have ~**, avoir des rapports (sexuels). **~y** *a.* sexy *invar.*

sexist *a. & n.* sexiste (*m./f.*).

sexual *a.* sexuel. **~ intercourse**, rapports sexuels *m. pl.*

shabb|**y** *a.* (*place, object*) minable, miteux; (*person*) pauvrement vêtu; (*mean*) mesquin.

shack *n.* cabane *f.*

shade *n.* ombre *f.*; (*of colour, opinion*) nuance *f.*; (*for lamp*) abat-jour m. —v.t. (of person etc.) abriter; (of tree) ombrager.

shadow n. ombre f. —v.t. (follow) filer.

shady a. ombragé; (dubious: fig.) louche.

shaft n. (of arrow) hampe f.; (axle) arbre m.; (of mine) puits m.; (of light) rayon m.

shaggy a. (beard) hirsute; (hair) broussailleux; (animal) à longs poils.

shake v.t. secouer; (bottle) agiter; (house, belief, etc.) ébranler. —v.i. trembler. —n. secousse f. ~ **hands with**, serrer la main à. ~ **one's head**, (in refusal) dire non de la tête.

shaky a. (hand, voice) tremblant; (table etc.) branlant; (weak: fig.) faible.

shall v. aux. **I** ~ **do**, je ferai.

shallot n. échalote f.

shallow a. peu profond; (fig.) superficiel.

sham n. comédie f.; (person) imposteur m.; (jewel) imitation f. —a. faux. —v.t. feindre.

shambles n.pl. (mess: fam.) désordre m., pagaille f.

shame n. honte f. —v.t. faire honte à. **it's a** ~, c'est dommage.

shampoo n. shampooing m. —v.t. shampooiner.

shandy n. panaché m.

shanty n. (shack) baraque f. ~ **town**, bidonville m.

shape n. forme f. —v.t. (fashion, mould) façonner; (future etc.: fig.) déterminer. ~**less** a. informe.

shapely a. bien tourné.

share n. part f.; (comm.) action f. —v.t./i. partager; (feature) avoir en commun.

shareholder n. actionnaire m./f.

shark n. requin m.

sharp a. (knife etc.) tranchant; (pin

etc.) pointu; (point) aigu; (acute) vif; (sudden) brusque; (dishonest) peu scrupuleux. —adv. (stop) net.

sharpen v.t. aiguiser; (pencil) tailler.

shatter v.t./i. (glass etc.) (faire) voler en éclats, (se) briser; (upset, ruin) anéantir.

shav|e v.t./i. (se) raser. —n. **have a** ~**e**, se raser. ~**er** n. rasoir électrique m. ~**ing-brush** n. blaireau m. ~**ing-cream** n. crème à raser f.

shaving n. copeau m.

shawl n. châle m.

she pron. elle. —n. femelle f.

sheaf n. gerbe f.

shears n.pl. cisaille(s) f. (pl.).

sheath n. gaine f., fourreau m.; (contraceptive) préservatif m.

sheathe v.t. rengainer.

shed[1] n. remise f.

shed[2] v.t. perdre; (light, tears) répandre.

sheen n. lustre m.

sheep n. invar. mouton m. ~**-dog** n. chien de berger m.

sheepskin n. peau de mouton f.

sheer a. pur (et simple); (steep) à pic; (fabric) très fin. —adv. à pic, verticalement.

sheet n. drap m.; (of paper) feuille f.; (of glass, ice) plaque f.

shelf n. (pl. **shelves**) rayon m., étagère f.

shell n. coquille f.; (on beach) coquillage m.; (of building) carcasse f.; (explosive) obus m. —v.t. (nut etc.) décortiquer; (peas) écosser; (mil.) bombarder.

shellfish n. invar. (lobster etc.) crustacé(s) m. (pl.); (mollusc) coquillage(s) m. (pl.).

shelter n. abri m. —v.t./i. (s')abriter; (give lodging to) donner asile à. ~**ed** a. (life etc.) protégé.

shelve v.t. (plan etc.) laisser en suspens, remettre à plus tard.

shepherd n. berger m. —v.t. (people) guider. **~'s pie**, hachis Parmentier m.

sheriff n. shérif m.

sherry n. xérès m.

shield n. bouclier m.; (screen) écran m. —v.t. protéger.

shift v.t./i. (se) déplacer, bouger; (exchange, alter) changer de. —n. changement m.; (workers) équipe f.; (work) poste m.

shilling n. shilling m.

shimmer v.i. chatoyer. —n. chatoiement m.

shin n. tibia m.

shine v.t./i. (faire) briller. —n. éclat m., brillant m. **~ one's torch** or **the light (on)**, éclairer.

shingle n. (pebbles) galets m. pl.; (on roof) bardeau m.

shingles n. pl. (med.) zona m.

shiny a. brillant.

ship n. bateau m., navire m. —v.t. transporter; (send) expédier; (load) embarquer. **~ping** n. (ships) navigation f.

shipyard n. chantier naval m.

shirk v.t. esquiver. **~er** n. tire-au-flanc m. invar.

shirt n. chemise f.; (of woman) chemisier m. **in ~-sleeves**, en bras de chemise.

shiver v.i. frissonner. —n. frisson m.

shoal n. (of fish) banc m.

shock n. choc m., secousse f.; (electr.) décharge f.; (med.) choc m. —a. (result) choc invar.; (tactics) de choc. —v.t. choquer. **~ absorber**, amortisseur m. **~ing** a. choquant.; (bad: fam.) affreux.

shoddy a. mauvais.

shoe n. chaussure f., soulier m.; (of horse) fer (à cheval) m.; (in vehicle) sabot (de frein) m. —v.t. (horse) ferrer. **~ repairer**, cordonnier m.

shoehorn n. chaussepied m.

shoelace n. lacet m.

shoot v.t. (gun) tirer un coup de; (missile, glance) lancer; (kill, wound) tuer, blesser (d'un coup de fusil, de pistolet, etc.); (execute) fusiller; (hunt) chasser; (film) tourner. —v.i. tirer (at, sur). —n. (bot.) pousse f. **~ down**, abattre. **~ out**, (rush) sortir en vitesse. **~ up**, (spurt) jaillir; (grow) pousser vite.

shop n. magasin m., boutique f.; (workshop) atelier m. —v.i. faire ses courses. **~ assistant**, vendeu|r, -se m., f. **~per** n. acheteu|r, -se m., f. **~-soiled** adjs. abîmé. **~ window**, vitrine f.

shopkeeper n. commerçant(e) m. (f.).

shoplift|er n. voleu|r|r, -se à l'étalage m., f. **~ing** n. vol à l'étalage m.

shopping n. (goods) achats m. pl. **go ~**, faire ses courses. **~ centre**, centre commercial m.

shore n. rivage m.

short a. court; (person) petit; (brief) court, bref; (curt) brusque. **be ~ (of)**, (lack) manquer (de). —adv. (stop) net. —n. (electr.) court-circuit m.; (film) court-metrage m. **~s**, (trousers) short m. **~ of money**, à court d'argent. **~ of doing sth.**, à moins de faire qch. **cut ~**, écourter. **in ~**, en bref. **~-circuit**, court-circuit m. **~-circuit** v.t. court-circuiter. **~-cut**, raccourci m. **~-lived** a. éphémère. **~-sighted** a. myope. **~-staffed** a. à court de personnel. **~ story**, nouvelle f. **~-term** a. à court terme. **~ wave**, ondes courtes f. pl.

shortage n. manque m.

shortbread n. sablé m.

shortcoming n. défaut m.

shorten v.t. raccourcir.

shortfall n. déficit m.

shorthand n. sténo-(graphie) f. ~ **typist,** sténodactylo f.

shortly adv. bientôt.

shot n. (firing, attempt, etc.) coup de feu m.; (person) tireur m.; (bullet) balle f.; (photograph) photo f.; (injection) piqûre f. **like a** ~, comme une flèche. ~ **-gun** n. fusil de chasse m.

should v.aux. devoir. **you** ~ **help me,** vous devriez m'aider. **I** ~ **have stayed,** j'aurais dû rester. **I** ~ **like to,** j'aimerais bien.

shoulder n. épaule f. —v.t. (responsibility) endosser; (burden) se charger de. ~ **-bag** n. sac à bandoulière m. ~ **-blade** n. omoplate f. ~ **-pad** n. épaulette f.

shout n. cri m. —v.t./i. crier.

shove n. poussée f. —v.t./i. pousser; (put: fam.) ficher.

shovel n. pelle f. —v.t. pelleter.

show v.t. montrer; (of dial, needle) indiquer; (put on display) exposer; (film) donner; (conduct) conduire. —v.i. (be visible) se voir. —n. démonstration f.; (ostentation) parade f.; (exhibition) exposition f., salon m.; (theatre) spectacle m.; (cinema) séance f. **for,** pour l'effet. **on** ~, exposé. ~ **-down** n. épreuve de force f. ~ **-jumping** n. concours hippique m. ~ **ing** n. performance f.; (cinema) séance f.

shower n. (of rain) averse f.; (for washing) douche f. —v.t. ~ **with,** couvrir de. —v.i. se doucher. ~ **y** a. pluvieux.

showerproof a. imperméable.

showroom n. salle d'exposition f.

showy a. voyant; (manner) prétentieux.

shrapnel n. éclats d'obus m. pl.

shred n. lambeau m.; (least amount: fig.) parcelle f. —v.t. déchiqueter; (culin.) râper. ~ **der** n. destructeur de documents m.

shrewd a. astucieux.

shriek n. hurlement m. —v.t./i. hurler.

shrill a. strident, aigu.

shrimp n. crevette f.

shrine n. (place) lieu saint m.; (tomb) châsse f.

shrink v.t./i. rétrécir; (lessen) diminuer.

shrivel v.t./i. (se) ratatiner.

shroud n. linceul m. —v.t. (veil) envelopper.

shrub n. arbuste m.

shrug v.t. ~ **one's shoulders,** hausser les épaules. —n. haussement d'épaules m.

shudder v.i. frémir. —n. frémissement m.

shuffle v.t. (feet) traîner; (cards) battre. —v.i. traîner les pieds. —n. démarche traînante f.

shun v.t. éviter, fuir.

shunt v.t. (train) aiguiller.

shut v.t. fermer. —v.i. se fermer; (of shop, bank, etc.) fermer. ~ **down** or **up,** fermer. ~ **up** v.i. (fam.) se taire; v.t. (fam.) faire taire.

shutter n. volet m.; (photo.) obturateur m.

shuttle n. (bus etc.) navette f. —v.i. faire la navette. —v.t. transporter. ~ **service,** navette f.

shuttlecock n. (badminton) volant m.

shy a. timide. —v.i. reculer. ~ **ness** n. timidité f.

sibling n. frère m., sœur f.

Sicily n. Sicile f.

sick *a.* malade; (*humour*) macabre. **be ~,** (*vomit*) vomir. **be ~ of,** en avoir assez *or* marre de. **feel ~,** avoir mal au cœur.

sickle *n.* faucille *f.*

sickly *a.* (*person*) maladif; (*taste, smell, etc.*) écœurant.

sickness *n.* maladie *f.*

side *n.* côté *m.*; (*of road, river*) bord *m.*; (*of hill*) flanc *m.*; (*sport*) équipe *f.* **—a.** latéral. **~-effect** *n.* effet secondaire *m.* **~-step** *v.t.* éviter. **~-street** *n.* rue latérale *f.* **~-track** *v.t.* faire dévier de son sujet.

sideboard *n.* buffet *m.* **~s,** (*whiskers: sl.*) pattes *f. pl.*

sidelight *n.* (*auto.*) veilleuse *f.*

sideline *n.* activité secondaire *f.*

side|ways *adv. & a.* de côté.

siding *n.* voie de garage *f.*

siege *n.* siège *m.*

siesta *n.* sieste *f.*

sieve *n.* tamis *m.*; (*for liquids*) passoire *f.* **—***v.t.* tamiser.

sift *v.t.* tamiser. **—***v.i.* ~ **through,** examiner.

sigh *n.* soupir *m.* **—***v.t./i.* soupirer.

sight *n.* vue *f.*; (*scene*) spectacle *m.* **—***v.t.* apercevoir.

sightsee|ing *n.* tourisme *m.* **~r** *n.* touriste *m./f.*

sign *n.* signe *m.*; (*notice*) panneau *m.* **—***v.t./i.* signer.

signal *n.* signal *m.* **—***v.t.* communiquer (par signaux); (*person*) faire signe à. **~-box** *n.* poste d'aiguillage *m.*

signalman *n.* aiguilleur *m.*

signature *n.* signature *f.*

significan|t *a.* important; (*meaningful*) significatif. **~ce** *n.* importance *f.*; (*meaning*) signification *f.* **~tly** *adv.* (*much*) sensiblement.

signify *v.t.* signifier.

signpost *n.* poteau indicateur *m.*

silence *n.* silence *m.* **—***v.t.* faire taire. **~r** *n.* (*on car*) silencieux *m.*

silent *a.* silencieux; (*film*) muet. **~ly** *adv.* silencieusement.

silhouette *n.* silhouette *f.*

silicon *n.* silicium *f.* **~ chip,** microplaquette *f.*

silk *n.* soie *f.*

sill *n.* rebord *m.*

silly *a.* bête, idiot.

silo *n.* silo *m.*

silt *n.* vase *f.*

silver *n.* argent *m.*; (*silverware*) argenterie *f.* **—a.** en argent, d'argent.

similar *a.* semblable (**to,** à). **~ity** *n.* ressemblance *f.* **~ly** *adv.* de même.

simile *n.* comparaison *f.*

simmer *v.t./i.* (*soup etc.*) mijoter; (*water*) (laisser) frémir; (*smoulder: fig.*) couver. **~ down,** se calmer.

simpl|e *a.* simple. **~e-minded** *a.* simple d'esprit. **~icity** *n.* simplicité *f.* **~y** *adv.* simplement; (*absolutely*) absolument.

simplif|y *v.t.* simplifier. **~ication** *n.* simplification *f.*

simplistic *a.* simpliste.

simulat|e *v.t.* simuler. **~ion** *n.* simulation *f.*

simultaneous *a.* simultané. **~ly** *adv.* simultanément.

sin *n.* péché *m.* **—***v.i.* pécher.

since *prep. & adv.* depuis. **—***conj.* depuis que; (*because*) puisque. **~ then,** depuis.

sincer|e *a.* sincère. **~ely** *adv.* sincèrement. **~ity** *n.* sincérité *f.*

sinew *n.* tendon *m.* **~s,** muscles *m. pl.*

sinful *a.* (*act*) coupable; (*shocking*) scandaleux.

sing *v.t./i.* chanter. **~er** *n.* chanteu|r, -se *m., f.*

singe v.t. roussir.

single a. seul; (not double) simple; (unmarried) célibataire; (room, bed) pour une personne; (ticket) simple. —n. (ticket) aller simple m.; (record) 45 tours m. invar. **~s**, (tennis) simple m. **~ out**, choisir. **in ~ file**, en file indienne. **~-handed** a. sans aide. **~ parent,** parent seul m.

singly adv. un à un.

singlet n. maillot de corps m.

singular n. singulier m. —a. (uncommon & gram.) singulier; (noun) au singulier. **~ly** adv. singulièrement.

sinister a. sinistre.

sink v.t./i. (faire) couler; (of ground, person) s'affaisser; (well) creuser; (money) investir. —n. (in kitchen) évier m.; (wash-basin) lavabo m. **~ in**, (fig.) être compris. **~ unit,** bloc-evier m.

sinner n. péch|eur, -eresse m., f.

sinus n. (anat.) sinus m.

sip n. petite gorgée f. —v.t. boire à petites gorgées.

siphon n. siphon m. —v.t. **~ off**, siphonner.

sir n. monsieur m.

siren n. sirène f.

sirloin n. faux-filet m.

sister n. sœur f.; (nurse) infirmière en chef f. **~-in-law** belle-sœur f. **~ly** a. fraternel.

sit v.t./i. (s')asseoir; (of committee etc.) siéger. **be ~ting,** être assis. **~ down,** s'asseoir. **~ting** n. séance f.; (in restaurant) service m. **~ting-room** n. salon m.

site n. emplacement m. **(building) ~,** chantier m. —v.t. placer, construire, situer.

situat|e v.t. situer. **be ~ed,** être situé. **~ion** n. situation f.

six a. & n. six (m.). **~th** a. & n. sixième (m./f.).

sixteen a. & n. seize (m.). **~th** a. & n. seizième (m./f.).

sixt|y a. & n. soixante (m.). **~ieth** a. & n. soixantième (m./f.).

size n. dimension f.; (of person, garment, etc.) taille f.; (of shoes) pointure f.; (of sum, salary) montant m.; (extent) ampleur f. **~able** a. assez grand.

sizzle v.i. grésiller.

skate[1] n. invar. (fish) raie f.

skat|e[2] n. patin m. —v.i. patiner. **~er** n. patineu|r, -se m., f. **~ing** n. patinage m. **~ing-rink** n. patinoire f.

skateboard n. skateboard m., planche à roulettes f.

skeleton n. squelette m.

sketch n. esquisse f., croquis m.; (theatre) sketch m. —v.t. faire un croquis de, esquisser. —v.i. faire des esquisses. **~ out**, esquisser. **~ pad,** bloc à dessins.

sketchy a. sommaire.

skewer n. brochette f.

ski n. ski m. —a. de ski. —v.i. skier; (go skiing) faire du ski. **~ jump,** saut à skis m. **~ lift,** remonte-pente m. **~er** n. skieu|r, -se m., f. **~ing** n. ski m.

skid v.i. déraper. —n. dérapage m.

skilful a. habile.

skill n. habileté f.; (craft) métier m. **~s,** aptitudes f. pl. **~ed** a. habile; (worker) qualifié.

skim v.t. écumer; (milk) écrémer; (pass or glide over) effleurer. —v.i. **~ through,** parcourir.

skimp v.t./i. **~ (on),** lésiner (sur).

skimpy a. (clothes) étriqué; (meal) chiche.

skin n. peau f. —v.t. (animal) écorcher; (fruit) éplucher. **~-diving** n. plongée sous-marine f.

skinny a. maigrichon.

skint a. (sl.) fauché.

skip[1] v.i. sautiller; (with rope) sauter à la corde. —v.t. (page, *class, etc.*) sauter. —*n.* petit saut *m.*

skip² *n.* (*container*) benne *f.*

skipper *n.* capitaine *m.*

skirt *n.* jupe *f.* —*v.t.* contourner. **∼ing-board** *n.* plinthe *f.*

skit *n.* sketch satirique *m.*

skittle *n.* quille *f.*

skulk *v.i.* (*move*) rôder furtivement; (*hide*) se cacher.

skull *n.* crâne *m.*

skunk *n.* (*animal*) mouffette *f.*; (*person: sl.*) salaud *m.*

sky *n.* ciel *m.* **∼-blue** a. & *n.* bleu ciel *a.* & *m. invar.*

skylight *n.* lucarne *f.*

skyscraper *n.* gratte-ciel *m. invar.*

slab *n.* plaque *f.*, bloc *m.*; (*of paving-stone*) dalle *f.*

slack *a.* (*rope*) lâche; (*person*) négligent; (*business*) stagnant; (*period*) creux. —*v.t./i.* (*se*) relâcher.

slacken *v.t./i.* (se) relâcher; (*slow*) (se) ralentir.

slacks *n. pl.* pantalon *m.*

slag *n.* scories *f. pl.* **∼-heap** *n.* crassier *m.*

slake *v.t.* étancher.

slalom *n.* slalom *m.*

slam *v.t./i.* (*door etc.*) claquer; (*throw*) flanquer; (*criticize: sl.*) critiquer. —*n.* (*noise*) claquement *m.*

slander *n.* diffamation *f.*, calomnie *f.* —*v.t.* diffamer, calomnier. **∼ous** *a.* diffamatoire.

slang *n.* argot *m.*

slant *v.t./i.* (faire) pencher; (*news*) présenter sous un certain jour. —*n.* inclinaison *f.*; (*bias*) angle *m.* **be ∼ing**, être penché.

slap *v.t.* (*strike*) donner une claque à; (*face*) gifler; (*put*) flanquer. —*n.* claque *f.*; gifle *f.* —*adv.* tout droit.

slash *v.t.* (*cut*) taillader; (*sever*)

trancher; (*fig.*) réduire (radicalement). —*n.* taillade *f.*

slat *n.* (*in blind*) lamelle *f.*; (*on bed*) latte *f.*

slate *n.* ardoise *f.* —*v.t.* (*fam.*) critiquer, éreinter.

slaughter *v.t.* massacrer; (*animals*) abattre. —*n.* massacre *m.*; abattage *m.*

slaughterhouse *n.* abattoir *m.*

Slav *a.* & *n.* slave (*m./f.*). **∼onic** *a.* (*lang.*) slave.

slave *n.* esclave *m./f.* —*v.i.* trimer. **∼ry** *n.* esclavage *m.*

slay *v.t.* tuer.

sleazy *a.* (*fam.*) sordide.

sledge *n.* luge *f.*; (*horse-drawn*) traineau *m.* **∼-hammer** *n.* marteau de forgeron *m.*

sleek *a.* lisse, brillant; (*manner*) onctueux.

sleep *n.* sommeil *m.* —*v.i.* dormir; (*spend the night*) coucher. —*v.t.* loger. **go to ∼**, s'endormir. **∼er** *n.* dormeu|r, -se *m.*, *f.*; (*beam: rail*) traverse *f.*; (*berth*) couchette *f.* **∼ing-bag** *n.* sac de couchage *m.* **∼ing pill**, somnifère *m.*

sleep|y *a.* somnolent. **be ∼y,** avoir sommeil. **∼ily** *adv.* à moitié endormi.

sleet *n.* neige fondue *f.*

sleeve *n.* manche *f.*; (*of record*) pochette *f.*

sleigh *n.* traineau *m.*

sleight *n.* **∼ of hand,** prestidigitation *f.*

slender *a.* mince, svelte; (*scanty: fig.*) faible.

sleuth *n.* limier *m.*

slew *v.i.* (*turn*) virer.

slice *n.* tranche *f.* —*v.t.* couper (en tranches).

slick *a.* (*unctuous*) mielleux; (*cunning*) astucieux. —*n.* (*oil*) **∼**, nappe de pétrole *f.*, marée noire *f.*

slide *v.t./i.* glisser. —*n.* glissade *f.*

(*fall: fig.*) baisse *f.*; (*in play-ground*) toboggan *m.*; (*for hair*) barrette *f.*; (*photo.*) diapositive *f.* **~-rule** *n.* règle à calcul *f.*

slight *a.* petit, léger; (*slender*) mince; (*frail*) frêle. —*v.t.* (*insult*) offenser. —*n.* affront *m.* **~est** *a.* moindre. **~ly** *adv.* légèrement, un peu.

slim *a.* mince. —*v.i.* maigrir. **~ness** *n.* minceur *f.*

slim|e *n.* boue (visqueuse) *f.*; (*on river-bed*) vase *f.* **~y** *a.* boueux; vaseux; (*sticky, servile*) visqueux.

sling *n.* (*weapon, toy*) fronde *f.*; (*bandage*) écharpe *f.* —*v.t.* jeter, lancer.

slip *v.t./i.* glisser. —*n.* faux pas *m.*; (*mistake*) erreur *f.*; (*petticoat*) combinaison *f.*; (*paper*) fiche *f.* **~ away**, s'esquiver. **~ped** disc, hernie discale *f.* **~-road** *n.* bretelle *f.* **~ s.o.'s mind**, échapper à qn. **~ up**, (*fam.*) gaffer. **~up** *n.* (*fam.*) gaffe *f.*

slipper *n.* pantoufle *f.*

slippery *a.* glissant.

slipshod *a.* (*person*) négligent; (*work*) négligé.

slit *n.* fente *f.* —*v.t.* couper.

slither *v.i.* glisser.

sliver *n.* (*of cheese etc.*) lamelle *f.*; (*splinter*) éclat *m.*

slob *n.* (*fam.*) rustre *m.*

slobber *v.i.* baver.

slog *v.t.* (*hit*) frapper dur. —*v.i.* (*work*) trimer. —*n.* (*work*) travail dur *m.*; (*effort*) gros effort *m.*

slogan *n.* slogan *m.*

slop *v.t./i.* (se) répandre. **~s** *n. pl.* eaux sales *f. pl.*

slop|e *v.i.* être en pente; (*of handwriting*) pencher. —*n.* pente *f.*; (*of mountain*) flanc *m.* **~ing** *a.* en pente.

sloppy *a.* (*ground*) détrempé;

(*food*) liquide; (*work*) négligé; (*person*) négligent; (*fig.*) sentimental.

slosh *v.t.* (*fam.*) répandre; (*hit: sl.*) frapper. —*v.i.* patauger.

slot *n.* fente *f.* —*v.t./i.* (s')insérer. **~-machine** *n.* distributeur automatique *m.*; (*for gambling*) machine à sous *f.*

sloth *n.* paresse *f.*

slouch *v.i.* avoir le dos voûté; (*move*) marcher le dos voûté.

slow *a.* lent. —*adv.* lentement. —*v.t./i.* ralentir. **be ~**, (*clock etc.*) retarder. **~ly** *adv.* lentement. **~ness** *n.* lenteur *f.*

sludge *n.* gadoue *f.*, boue *f.*

slug *n.* (*mollusc*) limace *f.*; (*bullet*) balle *f.*; (*blow*) coup *m.*

sluggish *a.* lent, mou.

sluice *n.* (*gate*) vanne *f.*

slum *n.* taudis *m.*

slumber *n.* sommeil. *m.* —*v.i.* dormir.

slump *n.* effondrement *m.*; baisse *f.*; (*in business*) marasme *m.* —*v.i.* (*collapse, fall limply*) s'effondrer; (*decrease*) baisser.

slur *v.t./i.* (*spoken words*) mal articuler. —*n.* bredouillement *m.*; (*discredit*) atteinte *f.* (on, à).

slush *n.* (*snow*) neige fondue *f.*

slut *n.* (*dirty*) souillon *f.*; (*immoral*) dévergondée *f.*

sly *a.* (*crafty*) rusé; (*secretive*) sournois. **~ on the ~**, en cachette. **~ly** *adv.* sournoisement.

smack[1] *n.* tape *f.*; (*on face*) gifle *f.* —*v.t.* donner une tape à; gifler. —*adv.* (*fam.*) tout droit.

smack[2] *v.i.* **~ of sth.**, (*have flavour*) sentir qch.

small *a.* petit. —*n.* **~ of the back**, creux des reins *m.* —*adv.* (*cut etc.*) menu. **~ ads**, petites annonces *f. pl.* **~ businesses**, les petites entreprises. **~ change**, petite monnaie f. **~ talk**, menus propos m. pl.

smallpox n. variole f.

smart a. élégant; (clever) astucieux, intelligent; (brisk) rapide. —v.i. (of wound etc.) brûler. **~ly** adv. élégamment.

smarten v.t./i. **~ (up)**, embellir. **~ (o.s.) up**, se faire beau; (tidy) s'arranger.

smash v.t./i. (se) briser, (se) fracasser; (opponent, record) pulvériser. —n. (noise) fracas m.; (blow) coup m.; (fig.) collision f.

smashing a. (fam.) épatant.

smattering n. a **~ of**, des notions de.

smear v.t. (stain) tacher; (coat) enduire; (discredit: fig.) entacher. —n. tache f. **~ test**, frottis m.

smell n. odeur f.; (sense) odorat m. —v.t./i. sentir. **~ of**, sentir. **~y** a. malodorant, qui pue.

smelt v.t. (ore) fondre.

smil|e n. sourire. —v.i. sourire. **~ing** a. souriant.

smirk n. sourire affecté m.

smith n. forgeron m.

smock n. blouse f.

smog n. brouillard mélangé de fumée m., smog m.

smoke n. fumée f. —v.t./i. fumer. **have a ~**, fumer. **~d** a. fumé. **~less** a. (fuel) non polluant. n. fumeu|r, -se m., f. **~-screen** n. écran de fumée m.; (fig.) manœuvre de diversion f. **smoky** a. (air) enfumé.

smooth a. lisse; (movement) régulier; (manners, cream) onctueux; (flight) sans turbulence; (changes) sans heurt. —v.t. lisser. **~ly** adv. doucement.

smother v.t. (stifle) étouffer; (cover) couvrir.

smoulder v.i. couver.

smudge n. tache f. —v.t./i. salir, (se) tacher.

smug a. suffisant. **~ly** adv. avec suffisance. **~ness** n. suffisance f.

smuggl|e v.t. passer (en contrebande). **~er** n. contreband|ier, -ière m., f. **~ing** n. contrebande f.

smut n. saleté f.

snack n. casse-croûte m. invar. **~bar** n. snack(-bar) m.

snag n. difficulté f., inconvénient m.; (in cloth) accroc m.

snail n. escargot m. **at a ~'s pace**, à un pas de tortue.

snake n. serpent m.

snap v.t./i. (whip, fingers, etc.) (faire) claquer; (break) (se) casser net; (say) dire sèchement. —n. claquement m.; (photograph) instantané m. —a. soudain.

snappy a. (brisk: fam.) prompt, rapide. **make it ~**, (fam.) se dépêcher.

snapshot n. instantané m.

snare n. piège m.

snarl v.i. gronder (en montrant les dents). —n. grondement m. **~up**, n. embouteillage m.

snarl v.i. gronder (en montrant les dents). —n. grondement m. **~-up** n. embouteillage m.

snatch v.t. (grab) saisir; (steal) voler. **~ from s.o.**, arracher à qn. —n. (theft) vol m.; (short part) fragment m.

sneak v.i. aller furtivement. —n. (schol., sl.) rapporteu|r, -se m., f. **~y** a. sournois.

sneer n. ricanement m. —v.i. ricaner.

sneeze n. éternuement m. —v.i. éternuer.

sniff v.t./i. renifler. —n. reniflement m.

snigger n. ricanement m. —v.i. ricaner.

snip v.t. couper. —n. morceau coupé m.; (bargain: sl.) bonne affaire f.

snipe v.i. canarder. **~r** n. tireur embusqué m.

snippet n. bribe f.

snivel v.i. pleurnicher.

snob n. snob m./f. **~bery** n. snobisme m. **~bish** a. snob invar.

snooker n. (sorte de) jeu de billard m.

snooze n. petit somme m. —v.i. faire un petit somme.

snore n. ronflement m. —v.i. ronfler.

snorkel n. tuba m.

snort n. grognement m. —v.i. (person) grogner.

snout n. museau m.

snow n. neige f. —v.i. neiger. **~y** a. neigeux.

snowball n. boule de neige f. —v.i. faire boule de neige.

snowdrop n. perceneige m./f. invar.

snowflake n. flocon de neige m.

snowman n. bonhomme de neige m.

snowstorm n. tempête de neige f.

snub v.t. (person) snober; (offer) repousser. —n. rebuffade f.

snub-nosed a. au nez retroussé.

snuffle v.i. renifler.

snug a. (cosy) comfortable; (tight) bien ajusté; (safe) sûr.

snuggle v.i. se pelotonner.

so adv. si, tellement; (thus) ainsi. —conj. donc, alors. **so am I,** moi aussi. **so good/etc. as,** aussi bon/etc. que. **so does he,** lui aussi. **I think so,** je pense que oui. **so as to,** de manière à. **so long!,** (fam.) à bientôt! **so many, so much,** tant (de). **so that,** pour que.

soak v.t./i. (faire) tremper (**in,** dans). **~ in** or **up,** absorber. **~ing** a. trempé.

soap n. savon m. —v.t. savonner. **~ powder,** lessive f. **~y** a. savonneux.

soar v.i. monter (en flèche).

sob n. sanglot m. —v.i. sangloter.

sober a. qui n'est pas ivre; (serious) sérieux.

soccer n. (fam.) football m.

sociable a. sociable.

social a. social; (gathering, life) mondain. —n. réunion (amicale) f., fête f. **~ security,** sécurité f. sociale. **~ worker,** assistant(e) social(e) m. (f.).

socialist n. socialiste m./f. **~m** n. socialisme m.

society n. société f.

sociolog|y n. sociologie f. **~ical** a. sociologique. **~ist** n. sociologue m./f.

sock n. chaussette f.

socket n. cavité f.; (for lamp) douille f.; (electr.) prise (de courant) f.; (of tooth) alvéole f.

soda n. soude f.; **~(-water),** soda m., eau de Seltz f.

sodden a. détrempé.

sodium n. sodium m.

sofa n. canapé m., sofa m.

soft a. (gentle, lenient) doux; (not hard) doux, mou; (heart, wood) tendre; (silly) ramolli; (easy: sl.) facile. **~ drink,** boisson non alcoolisée f. **~ly** adv. doucement. **~ness** n. douceur f.

soften v.t./i. (se) ramollir; (tone down, lessen) (s')adoucir.

software n. logiciel m.

softwood n. bois tendre m.

soggy a. détrempé; (bread etc.) ramolli.

soil¹ n. sol m., terre f.

soil² v.t./i. (se) salir.

solar a. solaire.

sold a. **~ out,** épuisé.

solder n. soudure f. —v.t. souder. ∼ing iron, fer à souder m.

soldier n. soldat m. —v.i. ∼ on, (fam.) persévérer.

sole[1] n. (of foot) plante f.; (of shoe) semelle f.

sole[2] n. (fish) sole f.

sole[3] a. unique, seul. ∼ly adv. uniquement.

solemn a. (formal) solennel; (not cheerful) grave. ∼ly adv. solennellement; gravement.

solicit v.t. (seek) solliciter. —v.i. (of prostitute) racoler.

solicitor n. avoué m.

solid a. solide; (not hollow) plein; (gold) massif; (mass) compact; (meal) substantiel. —n. solide m. ∼ly adv. solidement.

solidarity n. solidarité f.

solidify v.t./i. (se) solidifier.

solitary a. (alone, lonely) solitaire; (only, single) seul.

solitude n. solitude f.

solo n. solo m. —a. (mus.) solo invar.; (flight) en solitaire. ∼ist n. soliste m./f.

solstice n. solstice m.

soluble a. soluble.

solution n. solution f.

solve v.t. résoudre.

solvent a. (comm.) solvable. —n. (dis)solvant m.

sombre a. sombre.

some a. (quantity, number) du, de l'*, de la, des; (unspecified, some or other) un(e), quelque; (a little) un peu de; (a certain) un(e) certain(e), quelque; (contrasted with others) quelques, certain(e)s. —pron. quelques-un(e)s; (certain quantity of it or them) en; (a little) un peu. —adv. (approximately) quelque. ∼ of my friends, quelques amis à moi. **he wants** ∼, il en veut. ∼ **time ago**, il y a un certain temps.

somebody pron. quelqu'un.

somehow adv. d'une manière ou d'une autre; (for some reason) je ne sais pas pourquoi.

someone pron. & n. = **somebody**.

somersault n. culbute f. —v.i. faire la culbute.

something pron. & a. quelque chose m. ∼ **good**/etc. quelque chose de bon/etc. ∼ **like**, un peu comme.

sometime adv. un jour. —a. (former) ancien.

sometimes adv. parfois.

somewhat adv. un peu.

somewhere adv. quelque part.

son n. fils m. ∼-**in-law** n. beau-fils m.; gendre m.

sonar n. sonar m.

sonata n. sonate f.

song n. chanson f.

sonic a. ∼ **boom**, bang supersonique m.

sonnet n. sonnet m.

sonny n. (fam.) fiston m.

soon adv. bientôt; (early) tôt. ∼ **after**, peu après. ∼ **er or later**, tôt ou tard.

soot n. suie f. ∼y a. couvert de suie.

soothe v.t. calmer. ∼ing a. (remedy, words, etc.) calmant.

sophisticated a. raffiné; (machine etc.) sophistiqué.

soprano n. (voice) soprano m.; (singer) soprano m./f.

sordid a. sordide.

sore a. douloureux. —n. plaie f.

sorrow n. chagrin m.

sorry a. (regretful) désolé (**to**, de; **that**, que); (wretched) triste.

sort n. genre m., sorte f., espèce f.; (person: fam.) type m. —v.t. ∼ (**out**), (classify) trier. ∼ **out**, (tidy) ranger; (arrange) arranger; (problem) régler.

SOS n. SOS m.

soufflé n. soufflé m.

soul n. âme f. ～-destroying a. démoralisant.

sound[1] n. son m., bruit m. —v.t./i. sonner; (seem) sembler (as if, que). ～ like, sembler être. ～-proof a. insonorisé; v.t. insonoriser. ～-track n. bande sonore f.

sound[2] a. solide; (healthy) sain; (sensible) sensé. ～ asleep, profondément endormi.

sound[3] v.t. (test) sonder. ～ out, sonder.

soup n. soupe f., potage m.

sour a. aigre.

source n. source f.

south n. sud m. —a. sud invar., du sud. —adv. vers le sud. ～-east n. sud-est m. ～-erly a. du sud. ～wards adv. vers le sud. ～-west n. sud-ouest m.

southern a. du sud. ～er n. habitant(e) du sud m. (f.).

souvenir n. (thing) souvenir m.

sovereign n. & a. souverain(e) (m. (f.)). ～ty n. souveraineté f.

Soviet a. soviétique. the ～ Union, l'Union soviétique f.

sow[1] v.t. (seed etc.) semer; (land) ensemencer.

sow[2] n. (pig) truie f.

soya, soy n. ～ bean, graine de soja f. ～ sauce, sauce soja f.

spa n. station thermale f.

space n. espace m.; (room) place f.; (period) période f. a. (research etc.) spatial. —v.t. ～ (out), espacer.

spacious a. spacieux.

spade[1] n. (large, for garden) bêche f.; (child's) pelle f.

spade[2] n. (cards) pique m.

spaghetti n. spaghetti m. pl.

Spain n. Espagne f. ～niard n. Espagnol(e) m. (f.). ～nish a. espagnol; n. (lang.) espagnol m.

span n. (of arch) portée f.; (of wings) envergure f.; (of time) durée f. —v.t. enjamber; (in time) embrasser.

spaniel n. épagneul m.

spank v.t. donner une fessée à. ～ing n. fessée f.

spanner n. (tool) clé (plate) f.; (adjustable) clé à molette f.

spar v.i. s'entraîner (à la boxe).

spare v.t. épargner; (do without) se passer de; (afford to give) donner, accorder; (use with restraint) ménager. —a. en réserve; (surplus) de trop; (tyre, shoes, etc.) de rechange; (room, bed) d'ami. —n. ～ (part), pièce de rechange f. ～ time, loisirs m. pl.

spark n. étincelle f. —v.t. ～ off, (initiate) provoquer. ～(ing)-plug n. bougie f.

sparkle v.i. étinceler. —n. étincellement m.

sparkling a. (wine) mousseux, pétillant; (eyes) pétillant.

sparrow n. moineau m.

sparse a. clairsemé. ～ly adv. (furnished etc.) peu.

spartan a. spartiate.

spasm n. (of muscle) spasme m.; (of coughing, anger, etc.) accès m.

spasmodic a. intermittent.

spastic n. handicapé(e) moteur m. (f.).

spate n. a ～ of, (letters etc.) une avalanche de.

spatter v.t. éclabousser (with, de).

spatula n. spatule f.

spawn n. frai m., œufs m. pl. —v.t. pondre. —v.i. frayer.

speak v.i. parler. —v.t. (say) dire; (language) parler. ～ up, parler plus fort.

speaker n. (in public) orateur m.; (pol.) président; (loudspeaker) baffle m.

spear n. lance f.

spearhead n. fer de lance m. —v.t. (lead) mener.

spearmint n. menthe verte f. —a. à la menthe.

special a. spécial; (exceptional) exceptionnel. **~ity** n. spécialité f. **~ly** adv. spécialement.

specialist n. spécialiste m./f.

specialize v.i. se spécialiser (in, en). **~d** a. spécialisé.

species n. invar. espèce f.

specific a. précis, explicite. **~ally** adv. explicitement; (exactly) précisément.

specify v.t. spécifier. **~ication** n. spécification f.; (details) prescriptions f. pl.

specimen n. spécimen m.

speck n. (stain) (petite) tache f.; (particle) grain m.

speckled a. tacheté.

specs n. pl. (fam.) lunettes f. pl.

spectacle n. spectacle m. **~s**, lunettes f. pl.

spectacular a. spectaculaire.

spectator n. specta|teur, -trice m., f.

spectre n. spectre m.

spectrum n. spectre m.; (of ideas etc.) gamme f.

speculat|e v.i. s'interroger (about, sur); (comm.) spéculer. **~ion** n. conjectures f. pl.; (comm.) spéculation f. **~or** n. spécula|teur, -trice m., f.

speech n. (faculty) parole f.; (diction) élocution f.; (dialect) langage m.; (address) discours m. **~less** a. muet.

speed n. (of movement) vitesse f.; (swiftness) rapidité f. —v.i. aller vite; (too fast too fast) aller trop vite. **~ limit**, limitation de vitesse f. **~ up**, accélérer; (of pace) s'accélérer. **~ing** n. excès de vitesse m.

speedboat n. vedette f.

speedometer n. compteur (de vitesse) m.

speed|y a. rapide. **~ily** adv. rapidement.

spell[1] n. (magic) charme m., sortilège m.; (curse) sort m.

spell[2] v.t./i. écrire; (mean) signifier. **~ out**, épeler; (explain) expliquer. **~ing** n. orthographe f. **~ing mistake**, faute d'orthographe f.

spell[3] n. (courte) période f.

spend v.t. (money) dépenser (on, pour); (time, holiday) passer; (energy) consacrer (on, à). —v.i. dépenser.

spendthrift n. dépens|ier, -ière m., f.

spent a. (used) utilisé; (person) épuisé.

sperm n. (semen) sperme m.; (cell) spermatozoïde m. **~icide** n. spermicide m.

spew v.t./i. vomir.

sphere n. sphère f.

spherical a. sphérique.

spic|e n. épice f.; (fig.) piquant m. **~y** a. épicé; piquant.

spider n. araignée f.

spik|e n. (of metal etc.) pointe f. **~y** a. garni de pointes.

spill v.t. renverser, répandre. —v.i. se répandre. **~ over**, déborder.

spin v.t./i. (wool, web, of spinner) filer; (turn) (faire) tourner; (story) débiter. —n. (movement, excursion) tour m. **~ out**, faire durer. **~-drier** n. essoreuse f. **~-off** n. avantage accessoire m.; (by-product) dérivé m.

spinach n. (plant) épinard m.; (as food) épinards m. pl.

spinal a. vertébral. **~ cord**, moelle épinière f.

spindle n. fuseau m.

spine n. colonne vertébrale f.; (prickle) piquant m.

spiral a. en spirale; (staircase) en

colimaçon. —n. spirale f. —v.i. (prices) monter (en flèche).

spire n. flèche f.

spirit n. esprit m.; (boldness) courage m. ~s, (morale) moral m.; (drink) spiritueux m. pl. ~-level n. niveau à bulle m.

spirited a. fougueux.

spiritual a. spirituel. —n. (song) (negro-)spiritual m.

spit¹ v.t./i. cracher; (of rain) crachiner. —n. crachat(s) m. (pl.) ~ out, cracher.

spit² n. (for meat) broche f.

spite n. rancune f. —v.t. contrarier. **in** ~ **of**, malgré. ~**ful** a. méchant, rancunier.

spittle n. crachat(s) m. (pl.).

splash v.t. éclabousser. —v.i. faire des éclaboussures. —n. (act, mark) éclaboussure f.; (sound) plouf m.; (of colour) tache f.

spleen n. (anat.) rate f.

splendid a. magnifique.

splendour n. splendeur f.

splint n. (med.) attelle f.

splinter n. éclat m.; (in finger) écharde f. ~ **group**, groupe dissident m.

split v.t./i. (se) fendre; (tear) (se) déchirer; (divide) (se) diviser; (share) partager. —n. fente f.; déchirure f.; (share: fam.) part f., partage m.; (quarrel) rupture f.; (pol.) scission f. ~ **up**, (couple) rompre.

splutter v.i. crachoter; (stammer) bafouiller; (engine) tousser; (fat) crépiter.

spoil v.t. (pamper) gâter; (ruin) abîmer; (mar) gâcher, gâter. —n. ~(**s**), (plunder) butin m. ~-sport n. trouble-fête m. invar.

spoke n. rayon m.

spokesman n. porte-parole m. invar.

sponge n. éponge f. —v.t éponger.

—v.i. ~ **on**, vivre aux crochets de. ~-bag n. trousse de toilette f. ~-cake n. génoise f. ~r n. parasite m.

spongy a. spongieux.

sponsor n. (of concert) parrain m.; sponsor m.; (surety) garant m.; (for membership) parrain m., marraine f. —v.t. parrainer, sponsoriser; (member) parrainer. ~**ship** n. patronage m.; parrainage m.

spontaneous a. spontané. ~**ity** n. spontanéité f. ~**ously** adv. spontanément.

spool n. bobine f.

spoon n. cuiller f. ~**ful** n. cuillerée f.

sporadic a. sporadique.

sport n. sport m. —v.t. (display) exhiber, arborer. ~**s** car/coat, voiture/veste de sport f. ~**y** a. (fam.) sportif.

sports|**man** n. (pl. -**men**) sportif m. ~**woman** n. (pl. -**women**) sportive f.

spot n. (mark, stain) tache f.; (dot) point m.; (in pattern) pois m.; (drop) goutte f.; (place) endroit m.; (pimple) bouton m. —v.t. (p.t. **spotted**) (fam.) apercevoir. **a** ~ **of**, (fam.) un peu de. **on the** ~, sur place; (without delay) sur le coup. ~ **check**, contrôle à l'improviste m. ~**ted** a. tacheté; (fabric) à pois.

spotless a. impeccable.

spotlight n. (lamp) projecteur m., spot m.

spouse n. époux m., épouse f.

spout n. (of vessel) bec m.; (of liquid) jet m. —v.i. jaillir.

sprain n. entorse f., foulure f. —v.t. ~ **one's wrist**/ etc., se fouler le poignet/etc.

sprawl v.i. (town, person, etc.) s'étaler. —n. étalement m.

spray¹ *n.* (*of flowers*) gerbe *f.*

spray² *n.* (*water*) gerbe d'eau *f.*; (*from sea*) embruns *m. pl.*; (*device*) bombe *f.*, atomiseur *m.* —*v.t.* (*surface, insecticide*) vaporiser; (*plant etc.*) arroser; (*crops*) traiter.

spread *v.t./i.* (*stretch, extend*) (s')étendre; (*news, fear, etc.*) (se) répandre; (*illness*) (se) propager; (*butter etc.*) (s')étaler. —*n.* propagation *f.*; (*of population*) distribution *f.*; (*paste*) pâte à tartiner *f.*; (*food*) belle table *f.*

spreadsheet *n.* tableur *m.*

spree *n.* go on a ~, (*have fun: fam.*) faire la noce.

sprig *n.* (*shoot*) brin *m.*; (*twig*) brindille *f.*

sprightly *a.* alerte, vif.

spring *v.i.* bondir. —*v.t.* faire, annoncer, *etc.* à l'improviste (**on**, à). —*n.* bond *m.*; (*device*) ressort *m.*; (*season*) printemps *m.*; (*of water*) source *f.* ~ **onion**, oignon blanc *m.* ~ **up**, surgir.

springboard *n.* tremplin *m.*

sprinkle *v.t.* (*with liquid*) arroser (**with**, de); (*with salt, flour*) saupoudrer (**with**, de). ~ **sand**/*etc.*, répandre du sable/*etc.* ~**r** *n.* (*in garden*) arroseur *m.*; (*for fires*) extincteur *m.* (à déclenchement) automatique *m.*

sprint *v.i.* (*sport*) sprinter. —*n.* sprint *m.* ~**er** *n.* sprinteu|r, -se *m., f.*

sprout *v.t./i.* pousser. —*n.* (*on plant etc.*) pousse *f.* (**Brussels**) ~**s**, choux de Bruxelles *m. pl.*

spruce¹ *a.* pimpant. —*v.t.* ~ **o.s. up**, se faire beau.

spruce² *n.* (*tree*) épicéa *m.*

spry *a.* alerte, vif.

spud *n.* (*sl.*) patate *f.*

spur *n.* (*of rider, cock, etc.*) éperon *m.*; (*stimulus*) aiguillon *m.* —*v.t.*

éperonner. **on the** ~ **of the moment**, sous l'impulsion du moment.

spurious *a.* faux.

spurt *v.i.* jaillir; (*fig.*) accélérer. —*n.* jet *m.*; (*at work*) coup de collier *m.*

spy *n.* espion(ne) *m.* (*f.*). —*v.i.* espionner. —*v.t.* apercevoir. ~ **on**, espionner.

squabble *v.i.* se chamailler. —*n.* chamaillerie *f.*

squad *n.* (*of soldiers etc.*) escouade *f.*; (*sport*) équipe *f.*

squal|id *a.* sordide. ~**or** *n.* conditions sordides *f. pl.*

squall *n.* rafale *f.*

squander *v.t.* (*money, time, etc.*) gaspiller.

square *n.* carré *m.*; (*open space in town*) place *f.*; (*instrument*) équerre *f.* —*a.* carré; (*honest*) honnête; (*meal*) solide; (*fam.*) ringard. (**all**) ~, (*quits*) quitte. —*v.t.* (*settle*) régler. —*v.i.* (*agree*) cadrer (**with**, avec). ~ **metre**, mètre carré *m.*

squash *v.t.* écraser; (*crowd*) serrer. —*n.* (*game*) squash *m.* **orange** ~, orangeade *f.*

squat *v.i.* s'accroupir. —*a.* (*dumpy*) trapu. ~**ter** *n.* squatter *m.*

squawk *n.* cri rauque *m.* —*v.i.* pousser un cri rauque.

squeak *n.* petit cri *m.*; (*of door etc.*) grincement *m.* —*v.i.* crier; grincer. ~**y** *a.* grinçant.

squeal *n.* cri aigu *m.* —*v.i.* pousser un cri aigu. ~ **on**, (*inform on: sl.*) dénoncer.

squeamish *a.* (*trop*) délicat.

squeeze *v.t.* presser; (*hand, arm*) serrer; (*extract*) exprimer (**from**, de); (*extort*) soutirer (**from**, à). —*v.i.* (*force one's way*) se glisser.

squid *n.* calmar *m.*

squiggle *n.* ligne onduleuse *f.*

squint v.i. loucher; (with half-shut eyes) plisser les yeux. —n. (med.) strabisme m.

squirm v.i. se tortiller.

squirrel n. écureuil m.

squirt v.t./i. (faire) jaillir. —n. jet m.

stab v.t. (with knife etc.) poignarder. —n. coup (de couteau) m. **have a ~ at** sth., essayer de faire qch.

stabilize v.t. stabiliser.

stab|le¹ a. stable. **~ility** n. stabilité f.

stable² n. écurie f.; **~-boy** n. lad m.

stack n. tas m. —v.t. **~ (up)**, entasser, empiler.

stadium n. stade m.

staff n. personnel m.; (in school) professeurs n. pl.; (mil.) étatmajor m.; (stick) bâton m.

stag n. cerf m.

stage n. (theatre) scène f.; (phase) stade m., étape f.; (platform in hall) estrade f. —v.t. mettre en scène; (fig.) organiser. **~-manage** v.t. monter, organiser. **~manager** n. régisseur m.

stagger v.i. chanceler. —v.t. (shock) stupéfier; (holidays etc.) étaler. **~ing** a. stupéfiant.

stagnant a. stagnant.

stagnat|e v.i. stagner. **~ion** n. stagnation f.

staid a. sérieux.

stain v.t. tacher; (wood etc.) colorer. —n. tache f.; (colouring) colorant m. **~ed glass window**, vitrail m. **~less steel**, acier inoxydable m. **~ remover**, détachant m.

stair n. marche f. **the ~s**, l'escalier m.

staircase n. escalier m.

stake n. (post) pieu m.; (wager) enjeu m. —v.t. (area) jalonner; (wager) jouer. **at ~**, en jeu.

stale a. pas frais; (bread) rassis; (smell) de renfermé; (news) vieux.

stalemate n. (chess) pat m.; (fig.) impasse f.

stalk¹ n. (of plant) tige f.

stalk² v.i. marcher de façon guindée. —v.t. (prey) traquer.

stall n. (in stable) stalle f.; (in market) éventaire m. **~s**, (theatre) orchestre m. —v.t./i. (auto.) caler.

stallion n. étalon m.

stamina n. résistance f.

stammer v.t./i. bégayer. —n. bégaiement m.

stamp v.t. (for postage, marking) timbre m.; (mark: fig.) sceau m. **~ out**, supprimer.

stampede n. fuite désordonnée f.; (rush: fig.) ruée f. —v.i. s'enfuir en désordre; se ruer.

stance n. position f.

stand v.i. être or se tenir (debout); (rise) se lever; (be situated) se trouver; (rest) reposer; (pol.) être candidat (**for**, à). —v.t. mettre (debout); (tolerate) supporter. —n. position f.; (mil.) résistance f.; (for lamp etc.) support m.; (at fair) stand m.; (in street) kiosque m.; (for spectators) tribune f.; (jurid., Amer.) barre f. **make a ~**, prendre position. **~ back**, reculer. **~ by**, (be ready) se tenir prêt; (promise, person) rester fidèle à. **~ by** a. de réserve; **be a ~-by**, être de réserve. **~ for**, représenter; (fam.) supporter. **~ in for**, remplacer. **~-in** n. remplaçant(e) m. (f.). **~ up**, se lever. **~ up to**, résister à.

standard n. norme f.; (level) niveau (voulu) m.; (flag) étendard m. **~s**, (morals) principes m. pl. —a. ordinaire. **~ lamp**, lampadaire m. **~ of living**, niveau de vie m.

standardize *v.t.* standardiser.

standing *a.* debout *invar.*; (*army*, *offer*) permanent. —*n.* position *f.*, réputation *f.*; (*duration*) durée *f.* **~ order**, prélèvement bancaire *m.*

standpoint *n.* point de vue *m.*

standstill *n.* **at a ~**, immobile. **bring/come to a ~**, (s')immobiliser.

staple[1] *n.* agrafe *f.* —*v.t.* agrafer. **~r** *n.* agrafeuse *f.*

staple[2] *a.* de base.

star *n.* étoile *f.*; (*famous person*) vedette *f.* —*v.t.* (*of film*) avoir pour vedette. —*v.i.* **~ in**, être la vedette de.

starboard *n.* tribord *m.*

starch *n.* amidon *m.*; (*in food*) fécule *f.* —*v.t.* amidonner.

stare *v.i.* **~ at**, regarder fixement. —*n.* regard fixe *m.*

starfish *n.* étoile de mer *f.*

start *v.t./i.* commencer; (*machine*) (se) mettre en marche; (*fashion etc.*) lancer; (*cause*) provoquer; (*jump*) sursauter; (*of vehicle*) démarrer. —*n.* commencement *m.*, début *m.*; (*of race*) départ *m.*; (*lead*) avance *f.*; (*jump*) sursaut *m.* **~ to do**, commencer *or* se mettre à faire. **~ out**, partir. **~er** *n.* (*auto.*) démarreur *m.*; (*runner*) partant *m.*; (*culin.*) entrée *f.* **~ing point**, point de départ *m.*

startle *v.t.* (*make jump*) faire tressaillir; (*shock*) alarmer.

starv|e *v.i.* mourir de faim; —*v.t.* affamer; (*deprive*) priver.

stash *v.t.* (*hide: sl.*) cacher.

state *n.* état *m.* —*a.* d'État, de l'État; (*school*) public. —*v.t.* affirmer (**that**, que); (*views*) exprimer; (*fix*) fixer. **the S~s**, les États-Unis.

statement *n.* déclaration *f.*; (*of account*) relevé *m.*

statesman *n.* homme d'État *m.*

static *a.* statique. —*n.* (*radio*, *TV*) parasites *m. pl.*

station *n.* station *f.*; (*rail.*) gare *f.*; (*mil.*) poste *m.*; (*rank*) condition *f.* —*v.t.* poster, placer.

stationary *a.* immobile, stationnaire; (*vehicle*) à l'arrêt.

stationery *n.* papeterie *f.*

statistic *n.* statistique *f.* **~s**, statistique *f.* **~al** *a.* statistique.

statue *n.* statue *f.*

stature *n.* stature *f.*

status *n.* situation *f.*, statut *m.*; (*prestige*) standing *m.* **~ quo**, statu quo *m.*

statut|e *n.* loi *f.* **~es**, (*rules*) statuts *m. pl.* **~ory** *a.* statutaire; (*holiday*) légal.

stave *n.* (*mus.*) portée *f.* —*v.t.* **~ off**, éviter, conjurer.

stay *v.i.* rester; (*spend time*) séjourner; (*reside*) loger. —*v.t.* (*hunger*) tromper. —*n.* séjour *m.* **~ behind/on/late/etc.**, rester. **~ in/out**, rester à la maison/dehors.

steadfast *a.* ferme.

stead|y *a.* stable; (*hand*, *voice*) ferme; (*regular*) régulier; (*staid*) sérieux. —*v.t.* maintenir, assurer; (*calm*) calmer. **~ily** *adv.* fermement; régulièrement.

steak *n.* steak *m.*, bifteck *m.*; (*of fish*) darne *f.*

steal *v.t./i.* voler (**from s.o.**, à qn.).

stealth *n.* **by ~**, furtivement. **~y** *a.* furtif.

steam *n.* vapeur *f.*; (*on glass*) buée *f.* —*v.t.* (*cook*) cuire à la vapeur; (*window*) embuer. —*v.i.* fumer. **~ iron**, fer à vapeur *m.* **~y** *a.* humide.

steam|er *n.* (*culin.*) cuit-vapeur

m.; (*also* ～**ship**) (bateau à) vapeur *m.*
steamroller *n.* rouleau compresseur *m.*
steel *n.* acier *m.*
steep[1] *v.t.* (*soak*) tremper. ～**ed in,** (*fig.*) imprégné de.
steep[2] *a.* raide, rapide; (*price: fam.*) excessif.
steeple *n.* clocher *m.*
steer[1] *n.* (ox) bouvillon *m.*
steer[2] *v.t.* diriger; (*ship*) gouverner; (*fig.*) guider. —*v.i.* (*in ship*) gouverner. ～**ing** *n.* (*auto.*) direction *f.* ～**ing-wheel** *n.* volant *m.*
stem[1] *n.* tige *f.*; (*of glass*) pied *m.* —*v.i.* ～ **from,** provenir de.
stem[2] *v.t.* (*stop*) contenir.
stench *n.* puanteur *f.*
stencil *n.* pochoir *m.*; (*for typing*) stencil *m.*
step *v.i.* marcher, aller. —*v.t.* ～ **up,** augmenter. —*n.* pas *m.*; (*stair*) marche *f.*; (*of train*) marchepied *m.*; (*action*) mesure *f.* ～**s,** (*ladder*) escabeau *m.* ～ **down,** (*resign*) démissionner; (*from ladder*) descendre. ～ **forward,** (faire un) pas en avant. ～ **up,** (*pressure*) augmenter. ～ **in,** (*intervene*) intervenir. ～**ladder** *n.* escabeau *m.*
step|brother *n.* demi-frère *m.* ～**daughter** *n.* belle-fille *f.* ～**father** *n.* beau-père *m.* ～**mother** *n.* belle-mère *f.* ～**sister** *n.* demi-sœur *f.* ～**son** *n.* beau-fils *m.*
stereo *n.* stéréo *f.*; (*record-player*) chaîne stéréo *f.* —*a.* stéréo invar.
stereotype *n.* stéréotype *m.* ～**d** *a.* stéréotypé.
steril|e *a.* stérile. ～**ity** *n.* stérilité *f.*
steriliz|e *v.t.* stériliser. ～**ation** *n.* stérilisation *f.*

sterling *n.* livre(s) sterling *f.* (*pl.*). —*a.* sterling *invar.*; (*silver*) fin; (*fig.*) excellent.
stern[1] *a.* sévère.
stern[2] *n.* (*of ship*) arrière *m.*
steroid *n.* stéroïde *m.*
stethoscope *n.* stéthoscope *m.*
stew *v.t./i.* cuire à la casserole. —*n.* ragoût *m.*
steward *n.* (*of club etc.*) intendant *m.*; (*on ship etc.*) steward *m.* ～**ess** *n.* hôtesse *f.*
stick[1] *n.* bâton *m.*; (*for walking*) canne *f.*
stick[2] *v.t.* (*glue*) coller; (*thrust*) enfoncer; (*put: fam.*) mettre; (*endure: sl.*) supporter. —*v.i.* (*adhere*) coller, adhérer; (*to pan*) attacher; (*remain: fam.*) rester; (*be jammed*) être coincé. ～ **at,** persévérer dans. ～ **out** *v.t.* (*head etc.*) sortir; (*tongue*) tirer; *v.i.* (*protrude*) dépasser. ～ **to,** (*promise etc.*) rester fidèle à. ～**ing-plaster** *n.* sparadrap *m.*
sticker *n.* autocollant *m.*
sticky *a.* poisseux; (*label, tape*) adhésif.
stiff *a.* raide; (*limb, joint*) ankylosé; (*tough*) dur; (*drink*) fort; (*price*) élevé; (*manner*) guindé.
stifle *v.t./i.* étouffer.
stile *n.* échalier *m.*
stiletto *a. & n.* ～**s,** ～ **heels** talons aiguille.
still *a.* immobile; (*quiet*) calme, tranquille. —*n.* silence *m.* —*adv.* encore, toujours; (*even*) encore; (*nevertheless*) tout de même.
stilted *a.* guindé.
stilts *n. pl.* échasses *f. pl.*
stimul|ate *v.t.* stimuler. ～**ant** *n.* stimulant *m.* ～**ation** *n.* stimulation *f.*

stimulus n. stimulant m.

sting n. piqûre f.; (organ) dard m. —v.t./i. piquer.

stingy a. avare (**with**, de).

stink n. puanteur f. —v.i. ~ (**of**), puer.

stint v.i. ~ **on**, lésiner sur. —n. (work) tour m.

stipulat|e v.t. stipuler. ~**ion** n. stipulation f.

stir v.t./i. (move) remuer; (excite) exciter. —n. agitation f. ~ **up**, (trouble etc.) provoquer.

stirrup n. étrier m.

stitch n. point m.; (in knitting) maille f.; (med.) point de suture m.; (muscle pain) point de côté m. —v.t. coudre.

stock n. réserve f.; (comm.) stock m.; (financial) valeurs f. pl.; (family) souche f.; (soup) bouillon m. —a. (goods) courant. —v.t. (shop etc.) approvisionner; (sell) vendre. —v.i. ~ **up**, s'approvisionner (**with**, de). ~**-taking** n. (comm.) inventaire m. **in** ~, en stock.

stockbroker n. agent de change m.

stocking n. bas m.

stockist n. stockiste m.

stockpile n. stock m. —v.t. stocker; (arms) amasser.

stocky a. trapu.

stoic n. stoïque m./f. ~**al** a. stoïque.

stoke v.t. (boiler, fire) alimenter.

stole n. (garment) étole f.

stomach n. estomac m.; (abdomen) ventre m. —v.t. (put up with) supporter. ~**-ache** n. mal à l'estomac or au ventre m.

stone n. pierre f.; (pebble) caillou m.; (in fruit) noyau m.; (weight) 6.350 kg. —a. de pierre. —v.t. lapider; (fruit) dénoyauter.

stool n. tabouret m.

stoop v.i. (bend) se baisser; (condescend) s'abaisser. —n. **have a** ~, être voûté.

stop v.t./i. arrêter (**doing**, de faire); (moving, talking) s'arrêter; (prevent) empêcher (**from**, de); (hole, leak, etc.) boucher; (of pain, noise, etc.) cesser; (stay: fam.) rester. —n. arrêt m.; (full stop) point m. ~ **off**, s'arrêter. ~ **up**, boucher. ~**-watch** n. chronomètre m.

stopgap n. bouche-trou m. —a. intérimaire.

stoppage n. arrêt m.; (of work) arrêt de travail m.; (of pay) retenue f.

stopper n. bouchon m.

storage n. (of goods, food, etc.) emmagasinage m. ~ **heater**, radiateur électrique à accumulation m.

store n. réserve f.; (warehouse) entrepôt m.; (shop) grand magasin m.; (Amer.) magasin m. —v.t. (for future) mettre en réserve; (in warehouse, mind) emmagasiner. ~**-room** n. réserve f.

storey n. étage m.

stork n. cigogne f.

storm n. tempête f., orage m. —v.t. prendre d'assaut. —v.i. (rage) tempêter. ~**y** a. orageux.

story n. histoire f.; (in press) article m.

stout a. corpulent; (strong) solide. —n. bière brune f.

stove n. (for cooking) cuisinière f.; (heater) poêle m.

stow v.t. ~ **away**, (put away) ranger; (hide) cacher. —v.i. voyager clandestinement.

stowaway n. passager, -ère clandestin(e) m., f.

straddle v.t. être à cheval sur.

straggle v.i. (lag behind) traîner

en désordre. ∿r n. traînard(e) m. (f.).

straight a. droit; (tidy) en ordre; (frank) franc. —adv. (in straight line) droit; (direct) tout droit. ∿ ahead or on, tout droit. ∿ away, tout de suite.

straighten v.t. (nail, situation, etc.) redresser; (tidy) arranger.

straightforward a. honnête; (easy) simple.

strain[1] n. (breed) race f.; (streak) tendance f.

strain[2] v.t. (rope, ears) tendre; (limb) fouler; (eyes) fatiguer; (muscle) froisser; (filter) passer; (vegetables) égoutter. —n. tension f.; (fig.) effort m. ∿ed a. forcé; (relations) tendu. ∿er n. passoire f.

strait n. détroit m. ∿s, détroit m.; (fig.) embarras m.

strand n. (thread) fil m., brin m.; (lock of hair) mèche f.

stranded a. (person) en rade; (ship) échoué.

strange a. étrange; (unknown) inconnu. ∿ly adv. étrangement.

stranger n. inconnu(e) m. (f.).

strangle v.t. étrangler.

strap n. (of leather etc.) courroie f.; (of dress) bretelle f.; (of watch) bracelet m. —v.t. attacher.

strategic a. stratégique.

strategy n. stratégie f.

stratum n. couche f.

straw n. paille f.

strawberry n. fraise f.

stray v.i. s'égarer; (deviate) s'écarter. —a. perdu; (isolated) isolé. —n. animal perdu m.

streak n. raie f., bande f.; (trace) trace f.; (period) période f.; (tendency) tendance f. —v.t. (mark) strier. —v.i. filer à toute allure. ∿y a. strié.

stream n. ruisseau m.; (current) courant m.; (flow) flot m.; (in schools) classe (de niveau) f. —v.i. ruisseler (with, de); (eyes, nose) couler.

streamer n. (of paper) serpentin m.; (flag) banderole f.

streamline v.t. rationaliser. ∿d a. (shape) aérodynamique.

street n. rue f. ∿ map, plan des rues m.

strength n. force f.; (of wall, fabric, etc.) solidité f.

strengthen v.t. renforcer.

strenuous a. énergique; (arduous) ardu; (tiring) fatigant.

stress n. accent m.; (pressure) pression f.; (med.) stress m. —v.t. souligner, insister sur.

stretch v.t. (pull taut) tendre; (arm, leg) étendre; (neck) tendre; (clothes) étirer; (truth etc.) forcer. —v.i. s'étendre; (of person, clothes) s'étirer. —n. étendue f.; (period) période f.; (of road) tronçon m. —a. (fabric) extensible.

stretcher n. brancard m.

strew v.t. (scatter) répandre; (cover) joncher.

stricken a. ∿ with, frappé or atteint de.

strict a. strict. ∿ly adv. strictement.

stride v.i. faire de grands pas. —n. grand pas m.

strident a. strident.

strife n. conflit(s) m. (pl.).

strike v.t. frapper; (blow) donner; (match) frotter; (gold etc.) trouver. —v.i. faire grève; (attack) attaquer; (clock) sonner. —n. (of workers) grève f.; (mil.) attaque f.; (find) découverte f. on ∿, en grève.

striker n. gréviste m./f.; (football) buteur m.

striking a. frappant.

string n. ficelle f.; (of violin, racket, etc.) corde f.; (of pearls) collier m.; (of lies etc.) chapelet m. —v.t. (thread) enfiler. ~ **bean**, haricot vert m.

stringent a. rigoureux.

strip[1] v.t./i. (undress) (se) déshabiller; (machine) démonter; (deprive) dépouiller. ~**per** n. strip-teaseuse f.; (solvent) décapant m. ~**-tease** n. strip-tease m.

strip[2] n. bande f. ~ **light**, néon m.

stripe n. rayure f., raie f. ~**d** a. rayé.

strive v.i. s'efforcer (**to**, de).

stroke[1] n. coup m.; (of pen) trait m.; (swimming) nage f.; (med.) attaque f., congestion f.

stroke[2] v.t. (with hand) caresser. —n. caresse f.

stroll v.i. flâner. —n. petit tour m. ~ **in**/etc., entrer/etc. tranquillement.

strong a. fort; (shoes, fabric, etc.) solide. ~**-box** n. coffre-fort m. ~**ly** adv. (greatly) fortement; (with energy) avec force; (deeply) profondément.

stronghold n. bastion m.

structur|e n. (of cell, poem, etc.) structure f.; (building) construction f. ~**al** a. structural; de (la) construction.

struggle v.i. lutter, se battre. —n. lutte f.; (effort) effort m. **have a** ~ **to**, avoir du mal à.

strum v.t. gratter de.

strut n. (support) étai m. —v.i. se pavaner.

stub n. bout m.; (of tree) souche f.; (counterfoil) talon m. —v.t. ~ **one's toe**, se cogner le doigt de pied. ~ **out**, écraser.

stubble n. (on chin) barbe de plusieurs jours f.; (remains of wheat) chaume m.

stubborn a. opiniâtre, obstiné. ~**ly** adv. obstinément. ~**ness** n. opiniâtreté f.

stubby a. (finger) épais; (person) trapu.

stuck a. (jammed) coincé. **I'm** ~, (for answer) je suis sec.

stud[1] n. clou m.; (for collar) bouton m. —v.t. clouter. ~**ded with**, parsemé de.

stud[2] n. (horses) écurie f.

student n. (univ.) étudiant(e) m. (f.); (schol.) élève m./f. —a. (restaurant, life, residence) universitaire.

studio n. studio m. ~ **flat**, studio m.

studious a. (person) studieux; (deliberate) étudié.

study n. étude f.; (office) bureau m. —v.t./i. étudier.

stuff n. substance f.; (sl.) chose(s) f. (pl.). —v.t. rembourrer; (animal) empailler; (cram) bourrer; (culin.) farcir; (block up) boucher; (put) fourrer. ~**ing** n. bourre f.; (culin.) farce f.

stuffy a. mal aéré; (dull: fam.) vieux jeu invar.

stumble v.i. trébucher. ~ **across** or **on**, tomber sur.

stump n. (of tree) souche f.; (of limb) moignon m.; (of pencil) bout m.

stun v.t. étourdir; (bewilder) stupéfier.

stunning a. (delightful: fam.) sensationnel.

stunt[1] v.t. (growth) retarder. ~**ed** a. (person) rabougri.

stunt[2] n. (feat: fam.) tour de force m.; (dangerous) cascade f. ~**man** n. cascadeur m.

stupefy v.t. abrutir; (amaze) stupéfier.

stupid a. stupide, bête. ~**ity** n. stupidité f. ~**ly** adv. bêtement.

sturdy a. robuste.

stutter v.i. bégayer. —n. bégaiement m.

sty[1] n. (pigsty) porcherie f.

sty[2] n. (on eye) orgelet m.

styl|e n. style m.; (fashion) mode f.; (sort) genre m.; (pattern) modèle m. —v.t. (design) créer. ~ist n. (of hair) coiffeu|r, -se m., f.

stylish a. élégant.

stylized a. stylisé.

stylus n. saphir m.

suave a. (urbane) courtois; (smooth: pej.) doucereux.

sub- pref. sous-, sub-.

subconscious a. & n. inconscient (m.), subconscient (m.). ~ly adv. inconsciemment.

subcontract v.t. sous-traiter.

subdivide v.t. subdiviser.

subdue v.t. (feeling) maîtriser; (country) subjuguer. ~d a. (weak) faible; (light) tamisé; (person, criticism) retenu.

subject[1] a. (state etc.) soumis. —n. sujet m.; (schol., univ.) matière f.; (citizen) ressortissant(e) m. (f.), sujet(te) m. (f.). ~ to, soumis à; (liable to, dependent on) sujet à.

subject[2] v.t. soumettre. ~ion n. soumission f.

subjective a. subjectif.

subjunctive a. & n. subjonctif (m.).

sublet v.t. sous-louer.

sublime a. sublime.

submarine n. sous-marin m.

submerge v.t. submerger. —v.i. plonger.

submi|t v.t./i. (se) soumettre (to, à). ~ssion n. soumission f.

subordinate[1] a. subalterne; (gram.) subordonné. —n. subordonné(e) m. (f.).

subordinate[2] v.t. subordonner (to, à).

subroutine n. sous-programme m.

subscribe v.t./i. verser (de l'argent) (to, à). ~ to, (loan, theory) souscrire à; (newspaper) s'abonner à, être abonné à. ~r n. abonné(e) m. (f.).

subscription n. souscription f.; abonnement m.; (membership dues) cotisation f.

subsequent a. (later) ultérieur; (next) suivant. ~ly adv. par la suite.

subside v.i. (land etc.) s'affaisser; (flood, wind) baisser. ~nce n. affaissement m.

subsidiary a. accessoire. —n. (comm.) filiale f.

subsid|y n. subvention f. ~ize v.t. subventionner.

subsist v.i. subsister. ~ence n. subsistance f.

substance n. substance f.

substandard a. de qualité inférieure.

substantial a. considérable; (meal) substantiel.

substantiate v.t. prouver.

substitut|e n. succédané m.; (person) remplaçant(e) m. (f.). —v.t. substituer (for, à). ~ion n. substitution f.

subterfuge n. subterfuge m.

subtitle n. sous-titre m.

subtle a. subtil. ~ty n. subtilité f.

subtract v.t. soustraire. ~ion n. soustraction f.

suburb n. faubourg m., banlieue f. ~s, banlieue f. ~an a. de banlieue.

subversive a. subversif.

subway n. passage souterrain m.; (Amer.) métro m.

succeed v.i. réussir (in doing, à faire). —v.t. (follow) succéder à. ~ing a. suivant.

success n. succès m.

successful a. réussi, couronné de succès; (*favourable*) heureux; (*in exam*) reçu.

succession n. succession f. **in ~,** de suite.

successive a. successif. **six ~ days,** six jours consécutifs.

successor n. successeur m.

succinct a. succinct.

succulent a. succulent.

succumb v.i. succomber.

such a. & pron. tel(le), tel(le)s; (*so much*) tant (de). —adv. si. **~ a book**/*etc.*, un tel livre/*etc.* **~ books**/*etc.*, de tels livres/*etc.* **~ courage**/*etc.*, tant de courage/ *etc.* **~ a big house,** une si grande maison. **~ as,** comme, tel que. **as ~,** en tant que tel.

suck v.t. sucer. **~ in** or **up,** aspirer.

sudden a. soudain, subit. **all of a ~,** tout à coup. **~ly** adv. subitement, brusquement. **~ness** n. soudaineté f.

suds n. pl. (*froth*) mousse de savon f.

sue v.t. poursuivre (en justice).

suede n. daim m.

suet n. graisse de rognon f.

suffer v.t./i. souffrir; (*loss, attack, etc.*) subir.

sufficient a. (*enough*) suffisamment de; (*big enough*) suffisant. **~ly** adv. suffisamment.

suffix n. suffixe m.

suffocat|e v.t./i. suffoquer. **~ion** n. suffocation f.; (*med.*) asphyxie f.

sugar n. sucre m. —v.t. sucrer. **~y** a. sucré.

suggest v.t. suggérer. **~ion** n. suggestion f.

suggestive a. suggestif. **be ~ of,** suggérer.

suicide n. suicide m. **commit ~,** se suicider.

suit n. costume m.; (*woman's*) tailleur m.; (*cards*) couleur f. —v.t. convenir à; (*of garment, style, etc.*) aller à; (*adapt*) adapter. **~able** a. qui convient (**for,** à), convenable. **~ably** adv. convenablement.

suitcase n. valise f.

suite n. (*rooms, retinue*) suite f.; (*furniture*) mobilier m.

sulk v.i. bouder. **~y** a. boudeur.

sullen a. maussade. **~ly** adv. d'un air maussade.

sulphur n. soufre m. **~ic** a. **~ic acid,** acide sulfurique m.

sultana n. raisin de Smyrne m.

sultry a. étouffant, lourd; (*fig.*) sensuel.

sum n. somme f.; (*in arithmetic*) calcul m. —v.t./i. **~ up,** résumer, récapituler; (*assess*) évaluer.

summar|y n. résumé m. —a. sommaire. **~ize** v.t. résumer.

summer n. été m. —a. d'été.

summit n. sommet m.

summon v.t. appeler; (*meeting, s.o. to meeting*) convoquer.

summons n. (*jurid.*) assignation f. —v.t. assigner.

sump n. (*auto.*) carter m.

sumptuous a. somptueux.

sun n. soleil m. **~-glasses** n. pl. lunettes de soleil f. pl. **~-roof** n. toit ouvrant m. **~-tan** n. bronzage m. **~-tanned** a. bronzé.

sunbathe v.i. prendre un bain de soleil.

sunburn n. coup de soleil m. **~t** a. brûlé par le soleil.

Sunday n. dimanche m.

sundial n. cadran solaire m.

sundr|y a. divers. **~ies** n. pl. articles divers m. pl.

sunflower n. tournesol m.

sunlight n. soleil m.

sunny a. ensoleillé.

sunrise n. lever du soleil m.

sunset n. coucher du soleil m.

sunshade n. (lady's) ombrelle f.; (awning) parasol m.

sunshine n. soleil m.

sunstroke n. insolation f.

super a. (sl.) formidable.

superb a. superbe.

superficial a. superficiel.

superfluous a. superflu.

superimpose v.t. superposer (**on**, à).

superintendent n. direc|teur, -trice m., f.; (of police) commissaire m.

superior a. & n. supérieur(e) (m. (f.)). **~ity** n. supériorité f.

superlative a. suprême. —n. (gram.) superlatif m.

supermarket n. supermarché m.

supernatural a. surnaturel.

superpower n. superpuissance f.

supersede v.t. supplanter.

supersonic a. supersonique.

superstiti|on n. superstition f. **~ous** a. superstitieux.

superstore n. hypermarché m.

supertanker n. pétrolier géant m.

supervis|e v.t. surveiller, diriger. **~ion** n. surveillance f. **~or** n. surveillant(e) m. (f.); (shop) chef de rayon m.; (firm) chef de service m.

supper n. dîner m.; (late at night) souper m.

supple a. souple.

supplement[1] n. supplément m. **~ary** a. supplémentaire.

supplement[2] v.t. compléter.

supplier n. fournisseur m.

suppl|y v.t. fournir; (equip) pourvoir; (feed) alimenter (**with**, en). —n. provision f.; (of gas etc.) alimentation f. **~ies**, (food) vivres m. pl.; (material) fournitures f. pl.

support v.t. soutenir; (family) assurer la subsistance de; (endure) supporter. —n. soutien m., appui m.; (techn.) support m. **~er** n. partisan(e) m. (f.); (sport) supporter m.

suppos|e v.t./i. supposer. **be ~ed to do**, être censé faire, devoir faire. **~ing he comes**, supposons qu'il vienne.

supposedly adv. soi-disant.

suppress v.t. (put an end to) supprimer; (restrain) réprimer; (stifle) étouffer. **~ion** n. suppression f.; répression f.

supreme a. suprême.

surcharge n. prix supplémentaire m.; (tax) surtaxe f.; (on stamp) surcharge f.

sure a. sûr. —adv. (Amer., fam.) pour sûr. **make ~ of**, s'assurer de. **make ~ that**, vérifier que. **~ly** adv. sûrement.

surety n. caution f.

surf n. (waves) ressac m. **~ing** n. surf m.

surface n. surface f. —a. superficiel. —v.t. revêtir. —v.i. faire surface; (fig.) réapparaître.

surfboard n. planche de surf f.

surfeit n. excès m. (**of**, de).

surge v.i. (of crowd) déferler; (of waves) s'enfler; (increase) monter. —n. (wave) vague f.; (rise) montée f.

surgeon n. chirurgien m.

surg|ery n. chirurgie f.; (office) cabinet m.; (session) consultation f. **~ical** a. chirurgical. **~ical spirit**, alcool à 90 degrés m.

surly a. bourru.

surmount v.t. surmonter.

surname n. nom de famille m.

surpass v.t. surpasser.

surplus n. surplus m. —a. en surplus.

surpris|e n. surprise f. —v.t. surprendre. **~ed** a. surpris (**at**, de). **~ing** a. surprenant.

surrender v.i. se rendre. —v.t. (hand over) remettre; (mil.) rendre. —n. (mil.) reddition f.

surround v.t. entourer; (mil.) encercler. ~**ing** a. environnant. ~**ings** n. pl. environs m. pl.; (setting) cadre m.

surveillance n. surveillance f.

survey[1] v.t. (review) passer en revue; (inquire into) enquêter sur; (building) inspecter. ~**or** n. expert (géomètre) m.

survey[2] n. (inquiry) enquête f.; inspection f.; (general view) vue d'ensemble f.

survival n. survie f.

surviv|e v.t./i. survivre (à). ~**or** n. survivant(e) m. (f.).

susceptible a. sensible (**to**, à). ~**to**, (prone to) prédisposé à.

suspect[1] v.t. soupçonner; (doubt) douter de.

suspect[2] n. & a. suspect(e) (m. (f.)).

suspen|d v.t. (hang, stop) suspendre; (licence) retirer provisoirement. ~**ded sentence**, condamnation avec sursis f. ~**sion** n. suspension f.; retrait provisoire m.

suspender n. jarretelle f. ~ **belt**, porte-jarretelles m.

suspense n. attente f.; (in book etc.) suspense m.

suspicion n. soupçon m.; (distrust) méfiance f.

suspicious a. soupçonneux; (causing suspicion) suspect. **be ~of**, (distrust) se méfier de. ~**ly** adv. de façon suspecte.

sustain v.t. supporter; (effort etc.) soutenir; (suffer) subir.

swab n. (pad) tampon m.

swallow[1] v.t./i. avaler. ~ **up**, (absorb, engulf) engloutir.

swallow[2] n. hirondelle f.

swamp n. marais m. —v.t. (flood, overwhelm) submerger. ~**y** a. marécageux.

swan n. cygne m.

swank n. (behaviour: fam.) épate f., esbroufe f.; (person: fam.) crâneu|r, -se m., f. —v.i. (show off: fam.) crâner.

swap v.t./i. (fam.) échanger. —n. (fam.) échange m.

swarm n. (of insects, people) essaim m. —v.i. four-miller. ~ **into** or **round**, (crowd) envahir.

swat v.t. (fly etc.) écraser.

sway v.t./i. (se) balancer; (influence) influencer. —n. balancement m.; (rule) empire m.

swear v.t./i. jurer (**to sth.**, de qch.). ~ **at**, injurier.

sweat n. sueur f. —v.i. suer. ~**shirt** n. sweat-shirt m. ~**y** a. en sueur.

sweater n. pull-over m.

swede n. rutabaga m.

Swed|e n. Suédois(e) m. (f.). ~**en** n. Suède f. ~**ish** a. suédois; n. (lang.) suédois m.

sweep v.t./i. balayer; (carry away) emporter, entraîner; (chimney) ramoner. —n. coup de balai m.; (curve) courbe f.; (movement) geste m., mouvement m.; (for chimneys) ramoneur m. ~ **out**, balayer. ~**er** n. (for carpet) balai mécanique m.; (football) arrière volant m.

sweet a. (not sour, pleasant) doux; (not savoury) sucré; (charming: fam.) gentil. —n. bonbon m.; (dish) dessert m.; (person) chéri(e) m. (f.). ~ **corn**, maïs m. ~ **pea**, pois de senteur m. ~**shop**, confiserie f. ~**ly** adv. gentiment. ~**ness** n. douceur f.; goût sucré m.

sweeten v.t. sucrer; (fig.) adoucir. ~**er** n. édulcorant m.

swell v.t./i. (increase) grossir;

(*expand*) (se) gonfler; (*of hand, face*) enfler. —*n.* (*of sea*) houle *f.* —*a.* (*fam.*) formidable. **~ing** *n.* (*med.*) enflure *f.*

swerve *v.i.* faire un écart.

swift *a.* rapide. —*n.* (*bird*) martinet *m.* **~ly** *adv.* rapidement. **~ness** *n.* rapidité *f.*

swill *v.t.* rincer; (*drink*) lamper. —*n.* (*pig-food*) pâtée *f.*

swim *v.i.* nager; (*be dizzy*) tourner. —*v.t.* traverser à la nage; (*distance*) nager. —*n.* baignade *f.* **go for a ~,** aller se baigner. **~mer** *n.* nageu|r, -se *m., f.* **~ming** *n.* natation *f.* **~ming-pool** *n.* piscine *f.* **~-suit** *n.* maillot (de bain) *m.*

swindle *v.t.* escroquer. —*n.* escroquerie *f.* **~r** *n.* escroc *m.*

swine *n. pl.* (*pigs*) pourceaux *m. pl.* —*n. invar.* (*person: fam.*) salaud *m.*

swing *v.t./i.* (se) balancer; (*turn round*) tourner; (*of pendulum*) osciller. —*n.* balancement *m.*; (*seat*) balançoire *f.*; (*of opinion*) revirement *m.* **(towards,** en faveur de); (*mus.*) rythme *m.* **in ~, round,** (*of person*) se retourner.

swirl *v.i.* tourbillonner. —*n.* tourbillon *m.*

Swiss *a.* suisse. —*n. invar.* Suisse(sse) *m.* (*f.*).

switch *n.* bouton (électrique) *m.*, interrupteur *m.*; (*shift*) changement *m.*, revirement *m.*; (*transfer*) transférer; (*exchange*) échanger (**for,** contre); (*reverse positions of*) changer de place. **~ trains/**etc., (*change*) changer de train/*etc.* —*v.i.* (*go over*) passer. **~ off,** éteindre. **~ on,** mettre, allumer.

switchboard *n.* (*telephone*) standard *m.*

Switzerland *n.* Suisse *f.*

swivel *v.t./i.* (faire) pivoter.

swoon *v.i.* se pâmer.

swoop *v.i.* (*bird*) fondre; (*police*) faire une descente, foncer. —*n.* (*police raid*) descente *f.*

sword *n.* épée *f.*

swot *v.t./i.* (*study: sl.*) bûcher. —*n.* (*sl.*) bûcheu|r, -se *m., f.*

sycamore *n.* sycomore *m.*

syllable *n.* syllabe *f.*

syllabus *n.* programme *m.*

symbol *n.* symbole *m.* **~ic(al)** *a.* symbolique. **~ism** *n.* symbolisme *m.*

symbolize *v.t.* symboliser.

symmetr|y *n.* symétrie *f.* **~ical** *a.* symétrique.

sympath|ize *v.i.* **~ with,** (*pity*) plaindre; (*fig.*) comprendre les sentiments de. **~r** *n.* sympathisant(e) *m.* (*f.*).

sympath|y *n.* (*pity*) compassion *f.*; (*fig.*) compréhension *f.*; (*solidarity*) solidarité *f.*; (*condolences*) condoléances *f. pl.* **be in ~y with,** comprendre, être en accord avec. **~etic** *a.* compatissant; (*fig.*) compréhensif.

symphon|y *n.* symphonie *f.* —*a.* symphonique. **~ic** *a.* symphonique.

symptom *n.* symptôme *m.*

synagogue *n.* synagogue *f.*

synchronize *v.t.* synchroniser.

syndicate *n.* syndicat *m.*

syndrome *n.* syndrome *m.*

synonym *n.* synonyme *m.* **~ous** *a.* synonyme.

synopsis *n.* résumé *m.*

syntax *n.* syntaxe *f.*

synthesis *n.* synthèse *f.*

synthetic *a.* synthétique.

syphilis *n.* syphilis *f.*

Syria *n.* Syrie *f.* **~n** *a. & n.* syrien(ne) (*m.* (*f.*)).

syringe *n.* seringue *f.*

syrup *n.* (*liquid*) sirop *m.*; (*treacle*)

mélasse raffinée f. **~y** a. sirupeux.

system n. système m.; (*body*) organisme m.; (*order*) méthode f. **~s analyst**, analyste-programmeu|r, -se m., f. **~s disk**, disque système m.

systematic a. systématique.

T

tab n. (*flap*) languette f., patte f.; (*loop*) attache f.; (*label*) étiquette f.

table n. table f. —v.t. présenter; (*postpone*) ajourner. ~ a. (*lamp, wine*) de table. **at ~**, à table. **lay** or **set the ~**, mettre la table. **~cloth** n. nappe f. **~mat** n. dessous-de-plat m. invar.; (*cloth*) set m. **~ tennis**, ping-pong m.

tablespoon n. cuiller à soupe f. **~ful** n. cuillerée à soupe f.

tablet n. (*of stone*) plaque f.; (*drug*) comprimé m.

taboo n. & a. tabou (m.).

tabulator n. tabulateur m.

tacit a. tacite.

taciturn a. taciturne.

tack n. (*nail*) broquette f.; (*stitch*) point de bâti m.; (*course of action*) voie f. —v.t. (*nail*) clouer; (*stitch*) bâtir; (*add*) ajouter. —v.i. (*naut.*) louvoyer.

tackle n. équipement m., matériel m.; (*football*) plaquage m. —v.t. (*problem etc.*) s'attaquer à; (*football player*) plaquer.

tacky a. poisseux, pas sec; (*shabby, mean: Amer.*) moche.

tact n. tact m. **~ful** a. plein de tact. **~fully** adv. avec tact. **~less** a. qui manque de tact.

tactic n. tactique f. **~s** n. & n. pl. tactique f. **~al** a. tactique.

tadpole n. têtard m.

tag n. (*label*) étiquette f.; (*end piece*) bout m.; (*phrase*) cliché m. —v.t. étiqueter; (*join*) ajouter. —v.i. **~ along**, (*fam.*) suivre.

tail n. queue f.; (*of shirt*) pan m. —v.t. (*follow*) filer. —v.i. **~ away** or **off**, diminuer. **~back** n. (*traffic*) bouchon m. **~gate** n. hayon arrière m.

tailor n. tailleur m. —v.t. (*garment*) façonner; (*fig.*) adapter. **~-made for,** (*fig.*) fait pour.

take v.t./i. prendre; (*carry*) (ap)porter (**to**, à); (*escort*) accompagner, amener; (*contain*) contenir; (*tolerate*) supporter; (*prize*) remporter; (*exam*) passer; (*choice*) faire; (*precedence*) avoir. **~ sth. from s.o.**, prendre qch. à qn. **~ sth. from a place**, prendre qch. d'un endroit. **~ s.o. home**, ramener qn. chez lui. **it ~s time/courage/etc. to**, il faut du temps/du courage/etc. pour. **~ apart**, démonter. **~ away**, (*object*) emporter; (*person*) emmener; (*remove*) enlever (**from**, à). **~-away** n. (*meal*) plat à emporter m.; (*shop*) restaurant qui fait des plats à emporter m. **~ back**, reprendre; (*return*) rendre; (*accompany*) raccompagner; (*statement*) retirer. **~ down**, (*object*) descendre; (*notes*) prendre. **~ in**, (*object*) rentrer; (*include*) inclure; (*cheat*) tromper; (*grasp*) saisir. **~ on**, (*task, staff, passenger, etc.*) prendre. **~ out**, sortir; (*stain etc.*) enlever. **~ over** v.t. (*factory, country, etc.*) prendre la direction de; (*firm: comm.*) racheter; v.i. (*of dictator*) prendre le pouvoir. **~over** n. (*pol.*) prise de pouvoir f.;

(comm.) rachat m. **~ part,** participer (in, à). **~ place,** avoir lieu. **~ to doing,** se mettre à faire. **~ up,** (object) monter; (hobby) se mettre à; (occupy) prendre; (resume) reprendre.

takings n. pl. recette f.

talcum n. **~ (powder),** talc m.

tale n. conte m.; (report) récit m.; (lie) histoire f.

talent n. talent m. **~ed** a. doué.

talk v.t./i. parler; (say) dire; (chat) bavarder. —n. conversation f., entretien m.; (words) propos m. pl.; (lecture) exposé m.

talkative a. bavard.

tall a. (high) haut; (person) grand.

tally v.i. correspondre (with, avec).

tambourine n. tambourin m.

tame a. apprivoisé; (dull) insipide. —v.t. apprivoiser; (lion) dompter.

tamper v.i. **~ with,** toucher à, tripoter; (text) altérer.

tampon n. (med.) tampon hygiénique m.

tan v.t./i. bronzer; (hide) tanner. —n. bronzage m. —a. marron clair invar.

tang n. (taste) saveur forte f.; (smell) odeur forte f.

tangent n. tangente f.

tangerine n. mandarine f.

tangible a. tangible.

tangle v.t. enchevêtrer. —n. enchevêtrement m. **become ~d,** s'enchevêtrer.

tank n. réservoir m.; (vat) cuve f.; (for fish) aquarium m.; (mil.) char m., tank m.

tankard n. chope f.

tanker n. camionciterne m.; (ship) pétrolier m.

tantaliz|e v.t. tourmenter. **~ing** a. tentant.

tantamount a. be **~ to,** équivaloir à.

tantrum n. crise de rage f.

tap[1] n. (for water etc.) robinet m. —v.t. (resources) exploiter; (telephone) mettre sur table d'écoute.

tap[2] v.t./i. frapper (doucement). —n. petit coup m.

tape n. ruban m.; (sticky) ruban adhésif m. **(magnetic) ~,** bande (magnétique) f. —v.t. (tie) attacher; (stick) coller; (record) enregistrer. **~-measure,** mètre (à) ruban m. **~ recorder,** magnétophone m.

taper n. (for lighting) bougie f. —v.t./i. (s')effiler. **~ off,** (diminish) diminuer.

tapestry n. tapisserie f.

tar n. goudron m. —v.t. goudronner.

target n. cible f.; (objective) objectif m. —v.t. prendre pour cible.

tariff n. (charges) tarif m.; (on imports) tarif douanier m.

Tarmac n. (P.) macadam (goudronné) m.; (runway) piste f.

tarnish v.t./i. (se) ternir.

tarpaulin n. bâche goudronnée f.

tarragon n. estragon m.

tart[1] a. acide.

tart[2] n. tarte f.; (prostitute; sl.) poule f. —v.t. **~ up,** (pej.; sl.) embellir (sans le moindre goût).

tartan n. tartan m. —a. écossais.

tartar n. tartre m. **~ sauce,** sauce tartare f.

task n. tâche f., travail m. **~ force,** détachement spécial m.

taste n. goût m. —v.t. (eat, enjoy) goûter; (try) goûter à; (perceive taste of) sentir le goût de. —v.i. **~ of** or **like,** avoir un goût de. **~less** a. sans goût; (fig.) de mauvais goût.

tasteful a. de bon goût. **~ly** adv. avec goût.

tasty a. savoureux.

tattoo v.t. tatouer. —n. tatouage m.

tatty a. (fam.) minable.

taunt v.t. railler. —n. raillerie f. ∿ing a. railleur.

Taurus n. le Taureau.

taut a. tendu.

tavern n. taverne f.

tawdry a. (showy) tape-à-l'œil invar.

tax n. taxe f., impôt m.; (on income) impôts m. pl. —v.t. imposer; (put to test: fig.) mettre à l'épreuve. ∿able a. imposable. ∿ation n. imposition f.; (taxes) impôts m. pl. ∿-free a. exempt d'impôts. ∿ inspector, inspecteur des impôts m. ∿ relief, dégrèvement fiscal m. ∿ return, déclaration d'impôts f.

taxi n. taxi m. —v.i. ∿ rank, station de taxi f.

taxpayer n. contribuable m./f.

tea n. thé m.; (snack) goûter m. ∿ towel n. torchon m.

teach v.t. apprendre (s.o. sth., qch. à qn.); (in school) enseigner (s.o. sth., qch. à qn.). —v.t. enseigner. ∿er n. professeur m.; (primary) institu|teur, -trice m., f.

teacup n. tasse à thé f.

teak n. (wood) teck m.

team n. équipe f.; (of animals) attelage m. —v.i. ∿ up, faire équipe (with, avec).

teapot n. théière f.

tear[1] v.t./i. (se) déchirer; (snatch) arracher (from, à); (rush) aller à toute vitesse. —n. déchirure f.

tear[2] n. larme f.

tease v.t. taquiner. —n. (person: fam.) taquin(e) m. (f.).

teaspoon n. petite cuiller f. ∿ful n. cuillerée à café f.

teat n. tétine f.

technical a. technique. ∿ity n.

détail technique m. ∿ly adv. techniquement.

technician n. technicien(ne) m. (f.).

technique n. technique f.

technolog|y n. technologie f. ∿ical a. technologique.

teddy a. ∿ bear, nounours m.

tedious a. fastidieux.

tee n. (golf) tee m.

teem[1] v.i. (swarm) grouiller (with, de).

teem[2] v.i. ∿ (with rain), pleuvoir à torrents.

teenage a. (d')adolescent. ∿d a. adolescent. ∿r n. adolescent(e) m. (f.).

teeter v.i. chanceler.

teeth|e v.i. faire ses dents. ∿ing troubles, (fig.) difficultés initiales f. pl.

telecommunications n. pl. télécommunications f. pl.

telegram n. télégramme m.

telegraph n. télégraphe m.

telepath|y n. télépathie f. ∿ic a. télépathique.

telephone n. téléphone m. —v.t. (person) téléphoner à; (message) téléphoner. —v.i. téléphoner. ∿ book, annuaire m. ∿ booth, cabine téléphonique f. ∿ call, coup de téléphone m. ∿ number, numéro de téléphone m.

telephoto a. ∿ lens, téléobjectif m.

telescop|e n. télescope m. —v.t./i. (se) télescoper. ∿ic a. télescopique.

teletext n. télétexte m.

televise v.t. téléviser.

television n. télévision f.

telex n. télex m./i. —v.t. envoyer par télex.

tell v.t. dire (s.o. sth., qch. à qn.); (story) raconter; (distinguish) distinguer. —v.i. avoir un effet;

(*know*) savoir. **~** of, parler de. **~ off,** (*fam.*) gronder.

teller n. (*in bank*) caiss|ier, -ière m., f.

telling a. révélateur.

telly n. (*fam.*) télé f.

temerity n. témérité f.

temp n. (*temporary employee*: *fam.*) intérimaire m./f. —v.i. faire de l'intérim.

temper n. humeur f.; (*anger*) colère f. —v.t. (*metal*) tremper; (*fig.*) tempérer. **lose one's ~,** se mettre en colère.

temperament n. tempérament m. **~al** a. capricieux; (*innate*) inné.

temperate a. tempéré.

temperature n. température f. **have a ~,** avoir (de) la fièvre *or* de la température.

template n. patron m.

temple[1] n. temple m.

temple[2] n. (*of head*) tempe f.

tempo n. tempo m.

temporal a. temporel.

temporar|y a. temporaire, provisoire. **~ily** adv. temporairement, provisoirement.

tempt v.t. tenter. **~ s.o. to do,** donner envie à qn. de faire. **~ation** n. tentation f. **~ing** a. tentant.

ten a. & n. dix (m.).

tenable a. défendable.

tenac|ious a. tenace. **~ity** n. ténacité f.

tenant /ˈtenənt/ n. locataire m./f.

tend[1] v.t. s'occuper de.

tend[2] v.i. **~ to,** (*be apt to*) avoir tendance à.

tendency n. tendance f.

tender[1] a. tendre; (*sore, painful*) sensible. **~ly** adv. tendrement. **~ness** n. tendresse f.

tender[2] v.t. offrir, donner. —v.i. faire une soumission. —n. (*comm.*) soumission f. **put sth.**

out to ~, faire un appel d'offres pour qch.

tendon n. tendon m.

tenement n. maison de rapport f., H.L.M. m./f.

tenet n. principe m.

tennis n. tennis m. —a. de tennis **~ shoes,** tennis m. pl.

tenor n. (*meaning*) sens général m.; (*mus.*) ténor m.

tense[1] n. (*gram.*) temps m.

tense[2] a. tendu. —v.t. (*muscles*) tendre, raidir. —v.i. (*of face*) se crisper.

tension n. tension f.

tent n. tente f.

tentacle n. tentacule m.

tentative a. provisoire; (*hesitant*) timide.

tenth a. & n. dixième (m./f.).

tenuous a. ténu.

tepid a. tiède.

term n. (*word, limit*) terme m.; (*of imprisonment*) temps; (*in school etc.*) trimestre m.; (*Amer.*) semestre m. **~s,** conditions f. pl. —v.t. appeler, **on good/bad ~s,** en bons/mauvais termes. **in the short/long ~,** à court/long terme. **come to ~s with sth.,** accepter qch.

terminal a. terminal, final; (*med.*) en phase terminale. —n. (*oil, computer*) terminal m.; (*rail.*) terminus m.; (*electr.*) borne f. (*air*) **~,** aérogare f.

terminate v.t. mettre fin à. —v.i. prendre fin. **~ion** n. fin f.

terminology n. terminologie f.

terminus n. terminus m.

terrace n. terrasse f.; (*houses*) rangée de maisons contiguës f.

terracotta n. terre cuite f.

terrain n. terrain m.

terrib|le a. affreux, atroce. **~y** adv. (*very*) terriblement.

terrier n. (*dog*) terrier m.

terrific a. (fam.) terrible. **~ally** adv. (very: fam.) terriblement; (very well: fam.) terriblement bien.

terrif|y v.t. terrifier. **be ~ied of,** avoir très peur de.

territorial a. territorial.

territory n. territoire m.

terror n. terreur f.

terroris|t n. terroriste m./f. **~m** n. terrorisme m.

terrorize v.t. terroriser.

terse a. concis, laconique.

test n. examen m., analyse f.; (of goods) contrôle m.; (of machine etc.) essai m.; (in school) interrogation f.; (of strength etc.: fig.) épreuve f. —v.t. examiner, analyser; (check) contrôler; (try) essayer; (pupil) donner une interrogation à; (fig.) éprouver. **driving ~,** (épreuve f. du) permis de conduire m. **~tube** n. éprouvette f.

testament n. testament m. **Old/New T~,** Ancien/Nouveau Testament m.

testicle n. testicule m.

testify v.t./i. témoigner (**to,** de). **~ that,** témoigner que.

testimony n. témoignage m.

testy a. grincheux.

tetanus n. tétanos m.

tetchy a. grincheux.

tether v.t. attacher.

text n. texte m.

textbook n. manuel m.

textile n. & a. textile (m.).

texture n. (of paper etc.) grain m.; (of fabric) texture f.

Thai a. & n. thaïlandais(e)(n. (f.)). **~land** n. Thaïlande f.

Thames n. Tamise f.

than conj. que, qu'*; (with numbers) de. **more/less ~ ten,** plus/moins de dix.

thank v.t. remercier. **~s** n. pl.

remerciements m. pl. **~ you!,** merci! **~s!,** (fam.) merci! **~s to,** grâce à.

thankful a. reconnaissant (**for,** de). **~ly** adv. (happily) heureusement.

that a. ce or cet*, cette. **those,** ces. **—pron.** ce or c'*, cela, ça. **~ (one),** celui-là, celle-là. **those (ones),** ceux-là, celles-là. —adv. si, aussi. —rel. pron. (subject) qui; (object) que, qu'*. —conj. que, qu'*. **~ boy,** ce garçon. **~ one,** celui-là, celle-là. **those ones,** ceux-là, celles-là. **~ is,** c'est. **~ is (to say),** c'est-à-dire. **after ~,** après ça or cela. **~ big,** grand comme ça. **~ many, ~ much,** tant que ça.

thatch n. chaume m. **~ed** a. en chaume. **~ed cottage,** chaumière f.

thaw v.t./i. (faire) dégeler; (snow) (faire) fondre. —n. dégel m.

the a. le or l'*, la or l'*, pl. les. **of ~, from ~,** du, de l'*, de la, pl. des. **to ~, at ~,** au, à l'*, à la, pl. aux.

theatre n. théâtre m.

theatrical a. théâtral.

theft n. vol m.

their a. leur, pl. leurs.

theirs poss. pron. le or la leur, les leurs.

them pron. les; (after prep.) eux, elles. **(to) ~,** leur. **I know ~,** je les connais.

theme n. thème m.

themselves pron. eux-mêmes, elles-mêmes; (reflexive) se; (after prep.) eux, elles.

then adv. alors; (next) ensuite, puis; (therefore) alors, donc. —a. d'alors. **from ~ on,** dès lors.

theolog|y n. théologie f. **~ian** n. théologien(ne) m. (f.).

theorem n. théorème m.

theor|y n. théorie f. **∼etical** a. théorique.

therapy n. thérapie f.

there adv. là; (with verb) y; (over there) là-bas. —int. allez. **he goes ∼**, il y va. **on ∼**, là-dessus. **∼ is**, **∼ are**, il y a; (pointing) voilà. **∼, ∼!**, allons, allons! **∼by** adv. de cette manière.

therefore adv. donc.

thermal a. thermique.

thermometer n. thermomètre m.

Thermos n. (P.) thermos m./f. invar. (P.).

thermostat n. thermostat m.

thesis n. thèse f.

they pron. ils, elles; (emphatic) eux, elles; (people in general) on.

thick a. épais; (stupid) bête; (friends: fam.) très lié. **∼ly** adv. (grow) dru; (spread) en couche épaisse. **∼ness** n. épaisseur f.

thicken v.t./i. (s')épaissir.

thief n. voleu|r, -se m., f.

thigh n. cuisse f.

thimble n. dé (à coudre) m.

thin a. mince; (person) maigre, mince; (sparse) clairsemé; (fine) fin. —v.t./i. (p.t. **thinned**) (liquid) (s')éclaircir. **∼ out**, (in quantity) (s')éclaircir. **∼ly** adv. (slightly) légèrement. **∼ner** n. diluant m.

thing n. chose f. **∼s**, (belongings) affaires f. pl.

think v.t./i. penser (about, of, à); (carefully) réfléchir (about, of, à); (believe) croire. **I ∼ so**, je crois que oui. **∼ better of it**, se raviser. **∼ nothing of**, trouver naturel de. **∼ of**, (hold opinion of) penser de. **∼ over**, bien réfléchir à. **∼er** n. penseu|r, -se m., f.

third a. troisième. —n. troisième m./f.; (fraction) tiers m. **T∼ World**, Tiers-Monde m.

thirst n. soif f. **∼y** a. be **∼y**, avoir soif.

thirteen a. & n. treize (m.). **∼th** a. & n. treizième (m./f.).

thirt|y a. & n. trente (m.). **∼ieth** a. & n. trentième (m./f.).

this a. ce or cet*, cette. **these**, ces. —pron. ce or c*, ceci. **∼ (one)**, celui-ci, celle-ci. **these (ones)**, ceux-ci, celles-ci. **∼ boy**, ce garçon; (with emphasis) ce garçon-ci. **∼ is a mistake**, c'est une erreur. **∼ is the book**, voici le livre. **∼ is my son**, je vous présente mon fils. **after ∼**, après ceci.

thistle n. chardon m.

thorn n. épine f.

thorough a. consciencieux; (deep) profond; (cleaning, washing) à fond. **∼ly** adv. (clean, study, etc.) à fond; (very) tout à fait.

though conj. bien que. —adv. (fam.) cependant.

thought n. pensée f.; (idea) idée f.

thoughtful a. pensif; (considerate) attentionné.

thoughtless a. étourdi.

thousand a. & n. mille (m. invar.). **∼s of**, des milliers de.

thrash v.t. rosser; (defeat) écraser.

thread n. (yarn & fig.) fil m.; (of screw) pas m. —v.t. enfiler.

threadbare a. râpé.

threat n. menace f.

threaten v.t./i. menacer (with, de).

three a. & n. trois (m.). **∼-dimensional** a. en trois dimensions.

thresh v.t. (corn etc.) battre.

threshold n. seuil m.

thrift n. économie f. **∼y** a. économe.

thrill n. émotion f., frisson m. —v.t. transporter (de joie). —v.i. frissonner (de joie). **be ∼ed**, être ravi. **∼er** n. livre or film à suspense m. **∼ing** a. excitant.

thriv|e v.i. prospérer. **he ∼es on it,** cela lui réussit. **∼ing** a. prospère.

throat n. gorge f. **have a sore ∼,** avoir mal à la gorge.

throb v.i. (wound) causer des élancements; (heart) palpiter; (fig.) vibrer. —n. (pain) élancement m.; palpitation f. **∼bing** a. (pain) lancinant.

thrombosis n. thrombose f.

throne n. trône m.

throng n. foule f. —v.t. (streets/etc.) se presser dans. —v.i. (arrive) affluer.

throttle n. (auto.) accélérateur m. —v.t. étrangler.

through prep. à travers; (during) pendant; (by means or way of, out of) par; (by reason of) grâce à, à cause de. —adv. à travers; (entirely) jusqu'au bout. —a. (train etc.) direct. **be ∼,** (finished) avoir fini. **come** or **go ∼,** (cross, pierce) traverser.

throughout prep. **∼ the country**/etc., dans tout le pays/etc. **∼ the day**/etc., pendant toute la journée/etc. —adv. (place) partout; (time) tout le temps.

throw v.t. jeter, lancer; (baffle: fam.) déconcerter. —n. jet m.; (of dice) coup m. **∼ away,** jeter. **∼ away** a. à jeter. **∼ off,** (get rid of) se débarrasser de. **∼ out,** jeter; (person) expulser; (reject) rejeter.

thrush n. (bird) grive f.

thrust v.t. pousser. —n. poussée f. **∼ into,** (put) enfoncer dans, mettre dans.

thud n. bruit sourd m.

thug n. voyou m., bandit m.

thumb n. pouce m. —v.t. (book) feuilleter.

thump v.t./i. cogner (sur); (of heart) battre fort. —n. grand coup m. **∼ing** a. (fam.) énorme.

thunder n. tonnerre m. —v.i. (weather, person, etc.) tonner.

thunderstorm n. orage m.

Thursday n. jeudi m.

thus adv. ainsi.

thwart v.t. contrecarrer.

thyme n. thym m.

thyroid n. thyroïde f.

tiara n. diadème m.

tic n. tic (nerveux) m.

tick¹ n. (sound) tic-tac m.; (mark) coche f.; (moment: fam.) instant m. —v.i. faire tic-tac. —v.t. (off), cocher. **∼ off,** (fam.) réprimander. **∼ over,** (engine, factory) tourner au ralenti.

tick² n. (insect) tique f.

ticket n. billet m.; (for bus, cloakroom, etc.) ticket m.; (label) étiquette f. **∼-office** n. guichet m.

tickle v.t. chatouiller; (amuse: fig.) amuser. —n. chatouillement m.

tidal a. qui a des marées. **∼ wave,** raz-de-marée m. invar.

tide n. marée f.; (of events) cours m. —v.t. **∼ over,** dépanner.

tid|y a. (room) bien rangé; (appearance, work) soigné; (methodical) ordonné; (amount: fam.) joli. —v.t./i. ranger. **∼ily** adv. avec soin. **∼iness** n. ordre m.

tie v.t. attacher, nouer; (a knot) faire; (link) lier. —v.i. (football) faire match nul; (in race) être ex aequo. —n. attache f.; (necktie) cravate f.; (link) lien m.; égalité (de points) f.; match nul m. **∼ up,** attacher; (money) immobiliser; (occupy) occuper.

tier n. étage m., niveau m.; (in stadium etc.) gradin m.

tiger n. tigre m.

tight a. (*clothes*) étroit, juste; (*rope*) tendu; (*lid*) solidement fixé; (*control*) strict; (*knot, collar, schedule*) serré; (*drunk: fam.*) ivre. —adv. (*hold, sleep, etc.*) bien; (*squeeze*) fort.

tighten v.t./i. (se) tendre; (*bolt etc.*) (se) resserrer; (*control etc.*) renforcer. **~ up on**, se montrer plus strict à l'égard de.

tightrope n. corde raide f.

tights n. pl. collant m.

tile n. (on wall, floor) carreau m.; (on roof) tuile f. —v.t. carreler; couvrir de tuiles.

till[1] v.t. (*land*) cultiver.

till[2] prep. & conj. = **until**.

till[3] n. caisse (enregistreuse) f.

tilt v.i./t. pencher. —n. (*slope*) inclinaison f.

timber n. bois (de construction) m.; (*trees*) arbres m. pl.

time n. temps m.; (*moment*) moment m.; (*epoch*) époque f.; (*by clock*) heure f.; (*occasion*) fois f.; (*rhythm*) mesure f. **~s**, (*multiplying*) fois f. pl. —v.t. choisir le moment de; (*measure*) minuter; (*sport*) chronométrer. **have a good ~**, s'amuser. **in ~**, à temps; (*eventually*) avec le temps. **a long ~**, longtemps. **on ~**, à l'heure. **what's the ~?**, quelle heure est-il? **~ bomb**, bombe à retardement f. **~-lag** n. décalage m. **~-limit** n. délai m. **~-scale** n. délais fixés m. pl.

timeless a. éternel.

timely a. à propos.

timer n. (for cooker etc.) minuteur m.; (on video) programmateur; (culin.) compte-minutes m. invar.; (with sand) sablier m.

timetable n. horaire m.

timid a. timide; (fearful) peureux. **~ly** adv. timidement.

timing n. (measuring) minutage

m.; (*moment*) moment m.; (of artist) rythme m.

tin n. étain m.; (*container*) boîte f. **~(plate)**, fer-blanc m. **~-opener** n. ouvre-boîte(s) m.

tinge v.t. teinter (**with**, de). —n. teinte f.

tingle v.i. (*prickle*) picoter. —n. picotement m.

tinker v.i. **~ (with)**, bricoler.

tinkle n. tintement m.; (*fam.*) coup de téléphone m.

tinsel n. cheveux d'ange m. pl.

tint n. teinte f.; (for hair) shampooing colorant m. —v.t. (*glass, paper*) teinter.

tiny a. tout petit.

tip[1] n. bout m.; (*cover*) embout m. **~ped cigarette**, cigarette (à bout) filtre f.

tip[2] v.t./i. (*tilt*) pencher; (*overturn*) (faire) basculer; (*pour*) verser; (*empty*) déverser; (*give money*) donner un pourboire à. —n. (*money*) pourboire m.; (*advice*) tuyau m.; (for rubbish) décharge f. **~-off**, prévenir. **~-off** n. tuyau m. (*pour prévenir*).

tire v.t./i. (se) fatiguer. **~ing** a. fatigant.

tired a. fatigué. **be ~ of**, en avoir assez de.

tiresome a. ennuyeux.

tissue n. tissu m.; (*handkerchief*) mouchoir en papier m. **~-paper** n. papier de soie m.

tit n. (*bird*) mésange f.

titbit n. friandise f.

titillate v.t. exciter.

title n. titre m.

titter v.i. rigoler.

to prep. à; (*towards*) vers; (of attitude) envers. —adv. **to France/etc.**, en France/etc. **to town**, en ville. **to Canada/etc.**, au Canada/etc. **to the baker's/etc.**, chez le boulanger/etc. **the**

road/**door**/ etc. **to**, là route/ porte/etc. **de to me/her/**etc., me/lui/etc. **to do**/ **sit**/etc., faire/s'asseoir/etc. **I wrote to tell her**, j'ai écrit pour lui dire. **ten to six**, (by clock) six heures moins dix. **go to and fro**, aller et venir.

toad n. crapaud m.

toadstool n. champignon (vénéneux) m.

toast n. pain grillé m., toast m.; (drink) toast m. —v.t. (bread) faire griller; (drink to) porter un toast à; (event) arroser. **∼er** n. grille-pain m. invar.

tobacco n. tabac m.

toboggan n. toboggan m.

today n. & adv. aujourd'hui (m.).

toddler n. tout(e) petit(e) enfant m.(f).

toe n. orteil m.; (of shoe) bout m.

toffee n. caramel m. **∼-apple** n. pomme caramélisée f.

together adv. ensemble; (at same time) en même temps. **∼ with**, avec.

toil v.i. peiner. —n. labeur m.

toilet n. toilettes f. pl.; (grooming) toilette f. **∼-paper** n. papier hygiénique m. **∼-roll** n. rouleau de papier hygiénique m. **∼ water**, eau de toilette f.

toiletries n. pl. articles de toilette m. pl.

token n. témoignage m., marque f.; (voucher) bon m.; (coin) jeton m. —a. symbolique.

tolerabl|e a. tolérable; (not bad) passable. **∼y** adv. (work, play, etc.) passablement.

toleran|t a. tolérant (of, à l'égard de). **∼ce** n. tolérance f.

tolerate v.t. tolérer.

toll[1] n. péage m.

toll[2] v.i. (of bell) sonner.

tom, **∼-cat** n. matou m.

tomato n. tomate f.

tomb n. tombeau m.

tombola n. tombola f.

tomboy n. garçon manqué m.

tombstone n. pierre tombale f.

tomorrow n. & adv. demain (m.). **∼ morning/night**, demain matin/soir.

ton n. tonne f. (= 1016 kg.). **(metric) ∼**, tonne f. (= 1000 kg.). **∼s of**, (fam.) des masses de.

tone n. ton m.; (of radio, telephone, etc.) tonalité f. —v.t. **∼ down**, atténuer. —v.i. **∼ in**, s'harmoniser (**with**, avec).

tongs n. pl. pinces f. pl.; (for sugar) pince f.; (for hair) fer m.

tongue n. langue f.

tonic n. (med.) tonique m. —a. (effect, accent) tonique. **∼ (water)**, tonic m.

tonight n. & adv. cette nuit (f.); (evening) ce soir (m.).

tonne n. (metric) tonne f.

tonsil n. amygdale f.

tonsillitis n. amygdalite f.

too adv. trop; (also) aussi. **∼ many** a. trop de; n. trop. **∼ much** a. trop de; adv. & n. trop.

tool n. outil m. **∼-bag** n. trousse à outils f.

toot n. coup de klaxon m. —v.t./i. **∼ (the horn)**, klaxonner.

tooth n. dent f.

toothache n. mal de dents m.

toothbrush n. brosse à dents f.

toothpaste n. dentifrice m.

toothpick n. cure-dent m.

top n. (highest point) sommet m.; (upper part) haut m.; (upper surface) dessus m.; (lid) couvercle m.; (of bottle, tube) bouchon m.; (of beer bottle) capsule f.; (of list) tête f. —a. (shelf etc.) du haut; (floor) dernier; (in rank) premier; (best) meilleur; (distinguished) émi-nent; (maximum) maximum.

—*v.t.* (*exceed*) dépasser; (*list*) venir en tête de. **on ~ of**, sur; (*fig.*) en plus de. **~ secret**, ultrasecret. **~ up**, remplir. **~ped with**, surmonté de; (*cream etc.*: *culin.*) nappé de.

topic *n.* sujet *m.*

topical *a.* d'actualité.

topple *v.t./i.* (faire) basculer.

topsy-turvy *adv. & a.* sens dessus dessous.

torch *n.* (*electric*) lampe de poche *f.*; (*flaming*) torche *f.*

torment[1] *n.* tourment *m.*

torment[2] *v.t.* tourmenter; (*annoy*) agacer.

tornado *n.* tornade *f.*

torpedo *n.* torpille *f.* —*v.t.* torpiller.

torrent *n.* torrent *m.*

torrid *a.* (*climate etc.*) torride; (*fig.*) passionné.

torso *n.* torse *m.*

tortoise *n.* tortue *f.*

tortoiseshell *n.* écaille *f.*

tortuous *a.* tortueux.

torture *n.* torture *f.*, supplice *m.* —*v.t.* torturer.

Tory *n.* tory *m.* —*a.* tory (*f. invar.*).

toss *v.t.* jeter, lancer; (*shake*) agiter. —*v.i.* s'agiter. **~ a coin** tirer à pile ou face (**for**, pour).

tot[1] *n.* petit(e) enfant *m.(f.)*; (*glass*: *fam.*) petit verre *m.*

tot[2] *v.t.* **~ up**, (*fam.*) additionner.

total *a.* total. —*n.* total *m.* —*v.t.* (*find total of*) totaliser; (*amount to*) s'élever à. **~ly** *adv.* totalement.

totalitarian *a.* totalitaire.

totter *v.i.* chanceler.

touch *v.t./i.* toucher; (*of ends, gardens, etc.*) se toucher; (*tamper with*) toucher à. —*n.* (*sense*) toucher *m.*; (*contact*) contact *m.*; (*of colour*) touche *f.*; (*football*) touche *f.* **a ~ of**, (*small amount*)

un peu de. **get in ~ with**, contacter. **~ down**, (*aviat.*) atterrir. **~-line** *n.* (ligne de) touche *f.* **~ on**, (*mention*) aborder. **~ up**, retoucher.

touchdown *n.* atterrissage *m.*

touching *a.* touchant.

touchy *a.* susceptible.

tough *a.* (*hard, difficult*) dur; (*strong*) solide; (*relentless*) acharné. **~ness** *n.* dureté *f.*; solidité *f.*

toughen *v.t.* (*strengthen*) renforcer; (*person*) endurcir.

toupee *n.* postiche *m.*

tour *n.* voyage *m.*; (*visit*) visite *f.*; (*by team etc.*) tournée *f.* —*v.t.* visiter. **on ~**, en tournée. **~ operator**, voyagiste *m.*

tourism *n.* tourisme *m.*

tourist *n.* touriste *m./f.* —*a.* touristique. **~ office**, syndicat d'initiative *m.*

tournament *n.* tournoi *m.*

tousle *v.t.* ébouriffer.

tout *v.i.* **~ (for)**, racoler. —*v.t.* (*sell*) revendre. —*n.* racoleu|r, -se *m.,f.*; revendeu|r, -se *m., f.*

tow *v.t.* remorquer. —*n.* remorque *f.* **on ~**, en remorque. **~ away**, (*vehicle*) (faire) enlever. **~ truck**, dépanneuse *f.*

toward(s) *prep.* vers; (*of attitude*) envers.

towel *n.* serviette *f.*; (*teatowel*) torchon *m.* **~ling** *n.* tissu-éponge *m.*

tower *n.* tour *f.* —*v.i.* **~ above**, dominer. **~ block**, tour *f.*, immeuble *m.*

town *n.* ville *f.* **~ hall**, hôtel de ville *m.*

toxic *a.* toxique.

toxin *n.* toxine *f.*

toy *n.* jouet *m.* —*v.i.* **~ with**, (*object*) jouer avec; (*idea*) caresser.

trace n. trace f. —v.t. suivre or retrouver la trace de; (draw) tracer; (with tracing-paper) décalquer; (relate) retracer.

tracing n. calque m. **~-paper** n. papier-calque m. invar.

track n. (of person etc.) trace f., piste f.; (path, race-track & of tape) piste f.; (on disc) plage f.; (of rocket etc.) trajectoire f.; (rail.) voie f. —v.t. suivre la trace or la trajectoire de. **keep ~ of**, suivre. **~ down**, (find) retrouver; (hunt) traquer. **~ suit**, survêtement m.; (with sweatshirt) jogging m.

tract[1] n. (land) étendue f.; (anat.) appareil m.

tract[2] n. (pamphlet) tract m.

tractor n. tracteur m.

trade n. commerce m.; (job) métier m.; (swap) échange m. —v.i. faire du commerce. —v.t. échanger. **~ deficit**, déficit commercial m. **~ in**, (used article) faire reprendre. **~-in** n. reprise f. **~ mark**, marque de fabrique f.; (name) marque déposée f. **~ union**, syndicat m. **~-unionist** n. syndicaliste m./f. **~r** n. négociant(e) m. (f.), commerçant(e) m. (f.).

trading n. commerce m. **~ estate**, zone industrielle f.

tradition n. tradition f. **~al** a. traditionnel.

traffic n. trafic m.; (on road) circulation f. —v.i. trafiquer (**in**, de). **~ jam**, embouteillage m. **~ lights** n. pl. feux (de circulation) m. pl. **~ warden**, contractuel(le) m. (f.).

tragedy n. tragédie f.

tragic a. tragique.

trail v.t./i. traîner; (of plant) ramper; (track) suivre. —n. (of powder etc.) traînée f.; (track) piste f.; (beaten path) sentier m. **~ behind**, traîner.

trailer n. remorque f.; (film) bande-annonce f.

train n. (rail.) train m.; (underground) rame f. —v.t. (instruct, develop) former; (sportsman) entraîner; (animal) dresser; (aim) braquer. —v.i. recevoir une formation; s'entraîner. **~ed** a. (skilled) qualifié; (doctor etc.) diplômé. **~er** n. (sport) entraîneur|r, -se m., f. **~ers**, (shoes) chaussures de sport f. pl. **~ing** n. formation f.; entraînement m.; dressage m.

trainee n. stagiaire m./f.

trait n. trait m.

traitor n. traître m.

tram n. tram(way) m.

tramp v.i. marcher (d'un pas lourd). —v.t. parcourir. —n. pas lourds m. pl.; (vagrant) clochard(e) m. (f.); (hike) randonnée f.

trample v.t./i. (**on**), piétiner; (fig.) fouler aux pieds.

trampoline n. trampoline m.

trance n. transe f.

tranquil a. tranquille. **~lity** n. tranquillité f.

tranquillizer n. (drug) tranquillisant m.

transaction n. transaction f.

transatlantic a. transatlantique.

transcript n. transcription f.

transfer[1] v.t. transférer; (power) faire passer. —v.i. être transféré.

transfer[2] n. transfert m.; (of power) passation f.; (image) décalcomanie f.; (sticker) autocollant m.

transform v.t. transformer. **~ation** n. transformation f. **~er** n. (electr.) transformateur m.

transfusion n. transfusion f.

transient a. transitoire.

transistor n. transistor m.

transit n. transit m.

transition n. transition f.

transitive a. transitif.

transitory a. transitoire.

translat|e v.t. traduire. **~ion** n. traduction f. **~or** n. traduc|teur, -trice m., f.

transmit v.t. (pass on etc.) transmettre; (broadcast) émettre. **~ssion** n. transmission f.; émission f. **~tter** n. émetteur m.

transparen|t a. transparent. **~cy** n. transparence f.; (photo.) diapositive f.

transplant¹ v.t. transplanter; (med.) greffer.

transplant² n. transplantation f.; greffe f.

transport¹ v.t. (carry, delight) transporter. **~ation** n. transport m.

transport² n. (of goods, delight, etc.) transport m.

transvestite n. travesti(e) m. (f.).

trap n. piège m. —v.t. (jam, pin down) coincer; (cut off) bloquer; (snare) prendre au piège.

trapdoor n. trappe f.

trapeze n. trapèze m.

trash n. (junk) saleté(s) f. (pl.); (refuse) ordures f. pl.; (nonsense) idioties f. pl.

trauma n. traumatisme m. **~tic** a. traumatisant.

travel v.i. voyager; (of vehicle, bullet, etc.) aller. —v.t. parcourir. —n. voyage(s) m. (pl.). **~ agent**, agent de voyage m. **~ler** n. voyageu|r, -se m., f. **~ler's cheque**, chèque de voyage m. **~ sickness**, mal des transports m.

travesty n. parodie f.

trawler n. chalutier m.

tray n. plateau m.; (on office desk) corbeille f.

treacherous a. traître.

treachery n. traîtrise f.

treacle n. mélasse f.

tread v.i. marcher (on, sur). —n. démarche f.; (sound) bruit m. de pas m. pl.; (of tyre) chape f. **~ sth. into**, (carpet) étaler qch. sur (avec les pieds).

treason n. trahison f.

treasure n. trésor m. —v.t. attacher une grande valeur à; (store) conserver. **~r** n. trésor|ier, -ière m., f.

treasury n. trésorerie f. **the T~**, le ministère des Finances.

treat v.t. traiter; (consider) considérer. —n. (pleasure) plaisir m., régal m.; (present) gâterie f.; (food) régal m. **~ s.o. to sth.**, offrir qch. à qn.

treatment n. traitement m.

treaty n. (pact) traité m.

treble a. triple. —v.t./i. tripler. —n. (voice: mus.) soprano m.

tree n. arbre m.

trek n. voyage pénible m.; (sport) randonnée f. —v.i. voyager (péniblement); (sport) faire de la randonnée.

trellis n. treillage m.

tremble v.i. trembler.

tremendous a. énorme; (excellent: fam.) fantastique. **~ly** adv. fantastiquement.

tremor n. tremblement m.

trench n. tranchée f.

trend n. tendance f.; (fashion) mode f. **~y** a. (fam.) dans le vent.

trespass v.i. s'introduire sans autorisation (on, dans). **~er** n. intrus(e) m. (f.).

tresses n. pl. chevelure f.

trestle n. tréteau m. **~-table** n. table à tréteaux f.

trial n. (jurid.) procès m.; (test) essai m.; (ordeal) épreuve f. **go on ~**, passer en jugement. **~ run**, galop d'essai m.

triang|le n. triangle m. **~ular** a. triangulaire.

trib|e n. tribu f. **~al** a. tribal.

tribunal n. tribunal m.; (mil.) commission f.

tributary n. affluent m.

tribute n. tribut m. **pay ~ to**, rendre hommage à.

trick n. astuce f., ruse f.; (joke, feat of skill) tour m.; (habit) manie f. —v.t. tromper.

trickery n. ruse f.

trickle v.i. dégouliner. —n. filet m.; (fig.) petit nombre m.

tricky a. (crafty) rusé; (problem) délicat, difficile.

tricycle n. tricycle m.

trifle n. bagatelle f.; (cake) diplomate m. **a ~**, (small amount) un peu.

trigger n. (of gun) gâchette f., détente f. —v.t. **~ (off)**, (initiate) déclencher.

trim a. net, soigné; (figure) svelte. —v.t. (cut) couper légèrement; (hair) rafraîchir; (budget) réduire. —n. (cut) coupe légère f.; (decoration) garniture f. **~ming(s)** n. (pl.) garniture(s) f. (pl.).

Trinity n. Trinité f.

trinket n. colifichet m.

trio n. trio m.

trip v.t./i. (faire) trébucher —n. (journey) voyage m.; (outing) excursion f.; (stumble) faux pas m.

tripe n. (food) tripes f. pl.; (nonsense: sl.) bêtises f. pl.

triple a. triple. —v.t./i. tripler. **~ts** n. pl. triplé(e)s m. (f.) pl.

tripod n. trépied m.

trite a. banal.

triumph n. triomphe m. —v.i. triompher (over, de). **~ant** a. triomphant, triomphal.

trivial a. insignifiant.

trolley n. chariot m. **(tea-)~**, table roulante f.

trombone n. (mus.) trombone m.

troop n. bande f. **~s**, (mil.) troupes f. pl. —v.i. **~ in/out**, entrer/sortir en bande.

trophy n. trophée m.

tropic n. tropique m. **~s**, tropiques m. pl. **~al** a. tropical.

trot n. trot m. —v.i. trotter. **~ out**, (produce: fam.) sortir; (state: fam.) formuler.

trouble n. ennui(s) m. (pl.), difficulté(s) f. (pl.); (pains, effort) mal m., peine f. **~(s)**, (unrest) conflits m. pl. —v.t. (bother) (se) déranger; (worry) ennuyer. **be in ~**, avoir des ennuis. **what's the ~?**, quel est le problème? **~-maker** n. provoca|teur, -trice m., f.

troublesome a. pénible.

trough n. (drinking) abreuvoir m.; (feeding) auge f. **~ (of low pressure)**, dépression f.

troupe n. (theatre) troupe f.

trousers n. pl. pantalon m. **short ~**, culotte courte f.

trout n. invar. truite f.

trowel n. (garden) déplantoir m.; (for mortar) truelle f.

truan|t n. absentéiste m./f.; (schol.) élève absent(e) sans permission m.(f.). **play ~t**, sécher les cours.

truce n. trêve f.

truck n. (lorry) camion m.; (cart) chariot m.; (rail.) wagon m., plateforme f. **~-driver** n. camionneur m.

trudge v.i. se traîner.

true a. vrai; (accurate) exact; (faithful) fidèle.

truffle n. truffe f.

truly adv. vraiment; (faithfully) fidèlement; (truthfully) sincèrement.

trump n. atout m. —v.t. **~ up**, inventer. **~ card**, atout m.

trumpet n. trompette f.

trundle v.t./i. rouler bruyamment.

trunk n. (of tree, body) tronc m.; (of elephant) trompe f.; (box) malle f. ~s, (for swimming) slip de bain m.

truss n. (med.) bandage herniaire m. —v.t. (fowl) trousser.

trust n. confiance f.; (association) trust m. —v.t. avoir confiance en. —v.i. ~ in or to, s'en remettre à. on ~, de confiance. ~ s.o. with, confier à qn.

trustee n. administra|teur, -trice m., f.

truth n. vérité f. ~ful a. (account etc.) véridique; (person) qui dit la vérité.

try v.t./i. essayer; (be a strain on) éprouver; (jurid.) juger. —n. (attempt) essai m.; (Rugby) essai m. ~ on, essayer. ~ to do, essayer de faire.

T-shirt n. tee-shirt m.

tub n. baquet m., cuve f.; (bath: fam.) baignoire f.

tuba n. tuba m.

tubby a. dodu.

tube n. tube m.; (railway: fam.) métro m.; (in tyre) chambre à air f.

tuberculosis n. tuberculose f.

tubular a. tubulaire.

tuck n. (fold) rempli m., (re)pli m. —v.t. (put away, place) ranger; (hide) cacher. —v.i. ~ in or into, (eat: sl.) attaquer. ~ in, (shirt) rentrer; (person) border.

Tuesday n. mardi m.

tuft n. (of hair etc.) touffe f.

tug v.t. tirer fort (sur). —v.i. tirer fort. —n. (boat) remorqueur m. ~ of war, jeu de la corde tirée f.

tuition n. cours m. pl.

tulip n. tulipe f.

tumble v.i. (fall) dégringoler. —n. chute f. ~-drier n. séchoir à linge (à air chaud) m.

tumbler n. gobelet m.

tummy n. (fam.) ventre m.

tumour n. tumeur f.

tumult n. tumulte m. ~uous a. tumultueux.

tuna n. invar. thon m.

tune n. air m. —v.t. (engine) régler; (mus.) accorder. —v.i. ~ in (to), (radio, TV) écouter. be in ~/out of ~, (instrument) être accordé/désaccordé; (singer) chanter juste/faux.

tunic n. tunique f.

Tunisia n. Tunisie f. ~n a. & n. tunisien(ne) (m. (f.)).

tunnel n. tunnel m.; (in mine) galerie f.

turban n. turban m.

turbine n. turbine f.

turbo n. turbo m.

turbulen|t a. turbulent. ~ce n. turbulence f.

turf n. gazon m. —v.t. ~ out, (sl.) jeter dehors.

Turk n. Turc m., Turque f. ~ey n. Turquie f. ~ish a. turc; n. (lang.) turc m.

turkey n. dinde f.

turn v.t./i. tourner; (of person) (to other side) retourner; (change) (se) transformer (into, en); (become) devenir; (deflect) détourner; (milk) tourner. —n. tour m.; (in road) tournant m.; (of mind, events) tournure f.; (illness: fam.) crise f. in ~, à tour de rôle. take ~s, se relayer. ~ away v.i. se détourner; v.t. (avert) détourner; (refuse) refuser; (send back) renvoyer. ~ back v.i. (return) revenir; (vehicle) faire demi-tour; v.t. (fold) rabattre. ~ down, refuser; (fold) rabattre; (reduce) baisser. ~ off, (light etc.) éteindre; (engine) arrêter; (tap) fermer; (of driver) tourner. ~-off n. (auto.) embranchement m. ~

on, (*light etc.*) allumer; (*engine*) allumer; (*tap*) ouvrir; ~ **out** *v.t.* (*light*) éteindre; (*empty*) vider; (*produce*) produire; *v.i.* (*transpire*) s'avérer; (*come. fam.*) venir. ~ **over,** (se) retourner. ~ **round,** (*person*) se retourner. ~**-round** *n.* revirement *m.* ~ **up** *v.i.* arriver; (*be found*) se retrouver; *v.t.* (*find*) déterrer; (*collar*) remonter. ~**-up** *n.* (*of trousers*) revers *m.*

turning *n.* rue (latérale) *f.*; (*bend*) tournant *m.* ~**-point** *n.* tournant *m.*

turnip *n.* navet *m.*

turnover *n.* (*comm.*) chiffre d'affaires *m.*

turnstile *n.* (*gate*) tourniquet *m.*

turntable *n.* (*for record*) platine *f.*

turpentine *n.* térébenthine *f.*

turquoise *a.* turquoise *invar.*

turret *n.* tourelle *f.*

turtle *n.* tortue (de mer) *f.* ~**-neck** *a.* à col montant, roulé.

tusk *n.* (*tooth*) défense *f.*

tussle *n.* bagarre *f.*, lutte *f.*

tutor *n.* précep|teur, -trice *m.,f.*; (*univ.*) direc|teur, -trice d'études *m., f.*

TV *n.* télé *f.*

twang *n.* (*son: mus.*) pincement *m.*; (*in voice*) nasillement *m.* —*v.t./i.* (faire) vibrer.

tweed *n.* tweed *m.*

tweezers *n. pl.* pince (à épiler) *f.*

twel|ve *a. & n.* douze (*m.*). ~**fth** *a. & n.* douzième (*m./f.*). ~**ve (o'clock)** midi *m. or* minuit *m.*

twent|y *a. & n.* vingt (*m.*). ~**ieth** *a. & n.* vingtième (*m./f.*).

twice *adv.* deux fois.

twiddle *v.t./i.* ~ (**with**), (*fiddle with*) tripoter.

twig¹ *n.* brindille *f.*

twig² *v.t./i.* (*fam.*) piger.

twilight *n.* crépuscule *m.*

twin *n. & a.* jum|eau, -elle (*m., f.*).

twine *n.* ficelle *f.*

twinge *n.* élancement *m.*; (*remorse*) remords *m.*

twinkle *v.i.* (*star etc.*) scintiller; (*eye*) pétiller. —*n.* scintillement *m.*; pétillement *m.*

twirl *v.t./i.* (faire) tournoyer.

twist *v.t.* tordre; (*weave together*) entortiller; (*roll*) enrouler; (*distort*) déformer. —*v.i.* (*rope etc.*) s'entortiller; (*road*) zigzaguer. —*n.* torsion *f.*; (*in rope*) tortillon *m.*; (*in road*) tournant *m.*; (*of events*) tournure *f.*

twit *n.* (*fam.*) idiot(e) *m.* (*f.*).

twitch *v.t./i.* (se) contracter nerveusement. —*n.* (*tic*) tic *m.*; (*jerk*) secousse *f.*

two *a. & n.* deux (*m.*).

tycoon *n.* magnat *m.*

type *n.* (*example*) type *m.*; (*kind*) genre *m.*, sorte *f.*; (*person: fam.*) type *m.*; (*print*) caractères *m. pl.* —*v.t./i.* (*write*) taper (à la machine).

typewriter *n.* machine à écrire *f.*

typhoid *n.* ~ (**fever**), typhoïde *f.*

typhoon *n.* typhon *m.*

typical *a.* typique. ~**ly** *adv.* typiquement.

typing *n.* dactylo(graphie) *f.*

typist *n.* dactylo *f.*

tyrann|y *n.* tyrannie *f.* ~**ical** *a.* tyrannique.

tyrant *n.* tyran *m.*

tyre *n.* pneu *m.*

U

udder *n.* pis *m.*, mamelle *f.*

UFO *n.* OVNI *m.*

Uganda *n.* Ouganda *m.*

ugly *a.* laid.

UK *abbr. see* **United Kingdom.**

ulcer n. ulcère m.

ultimate a. dernier, ultime; (*definitive*) définitif; (*basic*) fondamental. **~ly** adv. à la fin; (*in the last analysis*) en fin de compte.

ultimatum n. ultimatum m.

ultrasound n. ultrason m.

ultraviolet a. ultraviolet.

umbilical a. **~ cord**, cordon ombilical m.

umbrella n. parapluie m.

umpire n. (*sport*) arbitre m. —v.t. arbitrer.

umpteen a. (*many: sl.*) un tas de. **~th** a. (*fam.*) énième.

UN abbr. (*United Nations*) ONU f.

un- pref. in-, dé(s)-, non, peu, mal, sans.

unable a. incapable; (*through circumstances*) dans l'impossibilité (**to do**, de faire).

unacceptable a. inacceptable.

unaccustomed a. inaccoutumé. **~ to**, peu habitué à.

unadulterated a. (*sheer*) pur.

unaided a. sans aide.

unanim|ous a. unanime. **~ity** n. unanimité f. **~ously** adv. à l'unanimité.

unarmed a. non armé.

unattainable a. inaccessible.

unattended a. (*laissé*) sans surveillance.

unattractive a. peu séduisant, laid; (*offer*) peu intéressant.

unauthorized a. non autorisé.

unavailable a. pas disponible.

unavoidab|le a. inévitable. **~y** adv. inévitablement.

unaware a. **be ~ of**, ignorer. **~s** adv. au dépourvu.

unbalanced a. déséquilibré.

unbearable a. insupportable.

unbeat|able a. imbattable. **~en** a. non battu.

unbelievable a. incroyable.

unbiased a. impartial.

unblock v.t. déboucher.

unborn a. futur, à venir.

unbounded a. illimité.

unbreakable a. incassable.

unbroken a. (*intact*) intact; (*continuous*) continu.

unbutton v.t. déboutonner.

uncanny a. étrange.

uncertain a. incertain. **be ~ whether**, ne pas savoir exactement si (**to do**, on doit faire). **~ty** n. incertitude f.

unchanged a. inchangé.

uncivilized a. barbare.

uncle n. oncle m.

uncomfortable a. (*thing*) peu confortable; (*unpleasant*) désagréable. **feel** or **be ~**, (*person*) être mal à l'aise.

uncommon a. rare.

uncompromising a. intransigeant.

unconcerned a. (*indifferent*) indifférent (**by**, à).

unconditional a. inconditionnel.

unconscious a. sans connaissance, inanimé; (*not aware*) inconscient (**of**, de) —n. inconscient m. **~ly** adv. inconsciemment.

unconventional a. peu conventionnel.

uncooperative a. peu coopératif.

uncork v.t. déboucher.

uncouth a. grossier.

uncover v.t. découvrir.

undecided a. indécis.

undeniable a. incontestable.

under prep. sous; (*less than*) moins de; (*according to*) selon. —adv. au-dessous. **~ age**, mineur. **~ it/there**, là-dessous. **~side** n. dessous m.

undercarriage n. (*aviat.*) train d'atterrissage m.

underclothes n. pl. sous-vêtements m. pl.

undercoat n. (of paint) couche de fond f.

undercover a. secret.

undercut v.t. (comm.) vendre moins cher que.

underdeveloped a. sous-développé.

underdog n. (pol.) opprimé(e) m. (f.); (socially) déshérité(e) m. (f.).

underdone a. pas assez cuit; (steak) saignant.

underestimate v.t. sous-estimer.

underfed a. sous-alimenté.

undergo v.t. subir.

undergraduate n. étudiant(e) m. (f.).

underground[1] adv. sous terre.

underground[2] a. souterrain; (secret) clandestin. —n. (rail.) métro m.

undergrowth n. sous-bois m. invar.

underhand a. sournois.

underlying a. fondamental.

underline v.t. souligner.

undermine v.t. miner.

underneath prep. sous. —adv. (en) dessous.

underpaid a. sous-payé.

underpants n. pl. slip m.

underpass n. (for cars, people) passage souterrain m.

underprivileged a. défavorisé.

underrate v.t. sous-estimer.

underskirt n. jupon m.

understand v.t./i. comprendre. ∼**able** a. compréhensible. ∼**ing** a. compréhensif; n. compréhension f.; (agreement) entente f.

understatement n. litote f.

understudy n. doublure f.

undertak|e v.t. entreprendre; (responsibility) assumer. ∼**e to**, s'engager à. ∼**ing** n. (task) entreprise f.; (promise) promesse f.

undertaker n. entrepreneur de pompes funèbres m.

undervalue v.t. sous-évaluer.

underwater a. sous-marin. —adv. sous l'eau.

underwear n. sous-vêtements m. pl.

underworld n. milieu m.

undeserved a. immérité.

undies n. pl. (female underwear; fam.) dessous m. pl.

undignified a. sans dignité.

undisputed a. incontesté.

undo v.t. défaire, détacher; (a wrong) réparer.

undoubted a. indubitable. ∼**ly** adv. indubitablement.

undress v.t./i. (se) déshabiller. get ∼**ed**, se déshabiller.

undue a. excessif. ∼**ly** adv. excessivement.

undulate v.i. onduler.

unearth v.t. déterrer.

unearthly a. mystérieux. ∼ hour, (fam.) heure indue f.

uneasy a. (ill at ease) mal à l'aise; (worried) inquiet; (situation) difficile.

uneducated a. (person) inculte; (speech) populaire.

unemploy|ed a. en chômage. ∼**ment** n. chômage m. ∼**ment benefit**, allocations de chômage f. pl.

unending a. sans fin.

unequal a. inégal. ∼**led** a. inégalé.

uneven a. inégal.

uneventful a. sans incident.

unexpected a. inattendu, imprévu. ∼**ly** adv. subitement; (arrive) à l'improviste.

unfailing a. constant, continuel; (loyal) fidèle.

unfair a. injuste. ∼**ness** n. injustice f.

unfaithful a. infidèle.

unfamiliar a. inconnu. be ∼ with, ne pas connaître.

unfashionable *a.* (*clothes*) démodé. **it's ~ to,** ce n'est pas à la mode de.

unfasten *v.t.* défaire.

unfavourable *a.* défavorable.

unfeeling *a.* insensible.

unfinished *a.* inachevé.

unfit *a.* (*med.*) peu en forme; (*unsuitable*) impropre (**for,** à). **~ to,** (*unable*) pas en état de.

unfold *v.t.* déplier; (*expose*) exposer. —*v.i.* se dérouler.

unforeseen *a.* imprévu.

unforgettable *a.* inoubliable.

unforgivable *a.* inexcusable.

unfortunate *a.* malheureux; (*event*) fâcheux. **~ly** *adv.* malheureusement.

unfounded *a.* sans fondement.

unfriendly *a.* peu amical.

ungainly *a.* gauche.

ungrateful *a.* ingrat.

unhapp|y *a.* malheureux, triste; (*not pleased*) mécontent (**with,** de). **~iness** *n.* tristesse *f.*

unharmed *a.* sain et sauf.

unhealthy *a.* (*climate etc.*) malsain; (*person*) en mauvaise santé.

unhook *v.t.* décrocher; (*dress*) dégrafer.

unhoped *a.* **~ for,** inespéré.

unhurt *a.* indemne.

unicorn *n.* licorne *f.*

uniform *n.* uniforme *m.* —*a.* uniforme. **~ity** *n.* uniformité *f.* **~ly** *adv.* uniformément.

unif|y *v.t.* unifier. **~ication** *n.* unification *f.*

unilateral *a.* unilatéral.

unimaginable *a.* inimaginable.

unimportant *a.* peu important.

uninhabited *a.* inhabité.

unintentional *a.* involontaire.

uninterest|ed *a.* indifférent (**in,** à). **~ing** *a.* peu intéressant.

union *n.* union *f.*; (*trade union*) syndicat *m.* **~ist** *n.* syndiqué(e) *m.* (*f.*). **U~ Jack,** drapeau britannique *m.*

unique *a.* unique. **~ly** *adv.* exceptionnellement.

unisex *a.* unisexe.

unison *n.* **in ~,** à l'unisson.

unit *n.* unité *f.*; (*of furniture etc.*) élément *m.,* bloc *m.* **~ trust,** (*équivalent d'une*) SICAV *f.*

unite *v.t./i.* (s')unir. **U~d Kingdom,** Royaume-Uni *m.* **U~d Nations,** Nations Unies *f. pl.* **U~d States (of America),** États-Unis (d'Amérique) *m. pl.*

unity *n.* unité *f.*; (*harmony: fig.*) harmonie *f.*

universal *a.* universel.

universe *n.* univers *m.*

university *n.* université *f.*

unjust *a.* injuste.

unkempt *a.* négligé.

unkind *a.* pas gentil, méchant. **~ly** *adv.* méchamment.

unknowingly *adv.* sans le savoir, inconsciemment.

unknown *a.* inconnu. —*n.* **the ~,** l'inconnu *m.*

unleash *v.t.* déchaîner.

unless *conj.* à moins que.

unlike *a.* (*brothers etc.*) différents. —*prep.* à la différence de; (*different from*) très différent de.

unlikel|y *a.* improbable. **~ihood** *n.* improbabilité *f.*

unlimited *a.* illimité.

unload *v.t.* décharger.

unlock *v.t.* ouvrir.

unlucky *a.* malheureux; (*number*) qui porte malheur.

unmarried *a.* célibataire.

unmask *v.t.* démasquer.

unmistakable *a.* (*voice etc.*) facilement reconnaissable; (*clear*) très net.

unmoved *a.* indifférent (**by,** à), insensible (**by,** à).

unnatural *a.* pas naturel.

unnecessary a. inutile; (*superfluous*) superflu.

unnerve v.t. troubler.

unnoticed a. inaperçu.

unobtainable n. impossible à obtenir.

unobtrusive a. discret.

unofficial a. officieux.

unorthodox a. peu orthodoxe.

unpack v.t. (*suitcase etc.*) défaire; (*contents*) déballer. —v.i. défaire sa valise.

unpalatable a. (*food, fact, etc.*) désagréable.

unparalleled a. incomparable.

unpleasant a. désagréable (**to**, avec).

unplug v.t. (*electr.*) débrancher; (*unblock*) déboucher.

unpopular a. impopulaire. ∼ **with**, mal vu de.

unprecedented a. sans précédent.

unpredictable a. imprévisible.

unprepared a. non préparé; (*person*) qui n'a rien préparé. **be** ∼ **for**, (*not expect*) ne pas s'attendre à.

unpretentious a. sans prétention(s).

unprofessional a. (*work*) d'amateur; (*conduct*) contraire au code professionel.

unqualified a. non diplômé; (*success etc.*) total.

unquestionabl|e a. incontestable. **∼y** adv. incontestablement.

unravel v.t. démêler, débrouiller.

unreal a. irréel.

unreasonable a. déraisonnable.

unrecognizable a. méconnaissable.

unrelated a. (*facts*) sans rapport (**to**, avec).

unreliable a. peu sérieux; (*machine*) peu fiable.

unreservedly adv. sans réserve.

unrest n. troubles m. pl.

unrivalled a. incomparable.

unroll v.t. dérouler.

unruly a. indiscipliné.

unsafe a. (*dangerous*) dangereux; (*person*) en danger.

unsatisfactory a. peu satisfaisant.

unsavoury a. répugnant.

unscathed a. indemne.

unscheduled a. pas prévu.

unscrew v.t. dévisser.

unscrupulous a. sans scrupules.

unseen a. inaperçu. —n. (*translation*) version f.

unsettle v.t. troubler. **∼d** a. (*weather*) instable.

unshakeable a. inébranlable.

unshaven a. pas rasé.

unsightly a. laid.

unskilled a. inexpert; (*worker*) non qualifié.

unsociable a. insociable.

unsophisticated a. simple.

unsound a. peu solide. **of** ∼ **mind**, fou.

unspecified a. indéterminé.

unstable a. instable.

unsteady a. (*step*) chancelant; (*ladder*) instable; (*hand*) mal assuré.

unsuccessful a. (*result, candidate*) malheureux; (*attempt*) infructueux. **be** ∼, ne pas réussir (**in doing**, à faire).

unsuitable a. qui ne convient pas (**for**, à), peu approprié.

unsure a. incertain.

unsuspecting a. qui ne se doute de rien.

unsympathetic a. (*unhelpful*) peu compréhensif; (*unpleasant*) antipathique.

untangle v.t. démêler.

untenable a. intenable.

unthinkable a. impensable.

untidy a. (*person*) désordonné;

(*clothes, hair, room*) en désordre; (*work*) mal soigné.

untie *v.t.* (*knot, parcel*) défaire; (*person*) détacher.

until *prep.* jusqu'à. **not ~**, pas avant. —*conj.* jusqu'à ce que; (*before*) avant que.

untimely *a.* inopportun; (*death*) prématuré.

untold *a.* incalculable.

untrue *a.* faux.

unused[1] *a.* (*new*) neuf; (*not in use*) inutilisé.

unused[2] *a.* **~ to**, peu habitué à.

unusual *a.* exceptionnel; (*strange*) insolite, étrange. **~ly** *adv.* exceptionnellement.

unveil *v.t.* dévoiler.

unwanted *a.* (*useless*) superflu; (*child*) non désiré.

unwelcome *a.* fâcheux; (*guest*) importun.

unwell *a.* indisposé.

unwieldy *a.* difficile à manier.

unwilling *a.* peu disposé (**to**, à); (*victim*) récalcitrant. **~ly** *adv.* à contrecœur.

unwind *v.t./i.* (se) dérouler; (*relax: fam.*) se détendre.

unwise *a.* imprudent.

unwittingly *adv.* involontairement.

unworthy *a.* indigne.

unwrap *v.t.* ouvrir.

unwritten *a.* (*agreement*) tacite.

up *adv.* en haut, en l'air; (*sun, curtain*) levé; (*out of bed*) levé, debout; (*finished*) fini. **be ~**, (*level, price*) avoir monté. —*prep.* (*a hill*) en haut de; (*a tree*) dans; (*a ladder*) sur. —*v.t.* augmenter. **come** *or* **go up**, monter. **up there**, là-haut. **up to**, jusqu'à; (*task*) à la hauteur de. **it is up to you**, ça dépend de vous (**to**, de). **be up to sth.**, (*able*) être capable de qch.; (*do*) faire qch.; (*plot*) préparer qch. **feel up to doing**, (*able*) être de taille à faire. **up-and-coming** *a.* prometteur. **up-market** *a.* haut-de-gamme. **up to date**, moderne; (*news*) récent.

upbringing *n.* éducation *f.*

update *v.t.* mettre à jour.

upgrade *v.t.* (*person*) promouvoir; (*job*) revaloriser.

upheaval *n.* bouleversement *m.*

uphill *a.* qui monte; (*fig.*) difficile. —*adv.* **go ~**, monter.

uphold *v.t.* maintenir.

upholster *v.t.* (*pad*) rembourrer; (*cover*) recouvrir. **~y** *n.* (*in vehicle*) garniture *f.*

upkeep *n.* entretien *m.*

upon *prep.* sur.

upper *a.* supérieur. —*n.* (*of shoe*) empeigne *f.*

upright *a.* droit. —*n.* (*post*) montant *m.*

uprising *n.* soulèvement *m.*

uproar *n.* tumulte *m.*

uproot *v.t.* déraciner.

upset[1] *v.t.* (*overturn*) renverser; (*plan, stomach*) déranger; (*person*) contrarier, affliger. —*a.* peiné.

upset[2] *n.* dérangement *m.*; (*distress*) chagrin *m.*

upshot *n.* résultat *m.*

upside-down *adv.* (*in position, in disorder*) à l'envers, sens dessus dessous.

upstairs *adv.* en haut. —*a.* (*flat etc.*) d'en haut.

upstart *n.* (*pej.*) parvenu(e) *m.* (*f.*).

upstream *adv.* en amont.

upsurge *n.* recrudescence *f.*; (*of anger*) accès *m.*

uptight *a.* (*tense: fam.*) crispé; (*angry: fam.*) en colère.

upturn *n.* amélioration *f.*

upward *a.* & *adv.*, **~s** *adv.* vers le haut.

uranium *n.* uranium *m.*

urban *a.* urbain.

urbane *a.* courtois.

urchin *n.* garnement *m.*

urge *v.t.* conseiller vivement (**to do**, de faire). —*n.* forte envie *f.*

urgen|t *a.* urgent; (*request*) pressant. **～cy** *n.* urgence *f.*; (*of request, tone*) insistance *f.* **～tly** *adv.* d'urgence.

urinal *n.* urinoir *m.*

urin|e *n.* urine *f.* **～ate** *v.i.* uriner.

urn *n.* urne *f.*; (*for tea, coffee*) fontaine *f.*

us *pron.* nous. **(to) us**, nous.

US *abbr. see* **United States.**

USA *abbr. see* **United States of America.**

usable *a.* utilisable.

usage *n.* usage *m.*

use[1] *v.t.* se servir de, utiliser; (*consume*) consommer. **～ up**, épuiser. **～r** *n.* usager *m.* **～-friendly** *a.* facile d'emploi.

use[2] *n.* usage *m.*, emploi *m.* **it is no ～ shouting**/*etc.*, ça ne sert à rien de crier/*etc.* **make ～ of**, se servir de.

used[1] *a.* (*second-hand*) d'occasion.

used[2] *p.t.* **he ～ to do**, il faisait (autrefois), il avait l'habitude de faire. —*a.* **～ to**, habitué à.

use|ful *a.* utile. **～fully** *adv.* utilement. **～less** *a.* inutile; (*person*) incompétent.

usher *n.* (*in theatre, hall*) placeur *m.* —*v.t.* **～ in**, faire entrer. **～ette** *n.* ouvreuse *f.*

USSR *abbr.* (*Union of Soviet Socialist Republics*) URSS *f.*

usual *a.* habituel, normal. **as ～**, comme d'habitude. **～ly** *adv.* d'habitude.

usurp *v.t.* usurper.

utensil *n.* ustensile *m.*

uterus *n.* utérus *m.*

utility *n.* utilité *f.* **(public) ～**, service public *m.*

utilize *v.t.* utiliser.

utmost *a.* (*furthest, most intense*) extrême. **the ～ care**/*etc.*, (*greatest*) le plus grand soin/*etc.* —*n.* **do one's ～**, faire tout son possible.

utter[1] *a.* complet, absolu. **～ly** *adv.* complètement.

utter[2] *v.t.* proférer; (*sigh, shout*) pousser. **～ance** *n.* déclaration *f.*

U-turn *n.* demi-tour *m.*

V

vacan|t *a.* (*post*) vacant; (*seat etc.*) libre; (*look*) vague. **～cy** *n.* (*post*) poste vacant *m.*; (*room*) chambre disponible *f.*

vacate *v.t.* quitter.

vacation *n.* vacances *f. pl.*

vaccinat|e *v.t.* vacciner. **～ion** *n.* vaccination *f.*

vaccine *n.* vaccin *m.*

vacuum *n.* vide *m.* **～ cleaner**, aspirateur *m.* **～ flask**, bouteille thermos *f.* (P.). **～-packed** *a.* emballé sous vide.

vagina *n.* vagin *m.*

vagrant *n.* clochard(e) *m.* (*f.*).

vague *a.* vague; (*outline*) flou. **be ～ about**, ne pas préciser. **～ly** *adv.* vaguement.

vain *a.* (*conceited*) vaniteux; (*useless*) vain. **in ～**, en vain. **～ly** *adv.* en vain.

valid *a.* valable.

validate *v.t.* valider.

valley *n.* vallée *f.*

valour *n.* courage *m.*

valuable *a.* (*object*) de valeur; (*help etc.*) précieux. **～s** *n. pl.* objets de valeur *m. pl.*

valuation *n.* expertise *f.*; (*of house*) évaluation *f.*

value n. valeur f. —v.t. (appraise) évaluer; (cherish) attacher de la valeur à.

valve n. (techn.) soupape f.; (of tyre) valve f.

vampire n. vampire m.

van n. (vehicle) camionnette f.; (rail.) fourgon m.

vandal n. vandale m./f. ～ism n. vandalisme m.

vandalize v.t. abimer.

vanilla n. vanille f.

vanish v.i. disparaitre.

vanity n. vanité f. ～ case, mallette de toilette f.

vapour n. vapeur f.

vari|able a. variable. ～ation n. variation f. ～ed a. varié.

variance n. at ～, en désaccord (with, avec).

varicose a. ～ veins, varices f. pl.

variety n. variété f.

various a. divers.

varnish n. vernis m. —v.t. vernir.

vary v.t./i. varier.

vase n. vase m.

vast a. vaste, immense.

vat n. cuve f.

VAT abbr. (value added tax) TVA f.

vault¹ n. (roof) voûte f.; (in bank) chambre forte f.; (tomb) caveau m.; (cellar) cave f.

vault² v.t./i. sauter. —n. saut m.

vaunt v.t. vanter.

VCR abbr. see **video cassette recorder**.

VDU abbr. see **visual display unit**.

veal n. (meat) veau m.

veer v.i. tourner, virer.

vegan a. & n. végétalien(-ne) (m. (f.)).

vegetable n. légume m. —a. végétal.

vegetarian a. & n. végétarien(ne) (m. (f.)).

vegetate v.i. végéter.

vegetation n. végétation f.

vehement a. véhément.

vehicle n. véhicule m.

veil n. voile m. —v.t. voiler.

vein n. (in body, rock) veine f.; (mood) esprit m.

velocity n. vélocité f.

velvet n. velours m.

veneer n. placage m.; (appearance: fig.) vernis m.

venerable a. vénérable.

venereal a. vénérien.

venetian a. ～ blind, store vénitien m.

vengeance n. vengeance f.

venison n. venaison f.

venom n. venin m. ～ous a. venimeux.

vent¹ n. (in coat) fente f.

vent² n. (hole) orifice m.; (for air) bouche d'aération f. —v.t. (anger) décharger (on, sur). **give ～ to**, donner libre cours à.

ventilat|e v.t. ventiler. ～ion n. ventilation f.

ventriloquist n. ventriloque m./f.

venture n. entreprise f. —v.t./i. (se) risquer.

veranda n. véranda f.

verb n. verbe m.

verbal a. verbal.

verbatim adv. mot pour mot.

verdict n. verdict m.

verge n. bord m. —v.i. ～ on, friser, frôler.

verif|y v.t. vérifier. ～ication n. vérification f.

vermicelli n. vermicelle(s) m. (pl.).

vermin n. vermine f.

vermouth n. vermouth m.

versatil|e a. (person) aux talents variés; (mind) souple. ～ity n. souplesse f.

verse n. strophe f.; (of Bible) verset m.; (poetry) vers m. pl.

versed *a.* ～ **in**, versé dans.

version *n.* version *f.*

versus *prep.* contre.

vertebra *n.* vertèbre *f.*

vertical *a.* vertical. ～**ly** *adv.* verticalement.

vertigo *n.* vertige *m.*

verve *n.* fougue *f.*

very *adv.* très. —*a.* (*actual*) même. **the** ～ **first**, le tout premier. ～ **much**, beaucoup.

vessel *n.* (*duct, ship*) vaisseau *m.*

vest *n.* maillot de corps *m.*

vet *n.* (*fam.*) vétérinaire *m./f.* —*v.t.* examiner (de près).

veteran *n.* vétéran *m.*

veterinary *a.* vétérinaire. ～ **surgeon**, vétérinaire *m./f.*

veto *n.* veto *m.*; (*right*) droit de veto *m.* —*v.t.* mettre son veto à.

vex *v.t.* contrarier, irriter.

via *prep.* via, par.

viable *a.* viable.

viaduct *n.* viaduc *m.*

vibrate *v.t./i.* (faire) vibrer. ～**ion** *n.* vibration *f.*

vicar *n.* pasteur *m.*

vice[1] *n.* (*depravity*) vice *m.*

vice[2] *n.* (*techn.*) étau *m.*

vice- *pref.* vice-.

vice versa *adv.* vice versa.

vicious *a.* (*spiteful*) méchant; (*violent*) brutal. ～ **circle**, cercle vicieux *m.* ～**ly** *adv.* méchamment; brutalement.

victim *n.* victime *f.*

victimize *v.t.* persécuter. ～**ation** *n.* persécution *f.*

victor *n.* vainqueur *m.*

Victorian *a. & n.* victorien(ne) (*m.* (*f.*)).

victory *n.* victoire *f.* ～**ious** *a.* victorieux.

video *a.* (*game, camera*) vidéo *invar.* —*n.* (*recorder*) magnétoscope *m.*; (*film*) vidéo *f.* ～ **cassette**, vidéocassette *f.* ～

(cassette) recorder, magnétoscope *m.* —*v.t.* (*programme*) enregistrer.

videotape *n.* bande vidéo *f.* —*v.t.* (*programme*) enregistrer.

vie *v.i.* rivaliser (**with**), avec).

view *n.* vue *f.* —*v.t.* (*watch*) regarder; (*consider*) considérer (**as**, comme); (*house*) visiter. **in** ～ **of**, compte tenu de. ～**er** *n.* (*TV*) téléspectateur, -trice *m.*, *f.*; (*for slides*) visionneuse *f.*

viewfinder *n.* viseur *m.*

viewpoint *n.* point de vue *m.*

vigilant *a.* vigilant. ～**ce** *n.* vigilance *f.*

vigour /ˈvɪgə(r)/ *n.* vigueur *f.* ～**orous** *a.* vigoureux.

vile *a.* exécrable.

villa *n.* pavillon *m.*

village *n.* village *m.*

villain *n.* scélérat *m.*, bandit *m.*; (*in story etc.*) méchant *m.*

vindicate *v.t.* justifier. ～**ion** *n.* justification *f.*

vindictive *a.* vindicatif.

vine *n.* vigne *f.*

vinegar *n.* vinaigre *m.*

vineyard *n.* vignoble *m.*

vintage *n.* (*year*) année *f.*, millésime *m.* —*a.* (*wine*) de grand cru; (*car*) d'époque.

vinyl *n.* vinyle *m.*

viola *n.* (*mus.*) alto *m.*

violate *v.t.* violer. ～**ion** *n.* violation *f.*

violent *a.* violent. ～**ce** *n.* violence *f.*

violet *n.* (*bot.*) violette *f.*; (*colour*) violet *m.* —*a.* violet.

violin *n.* violon *m.* ～**ist** *n.* violoniste *m./f.*

VIP *abbr.* (*very important person*) personnage de marque *m.*

viper *n.* vipère *f.*

virgin *n.* (*woman*) vierge *f.* —*a.* vierge.

Virgo *n.* la Vierge.

viril|**e** *a.* viril. **~ity** *n.* virilité *f.*

virtual *a.* vrai. **a ~ failure**/*etc.*, pratiquement un échec/*etc.* **~ly** *adv.* pratiquement.

virtue *n.* (*goodness, chastity*) vertu *f.*; (*merit*) mérite *m.*

virtuous *a.* vertueux.

virus *n.* virus *m.*

visa *n.* visa *m.*

viscount *n.* vicomte *m.*

viscous *a.* visqueux.

visib|**le** *a.* (*discernible, obvious*) visible. **~ility** *n.* visibilité *f.*

vision *n.* vision *f.*

visit *v.t.* (*person*) rendre visite à; (*place*) visiter. —*v.i.* être en visite. (*tour, call*) visite *f.*; (*stay*) séjour *m.* **~or** *n.* visiteu|r, -se *m., f.*; (*guest*) invité(e) *m.* (*f.*); (*in hotel*) client(e) *m.* (*f.*).

visor *n.* visière *f.*

vista *n.* perspective *f.*

visual *a.* visuel. **~ display unit**, visuel *m.*, console de visualisation *f.*

visualize *v.t.* se représenter; (*foresee*) envisager.

vital *a.* vital.

vitality *n.* vitalité *f.*

vitamin *n.* vitamine *f.*

vivac|**ious** *a.* plein d'entrain, animé. **~ity** *n.* vivacité *f.*

vivid *a.* vif; (*graphic*) vivant. **~ly** *adv.* vivement; (*describe*) de façon vivante.

vivisection *n.* vivisection *f.*

vocabulary *n.* vocabulaire *m.*

vocal *a.* vocal; (*person: fig.*) qui s'exprime franchement. **~ist** *n.* chanteu|r, -se *m., f.*

vocation *n.* vocation *f.*

vodka *n.* vodka *f.*

vogue *n.* (*fashion, popularity*) vogue *f.* **in ~**, en vogue.

voice *n.* voix *f.* —*v.t.* (*express*) formuler.

void *a.* vide (**of**, de); (*not valid*) nul. —*n.* vide *m.*

volatile *a.* (*person*) versatile; (*situation*) variable.

volcan|**o** *n.* volcan *m.* **~ic** *a.* volcanique.

volley *n.* (*of blows etc., in tennis*) volée *f.*; (*of gunfire*) salve *f.* **~ball** *n.* volley(-ball) *m.*

volt *n.* (*electr.*) volt *m.* **~age** *n.* voltage *m.*

volume *n.* volume *m.*

voluntar|**y** *a.* volontaire; (*unpaid*) bénévole. **~ily** *adv.* volontairement.

volunteer *n.* volontaire *m./f.* —*v.i.* s'offrir (**to do**, pour faire); (*mil.*) s'engager comme volontaire. —*v.t.* offrir.

vomit *v.t./i.* vomir. —*n.* vomi(ssement) *m.*

voracious *a.* vorace.

vot|**e** *n.* vote *m.*; (*right*) droit de vote *m.* —*v.t./i.* voter. **~er** *n.* élec|teur, -trice *m., f.* **~ing** *n.* vote *m.* (**of**, de); (*poll*) scrutin *m.*

vouch *v.i.* **~ for**, répondre de.

voucher *n.* bon *m.*

vow *n.* vœu *m.* —*v.t.* (*loyalty etc.*) jurer (**to**, à). **~ to do**, jurer de faire.

vowel *n.* voyelle *f.*

voyage *n.* voyage (par mer) *m.*

vulgar *a.* vulgaire. **~ity** *n.* vulgarité *f.*

vulnerab|**le** *a.* vulnérable. **~ility** *n.* vulnérabilité *f.*

vulture *n.* vautour *m.*

W

wad *n.* (*pad*) tampon *m.*; (*bundle*) liasse *f.*

wadding *n.* rembourrage *m.*

waddle *v.i.* se dandiner.

wade *v.i.* **~ through,** (*mud etc.*) patauger dans.

wafer *n.* (*biscuit*) gaufrette *f.*

waffle[1] *n.* (*talk: fam.*) verbiage *m.* —*v.i.* (*fam.*) divaguer.

waffle[2] *n.* (*cake*) gaufre *f.*

waft *v.i.* flotter. —*v.t.* porter.

wag *v.t./i.* (*tail*) remuer.

wage[1] *v.t.* (*campaign*) mener. **~ war,** faire la guerre.

wage[2] *n.* (*weekly, daily*) salaire *m.* **~s,** salaire *m.*

wager *n.* (*bet*) pari *m.* —*v.t.* parier (*that,* que).

waggle *v.t./i.* remuer.

wagon *n.* (*horse-drawn*) chariot *m.*; (*rail.*) wagon (de marchandises) *m.*

wail *v.i.* gémir. —*n.* gémissement *m.*

waist *n.* taille *f.*

waistcoat *n.* gilet *m.*

wait *v.t./i.* attendre. —*n.* attente *f.* **while you ~,** sur place. **~ for,** attendre. **~ on,** servir. **~ing-list** *n.* liste d'attente *f.*

wait|er *n.* garçon *m.*, serveur *m.* **~ress** *n.* serveuse *f.*

waive *v.t* renoncer à

wake[1] *v.t./i.* **~ (up),** (se) réveiller.

wake[2] *n.* (*track*) sillage *m.*

waken *v.t./i.* (se) réveiller.

Wales *n.* pays de Galles *m.*

walk *v.i.* marcher; (*not ride*) aller à pied; (*stroll*) se promener. —*v.t.* (*streets*) parcourir; (*distance*) faire à pied; (*dog*) promener. —*n.* promenade *f.*, tour *m.*; (*gait*) (dé)marche *f.*; (*pace*) marche *f.*, pas *m.*; (*path*) allée *f.*

walker *n.* (*person*) marcheu|r, -se *m.*, *f.*

walkie-talkie *n.* talkie-walkie *m.*

walking *n.* marche (à pied) *f.* —*a.* (*corpse, dictionary: fig.*) vivant. **~-stick** *n.* canne *f.*

Walkman *n.* (P.) Walkman (P.) *m.*, baladeur *m.*

wall *n.* mur *m.*; (*of tunnel, stomach, etc.*) paroi *f.* —*a.* mural.

wallet *n.* portefeuille *m.*

wallflower *n.* (*bot.*) giroflée *f.*

wallop *v.t.* (*hit: sl.*) taper sur. —*n.* (*blow: sl.*) grand coup *m.*

wallow *v.i.* se vautrer.

wallpaper *n.* papier peint *m.* —*v.t.* tapisser.

walnut *n.* (*nut*) noix *f.*; (*tree*) noyer *m.*

walrus *n.* morse *m.*

waltz *n.* valse *f.* —*v.i.* valser.

wand *n.* baguette (magique) *f.*

wander *v.i.* errer; (*stroll*) flâner; (*digress*) s'écarter du sujet; (*mind*) divaguer. **~er** *n.* vagabond(e) *m.* (*f.*).

wane *v.i.* décroître. —*n.* **on the ~,** (*strength, fame, etc.*) en déclin; (*person*) sur son déclin.

wangle *v.t.* (*obtain: sl.*) se débrouiller pour avoir.

want *v.t.* vouloir (**to do,** faire); (*need*) avoir besoin de (**doing,** d'être fait); (*ask for*) demander. —*v.i.* **~ for,** manquer de. —*n.* (*need, poverty*) besoin *m.*; (*desire*) désir *m.*; (*lack*) manque *m.* **I ~ you to do it,** je veux que vous le fassiez.

war *n.* guerre *f.* **at ~,** en guerre.

ward *n.* (*in hospital*) salle *f.*; (*minor: jurid.*) pupille *m./f.*; (*pol.*) division électorale *f.* —*v.t.* **~ off,** (*danger*) prévenir; (*blow, anger*) détourner.

warden *n.* direc|teur, -trice *m.*, *f.*; (*of park*) gardien(ne) *m.* (*f.*). **(traffic) ~,** contractuel(le) *m.* (*f.*).

warder *n.* gardien (de prison) *m.*

wardrobe *n.* (*place*) armoire *f.*; (*clothes*) garde-robe *f.*

warehouse *n.* entrepôt *m.*

warm *a.* chaud; (*hearty*) chaleureux. **be** *or* **feel** ∼, avoir chaud. **it is** ∼, il fait chaud. —*v.t./i.* ∼ **(up)**, (se) réchauffer; (*food*) chauffer; (*liven up*) (s')animer; (*exercise*) s'échauffer. ∼**th** *n.* chaleur *f.*

warn *v.t.* avertir, prévenir. ∼**ing** *n.* avertissement *m.; (notice)* avis *m.* **without** ∼**ing**, sans prévenir. ∼**ing light,** voyant *m.*

warp *v.t./i.* (*wood etc.*) (se) voiler; (*pervert*) pervertir.

warrant *n.* (*for arrest*) mandat (d'arrêt) *m.; (comm.)* autorisation *f.* —*v.t.* justifier.

warranty *n.* garantie *f.*

warrior *n.* guerr|ier, -ière *m., f.*

warship *n.* navire de guerre *m.*

wart *n.* verrue *f.*

wary *a.* prudent.

wash *v.t./i.* (se) laver; (*flow over*) baigner. —*n.* lavage *m.; (clothes*) lessive *f.; (of ship*) sillage *m.* **have a** ∼, se laver. ∼**basin** *n.* lavabo *m.* ∼ **out,** (*cup etc.*) laver; (*stain*) (faire) partir. ∼**out** *n.* (*sl.*) fiasco *m.* ∼ **up,** faire la vaisselle. ∼**able** *a.* lavable. ∼**ing** *n.* lessive *f.* ∼**ing-machine** *n.* machine à laver *f.* ∼**ing-powder** *n.* lessive *f.* ∼**ing-up** *n.* vaisselle *f.;* ∼**ing-up liquid,** produit pour la vaisselle *m.*

washer *n.* rondelle *f.*

wasp *n.* guêpe *f.*

wastage *n.* gaspillage *m.* **some** ∼, (*in goods, among candidates, etc.*) du déchet.

waste *v.t.* gaspiller; (*time*) perdre. —*v.i.* ∼ **away,** dépérir. —*a.* superflu; (*product*) de rebut. —*n.* gaspillage *m.; (of time*) perte *f.; (rubbish)* déchets *m. pl.* ∼**paper,** vieux papiers *m. pl.* ∼**paper basket,** corbeille (à papier) *f.*

wasteful *a.* peu économique; (*person*) gaspilleur.

watch *v.t./i.* (*television*) regarder; (*observe*) observer; (*guard, spy on*) surveiller; (*be careful about*) faire attention à. —*n.* (*for telling time*) montre *f.; (naut.*) quart. ∼ **out,** (*take care*) faire attention (*for,* à). ∼ **out for,** guetter.

water *n.* eau *f.* —*v.t.* arroser. —*v.i.* (*of eyes*) larmoyer. ∼**bottle** *n.* bouillotte *f.* ∼**colour** *n.* couleur pour aquarelle *f.; (painting*) aquarelle *f.* ∼ **down,** couper (d'eau); (*tone down*) édulcorer. ∼ **heater,** chauffe-eau *m.* ∼**ice** *n.* sorbet *m.* ∼**main** *n.* canalisation d'eau *f.* ∼**melon** *n.* pastèque *f.* ∼**skiing** *n.* ski nautique *m.*

watercress *n.* cresson (de fontaine) *m.*

waterfall *n.* cascade *f.*

watering-can *n.* arrosoir *m.*

waterlogged *a.* imprégné d'eau; (*land*) détrempé.

watermark *n.* filigrane *m.*

waterproof *a.* imperméable.

watershed *n.* (*in affairs*) tournant décisif *m.*

watertight *a.* étanche.

waterway *n.* voie navigable *f.*

watery *a.* (*colour*) délavé; (*eyes*) humide; (*soup*) trop liquide; (*tea*) faible.

watt *n.* watt *m.*

wav|e *n.* vague *f.; (in hair*) ondulation *f.; (radio*) onde *f.; (sign)* signe *m.* —*v.t.* agiter. —*v.i.* faire signe (de la main); (*move in wind*) flotter. ∼**y** *a.* (*line*) onduleux; (*hair*) ondulé.

wavelength *n.* (*radio & fig.*) longueur d'ondes *f.*

waver *v.i.* vaciller.

wax[1] *n.* cire *f.; (for skis*) fart *m.* —*v.t.* cirer; farter; (*car*) astiquer. ∼**en,** ∼**y** *adjs.* cireux.

wax[2] *v.i.* (*of moon*) croître.

way n. (*road, path*) chemin m. **(to,** de); (*distance*) distance f.; (*direction*) direction f.; (*manner*) façon f.; (*means*) moyen m.; (*particular*) égard m. **~s,** (*habits*) habitudes f. pl. —adv. (*fam.*) loin. **be in the ~,** bloquer le passage; (*hindrance: fig.*) gêner (qn.). **be on one's** or **the ~,** être sur son or le chemin. **by the ~,** à propos. **in a ~,** dans un sens. **make one's ~ somewhere,** se rendre quelque part. **that. ~,** par là. **this ~,** par ici. **~ in,** entrée f. **~ out,** sortie f.

wayward a. capricieux.

WC n. w.-c. m. pl.

we pron. nous.

weak a. faible; (*delicate*) fragile. **~ly** adv. faiblement; a. faible. **~ness** n. faiblesse f.; (*fault*) point faible m. **a ~ness for,** (*liking*) un faible pour.

weaken v.t. affaiblir —v.i. s'affaiblir, faiblir.

weakling n. gringalet m.

wealth n. richesse f.; (*riches, resources*) richesses f. pl.; (*quantity*) profusion f.

wealthy a. riche.

wean v.t. (*baby*) sevrer.

weapon n. arme f.

wear v.t. porter; (*put on*) mettre; (*expression etc.*) avoir. —v.i. (*last*) durer. **~ (out),** (s')user. —n. usage m.; (*damage*) usure f.; (*clothing*) vêtements m. pl. **~ off,** (*colour, pain*) passer. **~ on,** (*time*) passer. **~ out,** (*exhaust*) épuiser.

wear|y a. fatigué, las; (*tiring*) fatigant. —v.i. **~y of,** se lasser de. **~ily** adv. avec lassitude.

weasel n. belette f.

weather n. temps m. —v.t. (*survive*) réchapper de or à. **~ forecast,** météo f.

weave v.t./i. tisser; (*basket etc.*) tresser; (*move*) se faufiler. —n. (*style*) tissage m.

web n. (*of spider*) toile f.; (*fabric*) tissu m.; (*on foot*) palmure f. **~bed** a. (*foot*) palmé.

wed v.t. épouser. —v.i. se marier.

wedding n. mariage m. **~-ring** n. alliance f.

wedge n. coin m.; (*under wheel etc.*) cale f. —v.t. caler; (*push*) enfoncer; (*crowd*) coincer.

Wednesday n. mercredi m.

wee a. (*fam.*) tout petit.

weed n. mauvaise herbe f. —v.t./i. désherber. **~-killer** n. désherbant m. **~ out,** extirper.

week n. semaine f. **a ~ today/tomorrow,** aujourd'hui/demain en huit. **~ly** adv. toutes les semaines; a. & n. (*periodical*) hebdomadaire (m.).

weekday n. jour de semaine m.

weekend n. week-end m.

weep v.t./i. pleurer (**for s.o.,** qn.). **~ing willow,** saule pleureur m.

weigh v.t./i. peser. **~ down,** lester (avec un poids); (*bend*) faire plier; (*fig.*) accabler. **~ up,** (*examine: fam.*) calculer.

weight n. poids m. **lose/put on ~,** perdre/prendre du poids. **~-lifting** n. haltérophilie f. **~-weighting** n. indemnité f.

weir n. barrage m.

weird a. mystérieux; (*strange*) bizarre.

welcome a. agréable; (*timely*) opportun. **be ~,** être le or la bienvenu(e), être les bienvenu(e)s. **you're ~!,** (*after thank you*) il n'y a pas de quoi! **~ to do,** libre de faire. —*int.* soyez le or la bienvenu(e), soyez les bienvenu(e)s. —n. accueil m. —v.t. accueillir; (*as greeting*) souhaiter la bienvenue à; (*fig.*) se réjouir de.

weld v.t. souder. —n. soudure f. **~er** n. soudeur m.

welfare n. bien-être m.; (aid) aide sociale f.

well[1] n. (for water, oil) puits m.; (of stairs) cage f.

well[2] adv. bien. —a. bien invar. **as ~**, aussi. be **~**, (healthy) aller bien. —int. eh bien; (surprise) tiens. do **~**, (succeed) réussir. **~-behaved** a. sage. **~-being** n. bien-être m. **~-built** a. bien bâti. **~ done!**, bravo! **~-dressed** a. bien habillé. **~-known** a. (bien) connu. **~ off**, aisé, riche. **~-to-do** a. riche.

wellington n. (boot) botte de caoutchouc f.

Welsh a. gallois. —n. (lang.) gallois m. **~man** n. Gallois m. **~woman** n. Galloise f.

welsh v.i. **~ on**, (debt, promise) ne pas honorer.

wend v.t. **~ one's way**, se diriger, aller son chemin.

west n. ouest m. **the W~**, (pol.) l'Occident m. —a. d'ouest. —adv. vers l'ouest. **W~ Indian** a. & n. antillais(e) (m. (f.)). **the W~ Indies**, les Antilles f.pl. **~ern** a. de l'ouest; (pol.) occidental; (film) western m. **~ward** a. à l'ouest. **~wards** adv. vers l'ouest.

wet a. mouillé; (damp, rainy) humide; (paint) frais. —v.t. mouiller. **get ~**, se mouiller. **~ suit**, combinaison de plongée f.

whack n. (fam.) grand coup m. —v.t. (fam.) taper sur.

whale n. baleine f.

wharf n. quai m.

what a. (in questions) quel(le), quel(le)s. —pron. (in questions) qu'est-ce que; (object) qu'est-ce que or qu'*; (after prep.) quoi; (that which) ce qui; (object) ce

que, ce qu'*. —int. quoi, comment. **~ time?**, à quelle heure? **he said**, ce qu'il a dit. **~ is it?**, qu'est-ce que c'est? **~ you need**, ce dont vous avez besoin. **~ a fool**/etc., quel idiot/etc. **~ about me**/**him**/**etc.?**, et moi/lui/etc.? **~ about doing?**, si on faisait? **~ for?**, pourquoi?

whatever a. **~ book**/etc., quel que soit le livre/etc. —pron. (no matter what) quoi que, quoi qu'*; (anything that) tout ce qui; (object) tout ce que or qu'*. **~ happens**, quoi qu'il arrive. **~ you want**, tout ce que vous voulez. **nothing ~**, rien du tout.

whatsoever a. & pron. = **whatever**.

wheat n. blé m., froment m.

wheedle v.t. cajoler.

wheel n. roue f. —v.t. pousser. —v.i. tourner. **at the ~**, (of vehicle) au volant; (helm) au gouvernail.

wheelbarrow n. brouette f.

wheelchair n. fauteuil roulant m.

wheeze v.i. siffler (en respirant). —n. sifflement m.

when adv. & pron. quand. —conj. quand, lorsque. **the day**/**moment ~**, le jour/moment où.

whenever conj. & adv. (at whatever time) quand; (every time that) chaque fois que.

where adv., conj., & pron. où; (whereas) alors que; (the place that) là où.

whereas conj. alors que.

wherever conj. & adv. où que; (everywhere) partout où; (anywhere) (là) où; (emphatic where) où donc.

whet v.t. (appetite) aiguiser.

whether conj. si. **not know ~**, ne pas savoir si. **~ I go or not**, que j'aille ou non.

which *a.* (*in questions*) quel(le), quel(le)s. —*pron.* (*in questions*) lequel, laquelle, lesquel(le)s; (*the one or ones that*) celui (celle, ceux, celles) qui; (*object*) celui (celle, ceux, celles) que or qu'*; (*referring to whole sentence. = and that*) ce qui; (*object*) ce que, ce qu'*;(*after prep.*) lequel/*etc.* —*rel. pron.* qui; (*object*) que, qu'*. ~ **house?**, quelle maison? ~ (**one**) **do you want?**, lequel voulez-vous? **of ~, from ~,** lequel/*etc.* **to ~, at ~,** auquel/*etc.* **the book of ~,** le livre dont or duquel. **after ~,** après quoi.

whichever *a.* ~ **book**/*etc.*, quel que soit le livre/*etc.* que or qui. **take ~ book you wish,** prenez le livre que vous voulez. —*pron.* celui (celle, ceux, celles) qui or que.

whiff *n.* (*puff*) bouffée *f.*

while *n.* moment *m.* —*conj.* (*when*) pendant que; (*although*) bien que; (*as long as*) tant que. —*v.t.* ~ **away,** (*time*) passer.

whilst *conj.* = **while.**

whim *n.* caprice *m.*

whimper *v.i.* geindre, pleurnicher. —*n.* pleurnichement *m.*

whimsical *a.* (*person*) capricieux; (*odd*) bizarre.

whine *v.i.* gémir, se plaindre. —*n.* gémissement *m.*

whip *n.* fouet *m.* —*v.t.* fouetter; (*culin.*) fouetter, battre; (*seize*) enlever brusquement. ~**-round** *n.* (*fam.*) collecte *f.* ~ **out,** (*gun etc.*) sortir. ~ **up,** exciter; (*cause*) provoquer; (*meal: fam.*) préparer.

whirl *v.t./i.* (faire) tourbillonner. —*n.* tourbillon *m.*

whirlpool *n.* (*in sea etc.*) tourbillon *m.*

whirlwind *n.* tourbillon (de vent) *m.*

whirr *v.i.* vrombir.

whisk *v.t.* (*snatch*) enlever or emmener brusquement; (*culin.*) fouetter. —*n.* (*culin.*) fouet *m.*; (*broom, brush*) petit balai *m.*

whisker *n.* poil *m.* ~**s,** (*man's*) barbe *f.*, moustache *f.*; (*sideboards*) favoris *m. pl.*

whisky *n.* whisky *m.*

whisper *v.t./i.* chuchoter. —*n.* chuchotement *m.*

whistle *n.* sifflement *m.*; (*instrument*) sifflet *m.* —*v.t./i.* siffler. ~ **at** or **for,** siffler.

Whit *a.* ~ **Sunday,** dimanche de Pentecôte *m.*

white *a.* blanc. —*n.* blanc *m.*; (*person*) blanc(he) *m.* (*f.*). ~ **coffee,** café au lait *m.* ~**-collar worker,** employé(e) de bureau *m.* (*f.*).

whitewash *n.* blanc de chaux *m.* —*v.t.* blanchir à la chaux; (*person: fig.*) blanchir.

whiting *n. invar.* (*fish*) merlan *m.*

Whitsun *n.* la Pentecôte *f.*

whittle *v.t.* ~ **down,** tailler (au couteau); (*fig.*) réduire.

whiz *v.i.* (*through air*) fendre l'air; (*hiss*) siffler; (*rush*) aller à toute vitesse. ~**-kid** *n.* jeune prodige *m.*

who *pron.* qui.

whoever *pron.* (*no matter who*) qui que ce soit qui or que; (*the one who*) quiconque.

whole *a.* entier; (*intact*) intact. **the ~ house**/*etc.*, toute la maison/*etc.* —*n.* totalité *f.*; (*unit*) tout *m.* **on the ~,** dans l'ensemble. ~**-hearted** *a.*, ~**heartedly** *adv.* sans réserve.

wholefoods *n. pl.* aliments naturels et diététiques *m. pl.*

wholemeal *a.* ~ **bread,** pain complet *m.*

wholesale *n.* gros *m.* —*a.* (*firm*)

de gros; (*fig.*) systématique. —*adv.* (*in large quantities*) en gros; (*buy or sell one item*) au prix de gros; (*fig.*) en masse. **~r** *n.* grossiste *m./f.*

wholesome *a.* sain.

wholewheat *a.* = wholemeal.

whom *pron.* (*that*) que, qu'*; (*after prep. & in questions*) qui. **of ~**, dont. **with ~**, avec qui.

whooping cough *n.* coqueluche *f.*

whore *n.* putain *f.*

whose *pron. & a.* à qui, de qui. **~ hat is this?**, **~ is this hat?**, à qui est ce chapeau? **~ son are you?**, de qui êtes-vous le fils?

why *adv.* pourquoi. **the reason ~**, la raison pour laquelle.

wick *n.* (*of lamp etc.*) mèche *f.*

wicked *a.* méchant, mauvais, vilain.

wicker *n.* osier *m.* **~work** *n.* vannerie *f.*

wicket *n.* guichet *m.*

wide *a.* large; (*ocean etc.*) vaste. —*adv.* (*fall etc.*) loin du but. **open ~**, ouvrir tout grand. **~angle lens** grand-angle *m.* **~awake**, éveillé. **~ly** *adv.* (*spread, space*) largement; (*travel*) beaucoup; (*generally*) généralement; (*extremely*) extrêmement.

widen *v.t./i.* (s')élargir.

widespread *a.* très répandu.

widow *n.* veuve. *f.* **~er** *n.* veuf *m.*

width *n.* largeur *f.*

wield *v.t.* (*axe etc.*) manier; (*power: fig.*) exercer.

wife *n.* femme *f.*, épouse *f.*

wig *n.* perruque *f.*

wiggle *v.t./i.* remuer; (*hips*) tortiller; (*of worm*) se tortiller.

wild *a.* sauvage; (*sea, enthusiasm*) déchaîné; (*mad*) fou; (*furious*) furieux. —*adv.* (*grow*) à l'état sauvage. **~s** *n. pl.* régions

sauvages *f. pl.* **~-goose chase**, fausse piste *f.* **~ly** *adv.* violemment; (*madly*) follement.

wildcat *a.* **~ strike**, grève sauvage *f.*

wilderness *n.* désert *m.*

wildlife *n.* faune *f.*

wile *n.* ruse *f.*, artifice *m.*

wilful *a.* volontaire.

will[1] *v. aux.* **he ~ do/you ~ sing/**etc., (*future tense*) il fera/tu chanteras/etc. **~ you have a coffee?**, voulez-vous prendre un café?

will[2] *n.* volonté *f.*; (*document*) testament *m.* —*v.t.* (*wish*) vouloir. **at ~**, quand *or* comme on veut. **~-power** *n.* volonté *f.*

willing *a.* (*help, offer*) spontané; (*helper*) bien disposé. **~ to**, disposé à. **~ly** *adv.* (*with pleasure*) volontiers; (*not forced*) volontairement.

willow *n.* saule *m.*

wilt *v.i.* (*plant etc.*) dépérir.

wily *a.* rusé.

win *v.t./i.* gagner; (*victory, prize*) remporter; (*fame, fortune*) acquérir, trouver. —*n.* victoire *f.* **~ round**, convaincre.

wince *v.i.* se crisper, tressaillir.

winch *n.* treuil *m.* —*v.t.* hisser au treuil.

wind[1] *n.* vent *m.*; (*breath*) souffle *m.* —*v.t.* essouffler. **~cheater** *n.* blouson *m.* **~ instrument**, instrument à vent *m.*

wind[2] *v.t./i.* (s')enrouler; (*of path, river*) serpenter. **~ (up)**, (*clock etc.*) remonter. **~ up**, (*end*) (se) terminer. **~ up in hospital**, finir à l'hôpital. **~ing** *a.* (*path*) sinueux.

windfall *n.* fruit tombé *m.*; (*money: fig.*) aubaine *f.*

windmill *n.* moulin à vent *m.*

window *n.* fenêtre *f.*; (*glass pane*)

vitre f.; (in vehicle, train) vitre f.; (in shop) vitrine f.; (counter) guichet m. **~-cleaner** n. laveur de carreaux m. **~-shopping** n. lèche-vitrines m. **~-sill** n. (inside) appui de (la) fenêtre m.; (outside) rebord de (la) fenêtre m.

windscreen n. pare-brise m. invar. **~ washer**, lave-glace m. **~ wiper**, essuie-glace m.

windsurf|ing n. planche à voile f. **~er** n. véliplanchiste m./f.

windy a. venteux. **it is ~**, il y a du vent.

wine n. vin m. **~ list**, carte des vins f.

wineglass n. verre à vin m.

wing n. aile f. **~s**, (theatre) coulisses f. pl. **~ mirror**, rétroviseur extérieur m. **~er** n. (sport) ailier m.

wink v.i. faire un clin d'œil; (light, star) clignoter. —n. clin d'œil m.; clignotement m.

winner n. (of game) gagnant(e) m. (f.); (of fight) vainqueur m.

winning a. (number, horse) gagnant; (team) victorieux; (smile) engageant. **~s** n. pl. gains m. pl.

winter n. hiver m.

wipe v.t. essuyer. —v.i. **~ up**, essuyer la vaisselle. —n. coup de torchon or d'éponge m. **~ out**, (destroy) anéantir; (remove) effacer.

wir|e n. fil m. **~ing** n. (electr.) installation électrique f.

wireless n. radio f.

wiry a. (person) nerveux et maigre.

wisdom n. sagesse f.

wise a. prudent, sage; (look) averti. **~ly** adv. prudemment.

wish n. (specific) souhait m., vœu m.; (general) désir m. —v.t. souhaiter, vouloir, désirer (to do, faire); (bid) souhaiter. —v.i. **~**

for, souhaiter. **I ~ he'd leave**, je voudrais bien qu'il parte.

wisp n. (of smoke) volute f.

wit n. intelligence f.; (humour) esprit m.; (person) homme d'esprit m., femme d'esprit f.

witch n. sorcière f.

with prep. avec; (having) à; (because of) de; (at house of) chez. **the man ~ the beard**, l'homme à la barbe. **fill/etc. ~**, remplir/etc. de.

withdraw v.t./i. (se) retirer. **~al** n. retrait m. **~n** a. (person) renfermé.

wither v.t./i. (se) flétrir.

withhold v.t. refuser (de donner); (retain) retenir; (conceal, not tell) cacher (**from**, à).

within prep. & adv. à l'intérieur (de); (in distances) à moins de. **a month**, (before) avant un mois. **~ sight**, en vue.

without prep. sans. **~ my knowing**, sans que je sache.

withstand v.t. résister à.

witness n. témoin m.; (evidence) témoignage m. —v.t. être le témoin de, voir; (document) signer.

witty a. spirituel.

wizard n. magicien m.; (genius: fig.) génie m.

wobbl|e v.i. (of jelly, voice, hand) trembler; (stagger) chanceler; (of table, chair) branler. **~y** a. tremblant; branlant.

wolf n. loup m. —v.t. (food) engloutir. **~-whistle** n. sifflement admiratif m.

woman n. femme f. **~ doctor**, femme médecin f. **~ friend**, amie f.

womb n. utérus m.

wonder n. émerveillement m.; (thing) merveille f. —v.t. demander (**if**, si). —v.i. s'étonner (at, de); (reflect) songer (about, à). **it is no** ~, ce or il n'est pas étonnant (that, que).

wonderful a. merveilleux.

wood n. bois m. ~**en** a. en or de bois; (stiff: fig.) raide.

woodland n. région boisée f.

woodpecker n. pivert m.

woodwind n. (mus.) bois m. pl.

woodwork n. menuiserie f.

woodworm n. (larvae) vers (de bois) m. pl.

woody a. (wooded) boisé; (like wood) ligneux.

wool n. laine f. ~**len** a. de laine. ~**lens** n. pl. lainages m. pl. ~**ly** a. laineux; (vague) nébuleux; n. (garment: fam.) lainage m.

word n. mot m.; (spoken) parole f., mot m.; (promise) parole f.; (news) nouvelles f. pl. —v.t. rédiger. **give/keep one's** ~, donner/tenir sa parole. **have a** ~ **with**, parler à. ~ **processor**, machine de traitement de texte f.

work n. travail m.; (product, book, etc.) œuvre f.; (building etc. work) travaux m. pl. ~**s**, (techn.) mécanisme m.; (factory) usine f. —v.t./i. (of person) travailler; (shape, hammer, etc.) travailler; (techn.) (faire) fonctionner, (faire) marcher; (land, mine) exploiter; (of drug etc.) agir. ~**-force** n. main-d'œuvre f. ~ **out** v.t. (solve) résoudre; (calculate) calculer; (elaborate) élaborer; v.i. (succeed) marcher; (sport) s'entraîner. ~**-station** n. poste de travail m. ~**-to-rule** n. grève du zèle f. ~ **up** v.t. développer; v.i. (to climax) monter vers. ~**ed up**, (person) énervé.

worker n. travailleu|r, -se m., f.; (manual) ouvr|ier, -ière m., f.

working a. (day, lunch, etc.) de

travail. ~**s** n. pl. mécanisme m. ~ **class**, classe ouvrière f. ~**class** a. ouvrier.

workman n. ouvrier m.

workshop n. atelier m.

world n. monde m. —a. (power etc.) mondial; (record etc.) du monde. ~**-wide** a. universel.

worldly a. de ce monde, terrestre.

worm n. ver m.

worn a. usé. ~**-out** a. (thing) complètement usé; (person) épuisé.

worr|y v.t./i. (s')inquiéter. —n. souci m. ~**ied** a. inquiet.

worse a. pire, plus mauvais. —adv. plus mal. —n. pire m. **be** ~ **off**, perdre.

worsen v.t./i. empirer.

worship n. (adoration) culte m. —v.t. adorer. —v.i. faire ses dévotions.

worst a. pire, plus mauvais. —adv. (the) ~, (sing etc.) le plus mal. —n. **the** ~ **(one)**, (person, object) le or la pire.

worsted n. worsted m.

worth a. **be** ~, valoir. **it is** ~ **waiting**/etc., ça vaut la peine d'attendre/etc. —n. valeur f. **it is** ~ **(one's) while**, ça (en) vaut la peine. ~**less** a. qui ne vaut rien.

worthwhile a. qui (en) vaut la peine.

worthy a. digne (of, de); (laudable) louable.

would v. aux. **he** ~ **do/you** ~ **sing**/etc., (conditional tense) il ferait/tu chanterais/etc. **he** ~ **have done**, il aurait fait. **I** ~ **come every day**, (used to) je venais chaque jour. **I** ~ **like some tea**, je voudrais du thé. ~ **you come here?**, voulez-vous venir ici? **he** ~**n't come**, il a refusé de venir. ~**-be** a. soi-disant.

wound n. blessure f. —v.t. blesser.
wrangle v.i. se disputer. —n. dispute f.
wrap v.t. ∼ (up), envelopper. —v.i. ∼ up, (dress warmly) se couvrir. —n. châle m. ∼per n. (of book) jaquette f.; (of sweet) papier m. ∼ping n. emballage m.; ∼ping paper, papier d'emballage m.
wreath n. couronne f.
wreck n. (sinking) naufrage m.; (ship, remains, person) épave f.; (vehicle) voiture accidentée f. —v.t. détruire; (ship) provoquer le naufrage de. ∼age n. (pieces) débris m. pl.; (wrecked building) décombres m. pl.
wren n. roitelet m.
wrench v.t. (pull) tirer sur; (twist) tordre; (snatch) arracher (**from**, à). —n. (tool) clé f.
wrestl|e v.i. lutter, se débattre (**with**, contre). ∼er n. lutteu|r, -se m., f.; catcheu|r, -se m., f. ∼ing n. lutte f. (**all-in**) ∼ing, catch m.
wretch n. malheureu|x, -se m., f.; (rascal) misérable m./f.
wretched a. (pitiful, poor) misérable; (bad) affreux.
wriggle v.t./i. (se) tortiller.
wring v.t. (twist) tordre; (clothes) essorer.
wrinkle n. (crease) pli m.; (on skin) ride f. —v.t./i. (se) rider.
wrist n. poignet m. ∼-watch n. montre-bracelet f.
writ n. acte judiciaire m.
write v.t./i. écrire. ∼ down, noter. ∼ off, (debt) passer aux profits et pertes; (vehicle) considérer bon pour la casse. ∼-off n. perte totale f.
writer n. écrivain m.
writhe v.i. se tordre.
writing n. écriture f. **in** ∼, par écrit. ∼-paper n. papier à lettres m.

wrong a. (incorrect, mistaken) faux, mauvais; (unfair) injuste; (amiss) qui ne va pas; (clock) pas à l'heure. **be** ∼, (person) avoir tort (**to**, de); (be mistaken) se tromper. —adv. mal. —n. injustice f.; (evil) mal m. —v.t. faire (du) tort à. **what's** ∼?, qu'est-ce qui ne va pas?
wrought a. ∼ **iron**, fer forgé m.
wry a. (smile) désabusé.

X

xerox v.t. photocopier.
Xmas n. Noël m.
X-ray n. rayon X m.; (photograph) radio(graphie) f. —v.t. radiographier.
xylophone n. xylophone m.

Y

yacht n. yacht m. ∼ing n. yachting m.
yank v.t. tirer brusquement. —n. coup brusque m.
Yank n. (fam.) Américain(e) m. (f.), Amerloque m./f.
yap v.i. japper.
yard[1] n. (measure) yard m. (= 0.9144 metre).
yard[2] n. (of house etc.) cour f.; (for storage) dépôt m.
yarn n. (thread) fil m.; (tale: fam.) (longue) histoire f.
yawn v.i. bâiller. —n. bâillement m.
year n. an m., année f. **be ten**/etc. ∼**s old**, avoir dix/etc. ans. ∼**ly** a. annuel; adv. annuellement.
yearn v.i. avoir bien or très envie (**for**, **to**, de). ∼ing n. envie f.

yeast *n.* levure *f.*

yell *v.t./i.* hurler. —*n.* hurlement *m.*

yellow *a.* jaune —*n.* jaune *m.*

yelp *n.* (*of dog etc.*) petit jappement *m.* —*v.i.* japper.

yen *n.* (*desire*) grande envie *f.*

yes *adv.* oui; (*as answer to negative question*) si. —*n.* oui *m. invar.*

yesterday *n. & adv.* hier (*m.*).

yet *adv.* encore; (*already*) déjà. —*conj.* pourtant.

yew *n.* (*tree, wood*) if *m.*

Yiddish *n.* yiddish *m.*

yield *v.t.* (*produce*) produire, rendre; (*profit*) rapporter; (*surrender*) céder. —*v.i.* (*give way*) céder. —*n.* rendement *m.*

yoga *n.* yoga *m.*

yoghurt *n.* yaourt *m.*

yolk *n.* jaune (d'œuf) *m.*

yonder *adv.* là-bas.

you *pron.* (*familiar form*) tu, *pl.* vous; (*object*) te, t*****,*pl.* vous; (*polite*) vous; (*after prep.*) toi, *pl.* vous; (*polite*) vous; (*indefinite*) on; (*object*) vous. (**to** **∼**, te, t*****,*pl.* vous; (*polite*) vous. **I** **gave ∼ a pen**, je vous ai donné un stylo. **I know ∼**, je te connais; je vous connais.

young *a.* jeune. —*n.* (*people*) jeunes *m. pl.*; (*of animals*) petits *m. pl.*

youngster *n.* jeune *m./f.*

your *a.* (*familiar form*) ton, ta, *pl.* tes; (*polite form*, & *familiar form pl.*) votre, *pl.* vos.

yours *poss. pron.* (*familiar form*) le tien, la tienne, *pl.* les tien(ne)s; (*polite form*, & *familiar form pl.*) le or la vôtre, *pl.* les vôtres. **∼s faithfully/sincerely**, je vous prie d'agréer/de croire en l'expression de mes sentiments les meilleurs.

yourself *pron.* (*familiar form*) toi-même; (*polite form*) vous-même; (*reflexive & after prep.*) te, t*****; vous. **∼ves** *pron. pl.* vous-mêmes; (*reflexive*) vous.

youth *n.* jeunesse *f.*; (*young man*) jeune *m.* **∼ club**, centre de jeunes *m.* **∼ hostel**, auberge de jeunesse *f.*

Yugoslav *a. & n.* Yougoslave (*m./f.*) **∼ia** *n.* Yougoslavie *f.*

Z

zany *a.* farfelu.

zeal *n.* zèle *m.*

zebra *n.* zèbre *m.* **∼ crossing**, passage pour piétons *m.*

zenith *n.* zénith *m.*

zero *n.* zéro *m.* **∼ hour**, l'heure H *f.*

zest *n.* (*gusto*) entrain *m.*; (*spice: fig.*) piment *m.*; (*of orange or lemon peel*) zeste *m.*

zigzag *n.* zigzag *m.* —*a. & adv.* en zigzag. —*v.i.* zigzaguer.

zinc *n.* zinc *m.*

Zionism *n.* sionisme *m.*

zip *n.* (*vigour*) allant *m.* **∼(-fastener)**, fermeture éclair *f.* (P.). —*v.t.* fermer avec une fermeture éclair (P.). —*v.i.* aller à toute vitesse.

zodiac *n.* zodiaque *m.*

zone *n.* zone *f.*

zoo *n.* zoo *m.*

zoolog|y *n.* zoologie *f.* **∼ical** *a.* zoologique. **∼ist** *n.* zoologiste *m./f.*

zoom *v.i.* (*rush*) se précipiter. **∼ lens**, zoom *m.* **∼ off** *or* **past**, filer (comme une flèche).